Fodor's 26th Edition

The South

D0949109

Packed with details that will make your trip

The must-see sights, off and on the beaten path

What to see, what to skip

Mix-and-match vacation itineraries

City strolls, countryside adventures

Smart lodging and dining options

Essential local do's and taboos

Transportation tips, distances and directions

Key contacts, savvy travel tips

When to go, what to pack

Clear, accurate, easy-to-use maps

The complete guide, thoroughly up-to-date

Fodor's Travel Publications • New York, Toronto, London, Sydney, Auckland
www.fodors.com

Fodor's The South

EDITOR: Melissa Klurman

Editorial Contributors: Gene Bourg, Andrew Collins, Lauren Myers, Honey Naylor, Mary Sue Lawrence, Sam Starnes, Lisa H. Towle
Editorial Production: Tom Holton
Maps: David Lindroth, *cartographer*; Rebecca Baer, *map editor*
Design: Fabrizio La Rocca, *creative director*; Guido Caroti, *art director*; Jolie Novak, *photo editor*
Cover Design: Pentagram
Production/Manufacturing: Yexenia Markland
Cover Photograph: Peter Guttman (Roan Mountain, Blue Ridge Mountains)

Copyright

26th edition

ISBN 0–679–00671–0

ISSN 0147–8680

Special Sales

Fodor's Travel Publications are available at special discounts for bulk purchases for sales promotions or premiums. Special editions, including personalized covers, excerpts of existing guides, and corporate imprints, can be created in large quantities for special needs. For more information, contact your local bookseller or write to Special Markets, Fodor's Travel Publications, 280 Park Avenue, New York, NY 10017. Inquiries from Canada should be directed to your local Canadian bookseller or sent to Random House of Canada, Ltd., Marketing Department, 2775 Matheson Boulevard East, Mississauga, Ontario L4W 4P7. Inquiries from the United Kingdom should be sent to Fodor's Travel Publications, 20 Vauxhall Bridge Road, London SW1V 2SA, England.

PRINTED IN THE UNITED STATES OF AMERICA

10 9 8 7 6 5 4 3 2 1

CONTENTS

ON THE ROAD WITH FODOR'S

Every trip is a significant trip. Acutely aware of that fact, we've pulled out all stops in preparing *The South*. To guide you in putting together your South experience, we've created multiday itineraries and neighborhood walks. And to direct you to the places that are truly worth your time and money, we've rallied the team of endearingly picky know-it-alls we're pleased to call our writers. Having seen all corners of the South, they're real experts on the subjects they cover for us. If you knew them, you'd poll them for tips yourself.

About Our Writers

Born to a Creole-Acadian mother with an affinity for cooking, **Gene Bourg** maintains an acute interest in the unique cuisines of New Orleans. "Eating Out" columnist for the *Times-Picayune* from 1985 to 1994, he is currently a freelance food writer and host of *News You Can Eat*, a weekly program on New Orleans radio station WBYU. He adds his insight to our New Orleans dining reviews.

Karen Bryant, who updated the Mississippi chapter, was born and raised in South Mississippi. She lives on the Gulf Coast and is a freelance writer, editor, and marketing consultant. Her clients include magazines, newspapers, government entities, private businesses, and chambers of commerce.

Former Fodor's editor **Andrew Collins,** who updated and expanded the Smart Travel Tips A to Z section, writes a weekly syndicated column on gay travel for numerous newspapers as well as for the Web sites gay.com and planetout.com, and he's the travel columnist for *Fairfield County Magazine*, in Westport, Connecticut. He authored *Fodor's Gay Guide to the USA* and recently wrote the *Connecticut Handbook* for Avalon Travel Publishing; he is presently writing the *Rhode Island Handbook* and *CitySmart New Orleans* for the same publisher.

Hollis Gillespie, who updated and expanded the Georgia chapter, was born in Southern California but moved to Atlanta 11 years ago, and almost immediately swapped her Valley Girl accent for a Southern drawl. A prolific travel writer and foreign language interpreter, she also regularly pens humor pieces for *Atlanta Magazine* as well as the Atlanta-based Leader publications.

Mary Sue Lawrence, who added fresh insights to the South Carolina chapter, is a freelance writer and editor whose features on travel, entertainment, health, and business have appeared in national and British magazines. She is a South Carolina native and a proud descendant of Charlestonian General William Moultrie. She lives on Sullivan's Island near Charleston, and is a frequent contributor to Fodor's guides.

The Louisiana chapter was written and updated by the gregarious **Honey Naylor,** a Louisiana native who delights in exploring the bayous and byways and the treasures and trifles that make up her home state.

Alabama updater and new mother **Michelle Roberts** is a Mobile native and lifelong resident of the South. As editor of Mobile Bay Monthly and Coast magazines, she has written numerous features on food, travel, books, homes, and people. She also contributed to Fodor's *Road Guide USA*.

Sam Starnes—golfing aficionado, graduate of the University of Georgia, and a son of the South—wrote the Up-Close feature on the Robert Trent Jones golf trail in Alabama.

Lisa H. Towle, the author of the North Carolina chapter, remains fascinated by the diversity of her home state—a place she really grew to appreciate after living away from it for many years. When she's not exploring a scenic route, Lisa, a long-time journalist, writes for a number of national and regional publications or contributes to *Fodor's USA* and *The South's Best Bed & Breakfasts*.

Don't Forget to Write

Keeping a travel guide fresh and up-to-date is a big job. So we love your feedback—positive and negative—and follow up on all suggestions. Contact the South editor at editors@fodors.com or c/o Fodor's, 280 Park Avenue, 10th floor, New York, New York 10017. And have a wonderful trip!

Karen Cure

Karen Cure
Editorial Director

The South

Gulf of Mexico

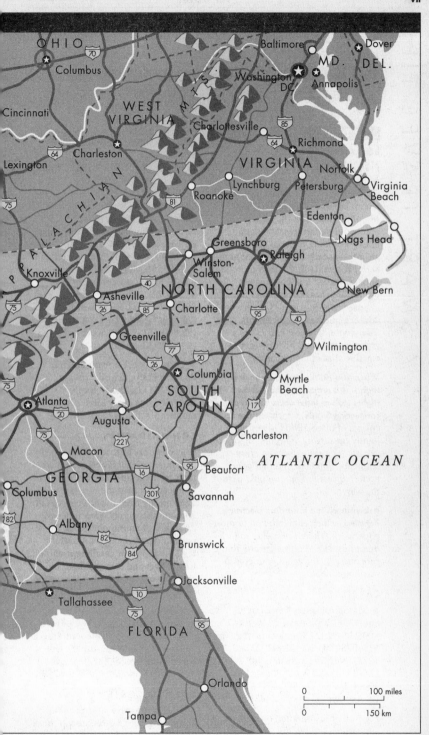

SMART TRAVEL TIPS A TO Z

Basic Information on Traveling in the South, Savvy Tips to Make Your Trip a Breeze, and Companies and Organizations to Contact

AIR TRAVEL

BOOKING YOUR FLIGHT

Price is just one factor to consider when booking a flight: frequency of service and even a carrier's safety record are often just as important. Major airlines offer the greatest number of departures. Smaller airlines—including regional and no-frills airlines—usually have a limited number of flights daily. On the other hand, so-called low-cost airlines usually are cheaper, and their fares impose fewer restrictions, such as advance-purchase requirements. Safety-wise, low-cost carriers as a group have a good history—about equal to that of major carriers.

When you book, **look for nonstop flights** and **remember that "direct" flights stop at least once.** Try to **avoid connecting flights,** which require a change of plane. Two airlines may jointly operate a connecting flight, so ask if your airline operates every segment—you may find that your preferred carrier flies you only part of the way.

Ask your airline if it offers electronic ticketing, which eliminates all or most paperwork. There's no ticket to pick up or misplace. You go directly to the gate and give the agent your confirmation number.

CARRIERS

➤ MAJOR AIRLINES: **American** (☎ 800/433–7300). **America West** (☎ 800/235–9292). **Continental** (☎ 800/525–0280). **Delta** (☎ 800/221–1212). **Northwest Airlines** (☎ 800/225–2525). **TWA** (☎ 800/221–2000). **United** (☎ 800/241–6522). **US Airways** (☎ 800/428–4322).

For further information on airports and airlines serving the South, see individual state chapters.

➤ SMALLER AIRLINES: **Air Canada** (☎ 800/776–3000). **AirTran** (☎ 770/994–8258 or 800/825–8538.) **American Eagle** (☎ 800/433–7300). **America West** (☎ 800/235–9292). **ASA/Delta Connection** (☎ 800/221–1212). **Atlantic Southeast** (☎ 800/221–1212 or 800/282–3424). **Co-mAir** (☎ 800/221–1212). **Continental Express** (☎ 800/525–0280). **Kiwi** (☎ 800/538–5494). **Markair** (☎ 800/521–9854). **Midway** (☎ 888/226–4392). **Midwest Express** (☎ 800/452–2022). **Northwest Airlink** (☎ 800/225–2525). **Southwest Airlines** (☎ 800/435–9792). **TWA Express** (☎ 800/221–2000). **Western Pacific** (☎ 800/930–3030).

➤ FROM THE U.K.: **American** (☎ 0345/789789), **British Airways** (☎ 0345/222111), and **Delta** (☎ 0800/414767) have direct service to a number of cities in the South.

CONSOLIDATORS

Consolidators buy tickets for scheduled international flights at reduced rates from the airlines, then sell them at prices that beat the best fare available directly from the airlines, usually without restrictions. Sometimes you can even get your money back if you need to return the ticket. Carefully read the fine print detailing penalties for changes and cancellations, and **confirm your consolidator reservation with the airline.**

➤ CONSOLIDATORS: **Cheap Tickets** (☎ 800/377–1000). **Up & Away Travel** (☎ 212/889–2345). **Discount Travel Network** (☎ 800/576–1600). **Unitravel** (☎ 800/325–2222). **World Travel Network** (☎ 800/409–6753).

CUTTING COSTS

The least expensive airfares to the South are priced for round-trip travel and usually must be purchased in advance. It's smart to **call a number of airlines, and when you are quoted**

a good price, book it on the spot—the same fare may not be available the next day. Airlines generally allow you to change your return date for a fee. If you don't use your ticket, you can apply the cost toward the purchase of a new ticket, again for a small charge. However, most low-fare tickets are nonrefundable. To get the lowest airfare, **check different routings.** Compare prices of flights to and from different airports if your destination or home city has more than one gateway. Also price off-peak flights.

When flying within the United States, **plan to stay over a Saturday night** and **travel during the middle of the week** to get the lowest fare. These low fares are usually priced for round-trip travel and are nonrefundable. You can, however, change your return date for a fee ($75 on most major airlines).

Travel agents, especially those who specialize in finding the lowest fares (☞ Discounts & Deals, *below*), can be especially helpful when booking a plane ticket. When you're quoted a price, **ask your agent if the price is likely to get any lower.** Good agents know the seasonal fluctuations of airfares and can usually anticipate a sale or fare war. However, waiting can be risky: the fare could go *up* as seats become scarce, and you may wait so long that your preferred flight sells out. A wait-and-see strategy works best if your plans are flexible.

CHECK-IN & BOARDING

Airlines routinely overbook planes, assuming that not everyone with a ticket will show up, but sometimes everyone does. When that happens, airlines ask for volunteers to give up their seats. In return, these volunteers usually get a certificate for a free flight and are rebooked on the next flight out. If there are not enough volunteers, the airline must choose who will be denied boarding. The first to get bumped are passengers who checked in late and those flying on discounted tickets, so **get to the gate and check in as early as possible,** especially during peak periods.

Always **bring a government-issued photo ID to the airport.** You may be asked to show it before you are allowed to check in.

FLYING TIMES

Flying time to Atlanta is 2½ hours from New York, 2 hours from Chicago, 4½ hours from Los Angeles, 2 hours from Dallas, and 9 hours from London. New Orleans is about 75 minutes southwest of Atlanta by plane, Jackson an hour west, Memphis 75 minutes northwest, Nashville an hour northwest, Knoxville an hour north, Charlotte an hour northeast, Raleigh 75 minutes northeast, Wilmington an hour and 45 minutes east, and Charleston, Hilton Head, and Savannah an hour east–southeast.

HOW TO COMPLAIN

If your baggage goes astray or your flight goes awry, complain right away. Most carriers require that you **file a claim immediately.**

➤ AIRLINE COMPLAINTS: U.S. Department of Transportation **Aviation Consumer Protection Division** (✉ C-75, Room 4107, Washington, DC 20590, ☎ 202/366–2220). **Federal Aviation Administration Consumer Hotline** (☎ 800/322–7873).

AIRPORTS

For information on airports serving the South, see the A to Z sections at the end of each regional section in the individual state chapters.

BIKE TRAVEL

Most of the South is great terrain for biking, in particular throughout South Louisiana, the Mississippi Delta, coastal Georgia, South Carolina, and North Carolina, where hills are few and the scenery remarkable. You'll find a number of extensive, in many cases marked, bike routes throughout North Carolina's Outer Banks, along southern Louisiana's Great River Road, around Savannah and Georgia's coastal islands, and throughout greater Charleston and coastal South Carolina's Low Country. There are dozens of local bike clubs throughout the South. To reach one of these groups, which generally welcome visitors and can provide detailed advice on local routes and rental

THE GOLD GUIDE / SMART TRAVEL TIPS

shops, contact the local tourist boards, many of which also distribute bike-trail maps.

BIKES IN FLIGHT

Most airlines will accommodate bikes as luggage, provided they are dismantled and put into a box. Call to see if your airline sells bike boxes (about $5; bike bags are at least $100), although you can often pick them up free at bike shops. International travelers can sometimes substitute a bike for a piece of checked luggage for free; otherwise, it will cost about $100. Domestic and Canadian airlines charge a $25–$50 fee.

BUS TRAVEL

Regional bus service, provided by Greyhound, is abundant throughout the South. It's a handy and affordable means of getting around; however, this style of travel prevents the sort of spontaneity and freedom to explore that you're afforded if traveling by car. Still, if it's a simple matter of getting from one city to another and you've got a bit of time on your hands, consider this option. Remember that buses sometimes make frequent stops, which may delay you but may also provide you the chance to see parts of the region you might not otherwise.

Within most large southern cities, it's possible to use municipal bus service to get around town, but relatively few nonlocals go this route—bus schedules and routes take a bit of learning, and many southern cities sprawl to a degree that sightseeing this way is impractical. *See* the A to Z sections within regional chapters for specific information on municipal buses.

➤ BUS INFORMATION: **Greyhound** (☎ 800/231–2222).

CUTTING COSTS

Greyhound offers the **Ameripass,** which allows unlimited travel in the United States within any 7-, 10-, 15-, 30-, 45-, or 60-day period ($169–$479, depending on length of the pass), and the similar International Ameripass (for non-U.S. residents only), which offers the same 7- to 60-day passes for $149–$429. Greyhound also has senior-citizen, children's, and student discounts.

FARES AND SCHEDULES

Approximate standard sample fares (based on 14-day advance purchase—prices can be 10% to 50% higher otherwise), times, and routes (note that times vary greatly depending on the number of stops): Atlanta to New Orleans, 9–11 hours, $40 one-way; Memphis to New Orleans, 9–10 hours, $37 one-way; Lafayette to Mobile, 5–8 hours, $55 one-way and Raleigh to Savannah, 6–9 hours, $70 one-way.

BUSINESS HOURS CAMERAS & PHOTOGRAPHY

EQUIPMENT PRECAUTIONS

Always **keep your film and tape out of the sun.** Carry an extra supply of batteries and **be prepared to turn on your camera or camcorder** to prove to airport security personnel that the device is real. Always **ask for hand inspection of film,** especially if your film is 800 speed or higher, as it can become cloudy after successive exposures to airport X-ray machines, and **keep videotapes away from metal detectors.**

TRAVEL PHOTOGRAPHY

➤ PHOTO HELP: **Kodak Information Center** (☎ 800/242–2424).

CAR RENTAL

Rates vary from city to city, generally being lowest in destinations with busy airports, where there's the greatest competition. Below is a range of actual sample rates, for both economy and luxury car rentals, quoted by the most popular agencies in three major southern cities (note that unlimited mileage is nearly always included):

In Atlanta daily rates range from about $32–$59 for an economy car to $65–$100 for a luxury car; weekly rates range from $170–$285 for economy to $290–$530 for luxury. Additionally in Atlanta there's a 7% sales tax, and at the airport location there's also a 10% "concession recoupment fee" and a 3% airport excise tax.

In Raleigh daily rates range from about $46–$65 for an economy car to

$78–$80 for a luxury car; weekly rates range from $209–$265 for economy to $345–$370 for luxury. Additionally, in Raleigh there's an 8% sales tax, a 5% local transportation tax, and at the airport location there's also the 10% "concession recoupment fee."

In New Orleans daily rates range from about $40–$53 for an economy car to $55–$86 for a luxury car; weekly rates range from $188–$265 for economy to $260–$390 for luxury. Additionally, in New Orleans there's an 8.75% sales tax, a 3% local transportation tax, and at the airport location there's also the 10% "concession recoupment fee."

Remember to **reserve a car well in advance of your expected arrival.**

➤ MAJOR AGENCIES: **Alamo** (☎ 800/327–9633; 020/8759–6200 in the U.K.). **Avis** (☎ 800/331–1212; 800/331–1084 in Canada; 02/9353–9000 in Australia). **Budget** (☎ 800/527–0700; 0144/227–6266 in the U.K.). **Dollar** (☎ 800/800–4000; 0124/622–0111 in the U.K., where it is known as Sixt). **Hertz** (☎ 800/654–3131; 800/263–0600 in Canada; 020/8897–2072 in the U.K.; 02/9669–2444 in Australia; 09/256–8690 in New Zealand). **National Car Rental** (☎ 800/227–7368; 0845/722–2525 in the U.K., where it is known as National Europe).

CUTTING COSTS

To get the best deal, **book through a travel agent who is willing to shop around.** When pricing cars, **ask about the location of the rental lot.** Some off-airport locations offer lower rates, and their lots are only minutes from the terminal via complimentary shuttle. Also ask whether certain frequent-flyer, AAA, corporate, or other such promotions are accepted and whether the rates might be lower the day before or after you had originally intended to travel. In some cases you'll find that the same agency offers a region's cheapest luxury car rates but priciest economy cars, or that the cheapest agency in one city may have high rates in another. It pays to check around. Think carefully about how much and where you'll be using the car before choosing among economy, compact, standard, luxury, or premium; it may be worth the extra few dollars per day for a more substantial vehicle if you're traveling long distances, driving up into the mountains or over rugged terrain, traveling with more than a couple of passengers, or using the car extensively.

Remember to ask about required deposits, cancellation penalties, and drop-off charges if you're planning to pick up the car in one city and leave it in another.

Also **ask your travel agent about a company's customer-service record.** How has the company responded to late plane arrivals and vehicle mishaps? Are there often lines at the rental counter? If you're traveling during a holiday period, does a confirmed reservation guarantee you a car?

INSURANCE

When driving a rented car, you are generally responsible for any damage to or loss of the vehicle. You also are liable for any property damage or personal injury that you may cause while driving. Before you rent, **see what coverage you already have** under the terms of your personal auto-insurance policy and credit cards.

For about $15 to $20 per day, rental companies sell protection known as a collision- or loss-damage waiver (CDW or LDW) that eliminates your liability for damage to the car; it's always optional and should never be automatically added to your bill.

In most states you don't need a CDW if you have personal auto insurance or other liability insurance. However, **make sure you have enough coverage to pay for the car.** If you do not have auto insurance or an umbrella policy that covers damage to third parties, purchasing liability insurance and a CDW or LDW is highly recommended.

REQUIREMENTS

In the South you must be 21 to rent a car, and rates may be higher if you're under 25. You'll pay extra for child seats (about $3 per day), which are compulsory for children under five, and for additional drivers (about $2 per day). Non-U.S. residents will need a reservation voucher, a passport, a driver's license, and a travel policy that covers each driver, in order to pick up a car.

SURCHARGES

Before you pick up a car in one city and leave it in another, **ask about drop-off charges or one-way service fees,** which can be substantial. Note, too, that some rental agencies charge extra if you return the car before the time specified in your contract. To avoid a hefty refueling fee, **fill the tank just before you turn in the car,** but be aware that gas stations near the rental outlet may overcharge.

CAR TRAVEL

A car is your most practical and economical means of traveling around the South, the only exception being a trip centered primarily in New Orleans, where you can get by with a combination of public transportation and cabs. In Atlanta a car works best because businesses and attractions tend to be far apart and mass-transit coverage spotty. Savannah, Charleston, Myrtle Beach, Nashville, Memphis, and Asheville can be explored fairly easily on foot or by using public transit and cabs, but a car is helpful to reach many of the most intriguing museums, parks, restaurants, and lodgings nearby. You really need a car to get around cities such as Birmingham, Mobile, Raleigh, Durham, Charlotte, and most others.

Although you'll make the best time traveling along the South's extensive network of interstate highways, keep in mind that U.S. and state highways offer some delightful scenery and the opportunity to stumble upon funky roadside diners, leafy state parks, and historic town squares. Although the South is rural, it's still densely populated, so you'll rarely drive for more than 20 or 30 mi—even on local roads—without passing roadside services, such as gas stations, restaurants, and ATM machines.

Among the most scenic highways in the South, consider the following: the **Natchez Trace,** from Natchez, Mississippi, to just south of Nashville, Tennessee; **U.S. 78** from Memphis, Tennessee, across northern Missis-

sippi and Alabama to near Augusta, Georgia; the **Great River Road** through southern Louisiana's Cajun Country; **U.S. 61** from New Orleans north through the Mississippi Delta to Memphis; **U.S. 441, 321, 25, 19, 74,** and **64** through the Smoky Mountains of eastern Tennessee and western North Carolina; **U.S. 17** from Brunswick, Georgia, along the coast through South Carolina and North Carolina; and the **Blue Ridge Parkway** from the eastern fringes of the Smoky Mountains through western North Carolina into Virginia.

Here are some common distances and approximate travel times between southern destinations: Atlanta to New Orleans is 475 mi and about 6½ hours; Nashville to Mobile is 450 mi and 6 hours; Memphis to Raleigh is 750 mi and 10 hours; Nags Head and the Outer Banks of North Carolina to Savannah is 515 mi and 7½ hours; Lake Charles (LA) to the North Carolina/Virginia border on I–95 is 1,150 mi and 15 hours; and Birmingham to Charleston is 465 mi and a little over six hours.

RULES OF THE ROAD

State lawmakers now set speed limits, even for federal interstate highways. Limits vary from state to state and from rural to urban areas, so **check posted speeds frequently.** The South is laced with busy interstate highways, where speed limits typically reach 65 mph, and gas is cheaper on average in these states than elsewhere in the country.

CHILDREN & TRAVEL

CHILDREN IN THE SOUTH

Most of the South is ideal for travel with kids. It's an enjoyable part of the country for family road trips, and it's also relatively affordable—you'll have no problem finding inexpensive kid-friendly hotels and family-style restaurants. Just keep in mind that a number of fine, antiques-filled B&Bs and inns punctuate the landscape, and these places are less suitable for kids—many flat-out refuse to accommodate children. Also, some of the quieter and more rural parts of the region—although exuding history—lack child-oriented attractions.

Favorite destinations for family vacations in the South include Cajun Country around Lafayette, the Gulf Coast from Mississippi to Alabama, the Atlantic seaboard from Georgia through the Carolinas (especially Myrtle Beach and the Outer Banks), Opryland and the country-music sites in Nashville, the outstanding zoo in Atlanta, the space and rocket center in Huntsville, Mud Island and the Civil Rights Museum in Memphis, and the many lively attractions strung throughout the Smoky Mountains from Chattanooga and Knoxville east to Asheville. You might guess that upscale historic cities like Charleston and Savannah cater predominantly to adults, but these towns also have plenty of museums and attractions geared toward children, as does New Orleans, although parts of the French Quarter are inappropriate—especially at night—for youth.

If you are renting a car, don't forget to **arrange for a car seat** when you reserve. Most hotels in the South allow children under a certain age to stay in their parents' room at no extra charge, but others charge them as extra adults; be sure to **ask about the cutoff age for children's discounts.**

FLYING

If your children are two or older, **ask about children's airfares.** As a general rule, infants under two not occupying a seat fly at greatly reduced fares or even for free.

In general the adult baggage allowance applies to children paying half or more of the adult fare.

Experts agree that it's a good idea to use safety seats aloft for children weighing less than 40 pounds. Airlines, however, can set their own policies: U.S. carriers allow FAA-approved models but usually require that you buy a ticket, even if your child would otherwise ride free, since the seats must be strapped into regular seats. Airline rules vary, so it's important to **check your airline's policy about using safety seats during takeoff and landing.** Safety seats cannot obstruct the movement of other passengers in the row, so get an appropriate seat assignment as early as possible.

When making your reservation, **request children's meals or a free-standing bassinet** if you need them; the latter is available only to those seated at the bulkhead, where there's enough legroom. Remember, however, that bulkhead seats may not have their own overhead bins, and there's no storage space in front of you—a major inconvenience.

GROUP TRAVEL

When planning to take your kids on a tour, look for companies that specialize in family travel.

➤ FAMILY-FRIENDLY TOUR OPERATORS: **Families Welcome!** (✉ 92 N. Main St., Ashland, OR 97520, ☎ 541/482–6121 or 800/326–0724, ℻ 541/482–0660).

CONSUMER PROTECTION

Whenever possible, **pay with a major credit card** so you can cancel payment or get reimbursed if there's a problem, provided that you can furnish documentation.

If you're doing business with a particular company for the first time, **contact your local Better Business Bureau and the attorney general's offices** in your state and the company's home state, as well. Have any complaints been filed?

Finally, if you're buying a package or tour, always **consider travel insurance** that includes default coverage (☞ Insurance, *below*).

➤ LOCAL BBBs: **Council of Better Business Bureaus** (✉ 4200 Wilson Blvd., Suite 800, Arlington, VA 22203, ☎ 703/276–0100, ℻ 703/525–8277).

DINING

Although certain ingredients and preparations are common in Southern cooking, the genre as a whole varies greatly not only from state to state but also from county to county. Nevertheless, in the South you'll often find restaurants serving black-eyed peas, catfish, chitlins (fried tripe), corn on the cob, crab claws, coleslaw, crawfish, fried chicken, hushpuppies, fried green tomatoes, grits, collared greens, chicken-fried steak, raw and fried shellfish (especially oysters and shrimp), and desserts infused with pecans, peaches, peanuts, caramelized bananas, or sweet potatoes.

More specific regional influences include similar but distinct Creole and Cajun cuisines of southern Louisiana, the soul food served in many African-American households, the coastal recipes of the Low Country in the Carolinas, and—of course—barbecue. However, the preparation of this latter delicacy differs tremendously depending on whether you're in the Mississippi Delta, central Tennessee, the pine flats of North Carolina, or some other part of the South. Depending on where you are, you might find it prepared with shredded pork in a tomato-vinegar-based sauce, or perhaps with a mustard-based sauce and chicken or beef. The South's myriad culinary disciplines intermingle and influence one another, but southern foodies are quite careful to recognize—and preserve—the localized distinctions among them.

A number of fast-food chain eateries are based in the South. These include the Krispy Kreme doughnut chain (Winston-Salem, North Carolina), Shoney's (Nashville, Tennessee), Cracker Barrel (Lebanon, Tennessee), Waffle House (Atlanta), Hardee's (Greenville, North Carolina), Popeye's (New Orleans), and Chick-fil-A (Atlanta). Indeed, Southerners take their fast food seriously, and you'll find that many branches of these chain restaurants offer not only simple, quick sustenance but also a colorful, aromatic, and more than likely fattening glimpse into regional identities.

DISABILITIES & ACCESSIBILITY

The South ranks on a par with the rest of America in its accessibility for persons with disabilities or special needs. A drawback is the abundance of historic accommodations, restaurants, and attractions with narrow staircases, doorways, and small rooms that fail to conform to American's with Disabilities Act's (ADA) guidelines. Increasingly, however, businesses throughout the South—especially those in densely populated areas—are changing to improve accessibility.

MAKING RESERVATIONS

When discussing accessibility with an operator or reservations agent, **ask hard questions.** Are there any stairs, inside *or* out? Are there grab bars next to the toilet *and* in the shower/tub? How wide is the doorway to the room? To the bathroom? For the most extensive facilities meeting the latest legal specifications, **opt for newer accommodations,** which are more likely to have been designed with access in mind. Older buildings or ships may have more limited facilities. Be sure to **discuss your needs before booking.**

➤ COMPLAINTS: **Disability Rights Section** (✉ U.S. Department of Justice, Civil Rights Division, ✉ Box 66738, Washington, DC 20035-6738, ☎ 202/514–0301; 800/514–0301; 202/514–0383 TTY; 800/514–0383 TTY, ℻ 202/307–1198) for general complaints. **Aviation Consumer Protection Division** (☞ Air Travel, *above*) for airline-related problems. **Civil Rights Office** (✉ U.S. Department of Transportation, Departmental Office of Civil Rights, S-30, ✉ 400 7th St. SW, Room 10215, Washington, DC, 20590, ☎ 202/366–4648, ℻ 202/366–9371) for problems with surface transportation.

TRAVEL AGENCIES & TOUR OPERATORS

As a whole, the travel industry has become more aware of the needs of travelers with disabilities. In the United States, the Americans with Disabilities Act requires that travel firms serve the needs of all travelers. Note, though, that some agencies and operators specialize in making travel arrangements for individuals and groups with disabilities.

➤ TRAVELERS WITH MOBILITY PROBLEMS: **Access Adventures** (✉ 206 Chestnut Ridge Rd., Rochester, NY 14624, ☎ 716/889–9096), run by a former physical-rehabilitation counselor. **Flying Wheels Travel** (✉ 143 W. Bridge St., Box 382, Owatonna, MN 55060, ☎ 507/451–5005 or 800/535–6790, ℻ 507/451–1685), a travel agency specializing in customized tours and itineraries world-wide.

➤ TRAVELERS WITH DEVELOPMENTAL DISABILITIES: **Sprout** (✉ 893 Amsterdam Ave., New York, NY 10025, ☎ 212/222–9575 or 888/222–9575, FAX 212/222–9768).

DISCOUNTS & DEALS

Be a smart shopper and **compare all your options** before making any choice. For high-price travel purchases, such as packages or tours, keep in mind that what you get is just as important as what you save.

CLUBS & COUPONS

Many companies sell discounts in the form of travel clubs and coupon books, but these cost money. You must use participating advertisers to get a deal.

➤ DISCOUNT CLUBS: **Entertainment Travel Editions** (✉ 2125 Butterfield Rd., Troy, MI 48084, ☎ 800/445–4137; $20–$51, depending on destination). **Great American Traveler** (✉ Box 27965, Salt Lake City, UT 84127, ☎ 801/974–3033 or 800/548–2812); $49.95 per year. **Moment's Notice Discount Travel Club** (✉ 7301 New Utrecht Ave., Brooklyn, NY 11204, ☎ 718/234–6295); $25 per year, single or family. **Privilege Card International** (✉ 237 E. Front St., Youngstown, OH 44503, ☎ 330/746–5211 or 800/236–9732); $74.95 per year. **Sears's Mature Outlook** (✉ Box 9390, Des Moines, IA 50306, ☎ 800/336–6330); $19.95 per year. **Travelers Advantage** (✉ CUC Travel Service, ✉ 3033 S. Parker Rd., Suite 1000, Aurora, CO 80014, ☎ 800/548–1116 or 800/648–4037); $59.95 per year, single or family. **Worldwide Discount Travel Club** (✉ 1674 Meridian Ave., Miami Beach, FL 33139, ☎ 305/534–2082); $50 per year family, $40 single.

CREDIT-CARD BENEFITS

When you use your credit card to make travel purchases, you may get free travel-accident insurance, collision-damage insurance, and medical or legal assistance, depending on the card and the bank that issued it.

American Express, MasterCard, and Visa provide one or more of these services, so **get a copy of your credit card's travel-benefits policy.** If you are a member of an auto club, always **ask hotel and car-rental reservations agents about auto-club discounts.** Some clubs offer additional discounts on tours, cruises, and admission to attractions.

DISCOUNT RESERVATIONS

To save money, **look into discount-reservations services** with toll-free numbers, which use their buying power to get a better price on hotels, airline tickets, even car rentals. When booking a room, always **call the hotel's local toll-free number** (if one is available) rather than the central reservations number—you'll often get a better price. Always ask about special packages or corporate rates.

➤ AIRLINE TICKETS: **800/FLY–4–LESS. 800/FLY–ASAP.**

➤ HOTEL ROOMS: **Central Reservation Service (CRS;** ☎ 800/548–3311). **Quickbook** (☎ 800/789–9887). **Room Finders USA** (☎ 800/473–7829). **RMC Travel** (☎ 800/245–5738).

PACKAGE DEALS

Packages and guided tours can save you money, but don't confuse the two. When you buy a package, your travel remains independent, just as though you had planned and booked the trip yourself. Fly/drive packages, which combine airfare and car rental, are often a good deal.

EMERGENCIES

In many areas of the South, **dial 911 for police, fire, and ambulance.** See the A to Z sections that follow each regional section in the individual state chapters for more information.

GAY & LESBIAN TRAVEL

Attitudes about gays and lesbians tend toward disapproving, if intolerant, throughout much of the South, especially outside urban areas. On the whole, however, despite a reputation for conservative-minded residents, this part of the country is not any more hostile or dangerous for lesbians and gays—traveling solo or together—than the rest of the United States. It's prudent, however, to show an awareness of your surroundings and exercise a degree of discretion whenever you're venturing into unfamiliar territory.

As for lesbian and gay resources, there are several major newspapers serving the community throughout the South, including *Southern Voice,* in Atlanta, and *Impact* and *Ambush,* in New Orleans, plus a host of smaller local papers in Memphis, Nashville, Birmingham, and in the Carolinas. The gay nightlife and social scenes in New Orleans and Atlanta rival those of virtually any comparably sized cities in North America, and you'll also find thriving gay communities of varying sizes in Savannah, Charlotte, Charleston, Raleigh/Durham, Nashville, Memphis, Birmingham, and Columbia. With a much lower profile than most cities with gay populations, Asheville is something of a well-kept secret, with sizable women's and gay communities and a high number of gay-friendly businesses and accommodations.

➤ RESOURCES: *Fodor's Gay Guide to the USA, 2nd edition,* by Andrew Collins, provides information on travel in Atlanta, Charleston, Memphis, Nashville, New Orleans, and Savannah (available in bookstores, or from Fodor's at ☎ 800/533–6478; $20 plus shipping). Also, the Web site www.gay.com offers a number of valuable resources and travel articles geared toward lesbian and gay travelers.

➤ GAY- AND LESBIAN-FRIENDLY TRAVEL AGENCIES: **Corniche Travel** (✉ 8721 Sunset Blvd., Suite 200, West Hollywood, CA 90069, ☎ 310/854–6000 or 800/429–8747, FAX 310/659–7441). **Islanders Kennedy Travel** (✉ 183 W. 10th St., New York, NY 10014, ☎ 212/242–3222 or 800/988–1181, FAX 212/929–8530). **Now Voyager** (✉ 4406 18th St., San Francisco, CA 94114, ☎ 415/626–1169 or 800/255–6951, FAX 415/626–8626). **Yellowbrick Road** (✉ 1500 W. Balmoral Ave., Chicago, IL 60640, ☎ 773/561–1800 or 800/642–2488, FAX 773/561–4497). **Skylink Travel and Tour**

(✉ 3577 Moorland Ave., Santa Rosa, CA 95407, ☎ 707/585–8355 or 800/225–5759, FAX 707/584–5637), serving lesbian travelers.

HEALTH

MEDICAL PLANS

No one plans to get sick while traveling, but it happens, so **consider signing up with a medical-assistance company.** Members get doctor referrals, emergency evacuation or repatriation, 24-hour telephone hot lines for medical consultation, cash for emergencies, and other personal and legal assistance. Coverage varies by plan, so **review the benefits of each carefully.**

➤ MEDICAL-ASSISTANCE COMPANIES: **International SOS Assistance** (✉ 8 Neshaminy Interplex, Suite 207, Trevose, PA 19053, ☎ 215/245–4707 or 800/523–6586, FAX 215/244–9617; ✉ 12 Chemin Riantbosson, 1217 Meyrin 1, Geneva, Switzerland, ☎ 4122/785–6464, FAX 4122/785–6424; ✉ 10 Anson Rd., 14–07/08 International Plaza, Singapore, 079903, ☎ 65/226–3936, FAX 65/226–3937).

PRECAUTIONS

There are relatively few health issues specific to the South. Hospitals are as common and medical care as proficient as elsewhere in the United States.

PESTS AND OTHER HAZARDS

In coastal regions, especially along the Atlantic seaboard, swimmers and boaters should be respectful of the at-times powerful surf. Adhere to posted riptide warnings, and to be perfectly safe, stick with areas that have lifeguards. Summers can be exceptionally hot and humid throughout much of the South—wear light-color, loose-fitting, practical clothing during the summer months, drink plenty of fluids (and bring along bottled water on hikes, boat trips, and bike rides), and stay indoors during the hottest times of the day.

Mosquitoes, seasonal black flies, and just about every other flitting and annoying insect known to North America proliferates in the humid and often lush Southern states. Exercise common precautions and wear lotions or sprays that keep away such pests.

Although you might associate Lyme disease with New England, where it was first well documented, this relatively common and potentially dangerous disease strikes frequently in the South, too. Lyme disease is spread by bites from infinitesimal deer ticks. Symptoms, unfortunately, vary considerably from victim to victim, and one common problem is delayed diagnosis—the longer you go without treating this problem, the more severe its effects.

Most victims show a red-ring-shape rash around the bite from the deer tick, somewhat resembling a little bull's eye and appearing from a week to many weeks after the incident. Flulike symptoms often follow—fever, achy joints, swelling, and if left untreated for more than a couple months, chronic arthritis may set in.

Unfortunately, testing for Lyme disease is a sketchy business at best, as no definitive method has yet been developed. Doctors typically rely on a series of blood tests and even more often on observation of various symptoms.

When spending time in areas **where tick infestation is a problem, wear long-sleeve clothing** and slacks, tuck your pant legs into your boots and/or socks, **apply tick and insect repellent generously,** and check yourself carefully for signs of ticks or bites. It's a good idea to don light-color clothing, as you'll have an easier time sighting ticks, which are dark. Remember that the more commonly found wood ticks do not carry the disease, and that deer ticks are extremely small—about the size of a pinhead.

HOLIDAYS

Major national holidays include: New Year's Day (Jan. 1); Martin Luther King Jr. Day (third Mon. in Jan.); President's Day (third Mon. in Feb.); Memorial Day (last Mon. in May); Independence Day (July 4); Labor Day (first Mon. in Sept.); Thanksgiving Day (fourth Thurs. in Nov.); Christmas Eve and Day (Dec. 24–25); and New Year's Eve (Dec. 31).

INSURANCE

Travel insurance is the best way to **protect yourself against financial loss.**

The most useful plan is a comprehensive policy that includes coverage for trip cancellation and interruption, default, trip delay, and medical expenses (with a waiver for preexisting conditions).

Without insurance, you will lose all or most of your money if you cancel your trip, regardless of the reason. Default insurance covers you if your tour operator, airline, or cruise line goes out of business. Trip-delay covers unforeseen expenses that you may incur due to bad weather or mechanical delays. It's important to **compare the fine print regarding trip-delay coverage** when comparing policies.

Always **buy travel insurance directly from the insurance company;** if you buy it from a cruise line, airline, or tour operator that goes out of business, you probably will not be covered for the agency or operator's default, a major risk. Before you make any purchase, **review your existing health and home-owner's policies** to find out whether they cover expenses incurred while traveling.

➤ TRAVEL INSURERS: In the U.S., Access America (⌧ 6600 W. Broad St., Richmond, VA 23230, ☎ 804/285–3300 or 800/284–8300). **Travel Guard International** (⌧ 1145 Clark St., Stevens Point, WI 54481, ☎ 715/345–0505 or 800/826–1300). In Canada, **Mutual of Omaha** (⌧ Travel Division, ⌧ 500 University Ave., Toronto, Ontario M5G 1V8, ☎ 416/598–4083; 800/268–8825 in Canada).

FOR INTERNATIONAL TRAVELERS

CURRENCY

The dollar is the basic unit of U.S. currency. It has 100 cents. Coins include the copper penny (1¢); the silvery nickel (5¢), dime (10¢), quarter (25¢), and half-dollar (50¢); and the golden $1 coin, replacing a now-rare silver dollar. Paper bills are in denominations of $1, $5, $10, $20, $50, and $100, all green and identical in size; designs vary. The exchange rate at press time was US$1.45 per British pound, US$.68 per Canadian dollar, US$.58 per Australian dollar, and US$.43 per New Zealand dollar.

CAR TRAVEL

In the South gasoline costs anywhere from $1.35–$1.79 a gallon. Stations are plentiful. Most stay open late (24 hours along large highways and in big cities), except in rural areas, where Sunday hours are limited and where you may drive long stretches without a refueling opportunity. Highways are well paved. Interstate highways—limited-access multilane highways whose numbers are prefixed by "I–"—are the fastest routes. Interstates with three-digit numbers encircle urban areas, which may have other limited-access expressways, freeways, and parkways as well. Tolls may be levied on limited-access highways. So-called U.S. highways and state highways are not necessarily limited-access but may have several lanes.

Along larger highways roadside stops with rest rooms, fast-food restaurants, and sundries stores are well spaced. State police and tow trucks patrol major highways and lend assistance. If your car breaks down on an interstate, pull onto the shoulder and wait for help, or have your passengers wait while you walk to an emergency phone. If you carry a cell phone, dial *55, noting your location on the small green roadside mileage markers.

Driving in the United States is on the right. Do **obey speed limits** posted along roads and highways. Watch for lower limits in small towns and on back roads. Most states require front-seat passengers to wear seat belts. Always **strap children under age 3 into approved child-safety seats.** *See* individual state chapter's A to Z sections for specific information.

Book stores, gas stations, convenience stores, and rest stops sell maps (about $3) and multiregion road atlases (about $10).

CUSTOMS & DUTIES

➤ IN AUSTRALIA: Australia residents who are 18 or older may bring back $A400 worth of souvenirs and gifts (including jewelry), 250 cigarettes or 250 grams of tobacco, and 1,125 milliliters of alcohol (including wine, beer, and spirits). Residents under 18 may bring back $A200 worth of goods. **Australian Customs Service** (Regional Director, ✉ Box 8, Sydney, New South Wales 2001, ☎ 02/9213–2000, FAX 02/9213–4000).

➤ IN CANADA: Canadian residents who have been out of Canada for at least seven days may bring in C$500 worth of goods duty-free. If you've been away less than seven days but more than 48 hours, the duty-free allowance drops to C$200; if your trip lasts 24–48 hours, the allowance is C$50. You may not pool allowances with family members. Goods claimed under the C$500 exemption may follow you by mail; those claimed under the lesser exemptions must accompany you. Alcohol and tobacco products may be included in the seven-day and 48-hour exemptions but not in the 24-hour exemption. If you meet the age requirements of the province or territory through which you reenter Canada, you may bring in, duty-free, 1.14 liters (40 imperial ounces) of wine or liquor *or* 24 12-ounce cans or bottles of beer or ale. If you are 16 or older, you may bring in, duty-free, 200 cigarettes and 50 cigars.

You may send an unlimited number of gifts worth up to C$60 each duty-free to Canada. Label the package UNSOLICITED GIFT—VALUE UNDER $60. Alcohol and tobacco are excluded. **Revenue Canada** (✉ 2265 St. Laurent Blvd. S, Ottawa, Ontario K1G 4K3, ☎ 613/993–0534; 800/461–9999 in Canada).

➤ IN NEW ZEALAND: Although greeted with a *Haere Mai* (Welcome to New Zealand), homeward-bound residents with goods to declare must present themselves for inspection. If you're 17 or older, you may bring back $700 worth of souvenirs and gifts. Your duty-free allowance also includes 4.5 liters of wine or beer; one 1,125-milliliter bottle of spirits; and either 200 cigarettes, 250 grams of tobacco, 50 cigars, or a combo of all three up to 250 grams. **New Zealand Customs** (✉ Custom House, ✉ 50 Anzac Ave., Box 29, Auckland, ☎ 09/

359–6655 or 09/309–2978, ☎ 09/
359–6655 or 09/309–2978).

➤ IN THE U.K.: From countries outside the EU you may import, duty-
free, 200 cigarettes or 50 cigars; 1
liter of spirits or 2 liters of fortified or
sparkling wine or liqueurs; 2 liters of
still table wine; 60 milliliters of perfume; 250 milliliters of toilet water;
plus £136 worth of other goods,
including gifts and souvenirs. **HM
Customs and Excise** (✉ Dorset
House, ✉ Stamford St., London SE1
9NG, ☎ 0171/202–4227).

ELECTRICITY

The U.S. standard is AC, 110 volts/60
cycles. Plugs have two flat pins set
parallel to each another.

INSURANCE

Britons and Australians need extra
medical coverage when traveling
overseas.

➤ INSURANCE INFORMATION: **Association of British Insurers** (✉ 51–55
Gresham St., London EC2V 7HQ, ☎
0171/600–3333, FAX 0171/696–8999).
Insurance Council of Australia (☎
03/9614–1077, FAX 03/9614–7924).

MAIL & SHIPPING

You can buy stamps and aerograms
and send letters and parcels in post
offices. Stamp-dispensing machines can
occasionally be found in airports, bus
and train stations, office buildings,
drugstores, and the like. You can also
deposit mail in the stout, dark-blue steel
bins at strategic locations everywhere
and in the mail chutes of large buildings; pickup schedules are posted.

For mail sent within the United
States, you need a 33¢ stamp for first-
class letters weighing up to 1 ounce
(22¢ for each additional ounce) and
20¢ for domestic postcards. For
overseas mail you pay 60¢ for ½-
ounce airmail letters, 50¢ for airmail
postcards, and 35¢ for surface-rate
postcards. For Canada you need a
52¢ stamp for a 1-ounce letter and
40¢ for a postcard. For 50¢ you can
buy an aerogram—a single sheet of
lightweight blue paper that folds into
its own envelope and is pre-stamped
for overseas airmail.

To receive mail on the road, have it
sent care of General Delivery at your
destination's main post office (use the
correct five-digit zip code). You must
pick up mail in person within 30 days
and show a driver's license or passport.

PASSPORTS & VISAS

Visitor visas are not necessary for
Canadian citizens or for citizens of
Australia, New Zealand, and the
United Kingdom staying fewer than
90 days.

➤ AUSTRALIAN CITIZENS: **Australian
Passport Office** (☎ 131–232). The
U.S. Office of Australia Affairs (✉
MLC Centre, 19–29 Martin Pl., 59th
floor, Sydney NSW 2000).

➤ CANADIAN CITIZENS: **Passport
Office** (☎ 819/994–3500 or 800/
567–6868).

➤ NEW ZEALAND CITIZENS: **New
Zealand Passport Office** (☎ 04/494–
0700 for application procedures;
0800/225–050 in New Zealand for
application-status updates). **U.S.
Office of New Zealand Affairs** (✉ 29
Fitzherbert Terr., Thorndon, Welling-
ton).

➤ U.K. CITIZENS: **London Passport
Office** (☎ 0990/210–410) for application procedures and emergency
passports. **U.S. Embassy Visa Information Line** (☎ 01891/200–290).
U.S. Embassy Visa Branch (✉ 5
Upper Grosvenor Sq., London W1A
1AE); send a self-addressed, stamped
envelope. **U.S. Consulate General** (✉
Queen's House, Queen St., Belfast
BT1 6EO).

TELEPHONES

All U.S. telephone numbers consist of
a three-digit area code and a seven-
digit local number. Within most local
calling areas, dial only the seven-digit
number. Within the same area code,
dial "1" first. To call between area-
code regions, dial "1," then all 10
digits; the same goes for calls to
numbers prefixed by "800," "888,"
and "877"—which are all toll-free.
For calls to numbers preceded by
"900" you must pay—usually dearly.

For international calls dial "011"
followed by the country code and the
local number. For help dial "0" and

ask for an overseas operator. The country code is 61 for Australia, 64 for New Zealand, 44 for the United Kingdom. Calling Canada is the same as calling within the United States. Most local phone books list country codes and U.S. area codes. The country code for the United States is 1.

For operator assistance dial "0." To obtain someone's phone number, call directory assistance, 555–1212 or occasionally 411 (free at public phones). To have the person you're calling foot the bill, phone collect; dial "0" instead of "1" before the 10-digit number.

At pay phones instructions are usually posted. Usually you insert coins in a slot (25¢–35¢ for local calls) and wait for a steady tone before dialing. When you call long distance, the operator will tell you how much to insert; prepaid phone cards, widely available in various denominations, are easier. Call the number on the back, punch in the card's personal identification number when prompted, then dial your number.

LODGING

With the exception of Atlanta, New Orleans, Savannah, and Charleston, most lodging rates in the South fall below the national average. All major chains are well represented in this part of the country, both in cities and suburbs, and interstates are lined with inexpensive to moderate chains. It's not uncommon to find clean but extremely basic discount chains offering double rooms for as little as $20 to $30 nightly along the busiest highways.

In cities and some large towns you might want to forego the usual cookie-cutter modern hotel in favor of a historic property—there are dozens of fine old hotels throughout the South, many of them fully restored and quite a few offering better rates than chain properties that may have comparable amenities but nowhere near the ambience.

Rates can vary a great deal seasonally. Gulf and Atlantic coastal regions as well as the Smoky Mountains tend to have significantly higher rates in summer, while New Orleans peaks in

fall and spring (especially during Mardi Gras). Many Southern cities, including New Orleans, drop their rates a bit during the extremely hot summer months, when vacationers are more likely to flock to the mountains or the sea.

APARTMENT & VILLA RENTALS

If you want a home base that's roomy enough for a family and comes with cooking facilities, **consider a furnished rental.** These can save you money, especially if you're traveling with a large group of people. Home-exchange directories list rentals (often second homes owned by prospective house swappers), and some services search for a house or apartment for you (even a castle if that's your fancy) and handle the paperwork. Some send an illustrated catalog; others send photographs only of specific properties, sometimes at a charge. Up-front registration fees may apply.

Property Rentals International (⊠ 1008 Mansfield Crossing Rd., Richmond, VA 23236, ☎ 804/378–6054 or 800/220–3332, ℻ 804/379–2073). **Rent-a-Home International** (⊠ 7200 34th Ave. NW, Seattle, WA 98117, ☎ 206/789–9377 or 800/488–7368, ℻ 206/789–9379). **Hideaways International** (⊠ 767 Islington St., Portsmouth, NH 03801, ☎ 603/430–4433 or 800/843–4433, ℻ 603/430–4444; membership $99) is a club for travelers who arrange rentals among themselves.

B&BS AND INNS

Historic bed-and-breakfasts and inns are found in just about every region in the South, including in quite a few former plantation houses and lavish Southern estates. In many rural or less touristy areas, B&Bs offer an affordable and homey alternative to chain properties, but in tourism-dependent destinations you can expect to pay about the same or more for a historic inn as for a full-service hotel. Many of the South's finest restaurants are also found in country inns. Although many B&Bs and smaller establishments offer a low-key, homey experience without TVs or numerous amenities, the scene has changed greatly in recent years, especially in cities and upscale resort areas, where many such properties now attempt to cater to business and luxury leisure travelers with in-room data ports, voice mail, whirlpool tubs, and VCRs. In keeping with the South's fondness for filling meals, quite a few inns and B&Bs serve substantial full breakfasts—the kind that may keep your appetite in check for the better part of the day.

CAMPING

The South is popular both for RVing and tent camping, with facilities found throughout the region, especially in state and national parks, and extensively throughout the Atlantic and Gulf coasts.

HOME EXCHANGES

If you would like to exchange your home for someone else's, **join a home-exchange organization,** which will send you its updated listings of available exchanges for a year and will include your own listing in at least one of them. It's up to you to make specific arrangements.

➤ EXCHANGE CLUBS: **HomeLink International** (✉ Box 650, Key West, FL 33041, ☎ 305/294–7766 or 800/638–3841, FAX 305/294–1148; $83 per year).

HOSTELS

No matter what your age, you can **save on lodging costs by staying at hostels.** In some 5,000 locations in more than 70 countries around the world, Hostelling International (HI), the umbrella group for a number of national youth hostel associations, offers beds in single-sex, dorm-style beds and, at many hostels, "couples" rooms and family accommodations. Membership in any HI national hostel association, open to travelers of all ages, allows you to stay in HI-affiliated hostels at member rates (one-year membership is about $25 for adults; hostels run about $10–$25 per night). Members also have priority if the hostel is full; they're also eligible for discounts around the world, even on rail and bus travel in some countries.

➤ HOSTEL ORGANIZATIONS: **Hostelling International–American Youth Hostels** (✉ 733 15th St. NW, Suite 840, Washington, DC 20005, ☎ 202/783–

6161, FAX 202/783–6171). **Hostelling International–Canada** (✉ 400–205 Catherine St., Ottawa, Ontario K2P 1C3, ☎ 613/237–7884, FAX 613/237–7868). **Youth Hostel Association of England and Wales** (✉ Trevelyan House, ✉ 8 St. Stephen's Hill, Hertfordshire, Hertfordshire AL1 2DY, ☎ 01727/855215 or 01727/845047, FAX 01727/844126); membership in the U.S. $25, in Canada C$26.75, in the U.K. £9.30).

HOTELS

Most hotels will hold your reservation until 6 PM; **call ahead if you plan to arrive late.** Hotels will be more willing to hold a late reservation if you reserve with a credit-card number.

➤ TOLL-FREE NUMBERS: **Adam's Mark** (☎ 800/444–2326). **Best Western** (☎ 800/528–1234). **Choice** (☎ 800/221–2222). **Clarion** (☎ 800/252–7466). **Comfort** (☎ 800/228–5150). **Days Inn** (☎ 800/325–2525). **Doubletree and Red Lion Hotels** (☎ 800/528–0444). **Embassy Suites** (☎ 800/362–2779). **Fairfield Inn** (☎ 800/228–2800). **Forte** (☎ 800/225–5843). **Four Seasons** (☎ 800/332–3442). **Hilton** (☎ 800/445–8667). **Holiday Inn** (☎ 800/465–4329). **Howard Johnson** (☎ 800/654–4656). **Hyatt Hotels & Resorts** (☎ 800/233–1234). **Inter-Continental** (☎ 800/327–0200). **La Quinta** (☎ 800/531–5900). **Marriott** (☎ 800/228–9290). **Le Meridien** (☎ 800/543–4300). **Nikko Hotels International** (☎ 800/645–5687). **Omni** (☎ 800/843–6664). **Quality Inn** (☎ 800/228–5151). **Radisson** (☎ 800/333–3333). **Ramada** (☎ 800/228–2828). **Renaissance Hotels & Resorts** (☎ 800/468–3571). **Ritz-Carlton** (☎ 800/241–3333). **ITT Sheraton** (☎ 800/325–3535). **Sleep Inn** (☎ 800/221–2222). **Westin Hotels & Resorts** (☎ 800/228–3000). **Wyndham Hotels & Resorts** (☎ 800/822–4200).

MOTELS

➤ TOLL-FREE NUMBERS: **Budget Hosts Inns** (☎ 800/283–4678). **Econo Lodge** (☎ 800/553–2666). **Friendship Inns** (☎ 800/453–4511). **Motel 6** (☎ 800/466–8356). **Rodeway** (☎ 800/228–2000). **Super 8** (☎ 800/848–8888).

THE GOLD GUIDE / SMART TRAVEL TIPS

MEDIA

There's no major regional newspaper that serves the South, but the *Atlanta Journal and Constitution* and New Orleans' *Times-Picayune* rank among the most influential dailies in the region; just about every city with a population of greater than 40,000 or 50,000 also publishes its own daily paper. Most major cities have very good alternative newsweeklies with useful Web sites and copious information on area dining, arts, and sightseeing—these are usually free and found in restaurants, coffeehouses, bookstores, tourism offices, hotel lobbies, and some nightclubs. Of particular note is Atlanta's *Creative Loafing,* which has separate editions for a number of additional southern cities and regions, including Gwinnett County, GA; Savannah, GA; Birmingham, AL; Charlotte, NC; and Greenville, SC. Its Web site (www.cln.com) has links to each of these editions, as well as to other alternative newsweeklies throughout the south.

Monthly *Southern Living* magazine gives a nice sense of travel, food, and lifestyle issues relevant to the region. And local lifestyles magazines—including *Atlanta, Louisiana Life, New Orleans, Charlotte's Best,* and *Memphis*—offer colorful stories and dining and entertainment coverage.

All the major television and radio networks are well represented throughout the South, and Ted Turner's omnipresent CNN empire is based in Atlanta.

MONEY

As with most of America, credit and debit cards are accepted at the vast majority of shops, restaurants, and accommodations in the South. Common exceptions include small, independent stores and also B&Bs in more rural areas. Banks—as well as convenience stores, groceries, and even nightclubs—with ATMs are easy to find in just about every community.

The cost of living and traveling throughout most of the South is either slightly lower or comparable to that of most of America and is significantly cheaper than in many urban areas such as metro San Francisco, New York, and Chicago. Although the cost of living remains fairly low in most parts of the South, travel-related costs (such as dining, lodging, museums, and transportation) have become increasingly steep in Nashville, New Orleans, and Atlanta over the years and can also be dear in resort communities throughout Georgia and the Carolinas.

CREDIT & DEBIT CARDS

Should you use a credit card or a debit card when traveling? Both have benefits. A credit card allows you to delay payment and gives you certain rights as a consumer (☞ Consumer Protection, *above*). A debit card, also known as a check card, deducts funds from your checking account and helps you stay within your budget.

Otherwise, the two types of plastic are virtually the same. Both will get you cash advances at ATMs worldwide if your card is properly programmed with your personal identification number (PIN).

➤ ATM LOCATIONS: **Cirrus** (☎ 800/424-7787). **Plus** (☎ 800/843-7587) for locations in the U.S. and Canada, or visit your local bank.

TRAVELER'S CHECKS

Do you need traveler's checks? It depends on where you're headed. If you're going to rural areas and small towns, go with cash; traveler's checks are best used in cities. Lost or stolen checks can usually be replaced within 24 hours. To ensure a speedy refund, buy your own traveler's checks—don't let someone else pay for them: irregularities like this can cause delays. The person who bought the checks should make the call to request a refund.

NATIONAL AND STATE PARKS

National and state parks abound in the South and offer a broad range of visitor facilities, including campgrounds, picnic grounds, hiking trails, boating, and ranger programs. State forests are usually somewhat less developed. For more information on any of these, contact the state tourism offices or parks departments (☞

Contacts and Resources, at the end of each state chapter).

NATIONAL PARKS OF THE SOUTH

This part of the country contains a number of well-visited national parks, monument, seashores, and forests. Probably the most famous is the swath of the Appalachians that comprises the 800-acre Great Smoky Mountains National Park—the park straddles the eastern Tennessee and western North Carolina borders and contains some 16 peaks higher than 6,000 ft. Hiking, camping, and boating are among the park visitors' favorite activities.

At the other extreme, at least vertically speaking, are the several national parks that lie along the Atlantic coastline, as well as the Gulf Islands National Seashore, which takes in several islands off the coast of Mississippi (as well as coastal points near Pensacola Florida). These three islands are accessible only by boat charter. In coastal Alabama birdwatchers flock to Bon Secour National Wildlife Refuge; the same is true at Louisiana's Sabine National Wildlife Refuge. The top Atlantic shore parks are Pea Island National Wildlife Refuge and Cape Hatteras and Cape Lookout national seashores, in North Carolina; Cumberland Island National Seashore, Fort Pulaski and Fort Frederica National Monuments, and Okefenokee National Wildlife Refuge, in Georgia; and Fort Sumter National Monument, in South Carolina.

NATIONAL PARK PASSES

Look into discount passes to **save money on park entrance fees.** The Golden Eagle Pass ($50) gets you and your companions free admission to all parks for one year (camping and parking are extra). Both the Golden Age Passport ($10), for those 62 and older, and the Golden Access Passport (free), for travelers with disabilities, entitle holders to free entry to all national parks, plus 50% off fees for the use of many park facilities and services. You must show proof of age and of U.S. citizenship or permanent residency (such as a U.S. passport, driver's license, or birth certificate) and, if requesting Golden Access, proof of disability. All three passes are available at all national park entrances where entrance fees are charged. Golden Eagle and Golden Access passes are available by mail.

➤ PASSES BY MAIL: **National Park Service** (✉ National Capitol Area Office, ✉ 1100 Ohio Dr. SW, Washington, DC 20242).

OUTDOORS AND SPORTS

With daytime temperatures rarely dipping below freezing and a plethora of waterways, mountains, forests, and swamps, the South makes for an ideal destination among outdoors enthusiasts. Fans of pro and college sports will also find the South rife with live athletic events and Southerners to be among the most passionate and knowledgeable of sports enthusiasts.

PARTICIPANT SPORTS AND RECREATION

It's tough to come up with an outdoor activity that isn't celebrated somewhere in this part of the country, but fishing, golf, and tennis lead in popularity among most vacationers. These pastimes are widespread and covered with detail within specific state chapters of this book, but bear in mind a few key destinations for certain sporting endeavors: **Golfers** will find an entire community of world-class courses in the Pinehurst region of North Carolina, the Hilton Head and Myrtle Beach regions of South Carolina, and the coastal islands off Georgia. These areas also have plenty to offer in the way of **tennis.** In the inland Appalachian regions, from the Carolinas to Tennessee, you'll find many excellent mountain courses.

Fishing diehards find plenty of freshwater action in every state in the South, with stocked lakes and rivers at many state and municipal parks. Deep-sea and surf fishing prevail (including crabbing and shrimping) all along the Atlantic seaboard and the Gulf Coast; you'll find that charter- and guided-fishing operators abound in these parts.

Other activities with a strong following in the South include bicycling (☞ Bike Travel, *above*), boating and rafting, bowling, camping and hiking (☞ National and State Parks, *above*), hang-gliding, and hunting.

SPECTATOR SPORTS

Several Southern cities have major pro sports teams. In **baseball** check out the Atlanta Braves; **basketball** fans cheer on the Atlanta Hawks and Charlotte Hornets; for **football** there are the Atlanta Falcons, Carolina Panthers, New Orleans Saints, and Tennessee Titans; and **hockey** fans watch the Atlanta Thrashers and Carolina Hurricanes. Just about every Southern city has at least one minor-league sports franchise, including baseball, and these are among the most enjoyable teams to watch. College sports are, in some cases, equally or even more popular than pro events, with basketball and football especially well regarded in the South. Among the most popular **college basketball** programs are those of Duke (North Carolina), LSU (Louisiana), North Carolina, North Carolina State, Tennessee, and Vanderbilt (Tennessee), to name a few. Hugely successful **college football** programs include Alabama, East Carolina, Georgia, Georgia Tech, Mississippi State, Southern Mississippi, Tennessee, and Wake Forest (North Carolina). Other major sporting events in the South include numerous pro **golf** tournaments, highlighted by the Masters in Augusta, Georgia, and the women's LPGA AFLAC Champions in Mobile, Alabama. A smattering of world **tennis** tournaments are held in the South, and **auto-racing** fans will find NASCAR events staged throughout the region.

PACKING

There was a time, not too long ago, when any traveler planning to enjoy fine dining or the cushy confines of a luxury hotel in the South had to pack semiformal attire. As with the rest of the country, however, restaurants or hotel lobbies that require or even appreciate men dressed in jackets and ties and women in dresses have nearly disappeared. With a few formal exceptions, most of them in New Orleans and Atlanta, smart but casual attire works fine wherever you go.

LUGGAGE

How many carry-on bags you can bring with you is up to the airline. Most allow two, but the limit is often reduced to one on certain flights. Gate agents will take excess baggage—including bags they deem oversize—from you as you board and add it to checked luggage. To avoid this situation, make sure that everything you carry aboard will fit under your seat. Also, get to the gate early and request a seat at the back of the plane; you'll probably board first, while the overhead bins are still empty. Since big, bulky baggage attracts the attention of gate agents and flight attendants on a busy flight, make sure your carry-on is really a carry-on.

Airline liability for baggage is limited to $1,250 per person on flights within the United States. On international flights it amounts to $9.07 per pound or $20 per kilogram for checked baggage (roughly $640 per 70-pound bag) and $400 per passenger for unchecked baggage. You can buy additional coverage at check-in for about $10 per $1,000 of coverage, but it excludes a rather extensive list of items, shown on your airline ticket.

Before departure, **itemize your bags' contents** and their worth, and label the bags with your name, address, and phone number. (If you use your home address, cover it so that potential thieves can't see it readily.) Inside each bag, **pack a copy of your itinerary.** At check-in, **make sure that each bag is correctly tagged** with the destination airport's three-letter code. If your bags arrive damaged or fail to arrive at all, file a written report with the airline before leaving the airport.

PACKING LIST

Much of the South has hot, humid summers and sunny, mild winters. For colder months, pack a lightweight coat, slacks, and sweaters; you'll need heavier clothing in the more northerly states, where cold, damp weather prevails and snow is not unusual. Keeping summer's humidity in mind,

pack absorbent natural fabrics that
breathe; bring an umbrella, but leave
the plastic raincoat at home. You'll
want a jacket or sweater for summer
evenings and for too-cool air-conditioning. And **don't forget insect repellent.**

In your carry-on luggage **bring an
extra pair of eyeglasses or contact
lenses** and **enough of any medication
you take** to last the entire trip. You
may also want your doctor to write a
spare prescription using the drug's
generic name, since brand names may
vary from country to country. **Never
put prescription drugs or valuables in
luggage to be checked.** To avoid
customs delays, carry medications in
their original packaging. And don't
forget to copy down and carry addresses of offices that handle refunds
of lost traveler's checks.

SAFETY

At the risk of generalizing, Southerners are more often willing and able to
offer assistance or at least a friendly
word of advice or direction than many
other Americans. Those old clichés you
might have heard about the South's
remarkable sense of hospitality hold
uniformly true in most places. Still,
economic disparity and poverty, which
are prevalent both in urban and rural
areas all over the South, can breed
crime. In certain tourist-dependent
destinations, you should be wary of
suspicious-looking figures, and you
should never leave valuables in your
car or in unsecured places.

About the only Southern destination
of note with a truly infamous reputation for crime, including an unfortu-
nate degree of murder and assault, is
New Orleans, which has cleaned up a
great deal in recent years but is still a
place where you should always walk
with your head up and an eye open
for potential trouble. Your most
prudent approach, here and in other
cities, is to avoid venturing out alone
and to rely on cabs when getting
around at night.

SENIOR-CITIZEN TRAVEL

To qualify for age-related discounts,
**mention your senior-citizen status up
front** when booking hotel reservations
(not when checking out) and before
you're seated in restaurants (not when

paying the bill). Note that discounts
may be limited to certain menus,
days, or hours. When renting a car,
**ask about promotional car-rental
discounts,** which can be cheaper than
senior-citizen rates.

➤ EDUCATIONAL PROGRAMS: **Elderhos-
tel** (✉ 75 Federal St., 3rd floor,
Boston, MA 02110, ☎ 617/426–
8056).

STUDENT TRAVEL

➤ STUDENT IDs & SERVICES: **Council
on International Educational Exchange** (✉ CIEE, ✉ 205 E. 42nd St.,
14th floor, New York, NY 10017, ☎
212/822–2600 or 888/268–6245, FAX
212/822–2699), for mail orders only,
in the United States. **Travel Cuts** (✉
187 College St., Toronto, Ontario
M5T 1P7, ☎ 416/979–2406 or 800/
667–2887), in Canada.

➤ STUDENT TOURS: **Contiki Holidays**
(✉ 300 Plaza Alicante, Suite 900,
Garden Grove, CA 92840, ☎ 714/
740–0808 or 800/266–8454, FAX 714/
740–2034).

TAXES

Sales taxes in the South are as follows: Alabama, Georgia, Louisiana,
and North Carolina, 4%; Mississippi,
7%; South Carolina, 5%; and Tennessee, 6%. Most municipalities also
levy a lodging tax (from which small
inns with only a few rooms are usually exempt, but rules vary regionally), and in some cases a restaurant
tax. The hotel taxes in the South can
be rather steep, greater than 10% in
Georgia, Tennessee, and many counties in North Carolina.

TELEPHONES

AREA & COUNTRY CODES

Some cities are now served by multiple
area codes; in these places it's often
necessary to dial the full 10-digit number (including area code), sometimes
preceding by "1," even when placing
local calls (if in doubt, dial "0" when
you arrive to check with an operator, or
ask your hotel's front desk). Just in the
past year or so new area codes have
been assigned to Lafayette and southwestern Louisiana (now 337), to Tupelo
and northern Mississippi (now 662),
and to Knoxville and eastern Tennessee (now 865).

CREDIT-CARD CALLS

To get a credit card, **contact your long-distance telephone carrier,** such as AT&T, MCI, or Sprint.

DIRECTORY & OPERATOR INFORMATION

For assistance from an operator, dial "0." To find out a telephone number, call directory assistance, 555–1212 in every locality—there's usually a small charge for this call, up to about 75¢.

LONG-DISTANCE CALLS

Competitive long-distance carriers make calling within the United States relatively convenient and let you avoid hotel surcharges. By dialing an "800" number, you can get connected to the long-distance company of your choice.

If you want to charge a long-distance call to the person you're calling, you can call collect by dialing "0" instead of "1" before the 10-digit number, and an operator will come on the line to assist you (the party you're calling, however, has the right to refuse the call). It's far less costly, however, to purchase a long-distance phone card—these are available in a wide range of denominations from convenience stores, gas stations, and newsstands and offer rates competitive with those set by most major long-distance carriers.

➤ LONG-DISTANCE CARRIERS: **AT&T** (☎ 800/225–5288). **MCI** (☎ 800/888–8000). **Sprint** (☎ 800/366–2255).

TOUR OPERATORS

Buying a prepackaged tour or independent vacation can make your trip to the South less expensive and more hassle-free. Because everything is prearranged, you'll spend less time planning.

Operators that handle several hundred thousand travelers per year can use their purchasing power to give you a good price. Their high volume may also indicate financial stability. But some small companies provide more personalized service; because they tend to specialize, they may also be more knowledgeable about a given area.

BOOKING WITH AN AGENT

Travel agents are excellent resources. In fact, large operators accept bookings made only through travel agents. But it's a good idea to **collect brochures from several agencies,** because some agents' suggestions may be influenced by relationships with tour and package firms that reward them for volume sales. If you have a special interest, **find an agent with expertise in that area;** ASTA (☞ Travel Agencies, *below*) has a database of specialists worldwide.

Make sure your travel agent knows the accommodations and other services. Ask about the hotel's location, room size, beds, and whether it has a pool, room service, or programs for children, if you care about these. Has your agent been there in person or sent others you can contact?

Do some homework on your own, too: Local tourism boards can provide information about lesser-known and small-niche operators, some of which may sell only direct.

BUYER BEWARE

Each year consumers are stranded or lose their money when tour operators—even very large ones with excellent reputations—go out of business. So **check out the operator.** Find out how long the company has been in business, and ask several travel agents about its reputation. If the package or tour you are considering is priced lower than in your wildest dreams, **be skeptical.** Try to **book with a company that has a consumer-protection program.** If the operator has such a program, you'll find information about it in the company's brochure. If the operator you are considering does not offer some kind of consumer protection, then ask for references from satisfied customers.

In the United States, members of the National Tour Association and United States Tour Operators Association are required to set aside funds to cover your payments and travel arrangements in case the company defaults. It's also a good idea to choose a company that participates in the American Society of Travel

Agent's Tour Operator Program (TOP). This gives you a forum if there are any disputes between you and your tour operator; ASTA will act as mediator.

➤ TOUR-OPERATOR RECOMMENDATIONS: **American Society of Travel Agents** (☞ Travel Agencies, *below*). **National Tour Association** (✉ NTA, ✉ 546 E. Main St., Lexington, KY 40508, ☎ 606/226–4444 or 800/755–8687). **United States Tour Operators Association** (✉ USTOA, ✉ 342 Madison Ave., Suite 1522, New York, NY 10173, ☎ 212/599–6599 or 800/468–7862, FAX 212/599–6744).

COSTS

The more your package or tour includes, the better you can predict the ultimate cost of your vacation. Make sure you know exactly what is covered and **beware of hidden costs.** Are taxes, tips, and service charges included? Transfers and baggage handling? Entertainment and excursions? These can add up.

Prices for packages and tours are usually quoted per person, based on two sharing a room. If traveling solo, you may be required to pay the full double-occupancy rate. Some operators eliminate this surcharge if you agree to be matched with a roommate of the same sex, even if one is not found by departure time.

GROUP TOURS

Among companies that sell tours to the South, the following are nationally known, have a proven reputation, and offer plenty of options. The classifications used below represent different price categories, and you'll probably encounter these terms when talking to a travel agent or tour operator. The key difference is usually in accommodations, which run from budget to better, and better-yet to best.

➤ DELUXE: **Globus** (✉ 5301 S. Federal Circle, Littleton, CO 80123-2980, ☎ 303/797–2800 or 800/221–0090, FAX 303/347–2080). **Maupintour** (✉ 1515 St. Andrews Dr., Lawrence, KS 66047, ☎ 7853/843–1211 or 800/255–4266, FAX 785/843–8351). **Tauck Tours** (✉ Box 5027, 276 Post Rd. W, Westport, CT 06881-5027, ☎ 203/226–6911 or 800/468–2825, FAX 203/221–6866).

➤ FIRST-CLASS: **Caravan Tours** (✉ 401 N. Michigan Ave., Chicago, IL 60611, ☎ 312/321–9800 or 800/227–2826, FAX 312/321–9845). **Collette Tours** (✉ 162 Middle St., Pawtucket, RI 02860, ☎ 401/728–3805 or 800/340–5158, FAX 401/728–4745). **Gadabout Tours** (✉ 700 E. Tahquitz Canyon Way, Palm Springs, CA 92262, ☎ 619/325–5556 or 800/952–5068). **Mayflower Tours** (✉ Box 490, 1225 Warren Ave., Downers Grove, IL 60515, ☎ 630/960–3793 or 800/323–7604, FAX 630/960–3575). **Trafalgar Tours** (✉ 11 E. 26th St., New York, NY 10010, ☎ 212/689–8977 or 800/854–0103, FAX 800/457–6644).

➤ BUDGET: **Cosmos** (☞ Globus, *above*).

PACKAGES

Like group tours, independent vacation packages are available from major tour operators and airlines. The companies listed below offer vacation packages in a broad price range.

➤ AIR/HOTEL: **Delta Vacations** (☎ 800/872–7786). **SuperCities** (✉ 139 Main St., Cambridge, MA 02142, ☎ 617/621–0099 or 800/333–1234). **US Airways Vacations** (☎ 800/455–0123).

➤ CUSTOM PACKAGES: **Amtrak Vacations** (☎ 800/321–8684).

THEME TRIPS

For additional operators and trips, see the individual state chapters.

➤ BICYCLING: **Backroads** (✉ 801 Cedar St., Berkeley, CA 94710-1800, ☎ 510/527–1555 or 800/462–2848, FAX 510-527–1444). **Classic Adventures** (✉ Box 153, Hamlin, NY 14464-0153, ☎ 716/964–8488 or 800/777–8090, FAX 716/964–7297). **Vermont Bicycle Touring** (✉ Box 711, Bristol, VT 05443-0711, ☎ 800/245–3868 or 802/453–4811, FAX 802/453–4806).

➤ GOLF: **Stine's Golftrips** (✉ 193 Towne Center Dr., Kissimmee, FL 34759, ☎ 407/933–0032, FAX 407/933–8857).

➤ HOMES AND GARDENS: **Expo Garden Tours** (⌧ 70 Great Oak, Redding, CT 06896, ☎ 203/938–0410 or 800/448–2685, ℻ 203/938–0427).

➤ LEARNING: **National Audubon Society** (⌧ 700 Broadway, New York, NY 10003, ☎ 212/979–3066, ℻ 212/353–0190). **Smithsonian Study Tours and Seminars** (⌧ 1100 Jefferson Dr. SW, Room 3045, MRC 702, Washington, DC 20560, ☎ 202/357–4700, ℻ 202/633–9250).

➤ PHOTOGRAPHY: **Joseph Van Os Photo Safaris** (⌧ Box 655, Vashen, WA 98070, ☎ 206/463–5383, ℻ 206/463–5484).

➤ SPAS: **Spa-Finders** (⌧ 91 5th Ave., #301, New York, NY 10003-3039, ☎ 212/924–6800 or 800/255–7727).

TRAIN TRAVEL

Amtrak has a number of routes that pass through the South; however, many regions are not served by train, and those cities that do have service usually only have one or two arrivals and departures each day. Major cities served in the South include Atlanta, Georgia; Biloxi, Mississippi; Birmingham, Alabama; Charleston, South Carolina; Charlotte, North Carolina; Columbia, South Carolina; Durham, North Carolina; Greenville, South Carolina; Hilton Head, South Carolina; Jackson, Mississippi; Memphis, Tennessee; Mobile, Alabama; Lafayette, Louisiana; New Orleans, Louisiana; Raleigh, North Carolina; Savannah, Georgia; and Winston-Salem, North Carolina. In addition, a number of additional cities—including Nashville, Tennessee, and Myrtle Beach, South Carolina—are handled by Amtrak connecting services (depending on the route, these services may be provided by train, bus, or van).

➤ TRAIN INFORMATION: **Amtrak** (☎ 800/872–7245).

CUTTING COSTS

Amtrak offers a **North America rail pass** that gives you unlimited travel within the United States and Canada within any 30-day period ($656 peak, $459 off-peak), and several kinds of **USA Rail passes** (for non-U.S. residents only) offering unlimited travel for 15 to 30 days. Amtrak also has

senior-citizen, children's, disability, and student discounts, as well as occasional deals that allow a second or third accompanying passenger to travel for half price or even free. The **Amtrak Vacations** program customizes entire vacations, including hotels, car rentals, and tours.

FARES AND SCHEDULES

Here are a few sample fares (these are regular fares; discount or special fares may be lower), times, and routes: Atlanta to New Orleans, 11 hours, $75 one-way; Memphis to New Orleans, nine hours, $60 one-way; Lafayette to Mobile, eight hours, $50 one-way; and Raleigh to Savannah, eight hours, $65 one-way.

TRANSPORTATION TO AND AROUND THE SOUTH

Although a car is your best bet for getting around the South, it's worth considering a few other strategies for convenient and economical travel.

If you're planning to spend more than several days and visit more than a couple of cities, you might consider driving your own car rather than flying in and renting one—especially if you live anywhere within 500 mi of the region (i.e., the mid-Atlantic states, the Midwest, the lower Plains states, and Texas) and you're traveling with three or more in your group. Even if you have to spend a night at a motel on your way there and back, you'll save a considerable amount of money on airfare and car rentals this way. If, however, you lease your car rather than own it outright, you might factor in the number of miles you're planning to burn up before deciding which strategy works best. And, of course, if time is tight, flying is your best bet.

If coming by plane, plan to fly into one of the South's major airports, to which fares tend to be considerably lower than to smaller regional facilities. For example, the sheer competition and wealth of connections at Atlanta's busy Hartsfield Airport makes it an excellent choice—car-rental rates here are also highly competitive, and Atlanta is less than 500 mi from virtually every town in the South and within 300 mi of Savannah, Charleston, Charlotte, Asheville, Knoxville, Nashville, Birmingham, and Montgomery. Charlotte-Douglas International Airport, in North Carolina, is probably the second most central airport geographically. Less central but also with a wide range of connections and generally reasonable fares are the airports in New Orleans, Memphis, and Nashville.

It's difficult to find direct flights to most of the additional airports in the South, especially if flying from outside the region. However, within the South, check to see what airfares are between some smaller cities—very often airlines offer specials between popular shorter routes such as Atlanta to New Orleans, Atlanta to Savannah, Charlotte to Hilton Head, and so forth.

If you're trying to save money, you have a fair amount of time, and you're interested in taking in the landscape without having to drive, consider getting around via bus—Greyhound (☞ Bus Travel, *above*) has frequent and regular service to virtually every city in the South. Some routes, near the coastal areas and over the mountainous interior section, can be quite breathtaking. And if you book at least a couple days ahead, you'll find the rates quite reasonable. A bit less practical is relying on Amtrak (☞ Train Travel, *above*), as coverage within the South is a bit spotty, and round-trip fares are sometimes quite a bit higher than comparable bus fares—occasionally even more than corresponding airfares. However, if you were planning a one-way or multisegment trip through the South, you'll likely find that train travel offers a better value with more flexibility and fewer restrictions than attempting such an endeavor by plane. And you'd generally find the ride more comfortable and pleasant by train than by bus.

TRAVEL AGENCIES

A good travel agent puts your needs first. Look for an agency that has been in business at least five years, emphasizes customer service, and has someone on staff who specializes in your destination. In addition, **make sure the agency belongs to a profes-**

sional trade organization, such as ASTA in the United States. If your travel agency is also acting as your tour operator, *see* Buyer Beware in Tour Operators, *above*).

➤ LOCAL AGENT REFERRALS: **American Society of Travel Agents** (ASTA, ☎ 800/965–2782 24-hr hot line, FAX 703/684–8319). **Association of Canadian Travel Agents** (✉ 1729 Bank St., Suite 201, Ottawa, Ontario K1V 7Z5, ☎ 613/521–0474, FAX 613/521–0805). **Association of British Travel Agents** (✉ 55–57 Newman St., London W1P 4AH, ☎ 0171/637–2444, FAX 0171/637–0713). **Australian Federation of Travel Agents** (☎ 02/9264–3299). **Travel Agents' Association of New Zealand** (☎ 04/499–0104).

VISITOR INFORMATION

For general information and brochures before you go, contact the state tourism bureaus below.

➤ STATE TOURISM BUREAUS: **Alabama Bureau of Tourism and Travel** (✉ 401 Adams Ave., Montgomery, AL 36104, ☎ 334/242–4169 or 800/252–2262, FAX 334/242–4554). **Georgia Department of Industry, Trade and Tourism** (✉ Box 1776, Atlanta, GA 30301, ☎ 404/656–3545 or 800/847–4842, FAX 404/651–9063). **Louisiana Office of Tourism** (✉ Box 94291, Baton Rouge, LA 70804–9291, ☎ 504/342–8119 or 800/334–8626, FAX 504/342–8390). **Mississippi Department of Economic and Community Development** (✉ Box 849, Jackson, MS 39205, ☎ 601/359–3449 or 800/927–6378, FAX 601/359–2832). **North Carolina Travel and Tourism Division** (✉ 301 N. Wilmington St., Raleigh, NC 27601, ☎ 800/847–4862, FAX 919/733–8582). **South Carolina Department of Parks, Recreation, and Tourism** (✉ 1205 Pendleton St., Suite 106, Columbia, SC 29201, ☎ 843/734–1700 or 800/872–3505, FAX 803/734–0133). **Tennessee Department of Tourist Development** (✉ 320 6th Ave. N, Rachel Jackson Bldg., 5th floor, Nashville, TN 37243, ☎ 800/836–6200, FAX 615/741–7225).

THE GOLD GUIDE / SMART TRAVEL TIPS

Do check out the World Wide Web when you're planning. You'll find everything from current weather forecasts to virtual tours of famous cities. Fodor's Web site, www.fodors. com, is a great place to start your on-line travels. When you see a 🌐 in this book, go to www.fodors.com/urls for an up-to-date link to that destination's site. For more information specifically on the South, take a look at the sites listed below.

➤ ALABAMA: www.touralabama.org (Alabama Bureau of Tourism and Travel); www.bcvb.org (Birmingham Convention and Visitors Bureau); www.mobile.org (Mobile Convention and Visitors Corps); www. montgomerychamber.org (Montgomery Area Chamber of Commerce CVB)

➤ GEORGIA: www.georgia.org (Georgia Department of Industry, Trade and Tourism); www.acvb.com (Atlanta Convention and Visitors Bureau); www. bgivb.com (Brunswick and the Golden Isles of Georgia Visitors Bureau); www.savcvb.com (Savannah Area Convention and Visitors Bureau)

➤ LOUISIANA: www.louisianatravel. com (Louisiana Office of Tourism); www.lafayettetravel.com (Lafayette Convention and Visitors Commission); www.neworleanscvb.com (New Orleans Metropolitan Convention and Visitors Bureau)

➤ MISSISSIPPI: www.mississippi.org (Mississippi Department of Economic and Community Development); www. visitjackson.com (Jackson Convention and Visitors Bureau); www.tupelo.net (Tupelo Convention and Visitors Bureau)

➤ NORTH CAROLINA: www.visitnc. com (North Carolina Tourism Division), www.ashevillechamber.org (Asheville Convention and Visitors Bureau); www.cape-fear.nc.us (Cape Fear Coast and Wilmington Convention and Visitors Bureau), www. charlottecvb.org (Charlotte Convention and Visitors Bureau), www.durham-nc. com (Durham Convention and Visitors Bureau), www.raleighcvb.org (Greater Raleigh Convention and Visitors Bureau), www.wscvb.com (Winston-Salem Convention and Visitors Bureau)

➤ SOUTH CAROLINA: www.travelsc.com (South Carolina Department of Parks, Recreation, and Tourism), www.charlestoncvb.com (Charleston Convention and Visitors Bureau), www.columbiasc.net (Columbia Metro Convention and Visitors Bureau), www. hiltonheadisland.org (Hilton Head Island Chamber of Commerce), www. myrtlebeachlive.com (Myrtle Beach Area Chamber of Commerce)

➤ TENNESSEE: www.tourism.state.tn.us (Tennessee Department of Tourist Development), www.chattanoogacvb. com (Chattanooga Area Convention and Visitors Bureau), www.knoxville. org (Knoxville Convention and Visitors Bureau), www.memphistravel. com (Memphis Convention and Visitors Bureau), www.nashvillecvb. com (Nashville Convention and Visitors Bureau)

WHEN TO GO

Spring is probably the most attractive season in this part of the United States. Throughout the region cherry blossoms are followed by azaleas, dogwood, and camellias from April into May and by apple blossoms in May. Summer can be hot and humid in many areas, but temperatures will be cooler along the coasts or in the mountains. Folk, crafts, art, and music festivals tend to take place in summer, as do sports events. State and local fairs are held mainly in August and September, though there are a few in early July and into October. Fall can be a delight, with spectacular foliage, particularly in the mountains. The region is large and conditions vary; see the individual state chapters for more information.

CLIMATE

In winter, temperatures generally average in the low 40s inland, in the 60s by the shore. Summer temperatures, modified by mountains in some areas, by water in others, range from the high 70s to the mid-80s, now and then the low 90s.

The following are average daily maximum and minimum temperatures for key Southern cities.

BIRMINGHAM, ALABAMA

Jan.	56F	13C	May	82F	28C	Sept.	86F	30C
	35	2		58	14		63	17
Feb.	58F	14C	June	89F	32C	Oct.	77F	25C
	37	3		66	19		51	11
Mar.	65F	18C	July	90F	32C	Nov.	64F	18C
	42	6		69	21		40	4
Apr.	74F	23C	Aug.	90F	32C	Dec.	56F	13C
	50	10		65	20		35	2

ATLANTA, GEORGIA

Jan.	52F	11C	May	79F	26C	Sept.	83F	28C
	36	2		61	16		65	18
Feb.	54F	12C	June	86F	30C	Oct.	72F	22C
	38	3		67	19		54	12
Mar.	63F	17C	July	88F	31C	Nov.	61F	16C
	43	6		70	21		43	6
Apr.	72F	22C	Aug.	86F	30C	Dec.	52F	11C
	52	11		70	21		38	3

NEW ORLEANS, LOUISIANA

Jan.	63F	17C	May	83F	28C	Sept.	86F	30C
	47	8		68	20		74	23
Feb.	65F	18C	June	88F	31C	Oct.	79F	26C
	50	10		74	23		65	18
Mar.	72F	22C	July	90F	32C	Nov.	70F	21C
	56	13		76	24		56	13
Apr.	77F	25C	Aug.	90F	32C	Dec.	65F	18C
	61	16		76	24		49	9

JACKSON, MISSISSIPPI

Jan.	59F	15C	May	85F	29C	Sept.	88F	31C
	38	3		63	17		65	18
Feb.	63F	17C	June	92F	33C	Oct.	81F	27C
	41	5		70	21		54	12
Mar.	68F	20C	July	94F	34C	Nov.	67F	19C
	47	8		72	22		43	6
Apr.	76F	24C	Aug.	94F	34C	Dec.	61F	16C
	54	12		70	21		40	4

RALEIGH, NORTH CAROLINA

Jan.	50F	10C	May	78F	26C	Sept.	81F	27C
	29	– 2		55	13		60	16
Feb.	52F	11C	June	85F	29C	Oct.	71F	22C
	30	– 1		62	17		47	8
Mar.	61F	16C	July	88F	31C	Nov.	61F	16C
	37	3		67	19		38	3
Apr.	72F	22C	Aug.	87F	31C	Dec.	52F	11C
	46	8		66	18		30	-1

CHARLESTON, SOUTH CAROLINA

Jan.	59F	15C	May	81F	27C	Sept.	84F	29C
	41	6		64	18		69	21
Feb.	60F	16C	June	86F	30C	Oct.	76F	24C
	43	7		71	22		59	15
Mar.	66F	19C	July	88F	31C	Nov.	67F	19C
	49	9		74	23		49	9
Apr.	73F	23C	Aug.	88F	31C	Dec.	59F	11C
	56	13		73	23		42	6

NASHVILLE, TENNESSEE

Jan.	46F	8C	May	79F	26C	Sept.	83F	28C
	28	– 2		57	14		61	16
Feb.	51F	11C	June	87F	31C	Oct.	72F	22C
	30	– 1		65	18		48	9
Mar.	60F	16C	July	90F	32C	Nov.	59F	15C
	38	3		69	21		32	3
Apr.	71F	22C	Aug.	89F	32C	Dec.	50F	10C
	48	9		68	20		31	– 1

➤ FORECASTS: Weather Channel Connection (☎ 900/932–8437), 95¢ per minute from a Touch-Tone phone.

1 DESTINATION: THE SOUTH

SOUTHERN CULTURE(S)

To TRAVEL THE SOUTH is to be overwhelmed by its variety. People who study such things for a living report that the region is home to one-third of the nation's people and, depending on who's doing the counting, as much as a quarter of its territory. They also say that its speech patterns are more diverse than those in other parts of the country, that it has given the nation much of its music, and that it abounds with mountains (the highest in the East), water (including one-half of the contiguous U.S. coastline), caves (spelunkers find heaven under earth), plant life (think Spanish moss, Southern magnolia, Venus flytrap, and the leafy, ubiquitous perennial, kudzu), formal gardens (at 2,500 acres, Georgia's Calloway Gardens is one of the country's biggest), golf courses (about half of the professional tournaments in the United States take place on premier Southern courses), barbecue (how best to prepare pork—dressed with vinegar and red pepper, a tomato sauce, or a sweet mustard-based sauce—leads to vehement disagreements and tasty annual cook-offs), and corn bread (in South Carolina alone there are more than 100 words for different kinds of corn bread).

And, yes, there are also splendiferous plantations—Oak Alley and Rosedown in Louisiana, Drayton Hall in South Carolina, to name just a few. There are paddlewheel steamboats and Civil War sites, including Vicksburg National Military Park, considered the best preserved battlefield in the United States. The first city museum built in America was the Charleston Museum (1773); it has relocated to more modern quarters. The South has civil rights museums in Memphis and Birmingham, and in Montgomery the First White House of the Confederacy. In stark contrast to the past stand monuments to the present and to the most powerful economy in the country. There are the tall skyscrapers of Charlotte, the nation's second-largest financial center; the World of Coca-Cola museum in Atlanta, headquarters for the company that makes the best-selling soft drink; and the U.S. Space and Rocket Center in Huntsville, Alabama, home to the Redstone Arsenal, a missile research facility.

The South's is a mosaic culture, past and present glued together by a sense of place. Mississippi's Eudora Welty wrote: "Southerners feel passionately about Place. Not simply in the historical or philosophical connotation of the word, but in the sensory thing, the experienced world of sight and sound and smell, in its earth and water and sky and in its seasons."

There's that, and then there's the legend. "One of the main ways the South is different from the rest of the country is that it's more thickly overlaid with mythologies, all these competing mythologies," lamented poet James Applewhite. The myths about Southern lives and character began in the colonial period and haven't slowed. It's gotten to the point, noted Southern comic writer William Price Fox, that, "no lie, the average Yankee knows about as much about the South as a hog knows about the Lord's plan for salvation." There was the new Eden idealism, followed by a romanticized moonlight-and-magnolias South, followed by the benighted South, followed by talk of the Sun Belt and yet another New South (a speech in 1886 by Henry Grady, editor of the Atlanta *Constitution,* first popularized the phrase). The fact is, each complex and contradictory myth contains some truth, and native Southerners, with the aid of Hollywood and prime time, have helped reinforce stereotypes and clichés.

Still and all, social scientists and other astute observers of the culture have documented some interesting regional differences. Helpfulness and delightfully old-fashioned chivalry do indeed appear to be Southern traits. Smiling among middle-class people on the street was most common in Atlanta, Memphis, and Nashville, for example, while five of the six top cities for behaviors such as picking up an "accidentally" dropped pen and making change were Southern. When a damsel was in distress, two-thirds of Georgia men stopped to help, while only a third of non-Southerners responded. Meanwhile, in *Southerners: Portrait of a People,* North

Carolinian and CBS correspondent Charles Kuralt wrote, "By contrast with the Yankee, the Southerner never uses one word when 10 or 20 will do."

Sometimes, such as when the supernatural is involved, no words are needed. Hoodoo (conjuring), or voodoo, as pronounced by whites, came to Louisiana with slaves and free blacks after the Haitian revolution in the early 19th century. An underground religion, it was practiced with intensity, and apparently still is—by blacks and whites alike. Addressing the subject's past and present is the New Orleans Historic Voodoo Museum. The *Wall Street Journal* has reported that A. Schwab's department store in Memphis sells 21 tons of hoodoo supplies annually. Voodoo, of course, was one of the themes in John Berendt's true-life thriller *Midnight in the Garden of Good and Evil*. Set in Savannah, a city whose principal role has been as leader in the effort to preserve the South's past, the book has given rise to a cottage industry—tours of haunts such as Bonaventure Cemetery. The Myrtles plantation in St. Francisville, Louisiana, has been called the most haunted house in America. And rumor has it that William Faulkner ("The past is never dead. It's not even past") heard ghostly piano music and footsteps at Rowan Oak, his Oxford, Mississippi, home.

THIS IS ALL A PART OF FOLKLIFE whose traditions, with roots in Anglo-American, African-American, ethnic, and Native American cultures, are intimately tied to the region. Ensuring the continuation of tradition is the purpose of many of the plethora of festivals held throughout the South every year. People will lay aside their work for a day to pay homage to a slice of life, the old times: Festivals celebrate everything from azaleas, bluegrass, collards, and crawfish to mules, storytelling, Scottish clans, yams, and woolly worms. It is to the South's credit that down-home cultural gatherings exist side by side, sometimes literally, with events that reflect an urbane sophistication, such as the American Dance Festival, held every summer in Durham, North Carolina, at Duke University. It has presented more than 400 premieres, including many works it commissioned. Each June in South Carolina, thousands head to

Charleston for the Spoleto Festival's big-name outpouring of drama, Dixie-nurtured jazz, dance, and classical music.

Here's a key to one of the doors that leads to the heart of the South: don't be afraid to stray from the major thoroughfares, for off the beaten paths—sometimes not too far off—are real jewels. Want to see antebellum homes? Then roam through Eufaula, Alabama; it's chock-full of them. Want to see folk art being created? Head for the small towns of the High Country of North Carolina.

Travel along the coast of the Carolinas and Georgia during the summer months, and you will hear the strains of beach music, sanctified oldies such as "Under the Boardwalk," made famous by the Drifters. The focal point of this music is a dance ritual, the shag, immortalized in the Pat Conroy novel *Beach Music.* Now the state dance of South Carolina, the ever-evolving shag—no relation to the shag of the Northeast in the 1940s—has been described as a more refined cousin of the jitterbug and a kind of cooled-down lindy hop. Shagging classes are offered year-round in cities such as Raleigh, and the dance has its own contests and festivals. The Society of Stranders (from the Grand Strand, the nickname for South Carolina's northeast coastal area) meets each year in North Myrtle Beach; thousands of people gather for several days of festivities; all skill levels are welcome.

If you'd rather just listen, then Macon and the Georgia Music Hall of Fame is the place to pass the day. From Georgia has come an amazing array of music industry leaders and artists. To name a few: gospel's Thomas Dorsey and R&B's Ma Rainey and Ray Charles, soul's Isaac Hayes, alternative rock's R.E.M., and urban contemporary's Babyface and Toni Braxton. Macon itself is where Little Richard and Otis Redding grew up, Lena Horne lived as a child, and James Brown began his career.

The $6 million shrine, filled with memorabilia loaned or donated by artists or their relatives, is divided according to musical styles. Scattered throughout are listening stations. Settle back, focus on the variety of stories set to melody, and you will understand what soul and gospel singer Al Green meant when he said of the South, "All I can say is that there's a sweetness here . . . that makes sweet music. . . . If I had to tell somebody who had never been to the South, who had never heard of soul music, what it was, I'd just have to tell him that it's music from the heart, from the pulse, from the innermost feeling. . . . That's the South."

–Lisa H. Towle

BOOKS & VIDEOS

Before your trip you may want to read some books or watch some movies about the South. The region has its own language, rich in metaphor and rooted in Elizabethan speech, and it has given rise to a substantial literary heritage: novels, drama, and poetry, as well as short stories and songs. Its authors have won Nobel prizes (William Faulkner, from Mississippi) and many a Pulitzer, among them Georgia-born Caroline Miller for fiction (*Lamb in His Bosom,* 1934). You can choose from works by Eudora Welty, Tennessee Williams, Walker Percy, Reynolds Price, Pat Conroy, and Flannery O'Connor, to name just a few. Charles Frazier's 1997 novel, *Cold Mountain,* about the journeys of a Confederate soldier in western North Carolina, won a National Book Award. The South has produced writers of popular fiction as varied as Margaret Mitchell (*Gone With the Wind*), Anne Rivers Siddons, Anne Rice, and John Grisham. Although it's not authored by a Southerner, John Berendt's nonfiction *Midnight in the Garden of Good and Evil* is a tale of modern-day mayhem in Savannah.

The other element important in Southern culture is the region's passion for history, defined as both personal, family history and regional history. To see the importance of the Civil War period, view Ken Burns's nine-episode PBS television documentary *The Civil War.* Shelby Foote's three-volume history, *The Civil War,* is excellent, as is James McPherson's one-volume *Battle Cry of Freedom,* another history of the war. *Confederates in the Attic,* by Tony Hurwitz, discusses the appeal of Civil War reenactments.

The classic treatise on the culture of the South is W. J. Cash's groundbreaking *The Mind of the South,* published more than 50 years ago. The *Oxford Book of the American South,* edited by Edward L. Ayers and Bradley C. Mittendorf, is an outstanding collection of Southern writing about the region from the 18th century to the present.

For a clear picture of classic Southern architecture, look at Mills B. Lane's series *The Architecture of the Old South,* from his Beehive Press. Each book is devoted to a single state and has black-and-white photographs. The definitive book on Southern food is sociologist John Egerton's *Southern Cooking: On the Road, at Home, and in History,* a veritable treatise on Southern culture that includes many fine recipes.

Alfred Uhry's *Driving Miss Daisy,* a Pulitzer Prize–winning play and award-winning film, portrays an aspect of relationships between races and religions in the South. The novel (and film) *To Kill a Mockingbird,* by Alabama writer Harper Lee, portrays the good and the ugly in race relations in Southern society. Black Southern writers, of both fiction and nonfiction, now get the recognition they deserve. Although well-known author Alice Walker now lives in San Francisco, she is originally from Eaton, Georgia; Walker made her mark with the book *The Color Purple,* later a film.

The most important resource for Southern culture produced in recent years is the work of the Center for Southern Culture at the University of Mississippi in Oxford. Its single-volume *Encyclopedia of Southern Culture* serves as a guide to all matters Southern.

NEW AND NOTEWORTHY

Alabama

As Mobile, one of the South's grandest old cities, gets ready to celebrate its 300th birthday in 2002, the port city's downtown revitalization continues, with plans for a new cruise-ship terminal, renovation of the once-stately Battle House Hotel, and the creation of a downtown transportation hub in the historic GM&O Building, on Water Street.

In 2001 the Museum of Mobile will move into new digs in the Southern Market/Old

City Hall building, on Royal Street adjacent to the Gulf Coast Exploreum Museum of Science. Meanwhile, at the museum's former Government Street location, a new Mardi Gras Museum will tell the story of how the American carnival began in Mobile (contrary to popular belief, Mardi Gras did not originate in New Orleans).

Georgia

In 2000 all **exit numbers** on Georgia's interstate highways were changed to bring them into line with those of other states. Nationwide, exits on interstates are numbered based on their distance from the nearest state line, while Georgia's were previously numbered consecutively from the time you entered the state. We refer to many exit names and provide their corresponding number in order to enable you to better negotiate Georgia's interstates. For more information consult the Georgia Department of Transportation Web Site: www.dot.state.ga.us.

Louisiana

The **National D-Day Museum** opened in the summer of 2000 in the Warehouse district of New Orleans. Thousands of vets donated memorabilia to this highly anticipated museum whose opening brought celebrities such as Tom Hanks, Tom Brokaw, and Steven Spielberg to the Big Easy. Also opening its doors in 2000 was the **New Orleans Arena,** where both the New Orleans Brass ice hockey team and the Tulane Green Wave basketball team play home games. In eastern New Orleans, **Jazzland,** a 140-acre theme park with amusement park rides (including a stupendous roller coaster), a large picnic area, and plenty of food and music, opened to much fanfare in the summer of 2000.

Mississippi

Gambling continues to be a major growth industry. New Las Vegas–style casinos are surfacing all over the state, particularly in Tunica County, in the northwest corner of the state; Biloxi, on the Gulf of Mexico; and Greenville, on the Mississippi.

In Biloxi the **George Ohr Arts and Cultural Center** is raising funds for a new museum to be called the Ohr-O'Keefe. Architect Frank Gehry, who designed the acclaimed Guggenheim Bilbao Museum, has been signed to the project, and Gulf Coast residents are hoping for the same international tourism boom in Biloxi that Bilbao, Spain, experienced when their Gehry-designed building opened.

North Carolina

In spring 2000 the transformation of the **North Carolina Museum of Natural Sciences,** in Raleigh, was completed. Now the largest museum of its kind in the Southeast, the building is an architectural and technological showplace for exhibits that include a two-story mountain waterfall, the world's only display of a 110-million-year-old skeleton of an acrocanthosaurus, as well as the only known dinosaur heart.

The **North Carolina Aquarium at Roanoke Island** reopened in summer 2000, at twice its former size, after a two-year renovation. Animals found in the diverse aquatic environment of the Outer Banks are at home in the aquarium, whose centerpiece is a 285,000-gallon ocean tank with reef fish and the skeletal remains of a re-created Civil War ironclad.

South Carolina

In April 2001 the **Family Circle Magazine Cup Tennis Tournament,** in which top women professionals compete, will be held on Daniel Island, a few miles out from downtown Charleston. The tournament was formerly held on Hilton Head Island.

In **Myrtle Beach** the Conway Bypass is scheduled to open fully at the end of 2001 (sections of it opened at the end of 2000). In **Chesnee,** about 15 minutes from Spartanburg, the Carolina Foothills Artisan Center opened in fall 2000; it showcases and sells the works of local artists.

Tennessee

In 2000, the **Memphis Redbirds,** a St. Louis Cardinals AAA farm team, play at AutoZone Park, a new downtown stadium near the Peabody Hotel. A few blocks down the street from the hotel sprawls the growing **Peabody Place,** a retail and restaurant complex in several historic buildings, with plans to add a 23-screen multiplex and an IMAX 3-D theater.

In Nashville, the amazing **Tennessee Fox Trot Carousel** now open in Riverfront Park is the creation of artist Red Grooms. Figures and panels depict people from the city's history—everyone from President Andrew Jackson to the Everly Brothers. The NFL's

Tennessee Oilers play in 2000 at the all-grass Adelphia Coliseum, across the Cumberland River from downtown Nashville.

WHAT'S WHERE

Alabama

From sites where Native Americans lived for 8,000 years before the arrival of European settlers, to forts occupied during French colonial settlement in the 1700s and the American Revolution in the 1800s, to antebellum mansions that survived the Civil War, Alabama is a state loaded with history. It also brims with natural beauty—wooded hills and vast caves in the northeast, expansive lakes and broad rivers in the interior, and snow-white beaches along the Gulf Coast—within an easy drive of thriving cities such as Birmingham, Montgomery, and Mobile.

Georgia

Georgia is notable for its contrasting landscapes and varied cities and towns, each reflecting its own special Southern charm. The northern part of the state has the Appalachian Mountains and their waterfalls; Dahlonega, the site of an early gold rush; and Alpine Helen, a re-created Bavarian village in the Blue Ridge Mountains. Also in the north is Atlanta, a fast-growing city that serves as a banking center; and Macon, an antebellum town with thousands of cherry trees. If you drive some five hours southeast from Atlanta, you'll reach Savannah, which has the nation's largest historic district, filled with restored colonial and 19th-century buildings. From Savannah, the state's 100-mi Atlantic coast runs south to the Florida border. Along this stretch is a string of lush, subtropical barrier islands, the Golden Isles, which include the elegant seaside communities of Jekyll, Sea, and St. Simons islands. Farther south is Cumberland Island National Seashore, a sanctuary of marshes, beaches, forests, lakes, and ponds. Much of southern Georgia consists of gator-infested swampland, including the mysterious rivers and lakes of the Okefenokee.

Louisiana

Louisiana is a state divided, both physically and philosophically, around mid-state in Alexandria. North Louisiana, with its rolling hills and piney woods, is strongly Southern in flavor and appeal, while flatter, marshy South Louisiana is considered Cajun Country, with sharp differences in food, music, and even language. Riverboats ply the mighty Mississippi and antebellum homes line the wayside in both regions, but it's New Orleans, home of the famous Mardi Gras festivities, great music, and fine restaurants, that garners the lion's share of attention, drawing most visitors to South Louisiana.

Mississippi

Filled with Civil War battlegrounds and slightly partisan tales of ancestors who fought valiantly for the Confederacy, Mississippi has some of the best-preserved examples of antebellum architecture in the South. The Natchez Trace, a beautiful string of magnolias and hilltop vistas, cuts across the heart of Dixie, passing through Tupelo (Elvis Presley's birthplace), Jackson (the capital), and antebellum Natchez. The mighty Mississippi provides the natural western border of the state, winding slowly through the Delta past the port towns of Greenville and Vicksburg. The Gulf Coast offers gambling, sun, sand, fishing, and general lazing, while in the north of the state Oxford, a sophisticated courthouse town, still vibrates with the words of William Faulkner, Eudora Welty, and Tennessee Williams.

North Carolina

Historic sights and natural wonders abound in North Carolina, from Old Salem, where the 1700s spring to life in modern-day Winston-Salem, to the Great Smoky and Blue Ridge mountains in the west, where waterfalls cascade over high cliffs into gorges thick with evergreens. On the Cape Hatteras and Cape Lookout national seashores, tides wash over the wooden skeletons of ancient shipwrecks, and lighthouses stand as they have for 200 years. Here, too, you'll find sophisticated cities such as Charlotte and Raleigh, world-class golf in the Pinehurst Sandhills, and the rich soil of the gently rolling Piedmont, which has supported generations of farmers and potters alike.

South Carolina

South Carolina's scenic Lowcountry shoreline is punctuated by the lively port city of Charleston, decked out with fine museums (several in restored antebellum homes) and anchored by the recreational resorts of Myrtle Beach and Hilton Head at either end of the coast. The state capital, Columbia, is set in the fertile interior, and the Blue Ridge Mountains form the western border of the state. Also to the west are the rolling fields of Thoroughbred Country, noted for top race-horses and sprawling mansions, and Up-country, at the state's northwestern tip, with incredible mountain scenery and white-water rafting.

Tennessee

Among Tennessee's dominating charac-teristics is its geography. Bordered by the Great Smoky Mountains on the east and the Mississippi River on the west, the state offers breathtaking scenery. Carved by rivers and mountains into three verti-cal regions, the state spans more than 500 mi east–west but only about 115 mi north–south. Here are forests, fields, and streams for the nature lover, outlet malls for the die-hard shopper, and an array of amusements for the whole family. Mem-phis and Nashville are musts for music lovers, and Chattanooga has attractions that range from a world-class aquarium to nearby Chickamauga/Chattanooga Na-tional Military Park.

PLEASURES AND PASTIMES

Dining

Southern dining comes in a variety of fla-vors: You can choose down-home cookin' like Mama used to make, with plenty of country ham, corn bread, and fried cat-fish, or you can savor the refined cre-ations of brash young chefs who use fresh local ingredients in inventive new ways. You'll find both styles of cooking in At-lanta and many other Southern cities. In Louisiana, try Creole food, with its French influences, and hearty, heavily seasoned Cajun dishes. South Carolina's Low-country cooking highlights such special-ties as she-crab soup, stuffed oysters, and pecan pie. And don't forget to sample the local barbecue, with seasonings that vary from state to state, or the fine fresh fish and seafood available at casual waterfront eater-ies or elegant dining rooms all along the coast. Your culinary explorations won't end with

Southern cuisines, though. The increasing sophistication of the South has spurred the growth of restaurants that offer everything from good French and Italian fare to Thai and Tex-Mex.

History

On and off the beaten path, the South is rich in history. The lives of Native Amer-icans, the area's first inhabitants, can be studied in such sites as Moundville Ar-chaeological Park in Alabama and the Museum of the Cherokee Indian in Chero-kee, North Carolina. You'll find evidence of early French settlers in New Orleans and Mobile, and Old Salem in Winston-Salem re-creates the world of Moravian immigrants. Colonial history comes alive at Revolutionary War sites, whether at Kings Mountain National Military Park in Up-country South Carolina or at Guilford Courthouse National Military Park near Greensboro, North Carolina. Throughout the South you can visit plantation houses or walk through historic districts in cities like Savannah that stand as testimony to the antebellum era. The Civil War is com-memorated on the great battlefields of Chickamauga, Shiloh, Vicksburg, and many others, but studying a Civil War mon-ument in a town square can also take you to the heart of that wrenching conflict. In a later era, the South was the birthplace of the civil rights movement, and its land-marks and memorials stand proudly across the region, from the Ebenezer Baptist Church in Atlanta to the Civil Rights Memorial in Montgomery.

Music

Many people would say that the South is inseparable from music, and no visit here would be complete without taking in some performances and exploring the area's music museums. New Orleans, the birth-place of jazz, has plenty of choices, and in South Louisiana you can dance to the beat of Cajun music. The Mississippi Delta and Memphis gave birth to the blues, and on Beale Street and at muse-ums or shrines such as Elvis's Graceland, you can trace the fortunes of the blues and rock and roll. Nashville, with the Grand Ole Opry, is the place for country music, but there's plenty of blues and rock, too. Myrtle Beach in South Carolina has a large number of country venues, too. For fine bluegrass, you can head to the moun-tains of western North Carolina. But whether you're in Atlanta or Asheville, clubs and an abundance of musical festivals celebrate a full range of sounds. Classical music isn't neglected, either: Spoleto Festival USA in Charleston is just one showcase, and many cities have fine orchestras and chamber groups.

Outdoor Activities and Sports

Name your sport, and you'll discover superb places to pursue it throughout the South. This is a golfer's paradise, from the courses of the Robert Trent Jones Golf Trail in Alabama to the resorts of North Carolina's Pinehills. Boaters can explore the lakes of South Carolina's Heartland or travel the Intracoastal Waterway, and rivers provide thrilling white-water rafting and excellent flat-water canoeing in every state. All this water holds challenges for anglers, whether in fresh water or out on the ocean. The region's mountains, from the Blue Ridge to the Great Smokies, have well-marked hiking trails, including the Appalachian Trail, to help you get away from it all. And if beaches are your passion, take your pick: the white sands of the Gulf Coast, the windswept shores of Cape Hatteras National Seashore in North Carolina, the bustling resorts at Myrtle Beach in South Carolina, or Georgia's lush barrier islands, known as the Golden Isles.

GREAT ITINERARIES

The following recommended itineraries, arranged by both theme and area, are offered as a guide to planning individual travel.

Prominent Sites of African-American History

Alabama Tour

Alabama's historic civil rights sites provide a close look at the long struggle for racial equality.

Duration: Five to seven days.

One day: In Mobile see the antebellum State Street A.M.E. (African Methodist Episcopal) Zion Church and the St. Louis Street Missionary Baptist Church, two of four black congregations established in Alabama prior to 1865. Check out the black heritage display at Fort Condé and the National African-American Archives and Museum.

Two or three days: Travel to Montgomery and visit the Civil Rights Memorial and Dexter Avenue King Memorial Baptist Church, considered by many the birthplace of the civil rights movement. Then move on to Selma and see the Edmund Pettus Bridge, famous during the 1960s for clashes between civil rights marchers and police. Near the bridge, don't miss the National Voting Rights Museum. Make an excursion east from Montgomery to the Tuskegee Institute National Historic Site, which consists of Booker T. Washington's home, the Oaks; the George Washington Carver Museum; and Tuskegee University.

One or two days: From Montgomery go north to Birmingham and visit its Civil Rights district, the centerpiece of which is the Birmingham Civil Rights Institute. A few blocks south is the Alabama Jazz Hall of Fame, where jazz greats with Alabama ties are spotlighted. Among those honored is Erskine Hawkins, who wrote "Tuxedo Junction." Next, take in the Alabama Sports Hall of Fame; it pays tribute to many of the state's great African-American athletes.

One day: Travel north to Decatur and visit the Old Courthouse, noted for the 1933 retrial of the Scottsboro Boys. Northwest is Florence, site of the W. C. Handy Home and Museum.

Information: ☞ Chapter 2.

Tennessee/Mississippi Tour

For a glimpse of African-American life in the Deep South, visit the cotton country of the Mississippi Delta.

Duration: Four or five days.

One day: Begin in Memphis with a stop at the National Civil Rights Museum, on the site of Martin Luther King Jr.'s 1968 assassination. After this, you can walk through the shops and blues clubs in the Beale Street Historic District. About 45 mi northeast is Henning, hometown of the late Alex Haley and setting for his novel *Roots*.

One or two days: Next stop is Jackson, to get an overview of the civil rights movement's history in Mississippi. See the Old

Capitol Historical Museum and Eudora Welty Library, which houses a number of exhibits on writers from the South.

Two days: Head to Oxford and the Ole Miss campus, where an African-American was first graduated in 1963; see the Center for the Study of Southern Culture, which focuses on Southern music and folklore. Then go 62 mi southwest to Clarksdale and tour the Delta Blues Museum, which honors famous blues musicians.

Information: ☞ Chapters 5 and 8.

Lowcountry Tour

Blacks and whites in South Carolina's Lowcountry have always lived side by side, though, as evidenced by the 1739 Stono Plantation Rebellion and the 1822 Denmark Vesey plot to take over Charleston, not always peaceably. This distrust also motivated blacks to develop a lilting dialect called Gullah to communicate exclusively with one another. Historic sites in the Lowcountry recall this unique black experience.

The new **African-American Trail,** outlined in a brochure put out by South Carolina Parks, Recreation and Tourism, highlights African and African-American sites in three Lowcountry counties. Divided into two parts—the Coastal Trail, which winds along the coast, and the Folkways & Communities Trail, which travels through rural and urban centers—the trail familiarizes visitors with the lifestyle, culture, and achievements of enslaved Africans and African-Americans in the counties of Charleston, Dorchester, and Colleton.

Duration: Two days.

One day: In Charleston, begin with a walking tour of Cabbage Row, home of DuBose Heyward and setting for his novel *Porgy*. Then see the Emanuel A.M.E. Church—the place of worship of the South's oldest A.M.E. congregation. Also here is the Old Exchange and Provost Dungeon, site of the city's busiest slave market. The Avery Research Center in the historic district has an archives and museum that document the heritage of Lowcountry blacks.

One day: Travel on to the Beaufort area, where you'll see the Penn Center Historic District and York W. Bailey Cultural Museum on St. Helena Island. This community center consists of 17 buildings on the campus of a school that was established in 1862 for freed slaves. Also in Beaufort County is Daufuskie Island, until recently inhabited exclusively by descendants of slaves.

Information: ☞ Chapter 7.

Prominent Civil War Sites

The Southeastern Tour

South Carolina seceded from the Union on December 20, 1860, and the first shot of the war was fired the following April. The following itinerary takes in the major sites and sights in South Carolina, Georgia, and Alabama.

Duration: Seven to nine days.

One day: Begin in Charleston, South Carolina, and visit the Fort Sumter National Monument. On April 12, 1861, Confederate general P. G. T. Beauregard ordered the first shot fired, and the bloody four-year struggle began.

Two or three days: Drive the 300 mi south to Atlanta, Georgia. See the Eternal Flame of the Confederacy and visit the Cyclorama, depicting the 1864 Battle of Atlanta. Finally, explore 3,200-acre Stone Mountain Park, where there's a Confederate Memorial carved into the mountain—the world's largest monument.

Two days: From Atlanta drive 160 mi southwest to Montgomery, Alabama, the Cradle of the Confederacy. Visit the State Capitol, which was the site of the first capital of the Confederacy, and the First White House of the Confederacy, which was occupied by President Jefferson Davis and his family.

Two or three days: From Montgomery head southwest toward Mobile. Next stop is Fort Morgan, about 20 mi from Gulf Shores. A museum in Fort Morgan describes the dramatic 1864 Battle of Mobile Bay, during which Admiral David Farragut shouted, "Damn the torpedoes! Full speed ahead!"

Information: ☞ Chapters 2, 3, and 7.

The South Central Tour

The long, colorful trek through Mississippi, Louisiana, and Tennessee offers Civil War–history buffs a wealth of well-preserved battle sites.

Duration: 8 to 10 days.

Two or three days: From Mobile, head west toward New Orleans (146 mi). Overlooking the Gulf of Mexico between Gulfport and Biloxi, Mississippi, is Beauvoir, the home of Confederate president Jefferson Davis. At the Louisiana–Mississippi border, turn off to Baton Rouge (bypassing New Orleans, which fell to the Union in 1862) and then north to the Port Hudson State Commemorative Area, a 650-acre area on the site where, in 1863, 6,800 Confederates held off between 30,000 and 40,000 Federals from May 23 till July 9. Continue north to Vicksburg, the Mississippi River city that withstood Grant's siege for 47 days and nights before falling in July 1863, a Northern victory that was a major turning point in the war. Here you can visit the Vicksburg National Military Park.

Three days: From Vicksburg make the 242-mi trip to Jackson; then head north to Memphis. Another 100 mi east is Shiloh National Military Park and Cemetery, commemorating those who died in the April 1862 battle, one of the bloodiest of the Civil War.

Three to four days: Head south to Chattanooga. See the Battles for Chattanooga Museum and Point Park and visit the eight locations of the Chickamauga-Chattanooga National Military Park, whose headquarters is 10 mi south of the city. This is one of the nation's largest and oldest national military parks.

Information: ☞ Chapters 4, 5, and 8.

FODOR'S CHOICE

No two people will agree on what makes a perfect vacation, but it's fun and helpful to know what others think. We hope you'll have a chance to experience some of Fodor's Choices yourself in the South. For detailed information about each entry, refer to the appropriate chapter.

Special Moments

★ **Birmingham Civil Rights Institute, Alabama.** Observing the multimedia exhibits covering the movement from the 1920s to today, you can't help but reflect on the civil rights struggle through the years.

★ **Okefenokee National Wildlife Refuge, southeastern Georgia.** Savor nature at its most primeval as alligators and frogs bellow their respective mating calls in spring.

★ **Martin Luther King Jr. Center, Atlanta, Georgia.** The eternal flame burning at Martin Luther King Jr.'s tomb in front of the downtown center inspires reflection.

★ **Historic District, Savannah, Georgia.** Architecture buffs will have a field day strolling by the hundreds of restored buildings within a 2½-square-mi area.

★ **Pirate's Alley, New Orleans, Louisiana.** Romance comes alive in this section of town, redolent of old New Orleans, especially when viewed through the early morning mists.

★ **French Quarter, New Orleans, Louisiana.** From the deck of a riverboat, colors and shapes draw the eye to this section of the shoreline.

★ **Elvis's birthplace, Tupelo, Mississippi.** You'll understand how meager and humble were the beginnings of the King of Rock and Roll when you step into this tiny, two-room cabin.

★ **Plantation dinner, Monmouth, Mississippi.** Diners step back 150 years in time to experience the graciousness and grandeur of a formal soiree at this beautiful plantation in Natchez.

★ **Old Salem, Winston-Salem, North Carolina.** A 1700s village of brick-and-wood structures peopled by tradesmen and gentlewomen in period costume provides a slice of living history.

★ **Cape Hatteras National Seashore, North Carolina.** Stretching from Oregon Inlet to Ocracoke Island, this scenic coastline is dotted with beach communities, historic lifesaving stations, wildlife refuges, and beaches cluttered only by wild sea oats.

★ **Cypress Gardens, South Carolina.** A boat tour among the spring blossoms reflecting in the black waters of the gardens is a visual dazzler.

★ **Viewing the Great Smokies from Lookout Tower at Clingmans Dome, East Tennessee.** Here you'll see forested mountains capped by a gray haze of clouds as the early morning mists melt into midday. The drive up is more difficult in the morning mists, but those mists impart the true Smokies feel.

Dining

★ **Voyagers, Orange Beach, Alabama.** The airy two-level dining room of the Perdido Beach Resort is one of the most elegant restaurants on Alabama's Gulf Coast. *$$$*

★ **Silvertron Café, Birmingham, Alabama.** Tin ceilings, fresh flowers, and historic photographs of Birmingham create a down-to-earth atmosphere for expertly prepared traditional poultry, fish, and pasta dishes. *$$*

★ **Bacchanalia, Atlanta, Georgia.** Mediterranean cuisine with Asian influences is served in a new, stunning location that matches its exquisite menu. *$$$–$$$$*

The 1838 Langston House at Henderson Village, Perry, Georgia. You'll dine on French-based fare made with local ingredients and interpretations of regional dishes in a restored early 19th-century Greek Revival house outside Macon. *$$$*

★ **Elizabeth on 37th, Savannah, Georgia.** In an elegant turn-of-the-century mansion in the city's Victorian district, the emphasis is on seafood enhanced by delicate sauces. *$$$*

★ **Mrs. Wilkes Dining Room, Savannah, Georgia.** Expect long lines waiting to devour the reasonably priced, well-prepared Southern food, served family style at big tables. *$*

★ **Commander's Palace.** New Orleans's gastronomic heritage and celebratory spirit are perfectly captured in the creatively prepared Creole dishes served in a stately Garden Distric mansion. *$$$–$$$$*

★ **Lafitte's Landing, Donaldsonville, Louisiana.** Celebrity chef John Folse (of PBS fame) serves his regional fare in this upscale Acadian cottage. *$$$–$$$$*

★ **Joe's "Dreyfus Store," Livonia, Louisiana.** The old general store is still outfitted with polished-wood cabinets and other period memorabilia, an interesting, relaxed setting for the South Louisiana cuisine featured here. *$$–$$$*

★ **Café des Amis, Beaux Bridge, Louisiana.** Cajun and Creole seafood specialties are served in this little Acadian cottage, whose walls are decorated with paintings and folk art by local artists. *$*

★ **Nick's, Jackson, Mississippi.** As any local who comes here to dine on the tasty seafood will tell you, no visit to Jackson is complete without a meal here. *$$–$$$$*

★ **City Grocery, Oxford, Mississippi.** Attentive service and inventive Southern cuisine are your reward for visiting this trendy bistro. *$$–$$$*

★ **Gabrielle's at Richmond Hill, Asheville, North Carolina.** The fabulous dinners at this Victorian inn are not to be missed—held by some to be the most imaginative (wild boar sausage and grilled antelope medallions) and delicious food in the state. *$$$$*

Second Empire, Raleigh, North Carolina. Elegance and epicurean innovation are the bywords at this renovated Victorian-era mansion just blocks from the capital building. *$$$$*

★ **Lamplighter, Charlotte, North Carolina.** Fine contemporary cuisine served in the softly lighted interior of an old Dilworth home is the hallmark of this favorite. *$$$–$$$$*

★ **Woodlands Inn, Summerville, South Carolina.** The restaurant at this luxurious inn continues to be the most sophisticated in the Charleston area. *$$$–$$$$*

★ **Collectors Cafe, Myrtle Beach, South Carolina.** This pleasantly arty spot includes a gallery, so you can shop after you try the barbecued duck or veal-stuffed ravioli. *$$–$$$*

★ **Magnolias, Charleston, South Carolina.** Lots of Lowcountry dishes and a magnolia theme infuse this refurbished warehouse with Southern charm. *$$–$$$*

★ **Chez Philippe, Memphis, Tennessee.** The art deco setting is incredible, and the sophisticated French food lives up to the surroundings. *$$$$*

★ **212 Market, Chattanooga, Tennessee.** Light, healthy cuisine—poached salmon in ginger-lime sauce or vegetable terrine—is served in a colorful, contemporary setting. *$$*

★ **Burning Bush Restaurant, Gatlinburg, Tennessee.** The atmosphere is colonial, the menu Continental at this pleaser. *$*

Lodging

★ **The Tutwiler, Birmingham, Alabama.** Marble floors, chandeliers, and period reproduction furnishings are fitting touches in this elegant National Historic Landmark. $$$$

Marriott's Grand Hotel, Point Clear, Alabama. For more than 150 years the Grand—in an enviable spot on Mobile Bay—has offered guests personal service and comfortable elegance. $$$–$$$$

★ **Perdido Beach Resort, Orange Beach, Alabama.** Fantastic views, a splendid beach location, and lovely Mediterranean style set this one apart. $$$–$$$$

★ **Malaga Inn, Mobile, Alabama.** Two antiques-furnished town houses built by a wealthy landowner in 1862 house this romantic retreat, and the intimate restaurant in the former carriage house is an added bonus. $$–$$$

★ **Ritz-Carlton, Buckhead, Atlanta, Georgia.** The Ritz's signature 18th- and 19th-century furnishings grace this discreetly elegant gem close to Lenox Mall and Phipps Plaza shopping. $$$$

★ **Kehoe House, Savannah, Georgia.** Elegance, refinement, and Victorian opulence make a stay at this bed-and-breakfast inn a grand experience in every way. $$$–$$$$

Henderson Village, Perry, Georgia. An elegant, rustic cluster of farmhouses with a fine restaurant, it's the perfect base for your visit to Macon. $$$

★ **Jekyll Island Club Hotel, Jekyll Island, Georgia.** This former private winter hunting retreat for the wealthy now has luxurious guest rooms for the public and an excellent restaurant. $$$

★ **Windsor Court Hotel, New Orleans, Louisiana.** The Windsor embodies elegance with its fine service and luxurious furnishings. $$$$

★ **Lloyd Hall Plantation, Cheneyville, Louisiana.** A quiet country retreat features surprisingly upscale accommodations furnished in grand 19th-century Louisiana antiques. $$–$$$

★ **Butler Greenwood, St. Francisville, Louisiana.** Seven individually decorated cottages, each with hot tub and kitchenette, dot the tree-shaded acreage of a historic 18th-century mansion. $$

★ **Cedar Grove, Vicksburg, Mississippi.** Civil War cannonballs are still visible in the walls of this enormous 1840s mansion set near the river in Vicksburg. $$–$$$$

★ **Millsaps-Buie House, Jackson, Mississippi.** This 1888 Queen Anne Victorian, complete with turret and columned porch, is a lovely bed-and-breakfast furnished with antiques. $$–$$$$

★ **Fearrington House, Chapel Hill, North Carolina.** This French-style country inn was once a working farm and looks like an English country village. You'll get top-notch service in a genteel atmosphere. $$$$

★ **Grove Park Inn, Asheville, North Carolina.** The city's premier resort, Grove Park Inn has Arts and Crafts furnishings. It has been the haunt of guests like Thomas Edison and F. Scott Fitzgerald since its opening in 1913. $$$$

★ **First Colony Inn, Nags Head, North Carolina.** Four-poster beds, English antiques, and whirlpool tubs lend an air of romance to this inn by the ocean, reminiscent of the beach hotels of years past. $$$–$$$$

★ **Charleston Place, Charleston, South Carolina.** The upscale address for Charleston, this full-service hotel is conveniently located in the historic district. $$$$

★ **Kingston Plantation, Myrtle Beach, South Carolina.** This self-contained resort, loaded with facilities such as a spa and a marina, has a great location on a broad beach well removed from the bustle of the pavilion area. $$$–$$$$

★ **Westin Resort, Hilton Head Island, South Carolina.** Top of the line for Hilton Head, the Westin concentrates on luxury and service. $$$–$$$$

★ **Opryland Hotel, Nashville, Tennessee.** Top flight and massive, this resort hotel includes a waterfall and indoor gardens. $$$$

★ **Peabody Hotel, Memphis, Tennessee.** Legendary in the Delta, this grande dame was a locale for movie scenes in *The Firm*. Observing the Peabody ducks on parade is a unique part of the experience. $$$$

★ **Buckhorn Inn, Gatlinburg, Tennessee.** This unassuming country inn set on 40 secluded acres has been a celebrity hideaway for decades. $$$–$$$$

Nightlife

★ **Blind Willie's, Atlanta, Georgia.** This is one of the country's best blues venues.

Only first-rate, nationally famous musicians get the nod.

★ **Dancing at Mulate's, Breaux Bridge, Louisiana.** Devote at least one night to the foot-stompin' fun at Mulate's.

★ **New Orleans funk at Tipitina's, New Orleans, Louisiana.** This music blends R&B and Afro-Caribbean rhythms to create a sound entirely unique to New Orleans. This is the music the locals prefer.

★ **Traditional jazz at Preservation Hall, New Orleans, Louisiana.** When most people think of the New Orleans sound, traditional jazz comes to mind, and there's no better showcase than Preservation Hall.

★ **The blues on Beale Street, Memphis, Tennessee.** Whether you're at B. B. King's Blues Club or the Rum Boogie, savor the atmosphere of this legendary street.

FESTIVALS AND SEASONAL EVENTS

Starting with Mardi Gras in New Orleans and ending with Christmas in Natchez, Mississippi, the Southern states hold a wide variety of festivals and special events throughout the year. Call local or state visitor information offices for further information.

➤ DECEMBER: **Christmas** is celebrated all over the South, with events in almost every city. Highlights include Creole Christmas in the French Quarter of New Orleans and Old Salem Christmas, which re-creates a Moravian Christmas in Winston-Salem, North Carolina. Tennessee holiday events of note are Christmas in the City in Knoxville, Smoky Mountain Christmas in Gatlinburg, and Nashville's Trees of Christmas. The annual Festival of Trees in Atlanta highlights specially decorated trees, and Savannah glows with candlelight tours of the Historic District. The **Festival of Lights** in Natchitoches, Louisiana, begins the first weekend of the month and continues through December. **New Year's** events include the Peach Bowl, played in Atlanta; the AXA/Equitable Liberty Bowl, played in Memphis; and the First Night Charlotte festival, held on the Town Square in Charlotte, North Carolina.

➤ JANUARY: The year begins with two major **college football competitions,** the Delchamps Senior Bowl in Mobile, Alabama, and the Sugar Bowl, played in New Orleans. In South Carolina, Orangeburg invites the country's finest coon dogs to compete in the **Grand American Coon Hunt.** Regional **runners race** in the Savannah Marathon and Half Marathon in Savannah, Georgia, and the Charlotte Observer Marathon and Runners' Expo in Charlotte, North Carolina. **Martin Luther King Jr. Week** is celebrated in Atlanta. The **New Orleans Classical Music Festival** takes place late in the month.

➤ FEBRUARY: The big event of the month is **Mardi Gras** in New Orleans—the South's biggest parade and party; the week is also celebrated in Mobile and Fairhope, Alabama, and Biloxi and Natchez, Mississippi. **Black History Month** is observed throughout the South, with special events at Tuskegee University in Tuskegee, Alabama, and the W. C. Handy home in Florence, Alabama. In North Carolina, Asheville welcomes visitors to its annual **Winterfest Arts and Crafts Show.** Wilmington stages the **North Carolina Jazz Festival.** In Jackson, Mississippi, the **Dixie National Livestock Show** runs most of the month in conjunction with the **Dixie National Rodeo** and the **Dixie National Western Festival.**

➤ MARCH: The Old South comes alive: **Antebellum mansion and garden tours** are given in Natchez, Port Gibson, Vicksburg, and Columbus, Mississippi, and in Charleston and Beaufort, South Carolina. A **Revolutionary War battle** is reenacted on the anniversary of the Battle of Guilford Courthouse in Greensboro, North Carolina. The Grand Village of the Natchez Indians in Mississippi hosts the **Natchez Pow-Wow. Spring is celebrated** with a Cherry Blossom Festival in Macon, Georgia; the Festival of Flowers, in Mobile, Alabama; the Spring Flower Show in Montgomery, Alabama; Springfest, on Hilton Head Island, South Carolina; and the Great Smoky Arts and Crafts Community Spring Show, in Gatlinburg, Tennessee. **St. Patrick's Day** in Savannah is one of the nation's largest celebrations of the day. In Louisiana, Ville Platte hosts the **Boggy Bayou Festival.** New Orleans celebrates its **Tennessee Williams/New Orleans Literary Festival.** In Aiken, South Carolina, horse racing's **Triple Crown** includes Thoroughbred trials, harness races, and steeplechases. Fairhope, on Mobile Bay in Alabama, hosts a large weekend **Arts and Crafts Festival.**

➤ APRIL: In Alabama a **Civil War reenactment** draws thousands to Selma in late April. Eufaula, Alabama, stages its annual **Pilgrimage and Antiques Show.** The **Festival International de la Louisiane** in Lafayette, Louisiana, celebrates Cajun Country with several days of music, food, and crafts. **Spring festivals** abound, including Dogwood festivals in Atlanta, Georgia, Fayetteville, North Carolina, and Knoxville, Tennessee. Also consider the Okefenokee Spring Fling, in Waycross, Georgia; the Strawberry Festival in Ponchatoula, Louisiana; the Festival of Flowers, at the Biltmore estate in Asheville, North Carolina; and the Spring Wildflower Pilgrimage, in Gatlinburg, Tennessee. **Fish and shellfish lovers** should take note of the World Catfish Festival in Belzoni, Mississippi; the self-described World's Biggest Fish Fry, in Paris, Tennessee; and the Louisiana Crawfish Festival in St. Bernard, Louisiana. The **World Grits Festival** is held in St. George, South Carolina. **Music festivals** include the New Orleans Jazz and Heritage Festival and, in Wilkesboro, North Carolina, the Merle Watson Memorial Festival, featuring Doc Watson's renowned bluegrass picking. The **Masters Golf Tournament** in Augusta, Georgia, attracts top pros and thousands of spectators. More than 40,000 participate in the **Cooper River Bridge Run and Walk,** in Charleston.

➤ MAY: Festivals take to the air this month with the **Alabama Jubilee Hot Air Balloon Classic,** in Decatur. The annual **Hang Gliding Spectacular** is in Nags Head, North Carolina. Over Memorial Day weekend Greenville, South Carolina, hosts **Freedom Weekend Aloft,** the second-largest balloon rally in the country. **Memphis in May** is a monthlong salute to the city that includes the World Championship Barbecue Cooking Contest. **Spoleto Festival USA,** in Charleston, South Carolina, is one of the world's biggest arts festivals; **Piccolo Spoleto,** which runs concurrently, showcases local and regional talent. Mississippi hosts **two music festivals,** the Atwood Music Festival, in Monticello, and the Jimmie Rodgers Country Music Festival, in Meridian. In South Carolina Beaufort's **Gullah Festival** highlights the fine arts, customs, language, and dress of Lowcountry African-Americans.

SUMMER

➤ JUNE: June is **food month** in Louisiana, with the Okra Festival in Kenner, the Jambalaya Festival in Gonzales, the Great French Market Tomato Festival, in New Orleans, the Louisiana Blueberry Festival, in Mansfield, the Feliciana Peach Festival, in Clinton, and the famed Louisiana Catfish Festival, in Des Allemands. Alabama hosts the **Gehart Chamber Music Festival,** in Guntersville, as well as a seafood festival in Bayou la Batre, south of Mobile.

Georgiana, Alabama, pays tribute to country music's legendary **Hank Williams Sr.** on the first Saturday in June. Also in Alabama, the **City Stages music festival** rocks the city of Birmingham with dozens of bands performing on stages throughout the downtown area. The nine-day juried **Arts Festival of Atlanta** is held downtown in Centennial Olympic Park and celebrates performance and visual arts. Mississippi hosts Biloxi's colorful **Black Heritage and Culture Juneteenth Celebration.** Monticello's **Pioneer Pilgrimage of Lawrence County** celebrates Southern pioneer life in Mississippi. June is the time for Durham, North Carolina's, renowned **American Dance Festival.** Summer gets under way at the **Sun Fun Festival** on Myrtle Beach's Grand Strand on the South Carolina coast. The **Summer Lights Music City Festival** is held in Nashville during the first weekend in June, while the second week in June brings the **International Country Music Fan Fair. Carnival Memphis,** a music festival, is a city highlight. Chattanooga's **Riverbend Festival** showcases music from rock to blues for nine days.

➤ JULY: **Independence Day** celebrations are annual traditions around the South. **Deep-sea fishing rodeos** take place at both Dauphin Island, Alabama, and Gulfport, Mississippi; the latter is one of the largest fishing contests in the South. **Cajun Bastille Day** is celebrated in Baton Rouge for three days. Both Franklinton, Louisiana, and Mize, Mississippi, host **water-**

melon festivals. In North Carolina clog and figure dancing are part of the **Shindig-on-the-Green,** in Asheville. The annual **Highland Games & Gathering of the Scottish Clans** is held on Grandfather Mountain near Linville, North Carolina.

➤ AUGUST: Memphis, Tennessee, is home to the biggest event this month, **Elvis International Tribute Week.** The **Georgia Mountain Fair,** a mountain crafts and music extravaganza, is held in Hiawasse. Smaller happenings around the South include the **Roscoe Turner Hot Air Balloon Race,** in Corinth, Mississippi. North Carolina holds an **apple festival** in Hendersonville. The **Louisiana Shrimp and Petroleum Festival** is in Morgan City. August **music festivals** include the Beach Music Festival, on Jekyll Island, Georgia, and the annual Mountain Dance and Folk Festival, in Asheville, North Carolina. For four days in mid-August, the **Highway 127 Corridor Sale** (☎ 800/327–3945) lures shoppers along 450 mi of road, including sections in Tennessee and Alabama, to a mammoth outdoor sale and community festivals.

AUTUMN

➤ SEPTEMBER: Truly a **festival month,** September welcomes local events throughout the South. In **Alabama** Greensboro stages the Alabama Catfish Festival, while Tus-

cumbia holds Harvest Jam at the Alabama Music Hall of Fame. In **Georgia** Stone Mountain Park is the site of both the Yellow Daisy Festival, celebrating both the flower and area arts and crafts, and the Highland Games, with events and foods in honor of the South's Scottish heritage. In **Louisiana** some of the best festivals are the Zydeco Music Festival in Plaisance, the Frog Festival, in Rayne, Festival Acadiens, in Lafayette, and the Louisiana Sugar Cane Festival, in New Iberia. In **Mississippi** Columbus has the Possum Town Pig Fest, Indianola the Indian Bayou Arts and Crafts Festival, Biloxi the Seafood Festival, and Greenville the Delta Blues Festival. The annual **Woolly Worm Festival** takes place in Banner Elk, North Carolina. The **Candlelight Tour of Houses and Gardens** is held in Charleston during this month and October. Nashville hosts the **Tennessee State Fair.** The **National Storytelling Festival** captivates audiences over a weekend in historic Jonesborough, Tennessee.

➤ OCTOBER: Autumn brings more **celebrations of food,** including Alabama's National Shrimp Festival, in Gulf Shores; the National Peanut Festival, in Dothan; and the Chitlin' Jamboree, in Clio. The **Big Pig Jig,** in Vienna, Georgia, celebrates the glories of authentic Southern barbecue. A barbecue and parade of pigs guarantee fun at the **Lexington Barbecue Festival,** in North Carolina. Gulf

Shores, in Alabama, hosts the annual **Orange Beach Fishing Rodeo.** The **South Carolina State Fair** is a Columbia highlight. Allart, Tennessee, hosts the two-day **Great Pumpkin Festival,** with contests, crafts, and gospel singing. **Oktoberfest** is celebrated in Helen, Georgia, in Myrtle Beach and Walhalla, South Carolina, and in Memphis and Clarkville, Tennessee. The "ghost capital of the world"—Georgetown, South Carolina—stages a ghost tour. In Mississippi the **Scottish Highland Games** are held in Biloxi. Natchez, Mississippi, stages the **Fall Pilgrimage,** highlighted by the prestigious Antiques Forum. In Canton, Mississippi, the **Canton Flea Market** features antiques and objets d'art on the Courthouse Square. During the last week of the month, Oneonta, Alabama, holds its annual **Covered Bridge Festival.**

➤ NOVEMBER: **Thanksgiving** celebrations take place all over: The Creek Indian Thanksgiving Day Homecoming and Pow-Wow is held in Poarch, Alabama, and the Richland Pumpkin Festival is held in Richland, Mississippi. **Christmas preparations** include mistletoe markets in Albany, Georgia, and Jackson, Mississippi. Autumn **food festivals** include the Taste of Montgomery, in Montgomery, Alabama, and the Pecan festivals in Theodore, Alabama, and Colfax, Louisiana. The Catfish Festival takes place in Society Hill, South Carolina, and the Chitlin' Strut in Salley, South Carolina.

2 ALABAMA

From the Civil War to civil rights, Alabama has experienced the upheavals in Southern society. Steeped in history, rich in culture and tradition, and possessing a wealth of natural beauty from forested mountains to lovely Gulf beaches, the Cotton State provides myriad opportunities to enjoy life in the heart of Dixie.

A LABAMA IS A STATE OF SURPRISES. Visitors marvel at its physical beauty: the rocky, wooded hills and vast caves of the northeast; the expansive lakes and broad rivers of the interior; and the snow-white beaches of the Gulf Coast. Venturing off the interstates, you'll find something unexpected at almost every turn—a cascading waterfall or showy stand of wildflowers, an archaeological excavation or colonial fort, perhaps one of Alabama's 13 covered bridges.

Updated by
Michelle
Roberts

Alabama has had its share of accomplished sons and daughters. Father of the Blues William Christopher Handy, son of a Methodist minister descended from slaves, was born at Florence in 1873. A teacher, bandleader, and author, Handy is best remembered for such songs as "Memphis Blues" and "St. Louis Blues." In nearby Tuscumbia, the tiny frame cottage where Helen Keller overcame her loss of hearing and sight sits as a monument to her inspirational life. Farther south, Tuskegee Institute, founded in 1881 by the distinguished black educator Booker T. Washington, was where the young botanist George Washington Carver headed the agricultural department and did his seminal work in plant derivatives and crop diversification.

History and Southern tradition are around every bend of the road, whether you follow the path of Civil War soldiers or that of civil rights marchers. Many sections of the state have preserved the elegant antebellum homes so typical of the 19th century, yet the cities have an eye on the future. At Huntsville's high-tech Space and Rocket Center, the Saturn rocket was designed. The state's largest city, Birmingham, is a major medical center. The new and progressive blend nicely with the old and historic—Montgomery's modern state government buildings stand just one block from the First White House of the Confederacy. And Mobile, a coastal port city whose downtown area has experienced a renaissance in recent years, celebrates its 300th birthday in 2002.

Pleasures and Pastimes

Beaches

Some people find it difficult to believe that a state filled with mountains also has beaches. Yet those who discover the coast will find pure white sand, a family atmosphere, outstanding seafood restaurants, amusement parks, and golf courses. In Bon Secour National Wildlife Refuge, you can hike an undisturbed pocket of coastline. Fishing boats, which are especially abundant in Orange Beach, are available for half- or full-day charters. Whether you visit Alabama's beaches to take in the sun or to fish and hike, you won't be disappointed.

Dining

From the tons of fresh seafood served along the coast to the traditional Southern dishes and vegetables found inland, there's something for every taste in Alabama. An abundance of catfish farms throughout the state provide fresh delicacies to be served with a hearty helping of hush puppies (deep-fried cornmeal dumplings). The state is rich in long-standing favorites such as barbecue and grits (and everyone knows who has the best barbecue in town, though opinions may vary), but you can also find sophisticated chefs working their magic at some of the best restaurants in the South.

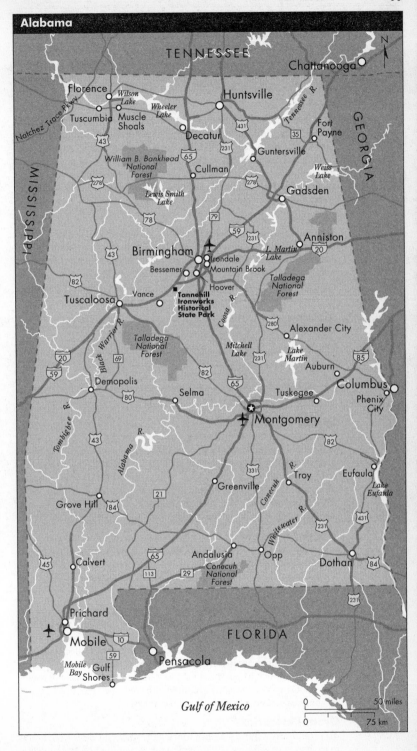

CATEGORY	COST*
$$$$	over $35
$$$	$25–$35
$$	$10–$25
$	under $10

per person for a three-course meal, excluding drinks, service, and 8% tax

Golf

Golf in Alabama is a popular pastime and can be played year-round, with spring and fall the ideal times. The state's wide-ranging topography offers various levels of hilly courses in the north and central parts of the state, fanning out to the flatland of the plains of south-central and lower Alabama. Greens fees are more reasonable than in Florida or Georgia, particularly the eight locations of the public Robert Trent Jones Golf Trail, which spans the state.

Lodging

Lodging around Alabama falls into several categories. There's a growing trend toward country inns and B&Bs in many of the rural northern counties, while the cities are a pleasant blend of remodeled older hotels and modern business complexes. Along the coast, full-service resorts with their own golf courses provide a relaxing stay with a spectacular view of the Gulf of Mexico.

CATEGORY	COST*
$$$$	over $130
$$$	$90–$130
$$	$60–$90
$	under $60

All prices are for a standard double room, excluding 4%–5% tax (depending on the county).

Spring Pilgrimage

Each spring a number of Alabama towns, among them Selma and Eufaula, hold "pilgrimages"—tours of historic homes (including many private residences not otherwise open to the public), mansions, plantations, churches, gardens, and even cemeteries. Hosts and hostesses in period costume greet visitors and tell tales of life in bygone days. It's a lovely time to visit, with the gardens decked out in dogwoods, azaleas, and magnolias. Candlelight tours add a romantic touch.

🕮 *following the text of a review is your signal that the property has a Web site, where you will find details and, usually, images; for a link, visit www.fodors.com/urls.*

Exploring Alabama

With the Appalachian Mountains stretching into the center of the state, Alabama has two very different types of terrain. The northern part of the state is quite mountainous, the southern part fairly flat and covered with extensive pine forests. Each, however, is filled with outdoor recreational opportunities, historic sites, and plenty of chances to sample a touch of Southern tradition and culture. The small towns and back roads of Alabama are often a throwback to earlier, less hectic times, when people knew their neighbors.

Great Itineraries

You could easily spend a month touring the state, but three to five days in each area of the state can provide a good sampling of Alabama life. If you have 10 days, you can cross from the mountains to the shore.

IF YOU HAVE 3 DAYS

You'll find historic sites mixed in with plenty of Southern culture on a short visit to Montgomery and Birmingham. In ⛶ **Montgomery,** you can stand on the steps of the State Capitol where Jefferson Davis took the oath of office as president of the Confederacy and look out at the Dexter Avenue King Memorial Baptist Church where Dr. Martin Luther King Jr. preached a hundred years later. Country music fans can trace the life of Hank Williams Sr. from his boyhood home in **Georgiana,** 60 mi south of Montgomery, to his final resting place at Montgomery's Oakwood Cemetery. Ninety minutes north via I–65 is the state's largest city, ⛶ **Birmingham.** Here you will find diverse sites including the Birmingham Civil Rights Institute, Birmingham Museum of Art, Birmingham Zoo, and the Alabama Sports Hall of Fame. Outside the city, Tannehill Ironworks Historical State Park is laced with hiking trails and steeped in Civil War history.

IF YOU HAVE 5 DAYS

You can spend two days seeing the sights of ⛶ **Birmingham,** then take a trip along the Tennessee River basin. You could begin along Alabama's portion of the Natchez Trace near the Mississippi border, then stop at ⛶ **The Shoals** (the quad cities of Tuscumbia, Sheffield, Muscle Shoals, and Florence) to visit Helen Keller's birthplace at Ivy Green, the Alabama Music Hall of Fame, and the W. C. Handy Home. Moving eastward, plan a day at ⛶ **Huntsville**'s U.S. Space and Rocket Center and EarlyWorks, a living-history center featuring Alabama Constitution Village. For your final day, venture farther eastward; stay near beautiful Lake Guntersville State Park in ⛶ **Guntersville** or in peaceful ⛶ **Mentone,** near the Georgia border.

Another five-day option is to explore Alabama's Gulf Coast, where you'll have to resist the temptation to do nothing more than sun yourself and sample seafood. Either ⛶ **Gulf Shores** or ⛶ **Orange Beach** is good for overnights on your first three days. You can have fun at Waterville, USA (a water park) or hike in Bon Secour National Wildlife Refuge. Another day's option is to explore Gulf State Park; you can fish there, too. You can charter a deep-sea fishing boat for a day or just a sailboat. If outlet shopping appeals, head for the Riviera Centre, just north of Foley. On your fourth day (if you're willing to leave the beach), drive 50 mi north to ⛶ **Mobile,** exploring Fort Morgan en route. In Mobile, Fort Condé, the USS *Alabama*, the Gulf Coast Exploreum and IMAX Dome Theater, and the Oakleigh Garden Historic District will occupy you, but save at least a half day for the spectacular Bellingrath Gardens and Home, in nearby **Theodore.**

IF YOU HAVE 10 DAYS

In 10 days you can travel across Alabama from The Shoals to the seashore. Begin in the northwest in ⛶ **The Shoals,** visiting the homes of Helen Keller and W. C. Handy. Spend the next day exploring ⛶ **Decatur**'s historic districts and Point Mallard Park or Wheeler Wildlife Refuge. On your third day, visit ⛶ **Huntsville**'s U.S. Space and Rocket Center and EarlyWorks living-history museum. Spend Day 4 relaxing at Lake Guntersville State Park, overnighting in ⛶ **Guntersville.** The next day wind your way south to **Childersburg** and DeSoto Caverns Park before heading to ⛶ **Birmingham.** Spend Day 6 exploring the city; the following morning, proceed southwest to ⛶ **Tuscaloosa,** where you can visit the Paul W. "Bear" Bryant Museum and the Warner Collection. At nearby Moundville Archaeological Park, native life has been preserved. On Day 8, drive south into what was plantation country, stopping to see the old homes in **Demopolis** before going to ⛶ **Selma,** with its Civil War and civil rights heritage. On Day 9 start early as you

head south on I–65 for 🏢 **Mobile.** You can tour historic Fort Condé
or the battleship USS *Alabama.* You may want to visit Bellingrath Gardens and Home in **Theodore** or drive south to the beaches of the 🏢
Gulf Coast, stopping en route in charming **Fairhope,** on Mobile Bay's
Eastern Shore.

When to Tour Alabama

Although the state is a year-round haven, be advised that sometimes
the summer heat and humidity can be a bit overpowering, especially
for those not used to it. The summer is, however, prime time for the
white-sand beaches and superb deep-sea fishing. The offshore breezes
along the Gulf Coast help keep you comfortable.

Spring, when the azaleas are in full bloom, is perhaps the most beautiful time of all, and late spring is perfect for the wildflowers of northern Alabama along the Tennessee River basin and atop Lookout
Mountain near Mentone. Fall visitors will find almost summerlike conditions along the coast until November. It may be a little cool at night,
but the warm sunny days are ideal for strolling along the sand dunes.

Winters, although not severe, do get a touch cold at times, but normally the temperatures moderate quickly. Golf is played year-round,
but wintertime golfers and bird-watchers might need a sweater or
jacket to ward off the chill.

BIRMINGHAM AND NORTH ALABAMA

Huntsville, The Shoals, Tuscaloosa

From the Tennessee border south to Birmingham and Tuscaloosa,
you'll find rolling hills, recreational paradises, natural beauty, and history all competing for your attention.

*Numbers in the margin correspond to points of interest on the Bir-
mingham and North Alabama maps.*

Birmingham

90 mi north of Montgomery.

Birmingham, set in a valley below the foothills of the Appalachians,
first blossomed around the coal mines and the iron industry in the late
1800s. Its rapid growth earned it a nickname: the Magic City. Today
the largest employer here is the University of Alabama at Birmingham,
with a fast-growing medical center. The city was a center for civil
rights activity; Dr. Martin Luther King Jr. was put in jail here for fighting racial inequality. A new city emerged after this turmoil, and in 1992
the city dedicated the Birmingham Civil Rights Institute. Today Birmingham is a glimmering, hospitable, thriving metropolis that has
some appealing historic areas and a number of museums.

★ ❶ Alabama has long been noted for its excellence in sports, and the **Alabama Sports Hall of Fame and Museum,** adjacent to the Convention
Complex, displays memorabilia of such Alabama heroes as coach Bear
Bryant, Jesse Owens, Willie Mays, Billy Williams, and Hank Aaron.
⊠ *2150 Civic Center Blvd.,* ☎ *205/323–6665.* ⌑ *$5.* ☉ *Mon.–Sat.
9–5, Sun. 1–5.* 🐾

❷ The **Birmingham Museum of Art,** with a multilevel sculpture garden,
has one of the world's largest collections of Wedgwood, the largest collection of contemporary Chinese paintings outside the People's Republic
of China, and some extraordinary examples of Western American art,

23

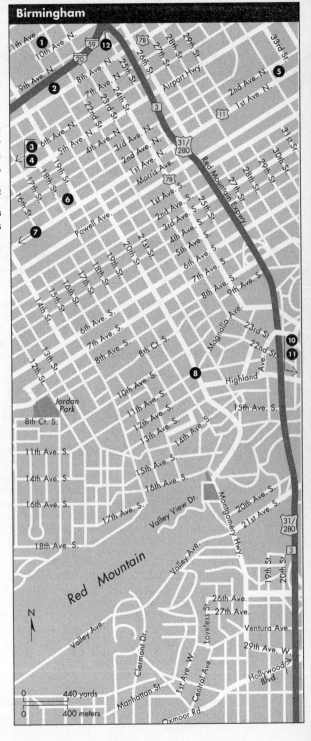

Birmingham

plus Italian Renaissance and pre-Columbian art. ⊠ *2000 8th Ave. N,* ☎ *205/254–2565.* ◱ *Free.* ☉ *Tues.–Sat. 10–5, Sun. noon–5.* ◈

❸ The **16th Street Baptist Church** was the site of one of the saddest and most memorable occurrences of the civil rights movement. On the morning of September 15, 1963, a bomb exploded, killing four young black girls who were attending Sunday school in the basement. A plaque erected to their memory bears this legend: MAY MEN LEARN TO REPLACE BITTERNESS AND VIOLENCE WITH LOVE AND UNDERSTANDING. The bombing is the subject of *4 Little Girls,* Spike Lee's 1997 documentary. ⊠ *1530 16th St.,* ☎ *205/251–9402.* ◱ *$2 for tour.* ☉ *Tues.–Fri. 10–4 (but it's best to call in advance), Sat. by appointment.*

★ ❹ The **Birmingham Civil Rights Institute** traces the civil rights movement from the 1920s through the present day, showing the changes from the segregated city of the past via exhibits, multimedia presentations, music, and storytelling. ⊠ *520 16th St. N,* ☎ *205/328–9696.* ◱ *$5.* ☉ *Tues.–Sat. 10–5, Sun. 1–5.* ◈

The **Alabama Jazz Hall of Fame,** two blocks from the Civil Rights Institute, has photos and memorabilia of the state's jazz greats, including Nat King Cole, Duke Ellington, and Lionel Hampton. ⊠ *1631 4th Ave. N,* ☎ *205/254–2720.* ◱ *Free.* ☉ *Tues.–Sat. 10–5, Sun. 1–5.* ◈

❺ **Sloss Furnaces,** a National Historic Landmark, is a massive ironworks that between 1882 and 1971 produced pig iron from ore dug from the hills surrounding Birmingham. Retired blast-furnace workers sometimes conduct tours of the plant. At other times tours are self-guided. ☎ *205/324–1911.* ◱ *Free.* ☉ *Tues.–Sat. 10–4, Sun. noon–4.*

☾ ❻ The **McWane Center** is a hands-on science learning center with an IMAX theater for large-screen movies. It's meant for kids, but adults will love it as well. ⊠ *200 19th St. N,* ☎ *205/558–2000.* ◱ *$7.50 for museum, $7.50 for IMAX, $11 for both.* ☉ *Sept.–May, weekdays 9–5, Sat. 9–6, Sun. noon–5; June–Aug., weekdays 9–6, Sat. 9–5, Sun. noon–6.* ◈

❼ **Arlington Antebellum Home and Gardens** is Birmingham's only remaining antebellum mansion (the city was not founded until after the Civil War). It was used as a headquarters by Union general James H. Wilson in March 1865, as he and his troops swept south through Alabama to Selma, destroying iron furnaces along the way. Today the classic Greek Revival structure houses Civil War memorabilia and some prime examples of 19th-century furniture. ⊠ *331 Cotton Ave. SW,* ☎ *205/780–5656.* ◱ *$3.* ☉ *Tues.–Sat. 10–4, Sun. 1–4.*

❽ The revitalized **Five Points South** area (⊠ Around 20th St., Magnolia Ave., and 11th Ave. S, just south of downtown) has quaint shops and a nice variety of restaurants. This historic neighborhood was originally one of Birmingham's first streetcar suburbs. Named for the landmark circle where five streets converge, Five Points South has a mix of architecture, including Spanish baroque as seen in the **Highlands United Methodist Church,** (⊠ 1045 20th St. S) and art deco.

★ ☾ ❾ The wooded **Birmingham Zoo** is home to some 800 exotic and endangered animals representing 202 species from around the world. Don't miss the white rhinoceroses, elephants, gorillas, giraffes, and llamas in outdoor exhibits; reptiles, tropical birds, and snow leopards are indoors. ⊠ *2630 Cahaba Rd.,* ☎ *205/879–0408.* ◱ *$5.* ☉ *Daily 9–5, with extended summer hrs.* ◈

❿ Under a great glass dome at the **Birmingham Botanical Gardens,** waterfalls cascade into pools with plants of every shade of green and flowers of every color imaginable. Outside, a quiet Japanese garden has small bridges over bubbling brooks and an authentic teahouse. Wear your best walking shoes: The gardens are as extensive as they are beautiful. The gardens are adjacent to the Birmingham Zoo. ⊠ *2612 Lane Park Rd.,* ☎ *205/414–3900.* ☑ *Free.* ☉ *Daily sunrise–sunset.* ☜

⑪ The **Southern Museum of Flight,** near the airport, has the Alabama Aviation Hall of Fame, the first Delta Air Lines plane, and World War II training planes. In addition to housing artifacts, this museum specializes in painstakingly renovating old aircraft. ⊠ *4343 73rd St. N,* ☎ *205/833–8226.* ☑ *$3.* ☉ *Tues.–Sat. 9:30–4:30, Sun. 1–4:30.*

⑫ The **Ruffner Mountain Nature Center** has 10 mi of well-marked nature trails and a wildflower garden. Bird-watchers can spot migratory birds and resident red-tailed hawks. ⊠ *1214 81st St. S (about 8 mi east of downtown via Exit 132 at 1st Ave. N from I–59),* ☎ *205/833–8264.* ☑ *Free.* ☉ *Tues.–Sat. 9–5, Sun. 1–5.* ☜

☾ Highlights of **VisionLand,** a 35-acre theme park that opened in 1998, are Celebration City, with games and thrill rides, and Steel Waters, a 7-acre water park. Special attractions include the Rampage, a wooden roller coaster, and Sky Wheel, a 106-ft-tall Ferris wheel. The park is 16 mi southwest of Birmingham. ⊠ *I–20/59, Exit 108, Bessemer,* ☎ *205/481–4750.* ☑ *$23, parking $4.* ☉ *Late May–late Aug., daily 10–10 (closing time may vary); late Aug.–Oct., weekends 10–10 (closing time may vary).* ☜

OFF THE
BEATEN PATH

MERCEDES-BENZ VISITORS CENTER – This center, some 30 mi west of Birmingham, is the first of its kind outside Germany. A museum contains historic Mercedes vehicles and offers a multimedia look at the past, present, and future of automotive technology. The adjacent factory produces M-Class sport-utility vehicles. ⊠ *Exit 89, off I–20/59, Vance,* ☎ *888/286–8762.* ☑ *$4.* ☉ *Weekdays 9–5, Sat. 10–5; factory tours weekdays by advance reservation.* ☜

TANNEHILL IRONWORKS HISTORICAL STATE PARK – Built around reconstructed ironworks and blast furnaces that produced munitions for the Confederacy, the park has a museum, crafts demonstrations, a pioneer farm, a country store, and a minitrain ride. There are also hiking trails, fishing opportunities, and a campground. The log-walled Furnace Master's Restaurant specializes in home cooking, with hot, fresh biscuits a morning favorite. ⊠ *Bucksville exit off I–59 (about 30 mi west of Birmingham),* ☎ *205/477–5711.* ☑ *$2.* ☉ *Daily 7–sunset.*

Dining and Lodging

$$$$ ✗ **Meadowlark Farms.** Owners Nick and Raphael Cairns have transformed this former farmhouse in suburban Alabaster, 20 minutes from downtown, into a European-style country inn. The intimate dining rooms gleam with fine china, silver, crystal, antiques, and fine art reproductions. Specialties include chateaubriand, rack of lamb, duck with brandied fruit sauce, and stuffed red snapper. ⊠ *I–65 to Exit 242, then south on U.S. 31 to County Rd. 66/Industrial Rd., Alabaster,* ☎ *205/ 663–3141. Reservations essential. D, MC, V. No lunch.*

$$$–$$$$ ✗ **Arman's at ParkLane.** In a brick former grocery store in Birmingham's elite English Village neighborhood, Arman's has a European feeling, with such touches as an 18th-century painting of a monk and a garden-scene mural and columns in the entrance foyer, and an elegant but not pretentious atmosphere. The market-driven menu changes weekly and features contemporary Italian dishes prepared with Southern ingredients. ⊠ *2117 Cahaba Rd.,* ☎ *205/871–5551. Reservations essential. AE, DC, MC, V. Closed Sun.*

$$$–$$$$ ✕ **Azalea.** The inventive menu at this casual yet upscale restaurant is "new American," fusing Southern, Southwestern, Asian, and French influences. The signature appetizer is not to be missed: prepared table-side and served with chopsticks, it's a whole pond-raised, grain-fed cat-fish stuffed with ginger and coated with rice flour, then lightly fried and served with black bean chili–soy sauce and wasabi. ⊠ *1218 20th St. S, ☎ 205/933–8600. AE, MC, V. No lunch weekends.*

$$$–$$$$ ✕ **Highlands Bar and Grill.** Owner-chef Frank Stitt continues to achieve
    ★ national acclaim with innovative Southern cooking influenced by rus-tic French cuisine. The dining room, reminiscent of a French bistro, has vintage posters and buttercup-yellow walls. The menu changes daily but may include pork rillettes with foie gras and spicy coleslaw; grilled grouper and Provençale pepper sauté on a bed of arugula with Niçoise olives and olive oil; and roast Carolina quail and pork tenderloin with creamy grits, blackstrap molasses, and mustard greens. ⊠ *2011 11th Ave. S, ☎ 205/939–1400. Reservations essential. AE, MC, V. Closed Sun.–Mon. No lunch.*

$$$–$$$$ ✕ **Bottega.** Birmingham's celebrated chef Frank Stitt's second restau-rant is housed in a beautiful Palladian limestone building with high ceil-ings and a dramatic mezzanine that overlooks the main dining room. Open for dinner only, the Italian-Mediterranean menu changes nightly to incorporate the freshest ingredients. An example of one of Stitt's cre-ations is lobster served with penne pasta and a saffron tomato sauce with garlic, chiles, and orange zest. ⊠ *2240 Highland Ave., ☎ 205/ 939–1000. Reservations essential. AE, MC, V. Closed Sun. No lunch.*

$$ ✕ **Fish Market Restaurant.** All kinds of fresh fish are served here, from West Indies salad (with lump crabmeat) and seafood gumbo to black-ened redfish, fried scallops, and raw oysters. Chef George Sarris is at his best with the Greek-style dishes. The decor is restaurant nautical: fishnets, lobster traps, and carved fish. The restaurant also functions as a fish market. ⊠ *611 21st St. S, ☎ 205/322–3330. Reservations not accepted. AE, D, MC, V. Closed Sun.*

$$ ✕ **Silvertron Café.** Since 1986 owner Alan Potts has been creating outstanding dishes with ingredients such as black Angus beef, chicken, pasta, and orange roughy. A specialty is the chicken salad, made from baked chicken breast and topped with almonds. This casual eatery has walls covered with photos of early Birmingham, fresh flowers on the tables, and ever-efficient service. Save room for a Bailey's brownie but ask for two spoons: Only the brave can eat this one alone. ⊠ *3813 Clairmont Ave., ☎ 205/591–3707. AE, DC, MC, V.*

$–$$ ✕ **Nabeel's Cafe.** Scattered tables and high-back booths give this
    ★ eatery the feel of a neighborhood spot you might find somewhere in the Mediterranean. Greek-born John Krontiras, his Italian-born wife, Ottavia, and their son, Anthony, prepare that region's foods with artistry, whether it's an eggplant casserole, spinach-and-feta croissant, or spinach pie. The adjacent gourmet market has most everything you can find in a Mediterranean market, and at modest prices. ⊠ *1706 Ox-moor Rd., ☎ 205/879–9292. AE, MC, V. Closed Sun.*

$ ✕ **Irondale Café.** Mary Jo and Bill McMichael's homey little restau-rant was the inspiration for the café in Fannie Flagg's *Fried Green Toma-toes at the Whistle Stop Café.* And, yes, fried green tomatoes are available, as well as a dozen other fresh vegetables, at least six entrées, and an array of desserts—all served cafeteria style. Unlike the tiny café in the book and movie, this now-sprawling restaurant has five dining rooms, the largest of which features photos and memorabilia of interest to Flagg fans. ⊠ *1906 1st Ave. N, Irondale (7 mi east of Birmingham), ☎ 205/956–5258. No credit cards. Closed Sat. No dinner.*

$ ✕ **Max's.** This is the spot for home-cooked foods like your mama used to make—chicken and dressing, meat loaf and mashed potatoes, and 25 kinds of pies, including banana cream. Take time to peruse the framed photos of the area and its people in early years. ✉ *2720 Pelham Pkwy.,* ☎ *205/664–0034. AE, D, MC, V. Closed weekends.*

$$$$ 🏨 **The Tutwiler.** A National Historic Landmark, the Tutwiler was built
★ in 1913 as luxury apartments and converted into a hotel in 1986. The elegant lobby has marble floors, chandeliers, brass banisters, antiques, and lots of flowers. Rooms feature period reproduction furnishings, including armoires and high-back chairs, plus velour love seats. ✉ *2021 Park Pl., 35203,* ☎ *205/322–2100 or 800/845–1787,* FAX *205/325–1183. 96 rooms, 52 suites. Restaurant, pub. AE, D, DC, MC, V.*

$$$–$$$$ 🏨 **Wynfrey Hotel.** The posh Wynfrey rises 15 stories above the Riverchase Galleria mall (☞ Shopping Districts and Malls, *below*). An Italian marble floor, Oriental rug, Chippendale furniture, fresh flowers, and a brass escalator set a formal tone in the lobby. Rooms are furnished in English and French traditional styles. The top three floors have two bi-level suites each. ✉ *U.S. 31, 1000 Riverchase Galleria, Hoover 35244,* ☎ *205/987–1600 or 800/996–3739,* FAX *205/988– 4597. 310 rooms, 19 suites. Restaurant, café, lounge, pool, hot tub, health club. AE, D, DC, MC, V.* ✎

$$–$$$$ 🏨 **Sheraton Birmingham Hotel.** This deluxe hotel, with a curved glass and concrete facade, is connected by a skywalk to the Birmingham Jefferson Convention Complex. A 17-story atrium overlooks public areas. Geared to business travelers, the spacious contemporary rooms are decorated in bright colors and have such extras as irons, coffeemakers, and large desks. ✉ *2101 Richard Arrington, Jr. Blvd., 35203,* ☎ *205/ 324–5000,* FAX *205/307–3045. 770 rooms, 51 suites. 2 restaurants, café, 2 lounges, indoor pool, sauna, health club, business services. AE, D, DC, MC, V.*

$$–$$$$ 🏨 **Sheraton Perimeter Park South.** On the southern edge of Birmingham, this hotel overlooks the Colonnade shopping center with its restaurants and specialty shops. Filled with traditional furniture including armoires and sofas, guest rooms have rich maroon, blue, and green color schemes; desks, data ports, and voice mail aid the business traveler. ✉ *8 Perimeter Dr., 35243,* ☎ *205/967–2700 or 800/567–6647,* FAX *205/ 972–8603. 205 rooms, 2 suites. Restaurant, 2 lounges, pool, exercise room, business services. AE, D, DC, MC, V.*

$$$ 🏨 **Mountain Brook Inn.** This spacious, comfortable hotel at the foot of Red Mountain has an eight-story glass exterior, a marble lobby, and bilevel suites with spiral staircases. ✉ *2800 U.S. 280, 35223,* ☎ *205/ 870–3100 or 800/523–7771,* FAX *205/414–2128. 170 rooms. Restaurant, pool. AE, D, DC, MC, V.* ✎

$$$ 🏨 **Pickwick Hotel.** Part of the Five Points South area, the eight-story
★ Pickwick was built in 1931 as an office building and converted in 1986 to a bed-and-breakfast hotel. Rooms are art deco style, with pink walls, green carpets, and elegant reproduction period furnishings. Suites have kitchenettes, wet bars, and dining tables. Afternoon tea is served Monday–Thursday from 3 to 5; wine and cheese from 5 to 7; both of which are complimentary. There are also free use of a nearby health club and a free shuttle to airport and to nearby attractions. ✉ *1023 20th St. S, 35205,* ☎ *205/933–9555 or 800/255–7304,* FAX *205/ 933–6918. 35 rooms, 28 suites. Breakfast room, lounge, airport shuttle. AE, DC, MC, V.*

$$$ 🏨 **Radisson Hotel.** This 14-story hotel is near the University Medical Center and Five Points South. The lobby has a marble floor, crystal chandeliers, and a piano lounge. Rooms are contemporary, in mauve and peach tones. ✉ *808 20th St. S, 35205,* ☎ *205/933–9000,* FAX *205/*

933–0920. *287 rooms, 11 suites. Restaurant, piano bar, pool, sauna, steam room. AE, D, DC, MC, V.*

$$–$$$ 🏨 **Ramada Hotel Airport.** This property, three minutes from the airport, has a lobby with a crystal chandelier, plants, sofas, and high-back upholstered chairs. Rooms, done in green and tan and with framed reproductions of Italian sites such as Pompeii, include hair dryers and coffeemakers. Executive Level rooms have three phones, marble baths, king-size beds, and 25-inch televisions. ⊠ *5216 Airport Hwy., 35212,* ☎ *205/591–7900 or 800/767–2426,* ℻ *205/592–6476. 186 rooms, 7 suites. Restaurant, bar, pool, exercise room, meeting rooms. AE, D, DC, MC, V.*

$–$$$ 🏨 **Historic Redmont Hotel.** The city's oldest hotel, dating from 1925, has modern conveniences as well as an art deco lobby and lounge that retain a sense of the past. The two-room suites, with parlors and large baths, are very popular. Rooms are decorated in blue and yellow with modern furnishings and small refrigerators. The free airport shuttle also serves nearby attractions such as the McWane Center and Five Points South. The property is one block from the financial district and four blocks from I–59. For a fee, guests can use the YMCA nearby. ⊠ *2101 5th Ave. N, 35203,* ☎ *205/324–2101,* ℻ *205/324–0610. 112 rooms, 8 suites. Restaurant, bar, airport shuttle. AE, D, DC, MC, V.*

$$ 🏨 **Courtyard by Marriott.** Built around a courtyard with a pool and a gazebo, the hotel has an outdoor feeling that is a pleasant alternative to properties that rise from sidewalks. Rooms, done in mauve and blue tones, have pine furniture; oversize desks and irons are standard. In-room data ports and a lounge-based printer for use with laptops are convenient for business travelers. The public areas are attractive, and the grounds are beautifully landscaped. ⊠ *500 Shades Creek Pkwy., 35209,* ☎ *205/879–0400 or 800/321–2211,* ℻ *205/879–6324. 126 rooms, 14 suites. Breakfast room, pool, hot tub, exercise room. AE, D, DC, MC, V.*

Nightlife and the Arts

For an up-to-date listing of happenings in the arts, get the current issue of *Birmingham* magazine on the newsstand. For ticket information contact the **Greater Birmingham Convention and Visitors Bureau** (☎ 205/458–8000 or 800/458–8085, ✍).

THE ARTS

The **Alabama Ballet** (☎ 205/322–4300) performs periodically at the Convention Complex from September through April.

Opera Birmingham (⊠ 1817 3rd Ave. N, ☎ 205/322–6737) presents two or three major productions each season, September–May, at Alabama Theatre.

The **Birmingham Jefferson Convention Complex and Arena** (⊠ Between 9th and 11th Aves. N, 19th and 22nd Sts., ☎ 205/458–8400)—a seven-block complex with an exhibition hall, a theater, a concert hall, a conference center, a hotel, and the Arena—presents touring Broadway shows, major rock concerts, and exhibitions. The **Terrific New Theatre** (⊠ 2821 2nd Ave. S, ☎ 205/328–0868) hosts touring drama groups. The **Birmingham Children's Theater** (☎ 205/458–8181), the nation's largest professional children's theatrical group, performs for children from September through May at the Convention Complex.

Rock concerts are held at the **Convention Complex Arena** (☎ 205/458–8400), the **Sloss Furnaces**'s covered amphitheater (⊠ 1st Ave. N and 32nd St., ☎ 205/324–1911), and the **Oak Mountain Amphitheater,** in Pelham (⊠ U.S. 119 off I–65, ☎ 205/985–0703). Organ shows on a "mighty Wurlitzer" accompany silent pictures and often precede other performances at the **Alabama Theatre** (⊠ 1817 3rd Ave. N, ☎ 205/252–2262).

For a month or more each spring, Birmingham celebrates culture, economic development, education, art, and music at its **Birmingham International Festival** (☎ 205/252–7652). Performances and exhibits are staged at various locations throughout the city, though the Civic Center is usually the hub. In June the city hosts a music festival, **City Stages** (☎ 205/251–1272), featuring 15 stages and performance areas in and around downtown's Linn Park.

NIGHTLIFE

The Comedy Club at the Stardome Theater (⊠ 1818 Data Dr., ☎ 205/444–0008) showcases nationally known and up-and-coming comedians nightly except Monday. **Park Place Lounge** (⊠ Sheraton Perimeter, U.S. 280 at I–459, ☎ 205/972–8606 or 205/967–2700) spins dance tunes nightly.

Music lovers frequent the **22nd Street Jazz Café and Brewery** (⊠ 710 22nd St. S, ☎ 205/252–0407).

Outdoor Activities and Sports

BASEBALL

The **Birmingham Barons,** a Chicago White Sox affiliate in the Southern League, play at Hoover Metropolitan Stadium (☎ 205/988–3200) in Hoover, southeast of Birmingham on AL 150.

CANOEING

North of Birmingham in Blount County, **Morgan Outfitters** (☎ 800/788–7070) offers canoeing and white-water rafting on the Black Warrior River. South of Birmingham, beginning and intermediate canoeing can be found on the Cahaba River, especially near Montevallo; call **Limestone Canoe Rental** (☎ 205/926–9672) or **Bulldog Bend Canoe Park** (☎ 205/926–7382) about rentals.

FISHING

Excellent crappie or bass fishing can be found about 30 mi east of Birmingham at **Logan Martin Lake** (⊠ Take I–20 east and look for numerous markers). There's fine fishing for crappie or bass at the lakes in **Oak Mountain State Park,** in Pelham (⊠ 15 mi south on I–65, Exit 246, Cahaba Valley Rd., ☎ 205/620–2520).

GOLF

In the Birmingham area, the Robert Trent Jones Golf Trail continues with the 18-hole, par-72 **Oxmoor Valley** (⊠ 100 Sunbelt Pkwy., ☎ 205/942–1177), where golfers can choose among three courses. The 18-hole, par-72 course in **Oak Mountain State Park** (☎ 205/620–2522; ☞ Fishing, *above*), just south of Birmingham, is both scenic and challenging.

HIKING AND JOGGING

Oak Mountain State Park (☞ Fishing, *above*), south of Birmingham in Pelham, is laced with trails for hiking or jogging. Joggers favor the quiet streets in and around the city's **Five Points South.**

TENNIS

Birmingham's **Park and Recreation Board** (☎ 205/458–8000) maintains a number of public courts.

Shopping

ANTIQUES

Hanna Antiques (⊠ 2424 7th Ave. S, ☎ 205/323–6036) is an antiques mall with European, English, American, and country items.

Mountain Brook Village (⊠ Cahaba Rd.), a small shopping area tucked away in the hollows of Birmingham's ritziest neighborhood, has a number of specialty shops, including Pappagallo.

Riverchase Galleria (⊠ Intersection of I–459 and U.S. 31, ☎ 205/985–3039) is one of the largest shopping malls in the Southeast. The bilevel mall has a huge food court and more than 200 stores, including Macy's, Rich's, JCPenney, McRae's, Sears, and Parisian department stores, plus such clothiers as Banana Republic.

The Summit (⊠ Intersection of I–459 and U.S. 280, ☎ 205/967–0111), one of Birmingham's newest malls, is a one-level shopping center with easy access to upscale stores like Restoration Hardware, Williams-Sonoma, and Eddie Bauer, as well as several restaurants.

Brookwood Village (⊠ 623 Brookwood Village, between U.S. 280 and U.S. 31S, ☎ 205/871–0406) is anchored by Rich's and McRae's and has 75 specialty stores, including some with upscale merchandise. There's also a food court.

OFF THE BEATEN PATH

ONEONTA – This rural community 35 mi north of Birmingham on Route 75 has three spectacular old wooden covered bridges. They're especially picturesque when the fall foliage brings the Blount County countryside into play as a backdrop. In late October Oneonta hosts its annual Covered Bridge Festival—four days of fun, entertainment, arts and crafts, and special tours to see the bridges and colorful leaves. For information contact the Blount County–Oneonta Chamber of Commerce (⊠ 227 2nd Ave. E, Oneonta 35121, ☎ 205/274–2153).

Cullman

50 mi north of Birmingham on I–65.

Besides an unusual collection of miniature buildings, this town in the heart of an agricultural area has the **Cullman County Museum** (⊠ 211 2nd Ave. N, ☎ 256/739–1258) and is near a number of parks.

⑬ At **Ave Maria Grotto** you'll see nearly 150 miniature churches, buildings, and shrines, painstakingly created in imitation of originals found in the United States and Europe by a Benedictine monk over the course of 50 years. Brother Joseph had never been to most of these places, but through books and pictures the monk created amazingly accurate copies of such structures as the Vatican in Rome and Notre-Dame in Paris. Only a few feet in height, these buildings were constructed from materials ranging from semiprecious stones to soup cans and building blocks. They are set in a landscaped garden. ⊠ *1600 St. Bernard Dr. SE,* ☎ *256/734–4110.* 🎟 *$5.* ☉ *Daily 7–5.*

Dining

$$–$$$$ ✕ **All Steak.** This locally owned restaurant, with a parking deck entrance, has kept diners happy for more than 65 years. The menu includes steaks, chicken, fish, fresh vegetables, and home-cooked cakes and pies. Tasty orange rolls are their trademark. ⊠ *314 2nd Ave. SW,* ☎ *205/734–4322. MC, V.*

Decatur

⑭ *30 mi north of Cullman on I–65 and U.S. 31, 80 mi north of Birmingham.*

Some of Decatur's appeal comes from two historic districts that hold the state's largest concentration of Victorian homes; the **Decatur Con-**

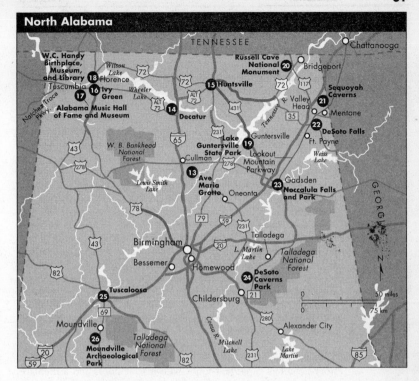

North Alabama

vention and Visitors Bureau (☎ 256/350–2028 or 800/524–6181) can provide information about these and about local festivals. The town is on Wheeler Lake, formed by a Tennessee Valley Authority (TVA) dam downstream, and has become a center for recreation in the mountain lakes region.

The **Monroe County Archives** (⊠ Corner of Vine and Bank Sts., ☎ 256/351–4726) holds county records dating to the 1800s as well as a small museum with 127 original photos from the 1933 retrial of the Scottsboro Boys, nine young black men falsely accused of raping two white women. The case, which was tried at the old Decatur courthouse, won international attention and led to the Supreme Court ruling that a jury of one's peers meant that blacks could not be excluded from serving as jurors.

☾ **Point Mallard Park** is a 750-acre spread with a swimming pool, wave pool, and water slide (open mid-May–Labor Day), plus the South's only open-air ice rink (open from mid-November–mid-March), campgrounds, an 18-hole championship golf course, miniature golf, a duck pond, and a 4-mi hiking and biking trail. ⊠ *1800 Point Mallard Dr.,* ☎ *256/350–3000 or 800/669–9283.* ⊠ *$11.* ☉ *Park year-round, activities daily 10–6 (until 9 Mon., Tues., and Thurs. in season).*

★ **Wheeler National Wildlife Refuge** is a haven for more than 300 species of waterfowl and other birds. You can sit in a building overlooking the lake and watch thousands of ducks and geese; special one-way glass and spotting scopes allow viewing without disturbing the birds. This is a wintering waterfowl refuge, so don't expect to see many ducks in summer. In winter, late afternoons are the best viewing time. Shaded walking trails provide a pleasant stroll through the natural beauty. The visitor center has outstanding displays. ⊠ *AL 67, 2 mi west of I–65,*

☎ 256/350–6639. ◻ *Free.* ☉ *Oct.–Feb., daily 9–5; Mar.–Sept., Tues.–Sat. 9–5.*

Dining and Lodging

$$–$$$ ✕ **Simp McGhee's.** Named after the riverboat captain who was a close
★   friend of Kate Lackner, a turn-of-the-century madam, this fish restaurant, one of Alabama's best, is in an early 1900s general-store building. The pub-style bar is original, the ceiling is pressed tin, and the old red-oak floor is stained dark. The downstairs dining room has a pub-like atmosphere; upstairs is more formal, with white linen tablecloths. Although steak and chicken dishes appear on the menu, most folks come for fish. The filé gumbo is popular, but the house specialty is the *Pontchartrain*: fresh fish of the day topped with shrimp and crabmeat, in a butter and wine sauce and served on a bed of wild rice. ⊠ *725 Bank St.,* ☎ *256/353–6284. AE, D, DC, MC, V.* ☉ *Closed Sun. No lunch Sat.*

$ ✕ **Big Bob Gibson's Bar-B-Q.** In response to friends who envied the tempting
★   smells rising from his backyard cooking, "Big" Bob Gibson opened his first restaurant in the 1930s. Some two decades later, he opened a second location that today is overseen by grandson Don McLemore; some staff have been with the eatery for years. Meats—tender, moist, and smoked—are doused in a red tomato sauce that in 1997 won first prize at a national barbecue cook-off. Chicken and turkey are served with Big Bob's secret white sauce. Pies—chocolate, coconut, and lemon icebox—are known far and wide. The drive-through opens daily at 7 AM. ⊠ *1715 6th Ave. SE,* ☎ *256/350–6969. AE, D, DC, MC, V.*

$$ 🏨 **Country Inns and Suites.** In historic downtown Decatur, this three-story hotel has an elegant lobby with marble floors and a fireplace, courtyards, and spacious two-room suites. Each suite comes with a sofa and swivel rocker, two televisions, an iron and ironing board, and a kitchenette complete with microwave, full-size refrigerator, and coffeemaker. Business travelers will appreciate the data ports. ⊠ *807 Bank St. NE, Decatur, 35601,* ☎ *256/355–6800 or 800/288–7332,* FAX *256350–0965. 110 suites. Restaurant, lounge, pool, hot tub, sauna, exercise room, coin laundry. AE, D, DC, MC, V.*

Huntsville

⑮   *90 mi north of Birmingham via I–65.*

The largest town in North Alabama, Huntsville is best known for the center that helped produce a rocket that took astronauts to the moon. Yet the Rocket City has a clutch of other attractions, including golf courses as well as historic homes and museums.

☼ ★   At the **U.S. Space and Rocket Center,** a NASA research facility, you can learn the fascinating story of space exploration and experience some of the training that real astronauts must undergo. The center offers a bus tour of the NASA labs and shuttle test sites; hands-on exhibits in the museum; space travel simulators; the IMAX Spacedome Theater, with large-format films photographed in space; and an outdoor park filled with spacecraft, including a full-size model of a space shuttle. ⊠ *1 Tranquility Base,* ☎ *256/837–3400 or 800/637–7223.* ◻ *$14; includes museum, film, NASA tour.* ☉ *Memorial Day–Labor Day, daily 9–6; Labor Day–Memorial Day, daily 9–5.*

☼   **EarlyWorks** is a hands-on history center comprising four properties. **Alabama Constitution Village** is the site of Alabama's 1819 Constitutional Convention. Craftspeople in period dress demonstrate skills here such as woodworking, printing, cooking, and weaving. At the **EarlyWorks Museum** visitors can hear stories from a talking tree, build a house at an interactive architectural exhibit, and examine a 46-ft keel-boat. The **Decorative Arts Center** features special exhibits in a restored 1848 home. A few blocks from the village, the **Historic Huntsville Depot**, built in 1860, offers a glimpse of railroad life in the mid-19th century. For an extra fee you can take a 30-minute trolley ride around town. ⊠ 404 Madison St., ☎ 800/678–1819 or 256/564–8100, ☒ $10. ☉ Apr.–Oct., Wed.–Sat. 9:30–2. Other times by appointment.

Dining and Lodging

$$ ✗ **Cafe Berlin.** Paintings and photographs of European café scenes adorn the walls, and crisp tablecloths and taped music emphasize the German theme. The menu is lighter than most Teutonic-style restaurants, and although schnitzel and wurst are prepared a number of ways, you can also order fish, chicken, and steak dishes, as well as enormous salads. The Black Forest gâteau is a favorite dessert. ⊠ *505 Airport Rd.,* ☎ *256/880–9920. AE, D, MC, V.*

$–$$ ✗ **Greenbrier Restaurant.** This rustic eatery in Madison was built by
★ hand in 1952 by the owner, Jack Webb. Many modern conveniences have been added, but the original hand-hewn decor makes eating at the Greenbrier fun. Good catfish, barbecue, ribs, and chicken have kept it a local favorite. The chicken is served with a special white barbecue sauce. Add generous portions, tasty coleslaw, and hot hush puppies, and you'll know why people drive long distances to eat here. ⊠ *27028 Old Hwy. 20, Madison (8 mi west of Huntsville, 2 mi off I–565),* ☎ *256/351–1800. AE, D, MC, V.*

$$–$$$ 🏨 **Huntsville Hilton.** Claiming the prize location in town, the Hilton is within walking distance of the historic district and museums, and many rooms overlook either Big Spring Park and Lake or the Von Braun Convention Center. The lobby has an upscale, classical ambience created by Oriental rugs, antique chairs and tables, and a grand piano, which provides entertainment most evenings. The spacious rooms have irons, hair dryers, and coffeemakers. ⊠ *401 Williams Ave., 35801,* ☎ *256/533–1400,* ℻ *256/534–7787. 268 rooms, 9 suites. Restaurant, bar, pool, hot tub, exercise room. AE, D, DC, MC, V.*

Outdoor Activities and Sports

GOLF

The three golf courses at **Hampton Cove** (⊠ 450 Old Hwy. 431S, Owens Cross Roads, ☎ 256/551–1818), part of the Robert Trent Jones Golf Trail, are 12 mi from Huntsville. All have 18 holes; two are par 72, and the third is par 54.

The Shoals

70 mi west of Huntsville.

The adjoining quad cities of Tuscumbia, Florence, Sheffield, and Muscle Shoals are known throughout Alabama simply as The Shoals. Spreading out on both sides of the Tennessee River basin, The Shoals is an attractive area rich in culture and history. Nearby Wilson Dam, begun in 1918 as a power supply center for munitions plants in World War I, later became the cornerstone of the Tennessee Valley Authority (TVA). This government agency, created in 1933, is involved with the integrated development of the region; its dams and reservoirs have greatly affected the economics of the area, providing both business and recreational opportunities.

★ ⑯ **Ivy Green** is the childhood home of Helen Keller. At the carriage house, behind the simple white frame main house, Annie Sullivan taught young Helen the meaning of language. This inspirational story, *The Miracle Worker,* is performed on the grounds Friday and Saturday nights at 8:15 from mid-June to mid-July; the grounds open at 7 so that ticket holders can tour the house (no extra charge). ✉ *300 W. North Commons, Tuscumbia,* ☎ *256/383–4066.* ✍ *$5; The Miracle Worker $5–$8.* ⊙ *Mon.–Sat. 8:30–4, Sun. 1–4.*

★ ⑰ At the **Alabama Music Hall of Fame and Museum,** you can wander through the history of Alabama's musical heritage and see the original contracts of Elvis Presley's deal with Sun Records, the actual touring bus of the country-music band Alabama, and exhibits on the likes of Hank Williams, Lionel Richie, and Nat "King" Cole. The annual September **Concert Series** festival draws performers and fans from across the country. ✉ *U.S. 72W, Tuscumbia,* ☎ *256/381–4417 or 800/239–2643.* ✍ *$6.* ⊙ *Mon.–Sat. 9–5, Sun. 1–5.* ⊛

⑱ The **W. C. Handy Birthplace, Museum and Library** is the birthplace of the internationally acclaimed Father of the Blues. Handy (1873–1958), a mainly self-taught songwriter and bandleader, was one of the first to write down the blues. The cabin has been furnished with items typical of the period when he grew up. In the museum, a treasure trove of his memorabilia has been preserved. Here you'll see his piano and famous golden trumpet, and testimonials to his genius by such contemporaries as George Gershwin and Louis Armstrong. The annual **W. C. Handy Music Festival** (☎ 256/766–7642), held during the first week in August, draws thousands. ✉ *620 W. College St., Florence,* ☎ *256/760–6434.* ✍ *$2.* ⊙ *Tues.–Sat. 10–4.*

Dining and Lodging

$$–$$$ ★ ✕ **Dale's Restaurant.** Dine in comfort as red-jacketed waiters serve flame-grilled steaks seasoned with Dale's famous marinade. A healthy variety of chicken and seafood dishes rounds out the menu. ✉ *1001 Mitchell Blvd., Florence,* ☎ *256/766–4961. AE, DC, MC, V.* ⊙ *Closed Sun. No lunch.*

$$–$$$ ✕ **Louisiana "The Restaurant."** New Orleans's French Quarter influences the large selection of specialties here. Seafood items, including shrimp and crawfish, can be fried, served in cream sauce, or wrapped in crepes. There are also grilled steaks, veal, lamb, chicken, and a Sunday Creole brunch. ✉ *1311 6th St., Muscle Shoals,* ☎ *256/386–0801. AE, D, DC, MC, V.* ⊙ *Closed Mon.*

$–$$ ✕ **Renaissance Grille.** In this casual restaurant atop the Renaissance Tower, you can choose from fine steaks, chicken, pasta dishes, or seafood as you watch the sun set from a vantage point 350 ft above the Tennessee River basin. ✉ *1 Hightower Pl., Florence,* ☎ *256/718–0092. AE, D, DC, MC, V.*

$$ ★ ▦ **Holiday Inn–The Shoals.** Serving both Florence and Sheffield, this motel has a courteous staff and spacious rooms that have traditional furniture, hair dryers, and computer jacks. A songwriters' showcase is hosted in the lounge on Thursday evening. ✉ *4900 Hatch Blvd., Sheffield 35660,* ☎ *256/381–4710,* ⅢX *256/381–4710, ext. 403. 201 rooms, 3 suites. Restaurant, lounge, pool, hot tub, exercise room. AE, D, MC, V.*

$$ ▦ **Joe Wheeler State Park Lodge.** At the center of a 3,400-acre state park, this three-story fieldstone-and-redwood lodge slopes down a hill, giving every room a view of Wheeler Lake. All rooms have balconies; suites have living rooms and tiny kitchenettes. Recreational opportunities abound: Boats are available for trips on the lake; countless hiking trails lead to secluded spots and picnic areas, and redwood walkways run from the guest rooms down to the pool area. Nearby are small, rustic log cabins, which are no-frills but comfortable. ✉ *U.S. 72, near Rogersville (between Athens and Florence), 4401 McLean Dr., Rogersville 35652,* ☎ *256/247–5461 or 800/544–5639,* ⅢX *256/247–*

5471. 69 rooms, 6 suites, 24 cabins. Restaurant, pool, 18-hole golf course, 4 tennis courts. AE, MC, V.

$ ⊞ **Homestead Executive Inn, Florence.** All the accommodations in Florence are basic motel style, and this renovated two-story gray-brick building near the center of town is the best of them. The Olympic-size pool is a pleasant extra. ⊠ *504 S. Court St., 35630,* ☎ *256/766–2331 or 800/248–5336,* FAX *256/766–3567. 119 rooms, 1 suite. Restaurant, bar, pool. AE, D, DC, MC, V.*

$ ⊞ **Key West Inn.** For those seeking a clean, comfortable motel at budget prices, this is the place. Rooms have microwaves and small refrigerators. ⊠ *1800 U.S. 72, Tuscumbia 35674,* ☎ *256/383–0700,* FAX *256/383–3191. 41 rooms. AE, D, DC, MC, V.*

Guntersville

40 mi southeast of Huntsville via U.S. 431.

The town of Guntersville, a TVA port, draws visitors with its parks and Lake Guntersville. The lake, with 949 mi of winding shoreline and 69,000 acres of water, was created by the Guntersville Lock and Dam. Eight public launch areas and eight full-service marinas make it ideal for all types of boating and fishing. You can rent everything from fishing boats to houseboats here.

★ ⑲ **Lake Guntersville State Park** lies along the southern bank of the Tennessee River just east of Guntersville and in the shadow of Sand Mountain. The natural beauty combines with a wealth of outdoor recreational opportunities, such as golf, hiking, camping, and world-class bass fishing, to make the park one of Alabama's most popular destinations. ⊠ *7966 AL 227,* ☎ *256/571–5444.* 🎟 *Free.*

Dining and Lodging

$–$$$ ✕⊞ **Lake Guntersville State Park Lodge.** People come here for the natural surroundings; the lodge itself is a fairly standard motel-type accommodation with simple furnishings. Rooms on the bluff side have balconies with great views of lake and forest. There are also lakefront two-bedroom cottages, which are as modern and plain as the lodge rooms but have a sitting room and a kitchen. The A-frame chalets have living rooms and two bedrooms. The Chandelier Dining Room overlooks the gigantic man-made lake and offers thick steaks and chicken and seafood dishes. Try the seafood divan, a casserole of shrimp, crabmeat, mushrooms, and broccoli. Fried mushrooms and fried zucchini are tasty starters. ⊠ *1155 Lodge Dr., 35976,* ☎ *256/571–5448 or 800/548–4553. 94 rooms, 6 suites, 20 chalets, 15 cottages. Restaurant, coffee shop, pool, 18-hole golf course, 2 tennis courts. AE, MC, V.*

Bridgeport

65 mi east of Huntsville via U.S. 72.

⑳ Seven miles outside Bridgeport is a cave with evidence of prehistoric settlement in the area. **Russell Cave National Monument,** an archaeological site, was occupied by Native Americans' prehistoric ancestors 8,000 years before the arrival of European settlers. You can tour the cave shelter—the entrance to more than 7 mi of cavernous passages—and view museum exhibits of prehistoric artifacts and a Native American burial ground. There are also tool demonstrations, a video program, a nature trail, a hiking trail, and picnic grounds. ⊠ *3729 County Rd. 98,* ☎ *256/495–2672.* 🎟 *Free.* ⊙ *Daily 8–4:30.*

Valley Head

25 mi southeast of Bridgeport on AL 117 to AL 11, 115 mi northeast of Birmingham via I–59.

Near the Georgia state line, this small town is a pleasant hideaway.

㉑ A half-mile guided tour through the **Sequoyah Caverns,** in Sand Mountain, brings visitors past rock formations mirrored in lakes. In the 1930s, dances were held in the largest room, now called the Ballroom. Outside, there's a picnic area, a small zoo, hiking trails, and a campground with a swimming pool and playground. ⊠ *Rte. 1,* ☎ *256/635–0024 or 800/843–5098.* ⊠ *$7.* ☉ *Mar.–Nov., daily 8:30–5; Dec.–Feb., weekends 8:30–5. Campgrounds open yr-round.*

Mentone

2 mi east of Valley Head on AL 117, 117 mi northeast of Birmingham via I–59.

Mentone, whose name means "musical valley spring," has narrow, twisting streets filled with shops, restaurants, and crafts places, many in historic buildings.

Dining and Lodging

$–$$ ✕ **Log Cabin Deli.** This early 1800s original pine-log cabin was once
★ used as a Native American fur-trading post. Dine on the open front porch, the screened back porch, or in the main dining room, with its great rock fireplace. The hand-cut cedar tables and rough wooden floors complete the rustic effect. Everything here is home-cooked, and the deli has become famous for its soups, hefty sandwiches (just try to finish the cabin roast beef special), country ham, and Southern-style vegetables. Desserts are a big hit; try the hot fudge nut cake with ice cream. ⊠ *AL 117,* ☎ *256/634–4560. No credit cards.* ☉ *Closed Mon.*

Fort Payne

15 mi south of Mentone via I–59, 100 mi northeast of Birmingham.

Fort Payne, known as the "sock capital of the world" because of the huge number of socks produced here, offers a pleasantly slow-paced lifestyle. It's near a lovely state park. The **Depot Museum** (⊠ 105 5th St. NE, ☎ 256/845–5714) has artifacts from local history. The **Alabama Museum** (⊠ 101 Glenn Blvd. SW, ☎ 256/845–1646) is dedicated to the music group Alabama.

㉒ **DeSoto Falls,** a 120-ft waterfall, is a mesmerizing attraction in the 5,000-acre **DeSoto State Resort Park.** Unsupervised swimming is allowed in DeSoto Lake, and the park has a supervised pool, picnic area, and campgrounds as well. **Little River Canyon,** one of the deepest canyons east of the Rocky Mountains, is just outside the park's boundary. The scenery is breathtaking at this 600-ft-deep and 16-mi-wide canyon. ⊠ *DeSoto State Resort Park, County Rd. 89,* ☎ *256/845–0051 or 800/252–7275.* ⊠ *Free; picnicking 50¢.* ☉ *Daily 7–dusk.*

Gadsden

35 mi south of Fort Payne via I–59, 63 mi northeast of Birmingham.

At the southern end of Lookout Mountain, Gadsden has an impressive waterfall. **Lookout Mountain Parkway,** a scenic 100-mi drive that ends in Chattanooga, also begins here (☎ 256/549–0351 for information). In mid-May the town hosts **Riverfest** (☎ 256/543–3472 for information), a three-day family-oriented event with good music and several blocks of food and arts and crafts. You can ride the Coosa River on the *Alabama Princess* riverboat (☎ 256/549–1111), too.

☾ ㉓ **Noccalula Falls and Park** is a 100-acre woodland area with a 90-ft waterfall, miniature golf, minitrain rides, a small zoo, a botanical garden, a covered bridge, and a 1776 pioneer homestead—four log cabins were moved here from the backwoods of Tennessee. There are also campgrounds and picnic areas. ⊠ *1500 Noccalula Rd.,* ☎ *256/549–4663.* ☒ *Homestead and garden $1.50; train ride $1.* ☉ *Daily 8–sunset.*

Talladega

40 mi south of Gadsden on AL 21.

Talladega's diverse attractions include a racing hall of fame and a nearby national forest. The town's **Silk Stocking Historic District** has homes built mainly from 1885 to 1915 for leading citizens such as textile merchants, lawyers, and doctors (whose wives could afford to wear the silk stockings that gave the district its name). The buildings range from simple cottages to elaborate Queen Anne homes.

Near the Talladega Superspeedway, the **International Motorsports Hall of Fame** (⊠ 3198 Speedway Blvd., ☎ 256/362–5002) has more than 100 racing vehicles and memorabilia.

Considered by many to be the state's best hiking experience, the trails of a nearby unit of the **Talladega National Forest** (☎ 256/362–2909 for district ranger) wind through the southernmost extension of the Appalachian Mountains. You'll discover hardwood trees, lakes, scenic overlooks, and mountain streams.

Outdoor Activities and Sports
The **Talladega Superspeedway** (⊠ 3366 Speedway Blvd., ☎ 256/ 362–2261) hosts two major NASCAR races each year.

Childersburg

72 mi southwest of Gadsden via U.S. 411/231, 40 mi southeast of Birmingham via U.S. 280.

Years before frontier settlers arrived here in the early 19th century, the area was a sacred Native American capital called Coosa. The town has evolved into a lumber and farming community, but visitors know it best for its caverns.

㉔ **DeSoto Caverns Park** is the site of a 2,000-year-old Native American burial ground. These vast onyx caves were rediscovered in 1540 by Hernando DeSoto and later served as a Confederate gunpowder mining center and a Prohibition speakeasy. Curious formations of stalagmites and stalactites allow the imagination free rein. Part of your cave tour includes a sound, laser, light, and water show in the largest cave, which is more than 12 stories high. A campground and picnic grove, gemstone mining, a water-fight maze, and other activities provide plenty of diversions. ⊠ *5181 DeSoto Caverns Pkwy.,* ☎ *256/378–7252 or 800/933–2283.* ☒ *$10.95; FunPac ticket (includes tour, maze, and gemstone mining) $13.75.* ☉ *Mon.–Sat. 9–5, Sun. 12:30–5; extended hrs spring and summer.*

Tuscaloosa

㉕ *50 mi west of Birmingham via I–20/I–59.*

Thanks to the teams of the University of Alabama, this city's leading export may well be football, but its wealth of cultural offerings cannot be overlooked.

The **Paul W. "Bear" Bryant Museum** follows the University of Alabama's 100-year tradition of football preeminence. The museum has many of Coach Bryant's personal belongings, as well as those of others who have laid the foundation for the University of Alabama football program. ✉ *300 Paul W. Bryant Dr.,* ☎ *205/348–4668.* ⌑ *$2.* ⊙ *Daily 9–4.*

★ The **Warner Collection,** displayed in two locations and comprising several hundred paintings as well as dozens of artifacts and sculptures, is quite possibly the nation's largest private collection of American painting. The Asian-style, beautifully landscaped **Gulf States Paper Corporation headquarters** (✉ 1400 River Rd. NE, ☎ 205/553–6200; ⌑ Free; ⊙ Sat. 10–5, Sun. 1–5; tours weekdays at 5:30 and 6:30) houses a range of art, including works by the Wyeths, Albert Bierstadt, Frederic Remington, Thomas Cole, and George Catlin. A short drive away is the even more impressive collection in the exquisitely furnished **Mildred Warner House** (✉ 1925 8th St., ☎ 205/345–4062; ⌑ Free; ⊙ Tours on the hr weekends 1–5), a log cabin built in 1822 (with an 1835 brick addition). William Aiken Walker's revealing Southern folk paintings, which depict 19th-century African-American life, are enough to make a visit worthwhile. There are works by such painters as Winslow Homer, John Singer Sargent, Childe Hassam, Georgia O'Keeffe, and James A. M. Whistler.

Information on the area can be obtained from the **Tuscaloosa Convention and Visitors Bureau** (✉ 1305 Greensboro Ave., ☎ 205/391–9200 or 800/538–8696), open weekdays 8–5. History and architecture aficionados can take a tour with the **Tuscaloosa County Preservation Society,** at the Battle-Friedman House (✉ 1010 Greensboro Ave., ☎ 205/758–2238 or 205/758–6138).

Dining

$$–$$$ ✕ **The Globe.** Ten minutes from downtown Tuscaloosa, across the Black Warrior River, you'll find the town of Northport and the big barnlike structure that once housed a dry goods store. Two actors have turned it into an adventurous dining establishment. Named after Shakespeare's first theater, the restaurant has a long English tavern–style bar in one of the two dining rooms; giant line drawings of scenes from Shakespeare's plays adorn the walls. But the international menu is the true star, including such entrées as pan-sautéed orange roughy, vegetarian quesadillas, Thai emerald curry, and broiled tilapia. The only thing that's typically Southern is the friendly service. ✉ *430 Main Ave., Northport,* ☎ *205/391–0949. Reservations not accepted. AE, D, MC, V.*

The Arts

Music lovers can stop in to hear the estimable **Tuscaloosa Symphony Orchestra** (✉ Battle-Friedman House, 1010 Greensboro Ave., ☎ 205/ 752–5515); and crafts collectors will enjoy October's outstanding **Kentuck Festival of the Arts** (☎ 205/758–1257), in nearby Northport, a town that has attracted many artists.

Moundville

14 mi south of Tuscaloosa on U.S. 69.

Near Moundville is a site that illuminates the lives of the area's prehistoric residents. **Moundville Archaeological Park** contains a number of artifacts that can be traced to the prehistoric forefathers of local Seminole, Creek, and Cherokee Native Americans. On the grounds are 20 earthen temple mounds (the largest of which supports a reconstructed Native American temple), an archaeological museum, a reconstructed native village, a nature trail leading to the Black Warrior River, picnic areas, and a campground. ⊠ *AL 69S*, ☎ *205/371–2572.* 🖭 *$4.* ☉ *Museum daily 9–5, park daily 8–8.*

Birmingham and North Alabama A to Z

Arriving and Departing

Birmingham's **Greyhound** (☎ 800/231–2222) terminal is on 19th Avenue North and Park Place. Greyhound also serves Huntsville, Decatur, and Florence.

I–59 goes northeast from Birmingham to Chattanooga, southwest to Tuscaloosa, and on into Mississippi. I–20 runs east to Anniston and Atlanta. I–65 goes north to Decatur and Nashville and south to Montgomery and Mobile. U.S. 72 and Alternate U.S. 72 run east–west across the northern part of the state and connect Florence, Tuscumbia, Decatur, and Huntsville.

For airline telephone numbers, *see* Air Travel *in* the Gold Guide. **Birmingham International Airport** (☎ 205/595–0533) is less than 3 mi from central downtown and is served by American, ComAir, Continental, Delta/Swissair, Northwest/KLM, Southwest, United/Lufthansa, US Airways, and US Airways Express. Taxis are readily available; the fare to most hotels is about $10 for one passenger, $5 for each additional passenger. Many hotels provide limousine service from the airport by prior arrangement. If you're traveling by car, follow the clearly marked signs downtown.

Huntsville International Airport (☎ 256/772–9395), at Exit 7 off I–565, is served by American, American Eagle, ComAir, Continental, Delta, Northwest, and US Airways.

Northwest Alabama Regional Airport (☎ 256/381–2869) is served by Northwest.

The only **Amtrak** station (☎ 205/324–3033 or 800/872–7245) in central Alabama is on Morris Avenue in downtown Birmingham. Trains run daily.

Getting Around

A car is a necessity in this region, where sights, accommodations, and restaurants are spread throughout the cities and towns.

The **Metro Area Express** (MAX) (☎ 205/521–0101) serves Birmingham. Buses require exact change—$1 fare, 25¢ transfer—and only run weekdays, typically 6–6.

Birmingham's **Yellow Cab** (☎ 205/252–1131) charges $1.75 plus $1.20 for each additional mile.

Contacts and Resources

Ambulance, police (☎ 911). **University Hospital** (⊠ 619 S. 19th St., ☎ 205/934–6500) has the all-night emergency room closest to downtown Birmingham.

GUIDED TOURS

The **Greater Birmingham Convention and Visitors Bureau** (☞ Visitor Information, *below*) has free brochures for self-guided tours of the downtown and Five Points South areas.

PHARMACY

CVS Pharmacy (⊠ 48 Green Springs Hwy., in Red Mountain Plaza, ☎ 205/942–1629) is open 24 hours.

RADIO STATIONS

AM: WERC 960, talk; WDJC 1260, Christian. **FM:** WBHM 90.3, public; WZZK 104.7, country; WODL 106.9, oldies; WRAX 107.7, modern rock.

VISITOR INFORMATION

Birmingham Convention and Visitors Bureau (⊠ 2200 9th Ave. N, 35203, ☎ 205/458–8000 or 800/458–8085). **Cullman Area Chamber of Commerce** (⊠ 211 2nd Ave. NE, 35056, ☎ 256/734–0454). **Decatur Convention and Visitors Bureau** (⊠ 719 6th Ave. SE, 35602, ☎ 256/350–2028 or 800/524–6181). **Huntsville/Madison County Convention and Visitors Bureau** (⊠ 700 Monroe St., 35801, ☎ 256/533–5723 or 800/772–2348). **Tuscaloosa Convention and Visitors Bureau** (⊠ 1305 Greensboro Ave., 35401, ☎ 205/391–9200 or 800/538–8696).

MONTGOMERY AND CENTRAL ALABAMA

Selma, Demopolis, Tuskegee

The flatlands of Alabama's central section provide the stage for life on Southern plantations of another century, the story of the Civil War, and the civil rights movement. Montgomery is a good base for exploring this region's Old South plantations, historic sites, and big fishing lakes.

Numbers in the margin correspond to points of interest on the Downtown Montgomery and Central and South Alabama maps.

Montgomery

From the days when the Civil War was the national preoccupation to another era when civil rights dominated the headlines, Montgomery has been in the forefront of Southern life. As you stand on the spot where Jefferson Davis took the oath of office as president of the Confederacy, you can gaze upon the Dexter Avenue King Memorial Baptist Church where Dr. Martin Luther King Jr. preached his message of freedom. A century apart in time and worlds apart in symbolism, the two landmarks are a mere block apart geographically.

Today Montgomery is the epitome of a progressive Southern business city. New hotels and restaurants spring up frequently, along with skyscraper office complexes. Still, many historic homes and buildings remain. Alabama's capital city is rich in its past and strives to become richer in its future.

★ ㉗ The **State Capitol** was built in 1851 and briefly (for a few months in 1861) served as the first capitol for the Confederate States of America. On the front portico, a bronze star marks the spot where Jefferson Davis stood to take the oath of office as president of the Confederacy. There is an amazing piece of interior design: The stairway curling up the sides of the circular hallway is freestanding, without visible support. The state's rich history has been caught by an artist's brush in great, colorful murals. In the large House chamber and smaller Sen-

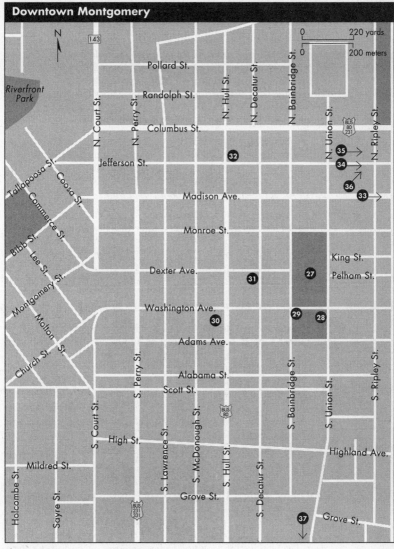

ate chamber, there are fireplaces with black Egyptian marble mantel pieces. ⊠ *600 Dexter Ave., at Bainbridge St.,* ☎ *334/242–3935.* ⊙ *Weekdays 9–5, Sat. 9–4.*

㉘ Built in 1840, the **First White House of the Confederacy** was occupied by Jefferson Davis and his family while the Confederacy was being organized. Today it contains many of their possessions, plus other artifacts of the Civil War period. The house is across the street from the State Capitol. ⊠ *644 Washington Ave.,* ☎ *334/242–1861.* ⊑ *Free.* ⊙ *Tours weekdays 8–4:30. Closed weekends.*

㉙ The **Alabama Department of Archives and History** houses the first state-funded archives in the United States as well as galleries with artifacts documenting the state's past, with an emphasis on 19th-century Alabama. ⊠ *624 Washington Ave.,* ☎ *334/242–4363.* ⊑ *Free.* ⊙ *Weekdays 8–5, Sat. 9–5. Reference room closed Mon.*

★ **㉚** On the grounds of the Southern Poverty Law Center, the **Civil Rights Memorial** has water flowing over a table that bears the names of 40 people who gave their lives for racial equality. On a wall behind this, over which water also flows, is a biblical quote used in a speech by Dr. Martin Luther King Jr.: UNTIL JUSTICE ROLLS DOWN LIKE WATERS AND RIGHTEOUSNESS LIKE A MIGHTY STREAM. The sculptor, Maya Lin, also created the Vietnam Veterans Memorial in Washington, D.C. ⊠ *400 Washington Ave.,* ☎ *334/264–0286.* ⊑ *Free.* ⊙ *24 hrs.* ✎

㉛ The **Dexter Avenue King Memorial Baptist Church** is where Dr. Martin Luther King Jr. began his career as a minister in 1955. From the church he directed the Montgomery bus boycott, which began after Rosa Parks was arrested for refusing to give up her seat to white people. The church's sanctuary and the basement Sunday-school rooms are open to visitors. A mural covering one basement wall depicts people and events associated with Dr. King and the civil rights movement. ⊠ *454 Dexter Ave.,* ☎ *334/263–3970.* ⊑ *Free.* ⊙ *Tours Mon.–Thurs. at 10 and 2, Fri. at 10.*

㉜ **Old Alabama Town,** about six blocks northwest of the capitol between Madison Avenue and Columbus Street, consists of 40 newly restored houses, barns, stores, and other structures from between 1818 and the turn of the century. The **Loeb Reception Center** has a self-guided cassette walking tour that covers the 10 house museums clustered in the Living Block. Volunteers give tours of the **Ordeman-Shaw House** (⊠ 230 N. Hull St.), an Italianate town house with restored outbuildings and gardens. The Working Block, just off Columbus Street on the district's north side, includes a gristmill, blacksmith shop, the **Cotton Gin and Cotton Museum,** the **Haigler Plantation Office,** and the **Rose-Morris Craft Center.** ⊠ *Loeb Reception Center, 301 Columbus St.,* ☎ *334/240–4500 or 888/240–1850.* ⊑ *Self-guided tour $7.* ⊙ *Mon.–Sat. 9–3.*

㉝ Alabama's oldest fine arts museum, the **Montgomery Museum of Fine Arts** has an impressive facility within the same park that houses the Alabama Shakespeare Festival Theatre. Highlights are works by Southern artists; ARTWORKS, a hands-on gallery for children and adults; a permanent gallery exhibiting the Blount, Inc., Corporate Collection of American Art; and a gift shop, auditorium, and print gallery, as well as galleries for changing exhibitions. You can dine in Cafe M. ⊠ *1 Museum Dr.,* ☎ *334/244–5700.* ⊑ *Free.* ⊙ *Tues.–Wed. and Fri.–Sat. 10–5, Thurs. 10–9, Sun. noon–5.* ✎

㉞ The 40-acre **Montgomery Zoo** is home to 800 animals from five continents. Dining, a gift shop, and a train ride are offered as well. Extensive renovations enable visitors to view the animals in natural habitat–like settings. Don't miss the bald eagles, black bears, and monkey island. ✉ *2301 Coliseum Pkwy.,* ☎ *334/240–4900.* 🎫 *$4.50.* ◷ *Daily 9–5.*

③⑤ The **Hank Williams Memorial** tombstone marks the burial place of one of Alabama's own, country-music singer and songwriter Hank Williams; after his untimely death at age 29 on New Year's Day 1953, he was brought here for one of the city's grandest funerals. It was held at City Hall, with top country stars delivering eulogies and singing sad songs. The memorial depicts him, along with sheet music from his most popular songs, including "Your Cheatin' Heart." ✉ *Oakwood Cemetery Annex, 1305 Upper Wetumpka Rd.,* ☎ *334/264–4938.* ◷ *Sunrise–sunset.*

③⑥ **Jasmine Hill Gardens and Outdoor Museum,** atop a wooded hill, are 20 acres of beautiful gardens with replicas of Greek sculptures and of the ruins of the Temple of Hera. The visitor center is an exact replica of the original temple facade as it once stood intact on Mt. Olympus. ✉ *3001 Jasmine Hill Rd.,* ☎ *334/567–6463.* 🎫 *$5.* ◷ *Tues.–Sun. 9–5.*

③⑦ The **F. Scott and Zelda Fitzgerald Museum** displays belongings of this colorful couple in their former home. Zelda Fitzgerald grew up in the area, and some of her artwork hangs at Montgomery's Museum of Fine Arts. Her husband, F. Scott, is famous for novels including *The Great Gatsby* and *Tender Is the Night* and numerous short stories. A 25-minute video on their life in Montgomery is shown. ✉ *919 Felder Ave.,* ☎ *334/264–4222.* 🎫 *Free.* ◷ *Wed.–Fri. 10–2, weekends 1–5, and by appointment.*

Dining and Lodging

$$$ ✕ **Vintage Year.** Chef Judy Martin's menu features snapper, tuna,
★   shrimp, salmon, and other fish prepared in the style of new American cuisine, with all ingredients as fresh as possible, including an assortment of fresh herbs. Lamb shank and duck are also popular items. The decor is elegant, and the neighborhood bar is a favorite meeting place. ✉ *405 Cloverdale Rd.,* ☎ *334/264–8463. Reservations essential. AE, MC, V. Closed Sun.–Mon. No lunch.*

$$–$$$ ✕ **Jubilee Seafood Company.** In a very pleasant small café, Bud Skinner cooks some of the finest and freshest seafood dishes in town, including snapper prepared in a variety of ways (including Greek style—sautéed in olive oil and spices and topped with roasted almonds), soft-shell crabs, crab claws, and other delicacies. For a real treat, try the barbecued shrimp, which are marinated in a secret red sauce, wrapped in bacon, and charbroiled. Bud also has a tasty West Indies salad with marinated crab. ✉ *1057 Woodley Rd., Cloverdale Plaza,* ☎ *334/262–6224. Reservations not accepted. AE, MC, V. Closed Sun.–Mon. No lunch.*

$$–$$$ ✕ **Sahara Restaurant.** Joe and Mike Deep's Sahara, in Cloverdale, is one of Montgomery's traditional Southern restaurants. Linen tablecloths and uniformed servers add to the charm. Fresh snapper, grouper, and scampi are broiled to taste, and succulent steaks are grilled over coals. The seafood gumbo is a specialty. ✉ *511 E. Edgemont Ave., Cloverdale,* ☎ *334/262–1215. AE, D, DC, MC, V. Closed Sun.*

$–$$ ✕ **Corsino's.** Serving Montgomery since 1954, family-run Corsino's is
★   one of the city's most popular restaurants. The noontime crowd gathers daily from state government offices and downtown businesses to enjoy some of the South's finest pasta dishes. You can also choose a savory, foot-long Italian sandwich served on hot, homemade Italian bread, or a hand-tossed New York–style pizza. The restaurant isn't fancy, just comfortable and friendly. ✉ *911 S. Court St.,* ☎ *334/263–9752. Reservations not accepted. No credit cards. Closed weekends.*

$-$$ ✕ **Sassafras Tearoom.** You can buy the table on which you ate and enjoy a superb meal in the Victorian atmosphere of this century-old shop-cum-eatery in the Cottage Hill district. Operated by retired colonel Jim Wallace and his wife, Mary, the restaurant draws professionals and antiques hunters. Sassafras tea, either hot or cold, accompanies crunchy chicken salad, buttermilk pie, and other home-cooked delectables. ✉ *532 Clay St.*, ☎ *334/265–7277. AE, D, DC, MC, V. Closed weekends. No dinner*

$ ✕ **Chris' Hot Dog Stand.** A Montgomery tradition for more than 80
★ years, this eatery has booths and an old-fashioned lunch counter with stools. The famous sauce combines chili peppers, onions, and a variety of herbs that give his hot dogs a one-of-a-kind flavor. Try the hot dog with "kitchen chili," a heavy, hot chili of beans and onions that you eat with a knife and fork. ✉ *138 Dexter Ave.*, ☎ *334/265–6850. Reservations not accepted. No credit cards. Closed Sun.*

$ ✕ **Farmer's Market Cafeteria.** In a downtown industrial building, the cafeteria is about as plain as restaurants get, except for the photos of past sports heroes on the wall. Fried chicken, catfish, country-style smothered steak, and fresh vegetables are served. The hearty breakfast with smoked bacon and homemade biscuits is a local tradition. ✉ *315 N. McDonough St.*, ☎ *334/262–9163. Reservations not accepted. No credit cards. Closed weekends. No dinner.*

$ ✕ **Martin's Restaurant.** Martin's is plain but comfortable. Here you'll find generous helpings of home-cooked fresh vegetables, Southern fried chicken, and delicious panfried catfish fresh from Alabama ponds. The corn-bread muffins literally melt in your mouth. ✉ *1796 Carter Hill Rd.*, ☎ *334/265–1767. No credit cards. Closed Sat.*

$$$ ☷ **Embassy Suites Hotel.** This downtown all-suite high-rise hotel between
★ the Civic Center and the old railroad station epitomizes Montgomery's new image. A spectacular atrium lobby resembles a tropical rain forest. Glass elevators give you a bird's-eye view. Included are a full cooked-to-order breakfast and a two-hour manager's reception each evening. ✉ *300 Tallapoosa St., 36104*, ☎ *334/269–5055*, 🖷 *334/269–0360. 237 suites. Restaurant, lounge, indoor pool, hot tub, sauna, steam room, exercise room, business services, meeting rooms. AE, D, DC, MC, V.*

$$-$$$ ☷ **Marriott Courtyard.** This handsome, contemporary low-rise motor inn with a sunny gardenlike courtyard offers amenities popular with business travelers—spacious rooms, king-size beds, oversize work desks, excellent lighting, and hot water dispensers for in-room coffee. ✉ *5555 Carmichael Rd., near I–85 Exit 6, 36117*, ☎ *334/272–5533*, 🖷 *334/279–0853. 134 rooms, 12 suites. Restaurant, bar, pool, hot tub, exercise room, meeting rooms. AE, D, DC, MC, V.*

$$ ☷ **Red Bluff Cottage.** In the heart of downtown and overlooking the
★ Alabama River plain, this cottage is bright and cheerful. Rooms are filled with antiques, some of them dating to the 18th century, collected by the Reverend Mark Waldo, who served an Episcopal parish in this city for many years, and his wife, Anne. The music room/library contains a harpsichord, a piano, and lots of books. ✉ *551 Clay St., Box 1026, 36101*, ☎ *334/264–0056*, 🖷 *334/263–3054. 4 rooms. Library. BP. AE, D, MC, V.*

$-$$ ☷ **Holiday Inn Hotel and Suites Historic Downtown.** The former Madison Hotel has an atrium lobby with a waterfall, plants and palm trees, maroon and burgundy chairs, and wrought-iron sofa sets that help establish a New Orleans theme. Elvis Presley once slept here, but you're more likely to run into legislators and businesspeople than rock stars. The Civic Center is two blocks away. ✉ *120 Madison Ave., 36104*, ☎ *334/264–2231*, 🖷 *334/263–3179. 153 rooms, 19 suites. Restaurant, 2 lounges, pool, meeting rooms. AE, D, DC, MC, V.*

$-$$ ⊡ **La Quinta Motor Inn.** The lobby of this chain property, just off I–85, is decorated in muted tones, with a terra-cotta-tile floor and silk flowers. Rooms are contemporary, in light earth tones. ⊠ *1280 Eastern Bypass, 36117-2231,* ☎ *334/271–1620,* ℻ *334/244–7919. 130 rooms. Pool. AE, D, DC, MC, V.*

$ ⊡ **Best Western–Montgomery Lodge.** This two-story hotel 3 mi from the airport has a lobby bookcase stocked for guests' use. Rooms have royal blue or cranberry hues; most have recliners and coffeemakers. ⊠ *977 W. South Blvd., 36105,* ☎ *334/288–5740,* ℻ *334/286–0042. 100 rooms, 1 suite. Restaurant, lounge, pool, meeting rooms. AE, D, DC, MC, V.*

The Arts

The **Montgomery Symphony Orchestra** (☎ 334/240–4004) performs at the **Davis Theatre for the Performing Arts** (⊠ 251 Montgomery St., ☎ 334/241–9567). Other arts-related events are held at the 1,200-plus-seat auditorium as well.

Shakespearean plays, modern drama, and musicals are performed on two stages at the **Alabama Shakespeare Festival** (⊠ Wynton Blount Cultural Park, 1 Festival Dr., ☎ 334/271–5353 or 800/841–4273), which is housed in the Carolyn Blount Theatre in a 250-acre park on the east side of Montgomery. The season runs from November through September; tickets cost $21–$30.

Concerts are hosted at the large auditorium at Montgomery's **Civic Center** (⊠ 300 Bibb St., ☎ 334/241–2100). At the campus theater of **Auburn University at Montgomery** (⊠ 7300 University Dr., ☎ 334/244–3632), student actors perform drama and comedy.

Outdoor Activities and Sports

DOG RACING

Greyhound races are held at **Victoryland,** about 20 mi east of Montgomery, just off I–85N in Shorter (☎ 334/269–6087 or 800/688–2946). There are racing and pari-mutuel betting every night but Sunday and several matinees during the week. Thoroughbred and greyhound events are also simulcast on race days. No one under 19 is admitted.

GOLF

Montgomery is home to **Lagoon Park** (⊠ 2855 Lagoon Park Dr., ☎ 334/271–7000), a very flat 18-hole, par-72 course with some water hazards and trees, consistently rated by *Golf Digest* as one of the top 50 public courses in the United States. **River Run** (⊠ AL 5, ☎ 334/271–2811) has a pro shop and putting greens. **Kolomi** (⊠ 800 Dozier Rd., ☎ 334/279–6686) is an 18-hole, par-72 course adjacent to the Tallapoosa River.

MINIATURE GOLF

Funtasia (⊠ 5761 Atlanta Hwy., ☎ 334/277–4653) takes golfers on a safari through and around a man-made mountain, complete with large model elephants and other animals, and a cave.

TENNIS

Lagoon Park (⊠ 2855 Lagoon Park Dr., ☎ 334/271–7001) has 17 lighted courts and is open daily.

Shopping

ANTIQUES

Herron House (⊠ 7834 Troy Hwy., ☎ 334/265–2063), Montgomery's oldest antiques shop, specializes in garden statuary as well as 18th- and 19th-century European furniture and accessories. **Bodiford's Antiques** (⊠ 919 Hampton St., ☎ 334/265–4220) has a variety of general antiques, including furniture and accessories.

MALLS

In addition to its anchor stores—Sears, Parisian, and Dillard's—**East-dale Mall** (✉ On Eastern Bypass and Atlanta Hwy., ☎ 334/277–7359) has a variety of specialty stores, record- and bookstores, restaurants, an eight-screen cinema complex, and Alabama's only ice-skating rink in a mall. **Montgomery Mall** (✉ 2925-A Montgomery Mall, at South Blvd. and McGehee Ave., ☎ 334/281–0242) is anchored by JCPenney, Parisian, and Dillard's and has a food court.

Selma

㊳ *45 mi west of Montgomery via U.S. 80.*

Selma has played major roles in both Civil War and civil rights history. With the Confederacy's second-largest arson and foundry, Selma was a target of Union attack in 1865. Almost 100 years after that fighting—Alabama's only major inland Civil War battle—Selma came again to the forefront on March 21, 1965, as the stage of "Bloody Sunday." Civil rights protesters seeking to draw attention to the voting rights issue set out on a 50-mi march to Montgomery, where they intended to present their plight to lawmakers. Marchers were beaten by state troopers with billy clubs as photographers captured the atrocities. The several hundred protesters on that failed march tried again three weeks later. Joined by some 20,000 supporters and led by civil rights leader Dr. Martin Luther King Jr., they accomplished a carefully guarded march to Montgomery, which resulted ultimately in the passing of the nation's Voting Rights Act. The path of that walk is a national All-American Road and an official National Trail, and the city honors the event every March.

Among the many sites worth visiting are **Old Town,** the largest historic district in the state, with more than 1,200 buildings, including the Greek Revival **Sturdivant Hall,** and **Martin Luther King Jr. Street,** a historic walking tour; the **Chamber of Commerce** (☎ 334/875–7241) has self-guided tours of these. The **National Voting Rights Museum and Institute** (✉ 1012 Water Ave., ☎ 334/418–0800) offers a record of the important role of voting rights in the civil rights struggle.

The **Old Depot Museum** (✉ 4 Martin Luther King Jr. St., ☎ 334/874–2197) offers history from the Civil War to civil rights. The **Smitherman Historic Building** (✉ 109 Union St., ☎ 334/874–2174) is an antebellum structure that houses the Art Lewis Civil War Collection.

In late March a **Historic Selma Pilgrimage** (☎ 800/457–3562) takes visitors through several antebellum homes, museums, and churches. In late April of every odd-number year, one of the largest biannual **Civil War reenactments** (☎ 334/875–7241 or 800/457–3562) in the nation draws thousands to the site of the Battle of Selma, on the Alabama River.

The **Visitor Information Center** (✉ 2207 Broad St., ☎ 334/875–7485) and the **Chamber of Commerce** (✉ 513 Lauderdale St., ☎ 334/875–7244 or 800/45–SELMA, ✎) have information about the city and festivals such as the Tale Tellin' Festival and Riverfront Market and the African Extravaganza, both in October.

Dining and Lodging

$$–$$$ ✕🏨 **St. James Hotel.** Parlors here bustled with wealthy cotton planters, merchants, and politicians in the 1830s. Later that century outlaws Jesse and Frank James were guests. One of the few remaining antebellum riverfront hotels in the country, the completely restored St. James has a lobby outfitted with antiques and rooms with 1800s plantation reproductions; suites have fireplaces and hot tubs. This is downtown

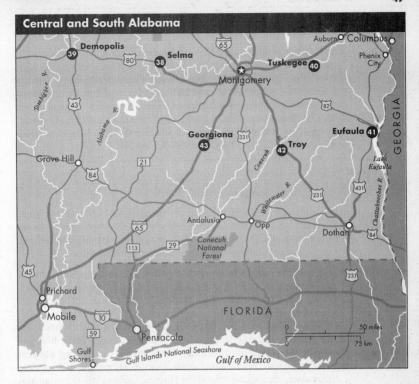

Central and South Alabama

Selma's only full-service hotel, and the adjacent St. James Place anchors the Water Avenue Historic District. ⌧ *1200 Water Ave., 36701,* ☎ *334/872–3234 or 888/264–6788,* FAX *334/872–0332. 38 rooms, 4 suites. Restaurant, lounge. AE, D, DC, MC, V.*

$$ ✕ **Major Grumbles** Named for a true Southern character—a self-appointed "major" in the Civil War—Major Grumbles is located in a circa-1830s former cotton warehouse. The casual, rustic atmosphere features photos of Selma's history. The restaurant is known for its marinated, chargrilled chicken breast. ⌧ *1 Grumbles Alley,* ☎ *334/872–2006. AE, DC, MC, V. Closed Sun.*

Demopolis

㊴ *40 mi west of Selma via U.S. 80.*

Demopolis takes great pride in its Southern heritage. Take time to ride past antebellum homes and 18th-century buildings in the historic downtown area. The 10,000-acre Demopolis Lake offers fishing, boating, swimming, picnicking, and campgrounds. For details contact the **Demopolis Area Chamber of Commerce** (⌧ 102 E. Washington St., ☎ 334/289–0270), open weekdays 8:30–5, or get brochures anytime at the **information center** (☎ 334/289–5772) at the Best Western Hotel on U.S. 80.

★ **Gaineswood,** built between 1843 and 1861, has been called one of the finest Greek Revival mansions in the South. The house has been extensively restored, down to reproductions of the original French wallpapers. It contains the original furnishings, such as carved four-posters and a flutina—a one-of-a-kind musical instrument invented by the original owner (who also designed Gaineswood itself). Interior architectural elements include elaborate columns and pilasters; friezes and medallions of wood, plaster, cast iron, and leather; and ceiling-dome window lanterns. ⊠ *805 S. Cedar Ave.,* ☎ *334/289–4846.* ⊠ *$5.* ⊘ *Mon.–Sat. 9–5, Sun. 1–5.*

Bluff Hall was built in 1832 as a Federal-style house and remodeled in the Greek Revival style several years later. It stands on a chalky cliff above the Tombigbee River and features a columned front portico, a huge double parlor with Corinthian columns, and Empire and Victorian furnishings donated by friends and descendants of the original owner. Also on display is a collection of period clothing. ⊠ *405 N. Commissioners Ave.,* ☎ *334/289–1666.* ⊠ *$5.* ⊘ *Jan.–Feb., Tues.–Sat. 10–4, Sun. 2–4; Mar.–Dec., Tues.–Sat. 10–5, Sun. 2–5.*

Tuskegee

④⓿ *35 mi east of Montgomery via U.S. 80.*

In addition to being the home of the historic Tuskegee Institute, Tuskegee has some antebellum houses and is near **Tuskegee National Forest** (☎ 334/727–2652), with fishing and hiking opportunities and a replica of the childhood home of Booker T. Washington.

The **Tuskegee Institute National Historic Site** includes the school founded by educator Booker T. Washington in 1881, one of America's first black universities; the institute's Victorian buildings, many designed and constructed by students; and Washington's actual redbrick Victorian home, **the Oaks.** The **George Washington Carver Museum** on the campus includes Carver's original laboratory and a historical study of the Tuskegee Institute. An agricultural chemist, Carver helped improve agricultural practices and also discovered hundreds of uses for the peanut, sweet potato, and soybean. A walking tour of the Historic Campus District originates at the Carver Museum. ⊠ *On Tuskegee College campus, off Old Montgomery Rd.,* ☎ *334/727–3200.* ⊠ *Free.* ⊘ *Daily 9–5.*

Eufaula

④① *90 mi east of Montgomery on U.S. 82.*

Eufaula is a town rich in Southern tradition and antebellum homes; it's also near a national wildlife refuge and has great fishing opportunities. Some homes built between 1834 and 1911 hold open house during the **Eufaula Spring Pilgrimage** (☎ 334/687–3793), in early April, featuring candlelight tours.

Open year-round, the **Shorter Mansion,** a white-columned house museum built in 1884, is a fine example of neoclassical architecture and a showplace of the Seth Lore National Historic District. ⊠ *340 N. Eufaula Ave.,* ☎ *334/687–3793.* ⊠ *$3. Weekdays 9–4, Sun. 1–5.*

Fendall Hall, one of the great 19th-century Italianate-style houses surviving in Alabama, has deep overhanging eaves, a hip roof topped with a cupola, and a long, wraparound porch. ⊠ *917 W. Barbour St.,* ☎ *334/687–8469.* ⊠ *$4.* ⊘ *Mon., Thurs., and Sat. 10–4.*

Outdoor Activities and Sports

Lake Eufaula is one of the best bass lakes in the country, with 8- to 10-pound largemouth bass caught with regularity.

Lakepoint State Park Resort (⊠ U.S. 431N, ☎ 334/687–6676), north of town, has six lighted tennis courts and an 18-hole, par-72 golf course.

Troy

42 *50 mi south of Montgomery on U.S. 231.*

This town is home to Troy State University and a fine pioneer museum. The **Pike Pioneer Museum** complex has more than 14,000 artifacts of the pioneer period—clothing, furniture, farm implements—plus spinning and weaving demonstrations. Don't miss the turn-of-the-century schoolhouse, log house, well-stocked general store, and 1883 steam logging locomotive. Special events—such as fall and spring Pioneer Days, and the Jean Lake Festival—take place throughout the year. Folklife artisans appear the first Saturday of the month from April through December. A picnic area is adjacent to the amphitheater. ⊠ *248 U.S. 231N,* ☎ *334/566–3597.* 🖾 *$3.* ⊘ *Mon.–Sat. 9–5, Sun. 1–5.*

Georgiana

43 *60 mi south of Montgomery on I–65.*

The small, rural community of Georgiana was the birthplace of one of country music's greatest performers—Hank Williams Sr. (1923–1953).

★ The city of Georgiana has established the **Hank Williams Sr. Boyhood Home and Museum,** and fans from around the world have donated Hank Williams memorabilia to fill the house to the brim. Rockers line the large wraparound porch, so you can relax as you listen to the songs of this country-music legend. Many of Williams's personal items are on display, along with an excellent collection of photographs. On the first Saturday in June, Georgiana comes alive for the **Hank Williams Sr. Festival,** as fans and performers pay tribute to their idol. The music goes on long into the night. ⊠ *127 Rose St.,* ☎ *334/376–2396.* 🖾 *$3.* ⊘ *Mon.–Sat. 10–5, Sun. 1–5.*

Montgomery and Central Alabama A to Z

Arriving and Departing

BY BUS

Greyhound (⊠ 950 W. South Blvd., Montgomery, ☎ 334/286–0953 or 800/231–2222).

BY CAR

I–65 runs north to Birmingham and south to Mobile. I–85 begins in Montgomery and runs northeast to Atlanta. U.S. 80 runs west past the airport to Selma.

BY PLANE

Dannelly Field (☎ 334/281–5040) is 7 mi southwest of downtown Montgomery. It is served by American Eagle, Atlantic Southeast, Delta, Northwest Airlink, and US Airways Express (☞ Air Travel *in* Smart Travel Tips A to Z for telephone numbers).

Taxis are readily available and relatively inexpensive at the airport. Many hotels provide transportation from the airport by prior arrangement. To get to the airport by **car** from downtown, take Exit 167 off I–65 to U.S. 80W and go 3 mi to airport entrance. To reach downtown from the airport, turn north onto I–65, follow signs to I–85, and take the first exit, Court Street.

BY TRAIN

The nearest **Amtrak** service to Montgomery and central Alabama is in Birmingham (☎ 800/872–7245). Montgomery has a **Thruway Intermodal Transit Terminal** (☎ 800/872–7245 for information) offering bus service to the Amtrak station in Atlanta, which is about 150 mi, or 2½ hours, northeast.

Getting Around

BY BUS

Montgomery has DART buses that run by request (☎ 334/262–7321) from 5 AM to 9:30 PM, although some routes may vary. Exact change is required for the $1.50 fare.

BY CAR

U.S. 80 cuts east–west across the state, connecting Demopolis, Selma, Montgomery, and Tuskegee. U.S. 82 runs east–west through Montgomery and Eufaula.

BY TAXI

Taxis in Montgomery charge $1.75 for the first ⅙ mi, $1.20 for each additional mile. Try **Yellow Cab** (☎ 334/262–5225).

Contacts and Resources

EMERGENCIES

Ambulance, police (☎ 911). For medical emergencies, contact the **Montgomery Baptist Medical Center** (✉ 2105 E. South Blvd., ☎ 334/288–2100).

GOLF

Several sections of Alabama's **Robert Trent Jones Golf Trail** are in this region: the **Grand National** course at Auburn/Opelika (✉ 3000 Sunbelt Pkwy., ☎ 205/749–9042), **Capitol Hill** (✉ 2600 Constitution Ave., ☎ 334/285–1114), at Prattville; **Highland Oaks** (✉ 704 Royal Pkwy., ☎ 334/712–2820), at Dothan; and **Cambrian Ridge** (✉ 101 Sunbelt Pkwy., ☎ 334/382–9787), at Greenville (considered by many golfers to be the most spectacular on the trail). The four sites offer 11 courses, all challenging and scenic. For reservations and information about any of the 18 trail courses, call ☎ 800/949–4444. Greens fees with cart run $54–$64.

GUIDED TOURS

Landmark Tours (☎ 334/262–4044) and **Whirlwind Tours** (☎ 334/272–5940) offer van and bus tours of area sights.

PHARMACY

Rite Aid (✉ Capitol Plaza Shopping Center, South Bypass, Montgomery, ☎ 334/281–1312) is open seven days a week from 8 AM to midnight.

RADIO STATIONS

AM: WACV 1170, talk; WXVI 1600, jazz. **FM:** WLWI 92.3, country; WZHT 105.7, soul.

VISITOR INFORMATION

Montgomery Visitors Center (✉ 401 Madison Ave., 36104, ☎ 334/262–0013). **Eufaula/Barbour County Chamber of Commerce** (✉ 102 N. Orange Ave., Eufaula 36027, ☎ 334/687–6664 or 800/524–7529).

MOBILE AND THE GULF COAST

Mobile, one of the oldest cities in Alabama—celebrating its 300th birthday in 2002—is also perhaps the most graceful. The city has profuse plantings of azaleas—a feature highlighted each spring with the Azalea Trail Festival. Nearby is Bellingrath Gardens, one of the most spectacular public gardens in the country, especially in spring, when more than 250,000 plants are indeed resplendent.

Mardi Gras began in Mobile, long before New Orleans ever celebrated Fat Tuesday, and today the city celebrates the pre-Lenten season, usually in February, with parades and merrymaking day and

TEE TIME: ALABAMA'S ROBERT TRENT JONES GOLF TRAIL

ALABAMA DOESN'T HAVE MUCH in the way of golf history, unlike Georgia, its neighbor to the east, which spawned golfing great Bobby Jones. Jones built the acclaimed Augusta National Golf Course and founded the Masters tournament which captures the golfing world's undivided attention each April. But another Jones, the legendary and prolific golf architect Robert Trent Jones Sr., a namesake of, but no relation to, Bobby Jones, has placed Alabama golf on the map in the past decade with a series of scenic, challenging public golf courses spanning the state.

The **Robert Trent Jones Golf Trail** comprises eight locations with 378 holes of golf stretching more than 100 mi through bucolic scenery. Jones, whose long storied career includes designing more than 500 courses, took on the ambitious project as an octogenarian in the late 1980s and met with rave reviews. Unlike most resort courses where you are routed through a developer's concocted maze of condos and town houses, only indigenous pines, oaks, rivers, streams, and lakes surround the Golf Trail courses. And more good news for golfers: wherever you are in Alabama, chances are you're not too far from one of the trail stops in Huntsville, Anniston/Gadsden, Birmingham, Montgomery, Greenville, Auburn, Dothan, or Mobile.

Courses on the trail are often described as challenging—a euphemism for just plain hard. It's recommended that you leave the championships tees to the pros, and move up one set of tees from your normal location, particularly for shorter hitters. Golf carts on the trail feature global positioning systems (GPS), providing yardage measurements on a small computer screen and limited information about the course. Purchasing a yardage book with suggestions on how to play each hole is a good idea. Tee shots that don't find the fairway are often severely punished by a forest, a splash in a lake or creek, or a difficult hillside lie. There are no breaks once you get to the green either, as almost every hole on the trail features gigantic undulating greens.

The three South Central Alabama locations make an excellent and convenient trip, with terrain much hillier than you might expect. **Capitol Hill** in Prattville, northwest of Montgomery, is not only the newest of the eight locations, but also the grandest and with the most layouts. There are three championship, 18-hole courses starting out from a fantastic clubhouse built with a view of downtown Montgomery. **Cambrian Ridge** in Greenville, about an hour south of Montgomery, is also one not to miss. Three challenging nines wind around the clubhouse, situated on the highest point in Butler County. Cambrian Ridge's Sherling Nine is stunningly serene and beautiful, particularly holes three through seven, which border placid, tree-lined Lake Sherling. Its Canyon Nine runs through an old deer-hunting site, starting off dramatically, with a 501-yard Par 4 that plays 200 ft straight downhill. The parallel finishing holes for both the Sherling and Canyon nines play uphill past unique geologic weathered brown boulders in a gully separating the two fairways. **Grand National** in Opeleika, near Auburn University, features two excellent championship courses that play along the banks of Lake Saughahatche. The Lakes Course at Grand National was home to the NCAA Golf Championships in 2000 as well as a regular stop on the professional Buy.com Tour.

These state-owned golf courses are much more economical than comparable lush resort courses of the Southeast, with greens fees ranging from as little as $29 to the peak rate of $49 in springtime at the busier tracks. The courses also are well managed, and the pace of play is steady, even in peak times in April. The only way you can go wrong here is to hit poor shots. Otherwise, Alabama can hold it's head up high knowing that there's more than one destination in the south worthy of a golfer's attention.

—Sam Starnes

night. In March the two-day Historic Mobile Homes Tour showcases the city's architecture, which includes Federal-style town houses, Creole cottages, and antebellum plantation homes. Springtime also brings the annual Festival of Flowers, a spectacular garden and flower show on the campus of Spring Hill College. In fall BayFest—a music festival covering several downtown blocks—rocks Mobile the first weekend in October.

The area of the Gulf Coast around Gulf Shores, to the south of Mobile, encompasses about 50 mi of pure white-sand beach, including a former peninsula called Pleasure Island and Dauphin Island to the west. Though hotels and condominiums take up a good deal of the beachfront, some of it remains public. Here you'll find small-town Southern beach life, with excellent deep-sea fishing as well as freshwater fishing in the bays and bayous, water sports of all types, and world-class golf.

Those with more time might explore the eastern shore of Mobile Bay—Spanish Fort, Daphne, and Fairhope—where, sometime between June and September, locals and tourists eagerly await the mythical phenomenon known as a Jubilee. During a Jubilee the bay's bounty—fish, crabs, shrimp, and more—scramble for shore and into the waiting nets of those who have usually stumbled out of bed in the middle of the night, awakened by their neighbors' excited cries. There are lots of explanations for the creatures' rush to the shore, the most popular having to do with a lack of available oxygen, but locals like to think of it more as a magical occurrence. The Eastern Shore revels in the laid-back atmosphere of yesteryear: live oaks hung with Spanish moss; sprawling clapboard houses with wide porches overlooking the lazy, dark water of the bay; and interesting watering holes where local artists and writers meet informally. At Point Clear, south of Fairhope, is the Victorian-style Marriott's Grand Hotel, host since the mid-19th century to the vacationing wealthy.

Numbers in the margin correspond to numbers on the Mobile and the Gulf Coast map.

Mobile

④④ *170 mi southwest of Montgomery on I–65.*

Fort Condé was the name given by the French in 1711 to the site known today as Mobile; around it blossomed the first white settlement in what is now Alabama. For eight years it was the capital of the French colonial empire, and it remained under French control until 1763, long after the capital had moved to New Orleans. This French connection survives in the area's strong Creole-flavor cuisine, which rivals New Orleans's in fieriness.

Mobile, a busy international port, is noted for its tree-lined boulevards fanning westward from the riverfront. In the heart of the revitalized downtown area is Bienville Square, a park shaded by moss-draped live oaks and has an ornate cast-iron fountain in the center. One of the city's main thoroughfares, Dauphin Street, experienced a renaissance in the 1990s and now is home to many thriving restaurant, bars, and shops.

In the center of town, **Fort Condé** survives as a reminder of the city's beginnings, thanks to a reconstruction (one-third of the original size) that preserved it when its remains were discovered—150 years after the fort was destroyed—during the building of the I–10 interchange (an I–10 tunnel now runs under the fort). A portion of the reconstructed French fort, originally built in 1724–35, houses the **visitor center** for the city, as well as a museum and several re-created rooms. Among the

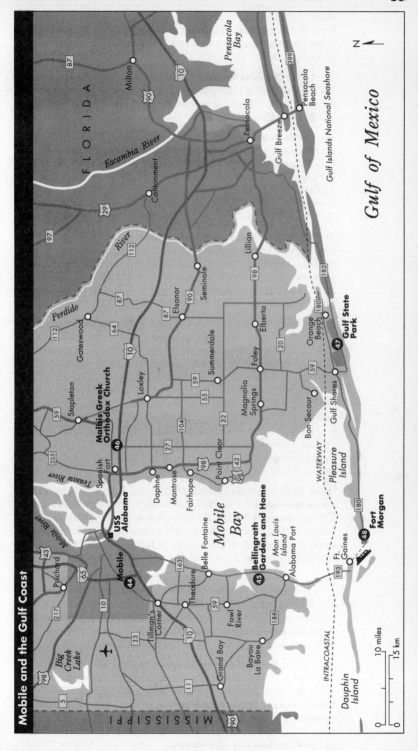

Mobile and the Gulf Coast

many brochures at the center are ones outlining excellent walking tours of the city's historic districts, including De Tonti Square, Church Street East, and Dauphin Street. ⊠ *150 S. Royal St.,* ☎ *334/434–7304.* ⚑ *Free.* ☉ *Daily 8–5.*

The **Condé-Charlotte Museum House,** next to Fort Condé, was built in 1822–24 as Mobile's first official jail and contains rooms furnished in the style from different periods of the city's history. ⊠ *104 Theatre St.,* ☎ *334/432–4722,* ⚑ *$3.* ☉ *Tues.–Sat. 10–4.*

The **Mobile Museum of Art** (⊠ 4850 Museum Dr., ☎ 334/343–2667) is undergoing a $15 million expansion and renovation at its Langan Park location in west Mobile. The new building is scheduled to open in early 2002. Meanwhile, the museum's permanent art collection is displayed at **Mobile Civic Center's Expo Hall** (⊠ 401 Civic Center Dr.). A branch gallery, **Mobile Museum of Art Downtown** (⊠ 300 Dauphin St., ☎ 334/343–2667), is near Cathedral Park in downtown Mobile.

At press time, the **Museum of Mobile** planned to move in early 2001 into the renovated Southern Market/Old City Hall building, at 111 S. Royal St., next to the Gulf Coast Exploreum. The museum's former location, in the historic Bernstein-Bush House at 355 Government St., will become the **Mardi Gras Museum of Mobile,** with a wide array of memorabilia from Carnival's long history in Mobile. ☎ *334/208–7569.*

The **Oakleigh Garden Historic District** begins 1 mi southwest of Fort Condé; signs lead to **Oakleigh,** an antebellum Greek Revival mansion with a stairway circling under ancient live oaks to a small portico. The high-ceiling half-timber house was built between 1833 and 1838 and is typical of the most expensive dwellings of its day. Fine period furniture, portraits, silver, jewelry, kitchen implements, toys, and more are displayed. Next door is the **Cox-Deasy House,** a raised Creole cottage built in 1850 that is a more typical middle-class home. Members of the Historic Mobile Preservation Society conduct tours of Oakleigh and the Cox-Deasy House. ⊠ *350 Oakleigh Pl.,* ☎ *334/432–1281.* ⚑ *$5 for both homes.* ☉ *Mon.–Sat. 10–4. Guided tours every ½ hr, last tour begins at 3:30.*

In the DeTonti Square Historic District, the Italianate **Richards–DAR House Museum,** built in 1860, holds magnificent period furnishings. The lace ironwork outside the house is notable. The Daughters of the American Revolution administer this welcoming museum, which even serves guests tea and cookies. ⊠ *256 N. Joachim St.,* ☎ *334/434–7320,* ⚑ *$4.* ☉ *Tues.–Sat. 10–4, Sun. 1–4.*

Several of Mobile's churches figure prominently in the area's rich African-American history: The **State Street A.M.E. Zion Church** (⊠ 502 State St., ☎ 334/432–3965) is one of the oldest and most striking African Methodist Episcopal Zion churches in town. The **St. Louis Street Missionary Baptist Church** (⊠ 108 N. Dearborn St., ☎ 334/438–3823) hosted the conference that established Selma University.

The modest **National African-American Archives and Museum,** a collection of items gathered locally, despite the word *national* in the name, holds portraits and biographies of well-known African-Americans. There is also a collection of carvings and artifacts, including Mardi Gras costumes, documents, and books. ⊠ *564 Dr. Martin Luther King Jr. Ave.,* ☎ *334/433–8511.* ⚑ *Donations accepted.* ☉ *Tues.–Fri. 9–noon and 1–4; weekends by appointment.*

☾ The **Gulf Coast Exploreum Museum of Science and IMAX Dome Theater,** across from the Mobile Convention Center downtown, is a science museum featuring the permanent Hands On Hall, where kids of all ages can have fun while learning through interactive exhibits, as well as traveling exhibitions. Films in the state-of-the-art IMAX Dome Theater change every few months; subjects have included Africa's elephant kingdom, Alaska, dolphins, and roller coasters. ⊠ *65 Government St.,* ☎ *334/208–6883 or 877/625–4FUN.* ⊡ *Exhibits $6; IMAX theater $6; both $11.* ☼ *Mon.–Thurs. 9–5, Fri. 9–9, Sat. 10–9, Sun. noon–5. Open Thurs. until 8 Memorial Day–Labor Day.* ✎

The **USS *Alabama*** is anchored in Mobile Bay just east of downtown Mobile off I–10. Public subscription saved the mighty gray battleship from being scrapped ignominiously after her heroic World War II service, which ranged from Scapa Flow to the South Pacific. A tour of the ship gives a fascinating look into the life of a 2,500-member crew. Anchored next to the battleship is the submarine **USS *Drum*,** another active battle weapon during World War II, also open to visitors. Other exhibits in the 100-acre **Battleship Memorial Park** include a B-52 bomber called *Calamity Jane* and a P-51 Mustang fighter plane. ⊠ *2703 Battleship Pkwy. (U.S. 90),* ☎ *334/433–2703 or 800/426–4929.* ⊡ *$8; parking $2.* ☼ *Daily 8–5.*

OFF THE BEATEN PATH

ESTUARIUM AT THE DAUPHIN ISLAND SEA LAB – This new facility about 40 mi south of Mobile spotlights the ecosystems of the Mobile Bay estuary, including the Mobile-Tensaw River Delta, Mobile Bay, the barrier islands, and the Gulf of Mexico. Outside, the Living Marsh Boardwalk has signs explaining the natural history of the state's marshes. Indoors, there are displays, interactive exhibits, a 9,000-gallon aquarium simulating the underwater environment of Mobile Bay, and a 16,000-gallon tank with sea life from the Gulf of Mexico. ⊠ *101 Bienville Blvd. Take I–10 to Exit 17A, then Rte. 193S to Dauphin Island; turn left at the water tower and proceed 2.2 mi,* ☎ *334/861–7500.* ⊡ *$6.* ☼ *Oct.–May, Mon.–Sat. 9–5, Sun. 1–5; June–Sept., Mon.–Sat. 9–6, Sun. 1–5.* ✎

Dining and Lodging

$$–$$$$ ✕ **Loretta's.** At a colorful corner just a block off Dauphin Street, Loretta's has its own dramatic flair. Hidden behind a wall of glass covered in creeping fig, this restaurant features gleaming silver palm trees and whimsically mismatched salt and pepper shakers. Owner/chef Christopher Hunter creates sophisticated, innovative comfort food, from a sausage-stuffed pork chop to pan-seared sashimi tuna steak. It's a good idea to make reservations for the popular Sunday brunch. ⊠ *19 S. Conception St.,* ☎ *334/432–2200. AE, D, DC, MC, V. Closed Mon. No dinner Tues. and Sun.*

$$ ✕ **Roussos Restaurant.** With a nautical look created by lots of fishnets and scenes of ships at sea, Roussos serves seafood fried, broiled, or served Greek style (a blend of spices and oils that helps bring out the fresh flavor). Steaks and chicken also are available. The appetizers are big favorites, too—especially the Roussos baked oysters and Mr. George's seafood gumbo. ⊠ *166 S. Royal St.,* ☎ *334/433–3322. AE, D, DC, MC, V. Closed Sun.*

$$ ✕ **Gus's Azalea Manor Restaurant and Courtyard.** Housed in a former storefront along Dauphin Street, Gus's is a popular gathering spot. The airy bar features a colorful mural and a street view; the comfortable dining room has a Mediterranean feeling. The lush courtyard behind the restaurant is a great place to dine alfresco on cool nights. Greek chef Gus Ravanos's menu highlights pastas, seafood, steaks, and chicken. ⊠ *751 Dauphin St.,* ☎ *334/433–4877. AE, D, DC, MC, V. Closed Sun.*

$–$$ ✕ **Dew Drop Inn.** Mobile's oldest restaurant, the Dew Drop Inn is also ★ one of the city's most popular places to meet and eat. It's first come, first served here, and the atmosphere is strictly no-frills. The menu's most popular item is the "world famous" Dew Drop Inn hot dog, which goes well with homemade onion rings or thick-cut steak fries. Daily specials include down-home favorites such as fried chicken or catfish, accompanied by perfectly seasoned vegetables. ⊠ *1808 Old Shell Rd.,* ☎ *334/473–7872. Reservations not accepted. MC, V. Closed Sun. No lunch Sat.*

$$–$$$$ ✕⚏ **Adam's Mark Mobile.** This 28-story waterfront hotel is connected to the Mobile Convention Center by a covered skywalk. The large guest rooms have floor-to-ceiling windows with views of downtown Mobile or Mobile Bay and a separate dressing area with a full-length mirror. The lobby and restaurants have oak paneling and are done in shades of rose and soft jade. The Riverview Cafe and Grill specializes in Gulf Coast seafood; there are lighter fare and live entertainment six nights a week in the Tiffany Rose Restaurant. ⊠ *64 S. Water St., 36602,* ☎ *334/438–4000,* 🖷 *334/415–3060. 375 rooms, 12 suites. 2 restaurants, bar, pool, hot tub, sauna, exercise room, meeting rooms. AE, D, DC, MC, V.*

$$–$$$ ⚏ **Radisson Admiral Semmes Hotel.** This restored 1940 hotel in the historic district is a favorite with local politicians. It's also popular with party goers, particularly during Mardi Gras, because of its excellent location directly on the parade route. The spacious, high-ceilinged rooms have a burgundy-and-green color scheme and are furnished in Queen Anne and Chippendale styles. ⊠ *251 Government St., 36602,* ☎ *334/432–8000,* 🖷 *334/405–5942. 148 rooms, 22 suites. Restaurant, bar, pool, business services. AE, D, DC, MC, V.*

$$ ⚏ **Malaga Inn.** A delightful, romantic getaway, the Malaga comprises
★ two town houses built by a wealthy landowner in 1862. The lobby is furnished with 19th-century antiques and opens onto a landscaped central courtyard with a fountain. The rooms are large, airy, and furnished with massive antiques. The front suite has 14-ft ceilings and crimson velveteen wallpaper. ⊠ *359 Church St., 36602,* ☎ *800/235–1586 or 334/438–4701,* ☎ 🖷 *334/438–4701. 36 rooms, 3 suites. Restaurant, lounge, pool. AE, D, MC, V.*

Nightlife and the Arts

The **Joe Jefferson Players** (☎ 334/471–1534), an amateur group started more than 50 years ago, performs plays and musicals at the Joe Jefferson Playhouse (⊠ 11 S. Carlen St.). The 1927 **Saenger Theater** (☎ 334/433–2787) hosts orchestras and touring companies. The **Mobile Civic Center** (⊠ 401 Civic Center Dr., ☎ 334/434–7381) presents theater groups, orchestras, and a variety of concerts. The new **Mitchell Center** at the University of South Alabama (⊠ Old Shell Rd., ☎ 334/460–6101), home to the university's Jaguars basketball team, also hosts concerts and other special events throughout the year. In the lobby the spectacular, restored 1940s Waterman Globe, 12 ft in diameter, rotates with the Earth's axis. The Playhouse in the Park's **Pixie Players** (☎ 334/344–1537) is a children's theater that puts on five shows annually.

Much of Mobile's nightlife centers around downtown's former commercial district, **Dauphin Street,** which today has a number of restaurants and nightspots. Occupying the space of a former pharmacy in a 1906 skyscraper, **Drayton Place** (⊠ 101 Dauphin St., ☎ 334/432–7438) is an atmospheric place for a full meal or a drink. You can visit the cigar bar or billiards room, or you can listen to live jazz (Thursday–Saturday nights). **Monsoon's** (⊠ 210 Dauphin St., ☎ 334/433–3500), **Grand Central** (⊠ 256 Dauphin St., ☎ 334/432–6999), and **Southside Music Hall** (⊠ 455 Dauphin St., ☎ 334/433–8080) are popular places to hear live bands perform. All three are housed in historic buildings with balconies overlooking Dauphin Street and all are filled with fun-loving, mostly college-age kids. As it's difficult to distinguish between them even before you've had a few cocktails, it's best to just wander down Dauphin and drop in at the place that appeals to you the most.

Outdoor Activities and Sports

DOG RACING

At the **Mobile Greyhound Park** (✉ Off I–10W, about 10 mi from Mobile, ☎ 334/653–5000), there are pari-mutuel betting and a restaurant overlooking the finish line. The track offers simulcasts.

BASEBALL

The **Mobile BayBears,** the AA affiliate of the San Diego Padres, play baseball from April through October at "the Hank"–Hank Aaron Stadium, named for the baseball legend and Mobile native (✉ 755 Bolling Brothers Blvd., just off I–65 at the Government Blvd. exit, ☎ 334/479–2327).

GOLF

Magnolia Grove (✉ 7000 Lamplighter Dr., ☎ 334/645–0075 or 800/949–4444) is the southernmost offering of Alabama's Robert Trent Jones Golf Trail. The facility has 54 holes of championship golf: two par-72 courses and an 18-hole, par-54 (all par-3) course that is anything but easy. The 18-hole, par-72 **Azalea City Golf Club** (✉ 1000 Gaillard Dr., ☎ 334/342–4221) is operated by the city of Mobile. **TimberCreek** (✉ 9650 TimberCreek Blvd., ☎ 334/621–9900), in Daphne, has 27 holes and is par 72. **Rock Creek** (✉ 140 Clubhouse Dr., ☎ 334/928–4223), in Fairhope, on the eastern shore of Mobile Bay, has 18 holes and is par 72.

NATURE-WATCHING

Wildland Expeditions, led by Captain Gene Burrell on the *Gator Bait,* explores the Mobile-Tensaw Delta on two-hour trips that leave from Chickasaw (just north of Mobile). You'll get close-up views of plants and animals, especially alligators during the warm weather months. ☎ *334/460–8206.* ✍ *$20.*

Shopping

Most shopping in Mobile is in malls and shopping centers in the suburban areas. Stores are generally open Monday–Saturday 10–9, Sunday 1–6. Sales tax is 9%.

ANTIQUES

Antiques buffs love Mobile because it offers more than 25 individual shops and malls that specialize in antiques. In the Loop area of midtown (where Government Street, Airport Boulevard, and Dauphin Island Parkway converge), several shops are within walking distance. The **Red Barn Antique Mall** (✉ 418 Dauphin Island Pkwy., ☎ 334/473–9227) has at least 15 shops with a variety of antiques, from glassware and books to furniture. The **Cotton City Antique Mall** (✉ 2012 Airport Blvd., ☎ 334/479–9747) features 12,000 square ft of antique furniture, vintage linens, clocks, and more. **Yellow House Antiques** ✉ 1902 Government St., ☎ 334/476–7382) is an upscale shop with 18th- and 19th-century English, Continental, and American furniture and accessories.

MALLS

Bel Air Mall (✉ 1 block east of I–65 Beltline off Airport Blvd., ☎ 334/478–1893) has 175 stores under one roof, including JCPenney, Parisian, Target, Dillard's, and Sears. **Springdale Mall-Plaza** (✉ Airport Blvd. and I–65, ☎ 334/479–9871), anchored by Dillard's and McRae's, has more than 100 stores. The **Pinebrook Shopping Center** (✉ At Airport Blvd. and McGregor Ave.) offers a variety of stores, including the Nuthouse, Stein Mart, Books-a-Million, and Petsmart.

Theodore

20 mi south of Mobile.

★ **45** One of the most popular gardens in the South is near the town of Theodore. **Bellingrath Gardens and Home** is famous for its magnificent azaleas, which are part of 65 acres of gardens set amid a 905-acre semitropical landscape. Show time for the azaleas is spring, when some 250,000 plantings of 200 different species are ablaze with color. But Bellingrath is a year-round wonder: In summer 2,500 rosebushes are in bloom; in autumn 60,000 chrysanthemum plants flourish; in winter fields of poinsettias provide color. During Christmas in Lights, in the month of December, holiday decorations throughout the gardens light up the night. Countless species and varieties of flowering plants spring up along Fowl River, a stream, and a lake populated by ducks and swans. Guides are on hand to assist or explain, but a free map lets you plan your own strolls along flagstone paths and across charming bridges. The gardens are also a sanctuary to more than 200 species of birds; in April and October, large numbers of migratory birds drop by.

Coca-Cola bottling pioneer Walter D. Bellingrath began the nucleus of the gardens in 1917, when he and his wife bought a large tract of land to use as a fishing camp. Their travels, however, prompted them to create, instead, a garden rivaling some they had seen in Europe, and before long they opened it to the public. Today the brick home they built is open to visitors and has one of the finest collections of antiques in the Southeast. On display in a separate building is the world's largest collection of Boehm porcelain birds. One-hour **boat cruises** on Fowl River aboard the *Southern Belle* leave from the dock next to the Bellingrath Home at regular intervals. ⊠ *12401 Bellingrath Rd.,* ☎ *334/973–2217 or 800/247–8420.* ☞ *Gardens $8; gardens and home $14; value pack (gardens, home, and cruise) $20.* ☉ *Gardens daily 8–sunset; home opens daily at 9 with closings varying by season.*

Malbis

10 mi east of Mobile on U.S. 90 via I–10.

Malbis is the outgrowth of a development begun in 1906 by a Greek immigrant and former monk who bought tracts of land and established a cannery, bakery, farm, and power plant; today it includes portions of a residential golf community, TimberCreek, as well as a new resi-

46 dential development known as Historic Malbis Plantation. The **Malbis Greek Orthodox Church** is a replica of a beautiful Byzantine church in Athens, Greece. It was built in 1965 as a memorial to the faith of Jason Malbis, founder of the community. The marble for the interior was imported from the same quarries that provided stone for the Parthenon, and a master painter was brought over from Greece to paint murals on the walls and the 75-ft dome of the rotunda. The stained-glass windows are stunning. ⊠ *County Rte. 27,* ☎ *334/626–3050.* ☞ *Free.* ☉ *Tours daily 9–noon and 2–5.*

Fairhope and Point Clear

12 mi south of Malbis on U.S. 98A.

Clinging to the eastern shore of Mobile Bay, the quiet towns of Fairhope and Point Clear have restored clapboard houses with wide porches overlooking the bay and live oak trees cloaked with Spanish moss. Fairhope was settled around 1900 by a group of Midwesterners, who established it as a utopian single-tax community (the system is still in use). Today Fairhope's streets are lined with seasonal flowers year-round—even the trash receptacles double as planters—and the downtown area has antiques shops, funky stores, art galleries, and bed-and-breakfasts, making it a relaxing weekend escape. With the Fairhope Municipal Pier as the centerpiece of town, it's also home to fishing, boating, and marine services. Fairhope's Arts and Crafts Festival, held each March, is a large juried show that draws more than 200 exhibitors for a weekend.

Point Clear's incomparable Grand Hotel, which has been in the same location since 1847, is a leading resort destination hidden away among million-dollar bayside estates. A walk along the hotel's boardwalk provides a glimpse at the summer homes that line Mobile Bay.

Lodging

$$$–$$$$ ★ 🏨 **Marriott's Grand Hotel.** Nestled amid 550 acres of beautifully landscaped grounds on Mobile Bay, the Grand has been a cherished tradition since 1847 and is one of the South's premier resorts. The octagonal, two-story cypress-paneled and -beamed lobby serves as the hub for several wings of rooms. Its large three-sided fireplace, armchairs, and pieces of porcelain evoke a casual elegance that is echoed in the half-moon dining room overlooking the bay. At press time, new owners were planning an extensive renovation of the hotel and golf courses. Rooms have resort or bay views. ⊠ *1 Grand Blvd., juts off Scenic 98, or 98A, Point Clear, 36564,* ☎ *334/928–9201 or 800/544–9933,* 🅵🅰🆇 *334/928–1149. 227 rooms, 24 suites. 5 restaurants, coffee shop, lounge, pool, hot tub, sauna, 2 18-hole golf courses, 8 tennis courts, horseback riding, beach, boating, fishing, bicycles, children's programs, playground. AE, D, DC, MC, V.*

$$$ 🏨 **Bay Breeze Bed & Breakfast.** A winding white-shell driveway leads through a camellia and azalea garden to the stucco-and-wood B&B owned by Bill and Becky Jones. This was Becky's childhood home, and it fronts Mobile Bay, not far from downtown Fairhope, and has a long fishing pier. Bedrooms in the main house have wooden floors, brass queen-size beds, old family portraits, antique furnishings, and large windows. Cottage suites are light and spacious, decorated with antiques, Oriental and hooked rugs, redbrick floors, and white pine paneling. ⊠ *742 S. Mobile St. (Box 526), 36533,* ☎ *334/928–8976,* 🅵🅰🆇 *334/928–0360. 3 rooms, 2 cottages. Air-conditioning, fans, game room, bicycles, fishing. AE, MC, V.*

The Gulf Coast

50 mi south of Mobile via U.S. 90E and AL 59.

With sugary white sand and gentle warm water, the beach along this coastal paradise is by far one of the state's greatest attractions. The cooling offshore breezes provide a nice respite from the normal hot, humid temperatures found around Alabama in the summer. Although the Gulf Shores beach area has plenty of concessions and is usually crowded, those seeking isolated beach walks need only venture a couple of miles west. To the east of Gulf Shores is Orange Beach, a heavily developed coastal strip between the Gulf of Mexico and Perdido Bay, with its peaceful bayous and creeks.

OFF THE BEATEN PATH **BURRIS FARM MARKET –** For a true sampling of Baldwin County's agricultural heritage, stop in at this sprawling family-owned market that features mostly local produce—much of it grown on the Burris family's farm. In the springtime you can pick your own strawberries. The huge open-air market topped by a tin roof is on the highway that leads to and from the beach. Burris Bakery, an air-conditioned area at the rear, will tempt you with freshly baked breads, pies, and cookies. In addition to the fresh fruit and vegetables, you'll also find a variety of homemade relishes, pickles, and dressings. ⊠ *Hwy. 59, Loxley (from I–10, take I–59 south 3 mi to Loxley),* ☎ *334/964–6464.* ☜ *Free.* ☉ *Feb.–Dec., daily 8–6.*

★ ㊲ **Gulf State Park** (⊠ 20115 AL 135, Gulf Shores, ☎ 334/948–7275, 800/544–4853, or 800/252–7275) covers more than 6,000 acres. Along with 2½ mi of pure white beaches and glimmering dunes, the park has two freshwater lakes with fishing, plus biking, hiking, and jogging trails through pine forests. Near the large beach pavilion, a concrete fishing pier juts about 800 ft into the Gulf. There is also a gulf-front resort lodge and convention center, 468 campsites, and 21 cottages, plus tennis courts and a golf course.

The 6,200 acres of the **Bon Secour National Wildlife Refuge** (⊠ AL 180W, ☎ 334/540–7720) are home to native and migratory birds and a number of endangered species, including the loggerhead sea turtle. You can hike or swim at some of the five units of the refuge.

Ⓒ **Waterville USA,** set on 17 acres, has a wave pool with 3-ft waves, eight exciting water slides, and a lazy river ride around the park. For younger children there are gentler rides in a supervised play area. There are also a 36-hole miniature golf course, a video-game arcade, and an amusement park with roller coaster, motion simulator, NASCAR go-karts, kiddie area, laser tag, and ride ejection seat—all priced per ride or game. ⊠ *906 Gulf Shores Pkwy. (AL 59), Gulf Shores,* ☎ *334/948–2106.* ☜ *$18.* ☉ *Water park, Memorial Day–Labor Day, daily 10–6; amusement park, daily 10–6.*

㊳ **Fort Morgan** was built in the early 1800s to guard the entrance to Mobile Bay. The fort saw fiery action during the Battle of Mobile Bay in 1864: Confederate torpedoes sank the ironclad *Tecumseh,* after Union admiral David Farragut gave his famous command: "Damn the torpedoes! Full speed ahead!" The original outer walls still stand; outside, a museum chronicles the fort's history and displays artifacts from Indian days through World War II, with an emphasis on the Civil War. ⊠ *51 Hwy. 180W, Gulf Shores,* ☎ *334/540–7125.* ☜ *$3.* ☉ *Weekdays 8–5, weekends 9–5.*

Dining and Lodging

$$$ ✕ **Voyagers.** Roses and art deco touches set the tone for this airy, el-
★   egant dining room. Two-level seating allows beach or poolside views from every table. Renowned chef Gerhard Brill, who describes his culinary style as "Gulf Coast creole," creates dishes such as trout with roasted pecans in creole meunière sauce and soft-shell crab topped with creole *choron* (a hollandaise sauce). Finish up with a fried-apple beignet with French vanilla sauce or crepe soufflé praline. Service is deft, and there's an extensive wine selection. ⊠ *Perdido Beach Resort, 27200 Perdido Beach Blvd., Orange Beach,* ☎ *334/981–9811. Reservations essential. AE, D, DC, MC, V.*

$$–$$$ ✕ **Bayside Grill.** For fine dining overlooking the back bays that channel to the Gulf, you can't beat this choice. Seafood is the New Orleans-born chef's specialty, along with pastas, steaks, salads, and chicken. The restaurant also offers a spectacular Sunday brunch. ⊠ *27842 Canal Rd., Orange Beach,* ☎ *334/981–4899. AE, D, DC, MC, V.*

$$–$$$ ✕ **Hazel's Family Restaurant.** This plain family-style restaurant with a full menu serves a good, hearty breakfast, soup-and-salad lunches, and buffet dinners with seafood dishes like flounder Florentine. There's also a self-service bar serving soft ice cream. ⊠ *Gulf View Square Shopping Center, AL 182, Orange Beach,* ☎ *334/981–4628. Reservations not accepted. AE, D, DC, MC, V.*

$$ ✕ **Mikee's.** The food at this popular, no-nonsense seafood restaurant in the heart of Gulf Shores will be worth the inevitable wait. There's no view—it's a couple of blocks north of the beach—but while you wait, you can check out the mounted fish and photos of the owners' biggest catches among the other local memorabilia decorating the walls. The menu features seafood dinners such as all-you-can-eat fried shrimp, steamed shrimp, barbecue shrimp, fried crab claws, and fried oysters, as well as po-boy sandwiches on New Orleans–style French bread. ⊠ *1st Ave. N and 2nd Ave. E,* ☎ *334/948–6452. Reservations not accepted. AE, D, DC, MC, V.*

$$–$$$$ 🏨 **Gulf Shores Plantation.** This 320-acre family resort, 12 mi west of
★ Gulf Shores, faces the Gulf and has condominiums with fully equipped kitchens in high-rises overlooking the pristine beach. Recreational activities abound, yet the remote location allows for peace and quiet. Kiva Dunes Golf Course is consistently ranked by magazines such as *Golf Digest* and *Golf* as being among the state's best. ⊠ *AL 180W, Box 1299, Gulf Shores 36547,* ☎ *334/540–5000 or 800/554–0344,* FAX *334/540–6055. 524 units. Café, lounge, pizzeria, indoor and outdoor pools, 8 tennis courts, beach, gift shop. AE, MC, V.*

$$–$$$$ 🏨 **Original Romar House.** This unassuming beach cottage is filled with surprises—from the Caribbean-style upstairs sitting area to the Purple Parrot Bar to the luxurious art-deco-style guest rooms. ⊠ *23500 Perdido Beach Blvd., Orange Beach 36561,* ☎ *334/981–6156 or 800/487–6627,* FAX *334/974–1163. 6 rooms. Bar, hot tub, bicycles. BP. AE, MC, V.*

$$–$$$$ 🏨 **Perdido Beach Resort.** The eight- and nine-story towers of the re-
★ sort are Mediterranean stucco and red tile. The lobby is tiled in terra-cotta and decorated with a brass sculpture of gulls in flight and mosaics by Venetian artists. Rooms are furnished in comfortable Mediterranean style, and all have a beach view and balcony. The location and scenic views here are outstanding. ⊠ *27200 Perdido Beach Blvd., Box 400, Orange Beach 36561,* ☎ *334/981–9811 or 800/634–8001,* FAX *334/981–5670. 333 rooms, 12 suites. Restaurant, café, piano bar, indoor-outdoor pool, 2 hot tubs, 4 tennis courts, exercise room, video games. AE, D, DC, MC, V.*

$–$$$$ 🏨 **Quality Inn Beachside.** This spacious hotel is made up of one three-story and one six-story building. The modern guest rooms are decorated in pastels and have private balconies and coffeemakers; most face the Gulf; half have kitchens. In the art deco–style atrium lobby, with glass-brick walls, is a 70-ft swimming pool and a waterfall. Glass-walled elevators rise six stories. ⊠ *931 W. Gulf Beach Blvd. (AL 182), Drawer 1013, Gulf Shores 36547,* ☎ *334/948–6874 or 800/844–6913,* FAX *334/948–5232. 158 rooms. Restaurant, food court, lounge, indoor and outdoor pools, hot tub. AE, D, DC, MC, V.*

$–$$ 🏨 **Lighthouse Resort Motel.** This complex of five two- to four-story buildings, surrounded by brightly colored exotic flowers, is set on a 680-ft private beach. The waterfront rooms have private balconies, and some units have kitchens. All have contemporary furnishings. ⊠ *455 E. Beach Blvd., Box 233, Gulf Shores 36547,* ☎ *334/948–6188,* FAX *334/948–6100. 200 rooms. 3 pools, beach. AE, D, DC, MC, V.*

Nightlife and the Arts

On the Alabama–Florida line is the sprawling **Flora-Bama Lounge** (⊠ Perdido Key Dr., Pensacola, FL, ☎ 334/980–5118 or 334/980–5119), home of the annual Interstate Mullet Toss, is open from 11 AM to 2:30 AM. The bar features live bands nightly and has outdoor seating in summer.

Outdoor Activities and Sports

BIKING

Gulf State Park (⊠ 20115 AL 135, ☎ 334/948–7275), in Gulf Shores, has biking trails through pine forests and rents bicycles. **Island Recre-**

ation Services (✉ 360 E. Beach Blvd., ☎ 334/948–7334) also in Gulf Shores, rents bikes and water-sports equipment.

FISHING

Freshwater and saltwater fishing in the Gulf area are excellent. **Gulf State Park** (✉ 20115 AL 135, ☎ 334/948–7275), in Gulf Shores, is highly recommended and has fishing from an 825-ft pier and rents flat-bottom boats for lake fishing. **Deep-sea fishing** from charter boats is very popular; in Gulf Shores, you can sign on board the *Moreno Queen* (☎ 334/981–8499 or 800/317–4850) or one of many other charter boats for a full- or half-day fishing expedition, and neighboring Orange Beach has more than 100 boats to choose from. For a brochure on Orange Beach's offerings, call 800/745–7263. Catches from these deep-sea expeditions include king mackerel, amberjack, tuna, white marlin, blue marlin, grouper, bonito, sailfish, and red snapper.

GOLF

In recent years, coastal Alabama has developed into one of the nicest golfing destinations in the Southeast. More courses are opening, and the names of their architects read like a who's who of the golfing world—Robert Trent Jones Sr., Arnold Palmer, and Jerry Pate, to name just a few. With winter temperatures averaging in the 60°F range and pleasant breezes, the area has become a true year-round-fun spot. Prices for all the courses range from about $32 to $70 for greens fees and a cart.

The spectacular 18-hole, par-72 **Kiva Dunes** course adjacent to Gulf Shores Plantation Resort (✉ 12 mi west of Gulf Shores on AL 180, ☎ 334/540–7000), designed by Jerry Pate, combines oceanfront dunes golf with Scottish-style links golf. The **Craft Farms** complex, off AL 59 just north of Gulf Shores (✉ 3840 Cotton Creek Blvd., ☎ 334/968–7500 or 800/327–2657), has three 18-hole, par-72 courses: the Arnold Palmer–designed course at Cotton Creek; Cypress Bend; and the Woodlands course designed by Larry Nelson. About 12 mi north of Gulf Shores in Foley, the **Glenlakes Golf Club** (✉ 9530 Clubhouse Dr., ☎ 334/955–1220 or 800/435–5253), a course designed by Bruce Devlin, has 18, par-72, challenging holes that play over 7,000 yards and another nine holes stretching 3,100 yards. The 18-hole, par-72 course at **Gulf State Park** (✉ 20115 AL 135, ☎ 334/948–7275), in Gulf Shores, isn't quite as new and challenging as others in the area, but it is one of the most scenic and best-maintained courses along the coast.

HORSEBACK RIDING

Country Trail Rides (☎ 334/943–7694 for reservations) offers guided group trail (minimum: two) rides for $20 per person; they're between Gulf Shores and Foley.

SAILING AND WATER SPORTS

Sailboats that can be rented with captain include the *T. J. Spithre,* a 53-ft catamaran (☎ 334/981–9706 for Island Sailing Center), and the *Daedalus* (☎ 334/986–7018) in Gulf Shores. For more private, customized tours of the Perdido Bay area and its sand islands, **Caribiana** (☎ 334/981-4442 or 888/203–4883) offers nature rides for up to six people aboard a 23-ft sea skiff.

Fun Marina (☎ 334/980–5122), in Orange Beach, offers parasailing and rents Jet Skis, pontoon boats, and 16-ft bay-fishing boats. In Gulf Shores, **Island Recreation Services** (✉ 360 E. Beach Blvd., ☎ 334/948–7334) rents Jet Skis, bikes, body boards, surfboards, and sailboats.

Shopping

The 120 outlet stores in the **Riviera Centre,** 8 mi north of Gulf Shores, offer savings of up to 75% off regular retail prices. Stores include Danskin, Calvin Klein, Liz Claiborne, Bose, Coach, Bass Shoes, and Pfaltz-graff. ⊠ *AL 59S, Foley,* ☎ *334/943–8888 or 800/523–6873.* ☉ *Mon.–Sat. 9–9, Sun. 10–6. Hrs vary Jan.–Feb.*

Mobile and the Gulf Coast A to Z

Arriving and Departing

BY BUS

Greyhound (☎ 800/231–2222) has stations in Mobile (⊠ 2545 Government Blvd., ☎ 334/478–6089) and in Pensacola, Florida (⊠ 505 W. Burgess Rd., ☎ 904/476–4800).

BY CAR

I–10 travels east from Mobile into Florida through Pensacola, west into Mississippi. I–65 slices Alabama in half vertically, passing through Birmingham and Montgomery and ending at Mobile. Gulf Shores is connected with Mobile via I–10 and AL 59; AL 180 and 182 are the main beach routes.

BY PLANE

For airline telephone numbers, *see* Air Travel *in* Smart Travel Tips A to Z. The **Mobile Regional Airport at Bates Field** (⊠ 8400 Airport Blvd., ☎ 334/633–0313), about 10 mi west of I–65, is served by Comair, Delta, Northwest Airlink, Continental Express, and United. **Pensacola Regional Airport** (⊠ 2430 Airport Blvd., ☎ 850/435–1746), some 40 mi east of Gulf Shores in Florida, is served by Continental, Delta, Northwest Airlink, and US Airways.

BY TRAIN

Amtrak (☎ 800/872–7245) service on the *Sunset Limited* links Mobile with both the East and West coasts. Westbound trains run Monday, Wednesday, and Saturday; eastbound trains run Sunday, Tuesday, and Thursday.

Getting Around

The most practical way to get around this area is by car.

Contacts and Resources

EMERGENCIES

Ambulance, police (☎ 911). The **University of South Alabama Hospital** (⊠ 2451 Fillingim St., ☎ 334/471–7000), in Mobile, offers 24-hour medical care in its emergency room.

GUIDED TOURS

Gray Line Tours (☎ 334/432–2229 or 800/338–5597), in Mobile, has excellent 1- to 3½-hour trolley or motor-coach tours, departing from Fort Condé daily, to Mobile's historic points of interest, as well as to Bellingrath Gardens and the USS *Alabama.*

Memorable Mobile Tours, Inc. (☎ 334/344–8687 or 800/441–1146) conducts customized guided tours of Mobile and Eastern Shore area attractions.

RADIO STATIONS

In Mobile, **AM:** WGOK 900, gospel and jazz; WKSJ 1270, country; WNTM 710, talk. **FM:** WZEW 92.1, modern rock; WABB 97.5, contemporary rock; WWRO 100.7, oldies; WKSJ 94.5, country.

VISITOR INFORMATION

Call the **Mobile Convention & Visitors Corporation** (☎ 334/208–2000 or 800/566–2453, ✍). You can visit **Fort Condé** (⊠ 150 S. Royal St., ☎ 334/434–7304), which has the official welcome center for Mobile. **Alabama Gulf Coast Area Convention and Visitors Bureau** (⊠ 23658

Perdido Beach Blvd., Orange Beach 36561, ☎ 334/968–7511 or 800/745–7263).

ALABAMA A TO Z

Arriving and Departing

By Car

Surrounded by Mississippi, Georgia, Tennessee, Florida, and the Gulf of Mexico, Alabama is accessible by a number of interstates. I–10 cuts across the southern tip of the state, providing direct route from Mississippi on the west and the Florida Panhandle on the east. From Atlanta, I–85 takes you to the central part of the state; I–20 takes you to Birmingham and points in North Alabama. The main north–south routes are I–65 coming down from Nashville and I–59 from the Chattanooga area. U.S. 80 cuts east–west across the state, connecting Demopolis, Selma, Montgomery, and Tuskegee. U.S. 82 runs northwest to southeast from Tuscaloosa through Montgomery and Eufaula.

Some sample mileages are: Birmingham to Huntsville, 95 mi; Birmingham to Mobile, 253 mi; Birmingham to Montgomery, 90 mi; Birmingham to Gulf Shores, 274 mi; Birmingham to Tuscaloosa, 57 mi.

By Plane

Major airports are **Birmingham International Airport** (☎ 205/599–0500), Montgomery's **Dannelly Field** (☎ 334/281–5040), **Huntsville International Airport** (☎ 256/772–9395), and **Mobile Municipal Airport** (☎ 334/633–0313). Many visitors to the Gulf Coast find it convenient to fly into the **Pensacola Regional Airport** (☎ 850/435–1746), an hour east in Florida, or the **Gulfport-Biloxi Regional Airport** (☎ 228/863–5953), an hour west in Mississippi.

By Train

Amtrak (☎ 800/872–7245) has daily service to Birmingham. Service into Mobile is on Sunday, Tuesday, and Thursday. East–west routes are serviced by Amtrak's *Sunset Limited* across the southern part of the state; north–south travelers board the *Crescent* from New York and Washington or New Orleans.

Getting Around

By Bus

Greyhound (☎ 800/231–2222) has service to the major cities—Birmingham, Huntsville, Mobile, and Montgomery—with intermediate stops at many of Alabama's smaller cities. Check for scheduled stops.

By Car

In Alabama, you can turn right during a red light unless otherwise noted by street signs. The speed limit on interstate highways is 70 mph in most places.

By Train

Montgomery has a **Thruway Intermodal Transit Terminal** (☎ 800/872–7245 for information) offering bus service to Amtrak service in Atlanta.

Contacts and Resources

B&B Reservation Agencies

Alabama has no central telephone number for bed-and-breakfasts. Use a B&B brochure available from the Alabama Bureau of Tourism and Travel (☞ Visitor Information, *below*) to make reservations at individual B&Bs.

Emergencies

In towns and cities, dial **911** for police, fire, and ambulance assistance.

Outdoor Activities and Sports

FISHING

Residents and nonresidents 16 or over need a valid fishing license to fish in Alabama; for information call 334/242–3826.

GOLF

Some of Alabama's most scenic and challenging courses are part of the **Robert Trent Jones Golf Trail,** 18 courses spread out among seven locations around the state, providing 324 holes of challenging golf. Call a toll-free number (☎ 800/949–4444, ✎) for reservations and information about any of the locations (*see also* Up-Close: Tee Time, *above*).

There's good golf in Alabama's **state parks** (☎ 800/252–7275). Greens fees with cart range from $26–$48.

State Parks

Alabama's 24 state parks include a wide variety of recreational activities and lodging accommodations. Choose among resort lodges, hotels, campgrounds, chalets, and cabins, both modern and rustic. Several parks have marinas, golf courses, and tennis facilities. Contact **Alabama State Parks** (✉ 64 N. Union St., Folsom Administrative Bldg., Suite 547, Montgomery 36130, ☎ 800/252–7275, ✎) for reservations or information.

Visitor Information

Alabama Bureau of Tourism and Travel (✉ 401 Adams Ave., Montgomery 36104, ☎ 334/242–4169 or 800/252–2262). **Welcome centers:** I–59 near Valley Head, I–59 at Cuba, I–65 at Elkmont, I–10 north of Seminole, I–10 at Grand Bay, I–20 east of Heflin, I–85 at Lanett, U.S. 231 south of Dothan.

Call the Alabama Bureau of Tourism and Travel (☎ 800/252–2262) for a free copy of **"Alabama's Black Heritage,"** a 56-page guide to African-American culture that includes hundreds of sites.

3 GEORGIA

Georgia is geographically the largest state east of the Mississippi River. Its varied terrain ranges from the foothills of the Appalachian Mountains in the north to the great coastal plain running from the state's center toward the shore to the beaches of the Golden Isles and the delicate ecology of the Okefenokee in the southeast. From progressive Atlanta to antebellum Macon and colonial Savannah, each of Georgia's cities and towns has its own special charm.

Updated by
Hollis Gillespie

EORGIA IS LIKE A CLEVERLY MADE PATCHWORK quilt. Its landscape encompasses the hazy blue foothills of the Appalachian Mountains in the north, the coastal plain connecting the heartland to the unspoiled beaches of the Atlantic, and the mysterious black-water swamps of the state's southern portion. Most visitors travel its interstate highways (I–75, I–85, I–95, and I–16), but the adventurous traveler who decides to explore the state's byways will be rewarded with pristine vistas and detours through charming towns.

Within the landscape lies a rich diversity of unusual flora, including mountain laurel, rhododendrons, azaleas, and camellias. Spanish moss drapes live oak trees in the southern and coastal areas, and flat fields of white puffy cotton line the horizon through the middle of the state. Known for its peaches, Georgia is also proud of its apples, and the fruit trees' soft blooms create splendid sights in spring. Hiking in the north Georgia mountains could reveal their wealth of deer charging through the forest. Along the coast, alligators, egrets, and herons take the visitor in stride.

As varied as its landscape, Georgia's citizens reflect the diversity of early settlers, native peoples, and new arrivals. During the 18th century, not only English and Scottish immigrants but also Jewish settlers, both Sephardic and Ashkenazic, and German religious refugees (the Salzburgers) arrived to take up positions of importance and prominence in the Georgia colony. Africans and native peoples—chiefly Cherokee and Creek—added their cultural spice to the mix, creating a state that is richer in ethnic character than is often recognized. Irish immigrants arriving throughout the 19th century and Greeks, Middle Easterners, and Asians during the late 19th and early 20th centuries contributed to the state's diversity. Georgians speak with accents that vary from the classic, slightly nasal mountain "twang" to the distinctive, soft coastal lilt of upper-crust Savannahians.

Georgia's towns each define in their own way that famous Southern charm of fable and film. Bustling Atlanta, the state capital since the Civil War ended in 1865, has been compared with Margaret Mitchell's heroine, Scarlett O'Hara, the classic Steel Magnolia: gentle in form but brash and tough in substance. Colonial Savannah, with the nation's largest Historic District, lures visitors to its 21 cobblestone squares, giant parterre gardens, waterfront gift shops, jazz bars, and parks. Dahlonega, site of the nation's early gold rush in 1828, is a typical example of the small Georgia town, with its central square dominated by a county courthouse. Macon, full of flowering Japanese cherry trees and images of both the antebellum and Victorian South, celebrates its heritage as home to poet and flutist Sidney Lanier. A few small towns are named for glittering foreign capitals that they resemble not in the slightest: Vienna (pronounced vy-*en*-ah), Madrid (may-*drid*), Rome, Athens, Cairo (*cay*-row), and so forth.

Georgia's 100-mi coast runs from the mouth of the Savannah River south to the mouth of the St. Marys River. The seaside resort communities blend Southern elegance with a casual sensibility. St. Simons Island, about 70 mi south of Savannah, attracts a laid-back crowd of anglers, beachgoers, golfers, and tennis players. On nearby Jekyll Island, the lavish lifestyle of America's early 19th-century rich and famous is still evident in their stately Victorian "cottages." Cumberland Island's protected forests and miles of sandy coastline, the rustically beautiful Sapelo Island, the isolated solitude of Little St. Simons Island, and the dark waters of the Okefenokee are favorite haunts of nature lovers.

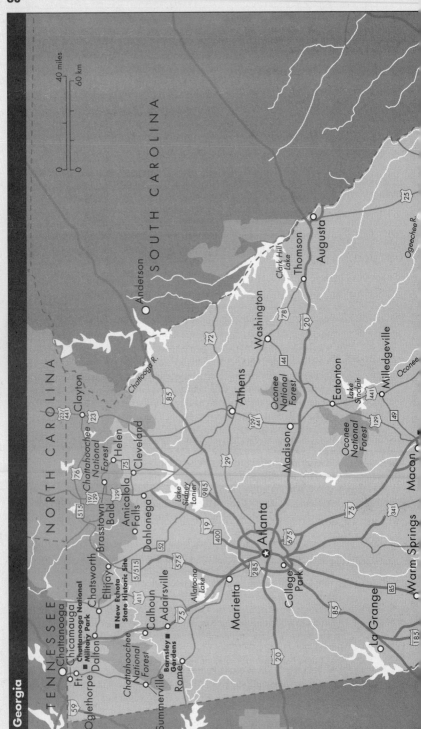

Georgia

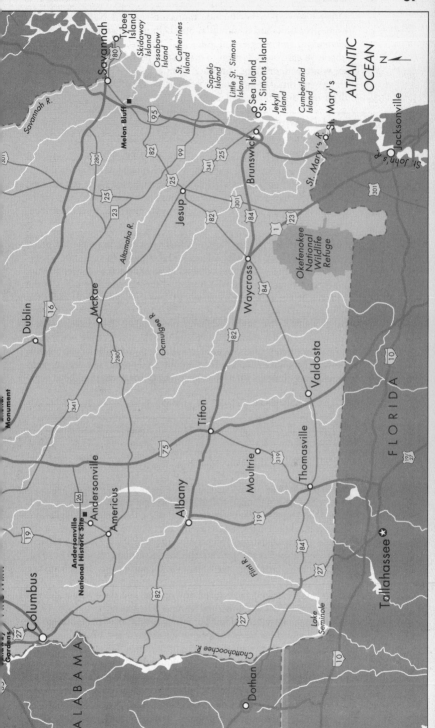

Other historical riches include thousand-year-old Native American homesites and burial mounds, antebellum mansions, war heroes' memorials, and intriguing monuments built by eccentric folk artists and obsessive gardeners. Georgia's many state parks have superb facilities for white-water rafting, canoeing, fishing, golf, and tennis; and nature trails wind through mountain forests delicately laced with wild rhododendrons, dogwoods, and azaleas.

Pleasures and Pastimes

Dining

Dining in Georgia has its ups and downs. Areas that have attracted substantial tourism have respectable to downright outstanding restaurants. Others lag far behind, their best offerings the chain restaurants, or the local barbecue joint. When dining in a small town, you might ask the fire department; firefighters often know which are the best local restaurants.

Atlanta sets the culinary pace, of course, with cutting-edge fare from outstanding chefs. Dress in Atlanta—and elsewhere in the state—is casual unless otherwise noted. Classic meat-and-threes—diners serving meat with three side dishes—are found throughout Georgia. On the byways of Georgia, barbecue stands and restaurants still cook the whole pig, serving customers its meat pulled off the bone for sandwiches or its tender ribs, both bathed in tangy sauce. Brunswick stew, a hunter's stew that traditionally contained the day's catch, is the standard accompaniment. Some of these places are full-fledged restaurants; others have no place to sit at all. If you're off the beaten path, these establishments offer your best chance for decent food.

CATEGORY	COST*
$$$$	over $50
$$$	$35–$50
$$	$25–$35
$	under $25
*per person for a three-course meal, excluding drinks, service, and 7% tax	

Historic Sites

You may want to plan your trip with Georgia's historic sites in mind. From the moment you enter the state along the interstate highways, brown markers with white lettering alert you to the locations of the state's principal historical sights along those routes. Georgia's towns constitute a special glimpse into the past. Savannah, founded in 1733, can be viewed from carriage or bus via specialty tours, by private car, or on foot; it's an excellent walking city. Augusta, founded in 1736, has a fine Riverwalk, a restored downtown, and the 19th- and 20th-century houses of Olde Town and Summerville. Macon, founded in 1823, is known for its wealth of fine antebellum and Victorian mansions that may be viewed by private car or on specialty tours. You'll find more than a fair share of battlefields to explore, including the dark woods and open fields of Chickamauga and unusual historic sites such as New Echota, the lost capital of the Cherokee Nation.

Lodging

Most national and some international hotel and motel chains have establishments in Georgia. Within the past decade, bed-and-breakfast inns have arisen throughout the state, some providing exquisite lodging, others doing a perfunctory job. Campsites are marked along the interstate highways, and the state has a fine network of parks, some of which offer campsites and overnight facilities. Always telephone ahead to bed-and-breakfast inns and campsites for reservations, as these are popular accommodations.

CATEGORY	ATLANTA AND SAVANNAH*	OTHER AREAS*
$$$$	over $230	over $170
$$$	$170–$230	$120–$170
$$	$100–$170	$75–$120
$	under $100	under $75

All prices are for a standard double room, excluding 13% tax and service.

Nightlife

No night in Georgia need ever be boring. Clubs, music venues, theater, film, symphony, and comedy revues all make nightlife hum. Blues and jazz, country and western and gospel, and rock and roll are all part of this region's—and Georgia's—homegrown musical tradition. Local composers and performers who made their marks on the national music scene include Savannah's Johnny Mercer; Macon's Otis Redding and the Allman Brothers; and Augusta's James Brown, the godfather of soul. Macon's Little Richard and Albany's Ray Charles still perform. Local groups that have gained national and international fame include R.E.M. and the B-52's from Athens, Indigo Girls from Decatur, and Black Crowes from Marietta. In country-and-western music, Travis Tritt started out in Marietta and Trisha Yearwood in Monticello. To hear rising new stars, call local radio stations for information about venues.

In the classical department, opera diva Jessye Norman is from Augusta, and violinist Robert McDuffie is from Macon. The state abounds in symphony orchestras, chamber groups, and classical and jazz ensembles, many of which perform on college campuses. For details, contact a local college campus or consult the local newspaper.

Theater is vital not only in Atlanta but also throughout the state, home to thespians Joanne Woodward (Thomasville), Julia and Eric Roberts (Smyrna), Holly Hunter (Conyers), Melvin Douglas (Macon), Pernell Roberts (Waycross), and playwright Alfred Uhry (Atlanta). If you can catch a performance of *Swamp Gravy,* by residents of Colquitt, Georgia, or *Reach of Song,* based on the poetry of mountain poet Byron Herbert Reece, you'll enjoy traditional local subject matter and music.

Outdoor Activities and Sports

For the sports enthusiast, Georgia has a full plate of activities—fishing, camping, golf and tennis, sailing and rowing. There's also a beloved baseball team, the Atlanta Braves. Hiking opportunities abound: At the Chattahoochee Nature Center outside Atlanta, you can see birds and other woodland animals in their natural habitat while hiking through 124 acres of lush forests and wetlands. Another outdoor favorite is Stone Mountain Park and its Walk Up Trail, an atmospheric jaunt up the west side of the mountain culminated by a rigorous 825-ft climb to the peak. It's well worth the challenge, as the ensuing panoramic view of Atlanta is stunning.

☙ *following the text of a review is your signal that the property has a Web site, where you will find details and, usually, images; for a link, visit www.fodors.com/urls.*

Exploring Georgia

Georgia has several distinct touring areas; the state is large, and you'd need more than a week to hit even some of the highlights. The Foothills of the Appalachian Mountains run from west to east in north Georgia, making this a popular destination for tourists, especially in spring and fall. Atlanta alone warrants serious exploration. The coast offers other opportunities, especially for the history aficionado; it's a good place to start if you have just a few days. From Savannah, Georgia's oldest city, to Augusta, its third oldest, colonial and Civil War history awaits at every turn. It's in east Georgia where you'll see most of the columned antebellum homes visitors have come to expect. The coastal islands have fine beaches and opportunities for nature-focused expeditions. The best spot for would-be naturalists, of course, is the Okefenokee Natural Wildlife Refuge.

Great Itineraries

IF YOU HAVE 3 DAYS

Explore the coast to get a true taste of what early Georgia was all about. Spend a day and night in ▦ **Augusta,** being sure to visit Meadow Garden, home of George Walton, youngest signer (at age 26) of the Declaration of Independence. Exhibits at the Morris Museum of Southern Art range from luminous 19th-century landscapes to folk art and the challenging abstracts of Augusta native Jasper Johns. Give the remaining two days over to an exploration of ▦ **Savannah.** Stay at a bed-and-breakfast inn (be sure to have reservations, especially for weekends) and view any of the fine restored homes the city offers. Spend some time along Riverfront Plaza, enjoying the waterfront, dining in restaurants, and just plain kicking back. Other must-see sights include the 1815 Isaiah Davenport House and the Colonial Park Cemetery, the final resting place for some of America's founders. Spring and fall are the best times to visit both these cities; in spring you may be able to catch a tour of Savannah's glorious private gardens.

IF YOU HAVE 7 DAYS

Add a trip to ▦ **Atlanta** to the three-day itinerary. History enthusiasts will want to visit the Atlanta History Center and its gardens, viewing those exhibits that focus on the history of the city and touring its two house museums. A fine small museum, the African-American Panoramic Experience, chronicles the history of blacks in America. In Grant Park, the Atlanta Cyclorama has a huge painting of the 1864 Battle of Atlanta. The Chattahoochee National Recreational Area is a great spot for joggers, walkers, hikers, and nature lovers. At Stone Mountain Park, you can see the Confederate Memorial (the world's largest sculpture), two Civil War museums, and the Road to Tara Museum. Atlanta is famous for its springtime, and no doubt this is a glorious time to visit. But fall is exquisite, too, as the hardwoods change color, beginning about early October.

IF YOU HAVE 10 DAYS

Follow the seven-day itinerary (☞ *above*). Then take a run up to the north Georgia mountains, visiting **Clayton,** with its many art and antiques shops; ▦ **Dahlonega,** where you can pan for gold in "them thar hills"; or **Chickamauga,** site of one of the Civil War's most important conflicts. The north Georgia mountains are glorious from spring through fall. A second option is to turn south and visit the heart of the state, taking in ▦ **Macon,** with its antebellum and Victorian homes and museums. Spring in middle Georgia is splendid, with azaleas and other flowers in full bloom. Many garden and historic home tours are scheduled at this time.

When to Tour Georgia

Spring is the best time to visit, although autumn, especially beginning in early October, is another glorious season.

ATLANTA

Founded in 1837 as the end of the Western & Atlantic railroad line and thus named Terminus, Atlanta today is a transportation hub, not just for the country but for the world: Hartsfield Atlanta International Airport is one of the nation's busiest in daily passenger flights. Direct flights to Europe, South America, and Asia have made Atlanta easily accessible to the more than 1,000 international businesses that operate here and the nearly 50 countries that have representation in the city through consulates, trade offices, and chambers of commerce. The city has emerged as a banking center and is the world headquarters for such Fortune 500 companies as CNN, Coca-Cola, Delta Airlines, Holiday Inn Worldwide, and United Parcel Service.

Atlanta's character has evolved from a mix of peoples: Transplanted Northerners and those from elsewhere account for 50% of the population and have undeniably affected the mood and character of the city. Irish immigrants had a major role in the city's early history, along with Germans and Austrians; the Hungarian-born Rich brothers founded Atlanta's principal department store. And the immigrants keep coming. In the past two decades, Atlanta has seen spirited growth in its Asian and Latin-American communities. Their restaurants, shops, and institutions have become part of the city's texture.

For more than four decades, Atlanta has been linked to the civil rights movement. Among the many accomplishments of Atlanta's African-American community is the Nobel Peace Prize that Martin Luther King Jr. won in 1964. Dr. King's widow, Coretta Scott King, continues to operate the King Center, which she founded after her husband's assassination in 1968. In 1972 Andrew Young was elected the first black congressman from the South since Reconstruction. After serving as ambassador to the United Nations during President Jimmy Carter's administration, Young was elected mayor of Atlanta. He is now a consultant with an international firm.

The traditional South—which in romantic versions consists of lacy moss dangling from tree limbs; thick, sugary Southern drawls; a leisurely pace; and luxurious antebellum mansions—is rarely found here. Even before the Civil War, the columned house was a rarity. The frenetic pace of construction that characterized the period after the Civil War continues unabated. Still viewed by die-hard Southerners as the heart of the Old Confederacy, Atlanta has become the best example of the New South, a fast-paced modern city proud of its heritage.

In the past two decades, Atlanta has experienced unprecedented growth. A good measure of that is its ever-changing downtown skyline, along with skyscrapers constructed in the Midtown, Buckhead, and outer perimeter (set by I–285) business districts. Since the late 1970s, dozens of dazzling skyscrapers designed by such luminaries as Philip Johnson, I. M. Pei, and Marcel Breuer have reshaped the city's profile. Residents, however, are less likely to measure the city's growth by skyscrapers than by increasing traffic jams, crowds, higher prices, and the ever-burgeoning subdivisions that continue to push urban sprawl farther and farther into surrounding rural areas. Although the Chamber of Commerce advertises Atlanta as a 20-county metropolitan area, the core of Atlanta revolves around five counties. The city of Atlanta is primarily in Fulton and DeKalb counties, with the southern part and the airport in Clayton County. Outside I–285, Cobb and Gwinnett counties on the northwest and northeast corners of the city, respectively, are experiencing much of Atlanta's population increase.

Atlanta's lack of grid system in most parts of the city will confuse some drivers. Some streets change their names along the same stretch of road, including the city's most famous thoroughfare, Peachtree Street, which follows a mountain ridge from downtown to suburban Norcross outside I–285N: It becomes Peachtree Road after crossing I–85 and then splits into Peachtree Industrial Boulevard beyond the Buckhead neighborhood and the original Peachtree Road, which heads into Chamblee. Adding to the confusion, 60 other streets in the metropolitan area use the word Peachtree in their names. Before setting out anywhere, get the complete street address of your destination, including landmarks, cross streets, or other guideposts, as street numbers and even street signs often are difficult to find.

Downtown Atlanta

Downtown Atlanta clusters around the hub known as Five Points. Here is the MARTA station that intersects north–south and east–west transit lines. On the surface, Five Points is formed by the intersection of Peachtree Street with Marietta, Broad, and Forsyth streets.

Numbers in the text correspond to numbers in the margin and on the Downtown Atlanta and Sweet Auburn map.

A Good Walk

This walk branches in three directions, which are most efficiently managed by taking MARTA trains to get quickly from one spot to the next. The valiant will, of course, prefer to go it on foot. Begin at **Woodruff Park** ①, and then proceed north on Peachtree Street, noting Atlanta's **Flatiron Building** ② on the west side of Peachtree and the **Candler Building** ③ on the east side of the street. Nearby on Peachtree Street at John Wesley Dobbs Avenue is the modern **Georgia-Pacific Center** ④, and across from it are **Margaret Mitchell Park** ⑤ and the **Atlanta-Fulton Public Library** ⑥. Continuing north up Peachtree Street, note the modern hotel **Ritz-Carlton, Atlanta** ⑦, the neo-Gothic **One-Ninety-One Peachtree Tower** ⑧, and **Peachtree Center** ⑨, which includes the small but worthwhile **Atlanta International Museum of Art and Design** ⑩. Walk east on Baker Street one block to Courtland Street; head north on Courtland until you reach Ralph McGill Boulevard. Here you'll find an open-air folk art exhibition known as the **Folk Art Park** ⑪.

Return to Peachtree Center and take the subway back one stop to the **Five Points MARTA station** ⑫, from which you can walk north on Peachtree Street to the **William-Oliver Building** ⑬, an award-winning restoration. (From Folk Art Park you can also follow Ralph McGill Boulevard west to Peachtree and then head south down to the William-Oliver Building.) From here, go east on Edgewood Avenue and just ahead you'll see the **Hurt Building** ⑭, a rare Atlanta example of Chicago-style architecture. Around the corner on Marietta Street at Broad Street is the handsome **Bank of America Building** ⑮, and nearby is the **Statue of Henry Grady** ⑯, right across from the building now housing the newspaper he founded, the *Atlanta Journal-Constitution* ⑰. A block west on Marietta Street is the **Federal Reserve Bank** ⑱, with its monetary museum. At Marietta Street and Techwood Drive, **Centennial Olympic Park** ⑲ hosts concerts and special events. Adjacent to the park is **CNN Center** ⑳, which you may tour if you make a reservation. At the rear of the center is the **Georgia Dome** ㉑.

At the CNN Center/Georgia Dome station, take MARTA one station back to the Five Points station and exit at the sign for **Underground Atlanta** ㉒. After taking a rest and a restorative snack in its food court, wander the maze of subterranean streets here and exit the doors of Underground

Atlanta, bearing slightly left toward the **Georgia Railroad Freight Depot** ㉓. Across the plaza from the depot is the **World of Coca-Cola** ㉔, with fun memorabilia on display. Across Martin Luther King Jr. Drive at Central Avenue is the historic **Shrine of the Immaculate Conception** ㉕, one of many historic churches still operating in downtown. Just south of the shrine are the neo-Gothic **City Hall** ㉖, with a modern addition housing a permanent art collection, which is on Mitchell Street, and the Renaissance-style **Georgia State Capitol** ㉗ on Washington Street.

TIMING

This walk requires at least a day, assuming you don't spend much time at any one location. If you plan to walk at a more leisurely pace, finish the first day at the Folk Art Park, and allow another half day for the rest of the walk. If you plan tours of CNN Center, the Georgia Dome, and World of Coca-Cola, you'll need an additional half day. If you tour these sights at length, it will probably take two full days to cover the territory. The terrain is fairly level and not too taxing, with sidewalks the entire distance.

Sights to See

OFF THE BEATEN PATH

★ **ATLANTA CYCLORAMA & CIVIL WAR MUSEUM** – In Grant Park (named for a New England–born Confederate colonel, not the U.S. president), you'll find a huge circular painting, completed by a team of expert European panorama artists shortly after the Civil War, depicting the 1864 Battle of Atlanta. The museum has one of the best Civil War bookstores anywhere. To reach the Cyclorama by car, take I–20 east to Exit 59A, turn right onto Boulevard, and then take a right at the next traffic light into Grant Park; follow signs to the Cyclorama. ✉ Grant Park, 800 Cherokee Ave., ☎ 404/624–1071 information. 💲 $5. ☉ June–Labor Day, daily 9:20–5:30; Labor Day–May, daily 9:20–4:30. 🐾

❻ Atlanta-Fulton Public Library. The Marcel Breuer–designed building houses on its fourth floor a large collection of *Gone With the Wind* memorabilia and newspapers from most major cities in the United States and elsewhere. ✉ 1 Margaret Mitchell Sq., ☎ 404/730–1700. ☉ Mon. and Fri.–Sat. 9–6, Tues.–Thurs. 9–8, Sun. 2–6.

★ **❿ Atlanta International Museum of Art and Design.** In the Peachtree Center in the Marriott Marquis Two Tower, this museum has mounted more than 30 major international exhibitions covering such subjects as textiles, puzzles, boxes, masks, and baskets. Exhibits focus on arts and crafts, design, and culture from around the globe. ✉ 285 Peachtree Center Ave., ☎ 404/688–2467. 💲 $3. ☉ Weekdays 11–5. 🐾

⓱ Atlanta Journal-Constitution. The building containing the business offices and printing plant for the city's—and the state's—dominant newspaper has a lobby that displays front-page news of historic events, an old printing press, and photographs of famous former employees. Tours must be scheduled at least two weeks in advance and are not open to children under six. ✉ 72 Marietta St., ☎ 404/614–2688. ☉ Tours of plant available by prior arrangement, weekdays at 11:30 and 12:30.

⓯ Bank of America Building. Originally known as the Chicago-style Empire Building and, more recently, as the NationsBank Building, this handsome 1901 classic was designed by Atlanta architect Phillip Trammel Shutze. In 1929 Shutze refashioned the first three floors, bestowing upon them a decidedly Renaissance look. This is one of the city's first steel-frame structures, and at 14 stories one of its tallest, but during the renovation Shutze resheathed the base with masonry. ✉ 35 Broad St.

③ Candler Building. Asa G. Candler, founder of the Coca-Cola Company, engaged the local firm of Murphy and Stewart to design this splendid terra-cotta and marble building in 1906. The ornate bronze and marble lobby shouldn't be missed. ⊠ *84 Peachtree St.* ⊙ *Daily 9–5.*

⑲ Centennial Olympic Park. This 21-acre urban landscape, the largest urban park to be developed in this country in more than two decades, was the central venue for Olympics entertainment in the summer of 1996. The park's Fountain of Rings (the world's largest using the Olympic symbol) centers a court of 24 flags, each of them representing the Olympic Games as well as the host countries of the modern Games. Seating in the fountain amphitheater allows you to enjoy the water and music spectacle (five tunes are programmed and timed to coincide with water displays). The park has a 6-acre great lawn and pathways formed by commemorative brick paving stones. ⊠ *Marietta St. and Techwood Dr.,* ☎ *404/223–4412; 404/223–4636 information.* ⊙ *Daily 8:30 AM–9 PM.*

㉖ City Hall. When the 14-story neo-Gothic building, designed by Atlanta architect G. Lloyd Preacher, was erected in 1929 critics dubbed it the Painted Lady of Mitchell Street. The newer wing, with its five-story glass atrium and beautiful marble entryway, houses a splendid permanent collection of art. ⊠ *68 Mitchell St.,* ☎ *404/330–6000.* ⊙ *Weekdays 8:15–5.*

⑳ CNN Center. The home of Ted Turner's Cable News Network occupies all 14 floors of this dramatic structure on the edge of downtown. The 40-minute CNN studio tour begins with a ride up the world's longest escalator to an eighth-floor exhibit about Turner's global broadcasting empire. Tours are not open to children under age six. ⊠ *1 CNN Center,* ☎ *404/827–2300. Reservations must be made at least 1 day in advance using credit card (AE, MC, V); walk-up tickets for same day only, if available, go on sale at 8:30 AM.* ▣ *45-min tour $7; 1¼-hr VIP tour $24.50.* ⊙ *Daily 9–5:30.*

⑱ Federal Reserve Bank. This bank sits on the site once occupied by Thrasherville, a settlement that predates the 1837 establishment of Atlanta. An exhibit explains the story of money as a medium of exchange and the history of the U.S. banking system. Items displayed include rare coins, uncut sheets of money, and a gold bar. There's a tour and a video, *Inside the Fed.* ⊠ *104 Marietta St.,* ☎ *404/521–8764.* ⊙ *Weekdays 9–4.*

⑫ Five Points MARTA Station. This MARTA station serves Underground Atlanta and nearby Woodruff Park, Georgia State University, and numerous businesses; the station is at the crossroads of MARTA's east–west and north–south lines. Stand on the corner of Peachtree and Alabama streets, outside the station, and notice the old-fashioned gas streetlight, with its historic marker proclaiming it the **Eternal Flame of the Confederacy.** ⊠ *Corner of Peachtree and Alabama Sts.*

② Flatiron Building. The English-American Building, as it was originally known, was designed by Bradford Gilbert. Similar to the famous New York City Flatiron Building, built after the turn of the 20th century, this one dates from 1897 and is the city's oldest high-rise. Its distinguishing features include a knife-sharp point that looks proudly up Peachtree Street. The rounded facade gazes toward Woodruff Park, and interesting bays within protrude out of the facade about 3 ft. ⊠ *74 Peachtree St.* ⊙ *Weekdays 8:15–5:30.*

⑪ Folk Art Park. Revitalizing an ignored part of the city, the park pays homage to an important American art form by gathering works that reflect the diverse styles of American (especially Southern) folk art. Work by more than a dozen different artists is on display, among them Harold Rittenberry, Howard Finster, and Eddie Owens Martin. Martin's brightly painted totems and snake-topped walls replicate portions of *Pasaquan* (the legendary visionary environment that Martin created at his farm near Columbus, Georgia). ⊠ *Ralph McGill Blvd. at Court-land St., Baker St., and Piedmont Ave.*

㉑ Georgia Dome. This arena accommodates 71,500 spectators with good visibility no matter where the seat is; it is the site of Atlanta Falcons football games, major rock concerts, conventions, and trade shows. The white, plum, and turquoise 1-million-square-ft facility is crowned with the world's largest cable-supported oval, giving the roof a circus-tent top. ⊠ *1 Georgia Dome Dr.,* ☎ *404/223–8687.* ☞ *Tour $2 (groups only).* ⊙ *Tours Wed.–Fri. every hr 10–4.*

④ Georgia-Pacific Center. The towering, 52-story structure occupies the site of the old Loew's Grand Theatre, where *Gone With the Wind* premiered in 1939. From certain angles, the red-marble high-rise appears to be flat against the sky. The **High Museum of Art, Folk Art and Photography Galleries** is inside the building. ⊠ *133 Peachtree St., at John Wesley Dobbs Ave. Museum:* ⊠ *30 John Wesley Dobbs Ave.,* ☎ *404/ 577–6940.* ⊙ *Mon.–Sat. 10–5.*

㉓ Georgia Railroad Freight Depot. After downtown's oldest extant building was constructed in 1869 to replace the one torched by Sherman's troops in 1864, it burned again in 1935 and was rebuilt in its present form. It is now used by several downtown companies as a banquet hall and for special events. It may be viewed only by appointment. ⊠ *65 Martin Luther King Jr. Dr.,* ☎ *404/656–3850.*

★ **㉗ Georgia State Capitol.** A Renaissance-style edifice, the capitol was dedicated on July 4, 1889. The gold leaf on its dome was mined in nearby Dahlonega. Inside, the **Georgia Capitol Museum** houses exhibits on the history of the Capitol Building. On the grounds, state historical markers commemorate the 1864 Battle of Atlanta, which destroyed 90% of the city. Statues memorialize a 19th-century Georgia governor and his wife (Joseph and Elizabeth Brown), a Confederate general (John B. Gordon), and a former senator (Richard B. Russell). Former governor and president Jimmy Carter is depicted with his sleeves rolled up, a man at work. ⊠ *Capitol Square,* ☎ *404/656–2844.* ⊙ *Guided tours weekdays at 10, 11, 1, and 2.* 🐾

OFF THE BEATEN PATH

HAMMONDS HOUSE GALLERIES AND RESOURCE CENTER – Dr. Otis Thrash Hammonds donated his handsome Eastlake Victorian house and his fine collection of Victorian furniture and paintings to the city of Atlanta as an art gallery and resource center. The permanent and visiting exhibitions are devoted chiefly to work by African-American artists, although art from anywhere in the African-influenced world can be a focus. ⊠ *503 Peeples St.,* ☎ *404/752-8730.* ☞ *$2.* ⊙ *Tues.–Fri. 10–6, weekends 1–5.*

HERNDON HOME – Alonzo Herndon, a former slave, emerged from slavery and founded both a chain of successful barber shops and the **Atlanta Life Insurance Company.** He traveled extensively and influenced the cultural life around Atlanta's traditionally black colleges. Alonzo's son, Norris, created a foundation to preserve the handsome Beaux Arts home as a museum and heritage center. ⊠ *587 University Pl., near Morris Brown College,* ☎ *404/581-9813.* ☞ *Donation.* ⊙ *Tues.–Sat. 10–4; tours every hr.*

⑭ Hurt Building. Named for Atlanta developer Joel Hurt, this restored 1913 Chicago-style high-rise, with its intricate grillwork and sweeping marble staircase, has a lower level of shops and art galleries. The excellent City Grill (☞ Dining, *below*) restaurant is at the top of the sweeping staircase. ☒ *50 Hurt Plaza.*

❺ Margaret Mitchell Park. A cascading waterfall and columned sculpture are highlights of this park named for Atlanta's most famous author, whose masterpiece and only novel is *Gone With the Wind.* ☒ *Margaret Mitchell Sq.*

❽ One-Ninety-One Peachtree Tower. Designed by John Burgee with Philip Johnson as a consultant, the 50-story neo-Gothic skyscraper, built in 1990, has a dazzling lobby with a seven-story-high atrium. ☒ *191 Peachtree St.*

❾ Peachtree Center. John Portman designed this skyscraper complex, built between 1960 and 1992, which contains shops, offices, and a variety of restaurants. Across the street, connected to Peachtree Center by skywalks, is the massive **Atlanta Market Center.** Two additional Portman creations, the **Atlanta Marriott Marquis** and the **Hyatt Regency Hotel,** are also connected to the center by skywalks. A MARTA stop is available at Peachtree Center. ☒ *225 Peachtree St.,* ☎ *404/654–1255.*

❼ Ritz-Carlton, Atlanta. The hotel (☞ Lodging, *below*) has a fabulous collection of hunting art, both paintings and sculptures, in the restaurant and the bar. ☒ *181 Peachtree St.,* ☎ *404/659–0400.*

㉕ Shrine of the Immaculate Conception. During the Battle of Atlanta, Thomas O'Reilly, the church's pastor, persuaded Union forces to spare his church and several others around the city. That 1848 structure was then replaced by this much grander building, whose cornerstone was laid in 1869. O'Reilly, a native of Ireland, was interred in the basement of the church. Now on the National Register, the church was nearly lost to fire in 1982 but has been exquisitely restored. The vestibule is always open, allowing visitors to view the interior, or you may contact the rectory for an appointment. ☒ *48 Martin Luther King Jr. Dr., at Central Ave.,* ☎ *404/521–1866.* ☉ *Weekdays 8:30–5, Sat. 9–7, Sun. 7–3.*

⓰ Statue of Henry Grady. New York artist Alexander Doyle's bronze sculpture honors the post–Civil War editor of the *Atlanta Constitution* and early advocate of the so-called New South. Much about Grady reminds one of Ted Turner, contemporary Atlanta media mogul. Among other things, Grady was an early booster of baseball. The memorial was raised in 1891, after Grady's untimely death at age 39. ☒ *Corner of Marietta and Forsyth Sts.*

㉒ Underground Atlanta. This six-block entertainment and shopping district, dotted with historic markers, was created from the web of underground brick streets, ornamental building facades, and tunnels that fell into disuse in 1929, when the city built viaducts over the train tracks. Merchants moved their storefronts to the new viaduct level, leaving the original street level for storage. Today it houses restaurants, clubs, art galleries, shopping emporiums, and a food court, making it a good stop on a walking tour. ☒ *50 Upper Alabama St.,* ☎ *404/523–2311.*

⓭ William-Oliver Building. Walk through the lobby of this Art Deco gem and admire the ceiling mural, brass grills, and elevator doors. Formerly an office building, it has been renovated for luxury downtown residences and won a 1997 award for historic preservation from the Atlanta Urban Design Commission. ☒ *32 Peachtree St.*

❶ Woodruff Park. Named for the city's great philanthropist Robert W. Woodruff, the late Coca-Cola magnate, the triangular park fills during lunchtime on weekdays with executives, street preachers, politicians,

Georgia State University students, and homeless people. ⊠ *Bordered by Pryor, Houston, and Peachtree Sts.*

⟲ ㉔ **World of Coca-Cola.** At this three-story, $15 million special-exhibit facility, you can sip samples of 38 Coca-Cola Company products from around the world and study memorabilia from more than a century's worth of corporate archives. Everything Coca-Cola, the renovated gift shop, sells everything from refrigerator magnets to evening bags. ⊠ *55 Martin Luther King Jr. Dr.,* ☎ *404/676–5151.* ⚅ *$6.* ⊙ *June–Aug., Mon.–Sat. 9–6, Sun. 11–6; Sept.–May, Mon.–Sat. 9–5, Sun. noon–6.*

OFF THE
BEATEN PATH

ZOO ATLANTA – This zoo has nearly 1,000 animals living in naturalistic habitats, such as the Ford African Rain Forest, Flamingo Lagoon, Masai Mara (re-created plains of Kenya), and Sumatran Tiger exhibits. Sibling gorillas Kudzoo and Olympia are always hits. To reach the zoo by car, take I–20 east to Exit 59A, turn right on Boulevard, then right again at the next light into Grant Park. Follow signs to the zoo. ⊠ *Grant Park, 800 Cherokee Ave.,* ☎ *404/624–5600.* ⚅ *$10.* ⊙ *Daily 9:30–4:30.*

Sweet Auburn

Between 1890 and 1930 the historic Sweet Auburn district was Atlanta's most active and prosperous center of black business, entertainment, and political life. Following the Depression, the area went into an economic decline that lasted until the 1980s, when the residential area where civil rights leader Rev. Martin Luther King Jr. was born, raised, and later lived was declared a National Historic District.

Numbers in the text correspond to numbers in the margin and on the Downtown Atlanta and Sweet Auburn map.

A Good Walk

Start your walk in the Martin Luther King Jr. National Historic District, the heart of Sweet Auburn, where you may get a sense of what the civil rights movement and its principal leader were all about. Here, first visit the **Martin Luther King Jr. Birth Home** ㉘ on Auburn Avenue, and on the next block west, the **Martin Luther King Jr. Center for Nonviolent Social Change** ㉙, where Dr. King is entombed. Next stop at the nearby **Ebenezer Baptist Church** ㉚, where Dr. King preached along with his grandfather, father, and brother. Proceed a few blocks west near the I–75/85 overpass to enjoy the **John Wesley Dobbs Plaza** ㉛, a good place to take a breather. The **Odd Fellows Building** ㉜, on the other side of Auburn Avenue just after you walk under the expressway, is a handsome structure not to be missed. At this point, go south on Bell Street and walk one block to Edgewood Avenue to visit the **Sweet Auburn Curb Market** ㉝. Walk three blocks west on Edgewood Avenue, and you'll reach the **Baptist Student Center** ㉞, a fine example of Victorian architecture. Returning north to Auburn Avenue, you'll see the **Atlanta Daily World Building** ㉟, and next to it the **African-American Panoramic Experience (APEX)** ㊱. Continue down Auburn Avenue just a few steps and enter the lobby of the **Atlanta Life Insurance Company** ㊲ to view its fabulous art collection. Now, proceed across the street and finish your walk with a stop at the **Auburn Avenue Research Library on African-American Culture and History** ㊳.

TIMING

This is a leisurely walk along level sidewalks, with shops and historic sites along the way. If you stop for tours, you'll fill an entire day. If you simply stroll and look, the walk should take an hour or two.

80

Downtown Atlanta and Sweet Auburn

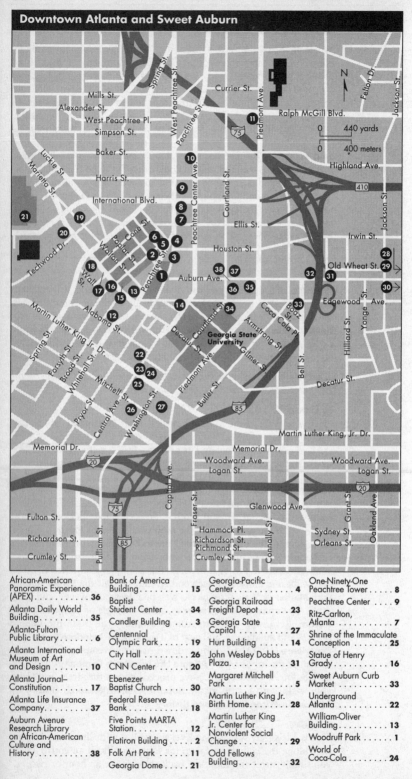

Sights to See

★ ㊱ **African-American Panoramic Experience (APEX).** The museum's quarterly exhibits chronicle the history of black people in America. Videos illustrate the history of Sweet Auburn, the name bestowed upon Auburn Avenue by businessman John Wesley Dobbs, who fostered business development for African-Americans on this street. ✉ *135 Auburn Ave., ☎ 404/521–2739. 💲 $3. ⊙ June–Aug., Tues.–Sat. 10–5, Sun. 1–5; Sept.– May, Tues.–Sat. 10–5.*🐾

㉟ **Atlanta Daily World Building.** This simple two-story brick building, banded with a white frieze of lion's heads, was constructed in the early 1900s; since 1945 it has housed one of the nation's oldest black newspapers. Despite its title, the publication is no longer a daily, although it was in the past. Alexis Reeves, publisher and CEO, is the granddaughter of William A. Scott II, who founded the paper as a weekly in 1928. ✉ *145 Auburn Ave., ☎ 404/659–1110.*

㊲ **Atlanta Life Insurance Company.** The landmark enterprise founded by Alonzo Herndon, a former slave, was in modest quarters at 148 Auburn Avenue until the modern complex at No. 100 was opened in 1980. The lobby holds an exhibition of art by black artists from the United States and Africa. ✉ *100 Auburn Ave., ☎ 404/659–2100. ⊙ Weekdays 8:30–5.*

㊳ **Auburn Avenue Research Library on African-American Culture and History.** This unit, added to the **Atlanta-Fulton Public Library** system (☞ *above*) in 1994, is a noncirculating library housing about 35,000 volumes devoted to African-American subjects. Special exhibits, programs, and tours are free and open to the public. The archives division contains art and artifacts, ephemera, oral histories, pamphlets, prints, rare periodicals, rare books, manuscript collections, photographs, and memorabilia. ✉ *101 Auburn Ave., ☎ 404/730–4001. ⊙ Mon. and Wed. 10–8, Tues. and Thurs. noon–8, Fri. 1–5, weekends 2–6.*

㉞ **Baptist Student Center.** Adjacent to the Georgia State University campus, this restored Victorian building once contained the Coca-Cola Company's first bottling plant. ✉ *125 Edgewood Ave., ☎ 404/659–8726.*

㉚ **Ebenezer Baptist Church.** A Gothic Revival–style building completed in 1922, the church became known as the spiritual center for the civil rights movement after Martin Luther King Jr. won the Nobel Peace Prize in 1964. Members of the King family have preached at the church for three generations; Dr. King's funeral was held here. A tour of the church includes an audiotape outlining the history of the building. Since 1999 the congregation has occupied the building across the street. ✉ *407 Auburn Ave., ☎ 404/688–7263. 💲 Tours free. ⊙ Tours Mon.– Sat. 9–5.*

㉛ **John Wesley Dobbs Plaza.** John Wesley Dobbs was an important civic leader whose legacy includes coining the name Sweet Auburn for Atlanta's black business and residential neighborhood. The plaza, which was built for the 1996 Olympic Games, has a life mask of Dobbs himself; children playing in the plaza may view the street through the mask's eyes. ✉ *Auburn Ave. adjacent to I–75/85 overpass.*

★ ㉘ **Martin Luther King Jr. Birth Home.** This modest Queen Anne–style historic home is managed by the National Park Service, which also has a visitor center across the street from the **Martin Luther King Jr. Center for Nonviolent Social Change** (☞ *below*). The visitor center contains a multimedia exhibit focused on the civil rights movement and Dr. King's role in it. To sign up for tours, go to the **fire station** (✉ 39 Boulevard).

✉ *501 Auburn Ave.,* ☎ *404/331–6922.* 🎫 *Tours free.* ☉ *Daily guided ½-hr tours every hr 10–5.* ✑

㉙ **Martin Luther King Jr. Center for Nonviolent Social Change.** The Martin Luther King Jr. National Historic District occupies several blocks on Auburn Avenue, a few blocks east of Peachtree Street in the black business and residential community of Sweet Auburn. The neighborhood was the birthplace of Martin Luther King Jr. in 1929. After King's assassination in 1968, his widow, Coretta Scott King, established the center, which exhibits personal items, such as King's Nobel Peace Prize, Bible, and tape recorder, along with memorabilia and photos chronicling the civil rights movement. In the courtyard in front of Freedom Hall, on a circular brick pad in the middle of the rectangular Meditation Pool, is King's white marble tomb; the inscription reads FREE AT LAST! Nearby, an eternal flame burns. A chapel of all faiths sits at one end of the reflecting pool. ✉ *449 Auburn Ave.,* ☎ *404/524–1956.* ☉ *Daily 9–5.*

㉜ **Odd Fellows Building.** The Georgia Chapter of the Grand United Order of Odd Fellows was a trade and social organization for African-Americans. In 1912 the membership erected this handsome Romanesque Revival–style building housing meeting rooms, a theater, commercial spaces, and a community center. African-featured terra-cotta figures adorn the splendid entrance. Now handsomely restored, the building houses offices. ✉ *250 Auburn Ave.*

㉝ **Sweet Auburn Curb Market.** The market, an institution on Edgewood Avenue since 1923, sells vegetables, fish, flowers, prepared foods, and meat. Individual stalls are operated by separate owners, making this a true public market. Don't miss the splendid totemic sculptures by young Atlanta artist Carl Joe Williams. The pieces were placed as part of Atlanta's Olympic art program. ✉ *209 Edgewood Ave.,* ☎ *404/659–1665.* ☉ *Mon.–Thurs. 8–5, Fri.–Sat. 8–7.*

Midtown

Just north of downtown lies this thriving area, a hippie hangout in the late '60s and '70s and now home to a large segment of the city's gay population, along with young families, young professionals, artists, and musicians. Formerly in decline, Midtown has evolved into one of the city's most interesting neighborhoods. Its gleaming new office towers give it a skyline to rival downtown's, and the renovated mansions and bungalows in its residential section have made it a city showcase.

Numbers in the text correspond to numbers in the margin and on the Atlanta Neighborhoods map.

A Good Drive

From downtown, take Piedmont Avenue about ½ mi to **SciTrek** ㊴, a science museum all ages will enjoy. Turn left from Piedmont Avenue onto Ponce de Leon Avenue and drive two blocks to Peachtree Street; then turn right and find the 1929 **Fox Theatre** ㊵ and, across the street, the **Georgian Terrace** ㊶, a luxury suites hotel. From Peachtree Street, circle around the block, turning right on 3rd Street to Juniper Street; then turn right on Juniper Street, continue two blocks, and turn right onto North Avenue. Turn right again onto Peachtree Street to view the **Bank of America Plaza Tower** ㊷. Continuing up Peachtree Street to Peachtree Place (one block south of 10th Street), you'll find the **Margaret Mitchell House** ㊸, the restored building where the Pulitzer Prize–winning author lived while completing *Gone With the Wind*. Continue one block up Peachtree Street and turn left onto 10th Street for four blocks to its intersection with 14th Street, where you'll find **One At-**

Atlanta Neighborhoods

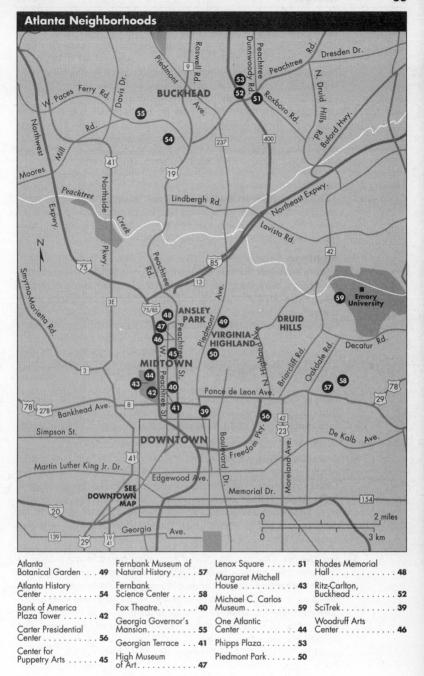

lantic Center ㊹, built for IBM. Turn left onto 18th Street to reach the **Center for Puppetry Arts** ㊺. Take 18th Street east back to Peachtree Street, turn left, and continue on to the **Woodruff Arts Center** ㊻, which includes the modern structure of the **High Museum of Art** ㊼. From this point, travel two blocks north on Peachtree Street to **Rhodes Memorial Hall** ㊽. From here, take Beverly Road east off Peachtree Street for about ¼ mi to Montgomery Ferry Drive; turn a quick dogleg left, then right, continuing on Beverly to Park Lane, and then turn right on Park Lane and drive about ¼ mi to where it intersects the Prado. Here, these two streets dead-end onto Piedmont Avenue, where you'll enter the **Atlanta Botanical Garden** ㊾, which adjoins **Piedmont Park** ㊿, bounded by Piedmont Avenue, 10th Street, and Westminster Drive.

TIMING

This drive is best accomplished between midmorning (about 9:30) and midafternoon (3:30) to avoid rush hour traffic. Give yourself between four and five hours to visit all the sights. Each place has parking no more than a few steps away, and often it's free.

Sights to See

㊾ **Atlanta Botanical Garden.** Occupying 30 acres inside Piedmont Park (☞ *below*), the grounds contain 15 acres of display gardens, including a serene Japanese garden, a 15-acre hardwood forest with walking trails, and the Fuqua Conservatory, which has unusual and threatened flora from tropical and desert climates. A permanent Fuqua Conservatory exhibit of tiny, brightly colored poison dart frogs is popular, especially with children. ⊠ *1345 Piedmont Ave., at the Prado,* ☎ *404/ 876–5859.* ☑ *$6; free Thurs. after 3.* ☉ *Mar.–Sept., Tues.–Sun. 9–7; Oct.–Feb., Tues.–Sun. 9–6.*

㊷ **Bank of America Plaza Tower.** Built in 1992, the skyscraper has a graceful birdcage roof easily visible from the interstate and is the South's tallest building, at 1,023 ft. Its elegant marble central lobby is worth seeing. ⊠ *600 Peachtree St.*

★ ㊺ **Center for Puppetry Arts.** At this interactive museum, you can see puppets from around the world and attend puppet-making workshops. Performances, which include original dramatic works and classics adapted for the museum theater, are presented by professional puppeteers who leave youngsters and adults alike spellbound. ⊠ *1404 Spring St., at 18th St.,* ☎ *404/873–3391.* ☑ *$5; special exhibits and programs extra.* ☉ *Mon.–Sat. 9–5.* ☜

㊵ **Fox Theatre.** One of a handful of remaining classic movie palaces in the nation, the Fox was built in 1929 in a fabulous Moorish-Egyptian style to be the headquarters of the Shriners Club. The interior's crowning glory is its skylike ceiling—complete with clouds and stars above Alhambra-like minarets. Threatened by demolition in the 1970s, the Fox was saved from the wrecker's ball by concerted civic action and is still a prime venue for musicals, rock concerts, dance performances, and film festivals. ⊠ *660 Peachtree St.,* ☎ *404/881–2100; 404/876– 2041 Atlanta Preservation Center.* ☑ *Tour conducted by Atlanta Preservation Center $5.* ☉ *Tours Mon., Wed., and Thurs. at 10, Sat. at 10 and 11.*

㊶ **Georgian Terrace.** Originally built in 1911 as a fine Beaux Arts–style hotel, the Georgian Terrace, designed by William L. Stoddart, housed the stars of the film *Gone With the Wind* when it premiered at the nearby Loew's Theater (now demolished) in 1939. President Calvin Coolidge also slept here. Stars of the Metropolitan Opera stayed at the hotel when the Met used to make its annual trek to Atlanta, and according to locals, Enrico Caruso routinely serenaded passersby from its balconies.

Renovated with style and historic sensitivity, the building is now a luxury hotel (☞ Lodging, *below*). ⊠ *459 Peachtree St.*, ☎ *404/897–1991.*

47 **High Museum of Art.** The permanent holdings of this high-tech museum built in 1983 focus on American decorative arts and African art. The Uhry Print Collection contains works by French Impressionists and other European artists. In 1991 the American Institute of Architects listed the sleek structure, designed by Richard Meier, among the 10 best works of American architecture in the 1980s. ⊠ *Woodruff Arts Center, 1280 Peachtree St., MARTA Arts Center station,* ☎ *404/733–4444 recorded information.* ⊡ *$6.* ⊙ *Tues.–Thurs. and Sat. 10–5, Fri. 10–9, Sun. noon–5.*

43 **Margaret Mitchell House.** Although the author of *Gone With the Wind* detested the turn-of-the-20th-century house (she called it "the Dump") where she lived when she wrote her masterpiece, determined volunteers got backing to restore the house and open it to the public. The visitor center exhibits photographs, archival material, and personal possessions, including her original typewriter. ⊠ *990 Peachtree St., at the corner of Peachtree Pl.,* ☎ *404/249–7012.* ⊡ *$10.* ⊙ *Daily 9–4.*

44 **One Atlantic Center.** You can see the unique profile of this pyramid-top office building, also known as the **IBM Tower,** from many parts of the city. It was designed by Philip Johnson and built in 1987. ⊠ *1201 W. Peachtree St.* ⊙ *Weekdays 9–5.*

50 **Piedmont Park.** The city's outdoor recreation center, this park is a major venue for special events. Tennis courts, a swimming pool, and paths for walking, jogging, and rollerblading are part of the attraction, but many retreat to the park's great lawn for picnics with a smashing view of the Midtown skyline. Each April the park hosts the popular Dogwood Festival (☞ Festivals and Seasonal Events *in* Chapter 1). ⊠ *Piedmont Ave. between 10th St. and the Prado.*

48 **Rhodes Memorial Hall.** Headquarters of the **Georgia Trust for Historic Preservation,** this former residence is one of the finest works of Atlanta architect Willis F. Denny II. Built at the northern edge of the city in 1904 for Amos Giles Rhodes, the wealthy founder of a Southern furniture chain, the hall has stained-glass windows that depict the heroes of the Confederacy. ⊠ *1516 Peachtree St.,* ☎ *404/881–9980.* ⊡ *$5.* ⊙ *Weekdays 11–4, Sun. noon–3.*

★ ☾ **39** **SciTrek.** The Science and Technology Museum of Atlanta covers 96,000 square ft and has rotating exhibitions and daily science demonstrations at the Coca-Cola Science Show Theater. About 150 hands-on exhibits occupy four environments: Simple Machines; Light, Color, and Perception; Electricity and Magnetism; and Kidspace, for children ages two–seven. The Information Petting Zoo exhibits "cybercritters." ⊠ *395 Piedmont Ave.,* ☎ *404/522–5500.* ⊡ *$7.50.* ⊙ *Mon.–Sat. 10–5, Sun. noon–5.*☜

46 **Woodruff Arts Center.** The center is home to the world-renowned **Atlanta Symphony Orchestra,** the **High Museum of Art** (☞ *above*), the **Alliance Theatre,** and the intimate **Studio Theater.** Both theaters present contemporary dramas, classics, and frequent world premieres. ⊠ *1280 Peachtree St.,* ☎ *404/733–4200.*

Buckhead

Atlanta's sprawl doesn't lend itself to walking between major neighborhoods, so take a car or MARTA to reach Buckhead. Many of Atlanta's trendy restaurants, music clubs, chic shops, and hip art galleries are concentrated in this neighborhood. Finding a parking spot on the weekends and at night can be a real headache, and waits of two hours or more are common in the hottest restaurants.

Numbers in the text correspond to numbers in the margin and on the Atlanta Neighborhoods map.

A Good Drive

Although the adventurous and high spirited may elect to walk this tour, most will prefer to drive. For one thing, the distance between the Atlanta History Center and the Georgia Governor's Mansion, while not great, entails walking where there are no sidewalks, a tricky proposition with traffic zooming just inches away. So begin the drive at the intersection of two splendid shopping malls. The older and larger of the two, **Lenox Square** ⑤①, sprawls from Peachtree Road down Lenox Road to East Paces Ferry Road. Across the street from Lenox Square is the **Ritz-Carlton, Buckhead** ⑤②, one of two Ritz hotels in Atlanta; across the Buckhead Loop from the hotel, you'll find the elegant shops of **Phipps Plaza** ⑤③. Leaving Phipps Plaza, exit onto Peachtree Road and turn right (south), traveling about ⅓ mi to West Paces Ferry Road. At this intersection, turn right and proceed about ¼ mi to Andrews Drive. Turn left, and the entrance to the **Atlanta History Center** ⑤④ is almost immediately on the left. Leaving the center, turn right from the entrance back to West Paces Ferry Road, and then turn left, driving about ½ mi to reach the **Georgia Governor's Mansion** ⑤⑤.

TIMING

As with other driving tours in this busy part of town, you are well advised to stick to the midmorning to midafternoon hours, or from about 9:30 to 3:30. In Buckhead, an additional wrinkle is the lunchtime traffic, which lasts from about 11:30 to 1:30. Simply driving the distance around the five sights, looking briefly at each one, will consume, generally, no more than 30 minutes. Allot several hours if you want to shop or tour the History Center and Governor's Mansion.

Sights to See

★ 54 **Atlanta History Center.** The museum highlights materials native to Georgia, with a floor of heart pine and polished Stone Mountain granite. Displays are provocative, juxtaposing *Gone With the Wind* romanticism with the grim reality of Ku Klux Klan racism. Also on the 33-acre site are the elegant 1928 **Swan House**; the **Tullie Smith Farm,** with a two-story plantation plain house (1840s); and **McElreath Hall,** an exhibition space for artifacts from Atlanta's history. ✉ *130 W. Paces Ferry Rd.,* ☎ *404/814–4000.* *$7.* ⏲ *Mon.–Sat. 10–5:30, Sun. noon–5:30.*

55 **Georgia Governor's Mansion.** Built in 1967, this 24,000-square-ft Greek Revival mansion contains 30 rooms and sits on 18 acres originally belonging to the Robert Maddox family (no relation to Georgia governor Lester Maddox, who was its first occupant). American Federal-period antiques fill the public rooms. ✉ *391 W. Paces Ferry Rd.,* ☎ *404/261–1858.* ⏲ *Free guided tours Tues.–Thurs. 10 AM–11:30 AM.*

51 **Lenox Square.** Local shoppers come for the more than 250 stores and several good restaurants at this mall (☞ Shopping, *below*). ✉ *3393 Peachtree Rd.,* ☎ *404/233–6767.*

53 **Phipps Plaza.** The mall is one of Atlanta's premier shopping areas, with upscale chain stores, specialty shops, and restaurants. It also includes a 14-screen movie theater (☞ Shopping, *below*). ✉ *3500 Peachtree Rd.,* ☎ *404/262–0992 or 800/810–7700.*

52 **Ritz-Carlton, Buckhead.** Among the finest hotels in the country, the Ritz contains one of the South's most valuable private art collections, pri-

marily 18th- and 19th-century American and European painting, sculpture, and porcelain. It's also home to the renowned **Dining Room** (☞ Dining, *below*). ✉ *3434 Peachtree Rd.,* ☎ *404/237–2700.*

Virginia-Highland and the Emory Area

Restaurants and art galleries are the backbone of Virginia-Highland/Morningside, northeast of Midtown. Like Midtown, this residential area was down-at-the-heels only 25 years ago. Reclaimed by writers, artists, and a few visionary developers, Virginia-Highland today offers intriguing shopping and delightful walking. Nightlife hums here as well.

Numbers in the text correspond to numbers in the margin and on the Atlanta Neighborhoods map.

A Good Drive

This tour meanders through some residential areas, such as Druid Hills, the location for the film *Driving Miss Daisy,* by local playwright Alfred Uhry. The neighborhood was designed by the firm of Frederick Law Olmsted, which also designed New York's Central Park. Begin at the **Carter Presidential Center** ⑤⑥, the central attraction in a sub-neighborhood called Poncey Highlands, because it lies south of Ponce de Leon Avenue and south of Virginia-Highland. The former president's center is bounded by Freedom Parkway, which splits and encircles the facility. To reach it from downtown, drive on Ralph McGill Boulevard about 1 mi east of I–75/85 (Exit 248C) to where the boulevard intersects with Freedom Parkway. Alternately, you can take North Avenue east from downtown about 1 mi to its intersection with North Highland Avenue, then turn right after a short distance and follow the signs.

From the center, take a left and drive only one short block on Highland Avenue to Ponce de Leon Avenue, and turn right (east), continuing for 1 mi to Clifton Road; next take a left onto Clifton and almost immediately enter the driveway for **Fernbank Museum of Natural History** ⑤⑦. On the east end of this extensive forest and recreational-educational preserve lies **Fernbank Science Center** ⑤⑧. To reach it, return via Clifton Road to Ponce de Leon Avenue and take a left. Drive east on Ponce de Leon Avenue about ½ mi and then turn left onto Artwood Road, which turns into Heaton Road. The center is on the left side of Heaton Road about ¼ mi from Ponce de Leon Avenue. Leaving the center, turn left and take Heaton a short way to Coventry Road, where you should go left again until you see East Clifton Road. Turn right on East Clifton and follow it around to Clifton Road, and continue north ¼ mi to North Decatur Road. The entrance to Emory University is directly in front of you. Enter the campus, bear right, and park in the lot if you wish to visit the **Michael C. Carlos Museum** ⑤⑨, an exquisite contemporary structure.

TIMING
You can drive this tour in about 15 minutes without stops. If you spend a few hours at each sight, it can easily take a full day.

Sights to See

★ ✋ ⑤⑥ **Carter Presidential Center.** This complex occupies the site where Union general William T. Sherman orchestrated the Battle of Atlanta (1864). The museum and archives detail the political career of former president Jimmy Carter. The center itself, which is not open to the public, focuses on conflict resolution and human rights issues. It sponsors foreign-affairs conferences and projects on such matters as world food supply. Outside, the Japanese-style garden is a serene spot to unwind. ✉ *1 Copenhill Ave.,* ☎ *404/331–3942.* 🎫 *$5.* ◷ *Mon.–Sat. 9–4:45, Sun. noon–4:45.* 🐾

🖑 ⑤⑦ **Fernbank Museum of Natural History.** The largest natural history museum south of the Smithsonian Institution in Washington, D.C., holds a permanent exhibit, *A Walk Through Time in Georgia*. Visitors meander through 15 galleries to explore the earth's natural history. The museum's IMAX theater shows films about the natural world. The café, with an exquisite view overlooking the forest, serves great food. ✉ 767 *Clifton Rd.,* ☎ *404/370–0960; 404/370–0019 IMAX; 404/370–0850 directions hot line.* ✑ *Museum $8.95, IMAX $6.95, both $13.95.* ☉ *Mon.–Sat. 10–5, Sun. noon–5, IMAX Fri. 6:30–10.*

🖑 ⑤⑧ **Fernbank Science Center.** The museum focuses on geology, space exploration, and ecology; it's best for younger children. Special seasonal programs for children under five, priced at 50¢, are offered weekends at 1:30 from October through November, early December through the first week of January, the end of January to March 15, and during the summer. ✉ *156 Heaton Park Dr.,* ☎ *404/378–4311.* ✑ *Museum free, planetarium shows $2.* ☉ *Mon. 8:30–5, Tues.–Fri. 8:30 AM–10 PM, Sat. 10–5, Sun. 1–5; planetarium shows Tues.–Fri. at 3:30 and 8, weekends at 3:30.*

★ 🖑 ⑤⑨ **Michael C. Carlos Museum.** Housing a permanent collection that embraces more than 16,000 objects, this excellent museum designed by renowned American architect Michael Graves exhibits artifacts from Egypt, Greece, Rome, the Near East, the Americas, and Africa. European and American prints and drawings cover the Middle Ages through the 20th century. The gift shop has rare art books, jewelry, and art-focused items for children. The museum's Caffé Antico is a good lunch spot. ✉ *Emory University, 571 S. Kilgo St.,* ☎ *404/727–4282.* ✑ *Suggested donation $3.* ☉ *Mon.–Sat. 10–5, Sun. noon–5.* ✑

Other Area Attractions

Atlanta's suburbs have excellent entertainment options. It is essential to drive to these venues, so plan your visits with Atlanta's notorious rush hours in mind.

★ **Château Élan.** A 16th-century-style French château has Georgia's best-known winery, set in 2,400 rolling acres about an hour north of downtown Atlanta. Winery tours and tastings are free. Château Élan is also a complete resort: European luxury blends with Southern hospitality at the 274-room inn and spa with private villas, golf courses, and an equestrian center. ✉ *100 Rue Charlemagne, Braselton, I–85 to GA 211, Exit 126 (Chestnut Mountain/Winder),* ☎ *770/932–0900 or 800/233–9463,* ☏ *770/271–6005.* ☉ *Wine market weekdays 11–3:30, weekends 11–4. Tours weekdays at 11, 12:15, 1:30, 2:45, and 4; Sat. hourly 11–5; Sun. at 12:30 and hourly 1–5.* ✑

🖑 **Chattahoochee Nature Center.** Birds and animals in their natural habitats may be seen from nature trails and a boardwalk winding through 124 acres of woodlands and wetlands. A gift shop, indoor exhibits, birds-of-prey aviaries, and a picnic area are on the property. Naturalist guides accompany evening canoe floats from May through August. ✉ *9135 Willeo Rd., Roswell,* ☎ *770/992–2055.* ✑ *$5.* ☉ *Mon.–Sat. 9–5, Sun. noon–5.*

Kennesaw Mountain National Battlefield. A must for Civil War buffs, this 2,884-acre park with 16 mi of hiking trails was the site of several crucial battles in June 1864. The visitor center contains a small museum with exhibits of Civil War weapons, uniforms, and other items recovered from the battlefield. A 10-minute slide presentation explains the battles. ✉ *Old U.S. 41 and Stilesboro Rd. (look for signs on I–75N), Kennesaw,* ☎ *770/427–4686.* ✑ *Free.* ☉ *Daily 7:30–dusk.*

🕭 **Six Flags over Georgia.** Atlanta's major theme park, with eight theme sections, heart-stopping roller coasters, and water rides (best saved for last to prevent being damp all day), is a child's ideal playground. The new Georgia Scorcher, a roller coaster that you ride standing up, moves at 54 mph. The park also has well-staged musical revues, concerts by top-name artists, and other performances. Take MARTA's west line to Hightower station and then the Six Flags bus. ⊠ *I–20W at 7561 Six Flags Pkwy., Austell,* ☎ *770/739–3400.* ☑ *All-inclusive 1-day pass $37, parking $6.* ☉ *June–Aug., daily 10 AM–11 PM; Mar.–May and Sept.–Oct., weekends from 10, closing times vary.*

🕭 **Stone Mountain Park.** This 3,200-acre state park has the largest exposed granite outcropping on earth. The Confederate Memorial on the north face of the 825-ft-high domed mountain is the world's largest sculpture, measuring 90 ft by 190 ft. The park has a skylift to the mountaintop, a steam locomotive ride around the mountain's base, an antebellum plantation, a swimming beach, a campground, a hotel, a resort, a wildlife preserve, restaurants, and two Civil War museums. Summer nights are capped with a laser light show, and annual events such as the Yellow Daisy Festival and the Scottish Highland Games draw visitors in the fall. ⊠ *U.S. 78E, Stone Mountain Pkwy.,* ☎ *770/498–5600.* ☑ *Per car $6; annual pass $30; day pass to all attractions $12.85 Georgia residents, $17.10 out-of-state residents; additional fees for special events.* ☉ *Daily 6 AM–midnight.*

Dining

Atlanta has sophisticated kitchens run by world-class chefs, myriad ethnic restaurants, and classic Southern establishments serving such regional favorites as fried chicken, Brunswick stew, fried catfish, and hush puppies. There's no shortage of urban chic in the dining scene, but traditional Southern fare—including Cajun and Creole, country-style and plantation cuisine, coastal and mountain dishes—continues to thrive.

The local taste for things sweet and fried holds true for restaurants serving traditional Southern food. Tea in the South comes iced and sweet; if you want hot tea, specify hot. Desserts in the region are legendary. Catch the flavor of the South at breakfast and lunch in modest establishments that serve only these meals. Reserve evenings for culinary exploration, including some of the new restaurants that present traditional ingredients and dishes in fresh ways. The influx of Asian immigrants makes Atlanta the perfect city to sample Thai, Vietnamese, Japanese, and authentic Chinese cuisines.

Downtown

$$$–$$$$ ✕ **Bacchanalia.** A favorite among dining critics, this swank restaurant
★ is newly situated in an impressive former industrial space. Dazzling dishes inspired by Mediterranean and occasionally regional cuisines fill the four-course prix-fixe menu. The plentiful options may include sautéed foie gras, Georgia white shrimp, veal sweetbreads, or American farmstead cheeses. Desserts are incredible—as are most items on the menu. ⊠ *1198 Howell Mill Rd.,* ☎ *404/365–0410. Reservations essential. AE, DC, MC, V. Closed Sun.–Mon. No lunch.*

$$–$$$$ ✕ **The Abbey.** Established in 1968, the restaurant is housed in a for-
★ mer church. Stained-glass windows and celestial music played by a harpist in the former choir loft reinforce the ambience. Dishes range from the dramatic lobster claw salad with mâche, mango, and apple to a grilled elk chop with dauphinoise potatoes and turnips. Desserts, such as the white chocolate and roasted banana napoleon, finish a meal with sweet abandon. ⊠ *163 Ponce de Leon Ave.,* ☎ *404/876–8532. Reservations essential. AE, D, DC, MC, V. No lunch.*

$$–$$$$ ✕ **Atlanta Grill.** With an outdoor veranda overlooking Peachtree Street, this restaurant in the Ritz-Carlton, Atlanta (☞ *below*), has taken dining in the hotel from formal to casual. Chef Peter Zampaglione focuses on regional Southern ingredients and specializes in grilled seafood and game. Sweet corn beignets are a nod to Creole cooking, while sweet-potato spoon bread acknowledges Southeastern traditions. ✉ *181 Peachtree St.,* ☎ *404/659–0403. AE, D, DC, MC, V.*

$$–$$$$ ✕ **City Grill.** This posh, breezy restaurant has made the most of its grand
★ location in the elegantly renovated historic Hurt Building. An impressive wine list accompanies the equally impressive menu. City Grill is a top Atlanta power-lunch spot. ✉ *50 Hurt Plaza,* ☎ *404/524–2489. AE, D, DC, MC, V. Closed Sun. No lunch Sat.*

$$–$$$ ✕ **Food Studio.** A piece of a former plow factory, this stylish restaurant
★ gleams with high-tech and industrial touches. From the same group that made South City Kitchen (☞ Midtown Dining, *below*) a success, the Studio is known for innovative American food, but has added a few more traditional dishes. The grilled veal chop with broccoli and spaghetti squash is a prime example. Desserts range from the parfaitlike frozen lemon basil bombe to chocolate gold mousse cake. ✉ *887 W. Marietta St., Studio K-102, King Plow Arts Center,* ☎ *404/815–6677. Reservations essential. AE, DC, MC, V. No lunch weekends.*

$$–$$$ ✕ **Mumbo Jumbo.** A long bar skirts the left side of the establishment,
★ guiding the eye to the rear dining room. Sleek young staffers conduct guests to tables. The menu emphasizes game in cool weather, fish and shellfish in summer, and regional ingredients and locally grown produce all year round. Dishes that tempt include heirloom tomatoes with milk-sweet buffalo mozzarella, rabbit, and the famous Mumbo Gumbo, a light seafood gumbo. ✉ *89 Park Pl.,* ☎ *404/523–0330. Reservations essential. AE, D, DC, MC, V. No lunch weekends.*

$–$$$ ✕ **Max Lager's American Grill & Brewery.** Line up a tasting of the house brews—the pale ale and brown ale are tops—and then order the Gulf Coast gumbo, the excellent fish-and-chips, or for lunch the vegetarian pita pocket. This lively brewpub near the city's major high-rise buildings is hopping after business hours. It brews its own root and ginger beers. ✉ *320 Peachtree St.,* ☎ *404/525–4400. AE, D, DC, MC, V.*

$ ✕ **ACE Barbecue Barn.** This slightly worn, down-home restaurant is right near the Martin Luther King Jr. Center (☞ Sweet Auburn, *above*). Delicious ribs and chopped rib tips, baked chicken and dressing, and sweet-potato pie are the draws. ✉ *30 Bell St. NE,* ☎ *404/659–6630. No credit cards. Closed Tues.*

$ ✕ **Thelma's Kitchen.** After losing her original location to the Centennial Olympic Park (☞ *above*), Thelma Grundy moved her operation down the road to the street level of the somewhat renovated Roxy Hotel. Brighter, spiffier, and more cheerful than the earlier spot, it has okra pancakes, fried catfish, "cold" slaw, and macaroni and cheese that are among the best in town. Thelma's desserts are stellar. *768 Marietta St. NW,* ☎ *404/688–5855. Reservations not accepted. No credit cards. Closed weekends. No dinner.*

Midtown

$$$–$$$$ ✕ **Le Saint Amour.** Bright colors—warm pink, orange, and teal—decorate this charming, intimate bistro. Young staff members, many still struggling with English, offer friendly service. The food is straight out of Provence, with such dishes as duck confit with sautéed truffles and coquilles St. Jacques (scallops) in wine sauce. ✉ *1620 Piedmont Ave.,* ☎ *404/881–0300. Reservations essential. AE, MC, V. Closed Sun. No lunch Sat.*

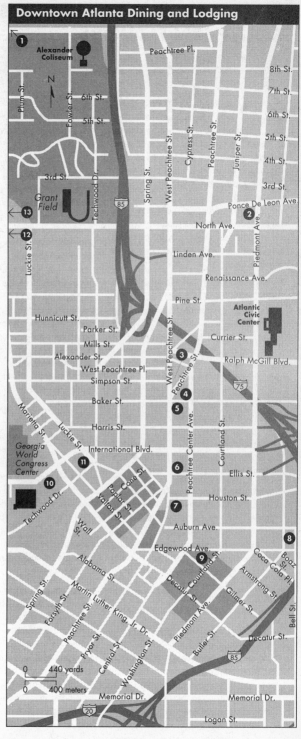

Downtown Atlanta Dining and Lodging

SOUTHERN FLAVORS

GEORGIA IS AN EXCELLENT PLACE to sample Southern food; cities such as Atlanta and Savannah have restaurants that serve the finest traditional fare as well as more innovative cooking. It helps to know that Southern food varies widely across the region and even within states. Nothing reflects this more than barbecue, and few culinary differences produce as many passionate opinions. Do your own tasting as you travel, and you can add to the debate.

Locals in Georgia and Mississippi generally prefer tomato-based sauces on ribs or chopped meat, although plenty of variations may be found. In North Carolina, barbecue is chopped pork piled on a bun with hand-cut coleslaw on top. The sauces range from vinegar and pepper (and little else) to Lexington style, with some tomato in the mix. And North Carolinians serve hush puppies (deep-fried ball-shape cornmeal fritters) with barbecue, which, for them, does not generally include ribs. For the rest of the South, the hush puppy is reserved for fried fish, whether fin or shell.

In South Carolina, mustard-based barbecue sauces are widely savored, whether on chopped meat or on ribs. In eastern Alabama (and the Florida Panhandle), you'll find a unique white sauce for barbecue. Memphis-style 'cue is famous for its dry rub, although there is also a "wet" style, in which the same spices, moistened, are rubbed on the ribs. In parts of Tennessee, barbecued mutton is traditional.

Prior to the Depression, there were two sorts of cooking in the South—country food and the elegant plantation fare drawn from French and English models. In recent years, country cooking, blending European, African, and Native American fare, has come to be the defining Southern cuisine in most people's minds. But many an elegant table was set with European-based dishes, especially along the coasts.

Gumbo, the spicy soup that is so clearly from this region, is a more apt metaphor for the South's demographics than the term *melting pot* because the word *gumbo* reflects all that comes to the Southern table (and to Southern culture) from its people. The term is West African, from *ngombo*, which meant okra in that part of the world. And what would gumbo be without okra? But gumbo is also European: A proper gumbo is based on a *roux*, a sauté of fat and flour cooked to the color of peanut butter. The cook might sauté vegetables for a gumbo, making a kind of *sofrito*, a legacy from the Spanish settlers in the lower part of Louisiana. Using sassafras or filé powder to thicken gumbo is a legacy of Southern Native Americans.

One defining ingredient in Southern cooking is corn, another Native American legacy. Parch the corn with lye, which swells the grains, and you make hominy. Grind the corn, white or yellow, and you have grits. Sift the grits, and you have cornmeal for making corn bread, fluffy spoon bread, cornpone, hoecakes, hush puppies, johnnycake (or Native American "journey" cake). Ferment the grain, and you have corn whiskey, also known as white lightning or moonshine (and arguably like Southern grappa).

In traveling Georgia and the rest of the South, you will find the area's diversity on its tables. Many of the region's chefs use the traditional ingredients to craft "new" Southern dishes as a way of restoring that sense of elegant dining to the region's cuisine. Others wouldn't get near that sort of fare, preferring to do the original dishes proud. Take your pick: Either way, you'll dine divinely.

Atlanta Neighborhoods Dining and Lodging

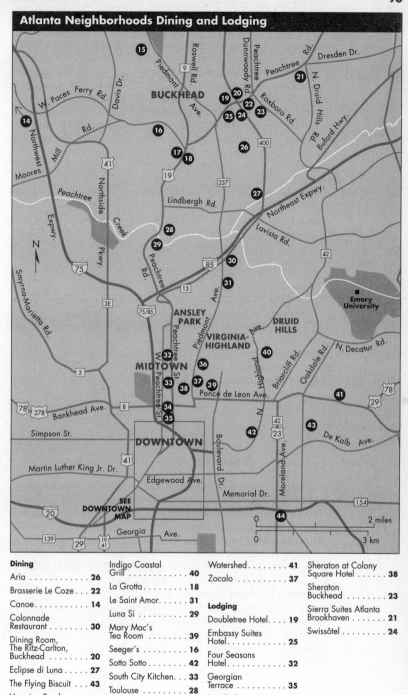

$$-$$$ ✕ **South City Kitchen.** The culinary traditions of South Carolina's Low-
★   country inspire the cooking at this bright restaurant. The clean, spare, art-filled interior attracts a hip crowd. This is the place for fried green tomatoes with goat cheese and she-crab soup. Catfish comes prepared in a variety of intriguing ways. The crab hash, served with poached eggs and chive hollandaise, is a classic. Don't miss the chocolate pecan pie. ✉ *1144 Crescent Ave.,* ☎ *404/873–7358. AE, MC, V.*

$–$$$ ✕ **Indigo Coastal Grill.** You can sample the world's coastal cuisines at this lively Virginia-Highland eatery. The menu has sushi and Thai food along with fresh deep-fried seafood, such as cornmeal-crusted oysters with jalapeño tartar sauce. For Sunday brunch there's jalapeño cheese grits, and for dessert, key lime pie. ✉ *1397 N. Highland Ave.,* ☎ *404/876–0676. AE, DC, MC, V. No lunch.*

$–$$$ ✕ **Veni Vidi Vici.** Gleaming woods, contemporary styling, and an out-
★   door boccie court and dining patio create the perfect setting for an indulgent Italian meal. Start with *Piatti piccoli,* savory small dishes such as veal meatballs or herbed goat cheese in marinara sauce. Then, try a pasta dish such as gnocchi with Gorgonzola cheese, or order one of the fragrant rotisserie meats. Finish with a dessert that will soothe the soul. ✉ *41 14th St.,* ☎ *404/875–8424. AE, D, DC, MC, V. No lunch weekends.*

$–$$ ✕ **Sotto Sotto.** Atlanta's hot spot close to downtown brings a fresh,
★   authentic approach to Italian food. The former commercial space hops with patrons dining on grilled scallops with white beans and truffle oil, spaghetti with sun-dried mullet roe, and perfect *panna cotta* (a custard of cooked cream). ✉ *313 N. Highland Ave.,* ☎ *404/523–6678. Reservations essential. AE, MC, V. No lunch.*

$–$$ ✕ **Watershed.** Indigo Girl Emily Saliers and three of her friends launched this casual restaurant–cum–gourmet shop. Chef Scott Peacock makes the planet's best shrimp salad, homemade flat bread, chicken salad with white truffles, homemade pimento cheese with sharp cheddar and egg, and desserts (these alone are worth the trip). Also an enoteca (wine bar), it sells wine both retail in bottles and by the glass at the comfy bar. When she's not in the recording studio, Saliers makes a fine sommelier and loves to talk about wine. ✉ *406 W. Ponce de Leon Ave., Decatur,* ☎ *404/378–4900. AE, MC, V. Closed Mon.*

$ ✕ **The Flying Biscuit.** This garage-sale-decorated spot was formerly an all-day breakfast café. Now open for dinner, its huge hits are egg dishes, turkey sausage and bean cakes with tomatilla salsa, as well as a side item called Pudge, a dense mound of mashed potatoes and rosemary. The biscuits, big and fluffy, are credited with the hour-long wait on weekends. ✉ *1655 McLendon Ave.,* ☎ *404/687–8888. Reservations not accepted. AE, D, MC, V. Closed Mon.*

$ ✕ **Heaping Bowl and Brew.** This eatery in the newly established, ultrahip East Atlanta Village has become a favorite. Meals are served in big, comfortable bowls, be it noodles, seared salmon, mashed potatoes, or Southwestern chicken. Specials often depend on what's growing fresh in the garden that day. ✉ *469 Flat Shoals Ave.,* ☎ *404/523–8030. AE, D, MC, V.*

$ ✕ **Mary Mac's Tea Room.** Local celebrities and ordinary folk line up for the country-fried steak, fried chicken, and fresh vegetables. Here, in the Southern tradition, lunch is called "dinner," and the evening meal is referred to as "supper." Waitresses will call you "honey" and pat your arm to assure you that everything's all right. It's a great way to plunge into Southern food and hospitality all at once. ✉ *224 Ponce de Leon Ave.,* ☎ *404/876–1800. No credit cards. No dinner Sun.*

$ ✕ **Zocalo.** A unique open-air patio restaurant (which manages to stay
★   warm in the frigid winter months with pillar-size heaters), it offers some of the best Mexican fare to be found in the city. Spicy chipotle-pepper

shrimp and creamy poblano pepper soup are just a sampling of the chef's culinary artworks. The bar has an excellent selection of epicurean tequilas. ⊠ *187 10th St.,* ☎ *404/249–7576. Reservations not accepted. AE, D, MC, V.*

Buckhead

$$$$ ✗ **Dining Room, The Ritz-Carlton, Buckhead.** This elegant, restrained dining room, with formal hunt scenes on the walls, romantic lighting, and generously spaced tables, comes across like an old gentlemen's club. Having worked in Bangkok, chef Joel Antunes brings an Asian touch to French fare. Lately though, such regional dishes as squab with collard greens have appeared on the menu. ⊠ *3434 Peachtree Rd.,* ☎ *404/ 237–2700. Reservations essential. Jacket and tie. AE, D, DC, MC, V. Closed Sun. No lunch.*

$$$$ ✗ **Seeger's.** Celebrated chef Guenter Seeger, formerly at the Dining
★ Room in the Ritz-Carlton (☞ *above*), presides over this sophisticated place. Some find the sleek space a bit noisy, but you'll forget about the volume after the first fragrant, flavorful bite. Dishes such as a roulade of foie gras and smoked salmon are outstanding. Local ingredients appear, as in grilled lamb chops with Vidalia onions. Prix fixes include a vegetable menu and, in season, an entire menu based on truffles. ⊠ *111 W. Paces Ferry Rd.,* ☎ *404/846–9779. Reservations essential. Jacket and tie. AE, D, DC, MC, V. Closed Sun. No lunch.*

$$$–$$$$ ✗ **Aria.** Formerly known as the ultraformal Hedgerose, this restaurant
★ was recently reinvented with a contemporary flair. Delectable entrées by chef Gerry Klaskala include pan-roasted salmon and lobster noodle soup. Don't miss the mouthwatering dessert menu created by renowned pastry chef Kathryn King. ⊠ *490 E. Paces Ferry Rd.,* ☎ *404/ 233–7673. Reservations essential. Jacket and tie. AE, D, DC, MC, V. Closed Sun. No lunch.*

$$–$$$$ ✗ **La Grotta.** Overlook the location in the ground level of a posh condominium: This is one of the best-managed dining rooms in town. The interior is elegant and sophisticated, with a burgundy and cream decor. Old northern Italian favorites are the core of the menu. Savor prosciutto with grilled pears and mascarpone cheese, then try roast quail stuffed with Italian sausage, and finish with zabaglione. ⊠ *2637 Peachtree Rd.,* ☎ *404/231–1368. Reservations essential. Jacket required. AE, D, DC, MC, V. Closed Sun., last wk in June, and first wk in July. No lunch.*

$$–$$$ ✗ **Horseradish Grill.** Once a red horse barn, this establishment is now
★ painted gray with white trim and has arched windows across the front that brighten the space. Some find it a bit noisy, but this place is a must for upscale Southern dishes that retain authenticity. Autumn venison stew and Carolina-style barbecue topped with coleslaw are examples from the seasonal menu. ⊠ *4320 Powers Ferry Rd.,* ☎ *404/255– 7277. Reservations not accepted. AE, D, DC, MC, V.*

$–$$$ ✗ **Brasserie Le Coze.** Shoppers stream into this glowing, wood-pan-
★ eled space with comfortable banquettes and comforting bistro-style fare. Traditional dishes include quiche, onion tart, mussels, coq au vin, and warm chocolate soufflé cake. *Vacherin* (meringue rings placed on a pastry base) filled with ice cream is just one of many extravagant desserts. ⊠ *3393 Peachtree Rd., Lenox Sq., near Neiman Marcus, Buckhead,* ☎ *404/266–1440. AE, DC, MC, V. Closed Sun.*

$–$$$ ✗ **Canoe.** This popular spot on the banks of the Chattahoochee River
★ brims with appreciative patrons nearly all day. In nice weather, the outdoor dining spaces allow the best view of the river. The restaurant's national reputation is based on such dishes as sea scallops with asparagus risotto, mushroom risotto with quail, and ravioli of roast rabbit. Sunday brunch is superb. ⊠ *4199 Paces Ferry Rd. NW,* ☎ *770/432– 2663. AE, D, DC, MC, V.*

$–$$$ ✗ **Luna Si.** The emphasis is on fun at this New York loft–style restaurant, where Latin music blares and customers are encouraged to write on the walls. The menu, which changes weekly, is dominated by seafood. Signature items include salmon with a ginger crust, roast chicken and mashed potatoes, excellent foie gras, and homemade biscotti. ✉ *1931 Peachtree Rd.,* ☎ *404/355–5993. Reservations essential. AE, D, DC, MC, V. Closed Sun. No lunch.*

$–$$ ✗ **Colonnade Restaurant.** For traditional Southern food such as oyster stew, ham steak, and turkey and dressing, insiders head for the Colonnade, an Atlanta institution since 1927. The interior, with patterned carpeting, feels like a stylish version of a classic 1950s restaurant. ✉ *1879 Cheshire Bridge Rd.,* ☎ *404/874–5642. Reservations not accepted. No credit cards.*
★

$–$$ ✗ **Toulouse.** Open spaces enclosed by warm, rough-brick walls characterize this attractive dining spot. The food is inspired in theory by the cooking of southwestern France but seems more American in execution. The country potato soup is a perfect cold weather meal. Especially wonderful are the roast chicken, duck confit with blueberry vinaigrette, and crème brûlée. ✉ *2293B Peachtree Rd., Peachtree Walk,* ☎ *404/351–9533. AE, D, DC, MC, V. No lunch.*

$–$$ ✗ **Vino!** Mediterranean colors create a warm, intimate atmosphere. The focus is on tapas and wines by the glass, but you can eat a full meal here, too. Tapas ($5–$6) are traditional; among the best are the meat-stuffed pastries called empanadas, and Serrano ham, a Spanish meat similar to prosciutto. ✉ *2900 Peachtree Rd.,* ☎ *404/816–0511. AE, DC, MC, V. Closed Sun.*

$ ✗ **Eclipse di Luna.** Tucked at the very end of Miami Circle, a "trade-only" design center, this hot spot has captured the fancy of twenty-somethings, who flock here on weekends. Lunch is sandwiches and salads, and evening fare is tapas ($3) and wine by the glass. *Patatas bravas* (potatoes with olive oil and spicy sauce), tender braised chicken with saffron and garlic, and flan will take you to Castile. ✉ *764 Miami Circle,* ☎ *404/846–0449. AE, DC, MC, V. Closed Mon.*
★

Lodging

One of America's three most popular convention destinations, Atlanta offers a broad range of lodgings. More than 12,000 rooms are in the compact downtown area, close to the Georgia World Congress Center, Atlanta Civic Center, Atlanta Merchandise Mart, and Omni Coliseum. Other clusters are in Buckhead, in the north I–285 perimeter, and around Hartsfield Atlanta International Airport.

Downtown

$$$$ 🏨 **Ritz-Carlton, Atlanta.** The mood here is set by traditional afternoon tea served in the intimate, sunken lobby beneath an 18th-century chandelier. Notice the 17th-century Flemish tapestry when you enter from Peachtree Street. Some guest rooms are luxuriously decorated with marble writing tables, plump sofas, four-poster beds, and white-marble bathrooms. The Atlanta Grill (☞ Dining, *above*) is one of downtown's only outdoor dining spots. ✉ *181 Peachtree St. (entrance to MARTA's Peachtree Center rail station is across the street), 30303,* ☎ *404/659–0400 or 800/241–3333,* 🖷 *404/688–0400. 425 rooms, 22 suites. Restaurant, bar, laundry service, business services, parking (fee). AE, D, DC, MC, V.* 🛎
★

$$$–$$$$ 🏨 **Hyatt Regency, Atlanta.** This Hyatt was John Portman's first atrium-centered building, and it became the model for other Portman-designed hotels, including the San Francisco Embarcadero and the Atlanta Marriott Marquis (☞ *below*). The blue-bubble top stands out against the Atlanta skyline. Expect the careful service and quality facilities typ-

ical of Hyatt hotels. ⊠ *265 Peachtree St. (connected by skywalk to Peachtree Center), 30303,* ☎ *404/577–1234 or 800/233–1234,* FAX *404/ 588–4137. 1,206 rooms, 58 suites. 3 restaurants, bar, pool, health club, business services, parking (fee). AE, D, DC, MC, V.* ⊛

$$$–$$$$ 🏨 **Omni Hotel at CNN Center.** The hotel is adjacent to the home of Ted Turner's Cable News Network. The lobby combines old-world and modern accents, with marble floors, Oriental rugs, and exotic floral and plant arrangements. Rooms have large windows and contemporary-style furniture, including a sofa. Guests have access to the Downtown Athletic Club and two small meeting rooms. ⊠ *100 CNN Center (MARTA's Omni rail station is adjacent to CNN Center), 30305,* ☎ *404/659–0000 or 800/843–6664,* FAX *404/525–5050. 455 rooms, 4 suites. 2 restaurants, lobby lounge, business services, parking (fee). AE, D, DC, MC, V.* ⊛

$$$ 🏨 **Atlanta Marriott Marquis.** Immense and coolly contemporary, the Marquis seems to go on forever as you stand under the lobby's huge fabric sculpture that hangs from the skylighted roof 47 stories above. Guest rooms, which open onto this atrium, are decorated in dark greens and neutral shades. Major suites have live plants and fresh flowers; two suites have grand pianos and ornamental fireplaces. ⊠ *265 Peachtree Center Ave., 30303,* ☎ *404/521–0000,* FAX *404/586–6299. 1,671 rooms, 60 suites. 5 restaurants, 2 bars, indoor-outdoor pool, health club, business services, parking (fee). AE, D, DC, MC, V.* ⊛

$–$$ 🏨 **Quality Hotel Downtown.** This quiet, older downtown hotel, two blocks off Peachtree Street, has a marble lobby with sofas and a grand piano that guests sometimes play. Modest-size rooms in teal and navy make the hotel inviting. The place is popular for conventions due to its proximity to the World Congress Center and the show marts; prices go up when conventions are in town. ⊠ *89 Luckie St., 30303,* ☎ *404/ 524–7991,* FAX *404/524–0672. 70 rooms, 5 suites. Pool. AE, D, DC, MC, V.* ⊛

Midtown

$$$$ 🏨 **Four Seasons Hotel.** A sweeping staircase leads up to a welcoming, refined bar and Park 75, the hotel's fine dining establishment. Rose-hue marble creates a warm feeling in the public spaces. Marble bathrooms, pale lemon or celadon color schemes, and polished brass chandeliers are among the guest room appointments. ⊠ *75 14th St., 30309,* ☎ *404/ 881–9898,* FAX *404/873–4692. 226 rooms, 18 suites. Restaurant, bar, pool, health club, business services. AE, D, DC, MC, V.* ⊛

$$$–$$$$ 🏨 **Georgian Terrace.** Spend a night where Enrico Caruso and the Metropolitan Opera stars once lodged. This fine old hotel across the street from the Fox Theatre (☞ Midtown, *above*) is on the National Register of Historic Places and housed the rich and famous in its heyday. Now restored, and with an added matching tower, all units are suites with kitchenettes or full kitchens. ⊠ *659 Peachtree St., 30308,* ☎ *404/897–1991 or 800/651–2316,* FAX *404/724–0642. 320 suites. Restaurant, pool, convention center, meeting rooms, parking (fee). AE, D, DC, MC, V.* ⊛

$$–$$$ 🏨 **Sheraton at Colony Square Hotel.** Theatricality and opulence are epitomized by the dimly lighted lobby with overhanging balconies, piano music, and fresh flowers. Rooms are modern, with muted tones; those on higher floors have city views. The hotel is two blocks from MARTA's Arts Center station and two blocks from the Woodruff Arts Center and the High Museum of Art (☞ Midtown, *above*); it anchors the Colony Square complex of office, residential, and retail buildings. ⊠ *188 14th St., 30361,* ☎ *404/892–6000 or 800/422–7895,* FAX *404/872–9192. 436 rooms, 31 suites. Restaurant, lobby lounge, pool, parking (fee). AE, D, DC, MC, V.* ⊛

INNS AND GUEST HOUSES

$$ 🏠 **Shellmont.** The Shellmont is named for the shell motif that adorns the house. Designed in 1891 by Massachusetts-born, Atlanta-reared architect Walter T. Downing for Dr. William Perrin Nicholson, the house has classical architectural elements, detailed stained-glass windows, and a reproduction of the original Victorian stenciling on the walls. Guest rooms have American Victorian antiques and CD players. ⊠ *821 Piedmont Ave., 30306,* 🕿 *404/872–9290 or 404/872–5379. 2 rooms, 2 suites, 1 carriage house. AE, D, DC, MC, V. BP.* 🐾

Buckhead

$$$$ 🏠 **Ritz-Carlton, Buckhead.** Decorated with the Ritz's signature 18th-
★ and 19th-century antiques and art, this elegant gem bids a discreet welcome. Shoppers from nearby Lenox Square mall and Phipps Plaza often revive here over afternoon tea or cocktails in the richly paneled Lobby Lounge. The **Dining Room** (☞ *Dining, above*) is one of the city's finest restaurants. The spacious rooms are furnished with traditional reproductions and have luxurious white-marble baths. From the hotel's club floors you get a view of Buckhead and an understanding of why Atlanta is known as a city of trees. Weekend musical performances are a delight. ⊠ *3434 Peachtree Rd., 30326,* 🕿 *404/237–2700 or 800/ 241–3333,* FAX *404/239–0078. 524 rooms, 29 suites. 2 restaurants, bar, pool, hot tub, health club, parking (fee). AE, D, DC, MC, V.* 🐾

$$–$$$$ 🏠 **Swissôtel.** Sleek and efficient, this stunner boasts a chic, modern glass and white-tile exterior with curved walls and Biedermeier-style interiors. Convenient to Lenox Square mall, a prime location for shopping and dining, the hotel is a favorite with business travelers. The restaurant, the Palm, is noted for its steaks. The full-service fitness center has everything from facials to fitness trainers. ⊠ *3391 Peachtree Rd., 30326,* 🕿 *404/365–0065 or 800/253–1397,* FAX *404/365–8787. 364 rooms, 16 suites. Restaurant, bar, pool, health club, business services, parking (fee). AE, D, DC, MC, V.* 🐾

$$–$$$ 🏠 **Embassy Suites Hotel.** This modern high-rise is just blocks from the Phipps Plaza and Lenox Square malls. A variety of suites ranging from deluxe presidential (with wet bars) to more basic sleeping- and sitting-room combinations are available. Rates include afternoon cocktails. ⊠ *3285 Peachtree Rd., 30305,* 🕿 *404/261–7733 or 800/362–2779,* FAX *404/261–6857. 313 suites. Restaurant, indoor pool, outdoor pool, exercise room, parking (fee). AE, D, DC, MC, V. BP.* 🐾

$$–$$$ 🏠 **Sheraton Buckhead.** This modern, eight-floor hotel has the advantage of being right across from Lenox Square mall. Rooms have contemporary furnishings; some have a desk and chair, others sofas. ⊠ *3405 Lenox Rd., 30326,* 🕿 *404/261–9250,* FAX *404/848–7391. 355 rooms, 7 suites. Restaurant, bar, pool. AE, D, DC, MC, V.* 🐾

$$ 🏠 **Doubletree Hotel.** It has spacious rooms and reasonable rates given the excellent location. Guests have access to a health club. The hotel offers complimentary transportation within 2 mi of the hotel and is adjacent to the Buckhead MARTA station. ⊠ *3340 Peachtree Rd., 30326,* 🕿 *404/231–1234 or 800/222–8733,* FAX *404/231–5236. 217 rooms, 4 suites. Restaurant, free parking. AE, D, DC, MC, V.* 🐾

$–$$ 🏠 **Sierra Suites Atlanta Brookhaven.** The feel is modern Southwestern at this comfortable hotel, just north of Lenox Square. Cream and green color schemes decorate the one-bedroom studio suites with kitchenettes (no ovens). ⊠ *3967 Peachtree Rd.,* 🕿 *404/237–9100,* FAX *404/237–0055. 92 suites. Pool, exercise room, laundry service. AE, D, DC, MC, V.* 🐾

Nightlife and the Arts

The Arts

For the most complete schedule of **cultural events,** check the *Atlanta Journal-Constitution*'s Friday "Weekend Preview" and Saturday "Leisure" sections. Also available for cultural and entertainment listings are two lively community weeklies, *Creative Loafing* and *Atlanta Press,* each distributed free at Atlanta restaurants, bars, and stores. You can also call the 24-hour **Arts Hotline** (☎ 404/853–3278).

Tickets for the Fox Theatre, Atlanta Civic Center, and other locations are handled by **TicketMaster** (☎ 404/249–6400 or 800/326–4000) and **Ticket-X-Press, Inc.** (☎ 404/231–5888). Some companies only sell tickets through their own box offices.

CONCERTS

The **Atlanta Symphony Orchestra (ASO),** under the new musical direction of Robert Spano, is now more than a half century old, with 14 Grammy Awards to its credit. It performs the fall–spring subscription series in the 1,800-seat Symphony Hall at Woodruff Arts Center (⊠ 1280 Peachtree St., ☎ 404/733–5000). During the summer, the orchestra regularly plays with big-name popular and country artists in Chastain Park's outdoor amphitheater (⊠ 4469 Stella Dr., ☎ 404/733–4800).

Emory University (⊠ N. Decatur Rd. at Clifton Rd., ☎ 404/727–6187, FAX 404/727–6421), an idyllic suburban campus, has four venues where both internationally renowned guest artists and faculty and student groups perform. Expect quality music from a variety of ensembles, including woodwinds, brass, jazz, and vocal.

Georgia State University (⊠ Art and Music Bldg., Peachtree Center Ave. and Gilmer St., ☎ 404/651–4636 or 404/651–3676), with the entrance on Gilmer Street and free parking at the corner of Edgewood and Peachtree Center avenues, sponsors many concerts (about 80%) that are free and open to the public. Performances by faculty, student, and local groups and guest artists focus on jazz and classical. There are also performances at the Rialto Center for the Performing Arts (☞ *below*), an old movie theater the university turned into a performance venue.

DANCE

The country's oldest continuously operating ballet company (founded in 1929), the **Atlanta Ballet** (⊠ 1400 W. Peachtree St., ☎ 404/873–5811) has received international recognition for its productions of classical and contemporary works. Performances are usually at the Fox Theatre (☞ *below*) but sometimes take place elsewhere. Artistic director John McFall, only the third in the company's history, brings new ideas and vision to the group.

FESTIVALS

The **Atlanta Jazz Festival,** held Memorial Day weekend, gathers the best local, national, and international musicians to give mostly free concerts at Atlanta's Piedmont Park. For information, contact the Atlanta Bureau of Cultural Affairs (☎ 404/817–6815, FAX 404/817–6827).

The **Montreux/Atlanta International Music Festival** began in 1988, when Atlanta joined with Montreux, Switzerland, to cohost a music festival featuring a variety of styles: jazz, blues, gospel, reggae, and classical. The festival typically starts during Labor Day weekend, with performances in Piedmont Park (free) and Chastain Park (expensive). For information, contact the Atlanta Bureau of Cultural Affairs (☎ 404/817–6815, FAX 404/817–6827).

OPERA

The **Atlanta Opera** (✉ 728 W. Peachtree St., ☎ 404/881–8801 or 800/ 356–7372) usually mounts four main-stage productions each year from spring through fall at the Fox Theatre (☞ *below*). Major roles are performed by national and international guest artists, while the chorus and orchestra come from the local community. Call TicketMaster (☎ 404/817–8700) for information.

PERFORMANCE VENUES

Atlanta Civic Center (✉ 395 Piedmont Ave., ☎ 404/523–6275) presents touring Broadway musicals, pop music, and dance concerts.

Fox Theatre (✉ 660 Peachtree St., ☎ 404/881–2100), a fine faux-Moorish theater (☞ Midtown, *above*), is the principal venue for touring Broadway shows and national productions, as well as the home of the Atlanta Opera (☞ *above*) and the Atlanta Ballet (☞ *above*).

Georgia Tech Center for the Performing Arts (✉ 349 Ferst Dr., ☎ 404/ 894–9600), at the Georgia Institute of Technology, offers performances that run the gamut, from classical to jazz, from dance to theater. The highly regarded student-operated theater, DramaTech, is in the James E. Dull Theatre. There's ample free parking on site.

Rialto Center for the Performing Arts (✉ 80 Forsyth St., ☎ 404/651– 4727), developed by Georgia State University in a beautifully renovated and restructured former movie theater, features film, theater, and dance, as well as musical performances by local and international performers.

Spivey Hall (campus: ✉ 5900 N. Lee St., ☎ 770/961–3683) is a gleaming, modern, acoustically magnificent performance center at Clayton College and State University, 15 mi south of Atlanta in Morrow. The hall is considered one of the country's finest concert venues. Internationally renowned musicians perform everything from chamber music to jazz.

Variety Playhouse (✉ 1099 Euclid Ave., ☎ 404/524–7354), a former movie theater, is one of the cultural anchors of the hip Little Five Points neighborhood. Its denizens don't don fancy frocks to listen to rock, bluegrass and country, blues, reggae, folk, jazz, and pop.

Woodruff Arts Center (✉ 1280 Peachtree St., ☎ 404/733–4200) is home to the Alliance Theatre and the Atlanta Symphony Orchestra (☞ *above*).

THEATER

Check local newspaper listings for information on the outstanding companies in Atlanta and its suburbs. Consult *Creative Loafing* and the *Atlanta Journal-Constitution* for performance information.

Actor's Express (✉ 887 W. Marietta St., ☎ 404/607–7469), an award-winning theater, presents an eclectic selection of classic and cutting-edge productions in the 150-seat theater of the King Plow Arts Center, a stylish artists' complex hailed by local critics as a showplace of industrial chic. For an evening of dining and theater, plan on dinner at the Food Studio (☞ Dining, *above*), at the King Plow Arts Center.

Alliance Theatre (✉ 1280 Peachtree St., ☎ 404/733–4200), Atlanta's premier professional theater, presents everything from Shakespeare to the latest Broadway and off-Broadway shows in the Woodruff Arts Center (☞ Midtown, *above*).

☝ **Atlanta Shakespeare Tavern** (✉ 499 Peachtree St., ☎ 404/874–5299) produces plays by the Bard, his peers, and more contemporary dramatists. Performances vary in quality but are always fun. The Elizabethan-style playhouse is a tavern, so alcohol and pub-style food are available. It's also home to the Kaleidoscope Children's Theater, which presents classics, such as *The New Adventures of the Three Musketeers,* on most weekends during the day.

14th Street Playhouse (⊠ 175 14th St., ☎ 404/733–4750 or 404/733–4754) is part of the Woodruff Arts Center (☞ Midtown, *above*). The house has three theaters, a 400-seat main stage, a 200-seat second stage, and an 80-seat stage, which are rented for special productions. There is no resident company. Musicals, plays, and sometimes opera are presented.

Horizon Theatre Co. (⊠ 1083 Austin Ave., Little Five Points, ☎ 404/584–7450) is a professional troupe that was established in 1983; it produces premieres of provocative and entertaining contemporary plays in its 185-seat theater.

Nightlife

The pursuit of entertainment—from Midtown to Buckhead—is known as the "Peachtree Shuffle." Atlanta's vibrant nightlife includes everything from coffee bars to sports bars, from country line dancing to high-energy dance clubs. Atlanta has long been known for having more bars than churches, and in the South, that's an oddity.

Most bars and clubs are open seven nights, until 2–4 AM. Those with live entertainment usually have a cover charge. Consult *Creative Loafing* and the *Atlanta Journal-Constitution* for information.

ACOUSTIC

Eddie's Attic (⊠ 515B N. McDonough St., Decatur, ☎ 404/377–4976) is a good spot for catching local and some national acoustic, folk, pop, and country-music acts. It has a full bar and restaurant and is right near the Decatur MARTA station. Covers range from $6 to $12.

BARS

The **Beluga Martini Bar** (⊠ 3115 Piedmont Rd., ☎ 404/869–1090) has caviar, smoked salmon, champagne by the glass, and other light fare in an intimate, comfortable space with live music.

For Irish atmosphere, food, beer, and music (both live and on CD), head straight over to **Fadó** (⊠ 3035 Peachtree Rd., ☎ 404/841–0066). The food ranges from *boxty* (potato pancakes with savory fillings) to Irish stew made with lamb, cottage pie, and whiskey trifle.

Limerick Junction (⊠ 822 N. Highland Ave., ☎ 404/874–7147), a lively Irish pub, features singers from the large Atlanta community that ably render traditional Irish music, as well as performers from the Old Sod itself. It has a rollicking, good-time atmosphere. Parking is dreadful, so consider a cab. A small cover may be charged.

Manuel's Tavern (⊠ 602 N. Highland Ave., ☎ 404/525–3447) is a neighborhood saloon where families, politicians, writers, students, and professionals gather for drinks, beer-steamed hot dogs, veggie soy burgers, and the like. When the Atlanta Braves play, the crowd gathers around the wide-screen TVs.

Mike n' Angelo's (⊠ 312 E. Paces Ferry Rd., ☎ 404/237–0949), with a friendly atmosphere, knowledgeable bartenders, live bands, and hearty pub fare, is a local favorite.

To make it through the door at **Tongue & Groove** (⊠ 3055 Peachtree Rd., ☎ 404/261–2325), you must dress up: long dresses for ladies and jackets for men. Live music—sometimes rock, sometimes salsa—alternates with recorded tunes. The light-fare menu is as chic as the atmosphere. Covers range from $5 to $10, depending on the program.

COMEDY

The **Punchline** (⊠ 280 Hilderbrand Dr., Sandy Springs, Balconies Shopping Center, ☎ 404/252–5233), Atlanta's oldest comedy club, books major national acts, among them Henry Cho, Craig Shoemaker, Tom Rhodes, and Judy Tenuta. The small club is popular, so you need a reservation. Cover charges vary and can be upwards of $20 for some acts, but it's usually worth it. The menu has light fare and sandwiches, and there's a one-item minimum, either food or beverage. To enter, you must be 21.

COUNTRY

Buckboard Country Music Showcase (⊠ 2080 Cobb Pkwy., Windy Hill Plaza, ☎ 770/955–7340), a 425-seat house, has a large dance floor, pool tables, and two full bars; it serves food of the hamburgers, nachos, and chicken fingers variety. The house band is the Buckboard Bandits, and Nashville-based bands play on Thursday night. The cover charge is $5–$10.

Cowboys Concert Hall (⊠ 1750 N. Roberts Rd., Kennesaw, ☎ 770/426–5006) attracts national talent twice monthly on Friday. On Wednesday, Thursday, Friday, and Sunday, line-dancing classes and couple-dancing lessons are taught. This 44,000-square-ft venue is north of the city. The cover is $5, unless an unusually high-profile act is slated.

DANCE

Cajun dancing is rapidly gaining favor as a weekend frolic. The **Atlanta Cajun Dance Association** (⊠ 2704 Laurelwood Rd., ☎ 770/451–6611) offers a one-hour lesson before the party, called a *fais do-do*. Although two local Cajun bands frequent the stage, nationally known bands from Louisiana often take over. Weekend dances usually take place at the Knights of Columbus Hall (⊠ 2620 Buford Hwy.).

Backstreet (⊠ 845 Peachtree St., ☎ 404/873–1986), drawing both men and women, has been Midtown's mainstay gay club for nearly two decades, but straight people enjoy the place, too. Downstairs is the dance floor with recorded music, and upstairs is Charlie Brown's Cabaret, with female impersonators. As the club is open 24 hours, membership is required; quarterly memberships cost $10, entitling cardholders to free admission Sunday through Thursday and $5 covers Friday and Saturday.

JAZZ AND BLUES

Blind Willie's (⊠ 828 N. Highland Ave., ☎ 404/873–2583) showcases New Orleans– and Chicago-style blues that sends crowds into a frenzy. The name honors Blind Willie McTell, a native of Thomson, Georgia, whose original compositions include "Statesboro Blues," made popular by the Macon, Georgia–based Allman Brothers. Cajun and zydeco are also on the agenda from time to time. Cover charges run in the $10 range.

Dante's Down the Hatch (⊠ 3380 Peachtree Rd., Buckhead, ☎ 404/266–1600) is popular for its music and sultry atmosphere. Regular entertainers include the Paul Mitchell Trio, which conjures silky-smooth jazz in the "hold" of a make-believe sailing ship.

Fuzzy's Place (⊠ 2015 N. Druid Hills Rd., ☎ 404/321–6166), a crowded and smoke-filled neighborhood bar, begins the day by serving lunch to the denizens of nearby office buildings. By night, it's a restaurant with a surprisingly sophisticated menu, sports bar, and blues room. The finest local talent holds forth on the stage, including the venerable Francine Reed, one of Atlanta's favorite entertainers. There's usually no cover.

Sambuca Jazz Cafe (⊠ 3102 Piedmont Rd., ☎ 404/237–5299), with decent dining, a lively bar, and good live jazz, attracts a trendy young set.

Whiskers (⊠ 8371 Roswell Rd., in shopping center at Roswell and Northridge Rds., ☎ 770/992–7445) hosts blues and rock groups, with some of the best local talent. There's no cover.

ROCK

Masquerade (⊠ 695 North Ave., ☎ 404/577–8178) is a grunge hangout with music, from disco to techno, from industrial rock to swing. Basic bar food is available. The mix of people reflects the club's three separate spaces, dubbed Heaven, Hell, and Purgatory. The cover is $2–$8.

Smith's Olde Bar (⊠ 1578 Piedmont Ave., ☎ 404/875–1522) schedules a wide variety of talent, both local and regional, in its acoustically fine performance space. Food is available in the downstairs restaurant. Covers vary depending on the act but are usually in the $5–$10 range.

Star Community Bar (⊠ 437 Moreland Ave., ☎ 404/681–9018) is highly recommended for those who enjoy garage bands and rockabilly. Bands are featured almost nightly, with covers varying depending on the act. The bar is fully equipped, with an all-Elvis jukebox and an Elvis shrine that must be seen to be believed.

Outdoor Activities and Sports

Participant Sports

At almost any time of the year, in parks, private clubs, and neighborhoods throughout the city, you'll find Atlantans pursuing everything from tennis to soccer to rollerblading. *Atlanta Sports & Fitness* magazine (☎ 404/843–2257), available free at many health clubs and sports and outdoors stores, is a good link to Atlanta's athletic community. At the same locations, you can pick up *Georgia Athlete,* a guide to individual sporting events.

AEROBICS

Jeanne's Body Tech (⊠ 334 E. Paces Ferry Rd., ☎ 404/261–0227) has a variety of exercise equipment and classes including step and spinning. The drop-in fee is $10.

BIKING AND ROLLERBLADING

Piedmont Park (⊠ Piedmont Ave. between 10th St. and the Prado) is closed to traffic and popular for rollerblading and other recreational activities. **Skate Escape** (⊠ 1086 Piedmont Ave., across from the park, ☎ 404/892–1292) rents bikes and skates.

GOLF

Golf is enormously popular here, as the large number of courses attest. The only public course within sight of downtown Atlanta is the **Bobby Jones Golf Course** (⊠ 384 Woodward Way, ☎ 404/355–1009), named after the famed golfer and Atlanta native and located on a portion of the site of the Battle of Peachtree Creek. Despite having some of the city's worst fairways and greens, the immensely popular 18-hole, par-71 course is always crowded. At Chastain Park, the 18-hole, par-71 **North Fulton Golf Course** (⊠ 216 W. Wieuca Rd., ☎ 404/255–0723) has one of the best layouts and lies within the I–285 perimeter.

Stone Mountain Park (⊠ U.S. 78, ☎ 770/498–5715) has two courses. Stonemont, an 18-hole, par-72 course with several challenging and scenic holes, is the better of the two. The other course, Lakemont, is also 18 holes and par 72.

HEALTH CLUBS

Crunch Fitness (✉ 3340 Peachtree Rd., ☎ 404/262–2120), with six other locations, has equipment and amenities that vary from one location to another. The Cobb location (✉ 1775 Water Pl., ☎ 770/952–2120), for instance, has indoor and outdoor tennis courts. Single visits cost $16. Select hotels, such as the Doubletree (☞ Lodging, *above*), offer complimentary visits to guests.

JOGGING AND RUNNING

Chattahoochee National Recreation Area contains different parcels of land that lie in 15 separate units spread along the banks of the Chattahoochee River, much of which has been protected from development. The area is crisscrossed by 70 mi of trails. ✉ *1978 Island Ford Pkwy.*, ☎ *770/399–8070.* ☉ *Daily 7–7.*

SWIMMING

Dynamo Community Swim Center (✉ 3119 Shallowford Rd., Chamblee, ☎ 770/451–3272) has an eight-lane, 165-ft outdoor pool; a 10-lane, 25-yard pool; and a five-lane, 25-yard pool. Locker facilities and a weight room are on site. The cost is $4 per visit. Take I–85 to Exit 93.

TENNIS

Bitsy Grant Tennis Center (✉ 2125 Northside Dr., ☎ 404/609–7193), named for one of Atlanta's best-known players, is the area's best public facility, with 13 clay courts (6 of which are lighted) and 10 lighted hard courts. Charges are $2 per person per hour for the hard courts during the day and $2.50 at night (courts close around 10 PM), $2.25–$2.75 for the clay courts, which close around 7 PM. The clubhouse closes at 8 PM.

Piedmont Park, Atlanta's most popular park, has 12 lighted hard courts. Access the tennis center from Park Drive off Monroe Drive; even though the sign says DO NOT ENTER, the security guard will show you the parking lot. Courts are always open, but personnel keep specific hours. Costs are $1.50 per person per hour before 6 PM and $1.75 after 6. ✉ *Piedmont Ave. between 10th St. and the Prado.* ☎ FAX *404/853–3461.* ☉ *Weekdays 9–9, weekends 9:30–6.*

Spectator Sports

BASEBALL

The **Atlanta Braves** (✉ Turner Field, I–75/85, Exit 246 [Fulton St.]; I–20, westbound Exit 58A [Capitol Ave.]; eastbound Exit 56B [Windsor St./Spring St.], ☎ 404/522–7630) play in Turner Field, formerly the 1996 Olympic Stadium.

BASKETBALL

The **Atlanta Hawks** (✉ Philips Arena, 1 CNN Center, ☎ 404/827–3800) had a proud Olympics moment when Coach Lenny Wilkenson was selected to coach the U.S. Olympic men's basketball team in Atlanta.

FOOTBALL

Under coach Dan Reeves, the **Atlanta Falcons** (✉ Georgia Dome, 1 Georgia Dome Dr., ☎ 404/223–9200) have brought on board many impressive new personnel, both on the coaching staff and on the team. The Falcons have made the playoffs seven times, most recently in 1995.

HOCKEY

The 1999–2000 season was the first for the NHL's **Atlanta Thrashers** (✉ Philips Arena, 1 CNN Center, ☎ 404/827–5300). Named for the state bird, the brown thrasher, the team is backed by Atlanta's sports and media guru Ted Turner.

Shopping

Atlanta's department stores, specialty shops, large enclosed malls, and antiques markets draw shoppers from across the Southeast. Most stores are open Monday–Saturday 10–9, Sunday noon–6. Many downtown stores close Sunday. Sales tax is 7% in the city of Atlanta and Fulton County and 6%–7% in the suburbs.

Shopping Centers

Brookwood Square (⊠ 2140 Peachtree Rd.) is an arrangement of unusual shops, including the Vespermann Gallery (☞ Art Galleries, *below*) and the Piano Gallery, Atlanta's Steinway dealership.

Buckhead has many specialty and strip malls. At Peachtree Plaza, at the intersection of Peachtree Road and Mathieson Drive, you'll find Beverly Bremer's Silver Shop, devoted to fine antique silver, and Irish Crystal Co., offering fine cut glass and linens. Down Maple Drive off Peachtree Road you'll find Yesteryear, dealing in antique books (☞ Books, *below*), next to the Atlanta Guitar Center. A raft of boutiques and gift shops, along with some fine restaurants, lines Grandview Avenue (off Peachtree Road), and another similar collection runs down East Shadowlawn Avenue. East Village Square (⊠ Buckhead Ave. and Bolling Way) has art galleries and restaurants. Across from Lenox Square, the Around Lenox Shopping Center includes Tower Records–Video–Books. Andrews Square, on East Andrews Drive, is a treasure trove of shops, eateries, nightspots, and galleries. Next to it, Cates Center has similar stores.

Lenox Square mall (⊠ 3393 Peachtree Rd., ☎ 404/233–6767), one of Atlanta's oldest and most popular shopping centers, has branches of Neiman Marcus, Rich's (the local department store), Crate & Barrel, and Macy's looming next to specialty shops such as Geode (fine art jewelry) and Mori's (luggage and travel gifts). You'll fare better at one of the several good restaurants here—even for a quick meal—than at the food court.

Peachtree Center Mall (⊠ 231 Peachtree St., ☎ 404/524–3787), downtown, does steady business. Stores here are chiefly specialty shops, such as International Records and Tapes, the Architectural Book Center, and the Atlanta International Museum gift shop.

Perimeter Mall (⊠ 4400 Ashford-Dunwoody Rd.), known for upscale family shopping, has stores such as Nordstrom, the High Museum of Art Gift Shop, Gap Kids, and the Nature Company, as well as branches of Rich's, Sears, and JCPenney, and a good food court.

Phipps Plaza (⊠ 3500 Peachtree Rd., ☎ 404/262–0992 or 800/810–7700) has branches of Tiffany & Co., Saks Fifth Avenue, Birmingham-based Parisian, Lord & Taylor, and Abercrombie & Fitch alongside such shops as Skippy Musket (unique jewelry, collectibles, and decorative items for the home).

Underground (⊠ 50 Upper Alabama St., ☎ 404/523–2311) has galleries such as African Pride, with objets d'art from Africa; specialty shops such as Hats Under Atlanta; and Habersham Vineyard & Winery, a tasting room for Georgia wines. The classic chicory-laced New Orleans coffee and beignets at Café du Monde are the perfect way to refuel.

Outlets

The interstate highways leading to Atlanta have discount malls similar to those found throughout the country. Worth noting is the huge cluster around both sides of Exit 149 off I–85, 60 mi north of the city. The **North Georgia Premium Outlets** mall (⊠ GA 400 at Dawson Forest Rd.) is worth the 45 minutes it takes to get there from Atlanta's northern perimeter. This shopping center has more than 70 stores, including Williams-Sonoma for cookware; OshKosh B'gosh, a clothing store for children; Music for a Song, dealing in discount CDs and tapes; Stone Mountain Handbags, specializing in quality leather goods; a Barneys New York; and numerous designer outlet shops not found in most malls.

Specialty Shops

ANTIQUES

Buckhead has several antiques shops, most of them along or near Peachtree Road; expect rare goods and high prices here. Venture into Virginia-Highland and the city's suburban towns to find treasures galore.

Bennett Street (⊠ 116 Bennett St., ☎ 404/352–4430) has art galleries such as Out of the Woods; antiques shops such as Kelim; and a good restaurant, Fratelli di Napoli (⊠ 2101B Tula St., ☎ 404/351–1533), making it easy to spend a whole day here. The Stalls is a fine antiques market.

Chamblee Antique Row, at the intersection of Peachtree Road and Broad Street in the suburban town of Chamblee just north of Buckhead and about 10 mi north of downtown, is a browser's delight. For information, contact the Chamblee Antique Dealers Association (☎ 770/458–1614).

Little Five Points (⊠ intersection of Moreland and Euclid Aves.) attracts "junking" addicts who find nirvana in Atlanta's version of Greenwich Village, characterized by vintage clothing stores, art galleries, used-record and -book shops, and some stores that defy description.

Miami Circle, off Piedmont Road, is an upscale enclave for antiques and decorative arts lovers. Drop in for a snack at Eclipse di Luna (⊠ Miami Circle, ☎ 404/846–0449).

Stone Mountain Village (⊠ Main St., Stone Mountain, ☎ 770/879–4971 visitor center) is a 19th-century village beside a railroad track at the foot of Stone Mountain (☞ Other Area Attractions, *above*). Storefronts are exquisitely decorated at holiday time. Shops of note include Stone Mountain Handbags Factory Store (☎ 770/498–1316) and the Stone Mountain General Store (☎ 770/469–9331). The village is 17 mi from downtown. For a quick snack, have a coffee milk shake at Continental Park Café (⊠ 941 Main St., ☎ 770/413–6448).

2300 Peachtree Road, one of Buckhead's most stylish complexes, has more than 25 antiques shops, art galleries, and enough home furnishing stores to fill multiple mansions.

Virginia-Highland is one of the city's gentrified areas, full of art galleries, restaurants, fashionable boutiques, antiques shops, and bookstores. Atlanta designer Bill Hallman (⊠ 792 N. Highland Ave., ☎ 404/876–6055) showcases his own designs at his eponymous boutique. There's a wide array of memorabilia from 20th Century Antiques (⊠ 1044 N. Highland Ave., ☎ 404/892–2065).

ART GALLERIES

The city bursts with art galleries, some well established, others new, some conservative, others cutting edge. For more information on the Atlanta art gallery scene, including openings and location maps, consult *Museums & Galleries* (☎ 770/992–7808), a magazine distributed free at welcome centers and select area galleries. **Fay Gold Gallery** (⊠ 247 Buckhead Ave., East Village Sq., ☎ 404/233–3843) displays works by nationally renowned contemporary artists. **Jackson Fine Art Gallery**

(3115 E. Shadowlawn Ave., 404/233–3739) exhibits fine art photography. **Modern Primitive** (1393 N. Highland Ave., Virginia-Highland, 404/892–0556) has a fascinating assembly of folk and visionary art from around the state and the region. **Ray's Indian Originals** (90 N. Avondale Rd., Avondale Estates, 404/292–4999) shows exquisite original work by Native American artists. **Vespermann Gallery** (2140 Peachtree Rd., Brookwood Sq., 404/350–9698) has lovely handblown glass objects.

BOOKS

Chapter 11 (6237 Roswell Rd., 404/256–5518) is a great place to find recently published titles at good prices. **Yesteryear** (3201 Maple Dr., 404/237–0163) is the destination of choice for antiquarians. Its strengths include military history, Georgiana, and old cookbooks.

FOOD

DeKalb Farmers Market (3000 E. Ponce de Leon Ave., Decatur, 404/377–6400) has 175,000 square ft of exotic fruits, cheeses, seafood, sausages, breads, and delicacies from around the world. **East 48th St. Market** (2462 Jett Ferry Rd., at Mt. Vernon Rd., Williams at Dunwoody Shopping Center, 770/392–1499) sells Italian deli meats, fabulous breads, cheeses, and Italian prepared foods. Shop at **Eatzi's Market & Bakery** (3221 Peachtree Rd., 404/237–2266) for prepared foods, imported cheeses, great breads, and fine wines. **Harry's Farmers Markets** (1180 Upper Hembree Rd., Roswell, 770/664–6300; 2025 Satellite Pointe, Duluth, 770/416–6900; 70 Powers Ferry Rd., Marietta, 770/578–4400) consists of three markets north of the city, spun off from the original (DeKalb Farmers Market, *above*) by the owner's brother; they sell quality fish, cheese, wine, produce, ethnic foods, meats, and deli items. To grab a quick picnic basket before a concert, find one of several **Harry's in a Hurry** shops (three locations are 1061 Ponce de Leon Ave., 404/439–1100; 1875 Peachtree St., 404/352–7800; and 2804 Roswell Rd., 404/266–0800). Homesick Parisians take comfort at **Paris Market** (1833 Peachtree Rd., 404/351–4212), with fresh pâté, imported cheese and wine, and great bread. For health food, go to **Whole Foods Market** (2111 Briarcliff Rd., at LaVista Rd., 404/634–7800).

Atlanta A to Z

Arriving and Departing

BY BUS

Greyhound Bus Lines (232 Forsyth St., 404/584–1731 or 800/231–2222) provides transportation to downtown Atlanta.

Amtrak (1688 Peachtree St., 404/881–3060 or 800/872–7245) operates its Thru-Way bus service daily from Birmingham and Mobile, Alabama, to Atlanta's Brookwood station. Another bus goes daily from the station to Macon.

BY CAR

The city is encircled by I–285. Three interstates—I–85, running northeast–southwest from Virginia to Alabama; I–75, north–south from Michigan to Florida; and I–20, east–west from South Carolina to Texas—also crisscross Atlanta.

BY PLANE

Hartsfield Atlanta International Airport (6000 N. Terminal Pkwy, 404/530–6600), 13 mi south of downtown, is served by Atlantic Southeast Airlines, America West, American, Continental, Delta, GP Express, Markair, Midwest Express, National, Northwest, TWA,

United, and US Airways, as well as many international carriers (☞ Air Travel *in* Smart Travel Tips A to Z for airline telephone numbers).

Atlanta Airport Shuttle (☎ 404/766–5312) operates vans every half hour between 7 AM and 11 PM daily. The downtown trip, $12 one-way, $20 round-trip, takes about 20 minutes and stops at major hotels. Vans also go to Emory University and the Lenox area; $18 one-way, $28 round-trip.

If your luggage is light, take **MARTA** (Metropolitan Atlanta Rapid Transit Authority; ☎ 404/848–4711) high-speed trains between the airport and downtown and other locations. Trains operate 5 AM–1 AM weekdays and 6 AM–12:30 AM weekends. The trip downtown takes about 15 minutes to the Five Points station, and the fare is $1.50.

From the airport to downtown, the **taxi** fare is $20 for one person, $22 for two, and $25 for three or more, including tax. From the airport to Buckhead, the fare is $30 for one and $32 for two or more. With a reasonable advance reservation, **Carey-Executive Limousine** (☎ 404/223–2000) will provide 24-hour service. **Buckhead Safety Cab** (☎ 404/233–1152) and **Checker Cab** (☎ 404/351–1111) offer 24-hour service.

BY TRAIN

Amtrak (✉ 1688 Peachtree St., ☎ 404/881–3060 or 800/872–7245) operates the *Crescent* train, with daily service to Atlanta's Brookwood station from New York; Philadelphia; Washington, D.C.; Baltimore; Charlotte; and Greenville. It also goes daily from New Orleans to New York through Atlanta.

Getting Around

BY BUS

The **Metropolitan Atlanta Rapid Transit Authority** (MARTA; ☎ 404/848–4711), with a fleet of 667 buses, operates 150 routes covering 1,500 mi. The fare is $1.50, and exact change is required. Weekly and monthly TransCards give you a slight discount. Service is very limited outside the perimeter set by I–285, except for a few areas in Clayton, DeKalb, and Fulton counties.

BY CAR

Some refer to Atlanta as the Los Angeles of the South, because driving is virtually the only way to get to most parts of the city. Although the congestion isn't comparable to that in Los Angeles yet, Atlantans have grown accustomed to frequent delays at rush hour. Beware: The South as a whole may be laid back, but Atlanta drivers are not; they tend to drive faster than drivers in other Southern cities. Drive with vigilance.

BY SUBWAY

MARTA (☎ 404/848–4711) has clean and safe rapid-rail subway trains with somewhat limited routes that link downtown with many major landmarks. The rail system's two main lines cross at the Five Points station downtown. Trains run 5 AM–1 AM, and large parking lots (free) are at most stations beyond downtown. Tokens ($1.50 each) can be bought from machines outside the station entrance. TransCards and information on public transportation are available at Rides Stores, open weekdays 7–7 and Saturday 8:30–5; Rides Stores are at the airport, the Five Points station, the headquarters building by the Lindbergh station, and the Lenox station. You can also buy TransCards at Kroger and Publix grocery stores. Free transfers, needed for some bus routes, are available by pressing a button on the subway turnstile or requesting one from the bus driver.

BY TAXI

Taxi service in Atlanta can be a mixed experience. Drivers often do not have correct change even for a small bill, so be prepared either to charge your fare (many accept credit cards) or insist that the driver obtain change. Drivers also appear as befuddled as visitors by Atlanta's notoriously winding and hilly streets, so if your destination is something other than a major hotel or popular sight, come armed with directions.

Taxi fares start at $1.60 for the first mile, with 20¢ for each additional ½ mile, 50¢ per extra passenger, and $12 per hour waiting time. Each additional person is charged another $1. Within the Downtown Convention Zone a flat rate of $5 for one person or $1 for each additional passenger will be charged for any destination. **Buckhead Safety Cab** (☎ 404/233–1152) and **Checker Cab** (☎ 404/351–1111) offer 24-hour service.

Contacts and Resources

B&B RESERVATIONS

Great Inns of Georgia (⊠ 541 Londonberry Rd., 30327, ☎ 404/843–0471 or 800/501–7328, FAX 404/252–8886) can provide brochures on inns in Atlanta.

EMERGENCIES

Emergency assistance (☎ 911). For **24-hour emergency rooms,** contact **Georgia Baptist Medical Center** (⊠ 303 Parkway Dr., ☎ 404/265–4000), **Grady Memorial Hospital** (⊠ 80 Butler St., ☎ 404/616–4307), **Northside Hospital** (⊠ 1000 Johnson Ferry Rd., ☎ 404/851–8000), and **Piedmont Hospital** (⊠ 1968 Peachtree Rd., ☎ 404/605–5000).

GUIDED TOURS

The **Atlanta Preservation Center** (⊠ 156 7th St., Suite 3, ☎ 404/876–2041, 404/876–2040 tour hot line) offers 10 walking tours of historic areas and neighborhoods for $5 each. Especially noteworthy are tours of Sweet Auburn, the neighborhood associated with Martin Luther King Jr. and other leaders in Atlanta's African-American community; Druid Hills, the verdant, genteel neighborhood where *Driving Miss Daisy* was filmed; and the Fox Theatre, the elaborate 1920s picture palace.

Gray Line of Atlanta (⊠ 705 Lively Ave., Norcross 30071, ☎ 770/449–1806 or 800/593–1818, FAX 770/249–9397) has tours of downtown, Midtown, Buckhead, and the King Center. Stone Mountain may be included on some tours.

RADIO STATIONS

AM: WGST 640, news/talk; WSB 750, news/talk; WQXI 790, sports/talk. **FM:** WABE 90.1, National Public Radio/classical; WCLK 91.9, jazz/soul; WZGC 92.9, classic rock; WPCH 94.9, light rock; WNNX 99.7, modern rock; WKHX 101.5, country; WVEE 103.3, urban contemporary.

24-HOUR PHARMACIES

CVS (⊠ 1943 Peachtree Rd., ☎ 404/351–7629; 1554 North Decatur Rd., ☎ 404/373–4192; 2350 Cheshire Bridge Rd., ☎ 404/486–7289).

VISITOR INFORMATION

The **Atlanta Convention & Visitors Bureau** (ACVB; ⊠ 233 Peachtree St., Suite 2000, 30303, ☎ 404/222–6688 or 800/285–2682, FAX 404/584–6331) has information on Atlanta only. The ACVB has several visitor information centers in Atlanta: Hartsfield Atlanta International Airport, in north terminal at west crossover; Underground Atlanta (⊠ 65 Upper Alabama St.); Georgia World Congress Center (⊠ 285 International Blvd.); and Lenox Square mall (⊠ 3393 Peachtree Rd.). Write to the **Georgia Department of Industry, Trade, and Tourism** (⊠ Box 1776, 30301, ☎ 404/656–3590 or 800/847–4842, FAX 404/651–9063).

SAVANNAH

The very sound of the name Savannah conjures up misty images of mint juleps, handsome mansions, and a somewhat decadent city moving at a lazy Southern pace. It's hard even to say "Savannah" without drawling. Well, brace yourself. The mint juleps are there all right, along with the moss and the mansions and the easygoing pace, but this Southern belle rings with surprises. Take, for example, St. Patrick's Day: Savannah has a St. Patrick's Day celebration second only to New York's. The greening of Savannah began more than 164 years ago and everybody in town talks a blue (green) streak about St. Patrick's Day. Everything turns green on March 17, including the faces of startled visitors when green scrambled eggs and green grits are put before them.

Savannah's beginning was February 12, 1733, when English general James Edward Oglethorpe and 120 colonists arrived at Yamacraw Bluff on the Savannah River to found the 13th and last colony in the New World. As the port city grew, people from England and Ireland, Scottish Highlanders, French Huguenots, Germans, Austrian Salzburgers, Sephardic and Ashkenazic Jews, Moravians, Italians, Swiss, Welsh, and Greeks all arrived to create what could be called a rich gumbo.

In 1793 Eli Whitney of Connecticut, who was tutoring on a plantation near Savannah, invented a mechanized means of "ginning" seeds from cotton bolls. Cotton soon became king, and Savannah, already a busy seaport, flourished under its reign. Waterfront warehouses were filled with "white gold," and brokers trading in the Savannah Cotton Exchange set world prices. The white gold brought in solid gold, and fine mansions were built in the prospering city.

In 1864 Savannahians surrendered their city to Union general Sherman rather than see it torched. Following World War I and the decline of the cotton market, the city's economy virtually collapsed, and its historic buildings languished for more than 30 years. Elegant mansions were razed or allowed to decay, and cobwebs replaced cotton in the dilapidated riverfront warehouses.

In 1955, Savannah's spirits rose again. News that the exquisite Isaiah Davenport House (⊠ 324 E. State St.) was to be destroyed prompted seven outraged ladies to raise money to buy the house. They saved it the day before the wrecking ball was to swing. Thus was born the Historic Savannah Foundation, the organization responsible for the restoration of downtown Savannah, where more than 1,000 restored buildings form the 2½-square-mi Historic District, the nation's largest. Many of these buildings are open to the public during the annual tour of homes, and today Savannah is one of the country's top 10 cities for walking tours.

John Berendt's wildly popular *Midnight in the Garden of Good and Evil,* published in 1994, has lured many new visitors to Savannah. A nonfiction account of a notorious 1980s shooting, the book brings to life such Savannah sites as Monterey Square, Mercer House, and Bonaventure Cemetery. Clint Eastwood's 1997 film version was not a box-office hit, but visitor interest in Savannah has remained intense, to the consternation of old-timers who find the story's characters less than savory and the nosy Northerners a nuisance. Other Savannahians have rolled out the welcome mat, while still others have hiked prices, profiting from the tourist dollars.

Georgia's founder, General James Oglethorpe, designed the original town of Savannah and laid it out in a perfect grid. The Historic District is neatly hemmed in by the Savannah River, Gaston Street, East Street, and Martin Luther King Jr. Boulevard. Streets are arrow-straight, public squares of varying sizes are tucked into the grid at precise intervals, and each block is sliced in half by narrow, often unpaved streets. Bull Street, anchored on the north by City Hall and the south by Forsyth Park, charges down the center of the grid and lunges around the five public squares that stand in its way.

Numbers in the text correspond to numbers in the margin and on the Savannah Historic District map.

The Historic District

A Good Walk and Drive

You can cover Historic Savannah on foot, but to save time and energy, you might want to drive part of this tour. Start at the **Savannah Visitors Center** ⑥⓪, on Martin Luther King Jr. Boulevard. In the same building, the **Savannah History Museum** ⑥① is an ideal introduction to the city's history. There is public parking next to the center and museum.

Exit the parking lot and turn left (north), walking or driving two short and one very long blocks on Martin Luther King Jr. Boulevard to the **Scarborough House** ⑥②, which contains the Ships of the Sea Museum. Cross Martin Luther King Jr. Boulevard and continue two blocks east on West Congress Street, past Franklin Square to **City Market** ⑥③. Skirting around Franklin Square north on Montgomery Street, go two blocks to West Bay Street and turn right.

From this point, continue east on West Bay Street four blocks to Bull Street. On your left, you'll see **City Hall** ⑥④. Continue east down West Bay Street (which now becomes East Bay Street) to **Factors Walk** ⑥⑤, which lies south of River Street and the Savannah River. If you're driving, leave your car here to continue on foot (be sure to park in long-term parking, as the short-term meters are carefully watched and tickets dispensed expeditiously). Step down from Factors Walk toward the river and visit **Riverfront Plaza** ⑥⑥, which is best seen on foot.

At this point, if you're driving, you'll probably want to get back in your car to continue the tour. Return to East Bay Street and head west two long blocks back to Bull Street. Walk or drive four blocks south on Bull Street to **Wright Square** ⑥⑦; then turn right (west) and go two blocks to Telfair Square, where you can stop at the **Telfair Mansion and Art Museum** ⑥⑧. Stroll around Telfair Square and then continue east on West York Street back toward Wright Square, and turn right on Bull Street, heading two blocks south to the **Juliette Gordon Low Birthplace/Girl Scout National Center** ⑥⑨. Two more short blocks south from the Low House on Bull Street, and you'll reach **Chippewa Square** ⑦⓪. Continue south on Bull Street to the Gothic Revival **Green-Meldrim House** ⑦①. Next, walk four blocks south on Bull Street to **Monterey Square** ⑦②. Proceed two blocks farther south from Monterey Square to **Forsyth Park** ⑦③, the divide between East and West Gaston streets.

From the park, walk east on East Gaston Street and go one block to Abercorn Street; then turn left (north) on Abercorn, to Calhoun Square, and note the **Wesley Monumental Church** ⑦④. Continue north on Abercorn four blocks to Lafayette Square and view the **Andrew Low House** ⑦⑤. Northeast of Lafayette Square looms the **Cathedral of St. John the Baptist** ⑦⑥ on East Harris Street. Two blocks north at the intersection of Abercorn and East Oglethorpe streets is the huge **Colonial Park Cemetery** ⑦⑦. Proceeding two blocks north on Abercorn from the cemetery takes you to Oglethorpe Square; across from the square is the **Owens-Thomas House and Museum** ⑦⑧. From the house, walk east on East President Street two blocks to Columbia Square. Northwest of the square

Savannah Historic District

on East State Street stands the **Isaiah Davenport House** ⑲. From here, continue north up Habersham Street to **Emmet Park** ⑳, a splendid park to relax in at the end of your tour.

TIMING

This is a long but comfortable walk, as Savannah has no taxing hills. Allow a full day to see everything along this route, especially if you plan to read all the historic markers and explore the sights thoroughly, stopping for tours. Driving around the squares can be slow—but you can drive the entire route in two hours, a pace that allows for some stopping along the way. Allow extra time if you want to linger in Riverfront Plaza for a half hour or so.

Sights to See

⑦⑤ **Andrew Low House.** This residence was built in 1848 for Andrew Low, a native of Scotland and one of Savannah's merchant princes. The home later belonged to his son William, who married Juliette Gordon. After her husband's death, she founded the Girl Scouts in this house on March 12, 1912. The house has 19th-century antiques, stunning silver, and some of the finest ornamental ironwork in Savannah. ☒ *329 Abercorn St.,* ☎ *912/233–6854.* ☒ *$7.* ☉ *Mon.–Sat. 10:30–4, Sun. noon–4; last tour at 3:30.*

Beach Institute African-American Cultural Center. It's in the building that housed the first school for African-American children in Savannah, established after emancipation (1867). The center exhibits work by African-American artists from the Savannah area and around the country. ☒ *502 E. Harris St.,* ☎ *912/234–8000.* ☒ *$3.50.* ☉ *Tues.– Sat. noon–5.*

㏄ Cathedral of St. John the Baptist. Soaring over the city, the French Gothic–style cathedral, with pointed arches and free-flowing traceries, is the seat of the Diocese of Savannah. It was founded in 1799 by the first French colonists to arrive in Savannah. Fire destroyed the early structures; the present cathedral dates from 1874. Most of the cathedral's impressive stained-glass windows were made by Austrian glassmakers and imported around the turn of the 20th century. The high altar is of Italian marble, and the stations of the cross were imported from Munich. ☒ *222 E. Harris St.,* ☎ *912/233–4709.* ☉ *Daily 9–5.*

㏅ Chippewa Square. Daniel Chester French's imposing bronze statue of General James Edward Oglethorpe, founder of Savannah and Georgia, anchors the square. Also note the **Savannah Theatre** on Bull Street, which claims to be the oldest continuously operated theater site in North America. ☒ *Bull St. between Hull and Perry Sts.*

㏆ City Hall. Built in 1905 on the site of the Old City Exchange (1799–1904), this imposing structure anchors Bay Street. Notice the bench commemorating Oglethorpe's landing on February 12, 1733. ☒ *1 Bay St.,* ☎ *912/651–6444.* ☉ *Weekdays 8:15–5.*

㏇ City Market. This popular pedestrian-only area encompasses galleries, nightclubs, restaurants, and shops. ☒ *Between Franklin Sq. and Johnson Sq. on W. St. Julian St.*

★ **㏒ Colonial Park Cemetery.** The park is the final resting place for Savannahians who died between 1750 and 1853. You may want to stroll the shaded pathways and read some of the old tombstone inscriptions. There are several historical plaques, one of which marks the grave of Button Gwinnett, a signer of the Declaration of Independence. ☒ *Oglethorpe and Abercorn Sts.*

Columbia Square. When Savannah was a walled city (1757–1790), Bethesda Gate (one of six) was here. The square was laid out in 1799. ☒ *Habersham St. between E. State and E. York Sts.*

㏓ Emmet Park. The lovely tree-shaded park is named for Robert Emmet, a late-18th-century Irish patriot and orator. ☒ *Borders Bay St.*

㏕ Factors Walk. A network of iron walkways connects Bay Street with the multistory buildings that rise up from the river level, and iron stairways descend from Bay Street to Factors Walk. Cobblestone ramps lead pedestrians down to River Street. (These are serious cobblestones, so wear comfortable shoes.)

㏖ Forsyth Park. The park forms the southern border of Bull Street. On its 20 acres it has a glorious white fountain dating from 1858, Confederate and Spanish-American War memorials, and the Fragrant Garden for the Blind, a project of Savannah garden clubs. There are tennis courts and a tree-shaded jogging path. Outdoor plays and concerts often take place here. At the northwest corner of the park, in **Hodgson Hall,** a 19th-century Italianate–Greek Revival building, you'll find the **Geor-**

gia Historical Society, which shows selections from its collection of artifacts and manuscripts. ⊠ *501 Whitaker St.,* ☎ *912/651–2128.* ☉ *Tues.–Sat. 10–5.*

★ ⓲ **Green-Meldrim House.** Designed by New York architect John Norris and built in 1850 for cotton merchant Charles Green, this Gothic Revival mansion cost $90,000 to build—a princely sum back then. The house was bought in 1892 by Judge Peter Meldrim, whose heirs sold it to **St. John's Episcopal Church** to use as a parish house. General Sherman lived here after taking the city in 1864. Sitting on **Madison Square** (☞ *below*), the house has such Gothic features as a crenellated roof, oriels, and an external gallery with filigree ironwork. Inside are mantels of Carrara marble, carved black-walnut woodwork, and doorknobs and hinges of either silver plate or porcelain. The house is furnished with donated 16th-, 17th-, and 18th-century antiques, although some original pieces have been reacquired. ⊠ *1 W. Macon St.,* ☎ *912/233–3845.* 🖭 *$5.* ☉ *Tues., Thurs., and Fri. 10–4; Sat. 10–4. Closed last 2 wks of Jan. and 2 wks before Easter.*

★ ⓴ **Isaiah Davenport House.** The proposed demolition of this historic Savannah structure galvanized the city's residents into action to save their treasured buildings. Semicircular stairs with wrought-iron trim lead to the recessed doorway of the redbrick Federal mansion that master builder Isaiah Davenport built for himself between 1815 and 1820. Three dormered windows poke through the sloping roof of the stately house, and the interior has polished hardwood floors, fine woodwork and plasterwork, and a soaring elliptical staircase. Furnishings, from the 1820s, are Hepplewhite, Chippendale, and Sheraton. ⊠ *324 E. State St.,* ☎ *912/236–8097.* 🖭 *$6.* ☉ *Mon.–Sat. 10–4, Sun. 1–4.* 🕮

Johnson Square. The oldest of James Oglethorpe's original 24 squares was laid out in 1733 and named for South Carolina governor Robert Johnson. A monument marks the grave of Nathanael Greene, a hero of the Revolutionary War. The square was once a popular gathering place: Savannahians came here to welcome President Monroe in 1819, to greet the Marquis de Lafayette in 1825, and to cheer for Georgia's secession in 1861. ⊠ *Bull St. between Bryan and Congress Sts.*

⓺ **Juliette Gordon Low Birthplace/Girl Scout National Center.** This majestic Regency town house, attributed to William Jay (built 1818–1821), was designated in 1965 as Savannah's first National Historic Landmark. "Daisy" Low, founder of the Girl Scouts, was born here in 1860, and the house is now owned and operated by the Girl Scouts of America. Mrs. Low's paintings and other artwork are on display in the house, restored to the style of 1886, the year of Mrs. Low's marriage. ⊠ *142 Bull St.,* ☎ *912/233–4501.* 🖭 *$6.* ☉ *Mon.–Tues. and Thurs.–Sat. 10–4, Sun. 12:30–4:30.*

OFF THE BEATEN PATH **KING-TISDELL COTTAGE –** Tucked behind a picket fence is this museum dedicated to the preservation of African-American history and culture. The Negro Heritage Trail Tour (☞ Beach Institute *in* Savannah A to Z, *below*) visits this little Victorian house. Broad steps lead to a porch, and dormered windows pop up through a steep roof. The interior is furnished to resemble a middle-class African-American coastal home of the 1890s. To reach the cottage by car, go east on East Bay Street to Price Street, and turn south (right) on this street; continue for about 30 blocks to East Huntington Street, and take a left (east). The building is in the middle of the block. ⊠ *514 E. Huntington St.,* ☎ *912/234–8000.* 🖭 *$3.* ☉ *By appointment only.*

Lafayette Square. Named for the Marquis de Lafayette, the square contains a graceful three-tier fountain donated by the Georgia chapter of the Colonial Dames of America. ✉ *Abercorn St. between E. Harris and E. Charlton Sts.*

Madison Square. A statue on the square, laid out in 1839 and named for President James Madison, depicts Sergeant William Jasper hoisting a flag and is a tribute to his bravery during the Siege of Savannah. Though mortally wounded, Jasper rescued the colors of his regiment in the assault on the British lines. ✉ *Bull St. between W. Harris and W. Charlton Sts.*

㉒ Monterey Square. Commemorating the victory of General Zachary Taylor's forces in Monterrey, Mexico, in 1846, this is the fifth and southernmost of Bull Street's squares. A monument honors General Casimir Pulaski, the Polish nobleman who lost his life in the Siege of Savannah during the Revolutionary War. Also on the square is **Temple Mickve Israel** (☞ *below*). ✉ *Bull St. between Taylor and Gordon Sts.*

★ ㉘ Owens-Thomas House and Museum. English architect William Jay's first Regency mansion in Savannah is the city's finest example of that architectural style. Built in 1816–1819, the English house was constructed mostly with local materials. Of particular note are the curving walls of the house, Greek-inspired ornamental molding, half-moon arches, stained-glass panels, and Duncan Phyfe furniture. In 1825, the Marquis de Lafayette bade a two-hour au revoir from a wrought-iron balcony to a crowd below. ✉ *124 Abercorn St.,* ☏ *912/233–9743.* 🎟 *$8.* ⊙ *Mon. noon–5, Tues.–Sat. 10–5, Sun. 2–5.* 🎟

OFF THE
BEATEN PATH
RALPH MARK GILBERT CIVIL RIGHTS MUSEUM – In Savannah's Historic District, this history museum has a series of 15 exhibits on segregation, from emancipation through the civil rights movement. The role of black and white Savannahians in ending segregation in their city is detailed in these exhibits, largely derived from archival photographs. The museum also has touring exhibits. ✉ *460 Martin Luther King Jr. Blvd.,* ☏ *912/ 231–8900,* 🗛 *912/234–2577.* 🎟 *$4.* ⊙ *Mon.–Sat. 9–5.*

Reynolds Square. John Wesley, who preached in Savannah and wrote the first English hymnal in Savannah in 1736, is remembered here. A monument to the founder of the Methodist Church is shaded by greenery and surrounded by park benches. The **Olde Pink House** (✉ 23 Abercorn St.), built in 1771, is one of the oldest buildings in town. Now a restaurant (☞ *Dining, below*), the porticoed pink-stucco Georgian mansion has been a private home, a bank, and headquarters for a Yankee general during the Civil War. ✉ *Abercorn St. between E. Bryant and E. Congress Sts.*

㉖ Riverfront Plaza. Here you can watch a parade of freighters and pugnose tugs; youngsters can play in the tugboat-shape sandboxes. River Street is the main venue for many of the city's celebrations, including the First Saturday festivals when flea marketeers, artists, and artisans display their wares and musicians entertain the crowds.

㉑ Savannah History Museum. In a restored railway station, the museum is an excellent introduction to the city. Exhibits range from old locomotives to a tribute to Savannah-born songwriter Johnny Mercer. Situated on top of the **site of the Siege of Savannah**, it marks the spot where in 1779 the colonial forces, led by Polish count Casimir Pulaski, laid siege to Savannah in an attempt to retake the city from the Redcoats. They were beaten back, and Pulaski was killed while leading a cavalry charge against the British. The dead lie underneath the building. ✉ *303*

Martin Luther King Jr. Blvd., ☎ *912/238–1779.* ☞ *$3.* ⊙ *Weekdays 8:30–5, weekends 9–5.*

⓺⓪ **Savannah Visitors Center.** Come here for free maps and brochures, friendly advice, and an audiovisual overview of the city. The starting point for a number of guided tours, the center is in a big 1860 red-brick building with high ceilings and sweeping arches. It was the old Central of Georgia railway station. The parking lot is a good spot to leave your car while you explore the nearby Historic District. ✉ *301 Martin Luther King Jr. Blvd.,* ☎ *912/944–0455.* ⊙ *Weekdays 8:30–5, weekends 9–5.*

⓺⓶ **Scarborough House.** This exuberant Greek Revival mansion, built during the 1819 cotton boom for Savannah merchant prince William Scarborough, was designed by English architect William Jay. Scarborough was a major investor in the steamship *Savannah.* The house has a Doric portico capped by one of Jay's characteristic half-moon windows. Four massive Doric columns form a peristyle in the atrium entrance hall. Inside is the **Ships of the Sea Museum,** with displays of ship models, including steamships, a nuclear-powered ship (the *Savannah*), China clippers with their sails unfurled, and Columbus's vessels. ✉ *41 Martin Luther King Jr. Blvd.,* ☎ *912/232–1511.* ☞ *$5.* ⊙ *Tues.–Sun. 10–5.*

⓺⓼ **Telfair Mansion and Art Museum.** The oldest public art museum in the Southeast was designed by William Jay in 1819 for Alexander Telfair and sits across the street from **Telfair Square.** Within its marble rooms are American, French, and Dutch Impressionist paintings; German tonalist paintings; a large collection of works by Kahlil Gibran; plaster casts of the Elgin Marbles, the Venus de Milo, and the Laocoön, among other classical sculptures; and some of the Telfair family furnishings, including a Duncan Phyfe sideboard and Savannah-made silver. ✉ *121 Barnard St.,* ☎ *912/232–1177.* ☞ *$6; free Sun.* ⊙ *Mon. noon–5, Tues.–Sat. 10–5, Sun. 1–5.*

Temple Mickve Israel. A Gothic Revival synagogue on Monterey Square is home to the third-oldest Jewish congregation in the United States; its founding members settled in town five months after the establishment of Savannah in 1733. The synagogue's collection includes documents and letters (some from George Washington, James Madison, and Thomas Jefferson) pertaining to early Jewish life in Savannah and Georgia. ✉ *20 E. Gordon St.,* ☎ *912/233–1547.* ⊙ *Weekdays 10–noon and 2–4.*

⓻⓸ **Wesley Monumental Church.** This Gothic Revival–style church memorializing the founders of Methodism is patterned after Queen's Kirk in Amsterdam. Noted for its magnificent stained-glass windows, the church celebrated a century of service in 1968. ✉ *429 Abercorn St.,* ☎ *912/232–0191.* ⊙ *By appointment only.*

⓺⓻ **Wright Square.** Named for James Wright, Georgia's last colonial governor, the square has an elaborate monument in its center that honors William Washington Gordon, founder of the Central of Georgia Railroad. A slab of granite from Stone Mountain (☞ *above*) adorns the grave of Tomo-Chi-Chi, the Yamacraw chief who befriended General Oglethorpe and the colonists. ✉ *Bull St. between W. State and W. York Sts.*

Midnight in the Garden of Good and Evil

Town gossips can give you the best introduction to a city, and as author John Berendt discovered, Savannah's not short on them. In his 1994 best-seller, *Midnight in the Garden of Good and Evil,* Berendt shares the juiciest of tales imparted to him during the eight years he spent here wining and dining with Savannah's high society and dancing with her Grand Empress, drag queen the Lady Chablis, among others. By the time he left, there had been a scandalous homicide and several trials: The wealthy Jim Williams was accused of killing his assistant, Danny Hansford.

Before you set out, find a copy of the book, pour yourself a cool drink, and enter an eccentric world of cutthroat killers and society backstabbers, voodoo witches, and garden-club ladies. Then, slip on a pair of comfortable shoes and head over to the Historic District to follow the characters' steps to their homes and haunts. By the end of this walking tour, you'll be hard-pressed to find the line between Berendt's creative nonfiction and Savannah's reality. Note: Unless otherwise indicated, the sights on this tour are not open to the public.

A Good Walk and Drive

Begin at the southwest corner of Monterey Square, site of the **Mercer House** ⑧, whose construction was begun by songwriter Johnny Mercer's great-grandfather just before the Civil War. Two blocks south on Bull Street is the **Armstrong House** ⑧, an earlier residence of Jim Williams, the main character in the book. Walk south through Forsyth Park to the corner of Park Avenue and Whitaker streets (or, if driving, turn right on East Gaston to West Gaston Street, then left onto Whitaker). The **Forsyth Park Apartments** ⑧, where author John Berendt lived, are on the southwest corner of Forsyth Park. Then, if you're walking, turn back north through the park (if driving, turn left onto Park Avenue, left onto Drayton Street at the park's southeast corner, then left again onto East Gaston Street). At the midpoint of the park's northern edge, turn north up Bull Street in the direction of Monterey Square. Turn left on West Gordon Street off Bull Street and walk toward the corner of West Gordon Street and Whitaker Street, where you'll reach **Serena Dawes's House** ⑧. Next, cross West Gordon Street, walk north on Bull Street in front of Mercer House, cross Wayne Street, and the first house on the left facing Bull Street at Wayne Street is **Lee Adler's Home** ⑧, which sits across from Monterey Square's northwest corner. (If you're driving, proceed around Monterey Square to West Taylor Street, and at its intersection with Whitaker Street, take a left and go two blocks to West Gordon Street. Take a left onto West Gordon Street; the house is on the left.)

Continue walking north on Bull Street and take a right (east) on East Jones Street. **Joe Odom's first house** ⑧ is the third house on the left before Drayton Street. (If you're driving, go around the square again onto Bull Street, and go north on Bull Street to East Jones Street. Take a right, and the house will be on the left.)

Continue on East Jones Street to Abercorn Street and turn left (north), walking two blocks on Abercorn Street to East Charlton Street and the **Hamilton-Turner House** ⑧, now a bed-and-breakfast inn. Then, swing around Lafayette Square to East Harris Street, and take it about six blocks west to Pulaski Square at Barnard Street; turn right (north) on Barnard Street through Orleans Square and continue north to Telfair Square. On foot, you may elect to head west down West York Street on the south side of Telfair Square to find the **Chatham County Courthouse** ⑧, scene of all those trials, two blocks away. Drivers will have to continue around the square to take a left (west) onto West State Street, two blocks from the courthouse. Finally, take either Whitaker Street or Abercorn Street south to Victory Drive and turn left. Go through Thunderbolt to Whatley Avenue, and turn left again. Whatley Avenue leads directly to Bonaventure Road, which curves in both directions;

bear left, and on your right about a quarter mile up the road is **Bonaventure Cemetery** ⑧.

Allow a leisurely two hours to walk the main points of the tour, plus another hour to visit the cemetery. If driving, you'll easily complete the tour in an hour, but remember to add time to meander around Bonaventure Cemetery.

Sights to See

⑧ **Armstrong House.** Antiques dealer Jim Williams lived and worked in this residence before purchasing the Mercer House. On a late-afternoon walk past the mansion, Berendt met Mr. Simon Glover, an 86-year-old singer and porter for the law firm of Bouhan, Williams, and Levy, occupants of the building. Glover confided that he earned a weekly $10 for walking one of the firm's former partner's deceased dogs up and down Bull Street. Baffled? So was the author. Behind the house's cast-iron gates are the offices of Frank Siler, Jim Williams's attorney, who doubles as keeper of Uga, the Georgia Bulldog mascot. ⊠ *447 Bull St.*

⑧ **Bonaventure Cemetery.** A cemetery east of downtown is the final resting place for Danny Hansford. The haunting female tombstone figure from the book's cover has been removed to protect surrounding graves from sightseers. Now you can view the figure at the Telfair Mansion (☞ The Historic District, *above*). ⊠ *330 Bonaventure Rd.,* ☎ *912/651–6843.*

⑧ **Chatham County Courthouse.** The courthouse was the scene of three of Williams's murder trials, which took place over the course of about eight years. An underground tunnel leads from the courthouse to the jail where Williams was held in a cell that was modified to allow him to conduct his antiques business. ⊠ *133 Montgomery St.*

⑧ **Forsyth Park Apartments.** Here was Berendt's second home in Savannah; from his fourth-floor rooms he pieced together the majority of the book. While parking his newly acquired 1973 Pontiac Grand Prix outside these apartments, Berendt met the Lady Chablis coming out of her nearby doctor's office, freshly feminine from a new round of hormone shots. ⊠ *Whitaker and Gwinnett Sts.*

⑧ **Hamilton-Turner House.** After one too many of Joe Odom's deals went sour, Mandy Nichols, his fourth fiancée-in-waiting, left him and took over his third residence, a Second Empire–style mansion dating from 1873. Mandy filled it with 17th- and 18th-century antiques and transformed it into a successful museum through which she led tour groups. The elegant towering hulk is at the southeast corner of Lafayette Square. Hillis sold the house in 1997, and the new owners turned it into a bed-and-breakfast inn (☞ Hamilton-Turner Inn *in* Lodging, *below*). ⊠ *330 Abercorn St.*

⑧ **Joe Odom's First House.** At this stucco town house, Odom, a combination tax lawyer, real-estate broker, and piano player, hosted a 24-hour stream of visitors. The author met Odom through Mandy Nichols, a former Miss Big Beautiful Woman, who stopped by to borrow ice when the power had been cut off, a frequent occurrence. ⊠ *16 E. Jones St.*

⑧ **Lee Adler's Home.** Just north of the Mercer House, in half of the double town house facing West Wayne Street, Lee Adler, the adversary of Jim Williams, runs his business of restoring historic Savannah properties. Adler's howling dogs drove Williams to his pipe organ, where he churned out a deafening version of César Franck's *Pièce Héroïque.*

Later, Adler stuck reelection signs in his front lawn, showing his support for the district attorney who prosecuted Williams three times before he was finally found not guilty. ⊠ *425 Bull St.*

⑧ Mercer House. This redbrick Italianate mansion on the southwest corner of Monterey Square became Jim Williams's Taj Mahal; here he ran a world-class antiques dealership and held *the* Christmas party of the season; here also his sometime house partner Danny Hansford was shot and died. Williams himself died here in 1990, near the very spot where Hansford fell. Today, his sister lives quietly among the remnants of his Fabergé collection and his Joshua Reynolds paintings, in rooms lighted by Waterford crystal chandeliers. ⊠ *429 Bull St.*

㏓ Serena Dawes's House. Near the intersection of West Gordon and Bull streets, this house was owned by Helen Driscoll, also known as Serena Dawes. A high-profile beauty in the 1930s and '40s, she married into a Pennsylvania steel family. After her husband accidentally and fatally shot himself in the head, she retired here, in her hometown. Dawes, Berendt writes, "spent most of her day in bed, holding court, drinking martinis and pink ladies, playing with her white toy poodle, Lulu." Chief among Serena's gentlemen callers was Luther Driggers, rumored to possess a poison strong enough to wipe out the entire city. ⊠ *17 W. Gordon St.*

Other Area Attractions

Ebenezer. When the Salzburgers arrived in Savannah in 1734, Oglethorpe sent them up the Savannah River to establish a settlement. The first effort was assailed by disease, and they sought his permission to move to better ground. Denied, they moved anyway and established Ebenezer. Here, they engaged in silkworm production and, in 1769, built the Jerusalem Church, which still stands. After the Revolution, the silkworm operation never resumed, and the town faded into history. Descendants of these Protestant religious refugees have preserved the church and assembled a few of the remaining buildings, moving them to this site from other locations. Be sure to follow GA 275 to its end and see Ebenezer Landing, where the Salzburgers came ashore. ⊠ *Ebenezer Rd., U.S. 21 to GA 275, Rincon.*

Fort Jackson. About a mile outside Savannah via President Street, you'll see a sign for the fort, which is 3 mi from the city. Purchased in 1808 by the federal government, this is the oldest standing fort in Georgia. It was garrisoned in 1812 and was the Confederate headquarters of the river batteries. The brick edifice is surrounded by a tidal moat, and there are 13 exhibit areas. Battle reenactments, blacksmithing demonstrations, and programs of 19th-century music are among the fort's activities for tour groups. ⊠ *1 Ft. Jackson Rd.,* ☎ *912/232–3945.* ⊡ *$3.50.* ♡ *Daily 9–5.*

★ ☾ **Fort Pulaski National Monument.** Named for Casimir Pulaski, a Polish count and Revolutionary War hero, this must-see sight for Civil War buffs was built on Cockspur Island between 1829 and 1847. Robert E. Lee's first assignment after graduating from West Point was as an engineer here. During the Civil War the fort fell on April 11, 1862, after a mere 30 hours of bombardment by newfangled rifled cannons. The restored fortification, operated by the National Park Service, has moats, drawbridges, massive ramparts, and towering walls. The park has trails and picnic areas. It's 14 mi east of downtown Savannah; you'll see the entrance on your left just before U.S. 80E reaches Tybee Island. ⊠ *U.S. 80,* ☎ *912/786–5787.* ⊡ *$2.* ♡ *Sept.–May, daily 9–5; June–Aug., daily 9–6.* ✤

Melon Bluff. On a centuries-old 3,000-acre plantation that has been in one family since 1735, Melon Bluff includes a nature center, facilities for canoeing, kayaking, bird-watching, hiking, and other outdoor activities. You can camp here or stay at one of the three bed-and-breakfast inns ($$–$$$): Palmyra Plantation, an 1850s cottage; the Ripley Farmhouse, a classic rural house with a tin-covered roof; and an old barn, renovated to contain nine guest rooms. From Melon Bluff you can visit nearby **Seabrook Village,** a small but growing cluster of rural buildings from an African-American historic community; **Old Sunbury,** whose port made it a viable competitor to Savannah until the Revolutionary War ended its heyday; **Fort Morris,** which protected Savannah during the Revolution; and **Midway,** an 18th-century village with a house museum and period cemetery. To get here, take I–95 south from Savannah (about 30 mi) to Exit 76 (Midway/Sunbury), turn left, and go east for 3 mi. ⊠ *2999 Islands Hwy., Midway, 31320,* ☎ *912/884–5779 or 888/246–8188,* ℻ *912/884–3046.*

Mighty Eighth Air Force Heritage Museum. The famous World War II squadron the Mighty Eighth Air Force was formed in Savannah in January 1942 and shipped out to the United Kingdom. Flying Royal Air Force aircraft, the Mighty Eighth became the largest air force of the period, with some 200,000 combat crew personnel. Many lost their lives during raids on enemy factories or were interned as prisoners of war. Exhibits begin with the prelude to World War II and the rise of Adolf Hitler and continue through Desert Storm. ⊠ *I–95 and U.S. 80, 175 Bourne Ave., Exit 102, Pooler,* ☎ *912/748–8888.* ☎ *$7.50.* ☉ *Daily 9–6.*

🔄 **Skidaway Marine Science Complex.** On the grounds of the former Modena Plantation, it has a 14-panel, 12,000-gallon aquarium with marine and plant life of the continental shelf. Other exhibits highlight coastal archaeology and fossils of the Georgia coast. Nature trails overlook marsh and water. ⊠ *30 Ocean Science Circle, Skidaway Island,* ☎ *912/598–2496.* ☎ *$1.* ☉ *Weekdays 9–4, Sat. noon–5.*

Tybee Island. *Tybee* is an Indian word meaning "salt." The Yamacraw Indians came to this island in the Atlantic Ocean to hunt and fish, and legend has it that pirates buried their treasure here. The island is about 5 mi long and 2 mi wide, with seafood restaurants, chain motels, condos, and shops—most of which sprang up during the 1950s and haven't changed much since. The entire expanse of white sand is divided into a number of public beaches, where visitors shell and crab, charter fishing boats, and swim. It's 18 mi east of Savannah; take Victory Drive (U.S. 80), sometimes called Tybee Road, onto the island. On your way here, stop by Fort Jackson and Fort Pulaski National Monument (☞ *above*). Nearby, the misnamed Little Tybee Island, actually larger than Tybee Island, is entirely undeveloped. Contact **Tybee Island Beach Visitor Information** (⊠ Box 491, Tybee Island 31328, ☎ 800/868–2322).

Dining

Savannah has excellent seafood restaurants, and locals have a passion for spicy barbecue. The Historic District yields culinary treasures, especially along River Street. Several of the city's restaurants—such as Elizabeth on 37th, 45 South, the Olde Pink House, and Il Pasticcio—can easily compete with Atlanta's best dining establishments. Savannahians often drive to restaurants in Thunderbolt, and on Skidaway, Tybee, and Wilmington islands.

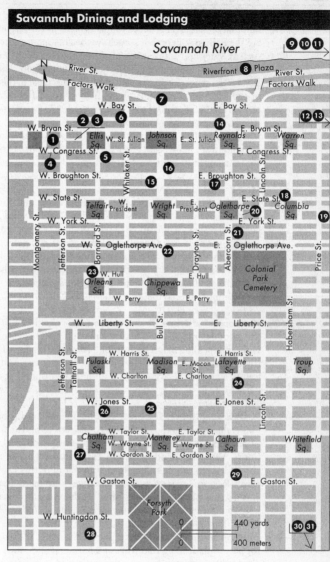

Savannah Dining and Lodging

Dining

Bistro Savannah **1**

Elizabeth on 37th **30**

45 South **13**

Georges' of Tybee **10**

Il Pasticcio **15**

Johnny Harris **31**

The Lady & Sons **4**

Mrs. Wilkes Dining Room . . . **26**

Nita's Place **21**

North Beach Grill **9**

Olde Pink House **14**

Sapphire Grill **2**

Seasons **3**

So' Soleil **16**

Trattoria Rivazza **5**

Wall's Bar-B-Q **19**

Lodging

Ballastone Inn **22**

Bed & Breakfast Inn **27**

Eliza Thompson House **25**

Foley House Inn **23**

Gastonian **29**

The Grande Toots Inn **28**

Hamilton-Turner Inn **24**

Hyatt Regency Savannah **7**

Kehoe House **18**

Marshall House **17**

Mulberry Inn **12**

The President's Quarters **20**

Quality Inn Heart of Savannah **6**

River Streeet Inn **8**

17th Streeet Inn **11**

$$$-$$$$ ✕ **Elizabeth on 37th.** There's something ingratiating about a restau-
  ★ rant that credits local produce suppliers on its menu. Regional specialties
     are the hallmark here, but somehow the chef manages to make dishes
     such as Maryland crab cakes and a Vermont blue cheese tamale sit com-
     fortably beside Southern fried grits and country ham. The extravagant
     Savannah cream cake is the way to finish your meal in this elegant turn-
     of-the-20th-century mansion with hardwood floors and spacious
     rooms. ⊠ 105 E. 37th St., ☎ 912/236–5547. Reservations essential.
     AE, D, DC, MC, V. No lunch.

$$$-$$$$ ✕ **45 South.** This popular south-side eatery is small and stylish, with
  ★ contemporary mauve and green decor. The game-heavy menu often in-
     cludes a confit of tender rabbit with morels and mashed potatoes. ⊠
     20 E. Broad St., ☎ 912/233–1881. Reservations essential. AE, D, DC,
     MC, V. Closed Sun. No lunch.

$$$-$$$$ ✕ **So' Soleil.** In the interior of a beautifully renovated downtown com-
     mercial building, former Atlanta chef Ian Winslade and partners have
     launched a slick, contemporary restaurant. Local ingredients, such as
     shrimp, get an Asian touch with lemongrass and ginger; the chicken
     with herbs and black olive sauce conjures Provence; and the crispy cala-
     mari in tomato rémoulade (dressing with mustard and herbs) brings a
     bit of the Mediterranean to this Southern establishment. The chef am-
     icably honors special dietary requests. ⊠ 1 W. Broughton St., ☎ 912/
     234–1212. AE, D, DC, MC, V. No dinner Sun.

$$-$$$ ✕ **Georges' of Tybee.** From the proprietors of the North Beach Grill
     (☞ below) comes Tybee's first fine restaurant. The warmly lit interior,
     with its appealing bar, is perfect for a romantic evening. Duck liver and
     frissee salad, roasted beets in sherry-ginger vinaigrette, and venison short
     loin in a cranberry reduction are among the dishes that delight diners
     here. ⊠ 1105 E. U.S. 80, Tybee Island, ☎ 912/786–9730. AE, MC,
     V. Closed Sun. No lunch.

$$-$$$ ✕ **Olde Pink House.** The brick Georgian mansion was built for James
     Habersham, one of the wealthiest Americans of his time, in 1771. One
     of Savannah's oldest buildings, the tavern has original Georgia pine
     floors, Venetian chandeliers, and 18th-century English antiques. The
     she-crab soup is a light but flavorful version of this Lowcountry spe-
     cialty. Regional ingredients find their way into many of the dishes, in-
     cluding the black grouper stuffed with blue crab and served with
     Vidalia onion sauce. ⊠ 23 Abercorn St., ☎ 912/232–4286. AE, MC,
     V. No lunch.

$-$$$ **Trattoria Rivazza.** Good for families with small children, it's the place
     for pastas made in myriad ways and hardier dishes, such as grilled veal
     chop with a vegetable stew, salmon braised in a fresh tomato broth,
     and grilled tuna steak with risotto. Fragrant coffee and decadent
     desserts round meals out nicely here. ⊠ 116 W. Congress St., ☎ 912/
     234–7300. AE, D, MC, V.

$$ ✕ **Bistro Savannah.** High ceilings, burnished heart-pine floors, and gray-
  ★ brick walls lined with artwork by local artists all contribute to the bistro
     atmosphere. The menu has such regional specialties as bouillabaisse
     of local seafood, crab cakes with lemon-caper aioli and chowchow, and
     shrimp and tasso (seasoned cured pork) on stone-ground grits. More
     cosmopolitan tastes are represented, too, in such treats as crispy roasted
     duck. The restaurant is near City Market. ⊠ 309 W. Congress St., ☎
     912/233–6266. AE, MC, V. No lunch.

$$ ✕ **Il Pasticcio.** Sicilian Pino Venetico turned this former department store
     into his dream restaurant. The bistro-style spot gleams with steel,
     glass, and tile and attracts a lively, hip, young crowd. The menu
     changes frequently, but fresh pastas and sauces are a constant. Don't
     miss the second-floor art gallery. Excellent desserts, including a supe-

rior tiramisu, make this one worth seeking out. ⊠ *2 E. Broughton St.,* ☎ *912/231–8888. AE, D, DC, MC, V. No lunch.*

$$ ✗ **Sapphire Grill.** Savannah's young and restless pack this popular bistro
★ every night. Chef Chris Nason focuses his seasonal menus on local ingredients, such as Georgia white shrimp, crab, and fish. Vegetarians will delight in his elegant vegetable presentations, such as a seasonal vegetable tart. The chocolate flan takes chocolate lovers to a new level of ecstasy. ⊠ *110 W. Congress St.,* ☎ *912/443–9962. Reservations essential. AE, D, DC, MC, V. No lunch.*

$$ ✗ **Seasons.** In the heart of City Market, Seasons is great for Sunday brunch, when so many of the downtown venues are closed. A complimentary glass of sparkling wine arrives at your table when you place your order. Brunch entrées include egg dishes, such as eggs Florentine with crabmeat. The lunch and dinner menus focus on seafood, including Georgia pecan grouper and Lowcountry shrimp and grits. ⊠ *315 W. St. Julian St.,* ☎ *912/233–2626. AE, D, DC, MC, V.*

$–$$ ✗ **Johnny Harris.** What started as a small roadside stand in 1924 has grown into one of the city's mainstays, with a menu that includes steaks, fried chicken, seafood, and a variety of meats spiced with the restaurant's famous tomato-and-mustard sauce. The lamb barbecue is a treat. There's live music Friday and Saturday night, except on the first Saturday night of the month, when there's dancing. ⊠ *1651 E. Victory Dr.,* ☎ *912/354–7810. AE, D, DC, MC, V. Closed Sun.*

$–$$ ✗ **North Beach Grill.** The tiny kitchen of this casual beachfront locale serves up a taste of the Caribbean. Diners will be tempted by dishes such as jerk-rubbed fish tacos with fruit salsa, grilled okra, and sea bass topped with caramelized onions and feta cream sauce. Come in a swimsuit for lunch but a bit more covered for dinner. ⊠ *41A Meddin Dr., Tybee Island,* ☎ *912/786–9003. Reservations not accepted. D, MC, V. Closed weekdays Dec.–Jan.*

$ ✗ **The Lady & Sons.** Visitors and locals stand in line at this eatery, patiently waiting to attack the buffet, laden at both lunch and dinner with such specials as moist, crispy fried chicken; the best baked spaghetti in the South; green beans cooked with ham and potatoes; tender sweet creamed corn; and homemade lemonade. The interior of this 1870s-era building, painted pale pink with faux ivy tendrils draped along its perimeter, is bright, cheerful, and busy. Owner Paula H. Deen's book, *The Lady & Sons: Savannah Country Cookbook,* includes recipes for many of the most popular dishes. Sons Bobby and Jamie work here with her. ⊠ *311 W. Congress St.,* ☎ *912/233–2600. AE, D, MC, V. No dinner Sun.*

$ ✗ **Mrs. Wilkes Dining Room.** Folks line up for a culinary orgy of fine
★ Southern food, served family style at big tables. For breakfast there are eggs, sausage, piping hot biscuits, and grits. At lunch, try fried or roast chicken, collard greens, okra, mashed potatoes, corn bread—the dishes just keep coming. ⊠ *107 W. Jones St.,* ☎ *912/232–5997. Reservations not accepted. No credit cards. Closed Jan. and weekends. No dinner.*

$ ✗ **Nita's Place.** Juanita Dixon has a reputation for perfectly preparing
★ down-home Southern cooking at this little steam-table operation. People come for salmon patties, baked chicken, perfectly cooked okra, outstanding squash casserole, and homemade desserts. The fresh vegetables alone are worth the trip. ⊠ *140 Abercorn St.,* ☎ *912/238–8233. Reservations not accepted. MC, V. Closed Sun. No dinner.*

$ ✗ **Wall's Bar-B-Q.** It's a bit hard to find this little hole in the wall, but the barbecue (get the tangy hot-but-not-too-hot mustard-and-tomato sauce), deviled crab, red rice, greens, sour cream pound cake, and layered red velvet cake are all worth the search. The perfect quick bite is the rib snack. ⊠ *515 E. York La.,* ☎ *912/232–9754. Reservations not accepted. No credit cards. Closed Sun.–Tues.*

Lodging

Although Savannah has its share of chain hotels and motels, the city's most distinctive lodgings are the more than two dozen historic inns, guest houses, and bed-and-breakfasts gracing the Historic District.

If "historic inn" brings to mind images of roughing it in shabby genteel mansions with antiquated plumbing, you're in for a surprise. Most inns are in mansions with the requisite high ceilings, spacious rooms, and ornate carved millwork. Most have canopy, four-poster, or Victorian brass beds. And amid antique surroundings, there is modern luxury: enormous baths, many with whirlpools or hot tubs; film libraries for in-room VCRs; and turndown service with a chocolate, praline, or even a discreet brandy on your nightstand. Continental breakfast and afternoon refreshments are often included in the rate. Prices have risen since the filming of *Midnight in the Garden of Good and Evil.* Special seasons and holidays, such as St. Patrick's Day, push prices up a bit as well. On the other hand, weekdays and the off-season can yield excellent bargains.

Inns and Guest Houses

$$$–$$$$ ★ **Ballastone Inn.** This sumptuous inn occupies an 1838 mansion that once served as a bordello. Rooms are handsomely furnished, with luxurious linens on canopy beds, antiques and fine reproductions, and a collection of original framed prints from *Harper's* scattered throughout. On the garden level, rooms are small and cozy, with exposed brick walls, beam ceilings, and, in some cases, windows at eye level with the lush courtyard. Most rooms have working gas fireplaces, and three have whirlpool tubs. ⊠ *14 E. Oglethorpe Ave., 31401,* ☎ *912/236–1484 or 800/822–4553,* ℻ *912/236–4626. 13 rooms, 3 suites. In-room VCRs, concierge. AE, MC, V. BP.* ✏

$$$–$$$$ ★ **Gastonian.** Guest rooms at this inn, built in 1868, have working fireplaces and antiques from the Georgian and Regency periods; most also have whirlpool tubs or Japanese soak tubs. The Caracalla Suite is named for the oversize whirlpool tub built in front of the fireplace. Breakfast features such specialty items as ginger pancakes. Afternoon tea, evening cordials, and complimentary wine are other treats. ⊠ *220 E. Gaston St., 31401,* ☎ *912/232–2869 or 800/671–0716,* ℻ *912/232–0710. 14 rooms, 3 suites. Outdoor hot tub, concierge. AE, D, MC, V. BP.* ✏

$$$–$$$$ **Kehoe House.** A fabulously appointed bed-and-breakfast inn, the Victorian-style Kehoe House has brass-and-marble chandeliers, a courtyard garden, and a music room. On the main floor, a double parlor holds two fireplaces and sweeps the eye upward with its 14-ft ceilings. Turndown service includes chocolates, wine, and bottled water. Rates include access to the Downtown Athletic Club. ⊠ *123 Habersham St., 31401,* ☎ *912/232–1020 or 800/820–1020,* ℻ *912/231–0208. 15 rooms. Concierge, meeting rooms. AE, D, DC, MC, V. BP.*

$$$ ★ **Foley House Inn.** Two town houses, built 50 years apart, form this elegant inn. Named for an Irish immigrant who made a fortune in Savannah, the original house was built by his widow for her five grandchildren, whose parents had died, leaving them in her care. Most rooms have antiques and reproductions; five rooms have whirlpool tubs. A carriage house to the rear of the property has less-expensive rooms. ⊠ *14 W. Hull St., 31401,* ☎ *912/232–6622 or 800/647–3708,* ℻ *912/231–1218. 17 rooms, 2 suites. Lounge, in-room VCRs, concierge. AE, MC, V. BP.* ✏

$$–$$$ **The Grande Toots Inn.** Delores Ellis, Savannah's only African-American innkeeper, spent six years refurbishing this fine old Victorian house, built in 1890. On the edge of Forsyth Park (☞ The Historic District, *above*), the neighborhood, inspired by her diligence, is slowly making a comeback. A grandmother, Ellis fusses over guests as if they were her own offspring. Amenities range from gas-log fireplaces to a whirl-pool tub. ⊠ *212 W. Hall St., 31401,* ☎ *912/236–2911 or 800/835–6831,* ℻ *912/236–4010. 4 rooms, 1 carriage house. D, MC, V. BP.* ✇

$$–$$$ ☷ **Hamilton-Turner Inn.** Experience *Midnight in the Garden of Good and Evil* with a stay in this 1873 mansion built by wealthy Savannah jeweler Samuel Hamilton. Until recently, the house belonged to Mandy Nichols, one of the principal figures in the book. It's furnished with fine Second Empire, Eastlake, and Renaissance antiques. Four rooms have large whirlpools, two have fireplaces, and two have both plus a balcony. Complimentary afternoon tea, robes, and a film library are among the amenities. ⊠ *330 Abercorn St., 31401,* ☎ *912/233–1833 or 888/448–8849,* ℻ *912/233–0291. 15 rooms. In-room data ports. AE, D, DC, MC, V. BP.* ✇

$–$$$ ☷ **Eliza Thompson House.** Eliza Thompson was a socially prominent widow when she built her fine town house around 1847. In 1995 Carol and Steve Day purchased the house and repainted, refinished, and re-furnished it in period style. Marble baths have been added. Continental breakfast and complimentary afternoon wine and cheese are served in the parlor or on the patio, with its fine Ivan Bailey sculpture. ⊠ *5 W. Jones St., 31401,* ☎ *912/236–3620 or 800/348–9378,* ℻ *912/238–1920. 25 rooms. Concierge. MC, V. CP.* ✇

$$ ☷ **The President's Quarters.** Each room in the classic Savannah inn is
★ named for an American president. Guests are greeted with wine and fruit, and the complimentary afternoon tea tempts with sweet cakes. Turndown service includes a glass of port or sherry. There are also rooms in an adjacent town house. ⊠ *225 E. President St., 31401,* ☎ *912/233–1600 or 800/233–1776,* ℻ *912/238–0849. 11 rooms, 8 suites. Concierge, free parking. D, DC, MC, V. BP.* ✇

$$ ☷ **17th Street Inn.** The inn's deck, adorned with plants, palms, and swings, is a gathering place for visitors to chat, sip wine, and enjoy breakfast with their hosts, Susie Morris and her spouse, Stuart Liles. Steps away from the beach, it has two-story porches and rooms with generous kitchenettes, double iron beds, and bright colors. ⊠ *12 17th St., Box 114, Tybee Island 31328,* ☎ *912/786–0607 or 888/909–0607,* ℻ *912/786–0601. 7 rooms. D, MC, V. CP.* ✇

$–$$ ☷ **Bed & Breakfast Inn.** So called, the owner claims, because it was the first such property to open in Savannah more than 20 years ago, the inn is a restored 1853 Federal-style row house on historic Gordon Row near Chatham Square. The courtyard garden is an oasis from a day's hectic events. Although much of the furniture suggests the period, the dining room is not as elegant as those of more expensive inns. One room has a private deck. Afternoon pastries, lemonade, coffee, and tea are served. ⊠ *117 W. Gordon St., 31401,* ☎ *912/238–0518,* ℻ *912/233–2537. 15 rooms. Kitchenettes (some). AE, D, MC, V. BP.* ✇

Hotels and Motels

$$$–$$$$ ☷ **Hyatt Regency Savannah.** When this riverfront hotel was built in 1981, preservationists opposed the construction of the seven-story modern structure in the Historic District. The main architectural fea-tures are the towering atrium and glass elevators. Rooms have mod-ern furnishings, marble baths, and balconies overlooking either the atrium or the Savannah River. MD's Lounge is the ideal spot to have a drink and watch the river traffic drift by. Windows, the hotel's restaurant, serves a great Sunday buffet. ⊠ *2 W. Bay St., 31401,* ☎ *912/238–1234 or 800/233–1234,* ℻ *912/944–3673. 325 rooms, 21 suites. Indoor pool, concierge, business services. AE, D, MC, V.* ✇

$$$ ⊞ **Mulberry Inn.** This Holiday Inn is ensconced in an 1860s livery sta-
★   ble that later became a cotton warehouse and then a Coca-Cola bot-
tling plant. Gleaming heart-pine floors and antiques, including a
handsome English grandfather clock and an exquisitely carved Victo-
rian mantel, make it unique. Guest rooms are traditionally decorated,
and suites have king-size beds and wet bars. The café is a notch nicer
than most other Holiday Inn restaurants. ⊠ *601 E. Bay St., 31401,*
☎ *912/238–1200 or 800/465–4329,* FAX *912/236–2184. 96 rooms, 26
suites. Bar, pool, outdoor hot tub. AE, D, DC, MC, V.* 🐾

$$–$$$ ⊞ **Marshall House.** This restored hotel, with original pine floors,
woodwork, and bricks, caters to business needs while providing the
intimacy of a bed-and-breakfast inn. Different spaces reflect different
parts of Savannah's history, from its founding to the Civil War. Artwork
is mostly by local artists. You can listen to live jazz on weekends in the
hotel lounge. Café M specializes in local cuisine such as Southern pot-
au-feu, a seafood-rich Lowcountry dish with okra and greens, and Geor-
gia smoked quail. ⊠ *123 E. Broughton St., 31401,* ☎ *912/644–7896
or 800/589–6304,* FAX *912/234–3334. 65 rooms, 3 suites. Café, lounge,
in-room data ports, meeting rooms. AE, D, MC, V.*

$$–$$$ ⊞ **River Street Inn.** The interior is so lavish that it's hard to believe the
building was once a vacant warehouse. Today, the structure, which dates
to 1817, houses guest rooms with antiques and reproductions from the
era of King Cotton. One floor has charming shops and a New Orleans–
style restaurant. ⊠ *115 E. River St., 31401,* ☎ *912/234–6400 or 800/
678–8946,* FAX *912/234–1478. 86 rooms. 3 restaurants, 3 bars, con-
cierge, business services. AE, D, DC, MC, V. BP.*

$ ⊞ **Quality Inn Heart of Savannah.** This basic, quality motel-style lodg-
ing is clean and very popular with the older budget-minded set. In the
Historic District, it offers convenience, a friendly staff, complimentary
coffee, and on-site parking at rock-bottom prices. ⊠ *300 W. Bay St.,*
☎ *912/236–6321 or 800/221–2222,* FAX *912/234–5317. 53 rooms. Free
parking. AE, D, DC, MC, V. CP.*

Nightlife and the Arts

Savannah's nightlife reflects its laid-back personality. Some clubs have
live reggae, hard rock, and other contemporary music, but most stick to
traditional blues, jazz, and piano-bar vocalists. After-dark merrymak-
ers usually head for watering holes on Riverfront Plaza or the south side.

Bars and Nightclubs

The **Bar Bar** (⊠ 219 W. St. Julian St., ☎ 912/231–1910), a neighbor-
hood hangout, has pool tables, games, and a varied beer selection. Once
a month at **Club One Jefferson** (⊠ 1 Jefferson St., ☎ 912/232–0200),
a gay bar, the Lady Chablis (☞ *Midnight in the Garden of Good and
Evil, above*) bumps and grinds her way down the catwalk, lip-synch-
ing disco tunes in a shimmer of sequin and satin gowns; the cover is
$5. **Kevin Barry's Irish Pub** (⊠ 117 W. River St., ☎ 912/233–9626)
has a friendly atmosphere, a full menu until 1:45 AM, and traditional
Irish music Wednesday to Sunday; it's *the* place to be on St. Patrick's
Day. The rest of the year there's a mix of tourists and locals, young
and old. **Malone's** (⊠ 27 Barnard St., ☎ 912/234–3059 or 912/237–
9862), a sports bar, has 13 TV screens and monitors. Pool tables and
a bar are downstairs, and a dance floor with live entertainment is up-
stairs. **Stogies** (⊠ 112 W. Congress St., ☎ 912/233–4277) has its own
humidor where patrons buy expensive cigars. It's a fun spot if you can
take the smoke.

Coffeehouses

Thanks to a substantial student population, the city has sprouted coffeehouses as if they were spring flowers. The **Savannah Coffee House and Café** (⊠ 102 W. Congress St., ☎ 912/233–5311) serves locally made bagels, croissants, and muffins and good coffee. Students cluster around tables and play chess or draw. **Ex Libris** (⊠ 228 Martin Luther King Jr. Blvd., ☎ 912/238–2427) is a handsome space where you can browse through new books over a sandwich, soup, salad, or an espresso. It's student managed and operated by the Savannah College of Art and Design (☞ Art Galleries *in* Shopping, *below*).

Jazz and Blues Clubs

Bayou Café and Blues Bar (⊠ 14 N. Abercorn St., at River St., ☎ 912/233–6414) has acoustic music during the week and the Bayou Blues Band on the weekend. The food has a Cajun flavor. **Cafe Loco** (⊠ 1 Old Hwy. 80, Tybee Island, ☎ 912/786–7810), a few miles outside Savannah, showcases local blues and acoustics acts. You can rollick with Emma Kelly, the undisputed "Lady of 6,000 Songs," at **Hard Hearted Hannah's East** (⊠ 20 E. Broad St., ☎ 912/233–2225) from Tuesday through Saturday.

Outdoor Activities and Sports

Boating

At the **Bull River Yacht Club Marina** (⊠ 8005 Old Tybee Rd., ☎ 912/897–7300), you can arrange a dolphin tour, a deep-sea fishing expedition, or a jaunt through the coastal islands. **Lake Mayer Park** (⊠ Montgomery Crossroads Rd. and Sallie Mood Dr., ☎ 912/652–6780) has paddleboats, sailing, canoeing, and an in-line skating and hockey facility. **Saltwater Charters** (⊠ 111 Wickersham Dr., ☎ 912/598–1814) provides packages ranging from 2-hour sightseeing tours to 13-hour deep-sea fishing expeditions. Water taxis to the coastal islands are also available. **Public boat ramps** are found at **Bell's Landing** (⊠ Apache Ave. off Abercorn St.) on the Forest River, **Islands Expressway** (⊠ Islands Expressway adjacent to Frank W. Spencer Park) on the Wilmington River, and **Savannah Marina** on the Wilmington River in the town of Thunderbolt.

Golf

Bacon Park (⊠ 1 Shorty Cooper Dr., ☎ 912/354–2625), a public course with 27 holes, is par 72 for 18 holes and has a lighted driving range. **Henderson Golf Club** (⊠ 1 Al Henderson Dr., at I–95 and GA 204 [Exit 94], ☎ 912/920–4653) is an 18-hole, par-71 course about 15 mi from downtown Savannah. **Mary Calder** (⊠ W. Lathrop Ave., ☎ 912/238–7100) is par 35 for its 9 holes.

Health Clubs

The **Jewish Educational Alliance** has racquetball courts, a gymnasium, weight room, sauna, whirlpool, outdoor pool, and aerobic dance classes. Call ahead to arrange admission. ⊠ *5111 Abercorn St.,* ☎ *912/ 355–8111.* ⌨ *Guest fee $10.*

Savannah Downtown Athletic Club has an exercise room, free-weight equipment, sauna, swimming pool, aerobics, tanning beds, and tae kwon do classes. ⊠ *7 E. Congress St.,* ☎ *912/236–4874.* ⌨ *Guest fee $7 daily, $25 weekly, $50 monthly.*

YMCA Family Center has a gymnasium, aerobics, racquetball, and a pool. ⊠ *6400 Habersham St.,* ☎ *912/354–6223.* ⌨ *Guest fee $10.*

Jogging and Running

Low-lying coastal terrain is ideal for jogging. **Forsyth Park** (⊠ Bull St. between Whitaker and Drayton Sts.) is a flat, pleasant place to walk, jog, or run. **Tybee Island** (☞ *above*) has a white-sand beach that is hard packed and relatively debris free, making it a favorite with runners. For **suburban jogging trails,** head for **Daffin Park** (⊠ 1500 E. Victory Dr.), with level sidewalks available during daylight hours, and **Lake Mayer Park** (⊠ Montgomery Crossroads Rd. and Sallie Mood Dr.), with 1½ mi of level asphalt available 24 hours a day.

Tennis

Bacon Park (⊠ 6262 Skidaway Rd., ☎ 912/351–3850) has 16 lighted asphalt courts. Fees are $1.75 per hour during the day and $2.25 after dark. **Forsyth Park** (⊠ Drayton St. and Park Ave., ☎ 912/351–3850) contains four lighted courts available until about 10 PM for free. **Lake Mayer Park** (⊠ Montgomery Crossroads Rd. and Sallie Mood Dr., ☎ 912/652–6780) has eight asphalt lighted courts available at no charge and open 8 AM–10 PM (until 11 PM May–Sept.).

Shopping

Find your own Lowcountry treasures among a bevy of handcrafted wares—handmade quilts and baskets; wreaths made from Chinese tallow trees and Spanish moss; preserves, jams, and jellies. The favorite Savannah snack, and a popular gift item, is the benne wafer. It's about the size of a quarter and comes in a variety of flavors. As once-empty downtown storefronts begin to fill with new businesses, a period of stagnation gives way to revitalization. Antiques malls and junk emporiums are still part of the scenario—but that's Savannah.

Shopping Districts

City Market, on West Saint Julian Street between Ellis and Franklin squares, has sidewalk cafés, jazz haunts, shops, and art galleries. **Riverfront Plaza/River Street** is nine blocks of shops in the renovated waterfront warehouses, where you can find everything from popcorn to pottery.

Specialty Shops

ANTIQUES

Alexandra's Antique Gallery (⊠ 320 W. Broughton St., ☎ 912/233–3999) is a four-level extravaganza of items from kitsch to fine antiques. **Arthur Smith Antiques** (⊠ 1 W. Jones St., ☎ 912/236–9701) has four floors showcasing 18th- and 19th-century European furniture, porcelain, rugs, and paintings.

ART GALLERIES

Compass Prints, Inc./Ray Ellis Gallery (⊠ 205 W. Congress St., ☎ 912/234–3537) sells original artwork, prints, and books by internationally acclaimed artist Ray Ellis. **Gallery Espresso** (⊠ 6 E. Liberty St., ☎ 912/233–5348) has a new show every two weeks focusing on work by local artists. A true coffeehouse, it stays open until the wee hours. **Gallery 209** (⊠ 209 E. River St., ☎ 912/236–4583) is a co-op gallery, with paintings, watercolors, pottery, jewelry, batik, stained glass, weavings, and sculpture by local artists. **Off the Wall** (⊠ 412 Whitaker St., ☎ 912/233–8840) exhibits artists from everywhere but Savannah. **Southern Images** (⊠ 132 E. Oglethorpe Ave., ☎ 912/234–6449) displays the work of Jack Leigh, whose photograph of Bonaventure Cemetery graces the cover of *Midnight in the Garden of Good and Evil.*

Savannah College of Art and Design (⊠ 26 W. Harris St., ☎ 912/525–5200), a privately owned school, has restored at least 40 historic buildings in the city, including 12 galleries. Work by faculty and students is often for sale, and touring exhibitions are frequently in the on-campus galleries. Stop by Exhibit A, Pinnacle Gallery, and the West Bank Gallery, and ask about other student galleries. Garden for the Arts has an amphitheater and shows performance art.

BENNE WAFERS

Byrd Cookie Company (⊠ 6700 Waters Ave., ☎ 912/355–1716), founded in 1924, is the best place to get the popular cookies that are also sold in numerous gift shops around town.

BOOKS

For regional to general Southern subjects and Americana, visit the **Book Lady** (⊠ 17 W. York St., ☎ 912/233–3628), in a two-centuries-old house for more than two decades. The shop also has a search service. **E. Shaver Booksellers** (⊠ 326 Bull St., ☎ 912/234–7257) is the source for 17th- and 18th-century maps and new books on regional subjects; the shop covers 12 rooms. **V. & J. Duncan** (⊠ 12 E. Taylor St., ☎ 912/232–0338) specializes in antique maps, prints, and books.

COUNTRY CRAFTS

Charlotte's Corner (⊠ 1 W. Liberty St., ☎ 912/233–8061) carries expensive and moderately priced Savannah souvenirs, children's clothes and toys, and beach wear.

Savannah A to Z

Arriving and Departing

BY BUS

Greyhound/Trailways (⊠ 610 W. Oglethorpe Ave., ☎ 912/233–8186 or 800/231–2222).

BY CAR

I–95 slices north–south along the eastern seaboard, intersecting 10 mi west of town with east–west I–16, which dead-ends in downtown Savannah. U.S. 17, the Coastal Highway, also runs north–south through town. U.S. 80, which connects the Atlantic to the Pacific, is another east–west route through Savannah.

BY PLANE

Savannah International Airport (⊠ 400 Airways Ave., ☎ 912/964–0514), 18 mi west of downtown, is served by Delta, US Airways, AirTran, and Continental Express for domestic flights (☞ Air Travel *in* Smart Travel Tips A to Z for telephone numbers). Despite the name, international flights are nonexistent. The foreign trade zone, a locus for importing, constitutes the "international" aspect.

Vans operated by **McCall's Limousine Service** (☎ 912/966–5364 or 800/673–9365) leave the airport daily for downtown locations. The trip takes 15 minutes, and the one-way fare is $15 for one person, $25 round-trip for one person; two-person rate is $10 per person one-way. Routes can include other destinations in addition to downtown. Advance reservation is required.

Taxi fare from the airport to downtown is $18 for one person, $5 for each additional person.

By car, take I–95 south to I–16 east into downtown Savannah.

BY TRAIN

Amtrak has regular service along the eastern seaboard, with daily stops in Savannah. The Amtrak station (⊠ 2611 Seaboard Coastline Dr., ☎ 912/234–2611 or 800/872–7245) is 4 mi southwest of downtown. Cab fare into the city is $5–$10, depending on the number of passengers.

Getting Around

Despite its size, much of the downtown Historic District can easily be explored on foot. Its grid shape makes getting around a breeze, and you'll find any number of places to stop and rest.

BY BUS

Chatham Area Transit (CAT; ☎ 912/233–5767) operates buses in Savannah and Chatham County Monday through Saturday from 6 AM to 11 PM, Sunday from 7 to 7. Some lines may stop running earlier or may not run on Sunday. The CAT Shuttle operates throughout the Historic District; the cost is 75¢ one-way. Buses require 75¢ in exact change.

BY TAXI

Adam Cab Co. (☎ 912/927–7466) is a reliable, 24-hour taxi service. Calling ahead for reservations could yield a flat rate. Taxis start at 60¢ and cost $1.20 for each mile.

Contacts and Resources

BED-AND-BREAKFAST RESERVATIONS

Great Inns of Georgia (✉ 541 Londonberry Rd., Atlanta 30327, ☎ 404/843–0471 or 800/501–7328, FAX 404/252–8886) can help you choose one of Savannah's many inns.

EMERGENCIES

Ambulance, police (☎ 911).

GUIDED TOURS

Carriage Tours of Savannah (✉ Box 2402, 31402, ☎ 912/236–6756) takes you through the Historic District by day or by night at a 19th-century clip-clop pace, with coachmen spinning tales and telling ghost stories along the way. A romantic evening tour in a private carriage costs $65 ($85 on Friday and Saturday evenings), and although champagne can no longer be included, guests may bring whatever refreshment they wish; regular tours are a more modest $17 per person.

Gray Line (✉ 215 W. Boundary St., 31401, ☎ 912/234–8687 or 800/426–2318) conducts a four-hour tour to Isle of Hope and the Lowcountry, including Thunderbolt (a shrimping community) and Wormsloe Plantation Site. Options include walking tours, minibus tours, and trolley tours. The cost ranges from $16 to $24.

Historic Savannah Foundation (✉ 117 W. Perry St., 31401, ☎ 912/234–4088 or 800/627–5030), a preservation organization, leads tours of the Historic District and the Lowcountry. Preservation, *Midnight in the Garden of Good and Evil,* the Golden Isles, group, and private tours also are available. In addition, the foundation leads excursions to the fishing village of Thunderbolt; the Isle of Hope, with stately mansions lining Bluff Drive; the much-photographed Bonaventure Cemetery on the banks of the Wilmington River; and Wormsloe Plantation Site, with its mile-long avenue of arching oaks. The cost depends on the number of people on the tour and its length.

Old Town Trolley Tours (☎ 912/233–0083) has narrated 90-minute tours traversing the Historic District. Trolleys go by 13 designated stops every half hour daily 9–4:30; you can hop on and off as you please. The cost ranges from $16 to $20.

HOSPITALS

Candler Hospital (✉ 5353 Reynolds St., ☎ 912/692–6000) and **Memorial Medical Center** (✉ 4700 Waters Ave., ☎ 912/350–8000) are area hospitals with 24-hour emergency rooms.

Beach Institute African-American Cultural Center (☞ The Historic District, *above*) is headquarters for the Negro Heritage Trail Tour. A knowledgeable guide traces the city's more than 250 years of black history. Tours, which begin at the Savannah Visitors Center (☞ The Historic District, *above*), are at 1 and 3 and cost $15.

Garden Club of Savannah (✉ Box 13892, 31416, ☎ 912/238–0248) runs spring tours of private gardens tucked behind old brick walls and wrought-iron gates. It costs $20 and finishes with tea at the Green-Meldrim House (☞ The Historic District, *above*).

A Ghost Talk Ghost Walk Tour (✉ 127 E. Congress St., ☎ 912/233–3896) should send chills down your spine during an easy 1-mi jaunt through the old colonial city. Tours, lasting an hour and a half, leave from Reynolds Square (✉ Congress and Abercorn Sts.) at the John Wesley Memorial, in the middle of the square. Call for dates, times, and reservations; cost is $10.

Square Routes (✉ 60 E. Broad St., Suite 11, ☎ 912/232–6866 or 800/868–6867) provides customized strolls and private driving tours that wend through the Historic District and other parts of the Lowcountry. In-town tours focus on the city's architecture and gardens, and specialized tours include the *Midnight in the Garden of Good and Evil* Walk. Tours usually last two hours and cost from $20 to $30.

CVS Pharmacy (✉ Medical Arts Shopping Center, 4725 Waters Ave., ☎ 912/355–7111).

Savannah Area Convention & Visitors Bureau (✉ 222 W. Oglethorpe Ave., 31401, ☎ 912/644–6401 or 877/728–2662, FAX 912/944–0468) provides maps and brochures about Savannah.

THE COASTAL ISLES AND THE OKEFENOKEE

Jekyll, St. Simons, and Sea Islands

The coastal isles are a string of lush, subtropical barrier islands meandering lazily down Georgia's Atlantic coast from Savannah to the Florida border. The islands have a long history of human habitation; Native American relics have been found here that date from about 2500 BC. The four designated Golden Isles—Little St. Simons, Sea, St. Simons, and Jekyll islands—are great vacation spots. The best way to appreciate the barrier islands' rare ecology is to visit Sapelo and Cumberland islands or take a guided tour.

Each coastal isle has a distinct personality, shaped by its history and ecology. All the Golden Isles but Little St. Simons are connected to the mainland by bridges in the vicinity of Brunswick; these are the only coastal isles accessible by automobile. Little St. Simons Island, a privately owned retreat with guest accommodations, is reached by a launch from St. Simons. Sapelo Island is accessible by ferry from the visitor center just north of Darien. The Cumberland Island National Seashore is reached by ferry from St. Marys. About 50 mi inland is the Okefenokee National Wildlife Refuge, which has a character all its own.

Lodging prices quoted here may be much lower during nonpeak seasons, and specials are often available during the week in high season. All Georgia beaches are in the public domain.

Numbers in the margin correspond to points of interest on the Coastal Isles map.

Sapelo Island

⑨ *8 mi from Darien.*

In Sapelo's fields, you'll find chips of Guale Indian pottery dating as far back as 2000 BC and shards of Spanish ceramics from the 16th century. On the northern end, remains of the Chocolate Plantation reveal the island's French heritage and role during the plantation days of the 19th century. Today, researchers occupy the southern sector of the island, studying ecology at the Sapelo Island National Estuarine Research Reserve and evaluating the marshland at the Marine Institute. The organizations' studies are instrumental to the preservation of Sapelo's delicate ecosystem and others like it throughout the world.

You can explore many historical periods and natural environments here, but facilities on the island are limited, for the most part, to drinking fountains and rest rooms. Bring insect repellent, especially in summer, and leave your pets at home.

Start your visit at the **Sapelo Island Visitors Center** (⊠ Rte. 1, Box 1500, Darien 31305, ☎ 912/437–3224, 912/485–2300 group tours, 912/485–2299 camping reservations), where you'll see an exhibition on the island's history, culture, and ecology. Here you can purchase a ticket good for a round-trip ferry ride and bus tour of the island. The bus tour views different sights on different days of the week but always includes the marsh, the sand dune ecosystem, and the wildlife management area. On Saturday, the tour views the 80-ft **Sapelo Lighthouse,** built in 1820, a symbol of the cotton and lumber industry once based out of Darien's port. To see the island's **Reynolds Mansion,** schedule your tour for Wednesday. Reservations are required for tours. If you wish to stay overnight on Sapelo, you can either camp or choose from several bed-and-breakfast inns. If you stay overnight (and only if you do), you may visit the beach and the **Hog Hammock Community,** one of the few remaining sites where ethnic African-American culture has been preserved on the south Atlantic coast. Hog Hammock's 65 residents are descendants of slaves who worked the island's plantations during the 19th century. You can rent a bicycle to tour the area but may not bring one on the ferry.

Dining and Lodging

$–$$ ✕ **Mudcat Charlie's.** It's plastic forks and plates all the way at this casual eatery. Local seafood—crab stew, fried oysters, and shrimp—is the specialty. The steaks, burgers, and pork chops are good, too. Peach and apple pies are made on the premises. It's between Brunswick and Darien on U.S. 17. ⊠ *250 Ricefield Way,* ☎ *912/261–0055. AE, D, DC, MC, V.*

$ ☷ **Open Gates.** This comfortable white frame Victorian house dates from 1876. Fine antiques fill the public spaces and guest rooms. Breakfast specialties include fresh fig preserves, plantation pancakes (puffed pancakes), and Hunter's casserole (a baked egg strata). Innkeeper Carolyn Hodges guides guests on tours of the Altamaha River. ⊠ *Vernon Sq., Box 1526, Darien 31305,* ☎ *912/437–6985,* ℻ *912/882–9427. 4 rooms, 2 with bath. Pool. No credit cards. BP.*

Little St. Simons Island

⑩ *10–15 mins by ferry from the Hampton River Club Marina on St. Simons Island.*

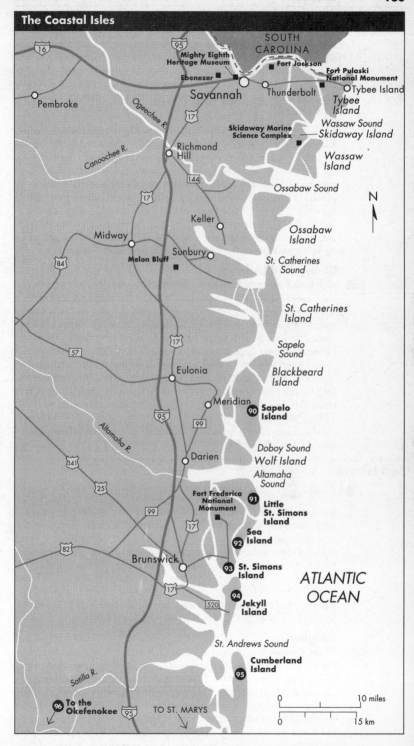

Six miles long, 2–3 mi wide, skirted by Atlantic beaches and salt marshes teeming with birds and wildlife, this privately owned resort is custom-made for Robinson Crusoe–style getaways. The island's only development is a rustic but comfortable guest compound. Guided tours, horseback rides, canoe trips, fly-fishing lessons, and other extras can be arranged, some for no additional charge. Inquire about children, as there are some limitations. In summer, day tours may be arranged.

The island's forests and marshes are inhabited by deer, armadillos, horses, raccoons, gators, otters, and more than 200 species of birds. Guests are free to walk the 6 mi of undisturbed beaches, swim in the mild surf, fish from the dock, and seine for shrimp and crabs in the marshes. There are also horses to ride, nature walks with experts, and other island explorations via boat or the back of a pickup truck. From June through September, up to 10 nonguests per day may visit the island by reservation; the $75 cost includes the ferry to the island, an island tour by truck, lunch at the lodge, and a beach walk. Contact the Lodge on Little St. Simons Island (☞ Lodging, *below*) for more information.

Dining and Lodging

$$$$ ✕☑ **Lodge on Little St. Simons Island.** The spacious, airy rooms are distributed among four buildings: the 1917 Hunting Lodge, with two antiques-filled guest rooms; a two-bedroom cottage; and two houses with four guest rooms each. In the houses, the four rooms each have private decks, and each house has a large living room with a fireplace. Houses also have large screened back porches, perfect for watching the sun set over the marshes. Meals are served family style in the main dining room and include platters heaped with fresh fish, homemade breads, and pies. Transportation from St. Simons Island, transportation on the island, and interpretive guides are included. ✉ *Box 21078, 31522,* ☎ *912/638–7472 or 888/733–5774,* 𝔽𝔸𝕏 *912/634–1811. 14 rooms, 1 suite. Pool, horseback riding, beach, boating, fishing, bicycles. AE, D, MC, V. FAP.* 🐾

Sea Island

92 *5 mi from St. Simons Island.*

Separated from St. Simons Island by a narrow waterway and a good many steps up the social ladder, Sea Island has been the domain of the well-heeled and the Cloister Hotel (☞ Lodging, *below*) since 1928. There is no entrance gate, and nonguests are free to admire the beautifully planted grounds and to drive past the mansions lining Sea Island Drive. The owners of the 180 or so private cottages and villas treat the hotel like a country club, and their tenants may use the hotel's facilities. For rentals, contact **Sea Island Cottage Rentals** (✉ Box 30351, 31561, ☎ 912/638–5112 or 800/732–4752, 𝔽𝔸𝕏 912/638–5824).

Lodging

$$$$ ☑ **The Cloister.** The Cloister still lives up to its celebrity status as a grand coastal resort. Guests lodge in spacious, comfortably appointed rooms and suites in the Spanish Mediterranean–style hotel, designed by Florida architect Addison Mizner. The hotel has its eccentricities; for example, gentlemen may not wear short-sleeved shirts in the dining rooms. Still, this classic coastal resort has kept up with the times. The spa is in a beautiful building of its own. Guests (and nonguests, space permitting) can play at the Sea Island Golf Course (on St. Simons). Other recreational options are skeet shooting, horseback riding, sailing, playing lawn games, and surf and deep-sea fishing. After dinner, you can dance to live music in the lounge. ✉ *Sea Island 31561,* ☎ *912/638–*

3611, 800/732–4752 reservations, FAX 912/638–5823. 254 rooms, 32 suites. 4 restaurants, 2 pools, spa, 54-hole golf course, 18 tennis courts, health club, bicycles, children's programs, concierge, business services, airport shuttle. AE, D, DC, MC, V. FAP. ✉

St. Simons Island

93 6 mi from Brunswick.

As large as Manhattan, with more than 14,000 year-round residents, St. Simons is the Golden Isles' most complete resort destination. Fortunately, accelerated development in recent years has failed to spoil the natural beauty of the island's regal live oaks, beaches, and salt marshes. Visits are highlighted by swimming and sunning, golfing, biking, hiking, fishing, horseback riding, touring historic sites, and feasting on fresh local seafood at more than 50 restaurants.

Many sights and activities are in the **village** area along Mallery Street at the more developed south end of the island, where there are shops, several restaurants, pubs, and a popular public pier. A quaint "trolley" takes visitors on a 1½-hour guided tour of the island, leaving from near the pier several times a day in high season, less frequently in winter; cost is $10.

☾ **Neptune Park** (✉ 550 Beachview Dr., ☎ 912/638–2393), on the island's south end, has picnic tables, a children's play park, miniature golf, and beach access. A swimming pool ($2 per person), with showers and rest rooms, is open each summer in the **Neptune Park Casino.**

St. Simons Lighthouse, a beacon since 1872, is virtually the symbol of St. Simons. The **Museum of Coastal History** in the lightkeeper's cottage has a permanent exhibit of coastal history. ✉ 101 12th St., ☎ 912/638–4666. ☜ $3, including lighthouse. ☉ Mon.–Sat. 10–5, Sun. 1:30–5.

At the burgeoning north end of the island there's a marina, a golf club, and a housing development, as well as **Fort Frederica National Monument,** the ruins of a fort built by English troops in the mid-1730s as a bulwark against a Spanish invasion from Florida. Around the fort are the foundations of homes and shops. Start at the **National Park Service Visitors Center,** which has a film and displays. ✉ Off Frederica Rd. just past Christ Episcopal Church, ☎ 912/638–3639. ☜ $4 per car. ☉ Daily 9–5.

Consecrated in 1886 following an earlier structure's desecration by Union troops, the white-frame Gothic-style **Christ Episcopal Church** is surrounded by live oaks, dogwoods, and azaleas. The interior has beautiful stained-glass windows. ✉ 6329 Frederica Rd., ☎ 912/638–8683. ☜ Donations welcome.

Dining and Lodging

$$ ✕ **The Redfern Café.** A popular spot with locals, the Redfern features 8–10 specials each night in addition to the regular menu. Fried oysters in a light cornmeal coating, shrimp and crab bisque with corn fritters, and the crab cakes are specialties. ✉ 200 Redfern Village, ☎ 912/634–1344. Reservations essential. MC, V. Closed Sun. No lunch.

$–$$ ✕ **Blanche's Courtyard.** In the village, this lively restaurant and nightclub has a "Bayou Victorian" style, with lots of antiques and memorabilia. The menu features seafood as well as basic steak and chicken dishes. Blue crab soup is a local favorite, and the huge seafood platter could easily feed two. Be sure to taste the popular apple fritters, known as "sweet puppies." ✉ 440 King's Way, ☎ 912/638–3030. AE, DC, MC, V. Closed Mon. No lunch.

$-$$ ✕ **Georgia Sea Grill.** This tiny and very popular place does a wide variety of fare, from such local dishes as the blue crab melt and key lime pie to pastas such as farfalle with spinach and feta cheese. ✉ *310B Mallory St., behind the kiosks,* ☎ *912/638–1197. MC, V. Closed Sun.–Mon. Oct.–Apr., Mon. June–Aug. No lunch.*

$$$ 🏨 **Sea Palms Golf and Tennis Resort.** Given the resort's emphasis on golf and tennis, it's an ideal location for the sports-minded visitor. It is a contemporary complex with fully furnished villas, most with kitchens, nestled on an 800-acre site. Guests also enjoy Beach Club privileges. ✉ *5445 Frederica Rd., 31522,* ☎ *912/638–3351 or 800/841–6268,* 🖷 *912/634–8029. 117 rooms, 37 suites. 2 restaurants, lounge, 2 pools, 27-hole golf course, 12 tennis courts, health club, volleyball, bicycles, children's programs, convention center. AE, DC, MC, V.* ✇

$$–$$$ 🏨 **King and Prince Beach and Golf Resort.** It's worth the trouble to get a room with easy beach access. Guest rooms are spacious, and villas have two or three bedrooms. The villas are owned by private individuals, so the total number available for rent varies from time to time. ✉ *201 Arnold Rd., Box 20798, 31522,* ☎ *912/638–3631 or 800/342–0212,* 🖷 *912/634–1720. 130 rooms, 10 suites, 43 villas. 2 restaurants, lounge, 1 indoor and 4 outdoor pools, hot tub, golf privileges, 4 tennis courts, bicycles, concierge. AE, D, MC, V.* ✇

$$ 🏨 **Holiday Inn Express.** With brightly decorated rooms at great prices, this nonsmoking facility is an excellent choice for the budget traveler. The six king executive rooms have sofas and desks. ✉ *Plantation Village, 299 Main St., 31522,* ☎ *912/634–2175 or 800/787–4666,* 🖷 *912/634–2174. 60 rooms. Pool, bicycles, coin laundry, meeting rooms. AE, D, MC, V. CP.*

RENTALS

For St. Simons condo and cottage rentals, contact **Golden Isles Realty** (✉ 330 Mallory St., 31522, ☎ 912/638–8623 or 800/337–3106, 🖷 912/638–6925) and **Trupp-Hodnett Enterprises** (✉ 520 Ocean Blvd., 31522, ☎ 912/638–5450 or 800/627–6850, 🖷 912/638–2983).

Jekyll Island

④ *90 mi from Savannah, 10 mi from Brunswick.*

For 56 winters, between 1886 and 1942, America's rich and famous faithfully came south to Jekyll Island. Through the Gilded Age, the Great War, the Roaring '20s, and the Great Depression, Vanderbilts and Rockefellers, Morgans and Astors, Macys, Pulitzers, and Goodyears shuttered their 5th Avenue castles and retreated to the serenity of this wild Georgia island. Here they built elegant "cottages," played golf and tennis, and socialized. Early in World War II, the millionaires departed for the last time. In 1947 the state of Georgia purchased the entire island for the bargain price of $675,000.

Jekyll Island is still a 7½-mi playground but no longer restricted to the rich and famous. The golf, tennis, fishing, biking, jogging, water park, and picnic grounds are open to all. One side of the island is lined by nearly 10 mi of hard-packed Atlantic beaches; the other, by the Intracoastal Waterway and picturesque salt marshes. Deer and wild turkeys inhabit interior forests of pine, magnolia, and moss-veiled live oaks. Egrets, pelicans, herons, and sandpipers skim the gentle surf. Jekyll's clean, mostly uncommercialized public beaches are free and open year-round. Bathhouses with rest rooms, changing areas, and showers are open at regular intervals along the beach. Beachwear, suntan lotion, rafts, snacks, and drinks are available at the **Jekyll Shopping Center,** facing the beach at Beachview Drive.

Jekyll Island Museum Visitor Center gives tram tours of the Jekyll Island National Historic Landmark District. Tours originate at the Museum Visitor Center on Stable Road and include several millionaires' residences in the 240-acre historic district. Faith Chapel, illuminated by Tiffany stained-glass windows, is open for meditation daily 2–4. ⊠ *I–95 to Exit 29, 375 Riverview Dr.,* ☎ *912/635–2119 group tours, 912/635–2762 daily tours, 800/841–6586,* ℻ *912/635–4004.* ⌨ *$10.* ☉ *Daily 9–5, tours daily 10–3.*

Dining and Lodging

$$-$$$ ✕ **Grand Dining Room.** In the Jekyll Island Club Hotel (☞ *below*), the
★ dining room sparkles with silver and crystal. The cuisine reflects the elegance of the private hunting club that flourished from the late 19th century to the World War II era and boasted a fine chef and staff brought in from New York's Delmonico's. Today, enjoy blue crab cakes, Georgia white shrimp, and other local fare. The restaurant has its own label pinot noir and chardonnay, made by Mountain View Vineyards. ⊠ *371 Riverview Dr.,* ☎ *912/635–2600. Reservations essential. Jacket required at dinner. AE, D, DC, MC, V.*

$$$-$$$$ 🏨 **The Beachview Club.** They literally raised the roof on an old motel
★ to build this luxury all-suites lodging in 1998. Stucco walls are painted light yellow, and big old oak trees shade the grounds. Efficiencies have either one king or two queen beds, a desk, and a kitchenette. More luxurious suites have full kitchens. ⊠ *721 N. Beachview Dr., 31527,* ☎ *912/635–2256 or 800/299–2228,* ℻ *912/635–3770. 26 efficiencies, 12 suites. Kitchenettes (some), pool, hot tub, meeting room. AE, D, DC, MC, V.*⌨

$$$ 🏨 **Jekyll Island Club Hotel.** Built in 1886, the four-story clubhouse with
★ wraparound verandas and Queen Anne–style towers and turrets once served as the winter hunting retreat for wealthy financiers. In 1985 a group of Georgia businessmen spent $17 million restoring it. The guest rooms and suites are custom-decorated with mahogany beds, armoires, and plush sofas and chairs. The nearby Sans Souci Apartments, built in 1896 by a group of club members, have been converted into spacious guest rooms. The hotel operates a free shuttle to area beaches. The bed-and-breakfast packages are a great deal. ⊠ *371 Riverview Dr., 31527,* ☎ *912/635–2600 or 800/535–9547,* ℻ *912/ 635–2818. 113 rooms, 21 suites. 2 restaurants, pool, 9 tennis courts, croquet, bicycles, meeting rooms. AE, D, DC, MC, V.*

$$-$$$ 🏨 **Holiday Inn Beach Resort.** Nestled amid natural dunes and oaks in a secluded oceanfront setting, this hotel has a private beach, but its rooms with balconies don't have an ocean view. The boardwalk out to the beach meanders through a lovely regional landscape, thick with palm trees and other native flora. ⊠ *200 S. Beachview Dr., 31527,* ☎ *912/635–3311 or 800/753–5955,* ℻ *912/635–2901. 200 rooms. Restaurant, lobby lounge, pool, 2 tennis courts, bicycles, playground. AE, D, DC, MC, V.*⌨

$$ 🏨 **Jekyll Inn.** Much of this popular oceanfront complex has been upgraded with modern conveniences like computer hookups in some rooms. The 15 acres of grounds space the buildings generously apart. Popular with families, the inn accommodates children under 17 free when they stay with parents or grandparents. Packages include summer family-focused arrangements and romantic getaways. The restaurant has an Italian theme. ⊠ *975 N. Beachview Dr., 31527,* ☎ *912/ 635–2531 or 800/431–5190,* ℻ *912/635–2332. 188 rooms, 76 villas. Restaurant, lobby lounge, in-room data ports, pool, volleyball, playground, coin laundry, meeting rooms. AE, D, DC, MC, V.*⌨

Jekyll's more than 200 rental cottages and condos are handled by **Jekyll Realty** (✉ Box 13096, 31527, ☎ 912/635–3301 or 888/333–5055, FAX 912/635–3303) and **Parker-Kaufman Realty** (✉ Box 13126, 31527, ☎ 912/635–2512 or 888/453–5955, FAX 912/635–2190).

Outdoor Activities and Sports

GOLF

The **Jekyll Island Golf Course** has 63 holes, including three 18-hole, par-72 courses with a main clubhouse (✉ 322 Capt. Wylly Rd., ☎ 912/635–2368) and a 9-hole, par-36 course known as the Historic Ocean-side Nine (✉ N. Beachview Dr., ☎ 912/635–2170), where the millionaires used to play. Greens fees are $26, good all day, and carts are $13.50 per person plus tax.

NATURE CENTER

The **Coastal Encounters Nature Center** runs summer programs for children and families on the ecology of the coastal islands. Programs and excursions are individually priced. At the center are exhibits about the fauna of the region. ✉ 100 S. Riverview Dr., ☎ 912/635–9102. 🎫 $2.

TENNIS

The **Jekyll Island Tennis Center** (✉ 400 Capt. Wylly Rd., ☎ 912/638–0221) has 13 clay courts, with 7 lighted for nighttime play; it hosts eight USTA-sanctioned tournaments throughout the year. Costs are $12 per hour daily 9–6 and $14 per hour for lighted courts; reservations for lighted courts are required and must be made prior to 6 PM on the day of reservation. Lighted courts are available until 10 PM.

WATER PARK

Summer Waves, an 11-acre water park, has an 18,000-square-ft wave pool, water slides, a children's activity pool with two slides, and a circular river for tubing and rafting. Guests are not permitted to bring their own equipment. ✉ 210 S. Riverview Dr., ☎ 912/635–2074. 🎫 $14.95. ☉ *Memorial Day–Labor Day, plus select weekends in May and Sept., Sun.–Fri. 10–6, Sat. 10–8 (hrs vary at beginning and end of season).*

Cumberland Island

95 *100 mi from Savannah to St. Marys via I–95, 45 mins by ferry from St. Marys.*

The largest, most southerly, and most accessible of Georgia's primitive coastal islands is Cumberland, a 16- by 3-mi sanctuary of marshes, dunes, beaches, forests, lakes and ponds, estuaries, and inlets. Waterways are home to gators, sea turtles, otters, snowy egrets, great blue herons, ibis, wood storks, and more than 300 other species of birds. In the forests are armadillos, wild horses, deer, raccoons, and an assortment of reptiles.

After the ancient Guale Indians came 16th-century Spanish missionaries, 18th-century English soldiers, and 19th-century planters. During the 1880s, the Thomas Carnegie family (he was the brother of industrialist Andrew) of Pittsburgh built several lavish homes here, but the island remained largely as nature created it. In the early 1970s, the federal government established the **Cumberland Island National Seashore** and opened this natural treasure to the public. There is no transportation on the island itself, and the only public access to the island is on the *Cumberland Queen*, a reservations-only, 146-passenger ferry based near the National Park Service Information Center at St. Marys. Ferry bookings are heavy in summer, but cancellations and no-shows often make last-minute space available. Reservations may be made up to 11 months in advance.

From the park-service docks at the island's south end, you can follow wooded nature trails, swim and sun on 18 mi of undeveloped beaches, go fishing and bird-watching, and view the ruins of Andrew Carnegie's great estate, **Dungeness.** You can also join history and nature walks led by park-service rangers. Bear in mind that summers are hot and humid and that you must bring everything you need, including your own food, soft drinks, sunscreen, and a reliable insect repellent. All trash must be transported back to the mainland. ⊠ *Cumberland Island National Seashore, Box 806, 31558,* ☎ *912/882–4335,* ⅨX *912/ 673–7747.* 🖃 *Round-trip ferry $10.17, day pass $4, annual pass $20.* ☉ *Mid-May–Sept., ferry departure from St. Marys daily at 9 AM and 11:45 AM, from Cumberland at 10:15 AM and 4:45 PM. No ferry service Oct.–May 14, Tues.–Wed.*

Dining and Lodging

ISLAND

$$$$ ✕🖿 **Greyfield Inn.** Cumberland Island's only accommodations are in a turn-of-the-20th-century Carnegie family home. Greyfield's public areas are filled with family mementos, furnishings, and portraits (you may feel as though you've stepped into one of Agatha Christie's mysterious Cornwall manors). Prices include all meals, transportation, tours led by a naturalist, and bike rentals. ⊠ *8 N. 2nd St., Box 900, Fernandina Beach, FL 32035,* ☎ *904/261–6408,* ⅨX *904/321–0666. 13 rooms, 4 suites. AE, D, MC, V. FAP.* ✎

$ ⚠ **Camping.** The island has three primitive camping sites in a National Wilderness Area. Reservations are required for all camping at these sites, and the rate is $2 per person per day. To reach the sites (Hickory Hill, Yankee Paradise, and Brickhill Bluff), start north of Sea Camp dock, and then hike (with all equipment) from 4 to 10 mi. Equipment must include rope to suspend provisions from trees for critter control. Non-wilderness Stafford Beach is good for novice backpackers. A half mi from the dock, with rest rooms and showers adjacent to campsites, Sea Camp is the ideal spot for first-time campers ($4 per person per day). A maximum of 16 campsites for 60 persons is available. Reservations are required (recommended at least two months in advance); no pets or fires are allowed; and a seven-day stay is the limit. Bring all required equipment. The beach is just beyond the dunes. To make a reservation, contact the Cumberland Island National Seashore (☞ *above*).

MAINLAND

$–$$ ✕ **Greek Mediterranean Grill.** It's a block from the St. Marys River, but the sky-blue murals and Greek proprietors make it seem more like the Mediterranean than the South. Traditional Greek dishes, such as *pastitso* (pasta and ground beef baked with cinnamon and white cream sauce) and moussaka, are the mainstay. ⊠ *122 Osborne St., St. Marys 31558,* ☎ *912/576–2000. No credit cards.*

$$–$$$ 🖿 **Spencer House Inn.** This comfortable Victorian inn dates from 1872 and is named for the sea captain who built it as a hotel. Innkeepers Mike and Mary Neff reside here and will prepare picnic lunches if you ask. The inn makes a perfect base for a tour of historic St. Marys and the waterfront and is convenient to the *Cumberland Queen* ferry. ⊠ *200 Osborne St., St. Marys 31558,* ☎ *912/882–1872,* ⅨX *912/882– 9427. 13 rooms, 1 suite. AE, D, MC, V. BP.* ✎

Okefenokee National Wildlife Refuge

40 mi from Brunswick, 38 mi from St. Marys.

Covering 730 square mi of southeast Georgia and spilling over into northeast Florida, the **Okefenokee,** with its mysterious rivers and lakes, bristles with seen and unseen life. Scientists agree that the Okefenokee, the largest intact freshwater wetlands in the contiguous United States, is not duplicated anywhere else on earth. The impenetrable Pinhook Swamp to the south, part of the same ecosystem, adds another 100 square mi. If the term *swamp* denotes a dark, dank place, the Okefenokee is never that. Instead, it is a vast peat bog with numerous and varied landscapes, including aquatic prairies, towering virgin cypress, sandy pine islands, and lush subtropical hammocks. During the last Ice Age 10,000 years ago, it was part of the ocean flow. Peat began building up 7,000 years ago atop a mound of clay, now 120 ft above sea level. Two rivers, the St. Marys and the Suwanee, flow out of the refuge, and it provides at least a part-time habitat for myriad species of birds, mammals, reptiles, amphibians, and fish.

As you travel by canoe or speedboat among the water lilies and the great stands of live oaks and cypress, be on the lookout for, among many others, alligators, otters, bobcats, raccoons, opossums, white-tailed deer, turtles, bald eagles, red-tailed hawks, egrets, muskrats, herons, cranes, and red-cockaded woodpeckers. The black bears tend to be more reclusive.

The Seminole people, in their migrations south toward Florida's Everglades, once took refuge in the Okefenokee. The last Native Americans to occupy the area, they were evicted by the army and Georgia's militia in the 1830s. When the Okefenokee acquired its present status of federal preserve (1937), the white homesteaders on its fringe were forced out.

Noting the many floating islands, the Seminole named this unique combination of land and water "Land of the Quivering Earth." If you have the rare fortune to walk one of these bogs, you will find the earth does indeed quiver, rather like fruit gelatin in a bowl.

The Okefenokee Swamp Park (☞ *below*), 8 mi south of Waycross, is a nonprofit development. The northern entrance to the refuge is here. There are two other gateways to the swamp: an eastern entrance at U.S. Fish & Wildlife Service Headquarters in the Suwanee Canal Recreation Area (☞ *below*), near Folkston; and a western entrance at Stephen C. Foster State Park (☞ *below*), outside the town of Fargo. You may take an overnight canoeing-camping trip into the interior, but the Okefenokee is a wildlife refuge and designated national wilderness, not a park. Access is restricted by permit. The best way to see the Okefenokee up close is to take a day trip at one of the three gateways. Plan your visit between September and April to avoid the biting insects that emerge in May, especially in the dense interior.

South of Waycross, via U.S. 1, **Okefenokee Swamp Park** has orientation programs, exhibits, a 1⅓-mi nature trail, observation areas, wilderness walkways, an outdoor museum of pioneer life, and boat tours into the swamp that reveal its unique ecology. A boardwalk and 90-ft tower are excellent places to glimpse cruising gators and a variety of birds. You may arrange for guided boat tours at an additional cost. A 1½-mi train tour passes by a Seminole village and stops at Pioneer Island, a re-created pioneer homestead, for a 30-minute walking tour. ⊠ *5700 Swamp Park Rd., Waycross 31501,* ☎ *912/283–0583,* ℻ *912/283– 0023.* 🎫 *$10, additional costs for tour packages.* ☉ *Daily 9–5:30.* 🐾

Stephen C. Foster State Park, 18 mi from Fargo via Route 177, is an 80-acre island park within the Okefenokee National Wildlife Refuge. The park encompasses a large cypress and black gum forest, a majestic backdrop for one of the thickest growths of vegetation in the southeastern United States. Park naturalists leading boat tours will spill out a wealth of Okefenokee lore while you observe alligators, birds, and native trees and plants. You may also take a self-guided excursion in rental canoes and a motorized, flat-bottom boat. Campsites and cabins are available (☞ Lodging, *below*). ✉ *Rte. 1, Box 131, Fargo 31631,* ☎ *912/637–5274.* ☒ *$5 per vehicle to National Wildlife Refuge.*

Suwanee Canal Recreation Area, 8 mi south of Folkston via GA 121/ 23, is administered by the U.S. Fish and Wildlife Service. Stop first at the visitor center, with exhibits on the Okefenokee's flora and fauna. A boardwalk takes you over the water to a 50-ft observation tower. The concession has equipment rentals and daily food service; you may sign up here for one- or two-hour guided boat tours. Hikers, bicyclists, and private motor vehicles are welcome on the Swamp Island Drive; several interpretive walking trails may be taken along the way. Picnicking is allowed. Wilderness canoeing and camping in the Okefenokee's interior are by reserved fee permit only. Permits are hard to get, especially in cool weather. Call refuge headquarters (☎ 912/496–3331) when it opens at 7 AM *exactly* two months in advance of the desired starting date. Guided overnight canoe trips can be arranged by refuge concessionaire Carl E. Glenn Jr. ✉ *Rte. 2, Box 3325, Folkston 31537,* ☎ *912/496–7156. Refuge headquarters:* ✉ *Rte. 2, Box 3330, Folkston 31537,* ☎ *912/496–7836.* ☒ *$5 per car; 1-hr tours $10.50; 2-hr tours $19.* ☉ *Refuge Mar.–Sept. 10, daily 6:30 AM–7:30 PM; Sept. 11–Feb., daily 8–6.*

Lodging

$$–$$$ 🏨 **The Inn at Folkston.** This craftsman-style inn has a huge front veranda and four working gas-log fireplaces. The inn is just 7 mi from the refuge, and guest rooms are individually decorated. The Garden Room has a king-size bed and whirlpool tub. ✉ *509 W. Main St., Folkston 31537,* ☎ *912/496–6256 or 888/509–6246. 4 rooms. AE, MC, V. BP.* ✍

$ 🏕 **Laura S. Walker State Park.** Named for a Waycross teacher who championed conservation, the park, 9 mi from Okefenokee Swamp Park, has campsites with electrical and water hookups. Be sure to pick up food and supplies on the way to the park. Boating and skiing are permitted on the 120-acre lake, and there's an 18-hole championship golf course, with all amenities. The cost is $20; carts are $10. ✉ *5500 Laura Walker Rd., Waycross 31503,* ☎ *912/287–4900 or 800/864–7275. Picnic areas, pool, fishing, playground.*

$ 🏕 **Stephen C. Foster State Park.** The park has two-room furnished cottages, each capable of sleeping eight, and campsites with water, electricity, rest rooms, and showers. Because of roaming wildlife and poachers and because of the park's location inside the refuge, the gates close between sunset and sunrise. If you're staying overnight, stop for groceries before you get here. ✉ *Fargo 31631,* ☎ *912/637–5274 or 800/864–7275.*

The Coastal Isles and the Okefenokee A to Z

Arriving, Departing, and Getting Around

`BY CAR`

From Brunswick, take the Jekyll Island Causeway ($2 per car) to Jekyll Island, and the Torras Causeway to St. Simons and Sea Island. You can get by without a car on Jekyll Island and Sea Island, but you'll need one on St. Simons. You cannot bring a car to Cumberland Island or Little St. Simons. To reach the Sapelo Island Visitors Center, take U.S. 17 north to Darien. At the courthouse, turn right onto GA 99 and take it for 8 mi. Then, make a right on Landing Road and follow the signs for the Sapelo Island National Estuarine Research Reserve.

BY FERRY

Cumberland Island and Little St. Simons are accessible only by ferry or private launch (☞ *above*). You can also get to Sapelo Island by ferry (☞ *above*).

BY PLANE

The coastal isles are served by Glynco Jetport, 6 mi north of Brunswick, which is served in turn by Delta affiliate **Atlantic Southeast Airlines** (ASA; ☎ 800/282–3424), with flights from Atlanta.

Visitor Information

The **Brunswick and the Golden Isles Visitors Center** (✉ 2000 Glynn Ave., Brunswick 31520, ☎ 912/264–5337 or 800/933–2627) provides helpful information on all of the Golden Isles. Georgia has centralized park reservations (Reservation Resource) for the state's **Department of Natural Resources** parks. For reservations, call ☎ 800/864–7275. In metropolitan Atlanta, the reservation number is ☎ 770/398–7275. For general park information, call ☎ 404/656–3530.

ATHENS TO AUGUSTA

If it's traces of the old South you crave, you'll want to take in Georgia's Antebellum Trail, a former stagecoach route that is now a highway, U.S. 441. It is dotted with small towns, like Madison, Eatonton, and Milledgeville, saturated in historic architecture: you'll find an abundance of white-columned mansions, shaded verandas, and magnolia gardens reminiscent of pre–Civil War days. Try to plan a visit in April or October, when these towns host community tours of their homes and gardens.

We begin in Athens—with its historic homes, thriving music and entertainment scene, and the University of Georgia—following the Antebellum Trail south to Macon. A visit to Washington and Augusta necessitates a side trip east along U.S. 78 and I–20, but both are well worth the detour, as they are steeped in history and tradition.

Athens

90 mi from Atlanta via I–85 north to GA 316.

Athens, the artistic jewel of the American South, is known as a breeding ground for such famed rock groups as the B-52's and R.E.M. Because of this distinction, creative types from all over the country flock to its trendy streets in hopes of becoming, or catching a glimpse of, the next big act to take the world by storm. At the center of this artistic melee is the University of Georgia (UGA). With more than 28,000 students, UGA lends its influential ingredient into the Athens mix, giving the quaint but compact city a distinct flavor that falls somewhere between a misty Southern enclave, a rollicking college town, and a smoky, jazz-club studded alleyway. It truly is a fascinating blend of Mayberry R.F.D. and MTV. The effect is as irresistible as it is authentic.

While the streets bustle at night with students taking in the coffee-house and concert life, Athens's quieter side also flourishes. The streets are lined with many gorgeous old homes, some of which are open to the public. Most prominent among them is the **Athens Welcome Center** (⊠ 280 E. Dougherty St., ☎ 706/353–1820) in the town's oldest surviving residence, the 1820 Church-Waddel-Brumby House. Athens also has several splendid Greek Revival buildings, including, on campus, the University Chapel, built in 1832, and the **university president's house** (⊠ 570 Prince Ave.), built in the late 1850s. The **Taylor-Grady House** (⊠ 634 Prince Ave.) was constructed in 1844. The 1844 **Franklin House** (⊠ 480 E. Broad St.) has been restored and reopened as an office building.

Just outside the Athens city limits is the **State Botanical Gardens of Georgia,** a tranquil, 313-acre wonderland of aromatic gardens and woodland paths. It has a massive conservatory overlooking the International Garden that functions as a welcome foyer and houses an art gallery, gift shop, and café. ⊠ 2450 S. Milledge Ave., off U.S. 129/441, ☎ 706/542–1244. ⌸ Free. ☉ Grounds: Apr.–Sept. weekdays 8–8, Oct.–Mar. weekdays 8–6; visitor center: Tues.–Sat. 9–4:30, Sun. 11:30–4:30.

Dining and Lodging

$–$$ ✕ **East West Bistro.** This popular bistro, one of the busiest spots in downtown Athens, has a bar, formal upstairs dining, and casual dining downstairs. The most interesting selections downstairs are the small plates that allow you to sample cuisines from around the world—from vegetable tempura to salmon bruschetta. The quieter upstairs dining room serves a more expensive classic Italian menu. ⊠ 351 E. Broad St., ☎ 706/546–4240. AE, D, MC, V.

$–$$ ✕ **Harry Bissett's.** One of the best restaurants in Athens, it serves sumptuous Cajun recipes straight from the streets of New Orleans. Wait for your table at the oyster bar, where they charge you by the shell. ⊠ 279 E. Broad St., ☎ 706/353–7065. AE, D, MC, V. No lunch Mon.

$ ✕ **Last Resort Grill.** It's a pleasant place to unwind with its cheery sidewalk café section. The cuisine is a cross between Tex-Mex and California, with items such as salmon and black bean quesadillas, roasted eggplant sandwiches, and grilled shiitake mushrooms and feta cheese tossed with pasta. ⊠ 174 W. Clayton St., ☎ 706/549–0810. AE, D, MC, V.

$ ✕ **Weaver D's Fine Foods.** This place not only serves some of the best soul food in Athens-Clarke County, it's also a piece of musical history; R.E.M. was so inspired by Weaver D's service motto, "Automatic for the People," that the band named its 1992 album after it. ⊠ 247 E. Washington St., ☎ 706/353–7797. No credit cards.

$$–$$$ ⊞ **Magnolia Terrace.** This bed-and-breakfast is housed in a 1912 mansion right in the middle of the historic district. Each room is decorated with a mishmash of antiques. It's within walking distance of the Grit, a popular vegetarian restaurant founded by one of Athens's musical prodigies, Michael Stipe of R.E.M., who himself lives close by in a house marked by big, opulent gates. ⊠ 288 Hill St., 30601, ☎ 706/548–3860, FAX 706/369–3439. 8 rooms, 1 suite. AE, D, MC, V. BP. ✎

$$ ⊞ **Nicholson House.** This 19th-century house, set on 6 acres of an 18th-century land grant originally deeded to William Few, one of Georgia's two signers of the U.S. Constitution, is, at its core, a two-over-two log house. Later additions and changes hide this original structure beneath a 1947 Colonial Revival exterior. The inn has a wide front veranda with rocking chairs. Rooms are decorated in rich colors, and furnishings are a mix of antiques and good reproductions. ⊠ 6295 Jefferson Rd., 30607, ☎ 706/353–2200, FAX 706/353–7799. 6 rooms, 3 suites. AE, D, MC, V. BP. ✎

$ ⊞ **Best Western Colonial Inn.** Just ½ mi from the UGA campus, it's a favorite among visiting relatives in town to attend graduation. Some rooms come with a microwave and refrigerator, and all rooms are equipped with a coffeemaker. Directly across the street is the Varsity Drive-In, where hungry students have been feasting on smothered hot dogs and heaps of fries for years. ⊠ *170 N. Milledge Ave., 30607,* ☎ *706/546–7311 or 800/528–1234,* FAX *706/546–7959. 69 rooms. Refrigerators (some), pool. AE, D, DC, MC, V.* ✆

Nightlife and the Arts

THE ARTS

The **Classic Center** (⊠ 300 N. Thomas St., ☎ 706/357–4444) features a splendid array of plays and other theatrical performances. The ultramod **Georgia Theater** (⊠ 215 N. Lumpkin St., ☎ 706/549–9918) doubles as a movie house and concert hall, showcasing edgy cinema and booking local bands. **UGA's Performing Arts Center** (⊠ South Campus on River Rd., ☎ 706/542–4400) routinely has world-class music recitals—by the Atlanta Symphony orchestra, for example—and modern dance shows.

NIGHTLIFE

For some boisterous rock-a-billy tunes, check out **Bumpers** (⊠ 1720 Commerce Dr., ☎ 706/369–7625). **40 Watt Club** (⊠ 285 W. Washington St., ☎ 706/549–7871) is the launching pad of numerous rock groups, such as R.E.M., that later went on to superstar status. Famed greats such as Bessie Smith and Cab Calloway regularly performed at **Morton Theatre** (⊠ 195 W. Washington St., ☎ 706/613–3770), listed on the National Register of Historic Places; it is now a performing arts center with musicals, concerts, and modern dance.

Madison

30 mi south of Athens via U.S. 129/441, 60 mi east of Atlanta via I–20 to U.S. 129/441.

Directly south of Athens is this small treasure filled with plenty of restaurants and irresistible antiques shops and gift boutiques. The town is a virtual odyssey of well-preserved examples of antebellum and Victorian architecture, a treat since so few buildings in Atlanta escaped the torches of the Union troops. Madison's homes are well preserved largely because of a curious stroke of luck: when Major General William Tecumseh Sherman (1820–91) burned a path through Georgia during the Civil War, he left Madison intact because of his friendship with U.S. Senator Joshua Hill, a Madison resident and Union sympathizer. That's how Madison earned the moniker "The Town that Sherman refused to burn." Hill's former home (not open to the public) is now one of Madison's most cherished mansions.

The **Madison-Morgan Cultural Center,** housed in an early 20th-century schoolhouse built in Romanesque Revival style, has tools and furniture from the late 19th century and a restored classroom of the period, plus information and printed guides on the Joshua Hill house and other historic sites in town. ⊠ *434 S. Main St.,* ☎ *706/342–4743.* ☞ *$3.* ☉ *Tues.–Sat. 10–5.*

At **Heritage Hall** (⊠ 277 S. Main St., ☎ 706/342–9627), you can take a guided tour of a preserved 1833 Greek Revival home and learn about aspects of antebellum high-brow society life.

The **welcome center** (⊠ 115 E. Jefferson St., ☎ 706/342–4454) provides maps for walking tours of historic neighborhoods and three house museums as well as information regarding annual events and celebrations.

Dining and Lodging

$ ✕ **Ye Olde Colonial Restaurant.** Housed in a renovated bank building (complete with seating accommodations in the former vault), this cafeteria-style restaurant is a must for hungry patrons passing through Madison. The buffet is a complete cornucopia of Southern faves: butterbeans, country-fried steak, sweet-potato casserole, fried chicken, corn bread, cobbler and, of course, iced tea. ⊠ *108 W. Washington St.,* ☎ *706/ 342–2211. AE, D, MC, V. Closed Sun.*

$ ✕ **Yesterday Cafe.** The brick walls of this former pharmacy are lined with archival black-and-white photographs. Drawing patrons from Atlanta to Eatonton and Athens, Teri Bragg has developed a following for her traditional but updated Southern fare: country fried steak with mashed red-skin potatoes, fresh vegetables, and buttermilk pie from an old recipe. The full Southern breakfast, served Tuesday through Sunday, is outstanding. It is 8 mi west of Madison. ⊠ *120 Fairplay St., Rutledge,* ☎ *706/557–9337. AE, MC, V. No dinner Sun.–Wed.*

$$ 🏨 **Burnett Place.** This charming bed-and-breakfast, right in the heart of town, is housed in a gorgeous Federal-style home built in the early 1800s. The guest rooms are spacious and inviting, and the proprietors are friendly and knowledgeable about the history of the region. ⊠ *317 Old Post Rd., 30650,* ☎ *706/342–4034. 3 rooms. MC, V. BP.* 🐾

$$ 🏨 **The Farmhouse Inn.** It is on a farm that has been in Melinda Hartney's family for generations. Guests have private entrances to their rooms, which are off a common area where they enjoy breakfast and late-afternoon gatherings. Over the barn is an apartment suite. The inn is 6 mi east of Madison. ⊠ *1051 Meadow La., Madison, 30650,* ☎ *706/ 342–7933. 5 rooms, 1 suite. AE, MC, V. BP.*

Eatonton

26 mi south of Madison on U.S. 129/441.

It's not your imagination—that really is a giant rabbit on the Eatonton courthouse lawn. This small town is the birthplace of celebrated novelist Joel Chandler Harris of Br'er Rabbit and Uncle Remus fame.

☾ The **Uncle Remus Museum,** built from authentic slave cabins, houses countless carvings, paintings, and other artwork depicting the characters made famous by the imaginative author. It's on the grounds of a park. ⊠ *Turner Park, U.S. 441,* ☎ *706/485–6856.* 🎟 *50¢.* ☉ *June– Aug., Mon.–Sat. 10–noon, Sun. 1–5; Sept.–May, Wed.–Mon. 10–noon, Sun. 1–5.*

The **Eatonton-Putnam Chamber of Commerce** (⊠ 105 Sumter St., ☎ 706/485–7701) provides printed maps detailing landmarks from the upbringing of Eatonton native Alice Walker, who won the Pulitzer Prize for her novel *The Color Purple*. It also has information on the many fine examples of antebellum architecture in Eatonton, including descriptions and photographs of the town's prize antebellum mansions, and a walking tour of homes.

Lodging

$$ 🏨 **Crockett House.** With its aromatic gardens, majestic wraparound porch, and in-room fireplaces, this bed-and-breakfast nestled in a restored 1895 Victorian home is perfect for a romantic getaway. Make sure to get a room with an old-fashioned, claw-foot bathtub. All rooms have working fireplaces. ⊠ *671 Madison Rd., 31024,* ☎ *706/485–2248. 6 rooms. AE, MC, V. BP.* 🐾

Milledgeville

17 mi south of Eatonton on U.S. 441.

Locals believe ghosts haunt what remains of the antebellum homes in Milledgeville. Formerly the state capital of Georgia (a title held for 64 years), the town was not as fortunate as Madison in terms of torch exposure. Sherman's troops stormed through with a vengeance after the general heard hardship stories from Union soldiers who had escaped from a prisoner-of-war camp in nearby Andersonville. The 1838 Greek Revival **Old Governor's Mansion** became Sherman's headquarters during the war. His soldiers are said to have tossed government documents out of the windows and fueled their fires with Confederate money. Guided tours of the building, now a museum home, are given daily. ⊠ *120 S. Clark St.*, ☎ *912/453–4545.* ⊡ *$5.* ⊙ *Tues.–Sat. 10–4, Sun. 2–4.*

On West Hancock Street is the Georgia College and State University campus. One of its most famous students was prolific Southern novelist Flannery O'Connor, author of such acclaimed novels as *Wise Blood* and *The Violent Bear It Away*. O'Connor did most of her writing at the family farm, Andalusia, just north of Milledgeville on U.S. 441. The **Flannery O'Connor Room**, inside the **Ina Russell Library**, has many of the author's hand-written manuscripts on display. It also contains O'Connor's typewriter and some of her furniture. ⊠ *231 West Hancock St.*, ☎ *912/445–4047.* ⊡ *Free.* ⊙ *Weekdays 9–4.*

Dining and Lodging

$ ✕ **The Brick.** This bar-restaurant has a comfortable, worn-at-the-elbows appeal, and comfort is important when you're about to consume massive pizzas with epicurean toppings like feta cheese and spinach. The menu also has salads and calzones. ⊠ *136 W. Hancock St.*, ☎ *912/452–0089. AE, D, MC, V. Closed Sun.*

$–$$ ⊡ **Antebellum Inn.** Each room of this pre–Civil War mansion is beautifully appointed with period antiques. Fabulous full Southern breakfasts are included in the rate. ⊠ *200 N. Columbia St., 31061*, ☎ *912/453–3993. 5 rooms. Pool. AE, MC, V. BP.* ⊛

Macon

30 mi southwest of Milledgeville via U.S. 441 to GA 49, 90 mi southeast of Atlanta via I–75.

At the state's geographic center, Macon, founded in 1823, has more than 100,000 flowering cherry trees, which it celebrates each March with a knockout festival. Its antebellum and Victorian homes are among the state's best preserved. Famous artists who have called Macon home include flutist and pre–Civil War poet laureate of the United States Sidney Lanier, violinist Robert McDuffie, Little Richard, the Allman Brothers, and Otis Redding.

To enjoy Macon at night, get a copy of the brochure *Lights on Macon* from the **Macon Convention and Visitors Bureau** (⊠ 200 Cherry St., ☎ 912/743–3401 or 800/768–3401) in the old train station.

★   Among the city's many sites to see is the **Georgia Music Hall of Fame**, appropriately located in Macon as a tribute to the city's extensive contribution to American music. The museum is a joint effort of state and private resources and is dedicated to Georgians who have helped define America's musical culture. Among the honorees are Ray Charles, James Brown, the Allman Brothers Band, Chet Atkins, R.E.M., and the B-52's. Exhibits pay homage to classical musicians including Robert Shaw, the late director emeritus of the Atlanta Symphony Orchestra;

opera singers Jessye Norman and James Melton; and violinist Robert McDuffie. ✉ *200 Martin Luther King Jr. Blvd.,* ☎ *912/750–8555.* ✉ *$8.* ☉ *Mon.–Sat. 9–4:30, Sun. 1–4:30.*

☾ The **Georgia Sports Hall of Fame,** with its old-style ticket booths, has the look and feel of an old ballpark. Exhibits honor sports at all levels, from prep and college teams to professional. ✉ *301 Cherry St.,* ☎ *912/752–1585.* ✉ *$6.* ☉ *Mon.–Sat. 9–5, Sun. 1–5.*

★ The unique **Hay House,** designed by the New York firm T. Thomas & Son, is a virtual study in fine Italianate architecture prior to the Civil War. The marvelous stained-glass windows and many technological advances, including indoor plumbing, make a tour worthwhile. ✉ *934 Georgia Ave.,* ☎ *912/742–8155.* ✉ *$6.* ☉ *Mon.–Sat. 10–4:30, Sun. 1–4:30.* ✍

African-American entrepreneur Charles H. Douglass built the **Douglass Theatre** in 1921. Great American musicians have performed here, among them Bessie Smith, Ma Rainey, Cab Calloway, Duke Ellington, and locals Little Richard and Otis Redding. It is currently a venue for movies, plays, and other performances. You can take a guided tour of the building. ✉ *355 Martin Luther King Jr. Blvd.,* ☎ *912/742–2000.* ✉ *$2.* ☉ *Tues.–Sat. 9–5.*

☾ The **Macon Museum of Arts and Sciences and Mark Smith Planetarium** displays everything from a whale skeleton to fine art. Discovery House, an interactive exhibit for children, is modeled after an artist's garret. ✉ *4182 Forsyth Rd.,* ☎ *912/477–3232.* ✉ *$5.* ☉ *Mon.–Thurs. and Sat. 9–5, Fri. 9–9, Sun. 1–5.*

Just 3 mi east of the city limits, the **Ocmulgee National Monument,** a significant archaeological site, was occupied for more than 10,000 years and was at its peak under the Mississippian peoples who lived here between AD 900 and 1100. There are a reconstructed earth lodge and displays of pottery, effigies, and jewelry of copper and shells discovered in the burial mound. ✉ *U.S. 80 east of Macon, 1207 Emery Hwy.,* ☎ *912/752–8257,* FAX *912/752–8259.* ✉ *Free.* ☉ *Daily 9–5.*

The **Tubman African American Museum** honors the former slave who led more than 300 people to freedom as one of the conductors on the Underground Railroad. A mural depicts several centuries of black history and culture. The museum also has an African artifacts gallery. ✉ *340 Walnut St.,* ☎ *912/743–8544.* ✉ *$3.* ☉ *Weekdays 9–5, Sat. 10–5, Sun. 2–5.*

OFF THE BEATEN PATH	**MUSEUM OF AVIATION** – This museum at Robins Air Force Base has an extraordinary collection of 90 vintage aircraft including a MIG, an SR-71 (Blackbird), a U-2, and assorted other flying machines from past campaigns. From Macon, take I–75 south to Exit 146 (Centerville/Warner Robins), and turn left onto Watson Boulevard, 7 mi to GA 247, then right for 2 mi. ✉ *GA 247 at Russell Pkwy., Warner Robins, 20 mi south of Macon,* ☎ *912/926–6870.* ✉ *Free; film $2.* ☉ *Daily 9–5.*

Dining and Lodging

$ ✕ **The Cherry Corner.** This taste of Italy is the perfect spot for lunch, a quick snack of pizza or soup, or coffee and a pastry. Dine at one of the sidewalk tables for a view of Macon's 19th-century buildings and blooming flowers. ✉ *502 Cherry St.,* ☎ *912/741–9525.* MC, V. *Closed Sun. No dinner Mon.–Thurs.*

$$$ ✕🏨 **Henderson Village.** Stunning 19th- and early 20th-century farm
★   buildings, some original to the site, are clustered around a green. Guest
rooms are rustic, but suites are more elegant, with fireplaces and whirl-
pool tubs. Buttermilk-yellow walls give the fine 1838 Langston House
restaurant a warm atmosphere, perfect for a meal of squab and foie
gras on a potato haystack or wild game on buckwheat polenta. Perry
is 30 mi south of Macon, 1 mi off I–75. ✉ *125 S. Langston Circle,
Perry 31069,* ☎ *912/988–8696 or 888/615–9722,* FAX *912/988–9009.
19 rooms, 5 suites. Restaurant, pool, in-room VCRs, hot tubs, con-
vention center. AE, MC, V. BP.* ✲

$$$–$$$$ 🏨 **1842 Inn.** With its grand, white-pillared front porch and period an-
tiques, this inn offers a taste of antebellum Macon. You can eat break-
fast in your room, in one of the parlors, or in the courtyard. It's an
easy walk to downtown and the historic district. ✉ *353 College St.,*
☎ *912/741–1842 or 800/336–1842,* FAX *912/741–1842. 21 rooms. In-
room data ports, hot tubs. AE, MC, V. BP.* ✲

Washington

38 mi east of Athens via U.S. 78, 100 mi east of Atlanta via I–20 to
Exit 154.

Washington, the first city chartered in honor of the country's first
president, is a living museum of Southern culture. Brick buildings, some
of which date back to the American Revolution, line the lively down-
town area, which bustles with shops, cafés, and antiques shops. Peo-
ple live and work downtown, giving Washington a little-city appeal
that separates it from most other small Southern towns. The Confed-
erate treasury was moved here from Richmond in 1865, and soon af-
terward the half-million dollars in gold vanished. This mysterious
event has been the inspiration for many a treasure hunt, since many
like to believe the gold is still buried somewhere in Wilkes County.

The **Washington-Wilkes Chamber of Commerce** (✉ 104 E. Liberty St.,
☎ 706/678–2013) is a good starting point for exploring the town. It
has information about antebellum life and architecture. The **Washington
Historical Museum** (✉ 308 E. Robert Toombs Ave., ☎ 706/678–2105)
houses a collection of Civil War relics, including the camp chest of Jef-
ferson Davis. The **Robert Toombs House** (216 E. Robert Toombs Ave.,
☎ 706/678–2226) is furnished with 19th-century antiques, some of
which are the personal items of former U.S. Senator Robert Toombs,
who served as secretary of state during the Civil War.

Be sure to stop by historic **Callaway Plantation.** Here you can experi-
ence the closest thing to an operating plantation, dating back to 1785.
Among a cluster of buildings on the estate you'll find a blacksmith's
house, school house, and weaving house. An ancient family cemetery
is also fun to explore. During the second week of April and October
the estate comes alive with Civil-War reenactments and activities such
as butter-churning and quilting demonstrations. ✉ *U.S. 78,* ☎ *706/
678–7060.* 💲 *$4.* 🕐 *Tues.–Sat. 10–5, Sun. 2–5.*

Dining and Lodging

$ ✕ **Another Thyme Cafe.** This café on the square in downtown Wash-
ington makes excellent salads and sandwiches. Try the grilled vegetables
on focaccia. Dinner goes upscale but stays regional with fried green toma-
toes, sweet-potato chips, and fried seafood. Homemade breads and
desserts (pecan pie) are worth the trip. ✉ *5 East Public Sq.,* ☎ *706/678–
1672. AE, D, MC, V. Closed Sun. No dinner Mon., Oct.–Mar.*

$$ ⊡ **Maynard's Manor.** This Classical Revival structure, originally built in 1820, was transformed into a B&B in 1998. Fireplaces in the main house warm the public spaces. Guests can gather in the library and parlor for conversation and light refreshments. The day begins with coffee, tea, and juice in the main hall at 7 AM, followed by a full breakfast in the morning rooms. ⊠ *219 E. Robert Toombs Ave., 30673,* ☎ *706/ 678–4303. 6 rooms, 1 guesthouse suite. MC, V. BP.* ✎

Augusta

60 mi east of Washington via U.S. 78 to I–20, 151 mi east of Atlanta via I–20.

Although Augusta escaped the ravages of Union troops during the Civil War, nature herself was not so kind. Situated on a river crossing along the Savannah River, the town was flooded many times before modern-day city planning redirected the water into a collection of small lakes and creeks. Now the current is so mild that citizens gather to send bathtub toys downstream every year in the annual Rubber Duck Race.

Augusta is Georgia's third-oldest city, founded in 1736 by James Edward Oglethorpe, who founded Savannah in 1733. The city was named for Augusta, Princess of Wales, wife of the future Frederick Louis, Prince of Wales. Augusta served as Georgia's capital from 1785 to 1795. The well-maintained paths of **Riverwalk** (⊠ between 5th and 10th Sts.) curve along the Savannah River and are the perfect place for a leisurely stroll. **Olde Town,** lying along Telfair and Greene streets, is a restored neighborhood of Victorian homes. The 1845 tree-lined **Augusta Canal** is another pleasant place for a walk.

Many antebellum and Victorian homes of interest are spread throughout the city. The **Ezekiel Harris House** dates from the late 18th century and is notable for its exterior staircase, a space-saving feature, and its gambrel roof. ⊠ *1840 Broad St.,* ☎ *706/737–2820.* ☞ *$2.* ☉ *Sat. 10– 1 or by appointment.*

Meadow Garden was the home of George Walton, one of Georgia's three signers of the Declaration of Independence and its youngest signer, at age 26. It is documented as Augusta's oldest extant residence. ⊠ *1320 Independence Dr.,* ☎ *706/724–4174.* ☞ *$3.* ☉ *Weekdays 10–4.*

The **Morris Museum of Southern Art** has a splendid collection of Southern art, from early landscapes and portraits through neo-Impressionism and native and modern art. ⊠ *Riverfront Center, 1 10th St., 2nd floor,* ☎ *706/724–7501.* ☞ *$3.* ☉ *Tues.–Sat. 10–5:30, Sun. noon–5:30.*

☾ Children love the National Science Center's **Fort Discovery,** an interactive museum with a moonwalk simulator, a bike on square wheels, a hot-air balloon, and a little car propelled by magnets. ⊠ *1 7th St.,* ☎ *706/821–0200 or 800/325–5445.* ☞ *$8.* ☉ *Mon.–Sat. 10–5, Sun. noon–5.*

Dining and Lodging

$$–$$$$ ✕ **La Maison on Telfair.** Augusta's best entry in the fine dining category, from owner and chef Heinz Sowinski, presents a classic menu of game, sweetbreads, and, with a nod to the chef's heritage, Wiener schnitzel. The experience is enhanced by the quiet and elegant atmosphere. ⊠ *404 Telfair St.,* ☎ *706/722–4805. AE, D, DC, MC, V. No lunch.*

$$–$$$ ⊡ **The Partridge Inn.** A National Trust Historic hotel, the restored inn sits at the gateway to Summerville, a hilltop neighborhood of summer homes dating to 1800. There's a splendid view of downtown Augusta from the rooftop concierge floor. Rooms are simple and sparsely decorated. Suites and some studios have full kitchens. ⊠ *2110 Walton Way,*

30904, ☎ 706/737–8888 or 800/476–6888, ⅋ⅹ 706/731–0826. *129 rooms, 27 suites. Restaurant, bar, lounge, pool, exercise room. AE, D, DC, MC, V. BP.* ✑

Athens to Augusta A to Z

Arriving and Departing

BY BUS

Greyhound Bus Lines (✉ 220 W. Broad St., Washington, ☎ 706/678–4479 or 800/231–2222) serves the entire area.

BY CAR

U.S. 441, known as the Antebellum Trail, runs north–south, merging with U.S. 129 for a stretch and connecting Athens, Madison, Eatonton, and Milledgeville. Macon is on GA 49, which splits off of U.S. 441 at Milledgeville. The total distance from Athens to Macon is approximately 98 mi. Washington lies at the intersection of U.S. 78, running east from Athens to Thomson, and GA 44, running south to Eatonton. I–20 runs east from Atlanta to Augusta, which is about 93 mi east of U.S. 441.

BY PLANE

Athens-Clarke Airport (✉ 1501 Aviation Way, ☎ 706/613–3420) is served by US Airways for domestic flights. **Augusta Ben Epps Airport** (✉ 1010 Ben Epps Ave., ☎ 706/798–3236) is served by both Delta and US Airways for domestic flights. (For airline telephone numbers, *see* Air Travel *in* Smart Travel Tips A to Z.)

Getting Around

BY BUS

Athens Transit (☎ 706/613–3430) operates buses throughout Athens-Clarke County from 6 AM to 6:45 PM Monday through Saturday, with no service on Sunday. The fare is $1 with free transfers; exact change is required.

The **Augusta Public Transit** (☎ 706/821–1719) runs bus service throughout Augusta-Richmond County from 6:30 AM to 8:30 PM Monday though Saturday, with no bus service on Sunday. The fare is 75¢, with an additional 35¢ for a transfer; exact change is required.

The **Macon Transit Authority** (☎ 912/746–1318) provides public transportation throughout the city from 5:30 AM to 6:45 PM Monday through Saturday, with no bus service on Sunday. The fare is 75¢; transfers cost 25¢.

BY TAXI

Augusta Cab Company (☎ 706/724–3543) provides transportation throughout Augusta-Richmond County. There is a $1.75 initial charge, plus $1.50 per mile. The fare from the airport to downtown Augusta, a distance of approximately 11 mi, is around $18.

Your Cab Company (☎ 706/546–5844) is a reliable, 24-hour taxi service in Athens. Calling ahead for reservations could yield a flat rate. Rates are determined by a grid of designated zones throughout the area, starting at $3. A trip from the airport to downtown costs $6.

Contacts and Resources

BED-AND-BREAKFAST RESERVATIONS

Great Inns of Georgia (✉ 541 Londonberry Rd., Atlanta 30327, ☎ 404/843–0471 or 800/501–7328, ⅋ⅹ 404/252–8886) can help you choose one of this area's many inns.

EMERGENCIES

Ambulance, police (☎ 911). **Doctors Hospital** (✉ 3651 Wheeler Rd., Augusta, ☎ 706/651–3232). **Macon Northside Hospital** (✉ 400 Charter Blvd., Macon, ☎ 912/757–8200). **Medical Center** (✉ 1199 Prince Ave., Athens, ☎ 706/549–9977).

GUIDED TOURS

Augusta Cotton Exchange (✉ 32 8th St., ☎ 706/724–4067) conducts free tours of its historic brick building, with exhibits from its past as an arbiter of cotton prices. It also has Saturday van tours throughout the historic district of Augusta with a fee of $10 per person.

Classic City Tours (✉ 280 E. Dougherty Way, ☎ 706/353–1820) conducts daily tours starting from the steps of the Athens Welcome Center (☞ Visitor Information, *below*) at 2 PM. The 1½-hour tour takes participants through the city's antebellum neighborhoods. The fee is $10 per person ($8 per person for groups of 10 or more).

24-HOUR PHARMACY

CVS (✉ 1520 Walton Way, Augusta, ☎ 706/724–0598; 1271 Gray Hwy., Macon, ☎ 912/743–6979 or 912/743–8936).

VISITOR INFORMATION

Athens Convention and Visitors Bureau (✉ 300 N. Thomas St., 30601, ☎ 706/357–4430 or 800/653–0603, FAX 706/549–5636). **Eatonton-Putnam Chamber of Commerce** (✉ 105 Sumter St., Eatonton 31024, ☎ 706/485–7701). **Macon Convention and Visitors Bureau** (✉ 200 Cherry St., 31201, ☎ 912/743–3401 or 800/768–3401). **Madison/Morgan County Chamber of Commerce** (✉ 115 E. Jefferson St., Madison 30605, ☎ 706/342–4454). **Milledgeville Convention and Visitors Bureau** (✉ 200 W. Hancock St., 31061, ☎ 912/452–4687). **Washington-Wilkes Chamber of Commerce** (✉ 104 E. Liberty St., Box 661, Washington 30673, ☎ 706/678–2013).

Georgia Welcome Center (✉ Box 211090, Martinez 30917, ☎ 706/737–1446) provides maps and brochures about prominent historical and recreational sites around the state.

NORTH GEORGIA

As an antidote to the congestion of city life, nothing beats the clear skies, cascading waterfalls, and tranquil town squares to be found in north Georgia. Within a half-day's drive from Atlanta, you'll find yourself in the middle of a refreshing cluster of old Southern towns and nature sites that pepper the northern region of the state, comprising the heart of Appalachia.

Dahlonega, Cleveland, Helen, Clayton, and Ellijay, directly to the north and northeast of Atlanta, abound in shops selling such Southern finds as handmade quilts, folk-art pottery, antiques, and loads of Grandma's chowchow in gingham-capped mason jars. They also offer a range of unusual experiences, from descending into a gold mine to exploring a re-created Alpine village to picking apples. To the northwest are two of Georgia's most important historic sites: New Echota State Historic Site and Chickamauga and Chattanooga National Military Park. And whether your preference is rustic or romantic, there are plenty of bed-and-breakfast inns and campgrounds to accommodate your sensibilities.

Dahlonega

60 mi north of Atlanta on GA 400/U.S. 19.

Hoards of fortune-seekers stormed the town of Dahlonega (named after the Cherokee word for "precious yellow metal") in the early 1800s in response to the discovery of gold in the hills nearby, but by 1849 miners were seeking riches elsewhere. In fact, the famous call, "There's gold in them thar hills!" originated as an enticement to miners in the Georgia mountains to keep their minds away from the lure of the gold rush in the West. It worked for a while, but government price fixing eventually made gold mining unprofitable, and by the early 1920s Dahlonega's mining operations had halted completely.

After that most mining villages would have become ghost towns, but not Dahlonega. Today it thrives as a rustic country outpost with an irresistible town square rife with country stores, art galleries, coffee houses, gem shops, old small-town businesses, and even a sophisticated restaurant or two. The gold mines are still there but are open mainly for show. **Consolidated Gold Mine** is open to the public for guided tours. You enter the mine, which has been reconstructed for safety, go through a breathtaking stone passage, and then begin a descent down 120 ft into the mine's depths to gaze at the geological wonders all around. Tour guides expound on historical mining techniques and tools, such as the "widowmaker," a drill that kicks up mining dust and caused disease among many of the miners. Before you leave you are invited to pan for gold prospector-style from a long wooden sluice. ⊠ *185 Consolidated Rd.,* ☎ *706/864–8473.* ⛶ *$10.* ☉ *Daily 10–4.*

A U.S. mint operated in this modest boomtown from 1838 to 1861. The **Gold Museum,** in the present-day courthouse on the square, has coins, tools, and a 5½-ounce nugget. The building is the oldest in north Georgia, and if you look closely at the bricks that form the building's foundation you'll notice a sprinkling of gold dust in their formation. Along with the exhibits, the museum shows a short film celebrating the region's history through interviews with Appalachian old-timers. ⊠ *Public Sq.,* ☎ *706/864–2257.* ⛶ *$2.50.* ☉ *Daily 10–5.*

OFF THE BEATEN PATH	**AMICALOLA FALLS –** Rushing waters will tumble your troubles away here in no time. This is the highest waterfall east of the Mississippi, with waters plunging an eye-popping 729 ft through a cluster of seven cascades. The surrounding state park is dotted with scenic campsites and cottages strategically situated near a network of nature trails, picnic sites, and fishing streams. ⊠ *Off GA 52, 18 mi west of Dahlonega,* ☎ *706/265–4703.* ⛶ *Parking $2.* ☉ *Daily 7–10.*

Dining and Lodging

$$ ✗ **Renée's Café & Wine Bar.** This fine, casual restaurant in a 19th-century restored residence is within walking distance of the village square. The contemporary cuisine has regional and Mediterranean accents, such as crawfish tails with spinach tortellini and Gorgonzola Alfredo sauce. Upstairs, patient patrons wait for their tables in a warmly lit bar or attend one of the monthly wine tastings hosted at the restaurant. ⊠ *136 N. Chestatee St.,* ☎ *706/864–6829. Reservations not accepted. MC, V. Closed Sun.–Mon. No lunch.*

$ ✗ **Smith House.** One of the most popular dining destinations in the north Georgia mountains, it has all-you-can-eat family-style meals that'll have the tables groaning under the weight of the heaping plates. Potatoes, fried chicken, peas, cobbler—you name a Southern dish and it's probably offered here. ⊠ *84 S. Chestatee St.,* ☎ *706/864–2348. Reservations not accepted. AE, D, MC, V. Closed Mon.*

$$ ⊡ **Worley Homestead.** This pristine bed-and-breakfast is housed in an 1845 mansion with two garden courtyards. Rates include a full country breakfast, and often on weekend evenings the proprietors arrange a wine table with cheese and crackers in the entry foyer. Each beautifully furnished room comes with a small TV. ⊠ *410 W. Main St., 30533,* ☎ *706/864–7002. 7 rooms. MC, V. BP.* ⊛

$–$$ ⊡ **Blueberry Inn & Gardens.** The inn, which crowns the crest of a low hill, takes its name from the wild blueberries growing on its 55 acres. Porch rocking chairs welcome guests at the end of a busy day of touring. Gracious hosts Phyllis and Harry Charnley have built a structure reminiscent of a 1920s farmhouse. Rooms are decorated with antiques and family pieces. On the grounds are mountain laurel, oaks, and dogwoods, along with flowering plants of all kinds. ⊠ *400 Blueberry Hill, 30533,* ☎ *706/219–4024 or 877/219–4024,* ℻ *706/219–4793. 12 rooms. MC, V. BP.* ⊛

Outdoor Activities and Sports
Appalachian Outfitters (⊠ Box 793, Dahlonega 30533, ☎ 800/426–7177) provide equipment and maps for self-guided canoeing and kayaking expeditions on the Chestatee River. River trails begin at their outpost in town and extend to GA 400.

Shopping
Golden Memories Antiques (⊠ 121 S. Public Sq., ☎ 706/864–7222) has an impressive array of local rocks and minerals as well as Coca-Cola collectibles for sale. **Pottery Plus** (⊠ 1127-B Hwy. 52E, ☎ 706/864–8362) has Southern folk art and traditional folk-art pottery; many pieces are one-of-a-kind. **Quigley's Antiques and Books** (⊠ 170-B North Public Sq., ☎ 706/864–0161) sells old and rare books, Blue Ridge china, vintage trunks, and old toys.

Cleveland

19 mi northeast of Dahlonega via U.S. 19 to U.S. 129, 60 mi northeast of Atlanta via I–985 and U.S. 129.

Cleveland's tiny town square has a number of antiques shops with some dusty steals. In the center of the square, look for the **Old White County Courthouse,** which was constructed by slaves in the mid-1800s and resembles Philadelphia's Independence Hall. ⊠ *1 Cleveland Sq.,* ☎ *706/865–3225.* ▦ *Free.* ☉ *Thurs.–Sat. 10–6.*

☾ By far Cleveland's biggest claim to fame is **Babyland General Hospital,** best known for starting the pandemoniac craze for Cabbage Patch Kids in the late 1970s; it was here that the dolls were first produced. The makeshift "hospital" is actually housed in a former clinic, and the dolls are displayed in a fake cabbage field. ⊠ *19 Underwood St.,* ☎ *706/865–5164.* ▦ *Free.* ☉ *Mon.–Sat. 9–6, Sun. 1–6.*

Shopping
Mary T's Auction and Antique (⊠ 233 Friendship Rd., ☎ 706/865–0575) has antique furniture, china and crystal, as well as Waverly fabrics and Sedgefield lamps. **Mount Yonah Gifts** (⊠ 3745 Helen Hwy., ☎ 706/865–5003) abounds in colorful curios such as pottery, birdhouses, ornamental concrete statuaries, and fountains. **Rocks Relics and Beads** (⊠ 5419 Hwy. 129N, ☎ 706/865–5003) sells minerals and rocks from local mines and from all over the world. It also has one of the best selections of antique and ornamental beads in the state.

Helen

13 mi north of Cleveland on GA 75, 85 mi northeast of Atlanta via I–985 and U.S. 129 to GA 75.

When Helen was founded at the turn of the 20th century, it was a simple little lumber outpost. By the 1960s it was in danger of turning into a ghost town because of a logging bust. Local business leaders came up with a plan to save the town: they transformed the tiny village of 300 into a virtual theme town, and "Alpine Helen" was born. Today all the businesses along Helen's central streets sport a distinctive German (as well as Swiss, Belgian, Danish, Dutch, and Scandinavian) facade, giving visitors the impression that they've stumbled upon a Bavarian vista in the middle of Appalachia. Everywhere you look are beer halls, steepled roofs, flowering window boxes, and billboards written in Renaissance script. As phony as it all is, the effect is contagious and makes you feel as if you've walked into a fairy tale.

The entrance to the village is particularly picturesque, with a narrow bridge traversing a pretty section of the Chattahoochee River. Along Main Street are a multitude of patio cafés lushly shaded by trees. A network of cobblestone walkways and plazas span a thicket of bakeries and little shops selling Bavarian-theme souvenirs. Costumed shop workers add to the charade. Housed in a faux castle that can't be missed is the **Museum of the Hills,** with an exhibit of "artifacts" that tell the tale of Helen's transformation. ⊠ *Main St.,* ☎ *706/878–3140.* ☞ *$5.* ☉ *Daily 10 AM–10 PM.*

OFF THE
BEATEN PATH

BRASSTOWN BALD – This is the highest mountain in Georgia, at 4,784 ft. In the heart of the Chattahoochee National Forest, it has a dramatic vantage from which you can view four different states (Tennessee, North Carolina, South Carolina, and Georgia). And sight is not the only sense that gets an aesthetic pick-me-up at Brasstown Bald: bushels of wildflowers in the spring and autumn give a boost to the nose as well. ⊠ *Off GA 180, 15 mi west of Helen,* ☎ *706/896–2556.* ☞ *Parking $3.* ☉ *Daily 9:30–5:30.*

Dining and Lodging

$ ✕ **Hofbrauhaus Inn.** This beer hall has the same name as Hitler's favorite hangout in Munich, but thankfully the patrons are decidedly more friendly here. The menu is saturated with hearty German fare, such as schnitzel, *bratkartoffeln* (fried potatoes), and wurst. ⊠ *Main St.,* ☎ *706/878–2248. AE, D, DC, MC, V.*

$$$ ☒ **Brasstown Valley Resort.** This resort has lodge-style accommodations, plus a full line of sports activities: tennis, golf, hiking trails, and a fitness center. The rooms are comfortable and spacious with an elegant but rustic decor, and some come with fireplaces and balconies overlooking the breathtaking valley. It's 32 mi west of Helen. ⊠ *6321 U.S. 76, Young Harris 30582,* ☎ *800/201–3205,* FAX *706/379–4615. Restaurant, bar. 129 rooms, 5 suites. AE, D, DC, MC, V. BP.* ☜

$$–$$$ ☒ **Fieldstone Inn.** Many of the beautifully appointed rooms, decorated with cherry-wood furniture, have a gorgeous view of Lake Chatuge. A nearby marina has a full array of boat rentals, including pontoons, paddle boats, sailboats, and kayaks. Sizable discounts are available in the winter months. It's 25 mi north of Helen. ⊠ *3499 U.S. 76, Hiawassi 30546,* ☎ *800/545–3408,* FAX *706/896–4128. 66 rooms. Restaurant, pool, tennis court. AE, D, DC, MC, V. BP.* ☜

Shopping

Gift World of Helen (⊠ 8614 Main St., ☎ 706/878–2504) sells a variety of candles, ceramics, knives, and T-shirts among other items. **Jolly's Toys** (⊠ 8800 Main St., ☎ 706/878–2262) is a wonderland of wooden American and European toys. **Kaiser Bill's II** (⊠ 8635 Main St., ☎ 706/878–2057) is the place to go for collectible beer steins. It also sells figurines.

Clayton

27 mi northeast of Helen on U.S. 23/441, 100 mi northeast of Atlanta via I–85 and I–985 to U.S. 23.

An unassuming mountain town, Clayton is near spectacular Tallulah Gorge, the deepest canyon in the United States after the Grand Canyon, and was a popular early 20th-century destination for Atlantans. The state of Georgia recently acquired the gorge for a state park and has created walking and mountain biking trails. Clayton is rich in art galleries, flea markets, and antiques shops; the **Main Street Gallery** (⊠ 641 Main St., ☎ 706/782–2440, FAX 706/782–2815), one of the state's best sources for folk art, features works by regional artists such as Sarah Rakes, O. L. Samuels, Jay Schuette, and Rudy Bostick. The nearby **Dillard House** (☞ *below*) is famous for its reasonably priced country food served family style. Be forewarned: as much as a two-hour wait can make getting in a bit of a chore.

Dining and Lodging

$$–$$$$ ✕⌂ **Glen-Ella Springs Country Inn.** This restored old hotel draws from
★ far and wide with its rustic charm, restful setting, and fine food emphasizing regional specialties, such as trout pecan, pickled shrimp, and Lowcountry shrimp on grits. Rooms have no TVs but plenty of reading material, and the splendid grounds invite hiking and exploring. The restaurant ($–$$$) does not serve alcohol, but you may bring your own (corkage $2.50). It is 15 mi south of Clayton. ⊠ *1789 Bear Gap Rd., Rte. 3 Box 3304, Clarkesville 30523,* ☎ *706/754–7295 or 877/456–7527,* FAX *706/754–1560. 14 rooms, 2 suites. Restaurant, pool, conference center. AE, MC, V. BP.* ✿

$–$$$ ✕⌂ **Dillard House.** Consisting of an inviting cluster of cottages and
★ motel-style rooms, this establishment sits on a plateau in the Little Tennessee River valley. Some rooms and the glass-walled Dillard House Restaurant ($) have vistas of the Blue Ridge Mountains. The restaurant serves all-you-can-eat, family-style platters overflowing with Southern favorites such as country ham, fried chicken, barbecue, corn on the cob, acorn squash, lima beans, and cabbage casserole. Breakfast is a gut buster: fresh muffins, piping hot biscuits, fresh eggs, and cottage fried potatoes are just the beginning. It is 7 mi north of Clayton. ⊠ *768 Franklin St., Box 10, Dillard 30537,* ☎ *706/746–5348 or 800/541–0671,* FAX *706/746–3680. 51 rooms, 6 suites. Restaurant, kitchenettes (some), hot tubs. AE, D, DC, MC, V.* ✿

Ellijay

73 mi west of Clayton via U.S. 76 to GA 5/515, 80 mi north of Atlanta via I–75, I–575, and GA 5/515 to GA 52.

Billed as "Georgia's Apple Capital," Ellijay is popular with antiques aficionados as well. The town, founded by Cherokee Indians, is home to a colorful cluster of crafts shops, antiques markets, and art galleries.

The most popular time to visit Ellijay is in the fall, when roadside stands brimming with delicious ripe apples dot the landscape. The annual **Georgia Apple Festival** takes place here in mid-October. In addition to showcasing the many manifestations of the crisp fruit—apple butter, apple pie, apple cider, and so on—the festival offers a host of arts and crafts shows. For more information, contact the **Gilmer County Chamber of Commerce** (☎ 706/635–7400).

During the apple festival, you can tour rows upon rows of ripening apple trees at **Hillcrest Orchards** (⊠ 9696 Hwy. 52E, ☎ 706/273–3838). Pick your own apples and then feast on homemade jellies, jams, breads, and doughnuts. Also on the orchard's premises are a petting zoo and picnic area.

Lodging

$$–$$$ 🏨 **Whitepath Lodge.** Set amid the tranquil scenery of the north Georgia mountains, this lodge has panoramic vistas from every room. The main lodge has seven suites, each with two bedrooms, three baths, and a fully-equipped kitchen. The Shenandoah Lodge has six two-floor suites that come with a fireplace and multilevel decks overlooking the woods. ⊠ 987 Shenandoah Dr., 30540, ☎ 706/276–7199 or 888/271–7199. 13 suites. AE, D, DC, MC, V. 🕸

Outdoor Activities and Sports

There are plenty of fishing, canoeing, and kayaking opportunities on the Cartecay River, which runs through town. **Mountaintown Expeditions** (⊠ GA Hwy. 52E, ☎ 706/273–3838) arranges outdoor adventures for people of all skill levels.

Shopping

Antiques & More (⊠ 6 River St., ☎ 706/365–7738) is a colorful collective of 45 dealers who sell everything from antique dolls and furniture to stained-glass windows and English china. **Crafts in the Cohuttas Pottery** (⊠ 1444 Zion Hill Rd., ☎ 706/636–2233) sells works by husband-and-wife team William Boerner and Ann Hofstadter; they host the Cohuttas Arts Studio Tour every fourth weekend in October.

New Echota State Historic Site

60 mi northwest of Atlanta via I–75 north to GA 225, 25 mi west of Ellijay.

From 1825 to 1838, New Echota was the capital of the Cherokee Nation, whose constitution was patterned after that of the United States. There was a council house, a printing office, a Supreme Court building, and the *Cherokee Phoenix,* a newspaper that utilized the Cherokee alphabet developed by Sequoyah. Some buildings have been reconstructed. ⊠ GA 225, 1 mi east of I–75N, near Calhoun, ☎ 706/624–1321. 🎟 $3. ☉ Tues.–Sat. 9–5, Sun. 2–5:30.

Just a few miles north of New Echota, the beautifully restored two-story brick **Chief Vann House,** with its intricately carved interior, was commissioned in 1805 by a leader of the Cherokee Nation, who hired Moravian artisans to construct it. Of mixed Scottish and Cherokee parentage, Chief James Vann owned numerous slaves who worked on the construction of the house. ⊠ GA 52A west of Chatsworth, 82 Hwy. 225N, Chatsworth, ☎ 706/695–2598. 🎟 $3. ☉ Tues.–Sat. 9–5, Sun. 2–5:30.

Dining and Lodging

$–$$ ✕ **La Scala.** Piero Barba from Capri, Italy, established this outpost of Italian cooking in 1996. The menu is dominated by classic dishes such as osso buco, braciola, and seafood and pasta. The wine list, which Barba claims is the largest in north Georgia, includes French, American, and Italian wines. The lunch buffet is a bargain. ⊠ 413 Broad St., Rome, ☎ 706/238–9000. AE, D, DC, MC, V. Closed Sun. No lunch Sat.

$$ 🏨 **Claremont House.** Jeff and Linda Williams's beautifully restored 1890s Victorian inn has huge rooms furnished with period antiques. Breakfast is sumptuous, with stuffed French toast and the like. Claremont House is about 30 minutes south of New Echota State Historic Site and the Chief Vann House. ⊠ 906 E. 2nd Ave., Rome 30161, ☎ 706/291–0900 or 800/254–4797, FAX 706/802–0551. 5 rooms, 1 suite. AE, D, MC, V. BP. 🕸

Chickamauga and Chattanooga National Military Park

93 mi northwest of Atlanta via I–75 to Hwy. 2 west to Fort Oglethorpe, 33 mi north of New Echota State Historic Site.

This site, established in 1890 as the nation's first military park, was the scene of one of the Civil War's bloodiest battles (30,000 casualties), which ended in the Union Capture of Chattanooga. The normally thick cedar groves and foliage covering Chickamauga were supposedly so trampled that the area resembled an open field, and so shot up were the trees that a sweet cedar smell mingled with the blood of fallen soldiers. The trees grew back in abundance, though, and today the park hosts battle-scene reenactments for spectators.

Monuments, battlements, and weapons adorn the road that traverses the 8,000-acre park, with markers explaining the action. An excellent visitor center has reproduction memorabilia, books, and a film on the battle. The center also provides trail maps and guides through the more than 80 mi of hiking trails. ⊠ *U.S. 27 off I–75, 12 mi south of Chattanooga,* ☎ *706/866–9241.* ⊡ *Free.* ☉ *Mid-Aug.–mid-June, daily 8–4:45; mid-June–mid-Aug., daily 8–5:45.*

Lodging

$$–$$$ ⊞ **Gordon-Lee Mansion.** To capture the feeling of the Civil War era, stay overnight at this antebellum mansion, which served as a field hospital during the battle. Guests in the log house, formerly Congressman Gordon Lee's office, have the run of two bedrooms, a living room with fireplace, and a full kitchen, where they prepare their own breakfast. ⊠ *217 Cove Rd., Chickamauga 30707,* ☎ *706/375–4728 or 800/487–4728,* ℻ *706/375–9499. 4 rooms, 1 cottage. MC, V. BP.* ☙

North Georgia A to Z

Arriving, Departing, and Getting Around

BY BUS

Greyhound Bus Lines (☎ 706/678-4479 or 800/231–2222) serves select cities and towns around the area. It has connections to Atlanta, Savannah, Athens, Augusta, and Macon.

BY CAR

U.S. 19 runs north–south, passing through Dahlonega and up into the north Georgia mountains. U.S. 129 runs northwest from Athens, passing through Cleveland and subsequently merging with U.S. 19. GA 75 stems off U.S. 129 and goes through Helen and up into the mountains. U.S. 23/441 runs north through Clayton; U.S. 76 runs west from Clayton to Dalton, merging for a stretch with GA 5/515. GA 52 runs along the edge of the Blue Ridge Mountains, passing through Ellijay. I–75 is the major artery in the northwesternmost part of the state and passes near the New Echota State Historic Site and Chickamauga and Chattanooga National Military Park.

BY TAXI

All of the small towns and villages in north Georgia can easily be explored by foot, but to get from town to town, call **A Rainbow Taxi** (☎ 706/219–3275), which is based in Cleveland and services the surrounding region.

Contacts and Resources

B&B RESERVATIONS

Great Inns of Georgia (⊠ 541 Londonberry Rd., Atlanta 30327, ☎ 404/843–0471 or 800/501–7328, ℻ 404/252–8886) can help you choose one of the region's many inns.

EMERGENCIES
Ambulance, police (☎ 911). **Laurelwood/Blairsville Hospital** (⊠ 214 Hospital Circle, Blairsville, ☎ 706/745–8641).

GUIDED TOURS
Upper Hi Fly Fishing and Outfitters (⊠ 257 Big Sky Dr., Hiawassee 30546, ☎ 706/896–9075) offer personalized guided trout and fly fishing trips in the Southern Appalachian Mountains. They also operate a full-service fly-fishing shop with state-of-the-art equipment.

OUTDOOR ACTIVITIES AND SPORTS
Fort Mountain State Park (⊠ 181 Fort Mountain Park Rd., Chatsworth 30705, ☎ 706/695–2621) has campgrounds amid prehistoric rock formations, plus hiking, mountain biking, horseback riding, miniature golf, fishing, boating, and swimming. It is 8 mi east of Chatsworth via GA 52. For more information, contact the Gilmer County Chamber of Commerce (☞ Visitor Information, *below*).

Trackrock Campground and Cabins (⊠ 4887 Trackrock Campground Rd., Blairsville 30512, ☎ 706/745–2420) offers camping accommodations throughout a network of hiking trails filled with ancient Indian carvings and historical markers. It also has fishing and horseback riding. It is 9 mi east of Blairsville via Hwy. 180E. For more information, contact the Blairsville/Union County Chamber of Commerce (☞ Visitor Information, *below*).

RADIO STATIONS
AM: WDGR 1210, country and gospel music, news, sports, and weather; WZCM 770, country. **FM**: WKHC 104.3, classical and country music, news, sports, and weather.

24-HOUR PHARMACIES
Kroger store pharmacies, select locations.

VISITOR INFORMATION
Alpine Helen–White County Convention and Visitors Bureau (⊠ Box 730, Helen 30545, ☎ 706/878–2181 or 800/858–8027). **Blairsville/Union County Chamber of Commerce** (⊠ 385 Blue Ridge Hwy., Blairsville 30512, ☎ 706/745–5789). **Clayton Chamber of Commerce** (⊠ Box 702, 30525-0702, ☎ 706/782–4512, FAX 706/782–4596). **Dahlonega-Lumpkin Chamber of Commerce** (⊠ 13 Park St. South, Dahlonega 30533, ☎ 706/864–3513 or 800/231–5543, FAX 706/864–7917). **Gilmer County Chamber of Commerce** (⊠ 5 Westside Sq., Ellijay 30540, ☎ 706/635–7400). **Helen Welcome Center** (⊠ 726 Bruckenstrasse, Box 730, 30545, ☎ 706/878–2181 or 800/858–8027, FAX 706/878–4032). **White County Chamber of Commerce** (⊠ 122 N. Main St., Cleveland 30528, ☎ 706/865–5356).

ELSEWHERE IN GEORGIA

Andersonville National Historic Site

110 mi south of Atlanta via I–75 to GA 49.

Andersonville, which opened in 1864, was the Civil War's most notorious prisoner-of-war site: 13,000 prisoners died here, and at war's end the Swiss-born commandant Captain Henry Wirz was tried, convicted, and hanged when he refused to exculpate himself by blaming Confederate president Jefferson Davis for the brutal treatment of the prisoners. Each state that had prisoners at Andersonville has a monument to their memory, and it is a place of active burial for U.S. veterans and their spouses. The National Prisoner of War Museum is also on the grounds. *Andersonville Welcome Center:* ⊠ *114 Church St.,* ☎ *912/924–2558; Andersonville National Historic Site:* ⊠ *Box 800, Andersonville 31711,* ☎ *912/924–0343.* ☎ *Free.* ☉ *Daily 8–5.*

Dining and Lodging

$$ ✕☎ **Windsor Hotel.** Just 10 mi from Andersonville, Americus is one of Georgia's most attractive regional towns. In its downtown lies a jewel of a National Trust Historic hotel, a veritable monument to Victorian architecture. All rooms have 12-ft ceilings and ceiling fans. The menu in this elegant white-and-eggplant-scheme dining room focuses on Southern fare, with such dishes as corn chowder, barbecued shrimp on linguine, crab cakes, and pecan-crusted salmon. ⊠ *125 W. Lamar St., Americus 31709,* ☎ *912/924–1555 or 888/297–9567,* ☎ *912/928–0533. 40 rooms, 5 suites. Restaurant. AE, D, MC, V. No dinner Sun.*

Callaway Gardens

70 mi south of Atlanta via I–85 to U.S. 27S.

This 14,000-acre family-style golf and tennis resort (you can also visit for the day) is best known for its impressive gardens developed in the 1930s by a couple determined to breathe new life into the area's dormant cotton fields. On the grounds are four nationally recognized golf courses, 17 tennis courts, bicycling trails, and a lakefront beach. The **Day Butterfly Center** has more than 1,000 varieties flying free. **Creek Lake** is well stocked with largemouth bass and bream. Dining and lodging are available at the gardens, as well as in nearby towns. ⊠ *U.S. 27S, Pine Mountain 31822,* ☎ *706/663–2281 or 800/282–8181.* ☎ *Day visit $12.* ☉ *Mar.–Aug., daily 7–7; Sept.–Feb., daily 8–5.*

For a nearby bed-and-breakfast inn, *see* Magnolia Hall *in* Warm Springs, *below.*

Warm Springs

63 mi south of Atlanta via I–85 to exit 41.

The **Little White House Historic Site** is the restored home of President Franklin Delano Roosevelt, who first visited Warm Springs in 1924 to take the therapeutic hot waters. In 1932 he built what became known as the Little White House, a simple three-bedroom cottage. It contains his personal effects and looks much as it did the day he died here. The pools where Roosevelt took his therapy are now open for tours. ⊠ *401 Little White House Rd.,* ☎ *706/655–5870.* ☎ *$5.* ☉ *Daily 9–4.*

Lodging

$$ ☎ **Magnolia Hall.** Painted green with taupe shutters, this handsome Victorian cottage 20 mi southwest of Warm Springs has gingerbread trim and a wraparound porch. Rooms are soundproof, and each has a thermostat. Breakfast, with such dishes as stuffed French toast, bacon pie, and lemon biscuits, is served in the formal dining room. ⊠ *127 Barnes Mill Rd., Hamilton 31811,* ☎ *706/628–4566. 3 rooms, 2 suites. No credit cards. BP.* ❧

GEORGIA A TO Z

Arriving and Departing

By Bus

Greyhound Bus Lines (⊠ 232 Forsyth St., Atlanta, ☎ 404/584–1731 or 800/231–2222) serves Atlanta and towns across the state, large and small.

By Car

Georgia is traversed east and west by several interstate highways. North and south are covered by I–75, running from northwest through the center of the state to the Florida line; I–85 runs from the northeastern part of the state through the west to Alabama; I–95 runs along the Georgia coast from South Carolina to Florida. I–85 and I–75 converge in Atlanta near its downtown; this nexus is called the Connector. Running east and west, I–20 stretches from Birmingham, Alabama, to Augusta, Georgia, running through the center of downtown Atlanta on its way. From Macon, I–16 leads directly east to Savannah, where it ends; along its route lie several interesting towns, including Vidalia (home of the famous onion). Scenic routes include U.S. 76, a good highway running east–west through the north Georgia mountains, and U.S. 441, running north–south from the mountains to the Florida line. Along the way, U.S. 441 links numerous charming small towns and is lined with barbecue joints of worth. On the west side of the state, various pleasant small towns are connected by U.S. 19, the north–south route of choice prior to development of the interstate and still a good option if I–75 comes to a standstill, as it routinely does. I–75 also runs through a number of quaint small towns.

By Plane

Numerous international and domestic airlines serve **Hartsfield Atlanta International Airport** (✉ 6000 N. Terminal Pkwy., ☎ 404/530–6600), 13 mi south of downtown (☞ Atlanta A to Z, *above*).

By Train

Amtrak serves Atlanta and the state from the Brookwood station (✉ 1688 Peachtree St., ☎ 404/881–3060 or 800/872–7245). The *Crescent* operates daily to Atlanta from New York; Philadelphia; Washington, D.C.; Baltimore; Charlotte; and Greenville; and daily from New Orleans to New York through Atlanta. Its Thru-Way bus service operates daily from Birmingham and Mobile, Alabama, to Atlanta's Brookwood station. Another bus goes from the train station to Macon.

Getting Around

By Bus

Greyhound (☎ 800/231–2222) serves select cities and towns around the state.

By Car

The speed limit on interstates is 50 mph in metropolitan areas and 70 mph elsewhere. Right turns on red lights are permitted unless otherwise indicated. Contact the **Georgia Department of Industry, Trade, and Tourism** (☞ Visitor Information, *below*) for brochures and maps, including the annual guide "Georgia on My Mind."

By Plane

Numerous regional airports serve the state. For airline telephone numbers, *see* Air Travel *in* Smart Travel Tips A to Z. **Glynco Jetport** (✉ 500 Connole St., ☎ 912/265–2070), 6 mi north of Brunswick near the coastal isles, is served by Atlantic Southeast Airlines, with flights from Atlanta. The **Macon Municipal Airport** (✉ 4000 Terminal Dr., GA 247 and I–75, ☎ 912/788–3760) is served by Atlantic Southeast Airlines. Eighteen miles west of downtown, **Savannah International Airport** (✉ 400 Airways Ave., ☎ 912/964–0514) is served by Delta, US Airways, and AirTran.

By Train

Amtrak has regular service along the eastern seaboard, with daily stops in Savannah (✉ 2611 Seaboard Coastline Dr., ☎ 912/234–2611 or 800/872–7245), where a station is 4 mi southwest of downtown.

Contacts and Resources

B&B Reservations

For home stays, **Bed & Breakfast Atlanta** (✉ 1608 Briarcliff Rd., Suite 5, Atlanta 30306, ☎ 404/875–0525 or 800/967–3224, FAX 404/875–8198) represents 80–100 homes and can find lodging in carriage houses, apartments, and bed-and-breakfast inns. **Great Inns of Georgia** (✉ 541 Londonberry Rd., Atlanta 30327, ☎ 404/843–0471 or 800/501–7328, FAX 404/252–8886) can provide information on inns throughout the state.

Biking

With a membership of about 3,000, the **Southern Bicycle League** (✉ Box 870387, Stone Mountain 30087, ☎ 770/594–8350) has promoted bicycling across Georgia and the South for more than 20 years. The **Bicycle Ride Across Georgia** (BRAG; ☎ 770/921–6166) is an annual event, and the same organization holds numerous shorter bicycling events throughout the year. Advance application is required.

Emergencies

For **ambulance and fire emergencies statewide,** call ☎ 911.

Fishing

The **Georgia Department of Natural Resources, Game and Fish Division** (✉ 2070 U.S. 278, Social Circle 30025, ☎ 770/918–6400) has free pamphlets covering Georgia's regulations and maps suggesting good fishing spots.

Road Conditions

For road information, call the **Georgia Department of Transportation** (☎ 404/656–1267).

State Parks

Housed under the Georgia Department of Natural Resources, the **Parks, Recreation & Historic Sites** division (✉ 205 Butler St. SE, Suite 1352, Atlanta 30334, ☎ 404/656–3530, 800/864–7275 reservations, 770/389–7275 local reservations) has information on Georgia's parks.

Visitor Information

The **Georgia Department of Industry, Trade, and Tourism** (✉ Box 1776, Atlanta 30301, ☎ 404/656–3590 or 800/847–4842, FAX 404/651–9063) is the best source for visitor information around the state.

4 LOUISIANA

Louisiana is a state divided, both physically and philosophically. North Louisiana, with its rolling hills and piney woods, is strongly Southern in flavor and appeal. The flatter, marshy land in South Louisiana is Cajun Country, with sharp differences in food, music, and even language. Riverboats ply the mighty Mississippi, and antebellum homes line the wayside in both regions, but it's New Orleans, home of the famous Mardi Gras festivities, that garners the lion's share of attention, drawing most visitors to South Louisiana.

Updated by
Honey Naylor

LOCALS GENERALLY DESCRIBE REGIONS of their states as "upstate," "to the south," and so on, but in Louisiana (also known as Sportsman's Paradise, the Bayou State, and the Pelican State), the land is clearly divided. There's a capitalized distinction: North Louisiana is Southern, and South Louisiana is not, and Louisianians never, ever, say "northern" or "southern" Louisiana. The two regions are at least connected physically through I–49, which runs between Shreveport, the unofficial capital of North Louisiana, and Lafayette, the so-called capital of French Louisiana, in the south.

North Louisiana was settled by English, Irish, and Scottish Protestants who moved to the region in the early 19th century from the eastern seaboard. In customs, culture, religion, and traits the region is very much akin to Southern states such as Mississippi and Alabama. Louisiana's Mason-Dixon line cuts through the state's midsection city of Alexandria, known as Alex and pronounced "Elleck" by most. North of Alexandria are rolling hills and piney woods, acres of hiking grounds, and lakes where you can fish and camp. The terrain flattens out and becomes marshy to the south.

South Louisiana is a region completely different from any other part of the country. New Orleans and its environs were settled by the French in the early 18th century, and 22 parishes (the state's term for counties) of South Louisiana were settled soon after by Cajuns. Cajuns are descendants of the French who colonized Acadia—present-day Nova Scotia and New Brunswick, Canada. In the mid-1700s the British expelled the Acadians, who resettled in the Louisiana Territory and became known as Cajuns. The exception to French influence in South Louisiana are the Feliciana parishes above Baton Rouge, which were settled by the English.

French colonists in the New Orleans area took the term *Creole* from the Spanish and Portuguese colonizers of the West Indies. *Criollo* designated a child born of full European parentage in the colonies, as opposed to a child of mixed race. Over time, Creole has come to define anything indigenous to the New Orleans region, from architecture to garlic. In 1999 the state celebrated its French influences with FrancoFête, a commemoration of the 300-year anniversary of the Le Moyne brothers' landing at the mouth of the Mississippi.

In 1803 President Thomas Jefferson purchased not just New Orleans, but the entire Louisiana Territory, from Napoléon Bonaparte. The territory encompassed all the land from the Alleghenies in the east to the Rockies in the west. A veritable flood of settlers came rafting down the Mississippi River from the Ohio Valley, adding yet more flavor to the state's rich gumbo of nationalities.

South Louisiana's uniqueness has brought it most of the state's tourist trade—the festivities of New Orleans's Mardi Gras pumps millions of dollars into the local economy. South Louisiana's success in luring tourists has prompted Mardi Gras celebrations even in Protestant North Louisiana. Outside New Orleans, in Cajun Country, you can ride a *pirogue* (a small, flat-bottom boat) poled through a bayou, kick your heels to fiddles, and eat at tables laden with crawfish, jambalaya, and gumbo. The Great River Road between Baton Rouge and New Orleans is decorated with stately antebellum homes and frilly riverboats plying the Mississippi; on a tour boat you can drift beneath lacy gray Spanish moss into mysterious cypress swamps and sloughs.

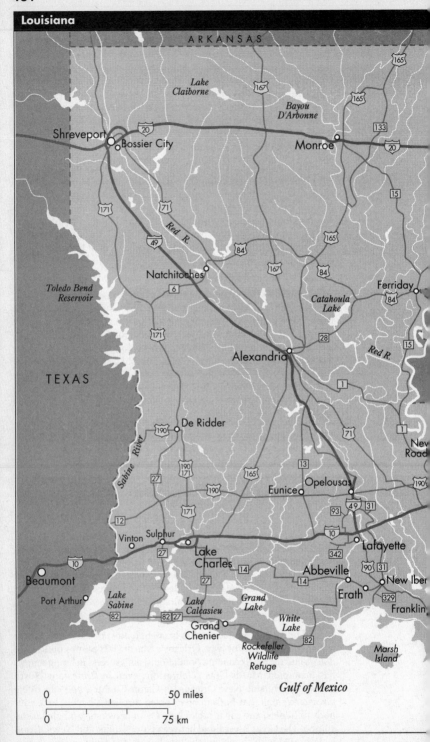

ARKANSAS

Lake Claiborne

Bayou D'Arbonne

165

165

133

Shreveport

20

Bossier City

Monroe

20

171

71

15

Red R.

49

84

84

165

Natchitoches

167

84

Ferriday

6

84

15

Toledo Bend Reservoir

Catahoula Lake

28

Red R.

171

Alexandria

TEXAS

1

De Ridder

71

1

190

New Road

Sabine River

190
171

27

13

New Road

165

12

190

Eunice

Opelousas

190

27

190

93

49

31

171

10

Vinton

Sulphur

342

Lafayette

27

Lake Charles

14

Abbeville

90

31

New Iber

Beaumont

27

14

Erath

329

Port Arthur

Lake Sabine

82

Lake Calcasieu

82
27

Grand Lake

White Lake

82

Franklin

Grand Chenier

Rockefeller Wildlife Refuge

Marsh Island

Gulf of Mexico

0 ———————— 50 miles

0 ———————— 75 km

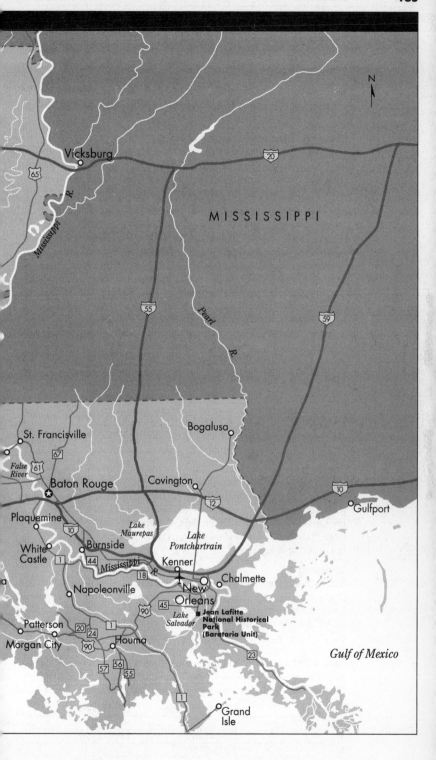

Vicksburg

65

MISSISSIPPI

20

55

Pearl R.

Mississippi R.

59

Bogalusa

St. Francisville

67

False River

61

Baton Rouge

Covington

10

12

Gulfport

Plaquemine

Lake Maurepas

10

Lake Pontchartrain

Burnside

White Castle

1

44

Mississippi R.

18

Kenner

Chalmette

Napoleonville

New Orleans

45

Lake Salvador

Jean Lafitte National Historical Park (Barataria Unit)

Patterson

20

24

1

90

Morgan City

90

Houma

57

56

55

23

Gulf of Mexico

1

Grand Isle

N

Pleasures and Pastimes

Biking

Bicycle trails honeycomb the state. The Kisatchie National Forest, near Natchitoches, has miles of trails through the piney woods. In flat-as-a-pancake South Louisiana, the area around Lafayette has more than 60 mi of marked trails. Some of the streets in New Orleans's French Quarter are blocked to all but bikers and pedestrians during the day. City Park and Audubon Park are great places for biking.

Birding, Boating, and Fishing

From north to south, the state is laced with waterways, making it an ideal destination for boaters and fisherfolk. Birders and fishers like to stalk the coastal marshes, and the Gulf of Mexico beckons those in search of big guys like blue marlin and wahoo.

Dining

Louisiana is perhaps the only state in the country that has a distinctive regional cuisine. The famed French Creole cuisine cooked up in New Orleans kitchens has blended over the years with Cajun cuisine born in the bayous and popularized by celebrity chef Paul Prudhomme, to produce what's known as South Louisiana Cooking. Cajun cooking, in particular, which usually means hot and spicy, has turned up on tables all over the world, but nobody does it like South Louisianans. Graced as the state is with waterways, Louisiana tables are also laden with seafood in every imaginable and innovative variety. Dress in restaurants is informal unless otherwise noted.

CATEGORY	COST*
$$$$	over $35
$$$	$25–$35
$$	$15–$25
$	under $15

*per person for a three-course meal, excluding drinks, service, and 9% sales tax

Festivals

Hardly a day goes by in Louisiana without a festival of some sort, saluting everything from the tomato to petroleum. New Orleans is home to North America's biggest bash—Mardi Gras—but Lafayette celebrates the same holiday with a Cajun flair. The New Orleans Jazz and Heritage Festival is a world-class event, as is the Festival International de la Louisiane in Lafayette.

Lodging

Accommodations in Louisiana run from homey bed-and-breakfasts to chain motels, from luxury hotels to elegant antebellum mansions. Louisiana has well over 100 bed-and-breakfasts; Cajun Country is loaded with charming ones, and Natchitoches alone has 16. Old and new blend in New Orleans, which also has many B&Bs in or near the city. Its French Quarter has a plethora of guest houses that emphasize old-world ambience in 19th-century town houses and carriage houses. As one of the nation's favorite convention cities, New Orleans has a Central Business District dominated by big and brassy high-rise, high-tech convention hotels.

CATEGORY	NEW ORLEANS*	OTHER AREAS*
$$$$	over $200	over $150
$$$	$150–$200	$110–$150
$$	$100–$150	$75–$110
$	under $100	under $75

*All prices are for a standard double room, excluding 6% tax.

Music

About a century ago, New Orleans gave birth to jazz, and the music has scarcely missed a beat since. It pours out of clubs along Bourbon Street in the French Quarter and floods the sightseeing riverboats on the Mississippi. It's everywhere. Southern as it is, North Louisiana favors country-and-western music, while in South Louisiana feet fly to the intoxicating Cajun and zydeco rhythms.

following the text of a review is your signal that the property has a Web site, where you will find details and, usually, images; for a link, visit www.fodors.com/urls.

Exploring Louisiana

South Louisiana encompasses all of the region south of Alexandria and extending east to the "instep" of this boot-shape state. Almost all of South Louisiana is considered Cajun Country, or French Louisiana, except for the region north of Baton Rouge. North of Alexandria hills start rolling, and the earth is red clay. By the time you reach Natchitoches, you're deep into North Louisiana, although the town also has rich Creole and Cajun textures. The state's main attraction, New Orleans, is in a class by itself, being characteristic of neither north nor south Louisiana. The city is a paradox in that it is both a major international port and an overgrown small town with an insouciant Caribbean flavor.

Great Itineraries

For a short visit of a few days, you'll want to focus on one area; for most visitors to Louisiana, this means New Orleans and, specifically, the French Quarter. If you have a few more days, you can get a taste of Plantation Country by touring restored plantations just 1½ hours west of the city.

With a week or more, you can explore key areas of the state outside New Orleans and Plantation Country. Lafayette, practically in the center of South Louisiana, is a good base from which to explore Cajun Country and is nearly as close to plantations as New Orleans. From here, you can also set out on direct routes west to Lake Charles and environs, or northwest to Natchitoches, the oldest permanent European settlement in the entire Louisiana Territory.

IF YOU HAVE 3 DAYS

Spend this time in ⊞ **New Orleans.** Many visitors never leave the French Quarter, even if they stay a week or more. One of the challenges of seeing New Orleans on a short visit is choosing among the city's vast number of outstanding restaurants. At least see the sights in and around Jackson Square, tour the Old Ursuline Convent, and stroll along Bourbon Street to hear the music pouring out of the jazz clubs. On your last day, spend a morning at the Aquarium of the Americas, and in the afternoon take the St. Charles Avenue streetcar to the Garden District and the Audubon Zoo.

IF YOU HAVE 5 DAYS

After a couple of days in ⊞ **New Orleans** (☞ *above*), travel 80 mi northwest to ⊞ **Baton Rouge,** the capital of Louisiana, with its museums and sites that pertain to state lore. On your way, you can tour the River Road plantations that lie between the cities, particularly Nottoway, Madewood, and Laura. Baton Rouge is in the heart of the area called Plantation Country; drive north of the city to quaint little **St. Francisville** where several of the restored estates are open for tours. Some of the plantations offer overnight accommodations.

Get to know 🏠 **New Orleans** and 🏠 **Baton Rouge** for a few days (☞ *above*), then take I–10 west out of Baton Rouge to spend at least a day in 🏠 **Lafayette,** whose many attractions focus on Cajun culture. Within a short drive south of Lafayette are colorful small towns and villages, such as **Erath** and **Abbeville,** that are typical of Cajun Country. Drive north to see the historic district in 🏠 **Natchitoches.** Although Natchitoches can be seen in a day and a half, it lies 142 mi north of Lafayette; en route Cane River Country has several sites that should be seen in a leisurely manner.

When to Tour Louisiana

The best times to visit Louisiana are in October and in the spring. During those times of the year temperatures and humidity are at bearable levels. Summers are scorchers throughout the state, with the mercury hovering above 90°F for much of June, July, and August. During those months, weather forecasters routinely predict "hot and humid, with a chance of afternoon thunder showers." In South Louisiana, hurricane season runs from June through November, and the coastline is sometimes battered with high winds and heavy rain. An ideal time for a first visit to New Orleans is Spring Fiesta (the weekend following Easter), when the city is dressed in springtime finery and many of the handsome homes are open for tours. Mardi Gras (February or March) is not recommended for a first visit to New Orleans. All of the city is given over to raucous revelry, and its quiet charms are buried beneath the mighty hordes of merrymakers.

NEW ORLEANS

New Orleans's reputation as one of the country's favorite good-time towns has remained intact over the years, and the city is forever finding something to celebrate. World-famous Mardi Gras aside, new festivals crop up at the drop of a Panama hat. New Orleans party animals even celebrate each new addition to the main zoo.

The city's most famous party place is the French Quarter, bordered by Canal Street, Esplanade Avenue, North Rampart Street, and the Mississippi River. Also called the Vieux Carré (Old Square), the Quarter is the original colony, founded in 1718 by French Creoles. As you explore its famous restaurants, antiques shops, and jazz haunts, try to imagine a handful of determined early 18th-century settlers living in crude palmetto huts and battling swamps, floods, hurricanes, and yellow fever. Two cataclysmic fires in the late 18th century virtually leveled the town. The Old Ursuline Convent on Chartres Street is the only remaining original French colonial structure. Survival was a struggle for the Creoles, and the sobriquet "the City That Care Forgot" stems from a determination not only to live life but to celebrate it.

In the early 19th century, the American Sector was just upriver of the French Quarter. For that reason, street names change as you cross Canal Street from the French Quarter: Bourbon Street to Carondelet Street, Royal Street to St. Charles Avenue, and so on.

The nerve center of the nation's second-largest port and main parade route during Mardi Gras, the CBD (Central Business District) cuts a wide swath between Uptown and Downtown, with Canal Street the official dividing line. Bordered by Canal Street, the river, Howard Avenue, and Loyola Avenue, the CBD has the city's newest convention hotels along with ritzy shopping malls, old department stores, international trade agencies and consulates, fast-food chains, monuments, and the monumental Superdome.

Nestled in between St. Charles Avenue, Louisiana Avenue, Jackson Avenue, and Magazine Street, the Garden District is aptly named. The Americans who built their estates upriver surrounded their homes with lavish lawns, forgoing the Creoles' preference for secluded courtyards. Magazine Street is heaven on earth for shoppers. Joggers, golfers, tennis buffs, bicyclists, and horseback riders head for Audubon Park.

Directions in New Orleans are described with respect to the Father of Waters: The Mississippi River moves in mysterious waves, looping around the city and wreaking havoc with ordinary routes. New Orleanians, ever resourceful, refer instead to lakeside (toward Lake Pontchartrain), riverside (toward the Mississippi), upriver (also called Uptown), and downriver (Downtown).

Some words of caution are necessary. Beneath New Orleans's exotic veneer is a high-crime city. The French Quarter and the Garden District can be very dangerous, even in broad daylight; walks at night can be particularly risky. Stay alert and streetwise, wherever and whenever you go—especially if you're carrying such obvious tourist trappings as cameras and opened maps.

Numbers in the text correspond to numbers in the margin and on the Downtown New Orleans map.

The French Quarter

The French Quarter is a carefully preserved historic district. It's also home to some 4,000 residents, some of the most famous French Creole restaurants, and many a jazz club. An eclectic crowd, which includes some of the world's best jazz musicians, ambles in and out of small two- and three-story frame, old-brick, and pastel-painted stucco buildings. Baskets of splashy subtropical plants dangle from the eaves of buildings with filigreed galleries, dollops of gingerbread, and dormer windows. Built flush with the banquettes (sidewalks), the houses, most of which date from the early to mid-19th century, front secluded courtyards awash with greenery and brilliant blossoms.

A Good Walk

A good place to begin a stroll around the Quarter is **Jackson Square** ①, which has been the heart and soul of the French Quarter. A flagstone pedestrian mall borders three sides of the square. As you face the statue, with St. Louis Cathedral behind you, the **New Orleans Welcome Center** ② is to your left, a few steps across the flagstones.

Turn right as you leave the visitor center to see the three historic buildings that sit on Chartres Street, facing the square. The white church in the middle is the late-18th-century **St. Louis Cathedral** ③. The two Spanish colonial buildings flanking the church are the **Cabildo** ④, on the left as you face the church, and the **Presbytère** ⑤, on the right. Alongside the church are Pirate's Alley and Père Antoine's Alley, cracked-flagstone passageways redolent of infamous plots and pirate intrigue—but, alas, the streets were laid long after Jean Lafitte and his Baratarian band had vanished. William Faulkner wrote his first novel, *A Soldier's Pay,* while living at 624 Pirate's Alley.

Lining Jackson Square, on St. Peter and St. Ann streets, the Pontalba Buildings are among the nation's oldest apartment buildings, built between 1849 and 1851. In the lower Pontalba (considered lower because it's downriver of the square) is the **1850 House** ⑥.

The promenade of **Washington Artillery Park** ⑦, opposite Jackson Square on Decatur Street, affords a splendid perspective of the square and the Mississippi River. On the Moon Walk promenade, across the

Downtown New Orleans

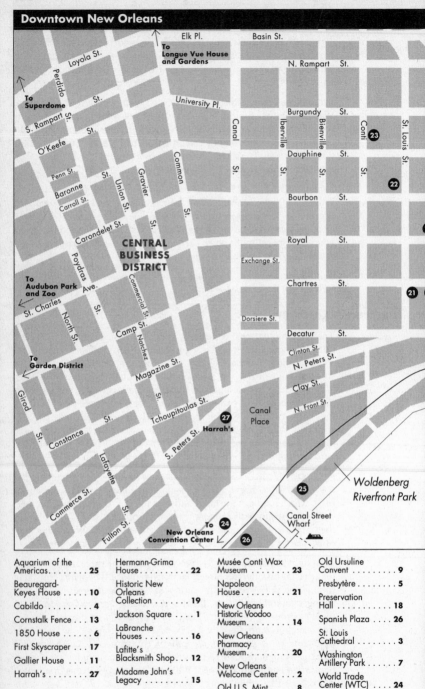

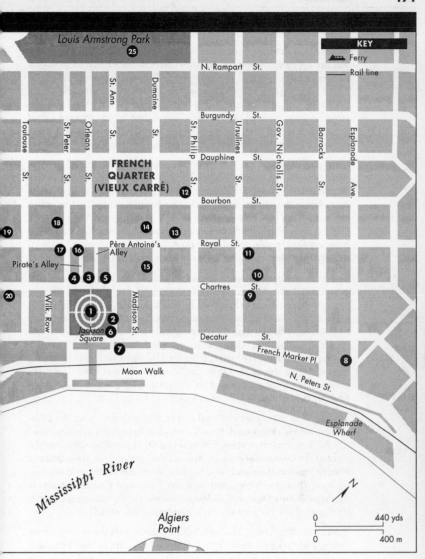

Louis Armstrong Park

25

KEY

Ferry

Rail line

N. Rampart St.

St. Ann St.

Dumaine St.

Burgundy St.

Toulouse St.

St. Peter St.

Orleans St.

St. Philip St.

Ursulines St.

Gov. Nicholls St.

Barracks St.

Esplanade Ave.

FRENCH QUARTER (VIEUX CARRÉ)

Dauphine St.

12

Bourbon St.

18

19

14

13

Père Antoine's Alley

Royal St.

11

17

16

15

10

Pirate's Alley

4

3

5

9

Chartres St.

20

Wilk. Row

1

2

Madison St.

Decatur St.

Jackson Square

6

7

French Market Pl.

8

Moon Walk

N. Peters St.

Esplanade Wharf

Mississippi River

N

Algiers Point

0   440 yds

0   400 m

tracks from the park, you can sit on a bench or stroll down the steps to the water's edge.

Washington Artillery Park is anchored on the upriver side by the Jackson Brewery and Millhouse, and downriver by the French Market. Jax Beer used to be made in the Brewery, and the market is on the site of a late-17th-century Indian trading post. Both sites are now filled with boutiques and restaurants, with Planet Hollywood and Virgin Megastore hogging most of the Brewery space. Two blocks toward Canal Street on Decatur Street is the Jackson Brewery Corporation's Marketplace, home of yet more restaurants and retail outlets.

On the same site for more than 100 years, Café du Monde at 800 Decatur Street is the upriver anchor for the French Market and is in one of its oldest buildings. Stretching from St. Ann Street downriver to Barracks Street, the market is alive with shops, outdoor cafés, and ice cream and candy stores. The downriver anchor of the French Market is the Old Farmers Market, where farmers from the countryside have been bringing their produce for more than 170 years, and where a Community Flea Market flourishes daily from dawn till dusk.

The area on the Esplanade Avenue fringe of the Quarter should be avoided at night, but you'll be safe during the day when you visit the jazz and Mardi Gras exhibits in the **Old U.S. Mint** ⑧. From the Mint, walk up tree-lined Esplanade Avenue to Chartres Street and turn left to reach the **Old Ursuline Convent** ⑨, within a walled complex at the corner of Chartres and Ursulines streets; it was built in 1749. The Greek Revival house across the street from the Ursuline Convent is the **Beauregard-Keyes House** ⑩. From the house, turn right onto Ursulines Street, walk one block to Royal Street, and turn right again, where you'll find the **Gallier House** ⑪, built around 1857.

Turn right at the corner of Royal and St. Philip streets to see the 18th-century **Lafitte's Blacksmith Shop** ⑫, which now houses a neighborhood bar. Back at the intersection of Royal and St. Philip streets, look to the right at the **Cornstalk Fence** ⑬. Around the corner is the **New Orleans Historic Voodoo Museum** ⑭ on Dumaine Street. From the museum, turn right on Dumaine Street, and between Royal and Chartres streets is **Madame John's Legacy** ⑮, a West Indies–style raised cottage that is similar to those built by the early planters in this area.

Turn right after leaving Madame John's Legacy, walk down to Chartres Street, and make another right. Continue on Chartres Street through Jackson Square to St. Peter Street, turn right again, and walk one block up to Royal Street. Here you'll see the 19th-century **LaBranche Houses** ⑯. Directly across St. Peter Street from the LaBranche Houses is the four-story **First Skyscraper** ⑰, constructed between 1795 and 1811.

Next, walk up St. Peter Street, away from Jackson Square. About midway between Royal and Bourbon streets, behind weathered walls, is **Preservation Hall** ⑱, where old-time legends of traditional jazz hold forth nightly. Not much happens here during the day, but you can peer through the gate to see the carriageway and the courtyard beyond it. Return to Royal Street, turn right, and cross Toulouse Street to reach the old Merieult House, which contains the **Historic New Orleans Collection** ⑲.

Walk toward the Mississippi River on Toulouse Street and turn right to find the **New Orleans Pharmacy Museum** ⑳. On the same side of the street, at the corner of Chartres and St. Louis streets, is the bar **Napoleon House** ㉑, a longtime favorite haunt of artists and writers.

Wrench yourself from the Napoleon House, walk away from the river, and cross Bourbon Street to reach the **Hermann-Grima House** ㉒, an

American-style town-house museum dating from the early 19th century. After you leave the residence, walk less than a block and turn left on Dauphine Street. Turn right at Conti Street to the **Musée Conti Wax Museum** ㉓.

TIMING

This old historic district is only about 1 square mi, and it can be walked easily in a half day. But that would mean you'd miss peeking into the plethora of shops and knocking back a Dixie beer, brewed locally, at Lafitte's Blacksmith Shop or a Pimm's Cup—a gin-based drink—at the Napoleon House. Allow yourself at least a full day (you could spend a week here) to enjoy the Quarter's main attractions: the Cabildo and St. Louis Cathedral at Jackson Square, the Old Ursuline Convent, and Gallier House. April and October are ideal times for strolling around the neighborhood. Be prepared for crowds: the neighborhood is almost always full of visitors and/or conventioneers, except perhaps during the worst dog days of summer. Ambling is simply impossible during Mardi Gras, when the streets are paved with people.

Sights to See

❿ **Beauregard-Keyes House.** A raised cottage with a Greek Revival portico, this house was built in 1826. For a brief period after the Civil War, it was home to Confederate general Pierre Gustav Toutant Beauregard, the Creole New Orleanian who ordered the first shot fired at Fort Sumter. In the mid-1940s the house was bought by novelist Frances Parkinson Keyes (author of *Dinner at Antoine's*), whose office was in the former slave quarters. Some of Keyes's books are sold in the gift shop. The pretty French garden adjacent to the house is part of the tour. ⊠ *1113 Chartres St.,* ☎ *504/523–7257.* ⊡ *$4.* ☉ *Mon.–Sat. 10–3; tours on the hr.*

❹ **Cabildo.** This colonial building dating from 1799 was named for the Spanish governing council that met here. Transfer papers for the Louisiana Purchase of 1803 were signed on the second floor, in the Sala Capitular, and in 1825, Lafayette, the French general who was a major leader alongside Washington in the American Revolution, stayed here on a welcome-back tour of the United States. Exhibits trace the multicultural historic contributions to the region. Among the artifacts is a death mask of Napoléon, who was a hero for many a New Orleanian. The Cabildo—along with the **Presbytère,** the **1850 House,** and the **Old U.S. Mint** (☞ *below* for all three)—is a property of the Louisiana State Museum. A 20% discount is available when you purchase tickets to two or more LSM properties at the same time. ⊠ *Jackson Sq.,* ☎ *504/568–6968.* ⊡ *$5.* ☉ *Tues.–Sun. 9–5.*

⓭ **Cornstalk Fence.** This heavy cast-iron fence, with its design of morning glories and ears of corn, is one of three such fences in the city; it dates from 1859. ⊠ *915 Royal St.*

❻ **1850 House.** You can see what life was like for upscale 19th-century Creole city dwellers on a guided tour of this restored apartment, which belongs to the Louisiana State Museum; it's filled with period furnishings, antique dolls, and plenty of evidence of cushy Creole living. This house was one of the first to have cast (or molded) ironwork, which would eventually replace much of the hand-wrought ironwork in the Quarter. ⊠ *523 St. Ann St., Jackson Sq.,* ☎ *504/568–6968.* ⊡ *$3.* ☉ *Tues.–Sun. 10–5.*

⓱ **First Skyscraper.** Also known as Maison LeMonnier, this "skyscraper" was so called because it was once the tallest building in the French Quarter. It was built between 1795 and 1811 for Dr. Yves LeMonnier, whose initials can be seen worked into the second-floor balcony. The edifice was originally a three-story high-rise; rumor has it that the fourth floor was added later so that it might retain its towering name. Shops on the ground floor are open to the public. ⊠ *640 St. Peter St.*

⑪ Gallier House. Irishman James Gallagher Sr. changed his name to Gallier before moving to New Orleans in order to fit in with the Creoles. This handsome house, which is exquisitely furnished, was designed by his renowned architect son, James Gallagher Jr., around 1857; the architect lived here with his family. The house has early Louisiana and Victorian antique furnishings upholstered in rich brocades and velvets, living room chandeliers made of etched glass and brass, marble mantels, and elaborate ceiling medallions. There are also short films on architectural crafts and exhibits on 19th-century life. The residence was one of the settings used in the 1994 film *Interview with the Vampire* (☞ *Anne Rice's New Orleans, below*). ⊠ *1118–1132 Royal St.,* ☎ *504/525–5661.* ☎ *$6; combination ticket with Hermann-Grima House is $10.* ☉ *Mon.–Sat. 10–4; tours 10:30–3:30 on ½ hr.*

㉒ Hermann-Grima House. William Brand designed this town house in 1831 for a wealthy merchant named Samuel Hermann, who later sold the house to attorney Felix Grima. It's one of the largest and best-preserved examples of American architecture in the Quarter. A guided tour takes in the first floor and the ancient rear kitchens, where Creole cooking demonstrations take place on Thursday from October through March. ⊠ *820 St. Louis St.,* ☎ *504/525–5661.* ☎ *$6; combination ticket with Gallier House is $10.* ☉ *Mon.–Sat. 10–4; last tour at 3:30.*

⑲ Historic New Orleans Collection. One of the nation's largest private collections of documents, paintings, blueprints, and artifacts is contained in the 18th-century Merieult House, one of the few buildings to survive the fire of 1794. The ground-floor Williams Gallery, with changing exhibits relating to the city's past, is free to the public; other galleries can be seen on a guided tour. ⊠ *533 Royal St.,* ☎ *504/523–4662.* ☎ *House tour $4, galleries tour $4.* ☉ *Tues.–Sat. 10–4:45.*

★ ♨ ❶ Jackson Square. Jackson Square, founded in 1718, was called Place d'Armes by the Creoles and was the center of all colonial life, home to parading militia, religious ceremonies, social gatherings, food vendors, entertainers, and pirates. Its sun-patterned landscaping was a popular design in the court of King Louis XIV, the Sun King. The square's focal point is a massive equestrian statue of General Andrew Jackson, hero of the 1815 Battle of New Orleans—in which he saved the city by defeating the British 5 mi downriver at Chalmette. Today the square remains a social hub. Pirate attire is not uncommon in the colorful crowd that flocks here.

The **Pontalba Buildings** that line either side of Jackson Square on St. Ann and St. Peter streets are among the oldest apartment houses in the country. Built between 1849 and 1851, they were constructed under the supervision of the baroness Micaela Pontalba, who occasionally lent the laborers a helping hand. ⊠ *Jackson Sq.: bordered by Chartres, St. Ann, Decatur, and St. Peter Sts.*

⑯ LaBranche Houses. This complex of lovely town houses, built in the 1830s by widow LaBranche, fills the half block between Pirate's Alley, Royal, and St. Peter streets behind the **Cabildo** (☞ *above*). The one at 700 Royal Street (on the corner of Royal and St. Peter streets) is one of the most photographed edifices in the French Quarter. Its filigreed double balconies bedecked with flowering plants are cast iron with an oak-leaf-and-acorn motif. Cast iron such as this was introduced into New Orleans in about 1850, so the balconies would have been a later addition. All the houses are privately owned. There are shops and restaurants on the ground floor.

⑫ **Lafitte's Blacksmith Shop.** In the mid-19th century, notorious free-booters Jean and Pierre Lafitte are said to have operated a blacksmith shop in this tattered cottage, which served as a front for their slave trading, smuggling, and sundry nefarious deeds. The building dates to 1772. For many years, it has served as a popular neighborhood bar, especially favored by artists and writers, both famous and obscure. ⊠ *941 Bourbon St.,* ☎ *504/523–0066.*

⑮ **Madame John's Legacy.** The 19th-century writer George Washington Cable, who lived in the Garden District, wrote often about New Orleans Creoles. He used several French Quarter homes as settings for his stories. This house is named for a character in his short story " 'Tite Poulette." The West Indies–style house was built in 1788 on the site of the birthplace of Renato Beluche, a Lafitte lieutenant who helped Andrew Jackson in the Battle of New Orleans. Owned by the Louisiana State Museum, the house, though unfurnished, is interesting architecturally and contains photographs and exhibits that pertain to this structure and to 18th-century New Orleans. It played a role in the film *Interview with the Vampire.* (☞ Anne Rice's New Orleans, *below.*) ⊠ *632 Dumaine St.* ☎ *504/568–6968.* ▣ *$3.* ☉ *Tues.–Sun. 10–5.*

↻ ㉓ **Musée Conti Wax Museum.** For a great introduction to New Orleans history, be sure to visit New Orleans's answer to Madame Tussaud's. Each of the 100 colorful tableaux depicts an event in the city's history, beginning with the 1682 arrival of LaSalle. Among the Louisiana luminaries captured in wax are Andrew Jackson, Jean Lafitte, Marie Laveau, and former governor Edwin Edwards. ⊠ *917 Conti St.,* ☎ *504/525–2605.* ▣ *$6.25.* ☉ *Mon.–Sat. 10–5, Sun. noon–5.*

★ ㉑ **Napoleon House.** Arguably the most popular bar of New Orleanians, this is a wonderfully atmospheric place with peeling sepia walls and Napoleonic memorabilia; the classical music, however, is canned. Napoléon never visited New Orleans, but he had many admirers. Among them was Mayor Nicholas Girod, whose house this was. Girod and cronies formed a syndicate whose purpose was to rescue the Little Corporal from incarceration on St. Helena and bring him to this house to live in an apartment Girod had added for that purpose. Alas, Napoléon died before the rescue could take place. ⊠ *500 Chartres St.,* ☎ *504/524–9752.* ☉ *Mon.–Sat. 11 AM–1 AM, Sun. 11–7.*

⑭ **New Orleans Historic Voodoo Museum.** An only–in–New Orleans attraction, this is a dimly lighted place with a prominently featured portrait of 19th-century voodoo queen Marie Laveau, a voodoo altar, sundry potions, and information about voodoo as it is practiced today in the Crescent City. ⊠ *724 Dumaine St.,* ☎ *504/523–7685.* ▣ *$6.25.* ☉ *Daily 10–8.*

⑳ **New Orleans Pharmacy Museum.** In 1823 Louis Dufilho, said to be the nation's first licensed pharmacist, had his pharmacy on the ground floor and lived upstairs. He grew medicinal herbs in the courtyard. This is a musty old place, full of ancient, mysterious medicinal items; there's also an Italian marble fountain used by 19th-century soda jerks. ⊠ *514 Chartres St.,* ☎ *504/565–8027.* ▣ *$2.* ☉ *Tues.–Sun. 10–5.*

❷ **New Orleans Welcome Center.** Before sallying forth on sightseeing forays, the New Orleans Welcome Center should be one of your first stops for maps, brochures, and friendly advice about the city. The welcome center shares space with an outlet of the Louisiana Office of Tourism, which offers information about attractions statewide. ⊠ *529 St. Ann St.,* ☎ *504/566–5068.* ☉ *Daily 9–5.*

⑧ Old U.S. Mint. Built in 1835, the massive Greek Revival building was the first branch of the U.S. Mint, and it turned out money hand over fist from 1838 until 1861 and the Civil War. During the war Confederate coins were stamped here until the Confederate States of America went broke, and afterward the Mint continued currency production until 1909. It's now a part of the Louisiana State Museum, housing jazz and Mardi Gras exhibits. Among many other artifacts, the jazz exhibit displays the first horn used by native son Louis Armstrong and some of his famous white handkerchiefs. Glittering Carnival gowns, crowns, and scepters are among the colorful Mardi Gras exhibits. ⊠ *400 Esplanade Ave.,* ☎ *504/568–6968.* ☜ *$4.* ☾ *Tues.–Sun. 9–5.*

★ **⑨ Old Ursuline Convent.** This handsome Greek Revival building is the oldest structure in the Lower Mississippi Valley and the only undisputed survivor of the late-18th-century fires. It was erected in 1749 by order of Louis XV, the second convent built on this site. The first Sisters of Ursula arrived in the colony in 1727, after surviving a torturous five-month voyage from France. The iron cross on the convent grounds came with the nuns from Rouen. The Ursulines stayed in another building until this one was completed; they occupied this convent from 1749 to 1824. The hand-hewn cypress spiral stairs inside are from the original convent. Guided tours of the complex include the lovely restored St. Mary's Church. ⊠ *1100 Chartres St.,* ☎ *504/529–3040.* ☜ *$5.* ☾ *Tours Tues.–Fri. 10, 11, 1, 2, and 3; weekends 11:15, 1, and 2.*

☾ ★ **⑤ Presbytère.** This building was constructed in 1795 to house priests of the church but was never used for this purpose. Like the **Cabildo** (☞ *above*), it's also a museum, but here the entire structure is given over to a permanent, and dazzling, Mardi Gras exhibit. The exhibits, unveiled in January 2000, trace the history of Mardi Gras around the world, showcase glittering costumes and crowns, and include kid-friendly interactive displays. The odd-shape structure in the arcade of the Presbytère is a Confederate submarine. ⊠ *Jackson Sq.,* ☎ *504/568–6968.* ☜ *Admission to each of the 4 state museums is $5, with a 20% discount on tickets to 2 or more museums purchased at the same time.* ☾ *Tues.–Sun. 9–5.*

★ **⑱ Preservation Hall.** The Hall, as it is known locally, may be the best-known attraction in town. Preservation Hall Jazz Bands tour around the world as ambassadors for New Orleans, for traditional jazz, and for the sight itself (☞ Nightlife and the Arts, *below*). In the years prior to World War I, the city was full of places like this, but over time they disappeared. In the 1960s, Allen Jaffe—Pennsylvanian, tuba player, and jazz aficionado—opened the Hall, providing a place for musicians to play and tourists to throng. Jaffe was revered by musicians; upon his death in 1987, thousands came from all over the world to pay their last respects and to march in a traditional jazz funeral. ⊠ *726 St. Peter St.,* ☎ *504/522–2841, www.preservationhall.com.* ☜ *$5 cover.* ☾ *Daily 8 PM–midnight.*

③ St. Louis Cathedral. Soaring above the earthly activity taking place right in its front yard, the small white church is a quiet reminder of the spiritual life of New Orleans citizens. The first church on this site was built in 1724 and named for Louis IX, France's saint-king. The present church dates from 1794 and was restored and enlarged in 1849. It was elevated to the status of minor basilica in 1964, and in honor of Pope John Paul II's 1987 visit, the mall in front of the cathedral was christened Place Jean Paul Deux. ⊠ *Jackson Sq., on 700 block of Chartres St.,* ☎ *504/525–9585.* ☾ *Tours daily every ½ hr 9–5.*

⑦ Washington Artillery Park. Named for the 141st Artillery, which has fought in every war since 1845, when its commander was General

Zachary Taylor, this small "park" is formed mostly of concrete. Ramps and steps lead from Decatur Street up to a promenade, where there are park benches, box trees, and a grand view of Jackson Square on one side and Old Man River on the other. Steps leading up to the promenade from Decatur Street form an amphitheater, with sundry jugglers and mimes entertaining on the sidewalk below. If you go down the steps on the river side of the park and cross the streetcar tracks, you'll reach Moon Walk. This promenade that stretches right along the Mississippi is lined with park benches, and stone steps lead down into the muddy water. Street musicians often play here. Beware the panhandlers. ⊠ *Decatur St. between St. Peter and St. Ann Sts.*

Foot of Canal

A walk around the foot of Canal Street in the Central Business District (CBD) takes in sights as varied as a trade center, an excellent aquarium, and a plaza anchored by a shopping mall.

A Good Walk

You can begin your walk atop the **World Trade Center** ㉔, where the 33rd-floor Top of the Mart cocktail lounge affords a 360-degree overview of the city. From the center, turn right, walk past the Canal Street Ferry landing, and cross Canal Street to reach the **Aquarium of the Americas** ㉕ in the 16-acre Woldenberg Riverfront Park.

To reach **Spanish Plaza** ㉖ behind the World Trade Center, backtrack across Canal Street to the ferry landing. Just to the right of the ferry landing is a large equestrian statue of Bernardo de Galvez, a governor of the Louisiana Territory during the Spanish colonial period. Behind the governor, a broad arch heralds Riverwalk. Spanish Plaza is across the tracks (watch out for the Riverfront Streetcar!), up the steps, and to the right.

The large Greek Revival–style building across from the World Trade Center is **Harrah's New Orleans Casino** ㉗, which opened in October 1999 after several years of legal problems.

TIMING

Allow at least a full morning or afternoon for a leisurely stroll around this riverfront area. Bear in mind, however, that assigning a time frame to either Top of the Mart or Harrah's is a tad difficult, what with one being a cocktail lounge and the other a gambling den. You can easily devote two hours to the aquarium. Spanish Plaza is a broad open area right by the Mississippi River, where the Riverwalk shopping mall can take up a few more hours of your time.

Sights to See

★ ♺ ㉕ **Aquarium of the Americas.** In this major family attraction, more than 7,000 aquatic creatures swim in 60 separate displays in four major environments—the Amazon River Basin, the Caribbean Reef, the Mississippi River, and the Gulf Coast. A $25 million wing contains galleries and an IMAX movie theater. The beautifully landscaped 16-acre **Woldenberg Riverfront Park** around the aquarium is a tranquil spot with many excellent views of the river. ⊠ *Foot of Canal St.,* ☎ *504/861–2538 aquarium; 504/581–4629 theater.* ☞ *Aquarium $13, IMAX $7.75; combination ticket $17.25.* ☉ *Aquarium Sun.–Thurs. 9:30–6, Fri.–Sat. 9:30–7; IMAX daily 10–8, shows on the hr.*

㉗ **Harrah's New Orleans Casino,** Louisiana's only land-based casino is this 100,000-square-ft facility with a slew of slots and gaming tables set in several themed "courts." The themes are all New Orleans–related—for instance, a Mardi Gras Court and a Jazz Court, as well as decorative schemes evocative of area plantations. Open 24 hours, seven days a week, the casino also features nightly entertainment, daily parades, and whatever else it takes to keep the dice rolling. ⊠ *4 Canal St. (Canal St. at the Mississippi River)*, ☎ *504/533–6000 or 877/277–4263.*

OFF THE
BEATEN PATH
WAREHOUSE DISTRICT – This burgeoning part of the CBD, bordered roughly by Poydras Street, Baronne Street, Howard Avenue, and the Mississippi River, was long characterized by a plethora of mostly abandoned warehouses. It began to blossom in the 1970s with the opening of the **Contemporary Arts Center** (⊠ 900 Camp St., ☎ 504/528–3800) in one of the restored buildings. It boasts an art gallery and two theaters; admission is $3. The CAC is virtually the mother church of the Warehouse District; its opening spawned a host of gallery openings in the area. Julia Street, known as Gallery Row, is lined with top-of-the-line expressionist galleries, and during the October Art for Arts Sake, arts aficionados gallery-hop from one opening to the next, ending with a gala at the CAC.

The **Louisiana Children's Museum** (420 Julia St., Warehouse District, ☎ 504/523–1357) is an excellent museum with a host of educational hands-on exhibits, including a market, a TV station, and a small port. You can reach the museum from Spanish Plaza (☞ *below*) by walking through Riverwalk and exiting at Julia Street. Admission is $5; the museum is open Tuesday to Saturday 9:30 to 4:30, Sunday noon to 4:30.

On June 6, 2000, the **National D-Day Museum** (⊠ 925 Magazine St., ☎ 504/527–6012) opened here. Inside the massive two-warehouse facility is the only museum dedicated to the 1944 D-Day invasion of Normandy and 18 other beach invasions during World War II. Exhibits include a replica of the Higgins boat troop-landing craft, which were made in New Orleans; British Spitfire and American Avenger fighter planes; a tank; and many other artifacts. The Louisiana Memorial Pavilion building has a theater that plays war footage and documentaries. Admission is $6; the museum is open daily from 9 to 5.

The former landmark Howard Memorial Library on Lee Circle will open as the **Ogden Museum of Southern Art** (615 Howard Ave., ☎ 504/539–9600) in early 2001. More than 500 works collected since the 1960s by local developer Robert Houston Ogden will form the center of the eclectic collection. A walkway leads to a second building.

㉖ **Spanish Plaza.** A gift to the city from the Spanish government in the 1970s, this broad open expanse paved with mosaic tile stretches from behind the World Trade Center to the Mississippi River. The centerpiece of the plaza is a splendid fountain emblazoned with Spanish coats of arms. Several excursion boats take on passengers at the plaza, and there are often food vendors. The area is anchored downriver by the ferry landing and upriver by **Riverwalk,** a ½-mi-long shopping mall that stretches right along the river from the plaza to Julia Street in the Warehouse District. There are some 200 shops and restaurants, along with local specialty shops, such as Yvonne LaFleur and Louisiana Opal. *Riverwalk:* ⊠ *Poydras St. at the river,* ☎ *504/522–1555.* ⊙ *Mon.–Sat. 10–9, Sun. 11–7.*

㉔ **World Trade Center (WTC).** This skyscraper contains offices of foreign consulates and trade agencies. At press time, negotiations were under way to convert the first 18 floors into a hotel, possibly operated by Crowne Plaza. Slated to remain in its 33rd-floor perch, the venerable **Top of the Mart** (☎ 504/522–9795, ⊙ Weekdays 10 AM–midnight, Sat. 11 AM–1 AM, Sun. 2 PM–midnight) is a revolving cocktail lounge with grand vistas of the river and the city. It's a good place to get an overview of the area. ⊠ *2 Canal St.*

The Garden District

The Americans who flocked to New Orleans after the 1803 Louisiana Purchase settled upriver of the French Quarter and built fine homes surrounded by luxuriant gardens. Many of the elegant Garden District homes were built during New Orleans's golden age, from 1830 until the Civil War. One of the nation's loveliest residential districts, the easily walkable area is bounded by Jackson, Louisiana, and St. Charles avenues and Magazine Street. Its grand mansions are private homes and closed to the public, but they are worth seeing from the outside.

A Good Walk

This walk begins following a short streetcar ride from Canal Street. Get off at 4th Street (Stop 16) and walk toward the river one block to Prytania Street. At the corner of 4th and Prytania, Colonel Short's Villa (⊠ 1448 4th St.) is a stunning Greek Revival–Italianate mansion. Walk down 4th Street to Coliseum Street, turn left, and go one block to 3rd Street. The Robinson House (⊠ 1415 3rd St.) is a lovely white house, said to have been among the first in New Orleans to have indoor plumbing. Continue on Coliseum Street to 1st Street. The home of novelist Anne Rice and husband Stan (⊠ 1239 1st St.) is a handsome Greek Revival house, which the writer restored and used as the setting for her novel *The Witching Hour*. Like other Garden District mansions, it is not open to the public, but there are often fans hanging out on the sidewalk, hoping for an author sighting.

Walk toward St. Charles Avenue on 1st Street; at the corner of 1st and Prytania streets is Toby's Corner (⊠ 2340 Prytania St.), which is said to be the oldest house in the Garden District, dating from about 1838. Across the street from it, the Bradish Johnson House (⊠ 2343 Prytania St.), now the Louise McGehee School, was built in the late 1860s.

TIMING

Allow about an hour and a half to leisurely stroll around the Garden District. The walk suggested above is highly selective; the neighborhood is filled with stunning mansions, and you might want to allow extra time for picture taking.

OFF THE BEATEN PATH
AUDUBON PARK AND ZOO – To reach the Audubon Park and Zoo from the Garden District, board the St. Charles streetcar once again to head to Uptown. The 340-acre park rolls out across St. Charles Avenue from Tulane and Loyola universities. With its live oaks and lush tropical plants, Audubon Park was once part of the plantation of Etienne de Boré, the father of Louisiana's granulated-sugar industry. In addition to the 18-hole golf course, there is a 2-mi jogging track with 18 exercise stations along the way, a stable that offers guided trail rides, and 10 tennis courts.

The Friends of the Zoo operate a free shuttle that boards in front of Tulane every 15 to 20 minutes for a ride to the zoo, which lies on the 58 acres of the park nearest the river. A wooden walkway strings through the zoo, a miniature train rings around a part of it, and it can take an entire day to explore. More than 1,800 animals roam about in natural habitats like the Australian exhibit, where kangaroos hobnob with wallabies. ⊠ *St. Charles Ave. (main entrance),* ☎ *504/861-2537.* ☞ *$9.* ☉ *Oct.–Mar., weekdays 9:30–5, weekends 9:30–6; Apr.–Sept., weekdays 9:30–5:30, weekends 9:30–6.*

Mid-City

This section of town stretches roughly lakeward from the French Quarter to City Park and from Esplanade Avenue to I–10. The early French

Creole settlers made camp near Bayou St. John, which forms the eastern border of City Park. The sights to be seen here are spread out, and you'll need a car to get from one to the other.

A Good Drive

To reach the **Pitot House** from the French Quarter, drive straight out Esplanade Avenue. Just before the Esplanade Avenue Bridge, turn left on Moss Street. Bayou St. John will be on your right, the Pitot House on your left. To reach the **New Orleans Museum of Art,** backtrack to Esplanade Avenue, cross the Esplanade Avenue Bridge, and go to the right of the equestrian statue of General P. G. T. Beauregard. At this entrance to **City Park,** Lelong Avenue, a long oak-lined drive, leads to the museum's entrance at Collins-Diboll Circle. Behind the museum, a half circle to the right and over a bridge takes you to the park's Victory Avenue. The New Orleans Botanical Garden is on the right, and past the garden is the Storyland playground. Next door is the 1906 merry-go-round of Carousel Gardens, and farther on you'll see tennis courts on the left. Turn left at the end of the courts, and left again onto Dreyfous Drive. The Casino building here (which doesn't have a casino) has a snack shop and rentals for pedal boats and canoes; fishing licenses are also issued here (you can't fish in the park without one). Turn left at the end of the road, then right onto Lelong Avenue and right again onto City Park Avenue. At I–10, City Park Avenue becomes Metairie Road. Continue on Metairie Road to the sign indicating **Longue Vue House and Gardens.**

TIMING

Plan to spend a minimum of two hours each at the New Orleans Museum of Art and Longue Vue House and Gardens. Both facilities hold treasures and should not be glossed over. A tour of the Pitot House takes about an hour. As for City Park, you can do a drive-through in a half hour or so, but this is a place to return time and again, for golfing, tennis, fishing, canoeing, and riding the carousel.

Sights to See

☺ **City Park.** With 1,500 luxuriant acres, this is one of the nation's largest urban parks. You can spend a great deal of time simply admiring the lagoons and majestic live oaks, whose gnarled branches bow and scrape to Mother Earth. But there is plenty to keep you busy if you are not an idler. There are four 18-hole golf courses, a double-deck driving range, 39 lighted courts in the Wisner Tennis Center, an ice-skating rink, baseball diamonds, stables, and the **New Orleans Botanical Garden** (☎ $3, ☉ Tues.–Sun. 10–4:30). The latter has a tropical conservatory, a water-lily pond, a formal rose garden, and azalea and camellia gardens. At the Casino concession building on Dreyfous Drive you can rent bikes, boats, and canoes—or just have a bite to eat. **Storyland** (☎ $1.50, ☉ Daily 10–4:30), a children's playground, has puppet shows, talking storybooks, story-book exhibits, and storytelling. Next door, **Carousel Gardens** (☎ $1, rides $1 per ride or $8 unlimited rides, ☉ Wed.–Fri. 10–2:30, weekends 11–5:30) has the Last Carousel, a restored 1906 merry-go-round replete with wooden horses, zebras, and other exotic creatures. Unfortunately, City Park is not safe at night. ⊠ *Main entrance at Lelong Ave.,* ☎ *504/482–4888.*

★ **Longue Vue House and Gardens.** Right on the border between Orleans and Jefferson parishes, the elegant estate was patterned after the great country manor houses of England. Once a private home, it is now a museum of decorative arts, furnished with European and Oriental antiques. Eight acres of landscaped gardens surround the house. ⊠ *7 Bamboo Rd.,* ☎ *504/488–5488. www.longuevue.com.* ☎ *$7.* ☉ *Mon.–Sat. 10–4:30, Sun. 1–5; last tour 45 mins before closing.*

OFF THE
BEATEN PATH

LOUISIANA NATURE AND SCIENCE CENTER – You can get a good in-town look at the surrounding swamps and bayous at this facility. There are nature trails, a children's discovery center, an interpretive center, and a planetarium. The center is in Joe W. Brown Memorial Park. To reach it from City Park, take I–10 east toward Slidell to Exit 244 (Read Boulevard) and turn right. At the third traffic light on Read Boulevard, turn left onto Nature Center Boulevard, which dead-ends at the facility. ⊠ *11000 Lake Forest Blvd. (East New Orleans),* ☎ *504/246–5672.* 🖃 *$4.75.* ☉ *Tues.–Fri. 9–5, Sat. 10–5, Sun. noon–5.*

New Orleans Museum of Art (NOMA). This white neoclassical building is large enough to exhibit virtually all of the museum's vast collections of 13th- to 18th-century Italian paintings, 20th-century European and American paintings and sculptures, Chinese jades, and the imperial treasures by Peter Carl Fabergé. ⊠ *City Park at 1 Collins-Diboll Circle,* ☎ *504/488–2631.* 🖃 *$6.* ☉ *Tues.–Sun. 10–5.*

Pitot House. This charming West Indies–style house was built in the late 18th century and bought in 1810 by New Orleans mayor James Pitot as a country home. It is furnished with Louisiana and other American 19th-century antiques. ⊠ *1440 Moss St.,* ☎ *504/482–0312.* 🖃 *$5.* ☉ *Wed.–Sat. 10–3; last tour at 2:15; sometimes closed Sat.*

Anne Rice's New Orleans

The eccentric charm and mystique of New Orleans have inspired many great fiction writers, but none has even approached the colossal commercial success enjoyed by Anne Rice. Her occult classics have spawned a cottage industry within New Orleans, as devoted readers seek to retrace the steps of her characters. Fans sporting vampire garb with pale makeup and black lipstick are just part of the scenery in this city with a penchant for pageantry. True diehards hang out in front of Rice's house waiting for a glimpse of their idol. Even if you eschew fangs and cape, the following tips may enhance your visit to the land of red beans and Rice. Each site appears in Rice's books and/or the 1994 film version of *Interview with the Vampire,* or relates to Rice herself.

Two neighborhoods predominate in Rice's writing set in New Orleans: the French Quarter, the figurative and literal center of the city; and the residential Garden District, some 3 mi upstream and ½ mi or so in from the river. The French Quarter sights discussed below are best visited on foot.

The Garden District sights may be visited on foot or by car; traffic and parking are both quite manageable. Anne Rice's tour operation has closed but look out for a possible new incarnation. Several tour companies do have Garden District tours, but don't focus on Rice sights (☞ Guided Tours *in* New Orleans A to Z, *below*).

Anne Rice has two ways to keep her fans updated on her busy life: her Web site, www.annerice.com, and her phone line (☎ 504/522–8634), on which she keeps a frequently updated, sincere-sounding recorded message.

French Quarter

In the French Quarter, New Orleans's sensory barrage reaches overload. There are live music on the streets and in the nightclubs, exquisite food at some of the world's best restaurants, and a visually intoxicating array of 17th- and 18th-century architecture. At night these old buildings—many of which are said to be haunted—take on a mysterious air that provides a plausible backdrop for the arcane activities of Anne Rice's fictional characters.

Start at **Gallier House** at 1118–1132 Royal Street, a mid-19th-century mansion that is perhaps the model for the fictional home of the vampires Lestat, Louis, and Claudia in the novel *Interview with the Vampire*. From Gallier House, turn left and walk two blocks along Royal Street to **Dumaine Street,** which often appears in Rice's writing. The house at 632 Dumaine Street, also known as Madame John's Legacy, appears in *Interview with the Vampire*. In Jackson Square, Lestat had his first encounter with Raglan James in *The Tale of the Body Thief*, and Lasher first appeared here in *The Witching Hour*. In *Interview with the Vampire*, Lestat drank the blood of a priest at St. Louis Cathedral.

The upper end of the French Quarter near Canal Street has several points of interest for Rice readers. Various characters in her books dine at **Galatoire's** and **Desire Oyster Bar.** The **St. Louis Hotel** is possibly the influence for the "new Spanish hotel" featured in *Interview with the Vampire*. Dolls used in the film of *Interview* were handmade in the Upper Quarter by Karl Boyer of **Boyer Antiques and Doll Shop** (⊠ 241 Chartres St., ☎ 504/522–4513); some interior footage was shot here as well.

Just outside the French Quarter are the historic and labyrinthine **St. Louis Cemeteries #1 and #2,** mentioned in both *Interview with the Vampire* and *Queen of the Damned*.

Timing. Allow a good three or four hours to take in the French Quarter sights. You may want to come for Halloween, when the author throws an annual bash that includes thousands of costumed guests. Bear in mind that New Orleans has a serious crime problem. You need to be careful strolling through the French Quarter, even during the day; at night, cemetery visits or walks, which may have special appeal for Rice readers, can be particularly dangerous. Be alert and streetwise.

Desire Oyster Bar. In *The Witching Hour* Michael Curry and Rowan Mayfair grab a bite here, as do Aaron Lightner and Rita Mae Lonigan. ⊠ 300 Bourbon St., ☎ 504/586–0300.

Dumaine Street. The French Quarter segment of Dumaine Street figures prominently in Rice's works: In *Interview with the Vampire* a musician friend of Lestat lives there; Lestat also resides on Dumaine in *The Vampire Lestat*, as does Julien Mayfair in *Lasher*.

The house known as **Madame John's Legacy** was finished in 1789 and is notable for its elements of West Indies plantation architecture; it appears in the film *Interview with the Vampire* during a voice-over by Louis, who describes Lestat's habit of dining on entire families, one member at a time. The house is a part of the Louisiana State Museum. ⊠ 632 Dumaine St., ☎ 504/568–6968. ☜ $3. ☉ Tues.–Sun. 9–5.

✗ **Galatoire's.** This is one of the best of the city's old-line restaurants (☞ Dining, *below*). Aaron Lightner and Llewelyn dine here in *The Witching Hour*. ⊠ 209 Bourbon St., ☎ 504/525–2021.

Gallier House. A restored mid-19th-century mansion, this residence is reputed to be the model for the fictional home of the vampires Lestat, Louis, and Claudia, as described in *Interview with the Vampire, The Queen of the Damned,* and *The Tale of the Body Thief*. A tour of the house may help Rice readers visualize scenes from these books and daily life in old New Orleans. ⊠ 1118–1132 Royal St., ☎ 504/525–5661. ☜ $6. ☉ Mon.–Sat. 10–4; tours 10:30–3:30 on ½ hr.

St. Louis Cemeteries #1 and #2. These historic and labyrinthine cemeteries lie just outside the French Quarter. St. Louis Cemetery #1 is mentioned in both *Interview with the Vampire* and *Queen of the Damned*; in the latter book it is the site of Louis's empty tomb. It's easy to get lost in the cemeteries' maze of aboveground graves; for this and other security reasons, as well as for maximum information, it's well worth your while to take a guided tour (☞ Guided Tours *in* New Orleans A to Z, *below*). ⊠ *400 Basin St.,* ☎ *504/482–5065 or 504/596–3050.* ⊙ *Mon.–Sat. 9–3, Sun. 9–noon.*

St. Louis Hotel. This is the reported prototype of the "new Spanish hotel" where several vivid blood-imbibing scenes unfold in *Interview with the Vampire*. For those who tire of a steady diet of crimson and claret, the hotel's restaurant **Louis XVI** serves exquisite French haute cuisine, at haute prices; if your budget allows splurging, this is a good place for it. ⊠ *730 Bienville St.,* ☎ *504/581–7300.*

Garden District

Several miles upriver from the French Quarter, the lovely residential Garden District is the other New Orleans neighborhood most closely associated with Anne Rice's novels. This is where the author grew up; she left the city around 1957 and lived in Dallas and San Francisco before returning to her hometown in 1988.

A GOOD WALK OR DRIVE

Start at Anne Rice's house, the Greek Revival–Italianate mansion at **1239 1st Street.** Next, walk one block on 1st Street in the direction of the streetcar tracks and turn left on Coliseum Street. Go four blocks on Coliseum to Washington Avenue and **Lafayette Cemetery #1,** which plays an important part in *Interview with the Vampire*. Across the street from the cemetery is **Commander's Palace,** another site appearing in Anne Rice's work. Just down the street, at the corner of Washington and Prytania streets, is an upscale minimall known as the Rink. This is the home of the **Garden District Book Shop** (⊠ 2727 Prytania St., ☎ 504/895–2266), which specializes in Rice's work and is the venue for the author's first signings of her new books.

Timing. Two to three hours should be ample here. One pleasant way to make the trip is via the St. Charles Avenue streetcar, stepping off around 1st Street. As in the French Quarter, you should be alert and streetwise when walking the streets, day or night; walking around at night, especially in the Lafayette Cemetery, can be dangerous.

SIGHTS TO SEE

Commander's Palace. This landmark restaurant (☞ Dining, *below*) is one of the city's more renowned spots for elegant regional cuisine. It is also the site of various Mayfair family dinners, especially after funerals, in *The Witching Hour*. ⊠ *1403 Washington Ave.,* ☎ *504/899–8221.*

Lafayette Cemetery #1. From the gates of the cemetery, you can see the lavish aboveground vaults and tombs of the families who built the surrounding Garden District mansions. Although the gates are generally open during working hours, it is not advisable to wander among the unguarded tombs. This sight serves as the burial ground for the fictional Mayfairs in *The Witching Hour*. The cemetery is also a major setting in *Interview with the Vampire*. Claudia Feeling requests a visit there to "roam the high marble tombs" in hopes of feasting on a sleeping vagrant, while Lestat uses the graveyard as a secret hiding place for his valuables. ⊠ *1400 Washington Ave.,* ☎ *504/588–9357.* ⊙ *Weekdays 7–2:30, Sat. 7–noon; closed Sun. except Mother's Day and Father's Day.*

1239 1st Street. Aspiring writers who gaze at Anne Rice's residence, a 19th-century Greek Revival–Italianate mansion, can imagine the potential rewards of creating a best-seller. Rice readers regard it as the obvious model for the Mayfair home in *The Witching Hour*. The building is not open to the public.

OFF THE
BEATEN PATH

ST. ELIZABETH'S HOME – In Uptown New Orleans, a mile upriver from the Garden District, St. Elizabeth's Home is a 19th-century three-building complex that Anne Rice owns. Rice has her extensive doll collection here. The former orphanage is open daily for guided tours. ⊠ *1314 Napoleon Ave.,* ☎ *504/899–6450.* ☞ *$7.* ☉ *Guided tours weekdays at 11, 1, and 3; weekends at 11 and 3.*

Scattered Grains of Rice

Some other neighborhoods and outlying rural areas are also significant to Rice's novels. The swamps and bayous that surround New Orleans have a distinct aura of mystery—making them ideal backdrops for such scenes as when Claudia and Louis dump the body of Lestat—and the fictional plantation homes, such as Oak Haven, Pointe du Lac, and Riverbend are based on a number of real-life residences.

Destrehan Plantation. The 1787 West Indies–style house was one of the film locations in *Interview with the Vampire*. The plantation is 23 mi from New Orleans (☞ Destrehan *in* Baton Rouge and Plantation Country, *below*). ⊠ *9999 River Rd. (LA 48),* ☎ *504/764–9315 or 504/524–5522.* ☞ *$8.* ☉ *Daily 9–4. Tours on the ½ hr.*

Madewood Plantation. Seventy miles southwest of New Orleans near Napoleonville, the impressive 21-room Greek Revival Madewood is the prototype for the Mayfair family's country home, Fontrevault, in *The Witching Hour* (☞ Napoleonville *in* Baton Rouge and Plantation Country, *below*). There are many other plantations up and down both sides of the river—some in idyllic settings and others butting up against oil refineries. The rural roads that lead to them are perfect for unloading those pesky corpses you've been lugging around. ⊠ *4250 Hwy. 308, Napoleonville,* ☎ *800/375–7151.* ☞ *$6.* ☉ *Daily 10–5.*

Oak Alley. Some 60 mi up and across the river near the town of Vacherie, this grand 1839 home was used as a film location in *Interview with the Vampire* (☞ Vacherie *in* Baton Rouge and Plantation Country, *below*). ⊠ *3645 Hwy. 18, Vacherie,* ☎ *800/442–5539.* ☞ *$8.* ☉ *Mar.–Oct., daily 9–5:30; Nov.–Feb., daily 9–5. Tours on the hr and ½ hr.*

Pitot House. This late-18th-century West Indian cottage on Bayou St. John inspired Louis's Pointe du Lac in *Interview with the Vampire*. ⊠ *1440 Moss St.,* ☎ *504/482–0312.* ☞ *$5.* ☉ *Wed.–Sat. 10–3. Final tour begins at 2:15.*

Dining

By Gene
Bourg

New Orleans usually means excellent dining. The Big Easy is recognized almost as much for zestily seasoned culinary delights as it is for hot and steamy jazz. Louisiana styles of cooking are becoming increasingly popular worldwide—but what is a fad elsewhere is a tradition here.

New Orleans is most renowned for Creole cuisine. A Creole, by definition, is a person of French or Spanish ancestry born in the New World. However, Creole is also a word of elastic implications, and in culinary terms, Creole refers to a distinctive cuisine indigenous to New Orleans with roots in European, African, and Caribbean dishes, enhanced by the liberal usage of local seasonings such as cayenne pepper and filé. The French influence is also strong, but the essence of Creole is in sauces, herbs, and the prominent use of seafood.

In recent years the term *nouvelle Créole* has been popularized by local restaurateurs. Instead of gumbo or jambalaya, a nouvelle menu might include hickory-grilled items, seafood served with pasta, or smoked meats and fish. There also has been a strong Italian influence in Creole cuisine, creating yet another marriage of styles.

Among the restaurant listings here are four Creole categories: Classic Creole, restaurants devoted to traditional Louisiana cuisine with minimal French overtones; French Creole, indicating a more expansive Continental accent; Soul Creole, black cuisine of Creole origin; and Creole-inspired, meaning the newer breed of cooking styles that incorporate nouvelle Creole dishes, new American cooking, and classic Creole. Please note that the categories often overlap; it is not unusual to find a blend of varying Creole cuisines on any given menu.

Cajun cuisine evolved from the farmhouse cooking brought from Nova Scotia to the bayou country by the Acadians more than 200 years ago, along with influences from the same French, African, Caribbean, and Spanish settlers who influenced Creole cookery. Cajun cooks generally use less expensive ingredients than their Creole counterparts, and they rely heavily on pork, game, and wild fowl. Cajun cuisine is rarely served in its purest form in New Orleans; rather it is often blended with Creole to create what's known as New Orleans–style cooking. There is a difference, though, between the two: Creole is distinguished by its classical French-inspired sauces; Cajun, by its tendency to be hearty and rustic.

The following terms appear frequently in the reviews and on menus:

Andouille (an-*dooey*)—a smoked Cajun sausage made with pork blade meat, onion, garlic, and other seasonings.

Bananas Foster—a dessert of bananas sautéed with butter, brown sugar, and cinnamon, flambéed in white rum and banana liqueur, and served on ice cream.

Barbecue shrimp—large shrimp baked in the shell, covered with butter, rosemary, herbs, and spices. They are not barbecued at all.

Boudin (boo-*dan*)—hot, spicy pork with onions, rice, and herbs stuffed in sausage casing.

Court-bouillon (coo-bee-*yon*)—a thick, hearty soup made with a roux, vegetables, and fish, and served over rice.

Crawfish—also known as mud-bugs, because in their wild state they live in the mud of freshwater streams. They resemble miniature lobsters and are served in a great variety of ways.

Étouffée (ay-too-*fay*)—crawfish étouffée is made with crawfish "fat" (actually, the liver), celery, and onion, then cooked for a short period of time and served over rice. Shrimp étouffée is heartier, made with an oil-and-flour roux or tomato paste, celery, onion, bell pepper, tomatoes, and chicken stock, cooked for approximately an hour and served over rice.

Filé (fee-*lay*)—ground sassafras, used to season gumbo and many other Creole and Cajun specialties.

Grillades (gree-*yads*)—bite-size pieces of veal round or beef chuck, braised in red wine, beef stock, garlic, herbs, and seasoning, served for breakfast with grits and with rice for dinner.

Gumbo—a hearty soup prepared in a variety of combinations (okra gumbo, shrimp gumbo, chicken gumbo, to name a few).

Jambalaya (jum-buh-*lie*-yah)—a spicy rice dish cooked with stock and chopped seasoning and made with any number of ingredients including sausage, shrimp, ham, and chicken.

Muffuletta—a large, round loaf of bread filled with cheese, ham, salami, and a garlicky olive salad.

Po'boy—also known as a poor boy; a large sandwich, similar to a hoagie or submarine, made on loaves of French bread and stuffed with roast beef and gravy, oysters, ham, shrimp, and other fillings.

Praline (*praw*-leen)—candy patty most commonly made from sugar, water or butter, and pecans. There are many flavors and kinds.

Rémoulade—a cold dressing that accompanies shrimp (sometimes crabmeat) over shredded lettuce, traditionally made of oil, Creole mustard, vinegar, horseradish, paprika, cayenne, celery, and green onion.

Brunch

Upscale restaurants on the tourist track often serve very reasonable, fixed-price brunch menus, many of them buffet style. A jazz group often supplies live music. Sunday, from late morning to early afternoon, is the prime time for brunch, although a few restaurants offer brunch on other days, too. Among the more reliable spots for these brunches are Commander's Palace, Palace Café, and Mr. B's Bistro, all for the festive atmosphere and food quality; Begué's in the Royal Sonesta Hotel, for the lavish buffet selections; Arnaud's, for the glittery main dining room; and the Praline Connection in the Warehouse District for the grand gospel brunch, with choirs from local churches.

Reservations and What to Wear

You are strongly advised to make reservations and to book well in advance for weekends, particularly during holiday periods or conventions. Pricey restaurants adhere to a moderate dress code—jackets for men, and in some places, a tie. New Orleans is a conservative city; dining out is an honored ritual, and people are expected to dress the part. A man in faded jeans and sports coat may be turned away, and even if he isn't, he may not feel entirely welcome.

Louisiana Cuisine

CAJUN-INSPIRED

$$$–$$$$ ✕ **K-Paul's Louisiana Kitchen.** It was in this rustic French Quarter café
  ★ that chef Paul Prudhomme started the blackening craze and added "Cajun" to America's culinary vocabulary. Two decades later thousands still consider a visit to New Orleans partly wasted without a trip to K-Paul's for his inventive gumbos, fried crawfish tails, blackened tuna, roast duck with rice dressing, and sweet-potato–pecan pie. Prices are steep at dinner but moderate at lunch; servings are generous. There's a second-floor balcony on Chartres Street and an upstairs room where diners can pass the time with cocktails before being seated. Reservations for dinner are also accepted (a recent change of policy). ⊠ *416 Chartres St., French Quarter,* ☎ *504/524–7394. AE, DC, MC, V. Closed Sun.*

CLASSIC CREOLE

$$$$ ✕ **Arnaud's.** This is a grande dame of classic Creole restaurants. The main dining room's outside wall of ornate etched glass reflects light from the charming old chandeliers. When that room fills up, the overflow spills over into a labyrinth of plush banquet rooms and bars. The big, ambitious menu includes classic dishes, as well as some new, more contemporary creations. Always reliable are the cold shrimp Arnaud in a superb rémoulade, the creamy oyster stew, and rich shrimp bisque, as well as the fine crème brûlée. Expect hurried service on especially crowded nights. ⊠ *813 Bienville St., French Quarter,* ☎ *504/523–5433. Reservations essential. Jacket required. AE, D, DC, MC, V.*

$$$–$$$$ ✕ **Gabrielle.** This bright and energetic restaurant, about five minutes
★ by taxi from the French Quarter, has remained a hit with locals thanks to chef Greg Sonnier's marvelous interpretations of earthy and spicy South Louisiana dishes. Seating has been expanded with the addition of a small dining room that has its own homey atmosphere, complete with lace curtains and framed still-life prints. Regulars come for the spicy rabbit and veal sausages, buttery oysters gratinéed with artichoke and Parmesan, a slew of excellent gumbos and étouffées, and Mary Sonnier's fresh-fruit cobblers and shortcakes. Servings are generous and sauces are rich. ⊠ *3201 Esplanade Ave., Mid-City,* ☎ *504/948–6233. AE, DC, MC, V. Closed Sun.–Mon. No lunch Tues.–Thurs. and Sat.*

$$$ ✕ **Brigtsen's.** Owner-chef Frank Brigtsen's fusion of Creole refinement and Acadian earthiness reflects his years as a protégé of Paul Prudhomme. His ever-changing menus add up to some of the best South Louisiana cooking you'll find anywhere. Everything is fresh and filled with the deep and complex tastes that characterize Creole-Cajun food. Rabbit and chicken dishes, usually involving rich sauces and gravies, are full of robust flavor. Fish dishes are elaborate, often showing up as crawfish, shrimp, or oysters in buttery, seasoned sauces. Trompe l'oeil murals add whimsy to the intimate spaces of a turn-of-the-century frame cottage. ⊠ *723 Dante St., Uptown,* ☎ *504/861–7610. Reservations essential. AE, MC, V. Closed Sun.–Mon.*

$$–$$$ ✕ **Clancy's.** Easy, sophisticated charm and a consistently classy menu
★ have made this minimally decorated bistro a favorite with professional and business types from nearby uptown neighborhoods. Most of the dishes are imaginative treatments of New Orleans favorites. Some of them, like the fresh sautéed fish in cream sauce flavored with crawfish stock and herbs, are exceptional. Simpler dishes such as fettuccine Alfredo and filet mignon in Madeira sauce benefit from careful and knowledgeable preparation. The decor is neutral, with gray walls and a few ceiling fans above bentwood chairs and white-linen cloths. ⊠ *6100 Annunciation St., Uptown,* ☎ *504/895–1111. Reservations essential. AE, MC, V. Closed Sun. No lunch Mon. and Sat.*

$$–$$$ ✕ **Mandich's.** This many-faceted locals' favorite resists categorizing.
★ It occupies a neat but unremarkable building in a blue-collar neighborhood. The decor—a mix of bright yellow paint, captain's chairs, and wood veneer—won't win prizes. The food ranges from straightforward and home style to ambitious trout and shellfish dishes. Fried oysters are swathed in a finely balanced butter sauce with garlic and parsley. The breaded trout Mandich has become a classic of the genre. ⊠ *3200 St. Claude Ave., 9th Ward,* ☎ *504/947–9533. MC, V. Closed Sun.–Mon. No dinner Tues.–Thurs.; no lunch Sat.*

CONTEMPORARY CREOLE

$$$–$$$$ ✕ **Commander's Palace.** No restaurant captures New Orleans's gas-
★ tronomic heritage and celebratory spirit as well as this one in a stately Garden District mansion. The upstairs Garden Room's glass walls have marvelous views of the giant oak trees on the patio below, and the other rooms promote conviviality with their bright pastels or delicate wall paintings. Chef Jamie Shannon's classics include poached oysters in a seasoned cream sauce with Oregon caviar; a spicy and meaty turtle soup; terrific crab cakes in an oyster sauce; and a wonderful sautéed trout coated with crunchy pecans. Among the addictive desserts are the bread pudding soufflé and chocolate Sheba, a wonderful Bavarian cream. The special weekend brunch menus are less ambitious but also less costly. ⊠ *1403 Washington Ave., Garden District,* ☎ *504/899–8221. Reservations essential. Jacket required. AE, D, DC, MC, V.*

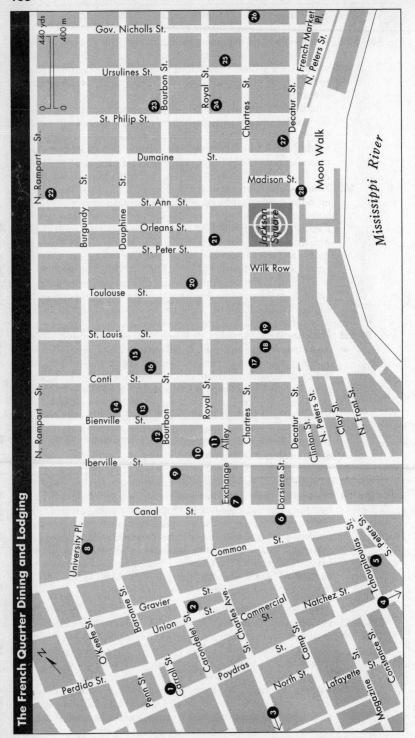

The French Quarter Dining and Lodging

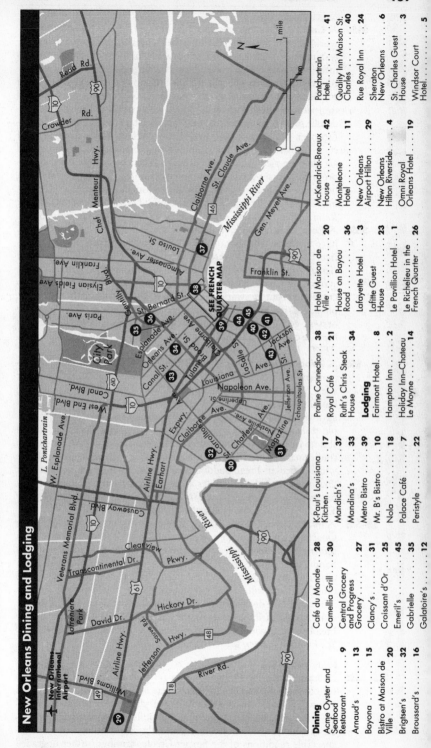

New Orleans Dining and Lodging

Dining

Acme Oyster and
Seafood
Restaurant **9**
Arnaud's **13**
Bayona **15**
Bistro at Maison de
Ville **20**
Brigtsen's **32**
Broussard's **16**
Café du Monde **28**
Camellia Grill **30**
Central Grocery
and Progress
Grocery **27**
Clancy's **31**
Croissant d'Or **25**
Emeril's **45**
Gabrielle **35**
Galatoire's **12**

K-Paul's Louisiana
Kitchen **17**
Mandich's **37**
Mandina's **33**
Metro Bistro **39**
Mr. B's Bistro. **10**
Nola **18**
Palace Café **7**
Peristyle **22**
Praline Connection . . **38**
Royal Café **21**
Ruth's Chris Steak
House **34**

Lodging

Fairmont Hotel. **8**
Hampton Inn **2**
Holiday Inn-Chateau
Le Moyne **14**

Hotel Maison de
Ville **20**
House on Bayou
Road **36**
Lafayette Hotel **3**
Lafitte Guest
House **23**
Le Pavillon Hotel . . **1**
Le Richelieu in the
French Quarter . . **26**

McKendrick-Breaux
House **42**
Monteleone
Hotel **11**
New Orleans
Airport Hilton . . **29**
New Orleans
Hilton Riverside. . **4**
Omni Royal
Orleans Hotel **19**

Pontchartrain
Hotel. **41**
Quality Inn Maison St.
Charles **40**
Rue Royal Inn **24**
Sheraton
New Orleans **6**
St. Charles Guest
House **3**
Windsor Court
Hotel **5**

CREOLE-INSPIRED

$$$$ ✕ **Emeril's.** Although celebrity chef Emeril Lagasse (of the Food Network's *Emeril Live*) makes rare appearances at his original namesake restaurant, you may spot a star or two from the sports and entertainment worlds in these always-jammed dining spaces. Noisy and decidedly contemporary, Emeril's has an ambitious menu that gives equal emphasis to Creole and modern American cooking. On the plate, this translates as a fresh corn crepe topped with Louisiana caviar, grilled andouille sausage in the chef's own Worcestershire sauce, a sauté of crawfish over jambalaya cakes, fresh-fruit cobblers, and a cornucopia of creative dishes. Singles and couples can grab a stool at a food bar and get close-up views of the chef at work. The looks of the place are appropriately avant-garde—brick and glass walls, gleaming wood floors, burnished-aluminum lamps, and a huge abstract-expressionist oil painting. ✉ *800 Tchoupitoulas St., Warehouse District,* ☏ *504/528–9393. Reservations essential. AE, DC, MC, V. Closed Sun. No lunch Sat.*

$$$–$$$$ ✕ **Nola.** Fans of chef Emeril Lagasse's who can't get a table at Emeril's
★ have this sassy and vibrant French Quarter restaurant as an alternative. Lagasse has not lowered his sights with Nola's menu, as lusty and rich as any in town. He stews boudin sausage with beer, onions, cane syrup, and Creole mustard before landing it all onto a sweet-potato crouton. Trout is swathed in a horseradish-citrus crust before it's plank-roasted in a wood oven. The combinations seem endless. For dessert, go for the coconut cream or apple-buttermilk pie with cinnamon ice cream. ✉ *534 St. Louis St., French Quarter,* ☏ *504/522–6652. AE, D, DC, MC, V. No lunch Sun.*

$$$ ✕ **Palace Café.** Members of the Commander's Palace branch of the Brennan family operate this big and colorful restaurant on Canal Street just a few blocks from the Mississippi riverfront. Crafted from a multistory building that was the city's oldest music store, the two-level Palace is a convivial spot to try some of the more imaginative contemporary Creole dishes. The crab chops, rabbit ravioli in sauce piquant, grilled shrimp with fettuccine, and seafood Napoleon represent the best in both traditional and modern New Orleans cookery. Desserts, especially the white-chocolate bread pudding and Mississippi mud pie, are luscious. Out front, the sidewalk tables are an excellent vantage point for people-watching. ✉ *605 Canal St., Central Business District,* ☏ *504/ 523–1661. Reservations essential. AE, DC, MC, V.*

$$–$$$ ✕ **Mr. B's Bistro.** The energy never subsides in this attractive, smart French Quarter restaurant, with waiters darting between the wood-and-glass screens that reduce the vastness of the dining room. In the green-vinyl banquettes, choose from a dependable contemporary-Creole menu centering on meats and seafood from a grill fueled with hickory and other aromatic woods. The barbecue shrimp is one of the best versions in town. Pasta dishes, especially the pasta jambalaya with andouille sausage and shrimp, are fresh and imaginative. The traditional-style bread pudding with Irish whiskey sauce is excellent, too. ✉ *201 Royal St., French Quarter,* ☏ *504/523–2078. AE, D, DC, MC, V.*

FRENCH CREOLE

$$$–$$$$ ✕ **Broussard's.** No French Quarter restaurant surpasses Broussard's for old-fashioned spectacle. A complete overhaul in the 1970s turned a dowdy Creole bistro into a soft-edged, glittery mix of elaborate wall coverings, chandeliers, porcelain, and polished woods, with a manicured courtyard to boot. If the menu blazes no trails, it contains respectable renditions of the fancier Creole standbys further upgraded with Continental touches. The savory cheesecake of crab and shrimp with dill and roasted sweet peppers is a star among the appetizers, along with lumps of backfin crab in a spicy sauce. Other luxurious sauces crown fillets of fresh pompano, braised quail, and a rack of lamb. ⊠ *819 Conti St., French Quarter,* ☎ *504/581–3866. AE, D, DC, MC, V. No lunch.*

$$$–$$$$ ✕ **Galatoire's.** Galatoire's always has epitomized the old-style French-Creole bistro, with a lengthy menu filled with sauces that can be humdrum in lesser restaurants. Many of the recipes date back to 1905. Fried oysters and bacon *en brochette* are worth every calorie, and the brick red rémoulade sauce sets the standard by which others should be measured. Others on the long list of winners include a Creole bouillabaisse (which must be ordered a couple of hours in advance), meaty veal or spring lamb chops in béarnaise sauce, and seafood-stuffed eggplant. The setting downstairs is a single, narrow dining room lighted with glistening brass chandeliers; the bentwood chairs at the white-cloth tables add to the timeless atmosphere. The quality of service varies from waiter to waiter. A recent renovation has produced second-floor dining rooms and a bar for those awaiting tables. ⊠ *209 Bourbon St., French Quarter,* ☎ *504/525–2021. Jacket required. AE, DC, MC, V. Closed Mon.*

$$–$$$ ✕ **Metro Bistro.** This cushy, smartly turned out spot just a block off Canal Street is a standout for its blend of attractiveness and practicality, as well as its good, hearty food. Near the mahogany bar, a huge, stylized mural suggests the New Orleans skyline. Above the burnished-wood chairs and banquette frames, the deep-gold walls rise to billows of sound-absorbing panels just below the 15-ft ceiling. Tiny cobalt blue lamps cast a soft light on the dishes, where traditional French and contemporary New Orleans styles meet. The *salade niçoise* holds bits of tuna carpaccio. Double-cut pork chops in a natural sauce, Burgundian beef stew, and a garlicky cassoulet with duck sausage, duck confit, and smoked pork are tailor-made for hefty appetites. Grilled fish lie between Creole stewed corn and a frizzle of sweet potato. And desserts are rich in flavor and creativity. ⊠ *200 Magazine St., in the Pelham Hotel, Central Business District,* ☎ *504/529–1900. AE, D, DC, MC, V.*

SOUL CREOLE

$–$$ ✕ **Praline Connection.** Down-home, Southern Creole–style cooking is the forte of this laid-back and likable restaurant a couple of blocks from the French Quarter (there's a branch in the Warehouse District, too). The food is the no-nonsense kind that has fueled generations of Southern families urban and rural, rich and poor. The fried or stewed chicken, smothered pork chops, barbecued ribs, and collard greens are definitively done. Add to this some of the lowest prices anywhere, a congenial service staff, and a neat-as-a-pin dining room, and the sum is a fine place to spend an hour or two. In the Warehouse District branch the Sunday gospel brunch is rousingly entertaining. ⊠ *542 Frenchmen St., Faubourg Marigny,* ☎ *504/943–3934;* ⊠ *901 S. Peters St., Warehouse District,* ☎ *504/523–3973. Reservations not accepted. AE, D, DC, MC, V.*

Avant-Garde

$$$–$$$$ ✕ **Bayona.** "New World" is the label chef Susan Spicer applies to her cooking style—such dishes as turnovers filled with spicy crawfish tails; a bisque of corn, leeks, and chicken; or fresh salmon fillet in white-wine sauce with sauerkraut. Her grilled duck breast with pepper-jelly glaze and shrimp with coriander sauce are among the creations that originally made Spicer's reputation. These and myriad other imaginative dishes are served in an early 19th-century Creole cottage on a quiet French Quarter street. The chef supervised the renovation of the handsome building, fairly glowing with oversize flower arrangements, elegant photographs, and, in one small dining room, trompe l'oeil murals suggesting Mediterranean landscapes. ⊠ *430 Dauphine St., French*

Quarter, ☎ *504/525–4455. Reservations essential. AE, DC, MC, V. Closed Sun.*

$$$–$$$$ ✕ **Peristyle.** Some of the most creative cooking in New Orleans em-
★ anates from the kitchen of this smartly turned-out yet very approach-
able little restaurant on the French Quarter's edge. Chef Anne Kearney
takes a thoroughly modern and personal approach to Continental
cooking on a small, ever-changing menu. In either the intimate bar, lined
with tables, or in the dining room proper, regulars dig into Kearney's
superb veal and sweetbreads ravioli, grilled sea bass with pickled
lemon vinaigrette, and veal chop with pickled cabbage. The look of
the place is intimate and simple, which makes concentrating on the great
food even easier. The wine list is small but nicely matched to the dishes.
✉ *1041 Dumaine St., French Quarter,* ☎ *504/593–9535. Reservations
essential. MC, V. Closed Sun.–Mon. No lunch Tues.–Thurs. and Sat.*

$$–$$$ ✕ **Bistro at Maison de Ville.** Small-scale chic has been the cachet of this
★ sleekly intimate spot, just a few steps from the raucous bawdiness of
Bourbon Street. Its fans certainly don't come in to stretch their limbs.
Only inches separate the tables, with those along the full-length ban-
quette close enough to become, in effect, a table for 20. But lustrous
mahogany and soft light from elegant wall lamps work their magic,
along with Impressionist-style oils reflected by the mirrors on the op-
posing wall. From the tiny kitchen come stylish, flavorful creations re-
flecting a modern approach to Creole and American cooking—barbecue
shrimp with New Orleans rice cakes, saffron-sage broth with quail ravi-
oli, and grilled salmon with a pecan-flavored wild rice. In accommo-
dating weather, umbrella-shaded tables await on the pleasant patio.
✉ *733 Toulouse St., French Quarter,* ☎ *504/528–9206. AE, DC, MC,
V. Closed Sun.*

$$–$$$ ✕ **Royal Café.** From the sidewalk at the corner of Royal and St. Peter
streets, you can almost hear the ceiling fans whirring overhead on the
café's three tiers of balconies, framed in lacy, gray cast iron. From the
second-floor tables, the ornate ironwork frames fascinating perspec-
tives along the French Quarter's main street. In the busily, colorfully dec-
orated downstairs room, the kitchen turns out dishes combining any
number of familiar New Orleans ingredients, such as a green salad with
fried okra, shrimp-and-crabmeat étouffée, oyster-and-artichoke soup, and
a Creole fricassee of duck and andouille sausage. At breakfast and
brunch, fancy sauces and garnishes make the omelets especially tempt-
ing. Reservations accepted for ground floor only. ✉ *706 Royal St.,
French Quarter,* ☎ *504/528–9086. AE, D, DC, MC, V. Closed Sun.*

Back to Basics

DESSERT

$ ✕ **Croissant d'Or.** Locals compete with visitors for a table in this col-
★ orful and pristine pastry shop that serves excellent and authentic
French croissants, pies, tarts, and custards, as well as an imaginative
selection of soups, salads, and sandwiches. Wash them down with real
French breakfast coffee, cappuccino, or espresso. In good weather, the
cheerful courtyard, with its quietly gurgling fountain, is the place to
sit. A filling lunch can be had for less than $10. Hours are 7–5 daily.
✉ *617 Ursulines St., French Quarter,* ☎ *504/524–4663. No credit cards.*

COFFEE SHOPS AND SANDWICHES

$ ✕ **Café du Monde.** For most visitors, a cup of chicory-laced café au
★ lait and a few sugar-dusted beignets in this venerable Creole institu-
tion are essential to their trip to New Orleans. The dozens of tables,
inside or out in the open air, are jammed at almost any hour (the café
is open 24 hours) with people feasting on the views of Jackson Square
and the hubbub on Decatur Street. The magical time to go is just be-
fore dawn, when the bustle subsides, and you can almost hear the birds

ONE LAST TRAVEL TIP:

Pack an easy way to reach the world.

Wherever you travel, the MCI WorldCom Card℠ is the easiest way to stay in touch. You can use it to call to and from more than 125 countries worldwide. And you can earn bonus miles every time you use your card. So go ahead, travel the world. MCI WorldCom℠ makes it even more rewarding. For additional access codes, visit **www.wcom.com/worldphone**.

MCI WORLDCOM.

EASY TO CALL WORLDWIDE

1. Just dial the WorldPhone® access number of the country you're calling from.

2. Dial or give the operator your MCI WorldCom Card number.

3. Dial or give the number you're calling.

Aruba (A) ⊹	800-888-8
Australia ◆	1-800-881-100
Bahamas ⊹	1-800-888-8000
Barbados (A) ⊹	1-800-888-8000
Bermuda ⊹	1-800-888-8000
British Virgin Islands (A) ⊹	1-800-888-8000
Canada	1-800-888-8000
Costa Rica (A) ◆	0800-012-2222
New Zealand	000-912
Puerto Rico	1-800-888-8000
United States	1-800-888-8000
U.S. Virgin Islands	1-800-888-8000

(A) Calls back to U.S. only. ⊹ Limited availability. ◆ Public phones may require deposit of coin or phone card for dial tone.

EARN FREQUENT FLIER MILES

When it Comes to Getting Cash at an ATM, Same Thing.

Whether you're in Yosemite or Yemen, using your Visa® card or ATM card with the PLUS symbol is the easiest and most convenient way to get cash. Even if your bank is in Minneapolis and you're in Miami, Visa/PLUS ATMs make getting cash so easy, you'll feel right at home. After all, Visa/PLUS ATMs are open 24 hours a day, 7 days a week, rain or shine. And if you need help finding one of Visa's 627,000 ATMs in 127 countries worldwide, visit **visa.com/pd/atm**. We'll make finding an ATM as easy as finding the Eiffel Tower, the Pyramids or even the Grand Canyon.

It's Everywhere You Want To Be®

in the crepe myrtles across the way. ✉ *French Market, Decatur and St. Ann Sts., French Quarter,* ☎ *504/525–4544. No credit cards.*

$ ✕ **Camellia Grill.** Every diner should be as classy as Camellia Grill, a one-of-a-kind eatery that deserves its following. Locals vie until early morning hours for one of the 29 stools at the gleaming counter, each place supplied with a large, fresh linen napkin. The 4-ounce hamburger is unsurpassed in the city. Other blue-ribbon dishes are the chili, the fruit and meringue pies, the garnished omelets, and the "cannibal special"—uncooked hamburger and egg with chopped onion on rye. Everything's made on the premises and served by bow-tied, white-waistcoated waiters with the fastest feet in the business. ✉ *626 S. Carrollton Ave., Uptown,* ☎ *504/866–9573. No credit cards.*

$ ✕ **Central Grocery.** This old-fashioned Italian grocery store in the French Quarter produces authentic muffulettas, one of the greatest gastronomic gifts of the city's Italian immigrants. They're good enough to challenge the po'boy as the local sandwich champ and are made by filling soft round loaves of seeded bread with ham, salami, mozzarella, and a salad of marinated chopped green olives. Each sandwich, about 10 inches in diameter, is sold in quarters and halves. Central is better known, but Progress comes up with a sandwich that many locals prefer because it's cheaper, more generous, and available in several varieties. You can eat your muffuletta at a counter, but some prefer to take theirs out to a bench on Jackson Square or the Moon Walk along the Mississippi riverfront, both just a few blocks away. ✉ *923 Decatur St.,* ☎ *504/523–1620.* ◷ *Daily 8–5:30.*

SEAFOOD

$$ ✕ **Mandina's.** The interior of this white-clapboard corner building is a study in 1940s nostalgia, with its functional bar facing a roomful of laminated tables set with sugar shakers, hot sauce, and salt and pepper. Regulars—a cross section of the population—endure a quarter-hour wait for a table under a 30-year-old newspaper clipping or the latest artwork from a St. Louis brewery. Butter, hearty seasonings, and tomato sauce are the staples. The shrimp rémoulade and old-fashioned gumbo are the logical appetizers. Broiled trout and shrimp, wading in seasoned butter, are tasty, as are the fried oysters and shrimp, the seafood or Italian-sausage po'boys, and the supersweet bread pudding. ✉ *3800 Canal St., Mid-City,* ☎ *504/482–9179. Reservations not accepted. No credit cards.*

$ ✕ **Acme Oyster and Seafood Restaurant.** A rough-edged classic in ★ every way, this no-nonsense eatery at the entrance to the French Quarter is a prime source of cool and salty raw oysters on the half shell; great shrimp, oyster, and roast beef po'boys; and state-of-the-art red beans and rice. Table service, once confined to the main dining room out front, is now provided in the rear room as well. Expect rather lengthy lines at the marble-top oyster bar. Crowds are sparser in the late afternoon. ✉ *724 Iberville St., French Quarter,* ☎ *504/522–5973. Reservations not accepted. AE, DC, MC, V.*

STEAK

$$$–$$$$ ✕ **Ruth's Chris Steak House.** Ruth's Chris is sacred to New Orleans ★ steak lovers. The all-American menu fairly drips with butter, and the main draw is aged U.S. prime beef in he-man portions, charbroiled and served atop a sizzling seasoned butter sauce. The hefty filet mignon is often taller than it is wide, the New York strip is usually packed with flavor, and a monstrous porterhouse serves several. If salads lack sparkle, the copious potato dishes are consistently first rate. The large, plush, but unfussy dining rooms of the flagship Mid-City restaurant are lined in pale wood paneling and understated landscape paintings. Politicians, both actual and aspiring, are everywhere. ✉ *711 N. Broad St., Mid-City,* ☎

504/486–0810; ✉ *3633 Veterans Blvd., Metairie,* ☎ *504/888–3600. Reservations essential on weekends. AE, D, DC, MC, V.*

Lodging

New Orleans has a wide variety of accommodations to choose from: posh high-rise hotels, antiques-filled antebellum homes, Creole cottages, and old slave quarters. Always try to reserve well ahead, especially during Mardi Gras or other seasonal events. Hotels frequently offer special packages at reduced rates, but during Mardi Gras almost every accommodation doubles its rates and many require a three- to five-day minimum stay.

Hotels

CENTRAL BUSINESS DISTRICT

The CBD will appeal to visitors who prefer accommodations in luxurious high-rise hotels. All the hotels listed are within walking distance of the French Quarter, but shuttles, taxis, buses, and the streetcar are readily available. Walking in this area after dark is not recommended.

$$$$ ⭐ 🏨 **Windsor Court Hotel.** Exquisite, gracious, elegant, eminently civilized—these words are frequently used to describe Windsor Court, but all fail to capture its wonderful quality. From Le Salon's scrumptious afternoon tea, served daily in the lobby, to the unbelievably large rooms, this is one of *the* places to stay in New Orleans. Four blocks from the French Quarter, the Windsor Court has plush carpeting, canopy and four-poster beds, stocked wet bars, marble vanities, oversize mirrors, and dressing areas. Phones have voice mail and data ports. The Windsor's Grill Room is an excellent restaurant choice. ✉ *300 Gravier St., 70130,* ☎ *504/523–6000 or 800/262–2662,* FAX *504/596–4513. 58 rooms, 266 suites, 2 penthouses. 2 restaurants, lobby lounge, pool, hot tub, sauna, steam room, health club, laundry service, parking (fee). AE, D, DC, MC, V.* ✇

$$$–$$$$ ⭐ 🏨 **Fairmont Hotel.** At this grand hotel built in 1893, the marble floor and Victorian splendor of the massive, busy lobby evoke a more elegant and gracious era. Rooms have special touches such as down pillows, terry robes, upscale toiletries, and bathroom scales; suites have fax machines. Impressive murals depicting life in the South enliven the walls of the famed Sazerac Bar; the lobby-level Sazerac Grill has an airy, cosmopolitan feel. Renovations have kept the Fairmont one of the finest hotels in the South. ✉ *123 Baronne St., 70140,* ☎ *504/529–7111 or 800/527–4727,* FAX *504/529–4764. 700 rooms, 85 suites. 3 restaurants, 2 bars, room service, pool, beauty salon, 2 tennis courts, exercise room, parking (fee). AE, D, DC, MC, V.* ✇

$$$–$$$$ 🏨 **New Orleans Hilton Riverside.** This sprawling, multilevel complex is right on the Mississippi River. Guest rooms have French Provincial furnishings and an iron and ironing board; the 180 rooms that share a concierge have fax machines. Rooms in the Riverside and Towers sections have superb views of the river. The hotel's health club is one of the best in the Gulf South, and there is an excellent business center. Pete Fountain's nightclub (☞ Nightlife, *below*) is here, and the Riverfront streetcar stops out front. The hotel has a resident golf pro and a four-hole putting green. ✉ *2 Poydras St., at Mississippi River, 70140,* ☎ *504/561–0500 or 800/445–8667,* FAX *504/568–1721. 1,600 rooms, 67 suites. 4 restaurants, 7 lounges, no-smoking floors, 2 pools, beauty salon, outdoor hot tub, massage, saunas, putting green, 8 tennis courts, aerobics, health club, jogging, racquetball, squash, nightclub, business services, parking (fee). AE, D, DC, MC, V.*

$$$–$$$$ ☆ 🏨 **Sheraton New Orleans.** On Canal Street, across from the French Quarter, this hotel has a lobby that's large and bright and usually bustling with conventioneers. A tropical atmosphere permeates the Pelican Bar, which features jazz nightly as well as a fine assortment of cigars. Café Promenade encircles the second level. Executive rooms on the top floors come with many special amenities, but even the regular guest rooms are spacious and well appointed. Expect top-quality service. ✉ *500 Canal St., 70130,* ☎ *504/525–2500 or 800/253–6156,* FAX *504/592–5615. 1,100 rooms, 72 suites. 3 restaurants, bar, lobby lounge, no-smoking rooms, pool, health club, parking (fee). AE, D, DC, MC, V.* 🐾

$$$ ☆ 🏨 **Lafayette Hotel.** This small brick building has housed the Lafayette Hotel ever since it was built in 1916. Special features are the handsome millwork, brass fittings, and marble baths throughout. The lobby is tiny but chic; rooms are spacious and sunny. Some rooms have four-poster beds; all have cushy easy chairs and ottomans. Brimming bookshelves are a homey touch. Some rooms on the second floor have floor-length windows opening onto a balcony; a number overlook Lafayette Square. ✉ *600 St. Charles Ave., 70130,* ☎ *504/524–4441 or 800/733–4754,* FAX *504/523–7327. 24 rooms, 20 suites. Restaurant, minibars, no-smoking rooms, dry cleaning, laundry service, concierge, parking (fee). AE, D, DC, MC, V.* 🐾

$$–$$$ ☆ 🏨 **Le Pavillon Hotel.** Magnificent chandeliers adorn the European-style lobby of this historic hotel (built in 1905), and a handsome display of artwork lines the corridors. Another pièce de résistance is the marble railing in the Gallery Lounge, originally from the Grand Hotel in Paris. Good-size rooms have high ceilings and identical traditional decor; suites are particularly elegant. ✉ *833 Poydras St., 70140,* ☎ *504/581–3111 or 800/535–9095,* FAX *504/522–5543. 219 rooms, 7 suites. Restaurant, bar, no-smoking floors, pool, hot tub, spa, exercise room, laundry service, parking (fee). AE, D, DC, MC, V.* 🐾

$–$$$ 🏨 **Hampton Inn.** This hotel is among several downtown office buildings that have either totally or partially converted to hotels (the UNO Downtown Center occupies the second and third floors). The lobby is Spartan, but rooms are large, all baths have hair dryers, and local phone calls and incoming faxes are free. Among its safety features are key-access elevators. Two blocks from Bourbon Street, the hotel is close to attractions. ✉ *226 Carondelet St., 70130,* ☎ *504/529–9990 or 800/ 426–7866,* FAX *504/529–9996. 186 rooms. Coffee shop, exercise room, concierge, parking (fee). AE, D, DC, MC, V. CP.*

FRENCH QUARTER

Most people who visit New Orleans stay in the Quarter, and the 96-square-block area has every type of accommodation. The selections that follow are all quality establishments chosen to provide variety in location, atmosphere, and price. Reservations are usually a must.

$$$–$$$$ ☆ 🏨 **Hotel Maison de Ville.** This small, romantic hotel lies in seclusion amid the hustle and bustle of the French Quarter. Tapestry-covered chairs, a gas fire burning in the sitting room, and antiques-furnished rooms all contribute to a 19th-century atmosphere. Some rooms are in former slave quarters in the courtyard; others are on the upper floors of the main house. Breakfast is served with a rose on a silver tray, and port and sherry are served in the afternoon. Other meals can be taken at a small adjacent restaurant called the Bistro. If you want a special hideaway, you'll love the hotel's Audubon Cottages, two blocks from the hotel, all are located off the street and have patios; the pool (for all guests) is here, too. Children under 12 are not accepted as guests. ✉ *727 Toulouse St., 70130,* ☎ *504/561–5858 or 800/634–1600,* FAX *504/528–9939. 14 rooms, 2 suites, 7 cottages. AE, D, DC, MC, V. CP. Restaurant, minibars, pool, parking (fee).*

$$$-$$$$ ⚑ **Monteleone Hotel.** The grande dame of French Quarter hotels, with
★ its ornate baroque facade, liveried doormen, and shimmering lobby chan-
deliers, was built in 1886 and was completely renovated in 1996. It's
the Quarter's oldest hotel and is operated by the fourth generation of
the Monteleone family. Rooms are extra large and luxurious. Fabrics
are rich, and there is a mix of four-poster beds, brass beds, and beds
with traditional headboards. Junior suites are spacious, and sumptu-
ous VIP suites come with extra pampering. The pool and exercise
room are on the roof; the slowly revolving Carousel Bar in the lobby
is a landmark. ⊠ *214 Royal St., 70140,* ☎ *504/523–3341 or 800/535–
9595,* ℻ *504/528–1019. 598 rooms, 28 suites. 3 restaurants, bar,
pool, exercise room, concierge, business services, meeting rooms. AE,
D, DC, MC, V.* ✎

$$-$$$$ ⚑ **Omni Royal Orleans Hotel.** This elegant white-marble hotel, built
★ in 1960 in the heart of the Vieux Carré, is a replica of the grand St.
Louis Hotel of the 1800s. Sconce-enhanced columns, gilt mirrors, fan
windows, and three magnificent chandeliers blend to re-create an aura
that reigned in New Orleans more than a century ago. Rooms are well
appointed, with marble baths and marble-top dressers and tables;
some have balconies. The old New Orleans map that covers one wall
of the lounge will fascinate anyone interested in history. The Rib Room
has been one of the city's culinary showpieces for 40 years. The rooftop
pool has the best overhead view of the French Quarter in the city. ⊠
621 St. Louis St., 70140, ☎ *504/529–5333 or 800/843–6664,* ℻ *504/
529–7089. 346 rooms, 16 suites. Restaurant, 3 lounges, pool, barbershop, beauty salon, exercise room, business services, meeting rooms,
parking (fee). AE, D, DC, MC, V.*

$-$$$$ ⚑ **Holiday Inn–Chateau Le Moyne.** Old-world atmosphere and decor
★ can be found just one block off Bourbon Street. Eight suites are in Cre-
ole cottages off a tropical courtyard; all rooms are furnished with an-
tiques and reproductions, and have coffeemakers, hair dryers, and
irons and ironing boards. ⊠ *301 Dauphine St., 70112,* ☎ *504/581–
1303 or 800/465–4329,* ℻ *504/523–5709. 160 rooms, 11 suites.
Restaurant, lounge, pool, parking (fee). AE, D, DC, MC, V.*

$$-$$$ ⚑ **Lafitte Guest House.** A four-story 1849 French-style manor house,
the Lafitte is meticulously restored, with rooms decorated with period
furnishings. Room 40 takes up the entire fourth floor and overlooks
French Quarter rooftops, and Room 5, the loft apartment, overlooks
the beautiful courtyard. Breakfast can be brought to your room, served
in the Victorian parlor, or enjoyed in the courtyard, and the owner serves
wine and hors d'oeuvres each evening. Smoking is not permitted. ⊠
1003 Bourbon St., 70116, ☎ *504/581–2678 or 800/331–7971,* ℻ *504/
581–2677. 16 rooms, 2 suites. AE, D, DC, MC, V. CP.* ✎

$-$$ ⚑ **Le Richelieu in the French Quarter.** Close to the Old Ursuline Con-
★ vent and the French Market, Le Richelieu combines the friendly, per-
sonal atmosphere of a small hotel with luxe touches (upscale toiletries,
hair dryers)—all at a moderate rate. Some rooms have mirrored walls
and large walk-in closets, many have refrigerators, and all have brass
ceiling fans and irons and ironing boards. Balcony rooms are the same
rates as standard rooms. There are an intimate bar and café off the
courtyard with tables on the terrace by the pool. ⊠ *1234 Chartres St.,
70116,* ☎ *504/529–2492 or 800/535–9653,* ℻ *504/524–8179. 69
rooms, 17 suites. Bar, café, pool, concierge, free parking. AE, D, DC,
MC, V.*

$-$$ ⚑ **Rue Royal Inn.** A pot of hot coffee and three Persian cats greet you
in the lobby. Many rooms are pleasantly oversize in this circa-1830
home; four have balconies overlooking Royal Street and a school playground, two have hot tubs, and each has a coffeemaker and a small
refrigerator. The complimentary Continental breakfast comes from the

nearby Croissant d'Or (☞ Dining, *above*). ✉ *1006 Royal St., 70116,* ☎ *504/524–3900 or 800/776–3901,* ⅨⅩ *504/558–0566. 17 rooms. Parking (fee). AE, D, DC, MC, V.*

GARDEN DISTRICT/UPTOWN

The Garden District is one of the city's ritziest residential areas. All the following are on or close to fashionable, mansion-lined St. Charles Avenue, where the St. Charles Avenue streetcar runs (24 hours), making the CBD and the French Quarter a mere 15–20 minutes away during the day. Take a taxi at night, as walking in this area after dark is not recommended.

$$–$$$ ★ 🏨 **Pontchartrain Hotel.** Maintaining the grand tradition is the hallmark of this quiet, elegant European-style hotel, which has reigned on St. Charles Avenue since 1927. Accommodations range from lavish sun-filled suites to small pension rooms with showers only (no tubs). The Pontchartrain has been the honeymoon hotel for such couples as Prince Aly Kahn and Rita Hayworth; suite names will tell you who else has stayed here. Nowadays more businesspeople than celebrities are guests. ✉ *2031 St. Charles Ave., 70140,* ☎ *504/524–0581 or 800/777–6193,* ⅨⅩ *504/524–7828. 84 rooms, 38 suites. 2 restaurants, piano bar, concierge, parking (fee). AE, D, DC, MC, V.* ✍

$–$$$ ★ 🏨 **Quality Inn Maison St. Charles.** This is a lovely property in six historic buildings that cluster around intimate courtyards. The tunnel entrance has an attractive mural. A complimentary shuttle to the convention center and 24-hour security are among the amenities. ✉ *1319 St. Charles Ave., 70130,* ☎ *504/522–0187 or 800/831–1783,* ⅨⅩ *504/528–9993. 129 rooms, 16 suites. Bar, no-smoking rooms, pool, hot tub, parking (fee). AE, D, DC, MC, V.*

$–$$ ★ 🏨 **McKendrick-Breaux House.** If you're looking for an alternative to the city's touristy quarters, this Greek Revival guest house in the Magazine Street antiques district is an excellent choice. In fact, the large rooms here, spread throughout the main house and a neighboring building, are one of the best values in the city. They have high ceilings, gorgeous wood floors, fresh flowers, TVs, telephones, and voice mail; many have their own entrances on the property's garden courtyard. ✉ *1474 Magazine St., 70130,* ☎ *504/586–1700 or 888/570–1700,* ⅨⅩ *504/522–7138. 7 rooms. Breakfast room, air-conditioning, free parking. AE, MC, V. CP.* ✍

$–$$ 🏨 **St. Charles Guest House.** Simple and affordable, this European-style pension is in four buildings one block from St. Charles Avenue. Rooms in the A and B buildings are larger. The small "backpacker" rooms share a bath and do not have air-conditioning. A pleasant surprise is the large swimming pool and deck. Proprietors Dennis and Joanne Hilton occasionally delight their guests with an impromptu crawfish boil or an introduction to New Orleans's red beans and rice. ✉ *1748 Prytania St., 70130,* ☎ *504/523–6556,* ⅨⅩ *504/522–6340. 36 rooms, 28 with bath. Pool. AE, MC, V. CP.* ✍

MID-CITY

$$–$$$$ ★ 🏨 **House on Bayou Road.** This circa-1798 West Indies–style Creole plantation home sits on 2 acres of lawns and gardens. All rooms have Louisiana antiques, including handsome four-poster feather beds. Accommodations are in the main house as well as in detached cottages. The suite in the private cottage is grand: There is a stunning skylight over the bed and a small kitchenette, bookshelves crammed with books, and a whirlpool bath. A full gourmet breakfast is served daily at umbrella tables around the pool. Wind chimes tinkle on the front porch, where there are rocking chairs for lolling. Smoking is allowed only on the porch or patio. A favorite of celebrities, this inn has hosted Dan Aykroyd,

Alfre Woodard, Fran Drescher, and Brad Pitt. A cooking school is conducted here by Chef Gerard Maras, a James Beard award–winning chef who leads small hands-on workshops. The house is in a remote setting, and walking in the area is not encouraged. ⊠ *2275 Bayou Rd., 70119,* ☎ *504/945–0992, 504/949–7711, or 800/882–2968;* ⨳ *504/945–0993. 5 rooms, 2 suites, 1 cottage. Pool. AE, DC.* ☟

KENNER/AIRPORT

$$–$$$ ☑ **New Orleans Airport Hilton.** Directly across from the New Orleans
★ International Airport is this upscale hotel offering unexpected elegance in this area of the city. The decor throughout is superb, with muted pastel colors that coordinate well with the soft pink Caribbean-style exterior. Rooms are spacious and sunny; the area rugs were handwoven in England. ⊠ *901 Airline Hwy., Kenner 70062,* ☎ *504/469–5000 or 800/872–5914,* ⨳ *504/466–5473. 317 rooms, 2 suites. Restaurant, bar, pool, putting green, tennis court, exercise room, business services, airport shuttle, parking (fee). AE, D, DC, MC, V.*

Nightlife and the Arts

The Arts

Comprehensive listings of events can be found in the weekly newspaper *Gambit,* which is distributed free at newsstands, supermarkets, and bookstores. The Friday edition of the daily *Times-Picayune* carries a "Lagniappe" tabloid that lists weekend events. The monthly *New Orleans* magazine also has a "Calendar" section. Credit-card purchases of tickets for events at the Theatre for Performing Arts, the Saenger Performing Arts Center, the Orpheum Theater, and Kiefer UNO Lakefront Arena can be made through TicketMaster (☎ 504/522–5555).

CONCERTS

Free **jazz concerts** are held on weekends during the day in Dutch Alley. Pick up a schedule at the French Market Visitor Center (⊠ French Market at Dumaine St., ☎ 504/596–3424). The **Louisiana Philharmonic Orchestra** (☎ 504/523–6530) performs at the Orpheum Theatre (⊠ 129 University Pl.).

DANCE AND OPERA

The **New Orleans Ballet Association** (⊠ 305 Baronne St., ☎ 504/522–0996) and the **New Orleans Opera Association** (⊠ 305 Baronne St., ☎ 504/529–2278) produce performances of visiting companies. Both ballet and opera productions take place at the New Orleans Theatre for the Performing Arts in Armstrong Park.

THEATER

The avant-garde, the offbeat, and the satirical are among the theatrical offerings at **Contemporary Arts Center** (⊠ 900 Camp St., ☎ 504/523–1216). At **Le Petit Théâtre du Vieux Carré** (⊠ 616 St. Peter St., ☎ 504/522–9958) classics, contemporary drama, children's theater, and musicals are presented. Touring Broadway shows, dance companies, and top-name talent appear at the **Saenger Performing Arts Center** (⊠ 143 N. Rampart St., ☎ 504/524–2490). The **Kiefer UNO Lakefront Arena** (⊠ 6801 Franklin Ave., ☎ 504/286–7222) is a venue for major concerts.

Festivals

During the annual **Jazz and Heritage Festival,** held from the last weekend in April through the first weekend in May, musicians from all over the world pour in to mix it up with local talent. Called the Jazzfest by its devotees, this festival draws thousands of fans and internationally acclaimed musicians. The weekend venue is the infield of the Fair Grounds; the week in between sees music venues all over town filled to bursting. In addition to homegrown talent such as Wynton and Branford Marsalis, Harry Connick, Jr., Allen Toussaint, and the Neville Brothers, look for such luminaries as B. B. King, Al Green, and Ray Charles.

North America's biggest bash—**Mardi Gras**—takes place in February or March (the date depends upon when Easter falls). Carnival season begins January 6 (Twelfth Night) and ends at midnight on Fat Tuesday, with the advent of Ash Wednesday and Lent. Mardi Gras means giant and fantastic floats rolling through downtown streets (though not in the French Quarter), eye-popping costumes, and the occasional exposed body parts. The last great push of the Carnival season is the weekend before Fat Tuesday (Mardi Gras Day), when parades roll day and night, and the city is given over to flat-out partying.

Nightlife

New Orleans is a 24-hour town, meaning there are no legal closing times, and it ain't over till it's over. Last call, especially on Bourbon Street, depends on how business is. Your best bet is to phone ahead before tooling out to barhop at 2 AM. It is also smart to ask ahead about current credit-card policy, cover, and minimum.

Gambit, the free weekly newspaper, has a complete listing of who's doing what where. Things can change between press and performance times, so if there's an artist you're especially eager to hear, it's wise to call and confirm before turning up.

BARS

With imbibing a favorite local pastime, New Orleans is loaded, so to speak, with good bars. The French Quarter has at least one on every block; touristy Bourbon Street is lined with bars of every sort, from oyster to bottomless. The University section, around Loyola and Tulane, is also a great place for barhopping.

One of the world's best-known bars and not incidentally home of the Hurricane (a sweetly potent concoction of rum and fruit juices) is **Pat O'Brien's** (⌧ 718 St. Peter St., ☏ 504/525–4823). There are three bars, including a lively piano bar and a large courtyard bar, and mobs of collegians and tourists line up to get in. Very lively, very loud, very late. The **Napoleon House** (⌧ 500 Chartres St., ☏ 504/524–9752), with sepia walls, taped classical music, and Napoleonic memorabilia, is a favored local haunt. **Lafitte's Blacksmith Shop** (⌧ 941 Bourbon St., ☏ 504/523–0066), in a tattered 18th-century cottage, has been a hangout for artists and writers for ages.

CASINOS

In 1999, after years of legal wrangling, a land-based casino finally opened at the foot of Canal Street. Operated by Harrah's, the downtown casino joins three gambling riverboats; all are open 24 hours daily, and all have a lounge and/or grill and live music, plus slots, video poker, and gaming tables for roulette, craps, blackjack, and big six.

Harrah's New Orleans Casino (⌧ 4 Canal St., ☏ 504/533–6000, 877/277–4263), a 100,000-square-ft gambling den at the foot of Canal Street, is housed in a Greek Revival–style structure dressed to the nines in New Orleans–themed decor. You'll find the Mardi Gras Court, a Jazz Court, and a Smugglers Court, among its diversions, as well as plenty of music and daily parades replete with Mardi Gras revelers. Oh, and it also has 2,900 slots and 117 table games.

Belle of Orleans (⌧ 1 Stars & Stripes Blvd., ☏ 504/248–3200 or 800/572–2559) is on Lake Pontchartrain adjacent to Lakefront Airport. **Boomtown Belle Casino** (⌧ 4132 Peters Rd., on the Harvey Canal, Westbank, ☏ 504/366–7711 or 800/366–7711) has a Wild West theme. **Trea-**

sure Chest (✉ 5050 Williams Blvd., Kenner, ☎ 504/443–8000 or 800/298–0711) is docked on Lake Pontchartrain, across from the Pontchartrain Center. It has a glitzy entertainment complex land-side.

DANCING

Two-stepping to a Cajun band is billed as the *"spécialité de la maison,"* but the **Maple Leaf Bar** moves with rock, R&B, reggae, and gospel as well. (Cajun nights are special.) ✉ *8316 Oak St.,* ☎ *504/866–9359.* ⊡ *$5 cover.* ☉ *3 PM; closing time varies.*

This is New Orleans, so it shouldn't surprise you that even a bowling alley has live music. Locals flock to the **Mid-City Lanes Rock-N-Bowl** and its ground-level sibling, **Bowl Me Under**, to dance to homegrown bands. Admission varies depending upon the bands. ✉ *4133 S. Carrollton Ave.,* ☎ *504/482–3133.* $ ⊡ *10–$15.* ☉ *Rock-N-Bowl, Wed.–Sat. 9:30 PM–2:30 AM; bowling alley, daily noon–midnight.*

JAZZ

Jazz was born in New Orleans, and the music isn't always at night. Weekend jazz brunches are enormously popular and pop up all over town. But a stroll down Bourbon Street will give you a taste of the city's eclectic rhythms—Cajun, gutbucket, R&B, rock, ragtime, new wave—you name it, and you'll hear it almost around the clock.

Aboard the **Creole Queen** you'll cruise on the river with a Dixieland jazz band, and there's a buffet to boot. If you've an ounce of romance racing through your veins, do it. ✉ *Poydras St. Wharf,* ☎ *504/524–0814. Daytime cruise:* ⊡ *$15.75.* ☉ *Daily 10:30 and 2. Dinner cruise:* ⊡ *$45.* ☉ *Daily 8–10, boards 7–8.*

There's live music five nights a week at the **Palm Court Jazz Café.** Traditional jazz is the rule, with blues thrown in on Wednesday. The fine Creole and international kitchen stays open until the music stops. ✉ *1204 Decatur St.,* ☎ *504/525–0200.* ⊡ *$5 cover to sit at tables, free at bar.* ☉ *7 PM–11 PM; live music Wed., Thurs., and Sun. at 8 PM, Fri.–Sat. at 7 PM. Closed Mon.–Tues.*

Pete Fountain's Club is a New Orleans legend with Pete's clarinet and his band, which plays in a plush 500-seat room on the third floor of the Hilton Hotel. This is Pete's home base, and the man's on the stand Tuesday, Wednesday, Friday, and Saturday when he's in town (he makes frequent appearances around the country, so it's wise to call ahead). ✉ *2 Poydras St.,* ☎ *504/523–4374.* ⊡ *$19 cover.* ☉ *Shows daily 10 PM–11:15 PM.*

Speaking of legends, the old-time jazz greats lay out the best traditional jazz in the world in a musty, funky hall that's short on comfort, long on talent. **Preservation Hall** is the place for traditional jazz. You may have to stand in line to get in (and it's often standing room only inside), but it will help if you get here about 7:30. ✉ *726 St. Peter St.,* ☎ *504/522–2841, www.preservationhall.com.* ⊡ *$5 cover.* ☉ *Daily 8 PM–midnight.*

★

Rambling, rustic, and raucous **Snug Harbor** is where graybeards and undergrads get a big bang out of the likes of the Dirty Dozen, Charmaine Neville, the David Torkanowsky Trio, and Maria Muldaur. ✉ *626 Frenchmen St.,* ☎ *504/949–0696.* ⊡ *Weekdays $8–$10 cover, weekends $12–$15 cover.* ☉ *Daily 5 PM–2 AM; show times 8 PM and 11 PM.*

R&B, CAJUN, ROCK, NEW WAVE

Industrial-strength rock rolls out of the sound system at the **Hard Rock Cafe.** Hard Rock Hurricanes are dispensed at a guitar-shape bar, and the place is filled with rock-and-roll memorabilia. Hamburgers, salads, and steaks are served. There's no cover. ✉ *440 N. Peters St.,* ☎ *504/529–8617.* ☉ *Weekdays 11–11, weekends 11 AM–midnight.*

House of Blues is a $7 million music venue with an awesome sound system where local and nationally known artists perform. There are also a recording studio, restaurant, and a shop. The cover and closing time vary depending on the show. ✉ *225 Decatur St.,* ☎ *504/529–2624.* ☉ *Restaurant daily 11 AM–midnight; nightclub daily from 8 PM, sets begin 9:30 PM.*

The college crowd raises the rafters at **Jimmy's Music Club.** The music, by national as well as local groups, is rock, new wave, reggae, R&B, whatever. ✉ *8200 Willow St.,* ☎ *504/861–8200.* ▣ *Cover $8–$15.* ☉ *Tues.–Sat. 9 PM, shows begin 9:30 PM; closing time varies.*

Fans of Jimmy Buffett flock to **Margaritaville Café,** where local funk and R&B acts perform, as occasionally does Buffett himself. The cover varies. ✉ *1104 Decatur St.,* ☎ *504/592–2565.* ☉ *Daily 11 AM, live band sets daily 2 PM, main stage weekend shows 10:30 PM; closing time varies.*

An institution, **Tipitina's** is a sort of microcosm of Jazzfest, featuring progressive jazz, reggae, ska, R&B, rock, new wave, blues—well, just about everything. Its name comes from a song by Professor Longhair, who was posthumously awarded a Grammy for Best Traditional Blues Recording, and the place is dedicated to his memory. It's funky, mellow, and loaded with laid-back locals. Tips also has a French Quarter branch, not far from the House of Blues. The **concert hot line** for both locations is ☎ 504/897–3943. *501 Napoleon Ave.,* ☎ *504/895–8477;* ✉ *233 N. Peters St., French Quarter,* ☎ *504/566–7095. Cover* ▣ *$3–$25.* ☉ *Daily 5 PM; closing time varies.*

Outdoor Activities and Sports

Baseball

The **AAA New Orleans Zephyrs** (☎ 504/734–5155), a farm team of the Houston Astros, play ball at the 10,000-seat Zephyr Field (✉ 6000 Airline Hwy. [Hwy. 61]), near David Drive and Transcontinental Drive, in Jefferson Parish, a 15-minute drive west of New Orleans. The **University of New Orleans Privateers** take on their foes in Privateers Park at the school's Lakefront campus (☎ 504/286–7240). **Tulane Green Wave** teams play home games at the New Orleans Arena (✉ 1501 Girod St., adjacent to Superdome) and at the school's St. Charles Avenue campus (☎ 504/861–3661).

Basketball

The **Sugar Bowl Basketball Classic** (☎ 504/525–8573) is played in the Superdome the week preceding the annual football classic.

Biking

Rentals are available at **Bicycle Michael's** (✉ 618 Frenchmen St., ☎ 504/945–9505) at $3.50 per hour and $12.50 per day. **French Quarter Bicycles** (✉ 522 Dumaine St., ☎ 504/529–3136) has mountain bikes ($4.50 per hour, $14 and up per day), baby strollers and baby carriages ($1 per hour, $4 per day), and one wheelchair ($4.50 per hour, $14 per day) for rent.

Guided bike tours of Plantation Country and Cajun Country are available from **French Louisiana Bike Tours** (✉ 3216 W. Esplanade Ave., PMB 302, Metairie, LA 70002, ☎ 504/488–9844 or 800/346–7989). Prices start at about $1,100 for a four-day tour that includes rental of a Cannondale hybrid (equipped with smooth tires, Avocet computer, back rack and handlebar pack), lodging, and meals.

Football

The **New Orleans Saints** (☎ 504/522–2600) play NFL games in the Superdome. Home games of **Tulane University** (☎ 504/861–3661) are played in the Dome. The annual **Sugar Bowl Football Classic** (☎ 504/525–8573) takes place in the Dome on New Year's Day. In late November the **Bayou Classic** (☎ 504/587–3663) pits Southern University against Grambling University. The Louisiana Superdome has hosted the **Super Bowl** eight times, more than any other city, and undoubtedly will do so again.

Horseback Riding

Cascade Stables (✉ 6500 Magazine St., ☎ 504/891–2246) has guided 45-minute trail rides, costing $20 per person, in Audubon Park.

Ice Hockey

The New Orleans Brass (1201 St. Peter St., ☎ 504/522–7825) of the East Coast Ice Hockey League play home games in the New Orleans Arena, the $84 million sports facility that opened in 1999 behind the Superdome.

Ice Skating

The city's only ice-skating rink opened in late 1999 in City Park, adjacent to the Wisner Tennis Center. **Holiday Ice Rink** (✉ Dreyfous Ave. at Victory Ave., ☎ 504/522–7465) has daily 90-minute skating sessions at 10, noon, 2, 4, 6, 8, and 10 (a bit later on weekends). The $9 admission price includes skate rental. The Olympic-size arena also offers lessons, figure skating exhibitions, and hockey demonstrations.

Tennis

There are 39 courts in the **City Park Wisner Tennis Center** (✉ 1 Dreyfous Ave., in City Park, ☎ 504/483–9383). **Audubon Park** (☎ 504/895–1042) has 10 courts near Tchoupitoulas Street.

Shopping

Pralines, chicory coffee, Mardi Gras masks, vintage clothing, and jazz records are usually hot tickets. The packaging of New Orleans food to go is a growing trend.

Shopping Districts

New Orleans shops string along the Mississippi all the way from the French Quarter to beyond Riverbend (at the Uptown bend in the river). The **French Quarter** is the place to search for antiques shops, art galleries, designer boutiques, bookstores, and all sorts of unique shops in all sorts of edifices. Among **Canal Place**'s (✉ 333 Canal St.) lofty tenants you'll find Saks Fifth Avenue, Laura Ashley, Gucci, Brooks Brothers, and the wares of New Orleans jewelry designer Mignon Faget. **Riverwalk** (✉ 1 Poydras St.) is a long, tunnel-like marketplace brightened by more than 200 splashy shops, restaurants, food courts, and huge windows overlooking the Mississippi. The tony **New Orleans Centre,** between the Hyatt Regency Hotel and the Superdome on Poydras Street, has more than 100 occupants, including Macy's and Lord & Taylor. Along 6 mi of **Magazine Street** are Victorian houses and small cottages filled with antiques and collectibles. Stop at the New Orleans Welcome Center for a copy of the shopper's guides published by the Magazine Street Merchants Association and the Royal Street Guild.

Turn-of-the-century Creole cottages cradle everything from toy shops to designer boutiques and delis in the **Riverbend** (✉ Maple St. and Carrollton Ave.). Macy's and Mervyn's are among the 155 shops in Metairie's glittering three-level **Esplanade Mall** (✉ 1401 W. Esplanade Ave.). The **Warehouse District** (✉ Bordered roughly by Girod St., Howard Ave., Camp

St., and the river), particularly Julia Street, has become a major center for the visual arts, not unlike New York City's SoHo.

Specialty Stores

ANTIQUES

Shoulder to shoulder along **Royal Street** are some of the finest—and oldest—antiques stores in New Orleans. **Adler & Waldhorn** (✉ 343 Royal St., ☎ 504/581–6379), the city's oldest antiques store, was established in 1881; specialties are English furniture, Victorian and Early American jewelry, and antique English porcelain and silver. **French Antique Shop** (✉ 225 Royal St., ☎ 504/524–9861) has a large selection of European chandeliers and furniture, as well as some Creole and local designs. **Lucullus** (✉ 610 Chartres St., ☎ 504/528–9620) carries fine Continental and English 17th- to 19th-century furniture, art, and cookware. **Manheim Galleries** (✉ 403–409 Royal St., ☎ 504/568–1901) has the city's largest collection of antique English, Continental, and Asian furnishings; porcelains; paintings; silver; and jade. This is the agent for Boehm Birds. **Moss Antiques** (✉ 411 Royal St., ☎ 504/522–3981) has a large selection of antique and estate jewels, as well as fine French and English furnishings, paintings, and bric-a-brac. **Patout Antiques** (✉ 920 Royal St., ☎ 504/522–0582) has high-quality antiques from Louisiana plantation houses. **Rothschild's Antiques** (✉ 241 Royal St., ☎ 504/523–5816; ✉ 321 Royal St., ☎ 504/523–2281) has a large collection of furniture, silver, jewelry, mantels, and clocks from the 18th through the 20th centuries. **Whisnant Galleries** (✉ 222 Chartres St., ☎ 504/524–9766) has delightfully eclectic antique jewelry, African sculptures, clocks, and unusual pieces.

ART

The **French Quarter** is known for its many art galleries, most of which are on Royal Street. **Bergen Galleries** (✉ 730 Royal St., ☎ 504/523–7882) offers posters and collectibles by local artists. The **Black Art Collection** (✉ 309 Chartres St., ☎ 504/529–3080) displays and sells works by local and national African-American artists. **Dyansen Gallery** (✉ 433 Royal St., ☎ 504/523–2902) features the work of modern and contemporary artists. **Rodrigue Gallery** (✉ 721 Royal St., ☎ 504/581–4244 or 800/899–4244) showcases artwork featuring the Blue Dog of internationally acclaimed Cajun artist George Rodrigue. **Southern Expressions** (✉ 521 St. Ann St., at Jackson Sq., ☎ 504/525–4530) shows the work of regional artists.

FLEA MARKET

Jazz is within earshot, and "junque" is at your fingertips at the **French Market Flea Market** (✉ French Market Pl., ☎ 504/522–2621) daily from 7 to 7.

FOOD TO GO

Battistella's Sea Foods, Inc. (✉ 910 Touro St., ☎ 504/949–2724) carries packaged seafood to go. The **New Orleans School of Cooking** (✉ Jax Brewery, 620 Decatur St., ☎ 504/525–2665) stocks packaged red beans and rice, beignet mixes, Cajun spices, pecans, and other Louisiana specialties. **Louisiana Products** (✉ 507 St. Ann St., on Jackson Sq., ☎ 504/524–7331) is another good source for Cajun and Creole foods and can ship anywhere in the country. **Foodies Kitchen** (✉ 720 Veterans Hwy, Metairie, ☎ 504/837–9695), opened in 1999, is a Commander's Palace operation that has take-out foods, including a deli and bakery, as well as tables for those who prefer to eat in.

JAZZ RECORDS

Louisiana Music Factory (✉ 225 N. Peters St., ☎ 504/523–1094) has a good selection of regional vinyl, CDs, and tapes.

MASKS

For exotic handmade masks to decorate your face or your wall, visit **Rumors** (⊠ 513 Royal St., ☎ 504/525–0292).

PRALINES

For the best pralines in town, try **Old Town Praline Shop** (⊠ 627 Royal St., ☎ 504/525–1413).

Side Trip from New Orleans

Jean Lafitte National Historical Park

20 mi south of downtown.

Just 45 minutes by car from the French Quarter, you can sample Louisiana's exotic natural splendors in the park's 8,000-acre Barataria Unit. Paved walkways lace alongside bayous, over which hang frayed canopies of Spanish moss and in which alligators, snakes, and other critters slither. Park rangers conduct free walking tours daily, but you can also wander along the trails on your own. At the **Bayou Barn** (⊠ Intersection of Rtes. 31, 34, and 45, ☎ 504/689–2663 or 800/862–2968, FAX 504/689–4554) the intrepid can rent a canoe and paddle off alone; it's $7.50 per person for two hours. The less adventuresome can take a Bayou Barn guided tour (six-person minimum, $20 for two hours); and all can enjoy the fresh gumbo and jambalaya dished up by the friendly folks at the shop. To reach the park, take U.S. 90 over the Crescent City Connection (bridge) across the river and turn left on Route 45. ⊠ *Just below Marrero on Lake Salvador (via U.S. 90, south of New Orleans, and Rte. 45),* ☎ *504/589–2330.*

New Orleans A to Z

Arriving and Departing

BY BOAT

You can arrive from northern ports in grand 19th-century style aboard one of the authentic overnight steamboats of the **Delta Queen Steamboat Company**—the *Delta Queen,* the *Mississippi Queen,* or the *American Queen*—which home-port in New Orleans (⊠ Robin St. Wharf, ☎ 800/543–1949, FAX 504/585–0630).

BY BUS

Greyhound (☎ 800/231–2222) operates out of Union Passenger Terminal (☞ By Train, *below*).

BY CAR

I–10 runs from Florida through New Orleans and on to California. I–55 is the north–south route, connecting with I–12 west of Ponchatoula and with I–10 a touch west of New Orleans; I–59 runs northeast into Mississippi and Alabama; and I–49 slashes diagonally through the state's midsection, from Lafayette to Shreveport. U.S. 61, from the west, and U.S. 90, from the east, also run through New Orleans.

BY PLANE

New Orleans International Airport (⊠ 900 Airline Dr., Kenner, ☎ 504/464–0831), 15 mi west of New Orleans, is served by American, Continental, Delta, Northwest, Southwest, TWA, United, and US Airways (☞ Air Travel *in* the Gold Guide for telephone numbers), as well as by a number of foreign carriers. Locals sometimes still call it Moissant Field, its former name.

Buses operated by **Louisiana Transit** (☎ 504/737–9611) run every 22 minutes between the airport and Elk Place in the CBD. Hours of operation are 6 AM–6:20 PM; the last bus leaves the airport at 5:40 PM. The $1.50 trip downtown takes about an hour.

The **Airport Shuttle** (☎ 504/522–3500 or 800/543–6332) leaves the airport every 5–10 minutes, 24 hours a day, for the 20- to 30-minute trip into town. Small vans drop passengers off at their hotels, so arrival time at your destination depends upon the van's number of stops. The fare is $10 per person.

Taxi fare is $21 for one or two passengers, $8 per additional person. The driver may offer three or four strangers together a rate comparable to the airport shuttle.

By **car** you can drive to New Orleans from Kenner via Airline Highway (U.S. 61) or I–10. Hertz, Avis, Budget, and other major car rental agencies have airport outlets (☞ Car Rental, *below*).

BY TRAIN
Amtrak (☎ 800/872–7245) trains pull into the CBD's **Union Passenger Terminal** (✉ 1001 Loyola Ave., ☎ 504/528–1610). New Orleans is connected via rail to California, Chicago, Florida, New York, and points in between.

Getting Around
BY BICYCLE
The flat terrain of the French Quarter invites bikers, and Royal and Bourbon streets in the Quarter are closed off during the day to all but bikers and pedestrians. Many cyclists make the trek from the Quarter to City Park or Audubon Park, both good places for easy wheeling.

BY BOAT AND FERRY
The **Canal Street Ferry** will take you across the Mississippi from the Canal Street Wharf to Algiers Ferry Landing; the ride takes 25 minutes round-trip. ☎ *504/364–8114.* ▨ *Free to pedestrians; motorists pay $1 for the return to Canal Street Wharf.* ◯ *Daily 5:30 AM–9:30 PM.*

The **New Orleans Steamboat Company** runs the mighty steamboat *Natchez,* which has two-hour cruises of the harbor during the day and two-hour dinner-jazz cruises in the evening, and the little *John James Audubon,* which cruises between the Aquarium and the Audubon Zoo. Aside from the view of the city and the water lapping at the sides of the boats, kids (and some adults) love to watch the big stern wheel turning. ☎ *504/586–8777 or 800/233–2628.* ▨ *Natchez harbor cruise $15.75, with lunch buffet $21.75; Natchez evening cruise $25.50, $45.50 with dinner; John James Audubon cruise $14.50 round-trip.* ◯ *Natchez harbor cruise daily 11:30, 2:30; Natchez evening cruise daily 7–9, boarding 6–7; John James Audubon cruise daily 10, noon, 2, and 4 from aquarium, daily 11, 1, 3, and 5 from zoo.*

BY BUS
Buses require $1.25 exact change or a token (sold only in banks). Transfers are 10¢ extra. The Vieux Carré shuttle operates weekdays from 5 AM to 7:30 PM. The **Regional Transit Authority** (RTA) has a 24-hour information service (☎ 504/248–3900; 504/248–3838 TTY). One- and three-day visitor passes, available at hotels, cost $5 and $12, respectively, and allow unlimited travel on buses and streetcars.

BY STREETCAR
The **St. Charles Streetcar** (☎ 504/248–3900; 504/248–3838 TTY), New Orleans's mobile Historic Landmark, clangs up St. Charles Avenue through the Garden District, past the Audubon Park and Zoo and other Uptown sights. The streetcar can be boarded in the CBD at Canal and Carondelet streets; the fare is $1.25. A round-trip self-guided sightseeing jaunt covers just over 13 mi and takes 90 minutes. The streetcar operates daily every five minutes from 7:30 AM to 6 PM, every 15–20 minutes from 6 PM to midnight, and hourly from midnight to 7 AM.

The **Riverfront Streetcar** (☎ 504/248–3900; 504/248–3838 TTY) follows the river between Esplanade Avenue and the Robin Street Wharf. It makes 10 stops, five above and five below Canal Street. The fare is $1.50, and it operates weekdays 6 AM–midnight; weekends 8 AM–midnight.

BY TAXI

Taxi fares start at $2.10, plus 75¢ per additional passenger and $1 per mi or 40 seconds stopped in traffic. For trips to special events, such as a ride to the fairgrounds during Jazzfest, cabs charge $3 per person or the meter rate, whichever is higher. Try **United Cabs** (☎ 504/522–9771) or **Yellow-Checker Cabs** (☎ 504/525–3311).

Contacts and Resources

B&B RESERVATION AGENCIES

Bed & Breakfast, Inc.–Reservations Service has a variety of accommodations in all areas of New Orleans. Some are 19th-century historic homes. Guest cottages, rooms, and suites are also available. Prices range from $40 to $150. Write or call Hazel Boyce: ✉ *1021 Moss St., Box 52257, 70152,* ☎ *504/488–4640 or 800/729–4640,* FAX *504/488–4639. No credit cards.*

New Orleans Bed & Breakfast lists private homes, apartments, and condos among 300 properties. Prices range from $45 to $250. Contact Sarah-Margaret Brown: ✉ *Box 8163, 70182,* ☎ *504/838–0071 or 504/838–0072,* FAX *504/838–0140. AE, D, MC, V.*

CAR RENTAL

National **car-rental services** in New Orleans include **Avis** (☎ 800/831–2847), **Budget** (☎ 800/527–0700), **Enterprise** (☎ 800/325–8007), **Hertz** (☎ 800/654–3131), and **National** (☎ 800/227–7568).

EMERGENCIES

Police, ambulance (☎ 911). All-night **hospital emergency rooms** include **Tulane Medical Center** (✉ 220 Lasalle St., ☎ 504/588–5711), in the CBD near the French Quarter, and **Touro Infirmary** (✉ 1401 Foucher St., ☎ 504/897–8250), near the Garden District.

GUIDED TOURS

Orientation:

You can hop aboard an air-conditioned 45-passenger **Gray Line** bus (☎ 504/587–0861) for a two-hour tour of New Orleans's major sights ($22). Gray Line also offers several options of combined city/harbor/attractions tours. **Tours by Isabelle** (☎ 504/391–3544) uses air-conditioned 14-passenger vans for a multilingual and more intimate three-hour tool around town ($35).
Special-Interest:

Classic Tours (☎ 504/862–7849) and **Jean Lafitte National Park** rangers (☎ 504/589–2636) both have Garden District walking tours. **Heritage Tours** (☎ 504/949–9805) conducts literary and historical walking tours of the French Quarter ($25). **Le 'Ob's Tours** (☎ 504/288–3478) runs a daily African-American heritage/city tour (✉ $35), as well as plantation, bayou, and Baton Rouge tours ($65–$80). **Pat Bernard's Classic Tours** (☎ 504/862–7849) is operated by a native New Orleanian who is in love with the city. Her chatty tours cover art, antiques, architecture, and history ($10). **Save Our Cemeteries** (☎ 504/525–3377) conducts lively guided tours of St. Louis Cemetery #1 ($12) and Lafayette Cemetery ($6). Statistics for the **Superdome** (☎ 504/587–3810) are staggering, and you can learn all about the huge facility during daily tours (✉ $6). **Tours by Isabelle** (☎ 504/391–3544) takes you around town ($35) to plantations, (✉ $85–$95 with lunch included), and to the bayous for a visit with a Cajun alligator hunter ($55). Voodoo haunts and such are covered by both **Magic Walking Tours** (☎ 504/588–9693; ✉ $13) and the **New Orleans Historic Voodoo Museum** (☎ 504/523–7685; ✉ $15). On the flatboats of **Wagner's Honey Island Swamp Tours** (☎ 504/641–1769), steered by a professional wetland ecologist, you can tour one of the country's best-preserved river swamps ($20, $40 with hotel pickup).

RADIO STATIONS
AM: WWL 870, talk, news; KGLA 1540, Spanish-language; WNOE 101.1, country music, news, weather; WGSO 990, CNN radio; WWNO 89.9, NPR, classical music, jazz. **FM:** WCKW 92.3, classic rock; WWOZ 90.7, community radio, New Orleans jazz; WNOE 101.1, country music, news, weather.

24-HOUR PHARMACIES
Eckerd (✉ 3400 Canal St., ☎ 504/488–6661). **Walgreen's** (✉ 3057 Gentilly Blvd., ☎ 504/282–2621; ✉ 9999 Lake Forest Blvd., ☎ 504/242–0981).

VISITOR INFORMATION
Write to the **New Orleans Metropolitan Convention and Visitors Bureau** (✉ 1520 Sugar Bowl Dr., New Orleans 70112, ☎ 504/566–5011 or 800/672–6124, FAX 504/566–5021, ✒). The **Tourist Commission** staffs a desk near the customs desk at New Orleans International Airport; its main outlet is the Louisiana State Office of Tourism, which shares space with the city at the New Orleans Welcome Center. ✉ 529 St. Ann St., French Quarter, ☎ 504/566–5068. ⊙ Daily 9–5.

CAJUN COUNTRY
Lafayette, Abbeville, Lake Charles, Opelousas

French Louisiana has become famous in the rest of the country through its food (po'boys and blackened fish) and music (zydeco). Many people who live here are Cajuns, descendants of 17th-century French settlers who established a colony they called l'Acadie in the present-day Canadian provinces of Nova Scotia and New Brunswick. The Acadians—"Cajun" is a corruption of "Acadian"—were expelled by the British in the mid-18th century. Their exile was described by Henry Wadsworth Longfellow in his epic poem "Evangeline." They eventually found a home in South Louisiana, and there they have been since 1762, imbuing the region, the state, and the nation with their unique cuisine and culture. The flavor of the region is summed up in the Cajun phrase *Laissez les bons temps rouler!* (Let the good times roll). Cajun Country is made for meandering. There are scenic routes and state highways, and you're encouraged to take to the country roads along the way to further explore the byways of bayou country.

U.S. 90 drops down from New Orleans into the marshlands of Houma, an area that abounds with campgrounds and charter freshwater and saltwater fishing boats. This route will take you through Morgan City, where the first Tarzan film was made; Franklin, an official Main Street USA town; and one of the state's Native American reservations. The rambling Bayou Teche (pronounced tesh) leads into St. Martinville in Evangeline Country, and next you'll head for Lafayette, which proudly calls itself, with some justification, the capital of French Louisiana. LA 14 is the scenic route to Lake Charles, which is fishing, camping, and bird-watching territory. Looping back toward Baton Rouge, you'll go through the area famed for the Courir de Mardi Gras, or Mardi Gras Run, during which masked and costumed horseback riders make a mad dash through the countryside. The trip ends near Baton Rouge on the Mississippi River.

While you're in Cajun Country, try to experience chank-a-chanking at a *fais do-do* (pronounced *fay* doh-doh). The little iron triangles in most Cajun bands make a rhythmic chank-a-chank sound, and most folks call dancing to the rhythm chank-a-chanking. As for fais do-do, that's the dance, or party, where you go to chank-a-chank. Fais do-dos crop up all over Cajun Country, sometimes in the town square, sometimes at somebody's house. There are also restaurants, dance halls, and lounges that regularly feature live Cajun music. The *Times of Acadiana* is a free newspaper that comes out every Wednesday and is available in hotels, restaurants, and shops. Check the "On the Town" section to see what's doing in the area.

Many restaurants and lounges regularly feature music for two-stepping, waltzing, and chank-a-chanking. Sunday afternoon is often devoted to dancing. Be sure to call to find out the schedule.

Numbers in the margin correspond to points of interest on the Cajun Country map.

Houma

㉗   *57 mi south of New Orleans on U.S. 90.*

Houma, in Terrebonne Parish, dates from 1795 and is in the heart of the old Hache Spanish Land Grant. The town is named for the Houmas Indians (the stressed first syllable of Houma sounds like "home"). Terrebonne Parish is a major center for shrimp and oyster fisheries, and the blessing of the shrimp fleets in Chauvin and Dulac is a colorful April event.

OFF THE   **WILDLIFE GARDENS** – The 1½-hr guided walking tour through this 30-acre
BEATEN PATH   park gives a real feel for swamp life. Creatures in the natural-habitat facility include bobcats, wild boar, turtles, peacocks, and a great-horned owl. There are twilight boat tours (year-round, by appointment) and a working alligator farm. Nature lovers can B&B in one of four rustic trapper's cabins. ⊠ *14 mi west of Houma on U.S. 90 in Gibson,* ☏ *504/ 575–3676.* ⊡ *$8, twilight boat tours $20.* ☉ *Grounds Tues.–Sat. 9–5; tours Sept.–May, Tues.–Sat. 10, 1, and 3:30; June–Aug., Tues.–Sat. 10 and 3:30.*

Morgan City

㉘   *37 mi northwest of Houma on U.S. 90.*

Morgan City, smack on the Atchafalaya River, struck it rich when the first oil-producing offshore well was completed on November 14, 1947, and the Kerr-McGee Rig No. 16 ushered in the black gold rush. Front Street runs alongside the 22-mi-long flood wall.

Atop the Great Wall, **Moonwalk** is a lookout with a great view of the Atchafalaya, as well as displays depicting the history of the region. At the **Morgan City Information Center** you can see a video of the first Tarzan movie, which was filmed here in 1917. ⊠ *725 Myrtle St.,* ☏ *504/384– 3343.* ☉ *Daily 8–5.*

Across from the information center, you can take a guided tour of 3½-acre **Swamp Gardens,** a heritage park that depicts the settlement of Atchafalaya Basin; displays include pirogues and other aspects of bayou life. ⊠ *725 Myrtle St.,* ☏ *504/384–3343.* ⊡ *$3.* ☉ *Tours Mon. 11, 1, 2, 3, and 4; Tues.–Sat. 10, 11, 1, 2, 3, and 4; Sun. 1, 2, 3, and 4.*

Cajun Country

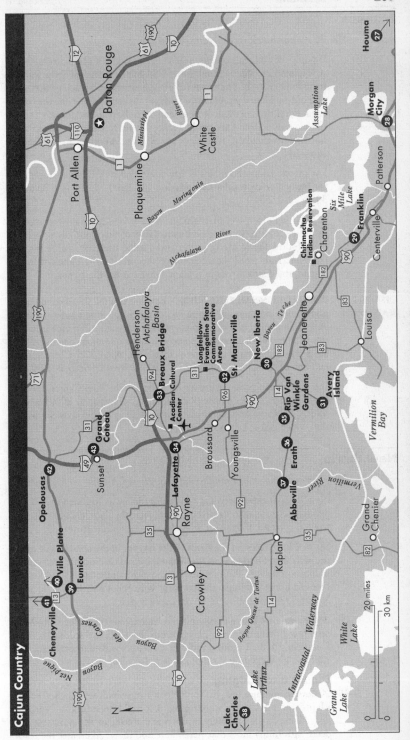

Franklin

 20 mi northwest of Morgan City on U.S. 90.

If you're of a nostalgic bent, you'll love Franklin's **Main Street,** which was named an official Main Street USA by the National Trust for Historic Preservation. The street rolls out beneath an arcade of live oaks, and old-fashioned street lamps with NO HITCHING signs line the boulevard. Franklin is nestled along a bend in the bayou, and there is a splendid view of it from **Parc sur le Teche.** (To reach the park as you drive north through town, turn right on Willow Street by the courthouse square.)

For information about this pretty town and its environs, stop at the **St. Mary Parish Tourist Commission** (⊠ 1600 Northwest Blvd., ☎ 337/828–2555).

A good way to travel to Franklin is via LA 182, which you pick up just outside Patterson. This is **Bayou Teche** country, and the state highways follow the writhing bayou along some stretches. *Teche* is a Native American word meaning snake. According to an ancient Indian legend, the death throes of a giant snake carved the bayou.

OFF THE BEATEN PATH

CHITIMACHA INDIAN RESERVATION – For centuries the Chitimacha flourished along the shores of Bayou Atchafalaya. The tribe's main settlement was in Charenton, site of the present-day reservation. The tribe is famous for its weaving, and Chitimacha baskets as well as other small items are sold in the reservation's crafts shop. ⊠ *LA 326, Charenton, 3 mi north of Franklin,* ☎ *337/923–4830.* ☞ *Free.* ☉ *Daily 8–4:30.*

The Chitimacha's main attraction these days is the busy Cypress Bayou Casino (⊠ 832 Martin Luther King Jr. Rd., Charenton, ☎ 800/284–4386). The large and seemingly ever-expanding facility is awash with slots, video poker, and gaming tables.

New Iberia

 25 mi northwest of Franklin via U.S. 90 or LA 182.

New Iberia—the Queen City of the Teche—was founded in 1779 by Spanish settlers, who named the town after the Iberian Peninsula. The town is a blend of Spanish, French, and Acadian cultures.

Set in 2 lush acres on the bank of the bayou, in the shadows of moss-draped oaks, **Shadows-on-the-Teche** is one of the South's best-known plantation homes. Built in 1834 for sugar planter David Weeks, this fine old home epitomizes what went with the wind. ⊠ *317 E. Main St.,* ☎ *337/369–6446.* ☞ *$8.* ☉ *Daily 9–4:30.*

☾ **City Park** is a 45-acre grassy playground across the Teche from Main Street, with tennis courts, playgrounds, baseball and softball fields, a fishing pond, boat ramps, and picnic shelters with barbecue facilities. ☞ *Free.* ☉ *Weekdays 8 AM–9 PM, Sat. 1–9, Sun. 1–5.*

Dining and Lodging

$–$$ ✕ **Café Lagniappe Too.** Just one block from Shadows-on-the-Teche is Elaine and Al Landry's charming, affordable restaurant. Not only does Elaine do the cooking, she also makes the huggable, oversize stuffed dolls with funny faces that perch here and there; Al creates the colorful paintings that hang on the walls. For lunch there are salads, soups, and sandwiches; the changing dinner menu might include medallions of veal, grilled quail, and trout meunière. ⊠ *204 E. Main St.,* ☎ *337/365–9419. AE, MC, V. Closed Sun. No lunch Sat.*

$$–$$$ ✕🏨 **leRosier.** Across the street from Shadows-on-the-Teche, set behind an antique rose garden, leRosier is a small family-run bed-and-breakfast whose dining room ($$$–$$$$) has won national acclaim. Chef Hallman Woods III has prepared his five-course crawfish degustation for the James Beard Foundation in New York. In addition to seafood there are specialties such as grilled marinated duck breast and rack of lamb. Rooms are quite small but are decorated with antiques or reproductions, and each has a minirefrigerator, phone, and TV. ⊠ *314 E. Main St., 70560,* ☎ *337/367–5306 or 888/804–7673,* FAX *337/365–1216. 6 rooms. AE, MC, V.* 🕭

Avery Island

③① *7 mi southwest of New Iberia via LA 329.*

Avery Island (it's actually a salt dome) is the birthplace of Tabasco sauce, and descendants of Edmund McIlhenny continue making the spicy condiment he invented in the mid-1800s. Other attractions are the 200-acre **Jungle Gardens,** lush with tropical plants, and **Bird City,** a sanctuary with flurries of snow-white egrets. There's a 50¢ toll to enter Avery Island. ⊠ *Off LA 329,* ☎ *337/369–6243 Jungle Gardens; 337/373–6129 Tabasco factory.* 🎟 *Gardens and sanctuary $5.75; Tabasco factory free.* ☉ *Gardens daily 9–5; factory daily 9–4.* 🕭

St. Martinville

③② *10 mi north of New Iberia via LA 31.*

St. Martinville is awash with legends. Longfellow's poem "Evangeline" was based on the story of Emmeline Labiche and Louis Arceneaux, two young lovers separated for years during Canada's Acadian exile (St. Martinville was a major entry point for Acadian refugees). Louis arrived in the town first and waited years hoping to find Emmeline, but eventually despaired of ever seeing her again and became engaged to another woman. Emmeline finally did reach St. Martinville, and, the story is told, Louis saw her by chance as she stepped ashore. Pale with shock, he told her that he was betrothed to another, turned on his heel, and disappeared. Their last, unhappy meeting place was beneath the Evangeline Oak (⊠ Evangeline Blvd. at Bayou Teche). *The Romance of Evangeline* was filmed in St. Martinville in 1929. Dolores Del Rio starred as Evangeline and posed for the bronze statue that the cast and crew donated to the town. You can see the statue in the cemetery behind the church of St. Martin de Tours (☞ *below*), near the grave of Emmeline Labiche. In the late 18th century, St. Martinville was known as Petit Paris because it was a major refuge for royalists who fled the French Revolution. Little Paris was the scene of many regal balls, soirees, and operas.

St. Martin de Tours (⊠ 123 S. Main St., ☎ 337/394–2233), mother church of the Acadians, is one of the oldest Catholic churches (early 18th century) in the country. Inside there is a replica of the Lourdes Grotto and a baptismal font said to have been a gift from Louis XVI.

La Remise, the St. Martinville visitor center, is across the street from the Evangeline Oak Park, just behind the Church Square. ⊠ *127 New Market St.,* ☎ *337/394–2233.* ☉ *Daily 9–5.*

La Maison Duchamp is a Classic Revival structure built as a private home in 1876. Here you can see a bedroom furnished with period antiques and turn-of-the-century photographs of the town. Tours are conducted in French and English. ⊠ *Main St. at Evangeline Blvd.,* ☎ *337/394–2229.* 🎟 *Free.* ☉ *Daily 9–3.*

OFF THE
BEATEN PATH   **LONGFELLOW–EVANGELINE STATE COMMEMORATIVE AREA** – Just north of the city limits, on LA 31 and the banks of the Teche, this 157-acre park is shaded by live oaks draped in shawls of Spanish moss. The park contains picnic tables and pavilions, a boat launch, and early Acadian houses. ☎ *337/394–3754.* ▨ *Grounds $2.* ◔ *Daily 9–5.*

Dining and Lodging

$–$$ ✕▦ **La Place d'Evangeline.** This historic redbrick inn, once the Old Castillo Hotel, rests on the banks of the Bayou Teche and beneath the branches of the Evangeline Oak. Eighteenth-century royalists once held lavish balls and operas in what is now the high-ceilinged dining room ($$–$$$). Seafood is king here, with the likes of corn and crab bisque, red snapper (broiled, fried, stuffed, or blackened), and frogs' legs. Don't pass up the homemade bread. Overnighters sleep in large antiques-filled rooms, some with a lovely view of Bayou Teche; all have private baths, and a full breakfast is included. ✉ *220 Evangeline Blvd., 70582,* ☎ *337/394–4010 or 800/621–3017,* ☎ *318/394–7983. 5 rooms. AE, MC, V.*

Breaux Bridge

③ *13 mi north of St. Martinville on LA 31.*

The little town of Breaux Bridge, which calls itself the Crawfish Capital of the World, is the home of the famous **Mulate's** restaurant. The **Crawfish Festival,** held in May, draws upwards of 100,000 people.

Dining

$–$$$ ✕ **Mulate's.** A roadhouse with flashing yellow lights outside and plas-
★   tic checkered cloths inside, Mulate's is an eatery, a dance hall, an age-old family gathering spot, and a celebrity, having been featured on the *Today Show* and *Good Morning, America,* among other programs. A dressed-down crowd digs into the likes of stuffed crabs and the Super Seafood Platters. There's live music at lunch and dinner. ✉ *325 Mills Ave.,* ☎ *800/634–9880; 800/422–2586 outside LA. AE, MC, V.*

$–$$ ✕▦ **Café des Amis.** Decorated with paintings and folk art by local artists,
★   this attractive and very popular restaurant specializes in sea creatures dressed in Cajun guise, such as crawfish and shrimp étouffée and gumbo. A zydeco band provides toe-tapping entertainment for Saturday-morning breakfasts. The adjacent Maison des Amis, in a small Acadian cottage with hardwood floors and front porch, is a B&B with four rooms for overnighters. Guest rooms have a four-poster, canopy, or tester bed; each has a private bath. There's a delightful gazebo overlooking Bayou Teche, a good site for building castles in the air. ✉ *140 E. Bridge St.,* ☎ *337/332–5273. AE, DC, MC, V.*

Nightlife and the Arts

La Poussière (✉ 1301 Grand Pointe Rd., Breaux Bridge, ☎ 337/332–1721) is one of the oldest dance halls around.

Lafayette

③ *9 mi west of Breaux Bridge on LA 94.*

Lafayette is a major center of Cajun lore and life, even if it does lack the charm and rusticity of smaller, outlying villages. Its plethora of excellent restaurants and B&Bs make it a good jumping-off point for exploring the region. In April the town hosts the Festival International de la Louisiane, several days of music, food, and crafts, and in the fall Festival Acadiens takes the spotlight. In preparation for a surge of visitors during the 1999 FrancoFete tricentennial celebrations, the downtown area was treated to a renovation that included new sidewalks and murals painted on exterior building walls. Stop in at the **Lafayette Convention and Visitors Bureau** (✉ Willow St. and Evangeline Thruway) and load up on maps and brochures.

The **Acadian Village,** a re-creation of an early 19th-century bayou settlement nestled in 10 wooded acres, has a general store, a blacksmith shop, a chapel, and houses representing different styles of Acadian architecture. In one of the houses, exhibits trace the life and works of native son and internationally renowned artist George Rodrigue, creator of the "Blue Dog." ✉ *200 Greenleaf Rd. (LA 342),* ☎ *337/981–2364.* ⊡ *$6.* ⊙ *Daily 10–5.*

The Louisiana Live Oak Society, founded in Lafayette more than 50 years ago, is on the grounds of the **Cathedral of St. John the Evangelist** (✉ 914 St. John St.), a Romanesque church with Byzantine touches. A charter member of that silent but leafy set of trees dominates the 900 block of St. John Street. The **St. John Oak** is 400 years old and has a matronly waistline of about 19 ft.

The **Lafayette Natural History Museum** is a busy place, with workshops, movies, concerts, and planetarium programs. It's also the venue for the annual September **Louisiana Native & Contemporary Crafts Festival.** ✉ *637 Girard Park Dr.,* ☎ *337/291–5544.* ⊡ *Free.* ⊙ *Mon. and Wed.–Fri. 9–5, Tues. 9–9, weekends 1–5.*

The natural history museum's sister facility is the **Acadiana Park Nature Station,** a three-story cypress-pole structure with an interpretive center and discovery boxes to help children get acquainted with the wildflowers, birds, and other things they'll see along a 3½-mi trail. ✉ *E. Alexandre St.,* ☎ *318/291–8448.* ⊡ *Free.* ⊙ *Weekdays 9–5, weekends 11–3.*

The **Lafayette Art Gallery** gives visitors a close look at local arts and crafts. ✉ *412 Travis St.,* ☎ *337/269–0363.* ⊡ *Free.* ⊙ *Tues.–Fri. noon–5, Sat. by appointment.*

OFF THE
BEATEN PATH

ACADIAN CULTURAL CENTER – The center, a unit of the Jean Lafitte National Historical Park and Preserve, traces the history of the Acadians through numerous audiovisual exhibits of Cajun music, food, and folklore. ✉ *501 Fisher Rd.,* ☎ *337/232–0789 or 337/232–0961.* ⊡ *Free.* ⊙ *Daily 8–5.*

Dining and Lodging

$$–$$$$ ✕ **Prejean's.** A local favorite, this cypress cottage has a cozy oyster bar, red-checkered cloths, live music nightly, and a jazz brunch on Sunday. Specialties include Prejean's Platter (seafood gumbo, fried shrimp, oysters, catfish, and seafood-stuffed bell peppers), as well as Cajun rack of elk, American buffalo au poivre, steak, and chicken. ✉ *3480 U.S. 167N, next to Evangeline Downs,* ☎ *337/896–3247. AE, DC, MC, V.*

$$–$$$ ✕ **Blue Dog Café.** In a little redbrick building with a snappy blue canopy, diners eat under the gaze of the wistful Blue Dog, paintings of which decorate the walls. Opened in 1999 by world-renowned artist and native son George Rodrigue, the upscale eatery features chef Britt Shockley's renditions of honey-glazed duck breast and seafood wontons, plus staples such as gumbo, seafood platters, étouffées, and sweet potato–pecan pie. ✉ *1211 W. Pinhook Rd.,* ☎ *337/237–0005. AE, DC, MC, V.*

$$–$$$ ✕ **Café Vermilionville.** This 19th-century inn with crisp white napery, old-brick fireplaces, and a casual elegance serves French and Cajun cuisine. Among the specialties are pecan-crusted tilapia, Louisiana crab madness (crabmeat prepared au gratin or étoufféed), and snapper Anna (filets of snapper sautéed in white wine and butter and laced with

crawfish tails, mushrooms, and artichoke hearts). ⊠ *1304 W. Pinhook Rd.,* ☎ *337/237–0100. AE, D, DC, MC, V.*

$ ✕ **Hub City Diner.** Quintessential diner fare—hearty breakfasts, chicken-fried steak with mashed potatoes and gravy, Mom's Famous Meat Loaf, plus milk shakes, malts, and sundaes—are served up in this '50s-style diner. You can eat in or take out. ⊠ *1412 S. College St.,* ☎ *337/235–5683. AE, MC, V.*

$$ ☷ **Best Western Hotel Acadiana.** This centrally located hotel has standard rooms with marble-top dressers, minirefrigerators, and wet bars. Rooms on the concierge floor have perks like Continental breakfast, evening hors d'oeuvres, and turndown service. Even-numbered rooms face the pool. ⊠ *1801 W. Pinhook Rd., 70508,* ☎ *337/233–8120 or 800/826–8386,* ℻ *337/234–9667. 301 rooms, 3 suites. Restaurant, bar, pool, 2 hot tubs, airport shuttle. AE, D, DC, MC, V.* ✆

$–$$ ☷ **Holiday Inn Central–Holidome.** These 17 acres contain virtually everything you'd ever need for a relaxing stay. Rooms with modern furnishings surround the large entertainment area. Ask for a second-floor room to avoid the noise of the pool area. ⊠ *2032 N.E. Evangeline Thruway, 70509,* ☎ *337/233–6815 or 800/942–4868,* ℻ *337/235–1954. 244 rooms, 6 suites. Restaurant, lobby lounge, indoor pool, hot tub, sauna, 2 tennis courts, jogging, recreation rooms, airport shuttle. AE, D, DC, MC, V.* ✆

Nightlife and the Arts

Randol's (⊠ 2320 Kaliste Saloom Rd., Lafayette, ☎ 337/981–7080) has hot dancing in a greenhouse setting. **Antler's** (⊠ 555 Jefferson St., ☎ 337/234–8877), in downtown Lafayette, is the city's oldest dancehall. It also has a lunchroom. Major concerts are held at the **Cajundome** (⊠ 444 Cajundome Blvd., ☎ 337/265–2100) and at the **Heymann Performing Arts Center** (⊠ 1373 S. College Rd., ☎ 337/291–5540).

Outdoor Activities and Sports

BIKING

These flatlands and lush parks make for easy riding. There are 60 mi of marked bike trails in Lafayette. Four-day to weeklong guided tours of Cajun Country are available through **French Louisiana Bike Tours** (⊠ 3216 W. Esplanade Ave., PMB 302, Metairie, 70002, ☎ 504/488–9844 or 800/346–7989).

GOLF

Play golf at the 18-hole, par-72 **City Park Golf Course** (80 acres) (⊠ Mudd Ave. and 8th St., Lafayette, ☎ 337/291–5557).

ICE HOCKEY

The **Ice Gators** (444 Cajundome Blvd., Lafayette, ☎ 337/265–2100) of the East Coast Ice Hockey League play home games in the Cajundome.

Rip Van Winkle Gardens

☙ ㉟ *15 mi south of Lafayette via U.S. 90 and LA 675.*

The 20 acres of formal and informal gardens that comprise Rip Van Winkle Gardens (formerly known as Live Oak Gardens) are part of a 5,000-acre tract that was purchased in the late 19th century by an American actor, Joseph Jefferson, who toured the country portraying Rip Van Winkle. On a hunting trip to South Louisiana, Jefferson fell in love with the area's groves of live oaks and lush countryside, and in 1870 he bought the land on which he built a winter home. His land came to be called **Jefferson Island.** The three-story **Jefferson house** is a comfortably opulent Southern Gothic home with Moorish touches. ⊠ *5505 Rip Van Winkle Rd., off LA 14,* ☎ *337/365–3332.* ☟ *House and gardens tour $9.* ☉ *Daily 9–5.*

Erath

36 *24 mi south of Lafayette via U.S. 90 and LA 89.*

Erath's earliest settlers were Acadians who migrated across the state from St. James Parish, near New Orleans. Its name, however, comes from an enterprising Swiss immigrant. In 1860, August Erath (pronounced Eee-rat) came to New Orleans and worked as a bookkeeper in a brewery. Later, he opened his own brewery in New Iberia, as well as a hardware business and soda-and-seltzer-water factory. Erath purchased land in the center of the present town, and when the railroad was built through his property, the town was officially named in honor of him.

You can poke through all sorts of Acadiana at the **Acadian Museum.** The several rooms are filled to the rafters with memorabilia donated by local folks—everything from antique radios and butter churns to patchwork quilts and yellowed newspaper clippings. ⊠ *203 S. Broadway,* ☎ *337/233–5832 or 337/937–5468.* ☑ *Free, but donations welcome.* ☉ *Weekdays 1–4.*

Abbeville

37 *5 mi west of Erath on LA 14.*

Abbeville is a charming town whose picturesque village square has a gazebo and moss-hung live oak trees. The vicinity of the square is the scene of the annual Giant Omelette Festival each November, when some 5,000 eggs go into the concoction. Pick up a self-guided walking tour brochure at the **Abbeville Main Street Program Office** in City Hall (⊠ 101 N. State St., ☎ 337/898–4110). Many buildings in the 20-block Main Street district are on the National Register of Historic Places. **St. Mary Magdalen Catholic Church,** adjacent to the village square, is a fine Romanesque Revival building with stunning stained-glass windows.

On an earthy note, Abbeville is home to **Cajun Downs** (⊠ On LA 338 off the LA 14 bypass, ☎ 337/893–8160 or 337/893–0421), a "bush" track cut smack through a cane field where all manner of critters race—horses, mules, maybe even pigs or chickens. The track is more than 100 years old and draws a Cajun Runyonesque crowd that cheers on the favorite with great enthusiasm. The track is open only on Sunday, when a half dozen or so races are run. Call first to see if the races are on; schedules tend to be pretty informal here.

OFF THE BEATEN PATH

ROCKEFELLER WILDLIFE REFUGE – Fifty-eight miles southwest of Abbeville via LA 82, you'll find an 84,000-acre tract where thousands of ducks, geese, gators, wading birds, otters, and others while away the winter months. ⊠ *On LA 82 between villages of Little Pecan Island and Grand Chenier (information center),* ☎ *337/538–2165.* ☑ *Free.* ☉ *Refuge daily sunrise–sunset, information center daily 7–4.*

Lake Charles

38 *74 mi west of Abbeville via LA 14, LA 13, and I–10.*

Lake Charles, the state's third-largest seaport, dates from the 1760s, when the first French settlers arrived. The first home was built by Charles Sallier on the shell beach by the lake, and the town was originally called Charlie's Lake. Today Lake Charles is a sprawling, not very attractive industrial town, whose wildly successful gambling riverboats (drawing in Texas money) have turned it into a boomtown. Nevertheless, the city has more than 50 mi of rivers, lakes, canals, and bayous, making it great for sailing, fishing, canoeing, shrimping, and crabbing. **North**

Beach is a white-sand beach on the north shore of the lake where you can loll in the sun, swim, or rent a Wave Runner during summer months. ⊠ *$1 per vehicle June–Aug.; free other times.*

Twelve miles north of the city, **Sam Houston Jones State Park** is a 1,068-acre recreation area that beckons sports and nature enthusiasts. ⊠ *LA 378,* ☎ *337/855–2665.* ⊠ *$2 per vehicle.* ☉ *Daily 7 AM–8 PM.*

The **Imperial Calcasieu Museum,** on the site of Charles Sallier's home, has an extensive collection pertaining to Lake Charles and Calcasieu Parish. The museum includes a photograph of the house built by town founder Charles Sallier, an old-fashioned pharmacy, an Audubon collection, and a Gay '90s barbershop. Adjacent to the museum, the Artisans Gallery has paintings, woodwork, ceramics, and jewelry made by local craftspeople. ⊠ *204 W. Sallier St., Lake Charles,* ☎ *318/439–3797.* ⊠ *$2.* ☉ *Tues.–Fri. 10–5, weekends 1–5.*

♻ The **Children's Museum** features interactive computers, a nature center, a TV station, a grocery store, and other hands-on exhibits as well as a toddlers' area. ⊠ *925 Enterprise Blvd., Lake Charles,* ☎ *318/433–9420.* ⊠ *$3.* ☉ *Tues.–Sat. 10–5.*

The **Mardi Gras Museum** is in the Central School Arts & Humanities Center, a restored schoolhouse that dates from 1912. The labyrinthine museum has a huge collection of costumes, headdresses, scepters, and glittering regalia, as well as photographs and exhibits—for example, on the art of costume making. New Orleans gets all the ink, but Carnival in Cajun Country is an event not to be sneezed at—the city boasts 33 krewes (carnival organizations). ⊠ *809 Kirby St.,* ☎ *337/430–0043.* ⊠ *$3.* ☉ *Tues.–Sat. 1–5.*

Dining and Lodging

$$$–$$$$ ✕ **Café Margaux.** Think candlelight, soft pinks, white linens, tuxedoed
★   waiters, and a 5,000-bottle mahogany wine cellar. Specialties include a marvelous lobster bisque, rack of lamb *en croute*, good steaks, and roasted quail with raspberry demiglace. ⊠ *765 Bayou Pines E,* ☎ *337/433–2902. Jacket and tie. AE, D, MC, V. Closed Sun.*

$–$$ ✕ **Steamboat Bill's.** In this busy, clattering country kitchen, you line up at the counter to place your order for fried, boiled, baked, or stuffed seafood platters. It couldn't be more casual. ⊠ *1004 Lakeshore Dr.,* ☎ *337/494–1070. AE, D, MC, V.*

$$ ☷ **Isle of Capri Casino & Hotel.** On the opposite side of the Lake from Players Island, this complex also boasts two floating gaming palaces that alternate cruising so that one is always dockside, as well as a flourishing entertainment pavilion. Top-name entertainers appear in the Flamingo Bay Ballroom, which also features boxing matches. The modern six-story all-suites hotel has accommodations done in blond woods, with good-quality muted pastel fabrics, cable TV with remote control, clock radios, and minirefrigerators. ⊠ *101 Westlake Ave., Westlake, 70669,* ☎ *337/430–2400 or 888/475–3847,* ℻ *337/430–0963. 241 suites. 3 restaurants, 2 bars, nightclub, deli, lobby lounge, room service, no-smoking rooms, pool, 2 casinos, video games, casino shuttle, airport shuttle. AE, D, MC, V.* ✥

$$ ☷ **Players Island Casino Hotel.** An 8-acre tropical extravaganza set between the lake and the interstate, this hotel/casino complex has a plethora of waterfalls, rockscapes, Animatronic tropical birds perched hither and yon, and activity aplenty. Gambling is done on two paddle-wheelers, which alternate cruising on Lake Charles. One is always dockside, and you can stroll from the hotel on an enclosed gangway without being aware you're walking on water, so to speak. In the accommodations portion of the property, rooms have traditional furni-

ture and are done in soothing earth tones. Suites and junior suites have refrigerators, wet bars, and well-lighted desks. There are seemingly endless buffets, as well as entertainment five nights a week. At press time negotiations were under way for the Players to be purchased by Harrah's. ⊠ 507 N. Lakeshore Dr., 70601, ☎ 337/437–1500 or 800/977–7529, FAX 337/437–6010. 394 rooms, 6 suites. 5 restaurants, 3 bars, coffee shop, lobby lounge, room service, no-smoking rooms, pool, exercise room, 2 casinos, video games, casino shuttle, airport shuttle. AE, D, MC, V. ✎

Nightlife and the Arts

Major concerts are held at the **Lake Charles Civic Center** (⊠ 900 Lakeshore Dr., ☎ 337/491–1256). The **Lake Charles Little Theater** (⊠ 813 Enterprise Blvd., ☎ 337/433–7988) puts on a variety of plays and musicals.

CASINOS

Wildly successful since it opened in 1994, **Grand Casino Coushatta** (⊠ 20 mins north of I-10 on U.S. 165, ☎ 800/584–7263), is on the Coushatta Indian Reservation near Lake Charles. **Players Island Casino** (☞ *above*; ⊠ 507 N. Lakeshore Dr., Lake Charles, ☎ 800/977–7529), done up like a tropical island, has two riverboat casinos with 1,650 one-armed bandits, 100 table games, and 24-hour entertainment. The **Isle of Capri Casino & Entertainment Pavilion** (⊠ Exit 27 off I-10, ☎ 800/843–4753) operates two triple-decker paddle-wheelers, open 24 hours, with table games and more than 900 slots.

Outdoor Activities and Sports

CANOEING

Paddling is almost a breeze on the easygoing **Whisky Chitto Creek.** Canoes can be rented at **Arrowhead Canoe Rentals** (☎ 337/639–2086 or 800/637–2086) and at **White Sand Canoe Rental** (☎ 800/621–9306), both in the Lake Charles area.

GOLF

You can tee off at the 18-hole, par-72 **Pine Shadows Golf Center** (⊠ 750 Goodman Rd., Lake Charles, ☎ 337/433–8681). Greens fees are $10.50 weekdays, $14 weekends; club rentals are $4.50. The 18-hole, par-72 **Mallard Cove** (⊠ Chennault Airpark, Lake Charles, ☎ 337/491–1241) is popular with locals. Greens fees are $11.25 weekdays, $14.50 weekends; club rentals are $10, and golf carts are $8.30.

HIKING AND NATURE TRAILS

The Old Stagecoach Road, in **Sam Houston Jones State Park** (⊠ 12 mi north of Lake Charles on LA 378, ☎ 337/855–2665), is a favorite for hikers who want to explore the park and the various tributaries of the Calcasieu River.

En Route The **Creole Nature Trail,** a 180-mi loop through exotic subtropical scenery, is one of only 14 rural roads in the country to be designated a National Scenic Byway by the Federal Highway Administration. Beginning on LA 27 in Sulphur, the state road dips south to the Gulf of Mexico on LA 82, and winds up LA 27 back to Lake Charles. Beautiful in the spring, this drive passes four wildlife refuges, including **Sabine National Wildlife Refuge,** 23 mi south of Sulphur, where interpretative displays include a diorama featuring the Cajun Man, an animated talking mannequin. Admission is free. A 1½-mi marsh trail 3 mi south of the center leads right into the wilds, and at its end an observation tower affords excellent views of the wilderness. Bring insect repellent. The Cajun Man's counterpart is the Animatronic Cajun Lady, who sits with her fishing pole and chats in the visitor center of the **Cameron Prairie National Wildlife Refuge,** also on the trail. For information call the Southwest

Louisiana Convention and Visitors Bureau (☎ 318/436–9588 or 800/456–7952). The interpretative centers of the **Sabine Wildlife Refuge** (☎ 337/762–3816) and the **Cameron Prairie National Wildlife Refuge** (☎ 337/598–2216) are open weekdays 7–4, Saturday 10–4.

Eunice

㊴ *66 mi northeast of Lake Charles via I–10 and LA 13.*

The tiny town of Eunice is home to the Cajun radio show *Rendez-Vous des Cajuns,* a live radio show, mostly in French, it has been described as a combination of the *Grand Ole Opry,* the *Louisiana Hayride,* and the *Prairie Home Companion.* ⊠ *Liberty Theatre, Park Ave. at 2nd St.,* ☎ *337/457–7389.* ⚏ *$5.* ⊙ *Sat. 6 PM–8 PM.*

The **Eunice Museum** is in a former railroad depot and contains displays on Cajun culture, including Cajun music and Cajun Mardi Gras. ⊠ *220 S. C. C. Duson Dr., Eunice,* ☎ *337/457–6540.* ⚏ *Free.* ⊙ *Tues.– Sat. 8–noon and 1–5.*

The **Prairie Acadian Cultural Center,** a large facility that's part of the Jean Lafitte National Historical Park, traces the history and culture of the Prairie Acadians, whose lore and mores differ from those of the Bayou Acadians around Lafayette. Food, crafts, and music demonstrations are held from time to time. ⊠ *250 W. Park Ave., Eunice,* ☎ *337/457–8490 or 337/457–8499.* ⚏ *Free.* ⊙ *Daily 8–5.*

A number of places in Cajun Country make not just music but instruments, too. Among them is the **Savoy Music Center Accordion Factory,** its front half a music store, its back a Cajun accordion workshop. Proprietor Marc Savoy's factory turns out about five accordions a month and fills orders all the way from Alaska to New Zealand. On Saturday morning, accordions and other instruments tune up during jam sessions held in the shop. There are beer and two-stepping, and musicians from all over the area drop in. The Monday before Mardi Gras— Lundi Gras, as it's known in these parts—the center has a big blowout, with a bonfire, music, and dancing. ⊠ *U.S. 190, 3 mi east of Eunice,* ☎ *337/457–9563.* ⚏ *Free.* ⊙ *Tues.–Fri. 9–5, Sat. 9–noon.*

The area surrounding Eunice is the major stomping ground for an annual event, **Courir de Mardi Gras,** which takes place the Sunday before Fat Tuesday (Mardi Gras Day). Le Capitain leads a band of masked and costumed horseback riders on a mad dash through the countryside, stopping at farmhouses along the way to shout, *"Voulez-vous recevoir cette bande de Mardi Gras* (Do you wish to receive the Mardi Gras band)?" The answer is always yes, and the group enlarges and continues, gathering food for the street festivals that wind things up. For information contact Lafayette Convention and Visitors Bureau (☎ 800/346–1958).

Ville Platte

㊵ *20 mi northeast of Eunice via LA 13 and LA 10.*

Ville Platte is home to the annual Cotton Festival, held in October, which features a medieval-style Tournoi with knights, steeds, and jousting.

The **Louisiana State Arboretum** is a 600-acre facility with 2½ mi of nature trails leading past a variety of plants native to the state. ⊠ *8 mi north of Ville Platte,* ☎ *337/363–2503.* ⚏ *Free.* ⊙ *Dawn–dusk.*

Cheneyville

㊶ *44 mi north of Eunice via LA 13 and I–49.*

At the turn of the 19th century, a group of immigrants, mostly of British ancestry, came from South Carolina to the area. Among them was a chap named Cheney, and the town was named for him.

$$–$$$ ⊞ **Loyd Hall Plantation.** This perfect quiet getaway is on 641 acres of
★ a working, historic cotton plantation. Outside the mansion are fully restored mid-1800s accommodations: a three-room cottage that once housed the commissary; two suites in the restored kitchens overlooking the pool; and one- or two-bedroom houses. All are furnished with a blend of antiques and modern comforts: wood-burning fireplaces, four-poster or tester beds, porch rockers, air-conditioning, TVs, and full modern kitchens stocked with breakfast fixings (two have washer-dryers). ⊠ *292 Lloyd Bridge Rd., 71325,* ☎ *318/776–5641 or 800/ 240–8135,* ℻ *318/776–5886. 4 cottages, 2 suites. Pool, bicycles. AE, MC, V.*

Opelousas

㊷ *51 mi south of Cheneyville on I–49.*

Opelousas is the third-oldest town in the state—Poste de Opelousas was founded in 1720 by the French as a trading post. The town is named for the Appalousa Indians, who lived in the area centuries before the French and Spanish arrived. For a brief period during the Civil War, Opelousas served as the state capital. At the intersection of I–49 and U.S. 190, look for the **Opelousas Tourist Information Center** (☎ 337/ 948–6263), where you can get plenty of information; arrange for tours of historic homes; and see memorabilia pertaining to Jim Bowie, the Alamo hero who spent his early years in Opelousas.

The **Opelousas Museum and Interpretive Center** has among its eclectic exhibits a washbasin in which celebrity chef (and native son) Paul Prudhomme bathed as a babe, a Civil War Room, adorable dollhouses, and an old-time barbershop replete with antique accoutrements. ⊠ *329 N. Main St.,* ☎ *337/948–2589.* 🎟 *Free.* ☉ *Tues.–Sat. 9–5.*

Dining
$ ✕ **Palace Café.** A down-home coffee shop on the town square run by the same family since 1927, this locals' favorite is famous for its home-made baklava. Among the eclectic specialties are cold fried-chicken salad, baked eggplant stuffed with Alaskan king crabmeat dressing, and Greek salad. There are also steaks, fried chicken, sandwiches, burgers, and seafood. ⊠ *167 W. Landry St.,* ☎ *337/942–2142. Reservations not accepted. MC, V.*

Nightlife and the Arts
Slim's Y-Ki-Ki (⊠ LA 167, Washington Rd., ☎ 337/942–9980), a rural club, is one of the best zydeco dancing places in the state.

Grand Coteau

㊸ *10 mi south of Opelousas via I–49, exiting on LA 93.*

Virtually every structure in peaceful little Grand Coteau, a religious and educational center, is on the National Register of Historic Places. The **Church of St. Charles Borromeo** is a simple wooden structure with an ornate high baroque interior. There are 36 works of art inside, most of which were done by Erasmus Humbrecht, whose works can also be seen in St. Louis Cathedral in New Orleans. The church's unusual bell tower is one of the area's most photographed sights. ☎ 337/662–5279. 🎟 *Tours $1 donation.* ☉ *Tours weekdays; you must call to make arrangements in advance.*

Established in 1821, the **Academy of the Sacred Heart** is the second-oldest institution of learning west of the Mississippi, remaining in operation through fire, epidemics, and war. The academy contains the **Shrine of St. John Berchmans,** in which the Miracle of Grand Coteau occurred. You'll hear all about the miracle on a guided tour. For tour information, contact the Academy office. ☎ *337/662–5275.* ☞ *$5.*

Chretien Point Plantation is noted not only for its grandeur but also for the role it played in *Gone With the Wind.* In the 1930s a photographer infatuated with the house took pictures of it and sent them to Hollywood. As a result, its staircase was the model for the one in Scarlett O'Hara's Tara. The house takes bed-and-breakfast guests, with rates ranging from $110 to $225 per night. ⊠ *About 4 mi from Sunset on the Bristol/Bosco Rd.,* ☎ *337/662–5876 or 800/880–7050,* FAX *337/662–5876* ☞ *$6.50.* ☉ *Daily 10–5; last tour at 4.* ☜

Cajun Country A to Z

Arriving and Departing

BY BUS

Greyhound Southeast Lines (☎ 800/231–2222) has frequent daily departures from New Orleans to Franklin, Houma, Lafayette, Lake Charles, Morgan City, New Iberia, Opelousas, and Thibodaux.

BY CAR

The fastest route from New Orleans through Cajun Country to Lafayette and Lake Charles is via I–10, which cuts coast to coast across the southern United States. However, if you have time, take the leisurely scenic drives for exploring.

Great Drives. LA 56 to LA 57 is a circular drive out of Houma, on which you can see shrimp and oyster boats docked along the bayous from May through December. Another circular drive is the Creole Nature Trail (LA 27) out of Lake Charles (☞ En Route, *above*). LA 82 (Hug-the-Coast Highway) runs through the coastal marshes along the Gulf of Mexico.

BY PLANE

For airline telephone numbers *see* Air Travel *in* Smart Travel Tips A to Z. **Lafayette Regional Airport** (⊠ 200 Terminal Dr., ☎ 337/266–4400) is served by American Eagle, Continental, Atlantic Southeast (a Delta connection), and Northwest Airlink. **Lake Charles Regional Airport** (⊠ 500 Airport Blvd., ☎ 337/477–6051) is served by American Eagle and Continental.

BY TRAIN

Amtrak (☎ 800/872–7245) serves Franklin, Schriever (12 mi from Houma), Lafayette, New Iberia, and Lake Charles.

Contacts and Resources

EMERGENCIES

Dial **911** for assistance. **Emergency rooms** include the **Medical Center of Southwest Louisiana** (⊠ 2810 Ambassador Caffery Pkwy., Lafayette, ☎ 337/981–2949) and **Lake Charles Area Medical Center** (⊠ 4200 Nelson Rd., Lake Charles, ☎ 337/474–6370).

GUIDED TOURS

Acadiana to Go (☎ 337/981–3918) gives guided tours of Acadiana, as well as the rest of Louisiana. **Allons à Lafayette** (☎ 337/269–9607) offers customized tours, with bilingual guides and itinerary planning for Lafayette and Cajun Country. **Terrebonne Swamp & Marsh Tours** (☎ 504/879–3934) is especially popular with kids. Annie Miller, who gets along great with gators, conducts daily tours March 1–November 1 out of Houma into the swamps. **Coerte Voorhies** (☎ 337/233–7816), based in Lafayette, conducts tours into the 800,000-acre Atchafalaya Basin for photographers, ornithologists, and all nature lovers. **Hammond's Flying Service** (☎ 504/876–0584) has air tours, which soar out of Houma over the swamps, marshlands, and the Gulf of Mexico. **McGee's Landing** (☎ 337/228–2384) conducts pontoon-boat tours from the levee in Henderson into the Atchafalaya Basin. **Airboat Tours** (☎ 337/229–4457) skims through the remote swamps, bayous, and sloughs of Lake Fausse Pointe.

Trips to fish, sightsee, or bird-watch can be arranged at **Gator Guide Service** (✉ Box 9224, New Iberia, ☎ 337/365–6400). **Sportsman's Paradise** (☎ 504/594–2414) is a charter-fishing facility 20 mi south of Houma, with eight boats available year-round. **Salt, Inc. Charter Fishing Service** (✉ Coco Marina, LA 56 south of Houma, ☎ 504/594–6626 or 504/594–7581) offers fishing trips in the bays and barrier islands of lower Terrebonne Parish, as well as into the Gulf of Mexico.

In the far southwestern part of the state, **Burgess Offshore, Inc.** (☎ 800/932–5077) conducts offshore fishing trips. **Hackberry Rod & Gun Club** (☎ 337/762–3391) is a charter saltwater fishing service.

RADIO STATIONS
AM: KROF 960, French/Cajun; KPEL 1420, news/talk; KEUN 1490, country/news/sports. **FM:** KROF 105.1, oldies; KTDY 99.9, adult contemporary; KYKZ 96.1, country.

24-HOUR PHARMACIES
In Lafayette, **Eckerd** (✉ 4406 Johnston St., ☎ 337/984–5220). In Lake Charles, **Walgreen's** (✉ 300 18th St., ☎ 337/433–4178).

VISITOR INFORMATION
The **Iberia Parish Tourist Commission** (✉ 2690 Centre St., New Iberia, 70560, ☎ 337/365–1540). The **Lafayette Convention and Visitors Commission** (✉ 1400 N.W. Evangeline Thruway, 70505, ☎ 337/232–3808; 800/346–1958; 800/543–5340 in Canada; ℻ 318/232–0161). For information from the visitors commission via fax, call 800/884–7329, ext. 610, main menu. www.lafayettetravel.com The **Southwest Louisiana Convention and Visitors Bureau** (✉ 1205 N. Lakeshore Dr., Lake Charles, 70601, ☎ 337/436–9588 or 800/456–7952, ℻ 337/494–7952 ✆) is open weekdays 8–5, weekends 9–3.

BATON ROUGE AND PLANTATION COUNTRY

St. Francisville, Livonia, White Castle, Napoleonville

Baton Rouge, one of South Louisiana's major cities, is the state capital. Legend has it that in 1699 French explorers observed that a red stick planted in the ground on a high bluff overlooking the Mississippi served as a boundary between two Indian tribes. Sieur d'Iberville, leader of the expedition, noted *le baton rouge*—the red stick—in his journal, and voilà! Baton Rouge.

This is the city from which colorful, cunning Huey P. Long ruled the state; it is also the site of his assassination. Even today, more than a half century after Long's death, legends about the controversial governor and U.S. senator abound.

The parishes to the north of Baton Rouge are quiet and bucolic, with gently rolling hills, high bluffs, and historic districts. John James Audubon lived in West Feliciana Parish in 1821, tutoring local children and painting 80 of his famous bird studies. In both terrain and traits, this region is more akin to North Louisiana than to South Louisiana—which is to say, the area is very Southern.

The area designated Plantation Country begins with a reservoir of fine old homes north of Baton Rouge that cascades all the way down the Great River Road to New Orleans. After touring the state capital, we recommend taking LA 61 to the historic districts and plantations in the parishes north of Baton Rouge, overnighting in one of the plantation bed-and-breakfasts. From St. Francisville, take the ferry for $1 at the tip of town and start south on LA 1 to the antebellum gems that grace the Great River Road.

Numbers in the margin correspond to points of interest on the Baton Rouge and Plantation Country map.

Baton Rouge

④④ *80 mi northwest of New Orleans via I–10.*

The **State Capitol Building** is a good place to start your tour; the **Visitor Information Center** in its lobby is loaded with maps and brochures. You can tour the first floor of the building, which includes the spot where Huey Long was shot in 1935. At 34 stories, this is America's tallest state capitol. An observation deck on the 27th floor affords a spectacular view of the Mississippi River and the city. ⊠ *State Capitol Dr.,* ☎ *225/342-7317.* ☑ *Free.* ⊘ *Daily 8–4:30; last tour at 4.*

A museum in the **Pentagon Barracks** has exhibits that acquaint visitors with the Capitol complex. The barracks were originally built in 1823–24 to quarter U.S. Army personnel, and when Louisiana State University moved from Pineville to Baton Rouge in 1869, it was to these buildings. ⊠ *959 3rd St., on State Capitol grounds,* ☎ *225/342–1866.* ☑ *Free.* ⊘ *Mon.–Sat. 10–4, Sun. noon–4.*

Only one Revolutionary War battle was fought outside the 13 original colonies, and it was fought on the State Capitol grounds. One of the historic buildings, the **Old Arsenal Museum,** a restored heavy-duty structure dating from about 1838, is a terrific place for children. The museum has hands-on exhibits set up inside powder kegs, displays on Louisiana's Native American history, and a giant jigsaw puzzle comparing the Capitol grounds as they appear today to 1865. ⊠ *State Capitol grounds,* ☎ *225/342–0401.* ☑ *$1.* ⊘ *Weekdays 9–4, Sat. 10–4, Sun. 1–4.*

★ When the castlelike, Gothic Revival **Old State Capitol** was built in 1849, the structure was considered by some to be a masterpiece, by others a monstrosity. No one can deny that the restored building is colorful and dramatic. In the entrance hall a stunning purple, gold, and green spiral staircase winds toward a stained-glass atrium. The building now holds the **Louisiana Center for Political and Government History,** an education and research facility with audiovisual exhibits. In the House chamber a multimedia show plays every hour beginning at 10:15, with the last show at 4. ⊠ *100 North Blvd., at River Rd.,* ☎ *225/342–0500.* ☑ *$4.* ⊘ *Tues.–Sat. 10–4, Sun. noon–4.*

Across the street from the Old State Capitol is the **Louisiana Arts & Science Center Riverside Museum,** housed in a 1925 Illinois Central railroad station. There is a fine-arts museum with changing exhibits, an Egyptian tomb exhibit, restored trains from the 1890s to the 1950s, and a Discovery Depot with a children's art gallery and workshop. Once

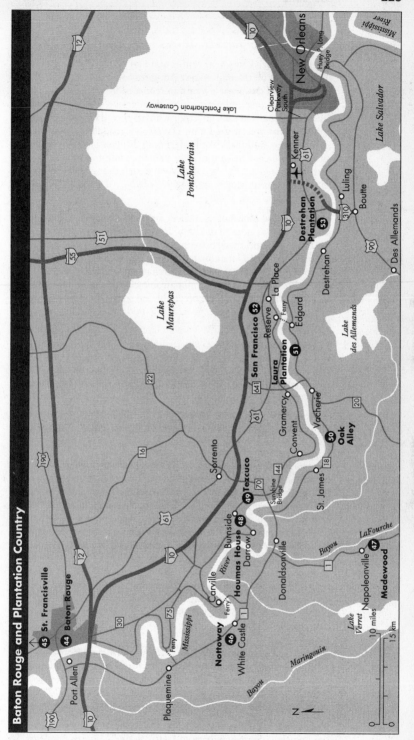

Baton Rouge and Plantation Country

a month the museum presents a hands-on *Challenger* simulated space flight. Call for specific times. ⊠ *100 S. River Rd.,* ☎ *225/344–5272.* ⛶ *$3; Sun. $1.* ⊙ *Tues.–Fri. 10–3, Sat. 10–4, Sun. 1–4.*

After an extensive two-year restoration that involved peeling multiple layers of paint off the walls to reveal original colors and handsome frieze work, the **Old Governor's Mansion** reopened in 1999. Built in 1930, during Huey Long's administration, the mansion showcases memorabilia that pertains to each governor who has served since the house was built—for example, in the Jimmy Davis room a saddle and cowboy hats are exhibited, and the Mike Foster room displays include wicker furniture used during his grandfather's administration. Each of the seven bathrooms is in a different, often vivid pastel (though some of the toilets are inexplicably missing). ⊠ *502 North Blvd.,* ☎ *225/343–3989.* ⛶ *$4.* ⊙ *Tues.–Fri. 10–4.*

☾ The **Enchanted Mansion** is, indeed, an enchanting place. Included in its collection of more than 2,000 dolls are Shirley Temple dolls from the 1930s, antiques made between 1850 and 1925, a white-haired Mark Twain replica, and an animated Huey Long making a stump speech. The oldest doll is St. Michael the Archangel, which dates from 1750. Perched here and there are Animatronic clocks and animals, as well as talking dolls. In the gift shop you'll find some of the most huggable baby dolls. ⊠ *190 Lee Dr.,* ☎ *225/769–0005.* ⛶ *$4.50.* ⊙ *Mon. and Wed.–Sat. 10–5, Sun. 1–4.*

★ The **USS** *Kidd,* a Fletcher-class destroyer, is a World War II survivor restored to its V-J Day configuration. A brochure details a self-guided tour that takes in more than 50 inner spaces of this ship and also the separate **Nautical History Museum.** Among its exhibits are articles from the 175 Fletcher-class ships that sailed for the United States, a collection of ship models, and a restored P-40 fighter plane hanging from the ceiling. ⊠ *305 S. River Rd. (Government St. at the levee),* ☎ *225/342–1942.* ⛶ *$6.* ⊙ *Daily 9–5.*

OFF THE
BEATEN PATH
Alligator Bayou – Eco-tours into a 900-acre backwater swampland are conducted aboard a 49-passenger covered barge by Frank Bonifay and Jim Ragland, who give lively commentary about the alligators, snakes, turtles, black bear, 250 species of birds, and giant cypress trees that abound here. Food, music, and Cajun and zydeco dance lessons are provided during regularly scheduled parties on a rustic bayou-side pavilion; canoe rentals and nature walks are available. To reach Alligator Bayou from downtown Baton Rouge, take I-10 to Exit 166 at Highland Road and go east for a half block; turn right on Old Perkins Road and right again at LA Hwy 928. Immediately after crossing over I-10, turn right on Alligator Bayou Road. ⊠ *35019 Alligator Bayou Rd.,* ☎ *225/642-8297 or 888/3SWAMPS (379–2677).* ⛶ *$15.* ⊙ *Tours daily by appointment.* ✍

About 1½ mi from the center of town, **Magnolia Mound Plantation** (circa 1791) is a raised cottage furnished with Federal antiques and Louisiana artifacts. On Tuesday and Thursday, from October through May, cooking demonstrations are conducted in the outbuildings. ⊠ *2161 Nicholson Dr.,* ☎ *225/343-4955.* ⛶ *$5.* ⊙ *Tues.–Sat. 10–4, Sun. 1–4.*

Louisiana State University (LSU) was founded in Pineville in 1860 as the Louisiana State Seminary of Learning and Military Academy. Its president was William Tecumseh Sherman, who resigned when war broke out and made his famous march through Georgia four years later. The 200-acre campus has several museums as well as Indian burial mounds that are of particular interest to archaeologists and archaeology buffs.

✉ *1 mi south of Magnolia Mound Plantation on Nicholson Dr.,* ☎ *225/388–3202.*

Spread over 5 acres of the 450-acre Burden Research Plantation, the LSU **Rural Life Museum** is an outdoor teaching and research facility. With three major areas—the Barn, the Working Plantation, and Folk Architecture—the compound's 20 or so rustic 19th-century structures represent the rural life of early Louisianians. Hundreds of items are displayed in the enormous barn, including a prairie schooner, ancient surreys and sulkies, antique cars, tools and dental implements, and African artifacts and masks. The working plantation's several buildings include a gristmill, a blacksmith's shop, and several outbuildings. ✉ *In Baton Rouge on Essen La. at I–10,* ☎ *225/765–2437.* ⊡ *$5.* ☉ *Daily 8:30–5.*

Baton Rouge's other major institution of higher learning besides Louisiana State University is **Southern University.** Founded in 1880, Southern U is the nation's largest predominantly black university. ✉ *About 5 mi north of town on U.S. 61,* ☎ *225/771–4500.*

OFF THE BEATEN PATH

PORT HUDSON STATE COMMEMORATIVE AREA – This 650-acre park is the site of a fiercely fought Civil War battle that was the longest siege in American military history. There are high viewing towers, gun trenches, and, on the first Sunday of each month, small arms demonstrations. Seven miles of hiking trails wend peacefully throughout the park, 14 mi north of Baton Rouge on U.S. 61. ✉ *756 W. Plains–Port Hudson Rd. (U.S. 61),* ☎ *225/654–3775.* ⊡ *$2.* ☉ *Wed.–Sun. 9–5.*

Dining and Lodging

$$–$$$ ✕ **Drusilla's.** This rambling restaurant has large rooms decorated with murals and paintings of sea scenes and sea creatures, setting the mood for the food served here. Munch on crisp onion rings while you study the extensive menu. Standout appetizers include escargot in mushroom caps, fried crab fingers, and oysters on the half shell. A Taste of Louisiana—a sampling of seafood gumbo, seafood eggplant casserole, shrimp au gratin, fried shrimp, fried catfish, french fries, and salad—is a good choice. There are several Cajun-fried sea critters and a lengthy list of broiled dishes. ✉ *3482 Drusilla La. (Drusilla Shopping Center),* ☎ *225/923–0896. AE, DC, MC, V.*

$$–$$$ ✕ **Juban's.** An upscale bistro with a lush courtyard and walls adorned
★ with art, Juban's is a family-owned and -operated restaurant that proudly presents its specialty—Hallelujah Crabs, a delectable concoction of stuffed soft-shell crabs dressed in a Creole sauce. The sophisticated menu offers oysters Rockefeller and Bienville, and tempting main courses of seafood, beef, and veal dishes, as well as roasted duck, rabbit, and quail. Vegetables are exceptionally tasty here, and Juban's own mango tea is delicious. The warm bread pudding is something to write home about. ✉ *3739 Perkins Rd. (Acadiana Shopping Center),* ☎ *225/346–8422. AE, DC MC, V. Closed Sun. No lunch Sat.*

$–$$$ ✕ **Mamacita's.** Gussied up with splashy murals of Mexican scenes, bright hues of pink and green, and sombreros hanging here and there, Mamacita's is very popular with locals. A whole raft of combination platters, fajitas, burritos, tacos, and enchiladas are on the list, and portions are huge. Gringos can order "Less-Mex" items, such as mesquite-grilled burgers, grilled red snapper, and barbecued pork ribs. ✉ *7524 Bluebonnet Blvd. (Bluebonnet Village),* ☎ *504/769–3850. AE, D, DC, MC, V.*

$ ✕ **Christina's.** Downtown businesspeople flock here for hearty, inexpensive breakfasts (two-fisted biscuits, pancakes, and the like) and lunches (spaghetti and meatballs is usually a special). In addition to plate lunches there are plenty of salads, sandwiches, and po'boys. The atmosphere couldn't be more casual, and the most expensive item is the rib eye for $7.95. ⊠ *320 St. Charles St., ☎ 504/336–9512. AE, MC, V. Closed Sun. No dinner.*

$$–$$$ 🏨 **Courtyard Baton Rouge Acadian Center.** Three miles from LSU, this three-story Marriott property has rooms in traditional decor complete with homey details such as a coffeemaker, a hair dryer, an iron and ironing board, and a desk with good lighting. Other amenities include phones with voice mail and data ports and a complimentary newspaper delivered to your door on weekdays. ⊠ *2421 S. Acadian Thruway, 70808, ☎ 225/924–6400 or 800/321–2211, ℻ 225/923–3041. 149 rooms, 12 suites. Cocktail lounge, valet service, business center, coin laundry. AE, D, DC, MC, V.*

$$–$$$ 🏨 **Embassy Suites.** This centrally located property has two-room suites, with peach-and-green decor, mahogany furniture, and a galley kitchen with microwave and coffeemaker. The complimentary full breakfast is cooked to order. ⊠ *4914 Constitution Ave., 70808, ☎ 225/924–6566 or 800/433–4600, ℻ 225/923–3712. 224 suites. Restaurant, bar, room service, indoor pool, sauna, steam room, shop, laundry service, airport shuttle. AE, D, DC, MC, V. embassysuites.com.*

$–$$$ 🏨 **Baton Rouge Hilton.** Conveniently located at I–10 and College Drive, this high-rise hotel has somewhat formal rooms and public spaces with traditional furnishings. Of the six suites, two are split-level; the top two floors offer VIP perks such as Continental breakfast and afternoon hors d'oeuvres and cocktails. ⊠ *5500 Hilton Ave., 70808, ☎ 225/924–5000, 800/621–5116, 800/221–2584 in LA; ℻ 225/925–1330. 292 rooms, 6 suites. Restaurant, coffee shop, lobby lounge, no-smoking rooms, room service, sauna, 2 tennis courts, health club, jogging, laundry service, concierge, business services, airport shuttle. AE, D, DC, MC, V.*

Nightlife and the Arts

BARS AND NIGHTCLUBS

In an old movie house, the **Varsity Theatre** (⊠ 3353 Highland Rd., ☎ 225/343–5267 or 225/383–7018) presents live shows, live music, and dancing. Pool tables along with blues, acoustic, and alternative bands attract a crowd to the **Caterie** (⊠ Acadian Perkins Plaza, 3617 Perkins Rd., ☎ 225/383–4178). The popular **Chimes** (⊠ 3357 Highland Rd., next to Varsity Theatre, ☎ 504/383–1754) has 40 draught beers; it draws businesspeople for lunch and happy hour, but after 10 PM the collegiates reign. **Gino's Restaurant** (⊠ 4542 Bennington Ave., ☎ 225/927–7156) has a piano bar and occasionally a jazz trio. **Tabby's Blues Box & Heritage Hall** (⊠ 244 Lafayette St., ☎ 225/387–9715) is the home court for local blues legend Tabby Thomas and his pals. There's live jazz on weekends at **M's Fine & Mellow Cafe** (⊠ 143 N. 3rd St., ☎ 225/344–5368).

CAJUN CLUBS

Mulate's (⊠ 8322 Bluebonnet Rd., ☎ 225/767–4794), in Baton Rouge, is a chip off the famed old Breaux Bridge block.

CONCERTS

Touring Broadway shows and top-name stars are booked into the **Centroplex Theatre for the Performing Arts** (☎ 225/389–3030). Guest soloists perform frequently with the **Baton Rouge Symphony Orchestra** (⊠ Centroplex Theatre for the Performing Arts, ☎ 225/387–6166). LSU's annual **Festival of Contemporary Music** (☎ 225/388–5128), which takes place in February, is more than 40 years old.

COUNTRY AND WESTERN

The **Texas Club** (⊠ 456 N. Donmoor Ave., ☎ 225/928–4655) is the hot spot for top-name country artists.

RIVERBOAT CASINOS

The **Casino Rouge** (☎ 800/447–6843) docks across from the capitol and is loaded up with games of chance and lively entertainment. The **Argosy Casino** (☎ 800/676–4847), formerly called the Belle of Baton Rouge, is a three-deck riverboat casino with all the games and entertainment you'd expect; it's berthed at Catfish Town, at the foot of South Boulevard.

THEATER

The **Swine Palace Theatre** (⊠ LSU Theater on Dalrymple Dr., LSU campus, ☎ 225/388–5128) is an Equity theater whose director is the estimable Barry Kyle. The **Baton Rouge Little Theatre** (⊠ 7155 Florida Blvd., ☎ 225/924–6496) has been presenting musicals, comedies, and dramas for more than 40 years. **Cabaret Theatre** (⊠ 3116 College Dr., ☎ 225/927–7529) presents productions by local groups.

Outdoor Activities and Sports

GOLF

Two championship 18-hole, par-72 **golf courses** open to the public are: **Santa Maria** (⊠ 1930 Perkins Rd., ☎ 225/752–9667), which does not offer rentals, and **Webb Park** (⊠ 1351 Country Club Dr., ☎ 225/383–4919), which is close to most hotels and rents clubs for $5.40.

SWIMMING

Blue Bayou Waterpark & Dixie Landin' Amusement Park, the state's largest water park, has a wave pool, a seven-story slide, and a lazy river. For the little ones there's a 7,000-square-ft pollywog pool. The amusement park includes roller coaster rides. There's also a seafood restaurant, a chicken restaurant, a pizzeria, and a fast-food facility. ⊠ *18142 Perkins Rd., off I–10, Baton Rouge, ☎ 225/753–3333. ☑ $18 for anyone over 4', $15 for under 4'. ☉ June–Labor Day, daily 10–6.*

TENNIS

You can lob and volley at the tennis courts of **City Park** (⊠ 1440 City Park Ave., ☎ 225/344–4501 or 504/923–2792), **Highland Road Park** (⊠ Highland and Amiss Rd., ☎ 225/766–0247), and **Independence Park** (⊠ 549 Lobdell Ave., ☎ 225/923–1792).

St. Francisville

45 *25 mi north of Baton Rouge on U.S. 61.*

Described as a town 2 mi long and 2 yards wide, much of long, skinny St. Francisville is listed on the National Register of Historic Places. You'll find a number of bed-and-breakfasts here.

Not to be confused with nearby Butler-Greenwood, **Greenwood Plantation** is a 1960s restoration of a grand 1830s Greek Revival mansion that burned. It's a working plantation that produces cattle, hay, and pecans. Fully furnished with some of the original antiques and portraits, the house, with its white columns and widow's walk, has a 70-ft hall with silver doorknobs and hinges. It has been the location for six movies, including *The North and The South.* ⊠ *LA 968, 3 mi. off LA 66, ☎ 225/655–4475. ☑ $4. ☉ Mar.–Oct., daily 9–5; Nov.–Feb., daily 10–4.*

The Myrtles is noted for its 110-ft gallery with Wedgwood-blue cast-iron grillwork, a lovely setting for the weddings and receptions frequently held here. The house was built around 1796 and has elegant formal parlors with rich molding and faux-marble paneling. Friday- and Saturday-night mystery tours buttress the Myrtles's claim to the title America's Most Haunted House. The Carriage House Restaurant is a fine place for dinner. ⊠ *7747 U.S. 61, about 1 mi north of downtown St. Francisville on U.S. 61,* ☎ *225/635–6277.* ☎ *$8, mystery tours $10.* ☉ *Daily 9–5.*

Rosedown Plantation and Gardens, an opulent house that dates from 1835, is beautifully restored, and nestles in 28 acres of exquisite formal gardens. At this time, only tours of the mansion's exterior are offered. *12501 LA 10, just off U.S. 61,* ☎ *504/635–3332.* ☎ *$10.* ☉ *Mar.–Oct. daily 9–5; Nov.–Feb., daily 10–4.*

OFF THE BEATEN PATH	**AUDUBON STATE COMMEMORATIVE AREA** – A few miles south of St. Francisville, off U.S. 61, you'll find the 100-acre park where Audubon did a major portion of his *Birds of America* studies. The three-story Oakley Plantation House on the grounds is where Audubon tutored the young Eliza Pirrie. ⊠ *LA 956,* ☎ *225/635–3739.* ☎ *Park and plantation $2.* ☉ *Daily 9–5.*

Lodging

$$ 🏠 **Butler Greenwood.** Shaded by live oaks draped with Spanish moss,
★   Anne Butler's home—a two-story frame house with a wraparound veranda, dormers, and gables—was built in the early 1800s. A house tour, which includes such items as a 12-piece set of rosewood Victorian furniture, is part of an overnight stay. The bed-and-breakfast accommodations are in seven uniquely decorated cottages. Each has a TV, a hot tub, and a kitchen or kitchenette stocked with a coffeemaker, toaster oven, fresh juice, croissants, cereal, and fruit so you can prepare breakfast at your leisure. ⊠ *8345 U.S. 61, 70775,* ☎ *225/635–6312,* ☎ *225/635–6370. 7 cottages. Air-conditioning, kitchenettes, pool. AE, MC, V.* ✾

Outdoor Activities and Sports

The Bluffs (⊠ LA 965, 6 mi east of U.S. 61, ☎ 225/634–5551) is an 18-hole, par-72 Arnold Palmer golf course. Reserve your tee time at least four days in advance. Club rentals are $20, golf carts are $12 per person, and greens fees are $60 ($70 from Friday through Sunday).

En Route   Drive aboard the **ferry** ($1 per car) just outside St. Francisville for a breezy ride across the Mississippi. Pick up LA 1 in New Roads and head south. You'll be driving right alongside False River, which was an abandoned riverbed that became a lake. In contrast to the muddy Mississippi, False River is dark blue. This is an excellent fishing area, and you'll see long piers and fishing boats tied up all along the route.

Livonia

24 mi west of Baton Rouge via U.S. 190 and LA 77.

In this part of the state, Cajun Country lies to the west, and English Louisiana is to the east in St. Francisville. Livonia and environs were settled by French Creoles who moved north from New Orleans in the early 18th century.

Dining

$$–$$$ ✗ **Joe's "Dreyfus Store."** This restaurant—off the beaten track, 35 mi
★   west of Baton Rouge—is simply one of Louisiana's best. The rustic frame house contained the Dreyfus Store from 1920 until 1989; shelves along the wall are still lined with relics from its general-store days, and the restaurant still uses many of the store's original chairs and cabinets. The atmosphere is quite casual. The highly creative cuisine includes

sherry-spiked turtle soup; bacon-wrapped, charbroiled quail; and a superb pork tenderloin, marinated, charbroiled, and served on a bed of braised red cabbage. ⊠ *2731 Maringouin Dr. (Rte. 77S),* ☎ *225/637–2625. Reservations not accepted. No credit cards. Closed Mon. No dinner Sun.*

White Castle

18 mi south of Baton Rouge on LA 1 on the east bank of the Mississippi.

46 White Castle is best known for **Nottoway,** the South's largest plantation home, built in 1859 by famed architect Henry Howard. Legend has it that the town, founded in 1885, was named for the plantation, which looked to residents like a magnificent castle. Others say the town was named for a grand plantation that no longer exists. The Greek Revival/Italianate mansion has 64 rooms filled with antiques and is noted for its white ballroom with original crystal chandeliers and hand-carved Corinthian columns. Some of the rooms are open for overnighters. Before you leave the lush grounds, walk across the road and go up on the levee for a splendid view of Old Man River. ⊠ *30970 LA 405, 2 mi north of White Castle,* ☎ *225/346–8263.* 🎟 *$10.* ☉ *Daily 9–5.*

Lodging

$$$–$$$$ 🏠 **Nottoway.** A massive Italianate mansion with elegant, antiques-filled rooms, this is reputed to be one of the most stunning B&Bs in the nation. Guests are welcomed with complimentary sherry upon arrival. Your first breakfast of the day—of croissants, juice, and coffee—is served in your room; the second breakfast a short while later is a full feast in the Magnolia Room. ⊠ *30970 LA 405, 2 mi north of White Castle, 70788,* ☎ *225/346–8263. 13 rooms. AE, D, MC, V.* 🐾

Donaldsonville

17 mi south of White Castle on LA 1.

In 1770 there was a settlement on this site called Fourche de Chitimacha. A town with the present name was founded in 1806; for a brief period in 1825 it was the state capital. A newspaper reporter at the time wrote that the capital was moved from New Orleans to Donaldsonville because the Crescent City was considered a "modern Sodom."

Dining

$$$–$$$$ ✕ **Lafitte's Landing at Bittersweet Plantation.** The Acadian cottage
★ that housed this stellar restaurant burned to the ground in 1998, and proprietor/chef John Folse—renowned the world over in culinary circles—immediately set about restoring his one-time residence in downtown Donaldsonville as the "new" Lafitte's Landing. Everything about the place is elegant, from the decor to the presentation of such Folse classics as Death by Gumbo, amberjack Magnolia Ridge (pan-seared and Jack Daniels–glazed) and sautéed fillet of trout on butternut beurre blanc topped with crawfish tails. There are two sumptuous suites for overnight guests. ⊠ *404 Claiborne Ave.,* ☎ *225/473–1232. Reservations essential. Jacket required. D, MC, V.* ☉ *Closed Mon. No lunch Tues.–Sat.*

Napoleonville

16 mi southeast of Donaldsonville: Take LA 70 and Spur 70 from Donaldsonville south to LA 308, and proceed southeast on LA 308 to Napoleonville.

Contrary to what many people think, Napoleonville was named not for the Little Corporal, but for a family of Napoleons who were early settlers. The town now has a population of just over 800.

★ **47** Henry Howard, of Nottoway fame, was also the architect for **Madewood,** a magnificent 21-room Greek Revival mansion with double galleries and white columns. *A Woman Called Moses,* starring Cicely Tyson, was filmed in the house. Visitors can opt for tea with a tour, or lunch with a tour, and—amazingly—reservations are not required for either. This is also an elegant antebellum bed-and-breakfast. ⊠ *4250 LA 308, 2 mi south of Napoleonville,* ☎ *504/369–7151.* ⌨ *$6; tour with tea $10.95; tour with lunch $18.* ☉ *Daily 10–5.*

Lodging

$$$$ ⊞ **Madewood.** Expect gracious Southern hospitality in this antiques-filled Greek Revival mansion. What sets Madewood apart is its warmth as well as its elegance. As the weekend country home of the Marshall family, it exudes a comfortably lived-in ambience lacking at other plantation mansions. There are five rooms in the main mansion, and three suites in a cottage behind it. The room or suite rate includes not only a full breakfast but wine and cheeses in the parlor, followed by a candlelighted Southern dinner in the stately dining room. ⊠ *4250 LA 308, 2 mi south of Napoleonville, 70390,* ☎ *504/369–7151 or 800/ 375–7151. 5 rooms, 3 suites. AE, D, MC, V.* ✇

Burnside

20 mi northwest of Napoleonville: Go 16 mi on LA 308 to Donaldsonville, then cross the Sunshine Bridge to LA 44 on the west bank and continue west for 4 mi.

The town is named for John Burnside who, in 1840, bought 20,000 acres of land and built Houmas House. On the east bank of the Mis-
48 sissippi River, docents in antebellum garb guide you through **Houmas House,** a Greek Revival masterpiece famed for its three-story spiral staircase. *Hush Hush, Sweet Charlotte,* with Bette Davis and Olivia de Havilland, was filmed here. ⊠ *LA 942, ½ mi off LA 44,* ☎ *888/323–8314.* ⌨ *$8.* ☉ *Feb.–Oct., daily 10–5; Nov.–Jan., daily 10–4.*

49 Built in 1835, **Tezcuco** is a graceful raised cottage with delicate wrought-iron galleries, ornate friezes, an antiques shop, a restaurant, and overnight cottages. Tezcuco is also home to the **River Road African American Museum and Gallery,** which examines this region's slave culture. ⊠ *LA 44, about 7 mi above Sunshine Bridge,* ☎ *225/562–3929.* ⌨ *$8.* ☉ *Daily 9–5.*

Vacherie

24 mi southeast of Burnside via the Sunshine Bridge and LA 18.

Although *vacherie* is a French word meaning pasturelands, this area was originally settled by Germans who came here shortly after the 1718 founding of New Orleans. Later inhabitants were Acadians.

50 Like many of its neighbors, the plantation **Oak Alley** is a movie star, having served as the setting for the Don Johnson/Cybill Shepherd TV remake of *The Long Hot Summer* and more recently for scenes in the Tom Cruise film *Interview with the Vampire.* The house dates from 1839, and the 28 gnarled and arching live oaks trees that give the house its name were planted in the early 1700s. There is a splendid view of those trees from the upper gallery. The plantation also has a restaurant and overnight accommodations on the grounds. ⊠ *3645 LA 18,*

*7½ mi upriver of Gramercy/Wallace Bridge, ☎ 225/265–2151 or 800/
442–5539. ☞ $8. ⊙ Nov.–Feb., daily 9–5; Mar.–Oct., daily 9–5:30.*

⑤ Different from the dressed-up River Road mansions, **Laura Plantation**
is an in-progress restoration of the main house and six slave cabins of
a former sugar plantation. The $1.3 million project, scheduled for com-
pletion in 2005, will include bed-and-breakfast accommodations.
Opened for tours in 1994, it is named for the 1805 owner/manager
Laura Locoul, and the restoration is based on historical documents that
include 100 pages of her diary. The Br'er Rabbit stories are said to have
first been told here by Senegalese slaves. ⊠ *2247 Hwy. 18, Vacherie,*
☎ *225/265–7690. ☞ $8. ⊙ Daily 9–5.*

Reserve

*12 mi east of Vacherie on the west bank: From Vacherie, take LA 18
on the east bank 4 mi to the Veterans Memorial Bridge; cross the bridge
to LA 44 on the west bank and go 5 mi east to Reserve.*

Local lore has it that a 19th-century peddler who went from plantation to plantation selling trinkets and such was turned away from a
particular home (not San Francisco) and vowed he'd "reserve" it for
his own. The story (probably apocryphal) continues that the plantation was later sold at auction, and the peddler purchased it for little
more than a song.

㉒ **San Francisco,** completed in 1856, is an elaborate Steamboat Gothic
house noted for its ornate millwork and ceiling frescoes. ⊠ *LA 44 near
Reserve,* ☎ *504/535–2341. ☞ $8. ⊙ Daily 10–4:30.*

Destrehan

*5 mi east of Reserve via LA 44 and LA 48 (the Great River Rd.), 23
mi from New Orleans via LA 48.*

This town was named in the 18th century for one d'Estrehan des Tours,
㉓ who was a royal treasurer when Louisiana was a French colony. **Destrehan
Plantation** is the oldest plantation left intact in the lower Mississippi Valley. The simple West Indies–style house, dating from 1787, is typical of
the homes built by the earliest planters in the region. ⊠ *9999 River Rd.,*
☎ *504/764–9315 or 504/764–9345. ☞ $8. ⊙ Daily 9–4.*

Baton Rouge and Plantation Country A to Z

Arriving and Departing

BY BUS

Greyhound Southeast Lines (☎ 800/231–2222) has frequent daily service from New Orleans to Baton Rouge and surrounding towns.

BY CAR

I–10 and U.S. 190 run east–west through Baton Rouge. I–12 heads east,
connecting with north–south I–55 and I–59. U.S. 61 leads from New
Orleans to Baton Rouge and north. Ferries across the Mississippi cost
$1 per car; most bridges are free.

Great Drives. LA 1 travels along False River, which is a blue oxbow
lake created ages ago when the mischievous, muddy Mississippi changed
its course. The route wanders past gracious homes and small lakeside
houses.

BY PLANE

Baton Rouge Metropolitan Airport (⊠ 9430 Jackie Cochran Dr., ☎ 225/
355–0333), 12 mi north of downtown, is served by American, Conti-

nental, Delta, and Northwest (☞ Air Travel *in* Smart Travel Tips A to Z for telephone numbers).

Contacts and Resources

EMERGENCIES

Dial **911** for assistance. Hospital **emergency rooms** are open 24 hours a day: **Baton Rouge General Medical Center** (✉ 3600 Florida Blvd., ☎ 225/387–7000) and **Our Lady of the Lake Medical Center** (✉ 5000 Hennessy Blvd., ☎ 225/765–6565).

GUIDED TOURS

Tiger Taxi & Tours (☎ 225/921–9199 or 225/635–4641) runs Baton Rouge city tours, tours of plantation country, and swamp tours. **Rachel Hall's St. Francisville Tours** (☎ 225/635–6283) conducts van tours of the Feliciana parishes north of Baton Rouge and of Cajun Country.

RADIO STATIONS

AM: KBRH 1260, CNN news/talk; WIBR 1300, news/talk/sports. **FM:** WYNK 101.5, country; WBRH 90.3, jazz/alternative.

24-HOUR PHARMACIES

Eckerd (✉ 4530 S. Sherwood Forest Blvd., ☎ 225/291–0596). **Walgreen's** (✉ 4747 S. Sherwood Forest Blvd., ☎ 225/292–8975).

VISITOR INFORMATION

Louisiana Visitor Information Center (✉ Louisiana State Capitol Bldg., State Capitol Dr., Box 94291, Baton Rouge 70808-9291, ☎ 225/342–7317, FAX 225/342–8390, ✇). **Baton Rouge Area Convention and Visitors Bureau** (✉ 730 North Blvd., Box 4149, Baton Rouge 70804, ☎ 225/383–1825 or 800/527–6843). **West Feliciana Historical Society Information Center** (✉ 364 Ferdinand St., St. Francisville, ☎ 225/635–6330).

NATCHITOCHES AND CANE RIVER COUNTRY

Natchitoches and environs have characteristics of both North and South Louisiana in terms of culture and cuisine. In this part of the state, barbecue is as popular as Cajun food, and country-and-western beats vie with zydeco for dancing feet. The terrain, however, is decidedly different. Here, the hills are alive with the scent of pine trees. Natchitoches is on the fringe of the Kisatchie National Forest, and although the area isn't exactly mountainous—the highest peak in all the state, the misnamed Driskill Mountain, farther north, soars to a dizzying 535 ft above sea level—it appears so after flat-as-a-pancake South Louisiana.

Natchitoches

264 mi northwest of New Orleans via I–10, U.S. 190, and I–49.

The earliest permanent European settlement in the Louisiana Purchase territory was not New Orleans but the little town of Natchitoches (pronounced Nak-uh-tish), which predates the Crescent City by four years. Nestled in rolling green hills and thick pine forests, Natchitoches has two other claims to fame. The town hosts a sparkling Christmas Festival of Lights, which was featured in the film *Steel Magnolias,* and it's the hometown of that film's screenwriter, Robert Harling. The friendly residents are happy to point out where Dolly Parton, Sally Field, Julia Roberts, and the other magnolias hung out during filming.

Front Street, which is lined with small, wrought-iron-faced buildings, lies alongside pretty Cane River Lake. The lake's sloping grass-green

banks are shaded by giant live oak trees. The downtown area is part
of a 33-block historic landmark district, which contains a number of
homes open to the public. Trolley tours, which focus on *Steel Magnolias* sites, are available through **Cane River Cruises** (☎ 318/352–2557).

The **Old Courthouse Museum,** in an 1896 Richardsonian Romanesque
building that originally housed several Natchitoches Parish offices, is
a facility of the Louisiana State Museum. Changing exhibits trace the
history and culture of the region. ⊠ *Corner of 2nd and Church Sts.,*
☎ *318/357–2270.* 🎫 *$3.* ☉ *Mon.–Sat. 9–5.*

Fort St. Jean Baptiste is a reconstruction of the outpost that stood near
this site in 1716. The several replica buildings were constructed using
18th-century hardware, including hand-forged door latches and hinges.
Structures include a church, powder magazine, and kitchen. ⊠ *Morrow and Jefferson Sts.,* ☎ *318/357–3101.* 🎫 *$2.* ☉ *Daily 9–5.*

Natchitoches is on the fringe of the 100,000-acre **Kisatchie National
Forest** (☎ 318/473–7160). In addition to its hardwood and pine forests,
it offers equestrian, hiking, and nature trails; picnic and camping sites;
and splendid vistas.

Dining and Lodging

$$–$$$ ✕ **Landing.** This large, noisy bistro with white tablecloths is one of the
★   town's most popular restaurants. The extensive menu includes shrimp
rémoulade, potato skins, and fried cheese sticks as starters. Pasta,
steak, chicken, and seafood entrées are prepared in a variety of ways.
The spicy country-fried steak is distinctive; the garlic bread is superb,
as is the bread pudding. ⊠ *530 Front St.,* ☎ *318/352–1579. AE, MC,
V. Closed Mon.*

$–$$ ✕ **Lasyone's Meat Pie Kitchen.** Natchitoches is famed for its succulent
meat pies, and the best place to sample them is this ultracasual coun-
try-kitchen café. Other offerings include meat, chicken, and seafood;
for dessert, select from a display of Cane River cream pies. The kitchen
closes at 7 PM. ⊠ *622 2nd St.,* ☎ *318/352–3353. Reservations not accepted. No credit cards. Closed Sun.*

$$–$$$ 🏠 **Levy-East House.** This elegant B&B dates from 1838 and is one of
Natchitoches's showplaces. Floors are heart pine, ceilings are 10½ ft,
and much of the furniture is Victorian. Queen-size beds are wood-carved,
with patchwork quilts and crocheted coverlets. Romantic taped music
wafts into each guest room (and can be volume-controlled in each);
armoires conceal TVs and phones. Guest baths have whirlpools and
terry robes. Amenities include sherry and coffeemakers in each guest
room, afternoon wine, and nightly turndown service with candy.
Gourmet breakfasts are served in a handsome formal dining room. The
upstairs porch, with rocking chairs, overlooks Jefferson Street. ⊠ *358
Jefferson St., 71457,* ☎ *318/352–0662 or 800/840–0662. 4 rooms. Dining room. AE, MC, V.*

$–$$$ 🏠 **Jefferson House.** A B&B near the historic district, Jefferson House
is a split-level frame structure in a serene setting. Guests occupy the
entire first floor, which is decorated in a tasteful blend of traditional
furnishings and East Asian objets d'art. A large, stately parlor has a
high beamed ceiling, brick fireplace, and doors opening to a veranda
with rocking chairs and a view of Cane River Lake. Bedrooms have
quilted spreads and matching drapes; baths are large and modern. The
downstairs room opens onto a patio that overlooks the lake. ⊠ *229
Jefferson St., 71457,* ☎ *318/352–3957. 4 rooms. MC, V.*

$ 🏠 **Fleur-de-Lis.** The granddaddy of local B&Bs expanded in 1999 and
now includes two houses: a 1903 rose-color Victorian and, next door,
a 1920s craftsman-style guest house. The Victorian features lovely
fringed and beaded lamp shades throughout, and guest rooms with a

four-poster, brass, or wicker beds. The guest house, with full kitchen and washer-dryer, has a living room/dining room in warm wood paneling and guest rooms in traditional furnishings. Each house has a front porch with rocking chairs and swing and and is decorated with family pictures and heirlooms. Baths in both houses are small but modern. There's a data port for laptops. Proprietors Tom and Harriette Palmer make guests feel right at home, with help from a friendly golden retriever named Ginger. Full breakfast is served family style in a simple dining room. ⊠ *336 2nd St., 71457,* ☎ *318/352–6621 or 800/ 489–6621. 8 rooms. AE, MC, V.*

$ ⌘ **Ryders Inn.** Comfortable and predictable rooms are available in this erstwhile Holiday Inn on the outskirts of town. It offers a restaurant, outdoor pool, and cable TV. ⊠ *Hwy. 1 South Bypass, 71457,* ☎ *318/ 357–8281 or 888/252–8281,* ℻ *318/352–9907. 143 rooms, 2 suites. Restaurant, bar, pool. AE, D, DC, MC, V.*

Nightlife and the Arts

The **Melrose Plantation Arts and Crafts Festival,** an annual event held the second weekend in June, showcases 135–150 regional craftsmen and -women displaying their arts beneath the canopy of live oaks on the picturesque grounds of Melrose Plantation. There are also food booths galore featuring Natchitoches meat pies and oodles of homemade desserts. For information, call the Natchitoches Parish Tourist Commission at ☎ 318/352–8072 or 800/259–1714.

Cane River Country

South of Natchitoches and nestled amid lush gardens is **Beau Fort Plantation,** constructed in the early 1800s of hand-hewn cypress and bousillage (an insulating material made of Spanish moss and mud). The handsome home, which is also a B&B, has an 84-ft gallery, and French doors line the front. The house is furnished with 19th-century Louisiana antiques and family heirlooms. ⊠ *Rte. 119, Bermuda, about 11 mi south of Natchitoches.* ☎ *318/352–5340 or 318/352–9580.* ⊡ *$5.* ☉ *Daily 1–4.*

The Cane River Lake drifts southward from Natchitoches, lined by tall trees, stately plantations, and humble cottages. Several plantation homes are open for tours. Eight miles south of Beau Fort Plantation, **Melrose Plantation** was the home of the late self-taught artist Clementine Hunter, who was known as the black Grandma Moses. The first owner of Melrose was a black freed slave who, with her family, began construction of the seven buildings in 1796. In this century, Melrose was the home of a patron of the arts whose guests included Erskine Caldwell, Lyle Saxon, and Alexander Woollcott. Particularly interesting is the African House, an unusual Congo-style structure, which has murals decorating the second floor. ⊠ *Rte. 119, Melrose,* ☎ *318/379– 0055.* ⊡ *$5.* ☉ *Daily noon–4.*

The still-working **Magnolia Plantation** is 6.2 mi south of Melrose. It is one of only two National Bicentennial farms west of the Mississippi River. The mansion's 27 rooms are furnished with an extensive collection of Louisiana and Southern Empire antiques. The outbuildings, which include brick cabins and a barn containing the only cotton press in the United States still in its original location, will become part of a projected Cane River Creole National Historical Park. Headquarters for the park will be a nearby Oakland Plantation, which at press time was undergoing a major restoration. ⊠ *Hwy. 119 near Derry, 22 mi south of Natchitoches,* ☎ *318/379–2221.* ⊡ *$5.* ☉ *Daily 1–4 or by appointment.*

Handmade bricks, heart cypress, and wooden pegs were used to build the **Kate Chopin House,** which houses the **Bayou Folk Museum.** Completed in 1809 and restored with new flooring in 1999, this raised cottage was the 1880s home of Kate Chopin, author of *The Awakening*. The museum contains photographs and memorabilia and a first edition of *Bayou Folk*, a collection of Chopin's short stories about Cane River Country. ⊠ *LA 491, 4 mi south of Magnolia Plantation in Cloutierville,* ☎ *318/379–2233.* 🖼 *$5.* ⊘ *Mon.–Sat. 9–5, Sun. 1–5.*

OFF THE BEATEN PATH **LECOMPTE –** This small town, 45 mi south of Cloutierville via I–49 and U.S. 71, was named for a racehorse famed in these parts in the 19th century. The horse's name was Lecomte (the town is pronounced le-count); according to an oft-told tale, an inebriated sign painter inserted the *p*, and the town became Lecompte.

Louisianians who make the trek from North to South Louisiana often plan to arrive in Lecompte at lunchtime. At **Lea's Lunch Room** there's nothing fancy, just a huge sun- and m̵̶-filled room where country food has been served since 1928. The corn bread and homemade pies are legendary. Expect brusque service and plate lunches of prodigious proportions. ⊠ *U.S. 71 S.,* ☎ *318/776–5178. Reservations not accepted. Credit cards not accepted. Closed Mon.*

Natchitoches and Cane River Country A to Z

Arriving and Departing

BY BUS
Natchitoches is served by **Greyhound** (☎ 800/231–2222).

BY CAR
Route 1 and I–49, which cut north–south through the state's midsection, bisect Natchitoches.

Contacts and Resources

EMERGENCIES
Ambulance, police (☎ 911). The **Natchitoches Parish Hospital** (⊠ 501 Keyser, ☎ 318/352–1200) offers help in medical emergencies.

GUIDED TOURS
Cane River Tours (☎ 318/352–2557) offers tours of Natchitoches by trolley, with the focus on sites featured in the film *Steel Magnolias*. **Tours by Jan** (☎ 318/352–2324 or 318/352–3802, FAX 318/352–0666) and **Ducournau Square, Inc.** (☎ 318/352–5242) both offer walking and driving tours of Natchitoches and the Cane River region.

RADIO STATION
KNWD 91.7, rock and alternative (FM).

VISITOR INFORMATION
The **Natchitoches Parish Tourist Office** (⊠ 781 Front St., ☎ 318/352–8072 or 800/259–1714) provides information about the region, including self-guided walking/driving-tour brochures.

SHREVEPORT AND NORTHERN LOUISIANA

Although southern Louisiana dances to Cajun tunes and dines on Creole and Cajun fare, most of northern Louisiana has more in common with Mississippi, Georgia, and other Southern states; Shreveport's ties are largely to neighboring Texas. It is not for nothing that Louisiana is known as Sportsman's Paradise. The northern region of the state is laced with rivers and lakes, with ample places for camping and fishing.

Shreveport and Bossier City

Shreveport and Bossier City, joined by the Red River, constitute the largest metropolitan area in northern Louisiana. A cultural center, **Shreveport** has a symphony orchestra, resident opera and ballet companies, and excellent community-theater productions.

This area, like Lake Charles in the southwest corner of the state, is booming as a result of the riverboat casinos that operate on the Red River.

★ The prestigious **R. W. Norton Art Gallery** has superb European and American art, including the area's largest permanent collection of works by Frederic Remington and Charles M. Russell. ⊠ *4747 Creswell Ave.,* ☎ *318/865–4201.* 🖭 *Free.* 🕙 *Tues.–Fri. 10–5, weekends 1–5.*

The **Louisiana State Exhibit Museum** has extensive displays and dioramas depicting the state's history, including a large collection of Native American artifacts from Poverty Point and other important excavations in Louisiana. ⊠ *Fairgrounds,* ☎ *318/632–2020.* 🖭 *$2.* 🕙 *Weekdays 9–4, Sat. noon–4.*

The **Ark-La-Tex Antique and Classic Vehicle Museum** traces automotive history in both classic and vintage models. ⊠ *601 Spring St.,* ☎ *318/222–0227.* 🖭 *$4.* 🕙 *Mon.–Sat. 10–5, Sun. 1–5.*

☾ The **Sci-Port Discovery Center** is a 67,000-square-ft science facility with hands-on interactive exhibits for all ages, as well as national traveling exhibitions and an IMAX theater. Admission is discounted the first Tuesday of each month. ⊠ *820 Clyde Fant Pkwy.,* ☎ *318/424–3466.* 🖭 *$6 museum, $6 IMAX theater, $10 combination ticket.* 🕙 *Daily 10–6.*

The **American Rose Center,** headquarters of the American Rose Society, is a 118-acre piney-woods park with more than 20,000 rosebushes in more than 60 individual gardens. The place lights up like a Christmas tree during the Christmas in Roseland show, which runs from the day after Thanksgiving through New Year's Eve. ⊠ *Jefferson-Paige Rd.,* ☎ *318/938–5402.* 🖭 *$4.* 🕙 *Apr.–Oct., weekdays 9–5, weekends 9–6; Christmas in Roseland, day after Thanksgiving–Dec 30., daily 5:30–10 PM.*

In Bossier City the **Eighth Air Force Museum** has World War II aircraft, dioramas, uniforms, and barracks of the Second Bomb Wing and the Eighth Air Force, which are headquartered at Barksdale Air Force Base. ⊠ *Barksdale Air Force Base,* ☎ *318/456–3067.* 🖭 *Free.* 🕙 *Daily 9:30–4.*

The Shreveport-Bossier area has, at press time, four **riverboat casinos** afloat on the Red River, with more scheduled to open soon. In 1999 Hollywood Casinos broke ground for a huge facility. All the casinos have a full complement of slot machines and table games, including roulette, blackjack, craps, baccarat, Caribbean stud, and big six; all have restaurants, and most have top-name entertainment, as well (*See also* hotels, *below*). Harrah's Casino, Shreveport (⊠ Shreveport, ☎ 800/427–7247); Isle of Capri Casino & Hotel (⊠ Bossier City, ☎ 318/747–2400 or 800/221–4095); the Horseshoe Riverboat Casino & Hotel (⊠ Bossier City, ☎ 800/895–0711); and Casino Magic (⊠ I–20, Exit 19B, ☎ 318/746–0711).

Louisiana Downs, one of the South's largest racetracks, has Thoroughbred racing from April through October. ⊠ *I–20, Bossier City,* ☎ *318/747–7223.*

South of Shreveport, the **Mansfield Battle Park** is the site of the last major Confederate victory of the Civil War. More than 30,000 men were involved in the bitter battle. The site contains monuments and an interpretive center with audiovisual displays. ⊠ *Rte. 2, 4 mi south of Mansfield,* ☎ *318/872–1474.* ☜ *Free.* ⊙ *Daily 9–5.*

Dining and Lodging

$$$$ ✕ **Monsieur Patout.** An enchanting jewel box of a restaurant, this small, prix fixe, *très intime* restaurant serves classic French cuisine. ⊠ *855 Pierremont Rd.,* ☎ *318/868–9822. Reservations essential. AE, D, DC, MC, V.*

$$–$$$ ✕ **Jack Binion's Steakhouse.** Two-fisted steaks are served in this handsome, always busy restaurant of the Horseshoe Hotel, which is named for its founding father. ⊠ *711 Horseshoe Blvd, Bossier City.,* ☎ *318/ 741–7870. Reservations essential. AE, D, DC, MC, V. No lunch.*

$$–$$$ ✕ **Superior Bar & Grill.** Even with a reservation you may have to hang out in the bar to wait for a table, but the fine mesquite-grilled steaks and Mexican food served here are worth the wait. ⊠ *6123 Line Ave.,* ☎ *318/869–3243. AE, D, MC, V.*

$ ✕ **Glenwood Drug Co.** This lovely Victorian tearoom, serving shepherd's pie and delicious salads, is a popular lunch spot. It's in a historic drugstore that's now a small mall whose several vendors offer china, silver, linens, books, scented candles, and such. It's a wonderful lunching, and browsing, place. ⊠ *3310 Line Ave.,* ☎ *318/868–3651. AE, MC, V.*

$$$ ⊞ **Horseshoe Hotel & Casino.** A $204 million, 26-story hotel, opened in 1999, this is a huge facility. Blimp-size crystal chandeliers hang over the sleek lobby, which is adjacent to the casino. The all-suites property has rooms with marble baths, coffeemakers, fridges, hair dryers, and modems. King-size–bed suites have three TVs, including one in the bath. The casino has nightly entertainment and top-name headliners appear in the Riverdome. ⊠ *711 Horseshoe Blvd., Bossier City, 71111,* ☎ *318/741–7870 or 800/895–0711,* ℻ *318/741–7870. 606 suites. 4 restaurants, lobby lounge, nightclub, casino, pool, health club, beauty salon. AE, D, DC, MC, V.* ✧

$$$ ⊞ **Isle of Capri Hotel & Casino.** The Isle features a tropical decor throughout. All accommodations are luxury suites, with whirlpool bath, three TVs, and phones with voice mail and modems. ⊠ *3033 Hilton Dr., Bossier City, 71111,* ☎ *318/747–2400 or 800/221–4095,* ℻ *318/ 747–6822. 230 suites. 3 restaurants, lobby lounge, nightclub, casino, pool, fitness center, childcare center, video arcade. AE, D, DC, MC, V. www.isleofcapricasino.com*

$$–$$$ ⊞ **Sheraton Shreveport Hotel.** In this luxury property near the convention center, every guest room has a wet bar, a refrigerator, three phones, and a modem line. ⊠ *1419 E. 70th St., 71105,* ☎ *318/797– 9900 or 800/325–3535,* ℻ *318/798–2923. 270 rooms. Restaurant, pool, health club. AE, D, DC, MC, V.* ✧

Shreveport and Northern Louisiana A to Z

Arriving and Departing

BY AIR

Shreveport Regional Airport (☎ 318/673–5370) is served by American Eagle, Continental Express, Delta, Northwest, TWA, and US Airways.

BY CAR

I–20 and U.S. 80 run east–west through the northern part of the state; Route 1 cuts diagonally from the northwest corner to the Gulf of Mexico; I–49 connects Shreveport with southern Louisiana. Other north–south routes are U.S. 171, 71, 165, and 167.

BY BUS

Greyhound/Trailways (☎ 800/231–2222) provides both interstate and intrastate bus service.

Contacts and Resources

EMERGENCIES

Police, ambulance (☎ 911). All-night **hospital emergency rooms** in Bossier City include **Christus Schumpert Bossier Healthplex** (⊠ 2541 Viking Dr., ☎ 318/681–4500); in Shreveport, **LSU Medical Center** (⊠ 1501 Kings Hwy., ☎ 318/675–6930).

RADIO STATIONS

AM: KEEL 710-AM, Talk. **FM:** KITT, 93.7 FM, country; KRUF 94.5 FM, Top 40.

VISITOR INFORMATION

Shreveport-Bossier Convention & Tourist Bureau (⊠ 629 Spring St., Shreveport 71166, ☎ 318/222–9391 or 800/551–8682, FAX 318/222–0056, ✇). There are four **visitor centers** (⊠ Southpark Mall, Jewella Rd., Shreveport; ⊠ Southpark Mall, Jewella Rd., Shreveport; ⊠ 100 John Wesley Blvd., Bossier City; and ⊠ Pierre Bossier Mall, Airline Dr., Bossier City; and Mall St. Vincent, St. Vincent and Southern Aves., Shreveport, ☎ 318/227–9880).

LOUISIANA A TO Z

Arriving and Departing

By Bus
Greyhound/Trailways (☎ 800/231–2222) provides both interstate and intrastate bus service.

By Car
Major east–west arteries through the state are Interstate 20 (I–20), which parallels U.S. 80 through North Louisiana, and Interstate 10 (I–10), which goes coast to coast, cutting through downtown New Orleans along the way. North–south routes include Interstate 49 (I–49), which goes diagonally through the state from Lafayette in the south through Shreveport and into Arkansas. Interstate 55 (I–55) comes south from Chicago and connects with I–10 about 20 mi west of New Orleans. LA Highway 1 is a scenic route, often over substandard roads, that goes diagonally from Grand Isle on the Gulf of Mexico to the farthest northwest tip of the state.

By Plane
All major domestic carriers and a number of foreign carriers fly into **New Orleans International Airport** (⊠ 900 Airline Dr., Kenner, ☎ 504/464–0831), the state's largest airport.

By Train
Amtrak trains (☎ 800/872–7245) from Miami, New York, Chicago, Los Angeles, and points in between pull into New Orleans's Union Terminal in the Central Business District.

Getting Around

By Bus
Greyhound/Trailways (☎ 800/231–2222) provides bus service between the state's cities and towns.

By Car
The speed limit on interstates is 70 mph. Right turns on red lights are permitted unless otherwise indicated. The Official State Map, available from the Louisiana Office of Tourism (☞ Visitor Information, *below*) and visitor centers, has a mileage chart as well as directories for each tourist area.

By Plane

There are **regional airports** served by commuter carriers in Baton Rouge (☎ 504/357–4165), Lafayette (☎ 318/232–2808), Alexandria (☎ 318/449–4642), Lake Charles (☎ 318/477–6051), Shreveport (☎ 318/673–5370), and Monroe (☎ 318/329–2461).

By Train

Amtrak (☎ 800/872–7245) serves South Louisiana with stops in Schriever (between Thibodaux and Houma), New Iberia, Lafayette, and Lake Charles. There is one train that operates westbound on Monday, Wednesday, and Saturday, and an eastbound train Tuesday, Thursday, and Sunday.

Contacts and Resources

Bed-and-Breakfasts

For a free illustrated brochure of statewide bed-and-breakfasts, contact **Louisiana Bed & Breakfast** (✉ Box 4003, Baton Rouge 70821–4003, ☎ 800/677–5597).

Emergencies

For **ambulance and fire** emergencies statewide, call ☎ 911.

Fishing

For information about licenses and lake maps, contact the **Louisiana Department of Wildlife & Fisheries** (✉ Box 98000, Baton Rouge 70898, ☎ 504/765–2800).

Road Conditions

Call the **24-hour Highway Safety Hotline** (☎ 800/259–4929 or 504/379–1541) for information.

Shopping

Louisiana is the first state to grant a sales tax rebate to foreign travelers. Look for shops, restaurants, and hotels that display the tax-free logo, then ask for a voucher for the tax, which varies from parish to parish, that's tacked onto most purchases. Present vouchers with your passport and airline ticket at the tax rebate office in New Orleans International Airport and receive up to $500 cash back. Rebates exceeding $500 will be mailed to your home address.

State Parks

Detailed information about campsites and facilities in the state parks can be obtained from the **Louisiana Office of State Parks** (✉ Box 44426, Baton Rouge 70804, ☎ 225/342–8111).

Visitor Information

For a copy of the free "Louisiana Tour Guide" brochure, contact the **Louisiana Office of Tourism** (✉ Box 94291, Baton Rouge 70804-9291, ☎ 225/342–8119 or 800/334–8626 FAX 225/342–8390, ✍).

5 MISSISSIPPI

Dotted with Civil War battlegrounds, Mississippi is a gold mine for history buffs and offers some of the best-preserved examples of antebellum architecture in the South. The Natchez Trace Parkway, strung with magnolia trees and hilltop vistas, cuts across the heart of Dixie, passing through Tupelo, Jackson, and antebellum Natchez. The mighty Mississippi forms the western border of the state, winding slowly through the Delta past the port towns of Greenville and Vicksburg. Along the Gulf Coast, the "Playground of the South" beckons with casinos, beaches, history, and cultural experiences.

Updated by
Karen S.
Bryant

A S YOU ENTER THE LUSH AND LOVELY Magnolia State, slow down, look around, and listen carefully so as not to miss a single one of the South's great treasures. Mississippi is, indeed, deep in the heart of Dixie, and Dixieland is steeped in legend and lore.

Listen, and hear the soft, gentle drawl of an authentic Southern welcome. Stop in small towns, rich with historic houses and museums, busy with locals eager to regale you with slightly partisan tales of the Civil War. Sit quietly and catch snippets of the gossip that permeates the air of any eatery redolent with country cooking. Gossip and good food get on famously down South.

Mississippians eat, sleep, and breathe history—so much so that they subconsciously perpetuate the presence of ancestors. Dyed-in-the-wool Mississippians honor tradition, which manifests itself in everything from the meticulous upkeep of stately old homes—you can tour many of them during special pilgrimage times—to the painstaking preservation of colorful front-porch stories passed down from generation to generation.

If you're looking for something a bit more fast-paced, Mississippi now has more gaming space than any other place outside Las Vegas. In fact, the largest single business investment in the state's history—a $600 million casino/hotel project called Beau Rivage—opened its doors in Biloxi in 1999. In Mississippi the past still endures, but at least part of the state's future is in gaming.

Whatever you do in Mississippi, you'll probably encounter evidence of the state's rich artistic heritage in one form or another. You'll feel exalted reading William Faulkner's Nobel Prize address, you'll laugh at the characters in Eudora Welty's short stories, and you'll find pathos aplenty in Tennessee Williams's plays and thrills in John Grisham's bestsellers. Hear the Delta Blues music of Robert Johnson and B. B. King, and roll to the rock of Tupelo native Elvis Presley. Mississippians all, they've contributed to a mystique no other state can touch.

Pleasures and Pastimes

Dining

Fresh Gulf seafood, particularly redfish, flounder, and speckled trout, stars in coast restaurants. Soft-shell crab is a coast specialty, and crab claws are a traditional appetizer. Coast locals are fond of quaffing Biloxi-born Barq's root beer with their seafood. In Tupelo, Jackson, and Natchez you can find everything from caviar to chitlins. Jackson has several elegant restaurants. Tupelo specializes in down-home cooking, but blue-plate dinners of fresh Mississippi vegetables are a widely available alternative. Southern breakfasts served in antebellum opulence are a Natchez trademark. All in all, good food and drink are required in the South; fancy surroundings aren't. Dress is casual unless otherwise noted.

CATEGORY	COST*
$$$$	over $35
$$$	$25–$35
$$	$15–$25
$	under $15

*per person for a three-course meal, excluding drinks, service, and 8%–10% sales tax (depending on the area)

Gambling

Sip a cocktail, enjoy a show, or maybe even strike it rich at the splashy, Las Vegas–style casinos permanently docked along the waterfront in Gulfport, Biloxi, and Bay St. Louis, on the Gulf Coast, or in the Delta's Tunica County. The casinos, built on huge barges that resemble land-based casinos more than actual boats all have numerous bars, lounges, and restaurants and are open 24 hours a day, so night owls are never at a loss for a place to go.

Lodging

With the advent of dockside casinos, the Gulf Coast hotel business is booming. Reserve a couple of weeks ahead—as gambling aficionados say, "The coast is cookin'." National hotel and motel chains are found throughout the Natchez Trace region, though Jackson's historic mansions add variety. In Natchez, travelers will find plantation homes that open their doors in bed-and-breakfast courtesy.

CATEGORY	COST*
$$$$	over $150
$$$	$110–$150
$$	$70–$110
$	under $70

*All prices are for a standard double room, excluding 8%–9% tax (depending on the area).

Pilgrimage Tours

Mississippians love to show their Southern hospitality by opening their antebellum and Victorian homes to the public in the form of spring and fall pilgrimages. Annual or biannual pilgrimages take place on the coast, in Columbus, Holly Springs, Port Gibson, Natchez, and Vicksburg, with the Natchez tours the crown jewel. Dates change year to year, so call the visitor centers in the towns for details.

✎ following the text of a review is your signal that the property has a Web site, where you will find details and, usually, images; for a link, visit www.fodors.com/urls.

Exploring Mississippi

Mississippi is a state of contrasts. The Gulf Coast and the areas as far north as Vicksburg and Natchez have a decidedly New Orleans flavor, while the Delta—the rich area of farmland periodically delivered by Mississippi River floods—is more like Memphis: genteel, polite, but all business. A trip along the Natchez Trace, which stretches from Natchez northeast through Jackson and Tupelo, then on to Nashville, will carry you back to a time of settlers, outlaws, traveling preachers, and post riders. Holly Springs and Oxford are sophisticated courthouse towns in northern Mississippi that don't fit neatly under the Gulf Coast, Delta, or Natchez Trace banners. They exemplify yet another dimension of Mississippi's diversity.

Great Itineraries

How you tour Mississippi depends largely on whether you start at the top or the bottom. You can experience a section of the Natchez Trace whether you're in north, central, or south Mississippi, since it cuts diagonally through the state. Driving the entire Trace takes about seven hours, but you could spend seven days if you have the time. The same goes for the rest of Mississippi. You could drive from top to bottom in six hours, but your only memory might be of row after row of roadside pine trees. Instead, take at least three days to explore any one of Mississippi's areas, or span the state for a nine-day vacation.

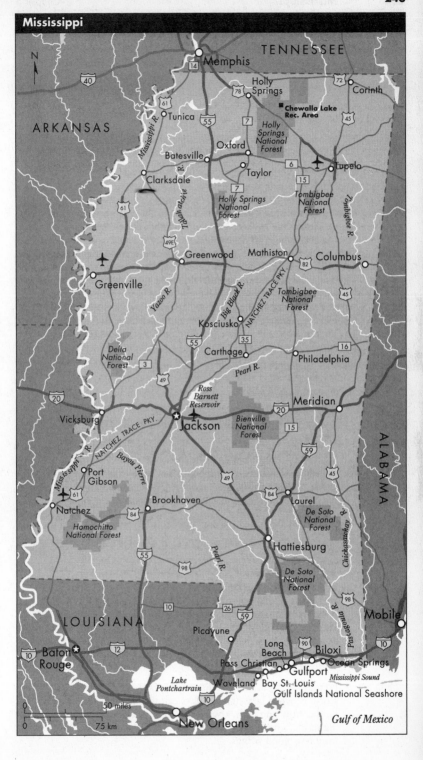

IF YOU HAVE 3 DAYS

Casinos docked all along the Gulf Coast have kept the area from Ocean Springs to Bay St. Louis packed with tourists, but there are other activities besides gambling to keep you busy. Start your Gulf Coast tour in **Ocean Springs,** which is worth at least an afternoon with its Walter Anderson Museum of Art, Shearwater Pottery, and unique shops. Overnight in ⊞ **Biloxi** and on Day 2 make an excursion to one of the barrier islands that separate the Gulf of Mexico from Mississippi Sound. On Day 3 head for ⊞ **Natchez,** where you might want to stay at one of the antebellum town's bed-and-breakfast establishments. Leave a full day for touring Natchez, more if you come during a pilgrimage time, when many of Natchez's lovely old homes are opened to visitors.

IF YOU HAVE 6 DAYS

Start out on the Gulf Coast, where you'll dine on some of the finest seafood in the nation. Overnight at either **Ocean Springs** or ⊞ **Biloxi.** On Day 2 head to ⊞ **Natchez,** worth at least an afternoon of exploration. On the third day enjoy a leisurely drive through **Port Gibson** to ⊞ **Jackson,** where you can spend your fourth day studying the city's notable architecture and admiring the regional and national artwork on display in its small museums. On the fifth day drive a long stretch of the Natchez Trace to ⊞ **Oxford,** where you can soak up the literary vibes set forth by such Southern heroes as William Faulkner, Eudora Welty, and Tennessee Williams. Visit Faulkner's Rowan Oak and the campus of the University of Mississippi, more commonly called Ole Miss, and the Eudora Welty Library where the region's rich literary history is felt most strongly.

IF YOU HAVE 9 DAYS

With nine days you'll have time to experience the Gulf Coast and a good portion of the Natchez Trace; see the itineraries above for suggested routes. Set aside the last three days to explore the Delta. Spend part of Day 7 in **Holly Springs,** which survived more than 50 raids during the Civil War. Though many of the town's historic homes are open to visitors only during pilgrimage time, their facades alone are worth seeing. Next morning, start toward ⊞ **Tunica County,** where you can try your luck at the slot machines and table games at any of several of the city's casino resorts. On your eighth day, head toward **Clarksdale,** home of the Delta Blues Museum. Stop for a hot tamale at Doe's in **Greenville** before continuing on to ⊞ **Vicksburg** at the south end of the Delta. Your ninth day can be spent touring Vicksburg's Civil War sights and cruising the Mississippi with Hydro-Jet Boat Tours.

When to Tour Mississippi

To be part of the action, hit the Gulf Coast's Mardi Gras celebrations in late January and February, Biloxi's Blessing of the Fleet in May, and Jackson's Jubilee! JAM, also in May. Fall brings historic house tours and antiques browsing in Natchez. The Mississippi Division of Tourism Development (☞ Visitor Information *in* Mississippi A to Z, *below*) will gladly send you a travel planner.

Prepare for the weather—Mississippi's fairly fickle. Spring and fall are glorious, while lazy summer days call for cool drinks on a shady veranda. Now and then, a winter cold snap sends porch sitters scurrying inside. Locals say it's tolerable here year-round, but be prepared for a few mood swings.

THE GULF COAST

Ocean Springs, Biloxi, Gulfport

The Mississippi Gulf Coast extends for about 80 mi from Alabama to Louisiana. Although I–10 runs along the coast, it's better to drive U.S. 90 in order to experience the coast. Restaurants, bars, hotels, motels, and souvenir shops jostle for space along its busy four lanes, and the riverboat casinos permanently docked at the water's edge welcome anyone seeking a good time. But don't let the clamor of this neon strip hide the coast's quieter treasures: the ancient land, sculpted by wind and water, continually changing; serene beachfront houses set on green and shady lawns; the teeming wildlife of Mississippi Sound and its adjacent bayous and marshes; the unspoiled natural beauty of the seven barrier islands that separate the Gulf of Mexico from Mississippi Sound.

On a clear day, if you have good eyesight or a good imagination, you can see these islands. Their names (from east to west) are Petit Bois (anglicized as "Petty Boy"), Horn, East and West Ship, and Cat. Two others, Round and Deer, lie within Mississippi Sound.

Three hundred years ago, France, England, and Spain ruled the area, according to their fortunes in international wars. Street names, family names, and traditions still reflect this colorful heritage. In the late 19th and early 20th centuries, the coast became a fashionable vacation spot for wealthy New Orleanians and Delta planters eager to escape yellow fever epidemics. Elegant hotels, imposing beachfront mansions, and smaller summer homes sprang up. Today the homes that have endured the vagaries of time and hurricanes stand along the beach—brave and beautiful survivors. Many of the homes along the coast are open for tours during pilgrimage time. The dates vary, so call the Mississippi Beach Convention and Visitors Bureau (☞ Visitor Information *in* The Gulf Coast A to Z, *below*).

Today the coast's people are known to be easygoing and tolerant, artistic and hardy. Add the local love of fun and frolic, and you'll understand why Las Vegas–style gaming has been a major coastal to-do since its inception in 1992. Dockside gambling's floating barges recall the days of riverboat gambling once rampant along the mighty Mississippi. Casino vessels today, however, are permanently moored and connected to dockside hotels and open round the clock. Restaurants, waterfront cafés, and Southern hospitality are also in abundance.

Enjoy wondrous walks along the water, but take your cue from the locals and ignore any urge to swim. The Mississippi Sound is murky (at best). Instead, admire the stately live oaks and frolic on the white sands. Go floundering and spear your supper. Above all, slow down. On the Mississippi Coast only the traffic on U.S. 90 moves quickly.

Ocean Springs

35 mi west of Mobile, 90 mi east of New Orleans.

To begin at the beginning, at least as far as Mississippi is concerned, start in Ocean Springs. Here, in 1699, the French commander Pierre LeMoyne Sieur d'Iberville established Fort Maurepas to shore up France's claim to the central part of North America. This first colony was temporary, but it's fondly remembered by Ocean Springs during its annual spring festival, which celebrates Iberville's landing. Magnificent oaks shade the sleepy town center, a pleasant area of small shops to explore on foot.

Walter Anderson (1903–65), an artist of genius and grand eccentricity, made his home in Ocean Springs. Drawings and watercolors, some not discovered until after his death, are on display at the **Walter Anderson Museum of Art,** built as an attachment to the **Old Community Center** where Anderson painted murals in 1951 (before it became the "Old" Community Center). The **Little Room** was extracted from Anderson's cottage home, loaded on a flatbed truck, and moved to the museum, with its murals intact. Anderson painted the intricate murals in the Old Community Center for a fee of $1; they are now appraised at $1 million. *Museum:* ⊠ *510 Washington Ave.,* ☎ *228/872–3164.* ☞ *$4.* ☼ *Mon.–Sat. 10–5, Sun. 1–5.*

The **Shearwater Pottery and Showroom** displays a wide selection of original Anderson family hand-thrown and hand-cast pottery. Potters demonstrate their craft in the Anderson family workshop; some pieces are for sale. ⊠ *102 Shearwater Dr.,* ☎ *228/875–7320.* ☞ *Free.* ☼ *Showroom Mon.–Sat. 9–5:30, Sun. 1–5:30; workshop weekdays 9–noon, 1–4.*

A brochure from the Ocean Springs Chamber of Commerce (☞ Visitor Information *in* The Gulf Coast A to Z, *below*) will guide you on a driving tour of the **d'Iberville Trail,** shaded by moss-draped trees and bordered by weathered but lovely summer houses. The route, which begins at Ocean Springs's train station, winds through the area first explored 300 years ago by Pierre LeMoyne Sieur d'Iberville.

☺ The **Doll House** displays a collection of contemporary and antique dolls, stuffed animals, and dollhouses. ⊠ *1201 Bienville Blvd. (U.S. 90),* ☎ *228/872–3971.* ☞ *$1 donation requested for YMCA Pet Shelter.* ☼ *Tues.–Sun. 1–5.*

★ **Gulf Islands National Seashore** (⊠ 3500 Park Rd., ☎ 228/875–9057)— which includes Ship, Horn, and Petit Bois islands—has its headquarters on Ocean Springs's Davis Bayou. When the heat and humidity aren't overwhelming, have a picnic and explore the nature trails. Wilderness camping is available on Horn and Petit Bois islands, accessible by charter and private boat; call for a list of charter boat operators. Gulf Islands National Seashore has 50 campsites for trailers and RVs, with electrical hookups available.

Dining

$$–$$$ ✕ **Germaine's.** Formerly Trilby's, this little house surrounded by live oaks has served many a great meal to its faithful clientele. The atmosphere is reminiscent of New Orleans, with unadorned wooden floors, walls decked in local art for sale, fireplaces, and attentive service. Specialties include crabmeat au gratin, broiled trout served with mushrooms and sautéed crabmeat, and sautéed veal in a creamy port wine sauce. ⊠ *1203 Bienville Blvd., U.S. 90E,* ☎ *228/875–4426. AE, D, MC, V. Closed Mon. No dinner Sun.*

$–$$ ✕ **Fisherman's Wharf.** A neighboring shrimp factory perfumes the parking lot here, but inside there are fresher air and views of oyster shuckers at work on the pier. You'll find soft-shell crab, gumbo, and oyster po'boys among the lunch specials; broiled catch of the day for dinner; and always, the only dessert Fisherman's Wharf pie, a top secret recipe that tastes a bit like a cross between a chess pie and a pecan pie (although there's no actual pecans in it). It's really very tasty. ⊠ *1409 Bienville Blvd. (Hwy. 90),* ☎ *228/872–6111. Reservations not accepted. AE, D, DC, MC, V. Closed Mon.*

$–$$ ✕ **Jocelyn's Restaurant.** Jocelyn is formerly of Trilby's kitchen, now
★   Germaine's (☞ *above*), and fans love her cooking just as much in this old frame house. This is as good as coast seafood gets. Specialties are fresh crabmeat fixed three or four ways. Trout, flounder, and, when

available, snapper are subtly seasoned and served with garnishes as bright and original as modern art. Stuffed eggplant is another favorite. ⊠ *U.S. 90E, opposite SouthTrust Bank,* ☎ *228/875–1925. Reservations not accepted. No credit cards.*

Shopping

At **Ballard's Pewter** (⊠ 1110 Government St., Ocean Springs, ☎ 228/875–7550) you'll find necklaces and earrings made from sand dollars, or have the pewterer fashion a bespoke (custom-made) piece.

At **Realizations** (⊠ 1000 Washington Ave., in the old Train Depot, ☎ 228/875–0503) you can buy Walter Anderson prints and clothing printed with his unique designs.

Biloxi

2 mi west of Ocean Springs.

Biloxi (pronounced bi-*lux*-i) is the oldest continuous settlement on the Gulf Coast and the third-largest city in Mississippi. When Pierre LeMoyne Sieur d'Iberville met the Native Americans who called themselves Biloxi, or "first people," he gave their name to the area and to the bay. The French constructed Fort Louis here; it served as the capital of the Louisiana Territory from 1720 until 1722, when the capital was moved to New Orleans. Today casinos bring the city plenty of action (☞ Dining and Lodging, *below*). Biloxi also has a number of museums and a white-sand beach for more sedate pursuits.

The **J. L. Scott Marine Education Center and Aquarium** has 48 live exhibits and aquariums brimming with reptiles and several species of fish from the Gulf. The centerpiece is a spectacular 42,000-gallon tank. ⊠ *115 Beach Blvd.,* ☎ *228/374–5550.* ⊡ *$4.* ☉ *Mon.–Sat. 9–4.* ☜

Across U.S. 90 is **Point Cadet Plaza,** a waterfront complex that in the 1880s housed European immigrants who flocked to Biloxi to work in seafood canneries. Exhibits at the **Maritime & Seafood Industry Museum** (⊡ $3) depict the growth and development of the Gulf Coast seafood industry. Two re-created **schooners,** which dock at Point Cadet's marina, are available for short trips and charters; call for fees and schedules. ⊠ *Point Cadet Plaza, Hwy. 90 and 1st St.,* ☎ *228/435–6320.* ☉ *Mon.–Sat. 9–4:30.* ☜

Biloxi's **Small Craft Harbor,** off U.S. 90 on the sound, captures the atmosphere of a lazy fishing village. Take the **Biloxi Shrimping Trip** aboard the *Sailfish* and experience 70 minutes as a shrimper as you pull the nets through the waters. ⊠ *Hwy. 90 and Main St.,* ☎ *228/385–1182.* ⊡ *$11.* ☉ *Mar.–Nov. (call for schedule).* ☜

Erected in 1848, the 48-ft-tall **Biloxi Lighthouse** is a landmark. During the Civil War, Union forces, operating from Ship Island, blockaded Mississippi Sound and cut Biloxi off from much-needed supplies. When the Yankees demanded that Biloxi submit or starve, they were told that the Union would have to "blockade the mullet" first. Ever since, mullet has been known as "Biloxi bacon" and honored with its own festival each October. The city defended itself with what appeared to be a formidable cannon array near the lighthouse but was actually only two cannons and many logs painted black. ⊠ *U.S. 90 at Porter Ave.,* ☎ *228/435–6293.* ⊡ *$2.* ☉ *Mon.–Sat. 10 AM–11 AM (closing time varies depending on number of visitors, it's best to arrive right at opening).*

Mardi Gras is almost as grand a celebration in Biloxi as in nearby New Orleans, and the Krewe costumes are equally festive. Costumes and crowns are housed in the **Mardi Gras Museum** in the old Magnolia Hotel, an 1847 structure listed on the National Register of Historic Places. ⊠ *119 Rue Magnolia,* ☎ *228/435–6245.* ▨ *$2.* ⊙ *Mon.–Sat. 11–4.*

★ **The Ohr/O'Keefe Museum of Art** houses a collection of intricate pottery crafted by the talented and eccentric Ohr, known as "the mad potter of Biloxi." To truly appreciate his great craftsmanship, take a few minutes to watch the film about his life. The center also exhibits the work of local artists. At press time there were plans to have a new center built by Frank Gehry, architect of the Guggenheim Bilboa Museum in Spain, to house the museum, so call ahead to confirm location. ⊠ *136 G. E. Ohr St.,* ☎ *228/374–5547.* ▨ *$3.* ⊙ *Mon.–Sat. 9–5.*

Dining and Lodging

$$–$$$ ✕ **Mary Mahoney's Old French House Restaurant.** Locals swear by it,
★   not only for the comfort of its old brick and age-darkened wood (the mansion Mary Mahoney's calls home dates to 1737) and for the memory of Mary herself (who always went from table to table, chatting with customers), but also for the food. Start off with a bowl of rich, dark gumbo or the shrimp Italienne salad with a lightly spicy dressing. The lightly breaded panfried veal Antonio, topped with cheese sauce and plenty of fresh crabmeat, the stuffed red snapper, and the sautéed shrimp are excellent main choices. The bread pudding drenched in rum sauce is unforgettable. ⊠ *110 Rue Magnolia,* ☎ *228/374–0163. AE, DC, MC, V. Closed Sun.*

$–$$ ✕ **McElroy's Harbor House Restaurant.** Biloxi locals and real shrimpers eat hearty breakfasts, lunches, and dinners as fishing boats come and go and fisherfolk load and unload their nets just outside. Notable are the po'boys, oysters on the half shell, broiled stuffed flounder, and stuffed crabs. ⊠ *Biloxi Small Craft Harbor, 695 Beach Blvd.,* ☎ *228/435–5001. Reservations not accepted. AE, D, DC, MC, V.*

$–$$ ✕ **Ole Biloxi Schooner.** Coast residents flock to this family-run restaurant on Biloxi's serene back bay. It's tiny—little more than a shack—but the food is good, especially the gumbo and the po'boys, which come "dressed" and wrapped in paper. ⊠ *159 E. Howard,* ☎ *228/374–8071. Reservations not accepted. No credit cards.*

$$–$$$$ ▦ **Beau Rivage.** The first grand Las Vegas–style hotel/casino on the
★   Gulf Coast, Mirage resorts pulled out all the stops when it built this impressive resort. In the lobby, majestic magnolia trees line the inside walkway that leads from the entrance to the mega-casino. The magnolia theme continues to the spacious modern rooms where the southern blooms decorate curtains and bedspreads. Among the eight restaurants on the property, Coral is the most spectacular, with floor-to-ceiling aquariums filled with schools of fish. For entertainment, there's the 72,000-square-ft casino with table games and slot machines. If a little r&r is what you're seeking, there's no better spot than the in-house salon that overlooks the beautiful pool. ⊠ *875 Beach Blvd.,* ☎ *228/386–7444 or 888/567–6667,* ℻ *228/386–7446. 1,780 rooms. 8 restaurants, bar, coffee shop, deli, ice cream parlor, no smoking floors, room service, pool, hot tub, beauty salon, spa, health club, dock, shops, casino. AE, D, DC, MC, V.* ⊛

$$–$$$$ **Palace Casino Resort.** A newcomer to the area, the Palace has standard, clean rooms that overlook Biloxi Bay and the Gulf of Mexico. The soaring atrium lobby has a 25-foot skylight and a cascading fountain that marks the entrance to the casino. Outside, elegant cabanas ring the pool and are adjacent to a sand beach. ⊠ *158 Howard Ave., 39530,* ☎ *228/432–8888 or 800/725–2239,* ℻ *228/386–2300. 236 rooms, 11 suites. 4 restaurants, 2 bars, 2 lounges, café, coffee shop, in-room modem lines, 2 pools, beauty salon, outdoor hot tub, massage, mineral baths, sauna, spa, golf privileges, exercise room, volleyball, beach, shops, casino, the-*

ater, video games, laundry service, concierge, concierge floor, airport shuttle, free parking. ☜

$$–$$$ ⚏ **Grand Casino Biloxi Hotel and Bayview Resort & Spa.** These two Grand Casino properties are located across the highway from one another on U.S. 90 and are connected by a climate-controlled, covered walkway. Together they offer 1,000 guest rooms and a full range of services including specialty shops, restaurants, a teen arcade, and a spa and salon. Both hotels have comfortable accommodations. The Bayview's rooms are particularly bright and airy, with a beach feel. The 1,600-seat Biloxi Grand Theatre hosts live stage shows, and both properties are adjacent to the Grand Casino, with Las Vegas–style gambling. Hotel guests are shuttled to and from the property's new Grand Bear golf course (☞ Outdoor Activities and Sports, *below*), an 18-hole championship course designed by Jack Nicklaus. ⊠ *265 Beach Blvd., 39530, ☎ 228/436–2946 or 800/354–2450. 1,000 rooms. 10 restaurants, 5 bars, 2 lounges, 2 pools, spa, beauty salon, exercise room, children's programs, shops, concierge, travel services, car rental, free parking. AE, D, DC, MC, V.* ☜

$$ ⚏ **Isle of Capri Casino Crowne Plaza Resort.** The Isle of Capri was the first gaming operation to open on the Gulf. Rooms are large, with ceiling fans; some have balconies with views of the Gulf. The casino, with slot machines, video poker, and table games, can be accessed through the mezzanine level. Weekends are usually packed here, so you might want to call ahead. ⊠ *151 Beach Blvd., 39530, ☎ 228/435–5400 or 800/843–4753, FAX 228/436–7834. 370 rooms, 4 suites. 3 restaurants, pool, health club, casino, meeting rooms. AE, D, DC, MC, V.*

$–$$ ⚏ **Casino Magic Bay St. Louis.** Though Casino Magic and the Casino Magic inn are not connected, they are within easy walking distance of each other. Rooms here are standard motel style; junior suites have refrigerators and microwaves. The 18-hole, Arnold Palmer–designed Bridges Golf Resort (☞ Outdoor Activities and Sports, *below*) provides challenging action for novices and low-handicappers alike. The casino offers slot machines and a full array of table games. The 24-hour entertainment complex showcases big-name talent. There is also a 100-site RV park on the premises with barbeque grills and laundry facilities. ⊠ *711 Casino Magic Dr., Bay St. Louis 39520, ☎ 228/467–9257 or 800/562–4425, FAX 228/466–2955. 201 rooms. 4 restaurants, 5 lounges, pool, dock, meeting rooms. AE, D, DC, MC, V.* ☜

$–$$ ⚏ **Casino Magic Biloxi.** This beachfront hotel is a sister property to Casino Magic hotel and casino in Bay St. Louis. It is adjacent to Las Vegas–style casino action and offers a host of amenities. Guests are shuttled to and from the 18-hole, Arnold Palmer–designed The Bridges Golf Resort (☞ Outdoor Activities and Sports, *below*) at the Bay St. Louis property. The course is challenging and well maintained. Players in the casino can wager on slot machines, blackjack, craps, roulette, and more. ⊠ *167 Beach Blvd., 39530, ☎ 228/386–4000 or 800/562–4425. 378 rooms. 4 restaurants, pool, spa, business services, meeting rooms. AE, D, DC, MC, V.* ☜

En Route On U.S. 90 between Biloxi and Gulfport is **Beauvoir,** the antebellum beachfront mansion where Jefferson Davis spent the last 12 years of his life. It was here that the president of the Confederacy wrote his memoirs and his book *The Rise and Fall of the Confederate Government.* The serene, raised-cottage-style house, with its sweeping front stairs, is flanked by pavilions and set on a broad lawn shaded by ancient live oaks. A Confederate cemetery on the grounds includes the Tomb of the Unknown Soldier of the Confederacy. A new presidential library holds materials about the era and about Davis. ⊠ *2244 Beach Blvd., ☎ 228/388–1313.* ☞ *$7.50.* ☉ *Daily 9–4.*

Gulfport

12 mi west of Biloxi.

A variety of activities for children plus access to one of the Gulf's most historic islands makes Gulfport a nice stop for families. If you have time for only one activity on this part of the coast, make it a getaway to **Ship Island** on the passenger ferry from the **Gulfport Small Craft Harbor**; the ferry runs twice a day from March through October; the trip takes about 90 minutes. At Ship Island, a part of Gulf Islands National Seashore, a U.S. park ranger will guide you through **Fort Massachusetts**, built in 1859 and used by Union troops to blockade Mississippi Sound during the Civil War. The rangers will treat you to tales of the island's colorful past, including the story of the *filles aux casquettes*—young women sent by the French government as brides for the lonely early colonists. Each girl (*fille*) carried a small hope chest (*casquette*). Spend the day sunning, swimming in the clear green water, and beachcombing for treasures washed up by the surf. ⊠ *Ticket office at Gulfport Harbor in Joseph T. Jones Memorial Park, east of intersection of U.S. 49 and U.S. 90,* ☎ *228/436–6010; 228/864–1014 after hrs for ferry schedule.* ⊠ *Ferry $16.* ☉ *Ferry runs Mar.–Oct.*

☾ With its playground, bumper boats, and cars, and more than 100 arcade games, **Funtime USA** provides hours of entertainment for children of all ages. ⊠ *U.S. 90 and Cowan Rd.,* ☎ *228/896–7315.* ⊠ *Grounds free; 75¢–$3 for rides and games.* ☉ *June–Aug., daily 9 AM–midnight; Sept.–May, daily 9 AM–10 PM.*

☾ **Marine Life Oceanarium** puts on continuous shows with performing dolphins, sea lions, and macaws. Plans are under way for a dolphin program that will allow visitors to interact with, and even swim beside, the intelligent mammals. ⊠ *Joseph T. Jones Memorial Park, east of intersection of U.S. 49 and U.S. 90,* ☎ *228/863–0651.* ⊠ *$13.75.* ☉ *Daily 9–6.*

Dining and Lodging

$$$ ✕ **Vrazel's.** The interior of this charming brick building has a soothing intimacy about it, with soft lighting and dining nooks with large windows facing the beach or overlooking exquisite gardens. Choose from a substantial list of coastal water fare: red snapper, Gulf trout, flounder, and shrimp prepared every which way. Try the eggplant La Rosa: baby Gulf shrimp and fresh crabmeat blended with eggplant, herbs, spices, and cheese in a casserole topped with Parmesan and baked. When amberjack is the special, it's a sure hit. ⊠ *3206 W. Beach Blvd. (U.S. 90), Gulfport,* ☎ *228/863–2229. AE, D, DC, MC, V. Closed Sun. No lunch Sat.*

$$ ✕ **Chappy's.** Special-occasion dining for coast residents often means a visit to this pleasant restaurant in Long Beach, just outside Gulfport. Specialties include rich gumbo, redfish panfried Cajun style, and barbecue shrimp. The fish, fresh from the Gulf, is cooked by chef Chappy himself. ⊠ *624 E. Beach Blvd., Long Beach,* ☎ *228/865–9755. AE, D, DC, MC, V.*

$$ ✕ **The Chimneys.** After establishing itself at the Long Beach Harbor as a favorite lunch and dinner place for locals and visitors alike, the Chimneys relocated to Gulfport in a renovated antebellum home that provides a gracious setting and stunning view of the Gulf. The kitchen serves up trout dishes, shrimp prepared a variety of ways, and blackened stuffed fillet filled with a savory blend of crabmeat and shrimp.

⌂ *1640 E. Beach Blvd., Gulfport,* ☎ *228/868–7020. AE, D, DC, MC, V. Closed Mon.*

$$–$$$$ ⊞ **Grand Casino Gulfport Hotel & Oasis Resort & Spa.** These two hotels are part of the Grand Casino Gulfport and are on either side of U.S. 49. They're connected by a covered, climate-controlled walkway. The Oasis, on the north side of the highway, has a lazy river pool that winds around the property where you can take a relaxing 15-minute tube float. Although accommodations are located in two separate buildings, the amenities and restaurants are easily accessible from both properties. Rooms at both locations have relatively standard decor; however, the ones at the Oasis have a slightly more laid-back, beachy feel that many people prefer. Kids Quest day care keeps the little ones entertained, and hotel guests are shuttled to and from the property's new Grand Bear golf course (☞ Outdoor Activities and Sports, *below*), an 18-hole championship course designed by Jack Nicklaus. You'll find that 24-hour casino action is never more than a few steps away. ⌂ *U.S. 90 at U.S. 49, Gulfport,* ☎ *228/870–7777 or 800/354–2450* ☏ *. 1,000 rooms. 6 restaurants, coffee shop, bar, in-room data ports, room service, 5 pools, beauty salon, spa, exercise room, video games, children's programs (ages 6 wks–11 yrs), concierge, car rental. AE, D, DC, MC, V.*☜

Shopping

Prime Outlets of Gulfport (⌂ Exit 34A off I–10, 1000 Factory Shops Blvd., ☎ 228/867–6100) has more than 80 famous-brand shops offering factory-outlet prices. The shops are connected by a covered walkway. A food court, tourist information booth, and playground are also on the premises.

En Route The landscape grows increasingly broad, wild, and lovely west of Gulfport. From Long Beach through to Pass Christian, U.S. 90 bisects stretches of stately homes to the north and shimmering water to the south. Be sure to slow down in Long Beach to admire the Friendship Oak on the campus of the University of Southern Mississippi. Legend has it that those who stroll under the massive branches of the more than 500-year-old oak will remain forever friends.

Pass Christian

10 mi west of Gulfport.

Sailboat racing in the South began here, and consequently the second yacht club in the country was formed in this town (it still exists today)— Louisiana landowner Zachary Taylor was at the yacht club when he was persuaded to run for the presidency.

Twenty-six miles of man-made beach extend from Biloxi to Pass Christian. Toward the west the beaches become less commercialized and less crowded; Pass Christian's is the best of all. Tan, sail, jet-ski, or beachcomb, but *don't swim:* The waters are shallow and murky.

On Pass Christian's scenic drive, which runs parallel to U.S. 90, is some of the most admired real estate in the country. When *Good Morning America* visited in 1999, the crew, impressed by the architectural elegance and beauty of the area, stopped unannounced at one of the antebellum mansions. They were invited inside by the gracious owner and went on to conduct an impromptu tour for the television audience. Most homes on the scenic drive are on the National Register of Historic Places, and you can tour many of them during the annual **Pass Christian Historical Society**'s home tour (☎ 228/452–0063).

OFF THE
BEATEN PATH

CROSBY ARBORETUM – Well worth a 30-mi detour northwest to the town of Picayune, the arboretum, with its 64-acre interpretive center, focuses on the ecosystems of the 16,000-square-mi Pearl River Drainage Basin of south Mississippi and Louisiana. ⊠ I–59, Exit 4 at Picayune, 370 Ridge Rd., ☎ 601/799–2311. ⊒ $4. ⊙ Wed.–Sun. 9–5.

Shopping

Hillyer House (⊠ 207 E. Scenic Dr., ☎ 601/452–4810) sells handmade jewelry, pottery, glass, and brass made by local and regional artists, plus packaged Southern delicacies.

Waveland

15 mi west of Pass Christian.

Travelers who think of Waveland as just a spot to get onto I–10 for New Orleans are missing one of the most accessible tourist information offices on the Gulf Coast, the **Hancock County Welcome Center** (⊠ I-10 Exit 2, at Highway 607, ☎ 228/533–5554). Waveland also offers great camping, and the residents throw a pretty snazzy Mardi Gras parade.

Buccaneer State Park (⊠ 1150 S. Beach Blvd., ☎ 228/467–3822) has an Olympic-size wave pool, open daily from Memorial Day through Labor Day 11–6:30, admission fee $9, that may lure you from the nature trail, the beach, and picnic sites. There are 129 campsites in a grove of live oaks streaming with moss. The park, open year-round, also has two tennis courts with lights, two basketball courts, and a seasonal camp store.

Dining

$$–$$$ ✕ **Armand's.** Chef Armand Jonte brings sophisticated cuisine to the coast in a small, intimate setting. You can't go wrong here, regardless of the menu choice; it's a place that's perfect for special occasions. The menu changes frequently to utilize the best fresh, local ingredients, but seafood always figures prominently, and Jonte's eggplant Eloise—a lightly breaded and fried slice of eggplant topped with shrimp, crab, and crawfish and drenched in decadent Choron sauce (a hollandaise/bernaise mix)—is always available.⊠ *141 Hwy. 90,* ☎ *228/467–8255. MC, V.*

$ ✕ **Lil Ray's.** Though the appointments are limited to trestle tables and benches, this is a place to dream about when you're hungry for seafood platters and po'boys. A waitress, asked by a customer for a diet drink, said it best: "Mister, this ain't no diet place." ⊠ *613 Hwy. 90,* ☎ *228/ 467–4566. Reservations not accepted. D, MC, V.*

The Gulf Coast A to Z

Arriving, Departing, and Getting Around

BY BUS

Coast Area Transit (⊠ 333 DeBuys Rd., Gulfport, ☎ 228/896–8080) provides coast-wide public transportation. **Greyhound** (☎ 800/231–2222) connects the coast with Jackson, New Orleans, and Mobile. Local service exists in Biloxi (⊠ 166 Main St., ☎ 228/436–4335 or 800/231–2222); Gulfport (⊠ 2805 13th St., ☎ 228/863–1022); and Bay St. Louis (⊠ 512 Ulman Ave., ☎ 228/467–4272).

BY CAR

You can drive across the Gulf Coast in 1½ hours via I–10 and U.S. 90. From Gulfport, it takes just over an hour to reach New Orleans and less than three hours to get to Jackson via U.S. 49.

BY PLANE

The **Gulfport-Biloxi Regional Airport** (✉ Airport Rd. off Washington Ave., Gulfport, ☎ 228/863–5953), 15 minutes from the beach, is served by AirTran, American Eagle, ASA/The Delta Connection, Casino Airlink (scheduled charter service), Continental Express, and Northwest Airlink (☞ Air Travel *in* the Gold Guide for telephone numbers).

Contacts and Resources

EMERGENCIES

Dial 911 or go to the emergency room at **Gulf Coast Medical Center** (✉ 180 DeBuys Rd., Biloxi, ☎ 228/388–6711).

GUIDED TOURS

Celebrity Limousine and Tours Service (✉ 2421 South Shore Dr., Biloxi, ☎ 228/388–1384) charters bus tours of the coastal area and New Orleans. **Magnolia Tours & Transportation** (✉ 14035 Airport Rd., Gulfport 39503, ☎ 228/863–9005 or 800/642–4684) custom-plans group tours in buses or vans.

OUTDOOR ACTIVITIES AND SPORTS

Charter boats for half-day, full-day, and overnight deep-sea **fishing** can be found at marinas and harbors all along the Gulf Coast. Prices start around $30 per person; group rates are usually available. The Mississippi Beach Convention and Visitors Bureau (☞ Visitor Information, *below*) can recommend charter services. Unless you're on a chartered boat (where the captain's license will cover you), you'll need a fishing license. Three-day licenses are available in many bait shops and other stores along the harbor.

The coast's climate allows for year-round **golfing,** and golf packages are offered by many coast hotels and motels. **The Bridges Golf Resort** (✉ The Bridges at Casino Magic Resort, 711 Casino Magic Dr., Bay St. Louis, ☎ 228/466–4991 or 800/562–4425) has an 18-hole course (par 72) designed by Arnold Palmer. The course encompasses more than 17 lakes and 14 acres of wetlands. Golf carts come equipped with computers that give pro tips on how to play each hole. The resort is also the site of the Arnold Palmer Golf Academy. Grand Casino's lavish **Grand Bear** (✉ North Harrison County, Grand Way, Gulfport, ☎ 228/604–7100) is a Jack Nicklaus–designed beauty that caters to resort guests only. The course (par 72) is on 650 acres that include natural wetland terrain, two rivers, and a man-made lake. **Diamondhead's Pine and Cardinal courses** (✉ 7600 Country Club Circle, ☎ 228/255–3910) has two 18-hole courses (both par 72) that challenge even the pros. Wooded, gently rolling, and well kept, they are ringed by the large, elegant houses and condominiums of the Diamondhead resort community. Beautifully landscaped **Mississippi National Golf Club** (✉ 900 Hickory Hill Dr., Gautier, ☎ 228/497–2372 or 800/477–4044) has fairways lined with whispering pines, tall oaks, magnolias, and dogwoods on an 18-hole course (par 72). **Pine Island Golf Course** (✉ Gulf Park Estates, 2¼ mi east of Ocean Springs, 3 mi south of U.S. 90, ☎ 228/875–1674) was designed by Pete Dye, who created the tournament players' course in Jacksonville. This 18-hole course, with a par of 71, spans three islands, and its abundant wildlife, beautiful setting, and clubhouse will lessen the bite of any double bogeys. The **Oaks Gulf Club** (✉ 24384 Club House Dr., off Menge Ave., Pass Christian, ☎ 228/452–0909), an 18-hole, par-72 championship course, has gotten rave reviews since its opening last year. It's the site of the annual Buy.Com Mississippi Gulf Coast Classic. **Windance Country Club** (✉ 19385 Champion Circle, Gulfport, ☎ 228/832–4871) has an 18-hole, par-72 course ranked by *Golf Digest* among the top 100 in the United States; nonmembers can play here through hotel golf packages.

PHARMACIES
Calvert-Gamble Pharmacy (✉ 2561 Pass Rd., Biloxi, ☎ 228/338–1411).
K&B Drug Store (✉ 292 Eisenhower Dr., Biloxi, ☎ 228/388–8500).
Sartin's Pharmacy (✉ 4300 15th St., Gulfport, ☎ 228/864–3514).

RADIO STATIONS
FM: KNN 99.1, country; WMJY 93.7, adult contemporary.

VISITOR INFORMATION
Get a free *Attractions and Accommodations* guide to the Gulf Coast
area at the **Mississippi Gulf Coast Convention and Visitors Bureau** (✉
Box 6128, Gulfport, 39506-6128, ☎ 228/896–6699 or 800/237–
9493), open weekdays from 8 to 5. **Ocean Springs Chamber of Commerce** (✉ 1000 Washington Ave., ☎ 228/875–4424), open from 8:30
to 5 weekdays, has racks of informational brochures on Ocean Springs
and the Gulf Coast area.

THE NATCHEZ TRACE

Corinth, Tupelo, Jackson, Natchez

The flower-sprigged and forested Natchez Trace Parkway is a vast and
verdant history lesson. This enchanted path between Nashville and
Natchez is said to be about 8,000 years old. It follows the early trails
worn by Choctaw and Chickasaw Native Americans, itinerant preachers, post riders, soldiers, and settlers. Landscaped by the National
Park Service, the Trace winds through straight pines, haunting cy-
presses, peaceful vistas of reeds, and still waters with dense woodlands.

Now virtually complete, the Trace is almost 450 mi long, with 313 mi
in Mississippi. The Mississippi segment of the Natchez Trace begins
as you enter the state's northeast corner, between Iuka and Belmont.
Mile markers are posted along the way to help drivers navigate. There
are no billboards on the parkway, and commercial vehicles are forbidden
to use it. Park rangers are serious about the 50 mph speed limit; you'll
probably get acquainted with one if you drive any faster.

*Numbers in the margin correspond to points of interest on the Natchez
Trace map.*

Corinth

❶ *90 mi southeast of Memphis.*

Settled just seven years before the Civil War, Corinth assumed military
importance because of its Memphis and Charleston Railroad. In April
1862, after the bloody Battle of Shiloh, near Shiloh Church in Tennessee,
21 mi to the north, the Confederates retreated to Corinth and turned
it into a vast medical center. In May 1862, the Confederates, under General P. G. T. Beauregard, were forced to withdraw farther. Their retreat
involved the most ingenious hoax of the war: To fool the Union forces,
campfires were lighted, dummy cannoneers were placed at fake cannons, empty trains were cheered as if they were carrying reinforcements,
and buglers moved along the deserted works, playing taps. The ploy
worked and was hailed as a triumph for Beauregard and a hollow victory for the Union forces who occupied the town. In October 1862, a
Confederate attempt to recapture the town failed.

Markers and displays throughout town commemorate the Battles of
Shiloh and Corinth. The **Northeast Mississippi Museum** displays Civil
War artifacts and distributes a free self-guided tour brochure to help
you explore the historic town. ✉ *4th St. at Washington St.,* ☎ *601/*

Natchez Trace

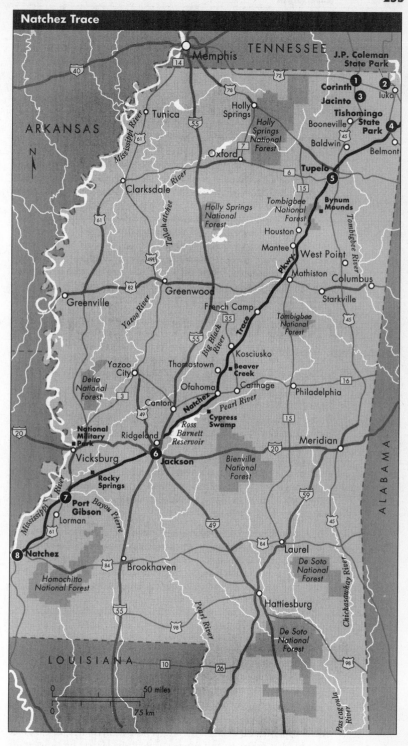

287–3120. ⌨ *Free.* ⊙ *Mar.–Oct., daily 10–5; Nov.–Feb., daily 10:30–4:30.*

J. P. Coleman State Park

❷ *13 mi north of Iuka off U.S. 25.*

With accommodations aplenty for overnighters, J. P. Coleman State Park (⊠ 613 County Rd. 321, Iuka 38852, ☎ 601/423–6515), open year-round, allows nature lovers ample time for exploring its various nature trails and playing in its waters. There are wooded campsites for tents and RVs, and 10 secluded cabins, some of them old and rustic, others from the 1970s with fireplaces and central air-conditioning and heat. Rooms at the balconied lodge overlook the shale beaches of serene Pickwick Lake. Visitors can rent canoes and boats, fish, swim, and water-ski.

Jacinto

❸ *9 mi east of U.S. 45.*

Between Corinth and Tupelo on MS 356 is Jacinto, with its restored Federal-style courthouse (1854). Nearby are a couple of pre-1870 buildings that are slowly being restored. Jacinto also has nature trails that lead to mineral springs, and a swinging bridge. For more information on Jacinto, call 601/286–8662.

Tishomingo State Park

❹ *15 mi south of Iuka.*

In the Appalachian foothills, Tishomingo State Park (⊠ Natchez Trace MM 304, Box 880, Tishomingo 38873, ☎ 601/438–6914) has a unique terrain for Mississippi. If you're feeling peppy, 13 mi of nature trails wind through a canyon along steep hills by waterfalls, granite outcrops, and a swinging bridge; otherwise, take the winding roads through shady forests. Eight-mile canoe trips and float trips are offered from mid-March through October. Around Haynes Lake are primitive campsites and hookups. Rustic cabins are another option. Bring your own food. The park has an outdoor swimming pool open during warmer months; there's a $2 charge.

En Route The **Natchez Trace Parkway Visitor Center** (☞ Visitor Information *in* Natchez Trace A to Z, *below*), 6 mi north of Tupelo on the Trace, distributes the 4-ft *Official Map and Guide,* which has mile-by-mile information from Nashville to Natchez. The center also displays exhibits, some of which are geared toward kids, and shows a 12-minute film relating to the Parkway.

Tupelo

❺ *90 mi southeast of Memphis, 70 mi east of Oxford.*

The largest city in north Mississippi, Tupelo (named after the tupelo gum tree), was founded in 1859 and is a city of accomplishment—it's here, after all, that Elvis Presley was born. Progressive leaders have successfully lured business and industry to an area that only 30 years ago was predominantly agricultural. The arts flourish here, and the North Mississippi Medical Center is the largest hospital in rural America. Twice each year, in February and August, one of the largest furniture trade shows in the country is held at the Tupelo Furniture Market. The four-day events draw nearly 25,000 buyers and exhibitors from around the world; room reservations are almost impossible to get at those times.

MISSISSIPPI MUSIC

IT MIGHT BE ENOUGH for most places to lay claim to a single musical genre—in this case, Mississippi Delta blues—but Mississippi went ahead and threw the King of Rock and Roll into the mix as well.

The musicians and storytellers who grew up in the Delta, a wedge-shaped piece of land lying in northern Mississippi between the Mississippi and Yazoo rivers, are typically credited with creating the blues around the turn of the 20th century. People like Robert Johnson, Blind Lemon Jefferson, Son House, and Turner Johnson helped push what was then known as "devil's music" to the forefront of musical acceptability.

It's been said that the blues were created out of necessity in the rural areas of the Deep South, particularly on large plantations and in industries that required heavy manual labor. The blues reflected not only the social isolation and lack of formal training of its creators—much of the music was handed down orally one generation to the next—but also their ability to make do with the most basic of resources and survive under the most oppressive circumstances. The basic vocal material for the early blues came from hollers (improvised work songs) that were sung by workers in the fields and in other occupations requiring just plain hard toil. The moody song style endures today in song, speech and music.

Locals say that if you find yourself in Mississippi and you're looking for a great juke joint, you might just check out the telephone poles. Over the years, they're proven to be a good informational source, since ads for the so-called chitlins circuit are often posted there.

Although the north end of the state upholds the tradition and culture of the blues, the bustling Mississippi Gulf Coast and Tunica County, with their numerous casinos, offer a variety of musical venues for other sounds. A random sampling of the nation's entertainers who have played

Tunica shows includes performers like Loretta Lynn, Tanya Tucker, Johnny Cash, and the Platters. Drawing heavily from the nearby musical hotbed of New Orleans, the Gulf Coast casinos have presented everyone from Dr. John to the Neville Brothers to Irma Thomas.

If you have a few days and you're interested in musical roots, you might consider the following rough itinerary, which begins just over the state border in Tennessee (☞ Chapter 8 and this chapter for more information; sights not in the book have telephone numbers). On Day 1 begin your Mississippi music heritage tour from Memphis—home of Beale Street and Graceland, Elvis Presley's mansion. Travel to Tupelo and tour the humble two-room house where the King was born. You can also see sites important to Elvis's early life—the school where he won his first talent contest singing "Old Shepp" and the hardware store where he bought his first guitar.

On Day 2 make your way to the Mississippi Delta and the area known as the Birthplace of the Blues. In Clarksdale visit the Delta Blues Museum with memorabilia of such music greats as Muddy Waters, Robert Johnson, and B. B. King. Take a ride down Highway 61 and see the famous crossroads where legend has it Johnson traded his soul for the unsurpassed talent that made him a star.

On Day 3 travel east across the state to Starkville, home of the **Templeton Music Museum** (✉ 46 Blackjack Rd., ☎ 601/325–8301), which has roller organs, player pianos, and music boxes from the ragtime era. Tours are by appointment. To the south is Meridian's Highland Park, home of the **Jimmie Rodgers Museum** (✉ Jimmie Rodgers Memorial Dr., ☎ 601/485–1808). This memorial to the father of Country Music includes Rodgers's original guitar and personal belongings.

Although the blues may be its past, the music of Mississippi is now as eclectic as the state itself.

For outdoors lovers, Tupelo's scenic hill country provides beautiful places to camp, swim, fish, jog, and bike.

★ The **Elvis Presley Park and Museum** is anchored by the tiny, two-room shotgun-style house built by Presley's father, Vernon, for just $180. Elvis Aaron Presley was born here on January 8, 1935. The home has been restored and furnished much as it was when the Presleys lived in it. The house is now surrounded by Elvis Presley Park, land purchased with proceeds from Elvis's 1956 concert at the Mississippi-Alabama Fair. The park includes a swimming pool, tennis courts, a playground, a youth center with a gift shop (stocked with Elvis souvenirs), and the Elvis Presley Museum, which stores more than 3,000 pieces of Elvis memorabilia. The **Elvis Presley Memorial Chapel**, suggested by the singer in 1971 as a place for his fans to meditate, was dedicated in 1979, two years after Presley's death. ✉ *306 Elvis Presley Dr., off E. Main St.,* ☎ *662/841–1245.* ▨ *Birthplace $2, museum $4.* ☉ *May–Sept., Mon.– Sat. 9–5:30, Sun. 1–5; Oct.–Apr., Mon.–Sat. 9–5, Sun. 1–5.*

The **Oren Dunn City Museum** displays Presley memorabilia along with other exhibits, including a turn-of-the-century Western Union office, a replica of a sorghum mill, a train depot and caboose, and an old-time country store. There are also space program–related displays, including space suits from the Apollo missions. ✉ *James J. Ballard Park, off MS 6W,* ☎ *662/841–6438.* ▨ *$1.* ☉ *June–Aug., weekdays 8–4, Sept.–May, weekends 1–5.*

The **Tupelo National Battlefield,** inside the city limits, commemorates the Civil War Battle of Tupelo with monuments and displays. In 1864 Union general A. J. Smith marched 14,000 troops against Nathan Bedford Forrest's forces near Tupelo. Smith's goal was to end the constant Confederate harassment of supply lines to Sherman's army and thereby secure the Union invasion of Atlanta. The battle, on July 14, 1864, was the last major battle in Mississippi and one of the bloodiest. ✉ *W. Main St. [MS 6].* ☉ *Daily sunrise–sunset.*

Dining and Lodging

$–$$$ ✗ **Vanelli's.** Family pictures and scenes of Greece adorn the walls at this comfortable restaurant. Lunch and dinner buffets include both Greek specialties and lighter fare. Vanelli's own bakery produces breads, strudels, and pastries. ✉ *1302 N. Gloster St.,* ☎ *662/844–4410. AE, D, DC, MC, V.*

$–$$ ✗ **Harvey's.** It's a favorite in four cities, and here's why: Harvey's restaurants have based their reputation on consistency and quality in food and service. Try the prime rib, seafood, steak, or, for lighter fare, the chicken Alpine or great garden salad. Lots of plants and warm wood tones add to the appeal. ✉ *424 S. Gloster St.,* ☎ *662/842–6763. AE, D, MC, V. Closed Sun.*

$–$$ ✗ **Jefferson Place.** Though this 19th-century house may look somewhat austere from the outside, red-checked tablecloths and bric-a-brac brighten its interior. The place is popular with the college crowd; short orders and steaks are the specialties. ✉ *823 Jefferson St.,* ☎ *662/844– 8696. Reservations not accepted. AE, MC, V. Closed Sun.*

$–$$$ ▥ **Mockingbird Inn Bed & Breakfast.** Each of the seven rooms in this tiny inn is decorated with the theme of a different country. The Athens Room comes with Greek columns and statues and sheer flowing fabrics. One has a fireplace, and one has a whirlpool tub. In summer you can take refuge from the hot Mississippi sun under the inn's gazebo or on its porch swing. ✉ *305 N. Gloster, 38801,* ☎ *662/841–0286,* FAX *662/840–4158. 7 rooms. AE, D, MC, V. BP.*

$-$$$ ▥ **Ramada Inn.** Near the Elvis Presley Park and Museum and the Natchez Trace Parkway Visitor Center, this modern hotel provides easy access to Tupelo's major areas of interest. Business travelers will appreciate the in-room modem lines. For families, there's a courtyard with a kiddie pool. Night owls can dance the night away in Bogart's Lounge every night except Sunday. ⊠ 854 N. Gloster, 38801, ☎ 800/228–2828 or 662/844–4111, ☎ FAX 662/844–4111. 230 rooms, 10 suites, 4 minisuites. Restaurant, in-room data ports, pool, spa, laundry service, meeting rooms. AE, D, DC, MC, V.

$-$$ ▥ **Executive Inn.** Guest rooms in this large, contemporary hotel are plain and functional, but clean. ⊠ 1011 N. Gloster St., 38801, ☎ 662/841–2222 or 800/533–3220, FAX 601/844–7836. 116 rooms, 4 suites. Restaurant, lounge, indoor pool, hot tub, sauna. AE, DC, MC, V.

$-$$ ▥ **Rex Plaza Suites.** Both short- and long-term stays can be arranged at this four-building hotel. There are a variety of suites, some of which have kitchens and washers and dryers. ⊠ 619 N. Gloster, 38804, ☎ 662/840–8000 or 800/203–5917, FAX 662/840–1116. 64 suites. Restaurant, lounge, pool, exercise room, meeting rooms. AE, D, DC, MC, V. ✎

$ ▥ **Trace Inn.** On 15 acres near the Natchez Trace, this old motel can accommodate the weary with neat rooms and friendly service. ⊠ 3400 W. Main St., 38801, ☎ 662/842–5555, FAX 662/844–3105. 134 rooms. Restaurant, pool, playground. AE, D, DC, MC, V.

From Tupelo to Jackson

From Tupelo the trip to Jackson takes three hours if you don't stop. It can easily take an entire day, however, if you pause to read the brown wooden markers, explore nature trails, and admire the neat fields, trees, and wildflower meadows. If you have the time, don't miss Columbus (☞ below) and environs, an hour or so east of the parkway near the Alabama line. The parkway is incomplete from Mile Marker 101.5 to 87.0. I–55, I–20, and I–220 are connecting routes. To reach Jackson, follow I–55 south from the Trace.

Bynum Mounds (Mile Marker 232.4) are ceremonial hills that were constructed between 100 BC and AD 200 by prehistoric people. Exhibits describe their daily existence.

At **French Camp** (Mile Marker 180.7), where Frenchman Louis LeFleur established a stand in 1812, you can watch sorghum molasses being made on Saturday in late September and October. Native American and French artifacts are housed inside the authentic dogtrot-style cabin.

Cypress Swamp (Mile Marker 122.0), a pleasure today, was a treacherous, mosquito-infested morass for early travelers. A 20-minute self-guided nature walk takes you through the tree-canopied tupelo/bald cypress swamp.

The **Mississippi Crafts Center at Ridgeland** (Mile Marker 102.4) displays and sells high-quality crafts in a dogtrot log cabin. Members of the Craftsmen's Guild of Mississippi have created pewter and silver jewelry, pottery, handwoven and hand-screened clothing, whimsical wooden toys, highly prized Choctaw baskets, and other interesting items. The center sponsors free demonstrations (usually on weekends) of basket weaving, wood carving, pottery, and quilting. There are rest rooms and picnic tables on site. ⊠ Natchez Trace at Ridgeland, ☎ 662/856–7546. ☑ Free. ☉ Daily 9–5. ✎

OFF THE
BEATEN PATH

COLUMBUS – Forty-five miles east of the Natchez Trace on U.S. 82 is one of Mississippi's most undisturbed antebellum towns. This river city (on the Tombigbee) contains 100 pre–Civil War mansions—some of which are open to the public as bed-and-breakfasts or for tours—and many historic sites. Columbus is called the town "where flowers healed a nation" because of a group of gracious women who, in 1866, placed flowers on the graves of both Confederate and Union soldiers in what is now called Friendship Cemetery. The gesture inspired the poem "The Blue and the Gray," written by Francis Miles Finch, and Columbus's Decoration Day at Friendship Cemetery is now observed as the nation's Memorial Day.

WAVERLY MANSION – This privately owned, immaculately restored showplace has been around since 1852. Outstanding antiques adorn each spacious room, and an antiques shop, Snow's Antiques, in on the premises. It's 10 mi northwest of Columbus off MS 50. ✉ *Rte. 2, West Point,* ☎ *601/494–1399.* 🎟 *$7.50.* ⏲ *Daily 9–5.*

Jackson

❻ *180 mi southwest of Tupelo, 45 mi west of Vicksburg.*

At its spangled edges, Jackson has little to distinguish it, but the state capital becomes increasingly original toward its shady heart. The downtown area has many small museums and most of the city's notable architecture.

The city is named for Andrew Jackson, who was popular with Mississippians long before he became president. As Major General Jackson, he helped negotiate the Treaty of Doak's Stand, according to which the Choctaw ceded large chunks of Mississippi to the United States on October 18, 1820. President Thomas Jefferson recommended that the town be laid out in a checkerboard pattern of alternating squares of buildings and parks. Peter A. Vandorn proposed the plan for Jackson and submitted a map for the new city in April 1822; today the Old Capitol, along with the Capitol Green on which it sits, is one of the few remaining examples of the scheme.

Jackson is also the county seat of Hinds County, named for another negotiator, Major General Thomas Hinds, an enterprising and daring hero of the Battle of New Orleans in the War of 1812.

The **Mississippi Agriculture and Forestry Museum** complex looks like an old farm marooned in the midst of expanding suburbs, but the city was actually here first. The 10 farm buildings were brought here to stand exactly as they once did in Jefferson Davis County, Mississippi. A crossroads town, similar to small Mississippi towns in the 1920s, has been assembled with a working blacksmith's shop and a cotton gin; meetings are held in the old Masonic Lodge, and weddings can be arranged at the 1897 Epiphany Episcopal Church building. The general store sells soft drinks, snacks, and souvenirs. A complete tour of the museum, which has fine exhibits on agriculture, forestry, and farm-related aviation, takes about 90 minutes. Also on the grounds is the **Jackson Visitor Information Center.** ✉ *1150 Lakeland Dr., 39216,* ☎ *601/354–6113 or 800/844–8687.* 🎟 *$4.* ⏲ *Memorial Day–Labor Day, Mon.–Sat. 9–5, Sun. 1–5; Labor Day–Memorial Day, Mon.–Sat. 9–5.*

The **Mississippi Sports Hall of Fame and Museum,** next to the Mississippi Agriculture and Forestry Museum off Lakeland Drive, honors Mississippi athletes past and present with interactive exhibits and films containing action-packed footage and interviews. Its recently expanded exhibits area showcases more than 200 sports figures. ✉ *Cool Papa*

Bell Dr. (¼ mi east of I–55), 39236-6021, ☎ 601/982–8264 or 800/ 280–FAME. ✉ $5. ☺ Mon.–Sat. 10–4. ⊛

The **Old Capitol,** flanked by the **War Memorial Building** (1940) to the north and the **Mississippi Archives Building** (1971) to the south, served as the state capitol from 1839 to 1903. Built between 1833 and 1838 with simple columns and elegant proportions, it's a tribute to Greek Revival architecture. The building was restored in 1959–61 to house the **State Historical Museum.** The Vandorn map, a blueprint of the city's original design, and other exhibits depicting Mississippi's history are on display in the museum. ✉ *100 S. State St.,* ☎ *601/359–6920.* ✉ *Free.* ☺ *Weekdays 8–5, Sat. 9:30–4:30, Sun. 12:30–4:30. ⊛*

The **Jackson Zoological Park** uses more than 100 acres to re-create a natural habitat for about 500 animals. Children love the petting zoo, complete with hands-on exhibits, and the miniature train ride. ✉ *2918 W. Capitol St.,* ☎ *601/352–2580.* ✉ *$4.* ☺ *Daily 9–5. ⊛*

Since its opening in 1847, **City Hall** (✉ 219 S. President St., ☎ 601/ 960–1035) has served continuously as Jackson's center of government. A Masonic Hall originally occupied the third floor of this stately white Greek Revival building. During the Civil War, City Hall was used as a hospital. Peek into the tiny City Council chamber with its black-and-white floors and heavy red-velvet curtains. On the west side of the building is the formal Josh Halbert Garden, with a 1968 statue of Andrew Jackson.

Within the **Mississippi Arts Center** is the Mississippi Museum of Art, dedicated to preserving Mississippi's artistic heritage. With its impressive permanent collection of both regional and national paintings, plus changing exhibits and a sculpture garden, you may want to set aside a few hours to explore each and every corner. ✉ *201 E. Pascagoula St.,* ☎ *601/960–1515.* ✉ *$3.* ☺ *Tues.–Sat. 10–5. ⊛*

The **Russell C. Davis Planetarium** offers breathtaking science and nature adventures every day (except Monday) in downtown Jackson. The planetarium's McNair Space Theater features a 60-ft domed screen (the largest in the mid-South), and a full complement of star, slide, special effect, and video shows. ✉ *201 E. Pascagoula St.,* ☎ *601/960–1550.* ✉ *$4.* ☺ *Hrs vary; call ahead.*

The **U.S. Federal Courthouse,** constructed of concrete and sandstone, exemplifies the streamlined art deco style that was popular between the world wars, a time when many Jackson buildings were erected. This building was completed in 1934 and served as Jackson's post office and as a Federal court building until 1988, when a new post office was built. The motifs of eagles, stars, and geometric designs on the exterior are repeated throughout the interior and on the freestanding light fixtures around the building. ✉ *245 E. Capitol St.*

St. Andrew's Episcopal Cathedral is an important example of Gothic Revival architecture and is enhanced by fine stained-glass windows. ✉ *305 E. Capitol St.,* ☎ *601/354–1535.* ☺ *Weekdays 8:30–5. ⊛*

The **Mississippi Governor's Mansion** has been the official home of the state's first family since its completion in 1842. At that time, Jackson was a tiny city, and this grand Greek Revival dwelling was an optimistic statement. General Sherman presumably lived here in 1863. The mansion is one of only two executive residences to be designated a National Historic Landmark. Invest 30 minutes in the lively tours, strong on legend as well as fact. ✉ *300 E. Capitol St.,* ☎ *601/359–6421.* ✉ *Free.* ☺ *Tours Tues.–Fri. 9:30–11:30.*

Smith Park is the only public square that remains from Thomas Jefferson's original plan for the city. The park was named after James Smith, a former Jacksonian (originally from Glasgow, Scotland), who donated $100 to fence and beautify the area. Eudora Welty used the park as the setting for her short story "The Winds." The park hosts frequent concerts, festivals, picnics, and art exhibits. ⊠ *At center of Smith Park Historic District.*

The **Cathedral of St. Peter the Apostle** (⊠ 203 N. West St.), built between 1897 and 1900, is the third building of the congregation, which organized in 1846. Their first building was burned by Union troops in 1863, as were many others in the city. Their second building, now in the very center of the downtown area, at the site of the present rectory (⊠ 123 N. West St.), was considered too remote from town. The cathedral is only open to the public for church services.

Mynelle Gardens is a 7-acre botanical showplace, with colorful paths surrounded by Southern flora and gentle streams. ⊠ *4736 Clinton Blvd.,* ☎ *601/960–1894.* 🎫 *$2.* ⊙ *Mar.–Oct., daily 9–5:15; Nov.–Feb., daily 8–4:15.*

The two-story Second Empire–style **Galloway House** was completed in 1889. It was built for Methodist bishop Charles Galloway, a distinguished churchman of international renown. In 1983 the house was renovated for use as a law office. ⊠ *304 N. Congress St.*

The **New Capitol** sits in beaux arts splendor at the junction of Mississippi and North Congress streets, its dome surmounted by a gold-plated copper eagle with a 15-ft wingspan. Completed in 1903 at what was then the enormous cost of $1 million, the capitol underwent a $19 million renovation from 1979 to 1983. It was designed by the German architect Theodore C. Link, who was influenced by the design of the Capitol in Washington, D.C. Among the elaborate architectural details inside the building is a Tiffany window. ⊠ *400 High St.,* ☎ *601/359–3114.* 🎫 *Free.* ⊙ *Weekdays 8–5; guided tours weekdays at 9, 10, 11, 1:30, 2:30, and 3:30.*

Eudora Welty Library, the largest public library in Mississippi, is named in honor of the city's famed short-story writer and novelist (*The Ponder Heart, Losing Battles, The Optimist's Daughter*). Opened in 1986, it houses a 42-ft-long circulation desk handcrafted in rosewood and maple by local craftsman Fletcher Cox. The Mississippi Writers' Room pays homage to the South's rich literary history with exhibits on Welty, as well as William Faulkner, Tennessee Williams, Margaret Walker Alexander, Ellen Douglas, and many others. ⊠ *300 N. State St.,* ☎ *601/968–5811.* ⊙ *Mon.–Thurs. 9–9, Fri.–Sat. 9–6, Sun. 1–5.* 📚

On North State Street between College and Fortification streets stand a few **Victorian homes,** the survivors of the many large houses that lined this street in its heyday as Jackson's best address. The **Morris House** (⊠ 505 N. State St.) is a classic Revival house built about 1900. The **Virden-Patton House** (⊠ 512 N. State St.), built about 1849, went undamaged through the Civil War, suggesting that Union officers may have used it as headquarters. The **Millsaps-Buie House** (⊠ 628 N. State St.), built in 1888, has been restored as a bed-and-breakfast inn (☞ Dining and Lodging, *below*). Two doors north is the **Garner Green House** (1910), with an imposing portico of Corinthian columns. This house was moved across the street from its original location and restored in 1988 as an office building. **Greenbrook Flowers** (⊠ 705 N. State St.), circa 1895–97, occupies the former St. Andrew's Episcopal rectory; it has been greatly altered. With the exception of the bed-and-breakfast, none of these homes is open to the public.

The **Manship House** was built about 1857 by Charles H. Manship, the Jackson mayor who surrendered the city to General William Tecumseh Sherman on July 16, 1863. The museum inside is a careful restoration of a small Gothic Revival cottage with wood graining painted by Manship himself. ✉ *420 E. Fortification St. (enter parking area from Congress St.),* ☎ *601/961–4724.* ☞ *Free.* ☉ *Tours Tues.–Fri. 9–4, Sat. 1–4.*

C. W. Welty and his wife, Chestina, built the house at **741 North Congress Street** in 1907. Their daughter, Eudora, was born in the master bedroom on the second floor in 1909. Welty used images of this house and neighborhood in many of her literary works, including *The Golden Apples.* It is now a law office.

The **Smith Robertson Museum and Cultural Center** has artifacts and exhibits depicting the history of black life in Mississippi. The building housed the first public school for black children in Jackson. ✉ *528 Bloom St.,* ☎ *601/960–1457.* ☞ *$1.* ☉ *Weekdays 9–5, Sat. 9–noon, Sun. 2–5.*

Jackson's neat, tree-shaded neighborhoods are excellent for walking, jogging, or Sunday driving, especially the **Belhaven area** bounded by Riverside Drive, I–55, Fortification Street, and North State Street. **Carlisle, Poplar, Peachtree,** and **Fairview streets** are distinguished by fine homes.

OFF THE
BEATEN PATH

MUSEUM OF THE SOUTHERN JEWISH EXPERIENCE – The history of Southern Jewry is captured in an orientation video, exhibits of religious artifacts, and photographs of the rural South by Bill Aron. The museum preserves the fascinating history of communities that have seen many of their members move on to larger cities or to the North. Temple B'nai Israel in Natchez is a satellite of the museum; call about tours. The museum also sponsors multiday tours of Jewish sites in the region. Utica is a 40-minute drive southwest of Jackson. ✉ *3863 Morrison Rd., Utica,* ☎ *601/362–6357.* ☞ *Free, except for special exhibitions.* ☉ *Daily 10–5.* ✎

Dining and Lodging

$$–$$$$ ✕ **Nick's.** Seafood is the main fare at this casually elegant restaurant. Grilled blackfish with crabmeat is one of the many luncheon specials, while dinner brings out more elaborate seafood masterpieces. Soup or salad and vegetable du jour are included with the entrée. Desserts are wonderful, too, especially the white-chocolate mousse with raspberry sauce. ✉ *1501 Lakeland Dr.,* ☎ *601/981–8017. AE, D, DC, MC, V. Closed Sun.*

$$–$$$ ✕ **BRAVO!** This cheery, bustling restaurant is set in a shopping mall, but that doesn't diminish its impact. Traditional regional Italian cuisine—zesty pastas, wood-fired pizza, homemade breads, and antipasti—shares the menu with grilled meats topped with unique sauces, chutneys, and herb rubs. The menu changes frequently but is consistently good. ✉ *244 Highland Village, South Plaza,* ☎ *601/982–8111. AE, D, DC, MC, V. Closed Mon.*

$–$$$ ✕ **Schimmel's.** Opened in 2000, this restaurant spruced up the local dining scene with creative and delicious menu choices such as breadless crab cakes, fried lobster tales, and an Asiago-crusted flounder. ✉ *2615 N. State St.,* ☎ *601/957–0702. AE, MC, V.*

$$ ✕ **Primos.** Since 1964 this cozy and comfy eatery has pleased local palates. The main dining room recalls a French country inn, while the patio is pure American South. House specialties are fresh seafood and

prime rib. ⊠ *4330 N. State St.,* ☎ *601/982–2064. AE, DC, MC, V. Closed Sun.*

$–$$ ✕ **Gridley's.** Mexican-tile tables and floors enhance small, sunny dining areas. Gridley's is famous for its spicy barbecued pork and ribs served with all the trimmings—coleslaw, baked beans, and potatoes. ⊠ *1428 Old Square Rd.,* ☎ *601/362–8600. AE, D, MC, V.*

$ ✕ **Broad Street Baking Co. & Café.** You can enjoy breakfast, lunch, or dinner here, where some dozen different breads are baked fresh daily using European and old family recipes. Specialties include pizzas, sandwiches, pastries, and croissants. ⊠ *101 Banner Hall, I–55 at Northside Dr.,* ☎ *601/362–2900. MC, V. No dinner Sun..*

$$$–$$$$ ☷ **Fairview Inn.** Listed on the National Register of Historic Places, this stately colonial Revival mansion is in Jackson's prestigious Belhaven section, conveniently situated near many of the major attractions yet secluded enough to suggest a country retreat. Period antiques fill the public rooms, and the guest rooms are decked out in chintz and Laura Ashley fabrics. ⊠ *734 Fairview St., 39202,* ☎ *601/948–3429 or 888/ 948–1908,* 🖷 *601/948–1203. 8 rooms. AE, D, MC, V. BP.* ✑

$$–$$$$ ☷ **Edison Walthall Hotel.** The cornerstone and huge brass mailbox near the elevators are almost all that remain of the original Walthall Hotel, but the marble floors, gleaming brass, paneled library/writing room, and cozy bar almost fool you into thinking this is a restoration of a 19th-century home. Rooms are decorated with mahogany furniture. ⊠ *225 E. Capitol St., 39201,* ☎ *601/948–6161 or 800/932–6161,* 🖷 *601/948–0088. 208 rooms, 6 suites. Restaurant, bar, barbershop, hot tub, exercise room, shop, airport shuttle. AE, D, DC, MC, V.* ✑

$$–$$$$ ☷ **Millsaps-Buie House.** This Queen Anne–style home, with its corner
★ turret and tall-columned porch, was built in 1888 for Jackson financier and philanthropist Major Reuben Webster Millsaps, founder of Millsaps College. It is listed on the National Register of Historic Places. Restored as a B&B in 1987, its guest rooms are individually decorated with antiques. A full Southern breakfast is served in the Victorian dining room. ⊠ *628 N. State St., 39202,* ☎ *800/784–0221,* 🖷 *601/352– 0221. 11 rooms. AE, DC, MC, V.* ✑

$$ ☷ **Hilton Jackson.** Just off I–55N, this sleek and contemporary high-rise convention motel underwent extensive renovations. Upgraded business facilities and a fitness center were among the additions. Rooms also got a full workout—all were appointed with brand-new mahogany furniture and data-port phones. ⊠ *1001 County Line Rd., 39211,* ☎ *601/957–2800,* 🖷 *601/957–3191. 300 rooms, 11 suites. 2 restaurants, 2 bars, pool, barbershop, exercise room, shop, airport shuttle. AE, DC, MC, V.*

Nightlife and the Arts

Live rock and roll and rhythm and blues beckon a mix of young and old to the **Dock** (⊠ Main Harbor Marina at Ross Barnett Reservoir, ☎ 601/856–7765) from Thursday through Sunday. **Hal and Mal's** (⊠ 200 S. Commerce St., ☎ 601/948–0888) often has live music, and there's always plenty of room to dance. **Poet's** (⊠ 1855 Lakeland Dr., ☎ 601/ 982–9711) presents food, drink, and dance bands in an old-fashioned atmosphere created by antiques, old signs, and a pressed-tin ceiling. **Rodeo's** (⊠ 6107 Ridgewood Rd., ☎ 601/957–9300) is an "in" spot, where live music and dancing attract big crowds.

Outdoor Activities and Sports

GOLF

Lefleur's Bluff Golf Course has nine holes (par 35) and a driving range. ⊠ *1205 Lakeland Dr.,* ☎ *601/362–3885.* ⌥ *$8 weekdays, $10 weekends.*

Jog on paths that curve under tall pines and stretch down to a sunny meadow in **Parham Bridges Park** (⊠ 5055 Old Canton Rd.).

TENNIS

Volley and lob on the 14 outdoor hard courts at **Tennis Center South** (⊠ 2827 Oak Forest Dr., off McDowell Rd., ☎ 601/960–1712) and at **Bridges Tennis Center** (⊠ 5055 Old Canton Rd., ☎ 601/956–1105), where there are 15 outdoor hard courts. Both centers have lights for night play.

Shopping

ANTIQUES

Bobbie King's (⊠ Woodland Hills Shopping Center, Old Canton Rd. at Duling Ave., ☎ 601/362–9803) specializes in new and heirloom textiles and exhibits them in lavish displays with one-of-a-kind accessories.

BOOKS

Books by Mississippi authors and about Mississippi are available from knowledgeable booksellers at **Lemuria** (⊠ 202 Banner Hall, 4465 I-55N, ☎ 601/366–7619). **Choctaw Books** (⊠ 926 North St., ☎ 601/352–7281) stocks first editions of Southern writers' works.

FLEA MARKET

If you're in the mood for a treasure hunt, the **Fairground Antique & Flea Market,** with 220 dealers, often harbors some fine pieces among the simply fun stuff. ⊠ 900 High St., ☎ 601/353–5327. ☉ Sat. 8–5, Sun. 10–5.

GIFTS

The **Chimneyville Crafts Gallery** (⊠ 1150 Lakeland Dr., ☎ 601/981–2499) sells the work of members of the Craftsmen's Guild of Mississippi. Pottery, jewelry, woodwork, glasswork, quilts, and paper are among the offerings. The Craftsmen's Guild's objets d'art can also be found in the Mississippi Crafts Center at Ridgeland (☞ From Tupelo to Jackson, *above*).

The **Everyday Gourmet** (⊠ 2905 Old Canton Rd., ☎ 601/362–0723; ⊠ 1625 County Line Rd., ☎ 601/977–9258) stocks local products, including pecan pie, bread, and biscuit mixes; muscadine jelly; jams and chutneys; cookbooks; fine ceramic tableware; and a complete selection of kitchenware and gourmet foods.

En Route Post riders stopped during the early 1800s at the Natchez Trace's **Rocky Springs** (Mile Marker 54.8). General Grant's army camped here on its march to Jackson and Vicksburg during the Civil War. Trails meander through the woods and up a steep hill to a tiny old cemetery and **Rocky Springs Methodist Church** (1837), where services are still held Sunday.

At Mile Marker 41.5 is a portion of the **Old Trace,** a short section of the original Native American Trace of loess soil (easily eroded and compacted earth). You can park and walk along it for a short way.

Port Gibson

❼ *Mile Marker 39.2; 60 mi southwest of Jackson.*

This is the earliest still-existent town on the Trace, with a large concentration of antebellum homes. The aptly named **Church Street** is a shady main thoroughfare lined with houses of worship and stately homes. The **First Presbyterian Church,** erected in 1859, has a spire topped by a 10-ft hand pointing heavenward. Also on Church Street are **Gage House** (⊠ 602 Church St.), circa 1830, with double galleries and a handsome brick dependency; **Temple Gemiluth Chassed** (⊠ 706 Church St.), circa 1892, a synagogue with Moorish Byzantine architecture unique in Mississippi; **St. James Episcopal Church** (⊠ 808 Church St.), circa 1897, a high Victorian Gothic structure designed by a Boston architect; **Port Gibson Methodist Church** (⊠ 901 Church St.), built in 1860 and Romanesque Revival in style; the **Hughes Home** (⊠ 907 Church St.), circa 1825, once owned by Henry Hughes, author of the first sociology textbook, and once the residence of poet Irvin Russell; and the Gothic **St. Joseph's Catholic Church** (⊠ 909 Church St.), built in 1849, with a hand-carved Communion rail. The palatial mid-19th century, 30-room mansion **Oak Square** (☞ Lodging, *below*) is open for tours by appointment. The **Port Gibson Chamber of Commerce** (☞ Visitor Information *in* The Natchez Trace A to Z, *below*), where you can get maps to local historic sites, is housed in a small 1805 home built by Port Gibson's founder, Samuel Gibson, and moved to this site in 1980.

Grand Gulf Military Monument, 7 mi northwest of Port Gibson, commemorates the town of Grand Gulf, site of an 1862 Civil War naval battle. On a steep hill, the old town site has become a museum with an 1863 cannon, a collection of carriages, an 1820s dogtrot cabin, an old Catholic church, and a Spanish house from the 1790s. ⊠ *North of Port Gibson off U.S. 61, Rte. 2,* ☎ *601/437–5911.* 🎫 *$1.50.* ☉ *Weekdays 8–5.*

Southwest of Port Gibson on MS 552 are the 23 vine-clad columns that are the romantic ruins of **Windsor,** a huge Greek Revival mansion built in 1861 that burned down in 1890. The remains of the largest plantation home ever built in Mississippi were featured in *Raintree County,* a late '50s film starring Elizabeth Taylor.

Lodging

$$–$$$ 🏨 **Oak Square.** Constructed circa 1850, this Greek Revival treasure, with its numerous outbuildings and lovely gardens, occupies an entire block on historic Church Street. It's now a bed-and-breakfast with comfortable rooms, each with private bath and color TV. Full Southern breakfasts are included in the room rate. ⊠ *1207 Church St., Port Gibson 39150,* ☎ *601/437–4350 or 800/729–0240,* ℻ *601/437–5768. 12 rooms. AE, D, MC, V.*

Shopping

Mississippi Cultural Crossroads (⊠ 507 Market St., ☎ 601/437–8905) has an enviable collection of quilts on display and for sale.

Lorman and Environs

12 mi south of Port Gibson.

On U.S. 61 and 1 mi east of the Natchez Trace Parkway, the sleepy settlement of Lorman is worth a stop for its Old South charm. Handmade bonnets swing in the breeze on the porch of the ✕ **Old Country Store** (⊠ 107 U.S. 61, Lorman, ☎ 601/437–3661), which was a plantation store built in 1875. You can buy souvenirs here, including handmade pewter, wooden toys, and antique dolls, and sample some down-home cooking at the property's restaurant (☞ Dining, *below*). On weekends there's a flea market.

About 12 mi southwest of Lorman is the restored **Rodney Presbyterian Church.** The town of Rodney, once home to wealthy plantation owners and river merchants, became a ghost town when the Mississippi River shifted its course. Your visit to Rodney will be enhanced by reading Eudora Welty's powerful essay "Some Notes on River Country" and her short story "At the Landing."

Dining and Lodging

$ ✕ **Old Country Store.** Checkered tablecloths, wallpaper with magnolia borders, antiques, and watercolors depicting local scenes create a pleasant, old-fashioned setting. Home-cooked Southern fare, such as hearty po'boys, fried chicken, and collard greens, is made to order and generously portioned. Try the peach cobbler for dessert. ✉ *107 U.S. 61, Lorman,* ☎ *601/437–3661. No credit cards.*

$$–$$$ ▦ **Rosswood Plantation.** Once a cotton plantation, Rosswood is now a bed-and-breakfast and a Christmas tree farm. Rooms have canopied beds, Oriental rugs, and antique furnishings. Silver coins and jewels are reportedly buried somewhere on the grounds. The "hidden treasure" dates to the Civil War when residents, fearing that the Union army would confiscate their possessions, hid them in the ground instead. The nearby nature trails are perfect for an easy hike. ✉ *Hwy. 552E, Lorman 39096-9701,* ☎ *601/437–4215 or 800/533–5889,* ℻ *601/437–6888. 4 rooms. AE, D, MC, V.* ✍

En Route **Emerald Mound** (Natchez Trace Mile Marker 10.3) is the second-largest Native American mound in the country, covering almost 8 acres. It was built around 1300 for religious ceremonies practiced by ancestors of the Natchez Native Americans.

As you near Natchez, the Natchez Trace Parkway abruptly ends, putting you on U.S. 61. You'll pass through the little town of Washington, capital of the Mississippi Territory from 1802 to 1817. In 1802 **Jefferson College** (☎ 601/442–2901) was chartered as the territory's first educational institution; its historic buildings have been meticulously restored.

Natchez

★ ❽ *40 mi southwest of Port Gibson.*

Antebellum Natchez is named for the Natchez Native Americans who lived here and worshiped the sun in small villages before the French built Fort Rosalie in 1716. Later the city came under British rule (1763–79), and the district known today as **Natchez-Under-the-Hill** grew up at the Mississippi River landing beneath the bluff. The Spanish took control in 1779 and left their mark on the city by establishing straight streets that intersect at right angles atop the bluff. The United States claimed Natchez by treaty, and the U.S. flag first flew over Natchez in March 1798. The city gave its name to the Natchez Trace and prospered as travelers heading for Nashville passed through with money in their pockets and a willingness to spend it on a rowdy good time.

Between 1819 and 1860, wealthy planters built stylish town houses and ringed the city with opulent plantation homes. Though Natchez survived the Civil War virtually unscathed, its economy suffered. Ironically, it was the city's decline that saved its architectural treasures—no one could afford to remodel or tear houses down. In 1932 the women of Natchez originated the idea of the pilgrimage, in which plantation families opened their homes for touring in hopes of raising money for preservation. The Natchez Pilgrimage is now held three times a year, in spring, fall, and around Christmas. During Pilgrimage, between 24 and 30 houses are open, and crowds flock to see them. Some houses are open year-round.

The following three **antebellum homes,** open daily from 9 to 5, are of particular note. All charge a $6 admission fee.

The 1857 **Stanton Hall** (✉ 401 High St., ☎ 601/442–6282 or 800/647–6742) is one of the most palatial and most photographed houses in America. Four giant fluted columns support double porticoes enclosed by delicate, lacy wrought-iron railings. This magnificent preservation project of the Pilgrimage Garden Club is furnished with Natchez antiques.

Rosalie (✉ 100 Orleans St., ☎ 601/445–4555), circa 1823, established what's considered the quintessential Southern plantation house, with its white columns, hipped roof, and red bricks. Restored by the Natchez Garden Club, the house serves as the state home of the Daughters of the American Revolution. Furnishings purchased for the house in 1858 include a famous Belter parlor set.

Magnolia Hall (✉ 215 S. Pearl St., ☎ 601/442–6672), circa 1858, was shelled by the Union gunboat *Essex* during the Civil War. A shell reportedly exploded in a soup tureen, scalding several diners at the table. The Greek Revival mansion has stucco walls and fluted columns topped with curving Ionic capitals. Note the plaster magnolia blossoms on the parlor ceiling. There is a costume museum on the second floor.

Natchez National Historical Park was established in 1988 to help preserve the city. Park headquarters are in **Fort Rosalie,** established in 1716 by French colonists. Currently, only one park property is open to the public: **Melrose,** circa 1845, a planter's estate that symbolizes the cotton era. A second property, the **William Johnson House,** circa 1841, is undergoing extensive renovation and at press time could be viewed only from the outside. When completed, the home will be a museum dedicated to African-American history. *Park headquarters:* ✉ *210 State St.,* ☎ *601/442–7047. Melrose:* ✉ *1 Melrose-Montebello Pkwy.,* ☎ *601/446–5790.* ☞ *$6.* ☉ *Daily 8:30–5. Tours on the hr.*

Longwood, circa 1860–61, is the largest octagonal house in the United States. Under construction during the Civil War, it was never completed. Preserved in its unfinished state, Longwood is now a museum for the Pilgrimage Garden Club and a National Historic Landmark. ✉ *140 Lower Woodville Rd.,* ☎ *601/442–5193.* ☞ *$6.* ☉ *Daily 9–5, except during pilgrimages, which take place in spring and fall. Call ahead to confirm hrs.*

Natchez in Historic Photographs offers a pictorial history of the city in the late 19th and early 20th centuries through the photography of Henry and Earl Norman. Several hundred prints made from the original glass negatives portray everything from river scenes to street scenes, leaving little to imagine about life in early Natchez. ✉ *117 S. Pearl St., 2nd floor,* ☎ *601/442–4741.* ☞ *Suggested donation $3.* ☉ *Mon.–Sat. 10–5, Sun. 1–5.*

Grand Village of the Natchez Indians. This archaeological park and museum depict the culture of the Natchez Native Americans, which reached its zenith in the 1500s. ✉ *400 Jefferson Davis Blvd.,* ☎ *601/446–6502.* ☞ *Free.* ☉ *Mon.–Sat. 9–5, Sun. 1:30–5.*

Dining and Lodging

$–$$ ✕ **Carriage House Restaurant.** On the grounds of Stanton Hall (☞ Natchez, *above*), the Carriage House serves up fried chicken, baked ham, and its famous mouthwatering miniature biscuits. The Victorian-parlor ambience is delightful. ✉ *401 High St.,* ☎ *601/445–5151. AE, MC, V. No dinner except during Pilgrimage wks.*

$–$$ ✕ **Cock of the Walk.** In a marvelous old train depot overlooking the Mississippi River, this famous original of a regional franchise specializes in fried catfish fillets, fried dill pickles, hush puppies, mustard greens, and coleslaw. There are also blackened or grilled catfish and chicken.

✉ *200 N. Broadway, on bluff,* ☎ *601/446–8920. AE, D, DC, MC, V. No lunch.*

$–$$ ✕ **John Martin's.** This fine dining restaurant is a favorite with locals. Signature dishes include seared breast of Muscovy duck topped with a three-pepper Mayhaw jelly, as well as redfish, lamb loin, and a 22-ounce bone-in rib-eye. ✉ *21 Silver St., Under-the-Hill,* ☎ *601/445–0605. AE, MC, V.*

$ ✕ **The Pig Out Inn Barbeque.** The menu at this funky, and extremely casual, place includes delectable chopped or sliced pork, beef, turkey, chicken, or hot sausage all topped by a crave-inducing BBQ sauce. Make room on your plate for sides such as baked beans, black bean and corn salad, or cole slaw. Top it all off with a slice of the homemade pecan or sweet potato pie and you'll truly know what it means to "pig out." ✉ *116 S. Canal St.,* ☎ *601/442–8050. Closed Sun.*

$$$–$$$$ 🏨 **The Briars Inn.** Once the home of Varina Howell, the wife of Jefferson Davis, the Briars sits on a promontory overlooking the Mississippi River. The 19 acres of landscaped grounds are a perfect place for peaceful strolling, and the inn's rooms are beautifully decorated with period furnishings imparting a gracious plantation feel. A Southern breakfast is served in the dining room. ✉ *31 Irving La. (behind Ramada Hilltop), 39121,* ☎ *601/446–9654 or 800/634–1818,* 𝔽𝔸𝕏 *601/445–6037. 14 rooms. Dining room. AE, D, MC, V.*

$$$–$$$$ 🏨 **The Burn.** Noted for its semispiral staircase, this elegant 1836 Greek Revival mansion is so lovely that its owners also offer private tours. The guest rooms are quiet and comfortable and furnished throughout with antiques. The Burn's verdant surroundings lend it the atmosphere of a country home, despite its size. Seated plantation breakfasts are included in the room rate. ✉ *712 N. Union St., 39120,* ☎ *601/442–1344 or 800/654–8859,* 𝔽𝔸𝕏 *601/445–0606. 7 rooms. Pool. AE, D, MC, V.*

$$–$$$ 🏨 **Dunleith.** Stately, colonnaded Dunleith is a popular Natchez bed-and-breakfast with elegant, plantation-style rooms furnished with four-poster beds and antiques. Guests are served lemonade upon arrival. The breakfast room is a former poultry house with old brick walls. Beautiful gardens enhance the grounds. ✉ *84 Homochitto St., 39120,* ☎ *601/446–8500 or 800/433–2445. 11 rooms. No children under 18. MC, V.*

$$ 🏨 **The Guest House Historic Inn.** A renovated home built in 1840, this cozy inn is in the heart of Natchez, on Antique Row. Its rooms are decorated with antiques and reproductions, giving the place the feel of a small European hotel. ✉ *201 N. Pearl St., 39120,* ☎ *601/442–1054,* 𝔽𝔸𝕏 *601/442–1374. 17 rooms. Meeting room. AE, D, DC, MC, V. CP.*

Nightlife and the Arts

King's Tavern (✉ 619 Jefferson St., ☎ 601/446–8845) is in the oldest house in the Natchez Territory (1789). The lounge is rustic and inviting, especially if you're an "Old Natchez" aficionado. The **Under-the-Hill Saloon** (✉ 25 Silver St., ☎ 601/446–8023) has live entertainment—from blues to folk—on weekends in one of the few original buildings left in Natchez-Under-the-Hill.

Outdoor Activities and Sports

There are eight outdoor tennis courts in **Duncan Park** (✉ Duncan St. at Auburn Ave., ☎ 601/442–1589), with lights for night play.

Natchez Trace A to Z

Arriving, Departing, and Getting Around

BY BUS

Greyhound (☎ 800/231–2222) offers daily service to Tupelo (✉ 201 Commerce St., ☎ 601/842–4557); Corinth (✉ 204 U.S. 72E, ☎ 601/

287–1466); Columbus (✉ 904 Main St., ☎ 601/328–4732); Philadelphia (✉ West Side Finance and Insurance Bldg., 270B W. Beacon St., ☎ 601/656–2851); Jackson (✉ 201 S. Jefferson St., ☎ 601/353–6342); Port Gibson (✉ 17 Church St., ☎ 601/431–5751); and Natchez (✉ 103 Lower Woodville Rd., ☎ 601/445–5291).

BY CAR

A car is the only way to tour the Natchez Trace properly, though you can reach major cities by plane and by bus. Corinth is at the intersection of U.S. 72 and U.S. 45, and Tupelo is 5 mi south of the Natchez Trace Parkway at the intersection of U.S. 45 and U.S. 78.

The Natchez Trace Parkway breaks at Jackson; pick up either I–55 or I–20, which run through the city. Jackson is accessed by U.S. 49 and U.S. 51. Natchez, at the beginning of the Natchez Trace Parkway, is served by U.S. 61.

BY PLANE

For airline telephone numbers, *see* Air Travel *in* the Gold Guide. **Golden Triangle Regional Airport** (✉ U.S. 82, 10 mi west of Columbus, ☎ 601/327–4422) is served by Northwest Airlink, American Eagle, and Atlantic Southeast Airlines, with connections nationwide through Memphis and Atlanta.

American Eagle, Continental Express, Delta, and Northwest Airlink make nonstop daily flights to Dallas, Atlanta, and New Orleans, with direct service available nationally. **Jackson International Airport** (✉ East of Jackson off I–20, ☎ 601/939–5631) is 10 minutes from downtown.

Tupelo Municipal Airport (✉ 631 Jackson Extended, 5 mi west of Tupelo, ☎ 601/841–6570) is served by Northwest Airlink and American Eagle.

Contacts and Resources

B&B RESERVATION AGENCIES

Natchez Pilgrimage Tours (☞ Guided Tours, *below*) can answer questions and handle reservations for bed-and-breakfasts.

EMERGENCIES

In towns and cities dial 911 for **police or ambulance.** For help on the Natchez Trace Parkway, dial 0 and ask for the nearest park ranger. Seek medical help at **North Mississippi Regional Medical Center** (✉ 830 S. Gloster St., Tupelo, ☎ 601/841–3000), **Mississippi Baptist Medical Center** (✉ 1225 N. State St., Jackson, ☎ 601/968–1776); and **Jefferson Davis Hospital** (✉ 54 Sgt. Prentiss Dr., Natchez, ☎ 601/442–2871).

GUIDED TOURS

Jackson Tour & Travel (✉ 1801 Crane Ridge Dr., Jackson 39216, ☎ 601/981–8415 or 800/873–8572), one of the South's premier tour operators, arranges independent departures to the state's prime attractions; Natchez and New Orleans are popular destinations.

Natchez Pilgrimage Tours (✉ 200 State St., Natchez 39121, ☎ 601/446–6631 or 800/647–6742) takes groups of 20 or more to tour about a dozen antebellum homes year-round. Carriage rides through downtown Natchez are also available.

RADIO STATIONS

AM: WKTS 95.5, country; WTUP 1490, all-sports talk. **FM:** WJMI 99.7, urban contemporary; WQNZ 95.1, country; WTRC 97.3, adult contemporary/news/sports.

Eckerd's (⊠ Deville Plaza, I–55, E. Frontage Rd., Jackson, ☎ 601/956–5143). **Super D Drugs** (⊠ 327 Meadowbrook, Meadowbrook Shopping Center, Jackson, ☎ 601/366–1449).

The **Alliance** (⊠ 810 Tate St., Corinth 38834, ☎ 601/287–5269 or 800/748–9048); open weekdays 8–5. **Metro Jackson Convention and Visitors Bureau** (⊠ Box 1450, Jackson 39215, ☎ 601/960–1891 or 800/354–7695); open weekdays 8:30–5. **Natchez Trace Parkway Visitor Center** (⊠ 2680 Natchez Trace Pkwy. [MM 266], Tupelo 38801, ☎ 601/680–4025 or 800/305–7417); open weekdays 8–5. **Natchez Convention & Visitors Bureau** (⊠ 640 S. Canal, Natchez 39120, ☎ 601/446–6345 or 800/647–6724); open weekdays 8–5. **Natchez Pilgrimage Tours** (tickets for tours and activities: ⊠ Canal St. at State St., Box 347, Natchez 39120, ☎ 601/446–6631 or 800/647–6742); open weekdays 8:30–5:30. **Port Gibson Chamber of Commerce** (⊠ Box 491, Port Gibson 39150, ☎ 601/437–4351); open weekdays 8–4, Saturday 9–4, Sunday noon–4. **Tupelo Convention and Visitors Bureau** (⊠ 399 E. Main St., Box 47, Tupelo 38802, ☎ 601/841–6521 or 800/533–0611); open weekdays 8–5, Saturday 9–5, Sunday 1–5.

HOLLY SPRINGS AND OXFORD

Holly Springs and Oxford, just east of I–55 in northern Mississippi, are sophisticated versions of the Mississippi small town; both are courthouse towns incorporated in 1837. They offer visitors historic architecture, arts and crafts, literary associations, and those unhurried pleasures of Southern life that remain constant from generation to generation—entertaining conversation, good food, and nostalgic walks at twilight.

Holly Springs

40 mi southeast of Memphis.

Holly Springs arose from a crossroads of old Native American trails originally called Spring Hollow. Chickasaw and travelers stopped to rest here and bathe in medicinal spring waters sheltered by holly trees. Settlers came from the Carolinas, Virginia, and Georgia in the 1830s, and Holly Springs became an educational, business, and cultural center as the newly arrived planters began to rake in profits. Cotton barons built palatial mansions and handsome commercial buildings. Today Holly Springs has more than 200 structures (61 of which are antebellum homes) listed on the National Register of Historic Places.

At least 50 raids befell Holly Springs during the Civil War. The worst took place in December 1862, when the Confederate army, under General Earl Van Dorn, destroyed $1 million worth of Union supplies intended to aid General Grant in his march against Vicksburg. Bent on reprisals against the city, Grant ordered General Benjamin Harrison Grierson to burn it to the ground. That's when a clever Holly Springs matron, Maria Mason, invited General Grierson into her home to chat. They discovered that they shared a love of music and that they had studied piano under the same teacher; so instead of destroying Holly Springs, Grierson enjoyed its hospitality at a series of afternoon gatherings and piano concerts.

Montrose (1858), which serves as headquarters for the Holly Springs Garden Club, has an elegant spiral staircase, elaborate cornices, and plaster ceiling medallions. The grounds have been designated a state arboretum. Tours are by appointment with the Holly Springs Chamber of Commerce (☞ Visitor Information in Holly Springs and Oxford A to Z, below). ⊠ *307 E. Salem Ave.,* ☎ *662/252–2943.* ⌐ *$5.*

Rust College (⊠ N. Memphis St., ☎ 662/252–4661), founded in 1866, contains **Oak View** (circa 1860), one of the oldest buildings in the area. Metropolitan Opera star Leontyne Price, a native of Laurel, Mississippi, gave a brief concert in 1966 that raised money to build the library named for her. It houses the extensive memorabilia of civil rights leader Roy Wilkins. The **Yellow Fever House** (⊠ 104 E. Gholson Ave.), built in 1836, was Holly Springs's first brick building. It was used as a hospital during the 1878 yellow fever epidemic. **Hill Crest Cemetery** (⊠ 380 S. Maury St.) contains the graves of 13 Confederate generals. Many of the iron fences surrounding the graves were made locally before the Civil War.

The **Kate Freeman Clark Art Gallery** is dedicated solely to the work of Holly Springs resident Kate Freeman Clark, who was trained as a painter in New York City during the 1890s. Clark completed more than 1,000 works on canvas and paper, including landscapes and portraits. She returned to Holly Springs in the 1920s and never painted again. Many of her friends did not know of her talent until her paintings were discovered after her death. In her will she left funds to establish a museum. ⊠ *292 E. College Ave.,* ☎ *662/252–4211.* ⌐ *$2.* ☉ *By appointment.*

Many of Holly Springs's **historic homes** are open only during Spring Pilgrimage (the third weekend in April), but their exteriors alone are quite spectacular. On Salem Avenue, you'll find **Cedarhurst** and **Airliewood,** brick houses constructed in the Gothic style popularized in the 1850s by Andrew Jackson Downing. General Grant used Airliewood as his headquarters during his occupation of Holly Springs.

Dining

$ ✕ **Phillips Grocery.** The building housing Phillips was constructed in 1882 as a saloon for railroad workers. Today it's decorated with antiques and crafts and serves big, old-fashioned hamburgers. ⊠ *541A Van Dorn St., across from old depot,* ☎ *662/252–4671. Reservations not accepted. No credit cards. Closed Sun. No dinner.*

Outdoor Activities and Sports

Holly Springs's **Chewalla Lake and Recreation Area** is part of Holly Springs National Forest and has nature trails, picnic areas, swimming, boating, camping, and fishing (license required). ⊠ *MS 4 to Higdon Rd., then turn east; 7 mi to entrance. Information:* ⊠ *National Forests Mississippi, 100 W. Capitol St., Suite 1141, Jackson 39269,* ☎ *601/965–4391.*

Oxford

60 mi southeast of Memphis, 50 mi east of Tupelo.

Oxford and Lafayette County were immortalized as the Jefferson and Yoknapatawpha County of the novels of Oxford native William Faulkner, but even if you're not a Faulkner fan, this is a great place to experience small-town living. You won't be bored: The characters who fascinated Faulkner still live here, and the University of Mississippi keeps things lively.

Faulkner received the Nobel Prize for literature in 1949, and his readers will enjoy exploring the town that inspired *The Hamlet, The Town,* and *The Mansion.* "I discovered that my own little postage stamp of native soil was worth writing about, and that I would never live long enough to exhaust it," said Faulkner. "I created a cosmos of my own."

Many people who knew the eccentric "Mr. Bill" still live in Oxford and are willing to share stories about him. You may encounter them around **Courthouse Square,** a National Historic Landmark in the center of town. At the center of the square is the white-sandstone **Lafayette** (pronounced luh-*fay*-it) **County Courthouse** named for the French Revolutionary War hero the Marquis de Lafayette. The courthouse was rebuilt in 1873 after Union troops burned it down; on its south side is a monument to Confederate soldiers. The courtroom on the second floor is original.

University Avenue, which runs from South Lamar Boulevard just south of the Courthouse Square to the University of Mississippi, is one of the state's most beautiful sights when the trees flame orange and gold in the fall or when the dogwoods blossom in the spring.

The **University Museums** display the brightly colored paintings of local artist Theora Hamblett. Hamblett gained international fame for her works depicting dreams and visions, Mississippi landscapes, and scenes from her childhood. Here, too, is a collection of Greek and Roman antiquities and what may perhaps be the country's quirkiest exhibit— a collection of fully dressed fleas. ⊠ *University Ave. at 5th St.,* ☎ *662/ 232-7073.* ▦ *Free.* ⊙ *Tues.–Sat. 10–4:30, Sun. 1–4.*

The state's beloved Ole Miss, or the **University of Mississippi,** opened in 1848 with 80 students. The **Grove,** the tree-shaded heart of the campus, is almost as important a meeting place as Courthouse Square (☞ *above*). (Supposedly, it was here that Faulkner, just fired from his position as postmaster for writing novels on the job, said, "Never again will I be at the beck and call of every son of a bitch who's got two cents to buy a stamp.") Contact the school's **public relations department** (☎ 662/232–7236) for information about university plays, lectures, sporting events, and special events.

The **Center for the Study of Southern Culture** (☎ 662/232–5993) is housed in antebellum Barnard Observatory, facing the Grove. The center has exhibits on Southern music, folklore, and literature and has the world's largest blues archives (40,000 records). Its annual Faulkner seminar attracts scholars from around the world, and its Oxford Conference for the Book (☞ Nightlife and the Arts, *below*), held each April, draws book lovers from all across the United States. The center's remarkable *Encyclopedia of Southern Culture* is on sale here.

The **Mississippi Room** (☎ 662/232–5855) in the John Davis Williams Library contains both a permanent exhibit on Faulkner, including his Nobel Prize medal, and first editions of other Mississippi authors.

★ **Rowan Oak** was William Faulkner's home from 1930 until his death in 1962. Although this is one of Mississippi's most famous attractions, there are no signs to direct you and only an unobtrusive historic marker at the site. The house and its surrounding 32 acres are as serene and private as they were when Faulkner lived and wrote here. Built about 1848 by Colonel Robert Sheegog, the two-story, white-frame house with square columns represents the primitive Greek Revival style of architecture common to many Mississippi antebellum homes. After the Civil War it fell into disrepair, but in 1930 it was purchased by Faulkner and his bride of one year, Estelle Oldham Franklin.

The house was both a sanctuary and a financial burden to the author; it is now a National Historic Landmark owned by the University of Mississippi. Faulkner made improvements and additions to the house, including a brick wall to shield him from curious strangers. After winning the Nobel Prize, he added the study where his bed, typewriter, desk, and other personal items—such as his sunglasses, a Colgate shave-stick refill, an ink bottle, and a can of dog repellent—still evoke his presence. Faulkner wrote an outline for his novel *The Fable* on the walls of the study, which is reputed to be the most photographed room in the state. The days of the week are neatly printed over the head and length of the bed, and to the right of the door leading into the room is the notation TOMORROW. ⊠ *Old Taylor Rd.,* ☎ 662/234–3284. FAX 601/232–5371. ⊑ *Free.* ⊙ *Tues.–Sat. 10–noon and 2–4, Sun. 2–4.*

Faulkner's funeral was held at Rowan Oak, and he was buried in the family plot in **St. Peter's Cemetery,** at Jefferson and North 16th streets, beside his relatives. Also buried here is Caroline Barr, "Mammy Callie," Faulkner's childhood nurse. The tomb of the author's brother, Dean Faulkner, who was killed in an airplane crash, bears the same epitaph as the one Faulkner had given to John Sartoris in the novel *Pylon.*

OFF THE
BEATEN PATH

COLLEGE HILL PRESBYTERIAN CHURCH – William Faulkner was married at this little church 8 mi northwest of Oxford on College Hill Road on June 20, 1929. The original pews are intact, although it's believed that Sherman stabled horses here during his occupation of College Hill in 1862. Behind the church is one of north Mississippi's oldest cemeteries.

TAYLOR – From Oxford take Old Taylor Road 9 mi (about 15 minutes by car) to the town of Taylor. Downtown Taylor comprises three buildings—two grocery stores and a potter's shop. The old **Taylor Grocery** (☎ 662/236–1716) has a restaurant in back where catfish and trimmin's are served Thursday through Sunday nights (at press time Taylor Grocery was closed for renovations, so be sure to call ahead). In sculptor William Beckwith's studio you can see his statue of Temple Drake, the character who waited for the train in Taylor in Faulkner's novel *Sanctuary.* Small as it is, Taylor is achieving cult status; it's proper to brag about coming here.

Dining and Lodging

$$–$$$ ✕ **City Grocery.** What was once a grocery store is now a trendy bistro
★ on Oxford's historic Courthouse Square. The chef's innovative menu is more suggestive of New Orleans than north Mississippi. A signature dish is the shrimp and grits, and the bananas Foster bread pudding is a showstopper. ⊠ *1118 Van Buren Ave.,* ☎ 662/232–8080. *AE, MC, V. Closed Sun.*

$–$$ ✕ **Downtown Grill.** With its comfortable plaid chairs and dark walls, the Grill's bar could be a club in Oxford, England. But then there's the light and airy balcony overlooking the square—pure Oxford, Mississippi. Downstairs in the restaurant, specialties include seafood gumbo; Mississippi catfish either grilled or Lafitte (topped with shrimp, julienned ham, and a savory cream sauce); and an array of rich desserts. ⊠ *110 Courthouse Sq.,* ☎ 662/234–2659. *AE, D, MC, V. Closed Sun.*

$ ✕ **Bottletree Bakery.** This is the closest to crusty European-style bread that you'll find in Mississippi and perhaps in all of the South. If that isn't reason enough to stop in, check out the saucer-size cinnamon rolls. The bakery serves breakfast and lunch as well as pastries and specialty coffees all day. ⊠ *923 Van Buren Ave.,* ☎ 662/236–5000. *MC, V. Closed Mon.*

$ ✕ **Smitty's.** Red-eye gravy and grits, biscuits with blackberry preserves, fried catfish, chicken and dumplings, corn bread, and black-eyed peas star on a menu of comfort food familiars. The menu reads, "If'n You Need Anything That Ain't on Here, Holler at the Cook." ⊠ *208 S. Lamar Blvd., south of square,* ☎ 662/234–9111. *MC, V.*

$$–$$$ 🛏 **Puddin' Place.** Near the Ole Miss campus, this Victorian house has a wonderful back porch with swings and rockers. The two suites—each with sitting room, separate bedroom, and private bath—are thoughtfully furnished with antiques and collectibles. The downstairs suite has its own washer and dryer as well as two working fireplaces; the upstairs suite has four working fireplaces—including one in the bathroom. A Southern breakfast is included in the room rate. ✉ *1008 University Ave., 38655,* ☎ *662/234–1250,* FAX *662/236–4285. 2 suites. No credit cards.*

$$ 🛏 **The Oliver-Britt House.** Each comfortable, pleasant room has its own bath and color TV in this restored Greek Revival built about 1900 and run as a casual B&B. The location, midway between the university and Courthouse Square, is convenient. A Southern breakfast is included in the room rate. ✉ *512 Van Buren Ave., 38655,* ☎ *662/234–8043,* FAX *662/281–8065. 5 rooms. AE, DC, MC, V.*

$–$$ 🛏 **Alumni Center Hotel.** The modern, hotel-style rooms bring a fresh look to a unique location on the Ole Miss campus. All rooms are done in rich dark colors, giving them a distinguished feel. ✉ *Alumni Dr., University of Mississippi, 38677,* ☎ *662/234–2331. 96 rooms. Snack bar, pool, 6 meeting rooms. MC, V.*

$–$$ 🛏 **Downtown Inn.** These functional rooms have no surprises. The restaurant, however, can do a remarkably good breakfast, though you'll probably choose nearby Smitty's (☞ *above*) for the biscuits. ✉ *400 N. Lamar, 38655,* ☎ *662/234–3031,* FAX *662/234–2834. 123 rooms, 2 suites. Restaurant, lounge, pool. AE, DC, MC, V.*

Nightlife and the Arts

The **Faulkner and Yoknapatawpha Conference,** held the first week in August, includes lectures by Faulkner scholars and field trips to the site of the fictional Yoknapatawpha County. The annual **Oxford Conference for the Book** is a meeting of bibliophiles with an emphasis on Southern authors.

Proud Larry's (211 S. Lamar Blvd., ☎ 662/236–0050) regularly schedules regional bands playing blues, folk, funk, jazz, and rock.

Outdoor Activities and Sports

Oxford's **Avent Park** (✉ Park Dr., the continuation of Bramlett Blvd., which runs north of E. Jackson Ave.) has tennis courts, a playground, picnic areas, and a jogging trail.

Holly Springs and Oxford A to Z

Arriving, Departing, and Getting Around

BY BUS

Greyhound (☎ 800/231–2222) has a station in Holly Springs (✉ 490 Craft St., ☎ 662/252–1353).

BY CAR

A 30-minute drive from Memphis, Holly Springs is in north Mississippi near the Tennessee state line on U.S. 78 and MS 4, MS 7, and MS 311.

Contacts and Resources

EMERGENCIES

In Holly Springs, dial 0 for assistance. In Oxford, dial 911. Medical help is available at **Baptist Memorial North Mississippi Hospital** (✉ Off I–55; take Batesville exit, 1 mi south of Oxford Sq. on S. Lamar Ave., Oxford, ☎ 662/232–8100).

RADIO STATIONS

AM: WSUH 1420, news/talk. **FM:** WOXD 95.5, oldies; WWMS 97.5, contemporary and country.

Holly Springs Chamber of Commerce (⊠ 154 S. Memphis St., ☎ 662/
252–2943); open weekdays 9–5. **Oxford Information Center** (⊠ Cottage next to city hall, ☎ 662/232–2419); open daily 9–5. **Oxford
Tourism Council** (⊠ 111 Courthouse Sq., Box 965, Oxford 38655, ☎
662/234–4680 or 800/758–9177); open weekdays 9–5. **Oxford-Lafayette
County Chamber of Commerce** (⊠ 299 W. Jackson Ave., ☎ 662/234–
4651); open weekdays 8:30–4.

THE DELTA

Clarksdale, Greenville, Vicksburg

"The Delta begins in the lobby of the Peabody Hotel in Memphis and
ends on Catfish Row in Vicksburg," said Greenville journalist David
Cohn. In between is a vast agricultural plain created by the Mississippi
River. If life should give you only one day in the Delta, use it to cruise
down U.S. 61 and the Great River Road (MS 1) from Memphis to Vicksburg. Gamble your way through Tunica. Time it right for lunch in Clarksdale, Merigold, or Boyle and for dinner at Doe's in Greenville. Then
on a Saturday night you'll be able to pick up public radio's *Highway
61,* which will be playing the blues about the time you glimpse the first
kudzu near Vicksburg.

*Numbers in the margin correspond to points of interest on the Mis-
sissippi Delta map.*

Tunica County

❾ *30 mi south of Memphis off U.S. 61.*

This region is a gambler's paradise. Las Vegas–style casinos have
sprung up all along the otherwise empty and somewhat barren strip
of Delta highway. The view of these garish entertainment and hotel
complexes emerging from the cotton fields is quite surreal, but step inside and you'll never know you're not in Vegas or Atlantic City.

Since the arrival of gaming in 1992, more than $2.5 billion has been
invested in the county, and the number of rooms for overnight accommodations has risen from 40 to more than 7,000 (☞ Lodging, *below,*
for descriptions of some casinos). Nine casinos fill the sky: Bally's Saloon, Fitzgeralds Casino & Hotel, the Gold Strike Casino Resort, Hollywood Casino & Hotel, Harrah's Tunica Casino & Hotel, Grand Casino
Tunica, Horseshoe Casino and Hotel, Sam's Town Hotel & Gambling
Hall, and the Sheraton Casino Hotel. The three listed below are the
best of the field. If you're not interested in gambling, you can still take
advantage of good entertainment at the hotels—everything from comedy acts to blues and country music.

Lodging

$$–$$$ 🏨 **Horseshoe Casino and Hotel.** One of the casino resorts that have
forever changed the North Mississippi Delta skyline, the Horsehoe plays
homage to the blues. You can stay in either the modern, 14-story, all-
suite hotel tower or in rooms above the casino, each of which is decorated in Victorian style. Players at the Horseshoe Casino can indulge
in 100% Las Vegas–style action: roulette, poker, slot machines, and
more. The Bluesville complex includes the Blues & Legends Hall of
Fame Museum, dedicated to the blues heritage of the Delta, and the
Bluesville Showcase Nightclub, which stages a variety of music. ⊠ *1021
Casino Center Dr., Robinsonville 38664,* ☎ *662/357–5500 or 800/363–*

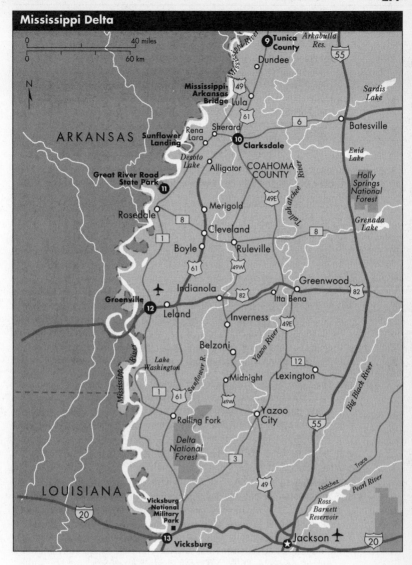

Mississippi Delta

7666, FAX 662/357–5600. *194 rooms, 311 suites. 4 restaurants, pool, massage, sauna, exercise room, meeting room. AE, D, DC, MC, V.* 🐾

$–$$ 🏨 **Sam's Town Hotel and Gambling Hall.** An Old West theme pervades this mammoth hotel-casino just south of the Memphis International Airport. Rooms and suites are adjacent to the casino, which contains more than 1,500 slot machines, 60 table games, and live poker and keno. Past performers at the resort's River Palace Arena have included Bill Cosby, Wynonna Judd, and Wayne Newton. Riverbend Links is the adjacent 18-hole championship golf course. Sam's five restaurants, including 24-hour Smokey Joe's, serve everything from juicy Angus steaks to spicy barbecue. ✉ *1477 Casino Strip Blvd., Robinsonville 38664,* ☎ *800/456–0711,* FAX *662/363–0746. 850 rooms, 44 suites. 5 restaurants, lounge, pool, golf, exercise room, 7 meeting rooms. AE, D, DC, MC, V.* 🐾

$ 🏨 **The Hollywood Casino and Hotel.** Movie memorabilia is everywhere at this full-service casino/hotel, including the model of the *Titanic* used in making the blockbuster film and the motorcycle driven by Peter Fonda in *Easy Rider*. Rooms are basic but spacious and tidy with amenities like coffeemakers and extras like video games. The Hollywood also has its own 72-space RV park with full hookups. Downstairs at the casino you can choose from more than 1,300 slot machines and video poker stations plus 44 table games. ☒ *1150 Casino Strip Blvd., Robinsonville 38664,* ☎ *662/357–7700 or 800/871–0711,* FAX *662/357–7895. 506 rooms, 26 suites. 6 restaurants, pool, exercise room, meeting room. AE, D, DC, MC, V.* 🐾

En Route At Rena Lara, turn west to **Sunflower Landing** on Desoto Lake. Near here, in May 1541, Hernando DeSoto "discovered" the Mississippi River.

At the town of Rich, swing west on U.S. 49 for a spectacular view of the Mississippi River from the **Mississippi—Arkansas Bridge.** Continue south on MS 1 to skirt serene Moon Lake and Friars Point. The levee parallels MS 1 for most of the southbound trip; park and climb up for a look at the Father of Waters.

Clarksdale

❿ *60 mi southwest of Memphis.*

As a child, author Tennessee Williams spent time in Clarksdale, visiting his grandfather, the rector of St. George's Episcopal Church. (In Williams's *Cat on a Hot Tin Roof,* Brick was running high hurdles at nearby Friars Point when he broke his leg.)

The **Delta Blues Museum** is a testament to the important role played by Clarksdale and Coahoma County in the history of the blues. Exhibits and programs trace the influence of the blues on rock, jazz, and pop music through videotapes, slides, records, and books. After 19 years in it's original location, the museum recently moved into the newly restored Illinois Central Freight Train Depot. ☒ *1 Blues Alley,* ☎ *662/627–6820.* 🎫 *$4.* 🕐 *Mon.–Sat. 9–5, Sun. noon–5.* 🐾

Dining

$–$$ ✕ **Rest Haven.** The Delta's large Lebanese community influences the food, which is considered regional fare. Among the favorites are *kibbe* (seasoned lean ground lamb with cracked wheat), spinach and meat pies, and cabbage rolls. Daily plate-lunch specials include chicken and dumplings, and red beans and sausage over rice. ☒ *419 State St. (Hwy. 61),* ☎ *662/624–8601. No credit cards. Closed Sun.*

En Route The McCartys of **Merigold** are famous throughout the state for their pale stoneware. Their shop showcases their pottery and handcrafted jewelry; in the spring and summer you may get a peek at their gardens. Around the corner from the shop is an eatery called the Gallery, where a choice of two entrées is offered for lunch. ☒ *Corner Goff and St. Mary Sts.,* ☎ *662/748–2293.* 🕐 *Feb.–Dec., Tues.–Sat. 10–4.*

Cleveland

30 mi southwest of Clarksdale.

Home to 15,000 residents plus the students at Delta State University, Cleveland is said to have inspired the music of W. C. Handy (1873–1958), who was among the first to write down the blues. It's a small town that has an outstanding restaurant, KC's.

Dining

$$$$ ✕ **KC's Restaurant.** A hidden treasure in the heart of the Delta, this funky and fabulous restaurant could hold its own anywhere. The eclectic and sophisticated menu changes every two weeks and has French, Italian, Asian, and Southwestern influences. Count on seeing wild game, fresh fish, free-range meats, and organic vegetables. There's a walk-in wine cellar (with a table for those who like to dine among the bottles) that offers evidence of the restaurant's amazing wine list. ✉ *U.S. 61N at 1st St.,* ☎ *662/843–5301. AE, MC, V. No lunch Sat. No dinner Sun.*

Rosedale

18 mi west of Cleveland.

This pastoral town on MS 8 offers sweeping views of the Mississippi River and an 800-acre park with the state's largest campground inside **⑪** the levee. The **Great River Road State Park,** on the bluffs of the Mississippi River, has a 75-ft-high overlook tower. There are also a boat ramp, both developed and primitive campsites, canoeing and tubing, fishing, nature trails, and picnic shelters. ✉ *Off MS 1, Box 292, 38769,* ☎ *662/759–6762.* ⊘ *Daily 8–5.*

Greenville

⑫ *35 mi southwest of Cleveland.*

Greenville, the seat of Washington County, is named for Revolutionary War hero General Nathaniel Greene, a close friend of George Washington. The city's history has been dominated by the Mississippi River. The river created the rich soil in which cotton flourished, and Greenville was—and is—the port used by the massive Delta plantations to ship their bales to market. During the Civil War battle for Vicksburg, Union troops burned Greenville to the ground. The citizens rebuilt the town only to suffer a yellow fever epidemic in 1877. Then, in 1890, the city experienced disastrous flooding; levees finally solved the problem after the great flood of 1927. At the turn of the century Greenville developed into a major river port.

Greenville probably has produced more writers than any other city of its size in the country, including William Alexander Percy (*Lanterns on the Levee*), his nephew Walker Percy (*The Last Gentleman, The Moviegoer*), Ellen Douglas (*A Family's Affair, The Magic Carpet*), Hodding Carter (Pulitzer Prize–winning crusading journalist), Shelby Foote (*The Civil War, Love in a Dry Season*), and Hodding Carter III (television news commentator and journalist). The best reason to visit Greenville, however, is to eat at Doe's (☞ Dining, *below*).

☾ The **Birthplace of the Frog Exhibit,** in Leland, on the outskirts of Greenville, is a tribute to the late Muppet creator Jim Henson and a must for Kermit fans. In the same building as the Leland Chamber of Commerce, the exhibit includes Henson family memorabilia, videos of Henson's first attempts at kiddie TV, three original Muppets on loan, and more. Henson was born in Greenville but grew up in Leland. ✉ *MS 82 at S. Deer Creek Dr. E,* ☎ *662/686–2687.* ▨ *Free.* ⊘ *Weekdays 10–4, tours on weekends by appointment.*

Dining

$$–$$$$ ✕ **Doe's.** Visually as uninspiring as any restaurant you'll find—Formica-top tables, mismatched chairs, mismatched cutlery, mismatched plates—Doe's isn't known for its ambience. But when you see that huge steak hanging off your plate, you'll know why this place is famous. Hot tamales

and the house salad dressing (olive oil, lemon juice, garlic) are specialties.
⊠ *502 Nelson St.,* ☎ *662/334–3315. MC, V. No lunch.*

OFF THE
BEATEN PATH

FLOREWOOD RIVER PLANTATION STATE PARK – It's worth straying from
the Delta path to visit this living-history park 2 mi west of Greenwood on
Highway 82. Near Greenwood, it's an exact replica of an 1850s working plantation, complete with reenactments in the school, blacksmith
shop, plantation store, and more. ⊠ *Box 680, Greenwood 38930,* ☎
662/455–3821. ☞ *$3.50.* ☉ *Tues.–Sat. 9–noon and 1–5, Sun. 1–5.*

MAMA'S DREAM WORLD – In Belzoni, 35 mi southeast of Greenville,
Mama's Dream World contains pictures embroidered by the late Ethel
Wright Mohamed, who took up needlework in her sixties to record her
life in the Delta with her storekeeper husband and eight children. Some
of Mrs. Mohamed's work is in the Smithsonian's permanent collection.
The gallery is in the Mohamed family home, and more than 125 pic-
tures cover the walls. ⊠ *307 Central St.,* ☎ *662/247–1433.* ☞ *$2.* ☉
By appointment.

Vicksburg

⑬ *75 mi south of Greenville, 35 mi west of Jackson.*

Vicksburg began as a mission founded by the Reverend Newitt Vick
in 1814. He chose a spot high on the bluffs above a bend in the Mississippi River, a location that would have important consequences for
the young city during the Civil War.

In June 1862 the Union had control of the Mississippi River, with the
exception of Vicksburg, which was in Confederate hands. Ulysses S.
Grant's men doggedly slogged through canals and bayous in five fu-
tile attempts to capture the city, which was called the Gibraltar of the
Confederacy because of its impregnable natural defenses. Then, in a
series of raids and battles, Grant laid waste the area between Vicksburg and Jackson to the east and Port Gibson to the south, before returning to Vicksburg. His attacks were repulsed once again; he then
laid siege to the city for 47 days as its citizens, hiding in caves, slowly
starved. On July 4, 1863, the city surrendered, giving the Union control of the river and a critical victory.

★ **Vicksburg National Military Park,** which nearly surrounds Vicksburg,
keeps the city's past close to today's constituents. The park comprises
1,800 acres of fortifications and earthworks lined with monuments and
markers tracing battle positions. The visitor center offers orientation
programs and exhibits. A guided tour is a good investment, should time
and money ($20 for two hours) permit. The self-guided driving tour
is well marked, however, and a cassette tape may be rented for $4.50.
About 7 mi into the park is the USS *Cairo,* a Union gunboat raised
from the Yazoo River and restored. Civil War artifacts recovered from
the *Cairo* are on display at the adjacent USS *Cairo* Museum. ⊠ *3201
Clay St.,* ☎ *601/636–0583 for main switchboard; 601/636–2199 for
USS Cairo.* ☞ *$4 per car.* ☉ *National Military Park grounds fall–spring,
daily 7–5; summer, daily 7–8; USS Cairo fall–spring, daily 8:30–5; summer, daily 9:30–6.*

The Vanishing Glory is a 15-projector, multimedia show portraying the
sights and sounds of Vicksburg under siege. ⊠ *717 Clay St.,* ☎ *601/
634–1863.* ☞ *$5.* ☉ *Daily 10–5. Shown on the hr.*

Vicksburg's **historic homes** may have cannonballs imbedded in their
walls, but they have been beautifully restored. Visit **Cedar Grove** (⊠
2200 Oak St.; ☞ Dining and Lodging, *below*), **Balfour House** (⊠

Crawford and Cherry Sts.), and the **Martha Vick House** (⊠ 1300 Grove St.), built by the daughter of the founder of Vicksburg, Newitt Vick.

Narrated one-hour **Hydro-Jet Boat tours** depart from Vicksburg for those longing for a Mississippi River adventure. ⊠ Box 506, 39181, ☎ 601/ 638–5443 or 800/521–4363. ➡ $16. ☉ Mar.–Nov., daily at 10, 2, and 5.

In 1894 Coca-Cola was bottled at the **Biedenharn Candy Company,** which is now a Coke museum. The history of one of the world's favorite soft drinks is documented through Coca-Cola advertisements and memorabilia. There's also an old-fashioned soda fountain on site. ⊠ 1107 Washington St., ☎ 601/638–6514. ➡ $2.25. ☉ Mon.–Sat. 10– 5, Sun. 1:30–4:30.

Dining and Lodging

$$ ✕ **Jacque's Café in the Park.** A popular spot with a good variety of menu choices, Jacque's has juicy steaks, veal, fresh seafood, and Cajun and Italian cuisine from which to choose. ⊠ 4137 I–20 Frontage Rd. (in Park Inn International), ☎ 601/638–5811. AE, DC, MC, V. No lunch.

$ ✕ **Walnut Hills.** If you're yearning for authentic regional cooking, this restaurant is a must. Don't miss the outstanding fried chicken, served with fresh snap beans or purple-hull peas. For dessert, try the blackberry cobbler. ⊠ 1214 Adams St., at Clay St., ☎ 601/638–4910. Reservations essential for large groups. AE, DC, MC, V. Closed Sat. No lunch weekdays.

$$–$$$$ 🏨 **Cedar Grove.** An entire city block is consumed by this 1840s man-
★ sion and its grounds. All rooms are furnished with period antiques and Civil War artifacts, the most impressive of which is the Union cannonball still lodged in the parlor wall. You can hear nearby river traffic at night from the otherwise quiet, gaslighted grounds, and survey the watery scene during the day from the rooftop veranda. A house tour and hearty Southern breakfast are included. ⊠ 2200 Oak St., 39180, ☎ 601/636– 1000 or 800/862–1300, FAX 601/634–6126. 35 rooms. Restaurant, piano bar, pool, tennis court, croquet, bicycles. AE, D, DC, MC, V.

$$–$$$$ 🏨 **Duff Green Mansion.** Used as a hospital during the Civil War, this man-
★ sion has been standing since 1856. Each guest room is decorated with antiques, including half-tester beds. A large, Southern-style breakfast and a tour of the home are included. ⊠ 1114 1st East St., 39180, ☎ 601/ 636–6968 or 800/992–0037. 4 rooms, 2 suites. Pool. AE, D, MC, V.

$$–$$$ 🏨 **Belle of the Bends.** Built in 1876 by Mississippi State senator Murray F. Smith and his wife, Kate, Belle of the Bends is a classic example of Victorian Italianate architecture. The mansion is decorated throughout with period antiques, oriental rugs, and memorabilia of the steamboats that plied the waters of the Mississippi River in the 1880s and early 1900s. A plantation-style breakfast and house tour are included in the room rate as is a tour of nearby **Cedar Grove.** The only downside is the nearby railroad line. ⊠ 508 Klein St., 39180, ☎ 601/634– 0737 or 800/844–2308. 4 rooms. AE, MC, V. 🐾

Nightlife and the Arts

Beechwood Restaurant & Lounge (⊠ 4449 Hwy. 80E, ☎ 601/636–3761) is a hot spot, with nightly country-and-western bands and a recently remodeled bar area.

Outdoor Activities and Sports

JOGGING

★ The hilly roads in the **Vicksburg National Military Park** (⊠ I–20, Exit 4-B, Clay St.) are a challenging course for joggers.

Clear Creek (✉ I–20, Bovina Exit 11, Vicksburg) has public courts.

Shopping

Climb up into the **Attic Gallery** (✉ 1101 Washington St., Vicksburg, ☎ 601/638–9221) to see regional art and fine crafts chosen with a discriminating eye—it's a Southern rival to New York galleries.

Delta A to Z

Arriving, Departing, and Getting Around

BY BUS

Greyhound (☎ 800/231–2222) stops in Belzoni (✉ West Side Grocery, 711 Francis St., ☎ 662/247–2150); Clarksdale (✉ 1604 State St., ☎ 662/627–7893); Cleveland (✉ U.S. 61N, ☎ 662/843–5113); Columbus (✉ 904 Main St., ☎ 601/328–4732); Greenville (✉ 1849 U.S. 82E, ☎ 662/335–2633); and Vicksburg (✉ 1295 S. Frontage Rd., ☎ 601/638–8389).

BY CAR

U.S. 61 runs from Memphis through the Delta to Vicksburg and Natchez and to Baton Rouge, Louisiana. The Great River Road (MS 1) parallels U.S. 61 and the river through part of this route.

BY PLANE

The **Greenville Municipal Airport** (✉ Air Base Rd., ☎ 662/334–3121) is served by Northwest Airlink.

Contacts and Resources

EMERGENCIES

In Greenville and Vicksburg dial 911 for **police and ambulance.** Seek medical help at **Delta Regional Medical Center** (✉ 1400 E. Union St., Greenville, ☎ 662/378–3783) and at **Vicksburg Medical Center** (✉ 1111 N. Frontage Rd., Vicksburg, ☎ 601/636–2611).

RADIO STATIONS

FM: WAID 106.5, urban contemporary; WBBV 101.1, country.

VISITOR INFORMATION

Clarksdale-Coahoma County Chamber of Commerce (✉ 1540 De Soto Ave., Box 160, Clarksdale 38614, ☎ 662/627–7337). **Cleveland-Bolivar County Chamber of Commerce** (✉ 600 3rd St., Box 490, Cleveland 38732, ☎ 662/843–2712). **Greenville-Washington County CVB** (✉ 410 Washington Ave., Greenville 38701, ☎ 662/334–2711 or 800/467–3582). **Greenwood Convention & Visitors Bureau** (✉ 1902 Le Flore Ave., Box 739, Greenwood 38935-0739, ☎ 662/453–9197 or 800/748–9064). **Mississippi Welcome Center** (✉ 4210 Washington St., Vicksburg 39180, ☎ 601/638–4269). **Vicksburg Convention & Visitors Bureau** (✉ Clay St. and Old Hwy. 27, Box 110, Vicksburg 39181, ☎ 601/636–9421 or 800/221–3536). **Washington County Welcome Center** (✉ U.S. 82 at Reed Rd., Box 6022, Greenville 38701, ☎ 662/332–2378).

MISSISSIPPI A TO Z

Arriving and Departing

By Bus

Greyhound (☎ 800/231–2222) serves most major cities in Mississippi.

By Car

The state's main north–south artery is I–55. I–20 crosses the state east–west from Meridian through Jackson to Vicksburg. I–10 crosses the Gulf Coast, and I–59 links Meridian with Picayune.

By Plane

Most visitors use **Jackson International Airport** (⊠ East of Jackson, off I–20, ☎ 601/939–5631) or **Memphis International Airport** (⊠ 2491 Winchester Rd., ☎ 901/922–8000).

Getting Around

By Bus

Coast Area Transit (⊠ 333 DeBuys Rd., Gulfport, ☎ 228/896–8080) provides a coast-wide public transportation system.

By Car

The speed limit on Mississippi interstate highways is 70 mph unless otherwise posted. The speed limit on the Natchez Trace Parkway is 50 mph. There's one service station on the Parkway, at Mile Marker 193.1. Right turns on red lights are permitted throughout the state unless otherwise indicated. Crash helmets approved by the American Association of Motor Vehicle Administrators are required for motorcycle riders. Drivers and front-seat passengers in any vehicle designed to carry 10 riders or less must wear seat belts. Children under four years of age must be in an approved child passenger restraint device.

By Train

Amtrak (☎ 800/872–7245) serves Batesville, Biloxi, Brookhaven, Canton, Durant, Grenada, Gulfport, Hattiesburg, Hazlehurst, Jackson, Laurel, McComb, Meridian, Pascagoula, Picayune, and Winona.

Contacts and Resources

Emergencies

In towns and cities, dial 911 for **police or ambulance.** Cellular calls to the Highway Patrol are free by dialing HP (47).

Visitor Information

The **Mississippi Division of Tourism** (⊠ Box 1705, Ocean Springs 39566, ☎ 601/359–3297 or 800/927–6378) will gladly send you a travel planner.

6 NORTH CAROLINA

Historical sites and natural wonders are plentiful in North Carolina, from Old Salem in Winston-Salem, where the 1700s spring to life today, to the Great Smoky and Blue Ridge mountains. On the Cape Hatteras and Cape Lookout national seashores, lighthouses stand as they have for 200 years, and unspoiled beaches stretch for miles. You'll find sophisticated shopping and dining in Charlotte; first-class golf in the Sandhills; and high technology, health care, and culture within the Triangle, a shape traced by Raleigh, Durham, and Chapel Hill.

By Lisa H.
Towle

THE FIRST STANZA OF NORTH CAROLINA'S OFFICIAL toast reads: "Here's to the land of the longleaf pine/ The summer land where the sun doth shine/ Where the weak grow strong and the strong grow great/ Here's to 'Down Home,' the Old North State!" Sure, it's a bit hyperbolic, but it's catchy and rhythmic. It also speaks to a deeper truth: as much as geography, people have shaped the state's landscape over the years. In a moving 1991 tribute that was both videotaped and printed, the late Charles Kuralt, television journalist, author, and inveterate traveler, noted that North Carolina—his "state of grace"—has been home to Whistler's mother, Billy Graham, Michael Jordan, Chief Manteo, and three U.S. presidents.

In 1524 explorer Giovanni da Verrazano landed on what is now North Carolina's shore and wrote in his log, ". . . as pleasant and delectable [a land] to behold as is possible to imagine." Sixty years later the New World's first English-speaking settlers found their way to the state's eastern edge, which is bordered by 300 mi of beaches, islands, and inlets. Hernando de Soto searched for gold in the western part of the state, an area bounded by two ranges of the southern Appalachians, the Blue Ridge Mountains and the Great Smoky Mountains. In 1540, he and his band of Spanish explorers met the centuries-long residents of the area, the Cherokee, at the ancient village of Guasili close by what is today the town of Murphy. Several centuries later, in 1799, the first gold rush in the United States got its start in the heartland, the Piedmont—near Concord, to be exact—when young Conrad Reed discovered a 17-pound nugget that would eventually be identified as gold. And although North Carolina was the last state to secede during the Civil War, the state provided more troops and supplies to the Confederacy than any other Southern state and suffered the most casualties.

Thanks to efforts of the state and many determined citizens, this history and more has been carefully preserved. A lot of it can be found along 1,500 mi of roadway designated by the state's Department of Transportation as Scenic Byways. Thirty-one such byways (all of them marked with signs) crisscross the state. The soul of North Carolina can be glimpsed on these meandering routes. Here the views can quickly shift from panoramic to intimate, and the jessamine and galax, azaleas and rhododendrons, magnolias and dogwoods, and soft Spanish moss grow undisturbed.

Unlike many other states, North Carolina does not have one city that stands head and shoulders above all others. Rather, due to a confluence of circumstance, custom, and capitalistic acuity, a number of centers of business, art, and education have grown up throughout the state. Citizens, from African-American to Quaker, are proud of their contributions to North Carolina's development and protective of the areas and unique cultures from which they sprang. Indeed, some have described the Old North State as a collection of fiercely independent city-states reminiscent of those in ancient Greece or 19th-century Italy. Taken as a whole, North Carolina is now more urban and suburban than rural. You won't find gritty, noisy, oversize cities here, though. Instead, the pace is a bit slower. Manners and smiles still count, and canopies of hardwoods and pine trees characterize cities and countryside alike.

Because it has a temperate climate, world-class schools, and one of the most dynamic economies in the nation, North Carolina is attracting new residents in record numbers. They come not just from around the country but from around the world, and their influence—through their arts, foods, faiths, and intellects—is unmistakable. Ultimately, how-

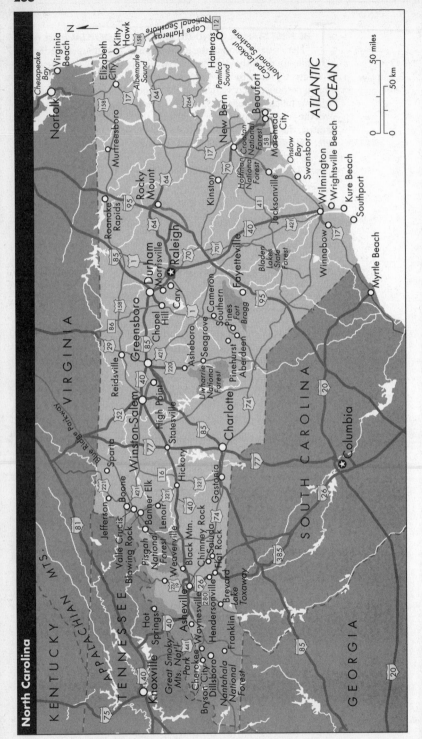

North Carolina

ever, what newcomers, both permanent and transitory, find is that one of the great appeals of North Carolina lies in its timelessness. In 1749, Peter Jefferson, the father of Thomas Jefferson, and his group of surveyors discovered a river in western North Carolina. Because they thought it was a large branch of the Mississippi River no one had seen before, they named it the New River. Later, archaeologists determined that it is actually the oldest river in the United States and the second oldest in the world, after the Nile. Today, amid majestic scenery, its two forks continue to flow.

Pleasures and Pastimes

Beaches

From the thin band of barrier islands known as the Outer Banks, along the northern coastline, to the area around Wilmington and the Cape Fear Coast, to the South Brunswick Islands near the South Carolina border, North Carolina's beaches are a year-round destination. You can visit national seashores or wildlife refuges, go surfing, diving, fishing, hiking, bird-watching, hang gliding—or just watch the waves. North Carolinians are proud that the nation's first national seashore, Cape Hatteras, is in their state, as is Roanoke Island, where the country's first European settlers landed more than 400 years ago.

Dining

In North Carolina's cities, risotto and dim sum are becoming as common as grits and corn bread. Ethnic specialties of all kinds are available, as well as contemporary American cuisine. The Sandhills, too, have a number of sophisticated restaurants. But you can find plenty of good old-fashioned Southern cooking, including Southern-fried chicken, Brunswick stew, ham, vegetables, biscuits, and fruit cobblers. Chopped or sliced pork barbecue is still a big item.

By far the best fare around the Outer Banks is fresh seafood. Raw bars serve oysters and clams on the half shell, and seafood houses offer fresh crabs (soft-shells in season, early in the summer) and whatever local fish—tuna, wahoo, mahimahi—have been hauled in that day. Cuisine in the Wilmington and Morehead City areas is strong on seafood, whether it's shrimp, Atlantic blue crab, or king mackerel, but pork barbecue and international cuisines are also options.

From Cherokee County to Asheville, the dining choices are many: upscale restaurants, middle-of-the-road country fare, and fast-food eateries. Fresh mountain trout, as well as such game meats as pheasant and venison, are regional specialties. Beer, wine, and liquor by the drink are permitted in Blowing Rock, Banner, Elk, and Beech Mountain; beer and wine only in Boone.

Unless otherwise noted, neat, casual wear (including golf wear in the Sandhills) is acceptable throughout North Carolina.

CATEGORY	COST*
$$$$	over $35
$$$	$25–$35
$$	$15–$25
$	under $15

*per person for a three-course meal, excluding drinks, service, and 6%–7% sales tax (depending on county)

Historic Places

Opportunities abound to get out of the fast lane and onto the back roads that lead to places where history is kept alive. Whether it's the site of a key battle in the Revolutionary War or the largest troop surrender of the Civil War, a Quaker settlement, or studios where artisans carry on a 200-year-old tradition in pottery, North Carolina cherishes its past. Places to visit are as varied as the site of man's first flight and the architectural legacies of America's industrial barons.

Lodging

In North Carolina's cities, you'll find everything from economy motels to convention hotels to bed-and-breakfasts in lovely historic districts. Most major chains are represented, and some hotels offer great weekend packages. A few warnings, though: During the twice-a-year furniture market in High Point, when 75,000 people descend on the city, empty hotel rooms and rental cars are almost impossible to find. May is graduation time for all of the Triangle's colleges and universities. Hotel rooms and restaurant seats are booked, in some cases, years in advance.

Most lodging options in the Sandhills are in the luxury resort category, with full amenities and services. Many of the prices quoted are for golf packages. However, there are some chain motels in Southern Pines and Aberdeen, as well as a variety of bed-and-breakfasts in the area.

Motels and hotels are clustered up and down the Outer Banks, with rental properties in all the towns that dot the Cape Hatteras National Seashore. Visitors to Wilmington and the Cape Fear Coast, and New Bern and the Central ("Crystal") Coast can choose from among a variety of chains, condos, and resorts overlooking water, whether it be rivers or the ocean. There are also in-town guest houses. Lodging options in the western mountains range from posh resorts to mountain cabins, country inns, and economy chain motels. There's a bed for virtually every pocketbook. When you're planning your trip, always ask about special packages and possible off-season rates.

CATEGORY	COST*
$$$$	over $170
$$$	$120–$170
$$	$75–$120
$	under $75

*All prices are for a standard double room, excluding 6%–12% tax (depending on county).

Outdoor Activities

North Carolina's unique geological and biological resources give outdoor enthusiasts a full spectrum of activities. There are hundreds of camping options, from primitive camping to family camping. Hikers and backpackers come here for the trails—one-day hikes to weeklong trips. Quite a few stables offer rental horses, and some have llama treks. Hard-core mountain bikers can ride a 27-mi loop through the Great Smoky Mountains National Park. Local outfitters regularly conduct white-water rafting trips. The state has eight ski resorts, and if you like height but not snow, there's hang gliding across the dunes at Nags Head.

☙ *following the text of a review is your signal that the property has a Web site, where you will find details and, usually, images; for a link, visit www.fodors.com/urls.*

Exploring North Carolina

Charlotte, the state's largest city, is known as a center of high finance in the South and prides itself on its cosmopolitan flair. The cities of the Triad (Greensboro, Winston-Salem, and High Point), in the upper Piedmont, showcase the legacies of some of the state's founding families. The Triangle (Raleigh, Durham, and Chapel Hill), in the central

Piedmont, is the hub of higher education, scientific research, and state-sponsored cultural resources. The Sandhills, on the Coastal Plain, is a favorite with antiques lovers and is recognized worldwide as a golf mecca. On the Outer Banks comes solitude in the form of miles of pristine shore and sea oats. Boating, scuba diving, and fishing are the main pastimes in Morehead City and the Central Coast, while history is alive in genteel New Bern. Wilmington and the Cape Fear Coast aren't just resort vacation spots—they're a thriving business and cultural center for the southeastern portion of North Carolina. In the western mountains, which are anchored by the city of Asheville, you'll find everything from hiking trails and Southern crafts to boot-scoot music and Brahms.

Great Itineraries

North Carolina is a large state and touring it comfortably from end to end could easily take two weeks, although you could whiz through in a week. Many people concentrate each trip on one region: mountains, Piedmont, or Coastal Plain. A week could be spent in each of these, but there are many worthwhile trips of shorter duration.

IF YOU HAVE 3 DAYS

Start your tour of the Outer Banks from its north end, coming in on U.S. 158. Drive north on NC 12 your first morning there to spend time in **Corolla,** visiting the Currituck Beach Lighthouse. After lunch head south through **Kitty Hawk, Kill Devil Hills,** and **Nags Head,** with a stop at the Wright Brothers National Memorial. Spend the first night (and the next) on ⊞ **Roanoke Island,** where you'll take the second day to visit historical locations and the North Carolina Aquarium. On Day 3, leave Roanoke and spend the day along the **Cape Hatteras National Seashore,** visiting sights on **Hatteras Island** in the morning and ⊞ **Ocracoke Island** in the afternoon.

IF YOU HAVE 5 DAYS

⊞ **Asheville** is the logical starting point for a tour of the North Carolina mountains. It will take a full first day to cover the Biltmore Estate and neighboring village. Day 2 should be devoted to the attractions south of Asheville, including **Chimney Rock** and the Carl Sandburg Home National Historical Site in **Flat Rock.** Another day back in Asheville will allow you to visit the remaining area attractions, including Pack Place. On the fourth morning begin your journey up the **Blue Ridge Parkway,** lingering at the many scenic stopping points along the way, and arrive in the ⊞ **Boone** area for the night. Day 5 will be occupied with High Country activities, including visiting the Tweetsie Railroad in **Blowing Rock.**

IF YOU HAVE 7 DAYS

With a full week at your disposal, you can do a whirlwind tour from one end of North Carolina to the other. Start your journey in ⊞ **Asheville,** touring the Biltmore Estate. Next head for ⊞ **Charlotte;** be sure to visit Discovery Place and the Mint Museum of Craft + Design during your day here. The Triad and the historical attractions of Old Salem are the focus of the third day; overnight in ⊞ **Winston-Salem.** The next two days will allow time for a taste of the Triangle, including the Duke University campus and Sarah Duke Gardens in **Durham,** the Morehead Planetarium and Franklin Street shopping in **Chapel Hill,** and the museums and capitol area of ⊞ **Raleigh.** Your sixth day should be spent in the Sandhills area enjoying antiques shops and the world-class golf in ⊞ **Pinehurst.** Wind up your visit in ⊞ **Wilmington,** where you can visit the historic downtown and USS *North Carolina* Battleship Memorial or just head for the nearby beaches.

When to Tour North Carolina

North Carolina particularly shines in the spring (April and May) and fall (September and October), when the weather is especially temperate and the trees and flowers burst with color. At these times, you'll avoid the peak tourist season. Summer trips are best spent in the mountains or at the coastal beaches, where temperatures are significantly cooler. In winter many mountain attractions close just as the ski resorts open for the season.

CHARLOTTE

Though Charlotte dates from Revolutionary War times (it is named for King George III's wife, Queen Charlotte), its Uptown is distinctively New South, with gleaming skyscrapers. Uptown encompasses all of downtown Charlotte, its business and cultural heart and soul. It's also home to the government center and some residential neighborhoods. More and more, public art is displayed in the city. Examples of this are the sculptures at the four corners of Trade and Tryon streets. Erected at Independence Square, they symbolize Charlotte's beginnings: a gold miner (commerce), a mill worker (the city's textile heritage), an African-American railroad builder (transportation), and a mother holding her baby aloft (the future). Residents of the Queen City won't hesitate to tell you that theirs is the largest city in the Carolinas and the second-largest banking center in the nation.

Heavy development has created some typical urban problems. Outdated road systems make traffic a nightmare during rush hour, and virtually all the city's restaurants are packed on weekends. But the locals' Southern courtesy is contagious, and people still love the traditional pleasure of picnicking in Freedom Park.

You'll be able to walk around Uptown and the Fourth Ward, and buses are adequate for getting around within the city limits; otherwise, you will need a car to tour.

Numbers in the text correspond to numbers in the margin and on the Charlotte map.

Uptown Charlotte

Uptown Charlotte is ideal for walking. The city was laid out in four wards around Independence Square, at Trade and Tryon streets. The Square, as it is known, is the center of the Uptown area.

A Good Walk

Stop first at **INFO! Charlotte** (⊠ 330 S. Tryon St., ☎ 704/331–2700) for information on a self-guided walking tour of the Fourth Ward (☞ *below*) and a historic tour of Uptown, as well as maps and brochures. You can park your car in an open lot a few blocks east of the Square. Take a stroll north on Tryon Street and enjoy the ambience of this revitalized area, noting the outdoor sculptures on the plazas and the creative architecture of some of the newer buildings, including the **Bank of America Corporate Center** ①.

Walk two blocks west on Trade Street from the Square to the **First Presbyterian Church** (⊠ 200 W. Trade St.) and begin exploring the **Fourth Ward** ②, Charlotte's new "old" city. It's a refreshing change from the newly developed parts of town. The brochure available at INFO! Charlotte (☞ Visitor Information *in* Charlotte A to Z, *below*) leads you to 18 historic sites.

Charlotte

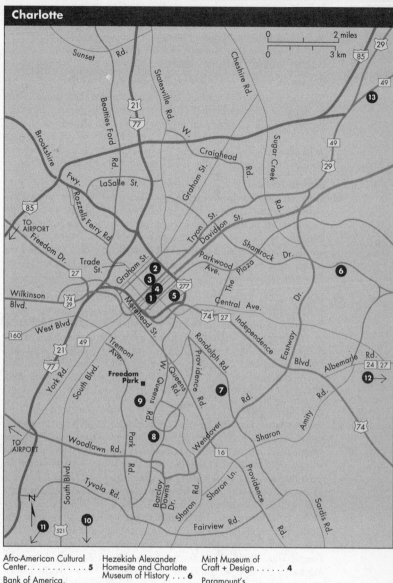

When you're done exploring the Fourth Ward, head south to North Tryon Street just above 6th Street, where you will find the science and technology museum **Discovery Place** ③, a leading attraction. Finish your walk at the new **Mint Museum of Craft + Design** ④, which showcases North Carolina's rich crafts tradition.

TIMING

You can spend a pleasant half day to a day touring these areas. Allow an hour to browse through the Bank of America Corporate Center and Founders Hall. You can tour the Fourth Ward in an hour or so. The bulk of your time will be spent in Discovery Place, which can occupy as much of the day as you wish. You can avoid the workday bustle by visiting on the weekend, but note Discovery Place's Sunday hours.

Sights to See

❶ **Bank of America Corporate Center.** This 60-story structure with a crown-like top designed by Cesar Pelli is one of the city's most striking buildings. Its main attraction is three philosophical frescoes by Ben Long that symbolize the city's past, present, and future. Also in the tower are the **North Carolina Blumenthal Performing Arts Center** and the restaurants, shops, and exhibition space of **Founders Hall.** ⊠ *100 N. Tryon St.*

★ ℃ ❸ **Discovery Place.** At Charlotte's premier attraction, the wonderful hands-on **Science Museum** is a priority; also allow at least two hours for the **aquariums,** the three-story **rain forest,** the **Omnimax theater,** and **Kelly Space Voyager Planetarium,** the largest in the United States. A ham radio room, a puppet theater, and a 10-ft model of an eyeball that you can walk through are other highlights. Check the schedule for special exhibits. ⊠ *301 N. Tryon St.,* ☎ *704/372–6261 or 800/935–0553.* 🎫 *$6.50 for 1 area, plus $3 for any additional area visited.* ☉ *Weekdays 9–5, Sat. 9–6, Sun. 1–6.* 🐾

❷ **Fourth Ward.** Charlotte's popular old neighborhood began as a political subsection created for electoral purposes in the mid-1800s. The architecture and atmosphere of this quiet, homespun neighborhood provide a feeling for life in a less hectic time. A brochure available at INFO! Charlotte (☞ Visitor Information *in* Charlotte A to Z, *below*) includes 18 historic places of interest. Be sure to stop by **Old Settlers Cemetery,** behind the **First Presbyterian Church** (⊠ 200 W. Trade St., ☎ 704/332–5123), which contains tombstones that date from the 1700s. The Gothic Revival church, which takes up a city block and faces West Trade Street, reflects the prosperity of the early settlers and their descendants. **Fourth Ward Park** is an oasis in the middle of the city. **Alexander Michael's** (⊠ 401 W. 9th St., ☎ 704/332–6789) is a favorite eatery. **Poplar Street Books** is housed in the Victorian Young-Morrison House (⊠ 226 W. 10th St.). U.S. president Taft spent the night in the **McNinch House** (⊠ 511 N. Church St.), now a restaurant, when he visited Charlotte in 1909. **Spirit Square** (⊠ 345 N. College St.), in a former church, includes galleries, a performing arts center, and classrooms that used to be the sanctuary for the First Baptist Church. The **public library** (⊠ 310 N. Tryon St.), which contains a mural reproducing a Romare Bearden painting, is open weekdays 9–9, Saturday 9–6, and Sunday 2–6.

❹ **Mint Museum of Craft + Design**. A sister to the Mint Museum of Art (☞ Greater Charlotte, *below*), the museum is in what used to be an upscale women's clothing store. The gallery alone is 16,000 square ft. Add on the permanent collections of ceramics, glass, fiber, metal, and wood, and you have one of the country's major crafts museums. You can use your receipt from the crafts museum to enter the Mint Museum of Art

free on the same day. ⊠ *220 N. Tryon St.,* ☎ *704/337–2000.* 🖾 *$6.*
🕘 *Tues.–Thurs. and Sat. 10–7, Fri. 10–9, Sun. noon–5.*

Greater Charlotte

Beyond Uptown and farther afield lie many of Charlotte's most interesting sights, from gardens to museums. You can reach the ones listed
below by car or by city bus; for visits elsewhere, a car is essential.

A Good Tour

From Uptown, follow 7th Street east and turn north on North Myers
Street to visit the galleries of the **Afro-American Cultural Center** ⑤. Continue east on 7th Street past I–277 to Central Avenue; go east on Central Avenue 3 mi to Eastway Drive, north on Eastway Drive 1½ mi to
Shamrock Drive, and east on Shamrock Drive to the **Hezekiah Alexander Homesite and Charlotte Museum of History** ⑥, where you can see
the county's oldest building. Return west on Shamrock Drive to Eastway Drive and travel south on Eastway Drive past Central Avenue until
it becomes Wendover Road. Continue on Wendover Road 1⅔ mi to
Randolph Road and then turn right on Randolph Road to visit the **Mint
Museum of Art** ⑦, a wide-ranging collection in a former mint. The next
stop, **Wing Haven Gardens and Bird Sanctuary** ⑧, is in Myers Park, a
handsome neighborhood. One approach to this area is to drive north
on Randolph Road to South Laurel Avenue, which leads south to
Providence Road (NC 16). Follow Providence Road south to Queens
Road to Selwyn Avenue and then turn west on Ridgewood Avenue.
More experience with nature can be found at the **Charlotte Nature Museum** ⑨, next to Freedom Park. To get here, continue west on Ridgewood Avenue to Westfield Road, take Westfield Road north to Sterling
Avenue, and then follow Sterling Avenue north to the museum.

TIMING
You can spend a leisurely day touring these sights, which are within a
few miles of each other.

Sights to See

⑤ **Afro-American Cultural Center.** In a historic former church, this center, with its galleries and theater, serves as a showcase for art, music,
drama, and dance. ⊠ *401 N. Myers St.,* ☎ *704/374–1565.* 🖾 *Free.*
🕘 *Tues.–Sat. 10–6, Sun. 1–5.*

🖐 ⑨ **Charlotte Nature Museum.** Though affiliated with Discovery Place, the
museum is in the southeast section of the city. You'll find a butterfly
exhibit, live animals, nature trails, nature films, and hands-on exhibits
just for children. ⊠ *1658 Sterling Ave. (next to Freedom Park),* ☎ *704/
372–0471.* 🖾 *$3.* 🕘 *Weekdays 9–5, Sat. 10–5, Sun. 1–5.*

⑥ **Hezekiah Alexander Homesite and Charlotte Museum of History.** The
stone house, built in 1774, is the oldest dwelling in the county. Alexander and his wife, Mary, reared 10 children in this house and farmed
the land. Costumed docents give guided tours weekdays at 1:15 and
3:15. Seasonal events commemorate the early days. Permanent and rotating exhibits in the museum span 300 years of southern Piedmont
history. ⊠ *3500 Shamrock Dr.,* ☎ *704/568–1774.* 🖾 *Museum $3,
homesite $4, combination ticket $6.* 🕘 *Tues. 10–9, Wed.–Sat. 10–5,
Sun. 1–5.*

★ ⑦ **Mint Museum of Art.** Built in 1836 as a U.S. Mint, this building has
served as a home for art since 1936. Among the holdings in its impressive
permanent collections are American and European paintings, furniture,
and decorative arts; African, pre-Columbian, and Spanish colonial
art; porcelain and pottery; and regional crafts and historic costumes.

You can use your receipt from this museum to enter the Mint Museum of Craft+Design (☞ Uptown Charlotte, *above*) free on the same day. ⊠ *2730 Randolph Rd.,* ☎ *704/337–2000.* ⊡ *$6.* ☉ *Tues. 10–10, Wed.–Sat. 10–5, Sun. noon–5.* ⊛

❽ Wing Haven Gardens and Bird Sanctuary. In Myers Park, one of Charlotte's loveliest neighborhoods, 4 acres of gardens developed by the Clarkson family are home to more than 135 species of birds. ⊠ *248 Ridgewood Ave.,* ☎ *704/331–0664.* ⊡ *Free.* ☉ *Sun. 2–5, Tues. 3–5, Wed. 10–noon, or by appointment.*

Other Area Attractions

Historic sites, a speedway, and a theme park provide plenty to explore beyond the city.

❿ James K. Polk Memorial. A state historic site south of Charlotte marks the humble 1795 birthplace and childhood home of the 11th president. Guided tours of the log cabins (replicas of the originals) are available. ⊠ *308 S. Polk St., Pineville,* ☎ *704/889–7145.* ⊡ *Free.* ☉ *Apr.–Oct., Mon.–Sat. 9–5, Sun. 1–5; Nov.–Mar., Tues.–Sat. 10–4, Sun. 1–4.*

⓭ Lowe's Motor Speedway. Learn all about NASCAR racing, one of the nation's fastest-growing sports, at this state-of-the-art, 167,000-seat facility; browse through the gift shop; or even take a "hot laps" (160 mph) lesson at the track through the **Richard Petty Driving Experience** (☎ *704/455–9443*) or **Fast Track Driving School** (☎ *704/455–1700*). Classes are given year-round except during event weeks in May and October. ⊠ *5555 U.S. 29, Harrisburg, northeast of Charlotte,* ☎ *704/455–3200.* ⊡ *$6.* ☉ *Mon.–Sat. 9–5, Sun. 1–5.*

☙ ⓫ Paramount's Carowinds. A 100-acre amusement park on the South Carolina state line has rides and attractions based on films. Costumed movie characters and actors greet visitors, and the Palladium offers musical concerts with star entertainers. Rides include the heart-stopping Drop Zone. ⊠ *14523 Carowinds Blvd.,* ☎ *704/588–2600 or 800/888–4386.* ⊡ *$35.* ☉ *Apr.–May weekends; June–mid-Aug. daily; mid-Aug.–early Oct., weekends. Park usually opens around 10; closing hrs vary.*

☙ ⓬ Reed Gold Mine State Historic Site. This area, east of Charlotte in Cabarrus County, is where America's first documented gold rush began, following Conrad Reed's discovery of a 17-pound nugget in 1799. Forty-minute guided underground tours of the gold mine are available, as well as seasonal gold panning, walking trails, and a stamp mill. ⊠ *9621 Reed Mine Rd., north of NC 24/27, Locust, follow signs beyond town,* ☎ *704/786–8337.* ⊡ *Free, gold panning $2 per pan.* ☉ *Apr.–Oct., Mon.–Sat. 9–5, Sun. 1–5; Nov.–Mar., Tues.–Sat. 10–4, Sun. 1–4; call for tour schedules.*

Dining

$$$–$$$$ ✕ **Campania.** Warmth is the byword for this restaurant in a country club community. The walls are golden and textured, there is richly toned wood and lots of candlelight, and the music is genuine Italian, from opera to contemporary. The food, too, is about as authentic as it gets outside southern Italy. The *gamberoni Mergellina,* shrimp sautéed in garlic butter and herbs, is sublime. Linguine Posillipo pairs clams with red or white sauce. Veal chops are another main category on the menu. ⊠ *6414 Rea Rd.,* ☎ *704/541–8505. AE, D, MC, V.*

$$$-$$$$ ✕ **Lamplighter.** For years one of Charlotte's destination restaurants,
★ the romantic, sophisticated Lamplighter is in a stucco-and-tile house
built in 1926. The wine list includes 550 vintages, and the menu is far-
ranging, with everything from sushi-grade blackened tuna to roast duck
and marinated ostrich fillet. The quiet, intimate lounge is good for cock-
tails. ✉ 1065 E. Morehead St., ☎ 704/372–5343. Reservations essential.
AE, DC, MC, V.

$$$-$$$$ ✕ **Townhouse.** Chef-owner Étienne Jaulin and his wife, Amanda, serve
exquisitely prepared American cuisine with a French twist. The atmo-
sphere is unassuming; walls are pale rose, and tables are covered with
white linens. The menu shifts frequently as Jaulin encourages sous-chefs
to go to the market and "come back with something fun." The end re-
sult may be thousand-layer salmon terrine or roasted Dover sole with
a sweet pea vanilla sauce. ✉ 1011 Providence Rd., ☎ 704/335–1546.
AE, D, DC, MC, V.

$$-$$$ ✕ **Atlantic Beer & Ice Co.** This Uptown eatery in a sprawling three-story
building has something for everyone: live entertainment, a cigar and
Scotch bar, and billiards tables. The building, with its exposed brick,
dark wood, and big windows, envelopes you. The seasonal menu is
broad: from knockwurst and pastrami sandwiches to beef Stroganoff.
Beef is the best bet. ✉ 330 N. Tryon St., ☎ 704/339–0566. AE, DC,
MC, V.

$$-$$$ ✕ **Providence Café.** The signature purple awnings and trendy fur-
nishings lend atmosphere. The menu may be comfortably predictable,
with chicken, beef, seafood, and pasta, but the focaccia baked daily
on the premises is a standout. It's a great place for Sunday brunch and
live jazz on Wednesday evenings. Two more Providence restaurants have
opened in the city. ✉ 110 Perrin Pl., ☎ 704/376–2008; 15205 John
Jay Delaney Dr., ☎ 704/540–2244; 8708 J. W. Clay Blvd., ☎ 704/549–
0050. AE, D, DC, MC, V.

$$-$$$ ✕ **Thai House.** Fiery pleasure awaits the adventurous diner who sam-
ples from a selection of vegetarian, seafood, and classic Thai dishes.
The food has proved so popular that two more branches have opened.
The satays (skewers of meat, fish, or poultry with peanut sauce) are
mild enough for any taste buds, and you can order many dishes as spicy
or mild as you wish. ✉ 3210 N. Sharon Amity Rd., ☎ 704/532–6868;
Tower Plaza Shopping Center, 8652 Pineville-Matthews Rd., No.
1000, ☎ 704/542–6300; 4918 Central Ave., ☎ 704/535–6716. AE,
D, DC, MC, V.

$-$$$ ✕ **Landmark Diner.** This spacious and informal place in the Eastland
Mall neighborhood is a cut above most other inexpensive restaurants,
and it's open until 3 AM on weeknights and 24 hours on weekends.
The chocolate cream pie is a must-try. ✉ 4429 Central Ave., ☎ 704/
532–1153. Reservations not accepted. AE, DC, MC, V.

$ ✕ **College Place Restaurant.** Simple down-home cookin' and plenty of
it is served for breakfast and lunch (7 AM–3 PM). You have to work to
spend more than $5. Breakfasts in particular are big and offer any com-
bination of eggs, pancakes, grits, bacon, and sausage, to name just a
few items. Lunch has lots of vegetable choices (12), meats, homemade
corn bread, and cobblers. This cafeteria and grill is close to the convention center. ✉ 300 S. College St., ☎ 704/343–9268. No credit cards.
Closed weekends. No dinner.

Lodging

Hotels and Motels

$$$$ ▦ **The Park.** Executives, entertainers, sports stars, and heads of state
★ appreciate the privacy and pampering as well as the parklike setting
of this hotel on a former estate in the southeast corner of the city. An-

tique furnishings, polished marble, and art grace the public areas, and the hotel owns more than 20 paintings by French artist Yolanda Ardisonne. Guest rooms have a residential feel; fabrics are lush and used generously. ⊠ *2200 Rexford Rd., 28211,* ☎ *704/364–8220 or 800/334–0331,* FAX *704/365–4712. 187 rooms, 7 suites. Restaurant, piano bar, in-room data ports, minibars, pool, spa, 18-hole golf course, health club, business services, meeting rooms, airport shuttle. AE, D, DC, MC, V.* ✥

$$$–$$$$ 🏨 **Adam's Mark.** This is the city's largest convention hotel, within walking distance of the convention center. The expansive main lobby, with its woodwork and shades of green and gray, has a clubby feel. Guest rooms are done in blues and plums. Bravo!, its popular signature restaurant, serving northern Italian cuisine, is known for its singing waiters. ⊠ *555 S. McDowell St., 28204,* ☎ *704/372–4100 or 800/444–2326,* FAX *704/348–4646. 631 rooms, 21 suites. Restaurant, bar, in-room data ports, indoor-outdoor pool, sauna, health club, racquetball, dry cleaning, laundry service, concierge, business services, meeting rooms, airport shuttle, free parking. AE, D, DC, MC, V.* ✥

$$–$$$$ 🏨 **Hyatt Charlotte at SouthPark.** The focal point of the four-story atrium is a Mexican water fountain surrounded by 25-ft olive trees. Scalini, the restaurant, serves northern Italian cuisine; the Club piano bar is a favorite. The hotel is within walking distance of the upscale SouthPark Mall (☞ Shopping, *below*). ⊠ *5501 Carnegie Blvd., 28209-3462,* ☎ *704/554–1234 or 800/233–1234,* FAX *704/554–8319. 258 rooms, 4 suites. Restaurant, piano bar, in-room data ports, indoor pool, hot tub, sauna, health club, business services, airport shuttle. AE, D, DC, MC, V.* ✥

$$ 🏨 **Comfort Inn–Lake Norman.** This economy motel, north of Charlotte on I–77 near Lake Norman and Davidson College, offers basic guest rooms with coffeemakers. Some rooms have VCRs, microwaves, and whirlpool baths. Jogging trails are nearby. ⊠ *20740 Torrence Chapel Rd., Cornelius 28031,* ☎ *704/892–3500 or 800/848–9751,* FAX *704/892–6473. 84 rooms, 6 suites. Pool, business services, meeting room. AE, D, DC, MC, V. CP.* ✥

$ 🏨 **Bradley Motel.** Clean and functional is what you get with this motel, which has been family-owned and -operated since 1959. Popular with families and NASCAR fans, the Bradley, near the airport and the coliseum, fills up on race weekends. The rooms are large, with full ceramic baths. Impromptu games of volleyball or horseshoes take place on the lawn outside. ⊠ *4200 S. I–85 Service Rd., 28214,* ☎ *704/392–3206,* FAX *704/392–5040. 21 rooms. AE, D, MC, V.*

Bed-and-Breakfasts

$$$–$$$$ 🏨 **Morehead Inn.** Though it's now a commercial venture catering to corporate clients, this B&B in the Dilworth neighborhood was once a private estate and still has all the comforts of a beautiful home. ⊠ *1122 E. Morehead St., 28204,* ☎ *704/376–3357 or 888/667–3432,* FAX *704/335–1110. 8 rooms, 2 suites, 1 2-bedroom apartment. In-room data ports, meeting rooms. AE, DC, MC, V. CP.* ✥

$$$ 🏨 **Inn Uptown.** The inn, an 1891 brick château on the edge of the historic Fourth Ward neighborhood, is popular because of its proximity to Uptown businesses and attractions. Many rooms have fireplaces. Most fun is the Tower Room, with its spiral staircase leading to a tower with a whirlpool bath and skyline view. ⊠ *129 N. Poplar St., 28202,* ☎ *704/342–2800 or 800/959–1990,* FAX *704/342–2222. 6 rooms. In-room data ports, business services. AE, D, DC, MC, V. BP.* ✥

$$ 🏨 **Homeplace.** This spotless early 20th-century Victorian gem in a res-
★ idential neighborhood has a wraparound porch, fireplaces, and 10-ft ceilings and is full of antiques and memorabilia. Rooms, with four-poster

beds, are country Victorian in style. The no-smoking inn is best for adults and older children. ⊠ *5901 Sardis Rd., 28270,* ☎ *704/365–1936,* 𝖥𝖠𝖷 *704/366–2729. 2 rooms, 1 suite. AE, MC, V. BP.* ❧

Nightlife and the Arts

The Arts

The key venue for performing arts is the **North Carolina Blumenthal Performing Arts Center,** or PAC (⊠ 130 N. Tryon St., ☎ 704/372–1000). It's home to several resident companies, including the Charlotte Symphony Orchestra, North Carolina Dance Theatre, Charlotte Repertory Theatre, and Opera Carolina. PAC also presents national tours of Broadway musicals. The **Spirit Square Center for the Arts & Education** (⊠ 345 N. College St., ☎ 704/372–7469) is an interdisciplinary arts center with classes, exhibits, and national acts such as Wynton Marsalis and Jerry Jeff Walker.

Blockbuster Pavilion (⊠ 707 Pavilion Blvd., ☎ 704/549–1292) spotlights a variety of big-name concerts (Tom Petty, Reba McEntire, N'Sync) from spring through fall. The **Paladium Amphitheater** at Paramount's Carowinds (⊠ 14523 Carowinds Blvd., ☎ 704/588–2600 or 800/888–4386) presents stars in concert from mid-spring through mid-fall.

Nightlife

Comedy Zone (⊠ 5317-A E. Independence Blvd., ☎ 704/568–4242) showcases live comedy nightly except Monday, with two shows Friday and two or three shows Saturday. The **Moon Room** (⊠ 433 S. Tryon St., ☎ 704/342–2003), a dimly lighted, funky bar with a coffeehouse atmosphere, presents a variety of entertainment. Friday and Saturday are reserved for live music. **Ri Ra** (⊠ 208 N. Tryon St., ☎ 704/333–5554), Gaelic for "uproar" or "a lot of fun," is filled with Irish food, ale, and, on Sunday night, live traditional Irish music.

Outdoor Activities and Sports

Participant Sports

CAMPING

Near Charlotte, camping can be found at **McDowell Park and Nature Reserve** (⊠ 15222 York Rd., ☎ 704/588–5224), **Paramount's Carowinds** (⊠ 14523 Carowinds Blvd., off I–77, ☎ 704/588–2600 or 800/888–4386), and **Duke Power State Park** (⊠ Rte. 2, Troutman, ☎ 704/528–6350).

CANOEING

Inlets on Lake Norman and Lake Wylie are ideal for canoeing, as are some spots of the Catawba River. The Pee Dee River east of Charlotte and the New River in the mountains offer other options.

FISHING

You'll find good fishing in Charlotte's neighboring lakes and streams. A mandatory state license can be bought at local bait and tackle shops or over the phone (with a credit card) from the **North Carolina Wildlife Commission** (☎ 919/715–4091).

GOLF

There are more than 50 golf courses within a 40-mi drive of Uptown Charlotte. The *Metrolina Golf Guide,* a free publication available at INFO! Charlotte (☞ *Visitor Information in* Charlotte A to Z, *below*), has a complete list. **Highland Creek Golf Club** (⊠ 7001 Highland Creek Pkwy., ☎ 704/875–9000), an 18-hole, par-72 course with a driving range, is considered by some to be the best public course in Charlotte.

Larkhaven Golf Club (✉ 4801 Camp Stewart Rd., ☎ 704/545–4653) is a championship 18-hole, par-72 course with clubhouse and pro shop. **Paradise Valley Golf Center** (✉ 9309 N. Tryon St., ☎ 704/548–1808), in the university area, has an 18-hole, all par-3 course. The driving range is ½ mi down the street (✉ 9615 N. Tryon St., ☎ 704/548–8114). **Woodbridge Golf Links** (✉ 922 New Camp Creek Church Rd., Kings Mountain, ☎ 704/482–0353), an attractive par-72 course, has 18 holes and a driving range.

SWIMMING

The **Mecklenburg County Aquatic Center** (✉ 800 E. 2nd St., ☎ 704/336–3483) has a 50-meter lap pool, hydrotherapy pool, fitness room, and whirlpool. Open swim times for visitors are 5:30–11 AM, 2–5 PM, and 7–10 PM. The fee is $4.

TENNIS

Tennis courts are available in several Charlotte city parks, including Freedom, Hornet's Nest, Park Road, and Veterans. For details, call the **Charlotte Park and Recreation Department** (☎ 704/336–3854).

Spectator Sports

AUTO RACING

NASCAR races, such as the Coca-Cola 600 and UAW/GM 500, draw huge crowds at the **Lowe's Motor Speedway** (✉ 5555 U.S. 29, Harrisburg, northeast of Charlotte, ☎ 704/455–3200).

BASEBALL

The AAA minor league **Charlotte Knights,** an affiliate of the Chicago White Sox, play from April through August at Knights Castle (✉ 2280 Deerfield Dr., at I–77 and Gold Hill Rd., Fort Mill, SC, ☎ 704/357–8071 or 803/548–8050).

BASKETBALL

The **Charlotte Hornets** NBA team plays from October through April at the Charlotte Coliseum (✉ 100 Hive Dr., ☎ 704/357–0252).

FOOTBALL

The NFL's **Carolina Panthers** play from September to mid-January in the 73,000-seat Ericsson Stadium (✉ 800 S. Mint St., ☎ 704/358–7800).

HOCKEY

The **Charlotte Checkers,** an East Coast Hockey League team, play from mid-October to mid-March at Independence Arena (✉ 2700 E. Independence Blvd., ☎ 704/342–4423).

Shopping

Charlotte is the largest retail center in the Carolinas. The majority of stores are in suburban malls, and villages and towns in outlying areas have regional specialties. Many of the Uptown shops, which can be found in the Overstreet Mall connected by a set of skywalks, are open Monday through Saturday 10–5:30. Most malls are open Monday through Saturday 10–9 and Sunday 1–6. Sales tax is 6%.

Shopping Malls

Carolina Place Mall (✉ 11025 Carolina Place Pkwy., off I–277 at Pineville, ☎ 704/543–9300) is the only Charlotte shopping center with five anchors and interstate access. Ask for a visitor discount card at the customer service center. **Eastland Mall** (✉ 5471 Central Ave., ☎ 704/537–2626), on the east side of town, has an ice-skating rink as well as Belk, Dillard's, JCPenney, Sears, and 112 other retail stores. **SouthPark Mall** (✉ 4400 Sharon Rd., ☎ 704/364–4411), in the most affluent section of the city, offers high-end stores such as Tiffany's, Pottery Barn, Coach, Eddie Bauer, and Godiva Chocolatier.

Concord Mills (⊠ 15 mi north of Charlotte, intersection of I–85 and Concord Mills Blvd., Concord, ☎ 704/979–3000 or 877/626–4557) has more than 200 stores and theme restaurants, a 24-screen movie theater, arcades, and even a waterfall and trout pond, arranged around a 1-mi oval walking lane.

The **Outlet Marketplace** (⊠ off I–77, Fort Mill, SC, 1 mi south of Charlotte, ☎ 704/377–8630) carries well-known brands at a discount.

Specialty Stores
ANTIQUES

The towns of Waxhaw, Pineville, and Matthews are the best places to find antiques. Waxhaw sponsors an annual antiques fair each February. Shops are usually open from Monday through Saturday in Pineville and Matthews. In Waxhaw, some shops are open on Sunday but closed on Monday. You can find a good selection of antiques and collectibles at the sprawling **Metrolina Expo** (⊠ off I–77N at 7100 N. Statesville Rd., ☎ 704/596–4643 or 800/824–3770) on the first and third weekends of the month.

BOOKS AND MAGAZINES

The locally owned and operated **Little Professor Book Center** (⊠ Park Road Shopping Center, 4139 Park Rd., ☎ 704/525–9239; South Lake Shopping Center, Lake Norman, ☎ 704/896–7323) has a good selection of contemporary fiction and classics. **Newsstand International** (⊠ 5622–128 E. Independence Blvd., ☎ 704/531–0199) carries hardbacks, newspapers, maps, and magazines from around the world.

CRAFTS

The best Charlotte crafts buys are in the **Metrolina Expo** (☞ Antiques, *above*). A number of shows, including the Carolina Craft Shows, held in the fall and spring at the convention center, as well as the Southern Christmas Show and the Southern Spring Show at the Merchandise Mart, showcase a wide variety of items.

FOOD AND PLANTS

The **Charlotte Regional Farmers Market** (⊠ 1801 Yorkmount Rd., ☎ 704/357–1269) sells produce, fish, plants, and crafts.

Charlotte A to Z

Arriving and Departing
BY BUS

Greyhound/Carolina Trailways (⊠ 601 W. Trade St., ☎ 704/372–0456 or 800/231–2222) serves the Charlotte area.

BY CAR

Charlotte is a transportation hub; I–77 comes in from Columbia, South Carolina, to the south and then continues north to Virginia, intersecting I–40 on the way. I–85 arrives from Greenville, South Carolina, to the southwest and then goes northeast to meet I–40 between Winston-Salem and the Triangle. From the Triangle, I–85 continues northeast to Petersburg, Virginia.

BY PLANE

Charlotte-Douglas International Airport (⊠ 5501 Josh Birmingham Blvd., ☎ 704/359–4013) is west of the city off I–85. American, British Airways, Delta, Northwest, TWA, United, US Airways, and their local affiliates serve the facility. For airline telephone numbers, *see* Air Travel *in* Smart Travel Tips A to Z.

Taxis from the airport cost about $15 ($2 each additional person), and airport vans are approximately $8 per person to Uptown. Most major hotels provide complimentary transportation. By car, take the Billy Graham Parkway, then Wilkinson Boulevard (U.S. 74) east to I–277, which leads to the heart of Uptown.

BY TRAIN

Amtrak (✉ 1914 N. Tryon St., ☎ 704/376–4416 or 800/872–7245) offers daily service from Charlotte to Washington, D.C., Atlanta, and points beyond, and there's daily service to cities in the Triangle.

Getting Around

BY BUS

Center City Circuit (☎ 704/332–2227) operates free shuttle service throughout Uptown on weekdays beginning at 7 and 7:30 AM. Look for the Uptown Circuit street signs. **Charlotte Transit** (☎ 704/336–3366) provides public transportation throughout the city. Fares are $1 for local rides and $1.40 for express service within Charlotte.

BY TAXI

Crown Cab (☎ 704/334–6666) and **Yellow Cab** (☎ 704/332–6161) have taxis and airport vans. **University Towncar** (☎ 704/553–2424 or 888/553–2424) caters to business travelers. You won't pay more for the company's flat rate than you would for a cab ride.

Contacts and Resources

EMERGENCIES

Ambulance, police (☎ 911).

GUIDED TOURS

The *Catawba Queen* paddle wheeler (✉ U.S. 150, Exit 36, Mooresville, ☎ 704/663–2628) gives dinner cruises and tours on Lake Norman. Reservations are essential.

HOSPITALS

Carolinas Medical Center (✉ 1001 Blythe Blvd., ☎ 704/355–2000). **Presbyterian Hospital** (✉ 200 Hawthorne La., ☎ 704/384–4000).

LATE-NIGHT PHARMACY

Eckerd Drugs (✉ Park Road Shopping Center, ☎ 704/523–3031; 3740 E. Independence Blvd., ☎ 704/536–3600).

RADIO STATIONS

AM: WBT 1110, news, talk, sports; WFNZ 610, all sports. **FM:** WSOC 103.7, country; WFAE 90.7, National Public Radio; WXRC 95.7, rock.

VISITOR INFORMATION

INFO! Charlotte (✉ 330 S. Tryon St., ☎ 704/331–2700 or 800/231–4636) is open weekdays 8:30–5, Saturday 10–4, and Sunday 1–4.

THE TRIAD

Greensboro, Winston-Salem, High Point

North Carolinians group six urban centers in the Piedmont into two threesomes: the Triad and the Triangle (☞ *below*). Although this shorthand is a verbal convenience, it's also testament that the whole can be greater than the sum of the parts. Make no mistake, though: Although they share geography and are scattered along the major arteries of the region, the Triad's major cities have very distinct personalities. Greensboro, to the east, bustles as a business center. Smaller Winston-Salem, to the west, will catch you by surprise with its eclectic arts scene. High

Point, to the south, has managed to fuse the simplicity of Quaker fore-bears with its role as a world-class furniture market.

Greensboro

96 mi northeast of Charlotte, 26 mi east of Winston-Salem, 58 mi west of Durham.

With 200,000 citizens, Greensboro is the largest population center in the Triad, and thanks to spacious convention facilities it's an increasingly popular destination for business travelers. Yet this city, named in honor of General Nathanael Greene, a Revolutionary War hero, takes pride in its role in American history and has taken great pains to preserve and showcase the sights of past eras.

With the exception of Old Greensborough and the downtown historic district, however, walking is not a comfortable sightseeing option. To tour the grand historic homes, glimpse monuments to famous native sons and daughters—Dolley Madison, Edward R. Murrow, O. Henry— or visit one of the many recreation areas, you'll need a car.

Guilford Courthouse National Military Park, the nation's first Revolutionary War park, has monuments, military memorabilia, and more than 200 acres with wooded hiking trails. It memorializes one of the earliest events in the city's history. On March 15, 1781, the Battle of Guilford Courthouse so weakened British troops that they surrendered seven months later at Yorktown. Today many families use the 3 mi of foot trails. ⊠ *2332 New Garden Rd.,* ☎ *336/288–1776.* ⚏ *Free.* ⚘ *Daily 8:30–5.*

Tannenbaum Park, a hands-on history experience near Guilford Courthouse National Military Park, draws you into the life of early settlers. With advance notice costumed re-enactors will escort you through exhibits at the **Colonial Heritage Center** in the visitor center. The restored **1778 Hoskins House** (tours by appointment) and a blacksmith shop and barn are on the property. The park has one of the most outstanding collections of original colonial settlement maps in the country. ⊠ *Visitor center, New Garden Rd. and Battleground Ave.,* ☎ *336/545–5315.* ⚏ *Free.* ⚘ *Tues.–Fri. 9–5, Sat. 10–5, Sun. 1–5.*

Roam through a dinosaur gallery, learn about gems and minerals, and see the lemurs, snakes, and amphibians at the **Natural Science Center of Greensboro.** There's also a planetarium and a petting zoo. ⊠ *4301 Lawndale Dr., adjacent to Country Park,* ☎ *336/288–3769.* ⚏ *$3.50, planetarium $1, prices subject to change for special exhibits and events.* ⚘ *Science center Mon.–Sat. 9–5, Sun. 12:30–5; zoo Mon.–Sat. 10–4:30, Sun. 12:30–4:30.*

The **Greensboro Historical Museum,** in a Romanesque church built in 1892, has exhibits about native son and daughter O. Henry and Dolley Madison, as well as one about the Woolworth sit-in that helped launch the national civil rights movement in the 1960s. ⊠ *130 Summit Ave.,* ☎ *336/373–2043.* ⚏ *Free.* ⚘ *Tues.–Sat. 10–5, Sun. 2–5.*

Greensboro Cultural Center at Festival Park, an architectural showplace, houses 25 visual and performing arts organizations, five art galleries, rehearsal halls, a sculpture garden, a restaurant with outdoor café-style seating, and an outdoor amphitheater. **ArtQuest,** developed by educators and artists, is North Carolina's only permanent interactive children's art gallery. ⊠ *200 N. Davie St.,* ☎ *336/373–2712.* ⚏ *Free.* ⚘ *Weekdays 8 AM–10 PM, Sat. 9–6, Sun. 1–6:30.*

☾ Exhibits and activities at the **Greensboro Children's Museum** are designed for children under 12. They can tour an airplane cockpit with an interactive screen, dig for buried treasure, or wrap themselves in a gigantic bubble. ✉ *220 N. Church St.,* ☎ *336/574–2898.* ☞ *$5.50.* ☺ *Labor Day–Memorial Day, Tues.–Sat. 9–5, Sun. 1–5; Memorial Day–Labor Day, Mon. 9–5.*

Elm Street, with its turn-of-the-20th-century architecture, is the heart of **Old Greensborough** (✉ 100 block of N. Elm St. to 600 block of S. Elm St., with portions of several other streets), which is listed on the National Register of Historic Places. Stop by the William Fields House, headquarters for the **Old Greensborough Preservation Society** (✉ 447 Arlington St., ☎ 336/272–6617), to collect your self-guided tour map. The entire tour may be walked in two hours.

In Old Greensborough, the elegant **Blandwood Mansion,** home of former governor John Motley Morehead, is considered the prototype of the Italian villa architecture that swept the country during the mid-19th century. Designed by noted architect Alexander Jackson Davis, the house still contains many of its original furnishings. ✉ *447 W. Washington St.,* ☎ *336/272–5003.* ☞ *$5.* ☺ *Tues.–Sat. 11–2, Sun. 2–5.*

The **Weatherspoon Art Gallery,** on the campus of the University of North Carolina–Greensboro, consists of six galleries and a sculpture courtyard. It is nationally recognized for its collection and changing exhibitions of 20th-century American art. The permanent collection includes lithographs and bronzes by Henri Matisse. ✉ *Corner of Tate and Spring Garden Sts.,* ☎ *336/334–5770.* ☞ *Free.* ☺ *Tues. and Thurs.–Fri. 10–5, Wed. 10–8, weekends 1–5.*

Dining and Lodging

$$$–$$$$ ✕ **Paisley Pineapple.** The dining is formal in this romantic Old Greensborough restaurant in a restored 1920s building. The fare on the extensive menu—rack of lamb, grilled veal tenderloin, and sautéed beef tenderloin—tends toward the hearty. On the lighter side are the soups (try the berry bisque if it's available) and seafood. Don't miss the cinnamon-seared salmon. Upstairs, there's a bar with sofas and background music. ✉ *345 S. Elm St.,* ☎ *336/279–8488. AE, MC, V.*

$$–$$$$ ✕ **Gate City Chop House.** This place has a lock on the upscale, everything-is-bigger-here steak house concept in the Triad. The look is masculine and clubby and the portions are geared toward large appetites. Beef is the star to be sure, but there's good to say about other menu items, such as seafood—try the shrimp bisque—and salads. The wine list is respectable. ✉ *106 S. Holden Rd.,* ☎ *336/294–9977. AE, D, DC, MC, V. Closed Sun.*

$$–$$$$ ✕ **Lo Spiedo di Noble.** Murals adorn some walls, and from the upstairs seating area you can see the wood-burning tile oven and the slowly turning spit that turn out Tuscan cuisine such as rack of pork with fresh peach-walnut-thyme compote on a bed of white beans and red chard. The piano bar on the lower level is a nice way to end the evening. A jazz trio plays Wednesday through Saturday evenings. ✉ *172 Battleground Ave.,* ☎ *336/333–9833. AE, D, MC, V.*

$$–$$$ ✕ **Casaldi's Cafe.** Light gray-green is the predominant color in this sleek little trattoria, appearing in the tile floors as well as marble countertops. Wildflowers decorate the tables, and display cases provide a powerful lure to sample the myriad pasta dishes. Particularly popular are the spinach and walnut ravioli and the bow-tie pasta with chicken and mushrooms. ✉ *1310 Westover Terr.,* ☎ *336/379–8191. Reservations not accepted. D, MC, V. Closed Sun.*

$$$$ ⚅ **O. Henry Hotel.** Named for a famous native son, this is one of the newest and grandest establishments on the city's lodging scene. The decor is somewhat evocative of the Arts and Crafts style, with wood, tapestries, and upholstery in warm tones. Particularly nice touches are the oversize rooms, tiled bathrooms with standing shower stalls and separate tubs, and bed coverlets that are laundered daily. A complimentary breakfast buffet is offered in a sunny pavilion overlooking a small garden. ✉ *624 Green Valley Rd., 27408,* ☎ *336/854–2000,* FAX *336/854–2223. 121 rooms, 10 suites. Restaurant, breakfast room, in-room data ports, in-room safes, refrigerators, room service, pool, exercise room, laundry service, business services, meeting rooms, airport shuttle. AE, D, DC, MC, V. BP.*

$$$ ⚅ **Sheraton Greensboro Hotel at Four Seasons/Joseph S. Koury Convention Center.** Business travelers are the mainstay here, at the state's largest hotel. Accommodations are standard fare, but the hotel and its nearby sister property, the Park Lane Hotel (☎ 336/294–4565), are convenient to major thoroughfares and the Four Seasons Town Centre (☞ Shopping, *below*), a three-story regional mall. ✉ *3121 High Point Rd., 27407,* ☎ *336/292–9161 or 800/242–6556,* FAX *336/292–1407. 1,014 rooms, 78 suites. 4 restaurants, 4 bars, in-room data ports, pool, wading pool, exercise room, racquetball, nightclub, video games, business services, convention center, meeting rooms, airport shuttle, kennel. AE, D, DC, MC, V.* ☻

$$ ⚅ **Biltmore Greensboro Hotel.** In the heart of the central business dis-
★ trict, the Biltmore has an old-world feel, with 16-ft ceilings, a cage elevator, and a lobby area with walnut-paneled walls and a fireplace. Some guest rooms have Victorian or Victorian-style furniture and electric candle sconces. Rates include evening wine and cheese. ✉ *111 W. Washington St., 27401,* ☎ *336/272–3474 or 800/332–0303,* FAX *336/275–2523. 21 rooms, 4 suites. In-room data ports, minibars, refrigerators, business services, meeting room, airport shuttle. AE, D, DC, MC, V. CP.* ☻

$$ ⚅ **Greenwood Bed and Breakfast.** Eclectic antiques, art, and various other collections fill this 1905 Craftsman-style home in historic Fisher Park. Owners Bob (a former New Orleans chef) and Dolly (a decorator) Guertin serve a full breakfast at the time of your choosing. Café au lait, French bread, eggs Benedict, and crepes suzette come with freshly squeezed orange juice and fruit. Desserts are set out in the evening. This no-smoking B&B is best for older children. ✉ *205 N. Park Dr., 27401,* ☎ *336/274–6350 or 800/535–9363,* FAX *336/274–9943. 5 rooms. Pool, meeting rooms. AE, D, DC, MC, V. BP.*

Nightlife and the Arts

The **Broach Theatre** (✉ 520 S. Elm St., ☎ 336/378–9300) has professional adult (March–June and September–December) and children's (September–June) theater in the Old Greensborough historic district. The **Carolina Theatre** (✉ 310 S. Greene St., ☎ 336/333–2600), a restored vaudeville venue, serves as one of the city's principal performing arts centers, showcasing dance, concerts, films, and plays. The **Greensboro Symphony** (☎ 336/333–7490) and the **Greensboro Opera Company** (☎ 336/273–9472) perform at the Greensboro Coliseum Complex (☞ *below*).

The vast **Greensboro Coliseum Complex** (✉ 1921 W. Lee St., ☎ 336/373–7474) hosts arts and entertainment events throughout the year as well as professional, college, and amateur sports.

The **Eastern Music Festival** (✉ 200 N. Davie St., ☎ 336/333–7450), whose alumni include Wynton Marsalis, brings six weeks of classical music concerts to Greensboro in summer.

Outdoor Activities and Sports

BASEBALL

The **Greensboro Bats,** the Class A farm club for the New York Yankees, play April through September at War Memorial Stadium (⊠ corner of Lindsay and Yanceyville Sts., ☎ 336/333–2287).

CAMPING

Some good choices are **Greensboro KOA** (⊠ 2300 Montreal Ave., ☎ 336/274–4143 or 800/562–4143), **Hagan-Stone Park** (⊠ 5920 Hagan-Stone Rd., ☎ 336/674–0472), and **Outdoor Center YMCA** (⊠ 4924 Tapawingo Trail, ☎ 336/697–0525).

GOLF

Golfers can choose from among 27 public courses and four driving ranges. **Bryan Park and Golf Club** (⊠ 6275 Bryan Park Rd., Browns Summit, ☎ 336/375–2200) is a highly regarded non-metal-spike, par-72 course north of Greensboro. The **Grandover Resort/Grandover Golf Club** (⊠ One Thousand Club Dr., ☎ 336/294–1800 or 800/472–6301) has two par-72 courses. The **Greensboro National Golf Club** (⊠ 330 Niblick Dr., Summerfield, ☎ 336/342–1113), 15 minutes north of Greensboro, is a par-72 course.

The PGA's **Greater Greensboro Chrysler Classic** is held each April at the Forest Oaks Country Club (⊠ U.S. 421S, ☎ 336/379–1570).

HIKING

The **Bog Garden** (⊠ on Hobbs Rd. north of Friendly Ave., ☎ 336/373–2199) has an elevated wooden walkway through a swampy area with more than 8,000 individually labeled trees, shrubs, ferns, and wildflowers. There are walking trails and an exercise course at the 120-acre **Oka T. Hester Park** (⊠ 910 Ailanthus St., ☎ 336/373–2937).

TENNIS

Greensboro Jaycee Park (⊠ Forest Lawn Dr. off Pisgah Church Rd., adjacent to Country Park, ☎ 336/545–5342) has sports facilities including a tennis center with 12 soft championship courts.

Shopping

OUTLET CENTERS

The 50 stores at the **Burlington Manufacturers Outlet Center** (⊠ off Exit 145 at I–85, ☎ 336/227–2872) make the area off I–85 near Burlington (about 20 mi east of Greensboro) a mecca for bargain hunters.

SHOPPING DISTRICTS AND MALLS

Four Seasons Town Centre (⊠ I–40 at High Point Rd., ☎ 336/292–0171) holds more than 200 major stores, specialty shops, restaurants, a first-run movie theater, a US Airways ticket office, and a post office. Head to **Old Greensborough** (☞ Greensboro, *above*) for antiques shops and bookstores.

SPECIALTY STORES

Replacements, Ltd. (⊠ I–85/40 at Mt. Hope Church Rd., Exit 132, ☎ 800/737–5223), the world's largest retailer of discontinued and active china, crystal, flatware, and collectibles, stocks nearly 6 million pieces of inventory and 125,000 patterns. The cavernous showroom is open 8–9 daily and free tours are given.

Side Trips from Greensboro

CHARLOTTE HAWKINS BROWN MEMORIAL STATE HISTORIC SITE
10 mi east of Greensboro.

On the site of the Palmer Institute, the memorial honors the African-American woman who founded the school in 1902. Before closing in 1971, this accredited preparatory school for African-Americans was recognized as one of the country's best and had expanded to more than 350 acres of land. There is a visitor center and a gift shop. ⊠ *6136 Burlington Rd., Sedalia, off I–85, Exit 135,* ☎ *336/449–4846.* 🖾 *Free.* ⊙ *Oct.–Apr., Tues.–Fri. 10–4, Sun. 1–4; May–Sept., Mon.–Sat. 9–5, Sun. 1–5.*

CHINQUA-PENN PLANTATION
★ *25 mi north of Greensboro.*

The **Chinqua-Penn Plantation,** a National Historic Register English-country mansion, was built by tobacco and utility magnates Jeff and Betsy Penn in 1925. The Penns, world travelers, filled the 27-room house with an eclectic collection of artifacts representing 30 countries. The estate also has a Chinese pagoda, a three-story clock tower, greenhouses, and formal gardens—even a cemetery for all the Penns' beloved dogs. ⊠ *2138 Wentworth St., Reidsville,* ☎ *336/349–4576 or 800/948–0947.* 🖾 *$13.* ⊙ *Mar.–Dec., Tues.–Sat. 9–5, Sun. noon–5.* 🐾

Winston-Salem

81 mi north of Charlotte, 26 mi west of Greensboro.

Winston-Salem residents' donations to the arts are among the highest per capita in the nation: The city bills itself as the City of the Arts, and its museums show the benefits of this support. The North Carolina School of the Arts commands international attention. Salem College, the oldest women's college in the country, is here, as is Wake Forest University, where writer Maya Angelou teaches. Old Salem, a restored 18th-century Moravian town within the city, has been a popular attraction since the early 1950s.

Staff at the **Winston-Salem Visitor Center** (⊠ 601 N. Cherry St., ☎ 336/777–3796 or 800/331–7018) will assist with directions and help you make dining and lodging reservations.

★ Founded in 1766 as a Moravian Congregation town and backcountry trading center, **Old Salem** has become one of the nation's most authentic and well-documented colonial sites. At this living history museum with more than 80 restored and original buildings, costumed interpreters re-create household activities and trades common in Salem in the late 18th and early 19th centuries. You can participate in African-American programs that include a stop by St. Philip's Church, the state's oldest-standing African-American church. Old Salem is home to museum shops, the Old Salem Furniture & Accessories Shop, the 1816 Salem Tavern restaurant, and the Winkler Bakery (don't pass up the Moravian sugar cake). The village is a few blocks from downtown Winston-Salem and near Business I–40 (take the Old Salem/Salem College exit). ⊠ *600 S. Main St.,* ☎ *336/721–7300 or 888/653–7253.* 🖾 *$15; combination ticket with Museum of Early Southern Decorative Arts (☞ below) $20.* ⊙ *Mon.–Sat. 9–5, Sun. 12:30–5.* 🐾

★ The **Museum of Early Southern Decorative Arts (MESDA),** on the southern edge of Old Salem, is the only museum dedicated to exhibiting and researching the regional decorative arts of the early South. Twenty-four intricately detailed period rooms and six galleries showcase the furniture, painting, ceramics, and metalware made and used regionally through 1820. The bookstore carries current and hard-to-find books on Southern decorative arts, culture, and history. ⊠ *924 S. Main St.,* ☎ *336/721–7360 or 888/653–7253.* 🖾 *$10; combination ticket with Old Salem (☞ above) $20.* ⊙ *Mon.–Sat. 10:30–4:30, Sun. 1:30–4:30.* 🐾

☾ The **SciWorks** complex includes a 120-seat planetarium, 15-acre Environmental Park, and 45,000 square ft of exhibits that are interactive or hands-on, including the Coastal Encounters wet lab. ⊠ *400 W. Hanes Mill Rd.,* ☎ *336/767–6730.* ⊠ *Museum $7, the Works (planetarium, park, and museum) $8.* ⊙ *Mon.–Sat. 10–5.*

You can take a guided tour through the exhibits on tobacco growing and auctioning at **R. J. Reynolds Whitaker Park,** view historical memorabilia related to the tobacco industry, and visit the gift shop. Tours of the factory floor are no longer offered, however. ⊠ *1100 Reynolds Blvd.,* ☎ *336/741–5718.* ⊠ *Free.* ⊙ *Weekdays 8–6.*

🕲 **Historic Bethabara Park,** set in a wooded 195 acres, is the site of the first Moravian settlement (1753) in North Carolina. Bethabara—meaning "house of passage"—was to be temporary until the town of Salem was established. You can tour restored buildings such as the 1788 congregation house and explore the foundations of the town. Children love the reconstructed fort from the French and Indian War and the wildlife preserve. ⊠ *2147 Bethabara Rd.,* ☎ *336/924–8191.* ⊠ *$1.* ⊙ *Exhibit buildings Apr.–Nov., weekdays 9:30–4:30, weekends 1:30–4:30; guided tours Apr.–Nov. or by appointment. Brochures for self-guided walking tour available year-round at visitor center.*

The **Museum of Anthropology** has exhibits of peoples and cultures of the Americas, Asia, Africa, and Oceania. The Museum Shop holds special sales in May and December. ⊠ *Wake Forest University, Reynolda campus, Wingate Rd.,* ☎ *336/758–5282.* ⊠ *Free.* ⊙ *Tues.–Sat. 10–4:30.*

Reynolda House Museum of American Art, formerly the home of tobacco magnate Richard Joshua Reynolds and his wife, Katherine, is filled with American paintings, prints, and sculptures by such artists as Thomas Eakins, Frederick Church, and Georgia O'Keeffe. There's also a costume collection, as well as vintage clothing and toys used by the Reynolds children. The museum is next to **Reynolda Village,** a collection of shops, restaurants, and gardens that fill the estate's original outer buildings. ⊠ *2250 Reynolda Rd.,* ☎ *336/725–5325.* ⊠ *$6.* ⊙ *Tues.–Sat. 9:30–4:30, Sun. 1:30–4:30.*

Exhibits at the **Southeastern Center for Contemporary Art (SECCA),** near Reynolda House, showcase regional arts and crafts as well as works by nationally known artists. The Centershop sells many one-of-a-kind pieces. ⊠ *750 Marguerite Dr.,* ☎ *336/725–1904.* ⊠ *$3.* ⊙ *Tues.–Sat. 10–5, Sun. 2–5.*

Just south of the city, **Tanglewood Park,** the home of the late William and Kate Reynolds, is now open to the public; in addition to golfing, boating, hiking, fishing, horseback riding, and swimming, it puts on a holiday lights festival, the largest such display in the Southeast. The **Tanglewood Festival of Lights** runs from mid-November to mid-January annually. ⊠ *U.S. 158 off I–40, Clemmons,* ☎ *336/778–6300.* ⊠ *$2 per car, separate fees for each activity.* ⊙ *Daily dawn–dusk.*

Dining and Lodging

$$$–$$$$ ✕ **Southbound Bistro and Grille.** Housed in a building erected in 1913 as the headquarters for Southbound Railway, this restaurant is anything but old-fashioned. It has a weekly-changing menu, with everything from grilled steak with fried sweet potatoes to grilled ostrich topped with honeyed onions and spicy cantaloupe chutney. ⊠ *300 S. Liberty St.,* ☎ *336/723–0322. AE, MC, V. Closed Sun. No lunch Sat.*

$$–$$$$ ✕ **Noble's Grille.** French and Mediterranean flavors influence the menu, which changes nightly. Entrées are grilled or roasted over an oak-and-hickory fire, from braised rabbit with black-pepper fettuccine to Carolina *poussin* (young chicken) with polenta. The dining room,

with tall windows and track lighting, has a view of the kitchen grill. ⊠ *380 Knollwood St.,* ☎ *336/777–8477. AE, DC, MC, V.*

$$$ ✕ **Leon's Café.** This eatery in a renovated building near Old Salem serves some of the best food in town—fresh seafood, chicken breasts with raspberry sauce, lamb, and other specialties. The restaurant's dark colors are set off by artwork and lacy window treatments. ⊠ *924 S. Marshall St.,* ☎ *336/725–9593. AE, D, MC, V.*

$$–$$$ ✕ **Old Salem Tavern Dining Room.** Although Moravian dishes such as chicken potpie and sauerbraten are the highlight of the lunch menu, dinner is more varied. In the warm months drinks are served under the arbor, and open-air seating draws diners to the covered back porch. ⊠ *736 S. Main St.,* ☎ *336/748–8585. AE, MC, V.*

$$–$$$ ✕ **The Vineyards.** The innovative seasonal menu, with such dishes as grilled swordfish on a bed of black-eyed-pea salsa, and stuffed eggplant, attracts diners to this Reynolda Village restaurant. Locals have voted the homemade bread pudding the best in town. ⊠ *120 Reynolda Village Rd.,* ☎ *336/748–0269. AE, MC, V.*

$$–$$$$ ☷ **Adam's Mark Winston Plaza Hotel.** Centrally located off I–40, the hotel is housed in two towers connected by a climate-controlled skywalk. The East Tower has a traditional look while the West Tower is a bit sleeker and more contemporary. The Cherry Street Bar, with its smoothly tailored living-room atmosphere, is a great place to relax. ⊠ *425 N. Cherry St., 27101,* ☎ *336/725–3500 or 800/444–2326,* ℻ *336/721–2240. 605 rooms, 26 suites. Restaurant, 2 bars, in-room data ports, room service, indoor pool, sauna, steam room, exercise room, dry cleaning, laundry service, business services, meeting rooms, parking (fee). AE, D, DC, MC, V.* ❧

$$–$$$$ ☷ **Henry F. Shaffner House.** Accessible to downtown and Old Salem, this B&B is a favorite with business travelers and honeymooning couples. The rooms in the restored English Tudor house are furnished in 19th-century Victorian elegance. Rates include breakfast as well as afternoon tea and evening wine and cheese. ⊠ *150 S. Marshall St., 27101,* ☎ *336/777–0052 or 800/952–2256,* ℻ *336/777–1188. 9 rooms. Restaurant, in-room data ports, business services, meeting room. AE, MC, V. BP, CP.*

$$$ ☷ **Brookstown Inn.** Handmade quilts, two-person tubs, and wine and cheese or freshly baked cookies in the lobby are amenities at this inn, built in 1837 as a textile mill. ⊠ *200 Brookstown Ave., 27101,* ☎ *336/725–1120 or 800/845–4262,* ℻ *336/773–0147. 40 rooms, 31 suites. In-room data ports, business services, meeting rooms. AE, DC, MC, V. CP.*

$–$$ ☷ **Tanglewood Manor House Bed & Breakfast.** The former home of a branch of the Reynolds family includes 10 rooms in the antiques-filled manor house, 18 rooms in a more contemporary motel behind the house, and four cottages on Mallard Lake in Tanglewood Park. Those staying in the motel can purchase the Continental breakfast served in the manor house. Admissions to the park and swimming pool are included; a fishing license is extra. Greens fees at park courses are discounted. ⊠ *U.S. 158 off I–40, Clemmons 27012,* ☎ *336/778–6300,* ℻ *336/778–6379. 28 rooms, 4 cottages, guest house. Picnic area, pool, wading pool, driving range, 2 18-hole golf courses, horseback riding, fishing, playground, meeting rooms. AE, DC, MC, V. CP.* ❧

$–$$ ☷ **Comfort Inn–Cloverdale.** Off I–40 Business near downtown and Old Salem, this immaculately kept property has rooms with microwaves and refrigerators. ⊠ *110 Miller St., 27103,* ☎ *336/721–0220 or 800/228–5150,* ℻ *336/723–2117. 122 rooms. In-room data ports, pool, sauna, exercise room, meeting room. AE, D, DC, MC, V. CP.* ❧

Nightlife and the Arts

THE ARTS

Many North Carolina School of the Arts musical and dramatic performances are held at the **Stevens Center** (⊠ 405 W. 4th St., ☎ 336/721–1945), a restored 1929 movie palace downtown that is part of the NCSA campus. The Broadway Preview Series shows first-run productions before they move on to Broadway engagements.

NIGHTLIFE

Burke Street Pub (⊠ 1110 Burke St., ☎ 336/750–0097) is an Irish-style pub with music, dancing, games, and sports TV. In the Adam's Mark Winston Plaza, the **Cherry Street Bar** (⊠ 425 N. Cherry St., ☎ 336/725–3500) has cozy chairs and smart decor. **Lucky 32** (⊠ 109 S. Stratford Rd., ☎ 336/777–0032), a fine bar adjoining a restaurant, caters to a professional crowd.

Outdoor Activities and Sports

BASEBALL

The **Winston-Salem Warthogs,** a Class A affiliate of the Chicago White Sox, play from April through August at Ernie Shore Field (⊠ 401 Deacon Blvd., ☎ 336/759–2233).

BASKETBALL

Winston-Salem's Atlantic Coast Conference entry is the Wake Forest University **Demon Deacons** (☎ 336/758–3322 or 888/758–3322).

GOLF

Tanglewood Park Golf Club (⊠ NC 158, Clemmons, ☎ 336/778–6320) has two fine 18-hole, par-72 courses, the Reynolds Course and the Championship Course, where the Vantage Championship is played each year. **Reynolds Park Golf Course** (⊠ 2931 Reynolds Park Rd., ☎ 336/650–7660) has 18 holes with a view of the city skyline and a par 71.

Shopping

SHOPPING DISTRICTS AND MALLS

The **Art District** at 6th and Trade streets (just behind the Winston-Salem Visitor Center) has several galleries and arts-and-crafts shops. **Reynolda Village** is near the Reynolda House Museum of American Art (☞ Winston-Salem, *above*). **Stratford Place,** a collection of upscale shops, restaurants, and cafés, is off I–40 Business in the Five Points area, where Country Club, Miller Road, and 1st Street converge.

At 1.8 million square ft, and with more than 200 stores, **Hanes Mall** (⊠ Silas Creek Pkwy. and Hanes Mall Blvd.) is one of the largest indoor malls in the Carolinas.

CRAFTS

All items at the **Piedmont Craftsmen's Shop and Gallery** (⊠ 1204 Reynolda Rd., ☎ 336/725–1516) are juried. An annual fair is held in November. **erl Originals** (⊠ 3069 Trenwest Dr., ☎ 336/760–4363), near I–40 and Hanes Mall, has 8,000 square ft of gallery space and represents more than 300 artists.

High Point

76 mi northeast of Charlotte, 20 mi southwest of Greensboro.

Originally settled by Quakers in the 1700s, High Point was incorporated in 1859. Its name is derived from its former position as the highest point on the railroad between Goldsboro and Charlotte. Today when people think of High Point, they think of furniture, for it is home to the twice-a-year (April and October) International Home Furnishings Market, the largest wholesale furniture market in the world (not open to the public). Tens of thousands of buyers and others associated with the trade "go to market" and in the process lend a sophistication to this warm and hospitable city. Retail outlets here offer furniture and home accessories at bargain prices.

The **High Point Museum/Historical Park,** focusing on Piedmont history and Quaker heritage, includes the 1786 Haley House and a mid-1700s blacksmith shop and weaving house. Exhibits highlight furniture, pottery, communication, transportation, and military artifacts. Tours of the buildings are available weekends and are conducted by costumed staff. ⊠ *1859 E. Lexington Ave.,* ☎ *336/885–6859.* ⌨ *Free.* ☉ *Museum Tues.–Sat. 10–4, Sun. 1–4; park buildings weekends 1–4.*

The **Furniture Discovery Center,** in a renovated fabric warehouse downtown, simulates the furniture design and manufacturing process. It has a Furniture Hall of Fame and an extensive miniature collection exhibited in room displays. ⊠ *101 W. Green Dr.,* ☎ *336/887–3876.* ⌨ *$5; combination ticket with Angela Peterson Doll and Miniature Museum (☞ below) $8.50.* ☉ *Apr.–Oct., weekdays 10–5, Sat. 9–5; Sun. 1–5; Nov.–Mar., Tues.–Fri. 10–5, Sat. 9–5, Sun. 1–5.*

The **Angela Peterson Doll and Miniature Museum** houses the collection of one woman: more than 1,700 dolls, costumes, miniatures, and dollhouses. ⊠ *101 W. Green Dr.,* ☎ *336/885–3655.* ⌨ *$4; combination ticket with Furniture Discovery Center (☞ above) $8.50.* ☉ *Apr.–Oct., weekdays 10–4:30, Sat. 9–4:30, Sun. 1–4:30; Nov.–Mar., Tues.–Sat. 10–4:30, Sun. 1–4:30.*

OFF THE BEATEN PATH

MENDENHALL PLANTATION – A few miles northwest of High Point is this well-preserved example of 19th-century Quaker domestic architecture. The Mendenhalls opposed slavery, and here you'll find one of the few surviving false-bottom wagons, used to help slaves escape to freedom on the Underground Railroad. ⊠ *603 W. Main St., Jamestown,* ☎ *336/454–3819.* ⌨ *$2.* ☉ *Mid-Apr.–Nov., weekdays 11–2, Sat. 1–4, Sun. 2–4.*

Dining and Lodging

$$$–$$$$ ✕ **J. Basul Noble's.** Locals hold Noble's in very high esteem, and it's not hard to see why. It's architecturally dramatic, with 10-ft pillars, a glass ceiling, and a river-rock wall. Veal dishes are recommended, and you could make a meal out of the fine breads (baked daily on the premises) and desserts served here. There's live jazz Thursday through Saturday. ⊠ *101 S. Main St.,* ☎ *336/889–3354. AE, DC, MC, V.*

$$–$$$ ✕ **Atrium Cafe.** Wall murals and a teal-and-peach color scheme create a casual and elegant atmosphere. Veal, duck, and fish dishes are standouts, but the pasta and mushrooms with marinara sauce proves the Atrium can appeal to vegetarians, too. It's near the top of the Atrium Furniture Mall (☞ Shopping, *below*). ⊠ *430 S. Main St.,* ☎ *336/889–9934. AE, D, DC, MC, V.*

$$–$$$ 🏨 **Radisson Hotel High Point.** The central location makes the Radisson a favorite with people coming to town for weekend shopping trips. Guest rooms are standard, but each suite is outfitted with furniture from the different manufacturers represented in the area. ⊠ *135 S. Main St., 27260,* ☎ *336/889–8888,* 䕶 *336/885–2737. 239 rooms, 13 suites. Restaurant, bar, in-room data ports, indoor pool, exercise room, business services, meeting rooms, airport shuttle, parking (fee). AE, D, DC, MC, V.* 🐾

$$ 🏨 **Premier Bed & Breakfast.** A local furniture designer owns this three-story B&B, a 1930s-era home in a historic neighborhood. It's just a mile north of downtown, near the furniture outlets and shopping. You

can relax while sipping wine by the fireplace or on the front porch swing. ⊠ *1001 Johnson St., 27262,* ☎ *336/889–8349. 6 rooms. Meeting room. MC, V. BP.*

Nightlife and the Arts

Headquartered in High Point is the **North Carolina Shakespeare Festival.** The professional troupe performs from August through October and in December at the High Point Theatre (⊠ 305 N. Main St., Suite 200, ☎ 336/841–2273).

Outdoor Activities and Sports

GOLF

There are four public golf courses in High Point: three have 18 holes and one has 9. Contact the High Point Convention and Visitors Bureau (☞ Visitor Information *in* The Triad A to Z, *below*) for information. Pete Dye designed the par-72 course at **Oak Hollow** (⊠ 3400 N. Centennial St., ☎ 336/883–3260).

HIKING

The 376-acre **Piedmont Environmental Center** (⊠ 1220 Penny Rd., ☎ 336/883–8531) has 11 mi of hiking trails adjacent to City Lake Park, with recreation opportunities and a nature preserve. There's also access to a 6-mi greenway trail.

SOCCER

The **Carolina Dynamo,** a United Soccer League team, play at A. J. Simeon Stadium (⊠ 2920 School Park Rd., ☎ 336/884–5255) from April to August.

TENNIS

In Oak Hollow Lake Park, the **Reitzel Tennis Center** (⊠ 3431 N. Centennial St., ☎ 336/883–3493) has four indoor courts, eight clay courts, and two hard courts. Reservations are a must.

Shopping

There are more than 60 retail **furniture stores** in and around High Point. The 36 stores in the **Atrium Furniture Mall** (⊠ 430 S. Main St., ☎ 336/882–5599) carry items by more than 700 manufacturers of furniture and home accessories.

Oak Hollow Mall (⊠ 921 Eastchester Dr., ☎ 336/886–6255) has 105 specialty stores, restaurants, and department stores.

Art shows rotate through the **Theatre Art Galleries** (⊠ 220 E. Commerce Ave., ☎ 336/887–3415), open weekdays noon–5 and weekends by appointment but closed during market weeks in April and October.

The Triad A to Z

Arriving, Departing, and Getting Around

BY BUS

Greyhound/Carolina Trailways (☎ 800/231–2222) has service in the area.

BY CAR

Greensboro and Winston-Salem are on I–40, which runs from Asheville in the west to Wilmington in southeastern North Carolina. I–40 and I–85 are combined coming into the Triad from the east, but in Greensboro, I–85 splits off to head southwest to Charlotte. High Point is off a business bypass of I–85 southwest of Greensboro.

BY PLANE

Just west of Greensboro, the **Piedmont Triad International Airport** (⊠ 6451 Bryan Blvd., Greensboro, ☎ 336/665–5666) is off NC 68 N from

I–40W; it's served by American, Continental, Atlantic Southeast Airlines, Eastwind, Northwest, United, and US Airways. For airline telephone numbers, *see* Air Travel *in* Smart Travel Tips A to Z.

Taxi service to and from the airport is provided by **Airport Express** (☎ 800/934–8779) and other tour, charter, limousine, and cab services, including the **Golden Eagle Cab Company** (☎ 336/724–6481) and **Piedmont Executive Transportation** (☎ 336/723–2179).

BY TRAIN
There are **Amtrak** stations in Greensboro (✉ 2603 Oakland Ave., ☎ 336/855–3382 or 800/872–7245) and High Point (✉ 100 W. High St., ☎ 336/841–7245 or 800/872–7245).

Contacts and Resources

EMERGENCIES
Ambulance, police (☎ 911).

GUIDED TOURS
Carolina Treasures and Tours (✉ 1031 Burke St., ☎ 336/631–9144) offers a look at historic Winston-Salem.

RADIO STATIONS
AM: WSJS 600, news, talk; WAAA 980, urban contemporary. **FM:** WFDD 88.5, National Public Radio; WKRR 92.3, rock; WJMH 102.1, urban contemporary; WTQR 104.1, country.

VISITOR INFORMATION
The following provide maps, brochures, and flyers on attractions, accommodations, and services. **Greensboro Area Convention & Visitors Bureau** (✉ 317 S. Greene St., 27401, ☎ 336/274–2282 or 800/344–2282). **High Point Convention & Visitors Bureau** (✉ 300 S. Main St., 27260, ☎ 336/884–5255 or 800/720–5255). **Winston-Salem Convention & Visitors Bureau** (✉ Box 1409, 27102, ☎ 336/728–4200 or 800/331–7018). In Winston-Salem, a visitor's **reception center** in the City Market building (✉ 601 N. Cherry St., ☎ 336/777–3796) is open daily.

THE TRIANGLE
Raleigh, Durham, Chapel Hill

The cities of Raleigh, Durham, and Chapel Hill make up the Triangle, with Raleigh to the east, Durham to the north, Chapel Hill to the west, and, in the center, Research Triangle Park—a renowned complex of corporations and public and private research facilities set in 6,800 acres of lake-dotted pineland that attracts scientists, academicians, and businesspeople from all over the world. Throughout the Triangle, an area that's been characterized as "trees, tees, and Ph.D.s," politics and basketball are always hot topics. The NCAA basketball championship has traded hands among the area's three schools.

Raleigh

143 mi northeast of Charlotte, 104 mi east of Winston-Salem.

Raleigh is Old South and New South, down-home and upscale, all in one. Named for Sir Walter Raleigh (who established the first English colony on the coast in 1585), it's the state capital and the biggest of the three cities. Many of the state's largest and best museums are here, as are North Carolina State University and six other universities and colleges.

312

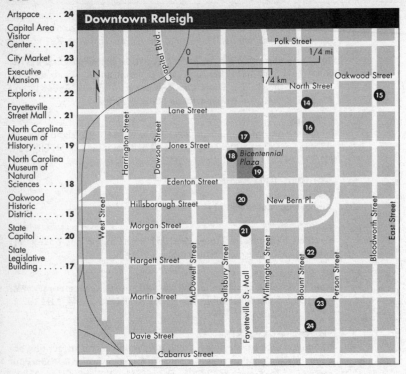

Downtown Raleigh

Numbers in the text correspond to numbers in the margin and on the Downtown Raleigh map.

A Good Walk

Downtown, the streets are laid out in an orderly grid with the State Capitol as the hub. Most downtown Raleigh attractions are state government buildings, historic buildings, and museums and are free to the public. Begin at the **Capital Area Visitor Center** ⑭, where you can pick up maps and brochures, including a self-guided walking tour of the **Oakwood Historic District** ⑮. To get to Oakwood, travel east from the visitor center on Lane Street. After finishing your walk through Oakwood, stroll by the **Executive Mansion** ⑯, home to governors since 1891. It's on Blount Street between Lane and Jones streets.

Follow Jones Street west past Wilmington Street to visit the **State Legislative Building** ⑰. Cross Jones to the Bicentennial Plaza, flanked by the **North Carolina Museum of Natural Sciences** ⑱ to the west and the **North Carolina Museum of History** ⑲ to the east. Continue south across Edenton Street to Capitol Square and the **State Capitol** ⑳.

Starting just south of the capitol across Morgan Street and continuing for four blocks is the **Fayetteville Street Mall** ㉑, a pedestrian-only walkway. From the mall, walk two blocks east on Hargett Street to **Exploris** ㉒, a children's museum. One block south is the **City Market** ㉓, a revitalized area between Blount and Person streets. Just south of the market are the studios and galleries of **Artspace** ㉔, at the corner of Blount and Davie streets.

TIMING

You'll need several hours just to hit the sights of this walk and even more time if you tend to get hooked on museums.

Sights to See

㉔ Artspace. Adjacent to the Moore Square art district, Artspace is a re-furbished auto dealership where the public can watch 40 artists work-ing in open studios and talk with them about their work. It has exhibition galleries and arts education programs. Most of the art is for sale. ✉ *201 E. Davie St.,* ☎ *919/821–2787.* ✒ *Free.* ☉ *Tues.–Sat. 10–6.*

⑭ Capital Area Visitor Center. Here, you can pick up maps and brochures and schedule tours of limited-access facilities such as the Executive Man-sion (☞ *below*). ✉ *301 N. Blount St.,* ☎ *919/733–3456.* ☉ *Week-days 8–5, Sat. 9–5, Sun. 1–5.*

㉓ City Market. This revitalized area with cobblestone streets is home to specialty shops, art galleries, restaurants, a comedy club, and a small farmers' market. The free Entertainment Trolley shuttles between the market and other downtown restaurant and nightlife locations from 6:40 PM to 1:40 AM Thursday through Saturday. ✉ *Martin St. and Moore Sq.,* ☎ *919/828–4555.* ☉ *Stores Mon.–Sat. 10–5:30, restaurants Mon.–Sat. 7 AM–1 AM and Sun. 11:30–10.*

⑯ Executive Mansion. The mansion is a brick early 20th-century Queen Anne cottage–style structure with gingerbread trim and manicured lawns. Tour hours vary; check with the **Capital Area Visitor Center** (☞ *above*). ✉ *200 N. Blount St.,* ☎ *919/733–3456.* ✒ *Free.*

Ⓒ ㉒ Exploris. This 84,000-square-ft architectural showplace is a learning center that stands apart from most other children's museums. It em-phasizes a global perspective, as opposed to specific health and natu-ral science topics. Exhibits explore language, culture, geography, global trade, and communications. ✉ *201 E. Hargett St.,* ☎ *919/834–4040.* ✒ *$7.* ☉ *Tues.–Sat. 9–5, Sun. noon–5.*

㉑ Fayetteville Street Mall. Extending from the State Capitol to the Raleigh Civic and Convention Center, this pedestrian walkway provides entrance to a number of high-rise office buildings. The shops and restaurants in the area cater to the weekday business crowd.

⑲ North Carolina Museum of History. Founded in 1898, the museum is now in a state-of-the-art facility on Bicentennial Plaza. It uses artifacts, audiovisual programs, and interactive exhibits to bring the state's his-tory to life. Exhibits include the *N.C. Sports Hall of Fame; N.C. Folk-life;* and *Militaria, Politics, and Society.* ✉ *5 E. Edenton St.,* ☎ *919/ 715–0200.* ✒ *Free.* ☉ *Tues.–Sat. 9–5, Sun. noon–5.*

★ Ⓒ ⑱ North Carolina Museum of Natural Sciences. At 200,000 square ft, the new museum is the largest of its kind in the Southeast. It has perma-nent exhibits and dioramas that celebrate the incredible diversity of species in the state. There are enough animals and insects—including butterflies, hummingbirds, snakes, and a two-toed sloth—to qualify for a small zoo. One signature exhibit contains rare whale skeletons. The pièce de résistance, however, is the *Terror of the South* exhibit, featuring the dinosaur skeleton of "Acro," a giant carnivore that lived in the South 110 million years ago. ✉ *11 W. Jones St.,* ☎ *919/733– 7450 or 877/462–8724.* ✒ *Free.* ☉ *Mon.–Sat. 9–5, Sun. 1–5.* ✑

⑮ Oakwood Historic District. Many fine examples of Victorian architec-ture can be seen in this tree-shaded neighborhood. Self-guided walk-ing tours of the area, which encompasses 20 blocks bordered by Person, Edenton, Franklin, and Watauga/Linden streets, are available at the **Cap-ital Area Visitor Center** (☞ *above*). Adjacent to historic Oakwood is **Oakwood Cemetery** (✉ *701 Oakwood Ave.,* ☎ *919/832–6077*). Es-tablished in 1869, it is the resting place of 2,800 Confederate soldiers,

Civil War generals, governors, and numerous U.S. senators. Free maps are available at the cemetery office.

㉒ State Capitol. A beautifully preserved example of Greek Revival architecture from 1840, the capitol once housed all the functions of state government. Today it's part museum, part executive offices. The capitol contains, under the domed rotunda, a copy of Antonio Canova's statue of George Washington depicted as a Roman general with tunic, tight-fitting body armor, and a short cape. ✉ *Capitol Sq. (1 E. Edenton St.),* ☎ *919/733–4994.* ☉ *Mon.–Sat. 9–5, Sun. 1–5.*

⑰ State Legislative Building. One block north of the State Capitol, this complex hums with lawmakers and lobbyists when the legislature is in session. It's fun to watch from the gallery. A free guided tour is also available through the **Capital Area Visitor Center** (☞ *above*). ✉ *Salisbury and Jones Sts.,* ☎ *919/733–7928.* ☉ *Weekdays 8–5, Sat. 9–5, Sun. 1–5.*

Other Area Attractions

The city is spread out, so a car is almost a necessity for museums and parks beyond downtown.

OFF THE BEATEN PATH

AVA GARDNER MUSEUM – This museum in the hometown of the legendary beauty and movie star has memorabilia that trace her life from childhood on the farm to Hollywood glory days. It's about 30 mi east of Raleigh in downtown Smithfield. ✉ *205 S. 3rd St., Smithfield,* ☎ *919/ 934–5830 or 919/934–0887.* ▨ *$3.* ☉ *Daily 1–5.*

Joel Lane House. The oldest dwelling in Raleigh was the home of the "father of Raleigh" and dates from the 1760s. Joel Lane sold the state the property on which the capital city grew. Costumed docents tell the story and show the restored house and beautiful period gardens. ✉ *720 W. Hargett St., at St. Mary's St.,* ☎ *919/833–3431.* ▨ *$3.* ☉ *Mar.– mid-Dec., Tues.–Fri. 10–2, 1st and 3rd Sat. of the month 1–4.*

Mordecai Historic Park. You can see the Mordecai family's plantation home and other structures, including the house where President Andrew Johnson was born in 1808. One-hour guided tours are given on the half hour. You can also board a trolley for a narrated 45-minute tour of historic Raleigh ($5). ✉ *1 Mimosa St., at Wake Forest Rd.,* ☎ *919/834–4844.* ▨ *$4.* ☉ *Mon. and Wed.–Sat. 10–3, Sun. 1–3.*

★ **North Carolina Museum of Art.** On the west side of Raleigh, the NCMA houses 5,000 years of artistic heritage, including one of the nation's largest collections of Jewish ceremonial art. Other exhibits range from ancient Egyptian times to the present, from the Old World to the New. The museum hosts touring exhibitions of works by such artists as Caravaggio and Rodin. The glass-wall **Museum Café** looks out on an outdoor performance center–cum–sculpture that when viewed from above spells the words PICTURE THIS. ✉ *2110 Blue Ridge Rd.,* ☎ *919/839– 6262, 919/833–3548 restaurant.* ▨ *Free.* ☉ *Tues.–Thurs. and Sat. 9– 5, Fri. 9–9, Sun. 11–6; Tues.–Sun. tours 1:30.* ✍

☾ **Pullen Park.** In summer crowds come to picnic and ride the 1911 Dentzel carousel, the train, and pedal boats. You can swim here in a large public aquatic center, explore an arts-and-crafts center, or, if the timing is right, see a play at the Theater in the Park. ✉ *520 Ashe Ave., near North Carolina State University,* ☎ *919/831–6468 or 919/831– 6640.* ▨ *Fees vary.* ☉ *Park daily dawn–dusk; rides Memorial Day– Labor Day, Mon.–Thurs. 10:30–6:30, Fri.–Sat. 10:30–8, Sun. 1–8.*

Dining and Lodging

$$$$ ✕ **Second Empire.** Wood paneling, crown molding and high ceilings,
★ floral arrangements, muted lighting, and well-spaced tables make for
a calming and elegant dining experience. The regularly changing menu
has a regional flavor; the food is best described as art on a plate, intricately styled so that colors, textures, and tastes fuse. For an entrée
you might get roasted mahimahi, paired with collard greens, butter-
nut squash, and garlic cream. A wood-and-brass tavern in the lower
level has a simpler and less expensive menu. ✉ *300 Hillsborough St.,*
☎ *919/829–3663. AE, MC, V. Closed Sun.*

$$$–$$$$ ✕ **Angus Barn.** A huge rustic barn houses a Raleigh tradition that has
won virtually every major dining award. The astonishing wine and beer
list is 35 pages. The restaurant is known for its steaks, baby-back ribs,
prime rib, and fresh seafood and for its clubby Wild Turkey lounge.
Desserts are heavenly. Reservations aren't accepted for Saturday din-
ner. ✉ *U.S. 70W (Glenwood Ave.) near Aviation Pkwy.,* ☎ *919/781–*
2444. AE, D, DC, MC, V.

$$$–$$$$ ✕ **Margaux's.** Eclectic is the key word for the cuisine at this north
Raleigh fixture, where a massive stone fireplace warms the intimate
setting. A blackboard lists the diverse specials, such as red chili fettuccine
with goat cheese, lamb with coconut curry sauce, or grilled shrimp and
crawfish tostada with roasted corn, black beans, and salsa *verde.* ✉
8111 Creedmoor Rd., ☎ *919/846–9846. AE, DC, MC, V.*

$$–$$$ ✕ **Tony's Bourbon Street Oyster Bar.** The atmosphere—already festive
with red walls, feather masks, and street lamps from New Orleans—
jumps up a notch with live music Thursday, Friday, and Saturday
evenings. Cajun and Creole dishes such as gumbo, jambalaya, and craw-
fish étouffée are served in the large, open dining room, or the oyster
bar. Cary, near the entrance to Research Triangle Park, is 25 minutes
from downtown Raleigh. ✉ *107 Edinburgh Dr., MacGregor Village*
Shopping Center, Cary, ☎ *919/462–6226. AE, MC, V.*

$–$$$ ✕ **Greenshields Brewery & Pub.** You can $ip beer and ale brewed on
the premises with your soup, salad, sandwich, or such entrées as fish-
and-chips, shepherd's pie, and steak in this English-style pub. Oak paneling and working fireplaces enhance the mood. ✉ *214 E. Martin St.,*
City Market, ☎ *919/829–0214. AE, D, MC, V.*

$ ✕ **Big Ed's City Market Restaurant.** A must for breakfast or lunch, Big
Ed's is filled with antique farm implements and the owner's political memorabilia, including pictures of presidential candidates who have stopped
at this landmark. Every Saturday morning a Dixieland band plays in front
of the restaurant. Come here for down-home cookin' and don't miss the
biscuits. ✉ *220 Wolfe St., City Market,* ☎ *919/836–9909. Reservations*
not accepted. No credit cards. Closed Sun. No dinner.

$$$ 🏨 **Courtyard by Marriott–Airport.** Convenient to the airport and Re-
search Triangle Park, this chain property offers many amenities with-
out hefty rates. Rooms are predictably modern. The dining room is for
guests only. ✉ *2001 Hospitality Ct., Morrisville, 27560,* ☎ *919/467–*
9444 or 800/321–2211, 🖷 *919/467–9332. 140 rooms, 12 suites. Din-*
ing room, in-room data ports, pool, hot tub, exercise room, airport
shuttle. AE, D, DC, MC, V. CP. ✍

$$$ 🏨 **North Raleigh Hilton.** This is a favorite spot for corporate meetings.
The standard rooms are done in mauve and green. You can dine in
Lofton's restaurant and listen to the piano afterward in the lobby bar.
Bowties (☞ Nightlife and the Arts, *below*) is a popular nightspot for
dancing. ✉ *3415 Wake Forest Rd., 27609,* ☎ *919/872–2323 or 800/*
445–8667, 🖷 *919/876–0890. 331 rooms, 7 suites. Restaurant, 2 bars,*
in-room data ports, indoor pool, exercise room, nightclub, business
services, meeting rooms, airport shuttle. AE, D, DC, MC, V. ✍

$$$ 🏨 **Quality Suites Hotel.** Minutes from downtown, Quality Suites has luxurious two-room suites equipped with cassette stereos, microwaves, and wet bars. The manager's evening reception and the cooked-to-order breakfast are included in the rate. ⊠ *4400 Capital Blvd., 27604,* ☎ *919/876–2211 or 800/543–5497,* FAX *919/790–1352. 114 suites. Breakfast room, in-room data ports, in-room VCRs, minibars, refrigerators, pool, exercise room, business services, meeting rooms. AE, D, DC, MC, V. BP.* 🐾

$$–$$$ 🏨 **Raleigh Marriott Crabtree Valley.** In one of the city's most luxurious hotels, fresh floral arrangements adorn the elegantly decorated public rooms. Standard rooms have soft colors such as cream, Asian floral prints, and dark cherry-wood furnishings. Guests can dine at J. W.'s Steakhouse and at Quinn's, a lounge where light fare and drinks are served daily. ⊠ *4500 Marriott Dr. (U.S. 70W near Crabtree Valley Mall), 27612,* ☎ *919/781–7000 or 800/228–9290,* FAX *919/781–3059. 375 rooms, 4 suites. Restaurant, bar, in-room data ports, indoor-outdoor pool, hot tub, exercise room, business services, meeting rooms, airport shuttle. AE, D, DC, MC, V.* 🐾

$$–$$$ 🏨 **William Thomas House.** A stately but not stuffy Victorian home is a B&B on the edge of downtown Raleigh a few blocks from the governor's mansion. Rooms, named for family members, are traditionally and elegantly decorated and have oversize windows and 12-ft ceilings. The richly hued common rooms are filled with heirlooms such as a grand piano from 1863 and antique china. ⊠ *530 N. Blount St., 27604,* ☎ *919/755–9400 or 800/653–3466,* FAX *919/755–3966. 4 rooms. Fans, in-room data ports, refrigerators. AE, D, DC, MC, V. BP.* 🐾

$ 🏨 **Hampton Inn & Suites.** In the southwest corner of Cary, right over the Raleigh line, this recently built hotel is just minutes from Raleigh's Entertainment & Sports Arena, the State Fairgrounds, and North Carolina State University. Rooms are typical of the chain; you'll need a car to get to restaurants. ⊠ *111 Hampton Woods La., Cary 27607,* ☎ *919/233–1798 or 800/426–7866,* FAX *919/854–1166. 126 rooms. In-room data ports, no-smoking floor, refrigerators, pool, exercise room, baby-sitting, laundry service, business services, meeting rooms. AE, D, DC, MC, V.* 🐾

$ 🏨 **Ramada Inn Crabtree.** Rooms are comfortable in familiar chain style at what may be the friendliest motel in town. It's also where football and basketball teams like to stay when they're here for a game, as evidenced by the sports memorabilia in the Brass Bell Lounge. ⊠ *3920 Arrow Dr. (U.S. 70 and Beltline/I–440), 27612,* ☎ *919/782–7525 or 800/441–4712,* FAX *919/781–0435. 157 rooms, 17 suites. Restaurant, bar, in-room data ports, pool, exercise room, business services, meeting rooms, airport shuttle. AE, D, DC, MC, V.* 🐾

Nightlife and the Arts

THE ARTS

The **North Carolina Theatre** (⊠ 1 E. South St., ☎ 919/831–6060), a professional nonprofit theater, produces five Broadway musicals a year. The **North Carolina Symphony** (⊠ 2 E. South St., ☎ 919/733–2750) gives more than 200 concerts throughout the state annually, but its home venue is the elegant Memorial Auditorium. The **Carolina Ballet** (⊠ 2914 Kildaire Farm Rd., Cary, ☎ 919/831–6060) performs from mid-October to mid-June in Memorial Auditorium and other venues. The **North Carolina State University Arts Programs** (☎ 919/515–1100) include the Center Stage series, host to professional touring productions and world-class artists. All arts program performances are open to the public.

Alltel Pavilion at Walnut Creek (⊠ 3801 Rock Quarry Rd., ☎ 919/831–6666), known as "The Creek," accommodates 20,000. Headliners appear from spring through mid-fall and cover the musical spectrum. This is the most attended amphitheater on the East Coast.

NIGHTLIFE

The **Berkeley Café** (✉ 217 W. Martin St., ☎ 919/821–0777) is one of the hottest gathering places in the Triangle for live music: rock and roll, R&B, and blues. **Bowties** (✉ North Raleigh Hilton, 3415 Wake Forest Rd., ☎ 919/878–4917) is a popular after-hours spot for dancing. **Charlie Goodnight's Comedy Club** (✉ 861 W. Morgan St., ☎ 919/828–5233) combines dinner with a night of laughs. Alumni include Jay Leno, Jerry Seinfeld, and Brett Butler. **Tir na nog** (✉ 218 S. Blount St., ☎ 919/833–7795) has Irish entertainers, Murphy's Irish Amber, Guinness, and even whiskey on tap. You can munch on simple Irish pub grub or contemporary fare. The owners and a good portion of the staff are Irish, so authenticity is what distinguishes this bar, whose name means "land of eternal youth." In the warehouse district is the **Warehouse Restaurant and Entertainment Center** (✉ 427 S. Dawson St., ☎ 919/836–9966), with a huge dance floor and game room.

Outdoor Activities and Sports

BASEBALL

The **Carolina Mudcats** (☎ 919/269–2287), the AA affiliate of the Colorado Rockies, play April through August at Five County Stadium in Zebulon, about 20 mi east of Raleigh.

BASKETBALL

Raleigh's Atlantic Coast Conference entry is the North Carolina State University **Wolfpack** (☎ 919/515–2106 or 800/310–7225).

BIKING

Raleigh has 40 mi of greenways for biking or walking, and maps are available through the **Raleigh Division of Transportation** (☎ 919/890–3430).

CAMPING

Try the North Carolina State Fairgrounds, William B. Umstead State Park, Clemmons State Forest near Clayton, or Jordan Lake between Apex and Pittsboro. For details, call the Greater Raleigh Convention and Visitors Bureau (☞ Visitor Information *in* The Triangle A to Z, *below*) or the North Carolina Division of Tourism, Film and Sports Development (☞ Visitor Information *in* North Carolina A to Z, *below*).

FISHING

Jordan Lake, a 13,900-acre reservoir in Apex, is a favorite fishing spot. Others are Lake Wheeler in Raleigh and the Falls Lake State Recreation Area in Wake Forest.

FITNESS

The **Central YMCA** (✉ 1601 Hillsborough St., ☎ 919/832–6601) will permit visitors to use its facilities for a few dollars provided they have a YMCA membership elsewhere. The **Cary Family YMCA** (✉ 101 YMCA Dr., at Cary Pkwy., Cary, ☎ 919/469–9622) doesn't charge if you are already a member of a Y elsewhere. It has an indoor lap track, two pools, high-tech exercise machines, and a weight room.

GOLF

There are 20 golf courses, either public or semiprivate, within a half-hour drive of downtown Raleigh. **Cheviot Hills Golf Course** (✉ 7301 Capitol Blvd., ☎ 919/876–9920) is a par-71 championship course. **Devil's Ridge Golf Club** (✉ Holly Springs Rd., Cary, ☎ 919/557–6100), about 15 mi from Raleigh, is a challenging par-72 course with large, rolling greens. **Lochmere Golf Club** (✉ Kildaire Farm Rd., Cary, ☎ 919/851–0611) provides a friendly atmosphere, good value, and a challenge at par-71. A 30-minute drive from Raleigh is the **Neuse Golf Club** (⊠ NC 42 E, Clayton, ☎ 919/550–0550), an attractive par-72 course on the banks of the Neuse River.

HOCKEY

The NHL's **Carolina Hurricanes** play in the 21,000-seat Raleigh Entertainment & Sports Arena (☎ 919/467–7825 or 888/645–8491).

JOGGING

Runners frequent Shelley Lake, the track at North Carolina State University, and the **Capital Area Greenway** system (☎ 919/831–6833 for a map).

SOCCER

The **Raleigh Capital Express** competes in the A League's Atlantic Conference April through September. Home games are played in the WRAL Soccer Center (⊠ 7700 Perry Creek Rd., ☎ 919/786–1313).

TENNIS

More than 80 courts in Raleigh city parks are available for use; call 919/872–4128 for details.

Shopping

SHOPPING MALLS AND OUTLET CENTERS

Cameron Village Shopping Center (⊠ 1900 Cameron St.), Raleigh's first shopping center, contains specialty shops and boutiques and restaurants. **Crabtree Valley Mall** (⊠ Glenwood Ave., U.S. 70) is one of the South's largest enclosed malls and has more than 240 specialty stores, including Pottery Barn, Abercrombie & Fitch, and Williams-Sonoma. Department stores include Lord & Taylor, Hudson-Belk, Hecht's, and Sears. **Prime Outlets** (⊠ Exit 284 off I–40, Airport Blvd., Morrisville, between Raleigh and Durham, ☎ 919/380–8700) is decidedly un-mall-like with its wooden floors and greenery. The area's only factory outlet center has more than 40 stores, including Off Fifth (Saks Fifth Avenue) and Geoffrey Beene.

ART AND ANTIQUES

City Market (☞ Sights to See, *above*) is a revitalized shopping area with an array of shops and art galleries. At **Artspace** (☞ Sights to See, *above*), you can visit artists' studios and purchase their works. The merchandise changes daily at **Carolina Antique Mall** in Cameron Village (☞ *above*), where 75 dealers stock the floor.

FOOD

Open year-round, the 60-acre **State Farmers' Market** (⊠ Lake Wheeler Rd. and I–40, ☎ 919/733–7417 market; 919/833–7973 restaurants) includes a garden center, seafood restaurant, and a down-home restaurant. **Wellspring Grocery** (⊠ 3540 Wade Ave., ☎ 919/828–5805) has outstanding produce, fresh-baked breads, health foods, and specialty items, as well as a place to sit and eat your purchases.

Durham

23 mi northwest of Raleigh on I–40 and NC 147 (Durham Freeway).

Durham has three of North Carolina's 22 National Historic Landmarks and long ago shed its tobacco-town image. It is now known as the City of Medicine for the medical and research centers at Duke University, one of the top schools in the nation. With more than 20,000 employees, Duke is not only the largest employer in Durham but also one of the largest in the state. Warehouses and mills around the city have been converted to chic shops, offices, and condos.

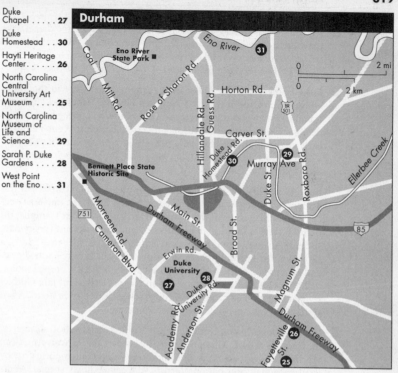

Numbers in the text correspond to numbers in the margin and on the Durham map.

A Good Drive

Durham has some areas appropriate for a good walk, such as Duke University's campus. However, to save time and ensure that you get the real flavor of this relatively compact, single-city county, it's best to drive. Start your tour 1½ mi south of downtown, exiting the Durham Freeway (NC 147) at Fayetteville Street, along which you will find the **North Carolina Central University Art Museum** ㉕ and the **Hayti Heritage Center** ㉖.

The next stop is about 3 mi away. Return to the Durham Freeway and continue northwest to the exit at Chapel Hill Street. Follow Chapel Hill west into the West Campus of **Duke University,** which includes the **Duke Chapel** ㉗ and the **Sarah P. Duke Gardens** ㉘. Return to Chapel Hill Street and take it past the Durham Freeway to Duke Street and turn left toward the northern sections of the city, about 3½ mi. Continue past I–85 and make a right at Murray Avenue, which will quickly bring you to the **North Carolina Museum of Life and Science** ㉙. Return to Duke Street, heading north a short distance, and turn left onto Carver Street, which leads to Duke Homestead Road, along which lies **Duke Homestead** ㉚. Retrace your path back to Duke Street, following it north until it merges with U.S. 501. Take U.S. 501 about 3½ mi to the conclusion of your tour at **West Point on the Eno** ㉛.

TIMING

You should allow 1 to 1½ days to explore these Durham highlights; select a number of sights that interest you if you have only a day.

Sights to See

★ ㉗ **Duke Chapel.** A Gothic-style gem built in the early 1930s, the chapel is the centerpiece of the campus. Modeled after Canterbury Cathedral, it has 77 stained-glass windows and a 210-ft bell tower. ⊠ *Chapel Dr., West Campus of Duke University,* ☎ *919/681–1704.* ⊙ *Daily 8 AM–9 PM.* ☙

㉚ **Duke Homestead.** The Duke family empire began here in the 1860s with tobacco, and it is now a National Historic Landmark. You can tour the small wood-frame factories, pack house, and curing barn; guides demonstrate early manufacturing processes. The visitor center exhibits early tobacco advertising. ⊠ *2828 Duke Homestead Rd.,* ☎ *919/ 477–5498.* 🎟 *Free.* ⊙ *Apr.–Oct., Mon.–Sat. 9–5, Sun. 1–5; Nov.–Mar., Tues.–Sat. 10–4, Sun. 1–4.*

Duke University. A stroll along the beautiful tree-lined streets of this campus is a lovely way to spend a few hours. In all, the university encompasses 525 acres in the heart of Durham. The East Campus, off Broad Street, has Georgian architecture and the **Duke University Museum of Art** (⊠ Buchanan Blvd. at Trinity Ave., ☎ 919/684–5135), a showcase for pre-Columbian, African, Russian, European medieval, and Renaissance art. A mile or so away is the West Campus, dominated by **Duke Chapel** (☞ *above*) on Chapel Drive and late-Gothic-style buildings. The sprawling medical school is on Erwin Road. A bus system and bike paths connect the campuses.

㉖ **Hayti Heritage Center.** One of Durham's oldest ecclesiastical structures, St. Joseph's A.M.E. Church houses this center for African-American art. In addition to exhibitions of traditional and contemporary art by local, regional, and national artists, the center hosts special events such as the Black Diaspora Film Festival. ⊠ *804 Old Fayetteville St.,* ☎ *919/683–1709 or 800/845–9835.* 🎟 *Free; fees for special events vary.* ⊙ *Weekdays 9–5, Sat. 10–2:30.*

㉕ **North Carolina Central University Art Museum.** African-American art is showcased at the nation's first liberal arts college for African-Americans. Besides the permanent collection you can see works by students and local artists. ⊠ *1801 Fayetteville St.,* ☎ *919/560–6211.* 🎟 *Free.* ⊙ *Tues.–Fri. 9–5, Sun. 2–5.*

☝ ㉙ **North Carolina Museum of Life and Science.** Here you can create a tornado, encounter dinosaurs on the prehistoric trail, view NASA artifacts, and ride a train through a wildlife sanctuary. The nature center has such native North Carolina animals as flying squirrels. The three-story **Magic Wings Butterfly House** has a tropical butterfly conservatory and includes the Insectarium, where you can see and hear live insects under high magnification and amplification. ⊠ *433 Murray Ave., off I–85,* ☎ *919/220–5429.* 🎟 *Museum $8, train ride $1.50.* ⊙ *Mon.–Sat. 10–5, Sun. noon–5.*

★ ㉘ **Sarah P. Duke Gardens.** These 55 acres, complete with a wisteria-draped gazebo and a Japanese garden with a lily pond teeming with fat goldfish, have more than 5 mi of pathways through formal plantings and woodlands. ⊠ *Main entrance on Anderson St., West Campus of Duke University,* ☎ *919/684–3698.* 🎟 *Free.* ⊙ *Daily 8–dusk.* ☙

㉛ **West Point on the Eno.** Included in a city park on the banks of the Eno River are a 19th-century blacksmith shop, an 1880s home, and a restored mill dating from 1778. It's the site of an annual three-day folklife festival surrounding the Fourth of July; musicians, artists, and craftspeople come from around the region. ⊠ *5101 N. Roxboro Rd. (U.S. 501N),* ☎ *919/471–1623.* 🎟 *Free.* ⊙ *Daily 8–sunset, historic buildings weekends only 1–5.*

Other Area Attractions

Bennett Place State Historic Site. In this farmhouse in April 1865, Confederate general Joseph E. Johnston surrendered to U.S. general William T. Sherman, 17 days after Lee's surrender to Grant at Appomattox. The two generals then set forth the terms for a "permanent peace" between the South and the North. Historical reenactments are held annually. ✉ *4409 Bennett Memorial Rd., 10 mi from downtown,* ☎ *919/ 383–4345.* 🎟 *Free.* ⊙ *Apr.–Oct., Mon.–Sat. 9–5, Sun. 1–5; Nov.–Mar., Tues.–Sat. 9–5, Sun. 1–5.*

Eno River State Park. The park's 2,733 acres include hiking trails, a picnic area, rough camping, and Class II rapids (after a heavy rain). ✉ *6101 Cole Mill Rd.,* ☎ *919/383–1686.* 🎟 *Free.* ⊙ *Daily 8–sunset.*

Dining and Lodging

$$$–$$$$ ✕ **Magnolia Grill.** This bistro is consistently one of the area's finest,
★ most innovative places to dine. The food is as eye-catching as the art on the walls. On the daily menu you may find grilled jumbo sea scallops on spicy black beans with blood-orange-and-onion marmalade or grilled hickory-smoked pork tenderloin in a sun-dried cherry sauce. ✉ *1002 9th St.,* ☎ *919/286–3609. MC, V. Closed Sun. No lunch.*

$$–$$$$ ✕ **Café Parizäde.** This Erwin Square Mediterranean restaurant gets high marks for its food and service. Soft lighting, white tablecloths, and ceiling murals give the place an elegant feel. One appetizer is fried calamari with jalapeño-tomato salsa; some entrées are fettuccine with fresh salmon and black-pepper dill cream, sesame pasta with scallops, and roast duck with fresh vegetables. ✉ *2200 W. Main St.,* ☎ *919/ 286–9712. AE, D, DC, MC, V. No lunch weekends.*

$$–$$$ ✕ **Pop's.** The roof is rough tin and the sculptures rusty industrial, while the lattice walls are covered in silk flowers and vines. Like the decor, the menu is eclectic, with Italian and contemporary cuisine. You can get a grilled pork chop with polenta or *fritto misto* calamari (batter-fried squid). Arrive early; it fills up quickly. ✉ *810 W. Peabody St.,* ☎ *919/956–7677. MC, V. Closed Mon.*

$$$–$$$$ ✕🏨 **Washington Duke Inn & Golf Club.** On the campus of Duke Uni-
★ versity, this luxurious hotel overlooks a Robert Trent Jones golf course. Rooms evoke the feeling of an English country inn, with floral bedspreads and creamy striped wall coverings. On display in the public rooms are memorabilia belonging to the Duke family, for whom the hotel and university are named. At the truly elegant Fairview restaurant, you can start with Moroccan spiced lamb sausage or chestnut soup with rosemary cream and then move on to entrées such as breast of Muscovy duck with mashed white beans, roasted garlic, and sweet-and-sour cranberry sauce. ✉ *3001 Cameron Blvd., 27706,* ☎ *919/490– 0999 or 800/443–3853,* 🗏 *919/688–0105. 164 rooms, 7 suites. Restaurant, bar, in-room data ports, pool, driving range, 18-hole golf course, putting green, 12 tennis courts, exercise room, jogging, business services, meeting rooms, airport shuttle. AE, D, DC, MC, V.* 🐾

$$–$$$$ 🏨 **Arrowhead Inn.** Brick chimneys and tall Doric columns distinguish this bed-and-breakfast inn in an 18th-century white-clapboard farmhouse. It's a few miles outside Durham and has a homelike setting, with antiques, old plantings, fireplaces, and a log cabin in the garden. ✉ *106 Mason Rd., 27712,* ☎ *919/477–8430 or 800/528–2207,* 🗏 *919/ 471–9538. 9 rooms, 2 suites. Picnic area, business services. AE, D, DC, MC, V. BP.* 🐾

$$–$$$$ 🏨 **Blooming Garden Inn.** Truly a bright spot in the Holloway Historic District, this B&B is painted yellow outside. Inside, the inn explodes with color and warmth, thanks to exuberant hosts Dolly and Frank Pokrass. Breakfast might be walnut crepes with ricotta cheese and warm raspberry sauce. A sister B&B, the Victorian Holly House across the

street, accommodates people on extended stays. ⊠ *513 Holloway St., 27701,* ☎ *919/687–0801 or 888/687–0801,* ℻ *919/688–1401. 4 rooms, 2 suites. AE, D, DC, MC, V. BP.* 🐾

Nightlife and the Arts

The 1926 Beaux Arts **Carolina Theatre** (⊠ 309 W. Morgan St., ☎ 919/ 560–3040) hosts film festivals, orchestras, and operas, as well as the International Jazz Festival (March) and the American Dance Festival (June).

Outdoor Activities and Sports

BASEBALL

The **Durham Bulls,** a tradition since 1902, were immortalized in the hit movie *Bull Durham.* The AAA team, an affiliate of the Tampa Bay Devil Rays, plays at their stadium near downtown (⊠ 409 Blackwell St., ☎ 919/687–6500).

BASKETBALL

Durham's Atlantic Coast Conference team is Duke's **Blue Devils** (☎ 919/681–2583 or 800/672–2583).

CAMPING

Try the **Eno River State Park** (⊠ 6101 Cole Mill Rd., ☎ 919/383–1686). For information, call the North Carolina Division of Tourism, Film and Sports Development (☞ Visitor Information *in* North Carolina A to Z, *below*).

GOLF

Durham has four 18-hole public golf courses. **Duke University** (⊠ Cameron Blvd. and Science Dr., ☎ 919/681–2288) has a Robert Trent Jones course, with a par 72. **Hillandale Golf Course** (⊠ Hillandale Rd., ☎ 919/286–4211) has a par-71 George Cobb course.

TENNIS

The city's **Parks and Recreation Department** (☎ 919/560–4355) has information on the city's 72 public tennis courts.

Shopping

SHOPPING DISTRICTS AND MALLS

Durham's **9th Street** has funky shops and restaurants. **Brightleaf Square** (⊠ 905 W. Main St., ☎ 919/682–9229) is an upscale shopping-entertainment complex housed in old tobacco warehouses in the heart of downtown. **Northgate Mall** (⊠ 1058 W. Club Blvd., ☎ 919/286– 4400) draws shoppers from all parts of the Triangle. Kids enjoy riding the old-fashioned carousel while adults can choose from among three department stores and nearly 200 specialty stores.

CRAFTS

One World Market (⊠ 1918 Perry St., ☎ 919/286–2457) carries unique, affordable gifts. One goal of the store is to provide increased self-employment for low-income crafters from around the world.

FOOD

Fowler's Gourmet (⊠ 112 S. Duke St., ☎ 919/683–2555) stocks everything from exotic spices to wines, fresh seafood, and European chocolates. Customized gift baskets are shipped all over the country. **Wellspring Grocery** (⊠ 621 Broad St., ☎ 919/286–2290) has outstanding fresh produce, soups, salads, and sandwiches prepared daily.

Chapel Hill

12 mi southwest of Durham on U.S. 15–501, 28 mi northwest of Raleigh.

Chapel Hill may be the smallest city in the Triangle, but its reputation as a seat of learning—and of liberalism—looms large. The home of the nation's first state university, the 208-year-old University of North Carolina (UNC), Chapel Hill retains the feel of a quiet, tree-shaded village while crowded with students and retirees.

Morehead Planetarium, where the original *Apollo* astronauts and many since have trained, is one of the largest in the country. You can learn about the constellations and take in laser-light shows. ⊠ *250 E. Franklin St.,* ☎ *919/962–1236, 919/549–6863 show information.* 🖾 *$4.* ⊗ *Mon. 12:30–5, Tues.–Fri. and Sun. 12:30–5 and 7–9:45, Sat. 10–5 and 7–9:45; call ahead for show times.*

★ **Franklin Street,** in the heart of downtown Chapel Hill, is lined with bicycle shops, bookstores, clothing stores, restaurants and coffee shops, and a movie theater.

Franklin Street runs along the northern edge of the **University of North Carolina** campus, which is filled with oak-shaded courtyards and stately old buildings. The **Louis Round Wilson Library** (⊠ South St., ☎ 919/962–0114) is home to the largest single collection of state literature in the nation. Its North Carolina Collection Gallery (919/962–1172) has exhibits of rare books, photos, and oil portraits. Several historic rooms highlight topics in the state's history, such as the Walter Raleigh Room. The university's **Ackland Art Museum** (⊠ Columbia and Franklin Sts., ☎ 919/406–9837) showcases some of the Southeast's strongest collections of art from India and of Western art, as well as old-master paintings and sculptures. Of special interest is North Carolina folk art.

Ⓒ The **ArtsCenter** (⊠ 300G E. Main St., Carrboro, ☎ 919/929–2787) has exhibits, offers classes of all kinds for children, and hosts dance, theater, and music events.

The **North Carolina Botanical Garden,** south of downtown via U.S. 15–501 Bypass, has the largest collection of native plants in the Southeast. Nature trails wind through a 300-acre Piedmont forest; the herb garden and carnivorous plant collection are impressive. ⊠ *Old Mason Farm Rd.,* ☎ *919/962–0522.* 🖾 *Free.* ⊗ *Apr.–Oct., weekdays 8–5, Sat. 10–5, Sun. 1–5; Nov.–Mar., weekdays 8–5, Sat. 9–6, Sun. 1–6.*

Dining and Lodging

$$$ ✕ **Il Palio Ristorante.** Tuscan cuisine and attentive service are the hallmarks of this restaurant in the sumptuous Siena Hotel (☞ *below*). You won't be hurried here, which is a good thing, since it takes a while just to get through the antipasto while you anticipate entrées such as *filetto di branzino*—black grouper filled with greens and wrapped with prosciutto, in a saffron broth. ⊠ *1505 E. Franklin St.,* ☎ *919/929–4000. AE, D, DC, MC, V.*

$$–$$$ ✕ **Aurora.** Northern Italian cuisine is the specialty. The changing menu may include succulent sea scallops and shiitake mushrooms in rosemary and white wine, fresh chive pasta stuffed with four cheeses and tossed with walnut sauce, or veal with apples. ⊠ *1350 Raleigh Rd. (NC 54 Bypass),* ☎ *919/942–2400. AE, MC, V.*

$$–$$$ ✕ **Crook's Corner.** This small, often noisy restaurant is an exemplar of Southern chic. It turns out such regional specialties as snapper with mint, pecans, and oranges, as well as hot pepper jelly, crab gumbo, and

buttermilk pie. A wall of bamboo and a waterfall fountain make the patio a delightful alfresco experience. Look for the pink pig atop the building. ✉ *610 W. Franklin St.,* ☎ *919/929–7643. AE, MC, V.*

$$–$$$ ✕ **Pyewacket Restaurant.** What began as a hole-in-the-wall vegetarian restaurant in 1977 has become one of Chapel Hill's most popular eateries. Now with bigger digs and courtyard dining, Pyewacket has added seafood and pasta specialties to its repertoire. Entrées range from southwestern grilled seafood to spinach lasagna. ✉ *431 W. Franklin St.,* ☎ *919/929–0297. AE, D, DC, MC, V.*

$$$$ ✕🏨 **Fearrington House.** A member of the prestigious Relais & Châteaux
★ group, this country inn is on a 200-year-old farm that has been remade into a residential community resembling a country village. The village mascots, the "Oreo cows" (black on the ends, snow white in the middle), roam the pasture at the entrance. The inn's modern guest rooms, overlooking a courtyard, gardens, and pasture, are furnished with antiques, original art, English pine, and floral print fabrics. The restaurant serves regional food, such as collard-pecan-pesto-stuffed chicken breast with Hoop cheddar grits over a chicory morel gravy. Dinner is prix-fixe. Guests can use the Fearrington Swim & Croquet Club. ✉ *2000 Fearrington Village Center, 8 mi south of Chapel Hill on U.S. 15–501, Pittsboro 27312,* ☎ *919/542–2121,* ℻ *919/542–4202. 30 rooms, 2 suites. 2 restaurants, pool, 2 tennis courts, croquet, business services, meeting rooms. AE, MC, V. BP.* ✆

$$$ 🏨 **Siena Hotel.** The love affair Sam and Susan Longiotti have with Siena, Italy, has carried over to their posh, European-style hotel, arguably the nicest in Chapel Hill. The lobby and rooms have imported furniture, and fabrics and artwork that conjure the Italian Renaissance. The friendly staff and the pleasant atmosphere more than make up for the location—off a main road, surrounded by the parking lot (and some trees). Rates include a breakfast buffet served by Il Palio, the in-house restaurant (☞ *above*). ✉ *1505 E. Franklin St., 27514,* ☎ *919/929–4000 or 800/223–7379,* ℻ *919/968–8527. 68 rooms, 12 suites. Restaurant, bar, picnic area, in-room data ports, business services, meeting rooms, airport shuttle. AE, DC, MC, V. BP.* ✆

Nightlife and the Arts

THE ARTS

The **Dean E. Smith Center** (✉ Skipper Bowles Dr., on the UNC campus, ☎ 919/962–7777) is the place to see the university's men's basketball games, special events, and concerts. **Playmakers Repertory Company** (✉ Country Club Dr., on the UNC campus, ☎ 919/962–7529), a non-profit professional theater, performs six plays annually (September–May) at the Paul Green Theatre.

NIGHTLIFE

The Chapel Hill area is the place to hear live rock and alternative bands. **Cat's Cradle** (✉ 300 E. Main St., Carrboro, ☎ 919/967–9053) is smoky and dark and presents entertainment nightly.

Outdoor Activities and Sports

BASKETBALL

The University of North Carolina's **Tarheels** (☎ 919/962–2296 or 800/722–4335) are Chapel Hill's Atlantic Coast Conference team.

BIKING

Chapel Hill is a great town for biking; for a bicycling map, contact the **Chapel Hill/Orange County Visitors Bureau** (☞ Visitor Information *in* the Triangle A to Z, *below*).

There are three public golf courses in Orange County; Chapel Hill has one of them: **Finley Golf Course** (⊠ Finley Golf Course Rd., off NC 54 on the UNC campus, ☎ 919/962–2349) is a championship par-72 course with a driving range and putting green.

There are 21 public courts in Chapel Hill. For information call the **Chapel Hill Parks and Recreation Department** (☎ 919/968–2784).

Shopping

Minutes from downtown, the lively **Eastgate Shopping Center** (⊠ between E. Franklin St. and U.S. 15–501) sells everything from antiques to wine. **Fearrington Village,** a planned community 8 mi south of Chapel Hill on U.S. 15–501 in Pittsboro, has upscale shops selling art, garden items, handmade jewelry, and more. **Franklin Street** in Chapel Hill has a wonderful collection of shops, including bookstores, art galleries, crafts shops, and clothing stores.

At **McIntyre's Fine Books and Bookends** (⊠ Fearrington Village, U.S. 15–501, Pittsboro, ☎ 919/542–3030), an independent operation, you can read by the fire in one of the cozy rooms. It has extensive collections of travel and gardening books.

A Southern Season (⊠ Eastgate Mall, ☎ 919/929–9466 or 800/253–3663) stocks everything from wine to such Tarheel treats as barbecue sauces, peanuts, and hams. The Weathervane Café has indoor and alfresco dining. **Wellspring Grocery** (⊠ 81 S. Elliott Rd., ☎ 919/968–1983) has fresh produce and health foods.

The Triangle A to Z

Arriving and Departing

Greyhound/Carolina Trailways (☎ 800/231–2222) serves Raleigh, Durham, and Chapel Hill.

U.S. 1, which runs north–south through the Triangle and the Sandhills, also links to I–85 going northeast. U.S. 64, which makes an east–west traverse across the Triangle, continues eastward all the way to the Outer Banks. I–95 runs northeast–southwest to the east of the Triangle and the Sandhills, crossing U.S. 64 and I–40 on its way from Virginia to South Carolina.

The **Raleigh-Durham International Airport** (⊠ 1600 Terminal Blvd., Morrisville, ☎ 919/840–2123), off I–40 between the two cities, is served by 19 airlines, including American, Continental, Delta, Northwest, TWA, United, US Airways, Midway, and Southwest. For airline telephone numbers, *see* Air Travel *in* Smart Travel Tips A to Z. If you're driving from the airport to Raleigh, take I–40 east to Exit 285; for Chapel Hill, take I–40 west to Exits 273, 270, and 266; for Durham, also take I–40 west to NC 147. It takes about 20 minutes to get to any of the three cities.

The **Amtrak** (⊠ 320 W. Cabarrus St., Raleigh, ☎ 919/833–7594 or 800/872–7245; 400 W. Chapel Hill St., Durham, ☎ 919/956–7932 or 800/872–7245; 211 N. Academy St., Cary, ☎ 800/872–7245) *Carolinian* has one daily train northbound and one southbound, with stops in

Raleigh, Cary, Durham, and 10 other Piedmont cities. The in-state *Piedmont* connects nine cities between Raleigh and Charlotte each day.

Getting Around

BY BUS

Capital Area Transit (☎ 919/833–5701) is Raleigh's public transport system. Fares are 75¢. **Chapel Hill Transit** (☎ 919/968–2769), at 75¢ a ride, takes you around the city. **Durham Area Transit Authority** (☎ 919/688–4587) is Durham's intracity bus system. Fares are 75¢, transfers 10¢. **Triangle Transit Authority** (☎ 919/549–9999), which links downtown Raleigh with Cary, Research Triangle Park, Durham, and Chapel Hill, runs weekdays except major holidays. Rates start at $1.

BY TAXI

More than 25 taxi companies serve the Triangle; fares are calculated by the mile. **City Taxi** (✉ Raleigh, ☎ 919/832–1489). **National Cab** (✉ Raleigh-Durham Airport, ☎ 919/469–1333). **Orange Cab** (✉ Durham, ☎ 919/682–6111).

Contacts and Resources

EMERGENCIES

Ambulance, police (☎ 911). For minor emergencies, go to one of the many urgent-care centers in Raleigh, Cary, Durham, and Chapel Hill.

GUIDED TOURS

The **Capital Area Visitor Center** (✉ 301 N. Blount St., 27611, ☎ 919/733–3456) in Raleigh offers maps, brochures, and free tours of government buildings; it's open weekdays 8–5, Saturday 9–5, Sunday 1–5.

The **Historic Chapel Hill/UNC Trolley Tour** (☎ 919/942–7818) operates April to November 15, Wednesday at 2. Fare is $5; call on weekdays for reservations.

LATE-NIGHT PHARMACIES

Eckerd Drug Store (✉ Lake Boone Shopping Center, Wycliff Rd., Raleigh, ☎ 919/781–4070) is open 24 hours. The **Wal-Mart** pharmacy (✉ 6600 Glenwood Ave., Raleigh, ☎ 919/783–9693) is open 24 hours. **Eckerd Drugs** (✉ 3527 Hillsborough Rd., Durham, ☎ 919/383–5591) is open 8 AM–midnight weekdays and 9 AM–11 PM weekends.

RADIO STATIONS

AM: WPTF 680, news, talk; WRBZ 850, talk. **FM:** WCPE 89.7, classical; WUNC 91.5, National Public Radio; WRAL 101.5, adult contemporary; WQDR 94.7, country; WRDU 106.1, rock.

VISITOR INFORMATION

Chapel Hill/Orange County Visitors Bureau (✉ 501 W. Franklin St., Suite 104, Chapel Hill 27516, ☎ 919/968–2060 or 888/968–2060). The **Downtown Chapel Hill Welcome Center** has maps, brochures, and flyers on attractions, accommodations, and services. ✉ *Bank of America Center, 137 E. Franklin St.,* ☎ *919/929–9700.* ⊙ *Tues.–Sat. 10–4.*

Durham Convention & Visitors Bureau (✉ 101 E. Morgan St., 27701, ☎ 919/687–0288 or 800/446–8604). The **Durham Bullhorn** provides 24-hour recorded information on events and activities (☎ 919/688–2855 or 800/772–2855).

Greater Raleigh Convention and Visitors Bureau (✉ Bank of America Bldg., 421 Fayetteville Street Mall, Suite 1505, 27601, ☎ 919/834–5900 or 800/849–8499).

THE SANDHILLS

Southern Pines, Pinehurst

Because of their sandy soil—they were once Atlantic beaches—the Sandhills weren't of much use to early farmers, most of whom switched to lumbering and making turpentine for a livelihood. Since the turn of the 20th century, however, this area with its gently undulating hills has proved ideal for golf and tennis. Promoters call it the Golf Capital of the World; the Tufts Archives honors the sport and the founding of Pinehurst. First-class resorts are centered on the 40 championship golf courses, including the famed Pinehurst Number 2. Public tennis courts can be found in many communities, and the area has also long been popular with horse owners.

The Highland Scots who settled the area left a rich heritage perpetuated through festivals and gatherings. In Colonial times, English potters were attracted to the rich clay deposits in the soil, and today their descendants and others turn out beautiful wares that are sold in more than 40 local shops.

Southern Pines

104 mi east of Charlotte, 71 mi southwest of Raleigh.

Southern Pines, the center of the Sandhills, is a good place to start your visit to the area.

Sandhills Horticultural Gardens has a wetland area that can be observed from elevated boardwalks. It's part of a 15-acre series of gardens showcasing roses, fruits and vegetables, herbs, conifers, hollies, a formal English garden, pools, and a waterfall. ⊠ *2200 Airport Rd., Sandhills Community College campus,* ☎ *910/695–3882 or 800/338–3944.* ☒ *Free.* ◷ *Daily sunrise–sunset.*

The **Shaw House,** the oldest structure in town (circa 1820), serves as headquarters for the Moore County Historical Association. There are three historic houses on the property and one about 15 mi away. ⊠ *S.W. Broad St. and Morganton Rd.,* ☎ *910/692–2051.* ☒ *Free.* ◷ *Apr.– Dec., Wed.–Sun. 1–4.*

Weymouth Center, former home of author and publisher James Boyd, hosts numerous concerts and lectures. Boyd, who died in 1944, was visited by many well-known writers; his home served as a cultural center for the area. The North Carolina Literary Hall of Fame is here, and a writer-in-residence program has hosted more than 600 writers. ⊠ *555 E. Connecticut Ave.,* ☎ *910/692–6261.* ☒ *Free.* ◷ *Weekdays 10– noon and 2–4; call ahead to arrange tours.*

Weymouth Woods Sandhills Nature Preserve, on the eastern outskirts of town, is a 571-acre wildlife preserve with 4 mi of hiking trails, a beaver pond, and a naturalist on staff. ⊠ *1024 N. Fort Bragg Rd. (off U.S. 1),* ☎ *910/692–2167.* ☒ *Free.* ◷ *Apr.–Oct., daily 9–7; Nov.–Mar., daily 9–6.*

OFF THE BEATEN PATH
CAMERON – Cameron, which hasn't changed much since the 19th century, is the place to shop for antiques. Approximately 60 antiques dealers operate out of several stores. The town itself, off U.S. 1, has been declared a historic district. Most shops are open Tuesday through Saturday 10–5, Sunday 1–5; call the historic district office (☎ 910/245–7001) for information. The town is 12 mi north of Southern Pines.

Dining and Lodging

$–$$$$ ✕ **Lob Steer Inn.** Salad and dessert bars complement generous broiled seafood and prime rib dinners at this casual, dimly lit steak house. ⊠ U.S. 1, ☎ 910/692–3503. *Reservations essential. AE, DC, MC, V. No lunch.*

$$$$ 🏨 **Pine Needles Lodge and Golf Club.** One of the bonuses of staying at this informal lodge is the chance to meet Peggy Kirk Bell, a champion golfer and golf instructor. She built the resort with her late husband and continues to help run it. It was host to the 1996 U.S. Women's Open and has been awarded the championship again for 2001. The rooms are done in a rustic style; many have exposed beams. ⊠ *1005 Midland Rd., Box 88, 28387,* ☎ *910/692–7111 or 800/747–7272,* FAX *910/692–5349. 71 rooms. Bar, dining room, snack bar, in-room data ports, pool, driving range, 18-hole golf course, putting green, 2 tennis courts, bicycles, business services, meeting rooms, airport shuttle. AE, MC, V. FAP.* ✎

$$$ 🏨 **Mid Pines Inn and Golf Club.** This resort community includes a Georgian-style clubhouse and a golf course designed by Donald Ross that has been the site of numerous tournaments. The spacious rooms in the 1921 inn are Wedgwood blue, with American antiques or good copies. Jackets are required in the dining room. ⊠ *1010 Midland Rd., 28387,* ☎ *910/692–2114 or 800/323–2114,* FAX *910/692–4615. 112 rooms, 5 houses, 7 villas. Bar, dining room, snack bar, pool, 18-hole golf course, putting green, 4 tennis courts, business services, meeting rooms, airport shuttle. AE, D, DC, MC, V.* ✎

Outdoor Activities and Sports

There are many excellent 18-hole golf courses here. **Club at Longleaf** (⊠ 2001 Midland Rd., ☎ 910/692–6100 or 800/889–5323) was built on a former horse farm. The front nine of the par-71 course plays through posts, rails, and turns of the old racetrack. **Mid Pines Golf Club** (⊠ 1010 Midland Rd., ☎ 910/692–2114 or 800/323–2114) is a golf getaway with a Donald Ross–designed par-72 course. **Pine Needles Resort** (⊠ 1005 Midland Rd., ☎ 910/692–7111 or 800/747–7272) has a Donald Ross–designed par-71 course complemented by practice facilities, grass tennis courts, and an outdoor swimming pool. **Talamore at Pinehurst** (⊠ 1595 Midland Rd., ☎ 910/692–5884 or 800/552–6292), with its unusual llama caddies, is a par-71 course designed by Rees Jones.

Shopping

Country Bookshop (⊠ 140 N.W. Broad St., ☎ 910/692–3211), in the historic downtown district, often has regional authors do readings and signings; the store stocks lots of children's books.

Pinehurst

6 mi west of Southern Pines.

Pinehurst, a New England–style village with quiet, shaded streets and immaculately kept cottages, was laid out in the late 1800s in a wagon-wheel design by landscape genius Frederick Law Olmsted. Annie Oakley lived here for a number of years and headed the gun club. Today, it is a mecca for sports enthusiasts, retirees, and tourists.

Tufts Archives recounts the founding of Pinehurst in the letters, pictures, and news clippings, dating from 1895, of James Walker Tufts, who served as president of the United States Golf Association. Golf memorabilia are on display. ⊠ *Given Memorial Library, 150 Cherokee Rd.,* ☎ *910/295–6022 or 910/295–3642.* ⊙ *Weekdays 9:30–5, Sat. 9:30–12:30.*

Dining and Lodging

$ ✗ **Pinehurst Playhouse Restaurant.** This casual eatery in the shop-filled Theater Building is in the heart of the village. It's *the* place to meet for soups and sandwiches. ✉ *W. Village Green,* ☎ *910/295–8873. Reservations not accepted. No credit cards. Closed Sun. No dinner.*

$$$$ ✗🏠 **Holly Inn.** Listed on the National Register of Historic Places, this hotel, affiliated with the Pinehurst Resort (☞ *below*), was the first in the village. Molding, lighting, and plumbing fixtures, based on research from local archives, recall the 1890s, the decade of its opening. Luxuries include silk hangers; embroidered robes; and afternoon sandwiches, cookies, and ice tea. A two-night stay is required. The menu at 1895, the bistro-style restaurant, changes with the seasons. Signature dinner entrées include pinecone-smoked free-range chicken with truffles, tarragon-scented roast tenderloin of veal, and Carolina blue-crab hash served with Madeira and orange basil hollandaise sauce. Jackets are required at the restaurant. ✉ *Cherokee Rd., 28374,* ☎ *910/295–2300 or 800/682–6901,* 🖷 *910/295–0988. 78 rooms, 7 suites. Restaurant, bar, in-room data ports, pool, golf and tennis privileges, croquet, business services, meeting rooms. AE, DC, MC, V. MAP.* 🐾

$$$–$$$$ ✗🏠 **Pinehurst Resort and Country Club.** The Pinehurst, a venerable re-
★ sort hotel in operation for nearly a century, has never lost the charm that founder James Tufts intended it to have. Civilized decorum rules in the spacious public rooms, on the rocker-lined wide verandas, and amid the gardens. Guest rooms are elegantly traditional. You can tee off on one of eight signature golf courses. Two blocks away the Manor Inn, a Pinehurst property with 45 rooms, has the feel of a cozy bed-and-breakfast. Manor Inn guests have access to all the resort and country club facilities, including the Carolina Dining Room. Known for its fine five-course meals, the restaurant is formal and requires a jacket. Try the veal medallions with applejack cream sauce, grilled apples, and caramelized Vidalia onions. ✉ *1 Carolina Vista Dr., Box 4000, 28374,* ☎ *910/295–6811 or 800/487–4653,* 🖷 *910/295–8503. 338 rooms, 130 condominiums. 2 restaurants, bar, in-room data ports, 5 pools, massage, 8 18-hole golf courses, 24 tennis courts, croquet, health club, windsurfing, boating, fishing, bicycles, children's programs, business services, meeting rooms. AE, D, DC, MC, V.* 🐾

$$$ ✗🏠 **Magnolia Inn.** This 102-year-old inn, once just a hangout for golfing buddies, is tastefully decorated with unusual antiques. Most guest rooms are in the Victorian style with wicker and brass beds; bathrooms have original fixtures such as claw-foot tubs. The inn's dining rooms ($$$–$$$$), with their dusty-rose wallpaper and fireplaces, have a cozy feel. Superb dinner choices are the grilled Norwegian salmon or roasted herb-crusted rack of lamb. There's also an English-style pub. ✉ *Magnolia and Chinquapin Rds., Box 818, 28370,* ☎ *910/ 295–6900 or 800/526–5562,* 🖷 *910/215–0858. 11 rooms. Dining room, pool, business services. AE, MC, V. BP.* 🐾

$$ 🏠 **Pine Crest Inn.** Chintz and mahogany fill the rooms of this slightly faded gem once owned by golfing great Donald Ross. The chefs whip up meals reminiscent of Sunday supper: homemade soups, fresh seafood dishes, and the house special, stuffed pork chops. Mr. B's Bar is the liveliest nightspot in town. Guests have golf and tennis privileges at local clubs. ✉ *Dogwood Rd., Box 879, 28370,* ☎ *910/295–6121 or 800/371–2545,* 🖷 *910/295–4880. 40 rooms. Dining room, bar. AE, D, DC, MC, V. MAP.* 🐾

Outdoor Activities and Sports

GOLF

Pinehurst Resort and Country Club (⊠ 1 Carolina Vista Dr., ☎ 910/295–6811 or 800/487–4653) has eight courses designed by masters such as Donald Ross, including the famed and challenging par-72 Number 2.

The par-71 **Pit Golf Links** (⊠ NC 5, ☎ 910/944–1600 or 800/574–4653) was designed by Dan Maples and sculpted from a 230-acre sand quarry.

HORSEBACK AND CARRIAGE RIDING

Riding instruction and carriage rides are available by appointment at **Pinehurst Stables** (⊠ NC 5, ☎ 910/295–8456).

TENNIS

The **Lawn and Tennis Club of North Carolina** (⊠ 1 Merrywood, ☎ 910/692–7270) and **Pinehurst Resort and Country Club** (⊠ Carolina Vista Dr., ☎ 910/295–8556) are known for their daily clinics.

Aberdeen

5 mi southeast of Pinehurst, 5 mi southwest of Southern Pines.

Aberdeen, a small town of Scottish ancestry, has a beautifully restored early 20th-century train station and plenty of shops with antiques and collectibles. The **Bethesda Presbyterian Church,** on Bethesda Road east of town, was founded in 1790. The present wooden structure, which is used for weddings, funerals, and reunions, was built in the 1860s and has bullet holes from a Civil War battle. The cemetery, where many early settlers are buried, is always open.

Malcolm Blue Farm, one of the few remaining examples of the 19th-century Scottish homes that dotted the area, has farm buildings and an old gristmill. A September festival recalls life here in the 1800s. The farm and museum are part of the North Carolina Civil War Theme Trail. ⊠ *Bethesda Rd.,* ☎ *910/944–7558, 910/944–9483 museum.* ✉ *Free.* ☉ *Thurs.–Sat. 1–4.*

OFF THE
BEATEN PATH

FORT BRAGG/POPE AIR FORCE BASE – This army–air force duo outside Fayetteville, 45 mi east of Aberdeen via NC 211 and U.S. 401, is one of the world's largest military complexes. Pope hosts an open house and air show annually (☎ 910/394–4183). Bragg, the biggest army post east of the Mississippi, is open year-round, and self-guided tours are available. The welcome center (☎ 910/907–2026) at the corner of Randolph and Knox streets on Fort Bragg has maps indicating public access areas. Free sites include the **82nd Airborne Division War Memorial Museum** (☎ 910/432–3443), which tells the story of this unit famous from World War I through Desert Storm. ⊠ *Off NC 24 or the All American Fwy. Some sites closed Mon.*

Lodging

$-$$ 🛏 **Inn at Bryant House.** One block east of U.S. 1, this charming downtown B&B, built in 1913, is a home away from home. All rooms are individually decorated; some have canopy beds. The inn has golf packages and arranges tennis and horseback riding. ⊠ *214 N. Poplar St., 28315,* ☎ *910/944–3300 or 800/453–4019,* FAX *910/944–8898. 9 rooms, 7 with bath. AE, D, MC, V. CP.* ✆

Outdoor Activities and Sports

Legacy Golf Links (⊠ U.S. 15–501S, ☎ 910/944–8825 or 800/344–8825) has the first American course designed by Jack Nicklaus II (par 72).

Seagrove

35 mi northwest of Pinehurst via NC 211 and U.S. 220.

★ Potters, some of whom are carrying on traditions that have been in their families for generations and others who are newer to the art, handcraft mugs, bowls, pitchers, platters, vases, and clay "face jugs" in the **Seagrove** area. More than 90 potteries are scattered along and off Route 705 and U.S. 220. Some of the work of local artisans is exhibited in national museums, including the Smithsonian. Most shops are open Tuesday through Saturday 10–5.

★ The **North Carolina Pottery Center,** a museum and educational facility, has exhibitions of pottery from around the state and maps locating the various studios around the area. ⊠ *250 East Ave.,* ☎ *336/873–8430.* ⊙ *Tues.–Sat. 10–4.* ✑

Asheboro

13 mi north of Seagrove, 23 mi south of Greensboro on U.S. 64.

Asheboro, the seat of Randolph County, sits in the Uwharrie National Forest, a haven for hikers, bikers, horseback riders, and fisherfolk. This part of the southern Piedmont is a lovely place to view scenery and visit crafts shops. You can also visit the **American Classic Motorcycle Museum** (⊠ 11740 U.S. 64W, ☎ 336/629–9564) or the **Foundation for Aircraft Conservation Flying Museum** (⊠ 2222 Pilot View Rd., ☎ 336/625–0170).

★ ♻ The **North Carolina Zoological Park,** a 1,500-acre home for more than 1,100 animals and 60,000 exotic and tropical plants, was the first zoo in the country designed from the get-go as a natural habitat facility. The park includes the 300-acre African Pavilion, an aviary, a gorilla habitat, a Sonoran Desert habitat, and a 200-acre North American habitat with polar bears and sea lions. You can take a tram between areas. ⊠ *4401 Zoo Pkwy.,* ☎ *336/879–7000 or 800/488–0444.* ⊞ *$8, including tram ride.* ⊙ *Apr.–Oct., daily 9–5; Nov.–Mar., daily 9–4.* ✑

Sandhills A to Z

Arriving, Departing, and Getting Around

BY CAR
U.S. 1 runs north–south through the Sandhills and is the recommended route from the Raleigh-Durham area, a distance of about 70 mi.

BY PLANE
US Airways Express (☎ 800/428–4322) serves the **Moore County Airport** (⊠ NC 22, Southern Pines, ☎ 910/692–3212), with connections from **Charlotte-Douglas International Airport** (☎ 704/359–4013), **Raleigh-Durham International Airport** (☎ 919/840–2123), and the **Piedmont Triad International Airport** (☎ 336/665–5666). Many lodging establishments run shuttle services.

BY TRAIN
Amtrak (☎ 910/692–6305 or 800/872–7245) southbound and northbound trains, one daily in each direction, stop in Southern Pines.

Contacts and Resources

EMERGENCIES
Ambulance, police (☎ 911). **Moore Regional Hospital** (⊠ 155 Memorial Dr., Pinehurst, ☎ 910/215–1111) has an emergency room.

RADIO STATIONS
AM: WKHO 550, easy listening; WEEB 990, news, talk; WQNX 1350, talk. **FM:** WIOZ 107, easy listening.

VISITOR INFORMATION
Pinehurst Area Convention and Visitors Bureau (⌧ 1480 U.S. 15–501N, Box 2270, Southern Pines 28388, ☎ 910/692–3330 or 800/346–5362) serves the Pinehurst, Southern Pines, and Aberdeen area. For details on local events, call the **events hot line** (☎ 910/692–1600). **Moore County Parks and Recreation Department** (☎ 910/947–2504) can provide recreation information.

THE OUTER BANKS
Cape Hatteras, Cape Lookout

North Carolina's Outer Banks, a series of barrier islands on the Atlantic Ocean, stretch from the Virginia state line south to Cape Lookout. Throughout history these waters have been the nemesis of shipping, gaining the nickname the Graveyard of the Atlantic; the network of lighthouses and lifesaving stations draws visitors today, and the many submerged wrecks attract scuba divers. The islands' coves and inlets offered privacy to pirates—the notorious Blackbeard lived and died here. For many years the Outer Banks remained isolated, home only to a few families who made their living by fishing. Today the islands, linked by bridges and ferries, have become popular destinations. Much of the area is included in the Cape Hatteras and Cape Lookout national seashores. The largest towns are Kitty Hawk, Kill Devil Hills, Nags Head, and Manteo.

On the inland side of the Outer Banks is the historic Albemarle region, a remote area of small villages and towns surrounding Albemarle Sound. Edenton was the colonial capital for a while, and many of its early structures are preserved.

You can tour the Outer Banks from the south end, by taking a car ferry to Ocracoke Island or, as in the following route, from the north end. You can drive the 120-mi stretch of NC 12 from Corolla to Ocracoke in a day, but be sure to allow plenty of time in summer to wait for the ferry connecting the islands and for exploring the undeveloped beaches, historic lifesaving stations, and charming beach communities stretched along the national seashores. Rentals are available throughout the area, with the highest concentration of accommodations between Kill Devil Hills and Nags Head. Mile markers (MM) indicate addresses for sites where there aren't many buildings. Be aware that during major storms and hurricanes the roads and bridges become clogged with traffic following the blue-and-white evacuation signs.

Numbers in the margin correspond to points of interest on the Outer Banks map.

Corolla, Duck, and Kitty Hawk

Kitty Hawk: 87 mi south of Norfolk, Va., via U.S. 17 and U.S. 158; 215 mi east of Raleigh via U.S. 64 and NC 12. Duck: 7 mi north of Kitty Hawk. Corolla: 19 mi north of Duck.

The small settlements of Corolla and Duck are largely seasonal residential enclaves full of summer rental condominiums. **Duck** has a growing number of restaurants and shopping outlets. The Currituck Beach Lighthouse in **Corolla** is the northernmost lighthouse on the Outer Banks. Drive slowly in Corolla; wild ponies wander free here and al-

The Outer Banks

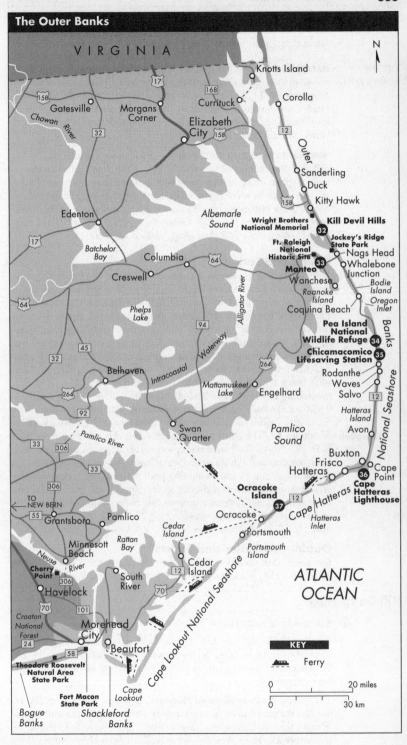

VIRGINIA

Knotts Island

17

168

Corolla

158

Gatesville

Morgans Corner

Currituck

12

Chowan River

32

Elizabeth City

158

Sanderling

Outer

Duck

158

Kitty Hawk

Edenton

Albemarle Sound

Wright Brothers National Memorial

Kill Devil Hills

32

Jockey's Ridge State Park

17

Batchelor Bay

Ft. Raleigh National Historic Site

Nags Head

Columbia

64

Manteo

33

Whalebone Junction

Creswell

Wanchese

Bodie Island

64

Roanoke Island

Oregon Inlet

Coquina Beach

Phelps Lake

94

Pea Island National Wildlife Refuge

34

45

Alligator River

Chicamacomico Lifesaving Station

35

32

Banks

Rodanthe

Belhaven

Intracoastal

Mattamuskeet Lake

Waves

Salvo

12

264

Engelhard

Hatteras Island

National Seashore

92

Pamlico Sound

Avon

33

306

Pamlico River

Swan Quarter

33

Buxton

306

Frisco

Cape Point

TO NEW BERN

Hatteras

36

55

Grantsboro

Pamlico

Ocracoke Island

12

Cape Hatteras

Cape Hatteras Lighthouse

Cedar Island

37

Ocracoke

Hatteras Inlet

Minnesott Beach

Rattan Bay

Portsmouth

Cherry Point

Neuse River

Portsmouth Island

306

South River

ATLANTIC OCEAN

Havelock

12

Cedar Island

70

101

70

Croatan National Forest

Morehead City

24

58

Beaufort

Theodore Roosevelt Natural Area State Park

Cape Lookout National Seashore

KEY

Ferry

Fort Macon State Park

Cape Lookout

0   20 miles

Bogue Banks

Shackleford Banks

0   30 km

ways have the right of way. **Kitty Hawk,** with a few thousand permanent residents, is among the quieter of the beach communities, with fewer rental accommodations.

OFF THE
BEATEN PATH

ELIZABETH CITY – This city's historic district has the largest number of pre–Civil War commercial buildings in the state. The **Museum of the Albemarle** (⊠ 1116 U.S. 17S, ☎ 252/335–1453), an affiliate of the North Carolina Museum of History (☞ Raleigh, *above*), has displays on local history; admission is free. Elizabeth City is 50 mi northwest of Kitty Hawk on the Albemarle Sound.

MERCHANTS MILLPOND STATE PARK – A 200-year-old man-made millpond and an ancient swamp form one of the state's rarest ecosystems. Cypress and gum trees hung with Spanish moss reach out of the still, dark waters, which are ideal for canoeing. Fishing, hiking, and camping are also available. The park is 80 mi northwest of Kitty Hawk, on the mainland. ⊠ *U.S. 158, Gatesville,* ☎ *252/357–1191.* ⊠ *Free.* ☺ *Sept.–May, daily 8–8; June–Aug., daily 8 AM–9 PM.*

Dining and Lodging

$$$$ ✕▥ **Sanderling Inn Resort & Conference Center.** The Sanderling, on a remote beach 5 mi north of Duck, is a fine place to be pampered. Recreation choices include tennis, swimming, and nature walks through the Pine Island Sanctuary. Though it has all the contemporary conveniences, the inn has the stately, mellow look of old Nags Head. Ceiling fans, wicker, and neutral tones give rooms a cool and casual feel. The ambitious restaurant ($$$; dinner reservations essential) is in a renovated lifesaving station; try the crab cakes, roast Carolina duckling with black cherry sauce, or fricassee of shrimp. ⊠ *1461 Duck Rd., Sanderling 27949,* ☎ *252/261–4111 or 800/701–4111,* 𝐅𝐀𝐗 *252/261–1638. 88 rooms, 29 efficiencies. Restaurant, bar, pool, hot tub, 2 tennis courts, health club, library, meeting rooms. AE, D, MC, V.* ☺

$$$–$$$$ ▥ **Advice 5¢.** The name may be quirky, but this contemporary B&B in Duck's North Beach area is very serious about guest care. Just a short walk from downtown shops and restaurants, Advice also offers the use of the tennis courts and swimming pool at Sea Pines, a nearby property. Beds in each room are dressed with crisp, colorful linens. All rooms have ceiling fans, shuttered windows, and baths stocked with thick cotton towels. ⊠ *111 Scarborough La., 27949,* ☎ *252/255–1050 or 800/238–4235. 4 rooms, 1 suite. MC, V. Closed Dec.–Jan. CP.* ☺

Outdoor Activities and Sports

Sea Scape Golf Course (⊠ 300 Eckner St., MM 2.5, Kitty Hawk, ☎ 252/261–2158) is a links course set amid the dunes. Par is 72.

Kill Devil Hills

32   *4 mi south of Kitty Hawk.*

Kill Devil Hills, on U.S. 158 Bypass, has been the site of rapid development over the last decade. Its population explodes in summer, and though many businesses are seasonal, you can find anything you need here year-round.

★   The **Wright Brothers National Memorial,** a granite monument that resembles the tail of an airplane, stands as a tribute to Wilbur and Orville Wright, the two bicycle mechanics from Ohio who took to the air on December 17, 1903. You can see a replica of the *Flyer* and stand on the spot where it made four takeoffs and landings, the longest flight a distance of 852 ft. Exhibits and an informative talk by a National Park Service ranger bring the event to life. The Wrights had to bring in the unassembled airplane by boat, along with all their food and supplies for building a camp. They made four trips to the site, beginning in 1900. The First Flight is commemorated annually. ⊠ *Off U.S. 158, between MM 7 and MM 8,* ☎ *252/441–7430.* 🖙 *$4 per car or $2 per person.* ☉ *Daily 9–5; extended hrs in summer.*

Kill Devil Hills has 5 mi of **beach** with 27 public access areas with limited parking off NC 12. Some have off-road vehicle access. Because of the number of rental cottages and hotels, this beach tends to have more people, but it is seldom uncomfortably crowded.

Dining and Lodging

$$–$$$ ✕ **Flying Fish Cafe.** While the interior of this downtown café is brightly colored and casual, the food and wine are taken very seriously. A perennial favorite entrée is shrimp on spinach fettuccine with feta cheese. ⊠ *2003 Croatan Hwy., off U.S. 158,* ☎ *252/441–6894. AE, D, MC, V. No lunch weekends.*

$$$–$$$$ 🏨 **Ramada Inn.** Guest rooms in this convention-style hotel have private balconies, some with ocean views. Peppercorns restaurant, overlooking the ocean, serves breakfast and dinner, and lunch is available on the sundeck next to the pool. ⊠ *1701 S. Virginia Dare Trail, off U.S. 158, MM 9.5, Box 2716, 27948,* ☎ *252/441–2151 or 800/635–1824,* 𝖥𝖠𝖷 *252/441–1830. 172 rooms. Restaurant, bar, in-room data ports, indoor pool, hot tub, shuffleboard, volleyball, business services, meeting rooms. AE, D, DC, MC, V.* 🏊

Nags Head

4 mi south of Kill Devil Hills.

Nags Head got its name because Outer Bankers hoping for shipwrecks would tie lanterns around the heads of their horses to lure merchant ships onto the shoals, thus profiting from the cargo that washed ashore. This is a very commercialized and congested area. On the upside, there are many restaurants, motels, hotels, and shops from which to choose.

Nags Head has 11 mi of **beach** with 33 public access areas, all with parking and some with rest rooms and showers. One point of interest is mile marker 11.5, the first North Carolina Historic Shipwreck Site. The USS *Huron* lies in 20 ft of water off the Nags Head Pier.

Coquina Beach (⊠ off NC 12, 8 mi south of U.S. 158) in the **Cape Hatteras National Seashore** (🖙 *below*) is considered by some to be the best swimming hole on the Outer Banks. The wide-beamed ribs of the shipwreck *Laura Barnes* rest in the dunes here. Picnic shelters are available.

🌀 **Jockey's Ridge State Park** still has the tallest sand dune in the East (about 88 ft), though it has lost some 22 ft since the 1930s thanks to the million visitors a year who carry sand away. It's a popular spot for hang gliding, kite flying, and sandboarding. ⊠ *U.S. 158 Bypass, MM 12,* ☎ *252/441–7132.* 🖙 *Free.* ☉ *Daily 8–sunset.*

Dining and Lodging

$$$–$$$$ ✕ **Owens' Restaurant.** In an old Nags Head–style clapboard cottage, Owens' has been in the same family since 1946. Though the menu features pasta and beef, the seafood is the star—especially the coconut shrimp and lobster bisque. The brass-and-glass Station Keeper's Lounge has entertainment. ⊠ *U.S. 158, MM 17,* ☎ *252/441–7309. Reservations not accepted. AE, D, DC, MC, V. Closed Jan.–Feb. No lunch.*

$$–$$$ ✕ **Windmill Point.** The menu changes but you can always count on the signature seafood trio: diners may choose any combination of three fish. The preparation is at the whim of the chef: lightly poached or grilled, and topped with roasted red pepper and capers, or shredded cucumber and dill, or a pineapple salsa. The restaurant has stunning views of the sound at sunset, eye-catching memorabilia from the luxury liner SS *United States,* and yes, a real windmill. ⊠ *U.S. 158 Bypass, MM 16½,* ☎ *252/441–1535. AE, D, DC, MC, V.*

$$$–$$$$ 🏨 **First Colony Inn.** This historic three-story B&B has encircling ve-
★ randas for great ocean views. Two rooms have wet bars, kitchenettes, and whirlpool baths; others have four-poster or canopy beds, hand-crafted armoires, and English antiques. The entire property is no-smoking. ⊠ *6720 S. Virginia Dare Trail, 27959,* ☎ *252/441–2343 or 800/368–9390,* 🖷 *252/441–9234. 26 rooms. Picnic area, in-room data ports, pool, beach, business services. AE, D, MC, V. CP.* 🕭

Outdoor Activities and Sports

GOLF

Nags Head Golf Links (⊠ 5615 S. Seachase Dr., MM 15, ☎ 252/441–8074 or 800/851–9404) has a par-71 course with ocean views.

HANG GLIDING

Lessons and gear are provided by **Kitty Hawk Kites** (⊠ U.S. 158, MM 13, ☎ 252/441–4124 or 800/334–4777), the oldest hang-gliding school on the East Coast.

Roanoke Island

10 mi southwest of Nags Head.

On a hot July day in 1587, 117 men, women, and children left their boat and set foot on Roanoke Island to make the first permanent En-glish settlement in the New World. Three years later they disappeared without a trace, leaving a mystery that continues to intrigue histori-ans. Today Roanoke Island is a sleepy, well-kept place that hasn't suc-cumbed to full-scale commercialism. Much of the 12-mi-long island remains wild. In summer, Roanoke and its two villages—picturesque Manteo, whose waterfront provides a pleasant combination of resi-dential and commercial development, and Wanchese, a commercial fish-ing community—come alive. The island is reached by U.S. 64/264 ③ from U.S. 158 Bypass. **Manteo** has some sights related to the island's history as well as an aquarium.

A history, education, and cultural arts complex opposite the waterfront in Manteo, **Roanoke Island Festival Park** includes the *Elizabeth II* State Historic Site. Costumed interpreters conduct tours of the 69-ft ship, a re-creation of a 16th-century vessel, except when it is on educational voyages in the off-season (call ahead). The complex also has plays, con-certs, arts and crafts exhibitions, and special programs. ⊠ *Downtown Manteo,* ☎ *252/473–1144.* 🖾 *$8.* ☉ *Mar., daily 10–5; Apr.–Oct., daily 9–6; Nov.–Dec., daily 10–5.*

Clustered together on the outskirts of Manteo are the lush **Elizabethan Gardens,** a re-creation of a 16th-century English garden, established as a memorial to the first English colonists. They are impeccably main-tained by the Garden Club of North Carolina. ⊠ *1411 U.S. 64/264, 3 mi north of downtown Manteo,* ☎ *252/473–3234.* 🖾 *$5.* ☉ *Apr.–May and Sept.–Oct., daily 9–6; June–Aug., daily 9–7; Dec.–Feb., week-days 10–4.*

Fort Raleigh National Historic Site is a restoration of the original 1585 earthworks that marks the beginning of English colonial history in Amer-ica. Be sure to see the orientation film and then take a guided tour of the fort. A nature trail leads to an outlook over Roanoke Sound. ⊠ *Off U.S. 64/264, 3 mi north of Manteo,* ☎ *252/473–5772.* 🖾 *Free.* ☉ *Daily 9–5; extended hrs in summer.*

The *Lost Colony,* begun in 1937, is the country's first and longest-running outdoor drama. It reenacts the story of the first colonists who settled here in 1587 and then disappeared, and it is staged at the Waterside Amphitheatre. ⊠ *1409 U.S. 64/264,* ☎ *252/473–3414 or 800/488–5012.* 🎫 *$16 (reservations essential).* ☉ *Performances June–Aug., Sun.–Fri. at 8:30 PM.*

� The **North Carolina Aquarium at Roanoke Island,** overlooking Croatan Sound, has been expanded to twice its former size. *The Graveyard of the Atlantic* is the centerpiece exhibit. It is a 285,000-gallon ocean tank containing the re-created remains of the USS *Monitor,* sunken off Hatteras Island (☞ *below*). ⊠ *Airport Rd., off U.S. 64,* ☎ *252/473–3493.* 🎫 *$3.* ☉ *Daily 9–5.*

<table>
<tr>
<td>OFF THE
BEATEN PATH</td>
<td>EDENTON – Rich with history, North Carolina's first permanent settlement and the colony's first capital is a placid, immensely scenic place on the north side of the Albemarle Sound (65 mi west of Manteo). Originally incorporated in 1715 with the name the Towne on Queen Anne's Creek, the spot was renamed Edenton seven years later in honor of Governor Charles Eden. A fine collection of 18th-century buildings has been well maintained. Stop by the visitor center (⊠ 108 N. Broad St., ☎ 252/482–2637) to hear tales about the colonists, such as the women of the Edenton Tea Party, who fought for liberty. An inexpensive pamphlet serves as a guide on a 1½-mi walking tour. Guided tours of the historic district are available and are recommended. Some highlights are the Jacobean-style Cupola House and Gardens, the Chowan County Courthouse (1767), and St. Paul's Episcopal Church.</td>
</tr>
</table>

Dining and Lodging

$$ ✕ **Weeping Radish Brewery and Restaurant.** This Bavarian-style restaurant and microbrewery is known for its German cuisine and the annual Octoberfest weekend held after Labor Day, which showcases German and blues bands. Brewery tours are offered free of charge upon request. The beer is superb. ⊠ *U.S. 64, Manteo,* ☎ *252/473–1157. D, MC, V.*

$$$ ✕🏠 **Tranquil House Inn.** This 19th-century-style waterfront inn is only a few steps from shops, restaurants, and the Roanoke Island Festival Park (☞ *above*), and bikes are provided for more distant adventures. Handmade comforters give rooms a cozy feel. Wine and cheese each evening are part of the rate. The restaurant, 1587 ($$$–$$$$), serves inventive entrées such as sesame-crusted tuna with wasabi vinaigrette and shiitake mushrooms. ⊠ *405 Queen Elizabeth Ave., Box 2045, Manteo 27954,* ☎ *252/473–1404 or 800/458–7069,* 🖷 *252/473–1526. 25 rooms. Restaurant, business services, meeting rooms. AE, D, MC, V. Closed Dec.–Jan. CP.* ✍

Cape Hatteras National Seashore

Extends 70 mi south of Nags Head.

★ **Cape Hatteras National Seashore** has more than 70 mi of unspoiled beaches stretching from south Nags Head to Ocracoke Inlet across three narrow islands: Bodie, Hatteras, and Ocracoke. The islands are linked by NC 12 and the Hatteras Inlet ferry. This coastal area is ideal for swimming, surfing, windsurfing, diving, boating, and other water activities. It's easy to find your own slice of beach as you drive south down NC 12, but park only in designated areas. If you want to swim, beware of strong tides and currents—there are no lifeguard stations. Fishing piers can be found in Rodanthe, Avon, and Frisco. For information, *see* Visitor Information *in* the Outer Banks A to Z, *below.*

Hatteras Island

15 mi south of Nags Head.

The Herbert C. Bonner Bridge arches for 3 mi over Oregon Inlet and carries traffic to Hatteras Island, known as the "blue marlin capital of the world." The island, a 33-mi-long ribbon of sand, juts out into the Atlantic Ocean; at its most distant point (Cape Hatteras), Hatteras is 25 mi from the mainland. About 85% of the island belongs to Cape Hatteras National Seashore, and the remainder is privately owned in seven small, quaint villages strung along NC 12, the island's fragile lifeline to points north.

㉞ **Pea Island National Wildlife Refuge,** between Oregon Inlet and Rodanthe, is made up of more than 5,000 acres of marsh. This birder's paradise, with observation platforms and spotting scopes, is on the Atlantic Flyway: More than 265 species are sighted regularly, including endangered peregrine falcons and piping plovers. NC 12 travels through marsh areas, and you can hike or drive, depending on the terrain. A visitor center, 5 mi south of Oregon Inlet on NC 12, has an informational display. ⊠ *Pea Island Refuge Headquarters, NC 12,* ☎ *252/473–1131.* 🎟 *Free.* ☉ *May–Sept., daily 9–4; Oct.–Apr., weekdays 9–4.*

㉟ In Rodanthe, the restored 1911 **Chicamacomico Lifesaving Station** has a museum that tells the story of the 24 stations that once lined the Outer Banks. Living-history reenactments are performed June–August. ⊠ *Off NC 12,* ☎ *252/987–1552.* 🎟 *Free.* ☉ *May–Oct., Tues., Thurs., and Sat. 11–5.*

㊱ **Cape Hatteras Lighthouse,** about 30 mi south of Rodanthe, is a beacon to ships offshore. At 208 ft this is the tallest brick lighthouse in the world, and it's painted with distinctive black and white spirals. During the summer the Principal Keeper's quarters are open for viewing. Offshore lie the remains of the USS *Monitor,* a Confederate ironclad ship that sank in 1862. The visitor center here provides information on the National Seashore. ⊠ *Hatteras Island Visitor Center, off NC 12 near Buxton,* ☎ *252/995–4474.* 🎟 *Free.* ☉ *Daily 9–5.*

Dining

$–$$$ ✕ **Tides.** Just south of the entrance for the Cape Hatteras Lighthouse, this place is popular for its good service, well-prepared food, and homey atmosphere. In addition to offering the usual seafood, the menu has chicken and ham. It's also a favorite breakfast spot. ⊠ *NC 12, Buxton,* ☎ *252/995–5988. MC, V. Closed Dec.–early Apr.*

Ocracoke Island

㊲ *Southwest of Hatteras Island.*

Much of Ocracoke Island is part of Cape Hatteras National Seashore. A free ferry that leaves every hour during the day will take you from Hatteras to the island in 40 minutes; other ferries leave from the mainland. Ocracoke was cut off from the world for so long that locals still speak in quasi-Elizabethan accents. Today, however, the island is a refuge for visitors. A village of shops, motels, and restaurants is around Silver Lake Harbor, where the pirate Blackbeard met his death in 1718. The **Ocracoke Lighthouse** is a photographer's dream. The **Ocracoke Island Visitor Center** (⊠ Ocracoke Village, south end of NC 12 on Silver Lake, ☎ 252/928–4531), run by the National Park Service, provides information.

Ocracoke Island **beaches** are among the least populated and most beautiful on the Cape Hatteras National Seashore. Four public access

NORTH CAROLINA'S PIRATES

NORTH CAROLINA'S COAST was a magnet for marauding sea dogs during the Golden Age of Piracy, a period that spanned the 17th and 18th centuries. Among its visitors was Stede Bonnet, captured in the Cape Fear region in 1718 but escaped; Anne Bonny, daughter of a plantation owner, wife of one pirate and lover of another; Charles Vane, whose crew mutinied; and Paul Williams, who accepted King George I's pardon, only to return to piracy.

The most notorious buccaneer of them all was Blackbeard, whose two-year reign of terror began in 1716: cultivating fear by strapping on six pistols and six knives, tying his luxuriant beard into pigtails and, legend has it, lighting matches under his hat to give the illusion that his head was smoking, Blackbeard attacked ships in the Caribbean and settlements along the coasts of Virginia and the Carolinas.

At least three of his ships sank in North Carolina's waters; archaeologists are retrieving artifacts from what is likely the flagship, *Queen Anne's Revenge,* which ran aground on a sandbar near Beaufort Inlet in May of 1718. The following November a seafaring posse caught Blackbeard in one his favorite playgrounds, Ocracoke Inlet. The pirate was decapitated and his head hung from a conquering ship. Still sought are the hulks of Blackbeard's lost ships and his treasure.

–By Lisa H. Towle

---

areas have parking, as well as off-road vehicle access. At the **Ocracoke Pony Pen** (⊠ NC 12, 6 mi southwest of the Hatteras–Ocracoke ferry landing), you can observe from a platform what some believe are the direct descendants of Spanish mustangs that once roamed wild on the island.

Dining and Lodging

$–$$ ✕⌨ **Island Inn and Dining Room.** The inn, built as a private lodge back in 1901, shows its age a bit but is full of Outer Banks character and is being upgraded gradually. Some rooms are in a modern wing, and these are good for families. The large rooms in the Crow's Nest on the third floor are the best; they have cathedral ceilings and look out over the island. The restaurant ($–$$) is known for its oyster omelet, crab cakes, and hush puppies. This is a no-smoking property. ⊠ *Corner of Lighthouse Rd. and NC 12, Box 9, 27960,* ☎ *252/928–4351, 877/ 456–3466 inn, 252/928–7821 dining room;* ﬁ *252/928–4352. 35 rooms, 4 villas. Restaurant, in-room data ports, pool, airport shuttle. D, MC, V.* ✎

Cape Lookout National Seashore

Southwest of Ocracoke Island via Cedar Island.

★ **Cape Lookout National Seashore** extends for 55 mi from Portsmouth Island to Shackleford Banks and includes 28,400 acres of uninhabited land and marsh. The remote, sandy islands are linked to the mainland by private ferries. Ferry service is available from Harkers Island to the Cape Lookout Light area, from Davis to Shingle Point, from Atlantic to an area north of Drum Inlet, and from Ocracoke to Portsmouth Village. Portsmouth, a deserted village that was inhabited from 1753 until the early 1970s, is being restored and is open to the public from April to early November. To the south, wild ponies roam Shackleford Banks. Four-wheel-drive vehicles are allowed on the beach, and primitive camping is available. For information, *see* Visitor Information *in* the Outer Banks A to Z, *below.*

The Outer Banks A to Z

Arriving, Departing, and Getting Around

BY BOAT

Seagoing visitors travel the Intracoastal Waterway through the Outer Banks and Albemarle region. Boats may dock at nearly 150 marinas, including **Elizabeth City** (☎ 252/338–2886), **Manteo Waterfront Docks** (☎ 252/473–3320), and **National Park Service Silver Lake Marina** (☎ 252/928–5111) in Ocracoke. For a complete list of facilities, see the *North Carolina Coastal Boating Guide,* compiled by the **North Carolina Department of Transportation** (☎ 919/733–2520).

BY CAR

U.S. 158 links the Outer Banks with U.S. 17 leading to Norfolk, Virginia, and other places north. NC 12 goes north toward Corolla and south toward Ocracoke. From Ocracoke there are **car ferries** to Cedar Island and Swan Quarter on the mainland. You need a reservation for the ferry (☎ 800/293–3779).

BY FERRY

For information about the state-run ferry system and its schedules and costs, call the North Carolina Department of Transportation's **Ferry Information Line** (☎ 800/293–3779).

BY PLANE

The closest commercial airports are the **Raleigh-Durham International Airport** (✉ 1600 Terminal Blvd., Morrisville, ☎ 919/840–2123), a five-hour drive, and, in Virginia, **Norfolk International** (✉ 2200 Norview Ave., ☎ 757/857–3351), a 1½-hour drive, both of which are served by major carriers, including American, Continental, Delta, and US Airways. For airline telephone numbers, *see* Air Travel *in* Smart Travel Tips A to Z. **Southeast Air** (☎ 252/473–3222 or 800/289–8202) and **Outer Banks Airways** (☎ 252/473–2227) provide charter service between the **Dare County Regional Airport** (✉ 410 Airport Rd., Manteo, ☎ 252/473–2600) and major cities along the East Coast.

BY TAXI

Beach Cabs (☎ 252/441–2500 or 800/441–2503), based in Nags Head, offers 24-hour service from Norfolk to Ocracoke and towns in between. **Outer Banks Limousine Service** (☎ 252/261–3133 or 800/828–5466), headquartered in Kill Devil Hills, serves the entire area and Norfolk International.

BY TRAIN

Amtrak service (☎ 800/872–7245) is available to Norfolk, Virginia, about 75 mi to the north.

Contacts and Resources

EMERGENCIES

Dial 911 for emergencies on Oregon Inlet, Roanoke Island, Hatteras Island, and Ocracoke Island. The **Healtheast/Outer Banks Medical Center** (✉ 2808 S. Croatan Hwy., Nags Head, ☎ 252/441–7111) is open 24 hours a day. **Beach Medical Care** (✉ 5200 N. Croatan Hwy., MM 1.5, Kitty Hawk, ☎ 252/261–4187) provides help around the clock. For **Coast Guard** assistance, dial ☎ 252/995–6411.

Historic Albemarle Tour, Inc. (⊠ 1 Harding Sq., Washington, ☎ 252/974–2950 or 800/734–1117) runs guided tours of Edenton and publishes a brochure on a self-guided tour of the Albemarle Region.

Kitty Hawk AeroTours leaves from the First Flight Airstrip or from Manteo for Kitty Hawk, Corolla, Cape Hatteras, Ocracoke, Portsmouth Island, and other areas along the Outer Banks. ⊠ *Behind Wright Brothers Monument, U.S. 158, MM 8, Kill Devil Hills,* ☎ *252/441–4460.* ⊙ *Tours Mar.–Labor Day.*

The **North Carolina Aquarium at Roanoke Island** (⊠ Airport Rd., Manteo, ☎ 252/473–3493) sponsors summer boat tours of the estuary and the sound.

OUTDOOR ACTIVITIES AND SPORTS

Camping is permitted in four designated areas along the **Cape Hatteras National Seashore** (⊠ Rte. 1, Box 675, Manteo 27954, ☎ 252/473–2111). These campgrounds can serve tents, trailers, and motor homes. All camping at **Cape Lookout National Seashore** (⊠ 131 Charles St., Harkers Island 28531, ☎ 252/728–2250) is in the primitive style and is allowed from mid-April through mid-October. Be sure to take extra-long tent stakes for sand, and don't forget insect repellent. All sites are available on a first-come, first-served basis, except Ocracoke, where reservations are accepted. For information about private campgrounds, contact the **Dare County Tourist Bureau** (☎ 252/473–2138 or 800/446–6262).

Fishing, whether surf casting or deep-sea, is wonderful here. You don't need a license for saltwater fishing. You can board a charter boat or head your own craft out of **Oregon Inlet Fishing Center** (☎ 252/441–6301 or 800/272–5199) or **Pirates Cove Yacht Club and Marina** (☎ 252/473–3906 or 800/367–4728) in Manteo. For fishing regulations, call the North Carolina Division of Marine Fisheries (☎ 252/726–7021).

With more than 1,500 known shipwrecks off the coast of the Outer Banks, **scuba-diving** opportunities are virtually unlimited. The USS *Monitor* is off-limits, however. The USS *Huron* Historic Shipwreck Preserve, which lies offshore between mile markers 11 and 12, is a popular diving site. Full-service dive shops include **Outer Banks Dive Center** (⊠ 3917 S. Croatan Hwy., Nags Head, ☎ 252/449–8349).

Surfing and **windsurfing** are excellent on the Outer Banks. For lessons and rentals, including windsurfing and kayaking, contact **Kitty Hawk Water Sports** (⊠ U.S. 158, MM 16.5, Nags Head, ☎ 252/441–6800 or 800/334–4777) or **Bert's Surf Shop** (⊠ U.S. 158, MM 10, Nags Head, ☎ 252/441–1939; U.S. 158, MM 4, Kitty Hawk, ☎ 252/261–7584).

RADIO STATIONS

AM: WGAI 560, adult contemporary; WOBR 1530, vacation information, news. **FM:** WNHW 92, country; WOBR 95.3, adult contemporary; WVOD 99.1, beach, Top 40; WRSF 105.7, country.

VISITOR INFORMATION

Dare County Tourist Bureau (⊠ 704 S. U.S. 64/264, Box 399, Manteo 27954, ☎ 252/473–2138 or 800/446–6262) operates two additional information centers. The **Aycock Brown Welcome Center** (⊠ U.S. 158, MM 1.25, Kitty Hawk, ☎ 252/261–4644) is open daily 8:30–6:30 and offers extensive resources including maps and ferry schedules. The smaller **Hatteras Island Welcome Center** (☎ no phone) is right before Bodie Island, just south of the Whalebone Junction intersection of NC 12 near Cape Hatteras National Seashore's northern entrance. This center is open from Memorial Day to October 1, daily 9–5, and on weekends in April, May, and November. The bureau can also direct you to agencies that arrange housing rentals.

The **National Park Service's Group Headquarters,** at Fort Raleigh National Historic Site in Manteo (⊠ Off U.S. 64/264), has a 24-hour general information line (☎ 252/473–2111) about Cape Hatteras National Seashore, or you can write the Superintendent (⊠ Rte. 1, Box 675, Manteo, 27954).

The **National Park Service, Cape Lookout National Seashore** (⊠ 131 Charles St., Harkers Island, 28531, ☎ 252/728–2250) has information about visiting Cape Lookout.

NEW BERN AND THE CENTRAL COAST

Craven County—home to New Bern; a good chunk of the 157,000-acre Croatan National Forest; and Cherry Point, the world's largest Marine Corps Air Station—is by turns genteel and historic, modern and commercialized, rural and wild. Golfers, boaters, and a growing number of retirees find the area a haven.

Neighboring Carteret County, with nearly 80 mi of ocean coastline, is known as the Central or "Crystal" Coast. It is composed of the south-facing beaches along the barrier island Bogue Banks (Atlantic Beach, Pine Knoll Shores, Indian Beach, Salter Path, and Emerald Isle), three mainland townships (Morehead City, Beaufort, and Newport), and a series of small, unincorporated "Down East" communities traversed by a portion of U.S. 70 that's a Scenic Byway.

New Bern

112 mi southeast of Raleigh.

The pace is quiet and slow in New Bern, the second oldest town in North Carolina. Settled in 1710 by Swiss and German colonists and named for Bern, Switzerland, the city has a heraldic Swiss black bear symbol that is everywhere. New Bern, the state capital from the period of English rule until immediately after the Revolution, is where North Carolina's first newspaper was printed and Pepsi Cola was invented. History is taken seriously here; there are more than 150 sites included in the National Register of Historic Places.

Sailors and sun seekers will enjoy the area, as the Neuse and Trent rivers are perfect for activities such as water-skiing and crabbing. The historic downtown area is filled with shops, many of them selling antiques. As in much of North Carolina, golf is a favorite New Bern pastime.

The reconstructed **Tryon Palace,** an elegant Georgian building, was the colonial capitol and the home of Royal Governor William Tryon during the 1770s. It was rebuilt according to architectural drawings of the original palace and furnished with English and American antiques according to Governor Tryon's inventory. An audiovisual orientation will prep you for a tour of the house led by costumed guides. In summer actors deliver monologues detailing a day in the life of the governor. Tours of the 18th-century formal gardens are self-guided. The stately **John Wright Stanly House** (circa 1783), the **Dixon-Stevenson House** (circa 1826), and **New Bern Academy** (circa 1809) are within or near the 13-acre Tryon Palace complex. ⊠ *610 Pollock St.,* ☎ *252/514–4900.* ⌨ *Palace and gardens $7, tour of all buildings and gardens $12.* ☉ *Mon.–Sat. 9–5, Sun. 1–5.*

Dining and Lodging

$$-$$$$ ✕ **The Flame.** The considerate staff at this dark, woodsy steak house, with decor that's vaguely reminiscent of the Victorian era, helps make dinners special. Steak, lobster, grilled shrimp, and teriyaki chicken are all good bets. ⊠ *2303 Neuse Blvd.,* ☎ *252/633–0262. AE, D, DC, MC, V. Closed Sun. No lunch.*

$ ✕ **Pollock Street Deli.** Good-size crowds gather in the tiny rooms of an authentic colonial house in the historic district and its sidewalk tables for a wide variety of classic deli treats or Sunday brunch. Service can be leisurely. ⊠ *208 Pollock St.,* ☎ *252/637–2480. AE, MC, V. No dinner Sun.*

$$-$$$ ✕▥ **Harvey Mansion Historic Inn.** The upstairs dining area at Beat and
★ Carolyn Zuttel's inn consists of six small dining rooms with 11½-ft ceilings and decorative fireplaces. Guest rooms have four-poster beds, plush carpeting, and extraplush mattresses. The mansion, a striking 1797 house, also serves as an art gallery, and the cellar, with its exposed beams, is a low-key pub. ⊠ *221 S. Front St., 28563,* ☎ *252/638–3205 or 800/638–3205,* ℻ *252/638–3206. 3 rooms. Restaurant, pub, meeting rooms. AE, D, DC, MC, V.* ✎

$$$ ▥ **Sheraton Grand.** At the confluence of the Neuse and Trent rivers, this Sheraton—with marina facilities—is actually two properties in one. A hotel has guest rooms overlooking the Trent River, and rooms at the inn have either waterfront or city views. An executive level contains suites. ⊠ *100 Middle St., 28560,* ☎ *252/638–3585,* ℻ *252/638–8112. 172 rooms. Restaurant, bar, in-room data ports, pool, business services, meeting rooms, airport shuttle. AE, D, DC, MC, V.* ✎

$$ ▥ **Harmony House Inn.** At this historic B&B convenient to all the at-
★ tractions, guests sleep in spacious rooms that once lodged Yankee soldiers during the Civil War. Today, rooms are furnished with a mix of antiques and reproductions. The inn serves complimentary white and dessert wines in the evening. ⊠ *215 Pollock St., 28560,* ☎ *252/636–3810 or 800/636–3113,* ℻ *252/636–3810. 10 rooms. In-room data ports, business services, airport shuttle. AE, D, MC, V. BP.* ✎

Morehead City

35 mi southeast of New Bern.

Morehead City is a fishing and boating center across Bogue Sound from the barrier island Bogue Banks. Popular family beaches on the island are **Atlantic Beach** and **Emerald Isle.** Among the more developed areas are these beach towns, as well as Pine Knoll Shores; all appeal to families.

ⓒ The **North Carolina Aquarium at Pine Knoll Shores,** in a maritime forest on Bogue Banks, has a 2,000-gallon salt-marsh tank with live alligators, a loggerhead turtle nursery, and a shipwreck exhibit. ⊠ *Salter Path Rd., MM 7, Atlantic Beach,* ☎ *252/247–4004.* ▨ *$3.* ☉ *Daily 9–5.*

Dining and Lodging

$$-$$$ ✕ **West Side Cafe.** A favorite among locals, this small café takes pride in serving fresh seafood any way you can eat it. Dinner is a delight here; sometimes there's live entertainment. ⊠ *4370-A Arendell St.,* ☎ *252/240–0588. MC, V.*

$-$$$ ✕ **Sanitary Fish Market & Restaurant.** Sixty-one years ago, when the Sanitary was founded, many fish houses were ill-kept. The owners wanted to signal their difference. Clean, simple, and generous are bywords at this waterfront place where diners sit on wooden benches. It can get noisy (the restaurant seats 600), but guests from around the world gush about the food. ⊠ *501 Evans St.,* ☎ *252/247–3111. D, MC, V.*

$$ 🏨 **Windjammer Inn.** This is the place for people focused on one thing: easy access to the ocean. What you get here is straightforward—a comfortable oversize room with a private balcony and ocean view. The five-story, glass-enclosed elevator sets the inn apart from typical beach lodging. A two-night minimum stay is required on summer weekends. ⊠ *Salter Path Rd. in Pine Knoll Shores, Atlantic Beach 28512,* ☎ *252/247–7123 or 800/233–6466,* 𝔽𝔸𝕏 *252/247–0133. 46 rooms. In-room data ports, refrigerators, pool. AE, D, MC, V.* ✎

$–$$ 🏨 **Best Western Buccaneer.** The inn sits beside the Morehead Plaza shopping center, a 10-minute drive from Atlantic Beach. Rooms are attractive and comfortable. ⊠ *2806 Arendell St., 28557,* ☎ *252/726–3115 or 800/682–4982,* 𝔽𝔸𝕏 *252/726–3864. 91 rooms. Restaurant, pool, business services, meeting room. AE, D, DC, MC, V. BP.* ✎

Beaufort

3 mi east of Morehead City.

Beaufort, a small seaport with a bustling boardwalk, brims with charm. The third-oldest town in North Carolina, it was named for Henry Somerset, Duke of Beaufort.

The **Beaufort Historic Site,** in the center of town, consists of restored buildings dating from 1767 to 1859, including the **Carteret County Courthouse** and the **Apothecary Shop and Doctor's Office.** Don't miss the **Old Burying Grounds** (1731). Here Otway Burns, a privateer in the War of 1812, is buried under his ship's cannon; a nine-year-old girl who died at sea is buried in a rum keg; and an English soldier saluting the king is buried upright in his grave. Tours on an English-style double-decker bus and guided walking tours depart from the visitor center. ⊠ *130 Turner St.,* ☎ *252/728–5225.* 🚌 *Bus tour $6, bus and walking tour $10.* ☉ *Visitor center Easter–Oct., Mon.–Sat. 9:30–5, Sun. 1:30–4; Nov.–Easter, Mon.–Sat. 10–4, Sun. 1:30–4.*

Beaufort's **North Carolina Maritime Museum** documents the state's seafaring and coastal history and includes an exhibit about the infamous pirate Blackbeard and the discovery of his flagship near Beaufort Inlet (☞ Close-Up: North Carolina's Pirates, *above*). The museum includes the **Watercrafts Center,** across the street, which gives boat-building classes. Its education staff also provides year-round programs, including trips to the marsh and barrier islands. ⊠ *315 Front St.,* ☎ *252/728–7317.* ☉ *Museum Mon.–Sat. 8–5, Sun. 1–5; watercrafts center Tues.–Fri. 9–5, Sat. 10–5, Sun. 1–5.* 🚌 *Free.*

Dining and Lodging

$–$$$ ✗ **Clawson's 1905 Restaurant and Pub.** Housed in what was a general store in the early 1900s, Clawson's serves hearty food such as ribs, steaks, pasta, and local seafood. It gets very crowded in summer, so arrive early for both lunch and dinner. The coffee bar opens at 7 AM. ⊠ *425 Front St.,* ☎ *252/728–2133. D, MC, V.*

$$–$$$ 🏨 **Langdon House.** You'll sleep surrounded by antiques at this B&B
★ built in 1733. The host provides everything from sightseeing suggestions to sumptuous Southern breakfasts and full beach baskets for picnics. ⊠ *135 Craven St., 28516,* ☎ *252/728–5499,* 𝔽𝔸𝕏 *252/728–1717. 4 rooms. No credit cards. BP.* ✎

New Bern and the Central Coast A to Z

Arriving, Departing, and Getting Around

BY BOAT

The Intracoastal Waterway provides access to many Central Coast destinations, including Beaufort, Morehead City, and Emerald Isle. Beaufort has plentiful anchorage and more than 35 marinas, including the **Beaufort Town Docks** (☎ 252/728–2053) and the **Morehead City Yacht Basin** (☎ 252/726–6862).

New Bern can be reached via the Neuse River from Pamlico Sound. Several marinas are available here, including the **Sheraton Grand Marina** (☎ 252/638–3585). You can dock for the day (but not overnight) at the public docks of **Union Point Park** (☎ 252/636–4060).

The *North Carolina Coastal Boating Guide,* compiled by the **North Carolina Department of Transportation** (☎ 919/733–2522), has a comprehensive list of facilities for boaters.

BY BUS
Greyhound/Carolina Trailways serves Morehead City (✉ 105 N. 13th St., ☎ 252/726–3029 or 800/231–2222) and New Bern (✉ 504 Guion St., ☎ 252/633–3100 or 800/231–2222).

BY CAR
U.S. 70 connects New Bern, Morehead City, and Beaufort with points to the west, including Raleigh and I–95. East of Beaufort, U.S. 70 connects to NC 12, which continues on the Outer Banks via ferry. U.S. 17 leads north from New Bern toward the Albemarle region and south to Wilmington. NC 58 runs the length of the Bogue Banks, while NC 24 follows the mainland shore from Morehead City south to Swansboro.

BY FERRY
For information about the state-run ferry system, call the North Carolina Department of Transportation's **ferry information line** (☎ 800/293–3779).

BY PLANE
US Airways Express (☎ 800/428–4322) flies into **Craven County Regional Airport** (✉ U.S. 70, New Bern, ☎ 252/638–8591), where charter service and car rentals are available.

BY TAXI
A-1 Yellow Cab Co. (☎ 252/728–3483) serves Atlantic Beach, Beaufort, Morehead City, and the airport. **Safeway Taxi Co.** (☎ 252/633–2828) operates in the New Bern area.

Contacts and Resources
BEACHES
NC 58 passes through all of the beach communities on the Bogue Banks, and locations are noted by mile markers (MM). Points of public access along the shoreline are marked by orange-and-blue signs. Lifeguards monitor some of the beaches. Contact the Carteret County Tourism Development Bureau (☞ Visitor Information, *below*) for information. You can fish, swim, picnic, and hike at **Fort Macon State Park** (☎ 252/726–3775), outside Morehead City.

EMERGENCIES
Ambulance, police (☎ 911). **Coast Guard assistance** (☎ 252/247–4598). For emergencies, contact **Carteret General Hospital** (✉ 3500 Arendell St., ☎ 252/247–1540) in Morehead City or **Craven Regional Medical Center** in New Bern (✉ 2300 Neuse Blvd., ☎ 252/633–8111).

OUTDOOR ACTIVITIES AND SPORTS
The Atlantic Beach King Mackerel Tournament is held on the Crystal Coast in September, and one of the largest and oldest **sportfishing** contests, the Big Rock Blue Marlin Tournament, is held in various locations each June. Fishing piers are found mostly on Bogue Banks and are closed during the winter. Dozens of charter boats operate year-round. In New Bern, bass fishing tournaments are popular, as is **crabbing** in

the Neuse River. For information on sportfishing and crabbing, contact the Craven County Convention and Visitors Bureau (☞ Visitor Information, *below*).

Golf courses are abundant, and locals prefer to play in the spring and fall months, when it's cooler. For a list of courses and help with reservations, contact **Crystal Coast Regional Golf Association** (⊠ 801 Arendell St., Box 1193, Morehead City 28557, ☎ 888/991–7529). Two notable courses are the par-72, 18-hole course at **Carolina Pines Gold and Country Club** (⊠ 390 Carolina Pines Blvd., off NC 70, between New Bern and Havelock, ☎ 252/444–1000) and the par-72, 18-hole course designed by Rees Jones at the **Emerald Golf Club** (⊠ 5000 Clubhouse Dr., on NC 70 Bypass, ☎ 252/633–4440).

Morehead City is consistently rated as a top **scuba diving** destination in North America. Two popular wreck sites are the *Schurz,* sunk in World War I, and the *Papoose,* a World War II tanker inhabited by docile sand sharks. **Olympus Dive Center** (⊠ 713 Shephard St., Morehead City, ☎ 252/726–9432) has five dive boats and offers full- and half-day charters, equipment rental, and lessons.

RADIO STATIONS

AM: WMBL 740, easy listening. **FM:** WRHT 96.3, Top 40; WMGV 103.3, adult contemporary; WTEB 89.3, National Public Radio.

VISITOR INFORMATION

The **Carteret County Tourism Development Bureau** operates two visitors centers, one in Morehead City (⊠ 3409 Arendell St., 28557, ☎ 800/786–6962) and one on NC 58 just north of the Cameron Langston Bridge to Emerald Isle (⊠ 263 NC 58, Swansboro 28584, ☎ 252/393–3100). **Craven County Convention and Visitors Bureau** (⊠ 314 S. Front St., New Bern 28560, ☎ 252/637–9400 or 800/437–5767) is open weekdays 8:30–5, Saturday 9–5, and Sunday 10–4.

WILMINGTON AND THE CAPE FEAR COAST

Wilmington and the Cape Fear Coast area, between the Cape Fear River and the Atlantic Ocean near the south end of the North Carolina coast, are simultaneously a beach resort and a shipping and trading center. Artists, golfers, history buffs, naturalists, and shoppers will all find something of interest here. The old seaport town of Wilmington has much to celebrate these days, including a once-decayed downtown that has been transformed with new places to shop and dine. On the surrounding Cape Fear Coast, you can tour old plantation houses and azalea gardens, study sea life at the state aquarium, or bask in the sun at nearby beaches.

Wilmington

130 mi south of Raleigh.

The city's long history, including its part in the American Revolution and its role as the main port of the Confederacy, is revealed in sights downtown and in the surrounding area. Chandler's Wharf, the Cotton Exchange, and Water Street Market are old buildings now used as shopping and entertainment centers. *Henrietta II,* a paddle wheeler similar to those that plied the waters of the Cape Fear River, has been put into service as a tourist vessel. Wilmington, also a college town, has special annual events such as the Azalea Festival, North Carolina Jazz Festival, Christmas candlelight tours, and fishing tournaments.

At the **USS *North Carolina* Battleship Memorial** you can tour a ship that participated in every major naval offensive in the Pacific during World War II. The self-guided tour takes about two hours, and a 10-minute film is shown throughout the day. Narrated tours on cassette can be rented. Warning: a climb down into the ship's interior is not for the claustrophobic. The ship can be reached by car or by taking the river taxi from Riverfront Park, Memorial Day through Labor Day, for a cost of $2. ⊠ *Junction of U.S. 74/76 and U.S. 17 and 421, west bank of Cape Fear River,* ☎ *910/251–5797.* ⚏ *$8.* ☉ *Mid-May –mid-Sept., daily 8–8; mid-Sept.–mid-May, daily 8–5.*

The **Cotton Exchange,** a shopping-dining complex, is in eight restored buildings on the Cape Fear River that have flourished as a trading center since pre–Civil War days. ⊠ *321 N. Front St.,* ☎ *910/343–9896.* ☉ *Mon.–Sat. 10–5:30; some stores also evenings and Sun. 1–5.*

The **Cape Fear Museum** traces the natural, cultural, and social history of the lower Cape Fear region from its beginnings to the present. One exhibit follows the youth of one of Wilmington's most famous native sons, basketball superstar Michael Jordan. ⊠ *814 Market St.,* ☎ *910/ 341–7413.* ⚏ *$4.* ☉ *Labor Day–Memorial Day, Tues.–Sat. 9–5, Sun. 2–5; Memorial Day–Labor Day, daily 9–5.*

Built in 1770 on the foundations of a jail, the **Burgwin-Wright Museum House** is a fine restoration of a colonial gentleman's town house and includes seven distinct period gardens. In April 1781 General Cornwallis used the house as his headquarters. ⊠ *224 Market St.,* ☎ *910/ 762–0570.* ⚏ *$5.* ☉ *Tues.–Sat. 10–3:30.*

St. John's Museum of Art is known for its 13 prints by Mary Cassatt, as well as for its works by North Carolina artists. The museum is housed in three buildings, including the 1804 Masonic Lodge Building, the oldest such lodge in the state. There is also a sculpture garden. ⊠ *114 Orange St.,* ☎ *910/763–0281.* ⚏ *$3.* ☉ *Tues.–Sat. 10–5, Sun. noon–4.*

The **Zebulon Latimer House,** built in 1852 in the Italianate style, is a reminder of opulent antebellum living. The Lower Cape Fear Historical Society is based here; it offers guided walking tours of the downtown historic district that depart from the house on Wednesday and Saturday mornings at 10. ⊠ *126 S. 3rd St.,* ☎ *910/762–0492.* ⚏ *$5.* ☉ *Weekdays 10–3:30, weekends noon–5.*

Chandler's Wharf (⊠ *225 S. Water St.*) contains shops and some seafood restaurants such as Elijah's. It's a great place to conclude a tour of downtown Wilmington.

Greenfield Lake and Gardens offers picnic spots and canoe and paddleboat rentals on a 180-acre lake bordered by cypress trees laden with Spanish moss. In April, the area is ablaze with azaleas. ⊠ *S. 3rd St. (U.S. 421), 2½ mi south of downtown,* ☎ *910/763–9371.* ⚏ *Free.* ☉ *Daily.*

At **Poplar Grove Historic Plantation,** an 1850 Greek Revival manor house 9 mi northeast of downtown, you can tour the manor house and outbuildings, see crafts demonstrations, shop in the country store, and pet the farm animals. ⊠ *10200 U.S. 17, Scotts Hill,* ☎ *910/686–9989.* ⚏ *Guided tours $7.* ☉ *Feb.–Dec., Mon.–Sat. 9–5, Sun. noon–5.*

The **New Hanover County Arboretum** has 33 exhibits, including magnolia and patio gardens, 100 varieties of shade-loving camellias, a salt-spray garden, and a children's garden with a maze. ⊠ *6206 Oleander Dr.,* ☎ *910/452–6393.* ⚏ *Free.* ☉ *Daily sunrise–sunset.*

OFF THE
BEATEN PATH

MOORE'S CREEK NATIONAL BATTLEFIELD – Military history buffs will appreciate this site, where American patriots defeated the Loyalists in 1776. ⊠ *200 Moores Creek Rd., Currie, 20 mi northwest of Wilmington on Rte. 210,* ☎ *910/283–5591.* ⊡ *Free.* ⊙ *Daily 8–5.*

Dining and Lodging

$$–$$$$ ✕ **Pilot House.** This Chandler's Wharf restaurant is known for its seafood, pastas, fresh vegetables, and Carolina seafood bisque. You can dine indoors at tables with linen tablecloths secured by vases of fresh flowers or outdoors overlooking the Cape Fear River. Sunday brunch, which starts at 11:30, is popular. ⊠ *2 Ann St.,* ☎ *910/343–0200. AE, D, DC, MC, V.*

$$–$$$ ✕ **Water Street Restaurant and Sidewalk Café.** A restored, two-story brick waterfront warehouse dating from 1835 holds an outdoor café and restaurant that serves up Greek, Mexican, Middle Eastern, and other ethnic cooking. Seafood chowder is made daily on the premises. ⊠ *5 Water St.,* ☎ *910/343–0042. AE, MC, V.*

$ ✕ **Mollye's.** Some people may recognize this little downtown restaurant from the *Dawson's Creek* television show. It specializes in salads, soups, roll-ups, and fruit dishes. The wine bar is open nightly and there's live music on weekends. ⊠ *118 Princess St.,* ☎ *910/772–9989. D, MC, V.*

$$$–$$$$ ⊞ **Inn at St. Thomas Court.** Many of the clients here are businesspeople and members of the entertainment community in the area to make movies or TV shows. In the heart of the historic district, former commercial buildings, an antebellum home, and a convent have been meticulously transformed into luxurious suites, each decorated in a different theme—classic movies, nautical heritage, and country French, for example. It's best for older children. ⊠ *101 S. 2nd St., 28401,* ☎ *910/ 343–1800 or 800/525–0909,* FAX *910/251–1149. 40 suites. In-room data ports, in-room VCRs, business services, meeting rooms. AE, D, DC, MC, V. CP.* ❧

$$$ ⊞ **Hilton-Riverside.** Overlooking the Cape Fear River on one side and the city on the other, the spacious Hilton is one of the most convenient places to stay in town. The lobby is plush; guest rooms are traditional, with dark woods and autumn colors. ⊠ *301 N. Water St., 28401,* ☎ *910/763–5900 or 800/445–8667,* FAX *910/763–0038. 262 rooms, 11 suites. Restaurant, bar, in-room data ports, pool, dock, business services, meeting rooms, airport shuttle. AE, D, DC, MC, V.* ❧

$$ ⊞ **Catherine's Inn.** This two-story Italianate home, built in 1883 in what is now a historic district overlooking the Cape Fear River, is a B&B with hardwood floors, a sunken garden, four-poster and canopy beds, and private phones in each room. Many items were collected by the innkeepers over the years. This is the only inn in the area with a direct view of the river. ⊠ *410 S. Front St., 28401,* ☎ *910/251–0863 or 800/ 476–0723,* FAX *910/772–9550. 5 rooms. MC, V. BP.* ❧

$$ ⊞ **Hampton Inn.** It's not luxurious, but this moderately priced chain motel is only 3 mi from downtown and 6 mi from Wrightsville Beach. It offers such extras as in-room movies and free local calls. ⊠ *5107 Market St., 28403,* ☎ *910/395–5045 or 800/426–7866,* FAX *910/799– 1974. 118 rooms. In-room data ports, pool, exercise room, business services, meeting room. AE, D, DC, MC, V. CP.* ❧

Nightlife and the Arts

THE ARTS

The city has its own symphony orchestra, oratorio society, civic ballet, and concert association; and the North Carolina Symphony makes four appearances here each year. For information, contact the Cape Fear Coast Convention and Visitors Bureau (☞ Visitor Information *in* Wilmington and the Cape Fear Coast A to Z, *below*). **Thalian Hall Center for the Performing Arts** (⊠ 310 Chestnut St., ☎ 910/343–3664 or 800/523–2820), an opera house built between 1855 and 1858 and restored to its former grandeur, hosts more than 250 theater, dance, and musical performances each year. Theatrical productions are staged by the Thalian Association, Opera House Productions, and Tapestry Players. The annual **Wilmington Jazz Festival,** held in February, and the **Blues Festival,** in August, draw crowds.

NIGHTLIFE

A favorite waterfront haunt is the **Ice House Beer Garden** (⊠ 115 S. Water St., ☎ 910/251–1158 or 910/763–2084), an indoor and outdoor bar with live rhythm and blues. **Rockit's Rhythm & Sports Grille** (⊠ 5025 Market St., ☎ 910/791–2001) is known for its music (rock, blues, beach). It's also a great place to play pool or watch a game.

Outdoor Activities and Sports

There are approximately 40 public-access golf courses in the Greater Wilmington area. **Beau Rivage Plantation Golf Club** (⊠ 6230 Carolina Beach Rd., ☎ 910/395–1300) is a par-72 course in a natural links setting. The **Cape Golf & Racquet Club** (⊠ 535 The Cape Blvd., ☎ 910/799–3110) is a par-72 resort course with a driving range.

South Brunswick County, about 30–40 mi from Wilmington on the coast, is golf heaven, especially the areas around Calabash, Sunset Beach, and Ocean Isle. **Lockwood Folly Golf Links** (⊠ 100 Club House Dr., Holden Beach, ☎ 910/842–5666 or 800/443–7891) is a highly rated par-72 resort course. **Marsh Harbour Golf Links** (⊠ NC 179, Calabash, ☎ 910/579–3161 or 800/552–2660) has a highly-rated par-71 course, offering views of marsh and marina activity. **Oyster Bay Golf Links** (⊠ NC 179, Sunset Beach, ☎ 910/579–3528 or 800/552–2660) is known for its oyster-shell hazards, gator sightings, and par 70. **Sea Trail Plantation** (⊠ 211 Clubhouse Rd., Sunset Beach, ☎ 910/579–4350 or 800/624–6601) has three courses designed by Dan Maples, Rees Jones, and Willard Byrd, respectively, with pars from 54 to 72.

Shopping

The city has fun shopping at Chandler's Wharf, the Cotton Exchange, and the Water Street Market; it also has shops in the downtown historic district, as well as shopping malls and outlets.

Wrightsville Beach

12 mi east of Wilmington.

Wrightsville Beach is a small, quiet island community that's very family oriented. It has a number of fine restaurants, and beaches good for swimming, boating, and surfing.

Dining and Lodging

$$$–$$$$ ✕ **Ocean Terrace Restaurant.** Part of the Blockade Runner Resort (☞ *below*), this restaurant attracts crowds with its weekend buffets and jazz brunch on Sunday. Regular dishes include grilled New York strip steak with bourbon-shallot butter; almond-breaded flounder with shrimp; and chicken breast with toasted pecans, pears, and apples. ⊠ *Blockade Runner Resort Hotel and Conference Center, 275 Waynick Blvd.,* ☎ *910/256–2251 or 800/541–1161. Reservations essential. AE, D, DC, MC, V.*

$$–$$$ ✕ **Oceanic Restaurant and Grill.** You'll have a panoramic view of the Atlantic for miles around—a great backdrop for the fresh seafood, steaks, and chicken. Dinner on the pier at sunset is a real treat. ⊠ *703 S. Lumina St.,* ☎ *910/256–5551. AE, MC, V.*

$$$$ 🖬 **Blockade Runner Resort Hotel and Conference Center.** This ocean-side complex is widely known for its Ocean Terrace Restaurant (☞ *above*) and supervised summer children's programs. Guest rooms, done in bright colors, overlook either the Intracoastal Waterway or, for a higher price, the ocean. Service can be uneven, especially at the height of the season, but the hotel's beachfront location and guaranteed parking keep them coming back. ⊠ *275 Waynick Blvd., 28480,* ☎ *910/256–2251 or 800/541–1161,* FAX *910/256–5502. 147 rooms, 3 suites. Restaurant, bar, indoor-outdoor pool, exercise room, beach, boating, bicycles, business services, meeting rooms, airport shuttle. AE, D, DC, MC, V.* 🕸

Kure Beach

17 mi south of Wilmington.

Kure Beach is a resort community that's a bit livelier than Wrightsville Beach (☞ *above*) as it's next to Carolina Beach, which has amusement parks and a boardwalk with bars. Historic site Fort Fisher and the North Carolina Aquarium provide further interest. In some places, twisted live oaks still grow behind the dunes. The community has miles of beaches; public access points are marked by orange-and-blue signs.

Fort Fisher State Historic Site marks the largest and one of the most important earthworks fortifications in the South during the Civil War. A reconstructed battery and Civil War relics and artifacts from sunken blockade-runners are on site. The fort is part of **Fort Fisher Recreation Area,** with 4 mi of undeveloped beach. ⊠ *U.S. 421,* ☎ *910/458–5538.* 🖼 *Free.* ☉ *Apr.–Oct., Mon.–Sat. 9–5, Sun. 1–5; Nov.–Mar., Tues.–Sat. 10–4, Sun. 1–4.*

Lodging

$$$–$$$$ 🖬 **Docksider Inn.** The nautical theme is no surprise given that this is a waterfront hotel. The inn is furnished in light-color beach-type furniture. Owners Kip and Maureen Darling have another property a block away on Atlantic Avenue. The five contemporary luxury suites of Darlings by the Sea are for adults only. Each has an expansive ocean view, custom-made drapes, bed skirting, and cabinetry. There are whirlpools for two and wet bars. ⊠ *202 Fort Fisher Blvd. (U.S. 421), 28449,* ☎ *910/458–4200 or 800/383–8111,* FAX *910/458–6468. 34 rooms. Pool, beach. AE, D, MC, V.* 🕸

Southport

30 mi south of Wilmington.

This small town, which sits quietly at the mouth of the Cape Fear River, is listed on the National Register of Historic Places. An increasingly desirable retirement spot, Southport retains its village charm and character. Stately and distinctive homes, antiques stores, gift shops, and restaurants line streets that veer to accommodate ancient oak trees. The town, portrayed in Robert Ruark's novel *The Old Man and the Boy,* is ideal for walking; it's also popular with moviemakers—*Crimes of the Heart* was filmed here.

If you're approaching the town from Fort Fisher and NC 421, the **Southport–Fort Fisher Ferry,** a state-operated car ferry, provides a river ride between Old Federal Point at the tip of the spit and the mainland. The Old Baldy lighthouse on Bald Head Island is seen en route. It's best to arrive 30 minutes prior to ferry departure, as it's first-come, first-served. ☎ *910/458–3329.* 🖼 *$3 per car.* ☉ *Ferries run mid-Mar.–mid-*

Nov., daily every 45 mins 6:15 AM–9:15 PM; mid-Nov.–mid-Mar., daily every 1½ hrs 6:15 AM–4:45 PM.

Lodging

$$–$$$ 🏨 **Bald Head Island Resort.** Reached by ferry from Southport, this private, self-contained, car-less community complete with grocery store and restaurants has bleached-wood villas and shingle cottages. You can explore the semitropical island on foot, by bicycle, or in a golf cart. Pastimes are watching the loggerhead turtles and taking a guided tour through the maritime forest. Accommodations include rental condos, villas, cottages, and a privately owned bed-and-breakfast; a two-night minimum stay is required. The **ferry** (☎ 910/457–5003) costs $15 per person round-trip and runs on the hour, 8–6 (except noon on weekdays), from Southport. Advance reservations are necessary for both the ferry and resort. ✉ *Bald Head Island, 28461,* ☎ *910/457–5000 or 800/ 234–1666,* FAX *910/457–9232. 195 condos, villas, and cottages; 15 rooms in B&B. 3 restaurants, pool, 18-hole golf course, 4 tennis courts, croquet, boating, fishing. AE, DC, MC, V.* 🐾

Outdoor Activities and Sports

For golf, the par-72 **Gauntlet at St. James Plantation** (✉ NC 211, ☎ 910/253–3008 or 800/247–4806) lives up to its reputation as a challenging course.

Winnabow

12 mi north of Southport, 18 mi south of Wilmington.

Winnabow is more of a crossroads than a town to visit; the draws here are gardens and a historic site, both off NC 133 near the Cape Fear
★ River. The house at **Orton Plantation Gardens** is not open to the public, but the 20 acres of beautiful, comprehensive gardens are great for strolling. The former rice plantation holds magnolias, ancient oaks, and all kinds of ornamental plants; the grounds are a refuge for waterfowl. ✉ *9149 Orton Rd. SE, off NC 133,* ☎ *910/371–6851.* 🎫 *$8.* 🕐 *Mar.– Aug., daily 8–6; Sept.–Nov., daily 10–5.* 🐾

At **Brunswick Town State Historic Site** you can explore the excavations of a colonial town; see Fort Anderson, a Civil War earthworks fort; and have a picnic. Special events include reenactments of Civil War encampments. ✉ *8884 St. Phillips Rd., off NC 133,* ☎ *910/371–6613.* 🎫 *Free.* 🕐 *Apr.–Oct., Mon.–Sat. 9–5, Sun. 1–5; Nov.–Mar., Tues.–Sat. 10–4, Sun. 1–4.*

Wilmington and the Cape Fear Coast A to Z

Arriving, Departing, and Getting Around

BY BOAT

A number of hotels provide docking facilities for guests. The Wilmington area has **public marinas** at **Carolina Beach State Park** (☎ 910/ 458–7770) and **Wrightsville Beach** (☎ 910/256–6666). Public boat access is also offered at Atlantic Marina, Masonboro Boat Yard and Marina, Seapath Transient Dock, and Wrightsville Gulf Terminal. The *North Carolina Coastal Boating Guide,* compiled by the **North Carolina Department of Transportation** (☎ 919/733–2522), has a comprehensive list of marinas and facilities for boaters. A state-run car ferry connects Fort Fisher with Southport on the coast.

BY BUS

Greyhound/Carolina Trailways serves the Union Bus terminal (✉ 201 Harnett St., ☎ 910/762–6625 or 800/231–2222). The **Wilmington**

Transit Authority (☎ 910/343–0106) provides service Monday–Saturday for 75¢ a ride.

BY CAR

Wilmington is linked to Raleigh by I–40 and to New Bern by U.S. 17.

BY PLANE

US Airways and Atlantic Southeast Airlines serve the **Wilmington International Airport** (⊠ 1740 Airport Blvd., ☎ 910/341–4125). For airline telephone numbers, *see* Air Travel *in* Smart Travel Tips A to Z.

Contacts and Resources

BEACHES

Three beaches—Wrightsville, Carolina, and Kure—are within a short drive from Wilmington, and miles and miles of sand stretch northward to the Outer Banks and southward to South Carolina. The beaches offer activities from fishing to sunbathing to scuba diving, and the towns here have a choice of accommodations. Approximately 100 points of public access along the shoreline are marked by orange-and-blue signs. Some of the smaller beaches have lifeguards on duty, and many are accessible to people with disabilities. Some fishing piers are open to the public. Contact the Cape Fear Coast Convention and Visitors Bureau (☞ Visitor Information, *below*) for more information. Camping, fishing, swimming, and picnicking are permitted at **Carolina Beach State Park** (☎ 910/458–8206, 910/458–7770 marina).

EMERGENCIES

Ambulance, police (☎ 911). **Coast Guard assistance** (☎ 910/343–4881). For emergency medical attention, contact the **Cape Fear Memorial Hospital** (⊠ 5301 Wrightsville Ave., ☎ 910/452–8100) or the **New Hanover Regional Medical Center** (⊠ 2131 S. 17th St., ☎ 910/343–7000), a regional trauma center.

GUIDED TOURS

From April through December, **Cape Fear Riverboats, Inc.** (⊠ docked at the Hilton in downtown Wilmington, ☎ 910/343–1611 or 800/676–0162) runs a variety of cruises aboard a stern-wheel riverboat, the *Henrietta II*, that departs from Riverfront Park. Cost is $9–$32. **Cape Fear Tours** (⊠ 8112 Sidbury Rd., Wilmington, ☎ 910/686–7744) gives walking and driving tours of the Wilmington Historic District, mansions, and the beaches. Individual tours are $20 per hour.

OUTDOOR ACTIVITIES AND SPORTS

There's surf **fishing** on the piers that dot the coast, and charter boats are available for off-shore fishing. Four major tournaments, for substantial prize money, are held each year—the Cape Fear Marlin Tournament, the Wrightsville Beach King Mackerel Tournament, the East Coast Open King Mackerel Tournament, and the U.S. Open King Mackerel Tournament. For information, contact the Cape Fear Coast Convention and Visitors Bureau (☞ Visitor Information, *below*).

Some top **golf** choices are listed in this section, but for more information contact the Cape Fear Coast Convention and Visitors Bureau (☞ Visitor Information, *below*) or the **South Brunswick Islands Chamber of Commerce** (⊠ 4948 Main St., Box 1380, Shalotte 28459, ☎ 910/754–6644).

Wrecks such as the World War II tanker *John D. Gill* make for exciting **scuba diving** off the coast. **Aquatic Safaris** (⊠ 5751–4 Oleander Dr., Wilmington, ☎ 910/392–4386) rents equipment and leads trips.

Surfing and **board sailing** are popular at area beaches, and rentals are available at shops in Wilmington, Wrightsville Beach, and Carolina Beach.

RADIO STATIONS

AM: WAAV 980, news, talk; WBMS 1340, news, talk, sports. **FM:** WHQR 91.3, National Public Radio; WGNI 102.7, adult contemporary and Top 40; WWQQ 101.3, country; WSFM 107.5, classic rock.

VISITOR INFORMATION

Cape Fear Coast Convention and Visitors Bureau (✉ 24 N. 3rd St., Wilmington 28401, ☎ 910/341–4030 or 800/222–4757) is in the Old Courthouse downtown and has an information center on the boardwalk along the Cape Fear River open weekdays 8:30–5, Saturday 9–4, Sunday 1–4.

THE MOUNTAINS

Cherokee, Asheville, and the High Country

The majestic peaks, meadows, and valleys of the Appalachian, Blue Ridge, and Smoky mountains characterize the western corner of the state, which is divided into three distinct regions: the southern mountains, home to the Cherokee reservation; the northern mountains, known as the High Country (Blowing Rock, Boone, Banner Elk); and the central mountains, anchored by Asheville, for decades a retreat for the wealthy and famous. National parks, national forests, handmade-crafts centers, and the Blue Ridge Parkway are the area's main draws, providing prime opportunities for shopping, skiing, hiking, bicycling, camping, fishing, canoeing, or just taking in the views.

At the southern terminus of the Blue Ridge Parkway and the North Carolina entrance to the Great Smoky Mountains lies the homeland of the Eastern Band of the Cherokee Indians. Through a blending of museums, dramas, assorted outdoor attractions, and everyday living, the Cherokee attempt to explain what's precious in their Land of the Blue Mist.

The biggest city in the mountains, Asheville has a lovely setting, a choice of hotels and restaurants, and a thriving arts community. The city's revitalized downtown has good shopping, galleries, museums, restaurants, and nightlife.

Picture-book towns such as Boone, Blowing Rock, and Banner Elk have boomed in the 30 years since the introduction of snowmaking equipment. Luxury resorts now dot the valleys and mountaintops, and you can take advantage of the many crafts shops, music festivals, and theater offerings. The passing of each season is a visual event here, and autumn is the star.

Cherokee

165 mi west of Charlotte, 50 mi west of Asheville.

The 56,000-acre Cherokee Indian Reservation is known as the Qualla Boundary, and the town of Cherokee is its capital. Truth be told, there are two Cherokees. There's the side with sometimes tacky pop culture, designed to appeal to mass numbers of tourists, many of whom are visiting nearby Great Smoky Mountains National Park. Another Cherokee explores the rich heritage of the tribe's Eastern Band. Though now relatively small in number—tribal enrollment is 11,000—these people and their ancestors have been responsible for keeping alive the Cherokee culture. They are the descendants of those who hid in the Great

Smoky Mountains to avoid the forced removal of the Cherokee Nation to Oklahoma in the 19th century, known as the Trail of Tears. They are survivors, extremely attached to the hiking, swimming, trout fishing, and natural beauty of their ancestral homeland.

The **Museum of the Cherokee Indian,** with displays and artifacts that cover 10,000 years, is one of the best Native American museums in the United States. Computer-generated images, lasers, specialty lighting, and sound effects help re-create events in the history of the Cherokee: children stop to play a butter bean game while adults shiver along the snowy Trail of Tears. The museum has an art gallery and an outdoor living exhibit of Cherokee life in the 15th century. ⊠ *U.S. 441 at Drama Rd.,* ☎ *828/497–3481.* 🎟 *$6.* ⊙ *June–Aug., Mon.–Sat. 9–8, Sun. 9–5; Sept.–May, daily 9–5.*

The **Qualla Arts and Crafts Mutual,** across the street from the Museum of the Cherokee Indian, is a cooperative that displays and sells items created by 300 Cherokee craftspeople. The store also has a large section of baskets, masks, and wood carvings. ⊠ *U.S. 441 at Drama Rd.,* ☎ *828/497–3103.* ⊙ *June–Aug., daily 8–8; Sept.–Oct., daily 8–6; Nov.–May, daily 8–4:30.*

At the historically accurate, re-created **Oconaluftee Indian Village,** guides in native costumes will lead you through a village of 225 years ago while others demonstrate traditional skills such as weaving, pottery, canoe construction, and hunting techniques. ⊠ *U.S. 441 at Drama Rd.,* ☎ *828/497–2315.* 🎟 *$10.* ⊙ *May 15–Oct. 25, daily 9–5:30.*

Every mountain county has significant deposits of gems and minerals, and at the **Smoky Mountain Gold and Ruby Mine,** on the Qualla Boundary, you can search for gems such as aquamarines. Children love panning precisely because it can be wet and messy. Here they're guaranteed a find. Gem ore can be purchased, too: gold ore costs $5 per bag. ⊠ *U.S. 441N,* ☎ *828/497–6574.* 🎟 *$4–$10, depending on the gems.* ⊙ *Mar., weekends 9–6; Apr.–Nov., daily 10–9.*

Dining and Lodging

$–$$ ✕ **Nantahala Village Restaurant.** This roomy rock-and-cedar restaurant with front-porch rocking chairs is about 10 mi southwest of Cherokee and is a local favorite. The food isn't fancy, but choices such as trout, chicken, and country ham are good and filling. Sunday brunch has some surprises: *huevos rancheros* (tortilla with fried eggs and salsa) and eggs Benedict, to name a couple. ⊠ *9400 U.S. 19W, Bryson City,* ☎ *828/488–9616 or 800/438–1507. D, MC, V. Closed Dec.–Mar.*

$$$–$$$$ ✕🏨 **Hemlock Inn.** Even if you're not a guest at the inn, which is built on a small mountain that overlooks three valleys, ̶ ̶ ̶ ̶ ̶ ̶ can make a reservation for dinner ($$) Monday through Satur̶ ̶ ̶ ̶ ̶ ̶ lunch on Sunday. The one-price, all-you-can-eat meals are ̶ ̶ ̶ ̶ ̶ ̶d with regional foods, including locally grown fruits and vegetab̶ ̶ ̶ ̶ mountain honey. Each cozy room is decorated with antiques and area crafts. ⊠ *Galbraith Creek Rd., 1 mi north of U.S. 19W, Bryson City 28713,* ☎ *828/488–2885, ℻ 828/488–8985. 29 rooms. Restaurant, recreation room. D, MC, V. Closed Nov.–mid-Apr. MAP.* 🐾

$–$$ 🏨 **Holiday Inn Cherokee.** Guest rooms are standard chain fare, but the staff at this well-equipped, full-service facility is very friendly. The Chestnut Tree restaurant has dinner buffets that are veritable groaning boards, and the native crafts shop, the Hunting Ground, with works by local artists, is a nice touch. ⊠ *U.S. 19S, 28719,* ☎ *828/497–9181 or 800/465–4329, ℻ 828/497–5973. 150 rooms, 4 suites. Restaurant, indoor pool, outdoor pool, wading pool, sauna, recreation room, playground, meeting room. AE, D, DC, MC, V.* 🐾

Nightlife and the Arts

THE ARTS

Unto These Hills Outdoor Drama (⊠ Mountainside Theater on Drama Rd., off U.S. 441N, ☎ 828/497–2111) is a colorful and well-staged history of the Cherokee from the time of Spanish explorer Hernando de Soto's visit in 1540 to the infamous Trail of Tears. It runs from mid-June to mid-August, and tickets are $11–$14.

NIGHTLIFE

The 175,000-square-ft **Harrah's Cherokee Casino** (⊠ U.S. 19 off U.S. 441 N, ☎ 828/497–7777) has action 24 hours a day. Its 2,400 gaming machines, video poker, video blackjack, and video craps make it the largest casino in a 500-mi radius. The complex also has a 1,500-seat concert hall, three restaurants, and a child-care area.

Outdoor Activities and Sports

FISHING

There are 30 mi of regularly stocked trout streams on the **Cherokee Indian Reservation.** To fish in tribal water, you need a tribal fishing permit, available at nearly two dozen reservation businesses. The $7 permit is valid for one day. For information, call ☎ 828/497–5201 or 800/438–1601.

HIKING

In the downtown area you can cross the Oconaluftee River on a footbridge to **Oconaluftee Islands Park & Trail** (⊠ across from Cherokee Elementary School on U.S. 441) and walk a trail around the perimeter of the Island Park, which also has picnic facilities. The flat 1½-mi **Oconaluftee River Trail** begins at the Great Smoky Mountains National Park entrance sign on U.S. 441 (near the entrance to the Blue Ridge Parkway) and ends at the Mountain Farm Museum/Park Visitor Center. A five-minute hike from the Mingo Falls Campground area (⊠ Big Cove Rd. about 4 mi north of Acquoni Rd.) will reward you with a view of the 200-ft-high **Mingo Falls.**

Great Smoky Mountains National Park

3 mi north of Cherokee.

★ Natural assets help make the **Great Smoky Mountains National Park** the most visited national park in the United States. No mountains in the world are older, and no place on earth can claim such biological diversity: more than 1,600 types of wildflowers and more than 140 species of trees flourish in this wildlife sanctuary. The Appalachian Trail runs along the crest of the mountains through the park, the largest protected land area east of the Rocky Mountains. Within its 800 square mi (276,000 acres lie in North Carolina, 244,000 in Tennessee) are 800 mi of trails, more than 600 mi of trout streams, and some 200,000 acres of virgin forest.

The Smokies are so named because of the frequently occurring smokelike blue mist that hovers in the air and can get so dense as to obscure mountaintops. In actuality, the "smoke" occurs when vegetation releases water vapor and natural oils produced by plants into the air. Along the twists and turns of the Blue Ridge Parkway are scores of scenic overlooks, and many byways lead to areas that grip the imagination.

U.S. Highway 441 is the only road that passes all the way through the park. Fishing permits and visitor information are available at ranger stations at the north and south entrances. Depending on your location, the **Oconaluftee Visitors Center** (☎ 828/497–1900) is the terminus of the Blue Ridge Parkway or its starting point. Adjacent to the visitor center, at mile marker 469.1, is **Mountain Farm Museum**, a re-created pioneer homestead. ⊠ *107 Park Headquarters Rd., Gatlinburg, TN 37738,* ☎ *423/436–5615.* ☞ *Free.* 🐾

Dillsboro

13 mi southeast of Cherokee on U.S. 441.

The tiny town of Dillsboro in Jackson County has a big reputation for good shopping, particularly if you favor folk art and crafts. The popular train rides of the **Great Smoky Mountains Railway** include six regular excursions and six special trips on diesel-electric or steam locomotives. Open-sided cars or cabooses are ideal for picture taking as the mountain scenery glides by. There's a train museum, too. ⊠ *119 Front St.,* ☎ *828/586–8811 or 800/872–4681.* ☞ *$21–$64; some rides include a meal.* ☉ *Mar.–Dec.; call for schedule.*

Franklin

32 mi south of Cherokee on U.S. 441.

Franklin, the Macon County seat, lies at the convergence of U.S. 441, U.S. 64, and NC 28. In the 1500s, Hernando de Soto came in search of gold and overlooked the wealth of gemstones for which this area is so famous. A dozen gem mines and nearly as many gem stores are nearby.

The **Scottish Tartans Museum** has the official registry of all publicly known tartans and is the American extension of the Scottish Tartans Society. Scottish heritage can be traced in the research library. ⊠ *86 E. Main St.,* ☎ *828/524–7472.* ☞ *$1.* ☉ *Mon.–Sat. 10–5, Sun. 1–5.*

Waynesville

17 mi east of Cherokee on U.S. 19.

This is where the Blue Ridge Parkway meets the Great Smokies. Pretty, arty Waynesville is the seat of Haywood County. About 40% of the county is occupied by the Great Smoky Mountains National Park, Pisgah National Forest, and the Harmon Den Wildlife Refuge.

The **Museum of North Carolina Handicrafts,** in the Shelton House (circa 1875), has a comprehensive exhibit of 19th-century heritage crafts as well as a working pioneer village and railroad memorabilia. ⊠ *307 Shelton St.,* ☎ *828/452–1551.* ☞ *$4.* ☉ *May–Oct., Tues.–Fri. 10–4.*

Cold Mountain, the vivid best-seller by Charles Frazier, has made a destination out of the real **Cold Mountain.** Located about 15 mi from Waynesville in the Shining Rock Wilderness Area of Pisgah National Forest, the 6,030-ft rise has until recently stood in relative isolation. But now, people want to see the region that Inman and Ada, the book's Civil War–era protagonists, called home.

There are different ways to experience Cold Mountain. For a view of the splendid mass—or at least of the surrounding area—stop at any of a number of overlooks off the Blue Ridge Parkway. Try the Cold Mountain Parking Overlook just past mile marker 411.9; the Wagon Road Gap parking area at mile marker 412.2; or the Waterrock Knob Interpretative Station at mile marker 451.2. You can climb the mountain, but beware, as the hike to the summit is rather strenuous. No campfires are allowed in Shining Rock, so you'll need a stove if you wish to cook. Inform the ranger station (☎ 828/877–3350) if you plan to hike or camp.

Those who want a more interpretive experience might consider Cold Mountain tours by **Southern Safari** (✉ Box 8237, Asheville 28814, ☎ 800/454–7374). In addition to the popular 11-mi guided hiking tours for small groups, which culminate in a "French country picnic" atop the mountain, this company has a historical driving tour. About six hours long, the tour includes visits to Waynesville and various points of interest along the Blue Ridge Parkway brought to life in the novel.

Lodging

$$$$ 🏨 **The Swag.** This exquisite, rustic inn sits high atop the Cataloochee Divide overlooking a swag—a deep depression in otherwise high ground. Its 250 wooded acres share a border with Great Smoky Mountains National Park and have access to the park's hiking trails. Guest rooms and cabins were assembled from six authentic log structures transported here. All have rough wooden walls, exposed beams, and wooden floors and are furnished with Early American crafts. A two-night minimum stay is required. ✉ *2300 Swag Rd., 28786,* ☎ *828/926–0430 or 800/789–7672,* 𝔽𝔸𝕏 *828/926–2036. 16 rooms, 3 cabins. Dining room, pond, massage, sauna, badminton, croquet, racquetball, library, business services. AE, D, MC, V. Closed Dec.–Apr. FAP.* 🍽

Asheville

50 mi east of Cherokee, 115 mi west of Charlotte.

The largest and most cosmopolitan city in the mountains, Asheville has been rated America's favorite place to live among cities of its size. It has scenic beauty, a good airport and road system, a moderate four-season climate, and a thriving arts community. Banjo pickers are as revered as violinists, and mountain folks mix with city slickers. Experience the renaissance of the city's downtown, a pedestrian-friendly place with upscale shopping, art galleries, museums, restaurants, and nightlife.

Downtown Asheville is noted for its eclectic architecture. The **Battery Park Hotel** (1924) is neo-Georgian; the **Flatiron Building** (1924) is neoclassical; the **Basilica of St. Lawrence** (1912) is Spanish Baroque; **Pack Place,** formerly known as Old Pack Library (1925), is in Italian Renaissance style; the **S&W Cafeteria** (1929) is Art Deco. In fact, the city has the largest collection of Art Deco buildings in the Southeast except for Miami.

The 92,000-square-ft **Pack Place Education, Arts & Science Center,** in downtown Asheville, houses the **Asheville Art Museum, Colburn Gem & Mineral Museum, Health Adventure,** and **Diana Wortham Theatre.** The **YMI Cultural Center,** also maintained by Pack Place, is across the street. ✉ *2 S. Pack Sq.,* ☎ *828/257–4500.* 🎟 *$4 per museum, $12 combination ticket.* 🕐 *June–Oct., Tues.–Sat. 10–5, Sun. 1–5; Nov.–May, Tues.–Sat. 10–5.*

Asheville's most famous son, Thomas Wolfe, grew up in a Queen Anne–style home that his mother ran as a boarding house. The home, a state historic site, burned as a result of arson. It is closed while undergoing restoration. However, the visitor center at the **Thomas Wolfe Memorial** remains open, showing a video about Wolfe and displaying photographs and other memorabilia related to the author and his career. Some items salvaged from the house are also here. ✉ *52 Market St.,* ☎ *828/253–8304.* 🎟 *$1.* 🕐 *Apr.–Oct., Mon.–Sat. 9–5, Sun. 1–5; Nov.–Mar., Tues.–Sat. 10–4, Sun. 1–4.*

★ The astonishing **Biltmore Estate,** which faces Biltmore Village, was built in the 1890s as the private home of George Vanderbilt. This 250-room French Renaissance château is America's largest private residence (some of Vanderbilt's descendants still live on the grounds but open the bulk of the home and grounds to visitors). Richard Morris Hunt designed it, and Frederick Law Olmsted landscaped the original 125,000-acre estate (now 8,000 acres). It took 1,000 men five years to complete the gargantuan project. On view are the priceless antiques and art collected by the Vanderbilts, and 75 acres of gardens and formally landscaped grounds. You can also see the state-of-the-art winery and take Christmas candlelight tours of the house. Allow a full day to tour the house and grounds. ⊠ *Exit 50 off I–40E,* ☎ *828/255–1700 or 800/624–1575.* ☞ *$32; prices for special events vary.* ۞ *Jan.–Mar., daily 9–5; Apr.–Dec., daily 8:30–5.* ✍

The **North Carolina Arboretum,** 426 acres that were part of the original Biltmore Estate, completes Frederick Law Olmsted's dream of creating a world-class arboretum in the western part of the state. It features southern Appalachian flora in a stunning number of settings, including the Blue Ridge Quilt Garden, with bedding plants that are arranged in patterns reminiscent of Appalachian quilts. There is also the formal Stream Garden, which capitalizes on the Bent Creek trout stream that runs through the grounds. An extensive network of trails is available for walking or mountain biking. ⊠ *100 Frederick Law Olmsted Way, 10 mi southwest of downtown Asheville, adjacent to Blue Ridge Pkwy. (near I–26 and I–40),* ☎ *828/665–2492.* ☞ *Free; call for group tour fees.* ۞ *Visitor education center Mon.–Sat. 9–5, Sun. noon–5; gardens and grounds daily 8 AM–9 PM.*

OFF THE BEATEN PATH	**PENLAND SCHOOL OF CRAFTS –** This world-famous institution about 45 mi northeast of Asheville on a remote mountaintop is the oldest and largest school for high-quality mixed-media arts and crafts in North America. It has classes in books and paper, glassblowing, ceramics, textile arts, and other media. A gallery displays works (some are for sale; call to check hours and winter closing). Classes aren't open to the public, but you can call about a free campus tour. ⊠ *Penland Rd. off NC 19/23, Penland,* ☎ *828/765–2359 school, 828/765–6211 gallery and campus tours.*

Dining and Lodging

$$$–$$$$ ✗ **Windmill European Grill.** The menu at this cool, dark, and cozy cellar restaurant is a mix of German, Italian, Middle Eastern, and Indian cuisines. ⊠ *85 Tunnel Rd.,* ☎ *828/253–5285. AE, D, MC, V. Closed Sun.–Mon. No lunch.*

$$–$$$$ ✗ **The Market Place.** Clean lines, neutral colors, and brushed steel mobiles create a sophisticated setting. The food offers refreshing twists on ingredients indigenous to the mountains (game and trout) and the South in general. Possible entrées are smoked trout and green apple salad, or tenderloin of pork with a sweet potato timbale. Iron gates open onto an exterior courtyard and dining patio. ⊠ *20 Wall St.,* ☎ *828/252–4162. AE, MC, V. Closed Sun. No lunch.*

$$ ✗ **Café on the Square.** When owners Bill and Shelagh Byrne moved to Asheville from San Francisco, they brought California-Continental cuisine with them. The local business crowd frequents this elegant and airy restaurant during lunch, but theatergoers favor it for dinner. The menu, which lists from four to eight specials at each meal, is heavy on fresh seafood and pastas cooked with salsas, chutneys, and simple marinades. The signature dishes are hickory-smoked chicken in a marsala-and-shiitake-mushroom sauce and a rich peanut-butter pie. ⊠ *1 Biltmore Ave.,* ☎ *828/251–5565. AE, D, MC, V. Closed Sun.*

$-$$ ✕ **The Laughing Seed Café.** You'll get more than brown rice and beans at this vegetarian eatery. The extensive menu ranges from fruit drinks to sandwiches and pizzas to dinner specialties influenced by the flavors of India, China, and Morocco. ✉ *40 Wall St.,* ☎ *828/252–3445. AE, D, MC, V. Closed Tues.*

$-$$ ✕ **West Side Grill.** A '50s-style diner, the West Side has a little bit of everything, including daily blue-plate specials, from Mile-High Meat Loaf to Southern-fried catfish. Vegetarians have a number of choices, including the focaccia veggie melt and the blackened garden burger. ✉ *1190 Patton Ave.,* ☎ *828/252–9605. Reservations not accepted. AE, D, MC, V.*

$$$$ ✕▥ **Grove Park Inn Resort.** With its supervised children's activities,
★ racquetball and tennis courts, special weekend packages, and views of the Blue Ridge Mountains, this is Asheville's premier resort. Since the resort's opening in 1913, the guest list has included Henry Ford, Thomas Edison, F. Scott Fitzgerald, and, more recently, Justice Sandra Day O'Conner and Michael Jordan. The inn is furnished with oak antiques in the Arts and Crafts style. The restaurants offer plenty of choices: Horizons specializes in game dishes from ostrich to boar; you can also order free-range chicken. ✉ *290 Macon Ave., 28804,* ☎ *828/252–2711 or 800/438–5800;* 𝔽𝔸𝕏 *828/253–7053 guests, 828/252–6102 reservations. 498 rooms, 12 suites. 4 restaurants, 3 bars, indoor pool, outdoor pool, hot tub, spa, 18-hole golf course, putting green, 9 tennis courts, health club, nightclub, playground, business services, meeting rooms. AE, D, DC, MC, V.* ✍

$$$$ ✕▥ **Richmond Hill Inn.** Once a private residence, this elegant Victo-
★ rian mansion is on the National Register of Historic Places. Many rooms in the mansion are furnished with canopy beds, Victorian sofas, and other antiques, while the more modern cottages have contemporary pine poster beds. Gabrielle's is known for its innovative cuisine, cherrywood paneling, and three-tier chandelier. Reservations are necessary here but not at the Arbor Grille, a glass-enclosed sun porch. Gabrielle's is only open to the public for dinner and Sunday brunch; jacket and tie are required. ✉ *87 Richmond Hill Dr., 28806,* ☎ *828/252–7313 or 888/742–4536,* 𝔽𝔸𝕏 *828/252–8726. 24 rooms, 3 suites, 9 cottages. 2 restaurants, croquet, library, business services, meeting rooms. AE, MC, V. BP.* ✍

$$$-$$$$ ▥ **Cedar Crest Victorian Inn.** Biltmore craftspeople constructed this beautiful cottage, with its leaded-glass front door and corbeled brick fireplaces, as a private residence in 1891. The lovingly restored guest rooms are furnished with period antiques. You are treated to afternoon tea, evening coffee or chocolate, and a breakfast of fruit, pastry, and coffee. It's best for older children. ✉ *674 Biltmore Ave., 28803,* ☎ *828/252–1389 or 800/252–0310,* 𝔽𝔸𝕏 *828/252–7667. 9 rooms, 2 cottage suites. Croquet, business services. AE, D, DC, MC, V.* ✍

$$$-$$$$ ✕▥ **Haywood Park Hotel.** The lobby of this Art Deco downtown hotel, once a department store, has golden oak woodwork accented with gleaming brass. The suites are spacious, with baths done in Spanish marble. The hotel's elegant restaurant, 23 Page, serves seafood and game. A favorite entrée is grilled lamb chop with radicchio and artichoke mousse. Adjoining the property is a shopping galleria. ✉ *1 Battery Park Ave., 28801,* ☎ *828/252–2522 or 800/228–2522,* 𝔽𝔸𝕏 *828/ 253–0481. 33 suites. Restaurant, bar, in-room data ports, sauna, exercise room, laundry service, business services, meeting rooms. AE, D, DC, MC, V. CP.* ✍

$$ ▥ **Comfort Inn.** This chain hotel, off I–240 near the River Ridge Outlet Mall, has a fireplace in a large sitting area. Most guest rooms are standard fare, but suites have private balconies and dinette areas. ✉ *800 Fairview Rd., 28803,* ☎ *828/298–9141,* 𝔽𝔸𝕏 *828/298–6629. 149*

rooms, 28 suites. Pool, business services, meeting rooms. AE, D, DC, MC, V. CP. ☙

$$ 🏨 **Hampton Inn.** You can relax beside the fire in the lobby at this motel off I–26 that's convenient to downtown. Some guest rooms have whirl-pool baths. ✉ *1 Rocky Ridge Rd., 28806,* ☎ *828/667–2022 or 800/426–7866,* ℻ *828/665–9680. 121 rooms. In-room data ports, indoor pool, sauna, exercise room, business services, meeting rooms, airport shuttle. AE, D, DC, MC, V. CP.* ☙

$–$$ 🏨 **Mountaineer Inn.** A fixture along Tunnel Road for nearly 40 years, the Mountaineer is ever popular with families and others who care less about fancy than they do about affordable, comfortable surroundings. ✉ *155 Tunnel Rd., 28805,* ☎ *828/254–5331 or 800/255–4080,* ℻ *828/254–5331. 79 rooms. In-room data ports, pool, business services, meeting rooms. AE, D, MC, V. CP.*

Nightlife and the Arts

An intimate, smoke-free listening room, **Be Here Now** (✉ 5 Biltmore Ave., ☎ 828/258–2071) has dancing and concerts. It's one of the region's premier music clubs, drawing a varied clientele and artists ranging from Doc Watson to the Second City comedy troupe. One of the best nightspots in town is **Gatsby's** (✉ 13 W. Walnut St., ☎ 828/254–4248), a cornerstone of the revitalized downtown. World-class acts range from blues to alternative rock.

Outdoor Activities and Sports

For other activities, *see* The Mountains A to Z, *below.*

GOLF

Colony Lake Lure Golf Resort (✉ 201 Blvd. of the Mountains, Lake Lure, ☎ 828/625–2888 or 800/260–1040), 5 mi from Asheville, has two 18-hole, par-72 courses known for their beauty. **Etowah Valley Country Club and Golf Lodge** (✉ U.S. 64, Etowah, ☎ 828/891–7141 or 800/451–8174), about 20 mi from Asheville, has three very different (one par-72, two par-73) 18-hole courses with good package deals. **Grove Park Inn Resort** (✉ 290 Macon Ave., ☎ 828/252–2711 or 800/438–5800) has a beautiful par-71 course.

HORSEBACK RIDING

Trail rides are offered by stables throughout the region between April and November, including **Pisgah View Ranch** (✉ Rte. 1, Candler, ☎ 828/667–9100) in the central mountains and **Cataloochee Ranch** (✉ Rte. 1, Maggie Valley, ☎ 828/926–1401 or 800/868–1401) in the southern mountains.

LLAMA TREKS

One-day and overnight hikes with llamas carrying your pack through local forests are arranged by **Windsong Llama Treks, Ltd.** (✉ 120 Ferguson Ridge Rd., Clyde, ☎ 828/627–6111). **Avalon Llama Trek** (✉ 310 Wilson Cove Rd., Swannanoa, ☎ 828/298–5637) leads trips on the lush trails of the Pisgah National Forest.

SKIING

Ski resorts in the Asheville area include **Cataloochee** (✉ Rte. 1, Maggie Valley, ☎ 828/926–0285 or 800/768–0285), **Fairfield-Sapphire Valley** (✉ 4000 U.S. 64W, Sapphire Valley, ☎ 828/743–3441 or 800/533–8268), and **Wolf Laurel** (✉ Rte. 3, Mars Hill, ☎ 828/689–4111).

Shopping

Biltmore Village (✉ Hendersonville Rd., ☎ 828/274–5570) on the Biltmore Estate is a cluster of specialty shops, restaurants, galleries, and hotels in a setting with a decided early 20th-century English-hamlet feel. Everything from children's books to music, antiques, and wearable art can be found.

Grovewood Gallery at the Homespun Shops (⊠ 111 Grovewood Rd., ☎ 828/253–7651), adjacent to the Grove Park Inn and established by Mrs. George Vanderbilt, sells furniture and contemporary and traditionally crafted woven goods made on the premises.

Side Trips from Asheville

Within 40 mi of Asheville are towns with parks and historic sites. Some are resort destinations in themselves.

BREVARD

40 mi southwest of Asheville on NC 280.

Plenty of nearby waterfalls and the **Brevard Music Center** (☎ 828/884–2011), which has a seven-week music festival each summer, are draws in this resort town. Nearby Pisgah National Forest has the **Cradle of Forestry in America National Historic Site** (⊠ 1001 Pisgah Hwy., ☎ 828/884–5823).

🕲 At **Sliding Rock** in summer, you can skid 150 ft on a natural water slide. Wear old jeans and tennis shoes and bring a towel. ⊠ *Pisgah National Forest, north of Brevard, off U.S. 276,* ☎ *828/877–3265.* 🎫 *Free.* ☉ *Memorial Day–Labor Day, daily 10–5:30.*

CHIMNEY ROCK

25 mi southeast of Asheville on U.S. 64/74A.

This town is deep in the Blue Ridge Mountains. At **Chimney Rock Park** an elevator travels through a 26-story shaft of rock for a staggering view of Hickory Nut Gorge and the surrounding mountains. Trails, open year-round, lead to 400-ft Hickory Nut Falls, where *The Last of the Mohicans* was filmed. ⊠ *U.S. 64/74A,* ☎ *828/625–9611 or 800/277–9611.* 🎫 *$11.* ☉ *Daily 8:30–4:30.*

FLAT ROCK

21 mi southwest of Chimney Rock, 25 mi south of Asheville via I–26.

Flat Rock has been a summer resort since the mid-19th century. The ★ **Carl Sandburg Home National Historic Site** is the spot to which the poet and Lincoln biographer Carl Sandburg moved with his wife, Lilian, in 1945. Guided tours of their house, Connemara, where Sandburg's papers still lie scattered on his desk, are given by the National Park Service. In summer, *The World of Carl Sandburg* and *Rootabaga Stories* are presented at the amphitheater. ⊠ *1928 Little River Rd.,* ☎ *828/693–4178.* 🎫 *$3.* ☉ *Daily 9–5.* 🐾

The **Flat Rock Playhouse** (⊠ Greenville Hwy., ☎ 828/693–0731) has a high reputation for summer stock theater. The season runs from May to mid-December.

SALUDA

30 mi southeast of Asheville.

At the top of the steepest railroad grade east of the Rockies, this salubrious town along the tracks is strung with antiques and crafts shops in 19th-century brick buildings. The surrounding area has apple orchards, woods, and waterfalls.

WEAVERVILLE

18 mi north of Asheville via U.S. 23/19.

This town's state historic site, the **Zebulon B. Vance Birthplace,** has a reconstructed two-story log cabin and several outbuildings. This is where Vance, governor of North Carolina during the Civil War and later a

ARTS AND CRAFTS IN THE MOUNTAINS

A CENTURY AGO, AS YOUNG GEORGE VANDERBILT prepared to build a retreat in then-bucolic Asheville, he and an architect traveled the French countryside looking for elements of designs that could be incorporated into the home he had modeled after a 16th-century Loire Valley château. A legion of craftspeople labored long to create the Biltmore Mansion, including its unlikely gargoyles and grotesques. Decades later, in the 1970s, two tiny Episcopal churches in Glendale Springs and West Jefferson became home to Ben Long frescoes stunning enough to be in a great cathedral.

The message is this: when it comes to arts and crafts in western North Carolina, expect the unexpected. (Note: if a place mentioned here isn't described elsewhere in the chapter, an address or telephone number is given.) There's so much more going on than first meets the eye. And that's the fun of it: the hunt. Sometimes handmade treasures are found out in the open: more than 85 crafts fairs are held annually throughout the rural 21-county region. At the Balsam Mountain Inn (✉ Off NC 23/74, Balsam, ☎ 828/456-9498) just off the Blue Ridge Parkway near Waynesville, the work of a range of artisans is tastefully showcased year-round.

More than 4,000 people here earn part or all of their living from crafts, and many of them can be found "around the bend" and in homes tucked back in forested hollows. They patiently coax form from clay and wood and metal, and because art is close to the heart, they are usually happy to talk about what they do. So go ahead—explore. Interesting roads that are off the map can lead to workshops. If hours are posted, however, it's best to respect them; time is precious.

In the beginning, it was practical function, not notions of folk art, behind all the quilting, weaving, woodworking, and pottery making. By the latter part of the 19th century, though, missionaries, social workers, and women of means—Frances Goodrich and Edith Vanderbilt among them—began to recognize that the things of day-to-day life contained artistry and thus economic salvation for a beautiful but isolated and impoverished area.

Today, utility and aesthetics have melded. From furnaces in the northwest counties of Mitchell and Yancey come gobs of hot liquid that are shaped by hand into art glass prized by collectors and dealers worldwide. Many glassblowers have perfected their métier at the prestigious Penland School of Crafts, whose courses include printmaking, wood, surface design, metals, drawing, clay, and fibers. The work of students and graduates, much of it contemporary, is on display in area galleries including Penland's own extensive gallery shop.

In the tiny village of Crossnore in southern Avery County, a rock cottage houses the Crossnore School's Weaving Room (✉ U.S. 221, ☎ 828/733-4660). Favored here are patterns used by the early settlers of the Appalachians; however, in a nod to modernity the ladies spin with easy-care rayon and synthetics as well as with cotton, wool, and linen.

On the Cherokee Reservation, in the shadow of the Smoky Mountains, elders pass on to children the secrets of finger weaving, wood carving, mask and beaded jewelry making. Their work, intricate and colorful and found in shops such as Medicine Man Crafts (✉ U.S. 441, ☎ 828/497-2202) in downtown Cherokee, is ageless, a connective thread to a time that predates the United States by thousands of years.

U.S. senator, grew up. Crafts and chores typical of his period are often demonstrated. Picnic facilities are available. An entrance to the Blue Ridge Parkway is nearby. ⊠ *911 Reems Creek Rd. (Rte. 1103),* ☎ *828/ 645–6706.* ⛭ *Free.* ☉ *Apr.–Oct., Mon.–Sat. 9–5, Sun. 1–5; Nov.–Mar., Tues.–Sat. 10–4, Sun. 1–4.*

Lake Toxaway

40 mi southwest of Asheville.

A century ago, a group called the Lake Toxaway Company created a 640-acre lake in the high mountains between Brevard and Cashiers. Nearby, a grand 500-room hotel built with the finest materials, providing the most modern conveniences, and serving European cuisine, attracted many of the country's elite. That hotel is long gone, but the scenic area, which some still call "America's Switzerland," has a number of fine resorts and some of the priciest real estate in the North Carolina mountains.

Those who love nature, even if it's just looking at it, will enjoy being in this mountain wilderness. And for those to whom shopping is a sport, a number of upscale stores—many specializing in antiques and regional arts and crafts—can be found.

Lodging

$$$$ 🏨 **Earthshine Mountain Lodge.** You can have as much solitude or adventure as you want at this spacious cedar log cabin with stone fireplaces. The lodge, which sits on 70 acres midway between Brevard and Cashiers on a ridge that adjoins the Pisgah National Forest, offers horseback riding, hiking, fishing, and even an opportunity to gather berries, feed the goats, or master some Cherokee skills. In the evening guests may gather around an open fire to sing songs, square dance, or exchange stories. A minimum stay of two nights is required. ⊠ *Golden Rd., off Silversteen Rd. off U.S. 64, Box 216C, 28747,* ☎ *828/862–4207. 10 rooms. Hiking, horseback riding, fishing, baby-sitting, children's programs (ages 6 and up), meeting rooms. D, MC, V. FAP.* ✎

$$$$ 🏨 **Greystone Inn.** In 1915, Savannah resident Lucy Molz built a second home in Lake Toxaway. Today, the six-level Swiss-style mansion is an inn listed on the National Register of Historic Places. Guest rooms have antiques or period reproductions, while suites that border the lake of this mountain resort are modern. Rates include breakfast and dinner, afternoon tea and cake, and cocktails. The inn is open January through March, weekends only. ⊠ *Greystone La., 28747,* ☎ *828/ 966–4700; 800/824–5766 outside NC,* 🖷 *828/862–5689. 33 rooms. Dining room, in-room VCRs, pool, lake, massage, driving range, 18-hole golf course, putting green, 5 tennis courts, children's programs, business services. AE, MC, V. MAP.* ✎

Hot Springs

30 mi northwest of Asheville via U.S. 23/19 and 25/70 past Marshall.

This picturesque village is a way station for hikers on the Appalachian Trail. The **Hot Springs Spa**'s mineral springs maintain a natural 100°F temperature year-round and have, since the turn of the 20th century, provided relief for visitors suffering a variety of ailments, including rheumatism and pelvic troubles. Massage therapy is also available. ⊠ *315 Bridge St.,* ☎ *828/622–7676 or 800/462–0933.* ⛭ *$12–$30 per hr, depending on time of day and number of people in tub.* ☉ *Daily 9 AM–11 PM; hrs variable Dec.–Jan. (call in advance).*

Dining and Lodging

$ ✕🏠 **Bridge Street Café & Inn.** This renovated storefront, circa 1922, is right on the Appalachian Trail and overlooks Spring Creek. Upstairs are brightly decorated rooms and two baths filled with antiques. One bathroom has a claw-foot tub. The café ($$–$$$) downstairs has a wood-fired oven and grill from which emerge delicious pizzas. ☒ *Bridge St., Box 502, 28743,* ☎ *828/622–0002,* FAX *828/622–7282. 4 rooms share 2 baths. Restaurant. AE, D, MC, V. Closed Nov.–mid-Mar.* 🐾

Blue Ridge Parkway

Entrance 2 mi east of Asheville, off I–40.

★ The beautiful **Blue Ridge Parkway** (☒ Superintendent, Blue Ridge Pkwy., 199 Hemphill Knob Rd., Asheville 28803, ☎ 828/298–0398, 🐾) gently winds through mountains and meadows and crosses mountain streams for more than 469 mi on its way from Cherokee, North Carolina, to Waynesboro, Virginia. This is the most scenic route from Asheville to Boone and Blowing Rock. The parkway is generally open year-round but often closes during inclement weather. Maps and information are available at visitor centers along the highway. Mile markers (MM) identify points of interest and indicate the distance from the parkway's starting point in Virginia.

The **Folk Art Center** sells authentic mountain crafts made by members of the Southern Highland Craft Guild. ☒ *Blue Ridge Pkwy., MM 382,* ☎ *828/298–7928.* ☉ *Daily 9–6.*

🐣 You can tour an underground mine or dig for gems of your own at **Emerald Village.** ☒ *McKinney Mine Rd. at Blue Ridge Pkwy., MM 334, Little Switzerland,* ☎ *828/765–6463 or 877/389–4653.* 🎫 *Mine $4, plus cost of gem bucket chosen ($3–$100). A $50 bucket guarantees you a stone, which will be cut free of charge; $100 guarantees 2.* ☉ *June–Labor Day, daily 9–6, May and Sept.–Oct., daily 9–5.*

Linville Caverns are the only caverns in the Carolinas. The caverns go 2,000 ft beneath Humpback Mountain and have a year-round temperature of 51°F. North of Asheville, exit the parkway at mile marker 317.4 and turn left onto U.S. 221. ☒ *U.S. 221 between Linville and Marion,* ☎ *828/756–4171.* 🎫 *$5.* ☉ *June–Labor Day, daily 9–6; Apr.–May and Sept.–Oct., daily 9–5; Nov. and Mar., daily 9–4:30; Dec.–Feb., weekends 9–4:30.*

From the **Linville Falls Visitor Center** (☒ Rte. 1, Spruce Pine, ☎ 828/765–1045), at mile marker 316.3, a ½-mi hike leads to one of North Carolina's most photographed waterfalls. The easy trail winds through evergreens and rhododendrons to overlooks with views of the series of cascades tumbling into Linville Gorge. There's also a campground and a picnic area.

Just off the parkway at mile marker 305, **Grandfather Mountain** soars to 6,000 ft and is famous for its Mile-High Swinging Bridge, a 228-ft-long bridge that sways over a 1,000-ft drop into the Linville Valley. There are also hiking and picnicking. The **Natural History Museum** has exhibits on native minerals, flora and fauna, and pioneer life. The annual **Singing on the Mountain** in June is an opportunity to hear old-time gospel music and preaching, and the **Highland Games in July** bring together Scottish clans from all over North America for athletic events and Highland dancing. ☒ *Blue Ridge Pkwy. and U.S. 221, Linville,* ☎ *828/733–4337 or 800/468–7325.* 🎫 *$10.* ☉ *Apr.–mid-Nov., daily 8–dusk; mid-Nov.–Mar., daily 8–5, weather permitting.*

Parks along the parkway include **Julian Price Park** (MM 295–298.1), which has hiking, canoeing on a mountain lake, trout fishing, and camping. The **Moses H. Cone Park** (MM 292.7–295) has a turn-of-the-20th-century manor house (home of a textile magnate) that's now the **Parkway Craft Center.** The center sells fine work by area craftspeople.

Dining and Lodging

$$$$ ✕☷ **Eseeola Lodge and Restaurant.** Rebuilt in 1936 after a fire, this
★ lakeside lodge, best described as dressed-up rustic, sits 3,800 ft above sea level and is one sure way to beat summer's heat. Golf is a passion here, but the diversions are many. The lovely grounds are manicured, and rich chestnut paneling and stonework grace the public areas. Entrées at the restaurant may include free-range chicken and rainbow trout; jacket and tie are required at dinner. ✉ *U.S. 221, Linville 28646,* ☎ *828/733–4311 or 800/742–6717,* ⅎ̄Ⅺ *828/733–3227. 19 rooms, 5 suites, 1 cottage. Restaurant, bar, pool, 18-hole golf course, putting green, 8 tennis courts, croquet, exercise room, boating, fishing, business services. MC, V. Closed late Oct.–mid-May. MAP.* ✇

Outdoor Activities and Sports

HIKING

More than 100 trails lead off the Blue Ridge Parkway, from easy strolls to strenuous hikes. For more information on parkway trails, contact the Blue Ridge Parkway (☞ *above*). Another good source is *Walking the Blue Ridge: A Guide to the Trails of the Blue Ridge Parkway,* by Leonard Adkins, available at most parkway visitor center gift shops. The **Bluff Mountain Trail** at Doughton Park (MM 238.5) is a moderately strenuous 7½-mi trail winding through forests, pastures, and valleys, and along the mountainside. Moses H. Cone Park's (MM 292.7) **Figure 8 Trail** is an easy and beautiful trail that the Cone family designed for their morning walks. The ½-mi loop winds through a tunnel of rhododendrons and a hardwood forest. Those who tackle the ½-mi, strenuous **Waterrock Knob Trail** (MM 451.2), near the south end of the parkway, will be rewarded with spectacular views from the 6,400-ft-high Waterrock Knob summit.

ROCK CLIMBING

One of the most challenging climbs in the country is the **Linville Gorge** (MM 317), often called "the Grand Canyon of North Carolina." Permits are available from the district forest ranger's office in Marion (☎ 828/652–2144) or from the Linville Falls Texaco station on U.S. 221.

SKIING

Cross-country skiing is offered at **Moses H. Cone Park** (☎ 828/295–7591) and at **Linville Falls** on the **Blue Ridge Parkway** and at **Roan Mountain** (☎ 615/772–3303). Tours and equipment are available from **High Country Ski Shop** (☎ 828/733–2008) in Pineola on U.S. 221.

Blowing Rock

86 mi northeast of Asheville, 93 mi west of Winston-Salem.

Blowing Rock, a mecca for mountain visitors since the 1880s, has retained the flavor of a quiet village. About a thousand people are permanent residents, but the population swells each summer. To retain the rural atmosphere, the community banded together to prohibit large hotels and motels. Blowing Rock is the inspiration for the small town in resident Jan Karon's novels about country life in the fictional town of Mitford. To get here from the Blue Ridge Parkway, take U.S. 221/321 to just north of the entrance to Moses H. Cone Park.

The **Blowing Rock** looms 4,000 ft over the Johns River Gorge. If you throw your hat over the sheer precipice, it may come back to you, should the wind gods be playful. The story goes that a Cherokee man and a Chickasaw maiden fell in love. Torn between his tribe and his love, he jumped from the cliff, but she prayed to the Great Spirit, and he was blown safely back to her. ⊠ *Off U.S. 321,* ☎ *828/295–7111.* ☜ *$4.* ⊙ *June–Oct., Sun.–Thurs. 8:30–7, Fri.–Sat. 8:30–8; Nov.–Dec. daily 9–5; Jan.–Feb. weekends 8–8; Mar.–May daily 9–5.*

The **Tweetsie Railroad** is a popular Wild West theme park centered on a steam locomotive beset by robbers. A petting zoo, a country fair, rides, gold panning, a saloon show, and concessions are also here. ⊠ *U.S. 321/221, off Blue Ridge Pkwy., MM 291,* ☎ *828/264–9061 or 800/526–5740.* ☜ *$20.* ⊙ *Mid-May–mid-Aug., daily 9–6; mid-Aug.–Oct., Fri.–Sun. 9–6.*

Lodging

$$$–$$$$ 🏨 **The Inn at Ragged Gardens.** With a grand stone staircase in the entry hall, colorful gardens, richly toned chestnut paneling, and the chestnut bark siding found on many older homes in the High Country, it's no wonder that this manor-style house in the heart of Blowing Rock gets rave reviews. Guests appreciate the attention to detail: the European and American antiques blended with contemporary art and the all-hours butler's pantry. All rooms have fireplaces and some have whirlpools and private balconies. It's best for older children. A two-night minimum is required on weekends. ⊠ *203 Sunset Dr., 28605,* ☎ *828/295–9703. 6 rooms, 2 suites. Meeting room. MC, V. BP.* ⊛

$$$ 🏨 **Chetola Resort.** This small resort, named for the Cherokee word meaning "haven of rest," grew out of an early 20th-century stone-and-wood lodge. The original building now houses the resort's restaurant and meeting rooms and is adjacent to the 1988 lodge. Guest rooms in the lodge have private balconies facing either the mountains, the lake, or both. Condominiums are spread among the hills. The property adjoins Moses H. Cone Park, with its hiking trails and riding facilities. ⊠ *N. Main St., Box 17, 28605,* ☎ *828/295–5500 or 800/243–8652,* FAX *828/295–5529. 37 rooms, 5 suites, 62 condominiums. 2 restaurants, piano bar, indoor pool, hot tub, massage, 5 tennis courts, exercise room, racquetball, boating, fishing, bicycles, playground, business services, meeting rooms. AE, D, MC, V.* ⊛

$$–$$$ 🏨 **Maple Lodge Bed & Breakfast.** Blowing Rock's oldest continuously operating bed-and-breakfast is just off Main Street, with its shops and restaurants. Built in 1946, the inn has a wonderful garden, pine paneling in the foyer and twin parlors, and pine ceilings and woodwork throughout. Some rooms are small, but most can hold a queen-size bed, antique dresser, table, and chair comfortably. The full breakfast, served in an enclosed porch, includes delicious homemade breads and muffins. ⊠ *152 Sunset Dr., 28605,* ☎ *828/295–3331,* FAX *828/295–9986. 10 rooms, 1 suite. Fans. AE, D, MC, V. Closed Jan.–Feb. BP.* ⊛

$–$$ 🏨 **Alpine Village Inn.** This motel in the heart of Blowing Rock harks back to a simpler time. Its rooms are neat as a pin and attractive in a homey way. Owners Rudy and Lynn Cutrera have decorated them with antiques, quilts, even flowers on holidays. Room refrigerators are available and morning coffee is served. ⊠ *297 Sunset Dr., 28605,* ☎ *828/295–7206. 15 rooms. AE, D, MC, V.* ⊛

Outdoor Activities and Sports

HORSEBACK RIDING

Blowing Rock Stables (⊠ U.S. 221, ☎ 828/295–7847) runs trail rides.

SKIING

There's downhill skiing at **Appalachian Ski Mountain** (⊠ 940 Ski Mountain Rd., ☎ 828/295–7828 or 800/322–2373).

Shopping

Bolick Pottery (⊠ NC 8 off U.S. 321, Lenoir, ☎ 828/295–3862), 3 mi southeast of Blowing Rock, sells mountain crafts and pottery hand-crafted by Glenn and Lula Bolick, fifth-generation potters. **Goodwin Weavers** (⊠ off U.S. 321 Bypass, ☎ 828/295–3394) sells bedspreads, afghans, and other goods woven in the traditional mountain style, plus home furnishings designed by North Carolina artist Bob Timberlake.

Boone

8 mi north of Blowing Rock.

Boone, named for frontiersman Daniel Boone, is a city of several thousand residents at the convergence of three major highways—U.S. 321, U.S. 421, and NC 105. You'll find mountain crafts in stores and at crafts fairs here. **Mast General Store** at the Old Boone Mercantile (⊠ 630 W. King St., ☎ 828/262–0000) is a classic general store.

Horn in the West, a project of the Southern Appalachian Historical Association, is an outdoor drama that traces the story of Daniel Boone's life. ⊠ *Amphitheater off U.S. 321,* ☎ *828/264–2120.* ☎ *$12.* ☉ *Performances nightly at 8, except Mon. mid-June–mid-Aug.*

The **Appalachian Cultural Museum** examines the lives of Native Americans and African-Americans in the High Country; showcases the successes of such mountain residents as stock-car racer Junior Johnson and country singers Lula Belle and Scotty Wiseman; and exhibits a vast collection of antique quilts, fiddles, and handcrafted furniture. ⊠ *University Hall near Greene's Motel, U.S. 321,* ☎ *828/262–3117.* ☎ *$4.* ☉ *Tues.–Sat. 10–5, Sun. 1–5.*

Dining and Lodging

$–$$$ ✕ **Mike's Inland Seafood.** Calabash-style (lightly battered and fried) or broiled, the seafood here couldn't taste better if it were served at the ocean. There's a branch in Banner Elk. ⊠ *U.S. 321,* ☎ *828/262–5605. AE, DC, MC, V. Closed Mon.*

$$$$ ☷ **Hound Ears Lodge and Club.** This alpine inn, overlooking Grandfather Mountain and a lush golf course, offers amenities such as a pool secluded in a natural grotto and comfortable, well-kept rooms dressed in Waverly print fabrics. From April through October, the room rate for special packages includes breakfast and dinner. The dining area is open only to guests and members; reservations are required, as are a jacket and tie for dinner. ⊠ *328 Shulls Mill Rd., off NC 105, 6 mi from Boone, Box 188, 28605,* ☎ *828/963–4321,* ℻ *828/963–8030. 29 rooms. Dining room, pool, 18-hole golf course, 6 tennis courts, business services, meeting rooms. AE, MC, V.* ☜

$–$$ ☷ **High Country Inn.** A honeymoon destination that draws skiers, golfers, and other groups interested in the discount packages, the inn, made of native stone and surrounded by ponds, has accommodations that range from luxurious to comfortable. Geno's, a popular sports bar and restaurant, is here. ⊠ *1785 NC 105 S, Box 1339, 28607,* ☎ *828/264–1000 or 800/334–5605,* ℻ *828/262–0073. 118 rooms, 2 suites, 2 log cabins. Restaurant, bar, indoor-outdoor pool, hot tub, sauna, exercise room, meeting rooms. AE, D, MC, V.* ☜

$–$$ ☷ **Smoketree Lodge.** Views of Grandfather Mountain and an in-house art gallery showing the work of local artists are highlights of this mountain inn near the ski slopes. All rooms are fully equipped and have a kitchenette; use of laundry facilities is free. ⊠ *11914 NC 105 S, Box*

*3407, 28607, ☎ 828/963–6505 or 800/422–1880, ℻ 828/963–7815.
46 rooms. Indoor pool, hot tub, exercise room. AE, D, MC, V.* ✏

OFF THE
BEATEN PATH

BLUE RIDGE MOUNTAIN FRESCOES – In the 1970s, North Carolina artist
Ben Long and his students painted four luminous big-as-life frescoes in
two churches about 45 mi northeast of Boone in Ashe County, past Blue
Ridge Parkway mile marker 258.6. *The Last Supper* is in the Glendale
Springs Holy Trinity Church; the others, including *Mary, Great with
Child*, are in St. Mary's Episcopal Church at Beaver Creek near West
Jefferson. Signs from the parkway lead to the churches. ☎ *336/982–
3076.* ▣ *Free.* ◷ *Freely accessible. Guide service available by prior
arrangement.*

Outdoor Activities and Sports

CANOEING AND WHITE-WATER RAFTING

Near Boone and Blowing Rock, the New River, a federally designated
Wild and Scenic River (Classes I and II rapids) provides excitement for
canoeists and rafters, as do the Watauga River, Wilson Creek, and the
Toe River. One outfitter is **Wahoo's Adventures** (☎ 828/262–5774 or
800/444–7238).

GOLF

Western North Carolina has many challenging courses. North Carolina
High Country Host (☞ Visitor Information *in* The Mountains A to
Z, *below*) has information on public courses in Boone, Seven Devils,
Newland, and West Jefferson. **Boone Golf Club** (⊠ Fairway Dr., ☎ 828/
264–8760) is a good par-71 course for the whole family. **Hound Ears
Club** (⊠ NC 105, ☎ 828/963–4312) has an 18-hole course with great
mountain views (par 72). **Linville Golf Club** (⊠ Linville, ☎ 828/733–
4363), 17 mi from Boone, has a par-72 Donald Ross course.

Valle Crucis

5 mi south of Boone.

This tiny mountain town has the state's first rural historic district; vintage stores line the downtown streets. Everything from ribbons and cal-
ico to brogans and overalls is sold in the **Mast General Store** (⊠ NC
194, ☎ 828/963–6511). Built in 1882, the store has plank floors worn
to a soft sheen and a potbellied stove.

Dining and Lodging

$$$–$$$$ ✕▥ **Mast Farm Inn.** You can turn back the clock and still enjoy mod-
ern amenities at this charming pastoral inn, built in the 1800s and now
on the National Register of Historic Places. Rooms are in the farm-
house or in log outbuildings. The restaurant uses locally and organi-
cally grown vegetables and local trout. Organic gardening demonstrations
are held in the Inn's gardens. ⊠ *2543 Broadstone Rd., Box 704,
28691, ☎ 828/963–5857, ℻ 828/963–6404 or 888/963–5857. 9
rooms, 6 cottages. Restaurant. MC, V. BP.* ✏

Banner Elk

6 mi southwest of Valle Crucis, 11 mi southwest of Boone.

Banner Elk is a popular ski resort town surrounded by the lofty peaks
of Grandfather, Hanging Rock, Beech, and Sugar mountains.

Dining and Lodging

$$–$$$$ ✕ **Stonewalls.** This contemporary rustic restaurant affords one of the
best views of Beech Mountain. Fare includes steak, prime rib, fresh
seafood, chicken, and homemade desserts. The salad bar is superb. ⊠
NC 184, ☎ 828/898–5550. AE, MC, V. No lunch.

$–$$$ 🛏 **The Inns of Beech Mountain.** As these two Appalachian Mountain resorts—the Beech Alpen Inn and the Top of Beech Inn—are in eastern America's highest town, they overlook the slopes of the Blue Ridge Mountains. The staff is friendly at these country inns, and some rooms have fireplaces and balconies. The restaurant at Beech Alpen is open for dinner only. ✉ *700 Beech Mountain Pkwy., 28604,* ☎ *828/387–2252. 50 rooms. Restaurant. AE, D, MC, V. CP.* ✧

Outdoor Activities and Sports

CANOEING AND WHITE-WATER RAFTING

The many rivers in the Banner Elk area provide a variety of possibilities. Outfitters include **Edge of the World Outfitters** (✉ NC 184, ☎ 828/898–9550 or 800/789–3343).

HORSEBACK RIDING

Banner Elk Riding Stables (✉ NC 184, ☎ 828/898–5424) runs trail rides.

SKIING

There's downhill skiing at **Ski Beech** (✉ NC 184, Beech Mountain, ☎ 828/387–2011 or 800/438–2093), **Sugar Mountain** (✉ off NC 184, Banner Elk, ☎ 828/898–4521 or 800/784–2768), and **Hawksnest Golf and Ski Resort** (✉ 1800 Skyland Dr., Seven Devils, ☎ 828/963–6561 or 800/822–4295). For **ski conditions,** call ☎ 800/962–2322.

The Mountains A to Z

Arriving, Departing, and Getting Around

BY BUS

Greyhound/Carolina Trailways (✉ 2 Tunnel Rd., ☎ 828/253–5353 or 800/231–2222) serves Asheville.

BY CAR

I–40 runs east and west through Asheville. I–26 runs from Charleston, South Carolina, to Asheville. I–240 forms a perimeter around the city. U.S. 23–19A is a major north and west route. The Blue Ridge Parkway runs northeast from Great Smoky Mountains National Park to Shenandoah National Park in Virginia, passing Cherokee, Asheville, and the High Country. U.S. 221 runs north to the Virginia border through Blowing Rock and Boone and intersects I–40 at Marion. U.S. 321 intersects I–40 at Hickory and heads to Blowing Rock/Boone.

BY PLANE

Asheville Regional Airport (✉ 708 Airport Rd., Fletcher, ☎ 828/684–2226) is served by Midway Connections, Atlantic Southeast Airlines, ComAir, and US Airways. For airline telephone numbers, *see* Air Travel *in* Smart Travel Tips A to Z. US Airways Express (☎ 800/428–4322) serves the **Hickory Airport** (✉ U.S. 321, ☎ 828/323–7408), about 40 mi from Blowing Rock.

Contacts and Resources

EMERGENCIES

Dial 911 for **police** and **ambulance** everywhere but the Cherokee Reservation, where the police can be reached at 828/497–4131 and the EMS service at 828/497–6402. **Memorial Mission** (✉ 509 Biltmore Ave., Asheville, ☎ 828/255–4000). **Watauga Medical Center** (✉ 336 Deerfield Rd., Boone, ☎ 828/262–4100). **Cannon Memorial Hospital** (✉ 805 Shawneehaw Ave., Banner Elk, ☎ 828/898–5111). **Blowing Rock Hospital** (✉ 416 Chestnut Dr., Blowing Rock, ☎ 828/295–3136).

GUIDED TOURS

A brochure entitled **"The Asheville Urban Trail,"** available at the Asheville Area Chamber of Commerce (✉ 151 Haywood St., ☎ 828/258–6100), provides a self-guided 1½-mi walking tour of downtown.

OUTDOOR ACTIVITIES AND SPORTS

There are **camping** opportunities at the five developed, or "frontcountry," campgrounds in the North Carolina part of Great Smoky Mountains National Park; one of these, Smokemont, accepts reservations through the **National Park Service Reservation Service** (☎ 800/365–2267). The remaining four campgrounds—Balsam Mountain, Big Creek, Cataloochee, and Deep Creek—are first-come, first-served only. All frontcountry camping in the park is primitive by design. For more information on campgrounds, including those in Tennessee, as well as regulations and restrictions, contact the **Great Smoky Mountains National Park Headquarters** (✉ 107 Park Headquarters Rd., Gatlinburg, TN 37738, ☎ 865/436–1230 or 865/436–1231 for inquiries about backcountry camping).

For **canoeing** and **whitewater rafting** in the Asheville area, the Chattooga, Nolichucky, French Broad, Nantahala, Ocoee, and Green rivers offer Class I–V rapids. One of the largest area outfitters is **Nantahala Outdoor Center** (✉ 13077 U.S. 19W, Bryson City, ☎ 828/488–2175 or 800/232–7238).

Western North Carolina offers many challenging **golf** courses. For a complete listing of public courses in Asheville, Black Mountain, Brevard, Hendersonville, Lake Lure, Old Fort, and Waynesville, contact the Asheville Convention and Visitors Bureau (☞ Visitor Information, *below*).

Anyone into serious **hiking** can explore the **Appalachian Trail,** which runs along the crest of the Appalachian Mountains at the North Carolina–Tennessee border. It can be picked up at several points, including the Newfound Gap parking area in **Great Smoky Mountains National Park** (☎ 615/436–5615) and **Grandfather Mountain** (☎ 828/733–4337), where you can get trail maps.

RADIO STATIONS

AM: WSKY 1230, talk; WZQR 1350, country. **FM:** WCQS 88.1, National Public Radio; WSPA 98.9, easy listening; WKSF 99.9, country.

VISITOR INFORMATION

In Asheville, the **Asheville Convention and Visitors Bureau** (✉ 151 Haywood St., Box 1010, 28802, ☎ 828/258–6102 or 800/257–1300) will answer questions and provide maps. The **Cherokee Visitors Center** (✉ U.S. 441 Business, ☎ 828/497–9195 or 800/438–1601) provides information on the reservation. **North Carolina High Country Host** (✉ 1701 Blowing Rock Rd., Boone 28607, ☎ 828/264–1299 or 800/438–7500) is a complete information center for the High Country counties of Watauga, Ashe, and Avery. **Smoky Mountain Host of NC** (✉ 4437 Georgia Rd., Franklin 28734, ☎ 828/369–9606 or 800/432–4678) has information about the state's seven westernmost counties.

NORTH CAROLINA A TO Z

Arriving and Departing

By Bus

Greyhound/Carolina Trailways (☎ 800/231–2222) links the cities of North Carolina with major cities in the southeastern United States.

By Car

I–40 traverses the state from Asheville in the west to Wilmington in the east. I–85 passes through the Triangle, the Triad, and Charlotte as it crosses from northeast to southwest. I–77 passes through the western part of the state from Virginia through Charlotte to South Carolina, and I–95 carries north–south traffic in the eastern part of the state.

By Plane

Among the major airports in the state are **Charlotte-Douglas International Airport** (⊠ 5501 Josh Birmingham Blvd., ☎ 704/359–4013), the **Piedmont Triad International Airport** (⊠ 6451 Bryan Blvd., Greensboro, ☎ 336/665–5666), and the **Raleigh-Durham International Airport** (⊠ 1600 Terminal Blvd., Morrisville, ☎ 919/840–2123).

By Train

Amtrak (☎ 800/872–7245) offers daily service from major cities on the eastern seaboard to the state's main population centers, including Charlotte, Greensboro, Raleigh, Durham, and Southern Pines.

Getting Around

By Bicycle

North Carolina has more than 5,000 mi of mapped and signed bicycle routes, many on scenic country roads. For maps and information, contact the **Division of Bicycle and Pedestrian Transportation** (⊠ Box 25201, Raleigh 27611, ☎ 919/733–2804).

By Bus

Greyhound/Carolina Trailways (☎ 800/231–2222) links cities and towns throughout the state.

By Car

The speed limit on interstates varies; it's generally 65 or 70 mph. Right turns on red are permitted unless otherwise indicated. The official *State Transportation Map* may be ordered from the **North Carolina Department of Transportation** (⊠ Public Affairs Division, Box 25201, Raleigh 27611, ☎ 919/733–7600, 800/847–4862 outside NC). Copies of the state's booklet about **Scenic Byways** are available at North Carolina welcome and visitor centers. To order a single copy, call ☎ 919/733–2920 or write to the Department of Transportation's (☞ *above*) Roadside Environmental Unit.

By Ferry

Ferries connect coastal communities. Routes and schedules are printed on the official North Carolina *State Transportation Map* (☞ By Car, *above*) and are available by phone from the Department of Transportation (☎ 800/293–3779).

By Train

Amtrak (☎ 800/872–7245) offers daily service between a number of cities and towns.

Contacts and Resources

Emergencies

In almost all cities and towns dial 911 for police or ambulance in an emergency. Most hospital emergency rooms are open 24 hours a day. Smaller ones are often connected by air evacuation systems to major trauma centers.

Fishing

A mandatory state license can be bought at local bait and tackle shops or over the phone (with a credit card) from the **North Carolina Wildlife**

Commission (☎ 919/715–4091). Cost for nonresidents is as follows: one day $10, three days $15, and year pass $30.

Visitor Information

The **North Carolina Division of Tourism, Film and Sports Development** (✉ 301 N. Wilmington St., Raleigh 27601, ☎ 919/733–4171 or 800/847–4862, FAX 919/733–8582) has information packets and an information line. Operators will answer questions about everything from beaches to snow conditions.

7 SOUTH CAROLINA

South Carolina's scenic Lowcountry shoreline is punctuated by the historic yet vibrant port city of Charleston, with its elegant homes and fine museums. The recreational resorts of Myrtle Beach and Hilton Head anchor each end of the coast. Columbia, the state capital, is set in the fertile interior of the state, which stretches toward the Blue Ridge Mountains. Also to the west are the rolling fields of Thoroughbred Country. Upcountry South Carolina, at the northwestern tip of the state, is noted for incredible mountain scenery and white-water rafting.

Updated by
Mary Sue
Lawrence

F ROM ITS LOWCOUNTRY SHORELINE, with wide sand beaches, spacious bays, and forests of palmettos and moss-draped live oaks, South Carolina extends into an undulating interior region rich with fertile farmlands, then reaches toward the Blue Ridge Mountains, whose foothills are studded with scenic lakes, forests, and wilderness hideaways. What this smallest of Southern states lacks in land area it makes up for in diversity and enthusiasm. People here like to celebrate. Every month of the year there's a local festival that turns on regional pride, feting critters such as jumping frogs, edibles such as peaches and watermelons, or rarefied delicacies such as okra and chitterlings. South Carolina owes much of its growth to the tourism industry, which brings more than $14 billion and 29 million people to the state each year.

The historic port city of Charleston, although lovingly preserved, is not a museum city. Many of its treasured double-galleried antebellum homes are authentically furnished house museums, just as many are home to Charlestonians and newcomers. Residents air their quilts over piazzas, walk their dogs down cobblestone streets, and tend their famous gardens in much the same way their ancestors did 300 years ago. Locals bravely rebounded from Hurricane Hugo, which hit in 1989, to painstakingly rebuild and renovate, making the city perhaps as gleaming and fresh as it was during the 18th century. Renovation continues to expand to the far reaches of the downtown historic district, extending across the Cooper River Bridge and out of the town of Mount Pleasant into Awendaw and McClellanville. Culturally vibrant, Charleston nurtures theater, dance, music, and visual arts, showcased each spring during the internationally acclaimed Spoleto Festival USA.

Myrtle Beach is the glitzy jewel of the Grand Strand, a 60-mi stretch of wide white-sand beaches and recreational activities, especially golf, a top attraction throughout the state. South from Myrtle Beach to Georgetown, it's almost one continuous community. Georgetown itself is enjoying a healthy tourism trade, offering a small-town respite smack-dab between the big-city sophistication of Charleston and amusement-park excitement of Myrtle Beach.

To the south, tasteful, low-key Hilton Head—divided into several self-contained resorts—also offers beautiful beaches and wonderful golf and tennis. A toll expressway was completed in 1997 to help handle traffic to the resort areas. Sun City, a large, newly developed retirement community, is attracting scores of fifty-somethings to the area.

Nearby is the port city of Beaufort, with lovely streets dotted with preserved 18th-century homes. A stopover popular with New York-to-Florida commuters, it's also the favorite of early retirees in search of small-town life and great deals on real estate; many have converted its historic houses into B&Bs.

Columbia, the state capital, is a busy and historic city blessed by three rushing rivers. Besides museums and a good minor-league baseball team, the city has one of the country's top zoos and a riverside botanical garden. The University of South Carolina, with a student body of 40,000, means that nightlife and cheap and cheerful restaurants are plentiful. Nearby lakes and state parks provide abundant outdoor recreation and first-rate fishing, and the Congaree Swamp National Monument has the oldest and largest trees east of the Mississippi.

Thoroughbred Country, centered on the town of Aiken, is a peaceful area of rolling pastures where top racehorses are trained. In this part of the state, charming, old-fashioned towns such as Abbeville and Cheraw draw more and more visitors with their history, abundant outdoor activities, sleepy main streets, and friendly residents.

Upcountry South Carolina, at the northwestern tip, is less visited than the rest of the state but repays time spent here with dramatic mountain scenery, excellent hiking, and challenging white-water rafting. Greenville has seen a dramatic growth spurt in the last few years. Downtown Greenville is changing rapidly; new cafés, shops, and boutiques, plus a newfound cultural diversity, are breathing fresh life into the old city.

Pleasures and Pastimes

Beaches

South Carolina's mild climate makes the surf enjoyable from April through October. The beaches are expanses of white sand—some serene and secluded, others bustling and lined with high-rises. You can choose the high-voltage action at busy Myrtle Beach or the more low-key scene on the resort island of Hilton Head, or just stroll the sands at Huntington Beach State Park.

Dining

South Carolinians love to cook and share good food, from dishes marinated in tradition to the creatively contemporary. Lowcountry specialties include she-crab soup, stuffed oysters, and infinite variations on pecan pie. Seafood—often the fresh catch of the day—is likely to be traditionally prepared on the Grand Strand and gussied up on Hilton Head. Elsewhere in the state, try barbecue and look for a variety of cuisine, from cosmopolitan to country cookery. And don't write off grits until you've tasted them laced with cheese, topped with *tasso* (spiced ham) gravy, or folded into a veal or quail entrée.

CATEGORY	COST*
$$$$	over $40
$$$	$30–$40
$$	$20–$30
$	under $20

per person for a three-course meal, excluding drinks, service, and 5% tax

Gardens

Gardening devotees can and do build vacations around South Carolina gardens, where camellias, azaleas, other flowering shrubs, and blooming trees abound. Along the coast are some of the nation's most famous, including Middleton Place, with the oldest landscaped garden in America; Cypress Gardens, where cypress trees tower in dark waters with azaleas on the banks; and Brookgreen Gardens, with a superb outdoor sculpture collection set amid giant oaks and colorful flowers. Inland, remarkable gardens planted with roses, irises, or mountain laurel make some small towns a worthwhile side trip. Along the way, you can see peach orchards in bloom in spring.

Lodging

From predictable but dependable chains to luxurious resort hotels and quaint B&Bs, accommodations are available for every budget. Reservations are a must, especially on the coast, and prices do vary with the seasons—in fact, winter rates in Charleston and along the coast can be a pleasant surprise. The charms of historic Charleston in particular can be enhanced by a stay at one of its many inns, most in restored structures. Some are reminiscent of European inns; others are tastefully contemporary.

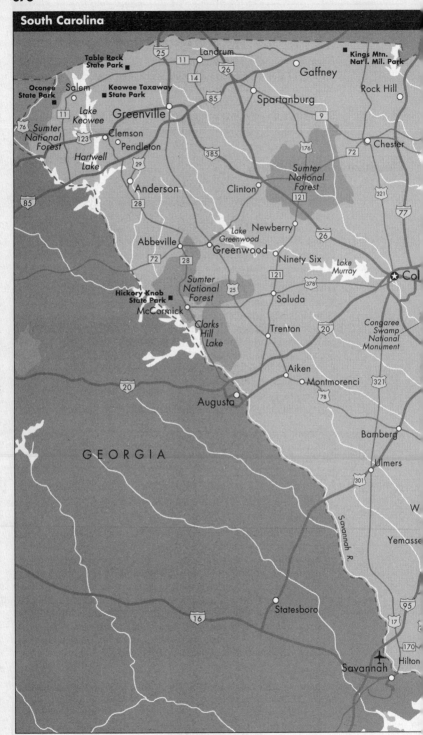

Landrum

Kings Mtn. Nat'l. Mil. Park

Gaffney

Table Rock State Park

Oconee State Park

Salem

Keowee Toxaway State Park

Rock Hill

Spartanburg

Lake Keowee

Greenville

Chester

Sumter National Forest

Clemson

Pendleton

Hartwell Lake

Sumter National Forest

Anderson

Clinton

Abbeville

Lake Greenwood

Newberry

Greenwood

Ninety Six

Lake Murray

Col

Hickory Knob State Park

Sumter National Forest

Saluda

McCormick

Congaree Swamp National Monument

Clarks Hill Lake

Trenton

Aiken

Montmorenci

Bamberg

Augusta

Ulmers

GEORGIA

W

Yemasse

Savannah R.

Statesboro

Hilton

Savannah

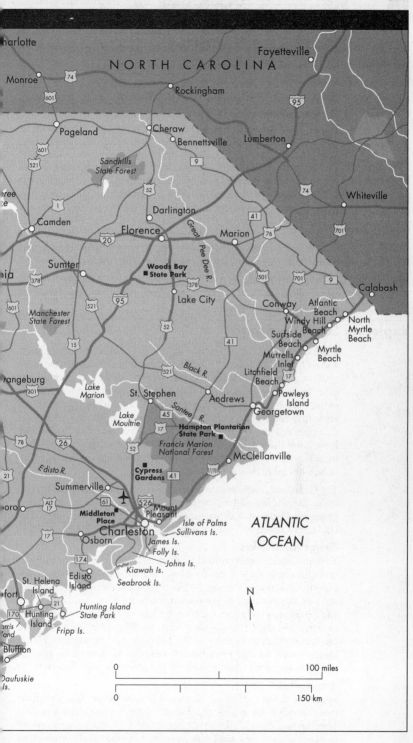

CATEGORY	CHARLESTON AND THE COAST*	OTHER AREAS*
$$$$	over $200	over $150
$$$	$150–$200	$110–$150
$$	$100–$150	$75–$110
$	under $100	under $75

*All prices are for a standard double room, excluding 7% tax.

Outdoor Activities

South Carolina's many rivers and lakes afford a range of activities, including boating, fly- and deep-water fishing, kayaking, sailboarding, sailing, tubing, and, in the Upcountry, whitewater rafting. Canoeing is popular on waters near Columbia. Anglers frequently break records with hauls of largemouth bass, stripers, crappie, and catfish caught in Lakes Marion and Moultrie. The first passages of the Palmetto Trail—a hiking, mountain biking, and horseback riding trail that will eventually wind 400 mi across the state—are open: the High Hills of Santee Passage, the Lake Moultrie Passage, and the Swamp Fox Passage in Francis Marion National Forest. Golfing, of course, reigns supreme practically year-round; the state has more than 380 courses.

following the text of a review is your signal that the property has a Web site, where you will find details and, usually, images; for a link, visit www.fodors.com/urls.

Exploring South Carolina

South Carolina has three regions—its 200-mi coastline, its interior heart, and its hilly north country. Charleston and points south are the Lowcountry, distinguished by aristocratic elegance and an accent unlike any other in the South. Because Hilton Head Island, in the southern part of the state, has become world renowned as a posh resort, it is treated separately here, along with the coastal towns near it. Natives consider the upper coasts part of what they call the Pee Dee (after the Pee Dee River), but the world knows Myrtle Beach and its environs by their more famous other name—the Grand Strand. It refers to the sandy strip of beaches more than 60 mi long.

The Heartland, including the Midlands core of the state, is an eclectic collection of towns and the capital city, Columbia. It also includes Thoroughbred Country, lush pasture for Triple Crown contenders. The Upcountry, noted for mountain scenery, is in the northwest.

Great Itineraries

To enjoy South Carolina to the fullest, you need a week or more to savor the coast and visit briefly inland. But you can have a memorable experience, however fleeting, by choosing sights that strike your fancy and promising yourself to return another time for more. The Lowcountry and Charleston are priorities; every traveler to South Carolina should visit that historic city—and most want to. With a bit more time, you can travel north from there to the Grand Strand or south to Hilton Head or west into the Heartland. If you have 10 days or so, you can add Thoroughbred Country and the Upcountry to your itinerary.

IF YOU HAVE 1 DAY

Spend the day in the historic district in ⊡ **Charleston.** Take a carriage ride through it for a look at some of the city's most elegant homes. Then browse through the shops in the Old City Market area, where most of the carriage tours begin and end. After that, walk south along East Bay Street or any side streets on your way to a couple of the area's museums. Here, wander the tree-shaded streets, discovering courtyard gardens and all the little surprises that reveal themselves to those who seek them out.

🏛 **Charleston** has so many charms—a rich antebellum and Civil War history, plantations and historic homes, beaches, golf, and superb restaurants—that you could spend a week here. Expand your itinerary on Day 2 by adding more sights within the historic district (it takes time to tour the house museums), by browsing in the Shops at Charleston Place or along King Street, and by including the Charleston Museum and other nearby museums. On the afternoon of Day 2 or Day 3, you could visit Mount Pleasant, with access to Fort Sumter National Monument, nice beaches, and Boone Hall Plantation to the north. Or you could head west of the Ashley River to visit Charles Towne Landing State Park and Magnolia Plantation and Gardens.

On Day 4, take a leisurely exit from Charleston along SC 61 and see **Drayton Hall** and **Middleton Place** as you make your way inland for a quick visit to 🏛 **Columbia,** with its State House, historic university campus, and zoo and botanical garden. Another choice is to take U.S. 17 north toward the beaches of the **Grand Strand,** where you can stay in busy 🏛 **Myrtle Beach** or more quiet 🏛 **Pawleys Island,** or south toward 🏛 **Beaufort** or 🏛 **Hilton Head Island.** There are beautiful gardens, stately plantations, and fine museums in both directions, or you may choose to go by boat on the ocean or Intracoastal Waterway.

Follow the itineraries above and then extend your time in 🏛 **Columbia.** Take a canoe ride on the scenic Saluda River or down the Congaree River, and visit Congaree Swamp National Monument. Browse in the South Carolina State Museum and enjoy shopping and dining in the Congaree Vista, a district stretching six blocks from the Congaree River. Take a day trip to historic, horsey **Camden** or **Aiken** to get the flavor of other Heartland towns. On Day 8, head to the Upcountry for magnificent scenery. You can explore 🏛 **Greenville,** perhaps driving north to the Cherokee Foothills Scenic Highway or to Kings Mountain National Military Park, a Revolutionary War site. You might head west and raft on the Chattooga River and spend your last night and day in 🏛 **Pendleton,** with its historic district and proximity to Clemson and the South Carolina State Botanical Garden.

When to Tour South Carolina

South Carolina is loveliest in spring, when azaleas, dogwood, and other flowering bushes and trees are in bloom, but flowers brighten every season—even winter, when pansies and camellias thrive. Between mid-March and mid-April, you can catch tours of private mansions in Charleston, and the city is alive with Spoleto events in May and June. Beaufort holds its Water Festival in mid-July. For price breaks on the coast, consider visiting in the off-season, October through February, but remember that some restaurants and a few attractions close around that time, and the water may be cool.

CHARLESTON

At first glimpse, Charleston resembles an 18th-century etching come to life. Its low-profile skyline is punctuated with the spires and steeples of 181 churches, representing 25 denominations—the reason that Charleston, known for religious freedom during its formation, is called the "Holy City." Parts of the city appear frozen in time; block after block of old downtown structures have been preserved and restored for residential and commercial use, and some brick and cobblestone streets remain. Charleston has survived three centuries of epidemics, earthquakes, fires, and hurricanes, and it is today one of the South's loveliest and best-preserved cities. It is not a museum, however: Throughout the year festivals (☞ Festivals *in* Nightlife and the Arts, *below*) add excitement and sophistication.

Besides the historic district (which we've divided, for ease of exploration, into two parts: the area north of Broad Street, and the Battery and area south of Broad Street), a visit to the city can easily include nearby towns, plantations and outstanding gardens, and historic sites, whether in Mount Pleasant or the area west of the Ashley River.

North of Broad

To really appreciate Charleston, you must walk its streets. The downtown historic district, roughly bounded by Calhoun Street to the north, the Cooper River to the east, the Battery to the south, and Legare Street to the west, is large, with 2,000 historic homes and buildings on the southeastern tip of the Charleston peninsula. In a fairly compact area you'll find churches, museums, and lovely views at every turn.

The area north of Broad Street has some of the finest historic homes and neighborhoods in the city, including Mazyck/Wraggborough neighborhood, where you'll find the Aiken-Rhett House. Large tracts of land made this area ideal for urban plantations during the early 1800s. While there are a number of pre-Revolutionary buildings here (including the Old Powder Magazine, the oldest public building in Charleston), in general, the farther north you travel on the peninsula, the newer the development. Still, because the peninsula was built-out by the early 1900s, North of Broad is rich with historic buildings from the 19th century and is often a treasure trove, as most tourists are busy conquering the waterfront area.

Numbers in the text correspond to numbers in the margin and on the Charleston map.

A Good Walk

Before you begin touring, drop by the **Visitor Information Center** ① on Meeting Street for an overview of the city, a map, and tickets for shuttle services if you want to give your feet a break. Start across the street at the **Charleston Museum** ②, with its large decorative arts collection; then turn right on Ann Street and follow it to Elizabeth Street to the palatial **Aiken-Rhett House** ③. After touring the house, head south down Elizabeth Street and turn right on John Street for the **Joseph Manigault Mansion** ④, another impressive house museum dating to the early 1800s. From here, return to Meeting Street and walk south toward Calhoun Street, passing the **Old Citadel Building** ⑤, converted into an Embassy Suites (☞ Lodging, *below*). Take a left on Calhoun Street; a half block down on your left is the **Emanuel African Methodist Episcopal Church** ⑥, where Denmark Vesey was a member. From here, you may want to use the shuttle bus DASH to give your feet a rest, or cross the street to Marion Square Mall for a drink and a break.

Retrace your steps on Calhoun Street (passing the Francis Marion Hotel, in the 1920s the highest building in the Carolinas) and continue two blocks west to St. Phillips Street, where you turn left to end up in the midst of the romantic campus of the **College of Charleston** ⑦, the oldest municipal college in the country. Enter through one of the gated openings on St. Phillips Street for a stroll under the many moss-draped trees. Then head east to King Street, Charleston's main shopping thoroughfare, and turn right; turn left on Hasell Street to see **Congregation Beth Elohim** ⑧, a Greek Revival building. Keep walking down Hasell Street, turn right on Meeting Street, and then turn left down Pinckney

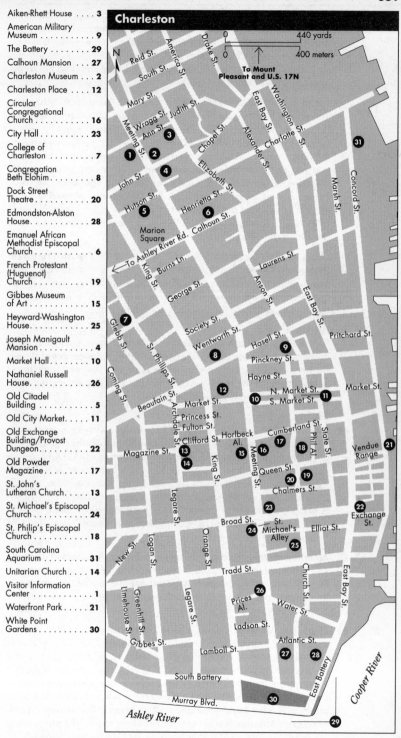

Charleston

Street to the **American Military Museum** ⑨. Two blocks to the south are **Market Hall** ⑩ and the bustling **Old City Market** ⑪. Now is a good time for a carriage tour, many of which leave from here (☞ Contacts and Resources *in* Charleston A to Z, *below*). Across Meeting Street is the classy **Charleston Place** ⑫, with its graceful hotel and cluster of shops. You can browse from one end to the other, exiting on King Street.

Facing you on the opposite corner is Saks Fifth Avenue; cross the street and walk a block down Market Street, turning left on quiet Archdale Street to wander through **St. John's Lutheran Church** ⑬ and the peaceful graveyard of the **Unitarian Church** ⑭. Turn left on Queen Street at the bottom of Archdale and walk two blocks to Meeting Street, where you turn left for the **Gibbes Museum of Art** ⑮, with its spectacular stained-glass dome. Across the street is the **Circular Congregational Church** ⑯. Behind it, on Cumberland Street, is the **Old Powder Magazine** ⑰. To the left as you face the building, you'll catch a glimpse of the steeple of **St. Philip's Episcopal Church** ⑱, famous in the city's skyline; it's around the corner on Church Street.

Cross over to picturesque Church Street to the **French Protestant (Huguenot) Church** ⑲ and the **Dock Street Theatre** ⑳ across the street. You might detour east here, down Queen Street and along Vendue Range to **Waterfront Park** ㉑ to relax in a bench swing overlooking beautiful river views, dramatic fountains, and a fishing pier.

TIMING

Set aside two to four hours for this walk, depending on your pace. Most of the house museum tours last about 40 minutes, so you might choose the two or three that interest you most. If it's high summer, you'll likely be moving with the speed of a Southern drawl, so pace yourself and make use of all those Charleston benches.

Sights to See

❸ **Aiken-Rhett House.** This stately 1819 mansion, with its original wallpaper, paint colors, and some of its furnishings, was the headquarters of Confederate general P. G. T. Beauregard during his 1864 Civil War defense of Charleston. The house, kitchen, slave quarters, and work yard are maintained much as they were when the original occupants lived here, making this one of the most complete examples of African-American urban life of the period. ⊠ *48 Elizabeth St.,* ☎ *843/723-1159.* ☜ *$7; combination ticket with Nathaniel Russell House and Old Powder Magazine (☞ below) $14.* ☉ *Mon.–Sat. 10–5, Sun. 2–5.*

❾ **American Military Museum.** The museum displays hundreds of uniforms and artifacts from all branches of service, beginning with the Revolutionary War. Its collections also include antique toy soldiers, war toys, miniatures, and weaponry. ⊠ *40 Pinckney St.,* ☎ *843/723-9620.* ☜ *$5.* ☉ *Mon.–Sat. 10–6, Sun. 1–6.*

★ ❷ **Charleston Museum.** Founded in 1773, the country's oldest city museum is in a contemporary complex. The 500,000 items in the collection—in addition to Charleston silver, fashions, toys, snuff boxes, and the like—include objects relating to natural history, archaeology, and ornithology. Its South Carolina decorative arts holdings are extraordinary. The Discover Me Room, designed just for children, has computers and other hands-on exhibits. Two historic homes—the **Joseph Manigault Mansion** (☞ *below*) and the **Heyward-Washington House** (☞ *below*)—are part of the museum. ⊠ *360 Meeting St.,* ☎ *843/722-2996.* ☜ *$8, museum and houses $18, 2 of the 3 sights $12.* ☉ *Mon.–Sat. 9–5, Sun. 1–5.*

⑫ Charleston Place. The city's only world-class hotel, this Orient Express property is flanked by a four-story complex of upscale boutiques and specialty shops (☞ Shopping, *below*). Peek into the lobby or have cocktails or tea in the intimate Lobby Lounge. Entrances for the garage and reception area are on Hasell Street between Meeting and King streets. ⊠ *130 Market St.,* ☎ *843/722–4900.*

⑯ Circular Congregational Church. The corners of this unusual Romanesque church were rounded off, they say, so the devil would have no place to hide. Simple but pretty, it has a beamed, vaulted ceiling. ⊠ *150 Meeting St.,* ☎ *843/577–6400.* ☉ *Call for tour schedule.*

⑦ College of Charleston. The lovely, tree-shaded campus of this college, founded in 1770, has a graceful main building, the Randolph House (1828), designed by Philadelphia architect William Strickland. It provides a romantic backdrop for the Cistern, often used as a grassy stage for concerts and other activities. Within the college, centered at the corner of George and St. Phillips streets, is the **Avery Research Center for African-American History and Culture,** which traces the heritage of Lowcountry African-Americans. ⊠ *Avery Research Center, 125 Bull St.,* ☎ *843/953–7609.* ☜ *Free. Mon.–Sat. noon–5, mornings by appointment.*

⑧ Congregation Beth Elohim. Considered one of the nation's finest examples of Greek Revival architecture, this temple was built in 1840 to replace an earlier one—the birthplace of American Reform Judaism in 1824—that was destroyed by fire. ⊠ *90 Hasell St.,* ☎ *843/723–1090.* ☉ *Weekdays 10–noon.*

NEED A BREAK?	On your way to the cluster of sights around Meeting Street, pick up a batch of Charleston's famed benne wafers at **Olde Colony Bakery** (⊠ 280 King St., between Society and Wentworth Sts., ☎ 843/722–2147). *Benne* is an African word used by slaves to describe the sesame seeds on these delicacies.

⑳ Dock Street Theatre. Built on the site of one of the nation's first playhouses, the building combines the reconstructed early Georgian playhouse and the preserved Old Planter's Hotel (circa 1809). The theater, which offers fascinating backstage views, welcomes visitors except when technical work for a show is under way. ⊠ *135 Church St.,* ☎ *843/720–3968.* ☜ *Free tours; call ahead for ticket prices and performance times.* ☉ *Weekdays 10–4.*

⑥ Emanuel African Methodist Episcopal Church. Home of the South's oldest A.M.E. congregation, the church had its beginnings in 1818. It was closed in 1822 when authorities learned that Denmark Vesey had used the sanctuary to plan his slave insurrection, but the church reopened in 1865 at the present site. ⊠ *110 Calhoun St.,* ☎ *843/722–2561.* ☉ *Daily 9–4.*

⑲ French Protestant (Huguenot) Church. This church is the only one in the country still using the original Huguenot liturgy, which can be heard in a special service held each spring. ⊠ *110 Church St.,* ☎ *843/722–4385.* ☉ *Weekdays 10–12:30 and 2–4.*

NEED A BREAK?	For a great view of the harbor and Waterfront Park, the **Vendue Inn** (☞ Lodging, *below*) on Vendue Range, at the end of Queen Street, serves lunch, drinks, and appetizers alfresco on the city's only Rooftop Lounge.

⑮ Gibbes Museum of Art. The collections of American art include notable 18th- and 19th-century portraits of Carolinians and an outstanding group of more than 400 miniature portraits. Don't miss the miniature rooms—intricately detailed with fabrics and furnishings and nicely displayed in shadow boxes inset in dark-paneled walls—or the Tiffany-style stained-glass dome in the rotunda. ⊠ *135 Meeting St.,* ☎ *843/722–2706.* *$5.* Tues.–Sat. 10–5, Sun.–Mon. 1–5.

❹ Joseph Manigault Mansion. A National Historic Landmark and an outstanding example of neoclassical architecture, this home was designed by Charleston architect Gabriel Manigault in 1803 and is noted for its carved-wood mantels and elaborate plasterwork. Some furnishings are British and French but most are Charleston antiques; some rare tricolor Wedgwood pieces are noteworthy. ⊠ *350 Meeting St.,* ☎ *843/723–2926.* *$7; for combination ticket, see the Charleston Museum (☞ above).* Mon.–Sat. 10–5, Sun. 1–5.

❿ Market Hall. Built in 1841 and modeled after the Temple of Nike in Athens, this imposing landmark building includes the **Confederate Museum,** where the Daughters of the Confederacy preserve and display flags, uniforms, swords, and other Civil War memorabilia. At press time, the museum, heavily damaged by Hurricane Hugo in 1989, was closed for renovation and may remain so into 2001; however, costumed guides sometimes stand outside and describe the facility for visitors. The collection is temporarily housed at 34 Pitt Street; admission is $2, and it's open Saturday noon–4, Sunday 1–4. ⊠ *88 Meeting St.,* ☎ *843/723–1541.*

❺ Old Citadel Building. Built in 1822 to house state troops and arms, the Old Citadel Building faces Marion Square. This is where the Carolina Military College—the Citadel—had its start. The fortresslike building is now the Embassy Suites Historic Charleston (☞ Lodging, *below*), and the Citadel is now on the Ashley River.

⓫ Old City Market. A series of low sheds that once housed produce and fish markets, this area is often called the Slave Market, although Charlestonians dispute that slaves ever were sold there. It now has restaurants, shops, gimcracks and gee-gaws for children, vegetable and fruit vendors, and local "basket ladies" weaving and selling sweet-grass, pine-straw, and palmetto-leaf baskets—a craft passed down through generations from their West African ancestors. ⊠ *Market St. between Meeting and E. Bay Sts.* Daily 9–sunset; hrs may vary.

NEED A
BREAK?

Just across the street from the Old City Market and Charleston Place, **Café Cafe** (⊠ 177 Meeting St., corner of Market, ☎ 843/723–3622) serves hearty sandwiches, inventive wraps, homemade soups, and great coffees and desserts throughout the day; some evenings there's live music, too.

⓱ Old Powder Magazine. This structure was built in 1713 and used during the Revolutionary War. It is now a museum with costumes, armor, and other artifacts from 18th-century Charleston, plus a fascinating audiovisual tour. ⊠ *79 Cumberland St.,* ☎ *843/805–6730.* *$2; combination ticket with Aiken-Rhett House (☞ above) and Nathaniel Russell House (☞ below) $14.* Mon.–Sat. 10–5, Sun. 2–5.

⓭ St. John's Lutheran Church. This Greek Revival church was built in 1817 for a congregation that celebrated its 250th anniversary in 1992. Notice the fine craftsmanship in the delicate wrought-iron gates and fence. Musicians may be interested in the 1823 Thomas Hall organ case. ⊠ *5 Clifford St.,* ☎ *843/723–2426.* Weekdays 9–3.

⓲ St. Philip's Episcopal Church. The graceful late-Georgian church is the second on its site; the congregation's first building burned down in 1838.

In the graveyard on the church's side of the street, Charlestonians are buried; in the graveyard on the other side, "foreigners" lie (including John C. Calhoun, who was from Abbeville, South Carolina). ✉ *146 Church St.,* ☎ *843/722–7734.* ◷ *By appointment.*

⑭ **Unitarian Church.** Completed in 1787, this church was remodeled in the mid-19th century using plans inspired by the Chapel of Henry VII in Westminster Abbey. The Gothic fan-tracery ceiling was added during that renovation. An entrance to the church grounds is on 161½–163 King Street, amid the antiques shops there. The secluded and romantically overgrown graveyard invites contemplation. ✉ *8 Archdale St.,* ☎ *843/723–4617 weekdays 8:30–2:30.* ◷ *Call ahead for hrs.*

❶ **Visitor Information Center.** The center gives a fine introduction to the city and sells tickets for shuttle services (☞ *Getting Around in Charleston A to Z, below*). Parking is 65¢ per hour; the first hour is free if you purchase a shuttle pass. Take time to see *Forever Charleston,* an insightful 20-minute film. ✉ *375 Meeting St.,* ☎ *843/853–8000 or 800/ 868–8118.* ▣ *Film $2.50.* ◷ *Mar.–Oct., daily 8:30–5:30; Nov.–Feb., daily 8:30–5; shows daily 9–5 on the ½ hr.*

㉑ **Waterfront Park.** A sprinkle from the park's interactive fountain will refresh you on hot summer days. Here, you'll also find swings, a fishing pier, picnic tables, and gardens overlooking Charleston Harbor. It's at the foot of Vendue Range, along the east side of Charleston Harbor. ☎ *843/724–7321.* ▣ *Free.*

The Battery and South of Broad

Along the Battery, on the point of a narrow peninsula bounded by the Ashley and Cooper rivers, handsome mansions, surrounded by gardens, face the harbor. Their distinctive look is reminiscent of the West Indies: before coming to the Carolinas in the late 17th century, many early British colonists had first settled on Barbados and other Caribbean isles, where they'd built houses with high ceilings and broad piazzas at each level to catch the sea breezes. In Charleston, they adapted these designs. One new type—narrow two- to four-story "single houses" built at right angles to the street—emerged partly because buildings were taxed according to the length of their frontage.

Heavily residential, the area south of Broad Street has many beautiful private homes, almost all of which have a plaque with a short written description of the home's history. You might get a peek at tucked-away, English-style gardens, too. An open gate in Charleston once signified that visitors were welcome to venture inside for a closer look at the owner's garden. Open gates are rare today, but keep an eye out, as you never know when you'll get lucky.

Numbers in the text correspond to numbers in the margin and on the Charleston map.

A Good Walk

Start at the top of Broad Street at the **Old Exchange Building/Provost Dungeon** ㉒, which held prisoners during the American Revolution. Two blocks down Broad Street are the Four Corners of Law, including **City Hall** ㉓, with some historical displays and portraits, and **St. Michael's Episcopal Church** ㉔, the city's oldest surviving church. In the famously affluent South of Broad neighborhood are several of the city's lavish house museums. The **Heyward-Washington House** ㉕ is a block south of Broad on Church Street. Next to it is the picturesque Cabbage Row, the inspiration for Catfish Row in *Porgy and Bess.* The **Nathaniel Russell House** ㉖ and the **Calhoun Mansion** ㉗ are on Meeting Street, about

ANTEBELLUM CHARLESTON: THE GOLDEN YEARS

CHARLESTON, CALLED CHARLES TOWNE until the British left in 1783, boomed with the plantation economy in the years before the Civil War. South Carolina's rice, indigo, and cotton crops produced an extraordinary concentration of wealth, making a few hundred plantation owners, merchants, and shippers rich. Rice was the most profitable export; the labor source used to grow the rice—slaves—was the most profitable import. Cotton, too, was a huge moneymaker; by the outbreak of the Civil War in 1861, cotton accounted for 57% of the nation's exports.

From Charleston's beginnings, the planter aristocracy set out to entertain itself in style, seeking a social and cultural lifestyle to match its financial success. By the mid-17th century, the city had a thriving musical community. The first playhouse, the original Dock Street Theatre, was open for business. There were dances and concerts; the town attracted some of the most important performers in colonial America. During the 1770s there were more than 23 singing and dancing masters teaching in the city, which also had a reputation for turning out the Colonies' best Shakespearean productions.

The city boasted talented goldsmiths, silversmiths, gunsmiths, tobacconists, brewers, and cabinetmakers and was one of the best shopping towns in North America. Immigrants and others seeking religious freedom poured into Charleston. More than 200 private residences were built during this boom. Though Charleston had half the population of New York during the early 1770s, its annual export trade exceeded the tonnage that passed through New York's port.

Until the Civil War, Charleston's fortunes continued to grow. The city's native sons played a huge part in the forming of the new national government; four Charlestonians signed the U.S. Constitution. Writers and artists filled the city. Charlestonian Robert Mills, who designed the Washington Monument, also designed many buildings in Charleston. George Washington toured Charleston in 1791, staying in many of the city's now historic homes.

Charleston thrived as the social and cultural center of planter families. The social season, from late January to March, was defined by balls, dinners, masquerades, concerts, plays, and horse races. The elite and their slaves moved from the plantations to their Charleston residences, embellished with silk curtains, Dutch linens, French china, English silver, and lavish ornamental gardens. They commissioned famous portrait artists and European craftsmen and gave extravagant dinners where guests were served by black slaves. Lowcountry gentlemen joined private clubs and favored fox hunts, races, and gambling. Lowcountry sons traveled to England for their education. By the 1840s, construction pervaded the city: City Hall was under renovation; the Battery was being made into a city park; and such buildings as the four-story Charleston Hotel had become part of the emerging cityscape. By 1850 the city's population had grown to nearly 43,000.

When the Union-held Fort Sumter was bombarded on April 11, 1861, Charlestonians celebrated. But the merriment, along with the years of splendor and luxury, was soon over; the collapse of slavery ended the plantation system, sending much of the state's economy into depression.

two blocks apart. Around the corner is the **Edmondston-Alston House** ㉘, overlooking Charleston's famous **Battery** ㉙ and the Charleston harbor. A park bench in the shade of **White Point Gardens** ㉚, so named because of the bleached whiteness of oyster shells left here by Native Americans, is a splendid spot for a rest. From here, go north along the Cooper River to the **South Carolina Aquarium** ㉛ by shuttle or by car.

TIMING

Plan to spend two to four hours doing this walk, depending on your pace and which buildings you visit. A trip to the aquarium can add two or so hours; you may wish to split the trip into two half-days.

Sights to See

㉙ **The Battery.** This sea wall and promenade has sweeping views of Charleston Harbor. ✉ *Murray Blvd.*

㉗ **Calhoun Mansion.** Opulent by Charleston standards, this is a no-holds barred example of Victorian taste. Built in 1876, it's notable for ornate plasterwork, fine wood moldings, and a 75-ft dome ceiling. ✉ *16 Meeting St.,* ☎ *843/722–8205.* 🎫 *$10.* ☉ *Feb.–Dec., Wed.–Sun. 10–4.*

㉓ **City Hall.** The intersection of Meeting and Broad streets is known as the Four Corners of Law, representing the laws of nation, state, city, and church. On the northeast corner is graceful City Hall, dating from 1801. The second-floor Council Chamber has a variety of historical displays and portraits, including John Trumbull's 1791 satirical portrait of George Washington and Samuel F. B. Morse's likeness of James Monroe. ✉ *80 Broad St.,* ☎ *843/577–6970 or 843/724–3799.* 🎫 *Free.* ☉ *Weekdays 10–5.*

OFF THE BEATEN PATH
COLONIAL LAKE – Joggers, walkers, and folks looking for a tranquil city spot flock to this small man-made lake circled by a wide sidewalk, trees, and benches. In the late 19th century, Colonial Common, as it was called at the time, was a popular gathering place for Victorian Charleston. Today it is surrounded by stately Victorian buildings. ✉ *Ashley and Rutledge Aves. to the east and west, Broad and Beaufain Sts. to the north and south,* ☎ *843/724–7327.*

㉘ **Edmondston-Alston House.** With commanding views of Charleston Harbor, this imposing home was built in 1825 in late Federal style and transformed into a Greek Revival structure during the 1840s. It is tastefully furnished with antiques, portraits, Piranesi prints, silver, and fine china. ✉ *21 E. Battery,* ☎ *843/722–7171.* 🎫 *$7; combination ticket with Middleton Place (☞ below) $24.* ☉ *Tues.–Sat. 10–4:30, Sun.–Mon. 1:30–4:30.*

㉕ **Heyward-Washington House.** Built in 1772 by rice king Daniel Heyward, this home was the backdrop for DuBose Heyward's book *Porgy,* which was the basis for the beloved folk opera *Porgy and Bess.* The neighborhood, known as Cabbage Row, is central to Charleston's African-American history. President George Washington stayed in the house during his 1791 visit. It is full of fine period furnishings by such local craftsmen as Thomas Elfe, and its restored 18th-century kitchen is the only one in Charleston open to visitors. ✉ *87 Church St.,* ☎ *843/722–0354.* 🎫 *$8; for combination ticket, see Charleston Museum (☞ above).* ☉ *Mon.–Sat. 10–5, Sun. 1–5.*

★ ㉖ **Nathaniel Russell House.** One of the nation's finest examples of Adamsstyle architecture, the Nathaniel Russell House was built in 1808. The interior is distinguished by its ornate detailing, its lavish period furnishings, and the "flying" circular staircase that spirals three stories with no apparent support. ⊠ *51 Meeting St.,* ☎ *843/724–8481.* 🌢 *$7; combination ticket with Aiken-Rhett House and Old Powder Magazine (☞ above) $14.* ☉ *Mon.–Sat. 10–5, Sun. 2–5.* 🍽

⛲ ㉒ **Old Exchange Building/Provost Dungeon.** Originally a customs house, the British used it for prisoners during the Revolutionary War. Today a tableau of lifelike mannequins recalls this era. ⊠ *122 E. Bay St.,* ☎ *843/727–2165.* 🌢 *$6.* ☉ *Daily 9–5.*

㉔ **St. Michael's Episcopal Church.** Modeled after London's St. Martin-in-the-Fields and completed in 1761, this is Charleston's oldest surviving church. Its steeple clock and bells were imported from England in 1764. ⊠ *14 St. Michael's Alley,* ☎ *843/723–0603.* ☉ *Weekdays 9–5, Sat. 9–noon.*

NEED A BREAK?
On your way down Broad Street toward Church Street, duck into the dark-paneled, tin-ceiling **Blind Tiger Pub** (⊠ 38 Broad St., ☎ 843/577–0088) for a drink or beer in the beer garden out back, or a meal from the Four Corners Cafe next door.

★ ⛲ ㉛ **South Carolina Aquarium.** The 322,000-gallon Great Ocean Tank has the tallest aquarium window in North America. Exhibits have more than 10,000 living organisms, representing more than 500 species. Visitors travel through the five major regions of the Southeast Appalachian Watershed as found in South Carolina: the Blue Ridge Mountains, the Piedmont, the Coastal Plain, the Coast, and the Ocean. Bring the little ones for the special toddler displays. ⊠ *3250 Concord St.,* ☎ *843/ 720–1990 or 800/722–6455.* 🌢 *$14.* ☉ *July–Aug., daily 9–7; Mar.– June and Sept.–Oct., daily 9–5; Nov.–Feb., daily 10–5.* 🍽

㉚ **White Point Gardens.** Pirates once hung from gallows here; now this small garden, with a gazebo, Charleston benches, and views of the harbor and Fort Sumter, is the number one marriage site in the city. Children love to climb on the cannon and cannonball replicas. ⊠ *Murray Blvd. and E. Battery,* ☎ *843/724–7327.* ☉ *Weekdays 9–5, Sat. 9–noon.*

Mount Pleasant and Vicinity

East of Charleston across the Cooper River bridges, via U.S. 17N, is the town of Mount Pleasant, named not for a mountain or a hill but for a plantation in England from which some of the area's settlers hailed. In its Old Village neighborhood are antebellum homes and a sleepy, old-time town center with shops and cafés. Along Shem Creek, where the local fishing fleet brings in the daily catch, are good seafood restaurants. Other attractions in the area are museums, plantations, and, farther north, the Cape Romain National Wildlife Refuge.

A Good Tour

There's enough adventure here to stretch over a number of days, especially if you're a war history buff. On the first day you might drive to **Patriots Point,** veering right off the Cooper River Bridge onto Coleman Boulevard in the direction of Sullivan's Island and the Isle of Palms. Turn right at the signs, and then board the museum ships for tours. From here you can catch the ferry for a harbor ride to **Fort Sumter National Monument.** Later, continue along Coleman Boulevard and, just after crossing the boat-lined docks and restaurants at Shem Creek, turn right at Whilden Street for a drive through the Old Village. Returning to Coleman Boulevard, you'll pass the Common, a cluster of shops on your left. Stop here for the **Museum on the Common,** featuring the *Hurricane Hugo Revisited* exhibit. As you make your way across the Ben Sawyer Bridge to Sullivan's Island and the Isle of Palms, you'll see how the area has recovered from Hugo. Follow the signs to **Fort Moultrie.** Spend the rest of the day relaxing on the beach or bicycling through Sullivan's Island, a residential community scattered with early 20th-century beach houses, or the Isle of Palms, which has a pavilion and more abundant parking.

Another day, drive out U.S. 17N 8 mi to **Boone Hall Plantation** and its famous Avenue of Oaks, stopping at nearby **Charles Pinckney National Historic Site,** with interpretations of African-American life on the plantation. Bring a picnic and rent bikes at **Palmetto Islands County Park,** across Boone Hall Creek from the plantation; you'll need a swimsuit for Splash Island, a mini–water park. Another option is a ferry ride and visit to Bull Island, part of the **Cape Romain National Wildlife Refuge,** one of the nation's most pristine wildlife areas. The Sewee Visitor & Environmental Education Center (on U.S. 17 heading north) has information and exhibits on the refuge as well as live birds of prey, red wolves, and trails.

TIMING

You need three days to see all the attractions here; if you have one day or less, choose a few based on your interests.

Sights to See

★ **Boone Hall Plantation.** This plantation is approached along one of the South's most majestic avenues of oaks, which was the model for the grounds of Tara in *Gone With the Wind*. You can tour the first floor of the classic columned mansion, which was built in 1935 incorporating woodwork and flooring from the original house. The primary attraction is the grounds, with formal azalea and camellia gardens, as well as the original slave quarters—the only "slave street" still intact in the Southeast—and the cotton-gin house used in the made-for-television movies *North and South* and *Queen*. ⊠ *1235 Long Point Rd., off U.S. 17N,* ☎ *843/884–4371.* ☞ *$12.50.* ◷ *Apr.–Labor Day, Mon.–Sat. 8:30–6:30, Sun. 1–5; Labor Day–Mar., Mon.–Sat. 9–5, Sun. 1–4.*

NEED A BREAK?	Driving north of Mount Pleasant along U.S. 17, you'll see **basket ladies** at roadside stands. If you have the heart to bargain, you *may* be able to purchase the baskets at somewhat lower prices than in Charleston. But remember that you are buying a nearly lost art, and sweet grass is no longer plentiful in the wild.

Cape Romain National Wildlife Refuge. A grouping of barrier islands and salt marshes, this 60,000-acre refuge is one of the most outstanding in the country. At the **Sewee Visitor & Environmental Education Center** you can view exhibits about the refuge and arrange to take a ferry to Bull Island for a day visit. The island is a nearly untouched wilderness; the beach here, strewn with bleached driftwood, is nicknamed Bone Beach. ⊠ *5821 U.S. 17N, Awendaw,* ☎ *843/928–3368.* ☞ *Free.* ◷ *Daily 9–5.*

Charles Pinckney National Historic Site. Across the street from Boone Hall, this is the only protected remnant of the country estate of Charles Pinckney, drafter and signer of the Constitution. A self-guided tour explores many fascinating interpretations of African-American life, including the plantation owner–slave relationship. You can also tour an 1820s tidewater cottage. ⊠ *1254 Long Point Rd., off U.S. 17N,* ☎ *843/881–5516,* ꜰꜳꭗ *843/881–7070.* ☞ *Free.* ◷ *Daily 9–5.* ✎

☾ **Fort Moultrie.** Here Colonel William Moultrie's South Carolinians repelled a British assault in one of the first Patriot victories of the Revolutionary War. Completed in 1809, this is the third fort on this site at **Sullivan's Island,** which you'll reach on SC 703 off U.S. 17N. A 20-minute film tells the history of the fort. ⊠ *W. Middle St., Sullivan's Island,* ☎ *843/883–3123.* ▣ *$2.* ☉ *Daily 9–5.*

★ ☾ **Fort Sumter National Monument.** It was here, on a man-made island in Charleston Harbor, that the first shot of the Civil War was fired, on April 12, 1861, by Confederate forces. After a 34-hour bombardment, Union forces surrendered and Confederate troops occupied Sumter, which became a symbol of Southern resistance. The Confederacy held the fort, despite almost continual bombardment, for nearly four years, and when it was finally evacuated, it was a heap of rubble. Today National Park Service rangers conduct free guided tours of the restored structure, which includes a free **museum** (☎ 843/883–3123) with historical displays. The fort is reached from either Charleston's Municipal Marina or Patriots Point. ☎ *843/722–1691.* ▣ *Ferry fare $11.* ☉ *Tours usually leave from Municipal Marina daily at 9:30, noon, and 2:30, but they vary by season. Tours leave from Patriots Point daily at 10:45 and 1:30; Apr.–Labor Day, additional tour at 4.* ✎

☾ **Museum on the Common.** This small museum has an outdoor maritime museum and a Hurricane Hugo exhibit prepared by the South Carolina State Museum; it shows the 1989 storm damage through video and photos. ⊠ *217 Lucas St., Shem Creek Village,* ☎ *843/849–9000.* ▣ *Free.* ☉ *Mon.–Sat. 10–4.*

☾ **Palmetto Islands County Park.** You'll find a Big Toy playground, 2-acre pond, paved trails, an observation tower, marsh boardwalks, and a "water island" at this park across Boone Hall Creek from Boone Hall Plantation. Bicycles and pedal boats can be rented in season. ⊠ *U.S. 17N, ½ mi past Snee Farm, turn left onto Long Point Rd.,* ☎ *843/884–0832.* ▣ *$1.* ☉ *Apr. and Sept.–Oct., daily 9–6; May–Aug., daily 9–7; Nov.–Feb., daily 10–5; Mar., daily 10–6.*

★ ☾ **Patriots Point.** Tours are available on all vessels here at the world's largest naval and maritime museum, now home to the Medal of Honor Society. Berthed here are the aircraft carrier *Yorktown,* the World War II submarine *Clamagore,* the destroyer *Laffey,* the nuclear merchant ship *Savannah,* and the cutter *Ingham,* responsible for sinking a U-boat during World War II. The film *The Fighting Lady* is shown regularly aboard the *Yorktown,* and there is a Vietnam exhibit. ⊠ *Foot of Cooper River Bridges,* ☎ *843/884–2727.* ▣ *$11.* ☉ *Labor Day–Mar., daily 9–6:30; Apr.–Labor Day, daily 9–7:30.* ✎

West of the Ashley River

A Good Tour

The sights covered here are each a few miles apart along Ashley River Road, SC 61, about 10 mi northwest of downtown Charleston over the Ashley River Bridge. Still, you'll need time to see them all. One day you could spend a few hours exploring **Charles Towne Landing State Park,** veering off SC 61 onto Old Towne Road (SC 171); then finish your day at **Middleton Gardens.** Another day you might tour the majestic simplicity of **Drayton Hall** before continuing on to **Magnolia Plantation and Gardens** and all their splendor.

TIMING

Nature and garden enthusiasts can easily spend a full day at Magnolia Gardens, Middleton Gardens, or Charles Towne Landing State Park, so budget your time accordingly. Spring is a peak time for the gardens, although they are lovely throughout the year.

Sights to See

★ ☙ **Charles Towne Landing State Park.** Commemorating the site of the original 1670 Charleston settlement, this park on SC 171N across the Ashley River Bridge has a reconstructed village and fortifications, English park gardens with bicycle trails and walkways, and a replica 17th-century vessel moored in the creek. In the animal park, native species roam freely—among them alligators, bison, pumas, bears, and wolves. Bicycle and kayak rentals and cassette and tram tours are available. ⊠ *1500 Old Towne Rd.,* ☎ *843/852–4200.* ⊡ *$5.* ☉ *Memorial Day–Labor Day, daily 9–6; Labor Day–Memorial Day, daily 9–5.* ⊛

★ **Drayton Hall.** Considered the nation's finest example of unspoiled Georgian-Palladian architecture, this mansion is the only plantation house on the Ashley River to have survived the Civil War. A National Historic Landmark, built between 1738 and 1742, it is an invaluable lesson in history as well as in architecture. Drayton Hall has been left unfurnished to highlight the original plaster moldings, opulent hand-carved woodwork, and other ornamental details. ⊠ *3380 Ashley River Rd.,* ☎ *843/766–0188.* ⊡ *$8; Mar.–Apr. and Sept.–Oct. $10.* ☉ *Guided tours Mar.–Oct., daily 10–4; Nov.–Feb., daily 10–3.* ⊛

☙ **Magnolia Plantation and Gardens.** The 50-acre informal garden, begun in 1685, has a huge collection of azaleas and camellias. A tram will take you for an overall tour with three stops. You can canoe through the 125-acre Waterfowl Refuge, explore the 30-acre **Audubon Swamp Garden** along boardwalks and bridges, or walk or bicycle more than 500 acres of wildlife trails. Tours of the manor house, built during Reconstruction, depict plantation life. The grounds also hold a petting zoo and a miniature-horse ranch. ⊠ *Ashley River Rd.,* ☎ *843/571–1266 or 800/367–3517.* ⊡ *$10; house tour $6 extra; tram tour $5 extra; swamp tour $5 extra.* ☉ *Daily 8–5:30.*

★ ☙ **Middleton Place.** The nation's oldest landscaped gardens, dating from 1741, are magnificently ablaze with camellias, magnolias, azaleas, roses, and flowers of all seasons planted in floral *allées* and terraced lawns and around ornamental lakes. Much of the mansion was destroyed during the Civil War, but the south wing has been restored and houses impressive collections of silver, furniture, paintings, and historic documents. In the stable yard craftspeople use authentic tools and equipment to demonstrate spinning, blacksmithing, and other domestic skills from the plantation era. Farm animals, peacocks, and other creatures roam freely. The Middleton Place restaurant serves Lowcountry specialties for lunch daily; a gift shop carries local arts, crafts, and souvenirs. Also on the grounds is a modern, Danish-style inn (access to the gardens is included in the room price) with floor-to-ceiling windows dramatizing views of the Ashley River; here you can sign up for kayaking and biking tours. ⊠ *Ashley River Rd.,* ☎ *843/556–6020 or 800/782–3608.* ⊡ *$14; house tours $7 extra.* ☉ *Daily 9–5; house tours Tues.–Sun. 10–4:30, Mon. 1:30–4:30.* ⊛

OFF THE BEATEN PATH

AMERICAN CLASSIC TEA PLANTATION – On a small rural island about 20 mi west of Charleston on SC 700 is the country's only commercial tea plantation. Tours run from May through October and cover tea history, harvesting, and production and include a discussion with the plantation's official tea-taster. The tour ends with tea and cookies. ⊠ *6617 Maybank Hwy., Wadmalaw Island,* ☎ *800/443–5987.* ⊡ *Free.* ☉ *May–Oct., 1st Sat. each month 10–1:30.*

☙ **ANGEL OAK –** This magnificent live oak has a massive canopy which creates 17,000 square ft of shade. Long a favorite with local children because of its bending branches that slope gently, armlike to the ground,

Angel Oak is believed to be more than 1,400 years old. It is about 15 mi west of Charleston off SC 700. ⊠ *3688 Angel Oak Rd., Johns Island,* ☎ *843/559–3496.* 🖃 *Free.* ◷ *Daily 9–4:45.*

Dining

She-crab soup, sautéed shrimp and grits, variations on pecan pie, and other Lowcountry specialties are served all over the Charleston area—as are creative contemporary dishes crafted by local chefs. Outstanding eateries, from seafood houses to elegant French restaurants, make Charleston a mecca for gastronomes. Trendy Mount Pleasant, across the East Cooper Bridge, has a number of good restaurants.

Contemporary

$$$–$$$$ ✗ **McCrady's.** This revamped restaurant, in a 1778 tavern, has locals raving over its potato gnocchi, tuna tartare, grouper with creamy leek sauce and truffle oil, herb-marinated rack of lamb with mint drizzle, and molten chocolate cake. ⊠ *2 Unity Alley,* ☎ *843/577–0025. No lunch. AE, MC, V.*

$$$–$$$$ ✗ **Peninsula Grill.** Surrounded by walls covered in olive-green velvet,
★ black iron chandeliers, and 18th-century-style portraits, diners at this busy spot in the Planters Inn (☞ Lodging, *below*) can feast on such delights as lobster citron, wild mushroom grits with oysters, and New Zealand benne-seed-encrusted rack of lamb. For dessert, try the divine lemon tart with lemon sorbet, lemon crisps, and candied lemon. ⊠ *112 N. Market St.,* ☎ *843/723–0700. No lunch. AE, D, DC, MC, V.*

$–$$$ ✗ **Sermet's Corner.** Colorful, bold artwork by chef Sermet Aslan decorates the walls of this lively eatery. The Mediterranean menu has *panini* (grilled Italian sandwiches), seafood, and flavorful pastas; the poached pear salad and lavender pork are favorites. ⊠ *276 King St.,* ☎ *843/ 853–7775. AE, MC, V.*

French

$$$$ ✗ **Robert's of Charleston.** After a 10-year sabbatical, Charleston's classically trained singer and chef reopened his restaurant. The special experience is much the same: four rich, generously portioned courses with lovely wines, impeccable service, and the best of Broadway tunes in a warm, intimate dining room. Signature dishes are scallop mousse with lobster sauce, duckling with grilled vegetables, and roast tenderloin with bordelaise (wine sauce with brown stock and herbs) sauce. ⊠ *182 E. Bay St.,* ☎ *843/577–7565. No lunch. MC, V.*

$–$$ ✗ **Gaulart and Maliclet Café Restaurant.** This casual, chic eatery serves Continental dishes—breads and pastries, soups, salads, sandwiches, and specials such as seafood Normandy and chicken sesame. ⊠ *98 Broad St.,* ☎ *843/577–9797. AE, D, MC, V. Closed Sun. No dinner Mon.*

Italian

$$$ ✗ **Fulton Five.** There are just 15 tables in this romantic restaurant on a side road off King Street. The chartreuse walls and antique brass accents provide the perfect setting to savor northern Italian specialties like risotto; lemon sherbet with Campari; and antipasto Spoleto, mozzarella and prosciutto wrapped in a romaine lettuce leaf and drizzled with olive oil and diced tomatoes. ⊠ *5 Fulton St.,* ☎ *843/853–5555. AE, DC, MC, V. Closed Sun., late Aug.–1st wk Sept. No lunch.*

$–$$ ✗ **Il Cortile del Re.** Great wines, hearty soups and pastas, and lovely cheeses and breads make it feel just like Tuscany. Tucked off King Street behind a women's clothing shop, this hard-to-find spot has a cozy back room and a romantic courtyard with a crumbling brick wall. ⊠ *193 King St.,* ☎ *843/853–1888. AE, DC, MC, V. Closed Mon.–Sun. No lunch Thurs.–Sat.*

Charleston Dining and Lodging

Lowcountry

$$–$$$$ ✕ **Carolina's.** Lively and bustling, Carolina's has long been a favorite. Black-and-white decor, terra-cotta tiles, and 1920s French posters create a casual bistro atmosphere. Fans return for the "appeteasers" such as crowder pea cakes (made with crowder peas, spices, egg, and bread crumbs) and fried calamari, plus smoked baby-back ribs and pasta with crawfish and tasso (spiced ham) in cream sauce. Dinner entrées are selections from the grill: among them, pork tenderloin with Jamaican seasoning and salmon with cilantro, ginger, and lime butter. ⊠ *10 Exchange St.,* ☎ *843/724–3800. Reservations essential. D, MC, V. No lunch.*

$$ ✕ **Slightly North of Broad.** This high-ceiling haunt with brick-and-stucco
★ walls has several seats looking directly into the exposed kitchen. From here you'll see chef Frank Lee laboring over his inventive dishes: sautéed quail filled with sausage, pad Thai noodles with shrimp or pork, and an incredible Southern vegetable plate. You can order most items as an appetizer or an entrée. The extensive wine list is moderately priced. A sister restaurant, Slightly Up the Creek (⊠ 130 Mill St., ☎ 843/884–5005), at Shem Creek in Mount Pleasant, has waterfront views and similarly fine food. ⊠ *192 E. Bay St.,* ☎ *843/723–3424. Reservations not accepted. AE, D, DC, MC, V. Closed Sun. No lunch Sat.*

Lowcountry/Southern

$$$–$$$$ ✕ **Charleston Grill.** With its clubby chairs and dark paneling, the restaurant at Charleston Place (☞ Lodging, *below*) is comfortably elegant. Chef Bob Waggoner's new South cuisine includes lobster tempura over lemon grits; salad with spicy fried oysters; and beef medallions over whipped black-eyed peas in a roasted pecan and shiitake mushroom sauce. Many nights there's live jazz. ⊠ *224 King St.,* ☎ *843/577–4522. AE, D, DC, MC, V.*

$$–$$$$ ✕ **High Cotton.** This brick-walled eatery studded with palm trees is the latest from the owners of Slightly North of Broad (☞ *above*) and Elliott's on the Square (☞ *below*). Diners enjoy spit-roasted and grilled meats and fish. The chocolate souffle with blackberry sauce and praline souffle are fabulous. ⊠ *199 East Bay St.,* ☎ *843/724–3815. AE, D, DC, MC, V. No lunch.*

$$–$$$$ ✕ **Louis's Restaurant.** Louis Osteen's fans followed him from his former restaurant at Charleston Place to this spot across the street. This place has a light, very contemporary Japanese feel, and serves the new South cuisine for which the chef is famous. Here you'll find his she-crab soup and crab and lobster cakes, as well as roasted Chilean sea bass, roasted duck, and lamb medallions. The inventive menu at the sleek bar, including fresh tuna burgers and pickled eggs, is inviting. ⊠ *200 Meeting St.,* ☎ *843/853–2550. AE, D, DC, MC, V. No lunch.*

$$–$$$ ✕ **Anson.** After an afternoon of strolling through the Old City Market, you can walk up Anson Street to this softly lighted, gilt-trimmed dining room. Framed by about a dozen French windows, Anson's has elegant booths anchored by marble-top tables. New South specialties include shrimp and grits, fried corn bread oysters, and barbecued grouper. The she-crab soup is some of the best around. ⊠ *12 Anson St.,* ☎ *843/577–0551. AE, D, DC, MC, V. No lunch.*

$$–$$$ ✕ **Magnolias.** This popular place, in an 1823 warehouse, is a local fa-
★ vorite, with a magnolia theme in vivid paintings, etched glass, wrought iron, and candlesticks. The uptown Down South cuisine shines in specialties such as an egg roll stuffed with chicken and collard greens with spicy mustard sauce and sweet pepper puree. Equally innovative appetizers are seared yellow grits cakes with tasso gravy and yellow corn relish, and sautéed greens. There's even fried chicken with mashed potatoes and mushroom gravy. You may also want to try the **Blossom Café** (⊠ 171 E. Bay St., ☎ 843/722–9200), owned by the same people but

with a more Continental menu, including pizzas cooked in a wood-burning oven, pastas, and fish. ⊠ *185 E. Bay St., ☏ 843/577–7771. Reservations essential. AE, DC, MC, V.*

$$ ✕ **Elliott's on the Square.** This bright and cheerful restaurant in the Francis Marion Hotel (☞ Lodging, *below*) serves Southern Sunday-dinner-style entrées for lunch and dinner, including black-eyed pea cakes, fried chicken, BBQ salmon over grits, and butter pound cake. The food may be down-home, but the service is not. ⊠ *387 King St., ☏ 843/ 724–8888. AE, D, DC, MC, V.*

$–$$$ ✕ **J. Bistro.** Funky steel cutouts liven up the outside and inside walls of this Mount Pleasant eatery. The lighting is whimsical and hangs low over tables lined up against a banquette. A varied list of appetizers and small plates makes this a great place to graze. Choose from such innovations as steamed lobster wontons, grouper with champagne crabmeat cream sauce, and pecan-crusted catfish over grits. The lamb chop is superb. ⊠ *819 Coleman Blvd., Mount Pleasant, ☏ 843/971–7778. Reservations essential. AE, MC, V. ⊘ Closed Mon. No lunch. No dinner Sun.*

$–$$ ✕ **Sticky Fingers.** Specializing in ribs six ways (Memphis-style wet and dry, Texas-style wet and dry, Carolina sweet, and Tennessee whiskey) and barbecue, this family-friendly restaurant has locations downtown and in Mount Pleasant and Summerville. Tuesday night is children's night, with supervised games and cartoons in a playroom. ⊠ *235 Meeting St., ☏ 843/853–7427 or 800/671–5966; U.S. 17 Bypass, Mount Pleasant, ☏ 843/856–9840; 1200 N. Main St., Summerville, ☏ 843/875–7969. AE, DC, MC, V.*

$ ✕ **Alice's Fine Foods.** The food Southerners crave is here in its origi-
★ nal, beloved form: baked or fried chicken, ribs, fried fish, and other entrées come with a choice of three home-cooked vegetables and side dishes, including green beans, collard greens, red rice, macaroni-and-cheese pie, okra and tomatoes, lima beans, rice and gravy, yams, and squash. ⊠ *468–470 King St., ☏ 843/853–9366. MC, V.*

$ ✕ **Hominy Grill.** Locals lunch and brunch at this breezy, café-style restaurant. Though a bit off the beaten path, it's worth a special trip. The young chef's Southern upbringing is evident in everything from the vegetable plate (collards, squash casserole, black-eyed-pea cakes with guacamole, and mushroom hominy) to the pimento cheese sandwich or turkey club with homemade french fries. The avocado and *wehani* rice salad with grilled vegetables is a refreshing don't-miss in the summer. Leave room for the excellent buttermilk pie or bread pudding. ⊠ *207 Rutledge Ave., ☏ 843/937–0930. AE, MC, V.*

Seafood

$$–$$$ ✕ **Barbadoes Room.** This large, airy plant- and light-filled space has a sophisticated island look and a view out to a cheery courtyard garden. The menu includes she-crab soup, blackened shrimp and scallops, and oyster and crab gratin. The extensive breakfast buffet and Sunday brunch are packed. ⊠ *115 Meeting St., in the Mills House Hotel, ☏ 843/577–2400. Reservations essential. D, DC, MC, V.*

$–$$$ ✕ **Boathouse Restaurant.** Large portions of fresh seafood at reason-
★ able prices make both locations of the Boathouse Restaurant wildly popular. The crab dip, fish specials, and lightly battered fried shrimp and oysters are irresistible. Entrées come with heaping helpings of mashed potatoes, grits, collard greens, or blue-cheese coleslaw. The original Isle of Palms location is right on the water. ⊠ *101 Palm Blvd., Isle of Palms, ☏ 843/886–8000; ⊠ 14 Chapel St., ☏ 843/886–8000. Reservations essential. AE, DC, MC, V.*

$-$$ ✕ **The Wreck.** Dockside and full of wacky character, this spot serves up such traditional dishes as boiled peanuts, fried shrimp, shrimp pilaf, deviled crab, and oyster platters in a shabby, candlelit screened-in porch and small dining area. ⊠ *106 Haddrell St., Mount Pleasant,* ☎ *843/884–0052. Reservations not accepted. No credit cards.*

Lodging

Rates tend to increase during the Spring Festival of Houses and Spoleto, when reservations are essential. The **Charleston Area Convention and Visitors Bureau** (⊠ Box 975, Charleston 29402, ☎ 843/853–8000 or 800/868–8118) distributes a Visitor Value Days Card entitling the bearer to 10%–50% off at many accommodations between December 1 and March 1.

Hotels and Motels

$$$$ ⛫ **Charleston Place.** This Orient Express property, a graceful low-rise
★   structure in the historic district, is surrounded by upscale boutiques and specialty shops. The lobby has a magnificent handblown Venetian-glass chandelier, an Italian marble floor, and antiques from Sotheby's. Rooms are furnished with period reproductions, linen sheets and robes, and fax machines. The hotel is world class. ⊠ *130 Market St., 29401,* ☎ *843/722–4900 or 800/611–5545,* 𝐅𝐀𝐗 *843/724–7215. 400 rooms, 40 suites. 2 restaurants, 2 lounges, minibars, indoor pool, hot tub, sauna, steam room, exercise room, concierge floors. AE, D, DC, MC, V.* ✦

$$$–$$$$ ⛫ **Embassy Suites Historic Charleston.** The courtyard of the Old Citadel military school where cadets once marched is now a skylighted atrium with stone flooring, armchairs, palm trees, and a fountain. The restored brick walls of the breakfast room and some guest rooms in this contemporary hotel contain original gun ports, reminders that the 1822 building was originally a fortification. Teak and mahogany furniture, safari motifs, and sisal carpeting recall the British colonial era. Breakfast and evening refreshments are complimentary. ⊠ *341 Meeting St., 29403,* ☎ *843/723–6900 or 800/362–2779,* 𝐅𝐀𝐗 *843/723–6938. 153 suites. Lounge, pool, exercise room. AE, D, DC, MC, V. BP.* ✦

$$$–$$$$ ⛫ **HarborView Inn.** Overlooking the harbor and Waterfront Park, this new inn is close to most downtown attractions. Calming earth tones and rattan are abundant; high ceilings, four poster beds, and sea-grass rugs complete the Lowcountry look. Some of the rooms are in a former 19th-century shipping warehouse with exposed brick walls; some have fireplaces and whirlpool tubs. Continental breakfast, afternoon wine and cheese, and evening cookies are included. ⊠ *2 Vendue Range, 29401,* ☎ *843/853–8439 or 888/853–8439,* 𝐅𝐀𝐗 *843/853–4034. 51 rooms, 1 suite. Concierge, business services. AE, D, DC, MC, V. CP.* ✦

$$$–$$$$ ⛫ **Mills House Hotel.** Antique furnishings and period decor give charm to a luxurious Holiday Inn property, a reconstruction of an old hostelry on its original site in the historic district. Though rooms are small and a bit standard, the hotel has a lounge with live entertainment and excellent dining in the Barbadoes Room (☞ Dining, *above*). ⊠ *115 Meeting St., 29401,* ☎ *843/577–2400 or 800/874–9600,* 𝐅𝐀𝐗 *843/722–0623. 199 rooms, 16 suites. Restaurant, 2 lounges. AE, D, DC, MC, V.* ✦

$$–$$$$ ⛫ **Doubletree Guest Suites Historic Charleston.** Across from the City Market, this hotel has a restored entrance portico from an 1874 bank, a refurbished 1866 firehouse, and three lush gardens. The spacious suites, all decorated with 18th-century reproductions and canopy beds, have full kitchens or wet bars with microwave ovens and refrigerators. ⊠ *181 Church St., 29401,* ☎ *843/577–2644 or 800/222–8733,* 𝐅𝐀𝐗 *843/ 577–2697. 182 suites. Lounge, hot tub, exercise room, business services, meeting rooms. AE, D, DC, MC, V.* ✦

$$–$$$ ☒ **Best Western King Charles Inn.** Renovated in 1997, this inn in the historic district is a cut above the typical chain, with a welcoming lobby and sitting area and spacious rooms furnished with 18th-century period reproductions. ✉ *237 Meeting St., 29401,* ☎ *843/723–7451 or 800/528–1234,* ℻ *843/723–2041. 91 rooms. Dining room, lounge, pool. AE, D, DC, MC, V.* ⊛

$$–$$$ ☒ **Francis Marion Hotel.** Built in 1924 as the largest hotel in the Car-
★ olinas, the restored Francis Marion is now a Westin property. It retains big-band and tea-dance glamour with its windowed ballrooms, wrought-iron railings, columns, high ceilings, crown moldings, decorative plasterwork, and views of Marion Square and the harbor. A few rooms have their original pedestal sinks and deep tubs. Excellent Southern cuisine can be had at Elliott's on the Square (☞ *Dining, above*). ✉ *387 King St., 29403,* ☎ *843/722–0600,* ℻ *843/723–4633. 160 rooms, 66 suites. Restaurant, lounge, health club, meeting rooms. AE, D, DC, MC, V.* ⊛

$$–$$$ ☒ **Meeting Street Inn.** Built in 1874, this salmon-color former tavern in the historic district overlooks a lovely courtyard with fountains and gardens. Spacious rooms have hardwood floors, high ceilings, and reproduction furniture including four-poster rice beds. ✉ *173 Meeting St., 29401,* ☎ *843/723–1882 or 800/842–8022,* ℻ *843/577–0851. 56 rooms. Meeting room. AE, D, DC, MC, V. CP.* ⊛

$$ ☒ **Holiday Inn Historic District.** Though this hotel changed hands and went through a major renovation, it still draws loyal repeat visitors because of its free parking and location a block from the Gaillard Municipal Auditorium and within walking distance of many must-see spots. Rooms are motel modern. ✉ *125 Calhoun St., 29401,* ☎ *843/805–7900,* ℻ *843/805–7700. 133 rooms. Restaurant, lounge, pool, meeting rooms. AE, D, DC, MC, V.* ⊛

$–$$ ☒ **Hampton Inn–Historic District.** This downtown chain has hardwood
★ floors and a fireplace in the elegant lobby, guest rooms with period reproductions, and a courtyard garden. It is a front-runner in its price category. ✉ *345 Meeting St., 29403,* ☎ *843/723–4000 or 800/426–7866,* ℻ *843/722–3725. 166 rooms, 5 suites. Pool. AE, D, DC, MC, V. CP.* ⊛

$–$$ ☒ **Holiday Inn Charleston/Mount Pleasant.** Just over the Cooper River Bridge, the Holiday Inn is a 10-minute drive from the downtown historic district. Everything has been gracefully done: brass lamps, crystal chandeliers, Queen Anne–style furniture. The suites designated as high-tech have PC cable hookups, large working areas, glossy ultramodern furniture, and refrigerators. ✉ *250 U.S. 17, Mount Pleasant 29464,* ☎ *843/884–6000 or 800/290–4004,* ℻ *843/881–1786. 158 rooms. Restaurant, lounge, pool, sauna, exercise room, concierge floor, meeting rooms. AE, D, DC, MC, V.* ⊛

$ ☒ **Hampton Inn Charleston Airport.** Near the airport in North Charleston, this chain motel is clean and quiet. Guests have access to a health club nearby. ✉ *4701 Saul White Blvd., North Charleston 29418,* ☎ *843/554–7154,* ℻ *843/566–9299. 125 rooms. Pool. AE, D, DC, MC, V.* ⊛

$ ☒ **Red Roof Inn.** At the foot of the Cooper River Bridge about 10 minutes from historic Charleston, this chain motel is clean and well lighted. Rooms have work areas. ✉ *301 Johnnie Dodds Blvd., 29403,* ☎ *843/884–1411 or 800/843–7663,* ℻ *843/884–1411. 126 rooms. Pool. AE, D, DC, MC, V.* ⊛

Inns and Guest Houses

$$$$ ☒ **John Rutledge House Inn.** This 1763 house, built by John Rutledge,
★ one of the framers of the U.S. Constitution, is one of Charleston's most luxurious inns. The ornate ironwork, original woodwork, plaster

moldings, parquet floors, marble fireplaces, and 14-ft ceilings are impressive. A lovely afternoon tea including wine is served in the ballroom, and Continental breakfast and newspapers are delivered to your room. Two charming period carriage houses also accommodate guests. There are whirlpool tubs and fireplaces in some guest rooms. ✉ *116 Broad St., 29401,* ☎ *843/723–7999 or 800/476–9741,* FAX *843/720–2615. 11 rooms in mansion, 4 in each of 2 carriage houses. In-room data ports, business services. AE, D, DC, MC, V. CP.* 🐾

$$$$ ⌂ **Wentworth Mansion.** This spectacular brick mansion, built around 1886 as a private home, is now a luxury inn. Hand-carved marble fireplaces, rich woodwork, Tiffany stained-glass windows, and Second Empire reproductions create an elegant atmosphere in the spacious guest rooms. Breakfast buffet, afternoon tea, wine tastings, evening cordials, turndown service, and on-site parking are included. Rooms have king-size beds and oversize whirlpools; most have gas fireplaces. Circa 1886, in the former carriage house, serves inventive food and is the perfect spot for a special occasion. ✉ *149 Wentworth St., 29403,* ☎ *843/853–1886 or 888/466–1886,* FAX *843/723–8634. 21 rooms. Restaurant, lounge. AE, D, DC, MC, V. BP.* 🐾

$$$–$$$$ ⌂ **Two Meeting Street.** As pretty as a wedding cake and just as romantic,
★ this early 20th-century inn near the Battery has very private honeymoon suites. There are Tiffany windows, carved English oak paneling, and a chandelier from the former Czechoslovakia. Guests are treated to afternoon high tea and Continental breakfast. ✉ *2 Meeting St., 29401,* ☎ *843/723–7322. 7 rooms, 2 suites. No credit cards. CP.* 🐾

$$–$$$$ ⌂ **Hayne House.** One block from the Battery in Charleston's prestigious South of Broad neighborhood, the Hayne house was built in 1755. It has old furnishings but a fresh, light spirit. Rooms are dominated by Federal antiques and other heirlooms from the proprietors' families. Two of the guest rooms are in the main house; the other four are in the kitchen house, with its narrow stairway, colonial brickwork, and chimney. ✉ *30 King St., 29401,* ☎ *843/577–2633,* FAX *843/577–5906. 4 rooms, 2 suites. MC, V. CP.* 🐾

$$$ ⌂ **Ansonborough Inn.** Formerly a stationer's warehouse dating from the early 1900s, this spacious all-suite inn is furnished in period reproductions. It offers hair dryers, irons, a morning newspaper, message service, wine reception, and Continental breakfast, but it's best known for its friendly staff. ✉ *21 Hasell St., 29401,* ☎ *843/723–1655 or 800/522–2073,* FAX *843/527–6888. 37 suites. Meeting room. AE, MC, V. CP.* 🐾

$$$ ⌂ **Planters Inn.** High-ceiling rooms and suites are beautifully appointed with opulent furnishings, including mahogany four-poster beds and marble baths. Twenty-one rooms have a piazza overlooking the garden courtyard. The inn's Peninsula Grill (☞ Dining, *above*) is wonderful. ✉ *112 N. Market St., 29401,* ☎ *843/722–2345 or 800/ 845–7082,* FAX *843/577–2125. 56 rooms, 6 suites. Restaurant, room service, concierge, business services. AE, D, DC, MC, V.* 🐾

$$$ ⌂ **Vendue Inn.** Many rooms of this elegant yet friendly inn look out over the harbor and Waterfront Park. Guest rooms have four-poster beds, cozy seating areas, and large bathrooms. A full buffet breakfast plus afternoon wine and cheese are complimentary. Climb up to the inn's rooftop terrace bar for sweeping views of the harbor along with drinks and appetizers from the inn's Library Restaurant. ✉ *19 Vendue Range, 29401,* ☎ *843/577–7970 or 800/845–7900. 22 rooms, 24 suites. Restaurant, lounge, exercise room, business services, meeting rooms. AE, D, DC, MC, V. BP.* 🐾

$$–$$$ ⌂ **Phoebe Pember House.** Built in 1807, the mansion still has its separate kitchen and slaves quarters, both of which now have two guest rooms upstairs and a living room, dining room, kitchenette, and garden downstairs. Colors and fabrics are cheerful yet refined; artwork is by Charleston artists. The inn is off a busy street, but the piazza is cocooned by a walled garden overlooking Charleston's port. A Continental breakfast of croissants and fruit is delivered to your room or the piazza. ✉ *26 Society St.,* ☎ *843/722–4186,* ℻ *843/722–0557. 7 rooms, carriage house. AE, MC, V. CP.* ✑

$$ ☷ **Cannonboro Inn and Ashley Inn.** Two of the most elegant inns in town, these B&B neighbors on the edge of the historic district near the Medical University have luxurious rooms, tastefully decorated in period furnishings. Guests are treated to a full English breakfast on piazzas overlooking Charleston gardens. Use of the bicycles, afternoon refreshments, and convenient parking in an off-street lot are all included. ✉ *Cannonboro: 184 Ashley Ave., 29403,* ☎ *843/723–8572,* ℻ *843/ 723–8007. 6 rooms. Bicycles, business services. MC, V. BP. Ashley: 201 Ashley Ave., 29403,* ☎ *843/723–1848,* ℻ *843/579–9080. 6 rooms, 1 suite. Bicycles, business services. AE, D, MC, V. BP.* ✑

$$ ☷ **1837 Bed and Breakfast and Tea Room.** Though not as fancy as some of the B&Bs in town, this inn is long on hospitality; you'll get a sense of what it's really like to live in one of Charleston's beloved homes. Restored and operated by two artists-teachers, the home and carriage house have rooms filled with antiques, including romantic canopied beds. A gourmet breakfast of homemade breads and hot entrées such as sausage pie or ham frittata is included in the rate, as is the afternoon tea (open to the public for a nominal price). ✉ *126 Wentworth St., 29401,* ☎ *843/723–7166. 8 rooms. AE, MC, V. BP.*

$$ ☷ **Elliott House Inn.** Listen to the chimes of St. Michael's Episcopal Church as you sip wine in the courtyard of this lovely old inn in the heart of the historic district. You can then retreat to a cozy room with period furniture, including canopied four-posters and Oriental carpets. ✉ *78 Queen St., 29401,* ☎ *843/723–1855 or 800/729–1855,* ℻ *843/ 722–1567. 26 rooms. Hot tub, bicycles. AE, D, MC, V. CP.* ✑

$$ ☷ **Guilds Inn.** There's no lack of charm at this place in Mount Pleasant's historic and scenic Old Village, a residential area with a soda fountain, antiques shop, and restaurant. The National Historic Register property has hardwood floors, traditional Lowcountry furnishings, and a mix of antiques and reproductions. Rooms have whirlpool tubs. ✉ *101 Pitt St., Mount Pleasant 29464,* ☎ *843/881–0510 or 800/331– 0510,* ℻ *843/884–5020. 6 rooms. AE, D, MC, V. CP.* ✑

Resort Islands

The semitropical islands dotting the South Carolina coast near Charleston are home to several sumptuous resorts that offer a wide variety of packages. Peak season rates (during spring and summer vacations) range from $140 to $300 per day, double occupancy. Costs drop considerably off-season.

$$$$ ☷ **Wild Dunes.** This serene 1,600-acre resort on the Isle of Palms has 250 one- to six-bedroom villas and homes for rent, each with a kitchen and washer and dryer. The plantation-style Boardwalk Inn at Wild Dunes is just a few yards from the beach; many rooms have balconies and overlook the ocean. There are two acclaimed golf courses, a racquet club, a yacht harbor on the Intracoastal Waterway, and a long list of recreational options. Tradewinds Restaurant has lovely views of the waterway; the Grill at the Boardwalk Inn has a piazza for alfresco dining from its Continental menu. ✉ *Box 20575, Charleston 29413,* ☎ *843/886–6000 or 800/845–8880,* ℻ *843/886–2916. 250 units, 93 rooms. 4 restaurants, lounge, 2 18-hole golf courses, 19 tennis courts, health club, boating, fishing, bicycles, rollerblading, children's programs. AE, D, DC, MC, V.* ✑

$$$–$$$$ ⊡ **Kiawah Island Resort.** Choose from 150 inn rooms and 430 completely equipped one- to five-bedroom villas and private homes in two luxurious resort villages on 10,000 wooded acres. There are 10 mi of fine broad beaches and an array of recreational opportunities. Dining options are many and varied. ⊠ *12 Kiawah Beach Dr., Kiawah Island 29455,* ☎ *843/768–2121 or 800/654–2924,* FAX *843/768–6099. 150 rooms, 430 villas and private homes. 8 restaurants, 5 18-hole golf courses, 28 tennis courts, boating, fishing, bicycles, shops, children's programs. AE, D, DC, MC, V.* ⌖

$$$–$$$$ ⊡ **Seabrook Island Resort.** A total of 175 completely equipped one- to three-bedroom villas, cottages, and beach houses dot this property. The Beach Club and Island House, open to all guests, are centers for dining and leisure activities. Bohicket Marina Village, the hub of activity around the island, offers three fine restaurants as well as pizza and sub shops. The marina area includes opportunities for shopping as well as scuba diving, deep-sea and inshore fishing charters, and small-boat rentals. ⊠ *1002 Landfall Way, Seabrook Island 29455,* ☎ *843/ 768–1000 or 800/845–2475,* FAX *843/768–3096. 175 units. 3 restaurants, 2 pools, 2 18-hole golf courses, 13 tennis courts, horseback riding, boating, parasailing, fishing, bicycles, children's programs. AE, D, DC, MC, V.* ⌖

Nightlife and the Arts

The Arts

CONCERTS

The **Charleston Concert Association** (☎ 843/722–7667) has information on visiting performing arts groups including symphonies, ballets, and operas. The **Charleston Symphony Orchestra** (843/723–7528) presents MasterWorks Series, Downtown Pops, First Union Family Series, and an annual holiday concert at Gaillard Municipal Auditorium (⊠ 77 Calhoun St., ☎ 843/577–4500). The orchestra also performs the Sotille Chamber Series at the Sotille Theater (⊠ 44 George St., ☎ 843/ 953–6340) and the Light and Lively Pops at Charleston Southern University (⊠ U.S. 78, ☎ 843/953–6340). The College of Charleston has a free **Monday Night Recital Series** (☎ 843/953–8228).

DANCE

Anonymity Dance Company (☎ 843/886–6104 or 800/215–6523), a modern dance troupe, performs throughout the city. The **Charleston Ballet Theatre** (⊠ 477 King St., ☎ 843/723–7334) performs everything from classical to contemporary dance at locations around the city. The **Robert Ivey Ballet Company** (☎ 843/556–1343), a semiprofessional company that includes several College of Charleston students, gives a fall and spring program of jazz, classical, and modern dance at the Sotille Theater.

FESTIVALS

The **Fall Candlelight Tours of Homes and Gardens** (⊠ Box 521, 29402, ☎ 843/722–4630), sponsored by the Preservation Society of Charleston in September and October, offers an inside look at Charleston's private buildings and gardens.

During the **Festival of Houses and Gardens** (⊠ Box 1120, 29202, ☎ 843/724–8484), held during March and April each year, more than 100 private homes, gardens, and historic churches are open to the public for tours sponsored by the Historic Charleston Foundation. There are also symphony galas in stately drawing rooms, plantation oyster roasts, and candlelight tours.

MOJA Arts Festival (✉ Office of Cultural Affairs, 133 Church St., 29401, ☎ 843/724–7305), which takes place during the last week of September and first week of October, celebrates the rich heritage of the African continent and Caribbean influences on African-American culture. It includes theater, dance, and music performances; art shows; films; lectures; and tours of the historic district.

Piccolo Spoleto Festival (✉ Office of Cultural Affairs, 133 Church St., 29401, ☎ 843/724–7305) is the spirited companion festival of Spoleto Festival USA, showcasing the best in local and regional talent from every artistic discipline. There are about 300 events—from jazz performances to puppet shows—held at 60 sites in 17 days from mid-May through early June, and most performances are free.

The **Southeastern Wildlife Exposition** (✉ 211 Meeting St., 29401, ☎ 843/723–1748 or 800/221–5273) in mid-February is one of Charleston's biggest annual events. It displays art by renowned wildlife artists.

Spoleto Festival USA (✉ Box 704, 29402, ☎ 843/722–2764), founded by the composer Gian Carlo Menotti in 1977, has become a world-famous celebration of the arts. For two weeks, from late May to early June, opera, dance, theater, symphonic and chamber music performances, jazz, and the visual arts are showcased in concert halls, theaters, parks, churches, streets, and gardens throughout the city.

The reasonably priced **Worldfest Charleston** (✉ Box 838, 29402, ☎ 843/723–7600 or 800/501–0111), held in mid-November, premieres new films from around the world, offers workshops and seminars, and provides opportunities to meet the producers, directors, and actors.

FILM

The **American Theater** (✉ 446 King St., ☎ 843/722–3456), a renovated theater from the 1940s, shows current movies in a table-and-chairs setting with pizza, burgers, finger foods, beer, and wine. Upstairs there's a virtual reality game center. The **Roxy** (✉ 245 E. Bay St., ☎ 843/853–7699) has films from around the world plus wine, beer, coffee drinks, pastries, sandwiches, and pasta.

THEATER

Several groups, including the Footlight Players and Charleston Stage Company, perform at the **Dock Street Theatre** (✉ 135 Church St., ☎ 843/723–5648). **Pluff Mud Productions** puts on comedies at the Isle of Palms' Windjammer (✉ 1000 Ocean Blvd., ☎ 843/886–8596). Performances by the College of Charleston's theater department and guest theatrical groups are presented during the school year at the **Simons Center for the Arts** (✉ 54 St. Phillips St., ☎ 843/953–5604).

The **Cavallaro** (✉ 1478 Savannah Hwy., ☎ 843/763–9222) is the home of several successful dinner theater productions.

Nightlife

DANCING AND MUSIC

Cumberland's (✉ 26 Cumberland St., ☎ 843/577–9469) has live blues, rock, reggae, and bluegrass Monday through Saturday; the place is also known for wings and cheap beer. Live bands entertain at the **Indigo Lounge** (✉ 5 Faber St., ☎ 843/577–7383) each weekend. The **Mills House Hotel** (✉ 115 Meeting St., ☎ 843/577–2400), favored by an elegant, older crowd, has a lively bar and either a live big band or swing music on Tuesday night. Most evenings **Momma's Blues Palace** (✉ 46 John St., ☎ 843/853–2221) has live music starting at 10 PM. The **Music Farm** (✉ 32 Ann St., ☎ 843/853–3276) features live national and local alternative bands. There's swing-dancing and funky '70s music at **Trio Club** (⊠ 139 Calhoun St., ☎ 843/965–5333) Wednesday through Saturday. The **Windjammer** (⊠ 1000 Ocean Blvd., ☎ 843/886–8596), on the Isle of Palms, is an oceanfront spot with live rock.

DINNER CRUISES

For an evening of dining and dancing, climb aboard the luxury yacht, *Spirit of Carolina* (☎ 843/722–2628). Reservations are essential; there are no cruises Sunday and Monday.

Breakfast, brunch, deli, and hot luncheons are prepared on board the *Charlestowne Princess* (☎ 843/722–1112), which also offers its Harborlites Dinner with live entertainment and dancing while cruising the harbor and rivers.

HOTEL AND JAZZ BARS

The **Best Friend Lounge** (⊠ 115 Meeting St., ☎ 843/577–2400), in the Mills House Hotel, has a guitarist playing light tunes most nights. The elegant **Charleston Grill** (⊠ 224 King St., ☎ 843/577–4522), in Charleston Place, offers live jazz nightly. In the **Lobby Lounge** (⊠ 130 Market St., ☎ 843/722–4900) in Charleston Place, cocktails and appetizers are accompanied by piano. At **Mistral Restaurant** (⊠ 99 S. Market St., ☎ 843/722–5709) there's a regular four-piece jazz band on weekends. **Mitchell's** (⊠ 102 N. Market St., ☎ 843/722–0732) has nightly, changing acts, from jazz pianists to bands.

LOUNGES AND BARS/BREWERIES

Charlie's Little Bar (⊠ 141 E. Bay St., ☎ 843/723–6242), above Saracen Restaurant, is intimate, cozy, and popular with young professionals. **Club Habana** (⊠ 177 Meeting St., ☎ 843/853–5900) is a chic, wood-paneled martini bar (open late) with a cigar shop downstairs. **Southend Brewery** (⊠ 161 E. Bay St., ☎ 843/853–4677) has a lively bar with beer brewed on the premises; the food is good, especially soups. You'll find authentic Irish music at **Tommy Condon's Irish Pub & Restaurant** (⊠ 160 Church St., ☎ 843/577–3818). **Vickery's Bar & Grill** (⊠ 139 Calhoun St., ☎ 843/723–1558) is a festive nightspot with a spacious outdoor patio and good, late-night food. There's another equally popular location in Mount Pleasant (⊠ 1205 Shrimp Boat La., ☎ 843/849–6770). **Zebo** (⊠ 275 King St., ☎ 843/577–7600) brews its beer here and offers tasty meals.

Outdoor Activities and Sports

Beaches

The Charleston area's mild climate generally is conducive to swimming from April through October. This is definitely not a "swingles" area; all public and private beaches are family oriented, providing a choice of water sports, sunbathing, shelling, fishing, or quiet moonlight strolling. The **Charleston County Parks and Recreation Commission** (☎ 843/762–2172) operates several public beach facilities.

Beachwalker Park on the west end of Kiawah Island (which is otherwise a private resort) has 300 ft of beach frontage, seasonal lifeguard service, rest rooms, outdoor showers, a picnic area, snack bar, and a 150-car parking lot. ⊠ *Kiawah Island,* ☎ *843/762–2172.* ᓂ *$4 per car (up to 8 passengers).* ☺ *June–Aug., daily 10–7; May and Sept., daily 10–6; Apr. and Oct., weekends 10–6.*

Folly Beach County Park, 12 mi south of Charleston via U.S. 17 and SC 171 (Folly Road), has 4,000 ft of ocean frontage and 2,000 ft of river frontage. Lifeguards are on duty seasonally along a 600-ft section of the beach. Facilities include dressing areas, outdoor showers, rest rooms, and picnicking areas; beach chairs, raft, and umbrella rentals; and a 400-vehicle parking lot. Pelican Watch shelter is available year-round for group picnics and day or night oyster roasts. ⌧ *Folly Island,* ☎ *843/588–2426.* ⌫ *$5 per car (up to 8 passengers).* ⊙ *May–Aug., daily 9–7; Apr. and Sept.–Oct., daily 10–6; Nov.–Mar., daily 10–5.*

Isle of Palms County Park is on the Isle of Palms at the foot of the Isle of Palms connector. Lifeguards are on duty seasonally along a 600-ft section of the beach. Facilities include dressing areas, outdoor showers, rest rooms, picnicking areas, beach chair and raft rentals, and a 350-vehicle parking lot. ⌧ *1 14th Ave., Isle of Palms,* ☎ *843/886–3863.* ⌫ *$5 per car (up to 8 passengers).* ⊙ *May–Aug., daily 9–7; Apr. and Sept.–Oct., daily 10–6; Nov.–Mar., daily 10–5.*

Private resorts with extensive beaches and amenities include **Fairfield Ocean Ridge** (☎ 843/869–2561), on Edisto Island; **Kiawah Island** (☎ 903/768–2121 or 800/654–2924); **Seabrook Island** (☎ 843/768–1000 or 800/845–5531); and **Wild Dunes** (☎ 843/886–6000 or 800/845–8880), on the Isle of Palms.

Participant Sports

BIKING

The historic district is ideal for bicycling, and many city parks have biking trails. Palmetto Islands County Park (☞ Mount Pleasant and Vicinity, *above*) also has trails. Bikes can be rented at the **Bicycle Shoppe** (⌧ 280 Meeting St., ☎ 843/722–8168; Kiawah Island, ☎ 843/768–9122). **Island Bike and Surf Shop** (⌧ Kiawah Island, ☎ 843/768–1158) has bikes, surfboards, and Rollerblades for rent. **Sea Island Cycle** (⌧ 4053 Rhett Ave., North Charleston, ☎ 843/747–2453) serves all the local islands.

GOLF

One of the most appealing aspects of golfing in the Charleston area is the relaxing pace. With fewer golfers playing the courses than in destinations that are primarily golf oriented, golfers find choice starting times and an unhurried atmosphere. For a listing of area golf packages, contact **Charleston Golf Inc.** (⌧ Box 975, 29402, ☎ 843/853–8000 or 800/774–4444).

Nonguests may play on a space-available basis at **private island resorts** such as Kiawah Island, Seabrook Island, and Wild Dunes. The prestigious Pete Dye–designed **Ocean Course at Kiawah Island Resort** (⌧ 1000 Ocean Course Dr., Kiawah Island, ☎ 843/768–7272) is an 18-hole, par-72 course that was the site of the 1991 Ryder Cup. Other championship **Kiawah courses,** all 18-hole and par 72, are the Gary Player–designed Marsh Point; Osprey Point, by Tom Fazio; and Turtle Point, a Jack Nicklaus layout (for all three: ⌧ 12 Kiawah Beach Dr., ☎ 843/768–2121). **Seabrook Island Resort,** a secluded hideaway on Johns Island, offers two more 18-hole, par-72 championship courses: Crooked Oaks, by Robert Trent Jones Sr., and Ocean Winds, designed by William Byrd (for both: ⌧ Seabrook Island Rd., ☎ 843/768–2529). **Wild Dunes Resort,** on the Isle of Palms, is home to two 18-hole, par-72 Tom Fazio designs: the Links (⌧ 10001 Back Bay Dr., ☎ 843/886–2180) and Harbor Course (⌧ 5881 Palmetto Dr., ☎ 843/886–2301).

Top **public courses** in the area include **Charleston Municipal** (⌧ 2110 Maybank Hwy., ☎ 843/795–6517), **Charleston National Country Club** (⌧ 1360 National Dr., Mount Pleasant, ☎ 843/884–7799), the **Dunes West Golf Club** (⌧ 3535 Wando Plantation Way, Mount Pleasant, ☎ 843/856–9000), **Links at Stono Ferry** (⌧ 5365 Forest Oaks Dr., Hollywood, ☎ 843/763–1817), **Oak Point Golf Course** (⌧ 4255 Bohicket

Rd., Johns Island, ☎ 843/768–7431), **Patriots Point** (✉ 1 Patriots Point Rd., Mount Pleasant, ☎ 843/881–0042), and **Shadowmoss Golf Club** (✉ 20 Dunvegan Dr., ☎ 843/556–8251). All the above are 18-hole, par-72 courses.

SCUBA DIVING

The **Cooper River Underwater Heritage Diving Trail** is more than 2 mi long and consists of six submerged sites including ships that date to the Revolutionary War. Contact the **East Coast Dive Connection** (✉ 206B E. 5th North St., Summerville, ☎ 843/821–0001) or **Charleston Scuba** (✉ 335 Savannah Hwy., ☎ 843/763–3483) for maps, rentals, and excursion information.

TENNIS

Courts are open to the public at **Kiawah Island** (☎ 843/768–2121), **Shadowmoss Plantation** (☎ 843/556–8251), and **Wild Dunes** (☎ 843/886–6000).

Spectator Sports

BASEBALL AND BASKETBALL

The minor-league **RiverDogs** (✉ 360 Fishburne St., ☎ 843/723–7241), a Class-A affiliate of the Tampa Bay Devil Rays, play at the Joseph P. Riley Jr. Ballpark from April through August.

The College of Charleston **Cougars** (✉ Johnson Gym, 30 George St., ☎ 843/953–5556) basketball team is consistently a top contender in the Southern Conference.

HOCKEY

The Charleston **Stingrays** (✉ North Charleston Coliseum, 3107 Firestone Rd., North Charleston, ☎ 843/744–2248) are a minor-league team affiliated with the NHL's Buffalo Sabres. They attract record-breaking crowds from October through March.

Shopping

Shopping Districts

The Market is a complex of specialty shops and restaurants. Don't miss the colorful produce market in the three-block **Old City Market** (✉ E. Bay and Market Sts.) and, adjacent to it, the open-air flea market, with crafts, antiques, and memorabilia. You'll find locally produced sweetgrass and other baskets here. Shopping complexes in the historic district are **Market Square** (Market St.); **Rainbow Market** (✉ 40 N. Market St.), in two interconnected 150-year-old buildings (don't miss the filled-to-the-hilt Good Scents in Rainbow Market, known for its perfume oils and lotions); **Shops at Charleston Place** (✉ 130 Market St.), with Gucci, Gap, and Brookstone; and **State Street Market** (✉ Market St.). **King Street** has some of Charleston's oldest and finest shops, including **Saks Fifth Avenue** (✉ 211 King St., ☎ 843/853–9888). From May until September, the festive **farmers' market** takes place each Saturday morning in Marion Square.

Antiques

King Street is the center for antiques shopping. **Birlant & Co.** (✉ 191 King St., ☎ 843/722–3842) presents fine 18th- and 19th-century English antiques, as well as the famous Charleston Battery bench, identical to those on Charleston Green. **Period Antiques** (✉ 194 King St., ☎ 843/723–2724) has 18th- and 19th-century pieces. **Petterson Antiques** (✉ 201 King St., ☎ 843/723–5714) offers curious objets d'art, books, furniture, porcelain, and glass. **Livingston & Sons Antiques,** dealers in 18th- and 19th-century English and Continental furniture, clocks, and bric-a-brac, has a large shop west of the Ashley River (✉ 2137

Savannah Hwy., ☎ 843/556–6162) and a smaller one on King Street (✉ 163 King St., ☎ 843/723–9697).

On James Island, a 10-minute drive from downtown, **Carolopolis Antiques** (✉ 2000 Wappoo Dr., ☎ 843/795–7724) has good bargains on country pieces, many of which are bought by downtown stores. On U.S. 17 in Mount Pleasant, **Hungryneck Mall** (✉ 401 Johnnie Dodds Blvd., ☎ 843/849–1744) has more than 60 dealers hawking sterling silver, oak and mahogany furnishings, linens, and Civil War memorabilia. In Mount Pleasant, **Page's Thieves Market** (✉ 1460 Ben Sawyer Blvd., ☎ 843/884–9672) has furniture, glassware, and "junque."

Art and Crafts Galleries

The **Birds I View Gallery** (✉ 119A Church St., ☎ 843/723–1276) sells bird paintings and prints by Anne Worsham Richardson. **Blink** (✉ 62B Queen St., ☎ 843/577–5688) has regionally and locally produced paintings, photos, pottery, jewelry, and garden art. **Charleston Crafts** (✉ 87 Hasell St., ☎ 843/723–2938) has a fine selection of pottery, quilts, weavings, sculptures, and jewelry fashioned mostly by local artists. **Charleston Gardens** (✉ 61 Queen St., ☎ 843/723–0252) has garden ornamentations and home accessories including English pottery, Charleston-style iron gates, urns, and contemporary lighting. The **Elizabeth O'Neill Verner Studio & Museum** (✉ 79 Church St., ☎ 843/722–4246), in a 17th-century house, is open to the public. Prints of Elizabeth O'Neill Verner's pastels and etchings are on sale at **Tradd Street Press** (✉ 38 Tradd St., ☎ 843/722–4246). The **Marty Whaley Adams Gallery** (✉ 2 Queen St., ☎ 843/853–8512) has original vivid watercolors and monotypes, plus prints and posters by this Charleston artist. At **Nina Liu and Friends** (✉ 24 State St., ☎ 843/722–2724), you'll find contemporary art objects including handblown glass, pottery, jewelry, and photographs. Famous for his Lowcountry beach scenes, local watercolorist Stephen Jordan displays his best at **Stephen Jordan Gallery** (✉ 192 King St., ☎ 843/722–8808). **Reflections South** (✉ 125 Meeting St., ☎ 843/577–9351) sells original paintings and limited-edition lithographs of Charleston and Lowcountry scenes.

Books

The independently owned **Chapter Two** (✉ 249 Meeting St., ☎ 843/722–4238), specializes in local and regional books; there's also a neat section for children. The **Preservation Society of Charleston** (✉ corner of King and Queen Sts., ☎ 843/722–4630) has books and tapes of historic and local interest, sweet-grass baskets, prints, and posters.

Gifts

Charleston's and London's own **Ben Silver** (✉ 149 King St., ☎ 843/577–4556), premier purveyor of blazer buttons, has more than 800 designs, including college and British regimental motifs. He also sells British neckties, embroidered polo shirts, and blazers. **Charleston Collections** (✉ Straw Market, Kiawah Island Resort, ☎ 843/768–7487; Quadrangle Center, ☎ 843/556–8911) has Charleston chimes, prints, candies, T-shirts, and more. **The Sugar Plantation** (✉ 48 N. Market St., ☎ 843/853–3924) has melt-in-your mouth pralines, fudge, Charleston chews, and Olde Colony Bakery benne-seed wafers. You can find Charleston foods, including peach leather, pepper jelly, and pickled okra, at area **Piggly Wiggly** grocery stores (two locations: ✉ 1501 U.S. 17N, Mount Pleasant, ☎ 843/881–7921; IOP Connector, Mount Pleasant, ☎ 843/881–8939).

Period Reproductions

Historic Charleston Reproductions (✉ 105 Broad St., ☎ 843/723–8292) has superb replicas of Charleston furniture and accessories, all authorized by the Historic Charleston Foundation. Royalties from sales contribute to restoration projects. At the **Old Charleston Joggling Board Co.** (⊠ 652 King St., ☎ 843/723–4331), these Lowcountry oddities (on which people bounce) can be purchased.

Side Trips from Charleston

Gardens, parks, and the charming town of Summerville are good reasons to travel a bit farther afield for some day trips.

Moncks Corner
30 mi north of Charleston on U.S. 52.

This town is a gateway to a number of attractions in Santee Cooper Country. Named for the two rivers that form a 171,000-acre basin, the area brims with outdoor pleasures centered on the basin and nearby Lakes Marion and Moultrie.

Cypress Gardens, a swamp garden created from what was once the freshwater reserve of the vast Dean Hall rice plantation, is about 24 mi north of Charleston via U.S. 52, between Goose Creek and Moncks Corner. You can explore the inky waters by boat or walk along paths lined with moss-draped cypress trees, azaleas, camellias, daffodils, wisteria, and dogwood. ⊠ *3030 Cypress Gardens Rd.,* ☎ *843/553–0515.* ☜ *$7.* ☉ *Daily 9–5.*

☙ On the banks of the Old Santee Canal is the **Old Santee Canal State Park,** reached via I–26 and U.S. 52. You can explore on foot or take a canoe. There's also an interpretive center. ⊠ *Rembert C. Dennis Blvd.,* ☎ *843/899–5200.* ☜ *$3 per car.* ☉ *Daily 9–5.*

Francis Marion National Forest consists of 250,000 acres of swamps, vast oaks and pines, and little lakes thought to have been formed by falling meteors. It's a good place for picnicking, camping, boating, and swimming. At the park's **Rembert Dennis Wildlife Center** (⊠ off U.S. 52 in Bonneau, north of Moncks Corner, ☎ 843/825–3387) deer, wild turkey, and striped bass are reared and studied. ⊠ *35 mi north of Charleston via U.S. 52,* ☎ *843/336–3248.* ☜ *Free.* ☉ *Daily 9–5.*

LODGING

$-$$ ⌂ **Rice Hope Plantation.** A former rice plantation in Moncks Corner, it consists of 11 acres of live oaks and gardens overlooking the Cooper River. The house has six working fireplaces and antiques and reproductions. Guest rooms have four-poster beds, comfortable seating, and private baths; the suite has a porch overlooking the river. ⊠ *206 Rice Hope Dr., 29461,* ☎ *843/761–4832 or 800/331–0510,* ℻ *843/884–5020. 4 rooms, 1 suite. Hot tub, tennis court, fishing, basketball. AE, MC, V. CP.* ☙

OUTDOOR ACTIVITIES AND SPORTS

Two good fishing spots are **Lakes Marion** and **Moultrie,** both full of bream, striped bass, catfish, and large- and smallmouth bass. For information, contact **Santee Cooper Counties Promotion Commission** (⊠ Drawer 40, Santee 29142, ☎ 843/854–2131; 800/227–8510 outside South Carolina).

Summerville
25 mi northwest of Charleston via I–26 (Exit 199), SC 78, or SC 61 and SC 165.

Built by wealthy planters, this picturesque town is a treasure trove of Victorian buildings, many of which are listed in the National Register of Historic Places. Colorful gardens of camellias, azaleas, and wisteria abound, and many streets curve around tall pines, as a local ordinance prohibits cutting them down. This is a good place for a bit of antiquing. To get oriented, stop by the **Summerville Chamber of Commerce** (⊠ 106 E. Doty Ave., Box 670, 29483, ☎ 843/873–2931). It's open weekdays 8:30–12:30 and 1:30–5, Saturday 10–3.

DINING AND LODGING

$$$$
★
✕🏠 **Woodlands Inn.** People drive from Charleston for superb meals ($$$–$$$$) at this luxury inn, part of the prestigious Relais & Châteaux group. A four-course menu and a five-course menu with wine are available at the restaurant. Delicate sauces and subtle touches are key in entrées such as Angus beef with Barolo wine reduction, potato-encrusted crabcakes, and Asian spiced lobster. Though the inn, built in 1906 as a winter home, backs up to a suburb, it's a first-rate getaway, with such niceties as fireplaces, whirlpool or claw-foot tubs, and heated towel racks. Rates include a split of champagne at arrival and afternoon tea. ⊠ *125 Parsons Rd., 29483,* ☎ *843/875–2600 or 800/774–9999,* 𝔽𝔸𝕏 *843/875–2603. 15 rooms, 4 suites. Restaurant, lounge, pool, spa, 2 tennis courts, croquet, bicycles. AE, D, DC, MC, V.* 🐾

Charleston A to Z

Arriving and Departing

BY BOAT

Boaters on the Intracoastal Waterway may dock at **Ashley Marina** (⊠ Lockwood Blvd., ☎ 843/722–1996) and **City Marina** (⊠ Lockwood Blvd., ☎ 843/723–5098) in Charleston Harbor, or at **Wild Dunes Yacht Harbor** (☎ 843/886–5100) on the Isle of Palms.

BY BUS

Greyhound (⊠ 3610 Dorchester Rd., N. Charleston, ☎ 800/231–2222 or 843/744–4247).

BY CAR

I–26 traverses the state from northwest to southeast and terminates at Charleston. U.S. 17, the coast road, passes through Charleston.

BY PLANE

Charleston International Airport (⊠ 5500 International Blvd., ☎ 843/767–1100) on I–26, 12 mi west of downtown, is served by Continental, Comair, Delta, Midway Express, United Express, Northwest, TWA, and US Airways. For airline telephone numbers, *see* Air Travel *in* Smart Travel Tips A to Z.

Lowcountry Limousine Service (☎ 843/767–7111 or 800/222–4771) charges $15 per person (or $10 per person for two or more) to downtown. If you're traveling from the airport by **car,** take I–26S into the city.

BY TRAIN

Amtrak (⊠ 4565 Gaynor Ave., N. Charleston, ☎ 843/744–8264 or 800/872–7245).

Getting Around

BY BOAT

CHARTS (⊠ 196A Concord, ☎ 843/853–4700) is the only full-service water taxi providing transportation to and from Patriots Point naval and maritime museum. It also offers harbor cruises.

BY BUS

Regular buses run in most of Charleston from 5:35 AM until 10 PM and to North Charleston until 1 AM. The cost is 75¢ exact change (free transfers). DASH (Downtown Area Shuttle) trolley-style buses provide fast service in the main downtown areas. The fare is 75¢, $2 for an all-day pass. For **schedule information,** call ☎ 843/747–0922.

Fares within the city average $3–$4 per trip. Companies include **Low-country Limousine Service** (☞ Arriving and Departing, *above*), **Safety Cab** (☎ 843/722–4066), and **Yellow Cab** (☎ 843/577–6565).

Contacts and Resources

Ambulance, police (☎ 911). The emergency rooms are open all night at **Charleston Memorial Hospital** (⊠ 326 Calhoun St., ☎ 843/577–0600) and **Roper Hospital** (⊠ 316 Calhoun St., ☎ 843/724–2000).

Charleston Harbor Tour (☎ 843/722–1691) and **Princess Gray Line Harbor Tours** (☎ 843/722–1112 or 800/344–4483) ply the harbor. **Fort Sumter Tours** (☎ 843/722–1691) includes a stop at Fort Sumter and also offers Starlight dinner cruises aboard a luxury yacht. **Flying High over Charleston** (☎ 843/569–6148) provides aerial tours. **Adventure Sightseeing** (☎ 843/762–0088 or 800/722–5394) and **Colonial Coach and Trolley Company** (☎ 843/795–3000) give motor-coach tours of the historic district. **Gray Line** (☎ 843/722–4444) has tours of the historic district, plus seasonal trips to gardens and plantations.

Lowcountry Carriage Co. (☎ 843/577–0042), **Old South Carriage Company** (☎ 843/723–9712), and **Palmetto Carriage Tours** (☎ 843/723–8145) run approximately one-hour horse- and mule-drawn carriage tours of the historic district, some conducted by guides in Confederate uniforms. Carriage tours have a set itinerary and cover one of four zones in the historic district; after the carriages have passengers, the drivers draw from a lottery to decide which zone each carriage will cover. **Doin' the Charleston** (☎ 843/763–1233 or 800/647–4487), a van tour, combines its narration with audiovisuals and makes a stop at the Battery.

Chai Y'All (☎ 843/556–0664) shares stories and sites of Jewish interest. **Gullah Tours** (☎ 843/763–7551) is an expert on local African-American culture. **Sweetgrass Tours** (☎ 843/556–0664 for groups) focus on African-American influences on Charleston architecture, history, and culture.

Walking tours are given by **Charleston Strolls** (☎ 843/766–2080); **Charleston Tea Party Walking Tour** (☎ 843/577–5896 or 843/722–1779), which includes tea in a private garden; **On the Market Get Set, Tour!** (☎ 843/853–8687); and the **Original Charleston Walks** (☎ 843/577–3800 or 800/729–3420). For a spookier view of the city, take the **Ghosts of Charleston** (☎ 843/723–1670 or 800/854–1670) walking tour. The same guides also celebrate the city in the Story of Charleston walking tour. The unique **Watercolors About Charleston** (☎ 843/889–6978 or 888/295–3574) combines a walking tour with a watercolor class and lunch.

Eckerds (⊠ 466 Savannah Hwy., ☎ 843/766–5593). **Henry's Conway Drug Store** (⊠ 517 King St., ☎ 843/577–5123). **Tellis Pharmacy** (⊠ 125 King St., ☎ 843/723–0682).

Rates tend to increase during the Spring Festival of Houses and Spoleto, when reservations are essential. For historic home rentals in Charleston, contact **Charleston Carriage Houses–Oceanfront Realty** (⊠ Box 6151, Hilton Head 29938, ☎ 843/785–8161). To find rooms in homes, cottages, and carriage houses, try **Historic Charleston Bed and Breakfast** (✉ 60 Broad St., Charleston 29401, ☎ 843/722–6606). For condo and house rentals on the Isle of Palms—some with private pools and tennis courts—try **Island Realty** (✉ Box 157, Isle of Palms 29451, ☎ 843/886–8144). **Southern Hospitality B&B Reservations** (✉ 110 Amelia Dr., Lexington 29072, ☎ 843/356–6238 or 800/374–7422) handles rooms in homes and carriage houses.

PERSONAL GUIDES

Contact **Associated Guides of Historic Charleston** (☎ 843/724–6419); **Cary Parker Limousine Service** (☎ 843/723–7601), which offers chauffeur-driven luxury limousine tours; or **Charleston Guide Service** (☎ 843/722–8240), the city's oldest guide service. **Janice Kahn** (☎ 843/556–0664) has done individualized guiding for more than 25 years.

RADIO STATIONS

AM: WQIZ 810, gospel; WTMA 1250, talk radio; WXTC 1390, sports. **FM:** WBUB 107.5, country; WXLY 102.5, oldies; WALC 100.5 contemporary rock; WJZK 96.9, smooth jazz; WSCI 89.3, news, classical, jazz, information line; WWWZ 93.4, urban contemporary; WYBB 98.1, classic rock.

VISITOR INFORMATION

You can pick up a schedule of events at the **visitor center** (✉ 375 Meeting St.) or at area hotels, inns, and restaurants. Also see "Tips for Tourists" each Saturday in the *Post & Courier*. **Charleston Area Convention and Visitors Bureau** (✉ Box 975, Charleston 29402, ☎ 843/853–8000 or 800/868–8118) has information on the city and also on Kiawah Island, Seabrook Island, Mount Pleasant, North Charleston, Edisto Island, Summerville, and the Isle of Palms. **Historic Charleston Foundation** (✉ Box 1120, Charleston 29402, ☎ 843/723–1623) and the **Preservation Society of Charleston** (✉ Box 521, 29402, ☎ 843/722–4630) have information on house tours.

MYRTLE BEACH AND THE GRAND STRAND

The lively, family-oriented Grand Strand, a booming resort area along the South Carolina coast, is one of the eastern seaboard's megavacation centers. Myrtle Beach alone accounts for about 40% of the state's tourism revenue. The main attraction, of course, is the broad, beckoning beach—60 mi of white sand, stretching from the North Carolina border south to Georgetown, with Myrtle Beach as the hub. All along the Strand you can enjoy shell hunting, fishing, swimming, sunbathing, sailing, surfing, jogging, or just strolling on the beach. And the Strand has something for everyone: more than 100 championship golf courses, designed by Arnold Palmer, Robert Trent Jones, Jack Nicklaus, and Tom and George Fazio, among others; excellent seafood restaurants; giant shopping malls and factory outlets; amusement parks, water slides, and arcades; a dozen shipwrecks for divers to explore; fine fishing; campgrounds, most of which are on the beach; plus antique-car and wax museums, the world's largest outdoor sculpture garden, an antique pipe organ and merry-go-round, and a museum dedicated entirely to rice. It has also emerged as a major center for country music, with an expanding number of theaters.

Myrtle Beach—whose population of 26,000 explodes to about 350,000 in summer—is the center of activity on the Grand Strand. It is here that you find the amusement parks and other children's activities that make the area so popular with families, as well as most of the nightlife that keeps parents and teenagers happy. On the North Strand, there is Little River, with a thriving fishing and charter industry, and the several communities that make up North Myrtle Beach. On the South Strand, the family retreats of Surfside Beach and Garden City offer more summer homes and condominiums. Farther south are towns as alluring to visit as are the sights along the way: Murrells Inlet, once a pirate's haven and now a scenic fishing village and port; and Pawleys Island, one of the East Coast's oldest resorts, which prides itself on being "arrogantly shabby." Historic Georgetown forms the southern tip.

Myrtle Beach

94 mi northeast of Charleston, 201 mi east of Columbia.

Myrtle Beach, with its high-rises and hyperdevelopment, is a swirl of seaside activity. To capture its flavor, start at the Myrtle Beach Pavilion Amusement Park and wind your way north on Ocean Boulevard. Here's where you'll find an eclectic assortment of gift and novelty shops—everything from T-shirts to perfect shells—a wax museum, and a museum of oddities. Turn east when it suits your fancy and make your way back on the beach amid children building sand castles and kids-at-heart flying kites. The sights included here are in Myrtle Beach and north to North Myrtle Beach, with a couple to the south.

Dozens of colorful streetlight displays around major intersections add yet a few more volts of energy to the already pulsating scene, and at Christmas, Myrtle Beach stages one of the largest, most colorful light shows in the South.

Ⓒ **Myrtle Beach Pavilion Amusement Park** has thrill and children's rides, the Carolinas' largest flume, a new wooden roller coaster, video games, a teen nightclub, specialty shops, antique cars, and sidewalk cafés. ⊠ *9th Ave. N and Ocean Blvd.,* ☎ *843/448–6456.* 🎟 *Fees for individual attractions; 1-day pass for unlimited access to most rides $23.60.* ☉ *Mid-Mar.–May and mid-Aug.–Sept., weekdays 6 PM–10 PM, Sat. 1–10, Sun. 1–8; June–mid-Aug., daily 1 PM–midnight. Operating hrs can vary, so call ahead.*

Ⓒ **Ripley's Believe It or Not Museum** is based on the drawings that adults used to see in the newspaper, translated into lively displays of odd facts and figures. Among the more than 750 exhibits is an 8-ft, 11-inch wax replica of the world's tallest man. ⊠ *901 N. Ocean Blvd.,* ☎ *843/448–2331.* 🎟 *$8.95.* ☉ *Daily 10–9.*

Myrtle Beach National Wax Museum offers drama, sound, and animation in sections highlighting religious, historical, and entertainment people and events. ⊠ *1000 N. Ocean Blvd.,* ☎ *843/448–9921.* 🎟 *$5.* ☉ *Late Feb.–May and Sept.–mid-Oct., daily 9 AM–11 PM; June–August, daily 9 AM–2 AM.*

Ⓒ **Hawaiian Rumble** is the crown jewel of Myrtle Beach, the minigolf capital of the world (other courses mimic Jurassic Park and Never-Never Land). The course has a smoking mountain that erupts fire and rumbles at timed intervals. ⊠ *3210 33rd Ave. S, U.S. 17,* ☎ *843/272–7812.* 🎟 *$8 all day (9–5), $6 per round after 5 PM.* ☉ *Mar.–Dec., daily 9 AM–10 PM.*

Ⓒ **Dragon's Lair** has a fire-breathing dragon and two 18-hole courses. ⊠ *U.S. 17 at Broadway at the Beach,* ☎ *843/444–3215.* 🎟 *$8.50 all day (10 AM–6 PM), $6.50 per round after 6 PM.* ☉ *Mar.–Dec., daily 9 AM–10 PM.*

★ Ⓒ **Alligator Adventure** has exciting interactive reptile shows, including an alligator-feeding demonstration. The boardwalks go through marshes and swamps on the 15-acre property, where you'll see wildlife of the wetlands, including the only known collection of rare white albino alligators; the gharial, an exotic crocodilian from Asia; giant Galápagos tortoises; and all manner of other reptiles, including boas, pythons, and anacondas. Unusual plants and exotic birds also thrive here. ⊠ *U.S. 17S at Barefoot Landing, North Myrtle Beach,* ☎ *843/361–0789,* ℻ *843/361–0742.* ⊞ *$10.95.* ☉ *Daily 10–9.* ✆

☽ **Myrtle Beach Grand Prix** is auto-mania heaven with Formula 1 race cars, go-carts, bumper boats, mini-go-carts, kids' cars, and mini–bumper boats for adults and children ages three and up. ⊠ *3201 U.S. 17,* ☎ *843/238–2421; Windy Hill, 3900 U.S. 17S, North Myrtle Beach,* ☎ *843/272–6010.* ⊞ *Rides $3–$5 each.* ☉ *Mar.–Oct., daily 10 AM–11 PM.*

☽ At **NASCAR Speedpark,** you can drive on seven different NASCAR-replica tracks; the 26-acre facility also has racing memorabilia, an arcade, and miniature golf. ⊠ *U.S. 17 Bypass and 21st Ave. N,* ☎ *843/626–8725.* ⊞ *$5 general admission, drives $3–$6 each.* ☉ *Mar.–Oct., weekdays 5 PM–midnight, weekends 12 PM–midnight; hrs vary, so call to confirm.*

☽ One of Myrtle Beach's newer attractions, **Ripley's Aquarium** has an underwater tunnel exhibit longer than a football field and exotic marine creatures from poisonous lionfish to moray eels and an octopus. Children can examine horseshoe crabs and eels in touch tanks. ⊠ *9th Ave. N and U.S. 17N Bypass,* ☎ *843/916–0888 or 800/734–8888.* ⊞ *$13.95.* ☉ *Sun.–Thurs. 9 AM–9 PM, Fri.–Sat. 9 AM–10 PM.*

☽ South of Myrtle Beach, **Wild Water** provides splashy family fun for all ages in 25 rides and activities. ⊠ *910 U.S. 17S, Surfside Beach,* ☎ *843/238–9453.* ⊞ *$17, $12 after 3 PM.* ☉ *Memorial Day weekend–Labor Day, daily 10–7.*

Dining and Lodging

MYRTLE BEACH

$$–$$$ ✕ **Collectors Cafe.** A successful restaurant, art gallery, and coffeehouse
★ rolled into one, this unpretentious arty spot has bright, funky paintings and tile work covering its walls and tabletops. You can shop for a painting while enjoying the veal-stuffed ravioli or barbecued duck over polenta cake with goat-cheese cream. ⊠ *7726 N. Kings Hwy.,* ☎ *843/449–9370. AE, D, DC, MC, V. Closed Sun.*

$$–$$$ ✕ **Villa Katrina's Underground Cantina.** Head downstairs into a fun, tavern-like space for Mexican fare of the elegant variety, including flaming coffees and desserts. ⊠ *821 Main St.,* ☎ *843/946–6216. AE, D, MC, V. Closed Sun.*

$$ ✕ **Sea Captain's House.** At this picturesque restaurant with nautical decor, the best seats are in the windowed porch room, which overlooks the ocean. The fireplace in the wood-paneled dining room inside is warmly welcoming on cool off-season evenings. Menu highlights include Lowcountry crab casserole and avocado-seafood salad. The breads and desserts are baked here. ⊠ *3000 N. Ocean Blvd.,* ☎ *843/448–8082. AE, D, MC, V.*

$–$$ ✕ **Croissants Bakery & Café.** The lunch crowd loves this spot, which has an on-site bakery. Try the chicken or broccoli salad, and the peanut butter cheesecake. ⊠ *504A 27th Ave. N,* ☎ *843/448–2253. D, MC, V. Closed Sun. No dinner.*

$–$$ ✕ **Vintage House Café.** Locals dine here on beef tips, smoked chicken ravioli, and homemade bananas Foster cheesecake. ⊠ *1210 N. Kings Hwy.,* ☎ *843/626–3918. AE, D, DC, MC, V. Closed Sun. No dinner Mon.*

$$$-$$$$ ☆ 🏨 **Kingston Plantation.** The Grand Strand's most luxurious property, the 20-story glass-sheathed tower is part of a complex of shops, restaurants, hotels, and one- to three-bedroom condominiums set amid 145 acres of oceanside woodlands. Guest rooms are highlighted by bleached-wood furnishings and an Art Deco theme; all have kitchenettes. ⊠ *9800 Lake Dr., 29572,* ☎ *843/449–0006 or 800/876–0010,* ℻ *843/497–1110. 255 suites; 510 villas and condos. 2 restaurants, lounge, indoor pool, 7 outdoor pools, sauna, tennis court, aerobics, health club, racquetball. AE, D, DC, MC, V.* 🐾

$$$ 🏨 **Breakers Resort Hotel.** The rooms in this oceanfront hotel are airy and spacious, with contemporary decor. Many have balconies and refrigerators. ⊠ *2006 N. Ocean Blvd., Box 485, 29578,* ☎ *843/444–4444 or 800/845–0688,* ℻ *843/626–5001. 204 rooms, 186 suites. 2 restaurants, lounge, indoor pool, 3 outdoor pools, 4 hot tubs, 3 saunas, exercise room, children's programs, laundry service. AE, D, DC, MC, V.* 🐾

$$-$$$ 🏨 **Holiday Inn Oceanfront.** This oceanfront inn is right at the heart of the action, and rates vary according to the season. The spacious rooms are done in cool sea tones. After beach basking, you can prolong the mood in the inn's spacious, plant-bedecked indoor recreation center. ⊠ *415 S. Ocean Blvd., 29577,* ☎ *843/448–4481 or 800/845–0313,* ℻ *843/448–0086. 306 rooms. 2 restaurants, lounge, snack bar, indoor pool, outdoor pool, hot tub, sauna, recreation room. AE, D, DC, MC, V.* 🐾

$$-$$$ 🏨 **Sheraton Myrtle Beach Resort.** All rooms and suites have a fresh, contemporary look. Oceanfront Lounge, highlighted by tropical colors and rattan furnishings, is a lively evening gathering spot. There are a lazy river (artificial stream) and an arcade nearby. ⊠ *2701 S. Ocean Blvd., 29577,* ☎ *843/448–2518 or 800/992–1055,* ℻ *843/449–1879. 211 rooms, 8 suites. Restaurant, indoor pool, outdoor pool, health club. AE, D, DC, MC, V.* 🐾

$-$$ 🏨 **Chesterfield Inn.** A remnant from the past, this oceanfront brick inn, hidden beneath the towers of Myrtle Beach's glitzier hotels, has been in operation for more than a half century. The rooms in the original building are plain and a bit worn, but many guests prefer them to those in the newer wing. The highlight: family-style meals are served on white tablecloths in the seafront dining room. ⊠ *700 N. Ocean Blvd., 29578,* ☎ *843/448–3177,* ℻ *843/626–4736. 57 rooms, 6 kitchenette units. Restaurant, pool, shuffleboard. AE, D, DC, MC, V.* 🐾

$ 🏨 **Days Inn at Waccamaw.** Relax by the pool or in the gazebo after a day of shopping at the nearby Waccamaw Pottery and Factory Shoppes. The theaters of the Fantasy Harbor complex are also close at hand. Rooms here are clean and functional, filled with contemporary furnishings, and most are equipped with a refrigerator. ⊠ *3650 U.S. 501, 29577,* ☎ *843/236–1950 or 800/325–2525,* ℻ *843/236–9415. 160 rooms. Restaurant, pool, hot tub. AE, D, DC, MC, V.* 🐾

$ 🏨 **Driftwood on the Oceanfront.** Under one ownership for more than 60 years, the Driftwood is popular with families. Some rooms are oceanfront; all are decorated in sea, sky, or earth tones. ⊠ *1600 N. Ocean Blvd., Box 275, 29578,* ☎ *843/448–1544 or 800/942–3456,* ℻ *843/448–2917. 90 rooms. 2 pools, exercise room. AE, D, DC, MC, V.* 🐾

$ 🏨 **Landmark Resort Hotel.** This high-rise oceanfront resort hotel, with a rooftop sundeck and artificial "lazy rivers" indoors and out, also has a building across the street. Rooms are colorfully decorated in a Caribbean motif, and some in the oceanfront building have balconies and refrigerators. ⊠ *1501 S. Ocean Blvd., 29577,* ☎ *843/448–9441 or 800/845–0658,* ℻ *843/448–6701. 313 rooms, 257 suites. Restaurant, pub, 2 pools. AE, D, DC, MC, V.* 🐾

NORTH MYRTLE BEACH

Dinner cruises are one dining option here. The cruise ship *Hurricane* and yachts of the Hurricane pleasure fleet (☎ 843/249–3571) depart from Vereen's Marina (✉ U.S. 17N and 11th Ave.). The *Barefoot Princess* (☎ 843/272–7743 or 800/685–6601), a replica of a side-wheel riverboat, offers dinner, sunset, and sightseeing cruises along the Intracoastal Waterway from Barefoot Landing (✉ 4898 U.S. 17S).

$$–$$$$ ✕ **Greg Norman's Australian Grille.** Overlooking the Intracoastal Waterway, this large restaurant in Barefoot Landing has leather booths, handpainted walls, an extensive wine list, outdoor seating, and even a piano bar. Much of the menu has an Asian flair; try the lobster dumplings or crispy duck. ✉ *4930 Hwy. 17S,* ☎ *843/361–0000. Reservations essential. AE, D, DC, MC, V.*

$–$$ ✕ **Horst Gasthaus.** Dine on knockwurst, bratwurst, sauerbraten, and other traditional German foods at this Bavarian-style restaurant, where there's music every night but Sunday. ✉ *802 37th Ave. S,* ☎ *843/272–3351. AE, D, MC, V.*

$$ ▥ **Sea Island Inn.** In the quiet residential end of Myrtle Beach, this inn has oceanfront rooms with comfortable, standard decor plus several social areas. Meals are served in the elegant oceanfront dining room. ✉ *6000 N. Ocean Blvd., 29577,* ☎ *843/449–6406 or 800-548-0767,* ℻ *843/449–4102. 113 rooms, 1 suite, 1 penthouse. Restaurant, 2 pools, Ping-Pong, children's programs. AE, D, MC, V. MAP.* ⌘

Nightlife and the Arts

CLUBS AND LOUNGES

Clubs offer varying fare, including beach music, the Grand Strand's unique '50s-style sound. Some clubs and resorts have sophisticated live entertainment during summer. Some hotels and resorts also have piano bars or lounges with easy-listening music.

South Carolina's only Hard Rock Cafe, Planet Hollywood, and NASCAR Cafe are just a few of the hot spots in **Broadway at the Beach** (✉ U.S. 17 Bypass between 21st and 29th Aves. N, ☎ 843/444–3200), which also has shopping. You can dance the shag (the state dance) at **Duck's** (✉ 229 Main St., North Myrtle Beach, ☎ 843/249–3858). **Gypsy's** (✉ 501 8th. Ave N, ☎ 843/916–2244) is great for late-night blues music and has a nice wine selection. **Sandals** (✉ 500 Shore Dr., ☎ 843/449–6461) is an intimate lounge with live entertainment. The shag is popular at **Studebaker's** (✉ 2000 N. Kings Hwy., ☎ 843/448–9747 or 843/626–3855).

FILM

The **IMAX Discovery Theater** at Broadway at the Beach (✉ U.S. 17 Bypass between 21st and 29th Aves. N, ☎ 843/448–4629) shows educational films on a six-story-high screen.

MUSIC AND LIVE SHOWS

Live acts, and country-and-western shows in particular, are a big draw at the Grand Strand. Music lovers have many family-oriented shows to choose from: the 2,250-seat **Alabama Theater** (✉ Barefoot Landing, 4750 U.S. 17, North Myrtle Beach, ☎ 843/272–1111); **Carolina Opry** (✉ 82nd Ave. N, Myrtle Beach, ☎ 843/238–8888 or 800/843–6779); **Dolly Parton's Dixie Stampede** (✉ 8901B U.S. 17 Business, next door to Carolina Opry, Myrtle Beach, ☎ 843/497–9700); **Legends in Concert** (✉ 301 U.S. 17 Business, Surfside Beach, ☎ 843/238–7827 or 800/843–6779). The elegant **Palace Theater** (✉ Broadway at the Beach, U.S. 17 Bypass between 21st and 29th Aves. N, ☎ 843/448–0588 or 800/905–4228) hosts performances by the likes of Aretha Franklin, Kenny Rogers, and the Radio City Rockettes.

The **Fantasy Harbor** complex (✉ SC 51, across from Waccamaw Factory Shoppes) includes several theaters: the 2,000-seat Crook and Chase Theater (☎ 843/236–8500 or 800/681–5209), The Savoy (☎ 843/236–2200 or 800/681–5209), Medieval Times Dinner & Tournament (☎ 843/236–8080 or 800/436–4386), and the 2,000-seat Forum Theater (☎ 843/236–8500).

The **House of Blues** (✉ 4640 U.S. 17S, North Myrtle Beach, ☎ 843/272–3000 for tickets), adjacent to Barefoot Landing, showcases big names and up-and-coming talent in blues, rock, jazz, country, and R&B on stages in its Southern-style restaurant and patio as well as in its 2,000-seat concert hall.

PERFORMING ARTS

Theater productions, concerts, art exhibits, and other cultural events are regularly offered at the **Myrtle Beach Convention Center** (✉ Oak and 21st Ave. N, ☎ 843/448–7166).

Outdoor Activities and Sports

BEACHES

All the region's beaches are family oriented, and most are public. The widest expanses are in North Myrtle Beach, where, at low tide, the sand stretches up to ⅛ mi from the dunes to the water. Those who wish to combine their sunning with enjoying nightlife and amusement-park attractions can enjoy it all at Myrtle Beach, the Strand's longtime hub. Vacationers seeking a quieter day in the sun head for the South Strand communities of Surfside Beach and Garden City.

Besides ocean swimming, **Myrtle Beach State Park** has surf fishing, a nature trail, and a pool; there's camping, too, but book in advance. ✉ *U.S. 17, 3 mi south of Myrtle Beach, ☎ 843/238–5325. ☎ $3 per car.*

FISHING

The Gulf Stream makes fishing usually good from early spring through December. Anglers can fish from 10 piers and jetties for amberjack, sea trout, and king mackerel. Surfcasters may snare bluefish, whiting, flounder, pompano, and channel bass. In the South Strand, salt marshes, inlets, and tidal creeks yield flounder, blues, croakers, spots, shrimp, clams, oysters, and blue crabs. The annual **Grand Strand Fishing Rodeo** (☎ 843/626–7444 Apr.–Oct.) hosts a "fish of the month" contest, with prizes for the largest catch of a designated species.

GOLF

Many of the Grand Strand's 91 courses are championship layouts; most are public. **Tee Times Central** (☎ 843/347–4653 or 800/344–5590) books tee times for eight courses, including 18-hole, par-72 **Long Bay** (✉ 350 Foxtail Dr., Longs, ☎ 843/399–2222); 18-hole, par-72 **Myrtle Beach National Golf Club** (✉ 4900 National Dr., ☎ 843/448–2308); and 9-hole, par-36 **Waterway Hills** (✉ U.S. 17N, ☎ 843/449–6488). Some popular courses include in Myrtle Beach, the 18-hole, par-72 **Arcadian Shores Golf Club** (✉ 701 Hilton Rd., ☎ 843/449–5217) and the three 18-hole, par-72 courses of the **Legends** (✉ U.S. 501, ☎ 843/236–9318); in North Myrtle Beach, the 18-hole, par-72 **Bay Tree Golf Plantation** (✉ SC 9, ☎ 843/249–1487 or 800/845–6191), **Gator Hole** (✉ 700 U.S. 17N, ☎ 843/249–3543 or 800/447–2668), **Heather Glen Golf Links** (✉ U.S. 17N, Little River, ☎ 843/249–9000), and **Robbers Roost Golf Club** (✉ 1400 U.S. 17N, North Myrtle Beach, ☎ 843/249–1471 or 800/352–2384); near Surfside Beach, the 18-hole, par-72 **Blackmoor Golf Club** (✉ SC 707, Murrells Inlet, ☎ 843/650–5555), one of the country's top female-friendly courses; and in Cherry Grove Beach, the much-touted 18-hole, par-72 **Tidewater** (✉ 4901 Little River Neck Rd., North Myrtle Beach, ☎ 800/446–5363).

SCUBA DIVING

In summer, a wide variety of warm-water tropical fish travel to the area from the Gulf Stream. Off the coast of Little River, near the North Carolina border, rock and coral ledges teem with coral, sea fans, sponges, reef fish, anemones, urchins, and crabs. Several outlying shipwrecks are home to schools of spadefish, amberjack, grouper, and barracuda. Instruction and equipment rentals are available from **Scuba Syndrome** (⊠ 2718 U.S. 501, ☎ 843/626–6740).

SPECTATOR SPORTS

The **Pelicans,** a single-A baseball team affiliated with the Atlanta Braves, play at the Coastal Federal Field (⊠ U.S. 17 Bypass, ☎ 843/918–6000) at Broadway at the Beach.

TENNIS

There are more than 200 courts on the Grand Strand. Facilities include hotel and resort courts, as well as free municipal courts in Myrtle Beach, North Myrtle Beach, and Surfside Beach. Among tennis clubs offering court time, rental equipment, and instruction are **Myrtle Beach Racquet Club** (☎ 843/449–4031) and **Myrtle Beach Tennis and Swim Club** (☎ 843/449–4486).

WATER SPORTS

Surfboards, Hobie Cats, Jet Skis, Windsurfers, and sailboats are available for rent at **Downwind Sails** (⊠ Ocean Blvd. at 29th Ave. S, ☎ 843/448–7245) and **Myrtle Beach Yacht Club** (⊠ Coquina Harbor, North Myrtle Beach, ☎ 843/249–5376).

Shopping

DISCOUNT OUTLETS

The **Factory Shoppes** (⊠ U.S. 501, ☎ 843/236–6152) is a large outlet center with Gap, Nike, Polo, and Off 5th (a division of Saks Fifth Avenue). In North Myrtle Beach head for the **Myrtle Beach Factory Stores** (⊠ Hwy. 501 and Waccamaw Pines Drive, ☎ 843/903–1614) for Brooks Brothers, Donna Karan, Banana Republic, and Eddie Bauer. At **Waccamaw Pottery and Linen** (⊠ U.S. 501 at the Waterway, ☎ 843/236–1100) more than 3 mi of shelves in several buildings are stocked with china, glassware, brass, pewter, and other items, and about 50 factory outlets sell clothing, furniture, books, jewelry, and more.

MALLS

Malls are generally open Monday–Saturday 10–9, Sunday 1–6. **Barefoot Landing** in North Myrtle Beach (⊠ 4898 S. Kings Hwy., ☎ 843/272–8349), built over marshland and water, has scores of shops and restaurants. There are 100 specialty shops at **Briarcliffe Mall** (⊠ 10177 N. Kings Hwy., ☎ 843/272–4040). **Broadway at the Beach** (⊠ U.S. 17 Bypass, ☎ 843/444–3200 or 800/819–2282) offers 75 shops with restaurants and nightlife venues. **Myrtle Square Mall** (⊠ 2501 N. Kings Hwy., ☎ 843/448–2513) has 71 upscale stores and restaurants, and a food court.

Murrells Inlet

15 mi south of Myrtle Beach on U.S. 17.

Murrells Inlet, a fishing village with some popular seafood restaurants, is a perfect place to rent a fishing boat or join an excursion. A notable garden and state park provide other diversions from the beach.

★ **Brookgreen Gardens,** begun in 1931 by railroad magnate–philanthropist Archer Huntington and his wife, Anna (herself a sculptor), displays more than 500 sculptures by such artists as Frederic Remington and Daniel Chester French. The works are set amid beautifully landscaped grounds, with avenues of live oaks, reflecting pools, and more than 2,000 plant species. Also on the site are a wildlife park, an aviary, a cypress swamp, nature trails, and an education center. Summer nights sculptures are illuminated. ☒ *West of U.S. 17, 3 mi south of Murrells Inlet,* ☎ *843/237–4218 or 800/849–1931.* ☒ *$8.50.* ☉ *Oct.–May, daily 9:30–5; June–Sept., Wed.–Fri. 9:30–9:30.* ☺

Huntington Beach State Park, the 2,500-acre former estate of Archer and Anna Huntington, lies east of U.S. 17, across from the couple's Brookgreen Gardens (☞ *above*). The park's focal point is **Atalaya** (circa 1933), their Moorish-style, 30-room home, open to visitors in season. In addition to the splendid beach, there are nature trails, fishing, an interpretive center, a marsh boardwalk, picnic areas, a playground, concessions, and a campground. ☒ *Off U.S. 17, 3 mi south of Murrells Inlet,* ☎ *843/237–4440.* ☒ *$4.* ☉ *Nov.–mid-Mar., daily 6 AM–6 PM; mid–Mar.–Oct., daily 6 AM–10 PM.*

Nightlife and the Arts

THE ARTS
In the fall, the **Atalaya Arts Festival** (☎ 843/237–4440) at Huntington Beach State Park is a big draw.

NIGHTLIFE
Drunken Jack's (☒ U.S. 17 Business, ☎ 843/651–2044 or 843/651–3232) is a popular restaurant with a lounge overlooking the docks.

Outdoor Activities and Sports
Capt. Dick's (☒ U.S. 17 Business, ☎ 843/651–3676) offers half- and full-day fishing and sightseeing trips.

Pawleys Island

10 mi south of Murrells Inlet.

About 4 mi long and ½ mi wide, this island, referred to as "arrogantly shabby" by locals, began as a resort before the Civil War, when wealthy planters and their families summered here. It's mostly made up of weathered old summer cottages nestled in groves of oleander and oak trees. You can watch the famous Pawleys Island hammocks being made and bicycle around admiring the beach houses, many dating to the early 1800s. Golf and tennis are nearby.

Dining and Lodging

$$–$$$ ✕ **Frank's.** Seasonal ingredients make this a local favorite. In a former 1930s grocery store with wood floors, framed French posters, and cozy fireside seating, diners indulge in large portions of fish, seafood, beef, and lamb cooked over an oak-burning grill. The roasted asparagus with prosciutto in phyllo and pork tenderloin with shiitake mushrooms and a Dijon cream sauce are just two highlights. Behind Frank's is the casual Outback at Frank's, specializing in rotisserie chicken, salads, and lighter fare. ☒ *10434 Ocean Hwy. (U.S. 17),* ☎ *843/237–3030. Reservations essential. D, MC, V. Closed Sun.*

$–$$ ✕ **Island Country Store.** This little eatery has terrific crab cakes, hickory-smoked barbecue, roasted chicken, and pizza (they deliver). Summer nights, tiki torches outside blaze and live music rocks the place. ☒ *The Island Shops, U.S. 17,* ☎ *843/237–8465. AE, MC, V.*

$$$–$$$$ ✕🛏 **Litchfield Plantation.** Period furnishings adorn four spacious suites of this impeccably restored 1750 rice-plantation manor house turned country inn. A beach-house club a short drive away is part of the package. After entrées of grouper or steak at the elegant Carriage House Club ($$–$$$), you can retire to the restaurant's book-lined library. The resort is approximately 2 mi south of Brookgreen Gardens on U.S.

17 (turn right at the Litchfield Country Club entrance and follow the signs). ✉ *River Rd., Box 290, 29585,* ☎ *843/237–9121 or 800/869–1410,* ꜰᴀx *843/237–8558. 26 rooms, 4 suites, 7 2- and 3-bedroom cottages. Restaurant, pool, 2 tennis courts, horseback riding, boating, concierge. AE, D, MC, V. CP.* ⊛

$$$$ ꙮ **Litchfield Beach and Golf Resort.** Rentals from one-bedroom condos to four-bedroom villas are within the resort's expansive gardenlike grounds, which include three private golf clubs and a racquet club open to guests. Suites are tastefully decorated in pastel tones and light woods, with marble baths, wet bars, refrigerators, and microwave ovens. The Country Club cottages and marsh-side villas are ideal for families or couples seeking extra privacy. The beachfront Litchfield Inn has standard motel-style rooms. ✉ *U.S. 17, 2 mi north of Pawleys Island (Drawer 320, 29585),* ☎ *843/237–3000 or 800/845–1897,* ꜰᴀx *843/237–4282. 124 rooms; 112 suites; 254 condominiums, cottages, and villas. Restaurant, 2 indoor pools, 12 outdoor pools, 3 18-hole golf courses, 4 tennis courts, health club. AE, D, DC, MC, V.* ⊛

$$$ ꙮ **Pelican Inn.** This unique inn, with the beach out back and creek out front, gives you a look at how families have idled away the summer at Pawleys for years. Rooms are no-fuss (some share baths) with hardwood floors and throw rugs. There's no air-conditioning, but with the breezes, ceiling fans, and relaxed lifestyle, you'll barely miss it. ✉ *500 Myrtle Ave., Box 15, 29585,* ☎ *843/237–2295 or 843/288–8255. 6 rooms. Dining room. 2-night minimum. Closed Nov.–Mar. No credit cards. MAP.*

$$–$$$ ꙮ **Sea View Inn.** A "barefoot paradise," Sea View is a no-frills beachside boardinghouse with long porches. Rooms, with views of the ocean or marsh, have half baths; showers are down the hall and outside. Three meals, served family style—with grits, gumbo, crab salad, pecan pie, and oyster pie—make this an unbeatable deal. ✉ *Myrtle Avenue, 29585,* ☎ *843/237–4253,* ꜰᴀx *843/237–7909. 20 rooms. Dining room. 2-night minimum May and Sept.; 1-wk minimum June–Aug. Closed Nov.–Mar. No credit cards. FAP.* ⊛

$ ꙮ **Ramada Inn Seagull.** This is a well-maintained inn on a golf course (excellent golf packages are available). Outfitted with motel-modern furnishings, the rooms are spacious, bright, and airy. ✉ *U.S. 17S, Box 2217, 29585,* ☎ *843/237–4261 or 800/272–6232,* ꜰᴀx *843/237–9703. 99 rooms. Dining room, lounge, pool. AE, D, DC, MC, V.* ⊛

Outdoor Activities and Sports

GOLF

Popular 18-hole, par-72 courses include **Litchfield Beach and Golf Resort** (✉ U.S. 17S, Litchfield Beach, ☎ 843/237–3000 or 800/845–1897), **Litchfield Plantation** (✉ U.S. 17S, Litchfield Beach, ☎ 843/237–9121 or 800/869–1410), and **Pawleys Plantation Golf & Country Club** (✉ U.S. 17S, Pawleys Island, ☎ 843/237–8497 or 800/367–9959). **Tee Times Central** (☎ 843/347–4653 or 800/344–5590) books tee times for **Litchfield Country Club** (✉ U.S. 17S, Pawleys Island, ☎ 843/237–3411), **River Club** (✉ U.S. 17S, Pawleys Island, ☎ 843/626–9069), and **Willbrook** (✉ U.S. 17S, Pawleys Island, ☎ 843/247–4900).

TENNIS

You can get court time, rental equipment, and instruction at **Litchfield Country Club** (☎ 843/237–3411).

Shopping

The **Hammock Shops at Pawleys Island** (✉ 10880 Ocean Hwy., ☎ 843/237–8448) is a complex of two dozen boutiques, gift shops, and restaurants built with old beams, timber, and ballast brick. Outside the Original Hammock Shop, in the Hammock Weavers' Pavilion, craftspeople demonstrate the more than 100-year-old art of weaving the famous cotton-rope Pawleys Island hammocks. Also look for jewelry, toys, antiques, and designer fashions.

Georgetown

10 mi south of Pawleys Island.

Founded on Winyah Bay in 1729, Georgetown became the center of America's colonial rice empire. A rich plantation culture developed on a scale comparable to Charleston's, and the historic district, which can be walked in a couple of hours, is among the prettiest in the state. Today, oceangoing vessels still come to Georgetown's busy port, and the **Harbor Walk,** the restored waterfront, hums with activity. For information on tours, *see* Contacts and Resources *in* Myrtle Beach and the Grand Strand A to Z, *below.*

The graceful market and meeting building in the heart of Georgetown, topped by an 1842 clock and tower, has been converted into the **Rice Museum,** with maps, tools, and dioramas. At the museum's Prevost Gallery next door, you can buy glass, jewelry, home accessories, and art made by South Carolina artisans. ⊠ *Front and Screven Sts.,* ☎ *843/546–7423.* ☞ *$2; combination ticket for Rice Museum, Harold Kaminski House (☞ below), and tour of Georgetown $13.50.* ☉ *Mon.–Sat. 9:30–4:30.*

Prince George Winyah Episcopal Church (named after King George II) still serves the parish established in 1721. It was built in 1737 with bricks brought from England. ⊠ *Broad and Highmarket Sts., Georgetown,* ☎ *843/546–4358.* ☞ *Donation suggested.* ☉ *Mar.–Oct., weekdays 11:30–4:30.*

Overlooking the Sampit River from a bluff is the **Harold Kaminski House** (circa 1769). It's especially notable for its collections of regional antiques and furnishings, its Chippendale and Duncan Phyfe furniture, Royal Doulton vases, and silver. ⊠ *1003 Front St.,* ☎ *843/546–7706.* ☞ *$4; combination ticket for Rice Museum (☞ above), Harold Kaminski House, and tour of Georgetown $13.50.* ☉ *Mon.–Sat. 10–5, Sun. 1–4.*

Bellefield Nature Center is at the entrance of Hobcaw Barony, on the vast estate of the late Bernard M. Baruch; Franklin D. Roosevelt and Winston Churchill came here to confer with him. The nature center is used for teaching and research in forestry and marine biology. There are aquariums, touch tanks, and video presentations. ⊠ *On U.S. 17, 2 mi north of Georgetown,* ☎ *843/546–4623.* ☞ *Nature center free, estate $15.* ☉ *Variety of nature tours and estate tours given yr-round; call at least 1 month in advance for schedules and fees.*

Hopsewee Plantation, surrounded by moss-draped live oaks, magnolias, and tree-size camellias, overlooks the North Santee River. The circa-1740 mansion has a fine Georgian staircase and hand-carved Adam lighted-candle moldings. ⊠ *U.S. 17, 12 mi south of Georgetown,* ☎ *843/546–7891.* ☞ *Mansion $6; grounds $2 per car; parking fees apply toward the tour if taken.* ☉ *Mansion Mar.–Nov., Tues.–Fri. 10–4; Dec.–Feb., by chance or appointment. Grounds, including nature trail, yr-round, daily dawn–dusk.*

Hampton Plantation State Park preserves the home of Archibald Rutledge, poet laureate of South Carolina for 39 years until his death in 1973. The 18th-century plantation house is a fine example of a Lowcountry mansion. The exterior has been restored; cutaway sections in the finely crafted interior show the changes made through the centuries. The grounds are landscaped, and there are picnic areas. ⊠ *Off U.S.*

17, at edge of Francis Marion National Forest, 16 mi south of George-town, ☎ *843/546–9361.* 🏛 *Mansion $2, grounds free.* ☉ *Mansion Thurs.–Mon. 1–4, grounds Thurs.–Mon. 9–6.*

Dining and Lodging

$$$ ✕ **Rice Paddy.** This riverfront Lowcountry restaurant can be crowded
★ at lunch, when locals flock in for vegetable soup, garden-fresh salads, and sandwiches. Dinner is more relaxed, and the menu might have broiled seafood, crabmeat casserole, or quail with ham cream grits. ⊠ *819 Front St.,* ☎ *843/546–2021. AE, D, MC, V. Closed Sun.*

$–$$ ✕ **River Room.** This restaurant on the Sampit River specializes in char-grilled fish, seafood pastas, and steaks. For lunch you can have shrimp and grits or a variety of sandwiches and salads. The dining room has river views from most tables. It's especially romantic at night, when the oil lamps and brass fixtures cast a warm glow on the dark wood and brick interior of the early 20th-century building. ⊠ *801 Front St.,* ☎ *843/527–4110. Reservations not accepted. AE, MC, V. Closed Sun.*

$ ✕ **Kudzu Bakery.** Here are some of the best desserts in town (includ-ing deep-dish pecan pie and Red Velvet cake), fresh bread and deli items, plus jams and jellies. There's a small counter space for a quick bite. ⊠ *714 Front St.,* ☎ *843/546–1847. MC, V. Closed Sun. No dinner.*

$$$$ 🏨 **Lodge at Lofton Landing.** You rent the entire lodge, a modern fa-cility overlooking the marshland of Cape Romain National Wildlife Refuge. It has a furnished kitchen, wraparound porch, and dock for fishing and crabbing. ⊠ *8889 U.S. 17, McClellanville 29458,* ☎ *843/720–7332,* 🖷 *843/856–8468. 3 rooms, 1 loft. Boating, fishing. AE, D, DC, MC, V.*

$–$$ 🏨 **Laurel Hill Plantation.** This plantation bed-and-breakfast home over-looks the marsh near the Intracoastal Waterway, near the quaint shrimping village of McClellanville. It's furnished with country antiques and folk art. Guests can read in the hammock, go fishing or crabbing, take a boat ride, or watch the birds. ⊠ *8913 U.S. 17N (22 mi south of Georgetown), Box 190, McClellanville 29458,* ☎ *843/887–3708. 4 rooms. Fishing. AE, D, DC, MC, V. BP.*

$–$$ 🏨 **1790 House.** Built in the center of town after the Revolution, at the peak of Georgetown's rice culture, this lovely restored white Georgian house with a wraparound porch contains colonial antique and repro-duction furnishings suitable to its age. A (very) full breakfast and evening refreshments are included in the rate. Guest rooms down-stairs in the former slave quarters have exposed brick walls. ⊠ *630 Highmarket St., 29440,* ☎ *843/546–4821 or 800/890–7432. 4 rooms, 1 suite, 1 cottage. Bicycles. AE, D, MC, V. BP.* 🐾

$ 🏨 **Mansfield Plantation.** As you drive up the unpaved road to the 760-acre plantation, past slave quarters and under the requisite canopy of moss-draped oaks, you'll sense what a plantation must have looked like 200 years ago. Guests stay in three historic redbrick outbuildings—the old kitchen, the former schoolhouse, and the 1930s guest house—which overlook the Black River. Rooms have hardwood pine floors, reproduction period antiques, and coal or wood-burning fireplaces. Both children and pets are welcome; guests can roam freely on the planta-tion grounds. ⊠ *U.S. 701N, (Rte. 8, Box 590), 29440,* ☎ *843/546–6961 or 800/355–3223,* 🖷 *843/546–5235. 8 rooms. In-room VCRs, boating, fishing, bicycles. No credit cards.* 🐾

Myrtle Beach and the Grand Strand A to Z

Arriving and Departing

Boaters traveling the Intracoastal Waterway may dock at **Hague Ma-rina** (⊠ Myrtle Beach, ☎ 843/293–2141), **Harbor Gate** (⊠ North Myrtle Beach, ☎ 843/249–8888), and **Marlin Quay** (✉ Murrells Inlet, ☎ 843/651–4444).

Greyhound Bus Lines (☎ 800/231–2222) serves Myrtle Beach.

Midway between New York and Miami, the Grand Strand can be reached from all directions via Interstates 20, 26, 40, 77, 85, and 95, which connect by other routes to U.S. 17, the major north–south coastal route through the Strand.

The **Myrtle Beach International Airport** (✉ 1100 Jetport Rd., ☎ 843/448–1580) is served by Air Canada, AirTran, ASA/Delta/Comair, Continental, Midway/Corporate, Spirit, Vanguard, and US Airways. For airline telephone numbers, *see* Air Travel *in* Smart Travel Tips A to Z.

Amtrak (☎ 800/872–7245) service for the Grand Strand is available through a terminal in Florence. Buses connect with Amtrak there for the 65-mi drive to Myrtle Beach.

Getting Around
Service in Myrtle Beach is provided by **Coastal Cab Service** (☎ 843/448–3360 or 843/448–4444) and **Orange Cab** (☎ 843/448–2941).

Contacts and Resources
Dial **911** for emergency assistance. The emergency room is open 24 hours a day at the **Columbia Grand Strand Regional Medical Center** (✉ 809 82nd Pkwy., off U.S. 17, Myrtle Beach, ☎ 843/692–1000) and the **Georgetown Memorial Hospital** (✉ 606 Black River Rd., Georgetown, ☎ 843/527–7000).

Spring and fall, with off-season rates, are the busiest seasons, and there are many packages available in the area; call **Golf Holiday** (☎ 843/448–5942 or 800/845–4653). **Tee Times Central** (☎ 843/347–4653 or 800/344–5590) books tee times at a number of area courses.

At the **Georgetown County Chamber of Commerce and Information Center** (✉ 1005 Front St., Georgetown, ☎ 843/546–8436 or 800/777–7705), you can arrange to tour historic areas March–October by tram, by 1840 horse-drawn carriage, or by boat. You can also pick up free driving- and walking-tour maps. **Georgetown Tour Company** (✉ 627 Front St., Georgetown, ☎ 843/546–6827) offers tram tours of the historic district, a Ghostbusting Tour, and an afternoon Tea 'n Tour. For an insider's view, hire Georgetown native Miss Nell to take you on one of **Miss Nell's "Real South" Tours** (✉ 308 Front St., Georgetown, ☎ 843/546–3975). **Palmetto Tour & Travel** (☎ 843/626–2660) and **Leisure Time Unlimited/Gray Line** (☎ 843/448–9483), both in Myrtle Beach, offer tour packages and guide services.

With about 60,000 rooms available along the Grand Strand, it's seldom difficult to find a place to stay, and discounting is rampant. Package deals are offered year-round, the most attractive of them between Labor Day and spring break. You can choose among cottages, villas, condominiums, and hotel-style high-rise units. For the free directory *Where to Stay and Play* write to the **Myrtle Beach Area Convention Bu-**

reau (⊠ 710 21st Ave. N, Suite J, Myrtle Beach 29577, ☎ 843/448–1629 or 800/356–3016). For Pawleys Island and Litchfield Beach, try **Pawleys Island Realty** (⊠ Box 306, Pawleys Island 29585, ☎ 843/237–4257 or 800/937–7352).

RADIO STATIONS

FM: WDAI 98.5, urban contemporary; WJXY 93.9, country; WJYR 92.1, easy listening; WKZQ 101.7, rock and roll; WNMB 105.9, best of the '60s–'80s; WRNN 94.5, talk; WSYN 106.5, oldies.

24-HOUR PHARMACY

The only all-night pharmacy in the area is at the **Columbia Grand Strand Regional Medical Center** (☞ Emergencies, *above*).

VISITOR INFORMATION

Georgetown County Chamber of Commerce and Information Center (☞ Guided Tours, *above*). **Myrtle Beach Area Chamber of Commerce and Information Center** (⊠ 1200 N. Oak St., Box 2115, Myrtle Beach 29578, ☎ 843/626–7444; 800/356–3016 brochures only). **Pawleys Island Chamber of Commerce** (⊠ U.S. 17, Box 569, Pawleys Island 29585, ☎ 843/237–1921).

HILTON HEAD AND BEYOND

Anchoring the southern tip of South Carolina's coastline is Hilton Head Island, named after English sea captain William Hilton, who claimed the 42 square mi for England in 1663. It was settled by planters in the 1700s and flourished until the Civil War. Thereafter, the economy declined and the island languished until Charles E. Fraser, a visionary South Carolina attorney, began developing the Sea Pines resort in 1956. Other developments followed, and today Hilton Head's casual pace, broad beaches, myriad activities, and genteel good life make it one of the East Coast's most popular vacation getaways.

Beaufort, some 40 mi north of Hilton Head, is a graceful antebellum town with a compact historic district preserving lavish 18th- and 19th-century homes from an era of immense prosperity, based on silky-textured Sea Island cotton. The *beau* in Beaufort is pronounced as in "beautiful," and Beaufort certainly is. Southeast, on the ocean, lies Fripp Island, a self-contained resort with controlled access. And midway between Beaufort and Charleston is Edisto (pronounced *ed*-is-toh) Island, settled in 1690, also once notable for its Sea Island cotton. Some of its elaborate mansions have been restored; others brood in disrepair.

Hilton Head Island

108 mi southwest of Charleston, 164 mi southeast of Columbia, over bridge on U.S. 278.

Lined by towering pines, palmetto trees, and wind-sculpted live oaks, Hilton Head's 12 mi of beaches are a major attraction, and the semitropical barrier island also has oak and pine woodlands and meandering lagoons. Choice stretches are occupied by various resorts, called "plantations," among them Sea Pines, Shipyard, Palmetto Dunes, and Port Royal. In these areas, accommodations range from rental villas and lavish private houses to luxury hotels. The resorts are also private residential communities, although many have public restaurants, marinas, shopping areas, and recreational facilities. All are secured, and visitors cannot tour them unless arrangements are made at the visitor office near the main gate of each plantation. A 5¾-mi Cross Island Parkway toll bridge ($1) makes it easy to bypass traffic and reach the south end of the island, where most of the resort areas and hotels are.

Hilton Head prides itself on its strict regulations that keep "light pollution" to a minimum; the lack of neon and streetlights also makes it difficult to find your way at night, so be sure to get good directions.

Audubon-Newhall Preserve, in the south of the island, is 50 acres of pristine forest, where you'll find native plant life identified and tagged. There are trails, a self-guided tour, and seasonal plant walks. ⊠ *Palmetto Bay Rd.,* ☎ *843/785–5775.* ☞ *Free.* ☉ *Daily dawn–dusk.*

Sea Pines Forest Preserve is a 605-acre public wilderness tract with walking trails, a well-stocked fishing pond, a waterfowl pond, and a 3,400-year-old Indian shell ring. Both guided and self-guided tours are available. ⊠ *At the southwest tip of the island, accessible via U.S. 278 (William Hilton Pkwy.),* ☎ *843/785–3333.* ☞ *Sea Pines Plantation $3 per car for nonguests, includes access to preserve.* ☉ *Daily dawn–dusk; closed during Heritage Golf Classic in Apr.*

The **Museum of Hilton Head Island** has a permanent collection depicting Native American life and hosts changing exhibits. Beach walks are conducted on weekdays, and tours of Native American sites, forts, and plantations are given randomly in season. ⊠ *100 William Hilton Pkwy.,* ☎ *843/689–6767.* ☞ *Free.* ☉ *Mon.–Sat. 10–5, Sun. noon–4.*

At the **James M. Waddell Jr. Mariculture Research & Development Center,** 3 mi west of Hilton Head Island, visitors may tour the 24 ponds and the research building to see how methods of raising seafood commercially are studied. ⊠ *Sawmill Creek Rd. near intersection of U.S. 278 and SC 46,* ☎ *843/837–3795.* ☞ *Free.* ☉ *Tours weekdays at 10 AM and by appointment.*

OFF THE
BEATEN PATH

DAUFUSKIE ISLAND – From Hilton Head, you can go by boat to nearby Daufuskie Island, the setting for Pat Conroy's novel *The Water Is Wide,* which was made into the movie *Conrack.* The Dafuskie Island Club & Resort—with an oceanfront inn, cottages, golf courses, tennis, pools, water sports, and several restaurants—is a wonderful getaway (☎ 843/ 341–4820 or ☎ 800/648–6778). Despite increasing development on the island, many inhabitants, descendants of former slaves, live on small farms among remnants of churches, homes, and schools—reminders of antebellum times. Excursions to Daufuskie are run out of Hilton Head by Adventure Cruises (⊠ Shelter Cove Marina, ☎ 843/785–4558), Calibogue Cruises (⊠ 164B Palmetto Bay Rd., ☎ 843/785–8242), and Vagabond Cruises (⊠ Harbour Town Marina, ☎ 843/842–4155).

Dining

$$$–$$$$ ✕ **Barony Grill.** This sophisticated yet unpretentious restaurant has a
★   high-beamed ceiling, high-back chairs, and French doors. Diners can try different wines in the Tasting Room before choosing a bottle or glass. The oak-smoked rack of lamb, seared tuna with shiitake mushroom risotto, and prime rib with bourbon jus are supreme; desserts are fantastic, too. ⊠ *Westin Resort, 135 S. Port Royal Dr.,* ☎ *843/681– 4000. Reservations essential. AE, D, DC, MC, V. Closed Sun.–Mon. No lunch.*

$$–$$$$ ✕ **Old Fort Pub.** Tucked away on a quiet site overlooking the marshlands of the Intracoastal Waterway and beside the Civil War ruins of Fort Mitchell, this rustic restaurant specializes in such dishes as oyster stew, corn-crusted pork chops, and mesquite-smoked filet mignon with mushroom cabernet sauce. The ambience is publike casual, but the service is not. Sunday brunch is wonderful. ⊠ *65 Skull Creek Dr.,* ☎ *843/681–2386. AE, D, DC, MC, V.*

$$–$$$$ ✕ **Starfire Contemporary Bistro.** Ultrafresh ingredients are served in a pleasingly unique way at this small bistro with a somewhat formal yet pleasant atmosphere. Try the wild mushroom soup with roasted rosemary; salmon with spiced seed crust atop a crunchy cucumber salad; and the intense chocolate sorbet with homemade biscotti. ⊠ *37 New Orleans Rd.,* ☎ *843/785–3434. AE, DC, MC, V. No lunch.*

$–$$$ ✕ **Two Eleven Park.** Choose from 75 wines by the glass and more than 200 by the bottle at this lively wine bar–bistro. Fans come here for the convivial atmosphere and specials like smothered shrimp over grits and beer-battered lobster tails. ⊠ *211 Park, Park Plaza,* ☎ *843/686–5212. AE, D, DC, MC, V. No lunch. Closed Sun.*

$–$$ ✕ **Brick Oven Café.** Velvet drapes, chandeliers, booths, and '40s lounge-style entertainment, on top of good, reasonably priced food served late, make this the trendy place to be. There's a nice wine selection. ⊠ *Park Plaza,* ☎ *843/686–2233. Reservations essential. No lunch. AE, D, DC, MC, V.*

$ ✕ **Antojitos.** At this basic little joint, you get the real taste of Mexico; try the *carne asada* (roasted meat). ⊠ *Suite 302A, Pineland Station, Hwy. 278,* ☎ *843/681–2233. Reservations essential. No lunch. AE, D, DC, MC, V.*

Lodging

Sea Pines, the oldest and best known of Hilton Head's resort developments, or plantations, occupies 4,500 thickly wooded acres with three golf courses, a fine beach, tennis clubs, stables, and shopping plazas. The focus of Sea Pines is **Harbour Town,** built around the charming marina, which has shops, restaurants, some condominiums, and the landmark Hilton Head Lighthouse. Accommodations are in luxurious houses and villas facing the ocean or the golf courses.

The **Crowne Plaza Resort** is the oceanfront centerpiece of **Shipyard Plantation,** which also has villa condominiums, three nine-hole golf courses, a tennis club, and a small beach club. **Palmetto Dunes Resort** has the oceanfront Hyatt Regency Hilton Head, Hilton Resort, and other accommodations, along with the renowned Rod Laver Tennis Center, a good stretch of beach, three golf courses, and several oceanfront rental villa complexes. At **Port Royal Plantation** there's the posh Westin Resort, which is on the beach and has three golf courses and a tennis club.

Hilton Head Central Reservations (⊠ Box 5312, Hilton Head Island 29938, ☎ 843/785–9050 or 800/845–7018, FAX 843/686–3255) represents almost every hotel, motel, and rental agency on the island. Other options are available through the **Hilton Head Condo Hotline** (☎ 843/785–2939), **Hilton Head Reservations and Golf Line** (☎ 843/444–4772), and **Island Rentals** (☎ 800/845–6134).

$$$$ 🏨 **Crowne Plaza Resort.** Holiday Inn Worldwide's first property of this caliber in the United States, the oceanfront resort glimmers with brass railings and accents, and shiny wood floors and trim. Decorated in a nautical theme and set in a luxuriant garden, the Crowne Plaza has access to all the amenities of Shipyard Plantation. ⊠ *130 Shipyard Dr., 29928,* ☎ *843/842–2400 or 800/465–4329, FAX 843/785–8463. 315 rooms, 25 suites. 2 restaurants, lounge, indoor pool, outdoor pool, sauna, 3 18-hole golf courses, health club, racquetball, business services, meeting rooms. AE, D, DC, MC, V.* ✏

$$$$ 🏨 **Hilton Oceanfront Resort.** There's a Caribbean feel to this five-story resort hotel, part of the Hilton chain. The grounds are beautifully landscaped, and the spacious rooms, all ocean side, are spacious and decorated with contemporary wood furniture and warm colors; all have kitchenettes. ⊠ *23 Ocean La., Box 6165, 29938,* ☎ *843/842–8000 or 800/845–8001, FAX 843/842–4988. 303 rooms, 20 suites. 2 restau-*

rants, deli, lounge, 2 pools, hot tubs, sauna, 3 18-hole golf courses, health club, Ping-Pong, volleyball, boating, fishing, bicycles, children's programs. AE, D, DC, MC, V. 🐢

$$$$ 🏨 **Holiday Inn Oceanfront Resort.** A handsome high-rise motor hotel, the Holiday Inn is on a broad, quiet stretch of beach. The rooms are spacious and well furnished in a contemporary style. The outdoor Tiki Hut lounge (☞ Nightlife, *below*) is hugely popular. ⊠ *S. Forest Beach Dr., Box 5728, 29938,* 🕿 *843/785–5126 or 800/465–4329,* 🖷 *843/785–6678. 202 rooms. Restaurant, lounge, pool. AE, D, DC, MC, V.* 🐢

$$$$ 🏨 **Main Street Inn.** The outside of this inn looks like an Italianate villa
★ or a Charleston Battery home, with gardens, shuttered French doors, and iron railings. Luxury abounds inside, too, in the antique furnishings and the heart-pine floors covered in Turkish and sisal rugs. Guest rooms have velvet and silk brocade linens, feather duvets, and porcelain and brass sinks. Included in the rate are a European breakfast of imported meats, cheeses, quiches, breads, and pastries, and afternoon tea with homemade scones and tea sandwiches. ⊠ *2200 Main St., 29926,* 🕿 *843/681–3001 or 800/471–3001,* 🖷 *843/681–5541. 34 rooms. Bar, breakfast room, pool, hot tub, spa, concierge. AE, MC, V. BP.* 🐢

$$$$ 🏨 **Marriott's Grande Ocean Resort.** It was built as a time-share property, but this beautiful oceanfront condo development, within walking distance of shops and restaurants, has a limited number of rentals. The luxurious, fully furnished two-bedroom, two-bath villas come with kitchens, whirlpool tubs, and maid service. ⊠ *51 S. Forest Beach Dr., 29929,* 🕿 *843/785–2000 or 800/527–3490,* 🖷 *843/842–3413. 140 villas. Deli, lounge, indoor pool, outdoor pool, exercise room. AE, D, DC, MC, V.* 🐢

$$$–$$$$ 🏨 **Disney's Hilton Head Island Resort.** More than 100 villas have fully
★ furnished kitchen, dining, living, and sleeping areas. The smallest is a studio villa, and the largest has three bedrooms and four baths and sleeping accommodations for up to 12; all have marsh or marina views. Decorated in blues, greens, and deep reds, villas have porches with rocking chairs and picnic tables and suggest the rusticity of Adirondack cabins. The resort offers golf, tennis, and romance packages, beach shuttle service, and access to a fishing pier. The resort's 13,000-square-ft beach house has a fireplace in the living room, a heated pool, and an arcade. ⊠ *22 Harbourside La., 29928,* 🕿 *843/341–4100 or 800/453–4911,* 🖷 *843/341–4130. 102 units. Restaurant, pool, boating, fishing, bicycles, children's programs. AE, MC, V.* 🐢

$$$–$$$$ 🏨 **Westin Resort, Hilton Head Island.** One of the area's most luxuri-
★ ous properties, the horseshoe-shape Westin sprawls in a lushly landscaped oceanfront setting. The guest rooms, most with ocean views, are decorated with a residential feel: down pillows, rich colors, and comfortable wicker and contemporary furniture. All have seating areas and desks, and baths have marble flooring and distinctive lighting. Public areas display fine Asian porcelains and paintings. ⊠ *2 Grass Lawn Ave., 29928,* 🕿 *843/681–4000 or 800/228–3000,* 🖷 *843/681–1087. 412 rooms, 38 suites. 3 restaurants, 2 lounges, indoor pool, 2 outdoor pools, health club, children's programs. AE, D, DC, MC, V.* 🐢

$ 🏨 **Best Western Inn.** Just a five-minute walk from the beach, it's a frontrunner in the budget category; rooms are clean with standard decor. ⊠ *40 Waterside Dr., 29928,* 🕿 *843/842–8888,* 🖷 *843/842–5948. 120 rooms. Pool. AE, D, DC, MC, V.* 🐢

$ 🏨 **Hampton Inn.** A short drive from the public beaches, it is clean, nicely landscaped, and sheltered from the noise and traffic; suites have kitchenettes. ⊠ *1 Dillon Rd., 29926,* 🕿 *843/681–7900,* 🖷 *843/681–4330. 124 rooms. Pool. AE, D, DC, MC, V.* 🐢

$ ⊞ **Red Roof Inn.** This two-story inn is popular with families. Clean and functional rooms are just a short drive from the public beaches. ⊠ *5 Regency Pkwy., 29928,* ☎ *843/686–6808 or 800/843–7663,* FAX *843/ 842–3352. 112 rooms. Pool. AE, D, DC, MC, V.* ⊛

Nightlife and the Arts

THE ARTS

The **Self Family Arts Center** (⊠ Shelter Cove La., ☎ 843/686–3945) has details on Hilton Head arts events; it includes an art gallery, a theater, and a theater program for youth. In warm weather, free **outdoor concerts** are held at Harbour Town and Shelter Cove. Concerts, plays, films, art shows, theater, sporting events, food fairs, and minitournaments make up Hilton Head's **SpringFest** (☎ 843/686–4944 or 800/ 424–3387), which runs for the month of March. A Winter Carnival and Winefest are held each year.

NIGHTLIFE

Bars, much like everything in Hilton Head, are often in strip malls. Try the **Blue Nite** (⊠ 4 Target Rd., ☎ 843/842–6683) for live music or **Hilton Head Brewing Co.** (⊠ Hilton Head Plaza, ☎ 843/785–2739) for late-night disco every Wednesday. The **Lodge** (⊠ Hilton Head Plaza, ☎ 843/ 842–8966) has pool tables and roaring fires in the stone fireplaces. **Moneypenny's** (⊠ Palmetto Bay Rd., Village Exchange, ☎ 843/785–7878) is a cozy spot with acoustic music. **Monkey Business** (⊠ Park Plaza, ☎ 843/686–3545) is a dance club popular with young professionals.

The **Pelican Poolside** (☎ 843/681–4000), an oceanfront lounge at the Westin Resort, offers informal entertainment every night but Sunday. **Regatta** (⊠ 23 Ocean La., ☎ 843/842–8000), a sophisticated oceanfront nightspot in the Hilton Resort, features live beach and jazz music nightly. **Tiki Hut** (⊠ S. Forest Beach Dr., ☎ 843/785–5126), a locally popular beachside bar at the Holiday Inn Oceanfront Resort, has live music during the season.

Outdoor Activities and Sports

BEACHES

Although the resort beaches are reserved for guests and residents, there are four public entrances to Hilton Head's 12 mi of ocean beach. Two main parking and changing areas are at Coligny Circle, near the Holiday Inn, and on Folly Field Road, off U.S. 278. Signs along U.S. 278 point the way to Bradley and Singleton beaches, where parking space is limited.

BIKING

There are pathways in several areas of Hilton Head (many in the resorts), and pedaling is popular along the firmly packed beach. Bicycles can be rented at most hotels and resorts and at **Hilton Head Bicycle Company** (⊠ 11B Archer Rd., ☎ 843/686–6888), **Harbour Town Bicycles** (⊠ Heritage Plaza, ☎ 843/785–3546), and **South Beach Cycles** (⊠ Sea Pines Plantation, ☎ 843/671–2453).

CANOEING AND KAYAKING

Outside Hilton Head (⊠ South Beach Marina, ☎ 843/671–2643; Shelter Cove Plaza, ☎ 843/686–6996) is an ecologically sensitive company that rents canoes, kayaks, bikes, and Rollerblades; it also has nature tours.

FISHING

On Hilton Head, you can pick oysters, dig for clams, or cast for shrimp; supplies are available at **Shelter Cove Marina** at Palmetto Dunes (☎ 843/842–7001). Local marinas offer in-shore and deep-sea fishing charters. Each year a billfishing tournament and two king mackerel tournaments attract anglers.

GOLF

Many of Hilton Head's 29 championship courses are open to the public, including 18-hole, par-72 **Island West Golf Course** (⊠ U.S. 278, 8 mi before the bridge to Hilton Head, ☎ 843/689–6660); 18-hole, par-72 **Old South Golf Links** (⊠ U.S. 278, ☎ 843/785–5353); 18-hole, par-72 **Palmetto Dunes** (⊠ Ocean La., ☎ 843/785–1138); 18-hole, par-72 and 9-hole, par-36 **Port Royal** (⊠ Grass Lawn Ave., ☎ 843/689–5600); and 18-hole, par-72 **Sea Pines** (⊠ William Hilton Pkwy., ☎ 843/842–8484). **Harbour Town Golf Links at Sea Pines** (⊠ 11 Lighthouse La., ☎ 843/671–2448 or 800/955–8337), 18 holes and par 71, hosts the MCI Classic every spring.

HORSEBACK RIDING

Many trails wind through woods and nature preserves. Some stables in and near Hilton Head are **Lawton Stables** (⊠ Sea Pines, ☎ 843/671–2586) and **Sandy Creek Stables** (⊠ Near Spanish Wells, ☎ 843/689–3423). At **Sea Horse Farms** (⊠ 34 Mitchellville Rd., ☎ 843/681–7749), you can ride on the beach. **Old South** (⊠ Fording Island Rd., Bluffton, ☎ 843/842–7433) offers landscape riding. Rates are generally per person by the hour. **Rose Hill Plantation** (⊠ 1 Equestrian Way, Bluffton, ☎ 843/757–3082) welcomes experienced riders only.

SUMMER CAMP

On Hilton Head Island, all major hotels offer summer youth activities; some have full-scale youth programs. The **Island Recreation Center** runs a summer camp that visiting youngsters can join. ⊠ *Hilton Head Island Recreation Association, Wilborn Rd., Box 22593, Hilton Head Island 29925,* ☎ *843/681–7273.* ☉ *Camp mid-June–late Aug., weekdays.*

TENNIS

There are more than 300 courts on Hilton Head. **Port Royal** (⊠ 15 Wimbledon Ct., ☎ 843/686–8803); **Sea Pines Racquet Club** (⊠ 32 Greenwood Dr., ☎ 843/842–8484), home of the Family Circle Tournament; and **Shipyard** (⊠ Shipyard Dr. next to Crowne Plaza Resort, ☎ 843/686–8804) are highly rated. Other clubs that welcome guests include **Palmetto Dunes** (⊠ 6 Trent Jones La., ☎ 843/785–1151) and **Van der Meer Tennis Center** (⊠ 19 deAllyon Rd., ☎ 843/785–8388).

WINDSURFING

Lessons and rentals are available from **Outside Hilton Head** (☞ Canoeing and Kayaking, *above*).

Shopping

MALLS AND OUTLETS

Coligny Plaza (⊠ Coligny Plaza, off Coligny Circle, ☎ 843/842–6050) has 60-plus shops, restaurants, a movie theater, and a supermarket. **Hilton Head Factory Stores 1 & 2** (⊠ U.S. 278 at the island gateway, ☎ 843/837–4339 or 888/746–7333) has more than 80 outlets, including J. Crew, Gap, Brooks Brothers, Harry & David, and Coach, selling clothing and housewares. The **Mall at Shelter Cove** (⊠ U.S. 278, ½ mi north of Palmetto Dunes Resort, ☎ 843/686–3090) has 55 shops and four restaurants. **Shoppes on the Parkway** (⊠ U.S. 278, 1 mi south of Palmetto Dunes Resort, ☎ 843/686–6233) comprises 30 outlets, including Dansk, Gorham, and Van Heusen.

ART GALLERIES

The **Red Piano Art Gallery** (⊠ 220 Cordillo Pkwy., ☎ 843/785–2318) showcases 19th- and 20th-century works by regional and national contemporary artists.

BOOKS

Authors Bookstore (⊠ The Village at Wexford, ☎ 843/686–5020) carries a good selection of books focusing on local history and culture.

JEWELRY

The **Bird's Nest** (⊠ Coligny Plaza, ☎ 843/785–3737) sells locally made shell and sand-dollar jewelry. The **Goldsmith Shop** (⊠ 3 Lagoon Rd., ☎ 843/785–2538) carries classic jewelry and island charms.

NATURE

The **Audubon Nature Store** (⊠ The Village at Wexford, ☎ 843/785–4311) has items with a nature theme. The **Hammock Company** (⊠ Coligny Plaza, ☎ 843/686–3636 or 800/344–4264) sells gifts and other items with an emphasis on nature.

Beaufort

43 mi north of Hilton Head.

Charming homes and churches from Beaufort's prosperous antebellum days as a cotton center grace this historic town on Port Royal Island. Although many private houses in **Old Point,** the historic district, are not usually open to visitors, some may be on the annual Fall House Tour in mid-October and the Spring Tour of Homes and Gardens in April or May. The **Greater Beaufort Chamber of Commerce** (☎ 843/524–3163) can provide more information about house-tour schedules. The Gullah Festival, which takes place Memorial Day weekend, celebrates Lowcountry and West African culture.

The **John Mark Verdier House Museum,** built about 1790 in the Federal style, has been restored and furnished as it would have been between 1790 and the visit of Lafayette in 1825. It was the headquarters for Union forces during the Civil War. ⊠ *801 Bay St.,* ☎ *843/524–6334.* ⊠ *$4.* ⊗ *Mon.–Sat. 10–4:30.*

Built in 1795 and remodeled in 1852, the Gothic-style arsenal that was home of the Beaufort Volunteer Artillery now houses the **Beaufort Museum,** with prehistoric relics, native pottery, and Revolutionary War and Civil War exhibits. ⊠ *713 Craven St.,* ☎ *843/525–7077.* ⊠ *$2.* ⊗ *Mon.–Tues. and Thurs.–Sat. 10–5.*

St. Helena's Episcopal Church (1724) was turned into a hospital during the Civil War, and gravestones were brought inside to serve as operating tables. ⊠ *501 Church St.,* ☎ *843/522–1712.* ⊗ *Mon.–Sat. 10–4.*

Henry C. Chambers Waterfront Park, off Bay Street, is a great place to survey the scene. Barbra Streisand filmed *Prince of Tides* here. Its 7 landscaped acres along the Beaufort River, part of the Intracoastal Waterway, include a seawall promenade, a crafts market, gardens, and a marina. Some events of the popular mid-July Beaufort Water Festival, as well as a seasonal farmers' and crafts market, take place here.

At **Parris Island,** 10 mi south of Beaufort via SC 802, you can observe U.S. Marine Corps recruit training and either take a guided tour or drive through the base on your own. There's a replica of the Iwo Jima flag-raising monument on the base. The **Parris Island Museum** exhibits uniforms, photographs, and weapons chronicling military history since 1562, when the French Huguenots built a fort on St. Helena. ☎ *843/525–2951.* ⊠ *Free.* ⊗ *Fri.–Wed. 10–4:30, Thurs. 10–7.*

THE WORLD OF GULLAH

I N THE LOWCOUNTRY, Gullah refers to several things: language, people, and a culture. Gullah (the word itself is believed to be a version of Angola), an English-based dialect rooted in African languages, is the unique language of the African-Americans of the Sea Islands of South Carolina and Georgia. More than 300 years old, this rhythmic language has survived, in part, because of the geographic isolation of the people who speak it; most locally born African-Americans of the area can understand, if not speak, Gullah.

Descended from thousands of slaves who were imported by planters in the Carolinas during the 18th century, the Gullah people have maintained not only their dialect but also their heritage. Much of Gullah culture traces back to the African rice-coast culture and survives today in the art forms and skills, including sweet-grass basket making, of Sea Islanders. During the colonial period, when rice was king, Africans from the West African rice kingdoms drew high premiums as slaves. Those with basket-making skills were extremely valuable because baskets were needed for agricultural and household use. Still made by hand, sweet-grass baskets are intricate coils of a marsh grass called sweet grass. Highly prized by residents and visitors alike, the baskets are named for the sweet, haylike aroma of the sweet grass. Other Gullah art forms can be seen in hand-carved bateaus and gourds and in hand-tied nets used to catch shrimp in local creeks and rivers.

Nowhere is Gullah culture more evident than in the foods of the region. Rice, of course, appears at nearly every meal. Africans taught planters how to grow rice and how to cook and serve it as well. Like many African dishes, Lowcountry dishes use okra, peanuts, benne (the African word for sesame seeds), field peas, and hot peppers. Gullah food reflects the bounty of the islands: shrimp, crabs, oysters, fish, and vegetables such as greens, tomatoes, and corn. Watermelons, indigenous to West Africa, are grown all over the Lowcountry.

Many dishes are prepared in one pot, similar to the stew-pot cooking of West Africa. Frogmore stew calls for cooking shrimp, potatoes, sausage, and corn together in one large pot. Hoppin' John— a one-pot mixture of rice and field peas traditionally served on New Year's Day— is similar to rice and pigeon peas, a mainstay in West Africa.

The practices of plantation owners unknowingly helped the Gullah culture survive: from praise houses—one-room houses of worship where Christianity was introduced to keep slaves from running away—came plantation melodies. These songs live on in performances by groups including the Hallelujah Singers, Sea Island Singers, Mt. Zion Spiritual Singers, and Ron and Natalie Daise, all of whom perform regularly in Charleston and Beaufort.

The Penn Center on St. Helena Island near Beaufort is the unofficial Gullah headquarters, preserving the culture and developing opportunities for Gullahs. Until 1927 or so, St. Helena felt little influence from the outside world. Blacks retained the land, their language, and their unique culture. Many still go shrimping with hand-tied nets, harvest oysters, and grow their own vegetables. Nearby on Daufuskie Island, as well as on Edisto, Wadmalaw and Johns islands near Charleston, Gullah communities can still be found, though development continues to encroach. A number of companies can help visitors explore this world (☞ Guided Tours in Charleston A to Z, above).

A famous Gullah proverb says: If oonuh ent kno weh oonuh dah gwine, oonuh should kno weh oonuh come f'um. Translation: If you don't know where you're going, you should know where you come from.

St. Helena Island, 9 mi southeast of Beaufort via U.S. 21, is the site of the **Penn Center Historic District** and **York W. Bailey Museum.** Penn Center, established in the middle of the Civil War as the South's first school for freed slaves, today provides community services and has cottages for rent. The **York W. Bailey Museum** (formerly a clinic) has displays reflecting the heritage of Sea Island blacks. These islands are where Gullah, a musical language that combines English and African languages, developed. ⊠ *Land's End Rd., St. Helena Island,* ☎ *843/838–2432.* ⊡ *Donation suggested.* ☉ *Tues.–Fri. 11–4 and by appointment.*

OFF THE
BEATEN PATH

HUNTING ISLAND STATE PARK – This secluded domain of beach, nature trails, and varied fishing has about 3 mi of public beaches. The 1,120-ft fishing pier is among the longest on the East Coast. You can climb the 181 steps of the 140-ft **Hunting Island Lighthouse** (built in 1859 and abandoned in 1933) for sweeping views. The park is 18 mi southeast of Beaufort via U.S. 21; write for cabin and camping reservations.
⊠ *1775 Sea Island Pkwy., St. Helena 29920,* ☎ *843/838–2011.*
⊡ *$3 per car Mar.–Oct.; free rest of yr; $2 to climb lighthouse.* ☉ *Lighthouse daily 10–5.*

Dining and Lodging

$–$$$ ✕ **Emily's.** Long, narrow, and wood-paneled, Emily's is a lively restaurant and tapas bar that serves until 11. The crowds linger over tapas including chicken spring rolls, lamb chops, and crab wontons. This is definitely *not* a no-smoking haven. ⊠ *906 Port Republic St.,* ☎ *843/ 522–1866. AE, MC, V.*

$–$$ ✕ **Bistro de Jong.** This light-filled spot, with a comfortable counter bar and indoor courtyard motif, is popular with the lunch crowd. The Belgian chef, originally with the Beaufort Inn, blends European styles with local ingredients; the result is peanut-and-cilantro fried shrimp with Cajun rémoulade (a mayonnaise-based sauce), chicken pecan salad on focaccia bread, or the yummy Peter's pasta with sun-dried tomatoes, artichokes, and Portobello mushrooms. The apple belly pastries are a must. ⊠ *205 West St.,* ☎ *843/524–4994. AE, D, MC, V. Closed Mon. No dinner Sun.*

$–$$ ✕ **11th Street Dockside.** The succulent fried oysters, shrimp, and fish here are some of the best around. Other seafood specialties are steamed seafood pot and, by request only, Frogmore stew (consisting of shrimp, potatoes, sausage, and corn). It's all served in a classic wharf-side environment with screened porch and water views from nearly every table. ⊠ *11th St. W, Port Royal,* ☎ *843/524–7433. AE, D, DC, MC, V. No lunch.*

$$–$$$ ✕▦ **Beaufort Inn and Restaurant.** This peach-color 1897 Victorian inn, with its many gables and porches, has a superb restaurant with two mahogany-paneled dining rooms, porch dining, and a wine bar. Among the classy seafood dishes are crispy flounder with yucca chips and sashimi tuna in peanut sauce. Guest rooms are decorated with period reproductions, tasteful florals and plaids, and comfortable chairs. All have pine floors; several have fireplaces and four-poster beds. Reservations are required for afternoon tea, complimentary for guests. ⊠ *809 Port Republic St., 29902,* ☎ *843/521–9000,* ℻ *843/521–9500. 11 rooms. Restaurant. AE, MC, V. BP.* ✍

$$$–$$$$ ▦ **Rhett House Inn.** A storybook inn (circa 1820) in the heart of the
★ historic district is filled with art and antiques and abounds in such luxuries as down pillows and duvets, cotton linens, CD players in each room, and fresh flowers. Breakfast, afternoon tea, evening hors d'oeuvres, and dessert are included in the rate. Celebrity visitors have included Barbra Streisand, Jeff Bridges, and Dennis Quaid. The remodeled house across the street has six rooms, each with gas fireplace, whirlpool tub, private entrance, and porch. ⊠ *1009 Craven St., 29902,* ☎

843/524–9030, FAX *843/524–1310. 15 rooms, 1 suite. Bicycles. AE, MC,
V. BP.* ⊗

$$–$$$ 🏨 **Craven Street Inn.** This double-piazzaed 1870 inn is decorated in
clean, Pottery Barn–style, with olive and neutral tones, hand-crafted
cabinets, wreaths and baskets. Spacious guest rooms in the main house
have pine floors, high ceilings, and fireplaces; those in the 1920s garden house are small but cozy and comfortable. Breakfast might be stuffed
French toast or ham and cheese omelette with homemade crumpets.
⊠ *1103 Craven St., 29902,* ☎ *888/522–0250 or 843/522–1668,* FAX
843/522–9975. 7 rooms, 2 suites, 1 cottage. AE, D, MC, V. BP. ⊗

$$–$$$ 🏨 **Cuthbert House Inn.** Overlooking the bay, this pillared 1790 home
has original Federal fireplaces and crown and rope molding. The owners have filled it with 18th- and 19th-century heirlooms; rooms are elegant yet comfortable, with Oriental rugs on pine floors, commanding
beds, quilts, and books. ⊠ *1203 Bay St., 29902,* ☎ *843/521–1315 or
800/327–9275,* FAX *843/521–1314. 7 rooms, 1 suite. Bicycles. AE, D,
MC, V. BP.* ⊗

$$–$$$ 🏨 **Fripp Island Resort.** The resort encompasses the entire island; ac-
cess is limited to guests only. Two- and three-bedroom villas and homes
are contemporary in decor. The island is 19 mi south of Beaufort via
U.S. 21, just beyond Hunting Island State Park. There's a pavilion with
shops, restaurants, and a marina. ⊠ *1 Tarpon Blvd., 29920,* ☎ *843/
838–3535 or 800/845–4100,* FAX *843/838–9079. 240 units. 5 restaurants, 4 pools, 2 18-hole golf courses, 10 tennis courts, jogging, boating, bicycles, children's programs. AE, D, DC, MC, V.* ⊗

$–$$ 🏨 **Best Western Sea Island Inn.** At this well-maintained but standard
inn in the downtown historic district, rooms are basic. ⊠ *1015 Bay
St., Box 532, 29902,* ☎ *843/522–2090 or 800/528–1234,* FAX *843/521–
4858. 43 rooms. Pool. AE, D, DC, MC, V. CP.* ⊗

$ 🏨 **Howard Johnson.** This clean and cheerfully staffed hotel sits on the
edge of the marsh a few miles from the historic district. Rooms are spacious and have desks; many have views of the river and marsh. ⊠ *3651
Trask Pkwy. (U.S. 21), 29902,* ☎ *843/524–6020 or 800/528–1234,*
FAX *843/521–4858. 43 rooms. Pool. AE, D, DC, MC, V. CP.*

Nightlife and the Arts

Bananas (⊠ 910 Bay St., ☎ 843/522–0910) has a late-night bar and
live music on weekends. **Plum's** (⊠ 904½ Bay St., ☎ 843/525–1946)
is good for a late drink and has live bands during the weekend.

Outdoor Activities and Sports

BIKING

Beaufort is great for bicycling. Rentals are available from **Lowcountry
Bicycles** (⊠ 904 Port Republic St., ☎ 843/524–9585).

GOLF

Most golf courses are about a 10- to 20-minute drive from Beaufort.
Try the 27 holes designed by Tom Fazio at **Callawassie Island Club** (⊠
SC 170, Callawassie Island, ☎ 800/221–8431); the challenging and
beautiful 18-hole, par-72 **Cat Island Golf Club** (⊠ 8 Waveland Ave.,
Port Royal, ☎ 843/524–0300); or **Dataw Island**'s two 18-hole, par-
72 courses (⊠ Dataw Club Rd., 6 mi east of Beaufort off U.S. 21, Dataw
Island, ☎ 843/838–8250).

Shopping

ANTIQUES

Den of Antiquity (⊠ SC 170W, ☎ 843/521–9990), the area's largest antiques shop, carries a wide assortment of Lowcountry and nautical pieces.

ART GALLERIES

On canvas and sculpture as well as on bits of tin roofing, rugs, frames, and furniture, the colorful, whimsical designs of Suzanne and Eric Longo decorate their **Longo Gallery** (✉ 407 Carteret St.; 103 Charles St.; ☎ 843/522–8933 for both). The **Rhett Gallery** (✉ 901 Bay St., ☎ 843/524–3339) sells Lowcountry art by members of the Rhett family and antique maps and prints, including Audubons. On nearby St. Helena Island, the **Red Piano Too Art Gallery** (✉ 853 Sea Island Pkwy., ☎ 843/838–2241), in a huge old wooden building, is filled with quirky folk and Southern art, beads, and pottery.

JEWELRY

The **Craftseller** (✉ 818 Bay St., ☎ 843/525–6104) displays jewelry and other items by Southern craftspeople.

En Route   The ruins of **Sheldon Church,** built in 1753, make an interesting stop en route from Beaufort to Edisto Island. The church was burned in 1779 and again in 1865. Only the brick walls and columns remain beside the old cemetery. Get here from Beaufort on U.S. 21 to Gardens Corner; then go west on U.S. 17 and north on SC 21.

Edisto Island

80 mi northeast of Beaufort; take U.S. 17N and then follow SC 174.

On this rural island, magnificent stands of age-old oaks festooned with Spanish moss border quiet streams and side roads; wild turkeys may still be spotted on open grasslands and amid palmetto palms. Many of the island's inhabitants are descendants of former slaves. **Edisto Beach State Park** has 3 mi of beach with excellent shelling, housekeeping cabins by the marsh, and campsites by the ocean (though severe erosion is limiting availability). Luxury resort development has begun to encroach around the edges of the park. For camping reservations, call ☎ 843/869–2156 or 843/869–3396.

OFF THE BEATEN PATH   **CAW CAW INTERPRETIVE CENTER –** If you're heading toward Charleston, you might consider stopping at this 654-acre tract, once part of an old rice plantation. The 250 acres of rice fields are home to as many as 60 species of migratory birds, including long-legged wader birds such as blue herons. Eight miles of nature trails extend along cypress swamp, oak forest, and salt and fresh water marsh. ✉ *5200 Savannah Hwy. (U.S. 17S), 15 mi from Charleston,* ☎ *843/889–8898 or 843/762–2172.* ⚲ *Free.* ☉ *May–Aug., Tues.–Sun. 8–7; Mar.–Apr. and Sept.–Oct., Tues.–Sun. 9–6; Nov.–Feb., Tues.–Sun. 9–5.*

Dining and Lodging

$$–$$$ ✕ **Old Post Office.** Try the fussed-over pork chop or the blue-crab-and-asparagus pie, served with the house salad, vegetables, and fresh-baked bread. The house specialty at this restaurant on Store Creek is shrimp and grits and, well, *anything* with grits, rumored to be the best around these parts. Once Bailey's General Store and U.S. Post Office, the building contains the original post office boxes. ✉ *1442 SC 174, 5 mi from Edisto Beach,* ☎ *843/869–2339. MC, V. Closed Sun. June–Sept., Sun.–Mon. Oct.–May. No lunch.*

$$ ⌂ **Seaside Plantation.** This Federal-style plantation house, built around 1810, has 12-ft ceilings, intricate crown molding, pine floors, and family antiques. Nestled among shady live oaks on 245 acres where cotton once grew, Seaside is about 1 mi from the beach. A full breakfast of French toast or egg, cheese, and ham casserole with fruit is included. ✉ *400 Hwy. 174, 29438,* ☎ *843/869–0971. 4 rooms. No credit cards. BP.*

$$ ⌂ **Fairfield Ocean Ridge Resort.** Although not on the beach, most accommodations are a short walk away and combine resort amenities with a get-away-from-it-all setting. Well-furnished one- to five-bedroom villas and homes tastefully decorated in contemporary style are available. A trolley transports guests to the resort's beach shelter. ⊠ *1 King Cotton Rd., Box 27, 29438,* ☎ *843/869–2561,* FAX *843/869–2384. 100 units. Restaurant, lounge, pool, wading pool, 18-hole golf course, miniature golf, 4 tennis courts, hiking, beach, boating, fishing. AE, D, MC, V.*

Hilton Head and Beyond A to Z

Arriving and Departing

BY BOAT

Hilton Head is accessible via the Intracoastal Waterway, with docking available at **Harbour Town Marina** (☎ 843/671–2704), **Schilling Boathouse** (☎ 843/681–2628), and **Shelter Cove Marina** (☎ 843/842–7001).

BY CAR

Hilton Head Island is 40 mi east of I–95 (⊠ Exit 28 off I–95S, Exit 5 off I–95N). Beaufort is 25 mi east of I–95, on U.S. 21.

BY PLANE

Hilton Head Island Airport (☎ 843/681–6386) is served by US Airways Express and Midway. Most travelers use the **Savannah International Airport** (⊠ 400 Airways Ave., ☎ 912/964–0514), about an hour from Hilton Head, which is served by US Airways and Colgan-Air. For airline telephone numbers, *see* Air Travel *in* Smart Travel Tips A to Z.

Getting Around

BY TAXI

Lowcountry Taxi and Limousine Service (☎ 843/681–8294) and **Yellow Cab** (☎ 843/686–6666) provide service in Hilton Head; other options include **At Your Service** (☎ 843/837–3783) and **Lowcountry Adventures** (☎ 843/681–8212). In Beaufort, the **Point** (☎ 843/522–3576) and **Yellow Cab** (☎ 843/522–1121) provide service.

Contacts and Resources

EMERGENCIES

Ambulance, fire, police (☎ 911). Emergency medical service is available at the **Hilton Head Medical Center and Clinics** (⊠ Hospital Center Blvd., ☎ 843/681–6122).

GUIDED TOURS

Hilton Head's **Adventure Cruises** (☎ 843/785–4558) offers dinner, sightseeing, and murder-mystery cruises. Several companies, including **Harbour Town Charters** in Hilton Head (☎ 843/363–2628), run dolphin sightseeing and environmental trips. **Lowcountry Adventures** (☎ 843/681–8212) offers tours of Hilton Head, Beaufort, and Charleston. **Steel Horse Helicopters** (☎ 843/689–6747) gives tours of Hilton Head with a bird's-eye view, starting at $20 for five minutes.

Carolina Buggy Tours (☎ 843/525–1300) will show you Beaufort's historic district. **Carriage Tours of Beaufort** (☎ 843/221–1651) has tours of the historic district by horse-drawn carriage. **Gullah 'n' Geechie Mahn Tours** (☎ 843/838–7516) provides tours of Beaufort and Sea Islands such as St. Helena that focus on the traditions of African-American culture. Costumed guides sing and act out history during walking tours by the **Spirit of Old Beaufort** (☎ 843/525–0459). Call the **Greater Beaufort Chamber of Commerce** (☎ 843/524–3163) to find out about self-guided walking or driving tours of Beaufort.

LATE-NIGHT PHARMACIES
CVS (⊠ 95 Matthews, Hilton Head, ☎ 843/681–8363) is open until 9.

RADIO STATIONS
AM: WFXH 1130, sports talk. **FM:** WFXH 106.1, classic rock; WAEV 97.3, adult contemporary; WHVZ 99.7, beach, boogie, and blues; WLVH 101.1, soft soul; WJCL 96.5, country; WOCW 92.1, oldies.

VISITOR INFORMATION
For information on Edisto, call **Edisto Island Chamber of Commerce** (⊠ Box 206, Edisto Island 29438, ☎ 843/869–3867 or 888/333–2781). **Greater Beaufort Chamber of Commerce** (⊠ 1006 Bay St., Box 910, Beaufort 29901, ☎ 843/524–3163) has information about Beaufort and the surrounding area. You can call the **Hilton Head Island Chamber of Commerce** (⊠ Box 5647, Hilton Head 29938, ☎ 843/785–3673) for information. Two **Hilton Head welcome centers,** run by a private real-estate firm, are on U.S. 278 next to the bridge to Hilton Head and at 6 Lagoon Road at the island's south end. The centers provide visitor information and also attempt to entice you into purchasing real estate. In Hilton Head, your best bet is to stop by the **Welcome Center and Museum of Hilton Head** (⊠ 100 William Hilton Pkwy.).

COLUMBIA AND THE HEARTLAND
Camden, Aiken, Abbeville

South Carolina's Heartland, between the coastal Lowcountry and the mountains, is a varied region of swamps and flowing rivers, fertile farmland, and vast forests of pines and hardwoods. Lakes Murray, Marion, and Moultrie have wonderful fishing, and the many state parks are popular for hiking, swimming, and camping. At the center of the region is the state capital, Columbia, an engaging contemporary city superimposed on cherished historic remnants. It has restored mansions, several museums, a university, a variety of restaurants, a lively arts scene, and a fine zoo and botanical garden.

In Aiken, the center of South Carolina's Thoroughbred Country, such champions as Sea Hero and Pleasant Colony were trained. The beautiful landscape is studded with the fine mansions of wealthy Northerners such as the Vanderbilts and Whitneys. Throughout the region, such towns as Ninety Six, Sumter, and Camden preserve and interpret the past, with historic re-creations, exhibits, and restorations. Several public gardens provide islands of color during most of the year.

Columbia

112 mi northwest of Charleston, 101 mi southeast of Greenville.

In 1786 South Carolina's capital was moved from Charleston to Columbia, in the center of the state along the banks of the Congaree River. One of the nation's first planned cities, Columbia has streets that are among the widest in America—because it was then thought that stagnant air in narrow streets fostered the spread of malaria. The city soon grew into a center of political, commercial, cultural, and social activity, but in early 1865 General William Tecumseh Sherman invaded South Carolina and incinerated two-thirds of Columbia. A few homes and public buildings were spared—as was the First Baptist Church, where secession was declared, because a janitor directed Sherman's troops to a Methodist church when asked directions. Today the city is a sprawling blend of modern office blocks, suburban neighborhoods, and the occasional antebellum home. Here, too, is the expansive main campus of the University of South Carolina, including the historic and scenic Horseshoe.

☾ The **Columbia Museum of Art** contains the Kress Foundation Collection of Renaissance and Baroque treasures, sculpture, decorative arts including art glass, and European and American paintings; there are also changing exhibitions. Children may enjoy the museum's doll collection. ⊠ *Main and Hampton Sts.,* ☎ *803/799–2810.* ⊡ *$4.* ☉ *Tues. and Thurs.–Sat. 10–5, Wed. 10–9, Sun. 1–5.*

Stop by the **Museum Shop** of the Historic Columbia Foundation in the Robert Mills House (⊠ 1616 Blanding St., ☎ 803/252–1770) in the historic district to get a map and buy tickets to tour four Columbia houses: the Hampton-Preston Mansion, the Robert Mills House, the Mann-Simons Cottage, and the Woodrow Wilson Boyhood Home. ⊡ *Each house $4.* ☉ *All houses Tues.–Sat. 10:15–3:15, Sun. 1:15–4:15.*

The **Hampton-Preston Mansion** (⊠ 1615 Blanding St., ☎ 803/252–1770), dating from 1818, is filled with lavish furnishings collected by three generations of two influential families (☞ Museum Shop, *above*). The classic, columned 1823 **Robert Mills House** (⊠ 1616 Blanding St., ☎ 803/252–1770) was named for its architect, who later designed the Washington Monument. It has opulent Regency furniture, marble mantels, and spacious grounds (☞ Museum Shop, *above*). The **Mann-Simons Cottage** (⊠ 1403 Richland St., ☎ 803/252–1770) was the home of Celia Mann, one of only 200 free African-Americans in Columbia in the mid-1800s (☞ Museum Shop, *above*). The **Woodrow Wilson Boyhood Home** (⊠ 1705 Hampton St., ☎ 803/252–1770) displays the gaslights, arched doorways, and ornate furnishings of the Victorian period (☞ Museum Shop, *above*).

The **Fort Jackson Museum,** on the grounds of the U.S. Army Training Center, displays heavy equipment from the two world wars and has exhibits on the history of the fort from 1917 to the present. ⊠ *Bldg. 4442, Jackson Blvd.,* ☎ *803/751–7419.* ⊡ *Free.* ☉ *Tues.–Fri. 10–4, Sat. 1–4.*

☾ Exhibits at the **South Carolina State Museum,** in a large, refurbished textile mill, interpret the state's natural history, archaeology, historical development, and technological and artistic accomplishments. One exhibit portrays noted black astronauts (dedicated to South Carolina native Dr. Ronald McNair, who died on the *Challenger*), and another focuses on the cotton industry and slavery. An iron gate made for the museum by Phillip Simmons, the "dean of Charleston blacksmiths," is on display, as is the surfboard that physicist Kary Mullis was riding when he heard he'd won the Nobel Prize. In the Stringer Discovery Center, an interactive display, children can check out microorganisms under a microscope and climb trees to observe the animals who live in the branches. ⊠ *301 Gervais St.,* ☎ *803/737–4921.* ⊡ *$4.* ☉ *Mon.–Sat. 10–5, Sun. 1–5.*

South Carolina's capitol, the **State House,** started in 1855 and completed in 1950, is made of native blue granite in the Italian Renaissance style. Six bronze stars on the outer western wall mark direct hits by Sherman's cannons. The interior is richly appointed with brass, marble, mahogany, and artwork. A replica of Jean-Antoine Houdon's statue of George Washington is on the grounds. ⊠ *Main and Gervais Sts.,* ☎ *803/734–9818.* ⊡ *Free.* ☉ *Weekdays 9–5, Sat. 10–5, 1st Sun. of month 1–5.*

Make sure it's dark out when you drive by **Tunnelvision,** an optical illusion painted on the wall of the Federal Land Bank Building by local artist Blue Sky. ⊠ *Taylor and Marion Sts.*

A highlight of the sprawling **University of South Carolina,** near the State House, is its original campus—the scenic, tree-lined **Horseshoe**—dating to 1801, when the school was first established. Researchers explore the special collections on state history and genealogy at the **South Caroliniana Library,** established in 1840 (✉ Sumter St., ☎ 803/777–3131). It's free and open Monday, Wednesday, and Friday 8:30 to 5, Tuesday and Thursday 8:30 to 8, Saturday 9 to 5 (9 to 1 mid-May through mid-August). Here, too, is the **McKissick Museum,** with geology and gemstone exhibits and a fine display of silver (✉ Sumter St., ☎ 803/777–7251). It's free and open weekdays 9–4, weekends 1–5.

☾ **Riverfront Park and Historic Columbia Canal,** where the Broad and Saluda rivers meet to form the Congaree River, was created around the city's original waterworks and hydroelectric plant. Interpretive markers describe the area's plant and animal life and tell the history of the buildings. ✉ *312 Laurel St.,* ☎ *803/733–8613.* ☞ *Free.* ☉ *Daily dawn–dusk.*

★ ☾ **Riverbanks Zoological Park and Botanical Garden** contains more than 2,000 animals and birds, some endangered, in natural habitats. Walk along pathways and through landscaped gardens to see sea lions, polar bears, Siberian tigers, and black rhinos. The South American primate collection has won international acclaim, and the park is noted for its success in breeding endangered and fragile species. The aquarium-reptile complex has South Carolina, desert, tropical, and marine specimens. A 70-acre botanical garden on the west bank of the Saluda River includes a forested section with trails past historic ruins and spectacular views of the river. At the Bird Pavilion, you can view birds and wildlife from a safarilike tent. ✉ *I–126 and U.S. 76 at Greystone Riverbanks exit,* ☎ *803/779–8717.* ☞ *$6.25.* ☉ *Apr.–Oct. weekdays 9–4, weekends 9–5; Nov.–Mar. daily 9–4.* ✍

Dining and Lodging

$$–$$$ ✕ **Motor Supply Co. Bistro.** Dine on cuisine from around the world at a restaurant in the heart of town. Fresh seafood and homemade desserts are among the many offerings; on Sunday there's a bountiful brunch. ✉ *920 Gervais St.,* ☎ *803/256–6687. AE, DC, MC, V.*

$–$$$ ✕ **Mangia! Mangia!** Earth tones, hammered copper, and mosaic tiles
★ transform an early 20th-century building into an elegant place to dine. Window-side tables have a view of the Columbia skyline across the Congaree River; there's a lively outdoor patio, too, with heaters for chilly nights. Try the mussels steamed in wine-garlic sauce, followed by wild mushroom pizza baked in the wood-burning oven. The Tuscan-influenced menu also includes lamb shank roasted in red wine with herbs. The entire restaurant, except for the bar, is no-smoking. ✉ *100 State St., West Columbia,* ☎ *803/791–3443. AE, MC, V.*

$–$$ ✕ **Blue Marlin.** With polished wood, lines of booths, artsy light fixtures, and an oceanic mural over the bar, this restaurant speaks of bygone years—fitting for an eatery that was once a train station. Start with deviled crab or oyster shooters (raw oysters with jalapeño peppers, each in its own shot glass). Seafood and pasta dishes, always served with steaming collard greens and grits, are the staples here. Fruit cobblers with liqueur-laced whipped cream are popular dessert items. ✉ *1200 Lincoln St.,* ☎ *803/799–3838. Reservations not accepted. AE, DC, MC, V.*

$–$$ ✕ **California Dreaming.** This airy, greenery-bedecked space is the renovated old Union Train Station. The only drawback: an echo that's noticeable when it's crowded. Specialties include prime rib, barbecued baby-back ribs, Mexican dishes, and homemade pasta. ✉ *401 S. Main St.,* ☎ *803/254–6767. AE, MC, V.*

$ ✕ **Maurice Gourmet Barbecue–Piggie Park.** One of the South's best-known barbecue chefs, Maurice Bessinger has a fervent national following for his mustard-sauce-based, pit-cooked ham barbecue. Fans also love the chicken, ribs, hash over rice, and thick-battered onion rings. ✉ *1600 Charleston Hwy.,* ☎ *803/796–0220; 800 Elmwood Ave.,* ☎ *803/256–4377; 1141 Lake Murray Blvd., Irmo,* ☎ *803/732–5555. Reservations not accepted. AE, D, MC, V.*

$$$–$$$$ 🏨 **Embassy Suites Hotel Columbia.** In the spacious seven-story atrium lobby with skylights, fountains, pools, and live plants, overnight guests enjoy sumptuous breakfasts and evening cocktails. The pleasing staff caters to a mostly business clientele. ✉ *200 Stoneridge Dr., 29210,* ☎ *803/252–8700 or 800/362–2779,* FAX *803/256–8749. 214 suites. Indoor pool, health club, billiards. AE, D, DC, MC, V. BP.* 🐾

$$$ 🏨 **Claussen's Inn.** A small hotel in a converted bakery warehouse in the attractive Five Points neighborhood, the inn is near lively nightlife and specialty shops. Claussen's has an open, airy lobby with a Mexican-tile floor; the rooms, some two-story, are arranged around the lobby. The eight loft suites have downstairs sitting rooms, period reproductions, and four-poster beds. ✉ *2003 Greene St., 29205,* ☎ *803/765–0440 or 800/622–3382,* FAX *803/799–7924. 21 rooms, 8 suites. Hot tub, meeting rooms. AE, D, MC, V. CP.*

$$–$$$ 🏨 **Adam's Mark.** This upscale downtown hotel is near state offices and the University of South Carolina. It has leather armchairs, suspended lights, and brass accents in public areas. Guest rooms are contemporary, with armoires and desks. Finlay's Restaurant, in a spectacular atrium with wood-wrapped columns, serves American fare; Players Sports Bar is also an option. ✉ *1200 Hampton St., 29201,* ☎ *803/771–7000 or 800/444–2326,* FAX *803/254–8307. 296 rooms, 4 suites. Restaurant, lounge, sports bar, indoor pool, hot tub, health club, business services. AE, D, DC, MC, V.* 🐾

$$–$$$ 🏨 **Richland Street B&B.** Relax on the front porch or in the spacious ★ common area of this no-smoking inn in the heart of Columbia's historic district. Each antiques-furnished room has its own personality; the suite has a whirlpool tub. The complimentary breakfast includes fresh fruit and Belgian waffles or French toast; there are also afternoon refreshments. ✉ *1425 Richland St., 29201,* ☎ *803/779–7001,* FAX *803/765–0370. 7 rooms, 1 suite. Library. AE, MC, V. CP.*

$ 🏨 **Best Western Riverside Inn.** Close to the University of South Carolina's Williams-Brice Stadium and Coliseum, this inn has comfortable rooms and a cheerful staff. Rates include a complimentary Continental breakfast of breads, fruit, yogurt, grits, and oatmeal. Golf packages are available. ✉ *111 Knox Abbott Dr., 29033,* ☎ *803/939–4688 or 800/528–1234,* FAX *803/926–5547. 64 rooms. Pool, putting green. AE, D, DC, MC, V. CP.* 🐾

$ 🏨 **La Quinta Motor Inn.** At this three-story inn on a quiet street near the zoo, the rooms are spacious and well lighted, with large working areas. ✉ *1335 Garner La., 29210,* ☎ *803/798–9590 or 800/531–5900,* FAX *803/731–5574. 122 rooms. Pool. AE, D, DC, MC, V.* 🐾

Nightlife and the Arts

THE ARTS

The **Columbia Music Festival Association** (☎ 803/771–6303) can inform callers about events of the Choral Society, the Opera, Opera Guild, Dance Theatre, Brass Band, Caroliers, and Cabaret Company. The **Koger Center for the Arts** (✉ Assembly St., ☎ 803/777–7500) presents national and international theater, ballet, and musical groups as well as individual performers. Call the **South Carolina Philharmonic** (☎ 803/254–7445) for information about scheduled concerts of the Philharmonic, the Chamber Orchestra, and the Youth Orchestra.

The **Town Theatre** (✉ 1012 Sumter St., ☎ 803/799–2510), founded in 1919, stages six plays a year from September to late May, plus a special summer show. The **Workshop Theatre of South Carolina** (✉ 1136 Bull St., ☎ 803/799–4876) produces a number of plays.

NIGHTLIFE

In the hopping Vista neighborhood, the **Art Bar** (✉ 1211 Park St., ☎ 803/254–4792) is funky, with splash-painted walls, lighted lunch boxes, and dancing to world music. At **Billy G's** (✉ 828 Gervais Rd., ☎ 803/806–8870) you'll find live bands. **Willy's Bar & Grill** (✉ 1200B Lincoln St., ☎ 803/799–3111), in a former train station waiting room, has live music and an outdoor patio. In Five Points, **Goatfeathers** (✉ 2017 Devine St., ☎ 803/256–3325 or 803/256–8133), popular with university and law school students, is a tradition; its bohemian atmosphere draws the late-night coffee and dessert seekers.

Outdoor Activities and Sports

BASEBALL

The **Capital City Bombers** (☎ 803/256–4110), a Class-A affiliate of the New York Mets, play from mid-April through August at Capital City Stadium (✉ 301 S. Assembly St.) downtown.

CANOEING, KAYAKING, RAFTING

Self-guided canoe trails traverse an alluvial floodplain bordered by high bluffs at the 22,200-acre **Congaree Swamp National Monument** (✉ 20 mi southeast of Columbia, off SC 48, ☎ 803/776–4396). The water and trees here, including many old-growth bottomland hardwoods, are full of wildlife. Canoe rentals are available in Columbia at **Adventure Carolina** (☎ 803/796–4505) and the **River Runner Outdoor Center** (☎ 803/771–0353).

Rafting, kayaking, and canoeing on the **Saluda River** near Columbia offer challenging Class III and Class IV rapids. Guided river and swamp excursions can be arranged through Adventure Carolina and River Runner Outdoor Center (☞ *above*).

GOLF

Sedgewood (✉ Sumter Hwy., ☎ 803/776–2177), 18-hole, par-72, is among the many fine area courses. Call **Golf Vacations of Columbia** (☎ 888/501–0954) for tee times.

HIKING

Congaree Swamp National Monument (☞ Canoeing, *above*) has 22 mi of trails for hikers and nature lovers and a ¾-mi boardwalk for visitors with disabilities. Guided nature walks leave Saturday at 1:30.

Shopping

ANTIQUES AND FLEA MARKETS

Many of Columbia's antiques outlets (as well as boutique shops) are in the **Congaree Vista** around Huger and Gervais streets, between the State House and the river. A number of intriguing shops and cafés are in **Five Points,** around the intersection of Blossom and Harden streets. There are antiques shops across the river on Meeting and State streets in **West Columbia**. The **Old Mill Antique Mall** (✉ 310 State St., West Columbia, ☎ 803/796–4229) has items from many dealers. The **Thieves Market Antique Flea Mall** (✉ 502 Gadsden St., ☎ 803/254–4997) shows off the wares of dozens of antiques and collectibles dealers.

FARMERS' MARKET

The **State Farmers' Market** (✉ Bluff Rd., ☎ 803/253–4664) is one of the 10 largest in the country. Fresh vegetables are sold each weekday, along with flowers, plants, seafood, and more, from 6 AM to 9 PM.

Camden

32 mi northeast of Columbia via I–20.

Charming Camden, a town with a horsey history and grand Southern colonial homes, has never paved its fanciest roads for the sake of the hooves of the horses who regularly trot over them. The Carolina Cup and Colonial Cup are run here; in addition to the horse races, you'll see champagne tailgate parties with elegant crystal and china.

Camden is South Carolina's oldest inland town, dating from 1732. British general Lord Cornwallis established a garrison here during the Revolutionary War and burned most of Camden before evacuating it. A center of textile trade from the late 19th century through the 1940s, Camden attracted Northerners escaping the cold winters; the DuPont family is today one of Camden's major employers. Because General Sherman spared the town during the Civil War, most of its antebellum homes still stand.

The **Historic Camden Revolutionary War Site** re-creates the British occupation of 1780 on the site of the early 19th-century village. Several house restorations display period furnishings, including Cornwallis's headquarters, the **Kershaw-Cornwallis House** (circa 1770). Nature trails, fortifications, a powder magazine, a picnic area, and a crafts shop are also here. ⊠ U.S. 521, 1½ mi north of I–20, ☎ 803/432–9841. ☞ $5. ☉ Guided tours Mon.–Sat. 10–4, Sun. 1–4; museum shop daily 10–5.

Dining and Lodging

$$$–$$$$ ✕ **Mill Pond Restaurant.** In a historic building overlooking a sprawl-
★   ing millpond, this restaurant, about a 10-minute drive south of Camden, specializes in Mediterranean-influenced dishes. Try the wild boar on grits, bacon-wrapped scallops, or garlic toast and crab cakes with shrimp tartar sauce. ⊠ 84 Boykin Mill Rd., Rembert, ☎ 803/424–0261. Jacket and tie. MC, V. Closed Sun.–Mon. No lunch.

$–$$ ✕ **Avanti's Restaurant.** Cane-back chairs, fox-hunting prints, and elaborately tiled fireplaces set the tone for an elegant meal in the Victorian Greenleaf Inn (☞ below), the site of this restaurant. Avanti's serves wonderful pastas and pork with Italian family-style side dishes, plus great cannoli. ⊠ 1308 Broad St., ☎ 803/713–0089. AE, D, MC, V. Closed Sun. No lunch.

$–$$$ ✕⌂ **Greenleaf Inn.** Alice Boykin, whose name is to Camden what
★   Carnegie's is to Pittsburgh, opened the Greenleaf in 1993. The inn consists of three buildings: the main inn, with four rooms on the second floor above Avanti's Restaurant (☞ above); a nearby carriage house with seven rooms; and a guest cottage, which is particularly good for families. The spacious rooms have classic Victorian furniture and floral wallpaper; all baths are modern. You won't find a nicer or better-value lodging in the region. ⊠ 1308 Broad St., 29020, ☎ 803/425–1806 or 800/437–5874, ℻ 803/425–5853. 8 rooms, 3 suites, 1 cottage. Restaurant. AE, MC, V. BP.

$–$$$ ⌂ **A Camden Bed & Breakfast.** This Federal-style 1920s home in Cam-
★   den's historic district has wood-burning fireplaces in every room, antiques, and Persian rugs. The full breakfast might include a Canadian ham casserole or French toast. ⊠ 127 Union St., 29020, ☎ 803/432–2366. 2 rooms, 1 cottage. AE, MC, V. BP.

$–$$ ⌂ **Holiday Inn.** This well-maintained chain offering is 3 mi west of downtown Camden. The restaurant is excellent. ⊠ U.S. 1/601S, Box 96, Lugoff 29078, ☎ 803/438–9441 or 800/465–4329, ℻ 803/438–9441. 117 rooms. Restaurant, lounge, pool. AE, D, DC, MC, V. ☜

Nightlife and the Arts

The **Paddock Restaurant & Pub** (⊠ 514 Rutledge St., ☎ 803/432–3222) has music and dancing weekends.

Outdoor Activities and Sports

EQUESTRIAN EVENTS

Camden puts on two steeplechase events at **Springdale Race Course** (⊠ 200 Knights Hill Rd., ☎ 803/432–6513): the Carolina Cup in late March or early April and the Colonial Cup in November.

GOLF

White Pines Golf Club (⊠ 615 Mary La., ☎ 803/432–7442) is an 18-hole, par-72 course.

OFF THE
BEATEN PATH

CHERAW – The town's well-preserved, 213-acre historic district holds the Town Green, part of the original 1768 plan. The district encompasses more than 50 antebellum public buildings and houses, as well as later structures, including the Market Hall, Town Hall, Lyceum Museum, and Inglis-McIver law office. Stop by the Greater Cheraw Chamber of Commerce (⊠ 221 Market St., ☎ 803/537–7681) for a brochure about the area. Cheraw is 55 mi northeast of Camden on U.S. 1; you pass the Carolina Sandhills National Wildlife Refuge en route.

Sumter

30 mi southeast of Camden on U.S. 521; 44 mi east of Columbia on U.S. 378.

Sumter—named for the Revolutionary War hero and statesman General Thomas Sumter—was settled about 1740 as the center of a cultivated plantation district. Today it is home to varied industries, lumbering, agricultural marketing, and nearby Shaw Air Force Base.

The **Sumter County Museum** (headquarters of the Sumter County Historical Society), in a lovely 1845 Victorian Gothic house, exhibits fine period furnishings, Oriental carpets, vintage carriages, dolls, and various memorabilia. ⊠ *122 N. Washington St.,* ☎ *803/775–0908.* ☞ *Free.* ☉ *Tues.–Sat. 10–1 and 2–5.*

Swan Lake Iris Gardens is like Eden when its 6 million irises are in bloom. Coscoroba, whooper, trumpeter, and black Australian swans paddle leisurely around the 45-acre lake. The 150-acre park also includes walking trails, picnic areas, tennis courts, a playground, and concessions. ⊠ *W. Liberty St.,* ☎ *803/775–1231.* ☞ *Free.* ☉ *Daily 8–sunset.*

Lodging

$$–$$$ 🏨 **Magnolia House.** In Sumter's historic district, this four-column Greek Revival structure is a nice alternative to the region's generic chain motels. Antiques, many of them French, furnish the rooms; there are also stained-glass windows, inlaid oak floors, and five fireplaces. ⊠ *230 Church St., 29150,* ☎ *803/775–6694. 3 rooms, 1 suite. AE, MC, V. BP.* ✎

$–$$ 🏨 **Holiday Inn.** This well-maintained motor inn is 4 mi west of town, near Shaw Air Force Base. Simple, clean rooms are as you would expect from this chain. ⊠ *2390 Broad St. Extension, 29150,* ☎ *803/469–9001 or 800/465–4329,* FAX *803/469–7001. 124 rooms. Café, pool, exercise room. AE, D, DC, MC, V.*

Outdoor Activities and Sports

About 30 mi from Sumter, a mysterious canoe trail leads into a remote swampy depression at **Woods Bay State Park** (⊠ from Sumter, take

U.S. 378E to U.S. 301N, ☎ 803/659–4445), where rentals are available for $3 per hour or $10 for a full day.

Aiken

64 mi south of Sumter via U.S. 301/601 and U.S. 78, 56 mi southwest of Columbia via I–20.

Aiken, in Thoroughbred Country, first earned its fame in the 1890s, when wealthy Northerners wintering here built stately mansions and entertained one another with lavish parties, horse shows, and hunts. Many of the mansions—some with up to 90 rooms—remain as a testament to this era of opulence. The town is still a center for all kinds of outdoor activity, including the equestrian events of the Triple Crown, as well as tennis and golf.

The area's horse farms have produced many national champions, which are commemorated at the **Aiken Thoroughbred Hall of Fame** with exhibitions of horse-related decorations, paintings, and sculptures, plus racing silks and trophies. The Hall of Fame is on the grounds of the 14-acre **Hopeland Gardens**, with winding paths, quiet terraces, and reflecting pools. There's a Touch and Scent Trail with Braille plaques. Open-air free concerts and plays are presented on Monday evening mid-July through August. ☒ *Corner of Dupree Pl. and Whiskey Rd.,* ☎ *803/642–7630.* ☒ *Free.* ☉ *Museum Oct.–May, Tues.–Sun. 2–5; grounds daily dawn–dusk.*

The **Aiken County Historical Museum,** in one wing of an 1860 estate, is devoted to early regional culture. It has Native American artifacts, firearms, an authentically furnished 1808 log cabin, and a one-room schoolhouse. ☒ *433 Newberry St. SW,* ☎ *803/642–2015.* ☒ *Donations accepted.* ☉ *Tues.–Fri. 9:30–4:30, weekends 2–5.*

Aiken surrounds the serene and wild **Hitchcock Woods** (☒ enter from junction of Clark Rd. and Whitney Dr., Berrie Rd., and Dibble Rd.), 2,000 acres of Southern forest with hiking trails and bridal paths.

Stop for a wine tasting at **Montmorenci Vineyards** (☒ U.S. 78, 2½ mi east of Aiken, ☎ 803/649–4870). Montmorenci wines are made from French-American hybrid grapes, many typical of the Southeast, and include rosés, blushes, whites, and reds. Tours are by appointment during February and March.

Dining and Lodging

$–$$ ✕ **Malia's.** At this busy lunch and dinner spot, you get international cuisine, including lamb soup with curry; veal with shiitake mushrooms and brandy demi-glace; and a baked ham, Brie, and Portobello mushroom sandwich. ☒ *120 Laurens St.,* ☎ *803/643–3086. D, MC, V. No lunch weekends, no dinner weekdays.*

$–$$ ✕ **No. 10 Downing Street.** This stately Southern colonial dates from
★ 1837 and serves some of the best—and most diverse—food in town. The menu changes regularly: one month might focus on such Italian fare as *pollo al prosciutto* (chicken wrapped in prosciutto and fresh herbs with fettuccine Alfredo) and baked beef tenderloin with tomatoes, garlic, and oregano; another month may salute country French or regional cuisine. The bakery here sells fantastic breads. ☒ *241 Laurens St.,* ☎ *803/642–9062. AE, D, DC, MC, V. Closed Sun.–Mon.*

$ ✕ **Track Kitchen.** The who's who of Aiken's horsey set can be found here most mornings, feasting on the heavy and hearty cooking of Carol and Pockets Curtis. The small dining room is unpretentious, with walls of mint-green cinder block and simple Formica counters. ☒ *420 Mead Ave.,* ☎ *803/641–9628. No credit cards. No dinner.*

$$–$$$ 🏠 **Willcox Inn.** Winston Churchill, Franklin D. Roosevelt, and the Astors have slept at this elegant inn, built in grand style in the early 1900s. The lobby is graced with massive stone fireplaces, rosewood woodwork, heart-pine floors, and Oriental rugs. Though rooms have fine furnishings such as high four-poster beds, the decor could use a touchup. ⊠ *100 Colleton Ave., 29801,* ☎ *803/649–1377 or 800/368–1047,* FAX *803/643–0971. 24 rooms, 6 suites. Bar, dining room. AE, D, DC, MC, V. CP.* 🐾

$ 🏠 **Briar Patch.** You can learn plenty about both the Old and New South
★   from the knowledgeable innkeepers of this terrific B&B, which was formerly tack rooms in Aiken's stable district. Choose either the frilly room with French provincial furniture or the less dramatic one with pine antiques and a weather vane. ⊠ *544 Magnolia La. SE, 29801,* ☎ *803/649–2010. 2 rooms. Tennis court. No credit cards. CP.*

Outdoor Activities and Sports

EQUESTRIAN EVENTS

In Aiken, **polo matches** are played at Whitney Field (☎ 803/648–7874) on Sunday afternoon September through November and March through July. Three weekends in late March and early April are set aside for the famed **Triple Crown** (☎ 803/641–1111)—Thoroughbred trials of promising yearlings, a steeplechase, and harness races by young horses making their debut.

GOLF

The many fine 18-hole, par-70 courses in the area include **Highland Park Country Club** (⊠ 555 Highland Park Ave., ☎ 803/649–6029).

Greenwood

55 mi northwest of Aiken via SC 19, U.S. 25, and SC 72; 75 mi west of Columbia via U.S. 378, U.S. 178, and SC 72.

Founded by Irish settlers in 1802, Greenwood received its name from the site's gently rolling landscape and dense forests. Andrew Johnson, the 17th U.S. president, operated a tailor shop at Courthouse Square before migrating to East Tennessee. Anglers, swimmers, and boaters head for nearby Lake Greenwood's 200-mi shore. Two sections of Sumter National Forest are nearby.

The **Greenwood Museum** has more than 7,000 items in eclectic displays: Native American artifacts, natural history and geology exhibits, and a replicated village street including a one-room school and a general store. ⊠ *106 Main St.,* ☎ *864/229–7093.* 🎟 *$2.* ⏰ *Wed.–Sat. 10–5.*

The **Gardens of Park Seed Co.,** one of the nation's largest seed supply houses, maintains colorful experimental gardens and greenhouses 6 mi north on U.S. 178 at Hodges. The flower beds are especially vivid June 15 through July, and seeds and bulbs are for sale in the company's store. The **South Carolina Festival of Flowers**—with a performing-artists contest, a beauty pageant, private house and garden tours, and live entertainment—is held at Park's headquarters annually at the end of June. ⊠ *On SC 254, 7 mi north of town,* ☎ *864/941–4213 or 800/845–3369.* 🎟 *Free.* ⏰ *Gardens daily dawn–dusk; store Mon.–Sat. 9–5.*

Lodging

$ 🏠 **Inn on the Square.** This inn was fashioned out of a warehouse in the heart of town. Though the rooms suffer from rather unremarkable views, they're bright and spacious, with reproduction 18th-century antiques, four-poster beds, writing desks, and such thoughtful touches as turndown service and complimentary morning newspapers. The staff is attuned to the needs of business travelers and vacationers alike. ⊠

104 Court St., 29648, ☎ 864/223–4488, FAX 864/223–7067. 48 rooms. Restaurant, lounge, pool. AE, D, DC, MC, V. ✆

Ninety Six

10 mi east of Greenwood on SC 248.

The town of Ninety Six, on an old Native American trade route, is so named for being 96 mi from the Cherokee village of Keowee in the Blue Ridge Mountains—the distance a young Cherokee maiden, Cateechee, is supposed to have ridden to warn her English lover of a threatened Native American massacre. The **Ninety Six National Historic Site** commemorates two Revolutionary War battles. The visitor center's museum has descriptive displays, and there are remnants of the old village, a reconstructed French and Indian War stockade, and Revolutionary-era fortifications. ⊠ *SC 248,* ☎ *864/543–4068.* 🎫 *Free.* ☉ *Daily 8–5.*

Abbeville

14 mi west of Greenwood on SC 72.

★ **Abbeville** may well be one of inland South Carolina's most satisfying, though lesser-known, small towns. An appealing historic district includes the old business district, early churches, and residential areas. The "Southern cause" was born and died here, where the first organized secession meeting was held and where, on May 2, 1865, Confederate president Jefferson Davis officially disbanded the defeated armies of the South in the last meeting of his war council. The 1830 house where the Confederate council met is the **Burt-Stark House.** ⊠ *306 N. Main St.,* ☎ *864/459–4297 or 864/459–2181.* 🎫 *$3.* ☉ *Sept.–May, Fri.–Sat. 1–5 or by appointment; June–Aug., Tues.–Sat. 1–5 or by appointment.*

An 1850s jail houses the **Abbeville County Museum,** which contains area memorabilia. It's adjacent to the 1837 log-cabin home of Marie Cromer Siegler, founder of 4-H clubs, and an educational garden. ⊠ *Poplar and Cherry Sts.,* ☎ *864/459–4600.* 🎫 *Free.* ☉ *Wed. and Sun. 3–5 or by appointment.*

The **Abbeville Opera House** (⊠ Town Sq., ☎ 864/459–2157) faces the historic town square. Built in 1908, it has been renovated to reflect the grandeur of the days when lavish road shows and stellar entertainers came center stage. Current productions range from light, contemporary comedies to Broadway-style musicals. Call about tours.

OFF THE BEATEN PATH

HICKORY KNOB STATE RESORT PARK – This park on the shore of Strom Thurmond Lake, about 20 mi south of Abbeville, has everything for a complete vacation: fishing, waterskiing, sailing, motorboating, a swimming pool, a tackle shop, nature trails, an 18-hole championship golf course, a pro shop, and tennis courts. A 1770s log cabin, an 80-room lodge, nine duplex lakeside cottages, campgrounds, and a restaurant round out Hickory Knob's offerings. You're also near a stretch of the Savannah River Scenic Highway, which follows the Savannah River along the Georgia border, winding 100 mi and past three lakes. ⊠ *Rte. 1, Box 199B, McCormick 29835,* ☎ *864/391–2450 or 800/491–1764.* 🎫 *Free; fees for some activities.* ☉ *Office daily 7 AM–11 PM.*

Dining and Lodging

$–$$ ✕ **Village Grille.** Locals come to this high-ceiling room with
★ pomegranate-color walls and antique mirrors for the herb rotisserie chicken. Other choices are the ribs, homemade pastas, and cordial-laced

desserts. The atmosphere is trendy and friendly; the staff bends over backward to please. ⊠ *114 Trinity St.,* ☎ *864/459–2500. AE, D, MC, V. Closed Sun.–Mon.*

$ ✕ **Yoder's Dutch Kitchen.** You'll find authentic Pennsylvania Dutch home cooking in an unassuming redbrick building with a mansard roof. There are a lunch buffet and evening smorgasbord with fried chicken, stuffed cabbage, Dutch meat loaf, breaded veal Parmesan, and plenty of vegetables. Shoofly pie, Dutch bread, and apple butter can be purchased to go. ⊠ *U.S. 72,* ☎ *864/459–5556. No credit cards. Closed Sun.–Tues. No dinner Wed.*

$–$$ 🏠 **Belmont Inn.** Built in the early 1900s, this restored Spanish-style structure is a popular overnight stop with Opera House visitors. Guest rooms are spacious, with high ceilings and pine floors. Theater-and-dining package plans are offered. ⊠ *106 E. Pickens St., 29620,* ☎ *864/459–9625 or 888/251–2000. 25 rooms. Restaurant, lounge, meeting rooms. AE, D, MC, V.* 🕭

Nightlife and the Arts

The **Abbeville Opera House** (⊠ Town Sq., ☎ 864/459–2157) stages high-caliber productions in an early 20th-century setting. Reservations are taken weekdays 10–5.

Shopping

Abbeville's **Town Square** is lined with attractive gift and specialty shops in restored historic buildings dating from the late 1800s.

Columbia and the Heartland A to Z

Arriving and Departing

BY BUS

Greyhound (☎ 800/231–2222) serves all of South Carolina.

BY CAR

I–77 leads into Columbia from the north. I–26, I–20, and U.S. 1 intersect at Columbia.

BY PLANE

Columbia Metro Airport (⊠ 3000 Aviation Way, ☎ 803/822–5000), 10 mi west of downtown, is served by American Eagle, ComAir/Delta, and US Airways. For airline telephone numbers, *see* Air Travel *in* Smart Travel Tips A to Z.

BY TRAIN

Amtrak (☎ 800/872–7245) makes stops at Camden, Columbia, Denmark, Dillon, Florence, and Kingstree in the Heartland.

Getting Around

BY BUS

A local utility provides city bus service in and around **Columbia** (☎ 803/748–3019).

BY TAXI

Companies providing service in Columbia include **AAA Airport Shuttle Service** (☎ 803/796–3626), **Blue Ribbon** (☎ 803/754–8163), and **Checker-Yellow** (☎ 803/799–3311). **Gamecock Cab Co.** (☎ 803/796–7700) offers service from Columbia to other cities statewide.

Contacts and Resources

EMERGENCIES

Ambulance, fire, police (☎ 911). Emergency room services are available at **Richland Memorial Hospital** (⊠ 5 Richland Medical Park, Columbia, ☎ 803/765–7561).

GUIDED TOURS

The **Aiken Chamber of Commerce** runs a 90-minute tour of the historic district and will customize tours to suit individual interests. In Sumter, the charismatic former mayor **"Bubba" McElveen** (☎ 803/775–2851) gives walking, bus, and auto tours of the area. Customized tours of Camden are available from **Greenleaf Tours** (contact Louise Burns, ☎ 803/432–1515) or through **Kershaw County Chamber of Commerce** (☎ 803/432–2525). **Richland County Historic Preservation Commission** (☎ 803/252–1770) runs guided tours and rents out historic properties.

LATE-NIGHT PHARMACIES

CVS (⊠ 3595 Harden St., ☎ 803/779–1217) and **Kroger Sav-On** (⊠ 817 St. Andrews Rd. and 6 other locations, ☎ 803/551–1145) are open 24 hours.

OUTDOOR ACTIVITIES AND SPORTS

The 41-mi-long **Lake Murray,** just 15 mi west of Columbia via I–26 (Irmo exit), has swimming, boating, picnicking, and superb fishing. There are many marinas and campgrounds in the area. For information, contact the **Lake Murray Tourism and Recreation Association** (⊠ 2184 N. Lake Dr., Irmo 29063, ☎ 803/781–5940).

For **fishing,** Lakes Marion and Moultrie attract anglers after bream, crappie, catfish, and several kinds of bass. Supplies, camps, guides, rentals, and accommodations abound. For information, contact **Santee Cooper Counties Promotion Commission** (⊠ Drawer 40, Santee 29142, ☎ 803/854–2131, 800/227–8510 outside SC).

For information on **hiking** trails in the Francis Marion National Forest and the Sumter National Forest, contact the **National Forest Service** (⊠ 4931 Broad River Rd., Columbia 29210-4021, ☎ 803/561–4000).

RADIO STATIONS

In Columbia: **AM:** WCOS 1400, country; WOMG 1320, oldies; WVOC 560, news/talk. **FM:** WLTR 91.3, classical; WMFX 102.3, classic rock; WNOK 104, Top 40 hits; WTCB 106.7, adult contemporary; WUSC 90.5, alternative (jazz, blues, folk, reggae); WWDM 101.3, urban hits.

VISITOR INFORMATION

The **Columbia Metropolitan Convention and Visitors Bureau** (⊠ Box 15, 29202; visitor center: ⊠ 1012 Gervais St., ☎ 803/254–0479 or 800/264–4884) has brochures, maps, and advice for travelers; the center also presents a short film on area history. In Abbeville, contact the **Greater Abbeville Chamber of Commerce** (⊠ 104 Pickens St., Abbeville 29620, ☎ 864/459–4600). **Greater Aiken Chamber of Commerce** (⊠ 400 Laurens St. NW, Box 892, Aiken 29802, ☎ 803/641–1111) serves the Aiken area. **Kershaw County Chamber of Commerce** (⊠ 724 S. Broad St., Box 605, Camden 29020, ☎ 803/432–2525) has information and advice on where to go in Camden. **Ninety Six Chamber of Commerce** (⊠ Box 8, 29666, ☎ 803/543–2900) provides information on the town and district of Ninety Six.

THE UPCOUNTRY

The Upcountry, in the northwest corner of the state, has long been a favorite for family vacations because of its temperate climate and natural beauty. The abundant lakes and waterfalls and several state parks (including Caesar's Head, Keowee-Toxaway, Oconee, Table Rock, and the Chattooga National Wild and Scenic River) provide all manner of recreational activities. Beautiful anytime, the 130-mi Cherokee Foothills Scenic Highway (SC 11), which goes through the Blue Ridge

Mountains, is especially delightful in spring (when the peach trees are in bloom) and autumn.

Greenville is growing fast and attracting lots of industry, much of it textile-related, in keeping with the area's history. Clemson, home of Clemson University and the "Orange Wave," is pretty much a university town. Pendleton, just a few miles away, has one of the nation's largest historic districts. With its village green, surrounded by shops and restaurants, it's a lovely step back in time. The comfortable communities of Spartanburg and Anderson are beginning to rejuvenate their downtown areas.

Greenville

100 mi northwest of Columbia.

Although known for its textile and other manufacturing plants, Greenville has many tree-lined streets and a number of attractions including a zoo and nearby state parks such as Caesar's Head and Table Rock. It's also home to Bob Jones University, which has a gallery of religious art and antiquities.

The renowned international collection of religious art at **Bob Jones University Art Gallery and Museum** includes works by Boticelli, Rembrandt, Rubens, and Titian. ⊠ *Bob Jones University, 1700 Wade Hampton Blvd.,* ☎ *864/242–1050.* ⌑ *Free.* ☉ *Tues.–Sun. 2–5.*

Housed in an innovative modern building, the **Greenville County Museum of Art** displays American art dating from the colonial era. Exhibited are works by Paul Jenkins, Jamie Wyeth, Jasper Johns, and noted Southern artists. ⊠ *420 College St.,* ☎ *864/271–7570.* ⌑ *Free.* ☉ *Tues.–Sat. 10–5, Sun. 1–5.*

★ Modeled after a 14th-century Japanese mansion, the **Nippon Center** is a cultural center with a rock garden and exquisite Japanese furnishings. It has an authentic Japanese restaurant and tea ceremony. ⊠ *500 Congaree Rd.,* ☎ *864/288–8471.* ⌑ *Tours $3, tea ceremony $5.* ☉ *Mon.–Sat. 10–3 or by appointment; tea ceremony 3rd Wed. of the month.*

Dining and Lodging

$$$–$$$$ ✕ **Palms Restaurant.** This restaurant, probably Greenville's best, is in the Phoenix–Greenville's Inn (☞ *below*). The modest dining room serves up sophisticated dishes including galantine of duck, sesame-crusted mahimahi, and chocolate truffle cake with espresso sauce. The dark, cozy piano bar with a fireplace and wing chairs is a great place to wait for your made-to-order hot apple tart with cinnamon ice cream. ⊠ *246 N. Pleasantburg Dr.,* ☎ *864/233–4651. AE, D, DC, MC, V.*

$$–$$$ ✕ **Seven Oaks.** The seven oaks on the property gave this 1895 home its name. Now a restaurant, it has seven dining rooms with 14-ft curved ceilings, stained glass, and parquet floors. The dinner selections are as elegant as the decor: veal scallopini, mustard-crusted rack of lamb, and sweet-potato bread pudding. ⊠ *104 Broadus Ave.,* ☎ *864/232–1895. AE, D, MC, V. Closed Sun. No lunch.*

$–$$ ✕ **Stax Omega Diner.** A contemporary diner with booths and a half-circle counter with stools serves everything from bacon and eggs and burgers to souvlaki, Greek-style chicken, and shrimp and grits. It's all good, and it's open almost around-the-clock. ⊠ *72 Orchard Park Dr.,* ☎ *864/297–6639. AE, MC, V.*

$$$$ ✕▥ **La Bastide Inn & Restaurant.** About 19 mi northwest (30 minutes) from Greenville in the sloping Piedmont hills, this French provincial–style inn with surrounding vineyard re-creates the French countryside experience. A winery opens in fall 2001, and an entire petite village

with a 300-year-old chapel is planned for 2002. Rooms have European linens, French antiques and reproductions, elaborate chandeliers, wrought iron, gas fireplaces, and hillside views. Elegant French country meals and wine are available at the restaurant ($$$–$$$$). ⊠ *10 Road of Vines, Travelers Rest 29690,* ☎ *864/836–8463 or 877/836– 8463,* ⅎⅫ *864/836–4820. 12 rooms, 2 suites. Restaurant, croquet. AE, D, MC. BP.* ✎

$$–$$$ ✕⌂ **Phoenix–Greenville's Inn.** Plantation shutters and four-poster beds adorn this transformed and renovated property, the former Thunderbird Motel. You'll enjoy the residential feel and hospitality of a Southern inn; the service is excellent. Ask for a room overlooking the courtyard pool area. Palms Restaurant (☞ *above*) serves Continental cuisine. ⊠ *246 N. Pleasantburg Dr., 29607,* ☎ *800/257–3529,* ☎ ⅎⅫ *864/233–4651. 185 rooms. Restaurant, pool. AE, D, DC, MC, V.* ✎

$$$–$$$$ ⌂ **Hyatt Regency Hotel.** This standard chain offering's best feature is its central location in the midst of the small, revitalized downtown area of shops and restaurants. Rooms overlooking the atrium are a must. Airport shuttle service is complimentary. ⊠ *220 N. Main St., 29601,* ☎ *864/235–1234,* ⅎⅫ *864/232–7584. 327 rooms. Restaurant, lounge, pool, hot tub, health club. AE, D, DC, MC, V.* ✎

$$–$$$ ⌂ **Westin Poinsett Hotel.** After years of being closed, this historic 12-story hotel, dating to 1925, reopened in fall 2000. The large guest rooms have down comforters, marble baths, and high ceilings. All public spaces are back in their original opulence, including ornate plaster details and mosaic tilework. ⊠ *120 South Main St., 29601,* ☎ *864/421– 9700,* ⅎⅫ *864/421–9719. 181 rooms, 9 suites. Restaurant, coffee shop, lounge, health club, concierge. AE, D, DC, MC, V.*

Nightlife and the Arts

The **Peace Center for the Arts** (⊠ 101 W. Broad St., ☎ 864/467– 3030), which sits along the Reedy River, presents star performers, touring Broadway shows, dance companies, chamber music, and local groups.

Outdoor Activities and Sports

GOLF

South Carolinians sometimes prefer Upcountry courses to those on the coast, as they're less crowded and have the slightly cooler climate of the state's northwestern region. The area's rolling hills provide challenging courses. **Discover Upcountry Carolina** (☎ 800/949–6576 or 800/ 344–5590) has information on golf and other recreation in the area. Upcountry courses include **Links O'Tryon** (⊠ 11250 New Cut Rd., Campobello, ☎ 864/468–4995) and **Table Rock Golf Club** (⊠ 171 Sliding Rock Rd., Pickens, ☎ 864/878–2030).

ICE-SKATING

The **Greenville Pavilion Ice Rink** (☎ 864/322–7529) is a public indoor rink.

Spartanburg

31 mi east of Greenville.

Spartanburg once produced the state's largest peach crop. Lovely country drives in the area meander through peach orchards, which delight with fragrant, papery blossoms each spring and juicy treats at roadside stands each summer. While it's still part of the state's largest peach-producing area, today the town is better known as an international business center. So many foreign corporations have plants here that some local attractions provide brochures in German, French, and Spanish. In Spartanburg county, 20 German (including the new BMW plant), Swiss, or Austrian companies are visible from I–85. The town's early 20th-century downtown is slowly being revitalized with trendy shops and cafés. The NFL's Carolina Panthers train here each summer; their practice sessions at Wofford College (☎ 704/358–7000) are free and open to the public.

The **BMW Zentrum** plant, the company's only one in North America, exhibits BMW engineering in the auto, motorcycle, and aviation industries. On display is the Z3 James Bond drove in the film *Golden Eye,* classics from the past 80 years, and BMWs painted by artists including Warhol and Lichtenstein. The video about the making of the BMW Z3 roadster takes visitors down the factory line. ⊠ *Exit 60 off I–85 on SC 101S, Greer,* ☎ *888/868–7269.* ☞ *Free, factory tour $5.* ☉ *Tues.–Sat. 9:30–5:30; factory tours by appointment.*

More than 10,000 plants make **Hatcher Gardens** a refuge for birds and wildlife. It also has walking trails and ponds. ⊠ *Reidville Rd., Spartanburg,* ☎ *864/574–7724.* ☞ *Free.* ☉ *Daily dawn–dusk.*

Dining and Lodging

$$–$$$ ✕ **Abby's Grill.** A classy addition to downtown, it has a lounge and live jazz most evenings. High ceilings make the dining room open and airy. Try the calamari or pork chop with mashed potatoes. ⊠ *149 W. Main St.,* ☎ *864/583–4660. AE, DC, MC, V. Closed Sun.*

$$–$$$ ✕ **Harry's on Morgan.** An old-city atmosphere reigns at this elegantly restored barbershop and pool hall. The ambience is upscale but relaxed. Specialties include steaks and seafood. ⊠ *116 Magnolia St.,* ☎ *864/ 583–8121. AE, DC, MC, V. Closed Sun.*

$ ✕ **Beacon Drive-In.** This Spartanburg institution—and some of its staff—has been around for 50 years. They'll serve you curbside, but the action is inside at the counter. Locals come for the Beacon burgers (hamburgers with all the fixins'), onion rings, hot dogs, fried fish sandwiches, and sundaes. ⊠ *255 Reidville Rd.,* ☎ *864/585–9387. AE, DC, MC, V. Closed Sun.*

$$ ☷ **Hampton Inn.** You'll find comfort and simple style here. It's at the intersection of I–26 and I–85 Business. ⊠ *4930 College Dr., 29301,* ☎ *864/576–6080,* ☒ *864/587–8901. 112 rooms. Pool, business services, meeting room. AE, D, DC, MC, V. CP.*☺

$$ ☷ **Inn at Merridun.** This antebellum 1855 home in Union, about 27 mi from Spartanburg, has country style and cozy floral rooms. Rates include a complimentary full breakfast and evening dessert; picnic lunches and dinners are available. ⊠ *100 Merridun Pl., off U.S. 176, Union 29379,* ☎ *864/427–7052 or 888/892–6020,* ☒ *864/429–0373. 5 rooms. AE, MC, V. BP.*☺

$$ ☷ **Red Horse Inn.** Victorian-style cottages with porches and hand-painted murals are scattered on 190 acres about 25 mi from Greenville. Each cottage has a sitting area and fireplace; some have lofts and whirlpools. In the small kitchen you'll find a basket of breakfast items. ⊠ *4930 College Dr., Landrum 29301,* ☎ *864/895–4968,* ☒ *864/587– 8901. 9 cottages. AE, D, DC, MC, V. BP.*☺

Shopping

The more than 90 outlets at the **Prime Outlets of Gaffney** include the Gap, Nike, Levi's, and Donna Karan. The playground will keep older kids busy while you shop. Gaffney is about 20 minutes from Spartanburg via I–85N. ⊠ *I–85, Exit 90, Gaffney,* ☎ *864/902–9900 information center.*

Pendleton

25 mi southwest of Greenville.

Charming Pendleton, a few miles from Clemson University, has a historic district and interesting architecture. The Farmers Hall, built in 1826, was originally a courthouse. The Square, a district of restaurants and shops, faces the Village Green.

The **South Carolina State Botanical Garden,** on the Clemson University campus in nearby Clemson, holds more than 2,000 varieties of plants on more than 256 acres, including wildflower, fern, and bog gardens as well as nature trails. The **Fran Hanson Discovery Center,** which opened in 2000, has information on regional history and cultural heritage. ☎ *864/656–3405.* ▨ *Free.* ☉ *Daily dawn–dusk.*

Lodging

$$ ▨ **Liberty Hall Inn.** There's great food and lodging at this country inn in the heart of town. The inn, built in the 1840s, caters to business travelers and vacationers. Rooms are furnished with antiques and family heirlooms; a breakfast of waffles, breads, fruit, and yogurt is included. ✉ *621 S. Mechanic St., 29670,* ☎ *800/643–7944,* ☎ FAX *864/646–7500. 10 rooms. Restaurant. AE, D, DC, MC, V. BP.* ✜

Kings Mountain National Military and State Park

70 mi northeast of Greenville.

A Revolutionary War battle considered an important turning point was fought here on October 7, 1780. Colonial Tories commanded by British major Patrick Ferguson were soundly defeated by ragtag patriot forces from the southern Appalachians. Visitor center exhibits, dioramas, and an orientation film describe the action. A paved self-guided trail leads through the battlefield. ✉ *20 mi northeast of Gaffney, SC, off I–85 via a marked side road in NC,* ☎ *864/936–7921.* ▨ *Free.* ☉ *Labor Day–Memorial Day, daily 9–5; Memorial Day–Labor Day, daily 9–6.*

The 6,000-acre **Kings Mountain State Park** (☎ *864/222–3209*), adjacent to the national military park, has camping, swimming, fishing, boating, and nature and hiking trails.

Upcountry A to Z

Arriving and Departing

BY BUS

Greyhound (☎ 800/231–2222) serves all of South Carolina.

BY CAR

I–85 provides access to Greenville, Spartanburg, Pendleton, and Anderson. I–26 runs from Charleston through Columbia to the Upcountry, connecting with I–385 into Greenville.

BY PLANE

Greenville-Spartanburg Airport (✉ 2000 G.S.P. Dr., ☎ 864/867–7426), off I–85 between the two cities, is served by US Airways, Delta, Northwest, American Eagle, Continental, and Midway. For airline telephone numbers, *see* Air Travel *in* Smart Travel Tips A to Z.

BY TRAIN

Amtrak (☎ 800/872–7245) stops in Greenville.

Contacts and Resources

OUTDOOR ACTIVITIES AND SPORTS

The **Chattooga National Wild and Scenic River,** on the border of South Carolina and Georgia, is excellent for guided rafting, canoeing, and kayaking trips. Contact **Nantahala Outdoor Center** (☎ 864/647–9014 or 800/232–7238), **Southeastern Expeditions** (☎ 800/868–7238), or **Wildwater Ltd.** (☎ 864/647–9587 or 800/451–9972).

STATE PARKS

For information about state parks in the area, contact the **South Carolina Division of Tourism** (✉ 1205 Pendleton St., Columbia 29201, ☎ 843/734–0122 or 800/872–3505). **Devils Fork State Park** (✉ 161 Holcombe Circle, Salem 29676, ☎ 864/944–2639), on Lake Jocassee, has luxurious new villas and facilities.

VISITOR INFORMATION

Contact **Discover Upcountry Carolina Association** (✉ Box 3116, Greenville 29602, ☎ 864/233–2690 or 800/849–4766). The **Greater Greenville Convention and Visitors Bureau** (✉ 206 S. Main St., Box 10527, 29603, ☎ 864/421–0000 or 800/717–0023) can provide information on accommodations, restaurants, and attractions in the Greenville area specifically.

SOUTH CAROLINA A TO Z

Arriving and Departing

By Boat

Boaters can reach most of South Carolina's coastal cities and towns by the Intracoastal Waterway.

By Bus

Greyhound (☎ 800/231–2222) serves all of South Carolina.

By Car

I–26 traverses the state from northwest to southeast and terminates at Charleston. I–77 leads into Columbia from the north. I–26, I–20, and U.S. 1 intersect at Columbia. I–85 provides access to Greenville, Spartanburg, Pendleton, and Anderson. U.S. 17, a north–south coastal route, runs along the coastal edge of the entire state.

By Plane

Major airports are **Charleston International Airport** (✉ 5500 International Blvd., ☎ 843/767–1100); **Columbia Metro Airport** (✉ 3000 Aviation Way, ☎ 803/822–5000); **Greenville-Spartanburg Airport** (✉ 2000 G.S.P. Dr., ☎ 864/867–7426); **Hilton Head Island Airport** (☎ 843/681–6386), served by US Airways Express; **Myrtle Beach International Airport** (✉ 1100 Jetport Rd., ☎ 843/448–1589); and **Savannah International Airport** (✉ 400 Airways Ave., ☎ 912/964–0514), about an hour's drive from Hilton Head.

By Train

Amtrak (☎ 800/872–7245) stops in Charleston, Camden, Columbia, Denmark, Dillon, Florence, Greenville, Kingstree, and Yemassee (near Beaufort).

Getting Around

By Bus

Greyhound (☎ 800/231–2222) links several cities and towns throughout South Carolina.

By Car

The speed limit on interstates is 65 mph. You can turn right at a red light unless otherwise noted by street signs.

Contacts and Resources

B&Bs

For reservation agencies in **Charleston,** *see* Contacts and Resources *in* Charleston A to Z, *above.* Write to the **South Carolina Bed and Breakfast Association** (⊠ Box 1275, Sumter 29150-1275, ☎ 888/599–1234) for a current state directory of member B&Bs. For a complete list of B&Bs, write to the **South Carolina Division of Tourism** (⊠ 1205 Pendleton St., Columbia 29201, ☎ 803/734–0122 or 800/872–3505) and ask for the pamphlet *Bed & Breakfasts of South Carolina.*

Emergencies

Ambulance, fire, police (☎ 911).

Guided Tours

Lowcountry Adventures (☎ 843/681–8212) offers tours of Hilton Head, Beaufort, and Charleston. For information about other specific tours, contact the **South Carolina Division of Tourism** (☞ Visitor Information, *below*).

National and State Parks

For information about South Carolina's national park areas, contact the **U.S. Forest Service** (⊠ 4931 Broad River Rd., Columbia 29210, ☎ 803/561–4000). Several of South Carolina's 48 state parks operate like resort communities, with everything from deluxe accommodations to golf. For information, contact the **South Carolina Division of Tourism** (☞ Visitor Information, *below*).

Visitor Information

South Carolina Division of Tourism (⊠ 1205 Pendleton St., Columbia 29201, ☎ 803/734–0122 or 800/872–3505) has information about the entire state.

Welcome centers: ⊠ U.S. 17, near Little River; I–95, near Dillon, Santee and Lake Marion, and Hardeeville; I–77, near Fort Mill; I–85, near Blacksburg and Fair Play; I–26, near Landrum; I–20, at North Augusta; and U.S. 301, near Allendale.

8 TENNESSEE

Tennessee's dominating characteristics are its music—the blues developed in Memphis; rock and roll was born and came into popularity with the rise of Elvis Presley; country music claims Nashville as its capital—and its scenic geographical borders, the Great Smoky Mountains on the east and the Mississippi River on the west. Here, too, are forests, fields, and streams for the nature lover, outlet malls for the die-hard shopper, and an array of entertainment for the whole family.

M OUNTAINS AND MUSIC—these gifts Tennessee was given in abundance and shares generously with millions of guests each year.

Updated by
Katherine Price

Memphis, home of the blues, rises out of the flat, cotton-kissed south-west corner of the state, on the banks of the Mississippi River. Beale Street, in the core of its downtown, nurtured some of the finest talents of the genre, from blues artists W. C. Handy and B. B. King to rock-ers Elvis Presley and Jerry Lee Lewis. Today, with live music in Handy Park, Beale Street again reverberates with the moody sounds that made it legendary.

Nashville, now Tennessee's largest city, retains its title as the country-music capital of the world. Music City, USA, as it is known, is also the state's capital. Here, in the heart of Tennessee's green, gently rolling hills, country music is king. The recording studios on Music Row are thriving, and the Grand Ole Opry continues to pack its auditorium. The long-running radio-show extravaganza has launched many a singer's and picker's career and is still a major attraction for Nashville visitors.

As for mountains, they don't come any more beautiful than the Great Smokies—site of the nation's most visited national park and part of the Appalachian chain; they're in East Tennessee and are shared with North Carolina. Covered with a dense carpet of wildflowers in spring and ablaze with foliage in autumn, the Smokies—named for the man-tle of blue haze that so often blankets them—are a joy to hike or drive through. Spend some time in the little mountain towns and villages dot-ting the hollows to experience homegrown bluegrass music and tra-ditional cooking, along with the natural warmth of the people.

Pleasures and Pastimes

Dining

If you expect Tennessee dining to be all corn bread, turnip greens, and grits, you're in for a staggering surprise. Two decades ago Memphis had little more than various neighborhood "home cooking" restaurants, several chop-suey houses, a handful of spaghetti-and-lasagna spots, and numerous establishments serving pork barbecue. Today, in addition to a number of restaurants offering imaginative American cuisine, Mem-phis claims many competent international dining rooms. As in other cities around the country, hotel dining has improved greatly.

Memphis's top culinary attraction, however, remains barbecue, and a visit to one of the 70-odd barbecue restaurants is a must. Memphians debate which is better: wet or dry ribs—a reference to the cooking style, not how moist the meat is. True fanciers should schedule their visit around the World Championship Barbecue Cooking Contest, held during the annual Memphis in May International Festival. This cook-off draws more than 400 teams from around the world for its three-day run.

Nashville dining patrons are often casual in dress and prone to linger over meals. The city's mix of politics, country music, conventions, sports, and business means deal making at every meal, lending prosperity and longevity to some of its best restaurants. Such tenure translates into quality dining. Nashville's restaurant scene has come a long way in 10 years, with an influx of different ethnic groups as well as transplants from both coasts. Nowadays it is a healthy mix of contemporary, eth-nic, and experimental eateries, as well as classic Southern favorites.

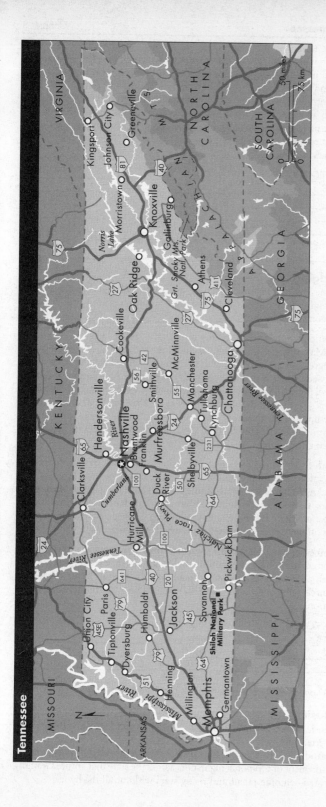

Tennessee

East Tennessee mountain cooks have long been noted for preparing fresh ingredients many different ways. Corn remains the old standby, used in the making of grits, luscious muffins, corn bread, and savory spoon bread. Barbecued ribs, thick pork chops, and generous slices of country ham with red-eye gravy rank as local favorites. Freshwater fish, such as varieties of trout, walleye, crappie, muskie, and catfish, will also be found in varied and delicious preparations (but remember to save room for home-baked pies and cobblers). Dress is casual unless otherwise noted.

CATEGORY	COST*
$$$$	over $50
$$$	$40–$50
$$	$20–$40
$	under $20

*per person for a three-course meal, excluding drinks, service, and 7%–8¾% tax

Lodging

Some restored historic hotels in larger cities offer lodging in settings reminiscent of earlier times. The major resort areas of Gatlinburg and Pigeon Forge have abundant choices.

Memphis hotels are especially busy in the spring, when the Memphis in May International Festival and June's Carnival Memphis are in progress; in mid-August, when pilgrims observe Elvis Presley's death; between Christmas and New Year's during the Axa/Equitable Liberty Bowl Football Classic; and in early January, when the faithful celebrate Elvis's birth. Another busy time is early November, when the city of Memphis hosts the Holy Convocation of God in Christ, a huge convention that virtually fills the city. Be sure to reserve well in advance during those times.

With more than 125 hotels and motels, Nashville has an impressive selection of accommodations in all price categories and levels of luxury. Although some establishments increase rates slightly during the peak summer travel season, especially Fan Fair week in mid-June, most maintain the same rates year-round. Some downtown luxury hotels offer lower rates on weekends, when the legislators have gone home.

Tennessee has 19 state parks with overnight accommodations ranging from rustic cabins to beautiful chalets. Prices vary from park to park, with a low of $45 a night for a cabin and a high of $140 a night for a three-bedroom chalet. Call 888/867–2757 for information and reservations.

CATEGORY	COST*
$$$$	over $160
$$$	$110–$160
$$	$70–$110
$	under $70

*All prices are for a standard double room, excluding 10%–11¾% tax.

Music

Music is everywhere in Tennessee. The blues and rock flood Beale Street in Memphis, while country is king on Nashville's Music Row, at the Grand Ole Opry, and in the District. Then there's Dollywood and an assortment of top-notch nightspots across the state that ensure Grammy Award–winning talent and rising stars without all the hype.

Outdoor Activities and Sports

Tennesseans take advantage of the state's generally mild climate and spend a lot of time outdoors. Many fish, hike, or swim at the abundant state parks that dot the landscape. Others prefer to enjoy a picnic or cool off under waterfalls or in caves. And Tennesseans like to cheer for their favorite teams. The NFL's Tennessee Titans (previously the Tennessee Oilers) moved into their new stadium on the banks of the Cumberland River in Nashville in 1999. The National Hockey League also has a Nashville franchise, the Nashville Predators, who play in the Gaylord Entertainment Center (formerly Nashville Arena). Both Memphis and Nashville have AAA baseball teams. Professional sports were slow to reach Tennessee, but fans have been demonstrating their love of football for decades, filling the University of Tennessee's Neyland Stadium in Knoxville to overflowing.

✎ *following the text of a review is your signal that the property has a Web site, where you will find details and, usually, images; for a link, visit www.fodors.com/urls.*

Exploring Tennessee

Tennessee spans more than 500 mi west to east but only about 115 mi north to south. Geographically, the state can be divided into West Tennessee, from the Mississippi River to the Tennessee River near Camden; Middle Tennessee, from the Tennessee River to the Cumberland Plateau at Crossville; and East Tennessee, to the Great Smoky Mountains and the border with North Carolina. All three sections are anchored by major cities with a wealth of cultural and historical attractions and first-rate lodging establishments.

Great Itineraries

Exploring Tennessee will require some time on the road. Fortunately, hopping on and off I–40, which crosses the state from east to west, will get you most places you want to go, whether west, middle, or east. Plan to spend at least two days to see the high points of any of Tennessee's major cities: Memphis, Nashville, Knoxville, or Chattanooga. Much of what's interesting about Tennessee is outside the major cities, however, so if you get to Memphis, for instance, allow some time for side trips.

IF YOU HAVE 3 DAYS

Explore ⊡ **Memphis,** home to Elvis Presley's Graceland. Be sure to see the morning or afternoon march of ducks to or from Peabody Hotel's lobby fountain. Listen to the blues on Beale Street and don't miss the barbecue. Study the history of the great Mississippi River at Mud Island and the history of music at the Memphis Music Hall of Fame. Take a day to make a side trip from Memphis, perhaps to the Casey Jones Museum in **Jackson,** to the northeast, or east to **Shiloh National Military Park** if you're a Civil War buff. Either of these could easily be visited on the way from Memphis to Nashville.

IF YOU HAVE 6 DAYS

After a few days in ⊡ **Memphis,** visit ⊡ **Nashville** and its surrounding area. Take in some country music at the Grand Ole Opry, or view the works of Georgia O'Keeffe, Picasso, and Renoir at Fisk University's Van Vechten Art Gallery. Combine Nashville's Music Row and the District and fill a day seeing the sights and museums such as the Country Music Hall of Fame, and do some shopping. At night, hear some live music, watch the stars come out at restaurants downtown, or take in a Broadway show at the Tennessee Performing Arts Center. Make time to venture to historic **Franklin** or to **Lynchburg** to see the home of Jack Daniel's sippin' whiskey. Try to work in a brief visit to 🏨 **Chattanooga,** a spruced-up, midsize city on the move.

IF YOU HAVE 9 DAYS

Start at one end of the state and head for the other, hitting the highlights. There's a lot to see and do after 🏨 **Memphis** and 🏨 **Nashville.** 🏨 **Chattanooga** has emerged as a fine family destination with its first-rate aquarium, IMAX theater, and fun museums, coupled with Civil War sites. Devote at least one full day here. Northeast of Chattanooga, **Great Smoky Mountains National Park** is spectacular; either its gateway, 🏨 **Gatlinburg,** or nearby 🏨 **Pigeon Forge,** a shopping and entertainment mecca with outlet malls, Dollywood, and theaters, is good for overnighting. Combine the three, trying a day of hiking and nature watching and then a day of shopping, sightseeing, and entertainment.

When to Tour Tennessee

Although spring and fall seem to be the most popular times to tour Tennessee, there is something going on all year. The Smokies and East Tennessee are especially beautiful but crowded during the fall color change. University of Tennessee home football games in Knoxville draw crowds exceeding 100,000, meaning road congestion. Temperatures stay mild until late June, when humidity begins to pick up. Late July and August heat can make outdoor activities trying.

May brings the W. C. Handy Awards and Blues Symposium to Memphis, when the blues are celebrated with musical performances and other activities centered on Beale Street. The highlight is the W. C. Handy Blues Awards, attended by luminaries of the music world. However, the blues emanate from Handy Park most weekends throughout the year. Many people plan their visit to coincide with the monthlong Memphis in May International Festival.

Christmas is a busy time, too, with Winterfest in Pigeon Forge, Gatlinburg, and Sevierville, and with the array of Christmas activities at the Opryland Hotel in Nashville.

MEMPHIS

Memphis was founded in 1819, but long before that, the Mississippi River, on whose banks it was built, exerted a powerful influence on the area. Both the river and the people who first appreciated it are celebrated in Memphis today. The Native American river culture that existed here from the 11th through the 15th centuries is documented in archaeological excavations, reconstructions, and exhibits at the Chucalissa Archaeological Museum. The river itself is celebrated with a museum dedicated to its history—part of Mud Island, a unique park occupying an island in the river.

The other significant influence on the city has been the music that has flowed through it. W. C. Handy moved from Alabama to Memphis in 1902–03, drawn by the long-thriving music scene, and it was here that he produced most of the blues songs that made him famous. The recent history of legendary Beale Street reflects that of all modern Memphis. Economic decline in the mid-20th century brought the city to its knees, and the unrest following the assassination in 1968 of Dr. Martin Luther King Jr. at the Lorraine Motel, just south of Beale, dealt a near-fatal blow. Today, thanks to public improvements and an economy built around such distribution giants as Federal Express, Memphis has been brought back to life, and Beale Street has numerous clubs and restaurants, as it did in its heyday.

When you mention Memphis, one name springs to most minds: Elvis, the undisputed king of rock and roll. Although he was actually born across the state line in Tupelo, Mississippi, Elvis put Memphis on the map, recording his first hits here in what came to be known as Sun Studio. His legacy burns bright at Graceland, the estate where he lived, died, and rests in peace. Each year hundreds of thousands of fans make the pilgrimage to pay homage to the man and his music. Elvis International Tribute Week, held each August at Graceland, has grown to match the myth.

Downtown Memphis

Numbers in the text correspond to numbers in the margin and on the Downtown Memphis map.

Old and new mingle as Memphis progresses with its riverfront development and urban renewal. Peabody Place, a collection of offices, shops, restaurants, and apartments, is a new development in the area surrounding the Peabody Hotel at 2nd Street and Union Avenue. For travelers who want to tour the area without parking worries, the downtown trolley system runs a north–south route down Main Street, connecting major attractions. A new loop adjacent to Riverside Drive completes the 5-mi circle.

A Good Walk and Drive

Pick up a map of the city at the **Tennessee Welcome Center** ① on Riverside Drive, where free parking is available. Take the Main Street trolley south to South Main Street to **Peabody Place** ③ to visit the **Center for Southern Folklore** ②, where the region's colorful past is chronicled in poignant exhibits. Continue south on foot to Beale Street and sneak a peak at the stately **Orpheum Theatre** ④; walk east to **A. Schwab Dry Goods Store** ⑤, a most unusual emporium. A few blocks east on Beale is **Handy Park** ⑥, where the father of the blues is immortalized. You can learn all about him at the nearby **W. C. Handy Memphis Home and Museum** ⑦. Walk farther east on Beale to the **Hunt-Phelan Home** ⑧ for a tour. Head for the south end of downtown (take the Main Street trolley five blocks) to tour the **National Civil Rights Museum** ⑨, on the site where Dr. Martin Luther King Jr. was assassinated in 1968, or north to the **Memphis Music Hall of Fame Museum** ⑩.

Take the Main Street trolley north to Adams Avenue and walk west to the **Mud Island** ⑪ Monorail to catch a ride over to the Mississippi River Park and Museum. When you come back, the **Pyramid** ⑫ is several blocks away from Mud Island parking and can be visited by trolley. Afterwards, pick up your car and drive east on Adams, first to the **Fire Museum of Memphis** ⑬, then on to the Victorian Village Historic District for tours of the **Magevney** ⑭, **Mallory Neely** ⑮, and **Woodruff-Fontaine** ⑯ houses. On the way out of downtown, stop at **Sun Studio** ⑰ for a dose of Memphis music history.

TIMING

Spend the morning in the Beale Street Historic District—the Hunt-Phelan Tour alone will take an hour—and work in lunch while you're there. The rest of downtown Memphis will take more than a day to cover, so depending on your schedule, you may want to pick and choose. Most of these attractions are closed Monday; the National Civil Rights Museum is closed Tuesday.

Sights to See

❺ **A. Schwab Dry Goods Store.** Step into the past at this highly eccentric shop where unusual odds and ends like voodoo potions stock the shelves, along with souvenirs, candy, and clothes. It's served many a

458

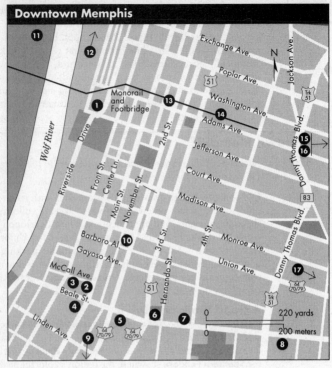

customer, including Elvis, since it was founded in 1876. ⊠ *163 Beale St.,* ☎ *901/523–9782.* ☉ *Mon.–Sat. 9–6.*

★ ❷ **Center for Southern Folklore.** These must-see exhibits on the people, music, food, crafts, and traditions of the South, particularly of the Mississippi Delta region, pay tribute to one of America's most flavorful cultural identities. Perhaps more than any other Memphis institution, the center has its finger on the pulse of local culture, and a visit here is both edifying and entertaining. After a recent move from Beale Street to its new home in nearby Peabody Place, the center's expanded facility includes more exhibit space; a restaurant with Southern food such as barbecue, greens, and cornbread; a bar and performance area; and videos about Memphis and Beale Street. Concerts daily at noon (free) and on weekend evenings ($5) feature blues, gospel, jazz, rockabilly, and folk music. Each year the center sponsors one of Memphis's finest music festivals, the three-day **Memphis Music Heritage Festival,** held Labor Day weekend. Tours of local interest are available (by reservation only). The gift shop carries regional folk art and handiwork, plus cassettes, videos, and books pertaining to the South. ⊠ *119 S. Main St.,* ☎ *901/525–3655.* ▣ *Free.* ☉ *Mon.–Wed. 11–7, Thurs.–Sat. 11–11, Sun. 11–7.*

☙ ❸ **Fire Museum of Memphis.** In Fire Engine House No. 1, a restored 1910 building, curiosity seekers of all ages can learn about the history of firefighting from the 19th-century bucket brigades to the present in an educational environment designed to increase fire safety awareness. An interactive center comes equipped with video games that teach safety tips and a fire truck that can be climbed. In the Fire Room, the *Fire*

Show uses visual and sound effects to simulate an actual fire. ⊠ *118 Adams Ave.,* ☎ *901/452–9973.* 🎟 *$5.* ⊘ *Tues.–Sat. 9–5, Sun. 1–5.*

⑥ Handy Park. The park holds a statue of W. C. Handy clutching his famed trumpet. In the core of the Beale Street Historic District, Handy Park is a prime venue for outdoor entertainment, including festivals and impromptu jam sessions. ⊠ *Between 3rd and 4th Sts.*

⑧ Hunt-Phelan Home. Costumed docents seem to transport guests to Memphis in the mid-1800s during tours of this restored antebellum home originally designed by Robert Mills. Ulysses S. Grant began the initial plans for the Battle of Vicksburg in the library, which contains an impressive collection of first-edition books. A rare 1874 rosewood piano from Steinway and Sons is another house treasure. ⊠ *533 Beale St.,* ☎ *901/344–3166 or 800/350–9009.* 🎟 *$10.* ⊘ *Mon. and Thurs.– Sat. 10–4, Sun. noon–4. Closed Tues.–Wed.*

⑭ Magevney House. This charming white-clapboard cottage, built in the 1830s, is one of Memphis's oldest dwellings. It's furnished with some of the original possessions of Eugene Magevney, a pioneer schoolteacher and ardent Catholic. The city's first Catholic church service was held in this house, and Magevney later helped build the church next door. ⊠ *198 Adams Ave.,* ☎ *901/526–4464.* 🎟 *Free.* ⊘ *Tues.–Fri. 10–2, Sat. 10–4.*

⑮ Mallory Neely House. Original family furnishings fill this 25-room Italianate Victorian. Note the hand-carved cornices and frescoed ceilings on the first floor, and the stained-glass panels in double front doors. ⊠ *652 Adams Ave.,* ☎ *901/523–1484.* 🎟 *$5.* ⊘ *Mar.–Dec., Tues.– Sat. 10–4, Sun. 1–4, last tour at 3:30.*

★ **⑩ Memphis Music Hall of Fame Museum.** For music buffs and pilgrims, this unassuming exhibit space in the shadow of the Peabody Hotel is not to be missed. Exhibits of rare photographs, film footage, audiotapes, and assorted memorabilia trace the birth and development of blues, country, and rock and roll—particularly Memphis's role in it all. Biographies of Memphis music legends such as W. C. Handy, Elvis Presley, and Charlie Rich are brought to life with original instruments and personal effects. On view are re-creations of the Sun Record Company's control room and Beale's P. Wee Saloon. Large memorabilia collections evoke the spirit of the famed STAX and HI record labels. ⊠ *97 S. 2nd St.,* ☎ *901/525–4007.* 🎟 *$7.50.* ⊘ *Mon.–Thurs. 10–6, Fri.–Sat. 10– 9, Sun. noon–6.*

☙ **⑪ Mud Island.** Accessible by monorail or pedestrian walkway, this 52-acre park on an island explores Memphis's intimate relationship with the Mississippi. At the **Mississippi River Museum,** galleries bring the history of the Mississippi to life with exhibits ranging from scale-model boats to life-size, animated river characters (Mark Twain spins his tales anew here) and the Theater of River Disasters. The most extraordinary exhibit is outside: **River Walk,** a five-block-long scale model of the Mississippi, which replicates its every twist, turn, and sandbar from Cairo, Illinois, to New Orleans, ending in a huge swimming pool bordered by a man-made, sandy beach. Also here are shops, restaurants serving regional foods, and a 5,400-seat amphitheater. The famed World War II B-17 bomber *Memphis Belle,* the first plane of its kind to complete 25 missions without casualties, is housed in an open pavilion topped by a gleaming white dome. Plans to move the plane off Mud Island have been discussed, so call ahead if it's of particular interest to you. ⊠ *125 Front St. (footbridge and monorail),* ☎ *901/ 576–6595 or 800/507–6507.* 🎟 *$8 for all attractions.* ⊘ *May–early Sept., daily 10–8; shorter hrs in Apr. and Oct.*

9 **National Civil Rights Museum.** The Lorraine Motel, where Dr. Martin Luther King Jr. was assassinated on April 4, 1968, has been transformed into a museum that documents the struggle of African-Americans and the civil rights movement. A Montgomery, Alabama, bus, like the one in which Rosa Parks refused to give up her seat, sparking an uprising against segregation; scenes of lunch-counter sit-ins; and audiovisual displays are among the exhibits. ⊠ *450 Mulberry St.,* ☎ *901/521–9699.* ⊑ *$6; free Mon. 3–5.* ☉ *Wed.–Mon. 9–5.*

4 **Orpheum Theatre.** This former vaudeville palace and movie theater, opened in 1928, has been refurbished as a center for the performing arts. Step inside to admire its crystal chandeliers, gilt decorations, and ornate tapestries. The theater hosts touring Broadway shows as well as performances by Opera Memphis and Ballet Memphis. At the Friday-night film series, moviegoers sink into the red-velvet seats to aim their gaze either on classics of the silver screen or on silent serial films accompanied by a pianist. ⊠ *203 S. Main St.,* ☎ *901/525–3000, 901/ 678–2706, or 901/737–7322.*

3 **Peabody Place.** This retail and entertainment center is the latest manifestation of downtown's ongoing revitalization. The complex between Front and Main streets near Beale includes apartments, shops, banks, bars, restaurants, entertainment venues, galleries, a 21-screen movie complex, an IMAX theater, and more. The Center for Southern Folklore (☞ *above*) makes its home here, as does the **Peabody Place Museum & Gallery** (☎ 901/523–2787; ⊑ $5; ☉ Tues.–Fri. 10–5:30, weekends noon–5), which has Chinese art from the Manchu dynasty. Gallery visitors enter through a round moon gate, and displays include 6-ft-tall cloisonné foo dogs, which stood watch over the Forbidden City. **Jillian's** features a sports-video café, seven bars, 12 billiard tables, private party and banquet rooms, a bowling alley, a dance club, and more than 200 electronic simulation games. ⊠ *119 Main St.,* ☎ *901/821– 7500.* ☉ *Hrs vary.*

12 **Pyramid Arena.** One of Memphis's downtown landmarks, the Pyramid, a gleaming, stainless-steel structure and the third-largest pyramid in the world, is at Front and Auction, six blocks north of Adams Avenue. This 32-story, 22,000-seat arena, covering the equivalent of six football fields, opened in 1991 and is home to the University of Memphis Tigers basketball team and a venue for concerts and other events. Guided tours are available. The **WONDERS: Memphis International Cultural Series** brings blockbuster art exhibitions to the Pyramid for five months out of the year; past exhibits explored the legacies of the *Titanic,* Catherine the Great, and Napoléon (☎ 901/576–1231 for details). ⊠ *1 Auction St., at Front St.,* ☎ *901/521–9675.* ⊑ *$4 for tour.* ☉ *Tours daily at noon, 1, and 2 but subject to change because of event schedules.*

Slavehaven/Burkle Estate Museum. This pre–Civil War era house was a stop on the Underground Railroad. A German immigrant built the modest middle-class home in 1849, when Memphis was a slave trade center. Displays of ads, auctions, and artifacts depict the history of slavery, while secret cellars and trapdoors reveal the escape route of runaway slaves; the dank basement sheltered the frightened runaways for weeks at a time. Heritage Tours operates the museum and provides guided tours by appointment. ⊠ *826 N. 2nd St.,* ☎ *901/527–3427.* ⊑ *$5.* ☉ *Tours by appointment only.*

17 **Sun Studio.** Sun Studio is still housed in the original, albeit modest, building into which Elvis himself wandered one day and recorded two songs—one in honor of his beloved mother—for producer Sam Phillips.

IF BEALE STREET COULD TALK. . .

HAILED AS THE BIRTHPLACE of the blues, the Delta's most famous street rises from the bluffs of Ole Man River and meanders for miles into Memphis's flat downtown. Among its brightly lighted bar fronts and barren lots lies a history of race and music, prosperity and decline, and, ultimately, renewal. Today's Beale is a chaotic, sometimes seamy mix of tourism and authenticity; a place where Old Beale's notorious bawdiness and prosperity have been reinvented in restored facades.

In the 1840s Beale Street was a thriving suburb, home to scores of Irish and Italian immigrants and at least 300 free African-Americans. Beale's Hunt-Phelan home is a relic of this early affluence. During the Civil War Ulysses S. Grant came to town and, with his keen eye for Southern properties, chose the Hunt-Phelan as his headquarters and mapped out his Vicksburg campaign from Beale.

Bloodshed and disease marred the street during Reconstruction. When an African-American boy was accused of killing an Irish boy, mob riots and fires ravaged the street for days. In the 1870s the entire city was besieged—and eventually bankrupted—by cholera and yellow fever epidemics; African-Americans, with a higher degree of immunity to these diseases, were able to remain in the Beale area and helped rebuild the community.

Soon Beale became "Main Street" for southern African-American life, with dentists, clothiers, dry goods and grocery stores, saloons, furniture stores, restaurants, loan offices, newspaper offices, photography studios, pawn shops, and tailors. The South's first black millionaire, Robert Church, known as the "Boss of Beale Street," owned land, stores, several saloons, and more. In 1905 he founded Memphis's first African-American bank, the Solvent Savings Bank and Trust, at 392 Beale.

Next door, at 391 Beale, he built a 6-acre park and concert hall, where peacocks roamed and children played among the planted trees; "Church's Park" became a social center.

Onto this street at the turn of the century stepped the young W. C. Handy, credited with writing the first blues song here, in 1909: "The Memphis Blues." Beale was a natural destination, home, during the Civil War era, to the Young Man's Brass Band, the first all-black musical group. During Reconstruction several bands rose to prominence here, playing violins and banjos, without written scores, in the honkytonks and juke joints. The Handy era was the street's heyday, when many distinguished musicians got their start, such as Muddy Waters, Furry Lewis, Albert King, Alberta Hunter, Bobby "Blue" Bland, Memphis Minnie McCoy, and Riley "Blues Boy" King, who became known as B. B. King.

After the Depression took its toll, the bustling neighborhood fell into decline, and in the late 1960s a ghostly version of Beale was named to the National Register of Historic Places. In the 1980s community and government revitalization efforts breathed life into the deserted blocks, and soon clubs, theaters, shops, and restaurants returned to the area, leading to today's somewhat self-conscious entertainment district and tourist playground.

Despite the tourism, Beale remains an excellent place to pay respects, catch a show, people-watch, and chow down. Venues like the New Daisy Theatre and B. B. King's Blues Club and festivals such as the Memphis Music Heritage Festival and Handy Awards Music Festival keep the history alive and continue to give Beale Street something worth talking about.

–Katherine Price

Pictures of Elvis and other well-loved musicians, from B. B. King to Jerry Lee Lewis to Roy Orbison, adorn the walls, and their hits play in the background during tours. At night, recording sessions crank up once again, with artists hoping to make it as big as their predecessors did. Upstairs there's a small gift shop with well-chosen paraphernalia (guitar picks, drinking glasses) and a hall-of-fame gallery. ⊠ 706 Union Ave., ☎ 901/521–0664. ☛ $8.50. ☉ Daily 10–6, tours every hr on the ½ hr, last tour at 5:30.

NEED A BREAK?
At the **Sun Studio Cafe** (⊠ 706 Union Ave., ☎ 901/521–0664), part of the Sun Studio building, eat like a king (of rock and roll, that is) or just look at the memorabilia. It was called Taylor's when Elvis ate here, and in his honor, the menu includes some of his favorite snacks, such as a fried peanut butter and banana sandwich. Burgers are around $5.

❶ **Tennessee Welcome Center and Memphis Visitors Center.** The center (☞ Memphis A to Z, *below*) is a good place to stock up on free maps, brochures, and other literature about Memphis and the Beale Street Historic District. ⊠ 119 N. Riverside Dr., ☎ 901/543–5333.

Victorian Village Historic District. This downtown Memphis district comprises some 25 blocks on Adams between Front and Manassas. Here, 18 houses ranging from neoclassical to Gothic Revival in style have been restored to their appearance in the days when cotton was king. Most are privately owned, but the ☞ **Magevney House,** the ☞ **Mallory Neely House,** and the ☞ **Woodruff-Fontaine House** are open to the public.

❼ **W. C. Handy Memphis Home and Museum.** Handy, who wrote some of his most famous blues pieces in this small wood-frame house, is recalled here through photographs, sheet music, and memorabilia. Visitors are treated to an inside look at the humble beginnings of the "Father of the Blues," who lived in this basic two-room house with his wife and six children. ⊠ 352 Beale St., ☎ 901/522–1556. ☛ $2. ☉ Apr.–Sept., Mon.–Sat. 10–5, Sun. 1–6; Oct.–Mar., Tues.–Sat. 11–4.

⓰ **Woodruff-Fontaine House.** This exquisite three-story French Victorian mansion was built in 1870 and has a grand drawing room graced with original parquet floors and large mirrors. Antique furnishings include Aubusson carpets, marble mantels, and a Venetian crystal chandelier. The formal garden still has its gingerbread playhouse, now the museum shop. ⊠ 680 Adams Ave., ☎ 901/526–1469. ☛ $5. ☉ Mon. and Wed.–Sat. 10–4, Sun. 1–4. Closed Tues.

Greater Memphis

Numbers in the text correspond to numbers in the margin and on the Greater Memphis map.

Graceland is the reason many visitors come to Memphis, but there are plenty of museums in the sprawling area outside downtown that range in appeal from the simply visual to the historical.

A Good Drive

The **National Ornamental Metal Museum** ⑱ is tricky to find (many a visitor has taken an unplanned detour to the first I–55 exit in Arkansas), but worth it. Loop south to **Chucalissa Archaeological Museum** ⑲, where the Native American culture of the mid-South is preserved. Continue east to **Graceland** ⑳, the must-see stop. After Elvis's Jungle Room, you can relax at **Dixon Gallery and Gardens** ㉑ in East Memphis on Park Avenue. Take Park Avenue west to Goodlett Street, then proceed north to Central Avenue. Turn left (west) on Central, and you'll be headed

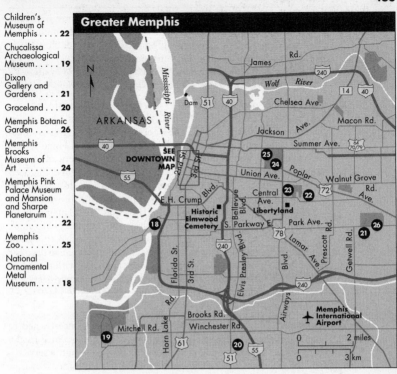

toward the imposing **Memphis Pink Palace Museum and Mansion and Sharpe Planetarium** ㉒. If you have kids in tow, head several blocks west on Central to the **Children's Museum of Memphis** ㉓. From there, continue west on Central to Airways Boulevard, turn right (north), then left (west) onto Poplar Avenue, where Overton Park is home to the **Memphis Brooks Museum of Art** ㉔ and to **Memphis Zoo** ㉕. Continue east down Poplar to Goodlett, take a right, then a left on Southern, and another right on Cherry, to visit the **Memphis Botanic Garden** ㉖.

TIMING

It would take several days to explore everything on the driving tour. Better to narrow down the choices according to your interests. Graceland is usually packed, and you'll probably have to wait in line for any of the tours. It's least crowded early in the morning, so try to arrive as it opens. Allot about an hour and a half for the house tour and at least two more hours for the rest of the Graceland attractions.

Sights to See

㉒ **Children's Museum of Memphis.** At Memphis's only children's museum, youngsters can touch, climb, and explore their way through a child-size city, including a food mart, recycling center, skyscraper, "time square," and house. An airplane displayed out front makes a favorite exploring ground. Seasonal events, such as an October pumpkin patch, weekend celebrations such as themed scavenger hunt parties, and interactive exhibits—about tools, castles, nature, and other topics—provide further fun and education. ✉ *2525 Central Ave.,* ☎ *901/458–2678.* ⌨ *$5.* ☉ *Tues.–Sat. 9–5, Sun. noon–5.*

㉙ **Chucalissa Archaeological Museum.** At the thought-provoking Chucalissa Archaeological Museum, about 10 mi southwest of downtown, a river culture that existed from AD 1000 to 1500 is immortalized. The 4-acre reconstruction is operated by the University of Memphis, and on-site archaeological excavations are often conducted in summer. In the museum, prehistoric tools, pottery, and weapons and a free 15-minute slide presentation describing Chucalissa life and culture provide clues to that world. Outside, skilled Choctaw craftspeople sell jewelry, weapons, and pottery. An annual August powwow is a highlight. ⊠ *1987 Indian Village Dr.,* ☎ *901/785–3160.* ☑ *$5.* ☉ *Tues.–Sat. 9–5, Sun. 1–4:40.*

㉑ Dixon Gallery and Gardens. Its 17 acres of formal and informal gardens and woodlands make Dixon Gallery and Gardens a bucolic enclave near the heart of the city. The Georgian-style estate and its superb art collections once belonged to the late Margaret and Hugo Dixon, philanthropists and cultural leaders. French and American Impressionist paintings, British portraiture and landscapes, and the Stout Collection of 18th-century German porcelain are on display. In special exhibitions impressionism reigns supreme, with previous highlights having included works by Raoul Dufy and Paul Gauguin. In the gardens, designed in the style of English parks, regional plants flourish. The two-acre Woodland Garden, a cutting garden, the Stout Camellia House conservatory, and ample statuary contribute to the oasis. At the summer outdoor film series, the back lawn fills with picnickers and fireflies. Other garden entertainment features jazz performances, symphonies, and more. ⊠ *4339 Park Ave.,* ☎ *901/761–5250.* ☑ *$5.* ☉ *Tues.–Sat. 10–5, Sun. 1–5.*

★ **⓴ Graceland.** The tour of the colonial-style mansion once owned by Elvis Presley reveals the spoils of stardom—from gold records to glittering show costumes—and a circuit of the grounds (shuttle service is available) leads to Meditation Garden, where Elvis is buried. Separate tours are available for additional fees. Among them is the **Elvis Presley Automobile Museum,** where a continuously run film montage of Elvis on the road is shown drive-in style as viewers sit in seats pulled from 1957 Chevys. Elvis's jet, the *Lisa Marie* (named for his daughter), complete with 24-karat gold-plated seat-belt buckles and a queen-size bed covered in light blue ultrasuede, stars in the **Airplanes Tour.** **Sincerely Elvis** is a small museum with personal items such as home movies, photos, and clothes. There are several restaurants and, of course, shops on the premises, along with a post office—few can resist the lure of a Graceland date stamp. ⊠ *3764 Elvis Presley Blvd. (off I–55), 12 mi southeast of downtown,* ☎ *901/332–3322; 800/238–2000 outside TN.* ☑ *Home tour $12, all attractions $22, parking $2.* ☉ *Mon.–Sat. 9–5, Sun. 10–4. Hrs may vary with season.*

Historic Elmwood Cemetery. Founded in 1852, the county's oldest active cemetery is home to a confederacy of 70,000 local ancestors—politicians, tycoons, "bosses," madams, Rebel soldiers, martyred nuns, and other notables. A stroll through its 8 landscaped acres, studded with Victorian statues and monuments, promises to enlighten and fascinate. Audio cassettes and walking maps are available at the Victorian gate cottage. ⊠ *824 S. Dudley St.,* ☎ *901/774–3212.* ☑ *Free; audio cassette $3; walking map $1.* ☉ *Cottage open weekdays 8–4, Sat. 8–2; cemetery grounds open daily 8–4.*

㉖ Memphis Botanic Garden. Across the street from the Dixon Gallery lie these 96 landscaped acres of outdoor gardens. A profusion of themes include Southern staples such as dogwoods, azaleas, irises, and roses, as well as wildflowers, herbs, perennials, daylilies, and cacti, and sculpture. All trails lead to the Japanese Garden of Tranquility, the crown jewel of the gardens, where a red bridge arcs over a pond and its audience of begging goldfish. In the Goldsmith Civic Garden Center special exhibits feature porcelain, art, and various horticultural shows such as bonsai, orchids, succulents, and roses. The botanic garden is part of East Memphis's main park—the **Audubon**—which includes a golf course, tennis courts, and walking trails. ✉ *750 Cherry Rd.,* ☎ *901/ 685–1566.* ☞ *$2; free on Tues. after 12:30.* ☉ *Nov.–Feb., Mon.–Sat. 9–4:30; Mar.–Oct., Mon.–Sat. 9–6, Sun. 11–6.*

㉔ Memphis Brooks Museum of Art. The collections of this museum in Overton Park span eight centuries and contain 7,000 pieces, including a notable collection of Italian Renaissance works, plus English portraiture, impressionist and American modernist paintings, decorative arts, prints, photographs, and one of the nation's largest displays of Doughty bird figurines. A popular exhibit upstairs gives a global survey of ancient art from Greece and the Mediterranean, the Americas, and Africa. Special exhibitions run the gamut from contemporary artists such as Duane Hanson to Renaissance-era decorative arts. Film buffs flock to the **Brooks Film Series** on Wednesday evening and Sunday afternoon for cinema classics and foreign films; the schedule varies, so call for details. ✉ *1934 Poplar Ave.,* ☎ *901/722–3500.* ☞ *$5; fees vary for major exhibits.* ☉ *Tues.–Fri. 10–4, Sat. 10–5, Sun. 11:30–5; first Wed. of month 10–8.*

NEED A
BREAK?

At the **Brushmark Restaurant** (☎ 901/722–3555), an elegant but casual eatery on the Memphis Brooks Museum of Art's first floor, art lovers can rest their feet while enjoying lunch, wine, and serene views of Overton Park. It's open Tuesday–Sunday 11:30–2:30.

☺ ㉒ Memphis Pink Palace Museum and Mansion and Sharpe Planetarium. Clarence Saunders, founder of the Piggly Wiggly self-service stores that are the predecessors of today's supermarkets, built this rambling pink-marble mansion in the 1920s. Exhibits, shown in both the mansion and an auxiliary museum, are eclectic, including natural and cultural history displays, a hand-carved miniature three-ring circus, and a replica of the original Piggly Wiggly. The Sharpe Planetarium explores the most current cosmic discoveries. The museum also has the Union Planters IMAX Theater. ✉ *3050 Central Ave.,* ☎ *901/320–6320.* ☞ *Planetarium $3.50, museum $6, IMAX theater $6.* ☉ *Mon.–Thurs. 9–4, Fri.–Sat. 9–9, Sun. noon–6.*

☺ ㉕ Memphis Zoo. One of the South's most notable zoos is home to more than 400 species living on 70 well-kept wooded acres in Overton Park. A recent large-scale renovation has resulted in state-of-the-art exhibits featuring larger, more natural habitats such as *Cat Country, Dragon's Lair, Primate Canyon, Madagascar, Animals of the Night,* a natural African veldt setting for larger creatures, a large reptile facility, and an animal-contact area. The zoo also has several eateries, shops, fountains, a farm discovery center, and a library. **Zoo Nights** offer summer family entertainment with live music and performances. ✉ *2000 Galloway St.,* ☎ *901/276–9453.* ☞ *$8, parking $2.* ☉ *Mar.–late Oct., daily 9–6 (last admission 5); late Oct.–Feb., daily 9–5 (last admission 4:30).*

⑱ National Ornamental Metal Museum. The nation's only museum preserving the art and the craft of metalworking—from wrought iron to gold—overlooks the Mississippi River. There are also a working blacksmith shop and changing exhibitions and demonstrations. The grounds hug the bluffs south of downtown and, with their vistas of river and skyline, have become a favorite spot for outdoor blues concerts, such as **Blues on the Bluffs,** held each September. ✉ *374 Metal Museum Dr. (via I–55N, last exit before bridge),* ☎ *901/774–6380.* ☞ *$4.* ☉ *Tues.– Sat. 10–5, Sun. noon–5.*

Dining

American

$$$ ✕ **Folk's Folly Prime Steak House.** Folk's is a Memphis favorite for one
simple reason: the juiciest sizzling-hot steaks in town. "Steak house"
is a bit misleading though—this restaurant resembles a suburban home,
with a lounge and five separate dining rooms, plus eight private rooms
for small parties. The generous vegetable side dishes, such as stuffed
baked potatoes and asparagus, are reliably fresh, and heaping portions
of seafood and whole lobster are always available. It's in East Mem-
phis, near some of the city's nicest residential areas. ⊠ *551 S. Menden-
hall St.,* ☎ *901/762–8200. AE, MC, V. No lunch.*

$$ ✕ **Café Society.** This sidewalk café in Midtown brings imagination and
a fresh range of choices to its lunch and dinner menu. Outdoor tables,
across the street from a small park, are popular with the happy-hour
crowd. Expect to find treats like coconut-fried shrimp with pineapple
chutney, grilled salmon with sesame- and poppy-seed crust and shrimp
Biscayne sauce, and veal and pasta dishes. The best dessert is the crème
brûlée. ⊠ *212 N. Evergreen St.,* ☎ *901/722–2177. AE, MC, V. No
lunch weekends.*

$ ✕ **Blues City Café.** This downtown restaurant specializes in huge steaks
and ribs, hamburgers, and hot tamales in a diner setting. ⊠ *138 Beale
St.,* ☎ *901/526–3637. AE, MC, V. ☉ Hrs vary; call ahead.*

Barbecue

$ ✕ **Charlie Vergos' Rendezvous.** Charlie Vergos, who has been in busi-
★ ness since 1948, has become something of a Memphis ambassador of
barbecued ribs: Not only does his downtown basement restaurant
draw thousands of tourists each year, but he also ships his ribs by air
express all over the country. The walls are filled with memorabilia and
bric-a-brac, from old newspaper cartoons to Essolene gas signs, but
what really packs in the crowds are the delicious pork loin plate and
the barbecued pork ribs. ⊠ *52 S. 2nd St.,* ☎ *901/523–2746. Reservations not accepted. AE, MC, V. ☉ Closed Sun.–Mon.*

$ ✕ **Corky's Bar-B-Q.** Expect to wait in line at this no-frills East Mem-
phis barbecue joint, a leader in sending ribs to loyal fans by air-express
service. One taste of the ribs or pork platter explains why. Letters from
customers and articles on Corky's cover the walls. ⊠ *5259 Poplar Ave.,*
☎ *901/685–9744. Reservations not accepted. AE, D, DC, MC, V.*

$ ✕ **Interstate Bar-B-Q.** The Neely family has barbecue sauce running
through its veins, and it all started here. Jim Neely's nephews have opened
their own places around town, but they all learned their secrets at this
restaurant. The long list of barbecue includes barbecued spaghetti, pork
sandwiches, beef ribs and links, and Polish and smoked sausage. Save
room for the homemade pecan pie. ⊠ *2265 S. 3rd St.,* ☎ *901/775–
2304. Reservations not accepted. AE, MC, V.*

Continental

$$ ✕ **Paulette's.** This Overton Square restaurant, which served bistro-style
cooking before it became popular in Memphis, has retained its vital-
ity for more than two decades. A crisp, fresh house salad and airy
popovers with strawberry butter help pack in the crowds for their sig-
nature Sunday brunch, along with lunch and dinner. Entrées include
several crepe dishes, along with grilled salmon, swordfish, chicken, baked
scallops, and brochettes of shrimp or beef. The hot chocolate dessert
crepes are sinful. On weekends a pianist plays requests ranging from
Gershwin to Beale Street blues. ⊠ *2110 Madison Ave.,* ☎ *901/726–
5128. AE, MC, V.*

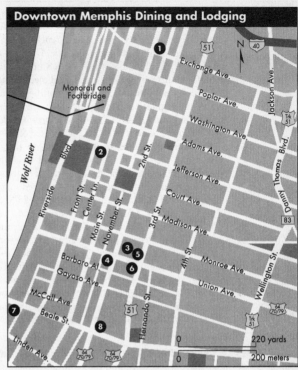

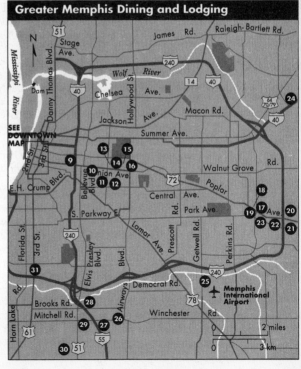

Eclectic

$$$–$$$$ ✕ **Restaurant Raji.** World-renowned chef and published author Raji
★   Jallepalli cooks in a style she calls a French-Indian fusion, using French
cooking techniques and Indian spices. The four-course prix-fixe din-
ner changes nightly, and always shows Raji's imagination in dishes such
as biryani with tea-smoked quail, veal medallions in lotus leaf, or an-
telope chop with blackberry-ginger chutney. There are several dining
rooms, all intimate and elegant, which attract culinary connoisseurs
from far and wide. ✉ *712 W. Brookhaven Circle,* ☎ *901/685–8723.
Reservations essential. AE, MC, V. Closed Sun.–Mon. No lunch.*

$$ ✕ **Automatic Slim's Tonga Club.** This hip restaurant is downtown
across from the Peabody Hotel. The split-level dining room is usually
crowded. Southwestern and Caribbean fare are served in thick, spicy
sauces; signature dishes include deep-fried red snapper with tomato and
jalapeño relish and Jamaican jerk duck. ✉ *83 S. 2nd St.,* ☎ *901/525–
7948. AE, MC, V. Closed Sun. No lunch Sat.*

$$ ✕ **Tsunami.** Newcomer Chef Ben Smith's informal restaurant in the
Cooper-Young District has been a hit since its inception in 1998. In a
city whose finer restaurants consistently look to Europe for inspira-
tion, Smith's exciting Asian-American–Pacific Rim cuisine adds new
vistas to the landscape. His ever-changing menu might include sea
bass on black Thai rice with soy beurre blanc one month and sake-
steamed mussels in a fiery Thai red curry sauce the next. ✉ *928 S. Cooper
St.,* ☎ *901/274–2556. AE, MC, V. Closed Sun. No lunch.*

French

$$$$ ✕ **Chez Philippe.** The setting is wonderfully lavish—high ceilings,
★   faux-marble columns, and huge murals depicting a masked ball. The
service is impeccable. Most important, the cuisine—among Memphis's
most innovative and sophisticated—lives up to its regal setting. The
menu ranges from delicate terrines to lamb tenderloin in puff pastry
to hot soufflés. The restaurant is immediately off the Grand Lobby of
the Peabody Hotel (☞ Lodging, *below*). ✉ *Peabody Hotel, 149 Union
Ave.,* ☎ *901/529–4188. Reservations essential. AE, DC, MC, V. Closed
Sun. No lunch.*

$$$$ ✕ **Erling Jensen.** Chef Jensen opened this restaurant in 1996 and has
★   been attracting crowds ever since. He characterizes his cuisine as
French with global influences, but to put it simply, his rack of lamb is
the best in town, and the orange roughy and veal tenderloin aren't bad
either. For years *Memphis Magazine* readers have voted Jensen Mem-
phis's best chef. ✉ *1044 S. Yates St., off Poplar,* ☎ *901/763–3700. Reser-
vations essential. AE, D, DC, MC, V. No lunch.*

$$$ ✕ **La Tourelle.** This quiet, turn-of-the-century bungalow with fine lace
★   curtains and wooden floors is reminiscent of a small country restau-
rant in France. The decor is as charming as the cuisine is acclaimed,
and many of the city's finest chefs have worked here. The menu varies,
but each night there's a special lobster creation as well as a game dish.
The five-course prix-fixe tasting menu is the best bet. ✉ *2146 Monroe Ave., near Overton Sq.,* ☎ *901/726–5771. Reservations essential.
MC, V. Closed Mon. No lunch Tues.–Sat.*

$$ ✕ **Owen Brennan's Restaurant.** This New Orleans–style eatery in an
upscale Memphis shopping center specializes in those fine Cajun and
Creole dishes that usually require a jaunt to the French Quarter. Fa-
vorite dishes include blackened chicken or seafood gumbo. The lavish
Sunday brunch is attended religiously, and easy banter, champagne, and
jazz flow freely. Best of all, an outdoor patio under towering shade trees
offers a cool respite from Memphis's sizzling summer sun. ✉ *6150 Poplar
Ave.,* ☎ *901/761–0990. AE, DC, MC, V.*

Mexican

✕ **Cafe Olé.** If Mexican with a healthy twist sounds intriguing, this popular Midtown hangout is for you. Specialties—cooked without the heavy animal fats used in most Mexican fare—include spinach enchiladas and chili *rellenos*. The exposed brick walls are decorated with Mexican paintings and ceremonial masks. ✉ *959 S. Cooper St.,* ☎ *901/274–1504. AE, D, DC, MC, V.*

Seafood

$$–$$$$ ✕ **Landry's Seafood House.** This remodeled riverfront eatery, one of Memphis's busiest restaurants, seats more than 300, but the wait can still be more than one hour. Patio dining is especially refreshing—if you can get a table. The fare—seafood, steaks, and Cajun—is simple but consistently good. Among the better offerings are shrimp in a brown-butter sauce, flounder stuffed with shrimp and crabmeat, and fried oysters and shrimp. ✉ *263 Wagner Pl.,* ☎ *901/526–1966. Reservations not accepted. AE, MC, V.*

Southern

$ ✕ **The Cupboard.** Owner Charles Cavallo knows fresh produce, and his cooks turn out masterful "meat-and-three" plates. Lucky is the soul who visits when both macaroni and cheese and fried green tomatoes are offered. ✉ *1495 Union Ave.,* ☎ *901/276–8015. AE, D, MC, V.*

Lodging

$$$$ ▥ **Peabody Hotel.** This 14-story Italian Renaissance Revival hostelry, ★ a city landmark since 1925, has been impeccably restored. The lobby preserves its original stained-glass skylights and ornate travertine marble fountain—home to the hotel's famed resident ducks, who waddle down each morning from their penthouse apartment and parade across a red carpet to the stirring sounds of Sousa's "King Cotton March"; the show is repeated each afternoon. Compared to the grandeur of the common areas, the small, simply furnished rooms are disappointing, but clean and comfortable. ✉ *149 Union Ave., 38103,* ☎ *901/529–4000 or 800/732–2639,* ℻ *901/529–3600. 468 rooms, 15 suites. 4 restaurants, bar, indoor pool, health club. AE, DC, MC, V.*

$$$–$$$$ ▥ **Adam's Mark Hotel.** This luxury property, a 27-story circular glass tower, is in the flourishing eastern suburbs of Memphis near I-240. From your glass-walled aerie, you'll have sweeping vistas of Memphis and its outskirts. Weekend nights the lounge comes alive with highly regarded visiting jazz performers and other musicians. ✉ *939 Ridge Lake Blvd., 38120,* ☎ *901/684–6664 or 800/444–2326,* ℻ *901/762–7411. 408 rooms, 5 suites. Restaurant, lounge, pool, health club. AE, D, DC, MC, V.*

$$–$$$$ ▥ **Elvis Presley's Heartbreak Hotel.** It had to happen sooner or later—a Memphis hotel named for the King and owned and operated by Elvis Presley Enterprises, Inc. Across from Graceland, the hotel features '50s-themed decor profuse with leopard prints and gold as well as a heart-shape swimming pool. Guest rooms include kitchenettes. Themed suites are more than 1,000 square ft and reflect aspects of Presley's career. ✉ *3677 Elvis Presley Blvd., 38116,* ☎ *901/332–1000, or 877/777–0606,* ℻ *901/332–2107. 124 guest rooms, 4 suites. Cocktail lounge, pool, health club, meeting rooms. AE, DC, MC, V.* ✍

$$–$$$$ ▥ **Marriott Memphis Downtown.** Adjacent to the downtown Convention Center, the sleek high-rise (18 floors) has a concierge floor and ample work space and lighting in the spacious guest rooms. The lobby lounge, a tasteful, greenery-filled retreat, is a pleasant spot to relax and listen to music from the grand piano. ✉ *250 N. Main St., 38103,* ☎ *901/527–7300,* ℻ *901/526–1561. 394 rooms, 8 suites. Restaurant,*

indoor pool, hot tub, sauna, health club, concierge floor, meeting rooms. AE, DC, MC, V.

$$$ 🏨 **Radisson Hotel.** Across the street from the Peabody is this downtown hotel with its own lobby fountain and waterfall. Glass-walled elevators whisk guests to rooms around a 10-story atrium. Rooms compare to the Peabody's across the street, for a better price. ✉ *185 Union Ave., 38103,* ☎ *901/528–1800,* FAX *901/526–3226. 280 rooms. Restaurant, pool. AE, D, DC, MC, V.* 🐾

$$–$$$ 🏨 **French Quarter Suites Hotel.** With its mellow rose-brick exterior and
★ classic architectural lines, this pleasant Overton Square hostelry is reminiscent of an older, New Orleans–style inn. All the one-bedroom suites have living rooms and whirlpool baths that accommodate two, and some are balconied. ✉ *2144 Madison Ave., 38104,* ☎ *901/728–4000 or 800/843–0353,* FAX *901/278–1262. 104 suites. Pool, exercise room. AE, DC, MC, V.*

$$–$$$ 🏨 **Holiday Inn East.** Close to I–240 and the bustling Poplar/Ridgeway office complex, this sleek 10-story hotel is popular with business travelers. The rooms are comfortable and well-maintained, but the hotel's main draw is its proximity to the I–240 loop, which provides easy access to the whole city. ✉ *5795 Poplar Ave., 38119,* ☎ *800/465–4329,* FAX *901/682–7881. 243 rooms. Restaurant, pool, health club. AE, D, DC, MC, V.* 🐾

$$ 🏨 **Guest House Inn & Suites.** This three-story hotel in East Memphis has many of the comforts of home. The two-room suites include bedrooms, kitchenettes, and living rooms, and sleep four. The decor includes teal carpeting and Aztec-pattern draperies. ✉ *4300 American Way, 38118,* ☎ *901/214–8378,* FAX *901/366–7835. 120 suites. Pool. AE, D, DC, MC, V. CP.*

$$ 🏨 **La Quinta Inn–Medical Center.** This two-story inn is convenient to midtown with its restaurants and shops, and has spacious, well-maintained rooms. ✉ *42 S. Camilla St., 38104,* ☎ *901/526–1050,* FAX *901/525–3219. 130 rooms. Pool. AE, D, DC, MC, V. CP.* 🐾

$$ 🏨 **Sleep Inn at Court Square.** This chain hotel is conveniently located near two highways and within walking distance of Mud Island and the Pyramid; Beale Street is a 15-minute walk or a quick trolley ride (there's a stop right out back) away. Extras include a free Continental breakfast, free parking, and free local phone calls. Business rooms have a desk, fax, data port, and VCR. ✉ *40 N. Front St., 38103,* ☎ *901/522–9700,* FAX *901/522–9710. 124 rooms. Exercise room, laundry service, business services. AE, D, MC, V.*

$–$$ 🏨 **Day's Inn Graceland.** Proximity to Graceland is this modest hotel's
★ claim to fame, and it makes the most of that with a guitar-shape swimming pool and free Elvis movies 'round the clock. ✉ *3839 Elvis Presley Blvd., 38116,* ☎ *901/346–5500,* FAX *901/345–7452. 61 rooms. Pool. AE, DC, MC, V.*

$–$$ 🏨 **Quality Inn.** This modern, typical chain-style hotel features private patios or balconies in all units; many have refrigerators and microwave ovens, and four have kitchens. There's a coin laundry on site. ✉ *1541 Sycamore View, 38134,* ☎ *901/388–1300,* FAX *901/388–1300. 96 rooms. Pool. AE, D, DC, MC, V. CP.* 🐾

$ 🏨 **Executive Inn.** This four-story motor lodge near Graceland has spacious, well-appointed rooms with tasteful touches of country decor. ✉ *3222 Airways Blvd., 38116,* ☎ *901/332–3800 or 800/221–2222,* FAX *901/345–8118. 118 rooms. Pool, exercise room. DC, MC, V. CP.*

$ 🏨 **Hampton Inn Airport.** This member of the economy-priced chain that
★ spun off from Holiday Inn has a pleasing contemporary design. Spacious, well-lighted rooms have Scandinavian-style teakwood furnishings. This is a front-runner in the moderate category. ✉ *2979 Millbranch*

Rd., 38116, ☎ 901/396–2200 or 800/426–7866, FAX 901/396–7034.
128 rooms. Pool. AE, DC, MC, V.

$ ⚠ **Memphis Graceland KOA.** This campground with tent and RV sites
as well as cabins is only a few yards from Graceland's entrance. ✉ *3691
Elvis Presley Blvd., 38116,* ☎ *901/396–7125 or 800/562–9386. 72
campsites, 4 cabins. Pool, playground, coin laundry. D, MC, V.*

Nightlife and the Arts

For a complete listing of weekly events, check the "Playbook" section
in the Friday *Memphis Commercial Appeal* or the *Memphis Flyer,* distributed free at newsstands around the city. The Tennessee Welcome
Center (☞ Memphis A to Z, *below*) will also provide an up-to-date
rundown of events.

The Arts

CONCERTS, DANCE, AND OPERA

The **Orpheum Theatre** (✉ 203 S. Main St., ☎ 901/525–3000) is the
scene of performances by **Ballet Memphis** (☎ 901/323–1947), which
features professional dancers and celebrity guest artists, and **Opera Memphis** (☎ 901/678–2706 for tickets), during fall, winter, and spring. Touring Broadway musicals are also staged here; past performances have
included *Cats, Chicago,* and *Phantom of the Opera.*

The **Germantown Performing Arts Centre** (✉ 1801 Exeter Rd., Germantown, 22 mi. east of downtown Memphis, ☎ 901/751–7514), celebrated for its acoustics, brings in world-class music, dance, theater
and opera. A sample of previous performances includes *Madame Butterfly,* Itzhak Perlman, Yo-Yo Ma, Mikhail Baryshnikov, and Ray
Charles.

The **Memphis Symphony Orchestra** (✉ 3100 Walnut Grove Rd., ☎
901/324–3627) is an 80-piece symphony that hosts world-renowned
soloists in a classical masterworks series and a pops series. The symphony holds concerts at Eudora Auditorium (at Poplar and Perkins),
outdoor concerts at Dixon Gallery and Gardens (☞ Sights to See, *above*),
and on the riverfront at the Sunset Symphony during Memphis in
May (☞ Festivals, *below*).

THEATER

Playhouse on the Square (✉ 51 S. Cooper St., ☎ 901/726–4656), open
September–July, has the city's only professional repertory company. **Center Stage,** at the Jewish Community Center (✉ 6560 Poplar Ave., ☎
901/761–0810), is used for musical performances and visiting authors
and lecturers. A professional acting group performs at **Circuit Playhouse**
(✉ 1705 Poplar Ave., ☎ 901/726–4656). At **Ewing's Children's Theatre** (✉ 2635 Avery Ave., ☎ 901/452–3968), performances are directed,
designed, and acted entirely by children under the guidance of the Ewing
Children's Theatre. **Theatre Memphis** (✉ 630 Perkins Extended, ☎ 901/
682–8323) has been acclaimed as one of the best community theaters
in the United States. At the University of Memphis, **University Theatre**
(✉ 3745 Central Ave., ☎ 901/678–2523) provides a venue for drama
students and visiting performers.

Festivals

The **Memphis in May International Festival** (☎ 901/525–4611) salutes
the cuisine, crafts, and other cultural offerings of a different country
each year over four consecutive weekends. This festival—Memphis's
largest—galvanizes the city each year and, with its **Beale Street Music
Fest** and **World Championship Barbecue Cooking Contest,** celebrates
Memphis as much as it does the honored country. Music Fest brings
in an exciting array of greats, from Bob Dylan to Bobby Bland to Delta

gospel artists. The month culminates with the **Sunset Symphony**, where picnickers watch the Memphis Symphony Orchestra perform Southern classics such as *Ole Man River* on the bluffs.

The **Africa in April Cultural Awareness Festival** (☎ 901/947–2133) is an annual downtown festival that celebrates the African diaspora with music, food, fashion, and workshops. **Arts in the Park** (✉ 750 Cherry Rd., ☎ 901/761–1278) was named Tennessee's number-one fine-arts festival by the Harris List. Held for four days each October in the Memphis Botanic Garden, the festival includes arts and crafts booths, music, dance, theater, and lots of children's activities. Sponsored by the Center for Southern Folklore, the **Memphis Music and Heritage Festival** (☎ 901/525–3655) in July showcases all kinds of music on the Main Street Mall and Beale Street downtown. As with all activities sponsored by the Center for Southern Folklore, this festival gives concertgoers a great opportunity for discovering Delta talent.

Nightlife

DOWNTOWN

A handful of areas make for good stepping out downtown. **Beale Street,** however touristy, tops the list, with more venues per square foot than any other place in town.

Alfred's on Beale (✉ 197 Beale St., ☎ 901/525–3711), one of the city's hottest dance clubs, also serves great food. Rock bands perform from Wednesday through Saturday, and a DJ—sometimes the legendary George Klein, Elvis's best man—spins popular dance tunes during the week. For quality blues, **B. B. King's Blues Club** (✉ 143 Beale St., ☎ 901/524–5464) sets the standard among Memphis's high-profile clubs, with infrequent appearances from the legendary blues artist for whom the club is named. You're more likely to see local legends such as Ruby Wilson than King. The food focuses on Southern specialties, naturally. The place can be packed; it's a favorite among locals and visitors alike.

Elvis Presley's Memphis (✉ 126 Beale St., ☎ 901/527–6900) has live bands Tuesday through Sunday. The menu—which boasts Elvis's favorites, such as fried peanut-butter-and-banana sandwiches—speaks for itself. Even for those who aren't diehard fans of the King, this venue is worth a trip for the kitsch. The decor features lots of red velvet, a retail counter hawking Elvis souvenirs, Vegas showroom-style booths, an ornate chandelier, and a large screen behind the stage. Upstairs guests can play pool at Elvis's personal billiard table. The live bands—usually rockabilly or gospel—put on a fun show. Of particular interest is the Sunday Gospel Brunch, from 11 AM to 3 PM.

At the **New Daisy Theatre** (✉ 330 Beale St., ☎ 901/525–8981)—the 900-seat venue where B. B. King got his start—blues, jazz, and (predominantly) rock bands perform. As an old stage theater turned music hall, the New Daisy has excellent acoustics. It's a great place to see musicians like Bob Dylan and Herbie Hancock up close. Professional boxing is held once a month.

The **Rum Boogie Cafe** (✉ 182 Beale St., ☎ 901/528–0150) stages live blues nightly, accompanied by Cajun cuisine and barbecue. The live jam sessions feature local blues artists.

Big-name entertainers and musical groups ranging from Harry Connick Jr. to Widespread Panic appear at the **Mud Island Amphitheatre** (☎ 901/576–7222) from April through October. With its backdrop of the downtown skyline, this outdoor theater is scenic, but on a breezeless summer night the heat is not for the faint of heart.

Among the offerings at the **Orpheum Theatre** (✉ 203 S. Main St., ☎ 901/525–3000) are easy-listening and jazz concerts, traveling Broadway shows, comedians, and a much-loved summer film series.

Other downtown points of interest include the historic **Pinch District,** north of downtown between North Front and North 3rd streets. The Main Street Trolley travels into the heart of this neighborhood. The **North End** (✉ 346 N. Main St., ☎ 901/527–3663) and the **High Point Pinch** (✉ 111 Jackson Ave., ☎ 901/525–4444) are two popular bars. The 32-story **Pyramid Arena** (☞ Sights to See *in* Downtown Memphis, *above*) hosts a variety of big-name country, rock, and R & B artists who draw large crowds.

OFF THE BEATEN PATH — The atmospheric blocks surrounding **South Main,** though often eerily quiet, are home to a handful of Memphis's most authentic clubs. **Earnestine & Hazel's** (✉ 531 S. Main St., ☎ 901/523–9754), an old-time juke joint, is cherished for its greasy-spoon cheeseburgers, jukebox, and occasional live blues and dancing. **Marmalade's Restaurant and Lounge** (✉ 153 Calhoun St., ☎ 901/522–8800) serves up soul food along with live performances by local jazz, blues, and R & B artists. **Raiford's** (✉ 115 Vance Ave., ☎ 901/525–9210) has become a Memphis institution, attracting patrons from all walks of life to its DJ-driven dance floor.

MIDTOWN

Among Midtown's nightlife offerings, **Overton Square** is the best known. With its concentration of theaters, restaurants, and bars within a few blocks, amblers are sure to stumble onto something lively. Wine lovers can enjoy a glass from the city's largest wine list at **Le Chardonnay Wine Bar** (✉ 2105 Overton Sq., ☎ 901/725–1375). Next door, at **Bayou Bar & Grill** (✉ 2105 Overton Sq. #1, ☎ 901/278–8626) Cajun specialties and lots of beer are served on an outdoor patio.

Another Midtown destination, the **Cooper-Young District,** can be found, appropriately, at the crossroads of Cooper Street and Young Avenue, several blocks down from Overton Square. Festive watering holes and eateries include **Cafe Olé** (✉ 959 S. Cooper St., ☎ 901/274–1504) and, next door, **Young Avenue Deli** (✉ 2119 Young Ave., ☎ 901/278–0034), which has one of the city's largest beer selections.

Elsewhere in Midtown, **Huey's** (✉ 1927 Madison Ave., ☎ 901/726–4372; ✉ 77 S. 2nd St., ☎ 901/527–2700) is famous locally for its burgers, live music on Sunday afternoon, and live blues or jazz on Sunday night. Relative newcomer **In the Grove** (✉ 2865 Walnut Grove Rd., ☎ 901/458–9955) is gaining a good reputation and large audiences for its quality live jazz performances. Year-round, the **Mid-South Coliseum** (✉ 996 Early Maxwell Blvd., ☎ 901/274–3982) draws its share of country and rock musicians, plus the occasional tractor pull or wrestling event. The atmosphere at the **P & H** (✉ 1532 Madison Ave., ☎ 901/726–0906) is one that some people may call unpretentious and others may call dive-y. Whatever your frame of mind, the P & H—which stands for the Poor & Hungry—is one of the best places in town for local color on weekend nights. The live music ranges from classical to rock to blues to jazz and then some, and the burgers can send a person into cardiac arrest.

Outdoor Activities and Sports

Auto Racing

The 600-acre **Memphis Motorsports Park** hosts weekly dirt-track and drag racing. Occasionally, amateurs can race their own cars on the track.

✉ *5500 Taylor Forge Rd., Millington,* ☎ *901/358–7223.* 🎫 *Prices vary.*
🕐 *Mar.–Nov.*

Baseball

The **Memphis Redbirds,** a St. Louis Cardinals AAA farm team and Memphis's highest-profile sports team, play at AutoZone Park (✉ 8 S. 3rd St., ☎ 901/721–6050), a new stadium, which opened downtown in April 2000.

Boating, Biking, and Hiking

Get back to nature at **Meeman-Shelby Forest State Park,** a 12,500-acre tract bordering the Mississippi with boat rental, hiking, and biking. ✉ *10 mi north of Memphis, off U.S. 51,* ☎ *901/876–5215.* 🎫 *Free.* 🕐 *Daily 7 AM–10 PM.*

There are hiking trails at **Shelby Farms Plough Recreation Area** (☎ 901/382–4250), **Lichterman Nature Center** (☎ 901/767–7322), and **T. O. Fuller State Park** (☎ 901/529–7581).

Football

Conference USA's top college team plays in the **AXA/Equitable Liberty Bowl** (☎ 901/274–4600) between Christmas and New Year's at Liberty Bowl Memorial Stadium (✉ 335 S. Hollywood) at the Mid-South Fairgrounds complex. The stadium also hosts the University of Memphis Tigers and other football teams. Every September fans flock from all over the South for the **Southern Heritage Classic** (☎ 901/398–6655), when Tennessee State University takes on Jackson State University at the Liberty Bowl the second Saturday of the month. Weekend festivities surrounding the event include receptions, luncheons, concerts, parties, a golf tournament, and a fashion show.

Golf

In June the Tournament Players Club at Southwind Country Club (✉ 3325 Club, at Southwind, ☎ 901/748–0534) hosts the **FedEx St. Jude Classic,** featuring top pros.

If you prefer playing to watching, the **Memphis Park Commission** (☎ 901/325–5966) operates two nine-hole and five 18-hole public golf courses; some good choices are **Galloway** (✉ 3815 Walnut Grove Rd., ☎ 901/685–7805), 18 holes, par 71; and **T. O. Fuller State Park** (✉ 1500 Mitchell Rd. W, ☎ 901/543–7771), 18 holes, par 72.

Hockey

The **Memphis RiverKings** (☎ 901/323–5525), a minor league club, play from November through March at the Mid-South Coliseum, in the Mid-South Fairgrounds complex.

Ice-Skating

The **Ice Chalet,** in the Mall of Memphis (✉ 4451 American Way, ☎ 901/362–8877), is open seven days a week.

Tennis

The **Kroger St. Jude Indoor Tennis Championship** (☎ 901/685–2237) brings top pros to the Racquet Club (✉ 5111 Sanderlin Avenue) in February.

The **Memphis Park Commission** (☎ 901/325–5766) operates nine facilities that offer tennis lessons, tournaments, and league play. **Leftwich** (☎ 901/685–7907), **Ridgeway** (☎ 901/767–2889), and **Whitehaven** (☎ 901/332–0546) have indoor courts.

Shopping

More than a dozen shopping centers and malls are scattered about Memphis. The **Mid America Mall,** on Main Street between Beale and Poplar streets, is one of the nation's longest pedestrian malls—better known for its trolley rides and people-watching than for shopping. Two antiques districts bracket Mid America Mall: **South Main,** on Main Street between Beale and Calhoun streets, and the **Pinch District,** just north of downtown between Front and 3rd streets, also known for its bars and restaurants. For more local color, midtown's **Cooper-Young District,** at the intersection of Cooper Street and Young Avenue, offers a handful of funky shops, vintage clothing stores and cafés. Also in midtown, **Overton Square** (⊠ 24 S. Cooper St., ☎ 901/278–6300)—a three-block shopping, restaurant, and entertainment complex in vintage buildings and newer structures—has upscale boutiques and specialty shops. **Oak Court Mall** (⊠ 4465 Poplar Ave., ☎ 901/682–8928), in the busy Poplar/Perkins area of East Memphis, has 70 specialty stores and two department stores. At **Wolfchase Galleria** (⊠ 2760 N. Germantown Pkwy., at U.S. 64, about 18 mi east of downtown Memphis, ☎ 901/381–2769), the four anchor stores are Goldsmith's, Dillard's, Sears, and JCPenney. A large carousel attracts scores of children, and a multiplex cinema shows a wide range of movies.

Belz Factory Outlet Mall (⊠ 3536 Canada Rd., Exit 20 off I–40, 20 mi east of downtown Memphis, Lakeland, ☎ 901/386–3180) includes 50 stores, from Bugle Boy to Van Heusen.

A. Schwab Dry Goods Store (⊠ 163 Beale St., ☎ 901/523–9782) is an old-fashioned store whose motto is "If you can't find it at A. Schwab's, you're better off without it!" Elvis shopped here, and you can, too—for top hats, spats, tambourines, bow ties, dresses to size 60, and men's trousers to size 74. **Davis-Kidd Booksellers** (⊠ 397 Perkins Ext., ☎ 901/683–9801) is a Tennessee-based chain with an expansive collection of titles as well as in-store cafés. The **Woman's Exchange** (⊠ 88 Racine St., ☎ 901/327–5681) specializes in children's wear and handcrafted items. There's a tearoom for weekday luncheons.

Side Trips from Memphis

The flatness of the northern tip of the Mississippi Delta is a sharp contrast to East Tennessee's mountains. Cotton and soybeans thrive in the rich dirt of West Tennessee, particularly around Henning, the home-town of Alex Haley, author of *Roots*. Those who love the great outdoors will want to make the two-hour trip north to Tiptonville's Reelfoot Lake, while points east of Memphis, such as Jackson and Shiloh National Military Park, will suit the Civil War buff.

Henning
50 mi north of Memphis.

The quiet, historic byways north of Memphis seem light-years away from the busy river city. Driving northward along U.S. 51 through the fertile Mississippi River bottomlands brings you into the heart of King Cotton's domain. Less than an hour from Memphis is Henning, a friendly little town remarkably untouched by its world acclaim as the boyhood home and burial place of Alex Haley, Pulitzer Prize–winning author of *Roots*. The **Alex Haley House Museum,** the only state-owned historic site in West Tennessee, displays family portraits, mementos, and furnishings. ⊠ *200 Church St., ☎ 901/738–2240. ☑ $2.50. ☺ Tues.–Sat. 10–5, Sun. 1–5.*

Tiptonville
105 mi north of Memphis.

Anglers and outdoors lovers of any sort are drawn to Tiptonville, in Tennessee's northwest corner, for its nearby bird and game refuge and spellbinding flora and fauna. The **Tiptonville Chamber of Commerce** (☎ 901/253–8144) can answer questions about dining and lodging.

Tiptonville's **Reelfoot Lake** gains a peculiar and mysterious beauty from a romantic scattering of cypress trees and charred stumps. The 13,000-acre lake was formed between 1811 and 1812, when the New Madrid earthquakes caused the Mississippi River to flood into the sinking land where a luxuriant forest once stood. From late November through mid-March the lake is a major sanctuary for American bald eagles. The quiet lake provides good fishing year-round for bass, crappie, trout, bream, and catfish. The Tennessee Department of Conservation conducts eagle-spotting tours at **Reelfoot Lake State Resort Park** (⊠ Rte. 1, Box 296, ☎ 901/253–7756).

Jackson
85 mi east of Memphis.

Jackson, site of several Civil War battles, was also a major railroad hub. It was home to John Luther "Casey" Jones, who was immortalized in the "Ballad of Casey Jones." The famed engineer became a hero by staying aboard his locomotive in a vain attempt to stop his engine from plowing into another train. For more information on Jackson, call the **Jackson/Madison County Convention & Visitors Bureau** (⊠ 400 S. Highland Ave., Jackson 38301, ☎ 901/425–8333 or 800/498–4748), open weekdays 8:30–4:30.

In **Casey Jones Village,** the **Casey Jones Home and Railroad Museum** (☎ 901/668–1223) contains a diverse assortment of railroad memorabilia. On the grounds is a replica of Old No. 382, Casey's steam engine. The **Casey Jones Village Old Country Store,** also in the village, has a restaurant, an 1890s-style ice cream parlor, and gift, souvenir, confectionery, and antiques shops. ⊠ *At U.S. 45 Bypass.* 🎟 *Museum $4.* ☉ *Jan.–Feb., daily 9–5; Mar.–Dec., daily 8 AM–9 PM.*

Savannah
110 mi east of Memphis on TN 57E.

Scenic Savannah, on the bluff of the Tennessee River, is a small, quiet town that exemplifies the charm and grace of Southern life. The historic **Cherry Mansion** (⊠ 101 Main St.), built in 1830, served as General Grant's headquarters during the Battle of Shiloh. The house is privately owned, but visitors are allowed to roam the grounds and to take pictures.

In the same building as the Chamber of Commerce, the **Tennessee River Museum** has exhibits on the Civil War, the river, and fossils from 65 million years ago, when this area was under water. ⊠ *507 Main St.,* ☎ *901/925–2363.* 🎟 *$2.* ☉ *Weekdays 9–5, Sat. 10–5, Sun. 1–5.*

Shiloh National Military Park
100 mi east of Memphis, 165 mi southwest of Nashville.

Site of one of the Civil War's grimmest and most pivotal battles, Shiloh National Military Park is the resting place of almost 4,000 soldiers, many unidentified, in the national cemetery. A self-guided auto tour (about 2½ hours) leads you past markers explaining monuments and battle sites. The visitor center runs a 25-minute film explaining the battle's strategy and has a display of Civil War artifacts. To get to Shiloh from Memphis, head east from Memphis on U.S. 64, then 10 mi south on TN 22. ⊠ *TN 22, Shiloh,* ☎ *901/689–5275.* 🎟 *$2.* ☉ *Visitor center daily 8–5.*

Pickwick Dam
110 mi southeast of Memphis.

Named after the eponymous character in Charles Dickens's *Pickwick Papers,* Pickwick Dam is considered by locals to be the playground of southwestern Tennessee's Hardin County.

Pickwick Landing State Resort Park (⊠ TN 57, ☎ 901/689–3135 or 800/250–8615) has a resort inn, a restaurant, playgrounds, swimming beaches, picnic areas, and a par-72, 18-hole golf course.

Memphis A to Z

Arriving and Departing

BY BOAT

The paddle-wheel steamers of the **Delta Queen Steamboat Company** (⊠ Robin St. Wharf, New Orleans, LA 70130, ☎ 800/543–1949) stop at Memphis and Nashville. The *Delta Queen,* the *Mississippi Queen,* and the *American Queen* travel between St. Louis and New Orleans.

BY BUS

Greyhound (☎ 800/231–2222) offers service throughout the region.

BY CAR

From Memphis, which is encircled by I–240, I–55 leads north to St. Louis and south to Jackson, Mississippi; I–40, east to Nashville and Knoxville.

BY PLANE

Memphis International Airport (⊠ 2491 Winchester Rd., ☎ 901/922–8000), served by American, Delta, Northwest, and Northwest Airlink, is 9 mi south of downtown. Taxi fare from the airport to downtown Memphis is about $20; try **Yellow Cab** (☎ 901/577–7700). By car, take I–240 to downtown.

BY TRAIN

Amtrak (⊠ 545 S. Main St., ☎ 901/526–0052 or 800/872–7245) operates the *City of New Orleans,* which stops in Memphis on the trip between New Orleans and Chicago.

Getting Around

BY BUS

Memphis Area Transit Authority (☎ 901/274–6282) buses cover the city and immediate suburbs; they run weekdays 4:30 AM–11:15 PM, Saturday 5 AM–6:15 PM, Sunday 9–6:15. The fare is $1.15, transfers 10¢. There is short-hop service on designated buses between Front, 3rd, and Exchange streets from 9 to 3 and between downtown and the Medical Center complex from 7 to 6. The fare is 35¢.

BY TAXI

The fare in **Memphis** is $2.90 for the first mile, $1.40 for each additional mile. There are stands at the airport and bus station. To order a taxi, call **Checker Cab** (☎ 901/577–7777).

BY TROLLEY

The Memphis Area Transit Authority (☞ *above*) operates the 2½-mi Main Street Trolley, fare 50¢ (25¢ during weekday lunch hours), in downtown Memphis. The recently completed Riverfront Loop extension, adjacent to Riverside Drive, connects with the Main Street Trolley.

Contacts and Resources

B&B RESERVATION SERVICES

Bed & Breakfast in Memphis Reservation Service (⊠ Box 111141, Memphis 38111-1141, ☎ 901/327–6129 or 800/336–2087, ℻ 901/458–1003).

EMERGENCIES

Ambulance, police (☎ 911). Near-downtown hospitals with 24-hour emergency service in Memphis include **Baptist Memorial Hospital Medical Center** (✉ 899 Madison Ave., ☎ 901/227–2727) and **Methodist Hospitals of Memphis** (✉ 1265 Union Ave., ☎ 901/726–7000).

GUIDED TOURS

Memphis Queen Line Riverboats (☎ 901/527–5694 or 800/221–6197) has 1½-hour sightseeing and two-hour dinner cruises. Sightseeing cruises run daily throughout the year, and dinner cruises run March–November from Wednesday through Sunday. **Blues City Tours** (☎ 901/ 522–9229) offers riverboat rides.

Carriage Tours of Memphis (☎ 901/527–7542) offers horse-drawn carriage rides.

Blues City Tours (☞ *above*) offers motor-coach tours to Memphis sites including Graceland, Mud Island, and Beale Street, plus nightly tours that include dinner and a show. The **Center for Southern Folklore** (☞ Sights to See *in* Downtown Memphis, *above*) gives tours of Beale Street, a farm on the Delta, and prominent areas of musical interest. **Gray Line/Stardust** (☎ 901/346–8687) operates day and night motor-coach tours to downtown and greater Memphis. **Heritage Tours** (☎ 901/527–3427) explores the area's rich African-American cultural heritage. **Unique Tours** (☎ 901/527–8876 or 800/235–1984) has three-day, two-night tours of Graceland, the National Civil Rights Museum, Mud Island, and other attractions.

PHARMACY

Walgreen's (✉ 1863 Union St., ☎ 901/272–1141).

RADIO STATIONS

AM: WMC 79, news and talk. **FM:** WEGR 103, adult contemporary and easy listening; WHRK 97, rhythm and blues.

VISITOR INFORMATION

Tennessee Welcome Center (✉ 119 N. Riverside Dr., 38103, ☎ 901/ 543–5333) is open 24 hours a day, seven days a week and is staffed daily from 9 to 6. **Memphis Convention & Visitors Bureau** (✉ 47 Union Ave., 38103, ☎ 901/543–5300 or 800/873–6282) is open weekdays 8:30–5.

NASHVILLE

Heralded as Music City, USA, and the country-music capital of the world, Tennessee's fast-growing capital city also shines as a leading center of higher education, appropriately known as the Athens of the South. Both labels fit. Nashville has prospered from them both, emerging as one of the South's most vibrant cities in the process. The Gaylor Entertainment Center (formerly Nashville Arena), a 20,000-seat facility spanning three blocks at 5th and Broadway, opened in 1996. Connected to the city's convention center by a tunnel, the Arena hosted the U.S. Figure Skating Championship in 1997. A successful drive to land both a National Football League and a National Hockey League franchise, coupled with a population gain that has pushed Nashville ahead of Memphis, has put Nashville into the major leagues of American cities.

Nashville's *Grand Ole Opry* radio program, which began as station WSM's *Barn Dance* in 1925 and thrived throughout the Great Depression right into today's MTV years, established the town as a music center. The Opry, which has added such popular newcomers as Alison Kraus, Steve Wariner, and Martina McBride to its cast, now performs in a sleek $15 million Opry House. The infusion of talent is attracting a new generation of fans. The Opry is still as gleeful and down-home informal as it was when ticket holders with handheld fans to combat the sweltering heat used to jam into the old Ryman Auditorium. Bolstering Nashville's reputation as a music town are dozens of clubs, performance stages (including the revitalized Ryman), and television tapings open to the public, as well as memorials to many country-music stars. The District, the downtown area along 2nd Avenue and historic Broadway, has emerged as another destination for tourists and locals alike, with restaurants, specialty shopping, and entertainment options. And, of course, legendary Music Row continues to beckon aspiring singers, musicians, and songwriters with stars in their eyes and lyrics tucked in their back pockets.

Much of Nashville's role as a cultural leader, enhanced by the presence of the Tennessee Performing Arts Center that opened in 1985, is derived from the presence of 16 colleges and universities, two medical schools, two law schools, and six graduate business schools. Several, including Vanderbilt University, have national or international reputations, and many have private art galleries. As ancient Athens was the "School of Hellas," so Nashville, where a full-size replica of the Parthenon graces Centennial Park, fills this role in the contemporary South. The historic sites throughout the city—such as the Hermitage, Belle Meade Plantation, and Travellers' Rest—add another dimension.

The Cumberland River horizontally bisects Nashville's central city. Numbered avenues, running north–south, are west of and parallel to the river; numbered streets are east of the river and parallel to it.

Downtown Nashville

Numbers in the text correspond to numbers in the margin and on the Downtown Nashville map.

Downtown Nashville has much to offer in the way of history, music, entertainment, dining, and specialty shopping. A walk through this compact area is a good way to take it all in.

A Good Walk

Begin at **Bicentennial Mall** ㉛, an outdoor history park, and the farmers' market. West of the park, on Harrison Street, is the **Museum of Tobacco Art and History** ㉜. Walk around James Robertson Parkway and turn left on Charlotte Avenue to visit the Greek Revival **State Capitol** ㉝. Across the avenue are the **War Memorial Auditorium** ㉞, the **Tennessee State Museum** ㉟, and the **Tennessee Performing Arts Center** ㊱.

Walk down 5th Avenue to **Downtown Presbyterian Church** ㊲ on Church Street and then go three blocks east to 2nd Avenue and the **District** ㊳, a good spot for lunch, dinner, or dancing. Nearby, toward the river, is a re-creation of historic **Fort Nashborough** ㊴. South on 1st Avenue is **Riverfront Park** ㊵, a fine place for resting before proceeding two blocks west to **Hatch Show Print** ㊶, a longtime poster print shop on Broadway, and on to the **Ryman Auditorium and Museum** ㊷, on 5th Avenue between Broadway and Commerce Street.

TIMING
Allow at least a day, depending on how long you tend to linger and whether you shop for souvenirs. Most of these attractions offer self-guided tours, so you can set your own pace. Keep in mind that the Tennessee State Museum is closed Monday.

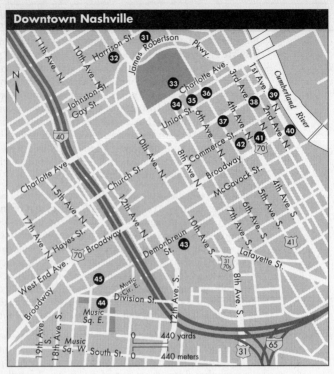

Downtown Nashville

Sights to See

31 Bicentennial Mall. This 19-acre outdoor history park, complete with a 200-ft granite map of Tennessee and the Walk of Counties, was built in 1996 in honor of the state's 200th birthday. The highlight of the park is a 2,000-seat amphitheater where community bands and children's shows are often staged. Staff at the welcome center can answer questions. The adjacent **farmers' market** (⊠ 900 8th Ave. N) contains 208 open-air stalls and a food court with local restaurants (most of which are open for lunch but not dinner). ⊠ *598 James Robertson Pkwy.,* ☎ *615/741–5800.* ☺ *Daily 7 AM–10 PM.*

38 The District. Thanks to an extensive preservation program begun in the early 1980s, this 16-square-block area between Church Street and Broadway is packed with handsomely restored 19th-century redbrick warehouses and storefronts. On Thursday, June–September, an after-work street party, Dancin' in the District, assembles with live music ranging from jazz to alternative rock. The Wildhorse Saloon, a huge country music dance hall, plus an array of popular local and chain restaurants and clubs, increases the festive atmosphere.

37 Downtown Presbyterian Church. This Egyptian Revival tabernacle (circa 1851) was designed by noted Philadelphia architect William Strickland. It's a National Historic Landmark. Docents are available weekdays 10–2. Other times, ring the buzzer for admittance. ⊠ *Corner of 5th Ave. and Church St.*

39 Fort Nashborough. High on limestone bluffs along the river, a crude log fort, whose original was built in 1779 to protect and shelter early settlers, overlooks Nashville. This painstaking re-creation, built in 1962, serves as a monument to courageous city founders. In five log cabins, costumed interpreters evoke the indomitable spirit of the American age of settlement. ✉ *170 1st Ave. N,* ☎ *615/862–8400.* 🎫 *Free.* ⊙ *Daily 9–5.*

👆 ㊸ **Frist Center for Visual Arts.** Set to open in the spring of 2001, this art gallery will boast 20,000 ft of exhibit space and offer the city an ambitious showcase of paintings, sculpture, and other visual art. The historic building, with its original art deco exterior, was formerly Nashville's downtown post office (some postal operations will still occur on site). In its current incarnation as the Frist Center, the building will house three art galleries, a children's discovery gallery, a 250-seat auditorium, gift shop, café, art workshops, and an art resource center. ✉ *209 10th Ave. S,* ☎ *615/244–3340.* 🎫 *Not available at press time.* ⊙ *Not available at press time.*

Gibson Bluegrass Showcase. The new Opry Mills complex is the setting for this bluegrass extravaganza, which provides an inside look at the music that gave country its roots. The Showcase is an all-in-one museum, performance venue, production facility, and retail center. From a sight-and-sound history of bluegrass to on-site crafting of bluegrass instruments like the Dobro (a kind of acoustic guitar) and banjo, this center explores the music to its fullest. Legendary bluegrass performers such as Earl Scruggs play live music nightly. Allow at least 45 minutes for a visit. ✉ *2802 Opryland Dr.,* ☎ *615/871–4500 or 615/514–2200.* 🎫 *Museum and store free; show $5.95, dinner and show $10.95.* ⊙ *Mon.–Sat. 10–9:30, Sun. 11–8. Shows Mon.–Sat. at 8* PM, *Sun at 4 and 6.*

㊶ **Hatch Show Print.** One of the nation's oldest poster print shops has been in business since 1879 and has printed posters for vaudeville shows, circuses, sporting events, and, most notably, Grand Ole Opry stars. The shop now makes posters and prints for contemporary artists and events. There's no formal tour, but this place is a slice of history which you can explore on your own. Hatch Show is now owned by the Country Music Hall of Fame and Museum (☞ Nashville's Music Row, *below*). ✉ *316 Broadway,* ☎ *615/265–1639.* ⊙ *Mon.–Sat. 10–6.*

㉜ **Museum of Tobacco Art and History.** This museum near the Bicentennial Mall (☞ *above*) uses art, antiques, and folk art to showcase the history of tobacco from Christopher Columbus to the 20th century. Meerschaum pipes, Delft tobacco jars, early advertising, Indian pipes, and cigar store figures make the collection intriguing. ✉ *800 Harrison St.,* ☎ *615/271–2291.* 🎫 *Free.* ⊙ *Mon.–Sat. 9–4.*

㊵ **Riverfront Park.** Though considerably smaller, the Cumberland River has been as important to Nashville as the Mississippi has been to Memphis. This welcoming green enclave on its banks has an expansive view of the busy barge traffic on the muddy river. The park serves as a popular venue for free summer concerts, block parties, and picnics, as well as a docking spot for riverboat excursions (☞ Contacts and Resources *in* Nashville A to Z, *below*). The Tennessee Fox Trot Carousel (☞ *below*) is a new addition. ✉ *100 1st Ave. N.*

㊷ **Ryman Auditorium and Museum.** A country-music shrine, the Ryman Auditorium and Museum was home to the Grand Ole Opry from 1943 to 1974. The auditorium seats 2,000 for live performances of classical, jazz, pop, gospel, and, of course, country. The museum displays photographs and memorabilia of past Ryman Auditorium performances that provide a history of both the facility and country music. ✉ *116 5th Ave. N, between Broadway and Commerce St.,* ☎ *615/254–1445 or 615/889–6611 for tickets.* 🎫 *Tours $8.* ⊙ *Daily 8:30–4; call for show schedules and ticket prices.*

③③ **State Capitol.** The state capitol was designed by noted Philadelphia architect William Strickland (1788–1854), who was so impressed with his Greek Revival creation that he requested—and received—entombment behind one of the building's walls. On the grounds—guarded by statues of such Tennessee heroes as Andrew Jackson—are buried the 11th U.S. president, James K. Polk, and his wife. ⊠ *Charlotte Ave. between 6th and 7th Aves.,* ☎ *615/741–1621.* ☐ *Free.* ☉ *Tours weekdays 9–4.*

🖱 ★**Tennessee Fox Trot Carousel.** A new attraction at Riverfront Park (☞ *above*), the carousel opened in summer 1998 and is a unique tribute to the state's culture and history. Nashville native and internationally renowned artist Red Grooms designed 37 riding figures for the carousel, from Andrew Jackson and Davy Crockett to Kitty Wells, Chet Atkins, and other country greats. There's even a figure for the spooky folk legend, the Bell Witch. The throngs of visitors attracted to this smash-hit addition to the park receive a fun history lesson that's hard to forget. ⊠ *Riverfront Park, 100 1st Ave. N.* ☐ *$2.* ☉ *Daily 8:30–5:30.*

③⑥ **Tennessee Performing Arts Center.** Part of the State Capitol (☞ *above*) complex, TPAC, as it's known, comprises Jackson Hall, Johnson Hall, and Polk Theater—named for the three U.S. presidents Tennessee has produced. **TPAC Friends** (☎ 615/298–3877) offers backstage tours of the center by appointment. ⊠ *505 Deaderick St.,* ☎ *615/255–9600.* ☐ *Free.* ☉ *Tues.–Sat. 10–5, Sun. 1–5.*

③⑤ **Tennessee State Museum.** More than 6,000 artifacts and rotating art and history exhibits trace the state's history from the days of Native American settlement through the Civil War and into the 20th century. ⊠ *505 Deaderick St.,* ☎ *615/741–2692.* ☐ *Free.* ☉ *Tues.–Sat. 10–5, Sun. 1–5.*

③④ **War Memorial Auditorium.** Inside this 1,900-seat venue for meetings, concerts, and theater, is a military museum honoring the state's World War I dead. ⊠ *Corner of 7th and Union Sts.,* ☎ *615/741–9277.* ☐ *Free.* ☉ *Mon.–Sat. 10–5, Sun. 1–5.*

Nashville's Music Row

Music Row, just a few miles from downtown, is where music is made. High-rise office buildings that hold publishing and licensing companies are mixed in with bungalows that house up-and-coming music entities. The main attraction is the Country Music Hall of Fame, where the admission price includes a trolley tour of Music Row and a very interesting tour of Studio B.

Numbers in the text correspond to numbers in the margin and on the Downtown Nashville map.

A Good Walk

Music Row is off I–40 (Demonbreun Street exit). The Row itself is along 16th Avenue, with music-publishing offices and recording studios stretching toward Belmont Boulevard. Park for free at the **Country Music Hall of Fame** ④④. Then walk up to 16th Avenue and up Demonbreun, where there are souvenir shops and other attractions, including the **Car Collectors Hall of Fame** ④⑤.

TIMING

Allow a half day to see Music Row attractions.

Sights to See

④⑤ **Car Collectors Hall of Fame.** One of Elvis's Cadillacs, Marty Robbins's Packard, and 40 other flashy vehicles with country origins are among

the displays. ⊠ *1534 Demonbreun St.,* ☎ *270/767–0947.* ⌨ *$4.95.*
☉ *Sept.–May, daily 9–5; June–Aug., daily 9–9.*

★ ㊹ **Country Music Hall of Fame and Museum.** Costumes, instruments,
films, and photos immortalize well-loved country music stars from Roy
Acuff to Patsy Cline to Vince Gill. A ticket for the Hall of Fame includes a guided trolley tour of Music Row and admission to the legendary RCA **Studio B,** two blocks away. Elvis, Dolly Parton, and
countless others recorded here; now the studio is a hands-on exhibit
area showing how records are produced. In late spring 2001 the country shrine is scheduled to move across from the Gaylord Entertainment
Center downtown. ⊠ *4 Music Sq. E,* ☎ *615/256–1639.* ⌨ *$10.75.*
☉ *June–Aug., daily 8–6; Sept.–May, daily 9–5.*

OFF THE
BEATEN PATH

CARL VAN VECHTEN GALLERY – Alfred Stieglitz rewarded Fisk University's
progressive arts program with a bequest from his collection of 20th-cen-
tury paintings and his own superb photographs. Stieglitz's wife, Georgia O'Keeffe, helped install the collection, which holds some of her own
paintings as well as works by Picasso and Renoir. The gallery also exhibits African sculpture. ⊠ *Fisk University at 18th Ave. N,* ☎ *615/329–
8543.* ⌨ *Donation suggested.* ☉ *Tues.–Fri. 9–5, weekends 1–5.*

AARON DOUGLAS GALLERY – Also at Fisk University, on the library's third
floor, this gallery features African-American art including paintings,
drawings, sculpture, watercolors, and prints. Artists on display include
William H. Johnson, Aaron Douglas, James Lesesne Wells, Malvin Gray
Johnson, and Henry Ossawa Tanner. In addition, you'll find African art
and pastel portraits by Winold Reiss on the first floor and Gregory Rid-
ley's abstract paintings and copper repoussé on the second floor. ⊠ *Fisk
University at 18th Ave. N, University Library,* ☎ *615/329–8720.* ⌨
Free. ☉ *Tues.–Fri. 11–1.*

Greater Nashville

To get a more complete feeling for the city, you'll want to explore the
area beyond downtown. Among the offerings are historic plantations,
a variety of museums covering everything from toys to science, and some
great places for kids, including the Nashville Zoo—not to mention the
Grand Ole Opry.

The Opryland theme park closed in 1997 and was replaced with a 200-
store shopping, dining, and entertainment complex in 2000. The complex includes the Opry Mills shopping complex, Cumberland Landing
(a riverside eating and entertainment venue), and the Grand Ole Opry.

*Numbers in the text correspond to numbers in the margin and on the
Greater Nashville map.*

A Good Drive

Nashville's attractions are like spokes on a wagon wheel, so expect to
spend a lot of time in the car. The **Grand Ole Opry** ㊻ is a good first
stop, northeast of downtown off Briley Parkway. Next door the **Opryland Hotel** ㊽ is worth a look. From the hotel you might choose to pursue the attractions in a clockwise fashion, starting at Donelson Pike
with Andrew Jackson's home, the **Hermitage** ㊾, and continuing along
Harding Place to **Travellers' Rest** ㊿ (a house built by one of Jackson's
friends), the botanical gardens at **Cheekwood** ㊿, and the lovely Greek
Revival **Belle Meade Plantation** ㉝. The Italianate **Belmont Mansion** ㉞
is off Hillsboro Road and is near the **Parthenon** ㉟, a copy of the Greek
original, on West End Avenue. The **Music Valley Wax Museum** ㊴, is a
good place to wind up the tour.

484

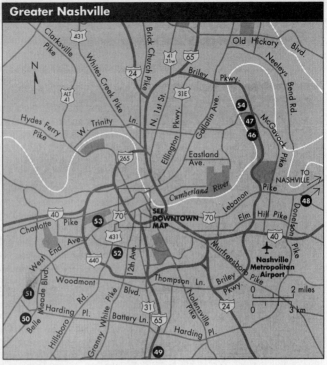

Greater Nashville

TIMING

Allow at least a day and a half to two days to tour these attractions. The guided tours at the homes can be more time-consuming than self-guided attractions.

Sights to See

★ ⑤ **Belle Meade Plantation.** Known as the "queen of the Tennessee plantations," this stunning Greek Revival house is recognized by the Civil War bullet holes that riddle its columns. Guides in period costumes lead you through the mansion, furnished in a pre-Civil War Victorian style, and the carriage house with its antique carriages. The mansion is the centerpiece of a 5,300-acre estate that was one of the nation's first and finest Thoroughbred breeding farms. It's also the site of the famous Iroquois, the oldest amateur steeplechase in America, a society event now run each May in nearby Percy Warner Park. A Victorian carriage museum with an impressive collection continues the equine theme. A new two-story **visitors center,** modeled after a traditional Southern paddock, has been added, as well as the **Cafe at Belle Meade,** whose menu comes courtesy of Nashville's renowned Loveless Cafe (☞ Dining, *below*). ⊠ *5025 Harding Rd.,* ☎ *615/356–0501.* ☞ *$8.* ⊙ *Mon.–Sat. 9–5, Sun. 1–5.*

⑤ **Belmont Mansion.** This 1850s Italianate villa was the home of Adelicia Acklen, Nashville's answer to Scarlett O'Hara, who married "once for money, once for love, and once for the hell of it." On Belmont College's campus, it's a gem right down to its sweeping staircase designed for grand entrances and cast-iron gazebos perfect for romance. ⊠ *1900 Belmont Blvd.,* ☎ *615/460–5459.* ☞ *$6.* ⊙ *June–Aug., Mon.–Sat. 10–4, Sun. 1–5; Sept.–May, Tues.–Sat. 10–4.*

⑤ **Cheekwood Botanical Garden and Museum of Art.** No visit to Nashville is complete without a trip to these 55 beautiful acres, which include the Botanical Garden, the mile-long Woodland Sculpture Trail, and the Pineapple Room restaurant. Among the displays are color, seasonal, water, and Japanese gardens, as well as herb, wildflower, and perennial gardens. Cheekwood, a Georgian-style mansion built in the late 1920s, was once the private residence of the Cheek family of Maxwell House Coffee fame. The mansion reopened in 1999 after extensive renovation and holds a collection of 19th- and 20th-century American art. The estate's former horse stables have been converted into art galleries devoted to permanent and traveling exhibits. A new series, the *Temporary Contemporary Series,* showcases the creations of local and regional artists. ⊠ *1200 Forrest Park Dr.,* ☎ *615/356–8000.* 🎫 *$8.* ☉ *Mon.–Sat. 9:30–4:30, Sun. 11–4:30.*

Ⓒ **Cumberland Science Museum and Sudekum Planetarium.** Children are invited to look, touch, smell, climb, and listen through interactive exhibits unveiling natural wonders. Exhibits include traveling national blockbusters such as *Star Trek* and *The Beat Goes On,* as well as the child-size Curiosity Corner. Daily live science demonstrations and animal shows add to the educational mix. The 40-ft-high planetarium has a variety of daily shows. ⊠ *800 Fort Negley Blvd.,* ☎ *615/862–5160.* 🎫 *$6; planetarium $1.* ☉ *June–Aug., Mon.–Sat. 10–5, Sun. 12:30–5:30; Sept.–May, Tues.–Sat. 10–5, Sun. 12:30–5:30.*

★ ㊻ **Grand Ole Opry.** This enormously popular radio show, performed in the Grand Ole Opry House, has been bringing America country music for more than 70 years. You can see superstars, legends, and up-and-coming stars on this stage. The Opry seats about 4,400 people and is broadcast live on WSM AM 650 every Friday and Saturday night at 6:30 and 9:30; buy tickets well in advance, particularly during Fan Fair week in June. ⊠ *2804 Opryland Dr.,* ☎ *615/889–6611 for ticket information.* 🎫 *$20.50–$22.50 for weekend lineups, $25–$75 for special shows.*

★ ㊽ **Hermitage.** The life and times of Andrew Jackson, known as Old Hickory, are reflected with great care at this house and museum. Jackson built the mansion on 600 acres for his wife, Rachel, for whose honor he fought and won a duel. Both are buried in the family graveyard. The **Andrew Jackson Center,** a 28,000-square-ft museum, visitor center, and education center, contains many Jackson artifacts never before exhibited. Knowledgeable guides take you through the mansion, furnished with many original pieces. An 18-minute film, *Old Hickory,* provides further background on the seventh president. Note the guitar-shape driveway designed to honor the "blue grass state." By the 1840s more than 140 African-American slaves lived and worked on the Hermitage Plantation, and archeological digs have uncovered the remains of many slave dwellings—**yard cabins, Alfred's cabin,** and **field quarters.** Across the road from the plantation stands the **Tulip Grove Mansion,** built by Mrs. Jackson's nephew, and the **Hermitage Church,** fondly known as "Rachel's church." ⊠ *4580 Rachel's La., Hermitage,* ☎ *615/889–2941; about 12 mi east of Nashville (I–40E to Old Hickory Blvd. exit).* 🎫 *$9.50.* ☉ *Daily 9–5.*

Music Valley Wax Museum. The lure of lifelike wax figures is as strong as ever, and certainly Nashville's country music stars make ripe material. Here fans can stroll among 50 of country music's brightest—including the most recent addition, Alan Jackson—all dressed in actual costumes. A stroll on the Sidewalk of the Stars yields the rewards of 250 entertainers' footprints, handprints, and signatures pressed in concrete. ⊠ *2515 McGavock Pike,* ☎ *615/883–3612.* 🎫 *$3.50.* ☉ *Memorial Day–Labor Day, daily 8 AM–10 PM; Labor Day–Memorial Day, daily 9–5.*

Ⓒ **Nashville Shores.** This sunny water theme park is a good place to exhaust the kids and have some fun while you're at it. The park offers a smorgasbord of outdoor entertainment, including 700 ft of water slides, giant lily-pad hops, sand dunes, dinosaur fossils, beaches, pools, miniature golf, boat and jet-ski rentals, and picnic areas. The *Nashville Shoreliner* offers cruises. ✉ *4001 Bell Rd., Hermitage,* ☎ *615/889–7050.* 💵 *$13.95; ½ price after 3 weekdays.* ◷ *May–Sept., Sun.–Fri. 10–7, Sat. 10–8.*

Ⓒ **Nashville Toy Museum.** The crowd-pleasing museum and train store houses one of America's most prestigious model train collections, with trains operating on enormous layouts. This attraction in the Grand Ole Opry area also has toy soldiers from around the world, a collection of vintage German teddy bears, giant ship models, early planes, farm tractors, dollhouses, and antique china dolls. The collections span 150 years and transport even the most curmudgeonly adults back to the joys of childhood. **Peterson's Train Store** is a hub for train enthusiasts and collectors, offering hundreds of new and vintage models, as well as opportunities for trade, repairs, and shoptalk. ✉ *2613 McGavock Pike,* ☎ *615/883–8870.* 💵 *$3.50.* ◷ *June–Aug., daily 9–9; Sept.–May, daily 9–5.*

Ⓒ **Nashville Zoo at Grassmere.** Since its recent merger with Grassmere's Wildlife Park, the zoo has relocated to take advantage of Grassmere's more than 200 spring-fed acres in the heart of Nashville. The zoo's transformation to its new home will be completed some time between 2003–2005, but in the meantime more than 600 exotic animals are on display in naturalistic environments, including clouded leopards, lions, white tigers, ring-tailed lemurs, giraffes, and red pandas. A new exhibit, the *Unseen New World,* features red-eyed tree frogs, rhino iguanas, leaf-nosed bats, and about 75 other species of reptiles, amphibians, insects, mammals, and birds, many of which have never before been exhibited in Nashville. At the **Jungle Gym Playground,** children can enjoy 66,000 square ft of play area, including a pond, cargo netting, slides, and climbers. The **Grassmere Historic Home and Farm** brings to life an 1880s-era working farm, with a barn, barnyard, livestock, hands-on demonstrations, and period gardens illustrating a typical variety of uses—culinary, medicinal, and decorative. The Italianate-style home, built in 1810, is the second-oldest residence in Davidson County open to the public. ✉ *3777 Nolensville Rd., 5 mi south of downtown,* ☎ *615/833–1534.* 💵 *$6; parking $2.* ◷ *Apr.–Sept., daily 9–6; Oct.–Mar., daily 9–4.*

④⑦ **Opryland Hotel.** Famous for its imaginative public spaces and displays of artwork, the Opryland Hotel (☞ Lodging, *below*) is a Nashville highlight. Three indoor garden areas covering acres of space are crowned by sparkling glass roofs. The newest is the Delta, which spreads over 4½ acres and has a river running through it. The hotel and convention center have numerous lounges with free music, as well as restaurants; parking is $5. ✉ *2800 Opryland Dr.,* ☎ *615/889–1000.*

★ ⑤③ **Parthenon.** An exact copy of the Athenian original, Nashville's Parthenon was constructed to commemorate Tennessee's 1897 centennial. Across the street from Vanderbilt University's campus, in Centennial Park, it's a magnificent sight, perched on a gentle green slope beside a duck pond. Inside are the Cowan Collection, with 63 works of art by American artists, traveling exhibits, and such exquisite statuary as the 42-ft *Athena Parthenos,* the tallest indoor sculpture in the Western world. ✉ *West End and 25th Aves.,* ☎ *615/862–8431.* 💵 *$2.50.* ◷ *Oct.–Mar., Tues.–Sat. 9–4:30; Apr.–Sept., Tues.–Sat. 9–4:30, Sun. 12:30–4:30.*

49 **Travellers' Rest.** Following the fortunes of pioneer landowner and judge John Overton—the law partner, mentor, campaign manager, and lifelong friend of Andrew Jackson, whose own home is nearby—this early 19th-century clapboard home metamorphosed from a 1799 four-room cottage to a 12-room mansion with Federal-influenced and Greek Revival additions. The mansion's interior has been restored to its mid-19th-century state with period furnishings. Also on the grounds are a restored smokehouse, kitchen house, and formal gardens. Travellers' Rest is off I-65S at the first of two Harding Place exits. ⊠ *636 Farrell Pkwy.,* ☎ *615/832–2962.* ⊡ *$6.* ⊘ *Tues.–Sat. 10–5, Sun. 1–5.*

☾ **Wave Country.** A mile from the Grand Ole Opry and a great place for a cooldown if you're visiting in the summer, Wave Country has a large wave pool and a three-flume water slide. ⊠ *2320 Two Rivers Pkwy., off Briley Pkwy.,* ☎ *615/885–1052.* ⊡ *$6.* ⊘ *Memorial Day–Labor Day, daily 10–7.*

Dining

American

$$ ✕ **Belle Meade Brasserie.** Nashville's poshest neighborhood welcomed this comfortable suburban restaurant with open arms in 1988. The menu is a symphony of best-loved recipes from all over the United States—an appetizer of corn fritters and pepper jelly, double pork chops with Thai barbecue sauce, oven-roasted grouper, and crawfish étouffée. Desserts are just as compelling, including a knockout Russian raspberry gratin. ⊠ *101 Page Rd.,* ☎ *615/356–5450. AE, DC, MC, V. Closed Sun. No lunch.*

$$ ✕ **Capitol Grille and Oak Bar.** This charming restaurant in down-★ town's historic Westin Hermitage Hotel serves cuisine with a regional flair, including sautéed grouper accompanied by garlic whipped potatoes. Another top pick is the filet mignon with a Portobello mushroom demiglace (a rich brown sauce) and crispy potatoes. The Capitol Grille is consistently ranked as one of Nashville's top restaurants by local food reviewers; one called it "opulent food." ⊠ *231 6th Ave. N,* ☎ *615/345–7116. AE, DC, MC, V.*

$$ ✕ **F. Scott's.** Contemporary American bistro cuisine is offered in this Green Hills spot, which has both the comfort of a neighborhood eatery and the sophistication of an upscale restaurant. The dining room is done in a warm version of art deco that uses mocha as the dominant color. Popular dishes on the seasonally changing menu are oven-roasted veal tenderloin with a tomato, artichoke, potato, and bacon ragout and braised lamb shank with rosemary tomato broth; lobster with ginger butter, sugar snap peas, and sticky rice is a summer choice. The wine list is extensive. There's live jazz nightly in the bar. ⊠ *2210 Crestmoor Rd.,* ☎ *615/269–5861. AE, D, DC, MC, V. No lunch.*

$$ ✕ **Mad Platter.** This local favorite in historic downtown Nashville blends traditional gourmet with California cuisine, using locally available ingredients from the nearby farmers' market. The baked salmon with red grapes and feta cheese, rack of lamb, and bananas Foster are favorites here. It's a popular spot for power lunches by day. Jazz music transforms the cozy 18th-century brownstone into a romantic nook at night. ⊠ *1239 6th Ave. N,* ☎ *615/242–2563. Reservations essential for dinner. AE, D, MC, V. No lunch weekends.*

$$ ✕ **Sunset Grill.** Seafood, pastas, steaks, and vegetarian and eclectic spe-★ cials highlight the menu of this postmodern restaurant that displays the work of local artist Paul Harmon. A good entrée choice is Voodoo pasta with andouille sausage, chicken, and shrimp in a roasted pepper sauce served with jalapeño-flavored fettuccine. Seventy wines are served by the glass. A tip: Food prices are slashed by 50% after 10 PM

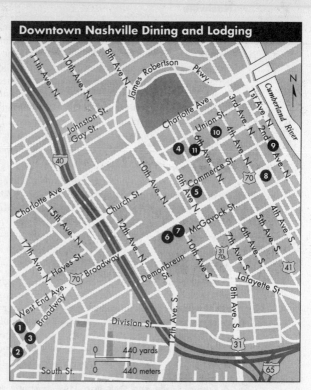

Downtown Nashville Dining and Lodging

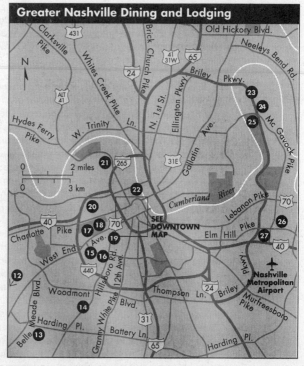

Greater Nashville Dining and Lodging

(midnight on weekends) until closing at 1:30 AM. ⊠ *2001A Belcourt Ave.,* ☎ *615/386–3663. AE, D, DC, MC, V. No lunch weekends.*

$ ✕ **NASCAR Cafe.** This is a theme chain restaurant with a standard menu, but many people (including kids) will appreciate this glimpse into the racing experience, which highlights the sounds, sights, and personalities of NASCAR. ⊠ *305 Broadway,* ☎ *615/313–7223. AE, DC, MC, V.*

Continental

$$–$$$$ ✕ **Arthur's.** This restaurant is in the stylishly renovated Union Station, where an upscale hotel has taken the place of the train terminal. The seven-course meals are dazzling (à la carte is also available) and the ambience romantic. The menu changes daily, but specialties include rainbow trout, duck, and lamb. Save room for dessert: the bananas Foster is especially good. The decor is lush, with lace curtains, velveteen-upholstered chairs, white linen, and fine silver service. ⊠ *Union Station, 1001 Broadway,* ☎ *615/255–1494. AE, DC, MC, V. No lunch.*

$$$ ✕ **Wild Boar.** Superb contemporary French cuisine is presented in an el-
★ egant setting that resembles a European hunting lodge. On the menu are Maine lobster, Canadian elk filet mignon, and seared guinea hen. The 15,000-bottle wine cellar gives the Wild Boar one of the top wine lists in the world, and 25 wines are available by the glass. ⊠ *2014 Broadway,* ☎ *615/329–1313. AE, D, DC, MC, V. Closed Sun.–Mon. No lunch Sat.*

$$–$$$ ✕ **Mère Bulles.** This restaurant in the heart of the District is known for elegant dinners and lavish Sunday brunch. The three intimate dining rooms all overlook the Cumberland River. Specialties include Colorado rack of lamb with a rosemary and thyme sauce, macadamia nut-crusted mahimahi with tropical citrus, and filet mignon with veal jus. There is music nightly in the Cabaret lounge. ⊠ *152 2nd Ave. N,* ☎ *615/256–1946. AE, DC, MC, V.*

Italian

$$$ ✕ **Mario's Ristorante Italiano.** Owner Mario Ferrari and his restaurant are a Nashville institution, consistently drawing political figures and celebrities for northern Italian food in an elegant atmosphere. The seafood and veal—such as the saltimbocca, veal medallions with mozzarella, prosciutto, mushrooms, and fresh sage—are enormously palate pleasing. ⊠ *2005 Broadway,* ☎ *615/327–3232. Reservations essential. Jacket and tie. AE, D, DC, MC, V. Closed Sun.*

Mediterranean

$$ ✕ **Cakewalk/Zola.** From the romantic interior to the adventurous menu, this restaurant re-creates a Mediterranean journey. A 27-ft mural graces the main dining room, while gauzy fabric billows in the Tent Room. Chef Debra Paquette, who owns the restaurant with her husband, Ernie, combines flavors from around the Mediterranean to create specialties such as Damascus duck, pomegranate pork, and seafood Operetta, a tasty bouillabaisse. ⊠ *3001 West End Ave.,* ☎ *615/ 320–7778. DC, MC, V.*

Southern

$ ✕ **Loveless.** This is an experience in true down-home Southern cook-
★ ing. Don't come for the decor—decidedly lax, with red-and-white-check tablecloths—but rather for the featherlight homemade biscuits and preserves, country ham and red-eye gravy, and fried chicken. ⊠ *8400 Hwy. 100,* ☎ *615/646–9700. MC, V.*

$ ✕ **Pancake Pantry.** This Nashville institution is the place to go for breakfast. It's a favorite haunt of celebrities like Garth Brooks and Alan Jackson and also popular with local politicos. Breakfast is the biggie, with 20 kinds of pancakes and homemade syrups, but there are soups and sandwiches for lunch. Expect to wait in line for breakfast on the weekends. ✉ *1796 21st Ave. S,* ☎ *615/383–9333. Reservations not accepted. AE, D, DC, MC, V. No dinner.*

$ **Swett's Restaurant.** A family-owned restaurant in business since 1954, Swett's offers some of the best meat-and-three meals in Nashville. Turnip greens, green beans, pork chops, fried chicken, and real mashed potatoes are all temptations. *2725 Clifton Ave.,* ☎ *615/329–4418. D, MC, V.*

Lodging

$$$$ ⊞ **Loew's Vanderbilt Plaza Hotel.** Celebrities and business travelers grav-
★ itate to this quiet European-style luxury hotel known for top-notch service and convenient to Music Row. The pristine white lobby is grand.
Musicians play nightly in the piano bar, and there's a cigar bar. Gracious guest rooms, some with skyline views, are done with dark cherry
furniture. Plaza suites are individually decorated, and the club-level rooms
have luxurious baths and extra phone and fax lines. ✉ *2100 West End
Ave., 37203,* ☎ *615/320–1700 or 800/235–6397,* FAX *615/320–5019.
327 rooms, 13 suites. 2 restaurants, piano bar, health club. AE, DC,
MC, V.* ✍

$$$$ ⊞ **Opryland Hotel.** This massive hostelry is one of the 25 largest in
★ the world. A 1996 addition called the Delta added nearly a thousand
rooms, plus an indoor river, a 110-ft-wide waterfall, and an amphitheater under a 4-acre glass dome. Harp music is played nightly at
the revolving bar at the Cascades, another skylighted interior space with
streams, waterfalls, and a half-acre lake. Rooms, which are fairly standard in size, have Victorian floral decor in beige and rose tones; request
one overlooking the gardens. The hotel claims to have more meeting space
than any other in the nation. The culinary staff is directed by a member
of the Culinary Olympics U.S. team. ✉ *2800 Opryland Dr., 37214,* ☎
615/889–1000, FAX *615/871–5728. 2,870 rooms, 200 suites. 5 restaurants, pool, wading pool, convention center. AE, D, DC, MC, V.* ✍

$$$$ ⊞ **Renaissance Nashville Hotel.** This luxurious, ultracontemporary
high-rise hotel adjoins the Nashville Convention Center. Spacious
rooms are furnished with period reproductions. Executive Club concierge floors offer extra privacy and personal services. ✉ *611 Commerce St., 37203,* ☎ *615/255–8400,* FAX *615/255–8202. 649 rooms,
24 suites. Restaurant, coffee shop, lounge, indoor pool, hot tub, sauna,
health club, concierge floors. AE, DC, MC, V.*

$$$$ ⊞ **Union Station Hotel.** This Victorian-era hotel in a convenient downtown location was reincarnated from a bustling train station. Late-19th-
century opulence is evoked in the 65-ft barrel-vaulted ceiling, gold-leaf
mirrors, and Tiffany stained glass. Standard rooms are handsomely appointed, and extra luxury awaits Heritage Club Level members, who
receive turndown service, shoe shines, Continental breakfast, and
cocktails. ✉ *1001 Broadway, 37203,* ☎ *615/726–1001 or 800/331–
2123. 124 rooms, 13 suites. Restaurant. AE, DC, MC, V.*

$$–$$$$ ⊞ **Sheraton Nashville Downtown.** Downtown, near the State Capitol
building, this 28-story tower has a vast, skylighted atrium lobby awash
with greenery and overseen by glassed-in elevators. Rooms are spacious
and contemporary, with great views of the growing Nashville skyline.
The hotel is topped by the Pinnacle, Nashville's only revolving rooftop
restaurant. ✉ *623 Union St., 37219,* ☎ *615/259–2000 or 800/447–
9825,* FAX *615/742–6057. 473 rooms, 14 suites. 2 restaurants, coffee
shop, lounge, no-smoking rooms. AE, DC, MC, V.*

$$$ ⊞ **The Inn at Opryland.** This contemporary-style, well-maintained
low-rise motor inn is across the street from, and now owned by, the
Opryland Hotel. ✉ *2401 Music Valley Dr., 37214,* ☎ *615/889–0800,*

FAX 615/883–1230. *303 rooms. Restaurant, lounge, indoor pool, hot tub, sauna. AE, DC, MC, V.*

$$$ ⊡ **Westin Hermitage.** Called the last of Nashville's grand hotels, this historic downtown building sits across from the capitol and the Tennessee Performing Arts Center. Built in 1910, the beaux-arts-style hotel once served as headquarters for both suffragist and antisuffragist groups in the 1920s. The elegant, old-world lobby soars three stories tall toward stained-glass ceilings. Guest suites feature living rooms with work desks and wet bars. ⊠ *231 6th Ave. N, 37219,* ☎ *615/244–3121 or 800/937–8461,* FAX *615/254–6909. 120 suites. Restaurant, refrigerators, meeting rooms. AE, DC, D, MC, V.* ⊛

$$–$$$ ⊡ **Hampton Inn Vanderbilt.** Near the Vanderbilt University campus and Music Row, this six-story inn is clean and contemporary and especially popular with visiting music executives and musicians. Rooms, done in shades of maroon, green, and cream, are spacious. A multipurpose hospitality suite has a conference table, chairs, and an audiovisual unit for meetings, making this a popular corporate choice. ⊠ *1919 West End Ave., 37203,* ☎ *615/329–1144 or 800/426–7866,* FAX *615/320–7112. 171 rooms. Pool, exercise room, meeting rooms. AE, D, DC, MC, V.*

$$ ⊡ **Courtyard by Marriott–Airport.** This handsome, freshly renovated low-rise motor inn with a sunny, gardenlike courtyard offers some amenities you'd expect in higher-price hotels: spacious rooms, king-size beds, oversize work desks, and hot-water dispensers for in-room coffee. ⊠ *2508 Elm Hill Pike, 37214,* ☎ *615/883–9500 or 800/321–2211,* FAX *615/883–0172. 133 rooms, 12 suites. Restaurant, lounge, no-smoking rooms, hot tub. AE, D, DC, MC, V.*

$ ⊡ **Shoney's Inn on Music Row.** On the Trolley Line and a guitar strum away from the Country Music Hall of Fame and other Music Row attractions, this is a typical, clean chain motel. The inn's namesake restaurant has a good, low-cost all-you-can-eat breakfast bar. ⊠ *1521 Demonbreun St., 37203,* ☎ *615/255–9977,* FAX *615/242–6127. 134 rooms, 13 suites. Restaurant. AE, DC, MC, V.*

$ ⊡ **La Quinta Inn–Metro Center.** Guest rooms here are spacious and well lighted, with a large working area and an oversize bed. ⊠ *2001 Metro Center Blvd., 37228,* ☎ *615/259–2130 or 800/531–5900,* FAX *615/242–2650. 121 rooms. Pool. AE, D, DC, MC, V. CP.* ⊛

$ ⊡ **Wilson Inn.** Three miles from the Grand Ole Opry, this five-story hotel is clean and convenient. Many rooms have kitchens. ⊠ *600 Ermac Dr. (Elm Hill Pike exit from Briley Pkwy.), 37214,* ☎ *615/889–4466 or 800/333–9457,* FAX *615/889–0484. 110 rooms. Pool. AE, D, DC, MC, V. CP.* ⊛

$ ⚠ **Opryland KOA.** This 27-acre campground is unique among KOAs, in that Opryland performers put on country music shows here from April through October. Its proximity to Opryland makes it a favorite destination for families. The campground is 11 mi from downtown Nashville. Rates vary with the season. ⊠ *2626 Music Valley Dr., 37214,* ☎ *615/889–0282 or 800/KOA–7789. 435 campsites, 25 cabins. Outdoor and indoor pool, playground, coin laundry. D, MC, V.*

Nightlife and the Arts

For a listing of weekly events, consult the **Visitor Information Center** (☎ 615/259–4747) or the local newspapers. For information on concerts and special events, call **WSM radio's entertainment line** (☎ 615/

737–9595). **TicketMaster** (☎ 615/255–9600) has information on events at various Nashville venues.

The Arts

Nashville has emerged as an arts center, with a full schedule of concerts and other performances; the city also has fine galleries for the visual arts.

LIVE TAPINGS

Anyone wanting to be part of an audience for a live taping of a television show has several options. **Prime Time Country with Gary Chapman** (☎ 615/889–6611 for information) tapes almost every weeknight in the Grand Ole Opry House. The regular free taping of the **Crook & Chase** show is on weekdays at Jim Owens Studios, between Music Row and downtown (✉ 1525 McGavock St., ☎ 615/256–7700). From time to time there are **special-event tapings**, such as the *Everly Brothers Show* (☎ 615/889–6611 for information and reservations). At the cable television network **TNN: The Nashville Network** (✉ 2806 Opryland Dr., ☎ 615/883–7000) opportunities abound to see shows in production.

MUSIC AND DANCE

The Nashville Symphony Orchestra's classical and pops series and concerts by visiting performers are staged at **Andrew Jackson Hall** (TicketMaster, ☎ 615/255–9600), part of the Tennessee Performing Arts Center (☞ Downtown Nashville, *above*). Chamber concerts, touring Broadway shows, and local theatrical performances take place at the Tennessee Performing Arts Center's (☞ Downtown Nashville, *above*) **Polk Theater** (☎ 615/255–9600). Rock and country events are held at the **Gaylord Entertainment Center** (✉ 501 Broadway, ☎ 615/770–2000). The **AmSouth Amphitheatre** (✉ 3839 Murfreesboro Rd., ☎ 615/641–5800) is the site of rock, pop, country, and jazz concerts, musicals, and special events; it also hosts some performances of the Nashville Symphony.

The **Nashville Ballet** (✉ 2976 Sidco Dr., ☎ 615/244–7233 or 800/333–4849) performs works accompanied by the Nashville Symphony Orchestra. Vanderbilt University stages music, dance, and drama productions (many free) at its **Blair School of Music** (✉ 2400 Blakemore Ave., ☎ 615/322–7651).

THEATER

The **Nashville Children's Theatre** (✉ 724 2nd Ave. S, ☎ 615/254–9103) is home to a professional children's theater troupe that performs September–May. At **Chaffin's Barn** (✉ 8204 Hwy. 100, ☎ 615/646–9977 or 800/282–2276) Nashville's first professional theater offers Southern buffet-style eating and Broadway plays year-round. **Circle Players** (✉ 505 Deaderick St., ☎ 615/254–0113), in operation for more than 50 seasons, is Nashville's oldest volunteer-run theater. The community troupe presents six shows a year, from September through May. The **Tennessee Repertory Theatre** (✉ 427 Chestnut St., ☎ 615/244–4878) is the state's largest professional theater company, staging four productions a year from September through May. For more experimental fare, the **Darkhorse Theater** (✉ 4610 Charlotte Ave., ☎ 615/297–7113) features original works and alternative theater and dance.

Nightlife

BARS

Big River Grille & Brewery Works (✉ 111 Broadway, ☎ 615/251–4677) is one of Nashville's hottest brew-pubs. The Nashville start-up **Boscos Nashville Brewing Company** (✉ 1805 21st Ave. S, ☎ 615/385–0050), in the heart of Hillsboro Village, serves Famous Flaming Stone Beer, a steinbier, or stone beer, brewed using hot granite (a method beloved among beer connoisseurs for the slightly caramel tone and taste it produces in the brew). Every weekday a cellarman taps the real ale keg, while pub food fare is cooked in wood-fired ovens. Nashville's version of the **Hard Rock Cafe** (✉ 100 Broadway, ☎ 615/742–9900) is great for burgers. **Planet Hollywood** (✉ 322 Broadway, ☎ 615/313–7827) offers pub grub amid the movie artifacts that have made the celebrity-owned chain famous.

COMEDY

For laughs, try **Zanies Comedy Showplace** (✉ 2025 8th Ave. S, ☎ 615/269–0221). The club hosts a variety of touring stand-up comedians.

COUNTRY MUSIC

Grammy Award–winning talent and Music City's up-and-coming stars often try out their latest material at **Bluebird Cafe** (✉ 4104 Hillsboro Rd., ☎ 615/383–1461), in the posh Green Hills neighborhood. **Douglas Corner Cafe** (✉ 2106A 8th Ave. S, ☎ 615/298–1688) is well known for everything from blues to country. The **Grand Ole Opry** (☞ Greater Nashville, *above*) is the site of country performances on Friday and Saturday evenings. **Nashville Nightlife Breakfast & Dinner Theater** (✉ 2620 Music Valley Dr., ☎ 615/885–5201 or 800/308–5779) presents a 1½-hour country music show accompanied by all the trimmings of a full Southern country buffet. Frequent musical guests include Grand Ole Opry stars such as Jack Greene, Jeannie Seely, and Del Reeves, as well as other recording artists. For those who stick it out, an autograph and photo session follows each show. **Robert's Western World** (✉ 416 Broadway, ☎ 615/248–4818) was originally a clothing store; cowboy boots adorn the walls, but today country music is what you come for. The **Texas Troubadour Theatre** (✉ 2414 Music Valley Dr., ☎ 615/885–0028) presents a country music lover's dream come true—a free midnight jam featuring Opry acts and country music newcomers alike. Audiences can attend the live broadcast of the **Ernest Tubb Midnite Jamboree** each Saturday night. The **Cowboy Church** features Sunday shows such as *A Closer Walk with Patsy Cline*. For honky-tonk atmosphere and all day/all night music, hit **Tootsie's Orchid Lounge** (✉ 422 Broadway, ☎ 615/726–0463). Boot-scoot over to the **Wildhorse Saloon** (✉ 120 2nd Ave. N, ☎ 615/251–1000), with its 3,300-ft dance floor and seating for 1,600.

JAZZ, BLUEGRASS, ROCK, AND VARIETY

Bluegrass lovers flock to the **Bluegrass Inn** (✉ 418 Broadway, ☎ 615/726–2799) for live performances by Buddy Goines and others. On board the **Broadway Dinner Train** (✉ 108 First Ave. S, ☎ 615/254–8000 or 800/274–8010), diners take a 2½-hour train ride while eating a four-course gourmet dinner. Dining cars have been restored to their former elegance, and two lounge cars offer live music.

Big-name pop artists can be found at **Exit/In** (✉ 2208 Elliston Pl., ☎ 615/321–4400). Past performers have included Jerry Lee Lewis, Chuck Mangione, Steve Martin, and the Allman Brothers. **Caffe Milano** (✉ 176 3rd Ave. N, ☎ /255–0073) presents fine food along with some of Nashville's best musicians. For the cigar and martini set, the **Havana Lounge** (✉ 154 2nd Ave., ☎ 615/313–7665) won't disappoint, especially on evenings featuring live swing music. For those who hanker for alternative rock, try **Indienet Record Shop** (✉ 1707 Church St., ☎ 615/321–0882). At this record store/club, rock bands such as Braid, Anti-Flag, and Fury 66 perform. No alcohol or smoking is allowed.

Festivals

Dancin' in The District (☎ 615/256–2073) is a huge, free street party held downtown every Thursday night from May through August; hours are 5–10.

The **International Country Music Fan Fair** (✉ 2804 Opryland Dr., 37214, ☎ 615/889–7503), held by the Grand Ole Opry and the Country Music Association during the second week in June at the Tennessee State Fairgrounds, is country music's premier event. Many tour companies offer packages, but plan ahead: Tickets sell out months in advance.

Outdoor Activities and Sports

Participant Sports

BOATING AND FISHING

You'll find boat rentals at lovely **J. Percy Priest Lake** (✉ 11 mi east of Nashville, off I–40, ☎ 615/889–1975) and **Old Hickory Reservoir** (✉ 15 mi northeast of Nashville via U.S. 31E). **Fun Boat Rentals** (☎ 615/399–7661) has everything from canoes and fishing boats to pontoons.

GOLF

Public courses open year-round are the 18-hole, par-72 **Harpeth Hills** (✉ 2424 Old Hickory Blvd., ☎ 615/862–8493); the 18-hole, par-72 **Hermitage Golf Course** (✉ 3939 Old Hickory Blvd., ☎ 615/847–4001); and the nine-hole, par-36 **Rhodes Golf Course** (✉ 1901 Ed Temple Blvd., ☎ 615/862–8463). Hermitage is the site each April of the LPGA Sara Lee Classic.

JOGGING

Centennial Park, the Vanderbilt University running track, J. Percy Priest Lake, and Percy Warner Park are great for jogging. The 1,000-member running club **Nashville Striders** (☎ 615/331–0111) can recommend choice spots and will provide information on many summer races.

HORSEBACK RIDING

You can jog or canter on gentle steeds at **Ramblin' Breeze Ranch** (✉ 3665 Knight Rd., White's Creek, ☎ 615/876–1029).

ICE-SKATING

Indoor skating is available at **Sportsplex** (✉ 25th Ave. N at Brandau Ave., ☎ 615/862–8480), near Centennial Park.

TENNIS

Several municipal tennis facilities offer good play. **Centennial Sportsplex Tennis Center** (✉ 224 25th Ave. N, ☎ 615/862–8490) has outdoor and indoor courts.

Spectactor Sports

AUTO RACING

NASCAR Winston Racing Series weekly stock-car racing takes place March through September at **Nashville Speedway USA** (✉ Tennessee State Fairgrounds, ☎ 615/726–1818).

BASEBALL

The **Nashville Sounds,** a AAA affiliate of the Chicago White Sox, play home games from mid-April through mid-September at Hershel Greer Stadium (☎ 615/242–4371).

FOOTBALL

Nashville's new **Adelphia Coliseum** (✉ 1 Titans Way, ☎ 615/565–4000 or 888/313–8326) is home to the NFL's **Tennessee Titans,** formerly the Houston Oilers. The 67,000-seat natural-grass stadium, which opened in 1999, sits on the banks of the Cumberland River.

The **Nashville Kats,** a professional indoor football franchise, bring the excitement of the 50-yard indoor war to the Gaylord Entertainment Center (✉ 501 Broadway, ☎ 615/254–KATS).

HOCKEY

The National Hockey League franchise team, the **Nashville Predators,** plays at the Gaylord Entertainment Center (⊠ 501 Broadway, ☎ 615/ 770–2000).

HORSE SHOW

For 10 days from late August to early September, Shelbyville, 50 mi southeast of Nashville, holds the **Tennessee Walking Horse National Celebration** (⊠ Box 1010, 37160, ☎ 615/684–5915), the world's greatest walking horse show.

Shopping

Antiques

Browse for distinctive 18th- and 19th-century English antiques and objets d'art east of downtown at **Madison Antique Mall** (⊠ 320 Gallatin Rd. S, ☎ 615/865–4677), close to Music Row at **Nashville Wedgewood Station Antique Mall** (⊠ 657 Wedgewood Ave., ☎ 615/259–0939), at **Tennessee Antique Mall** (654 Wedgewood Ave., ☎ 615/259–4077), **Goodlettsville Antique Mall** (⊠ 213 N. Main St., Goodlettsville, ☎ 615/ 859–7002), or in Andrew Jackson's stomping grounds at **Hermitage Antique Mall** (⊠ 4144-B Lebanon Rd., Hermitage, ☎ 615/883–5789). The shops along **8th Avenue South** make a good browsing ground.

Arts and Crafts

Cumberland Gallery (⊠ 4107 Hillsboro Circle, ☎ 615/297–0296) sells the works of major regional artists. **The Arts Company** (⊠ 215 5th Ave. N, ☎ 615/254–2040) carries photography, painting, sculpture, outsider art, and unexpected fun art.

The annual **Tennessee Crafts Fair** (☎ 615/665–0502), a juried crafts festival held on the grounds of the Parthenon in early May, is a great source for Tennessee crafts. There are works by 165 contemporary and traditional crafts artists, as well as demonstrations and children's activities.

Books

Bibliophiles appreciate the three-story **Davis-Kidd Booksellers and Cafe** (⊠ Grace's Plaza in Green Hills, 4007 Hillsboro Rd., ☎ 615/385– 2645), open late on weekends. Curl up in a chair with a glass of wine and the latest *New York Times* best-sellers.

Country-and-Western Wear

Nashville Cowboy (⊠ 2434 Music Valley Dr., ☎ 615/871–9448) carries the latest looks in country clothing.

Flea Market

From treasures to just plain "junque"—the **Nashville Flea Market** at the Tennessee State Fairgrounds has it all. Usually, 1,000 traders, craftspeople, and antiques dealers ply their wares the fourth weekend of every month except December (when it's the third weekend of the month). ⊠ *Wedgewood and Rains Aves.,* ☎ *615/862–5016.* ⊙ *Sat. 6–6, Sun. 7–5.*

Music

Country music fans can find the best of country tapes and CDs at **Ernest Tubb Record Shops** (⊠ 2416 Music Valley Dr., ☎ 615/889–2474; ⊠ 417 Broadway, ☎ 615/255–7503; ⊠ 1516 Demonbreun St., ☎ 615/ 244–2845). The **Great Escape** (⊠ 1925 Broadway, ☎ 615/327–0646; ⊠ 111 Gallatin Rd. N, Madison, ☎ 615/865–8052) has great used records of all kinds.

Shopping Centers

The new **Opry Mills** (✉ 2802 Opryland Dr.), consists of more than a million square ft of stores, restaurants, and entertainment spots. In addition to mall perennials such as Bass, Barnes & Noble, and and movie theaters, this supercomplex also houses the **Gibson Bluegrass Showcase**, a simulated racecar speedway, and an IMAX theater, among others. The **Bellevue Center Mall** (✉ 7620 Hwy. 70S, off Bellevue exit of I–40W, ☎ 615/646–8690) has more than 125 stores, including Abercrombie & Fitch and the Tennessee Museum Store. The **Mall at Green Hills** (✉ Hillsboro and Abbott Martin Rds., ☎ 615/298–5478), about 15 minutes from Music Row, has specialty stores such as Brookstone, Williams-Sonoma, Laura Ashley, and Brooks Brothers, plus a Dillard's department store. **100 Oaks** (✉ I–65 South to Exit 79, Armory Dr. to Powell, ☎ 615/383–6002) is one of Nashville's more upscale factory outlets. Twenty-five miles east of Nashville, the **Prime Outlets of Lebanon** (✉ Highway 231, Lebanon, ☎ 615/444–0433) is a favorite of locals looking for deals on Brooks Brothers, Ralph Lauren, Nike, and more.

Side Trips from Nashville

The middle Tennessee area surrounding Nashville is a pocket of gently rolling Cumberland Mountain foothills and bluegrass meadows. It is one of the state's richest farming areas. Such small towns as Lynchburg and Franklin, the latter of which historian Shelby Foote calls one of the nation's top Civil War sites, offer wonderful antiques shops and crafts boutiques.

The **Tennessee Antebellum Trail** (☎ 931/486–9055; 800/381–1865 for a map and admission prices), which has more than 54 historic sites, plantations, and Civil War battlefields, is a 90-mi loop tour that begins in Nashville and continues through historic Maury and Williamson counties. Nine sites are open to the public daily.

Loretta Lynn's Ranch
65 mi west of Nashville.

Loretta Lynn's Ranch encompasses the entire village of Hurricane Mills. The singer's personal museum is housed in an old restored gristmill. Tours are of the downstairs of the coal miner's daughter's stately antebellum home, a simulated coal mine, and a re-creation of her simple childhood home. Camping, canoeing, paddleboats, trout fishing, and swimming are among the many recreational activities available here. ✉ *44 Hurricane Mills Rd., Hurricane Mills,* ☎ *931/296–7700.* 🎟 *Tour $12.50, camping $13–$18 per night for 2 people.* ☉ *Mar.–Dec. for tours, Mar.–Oct. for camping.*

Franklin
18 mi south of Nashville.

The town of Franklin rivals Natchez, Mississippi, in charm and Civil War history. A self-guided walking tour begins at the town square and covers several antebellum homes plus the meticulously restored downtown business district, which has more than 50 shops, including several antiques shops and art galleries. The **Carnton Plantation,** where some of the Civil War's bloodiest battles were fought, and **Confederate Cemetery** are nearby. Also in the area is the entrance to the **Natchez Trace Parkway** (off I–40), which wends its way through gorgeous scenery in three states. For more information on Franklin and its attractions, contact **Williamson County Tourism** (✉ City Hall, Franklin 37065, ☎ 615/794–1225).

Lynchburg
75 mi southeast of Nashville.

Lynchburg has been depicted worldwide in ads for its best-known product, whiskey. The quaint town is home to the **Jack Daniel's Distillery,** the oldest registered distillery in the country, where you can observe every step of the art of making sour-mash whiskey. ⊠ *On TN 55,* ☎ *931/759–4221.* 🖼 *Free.* ☉ *Guided tours daily 8–4.*

DINING

$ ✕ **Miss Mary Bobo's Boarding House.** Diners flock to this two-story 1867 white-frame house with a white picket fence to feast family style at tables laden with fried chicken, roast beef, fried catfish, stuffed vegetables, and sliced tomatoes, along with corn on the cob, homemade biscuits, corn bread, pecan pie, lemon icebox pie, fruit cobblers, and strawberry shortcake. There's only one meal served Monday–Saturday, at 1. However, there is occasionally an 11 AM serving, so call ahead. ⊠ *Main St., ½ block from Public Sq.,* ☎ *931/759–7394. Reservations required. No credit cards.*

Nashville A to Z

Arriving and Departing

BY BUS

Greyhound (⊠ 200 8th Ave. S, at McGavock St., Nashville, ☎ 800/ 231–2222).

BY CAR

From Nashville I–65 leads north into Kentucky and south into Alabama, and I–24 leads northwest into Kentucky and Illinois and southeast into Chattanooga and Georgia. I–40 traverses the state east–west, connecting Knoxville with Nashville and Memphis. I–440 connects I–40, I–65, and I–24, and helps circumvent clogged major arteries during Nashville's rush hour. I–840, which will skirt Nashville's north side and connect I–40 with I–24N and I–65N, is under construction.

BY PLANE

Nashville International Airport (⊠ 1 Terminal Dr., ☎ 615/275–1600), approximately 12 mi east of downtown, is served by most major airlines. **Shuttle service** downtown (☎ 615/275–1180) costs $8–$10 per person. A cab costs about $20 plus tip. To reach downtown by car, take I–40W.

Getting Around

BY BOAT

Opryland River Taxis (☎ 615/871–6100), $12.99 round-trip, link Riverfront Park with Opryland, across the river.

BY BUS

Metropolitan Transit Authority (MTA) buses (☎ 615/862–5950) serve the entire county; the fare is $1.40 (exact change), and they run 4 AM– 11:15 PM.

BY TAXI

Try **Allied Taxi** (☎ 615/244–7433), **Music City Taxi** (☎ 615/262–0451 or 800/359–9692), or **Madison Rivergate Taxi** (☎ 615/865–4100).

BY TROLLEY

Nashville Trolley Co. (☎ 615/862–5950), fare $1 (exact change), runs regularly scheduled trolleys through downtown and along Music Row during summer months. All-day trolley tokens are sold at the visitor information center for $3.

Contacts and Resources

EMERGENCIES

Ambulance, police (☎ 911). Emergency rooms are open all night at centrally located **Baptist Hospital** (✉ 2000 Church St., ☎ 615/329–5555) and **Vanderbilt University Medical Center** (✉ 1211 22nd Ave. S, ☎ 615/322–7311).

GUIDED TOURS

The *General Jackson*, **Opryland's** four-deck paddle wheeler, has several two-hour cruises along the Cumberland River daily, including lunch and dinner cruises, with a music review in the Victorian Theater. Opryland's other boat is the *Music City Queen*, a 350-passenger paddle-wheel excursion boat on which there is a sightseeing lunch cruise every Tuesday.

Gray Line (☎ 615/227–2270 or 800/251–1864) and **Grand Ole Opry Tours** (☎ 615/889–9490) have tours that include drives past stars' homes and visits to the Grand Ole Opry, Music Row, and the District. **Johnny Walker Tours** (☎ 615/834–8585 or 800/722–1524) has three-hour sightseeing tours and special concert tours.

PHARMACY

Revco (✉ 303 E. Thompson La., ☎ 615/361–3636).

RADIO STATIONS

AM: WLAC 1510, news and talk. **FM:** WPLN 90.3, classical and jazz; WSIX 97.9, country; WSM 95, country.

VISITOR INFORMATION

The **Visitor Information Center** (✉ Arena Tower at 5th Ave. and Broadway, ☎ 615/259–4747) is loaded with information and has staffers who know Nashville.

EAST TENNESSEE

East Tennessee combines wholesome vacation ingredients much in the way a skilled mountain cook creates a sumptuous down-home feast, with bounty from forests, fields, ice-cold streams, and the family farm. From the misty heights of the Great Smoky Mountains to the Holston, French Broad, Nolichucky, and Tennessee rivers, this exquisitely beautiful part of the state beckons with a cornucopia of scenic grandeur and recreational possibilities from hiking to white-water rafting. The highest and most rugged elevations are in the Great Smoky Mountains National Park, a cool and scenic retreat for those seeking relief from the humidity of summer.

Numbers in the margin correspond to points of interest on the East Tennessee map.

Oak Ridge

162 mi east of Nashville.

The famous Atomic City was established secretly during World War II. Some of the original installations here include the **Oak Ridge National Laboratory,** still involved in programs of nuclear fission and magnetic fusion energy; the **Graphite Reactor,** 10 mi southwest, now a National Historic Landmark with a display area open to the public; and the **K-25 Visitors Overlook,** for views of the **Oak Ridge Gaseous Diffusion Plant,** where uranium is enriched for use in nuclear reactors.

The **American Museum of Science and Energy** focuses on uses of nuclear, solar, and geothermal energy, mainly for peaceful purposes. Exhibits in-

499

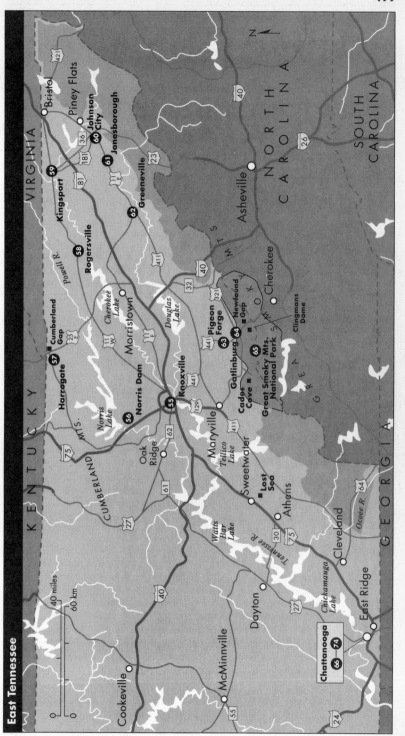

East Tennessee

clude hands-on experiments, demonstrations, and computer games. A slide show furnishes valuable background on Oak Ridge and the museum. ⊠ *300 S. Tulane Ave.,* ☎ *865/576–3200.* ☞ *Free.* ☉ *Daily 9–5.*

Outdoor Activities and Sports
South Hills Golf Club (⊠ 795 Tuskegee Dr., ☎ 865/483–5747) has an 18-hole, par-72 golf course open to the public.

Knoxville

⑤ *25 mi southeast of Oak Ridge.*

In 1786 patriot general James White and a few pioneer settlers built a fort beside the Tennessee River. A few years later, territorial governor William Blount selected White's fort as capital of the newly formed Territory of the United States South of the River Ohio and renamed the settlement Knoxville after his longtime friend, Secretary of War Henry Knox. It flourished from its beginning and became the state capital when Tennessee was admitted to the Union in 1796.

Throughout the 20th century, Knoxville has been synonymous with energy: The headquarters of the Tennessee Valley Authority (TVA), with its vast complex of hydroelectric dams and impounded recreational lakes, is here, and during World War II, atomic energy was secretly developed at nearby Oak Ridge (☞ *above*). Today the University of Tennessee adds its own energy—both intellectual and cultural—to this dynamic city, while a new riverfront development, Volunteer Landing, is alive with shops, restaurants, and residential space. The city's motto these days is "Where Nature and Technology Meet." Knoxville is surrounded by Oak Ridge National Laboratory and three national parks—Great Smoky Mountains National Park, Cumberland Gap National Historic Park, and Big South Fork National River and Recreation Area.

At the **Governor William Blount Mansion,** a modest white-frame structure dating from 1792, the governor and his associates planned the admission of Tennessee as the 16th state in the Union. The home is furnished with original and period antiques, along with memorabilia of Blount's checkered career. A **visitor center** adjacent to the 1818 **Craighead-Jackson House** presents an introductory slide program, museum exhibits, and a glass collection. ⊠ *200 W. Hill Ave.,* ☎ *865/525–2375.* ☞ *$4.95.* ☉ *Apr.–Dec., Mon.–Sat. 9:30–5, Sun. 1–5; Jan.–Mar., weekdays 9:30–5; last tour at 4.*

Different eras of Knoxville history are celebrated at **James White Fort** (⊠ 205 E. Hill Ave., ☎ 865/525–6514), a series of seven log cabins with authentic furnishings and pioneer artifacts. Marble Springs, the summer home of John Sevier, Tennessee's first governor, is preserved at the **John Sevier Historical Site** (⊠ 1220 John Sevier Hwy., ☎ 865/573–5508). The **Armstrong-Lockett House** (⊠ 2728 Kingston Pike, ☎ 865/637–3163), an elegant farm mansion dating from 1834, showcases American and British furniture, silver, and ornate appointments, along with terraces and fountains in Italianate gardens.

The **Mabry-Hazen House** served as headquarters for both Confederate and Union forces during the Civil War. It was built by a prominent Knoxvillian Joseph A. Mabry Jr. in 1858 and is now on the National Historic Register. ⊠ *1711 Dandridge Ave.,* ☎ *865/522–8661.* ☞ *$5.* ☉ *Tues.–Fri. 10–5, Sat. 10–2.*

The **McClung Museum,** on the University of Tennessee campus, has diverse collections in anthropology, natural history, geology, science, and fine arts. ⊠ *1327 Circle Park Dr.,* ☎ *865/974–2144.* 🖾 *Free.* ☉ *Mon.–Sat. 9–5, Sun. 1–5.*

The **Knoxville Museum of Art** is housed in a handsome 53,000-square-ft structure at World's Fair Park. Designed by renowned museum architect Edward Larrabee Barnes, the four-level concrete-and-steel building is faced in Tennessee pink marble. The museum includes four exhibition galleries, an exploratory gallery for children, a great hall, an auditorium, a museum store, and outdoor sculpture and educational program gardens. ⊠ *1050 World's Fair Park Dr.,* ☎ *865/525–6101.* 🖾 *Free, except special exhibits.* ☉ *Tues.–Thurs. and Sat. 10–5, Fri. 10–9, Sun. noon–5.*

The **East Tennessee Discovery Center and Akima Planetarium** contain pioneer tools and clothes, mounted animals, and fresh- and saltwater aquariums. Children love the hands-on and audiovisual exhibits. ⊠ *516 Beaman St., in Chilhowee Park,* ☎ *865/594–1480.* 🖾 *$3.* ☉ *Weekdays 9–5, Sat. 10–5; no admissions after 4; planetarium show times vary.*

You can spend a full day at the **Knoxville Zoological Park,** famous for breeding large-cat species and African elephants. Among the 1,100 animals are rare red pandas, wild creatures native to the African plains, polar bears, seals, and penguins. The working miniature steam train, elephant rides, and petting zoo will keep kids occupied for hours. Gorilla Valley, Cheetah Savanna, and Chimpanzee Ridge are among the best exhibits. ⊠ *In Chilhowee Park on Rutledge Pike S, 4½ mi east of I–40 Exit 392,* ☎ *865/637–5331.* 🖾 *$6.95; parking $2.* ☉ *Memorial Day–Labor Day, daily 9:30–6; Labor Day–Memorial Day, daily 10–4:30.*

Volunteer Landing, a festive development of shops, restaurants, houses, and a park along the Tennessee River, is being finished in phases. A new visitor center, the **Gateway Regional Center** (⊠ Neyland Dr., ☎ 865/523–7263 or 800/727–8045), offers an overview of the region. The mile-long development includes such restaurants as Calhoun's on the River and Regas Riverside Tavern.

Near Volunteer Landing, the new **Women's Basketball Hall of Fame** is the first Hall of Fame devoted exclusively to women's sports. Exhibits include a collection of 23 jerseys from the WNBA's inaugural all-star game, a modern locker rooms where you can listen to half-time talks by some of the country's top coaches, along with three practice courts where you can work on your dribble or try on historic uniforms. ⊠ *700 Hall of Fame Dr.,* ☎ *865/633–9000.* 🖾 *$7.95.* ☉ *Memorial Day–Labor Day, Mon.–Sat. 9–8, Sun. noon–8; Labor Day–Memorial Day, Mon.–Thurs. 10–6, Fri.–Sat. 10–8, Sun. noon–6.*

Dining and Lodging

$$ ✕ **Copper Cellar/Cumberland Grill.** A favorite of the college crowd and young professionals, the original downstairs Copper Cellar has an intimate atmosphere with friendly service. Upstairs, the Cumberland Grill serves aged Colorado beef, fresh seafood, salads, sandwiches, and award-winning desserts. There are a children's menu and a lavish Sunday brunch. ⊠ *1807 Cumberland Ave., across from University of Tennessee campus,* ☎ *865/673–3411. AE, D, DC, MC, V.*

$ ✕ **Calhoun's on the River.** Delicious barbecued ribs are served in a riverside setting at this sprawling rib house across the street from the site of one of Knoxville's original hot spots, the long-gone Chisholm's Tavern of pioneer days. Calhoun's ribs are famous throughout the South. ⊠ *400 Neyland Dr.,* ☎ *865/673–3399. Reservations not accepted. AE, D, DC, MC, V.*

$$$ 🖬 **Hyatt Regency Knoxville.** This is a handsome, contemporary adap-
★   tation of an Aztec pyramid atop a hill overlooking the Tennessee River,
the city, and mountainous hinterlands. The eight-story skylighted
atrium lobby blends modern furnishings and art in Meso-American mo-
tifs with abundant flora and colorful accessories. Rooms, done in light
woods and peach and blue pastels, have either windows or balconies
that open to fresh breezes. ⊠ *500 Hill Ave. SE, Box 88, 37915,* ☎
865/637–1234 or 800/233–1234, ℻ *865/522–5911. 360 rooms, 25
suites. Restaurant, coffee shop, sports bar, pool, exercise room, vol-
leyball. AE, D, DC, MC, V.*

$ 🖬 **La Quinta Motor Inn.** The rooms here are spacious and well lighted,
with convenient working areas. ⊠ *258 N. Peters Rd., 37923,* ☎ *865/
690–9777 or 800/531–5900,* ℻ *865/531–8304. 130 rooms. Pool.
AE, D, DC, MC, V.*

Outdoor Activities and Sports
Whittle Springs Municipal Golf Course (⊠ 3113 Valley View Dr., ☎
865/525–1022) is an 18-hole, par-72 golf course open to the public.

Nightlife and the Arts
The **Knoxville Opera Company** (☎ 865/524–0795) sponsors New
York Metropolitan Opera competitions each year, along with two lo-
cally produced operatic performances. The **Knoxville Symphony Or-
chestra** (☎ 865/523–1178) presents nearly 200 concerts a year, often
with esteemed guest artists. The **Lamar House Bijou Theater,** in Knoxville
(⊠ 803 S. Gay St., ☎ 865/522–0832), stages seasonal ballet, concerts,
and plays.

The Old City, on the north side of downtown, is the site of Knoxville's
most varied nightlife, with restaurants and clubs sharing space with
industries that have been in the warehouse district for decades.
Nightspots to check out are **Patrick Sullivan's** (⊠ 100 N. Central Ave.,
☎ 865/637–4255) for saloon shenanigans, **Hooray's** (⊠ 106 S. Cen-
tral Ave., ☎ 865/546–6729), and the lounge at the **Orangery Restau-
rant** (⊠ The Orangery, 5412 Kingston Pike, ☎ 865/588–2964).

Norris

25 mi northwest of Knoxville.

Scenic U.S. 441 leads to Norris, a delightful planned town built in 1933
as a workers' community during construction of the Tennessee Valley
🟢 Authority's first dam. The **Norris Dam,** which spans the Clinch River
and impounds a 72-mi-long lake, has a visitor lobby and two over-
looks. Some of the best views, though, are from **Norris Dam State Re-
sort Park** (☞ Outdoor Activities and Sports, *below*), which has cabins
and campsites.

Norris's prime attraction is the **Museum of Appalachia,** where about
35 log structures—among them a molasses mill powered by mules—
have been restored to reflect the hardscrabble life of the early moun-
taineers. More than 250,000 period furnishings and implements are
in the buildings, and there is a working farm. Locals sometimes bring
their musical instruments for an old-time hoedown. ⊠ *2819 Ander-
sonville Hwy.,* ☎ *865/494–7680.* 🎫 *$6.* ☉ *Daily 8–5; summer hrs vary.*

Outdoor Activities and Sports
At Norris Lake, there's seasonal angling for striped bass, walleye,
white bass, and muskie, as well as boat launch ramps (but no rentals)
at **Norris Dam State Resort Park** (⊠ 125 Village Green Circle, Lake
City, ☎ 865/426–7461). Largemouth and white bass swim in Chero-
kee, Douglas, and Fort Loudon lakes. Trout lovers do best at Tellico-

Chilhowee Lakes, especially at night in April and May. Fly-fishing is popular in the Smokies' many streams.

Harrogate

57 *50 mi northeast of Norris.*

Harrogate, by the Virginia border, is home to **Lincoln Memorial University.** Founded in 1896, the school celebrates the Great Emancipator's principles and philosophies. **Lincoln Memorial Museum** contains one of the world's largest collections of Lincolniana. ⊠ *On Lincoln Memorial University campus, on U.S. 25E,* ☎ *423/869–6235 or 800/ 325–0900.* 🎫 *$3.* ⊙ *Weekdays 9–4, Sat. 11–4, Sun. 1–4.*

Rogersville

58 *45 mi southeast of Harrogate.*

Along U.S. 11W, Rogersville is a little hideaway East Tennessee town established in 1786. All of downtown is on the National Register of Historic Places, and it has both the oldest courthouse and oldest inn in the state. A walking-tour brochure, available throughout town, points out the various sites of interest.

Kingsport

59 *30 mi northeast of Rogersville.*

Founded in 1761, Kingsport is along U.S. 11W, surrounded by rolling hills, meadows, and woodlands. At **Exchange Place, Gaines-Preston Farm,** a restored pioneer homestead, craftspeople demonstrate their skills in commodious log houses. Their handmade quilts, baskets, wood carvings, ceramics, and stuffed dolls are sold in nearby shops. ⊠ *4812 Orebank Rd.,* ☎ *423/288–6071.* 🎫 *Free.* ⊙ *May–Oct., Thurs.–Fri. 10–2, weekends 2–4:30.*

Outdoor Activities and Sports

The 18-hole, par-72 **Warrior's Path State Park Golf Course** (⊠ 1687 Fall Creek Rd., ☎ 423/323–4990) is open to the public.

Johnson City

60 *22 mi southeast of Kingsport.*

Reached via U.S. 23, Johnson City is an important center for agriculture, manufacturing, and education—it is home to **Washington College,** the oldest institution of higher education in the state, and **East Tennessee State University,** with more than 9,000 students. At **Tipton-Haynes Historic Site,** the 19th-century main house, granary, horse barn, and law office have been authentically restored. ⊠ *2620 S. Roan St., off I–181 Exit 31, 1 mi south via University Pkwy. and S. Roan St.,* ☎ *423/926–3631.* 🎫 *$3.* ⊙ *Apr.–Nov., Mon.–Sat. 10–5; Dec.–Mar., Mon.–Sat. 10–4.*

OFF THE BEATEN PATH
ROCKY MOUNT – This two-story log mansion, completed in 1772, was Governor William Blount's territorial capitol from 1790 until he moved to Knoxville two years later. Faithful restoration and careful selection of authentic furnishings testify eloquently to the simple pioneer lifestyle. The entire farmstead is presented as living history, and you get to see the kitchen, slave quarters, blacksmith shop, and even a flax house where there are often weaving demonstrations. ⊠ *4 mi northeast of Johnson City on U.S. 11E at Piney Flats, 200 Hyder Hill Rd.,* ☎ *423/538–7396*

or 888/538–1791, ℻ 423/538–1086. ☎ $5. ⊙ Mar.–Dec. 20, Mon.–Sat. 10–5, Sun. 1–5; Jan. 6–Feb., weekdays 10–5.

Jonesborough

⑥ *10 mi southwest of Johnson City.*

The state's oldest town beckons visitors to admire a trio of antebellum churches, lovely vintage houses, brick and wooden fretwork shops, and the courthouse, all dating from the late 1700s. During October's famous National Storytelling Festival, professional and amateur storytellers from throughout the world come for a weekend to spin their tales. At the **Visitor Center and History Museum** (⊠ 117 Boone St., ☎ 423/753–1010), a slide show and local art exhibit describe the town's history.

Greeneville

⑥ *25 mi southwest of Jonesborough.*

In 1826 a young Andrew Johnson (later 17th president of the United States) settled in Greeneville, which was founded in 1783. After his arduous trek over the mountains from North Carolina, Johnson opened a tailor shop and married. The **Andrew Johnson National Historic Site** preserves his primitive tailor shop, the homestead where he lived from 1851 until his death in 1875, and his hilltop grave site, marked by an elaborate monument. Displays in the visitor center include notes he made at his impeachment trial. ⊠ *Depot and College Sts.,* ☎ *423/638–3551.* ☎ *Homestead $2.* ⊙ *Daily 9–5.*

Pigeon Forge

⑥ *25 mi southeast of Knoxville.*

Pigeon Forge, home of mountain native Dolly Parton's namesake theme park, Dollywood, has exploded with enough heavy-duty outlet shopping and kids' entertainment (from indoor skydiving simulators to laser tag) to keep families busy for a few days. But the intentionally cornpone image can become wearing, and it fails to reflect the quiet folksiness of the Appalachian communities scattered throughout these parts. Pigeon Forge has more than 200 outlet specialty stores, crafts shops, country hoedown emporiums, and kid-friendly attractions that line the main thoroughfare for several miles.

Ⓒ A favorite with families is **Carbo's Smoky Mountain Police Museum,** housing police memorabilia such as badges, guns, and the car in which legendary West Tennessee sheriff Buford Pusser was killed in a traffic accident. ⊠ *3311 Pkwy.,* ☎ *865/453–1358.* ☎ *$6.50.* ⊙ *Apr., weekends 10–5; May, Fri.–Wed. 10–5; June–Aug., daily 10–5; Sept.–Oct., Fri.–Wed. 10–5.*

The 1830s-era **Old Mill,** beside the Little Pigeon River, still grinds corn, wheat, and rye on water-powered stone wheels. A 20-minute tour explains the process. Flour, meal, grits, and buckwheat are for sale. ⊠ *2944 Middle Creek Rd.,* ☎ *865/453–8741.* ☎ *$3.* ⊙ *Mon.–Sat. 8:30–6:30, Sun. 10–6.*

★ Ⓒ **Dollywood,** singer Dolly Parton's popular theme park, embodies the country superstar's own flamboyance—plenty of Hollywood flash mixed with simple country charm that you either love or hate. This endeavor brings to life the folklore, fun, food, and music of the Great Smokies, which inspired many of Parton's early songs. In a re-created 1880 mountain village, scores of talented and friendly craftspeople demonstrate their artistry. Museum exhibits trace Parton's rise to stardom from her backwoods upbringing. There are many amusement rides (including Daredevil Falls, a waterfall ride), but music, of course, is the park's underpinning: Live shows are performed on the park's seven stages, and several times per season, Dolly shows up for a surprise appearance. The gala Harvest Celebration, held from October to early November, features the Smokies' only outdoor crafts festival as well as the Southern Gospel Jubilee. Smoky Mountain Christmas is the star attraction from mid-November through December. When hunger strikes, try Aunt Granny's Restaurant for down-home mountain cookery. ⊠ *1020 Dollywood La.,* ☏ *865/428–9488 or 800/365–5996.* ☒ *$34.25; free next day on tickets purchased after 3.* ☉ *Mid-Apr.–Oct., daily 9–6; extended hrs mid-June–mid-Aug. Closed Tues. and Thurs. in May and Sept., Thurs. in Oct.; call for varying hrs Nov.–Dec.*

ℭ **Ogle's Water Park.** This family park has a giant wave pool, a kiddie play area, 10 water slides, and miniature golf. ⊠ *2530 Pkwy., Pigeon Forge,* ☏ *865/453–8741.* ☒ *$21.* ☉ *May, weekends 11–6; June–Labor Day, daily 10–7.*

Dining and Lodging

$ ✕ **Alan Jackson's Showcar Cafe.** This theme café, showcasing Jackson's music and his cars, serves a breakfast buffet and has full lunch and dinner menus with Alan's and Mama Ruth's favorite home-cooked recipes. You can choose from sandwiches, pizzas, burgers, and salads or more substantial entrées. Several cars, among them a Viper, are on display; giant TV screens, an old-fashioned soda bar, and a gift shop complete the scene. ⊠ *2293 Pkwy.,* ☏ *865/908–9007. AE, D, DC, MC, V.*

$ ✕ **Apple Tree Inn Restaurant.** A traditional East Tennessee menu is of-
★ fered here, including fried chicken and spoon bread, a regal soufflé of cornmeal, flour, eggs, buttermilk, and seasonings, served hot from the baking dish. Order family style or individually in this very relaxed dining room. ⊠ *3215 Pkwy.,* ☏ *865/453–4961. Reservations not accepted. AE, MC, V. Closed Dec.–Feb.*

$$ ⌸ **Best Western Plaza Inn.** Convenient to shops, restaurants, and attractions, the Best Western is a best bet for families. Rooms are spacious and well furnished, and all have refrigerators; some overlook mountain scenery, others an indoor swimming pool. ⊠ *3755 Pkwy., Box 626, 37868,* ☏ *865/453–5538 or 800/232–5656,* FAX *865/453–2619. 198 rooms, 2 suites. 1 indoor and 2 outdoor pools, wading pool, hot tub, sauna, recreation room. AE, DC, MC, V. CP.*

$$ ⌸ **Hampton Inn & Suites.** Conveniently located near shopping and across from restaurants and theaters, this chain property has double rooms as well as one- and two-bedroom suites with kitchens. ⊠ *2025 Pkwy.,* ☏ *865/428–1600 or 800/310–8082. 75 rooms, 26 suites. Pool, outdoor hot tub, exercise room, coin laundry. AE, D, DC, MC, V. CP.*

$$ ⌸ **Holiday Inn.** This inn is in the middle of the action. Its vast Holidome Indoor Recreation Center has something for everyone in the family. Rooms are spacious and include refrigerators, irons, and coffee makers. ⊠ *3230 Pkwy., 37863,* ☏ *865/428–2700 or 800/782–3119,* FAX *865/428–2700. 204 rooms, 4 suites. Restaurant, indoor pool, hot tub, sauna, health club. AE, DC, MC, V.*

$-$$ ⌸ **Grand Resort Hotel and Convention Center.** This centrally located five-story inn has some ultramodern rooms with water beds and fireplaces. A few rooms even have large whirlpool tubs. ⊠ *3171 Pkwy., 37863,* ☏ *865/453–1000 or 800/362–1188,* FAX *865/453–0056. 415 rooms, 10 suites. Restaurant, pool, hot tub. AE, DC, MC, V.*

Nightlife and the Arts

Pigeon Forge has a host of theaters—something for everyone, presumably. From March through October, hearty chicken-and-ribs dinners are accompanied by a colorful, Western-theme musical show and rodeo at **Dixie Stampede** (⊠ 3849 Pkwy., ☎ 865/453–4400 or 800/356–1676). The **Music Mansion** (⊠ 100 Music Rd., ☎ 865/428–7469) presents an electrifying country-music variety show featuring Dollywood's award-winning James Rogers.

The **Comedy Barn** (⊠ 2775 Pkwy., ☎ 865/428–5222) presents a family variety show. The **Country Tonight Theater** (⊠ 129 Showplace Blvd., ☎ 865/453–2003) has foot-stompin' country music mid-March through December. The **Louise Mandrell Theater** (⊠ 2046 Pkwy., ☎ 865/453–6263), open April–December, is a high-energy show starring Mandrell, who sings, dances, and plays many instruments.

Shopping

Every imaginable outlet store can be found somewhere in the maze of outlet centers at the heart of Pigeon Forge. Three major outlet malls are the **Belz Factory Outlet Mall** (⊠ 2655 Teaster La., ☎ 865/453–3503), the **Pigeon Forge Factory Outlet Mall** (⊠ 2850 Pkwy., ☎ 865/428–2828), and the **Tanger Factory Outlet Center** (⊠ 175 Davis Rd., ☎ 865/428–7002). The **Tanger Outlet Center at Five Oaks** (⊠ 1645 Pkwy., ☎ 865/453–1053) is in Sevierville, a few miles north of Pigeon Forge.

For mountain crafts, stop at **Old Mill Village** (⊠ Off Parkway, turn left at traffic light No. 7, next to Patriot Park), which has shops such as **Pigeon Forge Craft Center** (☎ 865/453–8891), **Pigeon Forge Pottery** (☎ 865/453–3883), and **Waynehouse Artcrafts** (☎ 865/453–6798).

Gatlinburg

㉔ *8 mi southeast of Pigeon Forge.*

Gateway city to Great Smoky Mountains National Park (☞ *below*), Gatlinburg, popular with honeymooners and families, has steadily expanded from a remote little town with a sprinkling of hotels, chalets, and mountain crafts shops to the sprawling network of minigolf courses and homemade-candy "shoppes" it is today. During the summer, the town is clogged with visitors, complete with the annoyances of traffic jams and packed restaurants. Nevertheless, Gatlinburg is Tennessee's premier mountain resort town and is set in the narrow valley of the Little Pigeon River—actually a turbulent mountain stream.

With more than 400 specialty shops, this town is also a browsing mecca. Family attractions include a number of local trout farms, the **Gatlinburg Sky Lift** (☎ 865/436–4307), via which you can reach the top of Crockett Mountain; the **Guinness World Record Museum** (☎ 865/436–9100); and the **Ober Gatlinburg Tramway** (☎ 865/436–5423), which leads to a mountaintop amusement park, ski center, and shopping mall/crafts market. **Arrowmont School of Arts & Crafts** (⊠ 556 Pkwy., ☎ 865/436–5860) is a nationally known visual arts complex. Gatlinburg also hosts numerous festivals, the longest of which is the Smoky Mountain Lights, which runs from November through February, when the town is decorated with more than 2 million lights.

Dining and Lodging

$–$$ ✕ **Burning Bush Restaurant.** Reproduction antique furnishings and accessories evoke a colonial atmosphere. Broiled Tennessee quail and beef Rossini—an 8-ounce fillet served on an English muffin with Madeira sauce—are house specialties. Bountiful breakfasts are also offered. ⊠ *1151 Pkwy.,* ☎ *865/436–4669. AE, D, MC, V.*

$–$$ ✕ **Heidelberg Restaurant.** German, Swiss, and American dishes are served at this eatery. There's German entertainment nightly. ✉ *148 Pkwy., near traffic Light #1,* ☎ *865/430–3094 or 800/726–3094. AE, D, DC, MC, V.*

$ ✕ **Pancake Pantry.** This restaurant, in business since 1960, is a family favorite of repeat guests to the Smokies. Austrian apple-walnut pancakes covered with apple cider compote, black walnuts, apple slices, sweet spices, powdered sugar, and whipped cream are a house specialty. Other selections include waffles, omelets, sandwiches, soups, and fresh salads. Century-old brick, polished-oak paneling, rustic copper accessories, and spacious windows create a delightful ambience. Box lunches are available for mountain picnics. ✉ *628 Pkwy.,* ☎ *865/436–4724. Reservations not accepted. No credit cards. No dinner.*

$ ✕ **Smoky Mountain Trout House.** Of the eight distinctive trout preparations to choose from at this cozy restaurant, an old favorite is trout Eisenhower: panfried, with cornmeal breading and bacon as flavorings, and served with bacon-and-butter sauce and a side dish of mushrooms. Prime rib, country ham, and grilled chicken are also on the menu. ✉ *410 N. Pkwy.,* ☎ *865/436–5416. Reservations not accepted. AE, DC, MC, V. No lunch.*

$$$–$$$$ ✕⌂ **Buckhorn Inn.** This small inn owned and operated by the Young ★ family is set on 40 acres of remote woodlands about 5 mi outside Gatlinburg. Guests—including seclusion-seeking diplomats, government officials, and celebrities—have been coming here for more than 40 years. The views of Mt. LeConte and the Great Smokies are spectacular, and the Great Smoky Arts and Crafts Community (☞ Shopping, *below*) is convenient to the inn. Inside, the country-inn atmosphere is reinforced by wicker rockers, paintings by local artists, a huge stone fireplace, and French doors that open onto a large stone porch. All rooms are spacious, and some have king-size beds. Full gourmet breakfasts are included in the rate. A four-course dinner, with such items as home-baked breads, creamed soups, marinated beef tenderloin, and fruit tortes, is available to guests and nonguests, by reservation only. ✉ *Off U.S. 321, 2140 Tudor Mountain Rd., 37738,* ☎ *865/436–4668. 6 rooms, 4 cottages, 1 2-bedroom house. Hiking, fishing. D, MC, V.*

$$–$$$ ⌂ **Park Vista Resort Hotel.** This large, handsome hotel on a mountain ledge has modern, lavishly decorated public areas and large, elegantly appointed guest rooms, each with a balcony overlooking colorful gardens, the town of Gatlinburg, the Little Pigeon River, and the mountains beyond. Nonetheless, this white, semicircular contemporary tower is a jarring sight in the Great Smoky Mountains. ✉ *705 Cherokee Orchard Rd., 37738,* ☎ *865/436–9211 or 800/421–7275,* ℻ *865/436–5141. 306 rooms, 6 suites. Restaurant, lounge, sports bar, 2 indoor pools, wading pool, hot tub, sauna, meeting rooms. AE, DC, MC, V.*

$$ ⌂ **Best Western Twin Islands Motel.** In the center of Gatlinburg, beside the surging Little Pigeon River, this motel is notable for its low-key contemporary architectural style. All rooms have balconies overlooking the river. Kitchenette units are also available. ✉ *539 Pkwy., 37738,* ☎ *865/436–5121 or 800/223–9299,* ℻ *865/436–6208. 97 rooms, 10 suites. Restaurant, pool, fishing, playground. AE, DC, MC, V.*

$–$$ ⌂ **Holiday Inn Sunspree Resort.** This complex offers kids and adults ★ plenty to do and has a variety of family programs. All rooms have a refrigerator and coffeemaker, and there is a general store. The hotel is two blocks from the convention center. ✉ *520 Airport Rd., 37738,* ☎ *865/436–9201 or 800/465–4329,* ℻ *865/436–7974. 400 rooms. 2 restaurants, indoor and outdoor pools, hot tub, sauna, putting green, nightclub, meeting rooms. AE, D, DC, MC, V.*

$ ⊞ **Rainbow Motel.** This small, neat, well-maintained lodging is a pleas-
ant choice for budget-minded vacationers. ⊠ *390 E. Pkwy. (3 blocks
east of U.S. 441), Box 1397, 37738,* ☎ *865/436–5887 or 800/422–
8922. 41 rooms, 1 efficiency, 2 2-bedroom units. Pool. D, MC, V.*

Nightlife and the Arts

Sweet Fanny Adams Theatre and Music Hall (⊠ 461 Pkwy., ☎ 865/
436–4038 or 865/436–4039) stages original musical comedies, Gay '90s
revues, and old-fashioned sing-alongs; reservations are advised.

Outdoor Activities and Sports

Bent Creek Mountain Inn and Country Club (⊠ 3919 E. Pkwy., ☎ 865/
436–3947) has an 18-hole, par-72 course that is open to the public.

Shopping

The mountain towns of East Tennessee are known for Appalachian folk
crafts, especially wood carvings, cornhusk dolls, pottery, dulcimers, and
beautiful handmade quilts. The **Great Smoky Arts and Crafts Community**
is a collection of 80 shops and craftspersons' studios along 8 mi of rambling country road. Begun in 1937, the community includes workers
in leather, pottery, weaving, hand-wrought pewter, stained glass, quilt
making, hand carving, marquetry, and more. Everything sold here is
made on the premises by the community members. Also here are two
restaurants and the popular Wild Plum Tearoom. ⊠ *Off U.S. 321, 3
mi east of Gatlinburg,* ☎ *865/671–3600. For more information:* ⊠
Box 807, Gatlinburg 37738.

Great Smoky Mountains National Park

★ ⑥⑤ *45 mi from Knoxville.*

At Great Smoky Mountains National Park, the southern Appalachians reach their ultimate grandeur as 16 peaks soar more than 6,000
ft. Fall brings an unparalleled fiesta of colors to these mountains, and
in the early springtime wild azaleas and rhododendrons lace the moun-
tainsides with delicate pinks, lavenders, and whites. No wonder hikers, campers, and boaters flock to this, America's most heavily visited
national park, according to the National Park Service, whose 800
acres are divided almost equally between Tennessee and North Carolina.

From Gatlinburg (☞ *above*), the northern gateway to the park, drive
south along the scenic Newfound Gap Road (U.S. 441) to the Sugar-
lands Visitor Center at park headquarters, which has informative films,
exhibits, maps, and brochures about the park. Driving along on the
Newfound Gap Road, be sure to stop often at scenic overlooks, perhaps taking time to explore one or more of the nature trails that lead
off from many of them. The road ascends to **Newfound Gap** on the
Tennessee–North Carolina border, a haunting viewpoint. From here,
a 7-mi spur road leads to **Clingmans Dome**—at 6,643 ft, the highest
point in Tennessee—where you can walk up a spiral pathway to an
observation tower for panoramic views of the Smokies. Autumn is the
favorite season for the spectacular foliage.

The isolated mountain valley of **Cades Cove**, at the junction of U.S.
321 and TN 73, has preserved 19th-century farmhouses, barns,
churches, and an old gristmill that make it one of the region's most worthwhile attractions. Drive through on the 11-mi loop road (which can be
very busy in season) or, better yet, walk the grounds to get a sense of the
area and its history. From spring through fall, special park ranger programs and demonstrations describe the pioneer agriculture, crafts, and
folkways in the Cove. At the old gristmill—open from April 5 through

October, daily 9:30–5—you can take a tour and purchase stone-ground cornmeal. For a deep-forest drive, take Parson Branch Road, a quiet, one-way trek out of the park to U.S. 129. The Foothills Parkway will get you back into the park. ⊠ *107 Park Headquarters Rd., Gatlinburg 37738,* ☎ *865/436–1200.* ⌦ *Free.* ⊙ *Apr.–May and Sept.–Oct., daily 8–6; June–Aug., daily 8–7; Nov.–Mar., daily 8–4:30.* ✍

Outdoor Activities and Sports

HIKING

An unusually elevated and scenic portion of the **Appalachian Trail** runs along high ridges in the Great Smoky Mountains National Park. The trail can be easily reached at Newfound Gap from U.S. 441.

HORSEBACK RIDING

Smoky Mountain Stables (⊠ U.S. 321 North, ☎ 865/436–5634), arranges guided horseback riding in Great Smoky Mountains National Park from March through November.

RAFTING

Rafting in the Smokies (☎ 865/436–5008 or 800/PRO–RAFT) offers guided white-water raft trips from March through October.

En Route Driving between Great Smoky Mountains National Park and Chattanooga along U.S. 321, U.S. 411, or TN 68 will give travelers a chance to visit the **Lost Sea,** outside Sweetwater, where you can explore a 41½-acre underground lake by glass-bottom boat. ⊠ *TN 68, 140 Lost Sea Rd.,* ☎ *865/337–6616.* ⌦ *$9.* ⊙ *Nov.–Feb., daily 9–5; Mar.–Apr., daily 9–6; May–June and Aug., daily 9–7; July, daily 9–8; Sept.–Oct., daily 9–6.*

East Tennessee A to Z

Arriving, Departing, and Getting Around

BY BUS

Greyhound (☎ 800/231–2222) has a station in Knoxville.

BY CAR

I–75 runs north–south from Kentucky through Knoxville, then to Chattanooga, where it enters Georgia. I–81 enters East Tennessee from Virginia at Bristol and continues southwest until it ends at the junction with I–40 northeast of Knoxville. I–40 enters from North Carolina, traces a northwesterly course to Knoxville, then heads west. U.S. 11 joins Chattanooga with Knoxville.

BY PLANE

Knoxville Airport (⊠ 2055 Alcoa Pkwy., ☎ 865/970–2773), 12 mi from downtown, is served by Airtran, American Eagle, Continental Express, Delta, Northwest, TWA, United, and US Airways.

Contacts and Resources

ACCOMMODATIONS

For reservations at hotels, motels, chalets, and condominiums throughout the Great Smoky Mountains area, contact **Smoky Mountain Accommodations Reservation Service** (⊠ 526 E. Pkwy., Suite 1, Gatlinburg 37738, ☎ 865/436–9700 or 800/231–2230).

EMERGENCIES

Ambulance, police (☎ 911). Medical assistance is available in Knoxville at **Baptist Hospital** (⊠ 137 Blount Ave., ☎ 865/632–5011).

GUIDED TOURS

Self-guided-tour maps and brochures are available at many local visitor information centers. In Pigeon Forge, **Smoky Mountain Tours** (☎ 800/953–7469) offers guided tours through East Tennessee back roads, the Smoky Mountains, and to major East Tennessee sites. The **Smoky Mountain Adventure Guide Service** (☎ 800/882–1061) offers custom guided trips for fishing, hiking, boating, camping, and other outdoor fun in the Smokies and along the Appalachian Trail.

A boat ride on the *Star of Knoxville* (✉ Neyland Dr., Knoxville, ☎ 865/522–4630) offers views of an especially scenic portion of the Tennessee River. Sightseeing excursions as well as lunch and dinner cruises are scheduled daily April–December.

PHARMACIES

The **Kroger Pharmacy** in Knoxville (✉ 4409 C.C. Chapman Hwy., ☎ 865/573–9906) is open 24 hours.

RADIO STATIONS

FM: WDEF 92.3, contemporary easy listening; WUSY 101.7, country; WIVK 107.7, country; WMYU 102.1, oldies; WMLB 97.5, adult contemporary.

VISITOR INFORMATION

Gatlinburg Convention and Visitors Bureau (✉ Box 527, Gatlinburg 37738, ☎ 800/822–1998). **Knoxville Area Convention and Visitors Bureau** (✉ 601 W. Summit Hill Dr., Knoxville 37901, ☎ 865/523–7263 or 800/727–8045), open daily 8:30–5. **Northeast Tennessee Tourism Association** (✉ Box 415, Jonesborough 37659, ☎ 423/753–4188), open weekdays 8–5. **Pigeon Forge Chamber of Commerce** (✉ Box 1278, Pigeon Forge 37868, ☎ 865/453–5700 or 800/221–9858), open weekdays 8–5, Saturday 8–8. **Rogersville Chamber of Commerce** (✉ 415 S. Depot, Rogersville 37857, ☎ 423/272–2186), open weekdays 9–4.

CHATTANOOGA

Chattanooga is an up-and-coming river and railroad town with an intriguing past. In less than 20 years, Chattanooga has transformed itself from a polluted city struggling to clean up its outmoded industries to a bright, revitalized community that's a model for any small city looking to reinvent itself. Chattanooga's Tennessee Aquarium, the world's largest freshwater aquarium, is a must-see.

Back in 1969, Chattanooga ranked among the nation's worst in air pollution. Since the mid-1980s, civic pride and unity, as well as an $850 million downtown revitalization effort, have continued to transform the ragged downtown area into a vibrant community. A rich Civil War history, a verdant mountainous countryside, and the presence of such unabashedly old-fashioned, but popular, tourist attractions as Rock City Gardens and Ruby Falls laid the promising foundation for the city's comeback. New specialty museums, a restored carousel and interactive play fountain in Coolidge Park, and expanded shopping have added further appeal, particularly for families.

Downtown Chattanooga

Numbers in the text correspond to numbers in the margin and on the Chattanooga map.

The city's revitalized downtown, still a work in progress, has museums and shopping, in addition to an attractive riverfront walk. A good place to start exploring is the Chattanooga Visitors Center, next to the Tennessee Aquarium, at 2 Broad Street. It has brochures for sights and self-guided walking tours of historic districts, as well as combination tickets to many attractions.

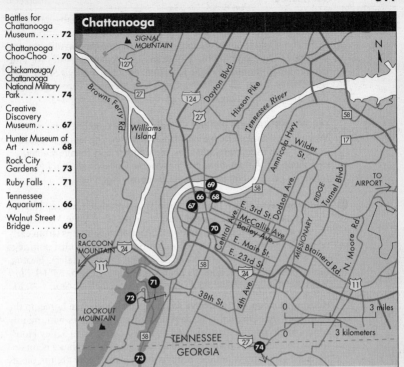

A Good Tour

The riverfront **Tennessee Aquarium** ⑥⑥, in **Ross's Landing Park and Plaza,**
and the **Creative Discovery Museum** ⑥⑦, two blocks south on Chestnut
Street, are both ideal for children. You can take the Riverwalk or drive
to the Bluff View Art District, near the **Hunter Museum of Art** ⑥⑧ and
the **Houston Museum of Decorative Art.** Retracing your steps on the
Riverwalk, the **Walnut Street Bridge** ⑥⑨ offers a chance to sit and rest
or to walk and cycle above the Tennessee River. Back downtown, you
can take a free electric bus shuttle south to the former train station,
now part of a hotel called the **Chattanooga Choo-Choo** ⑦⓪, and to
Warehouse Row, home to designer outlet stores.

TIMING

You could easily spend a day downtown visiting the Tennessee Aquarium (worth several hours), IMAX theater, Creative Discovery Museum,
and other museums. There is time ticketing for the Aquarium, and you
can make reservations for the IMAX.

Sights to See

⑦⓪ **Chattanooga Choo-Choo.** Chattanooga's turn-of-the-century terminal
station, immortalized in song by Glen Miller in the 1940s, is now a
Holiday Inn (☞ Lodging, *below*), but it's still one of the area's best-
loved attractions. Stop by if only to see the elegant lobby under the
original 85-ft freestanding dome, which appears much as it did before
trains stopped chugging into the terminal in 1970. Though the dining
room has a sense of grandeur about it, the food is standard. Save your
appetite and explore the area around the renovated train cars (now used
for lodging), the hotel's gardens, and a model railroad. ✉ *1400 Market St.,* ☎ *423/266–5000.*

💧 ⑥⑦ **Creative Discovery Museum.** Abundant, inventive hands-on activities
and displays in four exhibit areas—an artist's studio, a musician's

workshop, an inventor's studio, and a field scientist's lab—bring out the kid in visitors of all ages. In the artist's studio, for example, kids learn about and try printmaking, painting (including portraiture), and sculpture. The Little Yellow House play space has activities for children from 18 months to four years old. ✉ *321 Chestnut St., 37402,* ☎ *423/756–2738.* 🖼 *$7.75; parking $5.* ⊘ *Memorial Day–Labor Day, daily 10–6; Labor Day–May, Tues.–Sat. 10–5, Sun. noon–5.*

OFF THE
BEATEN PATH
FRAZIER AVENUE ARTS DISTRICT – Across the river (you can walk over the Walnut Street Bridge) from downtown is this emerging tourist and local hot spot, with restaurants, galleries, the Chattanooga Theatre Center, and shopping. A popular stop is the Mudpie Coffeehouse and Newsstand. It's about a half mile from the Tennessee Aquarium.

68 **Hunter Museum of Art.** Housed partially in a restored Classical Revival mansion, the riverside Hunter Museum, in the Bluff View Art District, houses an eclectic collection of mostly American paintings (from early portraits and Hudson River School works to Impressionist paintings and abstract pieces by artists such as Helen Frankenthaler), photography, and sculpture. There's also a sculpture garden. ✉ *10 Bluff View,* ☎ *423/267–0968.* 🖼 *$5.* ⊘ *Tues.–Sat. 10–4:30, Sun. 1–4:30.*

Houston Museum of Decorative Art. This small Victorian home, in the Bluff View Art District, is packed literally to the rafters with mainly American decorative arts collected by the eccentric Anna Safley Houston (who eventually owned 15,000 pitchers). The emphasis is on antique art glass and American pressed glass; also of note are the pieces of blue Staffordshire and English lusterware china. ✉ *201 High St.,* ☎ *423/267–7176.* 🖼 *$5.* ⊘ *Mon.–Sat. 9:30–4, Sun. noon–4.*

☖ **International Towing and Recovery Museum.** The first tow truck was created in Chattanooga, and this beguiling collection of shiny vehicles from the past and present may well grab the attention of adults as well as kids. ✉ *401 Broad St.,* ☎ *423/267–3132.* 🖼 *$3.50.* ⊘ *Weekdays 10–4:30, weekends 11–5.*

Ross's Landing Park and Plaza. This area includes the ☞ Tennessee Aquarium and ☞ Tennessee Aquarium 3-D IMAX Theater. World-class architects, artists, and landscape designers have provided an open-air retrospective of Chattanooga's long history as the starting point for the infamous Trail of Tears, the forced march of the Cherokee tribe from their home territories; the site of key Civil War battles; and a major railroad town. The Chattanooga Visitors Center is also here.

☖ ★ **66** **Tennessee Aquarium.** Chattanooga *is* river country and the world's largest freshwater facility of its kind, a 130,000-square-ft monument to the Tennessee River, tells the story. This aquarium displays the inhabitants behind glass in a spectacular 60-ft canyon with two living forests and 22 tanks. Five main areas, including explorations of the Tennessee River from its origin in the Appalachian highlands to midstream and on to the Mississippi Delta, contain habitats and tanks. *Rivers of the World* presents the flora and fauna of six freshwater rivers, from the St. Lawrence to the Zaire. A new exhibit, *VENOM: Striking Beauties,* on view until January 2002, displays nearly 50 venomous species such as Gila monsters, Black Widows, and scorpions in 22 realistic habitats, including a South American rainforest, African rainforest, and Southwestern desert. Designed by the Cambridge Seven Associates, who created Baltimore's National Aquarium, the aquarium's contemporary riverside structure, crowned with four glass rooftop pyramids, is a distinctive element in the city's low, sprawling skyline. A separate building holds the Tennessee Aquarium IMAX 3-D Theater (☞ *below*). ✉ *1 Broad*

St., ☎ *423/265–0695 or 800/262–0695.* ✍ *$11.95; $16.25 for joint ticket with IMAX 3-D theater.* ☉ *Daily 10–6, until 8 on summer weekends.*

🔄 **Tennessee Aquarium IMAX 3-D Theater.** The six-story-high screen, 3-D cameras, and special technology give viewers the feeling of being part of the movie. Educational films explore a variety of topics, such as dinosaurs, dolphins, and other wildlife. Each movie runs every two hours. An environmental learning lab is part of the theater. ⊠ *201 Chestnut St.,* ☎ *423/266–3467.* ✍ *$6.95; $16.25 for joint ticket with Tennessee Aquarium.* ☉ *Sept.–May, Sun.–Thurs. 11–6, Fri.–Sat. 11–9; June–Aug., daily 10–9.*

69 **Walnut Street Bridge.** The Tennessee Riverwalk promenade connects Ross's Landing Park and Plaza (☞ *above*) to the restored Walnut Street Bridge, the longest pedestrian bridge in the world. In 1978 the bridge was closed to vehicular traffic and slated for demolition, but a battle by preservationists culminated in its reopening as a pedestrian bridge in 1993. In 1991, the bridge was added to the National Register of Historic Places. Built in 1891, this 2,370-ft truss bridge spans the Tennessee River and has lovely views of the city and surrounding mountains. The bridge is popular for strolling and also as a site for special events and festivals.

Greater Chattanooga

Numbers in the text correspond to numbers in the margin and on the Chattanooga map.

Beyond downtown are a number of the area's longtime attractions, including some musts for Civil War buffs.

A Good Drive

A number of Chattanooga's attractions are clustered near **Lookout Mountain,** where most of the terrain isn't ideal for walking. Drive instead, taking Broad Street from downtown to **Ruby Falls** ⑦. From there, it's a short hop to the **Incline Railway** and **Point Park,** which is close to the **Battles for Chattanooga Museum** ⑫. Cross the Tennessee state line into Georgia for some old-fashioned fun at **Rock City Gardens** ⑬ and a history lesson at **Chickamauga/Chattanooga National Military Park** ⑭.

TIMING
A good day of sightseeing could be devoted to Lookout Mountain, whether your focus is family fun in places like Rock City and Ruby Falls or historical highlights such as Chickamauga/Chattanooga National Military Park.

Sights to See

⑫ **Battles for Chattanooga Museum.** Music, narration, and lights on an electric-map rendering of critical battles help you visualize key events in Chattanooga's Civil War history. There are also small displays of war artifacts and a good bookstore. The museum is near the entrance to ☞ **Point Park** on Lookout Mountain. ⊠ *1110 E. Brow Rd.,* ☎ *423/821–2812.* ✍ *$5.95.* ☉ *June–Labor Day, daily 9:30–6; Labor Day–May, daily 10–5.*

★ **⑭** **Chickamauga and Chattanooga National Military Park.** The 1863 battles for Chattanooga were some of the most violent ever fought—and they were a major turning point in the Civil War. The Union hoped to gain control of the area and the city, a rail center and a gateway to the Confederacy, but was defeated at nearby Chickamauga by General Bragg. Southern troops surrounded Union ones in Chattanooga before generals Thomas and Grant launched assaults that would lead to Union control of most of the state. In 1864, General Sherman would start from Chattanooga on his march to Atlanta and the sea. At this battlefield, apart from taking advantage of hiking and driving trails past monuments and acres of scenic beauty, you can explore a gun museum, check the bookstore, and watch a multimedia presentation about the battles. ✉ *U.S. 27, Chattanooga, GA,* ☎ *706/866–9241.* 🎫 *Free.* ☉ *Memorial Day–Labor Day, daily 8–5:45; Labor Day–Memorial Day, daily 8–4:45.*

OFF THE
BEATEN PATH

DAYTON – A 36-mi drive north along U.S. 27 from Chattanooga, this small town was the site of the famous Scopes "Monkey Trial" in 1925. The room where the trial took place has been preserved at the **Rhea County Courthouse.** A small museum has displays about the trial. ✉ *1475 New Market St.,* ☎ *423/775–7801.* 🎫 *Free.* ☉ *Mon.–Thurs. 8–4, Fri. 8–5:30.*

Incline Railway. The steepest passenger railway in the world, at a grade of 72.7 degrees, the Incline Railway seems to defy gravity as its tracks cut a swath straight up Lookout Mountain (☞ *below*). The view is spectacular. ✉ *827 E. Brow Rd., Lookout Mountain,* ☎ *423/821–4224.* 🎫 *$9.* ☉ *Labor Day–Memorial Day, daily 8:30 AM–9 PM; trains run every 15–20 mins.*

★ **Lookout Mountain.** Chattanooga's poshest homes sit atop Lookout Mountain, which extends into Georgia. Plan to visit Point Park (☞ *below*) and Rock City Gardens (☞ *below*). Though Lookout Mountain can be reached by car, Incline Railway (☞ *above*) is a thrilling alternative.

Point Park. Part of Chickamauga/Chattanooga National Military Park (☞ *above*), this breezy, wooded promontory atop Lookout Mountain (☞ *above*) has sweeping views of the outlying region. Markers remind you of the Union soldiers who scrambled up the craggy mountainside in a mad effort to escape the relentless showers of Confederate bullets during the 1863 "Battle Above the Clouds," part of the eventual Union victory. A visitor center has information; from June through August, rangers give tours and talks on the site. ✉ *E. Brow Rd.,* ☎ *423/821–7786.* 🎫 *Free.* ☉ *Visitor center daily 8–4:45.*

Reflection Riding. You can drive or walk through this lovely botanical garden near Lookout Mountain. Native American and Civil War history are part of the landscape, too. ✉ *400 Garden Rd.,* ☎ *423/821–9582.* 🎫 *$3.* ☉ *Mon.–Sat. 9–5, Sun. 1–5.*

❼❸ **Rock City Gardens.** At one time more than 900 barns throughout the Southeast were emblazoned with the words SEE ROCK CITY. Only a few remain, but visitors still come here for such simple pleasures as walking a swinging bridge. This craggy tribute to fairy tales and geology, just over the state line in Georgia, began in 1932 as a network of paths through rock formations with such names as Fat Man's Squeeze. The project grew, as exhibits depicting the tales of Mother Goose and Little Red Riding Hood were added. Walt Disney even consulted with Rock City's founders before designing his own magical kingdom. The garden's position atop Lookout Mountain (☞ *above*) provides views for hundreds of miles (a sign shows directions to seven states). Winter holiday displays of lights are popular. ✉ *1400 Patten Rd., Lookout Mountain, GA,* ☎ *706/820–2531.* 🎫 *$10.95.* ☉ *Summer, daily 8:30–5; fall–spring, daily 8:30–4.*

❼❶ **Ruby Falls.** There are two elements here: Above ground are a restaurant, souvenir shops, lookout tower, and children's playground, all contained within one castlelike structure. Inside, an elevator whisks groups of visitors several hundred feet below to a natural cave. A ½-mi path leads past formations such as stalagmites and stalactites to the deepest and highest underground waterfall (145 ft) in America. ⊠ *1720 Lookout Mountain Scenic Hwy.,* ☎ *423/821–2544.* ☒ *$9.50.* ☉ *Memorial Day–Labor Day, daily 8 AM–9 PM; Sept.–Oct. and Apr.–May, daily 8–8; Nov.–Mar., daily 8–6.*

☾ **Tennessee Valley Railroad.** Ride the rails of the largest historic railroad still operating in the South aboard a steam locomotive or diesel trains dating from World War II. Children love the train museum on premises. ⊠ *4119 Cromwell Rd.,* ☎ *423/894–8028.* ☒ *$9.50.* ☉ *May–Labor Day, Mon.–Sat. 10–5, Sun. noon–5; Apr. and Sept.–Nov., Sat. 10–5.*

Dining

$$–$$$ ✕ **Southside Grill.** This handsome downtown restaurant in a former meatpacking plant reinterprets the food of the region with a gourmet touch. Hardwood floors offset the dark paneled walls, which are hung with fine art. Smoked salmon on a crispy grits cake and grilled rib eye with crawfish cakes and chilled leek soup are just two possible choices on the seasonally changing menu. ⊠ *1400 Cowart St.,* ☎ *423/266–9211. AE, D, DC, MC, V.*

$$ ✕ **212 Market.** This terrific restaurant near the Tennessee Aquarium
★ (☞ Sights to See, *above*) serves new American cuisine, with an emphasis on healthy fare such as grilled salmon; the Taylor River enchilada has fresh spinach, black beans, cheeses, and salsa. The cavernous, contemporary dining room is bright and unpretentious. ⊠ *212 Market St.,* ☎ *423/265–1212. AE, MC, V. No dinner Sun.*

$–$$ ✕ **Town & Country.** This Chattanooga fixture, which has offered great food and service for 40 years, is across the bridge from the aquarium. The menu combines Southern cuisine with beef, chicken, prime rib, and seafood entrées. The atmosphere is casual and prices are reasonable. *110 N. Market St.,* ☎ *423/267–8544. AE, D, DC, MC, V.*

$ ✕ **Big River Grille & Brewing Works.** You can watch the brewing process through a soaring glass wall beside the bar of this restored trolley warehouse, handsomely designed with high ceilings, exposed brick walls, and hardwood floors. Order the sampler for a taste of this microbrewery's four different concoctions. The sandwiches and salads are generous and tasty. ⊠ *222 Broad St.,* ☎ *423/267–2739. Reservations not accepted. AE, D, DC, MC, V.*

Lodging

$$–$$$$ ⊞ **Bluff View Inn.** Painstakingly restored and tastefully decorated with
★ 18th-century English antiques and art, this colonial revival mansion was built in 1928 on a bluff overlooking the river. The River Gallery Sculpture Garden is beside the inn, near the Riverwalk, and the Tennessee Aquarium is within walking distance. There are also rooms in two other turn-of-the-20th-century mansions; a complimentary gourmet breakfast is made to order. The inn is part of the Bluff View Art District area of shops and restaurants. ⊠ *412 E. 2nd St., 37403,* ☎ *423/265–5033 or 800/725–8338,* ℻ *423/265–5944. 13 rooms, 3 suites. 3 restaurants, café. D, MC, V.*

$$$ ⊞ **Marriott at the Convention Center.** This 16-floor downtown convention hotel is the town's largest. Rooms are spacious, and those on the higher floors have a great view of either the Tennessee River or Lookout Mountain. Adjacent to the city's convention center, this hotel is the choice of many business travelers, but families will appreciate its baby-sitting service and health club. ⊠ *2 Carter Plaza, 37402,* ☎

423/756–0002 or 800/841–1674, FAX *423/266–2254. 341 rooms, 2 suites. 2 restaurants, 2 lounges, indoor and outdoor pools, health club, laundry service, airport shuttle. AE, D, DC, MC, V.*

$$–$$$ ▥ **Radisson Read House—A Plaza Hotel.** The Georgian-style Read House dates from the 1920s and has been restored to the original grandeur that drew heads of state to lodge here in its heyday. The lobby has a large archway, stately columns, and polished walnut panels. Mailboxes from the days when guests stayed for months still neatly line one passageway. Guest rooms in the main hotel continue the Georgian motif; rooms in the annex are more contemporary. ⊠ *827 Broad St., 37402,* ☎ *423/266–4121 or 800/333–3333,* FAX *423/267–6447. 140 rooms, 100 suites. Restaurant, coffee shop, dining room, lounge, pool, hot tub, sauna. AE, DC, MC, V.*

$$ ▥ **Chattanooga Choo-Choo Holiday Inn.** This hotel (☞ Downtown Chattanooga, *above*) incorporates the landmark 1905 Southern Railway terminal, one of the first to be salvaged in the South. It's been renewed with restaurants, lounges, shops, exhibits, well-groomed gardens, and an operating trolley on 30 acres. Trains are parked on the tracks. Besides standard rooms in three buildings, the hotel has Victorian parlor cars—replete with the brocade and red upholstery of the period—converted to overnight berths. ⊠ *1400 Market St., 37402,* ☎ *423/266–5000 or 800/872–2529,* FAX *423/265–4635. 303 rooms, 10 suites, 48 railcars. 5 restaurants, lounge, 1 indoor and 2 outdoor pools, hot tub, 3 tennis courts. AE, D, DC, MC, V.*

$$ ▥ **Chattanooga Clarion Hotel.** The Clarion has a convenient downtown location only two blocks from the Tennessee Aquarium and other downtown attractions. Popular among business travelers, the simply furnished rooms feature coffeemakers and irons and ironing boards. *407 Chestnut St.,* ☎ *423/756–5150 or 800/252–7466. 203 rooms, 2 suites. 2 restaurants, data ports, pool, exercise room. AE, DC, MC, V.*

$–$$ ▥ **Days Inn Rivergate.** A half block from the Chattanooga Trade and Convention Center, this hotel is not only a bargain but very convenient to downtown. Rooms are the chain's standard fare. ⊠ *910 Carter St., 37402,* ☎ *423/266–7331 or 800/329–7466. 140 rooms. Pool, meeting rooms. AE, D, DC, MC, V.*

$ ▥ **Econo Lodge East Ridge.** Rooms here are spacious, contemporary in style, clean, and well maintained. ⊠ *1417 St. Thomas St., 37412,* ☎ *423/894–1417 or 800/446–6900. 89 rooms. Pool. AE, D, DC, MC, V.*

Nightlife and the Arts

The Arts

The restored **Memorial Auditorium** (⊠ *399 McCallie Ave.,* ☎ *423/757–5042*) is a venue for concerts and operas. Throughout the summer free concerts from blues to Celtic play on **Miller Plaza** (⊠ *850 Market St.,* ☎ *423/265–0771*). The **Chattanooga Theatre Center** (⊠ *400 River St.,* ☎ *423/267–8534*) stages 32 productions a year.

A city highlight, the mid-June **Riverbend Festival** (☎ *423/265–4112*) brings live rock, country, blues, jazz, and folk music to five stages over nine days and nights. A $22 pin is good for admission to all the 100 or so acts.

Nightlife

The Southside Jazz Junction and Tapas Restaurant (⊠ *114 W. Main St.,* ☎ *423/267–9003*) tempts both the ear and the taste buds with live jazz performances three to five nights a week, along with a delectable array of hors d'oeuvres. Every Friday night between 8 and 11, the free **Mountain Opry** (⊠ Walden Ridge Civic Center, Fairmount Rd., Chattanooga) showcases traditional bluegrass and mountain music.

Outdoor Activities and Sports

Canoeing and Rafting

The Ocoee River, site of the 1996 Olympic kayaking events, has powerful Class III and IV rapids. **Outdoor Adventure Rafting** (☎ 800/627–7636) can take you for a ride on the Ocoee. The Sequatchie River, gentler than the Ocoee, is suitable for year-round floating; try **Canoe the Sequatchie** (☎ 423/949–4400), April–October, for equipment. **Hiwassee Outfitters** (☎ 423/338–8115), in Reliance, open from mid-March to early November, has canoes, rafts, and tubes for beginners and intermediates; the nearby Hiwassee has occasional rapids.

Golf

Six miles south of the city in Georgia, the 18-hole, par-72 **Windstone Golf Club** (⊠ 9230 Windstone Dr., Ringgold, ☎ 423/894–1231) is one of the area's best courses. It's a daily fee course within the private Windstone community.

Hang Gliding

At **Lookout Mountain Flight Park and Training Center** (⊠ 7201 Scenic Hwy., Rising Fawn, GA, ☎ 706/398–3541 or 800/688–5637), you can soar solo or tandem (with an instructor); a variety of lessons and packages are available.

Shopping

Hamilton Place (⊠ 2100 Hamilton Place Blvd., ☎ 423/894–7177) is one of Tennessee's largest malls, with five department stores, more than 200 other stores, 30 eateries, and 17 theaters. An outlet center, **Warehouse Row** (⊠ 12th and Market Sts., ☎ 423/267–1111) yields some of the region's best (and most chic) buys. More than 40 upscale shops—such as Ellen Tracy, Polo/Ralph Lauren, Coach, and J. Peterman—are in several attractive, restored redbrick railroad warehouses downtown.

River Gallery (⊠ 400 E. 2nd St., ☎ 423/267–7353), in the Bluff View Art District, carries lovely crafts, from pottery to wood and metal pieces, as well as paintings and sculpture.

Chattanooga A to Z

Arriving and Departing

BY BUS

Greyhound (☎ 800/231–2222) has a terminal in Chattanooga.

BY CAR

I–75 runs north–south from Kentucky through Chattanooga and on to Georgia. U.S. 11 joins Chattanooga with Knoxville.

BY PLANE

Chattanooga Metropolitan Airport (⊠ 1001 Airport Rd., ☎ 423/855–2200), 8 mi east of downtown, is served by ASA, ComAir, Delta, Northwest Airlink, United Express, and US Airways.

Getting Around

BY BUS

Carta (☎ 423/629–1473), a free downtown shuttle on electric buses, runs between the Chattanooga Choo-Choo Hotel and the Tennessee Aquarium, with stops in between.

Contacts and Resources

EMERGENCIES

Ambulance, police (☎ 911). Medical assistance is available at **Erlanger Medical Center** (⊠ 975 E. 3rd St., ☎ 423/778–7000).

PHARMACIES
Eckerd (⊠ 3569 Brainerd Rd., ☎ 615/629–7323).

VISITOR INFORMATION
Chattanooga Area Convention and Visitors Bureau (⊠ 2 Broad St., 37402, ☎ 423/756–8687 or 800/322–3344); the visitor center is open daily 8:30–5:30.

TENNESSEE A TO Z

Arriving and Departing

By Bus
Greyhound (☎ 800/231–2222) links most cities in Tennessee.

By Car
The state's main east–west artery is I–40. I–55 runs north–south in West Tennessee. In Middle Tennessee, I–65 and I–24 cross in Nashville. I–75 links Chattanooga to Knoxville in East Tennessee. I–81 runs from just east of Knoxville through upper East Tennessee.

By Plane
Most visitors use **Memphis International Airport** (☞ Memphis A to Z, *above*) or **Metropolitan Nashville Airport** (☞ Nashville A to Z, *above*).

Getting Around

By Car
The speed limit on interstate highways ranges from 65 to 70 mph, as indicated, unless otherwise posted. Right turns on red lights are allowed unless a sign indicates otherwise. Scenic highways within Tennessee are marked by a mockingbird sign above the sign giving the route number.

Contacts and Resources

B&B Reservation Service
Tennessee Bed & Breakfast Innkeepers' Association (⊠ Box 120428, Nashville, 37212, ☎ 800/820–8144).

Emergencies
In towns and cities, dial 911 for **police** or **ambulance.** Cellular calls to the Highway Patrol are free by dialing *THP (*847).

Visitor Information
To request brochures, call ☎ 800/836–6200. Contact the **Tennessee Department of Tourist Development** (⊠ 320 6th Ave. N, 5th floor, Nashville, 37243, ☎ 615/741–2159).

INDEX